Confessions of a Born-Again Pagan

Confessions of a Born-Again Pagan

Anthony T. Kronman

Yale UNIVERSITY PRESS

New Haven & London

Published with assistance from the Mary Cady Tew Memorial Fund.

Yale University Press books may be purchased in quantity for educational, business, or promotional use. For information, please e-mail sales.press@yale.edu (U.S. office) or sales@yaleup.co.uk (U.K. office).

Set in Adobe Garamond type by Westchester Publishing Services.
Printed in the United States of America.

Library of Congress Control Number: 2015955523
ISBN 978-0-300-20853-5 (hardcover: alk. paper)

A catalogue record for this book is available from the British Library.
This paper meets the requirements of ANSI/NISO Z39.48-1992 (Permanence of Paper).

10 9 8 7 6 5 4 3 2

For Matt, Emma, Hope, and Alex

The earth is not an echo.

WALT WHITMAN, *Leaves of Grass*

Contents

Acknowledgments

This book is in important part about gratitude. Writing it, I have been acutely aware of my own for the gifts of many people, beginning with those who taught me years ago.

To three of my teachers I am especially grateful.

One is Dan O'Connor. It was in Dan's class on ancient philosophy at Williams College in 1965 that I first began to glimpse the beauty of Aristotle's world and to sense the radical implications of the doctrine of creation that destroyed it. The questions he asked in that class, and his way of asking them, have been with me ever since.

At Williams and then later at Yale, I worked closely with Kenley Dove. Kenley's preoccupation with the meaning of the modern world became my own, and his utterly original interpretation of the history of Western philosophy has influenced my thinking in ways I could not summarize or disentangle. I have never left off being Kenley's student.

I must also say a word of thanks to Karsten Harries. I met Karsten when I came to Yale as a graduate student in 1968. The freshness and depth of his reading of the old books; the clarity with which he asked the most important questions; and his inspiring humanity have been for me, for nearly half a century, an example of what philosophy should be.

For most of this time, I have been on the faculty of the Yale Law School. There is no more encouraging environment on earth. I could not have written this book anywhere else.

My closest philosophical companion at the Law School is Paul Kahn. Paul generally disagrees with what I say. But I wouldn't want it otherwise. Every conversation with him is the start of an adventure.

I must also record my gratitude to my colleagues Bruce Ackerman and Owen Fiss. Their wisdom and encouragement have sustained me since I joined the faculty of the Law School almost forty years ago. More recently, I have benefitted from the friendship and support of three of my younger colleagues, David Grewal, Jed Rubenfeld and Daniel Markovits.

Beyond these, there are many others to whom I am grateful for their guidance and help. They include Jonathan Lear, who has taught me so much, about Aristotle and Freud in particular; Doug Stone, who patiently answered my questions about physics; Bryan Garsten, who encouraged my love of Whitman; Steven Smith, who shares my love of Spinoza; and Howard Bloch, whose passion for the tradition of Western thought has strengthened and enlightened my own.

In completing the book, I have had the help of several talented research assistants. David Kim, Joe Nawrocki and Erick Sam have all made important contributions.

I am especially grateful to Samuel Loncar. Samuel has for several years been an enthusiastic interlocutor. His knowledge of philosophy and theology is vast. He has taught me much and I value his friendship greatly.

I want also to thank my imaginative and unbelievably hard working assistant, Darcy Smith. Darcy has been my companion in the venture from start to finish.

My deepest gratitude is, as always, to my family.

My wife, Nancy, has shown a superhuman patience for my distractedness during the long time I have been writing this book. I have talked with her about it every day. She has made countless suggestions to improve it. Her mind is my surest guide; her love makes the world a home.

My children, Matt, Emma, Hope and Alex, have all offered improving comments as well. They have welcomed my book as a younger sibling. It is to them that it is dedicated. "You that shall cross from shore to shore years hence are more to me, and more in my meditations, than you might suppose."

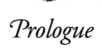

Prologue

The word "confession" has two meanings. The first is personal and intimate. To confess something in this sense means to share a thought or feeling that is peculiarly one's own—to reveal a secret of some kind.

Its second meaning is nearly the opposite. A confession in this sense is a public statement of belief. It is a formal declaration of the doctrines or ideas to which a community subscribes—those that distinguish it from other groups with different convictions. This is the sense in which we speak, for example, of the "Augsburg Confession," the collective statement that Luther and his followers submitted to the emperor Charles V in 1530, listing in precise terms the beliefs of those bound together in what would later be called the Lutheran Church. There is nothing personal about the document. It reveals no secrets. One searches it in vain for a glimpse of the private feelings of its authors. In this respect, it stands at the opposite pole from the most famous confession in Western literature—the long autobiographical essay that Augustine composed near the end of the fourth century C.E., in which even at this immense distance we can still hear the spoken secrets of his heart.

This book is a confession in the second sense. It is a doctrinal work, not a personal memoir. In it, I outline a system of ideas and present arguments on their behalf. Of course, I do not speak for a church but only for myself. To that extent, the book has an unavoidably personal character. But for the most part its tone is abstract and detached. I present its arguments, as best I can, from a third- rather than a first-personal point of view. They are meant to stand on their own, regardless of the private feelings of the man who made them.

And yet, though I have written the book in an impersonal voice, I know that my longings and fears will be apparent to those who accompany me to the end, for the topics I address touch on questions of living and dying that no one, not even the most abstracted philosopher, can approach without feelings of this kind. In this sense, the book is the cool deposit of an intensely personal quest and before setting out it is appropriate that I give the reader some account of the obsessions that have moved me for many years now, and that in retrospect I can see with a clarity that the act of writing this book has helped me achieve. Doing so may not only help to guide the reader through the arguments that follow, but meet, part way at least, the reasonable demand to know a little more about the guide himself before joining him on a journey of such length. Anyone who has picked up a book with the word "confession" in its title is owed as much.

The most lasting of my obsessions has been with the meaning of the modern world.

Since I first began to think about such things in even a modestly self-conscious way, I have been haunted by the thought that destiny has placed me in a world with a unique historical identity and been anxious to know what this is. That the modern age differs from those that preceded it is obvious. Indeed, it is *too* obvious. There are too many distinctions that set it apart. Some are political, others intellectual, scientific or aesthetic. But do all these have a common explanation? Is there some one thing that connects them? Putting aside the endlessly disputed questions of when and why it came into being, does the modern world have a *meaning* that joins its diverse parts in a single, intelligible whole? This is the question that has obsessed me for many years now and I have feared that unless I had an answer to it, I could never be more than a tourist in the world in which it was my fate to have been born.

I have come to think of this fear in religious terms, though not in the conventional sense. The word "religion" calls to mind churches, praying and the like. More importantly, in the modern West at least, it is difficult to separate the idea of religion from that of a God beyond the world, all-powerful and all-knowing, who watches over his human creatures with providential concern, rewarding and punishing them for their obedience or disobedience to his commands. Even those who say they do not believe in God generally have this God in mind.

I have never been a religious person in this sense. My father was trained as a rabbi and later became a screenwriter in Hollywood. My mother was raised as a fundamentalist Christian and worked for a time as an actress. Both repudiated organized religion of every kind. Indeed, they loathed it. To them, church and synagogue meant ignorance, superstition and the oppression of the human mind. They passed their skepticism on to me. I was taught that prayer is for weaklings and that anyone who wants to live an independent life must learn to do without it. I have never gotten over this feeling. I respect my orthodox friends and am interested in their beliefs. But I will never be able to share them. I will never be able to pray. The great German social historian Max Weber, who was also deeply interested in religious phenomena, was once asked if he was a religious man himself. He replied that he was not—that he was "unmusical" when it came to religion. That is how I would describe myself, so long as one has churches and praying and the God of Abraham in mind. And yet I would also say that my obsession with the meaning of the modern world has been a religious one in another, and I think legitimate, sense.

To understand the meaning of anything as a whole, one has to put it in a larger context of some kind—in an explanatory framework that is wider than the thing to be explained. But what could be wider than the modern world? Certainly nothing in it, for that is part of what needs to be explained. Perhaps the meaning of modernity can be grasped by placing it within the frame of human history as a whole. But then what explains *that?* Mustn't history too be placed within a wider frame of reference if any particular historical period is to be explained in a satisfying way?

This train of thought long ago led me to conclude (though I would not have put it this way at the time) that the meaning of the modern world can be adequately understood only if we are able to place it in the context of the one thing that is more encompassing than all of human history, indeed, than all of time—of what is not merely long lasting but eternal in the freighted and potent sense this word still retains.

I can now see that my anxious wish to master my world in thought has from the start been a longing to understand its relation to eternity, but without a God of the sort to whom Christians, Jews and Muslims pray. This is an intellectual longing, of course, but a spiritual one too. The desire to reach what lies beyond history and time, which Kant insists is an inextinguishable demand of the human mind, cannot be called by any other name without demeaning its ambition and converting it to a quest of a more prosaic and less disquieting but also less exalted kind. My youthful wish to understand the meaning of the modern world as a whole has always been a spiritual one in this sense, and if the field of theology is construed broadly to include *every* attempt to connect the world of human experience to what Aristotle calls "the eternal and divine" and not merely the familiar Abrahamic ways of doing so, then my obsession must be described as a theological one too.

This seems much clearer to me now than it did before. Perhaps the fiercely anticlerical environment in which I was raised made it difficult for me to acknowledge that my obsession with modernity had anything to do with theology. For a long time, I associated theology with the belief that at a crucial juncture one must be prepared to abandon reason for faith—to make what Weber calls "a sacrifice of the intellect." Viewed in this light, theology seemed to me to be the enemy of philosophy, which for as far back as I can recall has seemed to me the only intellectually self-respecting path to an understanding of the modern world (or anything else for that matter). My view of philosophy has not changed but my belief that it is at war with theology has. That is because I had not yet considered in a serious way the older theology, which the greatest philosophers of pagan antiquity shared, that declares the study of God to be the highest stage and completing phase in our campaign to comprehend the world by means of reason alone. Nor had I met the principal hero of this book, who shared this view and extended it in ways his pagan predecessors could not have imagined.

When I say that I had not met him, I mean that I had not studied the philosophy of Spinoza with any care. He was for me just a book on a shelf, though I have a dim and self-serving memory of saying to myself sometime in my sophomore year of college that Spinoza's *Ethics* might well contain the truth about things and that I would have to make a closer study of it later. In any case, none of this was apparent to me then. I thought of theology in the way most philosophers do, as a swamp of superstition, to be avoided at all costs. I now see how narrow this view is. I understand that it is hostage to a particular conception of God—the one that Augustine made decisive for the later tradition of Western philosophy. I know there is a different conception, which Aristotle embraced and Spinoza extended, that views the study of God as the culmination of the pursuit of knowledge in strictly rational terms for which no sacrifice of the intellect is required. And I can say without embarrassment, what my younger self would have greeted with astonishment, that this book is a work of theology in the latter sense.

As a theologian, I find myself unable to subscribe to either of the parties that struggle with such fury on so many fronts in the war over the meaning of religion today.

On the one side are the true believers—those who maintain their faith in the God of Abraham and his prophets. Their God is an obstacle to reason. He puts a sign in its path that reads, "No trespassing beyond this point." We should allow those who believe in such a God to worship him as they choose. But the demands of their religion cannot be reconciled with the rationalism of the modern world, whose governing principles and dominant practices are all based on the assumption that though its achievements remain forever incomplete, reason is never required to yield to faith. The belief that it must is a capitulation I cannot accept. It cannot be squared with the ambitions of philosophy or the deepest values and greatest achievements of the age in which we live.

On the other side are the self-professed atheists, who delight in mocking the true believers and pointing out that their God is dead. For them, theology is a mistake, or worse, a form of cowardice. They diagnose the longing for a connection to eternity as a childish wish, and advise us to grow up. In their view, this means abandoning the idea of God altogether. They insist that we must learn to live without a meaningful connection to the everlasting and divine—in a world where things come and go and nothing lasts forever, under the all-devouring dominion of time.

I cannot accept this either. That is not just because I feel the personal need for a connection to God, though I do. More fundamentally, it is because the thoroughness with which today's atheists deny the very intelligibility of the search for God is as antagonistic in its own way to the aims of philosophy as the true believers' insistence on the need for faith, and as contrary to the spirit of modern life, whose science, art and politics rest on a theology they fail to grasp.

This book offers a third alternative. I call it my born-again paganism to suggest the combination of classical and Abrahamic ideas that set it apart from other philosophies. Whether it or something like it will become the platform for a third-party movement in the fight over the spiritual meaning of the modern world, I cannot say. I have written these confessions mainly to understand my own mind in the matter, though if I did not believe that there are others who feel as I do, the task would have been a lonelier one than it has. I have had them in mind from the start, as a ghostly kind of audience, as I have had in mind that younger man who found himself obsessed with the question of modernity more than forty years ago, and has since followed various paths in an effort to answer it.

The first of these I began to explore as a college student in the 1960s. If I had been asked on the day I graduated from Williams College to describe my philosophy of life, I would have said, "I am a Marxist." This may be hard for some readers today to imagine. There are few committed Marxists left. But at the time, Marx's writings still had a tremendous authority and represented one of the main alternatives among which thoughtful people might be expected to choose in framing a view of life.

Part of the appeal of Marxism for me was political. I was a student activist and critical of halfhearted liberal attempts at reform. I believed that something more basic was needed. In the writings of Marx I found a system of ideas that justified this belief. But Marxism did more than give my politics coherence and direction. It satisfied my longing to understand the meaning of the modern world in a comprehensive way—to grasp its deepest structures in what Hegel calls the "grey on grey" of thought. Marxism was for me a philosophical science. This is the aspect of it that seems least plausible today. Marx's assault on the injustices of the capitalist system retains its moral urgency, and his writings are still a helpful guide to understanding the significance of that amorphous phenomenon we designate by the concept of class. But who now thinks of Marxism as a science in any sense of the term? Yet that is precisely what drew me to it.

The characterization of Marx's philosophy as a science rests on his claim to have amended Hegel's account of the modern world in a way that remains faithful to Hegel's own relentless commitment to reason. Unlike his contemporary Søren Kierkegaard, who regarded this commitment as a disease, Marx enthusiastically embraced it and sought to show that Hegel had failed to live up to its own demands. He claimed that a *fully* rational account of the modern world must explain the ways in which the emergence of what Hegel calls "Absolute Spirit" is conditioned by the material relations that embody the spiritual life of human beings at every stage of its development, and analyze more carefully than Hegel had the dynamic interplay between these two dimensions of human existence.

Hegel insists that Absolute Spirit has an intelligible history. He maintains that it sheds its preliminary and inadequate forms in a sequence we can comprehend completely, each stage taking the peculiar shape it does in response to its predecessor's failed attempt to live up to its own internal ideals. Hegel conceived each of these stages in abstract terms, as the representative of a certain imperfect view of the truth. But he also viewed each as a social structure of a particular kind, based on the implicit acceptance by those involved of a shared principle for determining what their roles or statuses shall be—the correlative of the conception of truth appropriate to the stage in question. In this latter connection, Hegel emphasized the essential role that various media of interaction (words and things, mainly) play in the constitution of the system of social relations that defines the public world of each of the earlier forms of life on the path to Absolute Spirit.

Following this method of philosophical analysis, Hegel arrived at the conclusion that the concept of right on which the modern state is based, together with the intellectual and material relations that correspond to it, represents the final stage in the restless, self-critical movement of Spirit toward a form of life that is adequate to its own aspirations—the last stop in the long history not merely of man but of the world itself, after which there can never again be a fundamental change of the sort that has marked the transition from each previous stage to the next. Those who follow the logic of Hegel's argument are thus rewarded with a view of the modern world as a form of life both necessary and final. For them, modernity is no longer a brute fact. It is a wholly explicable destiny, whose opacity reason has dispelled both in theory and practice—which now, at the end of history, become one and the same.

This was Marx's aim as well. But Hegel, he said, had failed to grasp the dialectical complications that arise as a result of the attempt to make our ideals real by means of the systems of production that alone give them a material presence in the world. These systems or "modes" of production, as Marx called them, also form an ordered series, each giving rise to the next through the transformative effect of its attempt to remain faithful to its own organizing principles. The sequence that Marx outlines is as necessary and therefore intelligible as the one that Hegel described, but according to Marx it has not yet come to an end. The capitalist mode of production that today forms the basic framework of all economic activity everywhere on earth is infected by the same instability as its predecessors. It is building a material world that no longer conforms to its own fundamental principle of organization (that things be valued according to the amount of labor time expended in their production), and therefore necessarily undermines its own foundations. Hence it cannot be the final stage in the history of man or the world. But the form of life to which it shall eventually give rise, out of its own self-defeat, *will be* the last one, after which nothing really fundamental can ever happen again. According to Marx, this is the deepest truth about the modern world, if we define its modernity not, as Hegel does, in abstract juridical terms as a free-standing system of right, but as a regime of law embedded in a particular mode of production that not only prevents the ideal of freedom associated with it from being fully achieved, but whose own self-destructive tendencies give rise to an alternative way of arranging our interactions with nature that will at last, after millennia of travail, bring to an end the struggle of the human spirit to fashion a proper home for itself.

On Marx's view, like Hegel's, history has a goal—it's just that we haven't quite reached it yet. We're one step away. Marxism seeks to explain the relation of the modern world to everything that came before, *and also* to account for its own internal strains in a transparently rational way. This was the main source of its appeal for me. I believed that if I could only master Marx's philosophy, I would eventually be able to understand my world as a "totality" whose intellectual and material elements form a single, intelligible whole. The fact that I was able to extract from Marx's writings a scientific blueprint for action, and quiet the doubts that haunt writers like Machiavelli who insists on the riskiness of every political act, was an added benefit for a young man in his twenties caught up in the passions of the greatest student movement the country has ever seen.

When I graduated from college in 1968 and enrolled in the Ph.D. program in philosophy at Yale, my ambition was to become a better Marxist. This required that I study the history of Western thought in greater detail. I felt that I needed to know it as well as my nineteenth-century hero. How else could I be his intelligent follower? The 1960s passed, the student movement subsided, and my own passion for politics waned. I began to prepare for a career. Still my most urgent ambition remained the same. I was now committed to becoming a professional philosopher. But what I wanted more than anything else was to validate and fortify the commanding point of view I had achieved as a young Marxist so that I might be able to survey my world with even greater assurance. It was with this goal in mind that I decided to write my doctoral dissertation on some aspect of Marx's philosophy. No other subject even occurred to me.

At Williams I had studied with Kenley Dove, a scholar of Hegel and Marx. In my senior year, he left Williams for Yale, and when I arrived in New Haven our relationship deepened. I just assumed that Kenley would be my dissertation advisor. I told him that I wanted to write on Marx, but he had another idea. Why not write on Max Weber instead? Many dissertations have been written on Marx, he said. Weber, on the other hand, was largely unknown in American philosophical circles. Yet Weber was also preoccupied with the meaning of modernity, and offers an account that differs in important ways from those of Hegel and Marx. In any case, Kenley said with a smile, I had no right to call myself a Marxist until I had wrestled with the ghost of Max Weber. And so the decision was made. I would write on Weber, and set out to learn as much as I could about the work of a man whose name I barely knew.

If I had given my dissertation a more accurate if somewhat longer title it would have been, "How the (good, progressive, more inclusively rational) Hegelian side of Weber's philosophy triumphs over its (bad, bourgeois, irrational) Kantian side and why it needs Marx's analysis of capitalism to be complete."

Let me explain.

In his writings on the methodological foundations of the social sciences, Weber asserts that all research is guided by value judgments; that these are plural and incommensurable; and that every judgment of this sort is the product of a free and ultimately unaccountable act of will that cannot be reduced to or justified in terms of an objective understanding of facts—the distinction between facts and values for which Weber is so famous. These ideas all have their roots in the neo-Kantian milieu that dominated German philosophy at the time.

In his substantive historical writings, Weber takes a different approach. His many, varied and detailed accounts of the forces that have contributed to the emergence in the modern West of a uniquely rational civilization rest not on Kantian but Hegelian presuppositions. Weber's starting point here is not the solitary self, willing values that others may reject but cannot refute. His analysis of modernity begins with the very different idea of a structure of authority in which individuals—even Kant's free and autonomous selves— have the identities they do solely on account of the organizing principles whose reciprocal recognition constitutes the essence of the structure in question. Moreover, Weber conceives the relation among the three pure forms of authority that he identifies (the traditional, charismatic and legal-rational) in dialectical terms that explain why the last of these enjoys a conceptual pre-eminence *vis-à-vis* the other two, and why the modern Western civilization that is founded on it has a "universal significance and validity" no other age or way of life possesses.

These are Hegelian themes and in my dissertation—how remote it seems to me now!—I underscored the tension between them and the Kantian outlook of Weber's more explicitly philosophical writings. I also tried to show that if Weber had been more self-consciously attentive to his own Hegelianism, he would have seen that the modern West cannot be defined in terms of what he calls the phenomenon of "rationalization" alone, but that the economic expression of this rationalism in the capitalist form of production is still tied to man's natural powers in a way that makes it incompletely rational. This is the heart of Marx's critique of Hegel. The aim of my dissertation was to vindicate Marx against Weber. I was twenty-seven when I finished.

In the course of writing it, however, something happened that I hadn't expected. My encounter with Weber produced a shift in mood that had lasting effects.

Broadly speaking, Weber is best known for three things: his insistence on the distinction between facts and values; his description of the process that has produced the institutions and ideals of the modern West as one of ever-increasing rationalization; and the anguish he expressed at the fate of being condemned to live in what he called "an iron cage" of reason.

For Weber, the modern world, with all its glittering attainments, is no longer a home for man. It may still be possible to find a measure of spiritual fulfillment in the recesses of private life—*in pianissimo,* as he puts it—but the governing apparatus of our lives is no longer connected to those larger structures of cosmic and religious meaning that once assured men that the world in which they live, and their lives themselves, have an ultimate significance of one kind or another. This is equally true in the realms of politics and economics. The first is characterized by bureaucratic rule and the second by impersonal markets. These have an unprecedented efficiency but are soulless machines that are incapable of satisfying our yearning to live in a world that has more meaning than we can put into it with our private and arbitrary valuations. The same is true of research science. It generates a continually expanding storehouse of knowledge, but only on the condition that the world be assumed to have no inherent meaning of its own.

Together these forces have resulted in what Weber calls the "disenchantment" of the world. This is the price of its rationalization. In return for the vast powers that reason affords us, we have been exiled—or rather, have exiled ourselves—from the world in which men always lived before, where it was still possible to have a direct connection to the eternal and divine. What we have gained is merely the other side of what we have lost. In this sense, our situation is a tragic one from which we can neither advance nor retreat. Weber ridicules the superficial cheerfulness of those who fail to grasp the spiritual gravity of our condition and the romanticism of those who think they can turn back the clock. The only alternative is honesty and courage. We must have the strength to accept the consequences of living in a godless age and conduct ourselves accordingly. That is hard to do, but everything else is cowardice.

These themes are most powerfully expressed in Weber's famous lecture, "Science as a Calling." They derive from certain of Nietzsche's ideas, which seem to have had a deep influence on Weber's general outlook. But whatever their source, the mood they convey is sharply opposed to that of every good Marxist. Marxism is an optimistic philosophy. It affirms that the modern world can be understood in its entirety and offers the peace of mind that comes with such knowledge. It is an antidote to despair. Weber's heroic existentialism offers no relief of this kind. It brings those who have grasped the inexorableness of the process of rationalization back to the personal question of how to live in a godless world, and drains philosophy of its salvific power. Even Weber, who understood this process with a breadth of learning that no one since has matched, could not avoid the question or rely on his intellect to answer it.

My own mood began to waver as I wrote my dissertation. I started in a spirit of optimism. Indeed, I sought to reinforce my confidence by demonstrating that Weber's challenge to Marx can comfortably be met. In retrospect, I think I must have already felt some anxiety in this regard. Why else should I have been so eager to protect my optimism by building a defensive shield around it? But if I sought to put my anxiety to rest, living with Max Weber for two years had exactly the opposite effect.

On the surface at least, the argument of my dissertation was belligerently hopeful. But by the time I finished it, my optimism had been largely hollowed out. I no longer felt that understanding Marx, or any philosopher for that matter, would bring me the peace that I sought. Even if I could somehow get my mind around the meaning of the modern world as a whole—even if I were able to understand everything about its origins and organizing principles— what good would that do me? I would still be living my life, hoping to make and keep a few friends, in the shadow of an all-too-imminent extinction from which there could be no escape—into the arms of God or anything else. My thesis was about the conflict between the Kantian and Hegelian strands in Weber's thought. But beneath this philosophical question, another of a more personal kind was becoming more urgent. What was philosophy to me? I had once felt confident that if I just pursued it far enough, to the point where I was able to see my world with panoptical completeness, I would be saved from the mortal perplexities of life. That confidence had now begun to fail, in part on account of the influence of Weber's ideas, but more fundamentally, I suspect, as the result of a seven-year psychoanalysis I began the year I came to Yale to study philosophy.

Still, the question of the meaning of the modern world never lost its fascination for me. I took it with me from graduate school to law school, and then into my career as a law teacher. Like Weber, I studied commercial law and taught its intricacies to my students at Minnesota, Chicago and Yale. But every year I offered a seminar on one or another of my beloved philosophers, who gave me the chance to continue to indulge my old obsession with modernity. The readings differed but the question was always the same. What distinguishes our modern ideas of law and justice, of personal identity and political authority, from their premodern counterparts, and how are these related? I had come to accept Weber's diagnosis of our condition as one of homelessness and made his lonely ethic of self-reliance my own. Still, I continued to believe, in a halfhearted way at least, that the modern world must be an intelligible whole. The search for an understanding of modernity remained at the center of my philosophical reflections, but now in place of the optimism that had once informed them, I took a kind of negative delight in Weber's pessimism instead—in the conviction that anyone who truly understands what modernity means will be forced to admit that we live in a "godless and prophetless" age. Of course (though I didn't see it at the time) this reversal of mood kept alive, in an inverted form, the longing for intellectual salvation that had been my motive from the start. Some, I suppose, simply have no interest in salvation of any kind. It isn't an issue for them. My fierce Weberian denial of the possibility of finding it should have made it clear to me how deep my own interest remained.

In these years, I gradually came to a third view about the meaning of the modern world that held my allegiance for a time. If the first was the Marxist view of my youth, and the second the Weberian one that displaced it, the third might be called Burkean, after the writer who helped me organize my thoughts about the profession of law to which in middle age I found myself happily wedded.

The law is not a philosophical discipline. There are many philosophies *of* law, of course, but the work of judging and representing clients is a practical activity that requires virtues different from those demanded in any strictly theoretical inquiry. The latter calls for a complete devotion to the requirements of reason and allows, indeed compels, an inattention to the peculiarities of particular people and events. Philosophers must lift their sights above these things. Judges and lawyers have to pay attention to them. Their task is to bring the generalities of the law into alignment with the specific circumstances of the cases and clients before them. This calls for a species of critical reflection resembling that of philosophy but constrained, as philosophy is not, by the requirements of precedent. To do this work well, judges and lawyers need what Aristotle calls practical wisdom and is commonly described as good judgment. This is a temperamental quality as much as an intellectual one, and cannot be acquired merely by thinking. It is the product of a process of habituation. As a law professor and then dean, I defended the virtue of practical wisdom against developments in legal education that had imported, I believed, an inappropriately theoretical attitude into the training of lawyers. I urged that the profession not cut its ties to the ideal of good judgment that had always anchored its self-understanding and self-respect, for the sake of a science of law which, valuable as it might be in the realm of scholarly thought, was an incomplete, indeed misleading guide in that of practice.

From this, I drew a more general conclusion about the nature of good government. I cautioned against the dangers of what Edmund Burke calls the "metaphysical" approach to politics—the view that human affairs can and should be arranged on the basis of abstract principles that deliberately ignore all the accidental circumstances that distinguish one concrete controversy from another. I recommended a more cautious approach, one that acknowledges the value of inherited traditions and the difficulty of beginning anything new in political life. Those who want to make a responsible contribution to law or politics, I said, must steer their course by the gathered wisdom of the past, which always requires improvement, but within limits that philosophy cannot abide. They should avoid the temptation, against which Burke warned, of thinking they can write on a blank sheet, unburdened by the weight of precedent, which to a philosopher must always seem an irrational constraint.

This was a deliberately, willfully antiphilosophical view, and I defended it with as much energy as I had the Marxist and Weberian philosophies that had once attracted me precisely because of their aspiration to that complete and rigorous knowledge of things that I now mocked as a dangerous pretention. It was also an antimodern view, insofar as one equates modernity with the self-conscious rationalization of every branch of human activity, including especially that of law.

Even to me, this looked and felt like a dramatic change of course, even, perhaps, a betrayal. I loved the law and had made it my home. But then how should I regard the tribe of philosophers, to which I had also once belonged? I might have said, "I was once a philosopher but no longer am." Instead, I turned against philosophy with a philosophical passion. Others had warned against the same developments in the profession that I now attacked on the grounds that they threatened the honor and stability of its traditional values. But my criticisms, unlike theirs, were pitched at a philosophical level that betrayed my inability to let philosophy go, and with it the younger man who had staked everything on it. This ought to have made it clear to me that I had never really left philosophy behind. And the emphatic antimodernism of my Burkean complaints ought to have suggested, by their very passion, that the question of the meaning of the modern world remained as much alive for me as it had been thirty years before, when I believed I had discovered the answer to it in the philosophies of Hegel and Marx.

I began to glimpse that this was so in the fall of 1993. I had just written a book on the legal profession defending what I called the lawyer-statesman ideal and found myself drawn to the question of where this ideal fits into the older and larger contest between the champions of reason, on the one hand, and those who have been more cautious about its claims on the other. I wanted to see whether my own doubts about these claims could be related to wider themes in Western philosophy and placed within the broader debate about the meaning of modernity as an age of enlightenment.

I had only fragmentary thoughts about this and no confidence that I had anything coherent to say. But I felt increasingly gripped by a stubborn obsession with questions about the source and scope of my Burkean beliefs that could not themselves be answered on Burkean grounds. Stumbling along, with no clear idea of where I was going, I began writing a new book that I titled *Amor Fati,* with Nietzsche's use of the phrase in mind. I still have the manuscript in my desk. Before I could get too far with it, however, my colleagues at the Yale Law School invited me to serve as their dean, and quite apart from the honor and pleasure of the assignment, I felt a deep sense of relief that I could now put the manuscript aside, for in truth I was over-whelmed by the subject, whose depth I guessed but had no line to fathom.

The deanship lasted ten years. When I finished, I was fifty-nine. After a year's leave, I returned to teaching and joined the faculty of Yale's Directed Studies Program, a great books course for freshman, where, in the company of my bright and intensely curious students I began to explore again the tradition of Western philosophical thought that I had studied as an undergraduate and graduate student. It was the best reeducation I could have had. Reading Plato and my other old friends in an organized and undistracted way at a stage of life when the questions of philosophy had a mortal salience that they inevitably lacked the first time around, not only helped me to a deeper knowledge of the works themselves, but of my own ideas about the nature and limits of human reason and of the relevance of these to an understanding of the modern world. This was the subject of the stillborn book I had begun a decade before. Now I had the chance to think it through afresh, and to come to a more mature answer to the question that had preoccupied me through my Marxist, Weberian and Burkean phases. This book is the result.

I call it a work of theology in the wider sense indicated before. It is an essay on the nature of God and God's place in the modern world. The God it describes and defends is not the familiar one of Abraham but what I call the "God of sufficient reason"—the timeless intelligibility of the world as a whole, by which I mean not some local portion of it, like our planet or solar system, or even the entire known universe, but reality as such, which includes parallel universes, if they exist, as well as those that precede and follow ours in time.

Some will say this is no God at all, but that, I think, is a mistake. The divinity of any God, including mine, lies in its eternality, whether one conceives this as the eternality of a God beyond the world, or of the world itself. I have given up on the first but not the second and in what follows seek to persuade the reader that this second God is more than an option we are free to embrace or reject. My central contention is that all our most distinctively modern beliefs and practices necessarily assume the existence of the eternal God of sufficient reason, and that none of our deepest convictions in the realms of science, art and politics can be sustained without it.

Others have observed, correctly I think, that Hegel and Marx transferred the God of Abraham to the world of human affairs, in which they found a fulcrum of ultimate meaning—of Absolute Knowledge or Communal Peace—that functions as a substitute for the now-dead God who spoke to Moses from the burning bush. That is why their philosophies are sometimes described as secularized theologies. My God fits this description too, though the inspiration for it comes from other sources. Still, I would not have felt the need to organize my story around this or any other conception of God if the yearning for a connection to eternity were not as strong in me today as when I thought that I had found the way to its fulfillment in the dialectics of Karl Marx.

There is also, however, a Burkean side to my born-again paganism. Burke was not a theologian. Indeed, he had an allergy to the sort of theological arguments I pursue at length in these pages. But my reflections on the God that animates our most cherished modern ideals is shaped by what I would call a Burkean appreciation of how far short of the eternal reality of the world all our efforts to explain, display and honor it are bound to fall. This is perhaps an overly elaborate way of saying something obvious. Human beings are finite and their lives come to an end. Between even their greatest achievements and the God of the world, an infinite gap always remains. This lesson can be learned in many ways, and life enforces it on us, whether we have learned it or not. In my case, it was Burke's sober reflections on our frailties and pretensions that helped bring its philosophical implications home.

Burke was of course in many ways an antirational thinker. He sought to put a limit to the claims of reason and hedged them about with the unreasoned requirements of tradition and prescriptive authority. My starting point is exactly the opposite. I accept these claims in their most extravagant form. I am not an antirationalist but a hyperrationalist, for whom the powers of reason are boundless. Yet our finitude always confines us within the narrowest of limits, and if we forget this, and confuse our paltry understanding of the world with its infinite intelligibility, we are likely to stumble and be tempted to commit terrible crimes. This is the note of Burkean caution that leavens my endorsement of the idea that for every question there is an answer, even if we shall never find it. Anyone who has reflected on the inevitable shortfall between what reason invites and what, even at our best, we are able to do with it, is bound to view the human condition as one of inevitable disappointment, and hence to regard it with a measure of pathos. That is how I see it, and from this point of view the optimism of my young romance with Marx, who held the key, I thought, to an understanding of the world more complete than any I now know I shall ever have, seems forgivably naive.

But pathos is not the same as despair. The spirit of my born-again paganism is one of joy—the exact opposite of the mood that colors Weber's despairing account of our homelessness in a world without God.

Weber was right to define the modern age as the result of a process of rationalization. He was also right to think that the intelligibility of what happens in time ultimately depends on our ability to relate it to an eternal reality of some kind. But he was wrong to equate the triumph of reason with the disaccreditation of every conception of eternity and to insist that the question of how best to live in such a world cannot be answered except in purely personal and arbitrary terms. That he did so was a consequence of his lingering attachment to the belief that the only God who can guarantee the meaning and intelligibility of the world is one beyond it—a God to whom the men and women of our disenchanted age are no longer able to relate without making a sacrifice of the intellect that is repugnant to the deepest values of the rationalized world in which we live. This self-defeating view is what Nietzsche calls nihilism. It inevitably leads to despair.

But there is an alternative to nihilism that demands no sacrifice of this kind. There is a conception of eternity that is adequate to sustain the intelligibility of the world and to define an ethic for living, without a God of the sort the Abrahamic religions require. Nietzsche understood this, and bent all his efforts toward what he calls the redivinization of the world. He believed that success in this regard leads beyond despair to joy. Joy is the highest value in Nietzsche's philosophy as it is in the writing of his American contemporary Walt Whitman, whose poetry is a sustained hymn to joy. And it is the highest value in the more traditional metaphysics of their seventeenth-century predecessor Baruch Spinoza, who defines joy as the experience of a finite being as it progresses toward an ever more complete embrace of the eternity of the world as a whole.

These are my three exemplary born-again pagans. For each the world is God itself—*deus sive natura,* in Spinoza's famous phrase—not merely with regard to its general structure or form, as Aristotle believed, but infinitely so, as the religions of Abraham first taught us to see, hence a God no finite being can ever fully know or express. This is the pathos of finitude, from which we are not exempt. It rules out the optimism of those, like Hegel and Marx, whose philosophies promise an absolute knowledge no longer confined by these limits. But it offers in return the joyful assurance that at each step toward the unreachable goal we seek, our share in the divinity of the world is real and growing.

This is all we can ask. It represents a genuine form of homecoming, not as complete, to be sure, as the one that Aristotle made the basis of his immensely comforting philosophy, but also not to be confused with the homelessness that Weber defines as the essence of our unhappy condition. It is a way of being at home in the world not despite but because of its rationalization, and the joy such knowledge brings, contrary to what the nihilist says, is the true spirit of the science, art and politics that distinguish the modern age from every other. We are already at home in the world. The challenge is to understand why.

Introduction

This book is divided into four parts, "Gratitude," "Pride," "Salvation" and "Joy." If I had to summarize its argument in a sentence, I would say that joy is pride transmuted by the self-defeating doctrine of salvation proclaimed by the religion of unrequited gratitude. I hope that a patient reader who accompanies me to the end will understand this Delphic formula. But at the start it is bound to be incomprehensible. A provisional sketch of the substance and structure of my argument is therefore in order.

The first part of the book is the shortest. It is meant to serve as an overture to the rest. It introduces the book's main themes and sets the stage for the more detailed argument that follows.

I have chosen to begin with the subject of gratitude because it offers a particularly helpful approach to understanding what Nietzsche and others mean when they describe the defining experience of the modern age as one of "homelessness." My book defends a different and more joyful conception of modernity—one suggested by Nietzsche himself, among others. At the end, I return to the subject of gratitude and reassess its meaning in light of this different conception. But first it is important to understand the nature of the illness that homelessness represents. The illness is spiritual and any cure for it must be so as well. To see what is at stake, it is useful to begin with some general reflections on the good of gratitude and its diminished place in public life today.

Gratitude is inseparable from love. It is what a well-adjusted person feels in response to the love of others. The capacity to acknowledge and accept their love awakens a longing to offer one's own in return. This capacity may be compromised or lost. A person may become so resentful of her reliance on the love of others that she recoils and looks for ways to make do without it. A certain degree of resentfulness at our dependence on what lies outside us, including the love of the human beings on whose care we depend completely in the first phase of life, is a permanent feature of the human condition. We all wish to be more independent than we ever are. But if this wish reaches a pathological intensity, it expresses itself as envy, the poisonous and self-destructive antithesis of gratitude, and puts an obstacle in the way of making an adequate return for the love one has received. The inability to do this is a source of disappointment and despair.

The love to which gratitude is a healthy response must be distinguished from both entitlement and luck. Love is never something to which we are entitled, and unlike mere good fortune, is a gift that comes with its recipient in mind. This is clearest in the case of the love of parents for their children. Parental love is always accompanied by feelings of hostility and resentment. But it is rarely missing altogether, and the good a child derives from it is neither an accident nor a benefit to which he or she has a claim of right. It is true that some philosophers have attempted to transform love into a claim of this kind by imagining a contract among the generations which provides that each shall be cared for by its predecessor on the condition that it care for its successor in turn. On this view, love becomes the repayment of a debt in disguise. But this contradicts the belief—on which our greatest hopes and deepest fears are founded—that the love of others is something real, and eliminates the opportunity to make a return for the gift of their love that is anything more than a *quid pro quo* for benefits received. It destroys the possibility of being a loving person oneself.

Without the gift of love, moreover, the world can never be a home. No amount of good fortune can make it one, nor can any system of rights, however elaborate and punctiliously enforced. My rights enhance my power. They increase my self-control. But in the absence of love, they leave me to face the world alone, in the company of other anxious and self-protective men and women, for each of whom the world is only a wilderness of opportunity and risk. Love alone has the power to make the world a home that welcomes and supports me, imperfectly at least, and to clear a space within it for the gratitude that is expressed in the simplest and most complex forms of thanks-giving, without which no human fulfillment is complete.

I develop these themes in chapter 1. In chapter 2, I add another.

The citizens of every modern Western state possess an ever-growing arse-nal of rights. As the realm of rights has grown, those of luck and gift have shrunk. More of the benefits that once were left to chance or charity are today viewed as entitlements to which their recipients have an enforceable claim. As a result, the idea that one should depend on the love of others for any of the things that are needed to lead a comfortable and fulfilling life has lost much of its legitimacy, in the public sphere at least.

The corresponding belief that gratitude is an important public virtue has become less credible as well. The opposing idea that citizens enjoy the bene-fits they do as a matter of right, and have no reason to be grateful to anyone for their enjoyment, has been gaining momentum since the French Revolu-tion. It is true that love and gratitude still figure importantly in our private lives, but even here their public devaluation casts a shadow over their place and importance in human experience generally. As a result, the very thing that makes the world a home, and releases our powers of creative thankful-ness in response, is today increasingly viewed as a merely private value that must be carefully confined lest it corrupt the system of entitlements that is the main repository of our highest and most widely shared ideals.

The growth of the realm of rights is motivated by a longing for control. Luck and love are forms of vulnerability. Each is a kind of dependence. Their conversion to rights represents an increase in our independence or autonomy. This is something that human beings have always desired. But the hypertro-phic expansion of the sphere of entitlements in the modern West is motivated by a desire for control of a peculiarly exaggerated kind. It is the result of spiri-tual as well as practical needs. It is driven by the longing to possess the abso-lute power of an omnipotent being that is able to produce any result it chooses merely by willing to do so—to create the world with a word. This is the God of the Christian religion, whose theology has been the nursery bed within which the civilization of the West has matured.

Along with many other features of modern Western civilization, the tri-umph of entitlement over luck and love is an expression of the urgent longing of the obedient but unhappy children of the Christian God to appropriate his heavenly powers. The assault on love and gratitude that has made us home-less in the world is the result of a centuries-long campaign to become the

God of the Christian religion. This goal can never be reached, of course, but that only intensifies its appeal. Moreover, it is not some force external to Christian belief that is responsible for the effort to unseat God but—paradoxically—the internal demands of its own theology. To be at home in the world again, we must release ourselves from these demands, which have outlived the authority of the religion that installed them at the heart of our now disenchanted civilization.

In chapter 3, I elaborate these ideas in a preliminary way by describing those features of Christian theology that account for its self-disenchantment.

All the Abrahamic religions make gratitude a central virtue. Each views the existence of the world as a divine gift motivated by God's infinite love. But Christianity attaches special importance to this virtue. That is because of the doctrine of the Incarnation. In addition to all his other gifts, Paul declares, God sacrificed his own son for our sake, so that we might be eligible for an immortality from which we would otherwise be excluded on account of our original parents' disobedience to God's first command. The only appropriate response to a gift so large, so intimate and shockingly vivid, is thankfulness even greater than any Adam had reason to feel before the Fall for the creation of himself and Eve and their location in the Garden of Eden.

This is one way in which Christianity differs from Judaism and Islam. Another is its essentially theological character. Judaism and Islam of course have theologies too. But their fundamental orientation is orthopractical. Both are religions whose adherents are distinguished, first and most importantly, by their observance of certain ritual and legal requirements, rather than by the affirmation of a set of rigorously prescribed beliefs. Christianity, by contrast, has always defined itself in orthodoxical terms. To be a Christian means to hold specific beliefs about man's relation to God. The correct identification of these beliefs has therefore been a matter of supreme importance from the very start for those who pray to the God on the cross.

Systematic reflection on the meaning of the crucifixion led Paul to a heightened emphasis on gift and gratitude. This eventually took the form of the doctrine of grace. The Christian concept of grace has only imperfect parallels in Jewish and Muslim thought. Rigorously interpreted, it compels the conclusion that no human gratitude can ever be adequate to the gift of God's self-imposed suffering. God's human creatures remain forever incapable of returning his love with one as good and great. Dwelling on the shortfall between these became at a very early stage the essence of Christian piety, and every suggestion that man's love and God's can somehow be made commensurable was rejected as an expression of pride—the root of all sin.

This conclusion condemns those who embrace it to incompetence in the love that matters most. None of us ever loves anyone or anything as well as we wish to do. But the Christian doctrine of grace not only burdens its proponents with an inadequacy greater than any they ever experience in their relations with other human beings. It also insists that they keep this inadequacy before their eyes at all times and make its affirmation their highest value—the key to salvation itself. The familiar human longing to give thanks for the love one has received with a love of an equal if necessarily imperfect kind is thus not merely denied but condemned by the doctrine of grace. The condemnation of this longing arouses anger at the one who makes it a sin to feel it, and stirs the jealous wish to take his place. By raising the value of gratitude to an unprecedented height, the Christian religion thereby becomes the breeding ground of pride in its most extravagant form. It drives those that it condemns to an unparalleled disappointment in love to take their revenge, as Satan sought to do, by usurping the place of the God who has done this to them. For this satanic wish, Christianity itself is responsible.

It is also responsible for easing the way to its fulfillment.

Like Jews and Muslims, Christians insist that God is separate from the world. This is a fundamental article of faith in all the Abrahamic religions. But the orthopractical orientation of Judaism and Islam helps keep God in touch with his human creatures. God may not be present in the world, but his laws ensure that he remains close by in the daily activities of eating, bathing and sex. The orthodoxical preoccupations of the Christian religion have exactly the opposite effect. They strengthen the resolve to place God at an ever-greater distance from the world. Paradoxically, this is true not despite but because of the doctrine of the Incarnation. This links the Christian God more closely to the world than his Jewish and Muslim counterparts. But just for that reason, it intensifies the need to defend God's supernatural status and motivates his followers to insist with growing passion on his remoteness from the world. In the end, the God of the Christian religion becomes an unknown and unknowable being, an "X," as Kant says, whose existence must be assumed but about which nothing can be said or even thought. When this happens, the place of God falls vacant, leaving an empty notional space for his envious human subjects to fill.

The theology of the Christian religion, with its distinctive emphasis on divine grace and its rigorous insistence on God's separation from the world, thus simultaneously intensifies man's rebellious wish to be God and creates the conceptual room for him to do so. The result is the occupation by man of God's role—or more exactly, since this can never happen in reality, the legitimation of the aspiration to do so. In this way, though the goal cannot be reached, it comes to function as a regulative ideal, from whose point of view every form of human dependence, including the one that love entails, seems an obstacle to surmount. From the standpoint of the omnipotent God whose powers we long to assume, and have given ourselves permission to strive to attain, the love of other human beings is just another of the countless dependencies we must struggle to overcome. The growth of the realm of rights at the expense of that of gift and love is one particularly telling expression of this ambition, to which Christian theology itself gives both energy and opportunity. Our loveless world of rights is the product of the religion of absolute love.

This is the poisonous fruit of the Christian religion. But if its own demands have been responsible for the disenchantment of the world and for the triumph of a political morality deformed by the insatiable demand to be a God in comparison with whose boundless powers our own seem not merely a limit but a disgrace, this same religion is also the source of the modern ideals to which we are most deeply attached. These all spring from a belief in the intelligibility and worth of the individual. This belief is a consequence of the idea of divine creation. All the Abrahamic religions affirm that God created the world from nothing. But it was the Christian proponents of this idea who, following the lead of Philo Judaeus, first worked out its implications in a rigorous way.

The great metaphysical systems of pagan antiquity all viewed the world as what Max Weber calls an "enchanted garden"—a cosmos suffused with the real presence of the eternal and divine. Judaism broke this cosmos apart. It separated the world from its creator and declared the first to be the gift of the second. The Christian interpretation of the meaning of this gift strengthened the demand that God be placed at an ever-greater distance from the world and intensified the yearning to escape the inhuman requirements of the doctrine of grace by seizing God's place. Yet this same theology also bequeathed to its disenchanted heirs a belief in the infinite value of every individual in the world, even after the God that created it had ceased to exist in their hearts and minds.

This is the premise on which modern science, art and politics all rest.

The assumption that the endless inquiries of science will be rewarded at each step by a deeper understanding of the world reflects the belief that its laws are merely provisional statements of the infinite intelligibility of every-thing that happens within it. The confidence that even ordinary things con-tain a boundless store of beauty is inspired by the same belief. So, too, is our commitment to diversity as a good in itself, and to a distinctively democratic form of political friendship founded upon it. All these ideals spring from the conviction that the intelligibility, beauty and worth of individuals can never be plumbed. The belief that this is so is entailed by the idea of creation from nothing and retains its validity even when the God that once sustained it is dead and gone. It is the precious and inspiring fruit of the Christian religion.

This leads to an obvious and important question. Is it possible to keep the good fruit without the bad? Put differently, can we ever be at home in the world on terms that are compatible with our modern ideals?

If we could return to Aristotle's divine cosmos, even in thought, it might be possible to be at home in the world again. But that is a cure no one today could accept. Aristotle's metaphysics denies the infinite value of the individ-ual. Like all the intellectualist philosophies of pagan antiquity his rests on the presumed validity of the distinction between form and matter, which ren-ders individuality as such worthless and unknowable. In this respect, it is at war with all our most cherished modern beliefs.

Aristotle's world was a home for man because it offered him an immedi-ate share in the eternal order of things. This was taken from us when eternity was transposed to a God beyond the world. At that point, we became, as Augustine says, pilgrims in the world, looking forward to a homecoming in heaven after death. And when this heaven was taken from us too, we became homeless in a final and complete sense.

Aristotle's world seems immensely comforting by comparison. But by equating its eternity with the forms of things alone, he rules out the possibil-ity that individuals can ever be knowable or valuable in their own right. This is what the doctrine of creation from nothing compels us to assume. It is what we still assume today. Hence, though Aristotle's world beckons us like a child-hood dream, it can never be a home of the kind we grownups require. To be at home in the world on the terms we now demand, it is not enough that the world be eternal, as Aristotle supposed. Its eternality must extend to the in-dividuality of every thing in it, even the most inconsequential and fleeting. Aristotle would have thought this idea absurd. But it is the key to overcoming the malaise of the modern age in a way that frees us from having to choose, as some say we must, between God, on the one hand, and science, art and democ-racy on the other.

There is a theology that avoids this terrible choice—one that reconciles the longing to be close to God with the ideals of our secular age. It is the theology neither of Aristotle nor of the Christian thinkers who transformed his cosmos into God's creation, though it resembles each in a certain way. Like both, it equates God with eternity, and like Aristotle's in particular, with the divinity of the world itself. In the latter respect, it differs fundamentally from the Christian conception of God as a personal deity defined by his separation from the world he creates. But unlike Aristotle's God, the one affirmed by this third theology is identical to the world in its entirety, and not merely its shape or form. It borrows this idea from Christian theology, whose God invests every particle of his creation with intelligibility, beauty and value. This is the most important metaphysical implication of the doctrine of creation from nothing, which erases all barriers to God's power and thereby dissolves the distinction between form and matter on which Aristotle's theology rests. One might therefore describe the relation among these three theologies by saying that for Aristotle, the world is inherently but not wholly divine; for Christians, it is not inherently divine, though God's divinity is omnipresent in it in a derivative way; and for the proponents of my third theology, the world is both inherently divine and infinitely so, down to the last jot and tittle.

This is what I mean by born-again paganism. Some may object that I have simply given pantheism a new name. There are two reasons for preferring the one I have chosen. The first is that the word "pantheism" carries too much baggage. It has too many familiar connotations. This makes a fresh approach to the subject more difficult. The second and more important reason is that it covers too much ground. "Pantheism" is a general term that may be applied to any metaphysics that identifies God with the world, Aristotle's included. By contrast, "born-again paganism" suggests the distinctive combination of classical and Christian ideas that sets this specifically modern form of pantheism apart from its ancient predecessors, and invites the question of how they can be joined.

Regardless of the name one chooses for it, a pantheism of this modern sort is possible only after two conditions have been met. The first is the dissolution of the distinction between form and matter on which Aristotle's metaphysics is based. The doctrine of creation from nothing accomplishes this result. The second is the disenchantment of the Christian religion, which draws the consequences of this doctrine with the greatest possible precision. What I call born-again paganism is therefore of necessity a post-Christian phenomenon. For it to be conceivable at all, the Christian theology that contributes one of its two essential ideas must first have undermined its own authority and with it, the idea of a God beyond the world.

In the last part of the book, I explore the implications of this third theology in some detail, inspired by the ideas of three writers in particular. The first and most important is Spinoza. The others are Nietzsche and Walt Whitman. The list could be expanded. I have chosen these three because I have found each to be a particularly helpful guide in understanding the possibilities for redivinizing the world in one of the three spheres I explore—those of science, art and politics respectively. With their help, I hope to persuade the reader that my born-again paganism is not merely an imaginable or even a plausible theology, but the one on whose basis work in all three spheres today actually proceeds, though the lingering Christian prejudices that Nietzsche diagnosed with such precision make this hard to see.

Those who follow the path to which my three born-again pagans show the way will be released from the grip of nihilistic despair, which is encouraged by the belief that eternity is nowhere to be found, either in this world or beyond it, however well-masked such feelings may be by a cheerful pragmatism that smirks at the mention of God. And they will be rewarded with some experience, at least, of the joy that is the highest value for all three, which springs from the knowledge that the infinite God of the world is present in all things.

The pagan philosopher and Christian saint know joy as well, and in their case too it is awakened by the presence of the eternal and divine. But the joy of the born-again pagan is different from theirs in one crucial respect. Both the philosopher and the saint affirm the possibility of crossing the divide that separates man from God—the first in this life, and the second in a life to come. For those who see the world as Spinoza, Nietzsche and Whitman do, this possibility no longer exists. There is no life after this one, and no finite being can ever adequately comprehend or represent all the truth and beauty that lies even in the least of things. That is something a finite being could do only in case it were able to view the world as a whole under what Spinoza calls "the aspect of eternity"—only in case it *were* the world and not a being within it. The reasons why both the philosopher and saint believe this gap can be closed are complex; we shall examine them in due course. For the moment, it is enough to note that the joy our born-again pagan writers promise by restoring our connection to God is tempered by a disappointment that can never be overcome. Its acknowledgment is a sign of maturity.

Accompanied by the joyful recognition that it is possible to live with an ever-deepening if always incomplete understanding of the infinite and eternal God of the world, it is the best way we have of preparing to die.

In this mortal enterprise, we shall forever be dependent on the love of other human beings, which is always a gift when it comes. If we are able to receive it as such, without resentment or envy or the wish to rid ourselves of the dependence that love by its nature entails, we may find fulfillment in the creative expressions of gratitude through which we give thanks to those who have cleared and held open a space in which we are able to approach the God of the world. We may find that we can be at home for a time in its overwhelming reality, without being angry because we are finite and it is not. We may find pleasure in working collaboratively with our predecessors and successors in an endless program of home improvement. And we may be happy in the knowledge that we are able to love as well as we are loved because the love in question is that of human beings for one another, and not of men for a God beyond the world whose gifts exceed our power to give thanks. To see and accept all this is what it means to be at home in the world on terms consistent with our modern ideals.

These are the main themes of my *Confessions*. I adumbrate some and anticipate others in part I ("Gratitude"). Everything that follows is an explication and defense. This is divided into three further parts.

The first consists of the seven chapters of part II ("Pride"). These are mainly devoted to a reconstruction of the pagan theology that underlies Aristotle's account of the world and man's place in it. Part II concludes by briefly exploring the ideas—advanced by Plato and increasingly prominent in late Stoic thought—that prepared the way for the radically different theology of Augustine and his Christian successors.

Part III ("Salvation") then traces the self-destructive arc of this theology, from Augustine's canonical formulation of it to Max Weber's nihilistic proclamation that we live in a "godless and prophetless" age.

Finally, in part IV ("Joy") I explore the meaning of the born-again pagan theology that fuses elements of these other two, and describe its relevance to the work of modern science, art and politics, using Spinoza, Nietzsche and Whitman as my guides. In the "Epilogue" I offer a few reflections on living and dying.

This broad outline may be filled in as follows.

I begin my discussion of Aristotle's theology with an account of what he calls "greatness of soul." Nothing reveals more clearly the distance between Aristotle's idea of human fulfillment and its Christian counterpart. The great-souled man is distinguished from others by the pride he takes in his independence from misfortune, honors, and the condescending generosity of those with superior power and wealth. For Aristotle, the pride that such a man takes in himself is a mark of his supreme well-being—the "crown of the virtues," as he puts it.

This is bound to seem perverse from a Christian point of view. For Christians, pride is the root of all sin. To them, Aristotle's celebration of it must therefore appear an inversion of the true order of values and the most telling symptom of the moral and spiritual deficiency of his pagan view of human flourishing, which amounts to a philosophy of pride (hence the title of part II).

I continue my discussion of Aristotle's ethics in chapter 5 by exploring his account of gifts and gratitude. The great-souled man is a lordly dispenser of favors. Others depend on him, not the other way around. He has more presence or reality than they, and this is the source of the pride he takes in himself. The idea that he should acknowledge his dependence on anyone else, let alone dwell on it obsessively as Christians are instructed to do, is hateful to a man of this sort. To him, it is the symptom of a servile attitude toward life, appropriate only in those who lack his self-possession.

This judgment rests on a theology that I begin to elaborate in chapter 6. Aristotle's great-souled man has more reality because the powers that make him a man are more actively at work in his life than in those of his inferiors. For Aristotle, reality is activity, and activity the energetic deployment of those powers that define one as a being of a certain kind—a man or fly or anything else.

The individual members of every kind, with the exception of the heavenly bodies, realize the powers peculiar to them to a greater or lesser degree and only for a limited time. Then they disappear and are replaced by others like them. But the form of their kind remains forever the same. To the extent that individuals succeed in actively realizing the form appropriate to them, they acquire at least a temporary share in the eternal and divine. According to Aristotle, everything in the world strives to do this, and does so within the limits its form allows. Human beings are no exception. We, too, yearn to share in the God of the world. What distinguishes us from other beings—from stones and drops of water at the lower end of things and the ever-circling stars above—is not the presence in us of this yearning but the fact that we have more than one way of fulfilling it.

The first is reproduction. Every plant and animal on earth seeks to participate in the eternal order of the world by making a copy of itself. Human beings of course do this as well. But we have two additional ways of pursuing immortality that are to unique to us alone. One is politics and the other is philosophy. I discuss these distinctively human forms of immortalization in chapter 7.

As between these two, the second is preeminent on account of the completeness with which it allows those who pursue it to achieve their goal. The philosophical life culminates in contemplation and the human beings who reach this peak attain the very highest level of activity that it is possible for a being of any kind to achieve. Aristotle calls this activity "thought thinking thought," by which he means the active being-at-work of the inherent mindedness or intelligibility of the world itself. This is a difficult but important idea. It holds the key to understanding the whole of Aristotle's philosophy, including his account of how it is best for human beings to live. Chapter 7 concludes with a portrait of the philosophical life and a description of the joy of contemplation, in which those who experience it become for a limited time, but as fully as any being can, the eternal intelligibility of the world, which is not the gift of a God beyond it but just the wonderful way things are.

The God of the world that a philosopher becomes in these moments of maximum lucidity is not one to whom he owes thanks. Does he then have no reason to be grateful to anyone? And does the great-souled man, who strives to give and never take, have no grounds for gratitude either? The lives of these two represent the pinnacles of human excellence in the realms of thought and action respectively. Each, moreover, is characterized by its supreme self-sufficiency. Yet each is attainable only within a human world that others have prepared and sustained. No one can lead a life of intellectual or practical virtue on his or her own. We all need the friendship of others to do this.

Friendship is the care of one human being for another for the latter's own sake. Without such selfless love—of parents for children, teachers for students and citizens for the cities to which they belong—the human world would collapse, and with it the possibility of attaining the highest states of excellence available to those within it. These states are defined by their independence, but the men and women who reach them have reason to be grateful to their friends, living and dead, for the love that enables them to do so. And because this is a human love and not that of a God who transcends our powers of reciprocation, it can be returned in a measure as good and great by teaching others to think and helping them acquire the virtues that are needed to live a proud and independent life in active service to the good of their communities. In this sense, though Aristotle's philosophy of pride exalts the value of self-sufficiency, it not only leaves room for a human ideal of friendship but requires one. I describe this ideal in chapter 8.

In the final chapters of part II, I explore a different tendency in pagan philosophy that begins with Plato and is powerfully evident in the Stoic tradition. Without repudiating Aristotle's fundamental equation of God with mind, or the value he assigned to self-sufficiency, these thinkers pioneered a view of the human soul that put increasing pressure on Aristotle's conception of divinity and helped to prepare the way for the appearance of a radically different theology that defines God not as mind but will.

Chapter 9 focuses on Plato, who I call the first cosmopolitan. In the *Republic* and elsewhere, Plato teaches us that we can be free anywhere in the world if we liberate ourselves from the seductive blandishments of opinion. Beyond the world of opinion and appearance, lies the realm of eternal forms. These cannot be seen with the eye of the body but only that of the mind, which is bound by a kind of kinship to the forms it strives to reach in thought. This is the most important task that any of us has and we must devote all our energies to it. If we succeed we shall be saved from the stupidities and torments of the world, as Socrates says at the end of the *Republic*.

The early books of the *Republic* constitute a sustained attack on Homer's theology. Homer's world is thoroughly enchanted. The gods occupy a high place in it, but are not outside of or beyond it. They appear and act within the realm of human affairs. The new Socratic teaching produces a sweeping disenchantment of the world. Now the sphere of deathless beings is no longer visible. The world that we see is a spectacle of unreal flux. We must learn to look through it to the true world beyond—to live as if we were already dead, as Socrates says in the *Phaedo*.

In Aristotle's theology, the world of moving, visible things becomes divine once again. In this sense, Aristotle may be said to vindicate Homer's world against Plato's attack, on a higher metaphysical plane. But the separation of God from the world, which Plato's philosophy inaugurates, could not be repaired. Many of the philosophers writing and teaching in the centuries between Aristotle and Augustine accepted this distinction and carried it to even greater extremes. The so-called Neoplatonists followed Plato explicitly in this regard. Others adopted core elements of his philosophy as well. One Platonic theme in particular was of great importance to writers in the Stoic tradition and became especially appealing to the Christian theologians who put their philosophy to use in constructing an entirely new conception of man's relation to God. This was the idea of an invisible interior life attuned to an invisible order of truth that lies beyond the realm of sense experience, in which men appear (but only appear!) to suffer and thrive on account of forces outside their control, and occupy a graded hierarchy of positions of power and authority defined by the false standards of the world.

In chapter 10, I explore the implications of this idea, focusing on the writings of Epictetus and Seneca. For the first, the key to human happiness lies in the notion of a power in the soul that rules over sense experience and enables us to detach ourselves from the care we normally feel for external things. For the second, the existence of this same power implies the equality of all human beings—even of masters and slaves. Together, the Stoic ideas of freedom and equality prepare the way for their reinterpretation in still more radical terms by later Christian thinkers. Yet for the Stoics themselves these ideas remained within the orbit of pagan thought, since the power in question continued to be conceived, even by late writers like Seneca, as that of reason or mind. In order for their views to be adapted to Augustine's new theology, a further, wholly unpagan idea was required—that of the will, which first enters Western philosophy as the human analogue to the divine power of creation that Augustine takes as his starting point in justifying God's ways to man.

Part III commences with the idea of creation. In chapter 11, I explain the difference between this idea and those of production and generation, the only two the Greeks and Romans had to account for the phenomena of beginning and change.

According to Aristotle, the idea that something can come from nothing is absurd. For Augustine, by contrast, it is essential. Without it, God's grandeur as a world-transcending creator cannot be adequately expressed. But this raises a problem that Aristotle never had to confront. If there is nothing in the world that God did not create, is he then responsible for the evil in it too? Augustine's famous answer, which I explore in chapter 12, is that man, not God, is responsible for the evil in the world. This requires, however, that human beings be radically free, since only then can they be held accountable for their acts. Augustine draws this conclusion and offers an analysis of human freedom that becomes foundational for the entire tradition of Western thought. The centerpiece of this analysis is his idea of the will, which Augustine defines as the cause of itself and models on God's power of creation from nothing.

But if the invention of the will solves one problem by relieving God of responsibility for the world's evil, it creates another. If human beings are truly free, how can God's omnipotence be complete? Either it is, in which case, having created beings with wills whose exact use he can foresee, God is responsible for the results, along with everything else. Alternatively, if human beings really have the power to initiate a new chain of events, the spontaneity of this power puts it beyond that of God to know or control in advance. Either God's own freedom is boundless, and there is no room in creation for any other will than his; or human beings have wills too and share responsibility for the world with God, making them junior partners in creation, which destroys the omnipotence his divinity demands. The problem is that Augustine's theology requires both divine omnipotence *and* human freedom, between which there can be no accommodation. In the end, it is necessary to give one of these two ideas priority over the other, and once one does, there is no stable resting point short of the complete obliteration of the idea that has been put in second place.

Augustine provides the resources for both strategies. He invents the idea of the will, whose later champions use it to depreciate and then eliminate God's role in the world altogether. He also extends and deepens the idea of grace, which in the rigorous formulation that he gives it in his late writings against the Pelagians, leads to the abolition of human freedom and an iron predestinarianism that saves God's dignity at man's expense. After Augustine, all Christian thought oscillates between these two poles, until the first decisively vanquishes the second, leaving behind a world engorged with human freedom in which God is nowhere to be found. I develop these themes in chapter 13.

In chapter 14, I introduce another. According to Aristotle, every individual is a combination of form and matter. The first makes it a kind of thing; the latter, an individual member of its kind. Aristotle's ethics, physics and metaphysics all assume the validity of this distinction. One of its implications is that the individuality of individuals is neither knowable nor valuable. For Aristotle, only the form of a thing is intelligible. It alone has beauty and is worthy of praise. As a result, Aristotle's epistemology, aesthetics and ethics are all necessarily formalistic.

But the distinction between form and matter cannot be reconciled with the idea of creation from nothing. This distinction may be a helpful guide to understanding the work of a craftsman who imposes a form on preexisting material. But God's creation of the world cannot be understood in these terms. God's creativity knows no bounds. There is absolutely nothing in God's creation that is not "informed" by God's will. The intelligibility, beauty and value of God's creatures are therefore not limited to their general properties but extend to their individuality too. The world is informed all the way down.

The idea of creation compels this conclusion, which conflicts with the most basic tendencies of Aristotle's philosophy. It thereby opens the way to a range of distinctively modern beliefs that all start from the assumption that the intelligibility and value of the world has no limit, and prepares the ground for a metaphysics whose fundamental premise is that the world is both inherently and infinitely divine. But to reach this metaphysics, the idea of creation, which first forces us to assume that the individuality of individuals is something real and hence knowable, must be abandoned. This idea is the cornerstone of the Christian religion. Its abandonment therefore means the end of Christianity as a serious metaphysical option. In the remaining chapters of part III, I explain how the demise of Christian belief is brought about by tensions inherent to it and already evident in the conflict between Augustine's doctrines of human freedom and divine grace.

According to Aristotle, the world not only has an order. Its order is both necessary and eternal. The world could not be other than it is. For anyone who accepts the idea of divine creation, this is a blasphemous proposition. The world may have exactly the order that Aristotle claims it does, and the motions of things in it may conform to the principles he elaborates in the *Physics* and elsewhere. But the fact that it does is a contingent one. God could have created a world different than the one he did, or none at all. Any other view compromises God's freedom in a way that no Abrahamic philosopher can accept. For any philosopher of this sort, the existence of the world as a whole must be viewed as a contingent state of affairs. This basic point came to be expressed in terms of the distinction between essence and existence. It is not of the essence of the world to exist (as it is of God). As best we can tell, Avicenna was the first to formulate this distinction in a rigorous way. By the time Aquinas wrote his *Summa Theologiae,* two and a half centuries later, it had become a basic premise of Christian thought. I discuss the meaning of the distinction in chapter 15.

In chapter 16, I examine Aquinas' theology in more detail. Like others of his generation and the one before, Aquinas was profoundly influenced by Aristotle's treatises on nature and human life, which had recently reappeared in the Latin-speaking West, after an absence of nearly six centuries. Indeed, he was *so* influenced by Aristotle's views, that he was tempted to embrace not only the latter's account of how things in the world actually work, but his necessitarianism as well—the belief that the existence of the world is as necessary as that of the God who creates it. I call this the "pagan temptation," and describe how close Aquinas came to yielding to it.

The following chapter recounts the powerful orthodox reaction against the creeping paganism of Aquinas and others, some of whom went even farther in this direction than he did. From the perspective of their critics, these neo-Aristotelian Christians threatened to destroy God's freedom by binding him in chains of reason. To liberate God, they claimed, the primacy of his will must be restored. This was the central ambition of the theologians who led the so-called "voluntarist" campaign against the necessaritarianism of the Latin Averroists. I outline some of the key metaphysical and moral implications of their movement in chapter 17, beginning with the Condemnation of 1277 and focusing on the theology of William of Ockham.

In chapters 18 and 19, I turn to Luther, whose Reformation theology represents the culmination of the voluntarist tradition. Luther exalts God's dignity to the greatest conceivable extent. He does this by reaffirming the Augustinian doctrine of grace in the most radical terms possible. The result is that human freedom disappears as completely in Luther's theology as in Augustine's later writings. For Luther, Aristotle is the worst of all philosophers, and the Christian theologians who follow him are as guilty of the sin of pride as the Roman Church, which teaches that men can bend God's will by supplicating him with offerings of one kind or another. Luther seeks to save the awesome freedom of the Christian God from these human entanglements, with a theology of grace as unyielding as Augustine's own.

Luther's antithesis in this respect is Kant. Kant grasped the other pole of Augustine's theology. He affirmed the value of human freedom with a rigor and consistency that has never been matched. Kant remained a religious man, of course. He never outgrew the devotional spirit of the Pietistic milieu in which he had been raised. But if Luther's problem was to reconcile human freedom with divine power, Kant's was precisely the opposite, and just as Luther solved his problem by abandoning the first of these ideas, Kant solved his by relinquishing the second—or rather, to put it in Kantian terms, by redefining our belief in an all-powerful "author" of the world as a "postulate" of practical reason that human beings require in order to make sense of the idea of the highest good, as morality itself delivers it to them. In Kant's philosophy, the presence of God dwindles down to an absolute minimum, preparing the way for his complete disappearance in the later secular philosophies that embraced Kant's ideal of human freedom without any dependence, even a notional one, on the God of the Christian religion. In chapters 20, 21 and 22, I follow Kant's reflections on freedom and grace, and explain his subordination of the second to the first.

Kant and Luther resolve what I call the Augustinian dilemma in opposite ways. It might seem that each of their solutions is as plausible as the other, and that one is therefore free to choose between them. But the Kantian or post-Kantian endorsement of human freedom at the expense of God's omnipotence has a built-in advantage over the Lutheran alternative. Or rather, it has two advantages, one psychological and the other logical.

Psychologically, Kant's philosophy of autonomy satisfies our envious longing to usurp God's position as an independent and all-powerful being. Logically, it carries to an absolute limit the principle that nothing can be known or said about God, thereby ensuring that God's position remains vacant so that this usurpation can proceed without hindrance. Together, these give Kant's radicalized version of human autonomy, which deepens and extends one of Augustine's defining values and obliterates the other, a leg up in its competition with Luther's reversed weighting of them. Shorn of the last remaining vestiges of Christian belief, the Kantian view has triumphed over the Lutheran, and today provides what many consider the best philosophical justification for the modern secular understanding of freedom, equality and human rights.

Its victory has not been easy or unopposed, however. The French Revolution gave the ideal of human freedom a practical authority as great as the philosophical one that Kant bestowed upon it. But some viewed the Revolution as a crime. To them its ideals represented the reassertion of pride on a world historical scale. This was how Joseph de Maistre interpreted its meaning. Maistre was the first great reactionary thinker of the modern age. As a Catholic, he loathed the Protestant reformers who in his view had done so much to undermine the authority of the established Church. But Maistre was closer to Luther than he thought. Like Luther, his chief ambition was to affirm the power and glory of God against man's prideful presumptions, now grown, he believed, to satanic proportions. This was the leitmotif of all his reactionary writings, which inaugurated the fourth great wave of Augustinian piety in Western thought (after Augustine himself, the voluntarist revolt of the fourteenth century, and Luther's radical restatement of the Augustinian doctrine of grace two centuries later).

Like Augustine and Luther before him, Maistre drew the contrast between human freedom and divine grace in uncompromising terms and gave the latter absolute precedence over the former. Indeed, in Maistre's theology, every assertion of human freedom becomes further proof of our utter lack of it. This is the heart of his attack on the French Revolution. According to Maistre, the revolutionaries believe they are acting freely, but all the while they are playing the parts assigned to them in God's preordained plan of redemption. Maistre extends this theological indictment of the Revolution to a wholesale condemnation of modernity as such. We live today, he says, in an age of universal pride. This is the defining characteristic of the Enlightenment, whose political and cultural assault on God must eventually be punished, as Adam's individual act was, by a measure of suffering commensurate with the crime.

Others followed in Maistre's footsteps. Like Maistre, they viewed the modern age as an apocalyptic war between freedom and grace—between man's sinful aspiration to be the master of his fate and God's endless and undeserved charity, for which we all ought to be abysmally grateful. One particularly influential follower was the nineteenth-century writer and diplomat, Juan Donoso Cortes. But Maistre's most important descendants are Carl Schmitt and Martin Heidegger. In Heidegger's writings especially, Maistre's Augustinian categories are deeply suppressed. They have been transmuted into abstract philosophical ideas whose Christian provenance is no longer apparent. But like Schmitt's political theology, Heidegger's account of what he calls "the oblivion of Being" is in essence a refined restatement of the old Augustinian drama of fall and redemption through grace, motivated by the same hatred of human pride that drove Maistre and Luther before him.

For a time at least, both Schmitt and Heidegger thought they saw in Nazism the rebuke to human pride for which their longing to restore man to a position of humility made them yearn with religious fervor. But the defeat of Nazism destroyed once and for all the authority of the reactionary political tradition whose foundations Augustine laid with his inhumane doctrine of grace, and Maistre revived in a modern guise to explain the cosmic wickedness of the French Revolution.

In Europe, a modest number of reactionaries survive and still exercise a measure of political power. In the Islamic world, an analogue to Maistre's radical teaching regarding the impotence of human freedom continues to gain support. But in the West, this way of resolving the Augustinian dilemma has no practical or intellectual future. That belongs entirely to the other way of doing so—to the equally radical affirmation of human freedom at the expense of divine grace that Kant made philosophically respectable and the French Revolution installed as a permanent fact of political life. The secularized version of this solution to the theological problem that Augustine's account of man's relation to God first presented, is today the ruling ideal of Western civilization and proclaims its legitimacy with growing confidence in every corner of the world (among other ways, through the doctrine of universal human rights). In chapters 23, 24 and 25, I trace the arc of the last, apocalyptic campaign on behalf of the doctrine of grace, beginning with Joseph de Maistre, up to the point of its defeat by the forces of freedom in reaction to which it was born, and the final loosening from every conceivable restraint of the belief that human beings are independent even of God.

In chapter 26, I return to Max Weber.

Weber believed that values exist only to the extent they are declared to be such by an act of will. This is true, according to Weber, even of those willful decisions that declare God to be the ground of the values they posit. In this sense, God too is a human creation.

But Weber also believed that although the human will is the only conceivable source of meaning and value, it is incapable of giving the values it posits a transcendent significance—one that is more objective than its own fleeting and changeable valuations. To have a significance of this sort, our decisions would have to be validated by a being uncorrupted by passion and time. They would have to be endorsed by God. But that is impossible, if God himself is merely a posit.

We are therefore in a terrible bind. We can neither affirm the existence of God without abandoning the belief that all values exist solely on account of the will, nor, without a God to verify and support them, can the values we affirm ever be more than our own private and arbitrary convictions. In Weber's view, this dilemma defines the spiritual predicament of our age. There can be no escape from it. A mature human being accepts it as his or her fate and has the strength to refuse all the easy but unavailing ways out. This is the unavoidable consequence, Weber claims, of the "disenchantment of the world," a uniquely Western phenomenon that is the result, in part at least, of the self-destruction of the Christian religion at the hands of its own ideals.

But Weber's stoic despair is still vestigially tied to Christian belief, for it rests on the assumption that only a God beyond the world could possibly save it, though none any longer exists. It rests on the self-defeating combination of beliefs that Nietzsche defines as nihilism and describes as the final stage of the Christian religion. If we are ever to find a way beyond Weber's religion of despair that leads forward and not back, as he puts it, into "the arms of the Church," the self-destructive theory of value that underlies it must be supplanted by a new and more positive theology that is neither pagan nor Christian, even in the attenuated, nihilistic form the latter still assumes in Weber's indictment of modernity.

The joyful teachings of this new theology are the subject of part IV.

One is that there is no logical obstacle to joining Aristotle's belief in the inherent divinity of the world with the Abrahamic belief that the uniqueness of every individual is infinitely knowable and precious. A second is that it is not only possible but necessary to join these beliefs if the working assumptions and guiding ambitions of modern science, art and politics are to make any sense at all. And a third is that, as finite beings, we shall never fully comprehend the divinity of the world as a whole, so that our experience of it is bound to disappoint us, though we can always make further progress toward this goal and become more divine as we do.

I first pursue these general themes in the realm of science.

The modern science of nature starts with a theological quarrel. The voluntarist reaction against the necessitarianism of Aristotle's physics opened the way to the empirical and experimental study of natural motion that culminates in the new physics of Galileo and Descartes. But in Descartes' case and Newton's as well, the laws of the physical world remain tied to an explicit belief in divine creation, which puts an absolute limit to the rationalizing ambitions of the physics whose foundations they helped to build. In order to set these ambitions free from this arbitrary but insuperable limit, the Christian conception of God as an omnipotent creator had to be replaced by the very different idea of God as the eternal intelligibility of the world itself, now expanded to include the whole of reality. Among the great philosophers of the seventeenth century, only Spinoza understood this, and he alone constructed a theology adequate to the aspirations of the new physics that was growing up around him. Einstein, among others, saw this quite clearly. I elaborate these ideas in chapter 27 and in chapter 28 explore the history of post-Newtonian physics in their light, examining in particular those recent developments in our understanding of physical motion, at the subatomic and cosmic levels, that seem to put the greatest pressure on Spinoza's theology.

In chapter 29, I discuss Darwin's idea of life, contrasting it with those of Aristotle and Descartes. My aim is to show that despite his attack on Aristotle's notion of the eternal species-being of plants and animals, and his rejection of Descartes' belief in a creator God, Darwin's account of natural selection can no more do without the idea of eternity than these other philosophies can. Darwin has a theology too. It is remarkably similar to Spinoza's.

Chapter 30 is devoted to Freud. Freud is sometimes thought of as a champion of irrationality. Nothing could be further from the truth. The discipline of psychoanalysis is predicated on the belief that everything in our mental lives is intelligible, however little of it we ever actually understand. This is what Freud means when he says that the "God" of psychoanalysis is "Logos" or reason. Freud's position is quite close to Spinoza's at this point. There is also a striking similarity in their ethical views. To the question of how one ought to live, they give parallel answers. In the first four chapters of part IV, Einstein, Darwin and Freud thus all emerge as thinkers of a Spinozistic cast whose otherwise different pursuits rest on the shared belief that the world is both inherently and infinitely knowable.

Chapter 31 concludes my reflections on the aims of modern science. In it, I discuss the modern research ideal. This affirms the need for a collaborative division of labor among those working to augment our ever-growing but always incomplete knowledge of the world. I describe this collaboration as a form of friendship that in certain ways exemplifies Aristotle's idea of it. But unlike the sort that exists between great-souled men, the friendship that joins the men and women engaged in an endless program of research is tied to the individuality of those involved as well as to that of the objects and events they seek to understand. In this respect it bears a resemblance to romantic love (though many will surely find the comparison surprising).

The next four chapters deal with art. Nietzsche is the central figure here. In *The Birth of Tragedy,* Nietzsche calls for a new "metaphysics of art." In chapter 32, I explain the meaning of his striking claim that the world can only be justified as "an aesthetic phenomenon." Then in chapter 33, I assemble the components of Nietzsche's own proposed justification in a more systematic way than he himself ever did. These include the concepts of drive, domination, perspective and the mysterious doctrine of eternal return—the key to Nietzsche's interpretation of the relation between being and becoming.

Throughout I stress the similarities between Nietzsche's metaphysics and Spinoza's. Both conceive the world to be eternal and divine, down to its smallest details—to the "spider" in the "moonlight," in Nietzsche's poetic formulation of the idea of eternal return. In Spinoza's case, this opens the way to a better understanding of the combination of ambition and humility that defines the spirit of modern science. In Nietzsche's, it illuminates the aims and limits of modern art, about which Spinoza has nothing to say.

In chapters 34 and 35, I illustrate the power of Nietzsche's metaphysics as a guide to modern art by considering two exemplary cases. The first is that of the novel, the most characteristically modern form of literary representation.

A novel, Henry James observes, is principally concerned with the individuality of its characters. Its plot, he says, is merely a device for bringing their unique personalities to light. This reverses the weight that Aristotle assigns these elements. Aristotle's literary theory (to give it an anachronistic title) rests on the same intellectualist metaphysics as every other branch of his philosophy. In chapter 34, I examine the very different metaphysics on which the genre of the novel is based. I develop its assumptions though a reading of five novels—*Middlemarch, Ulysses, In Search of Lost Time, The Death of Virgil,* and *Lolita.* The first of these makes it clear that the metaphysics that underlies the modern novel is as much a theology as the one on which Aristotle's analysis of the art of imitation is based. But it is a born-again pagan theology that joins a belief in the limitless beauty and worth of ordinary things to the conviction that the world itself, and not a God beyond it, is the source of their infinite value. My argument is inspired by Erich Auerbach's masterpiece, *Mimesis.*

In chapter 35, I focus on the plastic arts and on painting in particular. The painters of the Renaissance did more than merely revive certain ancient techniques and ideals. They reinterpreted these through the lens of Christian belief. In the process, the ancient understanding of art underwent a fundamental transformation. The classical idea of beauty was replaced by that of sublimity and the competence of the craftsman became the genius of the individual artist. The concepts of sublimity and genius are of Christian origin. They are the defining categories of all post-Renaissance art. In the centuries since Duccio and Cimabue began the process, in the West at least, of converting what Hans Belting calls "the sacred image" into a "work of art," the ideas of sublimity and genius have been loosened from the Christian theology that gave birth to them. They have come to be embedded in the very different theology that informs the work of Spinoza's contemporary Vermeer, as well as that of many other artists since. Chapter 35 traces this development.

It concludes with some observations about the unsettled state of contemporary art, whose ruling spirit veers between Vermeer's born-again paganism and a nihilistic metaphysics not unlike that of Max Weber.

In my final two chapters I consider again, in light of the argument of the book as a whole, the political order described in chapter 2.

There, I emphasized the connection between the ethic of entitlement and the ideal of personal autonomy. This ideal is a secular derivative of Christian theology. It expresses the supreme value that Augustine first assigned to freedom of the will, and reflects the aspiration to usurp God's place and become as self-sufficient as he.

The ideal of autonomy that is often invoked to justify the ethic of entitlement is the source of the hostility to love that deforms our public life today. It also cannot explain two other values that are of fundamental importance to the citizens of every liberal democratic state. One is that of diversity. The other is the value of the loyalty that joins them to their homeland in a special way.

If we respect the choices people make merely because they are the expression of their equal capacities for self-legislation, we have no reason to value the diverse content of these choices as something good in itself. An ethics of autonomy rules this out. Nor can it explain why the special loyalty we feel to the other members of the political community to which we happen to belong is of value in its own right. Patriotism will always be suspect from the vantage point of the secularized theology of the will that dominates the public morality of most liberal democracies today.

John Rawls' definition of political fraternity as a willingness on the part of the members of a political community to settle their disputes according to principles that would be agreed to in what he calls the "original position" illustrates the latter point, for there is no friendship in the original position and no way to generate it by resolving to view matters from its universalistic point of view. In chapter 36, I explore the limitations of the ethics of autonomy by examining the moral logic of Rawls' idea of the original position and exposing the supernaturalist theology on which it relies.

The key to solving these problems, as a philosophical matter at least, is a political theology based on the born-again pagan belief that the world is both inherently and infinitely divine. Only a theology of this sort can restore love to an honored place in public life and secure the value of diversity and democratic friendship in a lasting way.

This theology is remote from contemporary political thought. But it has a powerful champion in Walt Whitman, whose great poem has been called

America's "secular Scripture." Whitman's political theology is the subject of the last chapter of the book.

Whitman's poem is inspired by the belief that each of his fellow Americans is immortal in his or her own unique way. In Whitman's vision, every individual is a singular expression—a "mode," as Spinoza would say—of the one, all-comprehending God of the world. As such, each possesses a value that no one can ever entirely grasp, but whose infinite worth a poet like Whitman is able to glimpse and can help us more fully appreciate, despite the prejudicial conventions with which we box others in familiar categories that extinguish their individuality and obliterate their unique contribution to the divine order of things. Viewed in these terms, the idea that diversity is a good in itself is not merely plausible. It is inevitable.

But what about patriotism? The spirit of democracy is universal, indeed cosmic. It invites us to see the divinity in every human being. Yet the particular ones with whom I am joined in my country's experiment in democratic government have a special claim on my allegiance. How can this be combined with the cosmic inclusiveness that is the inspiration for Whitman's reverence for diversity?

I take up this question in the concluding sections of chapter 37. I liken democratic patriotism to romantic love and try to show that the one as much as the other only becomes intelligible when we view it from the vantage point of a theology that divinizes the distinctiveness of every individual. This allows for the reaffirmation of Aristotle's ancient ideal of political friendship, now loosed from its aristocratic limitations and widened to include every member of a diverse democratic community. The members of such a community feel a peculiarly intense friendship for one another, as all romantic lovers do. Yet their patriotism is unthreatened by the fact that others love their countries with equal passion too, unless their devotion is inspired by the belief that they have a monopoly on the divinity of our inexhaustibly diverse world and are therefore entitled to silence or suppress their neighbors' claims. Moreover, because it is a friendship of a wholly human kind, those who are bound together by it can adequately express the gratitude they feel for the care they have received, by giving as much and as good to others to keep the spirit of their democratic venture alive.

This way of looking at things puts the ethics of entitlement in a new perspective.

We assign rights to individuals to protect them against abuse. Most people are tempted to think that their interests are more important, and their view of the world more enlightened, than the interests and views of others. If given the power, they may enslave those they look down on, or take their property, or enact laws that express contempt for them. A system of rights protects against this.

But the best explanation for its existence is not that we all possess some supernatural power of self-legislation that qualifies us for membership in a "kingdom of ends." A better one is that we need a system of rights because our powers of self-restraint and sympathy are limited. It is true that the laws that establish our rights speak in general terms of "persons" and "entitlements." But that is only because the powers of observation and judgment of those who make and enforce such laws are severely confined, so that they are no more capable of determining, with any reliability, when the totality of his life circumstances ought to excuse a thief, than the thief is of viewing his victim in a more sympathetic light. A general system of entitlements is the best that we can do, even though it leaves out of account so much about the human beings whose conduct it controls.

Its establishment must also be our first priority. Until such a system is in place, a free democratic life is impossible. But it is not its highest goal. It is merely a preliminary to that, and the real shortcoming of every political morality that explains the need for a system of rights by appealing to the idea of autonomy, is that it hides this higher goal from view.

The true end of democracy is the celebration of the "amative" spirit of Walt Whitman's poem, with its love of diversity as something divine, and the cultivation of his ethic of individualized perfectionism, which invites us to develop the "special nativity" that makes each of us a one-of-a-kind expression of the immortal God of the world. These are the "democratic vistas" that open before us when we see that the establishment of even the most perfect system of rights can never be more than a prelude to something of still greater value. Yet to see this, we have to overcome the supernaturalist theology that lies behind the most widely accepted justifications of our modern world of rights. This theology is the decayed by-product of Christian belief. It blinds us to the value of the earth. To grasp the value of what it hides behind a veil of ignorance, we need to make the theological adjustment that Whitman invites and enacts. We must become born-again pagans like he.

In the "Epilogue," I turn from the political to the personal—or rather, I return to it, for it was with the personal meaning of love and gratitude that the book began. There my focus was on what Melanie Klein calls "the crisis of birth"—our expulsion from the womb into a condition of separateness and dependence. I end my *Confessions* with some reflections on the crisis of death, the second great rupture of existence.

None of us lives outside the shadow of death or can help thinking about it, infrequently perhaps, but at times with a feeling of loneliness unlike any other we ever experience. Does the born-again paganism whose implications I have followed through the realms of science, art and politics have any bearing on this most personal of all concerns?

I believe it does.

Spinoza seems to have been entirely unafraid of death. Few ever achieve his equanimity in this regard. But his *Ethics* is not a textbook for saints. It gives us all some guidance in how best to think about dying.

In Spinoza's view, the idea of a life after this one in which we shall live forever as our individual selves is an illusion. It conflates the finite and the infinite in a contradictory way. The belief in such a life is incoherent. It is the product of a childish wish.

Nor is it possible to become immortal in this life either, as Aristotle says we can, by contemplating the order of the world. That too is a mistake. It rests on the now no longer tenable assumption that the immortality of the world lies in its form alone, which when detached from the unintelligible matter in which it resides, can be fully grasped by finite minds like ours. Hence though we fear death, and hope to overcome it, there is no way to do so, either here on earth or in an imaginary heaven beyond.

Of course one can say, and many now do, that the search for eternity is a fool's errand, whether we pursue it in the way that Augustine or Aristotle recommends. They insist that we must learn to be grown-ups and get along without God. But this is not an alternative either, for a life without the yearning to reach the everlasting and divine is no longer recognizably human.

None of these answers to the question of the mystery of death, which is the mystery of life, can possibly satisfy any thoughtful person who asks it today. But that is not a reason for despair. There is another answer at hand. The main purpose of this book is to make it as credible to the reader as I have found it to be.

The answer is that although *we* cannot be immortal, the *world* is, and that every increase in our understanding of it, and in our power to sing its song, is a further, deeper experience of the deathlessness of the world, which as finite beings we can never fully possess but are never entirely excluded from either.

This thought is reinforced by another. I am part of the story of the world. Without me, its explanation would be incomplete. The same is true of everyone else. Each of us makes an indispensable contribution to the intelligibility of the world as a whole. If we could see ourselves under the aspect of eternity, we would see that this is true. We would see that everything in our lives belongs to the eternity of the world—that it is eternal already. We cannot do that, of course, but only because our finite powers of apprehension are inadequate to grasp the infinite and timeless intelligibility of our unique role in the order of things. To overcome the gap between these, we would have to be the world itself. Then we would indeed have conquered death. That is out of the question. But we can narrow the gap by living as thoughtfully and poetically as we are able. If we do, we come closer to the life everlasting that always lies beyond reach. This is the best life that a human being can live. Those that do soar in the light, so long as they can see it, toward the God of the world, and then "sink downward to darkness, on extended wings."

PART ONE

Gratitude

CHAPTER I

The Good of Gratitude

DEPENDENCE, ACCEPTANCE AND BEING
AT HOME IN THE WORLD

Gratitude is a social virtue. It is a way of treating other people. In this respect, it resembles the virtue of justice. A just man or woman acknowledges the rights of others and agrees to fair procedures for settling disputes. A grateful one appreciates their kindness and thanks them in return. Those who regard everything they receive as their due, and are unwilling or unable to say thank you when the occasion demands, are ingrates. They have a social vice. Perhaps a person can be grateful to him- or herself, but only in a secondary way. The primary sense of gratitude, as of all the social virtues, is that of a right relation to people other than oneself.[1]

Like justice, gratitude is also a powerful social bond. Justice has been called the "first virtue of social institutions,"[2] and no society, even one of thieves, is possible without it.[3] Gratitude plays a similar, if less formal, role in the maintenance of social order.[4] It may be possible to imagine a society of ingrates who never acknowledge the help they receive from one another. But whether such a society can exist for long is doubtful. Expressions of gratitude ease the frictions of social life and encourage people to be helpful to others in ways that no system of justice can fully anticipate or formally encode. Gratitude operates as a necessary supplement to the more formal requirements of justice and, like these, is an essential ingredient in social cohesion, as Seneca observed nearly twenty centuries ago.[5] Indeed, judging by the intensity with which we monitor the gratitude of others, and the ferocity with which we condemn its absence when we detect it, it would seem that the contribution that gratitude makes to the preservation of social order is only slightly less important to us than that of justice itself.

Because gratitude is a social virtue and a social bond, it is natural to look for the good of gratitude in its effects on other people. If Emma does Alex a favor and he thanks her for it, it is she who benefits; if he fails or refuses to do so, it is she who is hurt. In this respect, too, gratitude and justice are alike. When someone treats others unjustly, it is they who bear the cost. Indeed, those who act unjustly are often assumed to benefit from their injustice, if not detected in it. Plato needed the whole of the *Republic* to prove otherwise.[6] The good of gratitude appears external in a similar way. It seems to lie not in the welfare of the person whose gratitude it is, but in that of other people, and in the order and stability of society at large.

This way of thinking about gratitude is true as far as it goes. But it misses something important. A person's gratitude is good not only for others or for society in general. It is good for the grateful person too. It is a personal as well as a social good. Indeed, it is a personal good of an especially basic kind, on which many others depend. If a person lacks gratitude, that is bad for others. But for the man or woman in question, it is something worse. It is a malignancy of the soul that poisons many of life's greatest goods, including the two that Freud is said to have considered the very greatest, those of love and work.[7]

That gratitude is good for the soul of the grateful person and contributes to his or her own well-being is not an original observation.[8] Many understand this intuitively. The author of a recent book on the subject even suggests that people can increase their happiness by deliberately working to be more grateful than they are.[9] But why is gratitude good for one's soul? What is the connection of gratitude to love and creativity, and to human fulfillment more generally?

An essay by Melanie Klein gives us a point of departure.

THE CRISIS OF BIRTH

Klein was a psychoanalyst and follower of Freud's. She was the first to apply psychoanalytic methods to the treatment of young children and is best remembered for her pioneering work in this field.[10] Many of the insights she drew from her experience with children, and their implications for her understanding of the human condition in general, are contained in Klein's famous essay "Envy and Gratitude."[11]

For Klein, birth is a crisis we never overcome. Before we are born, we and the world are one, or more exactly, we and our mothers are one. We have no separate life apart from that of our mothers and experience no anxiety regarding our existence. Our condition is one of "prenatal unity" with our mothers and the world.[12]

There is a "universal longing" for this lost state, Klein says, and an equally universal anger at having been thrust out of it. From the moment of birth, we are on our own, in the world but no longer fully of it, until we die and are submerged in the world again. This separateness is the source of the primal anxiety that shadows our lives from beginning to end. And it is one source, at least, of all the literary, artistic and philosophical works of human culture that together represent our collective effort, through idealizations of one kind or another, to reshape a world we can never quite forgive for the "persecution"[13] of having been born.

The separate lives we begin at birth are wholly conditioned by the experience of dependence. Before birth, there can be no such experience. A fetus may of course die in the womb. Its continued existence is dependent on the life of its mother, in the same way that the existence of any other part of her body is. But because it has not yet been separated from its mother, and the world, and begun to live on its own, it cannot experience the anxious dependence we feel every moment of our lives from birth on. No other part of the mother's body has this fate. It is the unique privilege, and inescapable burden, of the one part that begins its career as a component of its mother's life and emerges, at birth, into a life of its own.

Vulnerability is another name for this experience. Throughout our lives, we remain exposed to countless dangers and have manifold needs, from the need for food to the need for recognition and love. The satisfaction of these needs is always partly out of our control since it depends on the availability of the objects of our desires, which exist independently of us, and on our limited ability to secure them. So long as we live, our desires are therefore always subject to frustration. We exist in a state of perpetually threatened disappointment and must constantly be on the lookout to avoid it.

The prenatal unity from which birth expels us is, by contrast, a condition of omnipotence. Our oneness with our mothers—with the world—means that there is nothing apart from us whose denial could be a disappointment. From omnipotence, birth propels us into finitude, into a state of dependence on what is no longer us but something—someone—that now exists apart: a state of anxious vulnerability, of worried searching and scheming, an endless

self-protective struggle to grasp and hold an other whose unity with us is rup-
tured at birth and restored only at life's end. This is the human condition
into which we are born. None of us can escape its travails or the feelings of
fear and anger that accompany it.

But if the world is for all of us a hostile place, it is for most of us a nurturing one as well that supports our struggle to exist by providing us with enough
to survive and grow, even, if we are lucky, to flourish.[14]

The world's nurturance takes many forms. Its natural fecundity is one.
The realm of cultural works that human beings have created to amuse and
inspire and enlighten themselves is another. These, too, support us in the enterprise of living. But our first support—the one on which we all depend decisively at the start—is the nourishment our parents provide us as infants. More
specifically, it is the nourishment our mothers provide, and more specifically
still, according to Klein, it is the milk that flows from the mother's breast.

The breast is the primal site of all worldly nurturance, the precursor and
emblem of every other form of support the world provides. For the infant,
the mother's breast is an object apart. It is not a part of the infant or the infant
a part of it. The breast belongs to the world, from which the infant has been
torn at birth. It is therefore a source of dependence and anxiety, of longing
and potential frustration. This cannot be avoided. But the good breast—the
available and fecund breast—is also a source of comfort and support. Nothing in this life can replicate the prenatal unity of the womb. But the experience
of what Klein calls a "happy feeding situation"[15] comes as close as possible. It
reassures the infant that the world is not a hopelessly hostile place, but in part
benign, and supportive of its struggle to exist as an independent being. A
good breast, a happy feed, suggests to the infant that the world is not merely
a wilderness, threatening and bare, but potentially at least, a home inhabited
by others who love the infant and wish to see it survive.

Not every feeding situation is a happy one, however. Some are a source of
frustration and aggravated anxiety instead. An unhappy feed may be the result of "external circumstances." If, for example, "birth has been difficult, and
in particular if it results in complications such as lack of oxygen, a disturbance in the adaptation to the external world occurs and the relation to the
breast starts at a great disadvantage."[16] Unhappiness may also be the result of
psychological factors such as the mother's own anxiety about her child and

her suppressed but communicated wish that the child not demand too much of her—of her breast, her milk, her love—perhaps even a wish that the child disappear.

Whatever the reasons for it, unhappiness in the primal relation of nurturance that exists between infant and breast accentuates and intensifies the anxiety that accompanies the rupture with the world that birth inaugurates. Instead of reassuring the infant that the world is a supportive as well as threatening place, an unhappy feeding situation strengthens the desire to hurt or punish the world whose withdrawal into separateness is the cause of the infant's anxiety in the first place. In this way, the mother's breast becomes a bad breast—a breast that withholds, denies, and keeps its nourishment for itself.

The infant confronting such a breast is likely, Klein says, to become envious of it, for the breast enjoys a fullness and satiety the infant desires but is denied. The infant's envy is a wish to have what the breast enjoys, to possess for itself the powers of the breast, and thus to be relieved of dependence upon it. But it is something more. It is—as envy always is—a vengeful desire to hurt the breast as well. "Envy is the angry feeling that another person possesses and enjoys something desirable—the envious impulse being to take it away or spoil it."[17]

The envious infant thus becomes filled with destructive impulses, with a desire not merely to "rob" the breast of what it has by "completely scooping [it] out, sucking [it] dry, and devouring the breast . . . but also to put badness, primarily bad excrements and bad parts of the self, into the mother, and first of all into her breast, in order to spoil and destroy her. In the deepest sense, this means destroying her creativeness."[18]

> As regards envy, it is not easy to explain how the mother who feeds the infant and looks after him can also be an object of envy. But whenever he is hungry or feels neglected, the child's frustration leads to the phantasy that the milk and love are deliberately withheld from him, or kept by the mother for her benefit. Such suspicions are the basis of envy. It is inherent in the feeling of envy not only that possession is desired, but that there is also a strong urge to spoil other people's enjoyment of the coveted object—an urge that tends to spoil the object itself. If envy is very strong, its spoiling quality results in a disturbed relation to the mother as well as later to other people; it also means that nothing can be fully enjoyed because the desired thing has already been spoiled by envy.[19]

Envy is therefore not merely a destructive impulse. It is a self-destructive one as well. To hurt the other who has what he wants, the envious person must wreck the "coveted object" the other possesses; in the process, he necessarily deprives himself of the thing he longs to enjoy. For the truly envious person, this is a price worth paying. Envy implies a willingness to sacrifice oneself for the sake of the pleasure of hurting someone else—indeed, not merely a willingness to do so, in the sense in which one may be prepared to pay a high price as the cost of attaining some goal, but the conversion of self-destruction into a source of pleasure itself, into a component of the pleasure the envious person derives from the destruction of the envied other, from whose suffering he can no longer distinguish his own enjoyment.

A bad breast (a mother whose milk and love are inadequate or interrupted or hoarded for the mother's own satisfaction) is, literally, the nursery bed of all envious feelings. Under the right conditions, these can grow into a generalized rage against the creativity of others and a wish to hurt their creations. At the highest level, this rage becomes a hostility to the very process of creation itself, a drive to tear things down and see them vanish.[20] This infantile wish, born of the envy of the mother's breast, can reach satanic proportions, and when it does, Klein says, it becomes the enemy of life and love themselves.

> The capacity to give and to preserve life is felt as the greatest gift and therefore creativeness becomes the deepest cause for envy. The spoiling of creativity implied in envy is illustrated in Milton's *Paradise Lost* where Satan, envious of God, decides to become the usurper of Heaven. He makes war on God in his attempt to spoil the heavenly life and falls out of Heaven. Fallen, he and his other fallen angels build Hell as a rival to Heaven, and become the destructive force which attempts to destroy what God creates. This theological idea seems to have come down from St. Augustine, who describes Life as a creative force opposed to Envy, a destructive force. In this connection, the First Letter to the Corinthians reads, "Love envieth not."[21]

AT HOME IN THE WORLD

The infant at the breast is the very image of human dependence. Without his mother's milk, he will soon die. Her milk has not been produced or earned by him, in the way a grown man produces his own food or earns it by "working" for a "living." The infant produces nothing (other than the waste products of bodily metabolism) and can do no work. The milk on which he depends thus comes to him as the purest of gifts.

There are two ways in which this gift may be received. If for whatever reason the infant is anxious about the availability of the nourishment he needs, or the reliability of his mother's love, he will receive the gift she offers in a spirit of envy, wishing to seize control of the situation and to hurt his benefactor for keeping what he wants. He will be driven by an angry and self-destructive longing for the omnipotence he once enjoyed. But if the infant is not deeply anxious in these ways—the condition of a good feed—he will receive his mother's gift with gratitude, accepting the dependence of his condition instead of railing against it, and acknowledging the presence of a loving other who has the infant's own welfare at heart. Klein calls this the "feeling of gratitude for goodness received." It is the source, she says, of our "capacity for enjoyment" in life, and the key to success in our search for fulfillment in love and work.[22]

A full gratification at the breast means that the infant feels he has received from his loved object a unique gift which he wants to keep. This is the basis of gratitude. Gratitude is closely linked with the trust in good figures. This includes first of all the ability to accept and assimilate the loved primal object (not only as a source of food) without greed and envy interfering too much. . . . [The greedy and envious infant] feels that he is controlling and exhausting, and therefore injuring it, whereas in a good relation to the external object, the wish to preserve and spare it predominates. . . . In this way, a good object is established, which loves and protects the self and is loved and protected by the self. This is the basis for trust in one's own goodness. . . . The more often gratification at the breast is experienced and fully accepted, the more often enjoyment and gratitude, and accordingly the wish to return pleasure are felt. This recurrent experience makes possible gratitude on the deepest level and plays an important role in the capacity to make reparation, and in all sublimations. . . . Gratitude is [thus] closely bound up with generosity. Inner wealth derives from having assimilated the good object so that the individual becomes able to share its gifts with others. This makes it possible to introject a more friendly outer world, and a feeling of enrichment ensues.[23]

For the infant who receives his mother's gift in this spirit, the entire world (which at the start is just his mother, indeed just his mother's breast) is more likely to be experienced as a generous and nurturing place that supplies the unearned help we need to live. Nothing can abolish our awful dependence on people and things that begins the minute we are born. Nothing can wholly eliminate the feelings of anxiety that attend our separation from the world and the irremediable vulnerability of our postnatal condition. But the infant's grateful acceptance of his mother's love gives grounds for the hope—and in time for the solid belief—that the world is, as Klein says, a "friendly" place that contains gifts as well as dangers.

Gratitude is the disposition to see the world in this light. A grateful person is one who is sufficiently released from the primal anxiety of life to recognize the gifts she receives for what they are and to accept them without wishing to be free of her dependence on any gifts at all—a fantasy of omnipotence that can only produce an envious and destructive desire to hurt our benefactors for not giving us even more. The ability to be thankful, and later on to say that one is, is thus the foundation and expression of a sense of being at home in the world—in a world that will not give me all I want, and in the end is bound to destroy me, but that gives me enough to flourish for a time, despite my finitude and vulnerability. In this sense, gratitude is not merely one good among others but a preeminent good that provides the key to a fulfilling life. For its presence or absence in a person's soul determines whether that person is at home in the world or at war with it, and either open or closed to the possibilities of happiness in love and work that being at home in the world invites.

Of course, even the happiest infant with the most loving mother never completely overcomes his envious anger at the world and the self-destructive wish to hurt it for the existential hurt of having been born. Even those who feel at home in the world never lose their sense of alienation from it. These are the indelible marks of finitude itself. They also contribute, in a basic way, to the human experience of love and work, for the longing to reach others in love, and to repair or beautify the world through work, is a consequence, in part, of our alienation from it and of the anxieties this arouses. But if the sense of alienation is too strong, its effect will be to close the openness to the world on which success in love and work depends. In the normally happy person, these destructive feelings are outweighed by those of gratitude for the gifts of others, uncorrupted by a desire to ruin them and oneself in the process. Indeed, it is precisely the predominance of gratitude over envy in the normally happy person that constitutes the source of her normal happiness—not of a happiness that is assured, or invulnerable to the accidents of life, for nothing can guarantee that, but of an adequately secure sense of being at home in the world, on which the possibility of happiness in love and work is founded.

LOVE

This is above all true of love. A person may be unlucky in love. He may lose those he loves, or be treated badly by them. But if he lacks the ability to feel and express love, he is entirely shut out from the chance to experience the greatest happiness a human being can know. Not everyone has this ability. But in the souls of those that do, their openness to love is rooted in the soil of gratitude for goodness received.

To love other people is to wish for their happiness—not derivatively as part of one's own, but directly and independently. It is to wish for the happiness of others for their own sake. But this requires that one be sufficiently secure about one's own well-being not to be anxiously preoccupied with it at every moment. Love requires that some space be opened in the field of self-regard within which the happiness of others can come to matter for itself, and this cannot happen so long as a person's thoughts and feelings are dominated by the belief that the world is a hostile place that means to hurt him whenever it can. A person who feels this way will be forever on the lookout to protect himself from danger and will want to hurt the world back when the opportunity arises. He will find it hard to love or be loved in return.

By contrast, the grateful person, who is as much at home in the world as a human being can be, will not be so constantly preoccupied with her own endangered well-being (though none of us can ever stop worrying about this for long). There will be room in her life to attend to the happiness of others, at least from time to time. There will be space in her life for love. Gratitude clears this space—in a real sense, it *is* this space—for by enabling us to experience the world as a place that is reasonably well disposed toward us, gratitude gives us the freedom to be well disposed toward others, in the selfless and noninstrumental way that love and its cognate feelings (charity, solidarity, friendship, and compassion) always are.

One may go further. Gratitude not only clears a space for love; it provides the motive for it as well. That is because the grateful person is moved by what Klein calls "the wish to return."[24] Nothing, perhaps, is more characteristic of gratitude than this. A gift that is meant for us arouses an affection for the one who has made it, so long as we are not crippled by envy. Of course, if the gift is spurious—if it has the outward form of a gift but is really meant to put us in debt, or humble our pride, and thus to serve the donor's interests rather than ours—we are likely to feel irritation or anger instead.[25] But in a person who is capable of gratitude, a true gift motivated by love cannot help but arouse feelings of affection toward the donor and a desire to express these feelings by making a reciprocal gift of one's own.

The gift may be as commonplace as saying thank you. It may be as exalted as marriage. It may express itself in creative work, through which the world is improved or embellished. All of these are bound to be shadowed by anxiety and envy, as are the gifts to which they respond. What human love is not? But where feelings of gratitude predominate in the soul of the recipient, a longing to reciprocate, to return love for love, will be the most natural and fulfilling expression of the thankfulness she feels. This longing is the root of the gift we make to those we love in return for the unearned gift of being loved by them (though the people we love and those who love us are often not the same). It is the root of the generative drive to create, to add to the world in some fashion, to make it a more lovely and comfortable place, the drive that characterizes all healthy and satisfying work, from the ordinary to the artistic. And it is the root of the "serenity" that is the greatest reward of old age, of the old person's ability "to take pleasure and interest in the lives of young people" while acknowledging "that youth cannot be regained": to affirm without bitterness "the continuity of life" and thus to accept, perhaps even with some sense of completion, the prospect of one's own extinction.[26]

Love, work, and the ability to face death without despair: these are possible only with the real, if incomplete, freedom from envy that gratitude allows and on account of the desire it awakens to make a gift to the world in return. The desire to do this is not the wish to repay a debt. A debt is a burden and repayment a relief. The joy of loving in return for love is something different. It is the joy of bringing a gift of one's own to those whose unbought love is the emblem and expression of a world that grateful human beings find a mostly congenial place, and embrace in the ambiguity of what Robert Frost called a "lover's quarrel."[27]

The freedom that characterizes love is the opposite of the compulsion that accompanies indebtedness in all its forms. Its disinterestedness is the opposite of the spirit of self-advancement that lies behind the discharge of every obligation. The freedom and disinterestedness of love enable us to draw as close to others and the world as our finitude permits. This is the supreme happiness that an unindentured love of the world brings those whose gratitude for goodness received opens a space in their lives where love can appear. It is the joy of loving and of being loved, which bears no resemblance to the bondsman's relief when his debt is paid.

If we follow Melanie Klein, therefore, we must think of gratitude not merely as a social virtue, and a binding force in human societies, whose good consists in the benefits it brings to other people. We are bound to view it as a personal good of great importance too, for without it the deepest sources of human happiness are harder to reach and in danger of conversion to their opposites through the corrosive power of envy—from love to hate, creation to destruction, serenity to despair. And if we follow her line of thought, we are also helped to see why, second only to an inability to feel gratitude, the worst disaster that can befall a human being is to be blocked in the desire to thank the world by making a reciprocating gift that is adequate to the one he or she has received.

GIFT AND LUCK

The special place of love in human life can be further clarified by contrasting its benefits with two other kinds. The first are those of good fortune and the second the benefits of entitlement. Both are real goods but neither provides an occasion for gratitude. This belongs to the realm of gift alone. Only here do we experience the world as a place occupied by others who love us and want to see us prosper for our own sake. No amount of good fortune, or system of entitlements, can ever make the world a home, or be a source of the gratitude for goodness received that moves us to love it in return.

Consider, first, the difference between gift and luck.

The care my parents gave me made me better off than I would otherwise have been. Finding ten dollars on the sidewalk improves my welfare too. In either case, things might have turned out differently. I might have been mistreated by my parents, or lost the money rather than found it. In addition, neither a gift nor a piece of good luck is something to which I am entitled. A gift is not the fruit of a bargain or a privilege I can claim as a matter of right. And of course my good luck is unearned as well. So gifts and happy accidents are alike in three respects. They work to my advantage, might have been otherwise, and are unearned by me.

Yet despite these similarities, there is an obvious difference between them. A gift is meant for me. The person who makes the gift intends that I be benefitted by it. Good luck just happens to come my way.

That a benefit be intentional is a necessary condition of its being a gift—though not of course a sufficient one, since entitlements are intentional too. But accidents, whether lucky or not, fail to satisfy this condition. There are no intentions behind them. Accidents are impersonal and therefore meaningless. By contrast, every gift happens only because some person means for it to happen. Gifts always come with this meaning attached.

Because the same benefit often has elements both of gift and good fortune, the difference between them can seem less fundamental than it is.[28] Consider the gift my parents gave me by caring for me as a child. This was the greatest gift I have ever received, yet from the very start it was conditioned by luck. To begin with, it was a piece of unaccountable good luck to have been conceived at all. If my mother had become pregnant a month sooner or later, she would have had another child, and since I only came into existence as a result of her conceiving when she did, her conception cannot possibly be regarded as a gift *to me*. At most, my mother intended to have *a* child. To that extent, any child my mother had (me included) might be thought of as having received the "gift" of life from "our" mother. But that this gift came to me rather than to another member of this class was a piece of blind good luck so far as *I* am concerned (though whether I can even say that it was *my* good luck is doubtful for the same reason).

Unlike the gift of conception, the many others I received from my parents after I was born were intended for me in a more obvious and straightforward sense. They were given to me, with me in mind. Yet luck played a role here too. If it was good luck to have been born at all, it was also good luck to have had parents who were temperamentally and materially equipped to care for me once I was alive. To some extent, their attitudes and resources were the product of deliberate effort on their part—of education, hard work and the like. But to some extent, they were the result of other, earlier accidents, of which my parents were themselves the beneficiaries—the endless chain of luck on which the gift of their care for me depended.

Indeed, in a general sense, every gift is conditioned by luck, for it depends on the willingness and ability of the donor to give it, and that is always—in part at least—a function of accidental factors in the donor's history and experience. Even the recipient's ability to receive and make use of the gift is always partly a matter of luck too. Whenever a gift is made, therefore, some luck lies in the background, and because of this it is always possible to shift attention from the gift to the luck that accompanies it and without which it would not have been given at all. And that in turn can make it seem that gift and luck are indistinguishable, or at least continuous—that the difference between them is merely one of degree.

But this is wrong, for though the effectiveness and even the existence of a gift always depend upon a background of luck, the distinction between them is fundamental. A gift is meant for me, and therefore always includes one benefit that no amount of good luck ever can. That is the benefit of being cared for by another person who intends for me to flourish. It is the benefit of being loved, which even the luckiest man or woman is not, so long as his or her good fortune is the result of impersonal forces alone.

Lucky as I was to have been born to parents who were willing and able to care for me, the care that I received from them was something more than an accident. My parents' care was meant for me and thus, in addition to supplying the requisites of life, assured me that there are others in the world who care for me specifically. It assured me that there are others whose generalized feelings of goodwill toward the world (which no doubt played a role in my parents' decision to have a child in the first place) had come to be focused on *me,* the lucky beneficiary of that decision and now the particularized object of their love. By itself, no amount of care-less good luck ever offers the least grounds for such assurance, and hence for the feeling of being at home in the world. It can never give its beneficiary a reason to be grateful to anyone, or provide a substitute for the experience of love that opens the way to the fulfillment of loving the world in return.

Indeed, good fortune often has the opposite effect. It deepens the anxiety that attends all human existence by underscoring the carelessness with which the world distributes their fates to the lucky and unlucky alike. That is why even those with the greatest good luck—those born to wealth and privilege and endowed with physical well-being—feel compelled to invent what Max Weber calls "theodicies" of good fortune that explain and justify their advantages.[29] Perhaps it is also why these theodicies so often imagine good fortune to be a gift. For most imaginative schemes of this sort not only convert luck, which is meaningless, to something with a meaning, but give it a meaning of an especially gratifying kind by reassuring the wealthy and privileged and strong that they are loved by a benevolent and protective power who takes an interest in their well-being.

Not every theodicy does this, of course. The Hindu doctrine of karma, which attributes all good and bad fortune in this life to a person's conduct in previous ones, is a theodicy of pure desert. The idea of gift is missing from it.[30] But in the West, this idea has played a prominent role in the interpretation of good fortune, from the very start of our literary and religious traditions.

When in the *Iliad,* for example, one of the heroes of the poem escapes disaster in battle or experiences some other kind of good luck, this is sometimes just an accident. Often, however, it is the result of the intervention of a divine champion. In book 3, Aphrodite intervenes to save Paris from destruction in his duel with Menelaus by spiriting him away to the safety of his bedroom at Troy.[31] This is a tremendous benefit to Paris. But his escape from death at Menelaus' hands is not merely a piece of good fortune; it is the gift of a god who loves him, and hence a source of solace that no amount of luck can ever supply.

The religion of Christianity deepens this idea and extends it to its logical limits. Homer's gods may love their human heroes, but their love is fickle and inconstant. They love different heroes and seek to hurt the ones their rivals favor. Eventually, they lose interest even in the fate of their own beloved champions. They become bored with the human spectacle of war and look for other entertainment.[32] By contrast, the God of the Christian religion never becomes bored or distracted and there is no other God to challenge his power and authority. His love is perfect and complete. Hence, every single bit of good fortune that human beings enjoy may be regarded as his gift, including first and most importantly the inestimable gift of a saving faith in God himself and of gratitude for his love. Even these are blessings that come as gifts from a loving God, who sent his son into the world to die for the sake of the sinful human creatures he loves beyond all desert—the greatest gift of all.

Christianity is the most perfect theodicy of love the world has even known—a conversion of luck to gift so complete as to render the very idea of luck unintelligible. In the end, its theology is unstable. Its highest values destroy themselves. The Christian religion is riven with logical and psychological contradictions that guarantee its own demise, and the "disenchantment" of the world.[33] How and why this has happened are among the central questions of this book. We shall explore them in detail later on. But for the moment it is enough to note that if Christianity has remained the religion of the West for more than eighty generations, that is in part because of its unparalleled success in satisfying a universal human longing that no amount of good luck ever can—the longing to be loved without first having had to earn the right to be so.

LUCK AND ENTITLEMENT

Luck and entitlement border the realm of love on opposing sides. They are not opposites in the strict sense, like night and day, or odd and even, since both luck and entitlement may be missing at once. But they cannot both be present at the same time, in the same way, and with respect to the very same thing. That is because every benefit that flows from an entitlement is earned or deserved, whereas the benefits of luck never are.

I am entitled, for example, to the undisturbed use of my home. If other people respect this right, they will not enter without permission. It is not just my good luck that they ask before coming in. I am entitled to be able to decide whether to admit them or not. There are reasons why I ought to be protected in the enjoyment of the benefits this entitlement affords. I can articulate these reasons and expect others to acknowledge them. Indeed, having this expectation is precisely what it means to be entitled to something in the first place.

Good luck, by contrast, is never backed by rights or supported by reasons. Before I found the ten dollars on the sidewalk, I had no claim to it and no reason why the good luck of finding it should be mine rather than anyone else's. If the bill had fallen out of my wallet a few moments earlier, I would have had a claim to it before it was found. It would have been *my* money. It would have belonged to me, and if someone else found it first, I would have had the right to get it back, assuming it could be identified as my own. It is good luck, of course, to recover a piece of property I have lost. But it is always something more as well. It is the assertion of a claim, backed by reasons, which in cases of pure luck do not exist at all. The presence of such a claim is the hallmark of every entitlement.

Prior ownership is one of the reasons I can give to support a claim to be entitled to a benefit. Another is that I have earned it. The check I receive each month from my employer is a benefit that I have earned with my labor. Or I may be entitled to something simply on account of being who I am, because I occupy a particular position or have certain characteristics. Citizens of the United States are entitled to vote merely on account of their status as citizens; it is not an entitlement they have to earn by prior service, or a piece of property, like the money in their wallets, that can be transferred or lost. Similarly, we are all entitled to a certain minimum of decent treatment by others. We all have certain basic human rights on account of the fact that we possess those characteristics (difficult, perhaps, to define but obvious enough in practice) that make us human beings.[34] These are entitlements too, backed by claims for which reasons can be given.

The differences among these various species of entitlement have important legal and moral implications. But all of them lie on one side of the line that separates entitlement from luck. It is not a piece of good luck that my employer pays me. It is not good luck when I go to the voting booth and am permitted to cast my ballot, or am treated by my government in a way that respects my human rights. None of these are accidents. I have a right to each and when I receive it am only getting my due. This is never true of luck, good or bad. I have no right to my good luck or grounds to complain about my misfortunes, and though people do grumble about their bad luck that is only because of the natural human tendency to view all accidental harms as wrongs (a first cousin of the tendency to view lucky benefits as either entitlements or gifts).

Of course, luck is always in the background of entitlement too. I may be entitled to the return of my money because it belongs to me. Still, it was good luck that someone found it, and further good luck that the person who did was willing to return it. It is good luck to have an employer who respects my contractual rights and to be the citizen of a country that respects my civil and human rights. After all, it might have been otherwise. I might have gone to work for a cheat or been born in a dictatorship. But though luck is always entangled with entitlement in these and other ways, it would be as great a mistake to conflate them as to confuse luck with gift. Every entitlement is supported by reasons; luck never is.

ENTITLEMENT AND GIFT

A benefit that I receive as a gift is accompanied by the intention to confer it. The recognition or fulfillment of an entitlement is likewise backed by an intention of some sort. The intention may be that of a specific individual or of an entire community, expressed in its laws and moral practices. It may be only implicit in some other commitment. It may not even be fully conscious in the mind of the person or persons whose intention it is. Still, the receipt of benefits to which one is entitled is always something deliberate. It happens "on purpose." In this respect, the benefits we enjoy on account of our entitlements and those that come to us as gifts resemble one another, for both have an intentionality that all luck lacks.

Yet despite this, gifts and entitlements differ in a basic way. We all recognize this intuitively. One indication is the sense of when it is appropriate to express our thanks for what we have received. When he hands me my paycheck, I may say "thank you" to my employer, but only to be polite. If he asks for a more sincere expression of gratitude I am likely to react with puzzlement or anger. After all, I have only gotten my due. "I have earned the money," I will say. "It belongs to me. It isn't a gift for which I should be grateful. In fact, if you hadn't given me my money I would have sued you for it." It is reported that Lyndon Johnson was disappointed when Martin Luther King failed to express more gratitude for all that Johnson had done for the cause of civil rights. Johnson's disappointment made King angry. For why should King have been grateful to anyone for finally getting what he was owed as an American and human being?[35]

Many relationships of course involve elements of both gift and entitlement. Even in a commercial transaction, one party may afford the other a measure of flexibility beyond anything demanded by their agreement, out of goodwill and not just because he expects the same treatment in return. His generosity is a gift—a benefit over and above what the contract requires. In a marriage, which is a contract too, gift and entitlement are both present as well, though in a healthy marriage their proportions are reversed. Yet despite the commingling of gift and entitlement, which is relatively common and in certain cases, like marriage, essential to the relation's success, the benefits we receive by way of gift and those that come to us in the form of entitlements differ in an essential way. The difference reflects the nature and extent of our dependence on those from whom these benefits come.

My entitlements of course depend on other people. If I am to receive what belongs to me, they must be willing and able to honor my rights. Others have the power to frustrate my rights by withholding what is mine. This happens all the time, and one of the central functions of law and morality is to minimize the extent to which others are able to exercise their power of frustration by keeping or stealing or refusing to give me what I am due.

The fact that others have this power is a consequence of the limits on mine. If my power were boundless, I could compel other people to respect my entitlements (as well as trample on theirs). The kind of dependence that entitlements presuppose thus arises from the finite power of human beings and their need to depend on others to get and keep what is theirs. This is a real and permanent dependence. But it is entirely compatible with the absence of love and a universal egoism in which every individual is exclusively preoccupied with his or her own well-being.[36]

The kind of dependence that gifts involve is different. To the extent that I depend on the gifts of others, I must rely on them to be concerned about my welfare for its own sake, and to be prepared to part with something that belongs to them so that I may flourish. I depend, in short, on their love, for if what they give me is truly a gift and not an entitlement in disguise—a familiar phenomenon that I discuss at length in the following chapter—the only motive they can have for giving it to me is that they take an interest in me, over and above whatever interest they take in themselves.

If my entitlements are to be honored, I need to depend on the enlightened self-interest of others, joined in a system of reciprocal respect driven by the egoistic desire of each to secure the possession of what he or she is owed. But if I am ever to receive a gift, I must depend on the love of other people, and this is a form of dependence different and deeper than any my entitlements involve. That is because the question of why others ought to love me is one I cannot answer. I am always able to answer the question of why others should respect my entitlements. I can answer it by appealing to their rational self-interest. The entire contractarian tradition in political thought is an explication of this answer. But the question of why someone should love me is unanswerable. To be dependent on the love of others is therefore to lack the power even to make a compelling argument on one's own behalf, regardless of whether others accept it or not.

Some may say, "Others should love me because I am loveable." But in the first place, it is unclear whether I am loveable on account of being loved or am loved because I am loveable. (Melanie Klein thought that the current runs in the first direction. Our deepest childhood anxiety is whether we are loveable, and only our parents' love can put it to rest.[37])

Second, and more importantly, the claim that one is loveable and ought therefore to be loved, is entirely within the power of one's lover (parent, spouse, or friend) to decide. There is no appeal from his or her judgment. There are no reasons that lovers are bound to respect, as an adjunct to their self-interest, like those that support my right to dispose of my property as I choose, or to vote, or to be treated as an equal by my fellow citizens. My claim to these rights rests on the assumption that my arguments have *de jure* validity—that I should, in principle at least, be able to persuade others of their soundness—

whether or not they are convinced as a matter of fact. But where love is concerned, I have no arguments even of this kind. I have, in fact, no arguments at all. I have no claim on anyone's love and no right to complain that I've been deprived of what is mine if I don't get it. Every gift thus reveals our abysmal dependence on the love of other people, which we want and need but cannot compel by reasons of any kind. The acceptance of this dependence is gratitude itself.

If every benefit that I need to live came in the form of an entitlement, the only reason I could ever have for being thankful to others would be my gratitude for the respect they show me by not taking what is mine, and that is no reason at all, since their respect is something I am owed—as much as the benefits themselves. That other people do not steal my property, or violate my civil rights, gives me a reason to be pleased, just as I am pleased when I find a ten-dollar bill on the sidewalk. But it gives me no reason to be grateful, as King's response to Johnson makes clear.

Even when others actively contribute to the enforcement of my rights in the way that a policeman or judge does, that is not a gift for which gratitude is owed since their actions merely render more secure the possession of what belongs to me already. The person who gives me what is mine, or helps me to protect it, is only doing what he ought. He is doing what I have reason to insist he do (whether he acknowledges my reasons or not). What he does is a benefit but not an act of love. It can therefore never cause me to believe that there are others in the world who care for me for my own sake, as opposed to supplying the measure of care they are duty-bound to provide. Good luck by itself can never cause me to believe this. Neither can the regard that others show for my entitlements. It is love alone that has the power to make the world a home, and to arouse in those who receive it a desire to love and create in return. This is the power of every true gift, and it exists only within the kingdom of love, which is bounded on one side by luck and on the other by entitlement, in neither of whose wide domains will we ever find anything for which to be grateful, and hence nothing to transform the world from a wilderness of happenstance and wary egos into a community of friends.

CHAPTER 2

◆━━◖◆◗◖◗◖◆◗◖◗━━◆

A World of Rights

THE EXPULSION OF LOVE AND
GRATITUDE FROM PUBLIC LIFE

Every modern Western state guarantees its citizens the right to a wide and diverse range of goods that once were left to charity or chance. These generally include the right to subsidized support for food, shelter, health care and education; to protection from domestic abuse and discrimination of all kinds; to compensation if they lose their jobs; to income when they retire; to clean air and water, help in case of fire or flood, and so on, nearly without limit. The growth in the number and variety of these rights is without historical precedent, and though it has been most pronounced in the West, the moral and political ideals on which it is based are increasingly acknowledged, rhetorically at least, in other parts of the world as well.

In an earlier age, many of the benefits that citizens today enjoy as a matter of right were the outcome of what John Rawls calls a "natural lottery"[1]—the accidental distribution of fortunes that determines whether a person is born to loving parents or neglectful ones, remains healthy or falls ill, is spared or ruined by fire, and the like. Others were conferred as gifts by family and friends, or by charitable and religious organizations. Gift and luck still play a large role in our lives. But it is a less public one than before. More of the benefits that we need to live and flourish are now provided by the state, and come to us in the form of entitlements. Ours is the age of rights. In the realm of public values, luck and gift have been pushed to the margin, and even in the sphere of private relations, they now operate under the shadow of the ethic of entitlement.

In different ways, luck and gift limit our ability to control our fates. The first makes us dependent on events we can neither predict nor prevent; the second, on the love of others, which we have no power to command or compel. By converting gifts to entitlements, and offsetting the effects of luck with compensating rights, we increase the range and effectiveness of our powers of control. The growth of the realm of rights represents a massive increase in the ability of human beings to control themselves and the world.

This is something we have always desired. The earliest human artifacts are mostly tools. But in the modern West, the longing for control has assumed a uniquely extravagant form. It is a longing for control without limits—for the ability to dispose of the world, ourselves included, in whatever way we wish, unhampered by constraints of any kind. This is of course an unattainable goal. We are bound to the earth and to each other by ties over which we can never have more than imperfect control. But today these limits no longer seem merely a challenge to our physical and social well-being. They appear as something more ominous—as an affront to our dignity as beings whose true worth is incompatible with the acceptance of any constraints on our powers of control. This is more than a practical judgment. It is a spiritual ideal, urgent and unyielding, and the source of the special energy that drives the modern Western longing for control, whose scale and intensity cannot be explained by the age-old desire for practical mastery alone.

The ideal in question rests on the conviction that our stature and value are compromised in an essential way so long as our control of the world is less than absolute. This is the kind of control that only an omnipotent God could possess. The longing for such control expresses the wish to be a God of this kind, and rests on the belief that our self-respect demands that we aspire to become one, even though we know we never can. More exactly, it expresses the wish to be the God of the Christian religion, whose control over the world is so complete that he has only to will something in order for it to exist.

The civilization of the West has been uniquely shaped by Christian belief. Today, the ideas and institutions of the Christian religion compete with secular forces that have been gaining strength for more than half a millennium. But among its lasting legacies is the longing of its disenchanted heirs to occupy the position of the God to whom their forebears prayed. The moral and political philosophies that today undergird and justify the ever-growing world of rights are an expression of this ambition.

Paradoxically, this ambition is the result of a revolt within Christianity itself. It is the product of a centuries-long campaign on the part of God's envious creatures to appropriate his powers for themselves—something that, despite its own intentions, Christian theology makes easier by widening the distance between man and God out of pious respect for his absolute power. Or so I shall claim in chapter 3 and argue at length in those that follow.

But before we begin to explore the issues this contentious claim presents, and start on a voyage that will bring us back to the disenchanted world of modern Western civilization only by a long and circuitous route, it is well to pause and briefly consider what the modern conception of rights implies for our understanding of gratitude and love. For only then will we be in a position to estimate, in a provisional way, what we have lost as well as gained by embracing a spiritual ideal that is modeled on the self-sufficiency of the otherworldly God of the Christian religion.

THE CONQUEST OF MISFORTUNE

Not all that long ago, most of the hardships of life were attributed to misfortune. If you were sick or poor, underfed or unemployed, that was simply bad luck. A person who suffered these things may have contributed to his own unhappiness, but in large part his suffering was a consequence of forces beyond his control—of the fates that decide which human beings flourish and which flounder or die. Today, many more of the bad things that happen to people are seen as the result of their not having gotten what they were entitled to, or of their not having been given a proper set of entitlements in the first place (the ones to which they are entitled). And conversely, more of the good things in their lives—the food on their tables, the health of their bodies, the wholesomeness of the air they breathe—are viewed as benefits to which they have a right, and not as a stroke of good fortune.

This represents a revolution in practice and expectations. It is the product of two factors. The first is our ability to control the occurrence and distribution of misfortune through technology. Certain diseases, for example, can now be prevented by means of medicine and machines. The cost of others can be distributed more evenly through insurance, which is a technology for increasing our control over the consequences of misfortune when these cannot be directly avoided.[2] Other technologies give us the means to control other forms of human suffering.

The second is the social character of these technologies. Many of them—insurance is a good example—can only be created and deployed by large aggregates of individuals working in coordination. Their very existence is a social artifact. Decisions about their design and use must therefore be made collectively; individuals cannot do this on their own. Some of these technologies remain in private hands. But the responsibility for managing a growing number of them has been taken over by the state, which today constitutes an all-encompassing authority within whose universal jurisdiction private individuals and groups are allowed to exercise the powers they possess only so far as the state permits.

Today, when a person suffers in some way, when she is homeless or hungry or sick or out of work, we are less quick than we would have been a century ago to attribute her suffering to misfortune. In the end, we may conclude that she is just a victim of fate. But before we do, we feel bound to ask whether her suffering could have been prevented; whether there is a law that entitles her to help; and if so, whether that law has been unfairly applied in her case. The answer to all these questions may be no. There may be no technology that can prevent her suffering, or allay its costs. The best imaginable scheme of entitlements may be one that gives her no claim to support. But the answers to these questions are not the important thing. It is the questions themselves that are significant, for the mere fact that we feel bound to ask them shows how far the realm of entitlements has intruded on that of luck in the public life of modern states.

SERVILITY

Something similar has happened in the relation of gift to entitlement.

Many forms of help that were once provided by private philanthropic organizations, especially religious ones, are now the responsibility of the state.[3] Income subsidies to the poor, hospital care and education—all at one time the province of charity—are today financed, to varying degrees, by the public treasury, and those who receive such help consider it a right, not a gift. To describe it as a gift would be demeaning to them. This is the premise of the modern welfare state, which has taken over many of the historic functions of the church and other private charities, and converted their gifts to entitlements.

The process of conversion has gone farther in Europe than in the United States, whose social welfare system is still comparatively weak. Private philanthropy continues to play a larger role in the provision of basic social goods on this side of the Atlantic than it does in Europe (in the realm of higher education, for example).[4] Yet even in America, the conversion of gift to entitlement has brought about a revolution in attitudes and expectations.

As more and more of the support one needs to live, in ordinary times and hard ones, has come to be provided by the state as a matter of right, instead of by one's family or friends or coreligionists in the form of a gift, the very idea that it is appropriate to feel and express one's gratitude for such support has been displaced from public life. It has come to be associated with an older, now discredited system of patronage, whose moral premises are incompatible with the ethic of entitlement. Gratitude is an acceptance of one's dependence on the love of others. But this is incompatible with the independence to which the political morality of rights attaches supreme importance. As a result, gratitude has become increasingly difficult to acknowledge or express as a public value, and been replaced by a different set of attitudes, characterized by an alertness on the part of each citizen to the vindication of his or her rights and by a readiness to demand their enforcement.

This marks a seismic shift in public sentiment whose repercussions may be felt in many quarters. One symptom, perhaps, is the thickening air of mistrust that now surrounds the most prominent public acts of thanksgiving—the building of monuments and memorials, for example. The Vietnam Memorial is a striking illustration. It contains no words of gratitude, of the sort one finds on earlier monuments. The memorial conveys, with matchless power, a sense of private loss. But the absence from it of any words of thanks betrays an unwillingness or inability on the part of its designers to express a public gratitude for the private sacrifice of those whose lives the memorial records, one by one. There are many reasons for this, including most obviously the unpopularity of the Vietnam War itself. But the awkwardness that now surrounds all expressions of gratitude in a public world dominated by the ethic of entitlement—which has room for rights and wrongs but less for thanks—may also have contributed to the design of the first public monument in American history that deliberately fails to thank those it honors.[5]

This awkwardness is nothing new. It has been a feature of modern political life since the French Revolution. Edmund Burke was the first to diagnose it.

Burke describes the leaders of the Revolution as "metaphysicians" inspired by a confidence in their ability to invent from whole cloth a new social order for whose existence they saw no reason to be thankful to anyone else.[6] The revolutionaries were determined, in Burke's view, to remove every shred of servility, and hence of gratitude, from public life.[7] He explains this as a consequence of the shift from a "prescriptive" understanding of politics to one based upon entitlement—to a belief in the "rights of man."[8]

The rights of man are not a gift. Every man and woman possesses them as a birthright; to be human is to be entitled to their benefits. Nor is the existence of a state committed to the protection of these rights a gift either. Such a state may or may not exist at a particular time, in a particular part of the world. But its establishment is as much a right of those within its territory as the rights it is created to protect. There is therefore no one the citizens of such a state ought to thank for its existence. If earlier generations worked to create and preserve it, that was merely what justice required. And if they failed to do so, it is the duty of the present generation to repair the injustice by doing what their predecessors did not. Charity, love, beneficence and gratitude do not come into the picture at all. They have no place in the definition of the rights of man, or of the obligations of citizens, or of the duties that succeeding generations owe to one another.

In the minds of the revolutionaries, the idea of gratitude was intimately associated with the *ancien régime* and the many degrading forms of dependence it encouraged. The new ideal of independence that inspired their own political program caused them to view every expression of gratitude as a kind of servile groveling, inappropriate to free men and women, which they sought to uproot by means of a systematic conversion of gift to entitlement.

Once begun, Burke says, the process of conversion acquires a momentum of its own. It moves forward at accelerating speed. As customs, privileges and traditions of all sorts are converted to rights the ancestral pieties associated with them lose respectability and are replaced by a sense of entitlement, leaving any remaining elements of piety and gratitude in an even more precarious position.

Burke grasped the logic of this process with prescient clarity and used his great rhetorical powers to defend the spirit of gratitude, without which, he believed, no human civilization is possible. But he was on the losing side of the struggle. In the more than two centuries that have passed since the French Revolution, the conversion of gift to entitlement has proceeded apace. The modern welfare state, swollen with rights of all sorts and marked by a principled hostility to gratitude which the champions of the Revolution were the first to make an axiom of political life, is its most fully developed expression.

GIFT, EXCHANGE AND JUSTICE

The conversion of gift to entitlement is facilitated by the absence of any natural distinction between them. Every gift can be redescribed, without much trouble, as a benefit to which its recipient is entitled as a participant in some mutually advantageous scheme of exchange. The theoretical convertibility of gift to entitlement has been exploited, in particular, by the discipline of economics. The explanations that economists offer of how to make such conversions in theory has eased the way to making them in practice, and thereby helped to provide intellectual support for the political expansion of the realm of entitlements.

Consider the following example. I am walking into the building where I work. My arms are filled with books. I hear a voice behind me say, "Please, let me help." A pleasant young woman opens the door. I say, "Thank you," and we part.

Encounters of this sort are a familiar part of our lives. We have many every day. Sometimes we supply the help, sometimes we receive it. Often these interactions have a ritualized character. There are set words that each participant is expected to speak. We have been brought up to know the script and to act as the situation demands, now playing one role, now the other. Knowing what to do when the situation arises—when to offer help and when to give thanks for it—is what we call politeness.

If the young woman, with no burden herself, had rushed ahead while I fumbled for my keys, I would have thought, "How rude." If I had not thanked her for her help, she would have thought the same. A lack of politeness in others is always a disappointment and sometimes a cause for anger. It leaves us feeling that we've been treated disrespectfully by being denied a benefit we were owed—something to which we were entitled.

In fact, it is quite reasonable to view my encounter at the door as an episode within a larger scheme of entitlements. Unlike those that guarantee my right to vote or to be paid by my employer, which are formally encoded in the law and enforced by courts and other institutions established for this purpose, my right to assistance in opening the door, and my helper's right to be thanked, belong to an informal system of entitlements enforced only by the diffuse social sanctions of disapproval, boycott and shame. Entitlements of the first kind (the formal sort) have an explicit rationale grounded in reciprocal self-interest. Entitlements of the second kind do not have, explicitly at least, the same justification. But a moment's reflection makes it plain that their aim and motive can easily be characterized in terms of self-interest as well.

The woman who opens the door for me does so because she expects that others will open the door for her when she needs their help. Her help now is the price she pays for theirs then. And my expression of gratitude is an acknowledgment that I recognize she has paid a price and is entitled to reciprocating help later on; it is also a declaration of my intention to provide this help to her or someone else, when the occasion arises.

Of course, none of this is said, or perhaps even thought. But it would be much too cumbersome to say it, given the number of times each day that I give help to a stranger or receive it in return. Even more obviously, it would be impossible to gather all the participants in this practice of mutual aid, or their delegates, in a legislative assembly to agree on the rules of politeness, in the way our elected representatives gather to vote on the rules of property law. The informal norms of politeness that we learn as children, and that are (re)enforced by the praise and chastisement of others, are a workable substitute for a formal system of rules—the least costly substitute we can devise. But their aim is essentially the same: to create a system of entitlements and expectations, of rights and duties, that works to the advantage of each of us in the long run, and leaves us better off than we would be if we never had to say "thank you" or offer a helping hand, but could not count on the help of others in return.

All of this makes perfect sense and helps to explain much social behavior. In particular, it helps to explain why gratitude is such an important social virtue, for on this view of it, gratitude is little different from our respect for the property of others. We do not reach over our neighbor's fence and take what is his. That would be theft. Similarly, it would be a kind of theft to accept the help of others when we need it, and not to say "thank you" or reciprocate when the occasion demands. In each case, we would be acting in a shortsightedly selfish way, indulging our self-interest in the short term but undermining it in the long, violating the rules of a system of entitlements that has been established to bring these two into alignment. A rational understanding of what promotes our self-interest will lead us, in both cases, to be respectful of the entitlements of others—of their legal right to the undisturbed possession of their property and their informal, social right to our help when they need it.

To be sure, the limits of the help we owe others are vague and subject to dispute. A stranger may think I've let him down by failing to stop and help with his flat tire. I may think that, under the circumstances, such help would be above and beyond anything he's owed—I'm late for an appointment; the road is dark; many drivers subscribe to commercial services that provide such assistance, and so on. But disagreements of this kind are no different than disputes over the meaning of an ambiguous term in a contract. In fact, that is precisely what they are, the only difference being that the contract in question is an implicit one to which we are all parties, and not an explicit agreement between specific individuals.

When we view the practice of politeness in this light, it is obvious why gratitude is an important social bond. For at bottom it represents a willingness to abide by the rules of reciprocation that lie at the foundation of all social order, which by restraining us increase our welfare beyond what it would be if we lived in an anarchy of rudeness and theft. It should therefore come as no surprise that Adam Smith, who understood as clearly as anyone the contribution the social virtues make to our collective well-being, gave gratitude an especially prominent place in his catalogue of moral traits.[9]

This way of thinking can be carried even farther.

In his famous book, *The Gift,* the anthropologist Marcel Mauss analyzed the economies of several primitive and premodern societies as systems of gift-giving arranged to produce an exchange of goods not unlike that achieved by a market economy.[10] In a market, goods are openly exchanged on the basis of self-interest. The parties have their own welfare in mind and if they benefit their trading partner, do so only as a condition of making themselves better off. What each gives to the other is not, in truth, a gift, but the price of what she receives in return (the "consideration" for it). In the economies that Mauss describes goods are also exchanged, but in the form of gifts. On the surface, these gifts appear to be motivated by generosity rather than self-interest. The donor's apparent intent is to show how generous he can be, and therefore how powerful, since generosity requires resources and the power to dispose of them as one chooses. But in fact, Mauss says, the principal motive for these gifts is to put the recipient in the uncomfortable position of being indebted to his donor, from which he can extract himself only by making a reciprocal gift of his own. Their real purpose is to sustain a system of exchange from which all the participants benefit.

In this respect, the gift economies of the Trobriand Islanders and Tlingit Indians do not differ fundamentally from the exchange economies of modern societies. Just as a participant in a modern-day market feels cheated if his contractual expectations are upset, an Indian chief who makes a gift to his counterpart from another tribe but receives no gift in return feels cheated too. He has not gotten his due. He has not gotten what he was entitled to, and though his entitlement takes the form of a gift, there is nothing gratuitous about it. From his point of view, the gift he is owed is not discretionary. In a manner of speaking, it belongs to him already, on account of the costs he has incurred as a result of his own participation in the system of gift-giving—just as the help the young woman gives me at the door already belongs to me on account of the similar help I've given others in the past and am prepared to give them in the future. Mauss himself draws this conclusion.[11] Our modern habits of generosity and gratitude should be understood, he says, in precisely the same terms as the archaic Indian potlatch and related ceremonies of exchange. In both cases, we must look through the superficial form of gift to the structure of entitlement that provides its true rationale.

This way of looking at things has no obvious limits. Even the primal gift relation of mother to child can be redescribed in such terms. The child receives her mother's gift of life on the condition that, when the child is grown, she will take care of her mother and then, when she has children of her own, do the same for them; the mother's gift is her fulfillment of the implicit pledge *she* made on the receipt of *her* mother's gift, and so on.

The result of these interlocking gifts is a durable human world, one that has continuity over time and lasts longer than a generation. Each generation presumably benefits from the existence of such a world. There are certain projects (building a cathedral) and ambitions (writing a book that will be read after one is dead) that are possible only on the assumption that the human world has a life longer than one's own. It is therefore in the interest of every member of each generation to do his or her part in sustaining this world by giving those in the next generation the help they need to survive, just as they were given similar help by those in the generation before.[12]

If all the generations, or their delegates, could be gathered in a council, they would presumably agree to some such arrangement. They would contract to support each other in sequence. That no such contract can be made is a consequence of the (accidental) fact that we exist in time and cannot meet with our great-grandparents and great-grandchildren face-to-face to fix our responsibilities. But that is really no different than the accidental fact that the number of people with whom we interact on a daily basis is so large and their identity so hard to determine in advance, that we cannot all gather to agree on rules of politeness. And it should not distract us from recognizing that the relation among generations is one of gift in form only. In reality, it is a relation of entitlement. Even the good breast is not really a gift but the ful-fillment of a contractual pledge.

If this seems far-fetched, it is useful to recall that the most influential work of political theory of the twentieth century defends precisely this view.

In *A Theory of Justice,* John Rawls devotes a number of pages to the sub-ject of what he calls justice between generations.[13] What do different genera-tions owe one another? What duties do they have to each other regarding the use of scarce resources? Rawls answers this question as he does every other: by asking what bargain the representatives of different generations would strike, if deprived of all information about their situation that might moti-vate them to choose some outcome other than the one that is fairest (in this case, most obviously, information about the particular generation to which they belong). The result is a view of the relation among generations from which the notion of gift is entirely absent. On Rawls' account, what each generation receives from its predecessors and conveys to its successors, it gets and gives in the form of an entitlement. From one generation to the next, the human world that Rawls describes is sustained not by love but right.

Rawls' concerns differ, of course, from those of an economist. Economists study efficiency—the characteristics of social arrangements that promote or retard the efficient use of resources. The power of economics as an instrument for the intellectual conversion of gift to entitlement derives from its ability to show that gift relations have efficiency-promoting properties and that the most enlightened way of viewing them is as the outcome of an implicit bargain.

Rawls' subject is justice, not efficiency. *A Theory of Justice* proposes a method for deciding which entitlements people should have in the first place, as a matter of fairness, even if some more efficient distribution can be imagined. The subject it explores is therefore anterior to that of economics, which always presupposes some answer to the question Rawls addresses.

The method Rawls adopts for answering this question, however, is a close cousin of the one the economist employs to study the efficiency of gift rela-tions. For Rawls, and for all those in the contractarian tradition of political philosophy to which he belongs, the nature of justice, like that of efficiency, is to be understood from the standpoint of a hypothetical bargain. From an economic point of view, an arrangement is efficient if those involved would have agreed to its terms, but for the transaction costs of actually doing so. From a contractarian perspective, a scheme of entitlements is fair if those subject to it would have agreed to the scheme beforehand.

Everything of course depends on a specification of the situation in which the parties are imagined to confront and decide the question of what entitlements they should have. Different specifications produce different bargains, and hence different answers to the question of what is fair. Rawls spends a great deal of time defending his own preferred description of what he calls the parties' "original position." The persuasiveness of his theory of justice, as compared with the accounts of other contractarian philosophers, depends very largely, if not entirely, on the plausibility of the description he gives.[14] But whether one finds his description compelling, or prefers some other to it, the result of *any* approach of the sort that Rawls employs is to enlarge the sphere of entitlement at the expense of that of gift, in a way that parallels the enlargement economics invites.

The individuals in Rawls' original position reach an agreement that settles the question of what basic rights and privileges the members of their society shall have. They do this on the basis of rational self-interest alone. There is no love among them. Their independence is so great, and their ignorance of themselves and one another so complete, that the very conditions of love are missing from the situation in which Rawls places them. None makes a gift to another, or receives one in return. All look to self-interest alone, and calculate accordingly. Each eyes his neighbors warily, conscious of the need to collaborate but looking for the best bargain possible.

This is a preposterously fictional condition, as Rawls himself concedes. But that is not the important point. Every abstract theory, of justice or anything else, is necessarily unrealistic. The important point is that by making the hypothetical agreement of those in his original position the benchmark by which to measure the justice of actual, existing arrangements, Rawls' theory necessarily elevates the legitimacy of entitlement and devalues that of gift, within the sphere of public life. For if the only way that one can justify existing arrangements is by appealing to an imaginary negotiation from which the very possibility of love has been excluded, every aspect of our public world that might be deemed a gift for which feelings of gratitude are appropriate will either lack legitimacy or be considered a threat to the only sort of legitimacy that such a theory allows.

The magic wand of economics has the power to convert every gift to a bargain. Economics makes it doubtful that gifts really exist. Rawls' theory of justice drains the very idea of gift of its public authority. Together, these provide theoretical support for the practical expansion of the realm of entitlement that has been underway since the French Revolution. They are the intellectual pillars of the modern welfare state, in whose vast arsenal of rights the revolutionaries' ambition to convert all gifts to entitlements, in the name of human freedom, is fulfilled to a degree that even Burke could not have imagined.[15]

A PRIVATE VIRTUE

The marginalization of gratitude is a pervasive feature of modern public life. It manifests itself in many ways. It colors Rawls' concept of justice as fairness, and motivates the economist's relentless campaign to recast every gift as a bargain. It shapes our attitude toward the work of public memorialization. It is in the background of debates about school prayer and the Pledge of Allegiance which, though framed in terms of the relation between church and state, are at least partly about the appropriateness of stylized acts of thanksgiving of any sort in a system of public education devoted to the production of independent-minded citizens who view the rights they possess as an entitlement, not a gift. And it perhaps even contributes to the support for abortion rights, or so one might infer from the antiabortion slogan that "a child is a gift, not a choice."

But the public devaluation of gratitude has not meant its disappearance from our lives. Outside the public realm, in the sphere of private life, love and charity and gratitude continue to thrive. Men and women still fall in love, and make gifts, and express their gratitude for the gifts of others. The growth of the realm of entitlements in the modern welfare state has not caused any of these things to vanish from the world. How could it? All that it has done is expel them from the public realm into that of private experience, where they are still very much alive. Indeed, one might wonder whether the public conversion of gift to entitlement has not left the number and intensity of people's feelings of thankfulness unchanged and merely reassigned them to a different arena.

This may well be true. There may be as many occasions (however one would measure such a thing) for the citizens of a modern state to express in private their gratitude for the love and generosity of family and friends, as the citizens of premodern political communities had to express in public their gratitude for the gifts of civic benefactors—those of the gods who favored them in war and peace, and of their human ancestors whose devotion and sacrifice created the possibility of a public life in the first place. But this misses the main point. The privatization of gratitude means more than its relocation from one sphere to another. It signifies its demotion as well, for a gratitude that can only be experienced and expressed in private is a *lesser* gratitude that lives under the disapproving shadow of the one morality we are all prepared to acknowledge as the only acceptable basis of our common life together, however we choose to live our private lives outside this sphere of shared agreement.

The ethic of entitlement is today the only one on which we all agree. Partly, this is for pragmatic reasons. Any principle of political morality that requires us to view important public benefits as a gift rather than a right, renders them less secure. As a result, it is unlikely to attract the support of those who depend upon these benefits. If we imagine the basic rules of public life to be the outcome of an agreement and seek, as Rawls does, to legitimate them by securing the consent of all involved, the ethic of entitlement is bound to enjoy a practical advantage over any morality based on gift.

But it is not for practical reasons alone that public moralities of the latter kind are now wholly discredited. We condemn them for ethical reasons too—because they are widely viewed as an offense to the dignity of those from whom gratitude is asked or expected, as a *humiliation* that others, even if they could, ought not to impose upon them. We have all grown used to this idea. It comes as close as any to being an unquestioned axiom of political life, and as such, cannot help but color our feelings about gratitude in general, even in the sphere of private relations. For however rigorously we separate the demands of public life from those of private experience, there is bound to be some seepage between them. The attitudes we regard as morally required in the first realm cannot be stopped at the door of the second. To some degree, they are bound to cross the threshold with us—since we are not, after all, separate persons but the same ones in different roles, and our ability to put on and take off the attitudes appropriate to each is at best incomplete.

Our imperfect ability to do this is the justification for the ancient observation that the public morality of a city is bound to inform the private morality of its citizens, and vice versa.[16] Today, our public morality is shaped by the belief that there is something humiliating about the gift relation and the gratitude that beneficiaries are expected to feel toward their donors, and by the assumption that all such relations, in the public sphere at least, ought to be converted to entitlements instead. Inevitably, this puts gratitude under a cloud in the private sphere as well. It does not abolish love, and gifts, and charity, or render gratitude for these things universally demeaning. But it sets them in opposition to the dominant public morality of our time, whose pressure to convert every gift to a right presents a hurdle which the experience and expression of gratitude even in private must now overcome.

In this sense, the privatization of gratitude is no mere relocation. It is a devaluation too. For if gratitude is *only* a private virtue, it is a lesser one whose dignity is rendered suspect by the sharply opposing values embodied in the ethic of entitlement that has displaced gift and gratitude from public life. The more its worth is challenged by the ruling public ideals of our time, which equate gratitude with humiliation, the harder it becomes to see the good of gratitude, and to honor it, even in those areas of life where it survives.

AUTONOMY

That the expansion of the realm of entitlement represents an immense increase of control is easiest to see in the case of luck. To be subject to luck is to be vulnerable to forces that are arbitrary or unknowable. When these are discovered to have an intelligible pattern that the mind can grasp, and technology can alter, they become subject to control instead. Once this happens, the question of whether we ought to control them arises. Indeed, it becomes unavoidable, for if we have the power to prevent a misfortune, like smallpox, and fail to do so, we are just as responsible for the consequences as if we chose to eradicate the disease instead. We may conclude that the preventive measures required to stop the spread of smallpox are too expensive, given our other needs, but this decision too is our responsibility. To meet the responsibilities that science and technology create, we must therefore decide which misfortunes people are entitled to be protected against, and which they must bear on their own. This leads to the establishment of countless entitlement programs. But even where it is decided that no right to protection exists, and that people should be left to the vagaries of fate, that decision itself is now the result of human planning—a triumph of control.

The conversion of gift to entitlement also entails an expansion of human control, though the reason is less obvious.

The fact that I am entitled to something does not mean, of course, that my control over it is assured. I have a right to the use of my property, but my neighbor may reach over the fence and take what is mine. We are all vulnerable to being robbed and cheated by others. That is why our entitlements can be secured only within a system of reciprocal restraints: "I will give you the

security you desire by respecting your rights if you give me the same in return." There is no escaping these mutual dependencies. They are a consequence
of the limits on our power to protect our rights by ourselves.

But there is another sense in which the holder of an entitlement possesses
all he needs to secure it, merely by virtue of the entitlement itself. The claim
that I have an entitlement implies that I have compelling reasons why others
should respect it. If in fact I have the right I claim I do, then others ought to
be persuaded by my reasons, even if they are not. The person who is entitled
to something already has what he needs to show why he should be treated in
a certain way. He already possesses the argumentative resources to demonstrate the validity of his claim, even if someone unjustly blocks or denies
it. The possession of these resources is itself an important form of control,
despite the fact that we depend on others to honor the arguments we construct with them.

The person who receives a gift depends on the generosity of his donor, just
as the owner of a piece of property depends on the respect and fair mindedness of his neighbor. But the recipient of a gift is dependent in another way
too, for he has no compelling argument why he should receive it. He has no
argument the donor is bound to respect, if he or she will only listen to reason. If the recipient *does* have such an argument, then the gift is not really a
gift but something else—a bargain, a trade, an entitlement in disguise—
one of those "gifts" that are really items in a system of mutually beneficial
exchange. By contrast, every true gift is an act of love, and that is something
we have no arguments to demand. There is no court of appeal to which those
disappointed in love can turn.

When a gift becomes a right, we are still not assured of receiving it, any
more than we are of receiving any of the other benefits to which we are entitled. But we are in greater control of our lives. The conversion of gift to entitlement expands the control we have over our lives by supplying us with
publicly recognized reasons for demanding that we be given what before we
received on account of the unforced generosity of others. It increases our independence by making us less dependent on love, which always remains beyond the power of reason to command.

The growth of the realm of entitlement at the expense of that of gift thus
broadly promotes human autonomy. This is not just because (as is often
remarked) the modern world of rights is premised on the equal capacity of
every citizen to be a self-*directing* agent. It is also because the conversion
of gift to entitlement makes our lives more self-*sufficient* as well. No system

of entitlements, however well-policed, can ever eliminate completely our dependence on others. But the conversion of gift to entitlement removes one
important source of dependence that cannot be policed at all, and by doing
so dramatically expands the domain of human autonomy understood as self-
sufficiency. To be perfectly self-sufficient, one would have to possess every resource needed to live and flourish—to be wholly self-contained, like a God
who requires no one and nothing but himself. The systematic conversion of
gift to entitlement represents an important step toward the attainment of this
godlike condition and is a powerful expression of the wish to achieve it.

We have met this wish before. It is the infant's wish to be restored to a
prenatal state of omnipotence in which the world no longer resists him as
something apart. This is a permanent feature of our constitution. It is inscribed
in the human heart. But in the civilization of the modern West, the universal
human longing for control has reached a pitch, and produced results, that have
no parallel in human history. To a degree their ancestors could not have
imagined, the inhabitants of this civilization have become, in Descartes'
phrase, "the masters and possessors of nature."[17] The replacement of luck and
gift by a system of entitlements is one expression of such mastery—in the
moral and political realm, perhaps the most important. Today, it is admired
and emulated on a global, if not quite universal, scale. But the development
and refinement of this system, and of all the other methods of control that
set the modern world apart, was pioneered in the West and has been carried
farther there than anywhere else. What explains this striking fact, given the
universality of the longing for control itself?

The answer of course is complex. Many factors are involved. But as Melanie Klein suggests, the desire for omnipotence can be aggravated by spiritual
longings, as in the case of Milton's Satan, whose passion for control reaches
cosmic proportions on account of his wounded pride and wish to punish God
for hurting him so badly. Max Weber makes a similar point in his famous
essay on capitalism and the Protestant ethic. The unique degree to which modern Western capitalism has succeeded in rationalizing, and thereby controlling, the production and exchange of goods, is to be explained, he claims, in
important part at least, by the religious attitudes of those who were responsible for the advancement of the capitalist system in the sixteenth and seventeenth centuries.

It therefore seems reasonable to look for an explanation of the exception-
alness of the modern Western pursuit of control in the tradition of spiritual
belief that sets the West apart from every other civilization in the world. The

longing for control is ubiquitous. So are the obstacles that oppose it and the opportunities for fulfilling it. But in the West, and there alone, these universal conditions have been shaped by the beliefs of the Christian religion, within whose matrix the civilization of the West has evolved. The West is a Christian civilization in a deeper sense than many, perhaps, suppose. Christian beliefs have played a decisive role in the development of Western science, politics and art. And these same beliefs have contributed in a crucial way to the amplification of the longing for omnipotence that in the modern West has reached unprecedented (some would say satanic) proportions.

The God of grace who has ruled the West for more than two thousand years makes unbearable demands on his subjects. He demands more gratitude than we can ever adequately express. He thus prevents us from returning his love with one as good and great. When we see ourselves in his eyes, we can only despise what we see. We can only feel contempt for our humanity and wish to overcome it—to be beings of a different kind. And so we have taken revenge on the God who has made our human condition so miserable by climbing up to Heaven and seizing his place, succeeding where Satan failed.

Every human child feels anger at the world for withholding what he wants. In a normally healthy child with a good enough mother, anger of this sort never gets the upper hand. It never disappears completely, but is overshadowed by a gratitude for goodness received that creates a space for love, and with it, for the fulfillment of loving the world in return. A child of this sort experiences the world as a place not wholly foreign or threatening. The foundation is laid for a generative and fulfilling life and for the acceptance of her own finitude, rather than an angry rebellion against it. But where anger and envy get the upper hand, the result is a pathological condition. The truly envious child is no longer at home in the world. And while, at an individual level, many factors determine which course a child takes, an entire civilization may also incline in one direction or the other on account of its ruling beliefs. The civilization of the modern West is distinguished by an envious longing for control that is the result of the religion that has directed its development for two thousand years, whose theology produces a resentment of God that leads to the religion's own destruction and leaves its disenchanted followers homeless in the world they have built.

I recognize that this will seem preposterous to many, Christians and non-Christians alike. How can a religion of boundless love produce a hatred of God? And how can it possibly destroy itself? That Christianity is threatened by forces external to it all will concede. But that it is its own worst enemy—how is that even thinkable? Only a close and sympathetic inspection of its own ideals, and of the metaphysical conflict among them, can provide an answer to these reasonable questions. The next chapter offers a preview and a starting point for the detailed explication that follows.

But even now, before we have begun in earnest, it may be possible to offer the following provisional judgment and to pose the question it invites.

The forms of control that in the modern West have been carried to such an extreme are responsible for much that is good in human life today. None of us would wish to live without the protections they afford. These include those guaranteed by the modern system of entitlements, which reduce our vulnerability to forces we cannot control and give public expression to the true belief that every human being is infinitely precious and therefore equally worthy of respect. And yet the moral and political philosophies that are most often invoked to vindicate this belief, and to provide a warrant for the expansion of the world of rights, have by and large proceeded on the basis of an ideal of self-sufficiency that makes it hard if not impossible to acknowledge, as a public matter at least, the place of love in human life and the good of the gratitude that is responsive to it. This is true, for example, of Rawls' theory of justice and of accounts that are similar to it, like Jürgen Habermas' defense of public norms by appeal to what he calls an "ideal speech situation." These philosophies and the attitudes they encourage make it more difficult to acknowledge, in a public way, an acceptance of our dependence on others, to whose love we have no right backed by reasons. They cause us to lose sight of the good of gratitude, and make us more likely to be, as envious children always are, unhappy in our condition. They validate our homelessness instead of offering an antidote to it. And that is because, though their vocabulary and method is entirely secular, they are the contemporary expression of a religious worldview that raises envy to the level of a cosmic force and through its own theology opens the way to its boundless expansion.

Is there any way of affirming the human longing for omnipotence without the envious and self-destructive wish to take the place of the God of the Christian religion, which in the West has given this universal longing both a uniquely effective and singularly destructive form? Of reconciling this longing, which is the source of so much that is wonderful in our lives, and of our reverence for the inventiveness and courage of human beings, with an acceptance of the human condition, in a way that restores love and gratitude to a valued place in the world—in today's world, enlightened by science and inspired by the belief that all human beings are worthy of respect? The answer is yes, but to reach it we need a different theology. We need a conception of what Aristotle calls "the eternal and divine" that is neither pagan, like his, nor Christian like the one that replaced it.[18] We need a different idea of God than either of these other two. To think that we can do without any such idea—that we can manage with no theology at all—is a terrible and inhuman mistake, encouraged by the nihilistic metaphysics that itself is merely the last, decayed remnant of the religion to which we owe both the glory and emptiness of our age. But that is a long story, and it is time we began.

CHAPTER 3

"Endless Gratitude So Burdensome"

CHRISTIAN THEOLOGY AND
WESTERN CIVILIZATION

The civilization of the modern West is the product of a long and complex historical development that Max Weber memorably describes as the "disenchantment" of the world.[1] Disenchantment implies a loss of religious belief or, at a minimum, its privatization—the expulsion of religion from the realm of public affairs into that of private experience. Today, Weber says, the disenchantment of the world is the universal "fate" of humankind.[2] But it began in the West and has gone farther there than anywhere else.

Many different forces have helped to shape what Weber calls our "godless and prophetless" age.[3] Any short list would include: the "creative destruction"[4] of the modern capitalist system of production, with its historically unique reliance on workers who neither own the means of production nor are owned by their employers; the rationally disciplined methods of public administration that first emerged in the states of early modern Europe, on the basis of a parallel separation of officeholders from the means of administration; and the new science of nature that in the sixteenth and seventeenth centuries transformed our understanding of the physical world, together with the immensely more powerful technologies of war and manufacture that it spawned. Weber discusses all these in detail.[5] But judging by the number of pages he devoted to it, the factor he considered most important in the disenchantment of the West was religion.[6]

More specifically, it was the Christian religion, which for nearly two millennia has supplied the framework of belief within which Western thought and culture have matured. Christianity has been the spiritual nursery bed of Western civilization. Its concepts of God, world, soul, and salvation have inspired the Western understanding of morality and politics and spurred the development of modern natural science.[7] Our answers to the questions of what it means to be a human being, to treat others in a just and responsible way, and to know why things happen as they do in the heavens and on earth, have all been shaped by Christian theology.

The intellectual legacy of pagan antiquity has of course played an important role too. But the philosophies of Plato and Aristotle, the mathematics of Euclid and the astronomy of Ptolemy have been filtered through the system of Christian ideas and interpreted from its point of view. The riches of the Hebrew Bible, and the great works of medieval Judaism and Islam, have had to pass through this same filter as well. Their reception in the West has likewise been conditioned by the metaphysical and moral commitments of the Christian religion, which since the age of Constantine has formed the bedrock of Western belief. From late antiquity on, the Christian understanding of God has provided the point of departure for all the most important and lasting developments in Western philosophy, politics and science. Even today, in an age of unbelief, our convictions about such elementary matters as the meaning of human dignity and the intelligibility of nature continue to be shaped, from the grave, by Christian assumptions.

Christianity affirms that the world was created from nothing by a transcendent God, who sent his son into the world to die on a cross, so that man, who had fallen through his own disobedience into a condition of otherwise irremediable disgrace, might be restored to the possibility of life everlasting by means of the redemptive suffering of Jesus Christ. This is the heart of the Christian message. It has no parallel in either Judaism or Islam, both of which emphatically reject the doctrine of Incarnation. The Christian theology of original sin and of salvation through God's sacrificial gift of himself to man is unique among the Abrahamic religions, and raises questions that neither Judaism nor Islam is compelled to address. The determined effort of Christianity's most brilliant apologists to answer these questions in a philosophically rigorous way, from the Church Fathers of the third and fourth centuries to the Protestant divines of the sixteenth and seventeenth, sets the Christian religion apart from every other in the world.

The paradoxical result of this effort has been the disenchantment of the civilization shaped by these very beliefs. In one sphere after another, the authority of God has been replaced by that of human beings and his divine direction of the world supplanted by human powers of control. But the displacement of God by man, as a normative and practical matter, is not the result, as many suppose, of an attack on religion by science and other secular forces. That is true only at a late stage of development. More fundamentally, the death of God and man's assumption of God's place is a Christian phenomenon whose roots lie in the unbearable demands that Christianity's own unique theology of grace makes on its adherents. Driven by their envious rage at a God for whose gifts they can never be thankful enough, his loving but unhappy children have relieved themselves of the torment of their unrequited gratitude by striving to make God's powers their own, with the result that we, who live in the world their rebellion has shaped, have lost the ability to give thanks in a public and philosophically supportable way for the gifts of the other human beings on whose love our existence depends, and to view the world as our home.

Homelessness is one dimension of disenchantment. Another is the loss of a shared sense of connection to the eternal and divine, and the relegation to the sphere of private life of what we today describe in a colorless way as "religious" belief. Many regard this, too, as the result of forces external to religion—of the practical need, for example, to find a nonsectarian basis for political authority. To a considerable extent this is true. But here again, the first and most important stimulus has been theological. The loss of a common and confident connection to God is also a product of Christian belief.

God's human subjects yearn to express their love for their creator. Yet they can never return his love with one as good and great. That is because he is too distant and different from them. This tempts them to draw God nearer and to make him more like themselves. But that is a sin. It is the work of pride. Christian piety demands that the abysmal gap between God and man be preserved against every attempt to reduce it. This in turn requires that God be set at an ever-greater distance from the world so that those who aspire to build a bridge between themselves and God are prevented from reaching their blasphemous goal. To preserve the dignity of the God to whom they pray, pious Christians are thus compelled to remove him to a position infinitely remote from the world. In the end, this makes it impossible even for his most ardent followers to have any relationship with him at all.

This is the result, I shall argue, of the logic of Christian belief. It is the conclusion to which we are led if we attempt to understand and explain the premises of Christian theology in a philosophically rigorous way. Many Christians—both laypersons and professional theologians—will of course object that to analyze their religion in this spirit is to do so from a point of view that is external, indeed hostile, to the life of faith that grounds it, which starts from an acceptance of the mystery of the Incarnation—something no philosopher who insists on proceeding by reason alone can accept. But the spirit of philosophy is not, in fact, foreign to that of the Christian religion. In contrast both to Judaism and Islam, Christianity has been driven from the start by a perceived need to justify its own doctrines in a philosophically disciplined fashion, thereby subjecting its central mysteries to a rationalizing pressure that in the end, as a logical matter at least, they have been unable to withstand.

Many Christians still refuse to accept this conclusion. But they are resisting a demand that is internal to their own theology, not repelling a threat from outside it. Others have given up the belief in a mystery that reason cannot condone—reluctantly or enthusiastically, as the case may be. But whether their number is larger or smaller than that of those who continue to hold to the faith, the refusal of these disenchanted Christians to give any normative or practical weight to the revealed truths of their religion is today in line with the deepest currents of Western civilization as a whole, for it represents one of the shared assumptions on which the science, morality and politics of the modern West all rest.

Yet even many of these modern unbelievers, whether they quietly concede or loudly proclaim that for them God is dead, still subscribe, implicitly at least, to one of the basic principles of the Christian religion. They continue to insist that *this* world could have meaning and value *only if* it were connected to *another* world beyond it, whose existence they deny. They remain committed to this metaphysical requirement while simultaneously maintaining that it cannot be met. As a result, they find themselves cut off from the only connection to the eternal and divine that the disenchanted heirs of two thousand years of Christian faith are able to conceive, homeless in this world with no prospect of a homecoming in any other. This is a hopeless and dispiriting condition whose inhabitants are condemned to a life interminably bleak, no matter how bravely they pretend to accept it. Nietzsche's term for the all-too-Christian philosophy that underlies it is "nihilism."[8]

Max Weber viewed this despairing condition as an inevitable consequence of disenchantment; indeed, he considered them the same. But that is a

peculiarly discouraging conclusion, for if Weber is right that disenchantment is the result of rationalization, then it would seem to follow that the
triumph of reason itself is bound to leave us homeless in a world without
God. But is that so? Is there no alternative to Weber's view? Is it possible to
understand the claims of reason in a way that restores our relation to God
and allows us to be at home in the world again, with the other human beings
whose love gives us the space we need to love the world in return? Is there a
cure for nihilism that embraces modernity too, instead of demanding that
we abandon reason for faith?

That is the principal question to which this book is addressed. But before
we consider where such a cure might be found, we need to inquire how we
became ill in the first place. In the chapters that follow, I shall attempt to
show, in some detail, that the source of our spiritual malaise lies in the
centuries-long struggle of Christianity's most determined advocates to remain
faithful to the dogmas of their own religion, and to defend these in a philosophically compelling way against enemies both within and without. Christianity is the religion that disenchants itself, and nihilism its final phase, as
Nietzsche understood more clearly than Weber.

THE WORD BECOME FLESH

The Christian God, like the Jewish and Muslim ones, exists apart from
the world and brings it into being from nothing in an act of uncompelled
love.[9] All three religions thus view the mere existence of the world as a divine
gift. And all three also recognize many other such gifts as well, including that
of moral life, which human beings alone enjoy on account of having been
endowed by God with the power to distinguish right from wrong, together
with the gift of his mercy and forgiveness for failing to use this power as we
should.

But Christianity recognizes another gift that Judaism and Islam do not—
God's gift of the life of his son,[10] sent into the world to pay a debt we had no
right to have discharged. This is a gift so large, so unexpected, so intimate
and vivid, as to eclipse all the others in its psychological effect. Indeed, even
saying that God gave his son for our sins fails to measure its magnitude, for
if Christ were just a man, like those he comes to save, his suffering could not
redeem their debt to God. To do this, Jesus himself must be divine. God and
his son must in some mysterious way be one. It must be God himself who
undergoes the sacrificial death required to lift the burden of original sin from

our shoulders. This is the central dogma of the Christian religion—the belief that God, who made us from nothing and gave us the gift of moral responsibility, took on flesh and died so that our abuse of all his other gifts might be forgiven.

Judaism and Islam of course teach their followers to be grateful to God for his blessings. But the gift of the Incarnation, which Christianity alone recognizes, is a uniquely impressive and humbling one, and the gratitude that Christians believe we ought to feel for it is commensurately great. In this way, Christianity brings the ideas of gift and gratitude, which are common to all the Abrahamic religions, to a higher pitch. As a result, the belief that God's gifts to man are so large that no expression of gratitude can ever be adequate to them acquires a salience in Christian thought that it lacks in either Judaism or Islam.

Both these religions rest on the assumption that human beings are able to express their gratitude to God in a more or less satisfactory way by living as his law requires. Both allow for the possibility of a life of piety whose rituals and routines, and spirit of devotion, fulfill the wish to thank God for his gifts. Fulfillment of this sort may be difficult, and rare, but it is not out of the question. It is not beyond human reach.

Christianity, by contrast, renders the very possibility of such fulfillment doubtful in a fundamental way. It requires its followers to acknowledge that any expression of thanks to God, whether in the form of prayer or ritual or anything else, always falls short of the mark. It compels them to accept that they can never be grateful enough for God's love. The most powerful expression of this belief is the Christian doctrine of grace.

The main function of the doctrine of grace is to underscore our utter dependence on God's gifts—most importantly, the gift of salvation through Jesus Christ. This is a gift we receive entirely by the grace of God, and not because we have earned it. To suggest otherwise is to convert our relation to God from one of benefaction to entitlement, which is a blasphemy against God, for if we can ever be entitled to anything from him (whether because we have obeyed his law or for any other reason), God's freedom is to that extent constrained. To suggest that this is possible, even in the smallest degree, is an insult to God. It is a prideful assertion of the sufficiency of our own human powers, which in truth require God's help to achieve even the smallest result.

The Israelites who covenanted with Yahweh were of course infinitely less powerful than he. But to the extent that he agreed to be bound by the terms of his covenant, he put the Israelites in the position of being able to complain—as they often did—that their partner had forgotten them or was neglecting his duties. Relations of entitlement are inherently egalitarian. Anyone who has a right, even against a vastly greater power, can defend it by appealing to a rule which, whether it be obeyed or not, applies with equal force to the holder of the right and the one against whom it is asserted. To think, therefore, that we can ever be entitled to anything from God is to imagine that we stand, incompletely perhaps, but meaningfully, on a par with him. It is to conceive of the gulf between us and God, however large, as something less than absolute. Hence, the only way to respect the chasm that separates us from God is to suppress the temptation to convert our relation to him into one of obligation and right. How to avoid this implication, while acknowledging that God can freely bind himself if he chooses, has been a perennial challenge to Christian philosophers from Augustine on.

Judaism and Islam both recoil at the suggestion that human beings can confine God's freedom by their actions—including even the most rigorous obedience to his law. They too insist on a gap between creator and creature that any assertion of rights against God threatens to narrow (though in the case of Judaism, its covenantal origins complicate matters considerably). But the Christian doctrine of the Incarnation makes the pressure to resist immeasurably stronger on account of the uniquely intense feelings of dependence on God's undeserved love that the image of Christ on the cross is bound to arouse.

Beginning with Paul, the principal weapon that Christian writers have used to defeat every proposal that would allow human beings to become, in however small a measure, the masters of their own salvation has been the doctrine of grace. The doctrine of grace is the antithesis of the idea of entitlement. Under the rationalizing influence of Greco-Roman thought, it became an abstract theological principle of cosmic importance, and through the writings of Augustine a foundational premise of the Western Christian tradition. The effect of the doctrine of grace has been to separate man from God in an ever more radical way, instead of drawing them closer together, as the idea of the Incarnation might seem to do. The only Abrahamic religion to teach that God became man has thus paradoxically been the one to drive them farthest apart, magnifying God's powers and belittling man's by means of a theological doctrine whose effect, though not of course its intention, has been to encourage the belief that we can never be grateful enough to the God who created and saves us.

A Christian who remains faithful to the idea of the Incarnation must refuse to believe that there is anything a follower of Christ can do to earn his or her salvation. To every suggestion that we have some power to compel God to recognize our goodness and reward us for it, here on earth or afterward in heaven, a true-believing Christian is bound to reply that everything we have, and are, and may hope to acquire, we possess by the grace of God alone, including our love of God himself. The history of Christian theology is punctuated by a series of such replies—from Paul's polemic against the rabbis, to Augustine's attack on Pelagius, to William of Ockham's metaphysical assault on the rationalizing philosophy of Thomas Aquinas, to Luther's condemnation of Erasmus' tepid endorsement of free will. What all these theologians teach, in different ways, is that the only proper attitude toward God is one of perfect gratitude, as limitless as the gifts of love he bestows upon us, summarized and represented by the gift of the cross: a gratitude that can never fulfill its own longing to thank God with a love as good and great, or even with one that is really our own to give, and not, like every other good thing we possess, a gift from God as well. The theological tradition represented by these writers has been carried forward in a deliberate, at times aggressive, way from Paul to Kierkegaard. It is as uniquely Christian as the doctrine of the Incarnation to whose meaning it is a response. In this sense, one might reasonably describe it as the most authentic strain in the complex skein of Christian belief.

SHORTFALL

The gratitude toward God that Christianity demands of its adherents resembles the thankfulness we feel toward other human beings. We are grateful to our parents for their care, which we did not earn or deserve. More generally, we are grateful to our predecessors in the various human communities to which we belong. Their help, too, is a gift and not an entitlement. The gratitude we feel toward our parents, toward earlier generations of citizens, toward those who have worked before us in the trades and professions and cultural communities to which we belong, is the human analogue of the gratitude a Christian feels for the gracious gifts of God.

But there is a crucial difference. My parents' care was a gift for which I can never make an adequate return *to them*. I can, however, make a gift of equal magnitude to someone else, for example, to the child on whom I bestow my care in turn. In the end, this is the only really adequate way I have of thanking my parents—by performing some comparably loving act of my own, which may take countless different forms, including that of having children. The same is true of my relation to my predecessors in the political community to which I belong. It is impossible for me to make a gift to them directly. They are dead and gone. But I can express my gratitude by making a gift of comparable value to those who follow me, and in that way reciprocate the care I have received with care as good and great.

This is not possible in the case of the gifts I receive from God. In the first place, there is no gift that I can make to God that compares with those I have received from him. To suggest otherwise implies that God depends on me, and needs my love, just as I need his. My relation with God is not merely asymmetrical in the way my relation with my parents is, on account of the irreversible order of our existence in time. It is *radically* asymmetrical. My dependence on God is absolute. My faith, my fate, my very existence, all depend completely and continuously on his unearned love. God's condition, by contrast, is one of perfect independence. He can never have any needs at all. God can never experience the neediness that alone makes a gift valuable to the one who receives it, as my neediness made the gift of my parents' love valuable to me, and the neediness of my children makes my gift to them of equal value.

Second, I can never make an adequate return to God by caring for other human beings and the world we inhabit together. My love for the men and women with whom I share this world may be commensurate with their own. But it cannot be commensurate with God's. That is because my love is finite and his is not. My human love is frail and flawed. It is easily overcome by other passions. But this can never happen to God. His love is perfect; it can never falter or fail. His gifts therefore radically outshine those I make to the human beings who are the objects of my limited solicitude and care—though my gifts to them shine just as brightly (or dimly!) as the gifts I receive from other, equally flawed mortals like my parents.

Third, and most important, the love that I would return to God in gratitude for his gifts is not even mine to give. Like every other good thing I possess, my love of God is a gift of the God to whom I would (re)give it. Some receive this gift and others do not. Those who do, experience the greatest happiness a human being can know. But the love of God in which their happiness consists is itself God's gift to them. To return God's love with a love of my own—in the way I return my parents' love with the love I show my children—is therefore out of the question. For my love is not merely weak and fallible by comparison with his; more fundamentally, it is not even something I possess with the independence that every true act of giving presupposes.

Indeed, *even to think* that I can adequately reciprocate God's gifts by making a return gift of my own is a form of pride. No such reciprocation is possible. Whatever gifts I make to other human beings or to God himself, in a spirit of thankfulness for the gifts I have received from him, can never measure up to those that he has given me. This is the central meaning of the cross. Many Christians, perhaps, have a more comforting view of its significance. But among those who, beginning with Paul, have thought about the matter most deeply, no other conclusion has seemed possible. The cross is the symbol of our incompetence ever to be adequately thankful to God.

For those who accept this conclusion, there will always be a shortfall between God's gifts and those they offer in return. A thoughtful Christian must strive to keep this in mind. He must dwell on the disproportion that exists between God's gifts and his own human powers of reciprocation. To forget this, even for a moment, is to put oneself on a par with God. It is to reenact the original sin of pride. For a follower of Christ who worships God in this spirit, a constant and unblinking insistence on his incapacity to be grateful enough for the gifts of God is the highest form of piety his religion invites.

In this sense, Christianity may be called the religion of unrequited gratitude, for it not only makes gratitude the virtue that most centrally defines our relationship to God, but also insists that no act or gesture of thankfulness, no return gift motivated by the love one feels for God, can ever be commensurate with the love that he has shown us. As a logical matter, at least, the Christian religion demands that we see in our incapacity to love God adequately the most perfect expression of our gratitude toward him.

This is the premise on which the philosophically refined theology of divine sacrifice that Paul was the first to expound is based. It is an idea that has been defended, and attacked, and reaffirmed countless times in the long history of Christian dogmatics. It is the premise of the doctrine of grace, which more than any other expresses the nature of man's relation to God, as the most thoughtful champions of the Christian religion conceive it. Christianity offers its followers a theodicy of infinite divine love—the love of a God who has given us everything, including himself, including even the gift of the love we feel for him. In return, it asks only that we be thankful for his gifts. Yet it bars the way to our ever expressing our gratitude to God with a love as good and great. It demands that we humbly acknowledge that God's gifts exceed all our human powers to make a return. Everything that denies this or departs from it, every attempt to explain how we might, after all, be adequately grateful to God, even in some modest and insignificant way, is pride. For a Christian, this is the greatest of all sins and the defining vice of the pagan conception of God, which rests on the antithetical premise that a proud self-sufficiency is the "crown" of human virtue instead.

ENVY

The grateful person knows herself to be loved. She accepts her lack of self-sufficiency and dependence on others, and receives their gifts of love without resentment or envy. She is at home in the world, and this frees her to love the world in return—to reciprocate the love she has received with loving acts of her own.

But if her efforts to reciprocate are blocked; if, having received the love of others, she is denied the chance to give hers back—not to them, perhaps, but to someone else, as much and as good; if she is frustrated in her attempt to express her gratitude in the only way she can, her sense of herself as a loving person will be compromised. She will feel less competent, less good, less loving, and more isolated in her dependence.

This is not the pain or disappointment of being unable to pay a debt. It is something worse. It is the deprivation of the greatest fulfillment a human being can know—the joy of returning the love of those on whose love one depends, with a love of a commensurate kind. The most miserable people on earth are those who are not loved at all. But a person who is loved, and moved to love in return, yet denied the chance to express her love in a way that is adequate to it, is miserable too, and perhaps even more so, for she has been brought to the threshold of the greatest of all human goods, only to be told she's not good enough to cross it.

A love for which there can be no adequate return is thus a source not merely of frustration but despair. Its effect is to intensify the feelings of loneliness and anxiety that attend our natal separation from the world. If gratitude is a condition of love and creativity, an unrequited gratitude is a cause of rage at the one who blocks or belittles it. Unrequited gratitude tends to become its opposite. It turns into anger at the one whose love is too large to be returned: a wish to punish or hurt him, and to appropriate his domineering power for oneself—to seize or absorb it, so that it can no longer be a source of despair.

In this way, the unrequited gratitude that Christianity demands of its adherents, not accidentally or intermittently, but constantly and as a matter of principle, becomes a cause of envy toward God. It arouses the wish to escape from the unhappiness of never being able adequately to thank God for his gifts, by seizing his powers.

This is how, with striking self-awareness, Satan describes the motives for his rebellion against God in book 4 of *Paradise Lost*.

Satan is not the hero of Milton's poem. He cannot create but only destroy. The only joy he knows is that of destruction, and that is not joy but its opposite—a tormenting condition of hatred for himself and everything else. "Which way I fly is Hell, myself am Hell, and in the lowest deep a lower deep still threat'ning to devour me opens wide, to which the Hell I suffer seems a Heav'n." No one could possibly wish to share his fate.

But what provoked Satan to rebel against God, with all the ruinous consequences that followed for him and us? Satan acknowledges that God "deserved no such return." The service that God demanded from Satan and the other angels in heaven was not "hard." "What could be less than to afford Him praise, the easiest recompense, and pay Him thanks? How due!"

And yet the very "good" that God had done by creating Satan, "wrought" in him "but malice." Among the angels, Satan stood at the very top. But as a creature, an infinite distance still remained between him and his creator. This radical asymmetry in their relation meant that Satan could never express his thanks to God in an adequate way. He could never love God as well or as much as God loved him.

For Satan, the experience of this inadequacy was intolerable. In a heaven otherwise so well arranged, his incapacity ever to be grateful enough to "Heav'n's matchless King," spoiled everything else. "Lifted up so high," Satan exclaims, "I 'sdeigned subjection and thought one step higher would set me highest and in a moment quit the debt immense of endless gratitude so burdensome—still paying! Still to owe!"[11]

God gives to all and owes gratitude to none. In this respect, his condition is one of perfect self-sufficiency, from which Satan's creaturely nature excludes him forever. Envious of God's freedom from the debt of gratitude under whose soul-crushing weight even the greatest of the angels groans with frustration and anger, and wounded in his pride, which cannot bear to accept his position of permanent "subjection," Satan seeks escape by the only route available. He mounts a war to "dispossess" God and "reign" in his place.[12] And when this fails, he pursues his vengeful campaign against the one who has put him in a position of awful servility, by corrupting his human creatures through a brilliant appeal to Eve to ignore God's command and indulge her wish to rise to "godhead" herself,[13] proudly aspiring to close the gap between creature and creator in the same way that Satan had sought but failed to do.

In this sense, the Fall in paradise is a reenactment of the first one in heaven. The Christian religion assigns this second act of criminal disobedience a pivotal place in its account of man's relation to God and gives it far greater weight than do either Judaism or Islam. Indeed, the doctrine of original sin might be called *the* Christian dogma *par excellence,* for it sets the terms on which the salvific meaning of Christ's sacrifice depends. The condemnation of the ungrateful assertion of independence that caused our fall from Eden—where as in heaven, God's creatures had nothing to do but thank their creator for his gifts—thus constitutes the distinctive essence of Christian piety.[14]

Milton's poem adopts this orthodox view. But its psychological genius lies in the poet's understanding that the motive for Satan's rebellion, which Milton makes the first cause of our own, is the unbearable burden of a gratitude that the Christian religion not only increases to an unprecedented degree, but demands that we affirmatively embrace as the most fitting expression of our devotion to God. Satan's joyless negativity is the very opposite of the attitude that a Christian should strive to achieve. Yet it is the understandable response to a need for self-esteem and for confidence in one's capacity to be adequately grateful for the love one has received, that Christianity itself simultaneously intensifies and frustrates in a way unique among the world's religions. Milton makes this clear. That is why, though Satan is not the hero of his poem, he is a more humanly familiar figure than either Adam or Eve.

DISTANCE

The Christian God is a lordly creator who brings the world into being from nothing. He is a God who exists apart from the world and before it. Like Judaism and Islam, Christianity assumes a separation between God and the world that is foreign to the sacred cosmologies of the East Asian religions and to the spirit of pagan philosophy.

But in contrast to Judaism, which remained a legalistic and orthopractical religion throughout the rabbinic period, Christianity quickly took a philosophical turn. Beginning already with the Gospel of John and the Letters of Paul, then even more aggressively and emphatically in the writings of the

Church Fathers, the proponents of the new Christian religion sought to explain and defend the idea of God's transcendence in a philosophically rigorous way. In contrast to Judaism, Christianity was a metaphysical religion from the start—one whose most characteristic expression, from its earliest days, was theology rather than law.[15] The result was a widening of the distance between man and God.

There were several reasons for Christianity's more philosophical orientation. One, perhaps, was the felt need to explain the postponement of the end of the world, which Jesus (unlike either Moses or Mohammed) had at certain moments seemed to promise. But the most important was the need of Christian apologists to meet the objections of their pagan critics on philosophical terms the latter respected. The Jews sought no converts among the gentiles and therefore had less need to do this. By contrast, the earliest Christian recruiters, beginning with Paul, were compelled to make the central teachings of their new religion intelligible to an audience that was heir to a five-hundred-year-old tradition of highly abstract metaphysical thought (just as they were forced to lower the ritual barriers to conversion). When Jews and Muslims eventually began to philosophize in a disciplined way, centuries later, they did so against the background of already-established traditions of practice and belief that gave their religions a very different, less metaphysical center of gravity. In Christianity, the need and impulse to philosophize was an original feature of the religion itself.

This applied, in particular, to the doctrine of the Incarnation. From the standpoint of pagan philosophy, nothing seemed more absurd than the idea that a simple, unlettered man like Jesus could be divine, or that God would take on human form and sacrifice himself for the followers of such a man. Human beings can become divine, the ancient philosophers taught, only by thinking. The proposition that any god would be willing to undergo the debasing pain of crucifixion so that his worshipers in this world might be restored to the hope of eternal life in the next seemed to them a ridiculously implausible idea.

In the cities where Paul and those who followed him sought their recruits, even the uneducated were familiar with the idea of the god-man—of the god (Zeus) who assumes a human form, and the man (Hercules) who becomes divine. They knew stories, too, of gods like Dionysus who allow themselves to be torn apart for the sake of their human worshipers. But these beliefs all rested on the assumption that men and gods belong to a single cosmos which, though graded in a hierarchy of power and prestige, is sufficiently continuous that even the line between the human and divine can be crossed from time to time.

This was of course precisely what Paul and the Church Fathers denied, as their Jewish forebears had done, centuries before, in an effort to distinguish their God from all the others known to man. The God of Paul and Clement and Tertullian was a creator God who brings the world into being from nothing. Between him and his creatures there exists a gap immeasurably wider than that between parent and child, or craftsman and artifact (the only two ways that pagan mythologists and philosophers had of conceiving God's relation to the world).[16] The special challenge that Christian apologists faced in their recruitment of literate gentiles was that of explaining how the God for whom they sought new followers could exist at a distance from the world incomparably greater than that of any Greek or Roman deity, *and yet at the same time* enter the world and take on the torn and bleeding flesh of a human being.

This is a challenge the Jews never faced, nor is it one that Muslim proselytizers had to confront six centuries later. It is a theological challenge peculiar to the Christian religion, and to meet it, those who brought the good news of the cross were forced, from a very early date, to place special emphasis on the distance of their God from the world precisely to avoid any implication of the wrong kind of intimacy between them, which the idea of the Incarnation might otherwise seem to invite. As a consequence, the very doctrine that involves the God of Christianity more directly in the world than his Jewish or Muslim counterparts, became a spur to the elaboration, in increasingly abstract terms inherited from the ancient tradition of pagan metaphysics, of the idea of God as a being whose distance from the world is greater than any that can be conceived. And that of course only intensified the symmetrical problem of explaining how the idea of such a God could be reconciled with his fleshly presence in Christ. The Christological and Trinitarian disputes of the early church were in important part motivated by these philosophical worries.

It is obvious that the God of Christianity cannot have worldly characteristics of the ordinary kind. He cannot have moods and passions, like the God of the ancient Israelites, or a body or a face. But a philosophically rigorous conception of God's distance from the world also requires that we accept our inability to search his mind or know his will. Any suggestion that God's mind must be sufficiently like ours to be intelligible is a slur against his transcendence. Even to say that God created our minds in the image of his own, as

Augustine for example maintains, so that we are able to have some "analogous" understanding of his thoughts, assumes—as later theologians observed—either an acquaintance with God's creative purposes, which we have no right to presume, or his subjection to the same principles of reason that constrain our human minds.

The wish to think that we can understand God and fathom his purposes; that we can grasp his providential design for the world; that we can know his laws and conform ourselves to them, and by doing so earn our salvation, is a strong, indeed irresistible longing. Many great Christian thinkers have fallen prey to it. But every time one has, another has arisen to insist that the assumption of any bridge of understanding between God and his human creatures depreciates God's otherworldliness and brings him closer to us than is permitted by the idea of a God whose transcendence of the world is complete. This is the only conception of God that a theologically consistent Christianity allows, and the only way to express it adequately is to remain resolute in the belief that there is nothing we can know about God's mind and nothing we can do to affect his will.

But if that is true, then we cannot have a practical or even intelligible relationship with God. The God of Christianity is bound to become, out of philosophical necessity, a bare postulate, Kant's "transcendental object = X,"[17] a being whose existence we must presume but about whom nothing can be known or said, and whose behavior we cannot affect in any way at all. This is the logical conclusion of the theological belief in a God whose dignity increases with his distance from the world—the assignment of God to a position so far beyond the world, so remote from human speech and thought that he is cut off completely from the human beings who worship him. The practical and intellectual evisceration of the idea of God in Western Christendom is the paradoxical result of a passionate longing to remain faithful to this very idea, carried to its self-destructive extreme by the striving for philosophical precision that sets Christianity apart from the other Abrahamic religions.

When this happens, the position occupied by God falls vacant. In Christian theology, God is the creator of the world and the guarantor of human salvation. The evacuation of the idea of God means that he can no longer perform these roles. But the roles themselves remain.[18] The assumption that something or someone must be the creator of the world and guarantee our salvation, survives, and to the extent it does, the Christian view of man and the world continues to shape our expectations, even after the hollowing out of the idea of God at the hands of his most devoted admirers.

But with God no longer available to create and save, a substitute must be found. The only credible candidate is man—the one creature who, on a Christian view, possesses God's power of creation from nothing. Man alone has freedom of the will. Kant calls this the power of "absolute spontaneity."[19] It is the "image" of the power traditionally ascribed to God as the creator of the world. Man is therefore the only creature qualified to fill the role left empty by the death of God. The ghostly demand that someone fill it leaves human beings no choice but to take up the responsibility of (re)creating the world and saving themselves.

But hard as this task may be, it is not one that falls on man's shoulders unwanted. It is an assignment he eagerly seeks, driven by the wish to avenge himself against a God who demands that his human creatures acknowledge the inadequacy of every attempt they could conceivably make to express their thankfulness to him. With this demand, God cuts man off from the happiness of making an adequate return to the world in gratitude for goodness received. He denies him the happiness of being at home in the world. The Christian doctrine of the Incarnation causes such unhappiness to a unique degree by dramatizing our incapacity ever to be grateful enough to the God who suffers agonies for our sake. It thereby strengthens the envious wish to seize God's powers to an unprecedented extent. At the same time, the drive to put the creedal premises of the Christian religion on a philosophically solid foundation empties the very idea of God of all expressible meaning. An opening is thereby created for man to act on his wish to take God's place. In this way, Christian theology gives man both a motive to assume God's powers and the opportunity to do so. The other Abrahamic religions, which are neither as strongly motivated by philosophical anxieties, nor as obsessed with the idea of grace, do so to a lesser degree.

This of course puts tremendous pressure on the doctrine of the Incarnation itself, which is the source both of the radicalized understanding of God's gifts to man, and of the peculiarly intense need to explain man's relation to God in intellectually rigorous terms, that set Christianity apart from Judaism and Islam.

In the end, only two alternatives remain. One is to acknowledge that Jesus was a sage but to deny that he was divine and accept the view of those who say he was only a teacher and a man. This is a perfectly respectable view, but not one that an orthodox Christian can embrace.

The other is to concede that the Incarnation is a mystery that human beings can never unravel. This is a respectable view too, and one that many

Christians accept. But it amounts to an admission of defeat in the centuries-long campaign that the greatest minds of Christendom have waged to make their God intelligible to themselves and others. If the Incarnation is a mystery about which nothing can be known or said, then it must be passed over in silence. The conversation the Church Fathers long ago began with the rationalist philosophers of pagan antiquity must come to an end. To concede this may perhaps be unavoidable. But one who does should have the courage to acknowledge that it marks the final failure of the mission on which Paul embarked in the shadow of the cross, and that has been the ambition ever since of what Kant calls the "universal religion of reason."[20]

LOVELESS AND GODLESS

The psychologically unbearable demand that we acknowledge our complete dependence on a God for whose gifts we can never be grateful enough produces an irrepressible wish to seize his powers. The radical separation of God from the world makes this possible. The religion of unrequited gratitude, which demands an inexpressible thankfulness toward an incomprehensible God, is thus for a combination of psychological and theological reasons a religion that disenchants itself. It drives its adherents, and all whose fate is tied to the civilization their beliefs have shaped, toward the loveless and godless world we inhabit.

By providing both the motive and the opportunity to claim God's power of creation for themselves Christianity reinforces in its followers the universal infantile desire for omnipotence and encourages them to assess their vulnerabilities from the standpoint of the self-sufficient deity whose place they long to assume. From this point of view, their weaknesses can only appear loathsome and humiliating—something to be shed or overcome. This applies even to love. The love that human beings receive from one another is a vulnerability too, perhaps the most poignant of all. The expansion of the realm of rights at the expense of that of gift reflects our wish to be free of the vulnerability of love, or rather, since we can never live without it, to expel love and the gratitude that is our most empowering response to it, from public life to the sphere of private relations, where they continue to survive, but only, as Weber says, *in pianissimo,* and under a cloud of mistrust.[21] The religion of Christianity, which demands a boundless gratitude toward God, thus leads to a world in which our gratitude for the love of other human beings is systematically devalued. Ours is the most powerful but least grateful civilization the world has ever known. Yet paradoxically, it has been inspired by, and drawn its spiritual energy from, a religion that raises the value of gratitude to the highest imaginable level. Our loveless world is the product of the religion of absolute love.

It is also a world haunted by the specter of nihilism.

Nihilism is something worse than skepticism or disbelief. It is the condition of those who maintain that the world could have meaning and value only in case it were connected to a ground or norm whose existence they simultaneously deny—a self-defeating condition that acknowledges the deepest longings of human beings only to insist they can never be met.

That the world have meaning and value is a demand we make on it and on ourselves. There is no way of extinguishing or even suppressing this demand. It is part of our human nature. To meet it, we must find a way of relating what changes and disappears to something that does not, either in the world or beyond it. This requirement too is part of human nature. Kant puts the point succinctly. In the introduction to the second edition of the *Critique of Pure Reason,* he speaks of "a remarkable predisposition, noticeable to every human being, never to be capable of being satisfied by what is temporal."[22] Without a connection to eternity, we can never be at peace with our mortality or at home in a world of people and things that are constantly changing and dying. Even Heraclitus would agree. The debate between Heraclitus and Parmenides is not about the reality of eternity as such, but the best way to conceive it. Every philosopher from Plato to Kant (to Nietzsche, even) is a participant in this debate.

Every religion also seeks to secure our relation to eternity in one way or another. Christianity is no exception. It too assumes that there is something that lasts forever, and because of this has the power to "save" the world from pointlessness and disorder. For Christians, this is the eternal God, beyond the world, who creates "what is temporal" from nothing. But the Christian religion satisfies the human longing for eternity in a radically negative way. It completely separates eternity from time and interprets the relation between them in a way that drains the world of all inherent value. It converts the world into a temporary residence in which we can never be anything but pilgrims. On the Christian view of the relation of eternity to time, the world is no longer our home, and when this view loses its grip on the souls and minds of men, there ceases to be any other home to which we might return. The continuing belief that only that other, heavenly home could have given the world in which we live its order and value—the spectral shadow of Christian belief—coupled with the conviction that we have lost that other home forever—the disbelief that follows the self-disenchantment of the Christian religion—is the very essence of the nihilism that quietly, loudly, deeply, superficially, despairingly and cheerfully poisons our spiritual lives today.

In the civilization of the modern West, for whose disenchantment it is largely responsible, the Christian religion has lost the authority it once possessed. It has ceased to be a unifying force in our public lives. Yet it has bequeathed to its secular heirs its own religiously conditioned understanding of man's homelessness in the world, and left human love under indictment. This is the true legacy of the Christian religion—the residue of its theology of grace, now drained of its power to inspire. If we are ever to be at home in the world again, and restore love to a place of public honor in our lives, we must find another way to satisfy our longing for eternity, and be persuaded that human friendship is the gateway to it.

ONCE UPON A TIME

Everything in the world exists in time. Every blade of grass has its hour in the sun, then withers and disappears. Human beings are born, grow up and die. Empires rise and fall. We now know that even species come and go, and that the earth and stars have histories of their own. The world is a great theater of time. Strictly speaking, it *is* time, what Christians call the "temporal" realm. But the thought that nothing lasts, that everything is eventually swallowed up by time, and lost and forgotten, is an unbearable and indeed unintelligible idea. We could not stand to live in such a world, or even comprehend it.

But this is the world we inhabit today. In our world, time has acquired a despotic power. We have grown used to the idea that everything is subject to the universal dominion of time, and smile with the amusement of grown-ups at childish words like "eternity" and "God." We bravely declare that we do not need anything beyond the realm of time in order to live meaningful lives within it. Some even say that the strength to do without eternity is the sign of a real, or authentic, human being. That is one of the secular dogmas of our age. But it is an inhuman mistake. For the thought that nothing outlasts time's dissolving powers, that eternity is an empty, foolish word, is a thought we can neither bear nor understand. It is a thought at war with our humanity, and to say that we can live without eternity is not real courage but a false bravado that only conceals the despair of those whose fate it is to live in a kingdom of transience and change from which no migration is ever allowed.

Once upon a time, before the advent of Christianity and the loveless, godless world it has bequeathed us, there was another world, shaped by a very different understanding of the relation between time and eternity. This was the pagan world that Christianity challenged and eventually destroyed. Its metaphysical foundations are described with matchless clarity and depth in the writings of Aristotle, the pagan philosopher *par excellence.*

In Aristotle's world, there is no room for the despair produced by the nihilistic belief that we must now find a way to live without a God beyond the world—the only eternity the disenchanted heirs of Christianity can imagine. That is because Aristotle's world is itself eternal.

Like ours, his world is a vast complex of motions. Everything in it is constantly changing. But the comings and goings of the weather, the seasons, the mortal individuals that belong to every kind of living thing, all have a pattern or shape that lasts forever. For Aristotle, eternity is just the form of the cosmos, the one and only world there is. It has no existence apart from the world and hence no existence apart from time. The human longing for a connection with the eternal and divine can therefore be satisfied simply by observing the form of the moving world we inhabit, as scientists and philosophers do when they inspect its order with their minds.

In Aristotle's pagan world, no human being, not even a philosopher, is personally immortal. No one can hope for a life after death, as an individual, in a heaven beyond this world and time. Only my form, which is not personal to me, survives my death—as the form of my children, and theirs, and so on forever. But Aristotle's world is nonetheless suffused with immortality and to be connected to it, to participate in it, all I need to do is open my eyes and look. Indeed, I don't even have to do that. For even the simplest human being, without a tincture of philosophy, is already a participant in the immortality of the world simply by virtue of having the human form that he or she does. In the history of Western thought, there has never been a world in which the human connection to immortality was more direct, or one in which man was more at home.[23] The sense of homelessness that followed the destruction of this world, under the pressure of Christian ideas, is the source of the longing to recover it that has been felt in every age since.

The most important of these ideas is that of creation from nothing.

The belief that God created the world entails its historicity and hence mortality. It enforces a rigorous separation between time and eternity. It drains the world of all meaning and value, and transfers these to God's will, which is the name of the power through which he brings the world into being. Aristotle had no concept either of will or creation. He thought of eternity and time as a composite, a unified whole, joined in the way the form and matter of any animal or artifact are, and just as incapable of existing separately. Christianity broke this unity apart. It relocated eternity to a heavenly city beyond the world, which became, as a result, a realm of pure becoming, a merely created thing with a beginning and end in time, within whose horizon nothing eternal can be found. In the West, Augustine was the first to develop these ideas in a philosophically organized way.

In the Christian world that displaced the Aristotelian one, the human longing for eternity could be satisfied only by maintaining a connection to a God separated from the world by a gulf greater than any Aristotle could have imagined. When this idea lost its power as a result of the self-imposed disenchantment of the Christian religion, what remained was a world of time with nothing eternal in it and nothing eternal beyond it to which the ever-moving spectacle of mortal change could be related in order to save it from senselessness and disorder. Because Aristotle's world is itself eternal and unchanging, there is no room in it for such nihilistic despair. Nor is there room for the Christian doctrine of grace and the unrequited gratitude that follows from it, for these make sense only on the assumption that the world is God's contingent creation.

According to Aristotle, the scientists and philosophers who contemplate the eternal order of the world realize this order in their work. They fulfill the world's potential to be understood by understanding it, and thereby join directly, for a time at least, in the eternal and divine. That is for them a cause of great happiness—the greatest a human being can know. Aristotle calls it "blessedness" or joy. But the happiness they experience is not the gift of a God beyond the world. It is the culmination of the world itself. That such happiness is possible for men is just the joyful way things are.

In this sense, Aristotle's understanding of what human beings should strive to be, and may hope to accomplish, is characterized by the absence of a demand for the kind of gratitude that is the defining mark of the Christian religion. Its absence relieves the pressure to revenge ourselves against the God who imposed it. This in turn makes it easier to recognize and value, as

Aristotle does, those loving relations among friends that establish and sustain a human world in the first place. Aristotle's freedom from the self-defeating demand that we love our creator for gifts for which there can be no adequate return, allows him to acknowledge the value of the love that human beings within the world show for one other, as finite but caring beings, joined in a collaboration to maintain their common home, whose occupants are helped by their friends to partake, so far as their nature allows, of the eternity of the world in which, like everything else, they pass their mortal careers.

In Aristotle's pagan philosophy, one therefore finds the resources both for a reconstructed understanding of our relation to the eternal and divine and for the restoration of love and gratitude to a place of public honor in our lives. It might therefore seem that Aristotle's philosophy contains all we need to cure ourselves of the lovelessness and godlessness that haunt our modern world, the twin scourges of the religion of unrequited gratitude, in whose shadow we still live. It might seem that to be at home in the world again, all we need to do is learn to see it through Aristotle's pagan eyes. But if, as Spinoza says, salvation were that easy, many would have found their way to it already.[24]

There is, in fact, a great deal in Aristotle's philosophy that is either silly or appalling—certain of the details of his science of nature, for example, and his endorsement of natural slavery. And there are other ideas missing from his account of the world that we can no longer do without—for example, that a work of art is beautiful partly on account of its individuality and not just because it conforms to a pattern of some sort. Aristotle's philosophy cannot be resurrected without being revised in these and other respects. If we are to preserve his ideas of joy and friendship, and make meaningful use of them, we must find a way to bring them into harmony with our deepest convictions in the realms of science, politics and art.

To do this, Aristotle's metaphysics must be rebuilt to accommodate the belief that individuals are intelligible and lovely in their own right—that their uniqueness is something we can understand and admire. This is a central teaching of the Abrahamic religions, and one that retains its authority even after we have given up on the idea of a divine creator beyond the world, and rejected the demand for a gratitude to God that always fall short of the mark.

Modern science, politics and art all rest on this Abrahamic premise. Their commitment to it distinguishes them from their premodern counterparts and from Aristotle's philosophy in particular. That is because his metaphysics excludes the possibility that the individuality of individuals is something knowable, beautiful and worthy of respect. If Aristotle's unification of time and eternity and his philosophy of human friendship are again to enjoy the intellectual and spiritual authority they once possessed, and to give us the help we need to cure ourselves of the godlessness and lovelessness from which we suffer, then his pagan philosophy must be joined to this Abrahamic idea, which today shapes our understanding of the nature of truth in science, beauty in art and goodness in human relations. Aristotle's paganism cannot be restored. It must be transfigured and reborn.

PART TWO

Pride

CHAPTER 4

Greatness of Soul

ARISTOTLE'S PHILOSOPHY OF PRIDE

Aristotle identifies a number of basic human virtues, including justice, courage, temperance, generosity and practical wisdom. A good man[1] possesses these qualities and his actions are guided by them. Their exercise is happiness itself.[2]

But gratitude is not among the virtues on Aristotle's list. For a Christian, gratitude is the cornerstone of human ethics. Good Christians acknowledge their dependence on God and strive to express their thankfulness for his gifts, above all for the saving grace of Jesus Christ. Their life is a meditation on their incompetence ever to be grateful enough. Aristotle does not mention gratitude as one of the virtues that a good man must possess, let alone assign it such special importance. Indeed, the few remarks he makes on the subject are of a generally disparaging kind.

From a Christian point of view, this is bad enough. But matters are in fact much worse, for Aristotle not only fails to give gratitude a significant place in his ethical scheme. He inverts the Christian order of values by making a supreme virtue of the trait that Christianity anathematizes as the worst of all sins.

Christian ethics condemns pride as the root of every human evil.[3] Pride is the assertion of man's self-sufficiency *vis-à-vis* God—the original sin from which all others spring. For Aristotle, by contrast, human self-sufficiency is a positive, indeed cardinal, value.

The greatest human beings possess a quality that Aristotle calls *megalopsychia,* or "greatness of soul."[4] This is not merely one virtue among many, but the summary and completion of all the rest. Greatness of soul is the "crown"[5] of the virtues, and the man who possesses it is distinguished by his outstanding independence. He is a supremely self-sufficient human being. He has the attributes and resources he needs to live a complete and fulfilling life, and the knowledge that he does is the source of the pride he takes in himself and of his sense of superiority to others less self-sufficient than he. For Aristotle, the pride of such a man is not something bad at all. To the contrary: it is a natural expression of the condition of power and well-being that in his view represents the highest goal of human living—the glowing look of happiness itself.

For anyone who starts with Christian beliefs, this is more than an error or oversight. It is a moral perversion, a complete reversal of the proper order of things. Aristotle's pagan ethics of pride stands the morality of Christianity on its head. Or rather, Christianity stands Aristotle's ethics on *its* head. For it is the revolution in values that Christianity wrought that separates our disenchanted world, still shaped by the nihilistic remnants of Christian belief, from the pagan world whose portrait Aristotle paints in philosophical shades of gray.

GENEROSITY

Though Aristotle has little to say about gratitude, he offers a lengthy account of the complementary virtue of generosity (*eleutheriotes*).

Gratitude and generosity are linked, both conceptually and psychologically. The first is what the recipient of a gift feels toward a donor who is motivated by the second. A gift that is made not in a spirit of generosity but for some other reason—to spite the recipient by placing him in a position of dependence, or merely to show off the donor's wealth[6]—gives the recipient less reason to be grateful for it. Generosity and gratitude are the two poles of a single relation, and it is characteristic of Aristotle's whole approach to the question of human happiness that he focuses on the first while largely ignoring the second.

Like other virtues, generosity is a mean between extremes of deficiency and excess. The first Aristotle calls stinginess, and the second extravagance.

A stingy man fails to give others as much as he can and should. This is of course a relative standard. The more a person has, the more he can afford to give away.[7] But all stinginess springs from the same defect of character. A stingy man loves material things more than is fitting or proper.

One ought not to be indifferent to material things. But it is important to care about them in the right way. The stingy person's defect is that he cares about such things as ends in themselves. He makes a fetish of money and goods. He treats them as inherently valuable, rather than as "useful things"[8] that "provide the means for living."[9] Because he views them in this way, the stingy man becomes a slave to his possessions, anxious to acquire and keep them, forever on the outlook to make sure that no one takes them away. He becomes dependent on his wealth, rather than the other way around, and in extreme cases comes to view himself as a means for protecting his possessions, rather than his possessions as a means for securing his life. A generous man, by contrast, "values material goods not for their own sake"[10] but for the sake of what he can do with them. His views wealth as a means to an end, and in this sense may be said to hold "material goods in low esteem."[11] He has the right attitude toward his resources, regardless of how large or small they happen to be.

Stinginess is a deficiency because it lacks—is "deficient in"—the attitude toward wealth from which all generous giving starts. An extravagant man possesses this same attitude to an excessive and self-destructive degree. Like a generous man, an extravagant one does not care about wealth for its own sake. But his lack of care has grown into a full blown carelessness. He "wastes" his wealth and by doing so destroys himself.[12] The extravagant man makes the mistake of forgetting that, even though wealth is *only* a useful thing, it is also a *necessary* thing, without which we cannot live, let alone live well.

To live well, one needs material resources—not great wealth, perhaps, but enough to care for one's family, to participate in the life of one's city, and to be generous to one's friends. Though valueless in itself, wealth is the indispensable means of noble living. The extravagant man forgets this. He spends his resources recklessly, failing to assure that he retains enough to live a life of nobility and freedom. In the end, he bankrupts himself and by doing so loses his independence. His life declines to a state of servility, driven by need and directed by others whose responsibility it now is to look after his affairs.

In this respect, the extravagant man ends up in a position of dependence that resembles that of the stingy man. In different ways, both lack the freedom that distinguishes the life of a generous man, who is a kind of mean between them. His freedom is that of a man who possesses wealth yet remains detached from it. To be sure, extravagance is the result of "foolishness," which is less ignoble than stinginess.[13] We therefore judge stingy and extravagant men differently. We say the first lack virtue, and criticize the second for their lack of caution or prudence. But extravagance, though not ignoble in itself, produces a life that *is* ignoble because unfree, and which therefore resembles the life of a stingy man, who is slavishly attached to his wealth. The free and self-sufficient life of a generous man lies between these two poles of dependence.

MAGNIFICENCE

Among the various forms of generosity, one is of special interest to Aristotle. He calls it "magnificence" (*megaloprepeia*). Magnificent giving "surpasses" other sorts of generosity "in scale"[14] and thus brings out, with special clarity, the nature of generosity in general.

Magnificent expenditures are "suited to persons who have the requisite means either by dint of their own effort or from ancestors or their connections."[15] Those who attempt to make such gifts without the means to do so risk embarrassing and impoverishing themselves. But it is not the magnitude of the means required for magnificent giving that Aristotle emphasizes. To be magnificent, a gift must have a certain kind of object. It must have a "great and noble" aim.[16] It must be spent on something "admirable" that can be looked upon with appreciation and wonder. Magnificent gifts possess an inherent brilliance. Merely to "look" at such a gift is "to admire it" and to be impressed by the character of the man who makes it.[17] All truly magnificent giving consists in a kind of visible greatness.[18]

A poor man, who lacks the means to make such gifts, may be a man of virtue. He may be generous, within the limits his resources allow. But his lack of wealth assures that he and his generosity are bound to remain invisible to all but a few. His poverty condemns him to a condition of anonymity, out of the view of others. The wealthy man possesses the means to make gifts that will catch the eye of a larger audience and be widely admired, so long as they are gifts of an admirable kind.

Of course, the mere fact that a man is rich is no guarantee he will do this. He may choose to make no gifts at all, or to spend his wealth "on insignificant or only moderately important occasions."[19] Indeed, even if he spends a great deal on his gifts, a wealthy man is not for that reason alone to be considered magnificent. His gifts may show that he is not a magnificent but a vulgar man, who "spends much where small expenditures are called for and makes an improper show of himself," for example, "by giving a dinner to his club on the scale of a wedding banquet . . . and similar things, not for a noble motive, but to show off his wealth, and in the belief that he will be admired for doing so."[20] Such gifts bring a man notoriety. They make him visible to others. But they show him to be a man with poor judgment and values. They show him to be a show-off.

Something similar may be said about the donor who makes large gifts on appropriate occasions, but in a spirit of what Aristotle calls "niggardliness," always concerned to economize, grumbling about how much he has to spend and "thinking that he is doing everything on a greater scale than he ought."[21] The niggardly man also makes a spectacle of himself in a way no poor man can, but it is a repulsive one, for the niggardly man spends "tremendous sums" yet "spoils the beauty of his achievement"[22] by monitoring his expenses in a spirit of "exact bookkeeping."[23]

The vulgar man gives in order to display his wealth, and by doing so shows that what he cares most about is being seen by others to be rich. The niggardly man's complaints and obsession with trifling sums reveal that he, too, attaches more importance to his money than he should. Wealth is for him also the thing that matters most. Unlike these others, a magnificent man spends "with pleasure and a free hand" and "because it is noble to do so."[24] He shows by the kind of gifts he makes that he views his wealth in the proper way, as an instrument for achieving noble ends. He reveals himself to be free from a servile and debasing attachment to wealth for its own sake.

The relation of magnificence to vulgarity and niggardliness is therefore exactly the same as that of generosity to extravagance and stinginess, for both magnificence and generosity are forms of freedom that lie in a mean between contrasting types of dependence whose servility springs from the enslavement to need that results from an overattachment to wealth.

A man's wealth enables him to meet his needs,[25] but the man who values his wealth for its own sake is led around by his needs, like a prisoner on a chain. A free man rises above his needs. He cannot escape them entirely, but keeps them in proper perspective and refuses to be defined by them. He presents himself to the world as a man for whom there are more important things, who lives for the sake of nobility and greatness and not merely that of living itself. In this way, he transcends the bodily requirements to which every human being is subject and defines himself as a man who is not a slave to life, or money, or need.

Ordinarily generous and truly magnificent men share this higher conception of themselves, and the gifts they make show they do. The difference between them is one of relative visibility. The magnificent man makes a more impressive appearance in the world than the man who possesses the same virtuous detachment from money and need, but lacks the means to make gifts on a similar scale. Like every generous donor, a magnificent man observes the standards of "correct giving." But the sheer scale of his gifts compels others to take notice. That is the special privilege of the magnificent man, in whom nobility of soul and the means to display it on a grand and impressive scale are happily joined.

This helps to explain a striking feature of Aristotle's account of magnificence. The gifts a magnificent man makes are typically public in nature. Aristotle acknowledges that magnificence can be shown in "private affairs," for example by the expenditures a man makes on a wedding or the furnishings in his home. But in the case of a truly magnificent man, even these private expenditures generally have a public dimension as well. They are likely to be spent on events that are "of interest to the whole city or to eminent people," like the receipt "of foreign guests."[26] And the gifts that are *most* characteristic of a magnificent man have a straightforwardly public purpose: "equipping a trireme," "heading a sacred embassy," outfitting a "chorus," giving "a feast for the city in a brilliant fashion," paying for "votive offerings, buildings, sacrifices" and the like.[27]

These are the most "honorable" sorts of gifts because they are made for "the common good,"[28] not the private welfare of the man who makes them. Broadly speaking, this distinction corresponds to that between a man's household and his city.[29] In his home, even a magnificent man is concerned with his own welfare and that of his dependents. He is preoccupied with the repetitive and transient activities of material life—the routines of eating and sleeping and laboring in which every human being must engage merely to live, and that leave no lasting trace behind.[30] In his civic life, by contrast, his attention is focused on the well-being of a much larger group that includes many of his equals and on the stature and safety of a political community that is more long-lived than any of its inhabitants. This gives his public actions a wider scope than the demands of domestic life allow. His public actions touch more people, and touch them in a more lasting way, and that is what makes such actions especially honorable, since "works that endure are the noblest."[31]

The public realm is one of heightened visibility. In it, things appear more clearly and can be seen by a greater number of people. In part, this is the result of purely physical considerations. What happens in a household takes place behind closed doors. What occurs in public transpires in the open, where others can observe and judge it. But in part, the idea of public visibility—of "publicity"—must be understood in intellectual and cultural terms. For the works that a man performs in public can be "seen" even by those who are not present to witness it, through the medium of memory. A great public deed—a singular act of courage or an especially magnificent gift—is likely to be remembered for a long time afterward, unlike the ordinary and repetitive actions of private life, which tend to be forgotten as soon as they are performed. The memorialization of public actions enhances their visibility by giving them an audience that, in principle at least, knows no limits in time. It lifts a few great deeds out of the obscurity to which our private lives are largely consigned and confers on them a lasting visibility that is the privilege of the public space alone.

To step out of the household into this space is to move from a region of darkness to one of light. It is to invite the admiration of one's peers, present and to come. To earn their recognition one must do something that is memorable on account of its nobility and grandeur. Statesmen do this with their words and warriors with their deeds. A magnificent man does it with his gifts. The monuments he builds and the celebrations he sponsors are as memorable as the speeches of Pericles and the actions of Achilles. Only a man of great wealth can do this. The privilege of publicity thus belongs to the rich in a special way. Merely being rich, and spending lavishly, is not enough by itself to win the prize this privilege affords. But a wealthy man who spends nobly—on the right occasions, for the right ends, and in the right spirit—wins a prize from which men of more moderate means are permanently excluded. He wins the prize of being recognized and honored, in the light of the public space, now and later, as a man of noble character who through the magnificence of his gifts shows the world his independence from the very wealth that enables him to pursue this prize in the first place.

SELF-SUFFICIENCY

Generosity (*eleutheriotes*) leads Aristotle to magnificence (*megaloprepeia*) and magnificence in turn to "greatness of soul" (*megalopsychia*). This is not merely one of several virtues that a noble man possesses, along with courage, temperance, justice and the like, but a comprehensive excellence that includes all the rest.[32]

The individual virtues are appropriate to different spheres of action, or to different human relationships. Thus, justice is the virtue appropriate to relations of exchange; temperance to the metabolic processes of eating and sex; courage to war, and so on. But all these virtues share something in common. Each exhibits greatness in some form or other. A great-souled man is one who possesses the spirit of greatness from which all the virtues spring. He also knows that he does and expects others to treat him accordingly. Unlike a good but overly modest man, who suffers from a deficiency of pride, a great-souled man values his character in accordance with its true worth. And unlike a vain man, who thinks he deserves to be honored for possessing a character of more value than he does, the pride of a great-souled man is justified by his being, in fact, the remarkable man he thinks he is.

A man who is good but not great also deserves to take pride in himself. But just as magnificence is generosity raised to a higher and more visible level, the pride of a great man is larger and easier to see. In a truly great man and in the commensurately great pride he takes in himself, human excellence reaches a luminous peak from whose vantage point the whole field of virtue can be surveyed. The great-souled man is a *summa* of human achievement. Aristotle's account of his character is a key to understanding what he considers most valuable in human life, and why.

The defining characteristic of a great-souled man is his "self-sufficiency."[33] Those who lack greatness, and on whom a high-minded man is therefore "justified in looking down,"[34] all depend on something or someone else in ways that make them less self-sufficient than he.

The self-sufficiency of a great-souled man manifests itself in things as trivial as his tone of voice and manner of walking. A man with a great soul has "a deliberate way of speaking" and walks "with a slow gait."[35] It is easy to make fun of this claim. Isn't it silly to think that a man's greatness should show itself in the speed with which he walks and talks? But there is a reason for this. A great man "takes few things seriously" and is therefore "unlikely to be in a hurry." He is "not one to be excitable." He knows that his dignity cannot be compromised by events beyond his control. This is reflected in his characteristic calmness—the mood of a man who is assured of his own worth and knows that it can neither be increased nor decreased by the ups and downs of life, to which the self-worth of smaller men is tied. A small man weighs his worth according to the twists and turns of fate. One day he is up, the next day he is down, depending on modest variations of fortune. As a result, he is always worrying about things. He is always in a state of excitement, concerned about what may happen next. He is an anxious man, who speaks with "a shrill voice" and walks with "a swift gait."[36] The speed with which he talks and walks reveals the insecurity that is the hallmark of every small-souled human being—just as the calmness of a great man's words and motions express the self-assurance that only those whose sense of self-worth is truly independent of events can ever possess.

This helps explain the attitude that a high-minded man takes toward the "gifts of fortune" generally.[37]

No one disputes that it is better to be rich and good than good alone. Among other things, a good man who is rich has the resources to be generous on a grand scale. He has the means to make magnificent gifts, which virtuous men of lesser wealth cannot do. It does not follow, of course, that good fortune is itself a source of honor. But one must be very high minded to resist the temptation to think that it is. "Without virtue it is not easy to bear the gifts of fortune gracefully."[38] A rich and powerful man whose virtue is imperfect will be tempted to think that he should be honored because of his wealth and power, and to look down on those who lack these gifts merely because they do. Others will encourage him in this belief. They will flatter him and praise him for his good fortune. But the truth is that there is nothing honorable about good fortune itself. Good fortune is instrumentally but not intrinsically valuable. The only thing that is intrinsically valuable is goodness of character, and only the man who possesses greatness of soul will be immune to the flattery of others and the seductive thought that he deserves to be honored on account of his wealth and power. Similarly, only a great-souled man stands any chance of retaining his sense of dignity and worth if his good fortune turns to bad. A high-minded man "will not be overjoyed when his luck is good, nor will bad luck be very painful to him."[39] He is protected against the false equation of honor with wealth and power when he has them, and their equally false equation when they are lost. And that is because a great-souled man's belief in the self-sufficient value of his character makes him (relatively) invulnerable to such swings of fortune.

Greatness of soul manifests itself in a person's attitude toward risk as well.

A high-minded man "does not take small risks and, since there are only a few things which he honors, he is not even fond of risks. But he will face great risks, and in the midst of them he will not spare his life, aware that life at any cost is not worth living."[40] Some men take risks for the sheer pleasure of doing so. They want to show off their courage or nerve. They are daredevils who love risk for its own sake, and the sign that they do is that they take risks for unworthy ends, whose value or importance is not commensurate with the risk involved. We call such men "reckless."[41] But their recklessness is itself a kind of dependence, for like other show-offs, the reckless man reveals by his behavior how important the opinions of others are to his own estimate of self-worth. He shows himself to be dependent on their judgments; his recklessness is a species of anxiety. By contrast, a great-souled man takes great risks only for great ends and thereby shows that what he considers worthy of honor in his actions and character is not his willingness to expose himself to danger merely for the thrill and notoriety of doing so, but his commitment to the end for whose sake he takes the risk he does.

Yet at the same time, if the end is great enough, a high-minded man will be willing to risk everything, even life itself, in order to reach it—making clear by his actions that he is no more moved by an anxious desire to save his life at all costs than by the equally anxious wish to win the applause of others for his bravado. The risks that a great man takes show that he is detached both from a fearful love of life and an anxious love of the crowd. Those who fear death too much are paralyzed from taking the risks that one sometimes must to achieve a noble end or to avoid a shameful one. They are, in a manner of speaking, slaves to life. Those who are so insecure about their courage that they must forever be demonstrating it to others, even for inappropriately small ends, are slaves to opinion. Both reveal in their actions a spirit of servile dependence that a great-souled man disdains, for he possesses, as they do not, a sense of self-sufficient worth that even death cannot destroy.

The same spirit of self-sufficiency manifests itself in the realm of gift-giving. All gifts involve two parties, a benefactor and a recipient. The great-souled man has a constitutional preference for the former role. Indeed, he has an abhorrence of the latter. "He is the kind of man who will do good but is ashamed to accept a good turn, because the former marks a man as superior, the latter as inferior."[42] If he does receive a gift from someone else, he will quickly "requite good with a greater good" and thereby "not only repay the original benefactor but put him in his debt at the same time by making him the recipient of an added benefit."[43] Indeed, to a man with a great soul, being the recipient of a gift is so shameful that he expunges it from his memory. He forgets such experiences; they are too painful to recall. Men of this sort "remember the good turns they have done," and listen with pleasure to those who recount them.[44] But they forget the gifts they have received and it causes them "displeasure" to be reminded of them. In sum, they do not "ask for any favors," and accept them only "reluctantly," but "offer aid readily."[45] "For," as

Aristotle says summarily, "the recipient is inferior to the benefactor," whereas a high-minded man "wishes to be his superior."[46]

The reason for this is obvious. A recipient is a dependent. Whatever good a gift may bring comes from a source outside himself. It comes from another person, for whose generosity the recipient has cause to be grateful. The experience and expression of gratitude are therefore bound to be humbling, for they entail an acknowledgment of the dependence of the person who feels or expresses it. A high-minded man finds this intolerable. It is an offense to his sense of self-sufficiency. To be put in the position of having to be grateful is, for a man with a truly noble soul, a kind of degradation, the reduction to a position of servility, characterized, as all forms of servility are, by its lack of independence—which is why men of this kind recoil at the prospect of being on the receiving end of a gift and, when they are, quickly forget what is for them a humiliating experience.

From the point of view of such a man, receiving instead of giving and the gratitude that goes with it define the shameful condition of those whose dependence bars them from ever doing or being anything great. A great man reacts with visceral disgust to the spectacle of such dependence. He tends to stay as far away from it as he can. He wants to be a sustaining force in the lives of other people, not the reverse. He longs to let his own rich soul spill over, like an overflowing cup, so that its noble contents can be seen and admired by all.

To want to be in this position of superiority is pride. The man who "adjusts his life to another"[47] shows by his behavior that he lacks pride or is incapable of it. The flatterer is such a man. So is one whose sense of self-worth depends on the opinions of others (like the arrogant man to whom the flatterer addresses his praise). Both show that they lack the spirit of self-sufficiency that is the mark of a great-souled man, whose pride forbids him to adjust his life to anyone "except a friend."[48]

OMNIPOTENCE

Aristotle's acknowledgment that even a great-souled man needs friends is an important reminder that the self-sufficiency of such a man, impressive as it is, falls short of complete omnipotence. A man who through good fortune has had the kind of upbringing one needs to acquire a noble character and who through further good fortune possesses the resources he requires to display his nobility on a grand public scale, will still want friends with whom to spend his time and share his happiness. No matter how much independence he achieves in his life, inwardly and outwardly, even the noblest human being can never reach a state of perfect self-containment that would allow him to live—or even to want to live—without friends.

For brief periods of time, perhaps, those who engage in philosophy, which Aristotle considers the highest of all human pursuits, may be able to attain a kind of self-sufficiency that might be compared to that of a god. Yet these moments are rare and short-lived, and the few who experience them yearn, as others do, to spend most of their time with friends of similar outlook and character, sharing pursuits and pleasures in common. To that extent, even the most independent life that Aristotle can imagine is one that depends on the presence of like-minded friends and hence its happiness, though proximate to the divine, is for the human beings that enjoy it never fully self-contained.

Their condition therefore differs in an essential way from that of the God of the Christian religion. The God to whom Christians pray is more than independent in Aristotle's sense. He is completely omnipotent. There is nothing outside of him that can resist his power. His being is fully and eternally self-contained. If God decides to create human beings in his image, that is not because he is lonely and needs friends. To assume that God needs anything is incompatible with his nature. God spontaneously brings the world and everything in it into being from nothing. Christians call this spontaneous act "creation" and the power that lies behind it "will." These are the essential categories of Christian metaphysics. They have no counterpart in the philosophy of Aristotle, for whom the idea that something can come from nothing is unintelligible.

The Christian religion teaches that human beings have wills as well. It asserts that God freely gave us a freedom that sets us apart from all other creatures (with the exception of angels).[49] We are not, of course, omnipotent like God. We are mortal and needy and subject to passions of all sorts. These put limits on what we are able freely to will. But within their range of operation, our wills are just as free as God's, for we can exercise them however we choose. If we could not, they would not be free, and hence would not be wills at all. Every act of will, whether human or divine, is an act of pure spontaneity, and in this sense a creation from nothing. This leads to the conclusion that human beings are omnipotent too, though, to put it paradoxically, in a more limited way.

The fact that we, like God, possess a power of creation from nothing gives the human ambition to assume God's place its metaphysical plausibility. The wish to be God is motivated by our anger at him for condemning us to a condition of permanently unrequited gratitude. This wish is the desire to exchange the constrained omnipotence we already possess, as finite beings with wills, for the omnipotence of a divine creator who is able, as Kant says, to cause things to exist merely by thinking about them. The modern ideal of autonomy, augmented by technology, expresses the longing to make this exchange and to seize God's boundless power of creation for ourselves.

Those who adopt this ideal do not deny that human beings are finite. That would be absurd. But they do regard the limits within which we are constrained to exercise our freedom as something more than a mere inconvenience. They view these limits as an offense to our sense of self-worth and feel a moral and spiritual obligation to do whatever they can to abolish them. From this vantage point, all the many forms of human dependence are suspect and subject to attack. Every one of them, including our dependence on the love of our friends, is something whose value we have reason to doubt—of which, indeed, we have reason to feel ashamed—when viewed from the perspective of the ideal of omnipotence that the Christian religion invites with its concepts of creation and will.

Aristotle knows nothing of these ideas. His account of the life of a great-souled man, and of the pride he takes in himself, rests on metaphysical premises entirely different from those that underlie the Christian view of the world. The crucial categories for Aristotle are not those of creation and will but action and power (*energeia* and *dunamis*). On the basis of these he constructs an ideal of human living that is not shadowed by feelings of defeat or disgust when measured against the omnipotence of an otherworldly God who is able to create whatever he wishes from nothing. Aristotle's ideal is adjusted to the human condition in a way the Christian ideal is not, and because of this it allows for the acceptance, without embarrassment or shame, of needs that even the most self-sufficient human being must experience—including, above all, his desire for the company of friends.

According to Aristotle, every kind of being has special powers of its own, and yearns to realize them to the fullest extent it can. These powers, and this yearning, give its movements their distinctive form. The form of a thing—of a frog, for example—shows what it can be even before it has become it. But at the same time, it sets limits to its becoming. A tadpole cannot grow into a dog or rose. In this sense, the forms of things both empower and constrain. This is true of frogs and dogs and flowers and stars and drops of water. It is true of human beings as well. They too have distinctive powers, and hence a special form, which "specifies" what a man can be and limits his endeavors by defining the state of maximal activity toward which all men strive, just as other beings strive toward the state of full display peculiar to things of their kind.

A great-souled man is an outstanding human being. He shows us what a man is capable of doing. His life displays the powers that human beings possess, at their zenith of deployment. He is the realization of what lesser men are potentially. In Aristotle's view, he possesses more reality than they—he *is* to a greater degree—and his pride is the acknowledgment of his own superior being.

But it is a greater *human* being. A great-souled man takes pride in himself because he has made the most of his human potential. His is the most self-sufficient life a man can live, within the bounds fixed by the form that makes him the kind of being he is. It represents the fulfillment of the human nature he shares with other men, and because only a few attain the state of maturity and independence in which the highest level of human being consists, they are entitled to look down on the many who fail to reach it.

The man who does has reason to be proud, for he knows that his life is a benchmark by which the lives of others must be judged. He knows that most men struggle to achieve the composure and self-reliance, and confident belief in their own worth, that he so serenely possesses. That is why he neither flatters, as some men do, nor like the vulgar rich, displays his wealth as if it were something honorable in its own right. It is why he takes risks only when they are warranted. It is why he finds repugnant even the appearance of dependence that being the recipient of a gift entails and tries, whenever he can, to be a benefactor instead. These are the emblems of pride, in which a great-souled man displays the glorious self-sufficiency that marks the life of a human being who has become all that a man can be.

But because it is the life of a man and not that of a star, let alone of a transcendent creator who can cause things to exist merely by willing them into being, the independence even of a great-souled man must be judged by human standards, and not found wanting because it fails to achieve the perfect self-sufficiency of the God of the Christian religion. This is a standard that Aristotle would have thought insane, had he been able to conceive it. For it contradicts the most elementary truths of his metaphysics—that being is power, that form is being, and that form limits as well as directs, so that the state of full empowerment in which the life of a justifiably proud man consists, like that of every fully realized being of any kind, is constituted by the form peculiar to it, and cannot be measured, or even conceived, apart from its requirements. That a great-souled man may be proud of his self-sufficiency, and contemptuous of those who are forced to be grateful to him, yet happily accept his dependence on friends of similar character, is a consequence of these beliefs, so distant from the Christian metaphysics of creation and will, which converts the pagan virtue of pride to a sin, and compels men to measure their always incomplete independence by a standard of omnipotence foreign to the human condition.

CHAPTER 5

Givers and Takers

THE GOOD OF SELF-SUFFICIENCY

A great-souled man has reached the peak of human excellence. His sense of self-worth is secure. He is distinguished from other, lesser men by his remarkable self-sufficiency, in which he properly takes pride. He wants to be a giver, not a taker, and considers gratitude a virtue only in the slavish and weak.

This is the heart of Aristotle's account of greatness of soul. Many will dismiss it as an expression of social prejudice unworthy of serious philosophical consideration. The Christian revolution in ethics encourages such a response. But if we reject Aristotle's defense of pride on these grounds, we miss something important. For however closely tied to the outlook of his own class and time Aristotle's views may have been, he himself did not regard the value of self-sufficiency or the nobility of those that possess it as mere social conventions. He believed their value to be anchored in the very nature of things—in what in his lectures on the most basic problems of philosophy he calls "the being of beings."[1]

The question of what it means for something to be, not this or that particular thing (a man rather than a statue or horse) but anything at all, is among the deepest questions of philosophy. In the *Metaphysics,* Aristotle addresses this question in a general and abstract way. But the answer he gives there is based on concepts that inform all his more concrete inquiries, including his investigation of the nature of human excellence and of the happiness it affords those who attain it.

In particular, these concepts provide the point of departure for his explanation of why a properly proud man wants to be a donor rather than a beneficiary. According to Aristotle, the attraction that such a man feels to the first role and his repulsion at the second is grounded in his desire to move as far as he can in the direction of what is most real—to realize himself to the greatest possible degree. The great-souled man's pride is at bottom a passion for being. Even Aristotle's account of the familiar experience of giving and taking thus has a decidedly metaphysical cast. The conversion of pride from the crown of the virtues to the worst of all sins is the result of Christianity's rejection of the concept of being on which Aristotle's analysis of this experience rests. A striking passage toward the end of his long discussion of friendship brings this concept into view.[2]

"THE WORK OF HIS OWN HANDS"

Many have wondered whether donors care more about the recipients of their gifts, or vice versa. It is commonly believed "that benefactors have a greater affection for those they benefit than recipients do for those who have done some good to them."[3] But this seems "unreasonable." Shouldn't it be the other way around? After all, if the benefactor had not made the gift, its recipient would be worse off. By contrast, a donor who has given something away has less than he did before. His wealth is depleted by the amount of the gift. And if that is true, what reason does he have to feel affection for the one to whom he makes it? The widespread belief that benefactors have more reason to love those they help than their recipients do to love them in return is a puzzle that needs to be explained.

"In the view of the majority," the explanation "is that one partner [to the gift relation] is a debtor and the other a creditor."[4] A man who has made another a loan will be "concerned for his debtor's safety." He will want his debtor to prosper so that the loan can be repaid. By contrast, the debtor will "wish that his creditor did not exist." If his creditor were to disappear, the debt he owes him would vanish too, and a burden be lifted from the debtor's shoulders. Far from caring about the welfare of his creditor, a debtor prefers to see him dead. In this sense, creditors care more about their debtors than their debtors do about them. Noticing this, men have generalized to other relations of indebtedness, including those that arise from the making of gifts, and have concluded that benefactors "who have done a good deed wish for the existence of its recipients in order to receive their gratitude in return, whereas the recipients have no interest in making a return."[5]

"But it would seem," Aristotle says, that "the true cause lies more deeply in the nature of things."[6] To begin with, the analogy between giving and lending is misplaced, for "there is no affection between creditor and debtor." Indeed, just the opposite is true. Debtors often feel something more like hate for their creditors, and a creditor's own anxiety about his debtor's welfare can hardly be called affectionate, since he takes no pleasure in the debtor's well-being for its own sake. The creditor's attitude toward his debtor is entirely instrumental. He wishes for the preservation of the debtor only "in order that something may be got out of him." By contrast, those who make gifts "have affection and love for those they have benefitted, even if they are not useful to them at the moment and are unlikely to be useful at a later time."[7] Hence, the fact that benefactors care more about their recipients than their recipients do about them cannot be explained on the grounds that their relation resembles that of creditor and debtor, for the first relation (of benefaction) is characterized by the presence of an affectionate regard whose absence is the hallmark of relations of the second kind (those of indebtedness).

At this point, Aristotle introduces another analogy. The relation of benefactor to recipient can better be understood, he says, if we think of it as resembling the relation between a craftsman and his handiwork. "Every craftsman loves the work of his own hands more than he would be loved by it, if it were to come to life." This attitude is particularly pronounced in the case of poets, who are craftsmen of an especially refined sort. Indeed, poets are often so attached "to their own poems" that they "love them as if they were their children." This gives us a clue to understanding the deeper source of the special affection that benefactors feel toward their recipients, for "the recipient" of a gift is the donor's own "handiwork," which the donor loves "more than it loves its maker."[8]

The relation of a craftsman to his work is asymmetrical in two respects. A maker must exist before the thing he makes, and though he can exist independently of it, the reverse is not the case. A bed, for example, cannot come into being before its maker does, nor can we imagine a bed existing by itself, without a bed maker, but a bed maker without beds (one who perhaps lacks the time or material or inclination to make them) is entirely conceivable. That is why a maker's relation to his handiwork is like that of a parent to his child, for the relation of parent to child is asymmetrical in these same two ways as well: a man exists before his child does and can exist without him, but the idea of a child without the man (or woman) who made him is absurd.

Another way of putting this is to say that the relation of work to maker, like that of child to parent, is one of existential dependence. A poem or child only comes into being through the productive work of the poet or parent who makes it. But the would-be maker will still exist even if he does no work at all.

Or so it would appear. But the appearance is misleading. The relation of a craftsman to his work is in reality more complex, and the complications explain why he loves the things he makes more than they could ever love him in return.

FORM AND MATTER

No poet or craftsman ever makes what he does entirely "from scratch." Every maker always starts with some materials, on which he works to produce an artifact of one kind or another. In the case of a bed maker, for example, these materials consist of wood, glue, and the like, along with the tools he needs to make a bed. In the case of a poet, they consist of words, sounds, and the conventionally established genres of poetry (tragedy, epic, etc.).

A maker shapes his materials in accordance with a design. They do not already possess the shape he gives them. His materials are not, of course, completely shapeless. The wood on which a bed maker works has a shape or form of its own. The form of wood is different from that of other materials—iron, for example. There are things that one can do with wood that cannot be done with iron, and vice versa. But the shape of the wood in the bed maker's shop is sufficiently flexible that it will accept the imposition of many other shapes upon it—the shape of a table or chair, as well as that of a bed. In relation to any of these shapes, the shape of the wood is relatively shapeless, that is, equally capable of receiving any of them or none.

Every worker starts with materials that are shapeless in this relative sense. He then shapes or forms them in a certain way. He "informs" his materials and the result is a work defined by the presence in it of a higher-order form than any that exists in the materials themselves. The form of a poem is more complex than those of the linguistic elements of which it is composed and the form of a bed more complex than that of wood. The latter, of course, continues to be recognizable in the finished artifact. A bed made from wood never loses its woodiness completely. To illustrate the point, Aristotle repeats the story of a bed that once sprouted shoots.[9] But the forms of the bed's materials are submerged in a new, synthetic arrangement of greater complexity. The same is true of the forms of the words that are shaped into a poem. In both cases, the maker takes his materials to a higher level of organization.

This is possible, however, only because the materials on which a craftsman works can be made into the thing that he makes from them. This is not true of all materials. Air, for example, cannot be made into a bed, nor can fire. And some materials, like stone, can be made into a bed only with great difficulty. They resist being made into a bed. Wood, by contrast, "lends itself" to being made into a bed (or a table or chair) just as words lend themselves to being made into a poem (or funeral oration). To use Aristotle's term, each is *potentially* the thing its maker makes it.

Of course, wood is not potentially a bed in the same way that a puppy is potentially a dog. A puppy will grow into a dog by itself, if properly nourished, so long as nothing prevents it from doing so. It is, as Aristotle says, in a puppy's nature to become a dog. It is not in the nature of wood to become a bed, or in the nature of words to become a poem. For either to happen, an extrinsic form must be imposed on these materials by someone else. But the nature of a craftsman's materials (if they have been properly chosen) allows and perhaps even invites him to do this. Other materials do not. In this sense, the materials on which a craftsman works have the potential to be shaped into the artifact he makes from them. They have the potential to be given a higher-order form that incorporates their lower-order forms in a more complex work of human construction.

The process in which every maker is engaged is therefore one of realization. It is a process in which his materials move from a state of potentiality to one of achieved or actual being. Living things follow a path of this sort on their own. A puppy is potentially a dog and becomes one in reality by growing up. The source of this movement lies in the puppy itself.[10] Artifacts do not have a similar source of movement in themselves. A bed is not a grown-up pile of wood. In order to become what it is, an artifact requires the shaping hand of its maker. But its construction is nevertheless a process of realization in an analogous way. As a puppy moves to adulthood, it shows what it can be. It shows what kind of creature it is—what sort of being it has. As wood and words "move" toward bed and poem, under the direction of their makers, they, too, show what they can be. They reveal what kind of thing they are—one that is capable of being shaped into an artifact with the particular sort of higher-order unity that a bed or poem displays. The potential that wood and words possess to become things with the specific sorts of higher-order unity these artifacts display is realized in the process of making them. The maker who makes them "brings out" their potential and transforms it from a mere possibility into something that actually exists.

These two states do not differ, however, merely in terms of their temporal order—in the way, for example, that a sunny day follows a cloudy one. It is true that potentiality always precedes actuality in time, but this is not the most important difference between them. Potentiality differs from actuality in the degree of being it possesses. Cloudy days are just as real as sunny ones. But a state of potentiality has less reality than a fully actualized one.

To be sure, it has *some* reality. To be potentially anything is to be something, indeed something definite. Wood is potentially a bed but not potentially a poem. The potentiality of wood to be made into a bed is a real property of wood. It is part of its makeup, part of what it is for wood to be the kind of thing it is and not something else. But a potential state has less being than the state of actuality in which it is realized. That is because both the definition and nature of every potentiality depend on its actualization. You cannot say what a potentiality is except by reference to the state or condition or thing in which it is fulfilled. And its very nature—the kind of reality it possesses as a potentiality to be something or other—consists in its capacity for becoming what its realized expression actually is. It *is* nothing but this capacity itself, which depends, both logically and ontologically, on the state of actualization to which it refers.

Thus, a puppy *is* an immature dog—that is how we define puppies and what it means for an animal to *be* a puppy, as opposed to a kitten or duckling. The movement from puppy to dog is more than a mere succession of states. It is a process of maturation, in which a puppy moves to a state of physical and behavioral adulthood that explains what it means for it to have been a puppy in the first place. It is a movement to a state in which the active exercise of the animal's powers gives us the standpoint we need to define these powers and to understand their nature. In this sense, the adult dog's state of being has a logical and ontological priority over that of the puppy from which it grew. The growth of the puppy toward this state represents an increase in being. It is a process of realization.

Something similar may be said about the process of making a bed or a poem. The construction of a bed from pieces of wood and other materials, or of a poem from the existing words of a language, takes these materials to a higher level of reality. It organizes them in accordance with a design more complex than any they exhibit on their own, but which they have the potential to assume. The process of making a bed or a poem realizes this potential. It shows us that latent in the wood of the bed, and in the words of the poem, is a power to become something more complex and refined. The bed and the poem thus occupy a position of logical and ontological priority *vis-à-vis* their materials that is analogous to the position an adult dog occupies in relation to a puppy, and the movement that takes place in the workshop of a bed maker or poet, like that from puppy to dog, is also a movement from a lower level of being to a higher one.

Of course, the finished form of an artifact is not already present in the materials from which it is made in the definitive way a dog's form is present in the puppy. If a puppy becomes anything at all, it can only become a dog. By contrast, wood and words can be made into many different sorts of things, though not an infinite variety since their own forms limit the range of forms a craftsman can impose upon them. The form of a bed or poem thus exists in its materials only in an indefinite way.

But though the form of the finished work does not already have a determinate existence in the "stuff" from which it is made, it does have an existence of this sort somewhere else, namely in the mind of the person who makes it. The form of a bed or poem, which gives it a more complex order, and higher level of being, than the materials used in its construction already possess, first exists as a specific idea in the mind of its maker. It exists as a concept before it becomes a reality, and the process of making an artifact is the realization of the idea its maker has of it beforehand, as well as of the potential of its materials to be shaped into a thing of this kind.

Hence, it is not just the materials a craftsman uses that move to a higher level of reality through their artful organization in the finished work. The maker himself moves to a higher level of being as well. He realizes himself by turning his design, which to begin with is "just" an idea, into something real. Before he starts, the man who makes a bed or poem already possesses the design for it in his mind. It is part of him. But it is part of him only in the way that any idea is—as a mere abstraction. As he sets about the work of making his bed or poem, the abstraction slowly becomes visible to himself and others. It takes on flesh in the shape of the work emerging under his watchful eye. In this sense, the construction of an artifact is a realization of the craftsman who makes it. Every act of craftsmanship produces an object distinct from itself—

some independently existing thing that survives the process of its production. This is what distinguishes making (*poesis*) from action (*praxis*)—from a theatrical performance, for example, or a political speech—which produces nothing apart from the action. In the object he makes, a maker sees his idea move from an abstraction in his soul to the informing shape of a real thing with an independent existence of its own. He sees his idea—and therefore himself—move to a higher level of being at which the promise of the idea is fulfilled in the shape of the finished work that displays his plan as a piece of accomplished mind, brought into the world and given a life of its own in the "mindful" product of his making. The construction of an artifact is therefore always a realization of its maker's mind as well as of the materials from which it is made, and of these two processes of realization, the first has priority over the second because it provides the occasion, means and motive for it.

BEING AND PRIDE

In the mind of a maker, the thing he makes exists already, but only prospectively or potentially. The artifact he constructs is the realization of this potential. Its construction is therefore a movement toward a greater quantum of being for the maker himself. In his product, he exists more fully than he did before, when his handiwork was just a "twinkle in his eye." This explains why he loves it as much as he does, for all men desire to be as fully as they can. The special intensity with which a maker loves the thing he makes reflects the greater being he achieves in it, since love and being are correlates and always increase in tandem. "Existence is for all men desirable and worthy of affection; but we exist in activity, i.e., by living and acting, and in his activity the maker is, in a sense, the work produced. He therefore loves his work, because he loves existence. And this lies in the nature of things: what a thing is potentially is revealed in actuality by what it produces."[11] The deeper explanation for why benefactors love their recipients more than their recipients love them rests on this metaphysical truth.

From the vantage point of its recipient, a gift is often of "use."[12] There are things the recipient can do with the gift that might otherwise be impossible, or prohibitively expensive. It expands his powers and advances his plans. For the recipient, the gift is an instrument of self-realization.

But the donor also has a plan that his gift helps to fulfill. His plan is to make the recipient better off (assuming the gift is motivated by real generosity, rather than a wish to put its recipient in debt), and the fulfillment of this plan (the donor's) is for the latter a self-realization as well. If the donor's plan (which has as its goal the advancement of the recipient's plan) is fulfilled, *he also* moves to a higher level of being. His design is accomplished; his powers are actualized; he becomes, in reality, what before he was only potentially—a generous enabler of others. But it is in the person of his recipient that this actualization takes place. His recipient is the locus of his generosity, and it is here—in the life of the recipient—that the benefactor's plan or design, his "idea" of generosity, comes to fruition.

The relation between benefactor and recipient thus resembles that between any maker and the thing he makes, and the affection the first feels for the second has the same source as the love that all makers feel for the things in which their ideas are fulfilled. The affection is asymmetrical because the benefactor does not play an analogous role in the plans of his recipient. The gift he receives enables the latter to do more—to live more fully and go further toward the attainment of his goals. But these goals are not themselves defined in terms of the benefactor's own plans. The empowerment of his benefactor is not, for the recipient, a part of the plan he is pursuing, in the way that the empowerment of the recipient *is* a part of the plan the benefactor has in mind.

The recipient may, of course, make gifts to others in turn. He may be a benefactor as well. In that case, he will love his recipients in the same way, and for the same reasons, that his own benefactor loves him. But every relation of benefaction is asymmetrical in the sense that the fulfillment of one of the parties to it is the means or medium of the other's fulfillment, and hence of his attainment of a higher level of existence, but not the other way around. And because "existence is for all men desirable and worthy of affection," a benefactor will love his recipient, in whose fulfillment his own realization lies, more than a recipient loves his benefactor, whose plans are not, in a symmetrical way, the handiwork in which the recipient's ambitions are achieved.

In this sense, the life of the recipient is subsumed in that of his benefactor. The recipient is an extension or expression of his benefactor's mind. His life shows that (other) mind at work—it is one of the places where the benefactor's mind is actively deployed. The recipient's life therefore constitutes an enlargement of his donor's being in the same way that a craftsman's handiwork constitutes an enlargement of his. But the reverse is not the case. The donor's life is not subsumed in the recipient's nor does it constitute an expression of it.

The relation of recipient to donor is thus one of part to whole. An organ is an inseparable part of the body to which it belongs. An artifact is a freestanding part of its maker's mind and belongs to him as intimately as a bodily organ, despite its physical separation. In an analogous way, the recipient of a gift is a separate and freestanding part of his donor's being and their relation is asymmetrical because no whole can be a part of any part that belongs to it.[13]

Every relation of part to whole is one of dependence. A part has no existence apart from the whole to which it belongs. Organs do not exist independently, nor do artifacts. It is true that a body depends on its organs. If they fail, it will die. It is also true that a craftsman "depends" on the things he makes, for if they are lost or destroyed, his talent will no longer be visible in the finished form of his works. But this dependence (of whole on part) is in the service of a greater independence that no part can ever achieve—the kind of independence that is enjoyed by an organism whose well-functioning parts enable it to move about and to react to things, which none of its parts can do by themselves, and by a craftsman who enjoys the appreciative reactions of others to the things that he has made, something they can never do on their own. A whole always possesses greater independence *vis-à-vis* its parts than its parts do in relation to it.

The relation of whole to part can also be described as one of greater reality. A whole exists at a higher level of being than its parts. There is more to a whole than its parts. The organs of an animal, spread out on the dissectionist's table, each have a certain degree of reality. But the living organism to which they belong exists at a higher level of being. It has powers over and above those of its parts, considered one by one. In a similar way, the maker of an artifact has more reality than the thing he makes. His powers are displayed in his works but not exhausted by them. Like an organism's vital powers, a craftsman's powers of construction represent a kind of ontological surplus—a measure of being over and above that of his artifacts. The relation between a benefactor and his recipient is like this. A benefactor of course depends on his recipient in the way that a craftsman depends on his artifacts. How else can a benefactor show his generosity except though the recipient whose ambitions he helps to fulfill? But the recipient's dependence on his benefactor is greater. For the benefactor already possesses the means to fulfill his ambitions, but the recipient must look to someone else for the resources he needs to achieve his. In this sense, the benefactor is the more independent, or self-sufficient, man.

He is also, for the same reason, the more real one. To modern ears, this sounds strange. How can one man be more real than another? But it captures the essence of Aristotle's view of the relation between givers and takers. A benefactor helps his recipient move from potentiality to actuality. For the recipient, this is a movement toward a higher level of being. But the recipient's fulfillment of his plans is a lesser included part of the donor's, whose realization also represents a movement to a higher level of reality—in the donor's own life. And this latter process of realization is one that takes place on a higher plane of being than the recipient's fulfillment, which is related to the donor's own as part to whole—just as the maturation of an organism occurs on a higher plane of being than the development of its various organs, and the refinement of a craftsman's skills on a higher plane than the construction of any of his individual works.

The life of a recipient is thus both less self-sufficient and less real than the life of his benefactor. That is because the recipient's life "belongs" to that of his benefactor in a way the benefactor's does not belong to him. A benefactor can legitimately say of his recipient, "I made him who he is." But it would be an absurd presumption on the part of a recipient to say the same of his donor, as absurd as if an artifact, could it speak, were to say, "I made my maker who he is"—a ridiculous reversal, on Aristotle's view, of the natural order of things.

The pride of a great-souled man is founded on this natural fact. It is a function of his greater independence and reality. He exists at a higher level of being than other men—in particular, than those who are the beneficiaries of his generosity. When they express their gratitude to him, they recognize their inferiority. They acknowledge that they are more dependent than he, and therefore less real. Gratitude is an expression of ontological inferiority. It is not just a sign of social inferiority, though of course it is that too. More fundamentally, it is the recognition of a relative lack of being. A man with a great soul exists at a higher level of reality than those to whom he makes his gifts, and both his pride and their gratitude reflect their relative positions on the great chain of being.

According to Aristotle, being is what men most want and admire. A properly proud man admires himself, and is admired by others, because he has gone further toward achieving this universally desired end. He is a paragon of being whose superiority is as obvious as that of a parent to a child, or of an educated man to an ignorant one. In him, the possibilities of human existence reach a visible peak of fulfillment. Everyone can see that he is the most a man can be. That is why he takes pride in himself, and avoids putting himself in the position of having to express his gratitude to others for their gifts—something that represents, for him, a hateful diminishment of being.

The central value that Aristotle assigns to pride, and his failure to include gratitude on his list of virtues, is thus more than a social prejudice. It is more than a reflection of prevailing opinion. It is the expression of a system of metaphysical beliefs that portrays in abstract terms the deepest convictions of the pagan world to which Aristotle belonged, whose orienting values he defines, with characteristic compression, in his laconic statement that "excellence consists in doing good rather than in having good done to one."[14] How this metaphysics was upset by the Christian concepts of creation and will, and undermined by the doctrine of grace, and why this led to the transformation of pride from a virtue to a sin, are questions I shall address in due course. But to understand the meaning and magnitude of this great revolution in thought, we need first to follow the metaphysical roots of Aristotle's ethics of pride to a still deeper level.

CHAPTER 6

The Eternal and Divine

WHAT EVERYTHING DESIRES

All men want to be, but fulfill this desire to different degrees. That is because being is not the same as living. If it were, each would have as much as every other. Being is activity. It is the exercise of a power of some sort. A power that is dormant or undeveloped is present in the thing whose power it is, but only as that special kind of directed and aspiring possibility that Aristotle calls "potential."[1] Its development represents a movement from potential to fulfillment, hence from a lower grade of being to a higher one.

Human beings possess certain distinctive powers that set them apart from other living things. A man who puts these powers to work in his life exists at a higher level of reality than those who do not. A truly great-souled man is one who realizes his human potential to an exceptional degree and the surplus of being he enjoys, relative to others, is the source and warrant of his pride.

BEING AND BECOMING

The desire to be is the metaphysical ground of human pride. But men are not alone in having this desire. Other animals have it too. Frogs, for example, yearn to be as fully as they can. For a frog, this means the active exercise of *its* distinctive powers. The movement from tadpole to frog represents an increase in reality, like that from child to man.[2] Not all frogs make this transition with equal success. A frog that loses a leg along the way is compromised in the exercise of its particular powers, just as a child who is badly educated is compromised in the exercise of his. A frog without a leg is like a man without an education: each is unable to be as active as others of its kind, and hence exists at a lower level of reality than they. The desire to be is in their case fulfilled to a lesser degree. Theirs are lives of thwarted desire.

The movement of a plant from seed to flower marks an increase in being too. When a lily reaches down into the earth, and stretches up toward the sun, it is actively striving to move from a lower level of reality to a higher one. Even certain inanimate things, like stones and drops of water, move naturally from potential to fulfillment. Their movement is not a kind of growth, like that of living things. Nor is it motivated by a purposeful (let alone conscious) longing for fulfillment. It is only a change of position. Yet even this represents a process of realization analogous to the more active striving characteristic of things with souls.

Consider the movement of water, one of the four elements of which Aristotle believed all things under the moon are composed. Water has its proper place in the order of things. It has a density (a "specific gravity") that causes it to settle between earth and air. This is where water belongs. When a drop of water is forcibly moved out of place—when it is gathered in a rain cloud and held there by constraint—it tends to move back to its proper place once the constraint is relaxed. In doing so, it realizes its potential to be a distinctive kind of matter occupying a particular place in the world, by actually coming to occupy that place again. In this sense, even the motion of the elements, and of the soulless objects composed of them, is a movement toward the highest state of being available to things of this kind: a cosmological principle that governs every motion in the world, from falling rain to the growth of a human child.

Each of these movements is a striving to be active in the exercise of some potential power, hence to be no longer moving but (actively!) at rest. In some cases, this striving takes the form of a desire.[3] In others, it is something simpler—a tendency to move in a certain direction if not impeded from without. But all these motions are toward a state of motionlessness in which there is nothing left to do or to become. Each is a striving to arrive at the motionless terminus of movement. Every becoming is in this sense a striving for being. That is the end toward which, and for the sake of which, all motions move.[4]

This striving is motivated by a love of being. Love is a longing for what one lacks and needs to be complete. It comes in many shapes and grades, from a plant's love of the sun to a man's love for his friends. It even includes, at the simplest level, the tendency of water to return to its proper place in the world. The love that becoming has for being is the organizing principle of Aristotle's world. Everything in his world is moving, from the elements to the stars, but all of their diverse motions are motivated by the same longing to reach a state of being in which their potential is realized and their striving finally fulfilled.

Everything that moves exists in time. That is because time is simply the measure of motion.[5] But the state toward which things strive is not itself moving and hence cannot possibly exist in time. The love of motionlessness that motivates their movements is thus necessarily a love of the eternal. This is what all moving things desire most of all. The deepest longing of everything in the world of time is to "partake of the eternal and divine," and each pursues this goal in the manner and within the limits its particular nature allows.[6]

Nothing could be further from the belief, to which many today subscribe, that human beings are able to live meaningful lives without a connection to eternity. On Aristotle's view, the love of eternity is the organizing principle of all human striving. That is because, at the deepest level, it is the motive of every striving, human and nonhuman alike. The world is a vast theater of motions, each of which is measured by time. But it is the love of eternity that gives all of these movements their shape and direction. Only this makes the world a cosmos—an ordered and intelligible whole. Without it, the world would be not a cosmos but a chaos, and nothing in it, man included, would make any sense at all.

The Christian religion also puts the longing for eternity at the center of its account of human life. For a Christian, salvation is the greatest good a human being can know. To be saved means to be rescued from the pointlessness of change, motion, time. Salvation is eternity—life everlasting. But on a Christian view, salvation is not to be found in this world. The eternity for which a Christian longs, and that gives our mortal lives their meaning, lies beyond this world, in heaven, with God who abides forever. To be saved means to be redeemed from the world, to be carried beyond it to another realm, to the "city of God." And this redemption is always a gift that comes from the God who made the world and bestows salvation on those he chooses as an act of grace, for which the only appropriate response is one of boundless thanks.

Aristotle's view is strikingly different. The eternity that everything in the world strives to reach is not something apart from the world. It is not a heaven above the world, or beyond it. Aristotle's eternity is the everlasting order *of* the world, whose never-changing form informs the varied and endless processes of change in which everything in the world is continually engaged. To participate in eternity thus means to be part of what never changes in the world, not to be transported beyond it. According to Aristotle, everything is equipped to do this in some fashion. The love of eternity that moves them all is satisfied by different things in different ways, as their natures dictate and allow. Yet in every case it is fulfilled, not outside the world but within it.

This is true of human beings as well. Frogs and lilies and even drops of water are able to participate in eternity, and so are we. This is part of our nature too. It is the just the way things are for us and them. It is not the gift of a God beyond the world, whose own eternal being stands opposed to the transience of the world in which we live. There is no God beyond the world, whose creation this world is, and who offers salvation from the world as a gift to the human beings he has made in his image. There is only this world, the one all-encompassing cosmos whose eternal order human beings are able to experience directly in their lives, if only in a limited way. And because our ability to do this is not a gift but a feature of the world itself, those men who realize their potential to participate in the eternal and divine have every reason to be joyful, but none at all to be grateful to a God by whose grace alone they have been given a share in the everlasting, for the world is our home, and we are equipped by nature to experience its immortality in thought and deed.

The human potential for such fulfillment is distinguished from that of other things in one important respect, however. Every other kind of thing has the power to participate in eternity, but only in one way. Drops of water share in eternity, but only by falling down. Frogs do so only by making other frogs like themselves. Even the stars, whose participation is the least limited of all moving things, experience eternity only by going around in their unchanging circles. We alone partake of the eternal and divine in different ways. Only our form, uniquely among those of all the things in the world, permits a variety of such fulfillments, and it would not be wrong to say that, for Aristotle, this plasticity *is* our human nature.[7]

HAPPINESS

The *Nicomachean Ethics* begins with some general reflections on the end or aim of human living. Human beings pursue many different goals, but most of these are for the sake of something else. A man may work to make money, for example, but does so in order to support his family, entertain his friends, and become an honored benefactor in his community. There is only one goal that men always pursue for its own sake. Aristotle calls this *eudaimonia,* a word that can be translated as "happiness," "flourishing" or "well-being." Happiness is the final goal of human striving—that for the sake of which all other goals are pursued.

"Both the common run of people and cultivated men"[8] agree that this is so. But there is disagreement about the nature of human happiness. In what does it consist? "Some say it is one thing and others another, and often the very same person identifies it with different things at different times; when he is sick he thinks it is health, and when he is poor he says it is wealth; and when people are conscious of their own ignorance, they admire those who talk above their heads in accents of greatness."[9]

The final end that men pursue thus appears to be indeterminate. Other beings strive to flourish, just as we do. Frogs strive to catch flies and reproduce. Lilies strive to grow and make a flower. Even water strives to reach its natural resting place. But each of these has only a single, determinate goal. Man alone pursues different forms of happiness. Hence, only for him does the question arise as to which of these is best. This is the first question that any study of the good for man must answer. Man is therefore the only ethical being in the world, since he alone confronts multiple possibilities of flourishing whose variety compels him to ask the question with which all ethical inquiry starts.

Of the different conceptions of human happiness, three have had the most lasting appeal. One equates happiness with bodily pleasure, another with political virtue, and a third with thought or contemplation. Each way of life has its followers and defenders. But how are we to choose among them? Is there a way of deciding which is best for human beings? We can make a start, Aristotle says, "by first ascertaining the proper function or 'work' [*ergon*] of man."[10] He begins his own account of man's work with some reflections on the simpler work of playing the flute.

Every art or skill has a distinctive function. Its possession enables one to perform a specific task in a certain way. A man who possesses the skill of flute playing can play music on the flute. He is able to "work" as a flute player. Of course, his work may be poor. He may play badly (something that, strictly speaking, a person without flute training cannot do, since even playing badly is a kind of playing). When he does play badly, a flute player's skills are not on display. They are not actively deployed in a way that he and others can recognize and appreciate. Considered just as a flute player, he is "underachieving." His playing falls short of the level reached by the player who is actively at work playing the flute and playing it well. The latter's performance has more "substance," or to use the Greek word from which this Latinized term derives, more "presence" (*ousia*). It "exists" to a greater degree. If being human is a kind of work too, then those who are actively engaged in it, and perform it well, are by analogy living lives that are more real, and hence fulfilled, than the lives of those who are inactive or whose work is marred in some fashion.

Flute playing is an acquired capacity. One is not born being able to play the flute. At most, one is born being able to learn to play the flute, but a capacity for flute playing is a second-order ability that can be acquired only through study and practice. The capacity for being human is like this too. Unlike other living things, we are born with a capacity to acquire the capacity for being human. But the latter capacity—for speech, politics, trade, music, philosophy and everything else unique to human life—must be awakened through instruction and training. It does not arise on its own, by nature. Outside the civilizing world of law and culture, we would never acquire it. Like the skill of flute playing, a capacity for being human arises only through education. A creature that is born with the capacity for acquiring this capacity but never does (like a child reared by wolves), is shut out from the special fulfillment of human living, just as a man who never learns to play the flute cannot be fulfilled as a flute player, however accomplished he may be in other respects.

The fact that a person has learned to play the flute is of course no guarantee that he will play it well. Even a skilled flute player can make mistakes, or be deprived of opportunities to play, or lose interest in doing so, or forget how. Being human is like flute playing in this regard as well. There are as many ways in which a person who has acquired the capacity for living a human life may fail to exercise this power and thus be unfulfilled as a human being, as there are ways in which a trained flute player may be unfulfilled in his art. By the same token, just as a man who learns to play the flute and neither makes mistakes nor lets his skill lie idle is more fully realized as a flute player, so too one who exercises his capacity for being human in the proper way is more fully realized as a human being than a man who allows this capacity to languish or performs "off-key."

But what is the work of a human being, and what does it mean to do it well? Or "is it then possible," Aristotle asks rhetorically, "that while a carpenter and a shoemaker have their own proper functions and spheres of action, man as man has none, but was left by nature a good-for-nothing without a function"?[11] To identify man's function, we need to define what it means to be human, and this requires that we specify the powers peculiar to man, for it is in the exercise of these that the work of being human presumably consists, just as the work of flute playing consists in the ability to play an instrument with the properties that flutes alone possess.

Human beings are living things. But there is nothing specifically human about being alive. Other animals and plants are alive as well. Man's work can therefore not be that of "simply living."[12] Men also belong to the narrower class of living beings that have perception and move about in pursuit of things they see and want. But every other terrestrial animal does this too. Even a worm lives a "life of sense perception."[13] So again, the work of being human cannot consist merely in living a life of this sort.

What sets man apart from other animals is his possession of reason. No other animal on earth possesses the power that manifests itself in thinking and speaking. However different human beings may be in other ways, the power of reason is one they share in common. Even a master and his slave share a bond of reason, for without it they could not communicate, and the slave would be no more useful to his master than a well-trained dog.[14]

Reason is therefore man's specific characteristic. It is the defining mark of the human species. A capacity for rational action (which must be awakened through education) is what empowers a human being to live a human life, in the same way that an ability to play the flute empowers one to play it. And just as the flute player's exercise of his ability constitutes his distinctive work, a human being's exercise of his capacity for rational action constitutes the work of "man as man." The work of man may therefore be defined as "an active life of the rational element."[15] A human being who lives such a life experiences a fulfillment analogous to that of a flute player who plays his instrument properly, and the person who lives this life in the best and most complete way experiences to the highest degree the happiness at which all men aim.

It would therefore seem that in order to decide whether the happiest life is one of bodily pleasure, or political virtue or contemplation, all we need to do is determine which of these allows for the active exercise of reason to the greatest degree. But this is more difficult than it appears. That is because reason does not occupy a separate compartment in human life, walled off from the capacities that men share with other living things, including the capacity for "nutrition and growth"[16] that even plants possess, and the power of perception and movement that "man has in common with the horse, the ox, and every animal."[17] The distinctively human power of reason is not a power apart. It informs all of human living and conditions every human activity, even those that are not themselves distinctively human.

Thus, human beings take in food, digest and excrete it, just as plants and animals do. But only men grow crops, develop cuisines, and build toilets and sewers. Man's entire metabolic existence is suffused with reason. Even his sex life is distinguished from that of other animals by the pervasive presence in it of those "mindful" projections we call fantasies, which are more than brute desires. Even more obviously, the cities in which men live, though established to satisfy their needs, are organized on the basis of rationally self-imposed laws, which distinguish them from the communities of other social animals, like ants or bees, and create a space for the leisured pursuit of all the many activities we gather under the rubric of culture. The political dimension of human existence, like the metabolic, is thus distinguished by its rational character, for it involves the transformation of something animalic (the social instinct) into a uniquely human enterprise through the informing work of reason.

In all these cases, one can think of reason as a form imposed on some non-human material (digestion, sexual desire, sociality), in such a way as to give the resulting product (cuisine, fantasy, culture and law) a distinctly human appearance. It follows that a life devoted to anything, including physical pleasure, can potentially be "an active life of the rational element." And if that is true, then the lives of an accomplished pastry chef, a distinguished statesman, and a philosopher who grasps the first principles of being, might all seem to stand on a par, so far as Aristotle's criterion of success in the work of being human is concerned.

But this is not Aristotle's view. He is emphatic that a life dedicated to physical pleasure is less fulfilling and happy than one devoted either to political virtue or contemplation. And as between the latter two, though he seems at times to waver, in the end he gives the prize to contemplation. Only a life of thought is "an active life of the rational element" in the fullest and most complete sense. Only in a life of this sort is man fully at work, and hence as happy as he can be. For Aristotle, these three lives do not stand on a par. They can be ranked in a hierarchy of excellence or worth. What explains Aristotle's ranking of these lives and his judgment that a life of contemplation is the happiest of all?

The answer lies in the longing for eternity that explains every movement in the world, including the human pursuit of happiness, whether men seek it in a life devoted to pleasure, politics or philosophy. The place that Aristotle assigns these lives in his hierarchical ordering of them is a function of how fully they satisfy this longing.

SPECIES AND SEASONS

The view that a happy life consists in bodily pleasure—a life like that of Sardanapallus, an Assyrian king famous for his sensual excesses[18]—is the most widely held view of happiness, and the one that Aristotle considers least plausible. Indeed, he treats it with contempt. "The common run of people and the most vulgar identify [a happy life] with pleasure, and are for that reason satisfied with a life of enjoyment." In doing so, they "betray their utter slavishness in their preference for a life suitable to cattle."[19]

But Aristotle's curt dismissal of this first conception of happiness ignores the fact that in one respect a human life devoted to pleasure is not like a cow's at all. No cow has ever prepared a five-course meal or put on lipstick to make herself attractive. Human beings do these and countless other things in the pursuit of bodily pleasure. Even a life completely devoted to such pleasures is shot through with thinking, planning, recollecting, and imagining—in short, with reason.

Aristotle's scornful contempt of those who consider this the best life for man therefore cannot be explained by the absence of reason from it. The real deficiency of the life of bodily pleasure is not its irrationality, but its confinement of the person living it to the sphere of metabolic routine. All plants and animals on earth, man included, pursue their love of eternity within and through these routines. But man's reason equips him for a different and higher fulfillment of the same desire—or rather, for two fulfillments, one in a life of politics and the other in a life devoted to thought. Each of these allows the human beings engaged in it to partake of the eternal and divine in a way no other earthly animal can.

Reason is not absent from the life of bodily pleasure. But in the lives of those who devote themselves to politics and contemplation, the reason that is present in human eating and sex is used to achieve a more intimate and self-sufficient connection to eternity. In the lives of statesmen and philosophers, the power of reason is therefore more fully at work in the pursuit of a goal that men and cattle share, but which can be achieved only in a less direct way within the domain of metabolic life to which cows are by nature confined. The man who makes bodily pleasure his aim degrades himself by limiting his pursuit of immortality to this domain, when better opportunities for doing so exist.

To see why these other opportunities are better, we need first to understand how the goal of sharing in the eternal and divine can be attained within the realm of metabolic life, and appreciate the limits to which its attainment is subject so long as one pursues it here. A remark that Aristotle makes in *De Anima* gives us a start.

The most "natural act" for every living thing, he says,

> is the production of another like itself, an animal producing an animal, a plant a plant, in order that, so far as its nature allows, it may partake in the eternal and divine. That is the goal toward which all things strive, that for the sake of which they do whatsoever their nature renders possible. . . . Since then no living thing is able to partake in what is eternal and divine by uninterrupted continuance (for nothing perishable can for ever remain one and the same), it tries to achieve that end in the only way possible to it, and success is possible in varying degrees; so it remains not indeed as the self-same individual but continues as something like itself—not numerically but specifically one.[20]

Every plant and animal is constantly changing. It is continually in motion, from conception to death. Its existence at every stage is therefore accompanied by nonexistence—by the no-longer of what it once was, and the not-yet of what it will be. And of course its entire career is shadowed by the prospect of its inevitable demise. Every living thing on earth is thus, in its essence, a compound of being and nonbeing, for the impermanence of each of its stages, and of its career as a whole, is not something accidental that just happens to befall it, but part of its nature.

As a living thing moves from birth to adulthood, barring any accidents in the normal course of development, its potential to be the sort of thing it is—a man, a frog, a lily—is realized to an ever greater degree. Its reality progressively increases. But if the normal process of maturation that a living thing undergoes represents a movement to a higher level of being, the fact that it is fated to decline and die limits the "amount" of being it can attain within the bounds of its own transient career. No matter how fully it realizes the powers peculiar to its kind, the life of a living thing can never escape the nonbeing that lies at its heart. And because of this, its love of being can be satisfied only up to a point, within the limits its mortality allows.

To satisfy this longing more completely, every living thing must find a way to participate in something that lasts forever, unlike itself. For only what lasts forever *is* in the fullest and most complete sense. Only its being is not diluted by the presence of any element of nonbeing. The love of being that every living thing experiences can therefore be fully satisfied only when it comes to rest in something that is never born or dies, that never changes and is always the same. In the case of living things, this longing is fulfilled by participating reproductively in the immortal life of their kind. By going out of themselves into their offspring, living things, which are mortal by nature, reach the immortality they seek. All plants and animals do this, man included.

Even natural but inanimate things participate in immortality in an analogous way, though not by means of reproduction, for unlike plants and animals they lack the power to make copies of themselves.

The four elements of earth, water, air, and fire are the most primitive types of organized stuff in the sublunary world. All more complex things, living and not, are composed of them, and eventually decompose into them again. "Beneath" the elements there is only "prime matter,"[21] which has no definite form of its own but is merely the potential the elements themselves possess to change into one another, as water changes to air when heated by the sun. Unlike other potentialities, however, that of prime matter is a *pure* potentiality with no determinate direction, about which we can therefore know nothing at all since our knowledge of any power depends on our ability to relate it to some determinately organized thing which it is the power to become.[22]

In contrast to prime matter, the elements all possess distinctive forms of their own. Each has a specific nature, a tendency (unless impeded) to act in a particular way—to move to the place in the world that is properly its own, to its "natural" location. Its tendency to do this is a potential that is realized by its arrival at the place it belongs, like the growth of a tadpole into a frog. Both are movements toward a state of motionlessness—the goal that every moving thing strives to reach. And just as plants and animals can reach this goal only by participating in the eternal life of their kind, the elements are able to do so only through the incorporation of their movements into an endless circle too.

None of the four elements is ever all together in an undivided whole. Each is always separated into individual bits. The dislodgement of bits of matter from their proper places and their natural movement back toward them is a ceaseless process that manifests itself in the ever-changing weather, which varies from one day to the next.[23] But it is also a cyclical process, for the external force that moves these bits out of place, and thus creates the condition for their return, is the regularly varying warmth of the ever-circling sun. In the spring, the sun causes water to rise out of its proper place. When the displacing power of the sun's heat dissipates in the fall, the water it "forced" to rise falls back again as rain. The sun moves round every year in a circle. The motion of the elements is rectilinear. They always move up or down, depending on where they happen to be and where they belong.[24] But through the regularity of its effects upon the elements, the sun communicates the eternality of its own circular motion to them, so that the elements themselves go up and down forever in a cyclical way. We call this the "wheel" of the seasons—the endlessly returning sequence of warm and cool, moist and dry, that sets the scene for life on earth and makes it possible in the first place. In the procession of the seasons, which follow one another in a fixed sequence with neither beginning nor end, the elements participate in eternity in the most complete way their nature allows. For in their motions of displacement and return, they have a share in the eternal cycle of the weather and the seasons, which in the tempestuous realm beneath the moon is the image of the sun's serener circle.

In this respect, living and nonliving things are alike. An individual plant or animal is in motion as long as it lives and can satisfy its yearning for motionlessness only by participating in the unchanging life of its species. A bit of water or earth is constantly in motion too, and its tendency toward stability can be fulfilled only by participating in the eternal cycle of the seasons. What the seasons are to the elements, the life of each species is to the mortal careers of its members. Just as the linear motion of the elements is incorporated within a larger seasonal cycle, the line that every living thing on earth draws from birth to death is placed within the encircling life of its kind, which is always beginning afresh with new copies. In this way, individuals of both sorts, living and not, partake of the eternal and divine. This is the condition of drops of water, of frogs and even of men, considered as metabolic beings only.

LIFE

Living things nevertheless differ from nonliving ones with respect to the *kind* of individuality they possess, and this has implications for the depth and intimacy of the connection they are able to establish to the immortality that all things in the natural world seek to attain.

The parts of a living thing are held together in a vital whole. They do not merely exist side by side, like those of a clump of earth or drop of water. They are organized in a dynamic unity that is more than the sum of its parts. Aristotle calls this the "soul" (*psyche*) of a living thing. Indeed, such things do not just *have* souls, in the way they have parts and capacities. The distinctive nature of a living thing—what makes it alive rather than dead—is nothing but the special sort of unity it possesses as an ensouled being. This distinctive kind of unity, which bits of earth and water lack, is what we mean when we say that something is alive.

When the parts of a plant or animal are separated from the living thing to which they belong, they disintegrate or decompose. They lose the animation they possess so long as they are integrated into the organism as a whole. By the same token, things outside a plant or animal—bits of inanimate matter, like water, and other living things—do not belong to its own functional organization, but to the world instead, unless and until they are absorbed into the organism through eating or drinking, in which case they lose the shape they had before and take on that of the plant or animal that consumes them. This is what we call metabolism (literally, a change of form).[25] So long as the parts of a living being continue to be held together in a vital unity through its successful metabolic interaction with the world, it retains the special kind of individuality that distinguishes plants and animals from lifeless things.

Death is the loss of this unity and of the individuality associated with it. A clump of earth can never be an individual in the way a living plant or animal is. It can never be more than a heap and therefore cannot die. It may be broken up, but its disintegration is not death. It is the unique privilege of all living things on earth to be individuals in a more complex way, and their correspondingly unique burden to die.

The basic condition of every plant and animal is thus defined by two characteristics—the possession of a special kind of unity, not shared by inanimate things, and the impermanence of this unity itself. Because they are mortal, plants and animals must transcend their individuality in order to participate in the eternal and divine. They have to go outside themselves, just as bits of elemental stuff must disintegrate and re-form in order to participate in the cycle of the seasons. But because they are alive, and have the kind of holistic and directed unity that only living things possess, they are able to transcend themselves in a special way, by means of reproduction. Moreover, unlike bits of earth and water, plants and animals actively desire such transcendence and thus experience within their own lives an *inner* connection to eternity that is deeper and more direct than any inanimate object can ever achieve. In them, the pursuit of this common goal may therefore be said to reach a higher and more active level of organization.

The active desire for immortality that defines the lives of living things is more than just a tendency, like that of water to fall from the sky. It is a purposeful (though generally unconscious) striving. The most potent expression of this striving is the desire to make a copy of oneself. Every other desire is subordinate to this one, including even the desire for nourishment, which along with the desire to reproduce is the only one that all plants and animals share. The desire for nourishment protects the integrity of living things against the world outside them. It is only by satisfying this desire that living things are able to survive at all. But survival is not the goal of life. It is not an end in itself. Survival is for the sake of reproduction. The preservation of the mortal life of the individual is for the sake of its transcendence through participation in the immortal life of its kind. All the other desires of plants and animals culminate in their longing for the eternal and divine, which living things, in contrast to inanimate ones, are equipped to pursue in a distinctively active and organized way.

Man is no exception. Like every other living thing, on earth at least, he seeks immortality through reproduction. Individual men and women actively strive to participate in the eternal life of humankind by leaving copies of themselves behind—something no mere bit of elemental stuff can ever do. But this is neither the only nor the best way men have of seeking the everlasting and divine, and those who claim, as many do, that happiness consists in physical pleasure, make the mistake of assuming that it is.

BETWEEN HEAVEN AND EARTH

For a modern reader, the most puzzling feature of Aristotle's cosmic taxonomy is his inclusion of the moon, sun, planets and stars in the category of living things.[26] The astrophysics that for centuries has shaped our understanding of the heavens teaches us to think of these bodies as inanimate objects, like bits of earth and water. But Aristotle insisted that the sun and moon and other heavenly bodies are alive—that they have souls, like the plants and animals on earth. Many have dismissed this as a symptom of Aristotle's scientific ignorance and have invoked it to impeach his philosophy in general.[27] But it is important to understand why he classified the heavenly bodies as living beings, since his reasons for doing are not just the product of primitive beliefs, or of poor observation with limited tools, but of Aristotle's deepest metaphysical commitments, on which his conception of man's place in the world, and his assessment of the relative worth of the three lives traditionally proposed as the best for man, are based.

Two things impressed Aristotle about the bodies he saw in the heavens. The first is that they are individuals. The sun is one body, the moon another. Like every individual, the heavenly bodies are bounded and therefore finite. In this regard, they are no different from individuals of any other kind.

The second is that they are immortal. Unlike clods of earth, which disintegrate, and terrestrial plants and animals, which die, the heavenly bodies last forever (or so Aristotle believed).

Their nature is defined by the conjunction of these two things. The sun and moon and planets and stars are immortal individuals, unlike the living and nonliving things we see about us in the world below the moon, all of which eventually perish and can therefore participate in the eternal and divine only by transcending their individuality in some fashion. The heavenly bodies do not need to do this. Immortality is inscribed in their individual being in a way it is in nothing else the eye can see. The conjunction of immorality and individuality is therefore even closer in their case than in that of plants and animals, in whom it is closer than in natural but inanimate things, which lack the active desire for immortality that constitutes the individuality of every living being.

Plants and animals reach immortality by going out of themselves through reproduction. The heavenly bodies are immortal already. Like clods of earth and drops of water, they do not reproduce. But that is not because they are inferior to plants and animals, whose power of reproduction puts them in closer touch with the divine than any bit of earth can ever be. It is because they have no need for this power, since they already enjoy what plants and animals are able to attain only by means of it. The love of being is therefore satisfied more fully and directly within the bounds of their individual lives than in those of other living beings. Because this is the benchmark by which the relative proximity of anything to the eternal and divine must be measured, and because, according to it, the heavenly bodies are closer to eternity than plants and animals, which are closer than inanimate things, it would be absurd to classify the moon and sun and planets and stars with the latter rather than the former. The only metaphysically plausible position for them in Aristotle's world is at the very top of the register of living beings. And this is where he puts them. The heavenly bodies are alive, he says, and among living things they are the very best of all.

But though the stars and planets come closer to immortality than anything else in the world, they nevertheless fall short of it in one obvious way. What is eternal must be forever exactly the same. *Any* change in a thing's condition therefore means that whatever kind of immortality it possesses is less perfect than that of something that does not change at all. But the heavenly bodies do change in one way (though only one). They move from place to place in an annual rotation. Hence even they, though their individual lives are everlasting, are not eternity itself—eternity in the perfect and unqualified sense. Even the sun and moon and planets and stars must therefore strive for an eternity they do not quite possess, and they do so by imitating the motionlessness of pure being in the best way that it can be imitated within the realm of moving things—by moving in a circle. This is the heavenly counterpart of the circle of the seasons, in which the soulless elements move, and of the round dance of reproductive life in which every plant and animal on earth is engaged.

The living beings we see above us in the heavens have a material nature too, like living and nonliving things in the sublunary sphere. If they didn't, we would not be able to see them at all. But the matter of which they consist is incorruptible. It never turns into anything else in the way that water turns to air.[28] Because they have a material existence, each of the heavenly bodies occupies a determinate place in space and time and is subject to the forces of motion—to moving and being moved. The materiality of the heavenly bodies is therefore the source of their finitude, for anything that is subject to motion is subject to change, and hence not unchanging itself. It follows that the planets and stars are able to partake of the motionlessness of the eternal and divine only by means of motion, and thus in an imitative and indirect way.

But unlike bits of earth and water, and individual plants and animals, whose linear movements share in eternity only through their incorporation in a larger circle of some kind, the heavenly bodies experience the endlessness of a circular existence directly. They experience it firsthand. This is possible because, though they belong to the realm of moving things, the heavenly bodies possess an individual identity that is organized around a yearning for immortality that remains undiminished forever, untouched by the passage of time—in contrast to the elements, whose separate bits have no psychic identity at all, and to other living things whose souls provide only a temporary principle of organization that always eventually yields to the forces of disintegration that press on them from within and without. Like everything else in the world of moving things, even the beautiful, glittering souls we see in the sky above us are in pursuit of an immortality they do not fully possess. But their special nature as living beings that live forever enables them to partake of it with a directness that is their privilege alone. By contrast, the souls of other living things—with the one exception of man—have a share in immortality only to the extent their individual lives are submerged in the wheel of birth and death that constitutes the life of their species. There is not a single moment in their lives in which eternity is directly present in them in the way it is in the lives of the heavenly bodies, where it is present forever.

Man's position in the chain of living things is therefore unique. Like the plants and animals around him, he lives only for a time. Individual men and women come and go; mankind alone is eternal. In this respect, the life of every human being differs from that of the immortal individuals he sees in the heavens above. But like them, he is able to have a direct if short-lived experience of immortality within the confines of his own individual life, and not just the indirect kind that every animal on earth enjoys by participating in the reproductive life of its species.

This experience is temporary. It is not the uninterrupted experience of immortality that the stars and planets enjoy. But though human beings have only a limited capacity for such experiences, it offers them the opportunity to participate in the eternal and divine in a more self-sufficient way than other terrestrial animals are able to do. Metaphorically, one might say that among the earthly animals, man alone is capable of enjoying, for brief periods at least, a starlike existence in which individuality and immortality are fused, though his animal nature, whose demands he can never escape, prevents him from living such a life without interruption.

As we shall see in the following chapter, both the life of politics and that of contemplation allow for the possibility of an experience of immortality that reproduction does not afford. In them, the individuality of the person living the life and the immortality he desires are temporarily joined in an especially intimate way. In each case, moreover, it is the power of reason, which among all the animals on earth man alone possesses, that creates the possibility of such a life. A human being who uses his reason to live a life of this kind is using it to forge the closest possible connection that a rational animal can hope to achieve between his own mortal existence and the motionlessness he longs to attain. He is using his reason to best advantage, as measured by the metaphysical yardstick that ranks everything in the world, human lives included, according to their success in satisfying the love of being that inspires them all.

By contrast, the man who makes bodily pleasure his goal, and says that a life spent pursuing such pleasures is the happiest there is, wastes his reason on an inferior grade of immortality. It is true that the human pursuit of bodily pleasure is rationalized throughout and achieves levels of refinement that exist nowhere else in the animal world. But every pleasure of this kind is built upon physical need, and these are all reducible to the drives for food and sex, which in turn serve the process of reproduction that satisfies the longing for eternity only indirectly, outside the individual, in the immortal life of the species to which he belongs.

The man who values physical pleasure above all else uses his reason as an aid or adjunct to these drives and thus chains himself to the metabolic routines that condition our lives but do not fully or finally constrain them, as they do the lives of other animals. And that is not merely to miss an opportunity for something exciting. It is to leave our human nature unfulfilled. It is to permit the highest power we possess to be squandered on something less than its best use. The lives of the politician and thinker allow for an experience of eternity which, brief though it may be, is more self-contained than any afforded by a life of physical pleasures, for however refined these become their satisfaction can never fulfill our longing to partake of the eternal and divine except in the indirect way that other animals do. The view that the best and happiest life for a human being is one devoted to sensual pleasure is therefore more than a mistake. It is a perversion, and when Aristotle contemptuously calls it a life fit for cattle, this is what he means.

CHAPTER 7

The Best Life of All

POLITICS AND CONTEMPLATION

Many believe that happiness consists in physical pleasure. But Aristotle gives no credence to this view. He dismisses it with a wave of the hand. Those who equate happiness with pleasure fail to understand that our longing to share in the eternal and divine can be better satisfied in the uniquely human activities of politics and philosophy than in the common metabolic routines of animal life. They make a metaphysical mistake.

That the happiest life is one devoted to the exercise of political virtue is a view Aristotle takes far more seriously. After introducing the general subject of happiness in book 1 of the *Ethics,* he devotes most of his remaining lectures to an examination of this way of life. Only at the very end of the *Ethics,* and very briefly, does he consider the possibility that the best life of all is one devoted neither to pleasure nor politics but to philosophy instead.

Among the different views that men hold about the nature of happiness, the belief that it consists in the active exercise of political virtue is both honorable and widely held, unlike the identification of happiness with pleasure, which is not honorable, and the view that it consists in thinking, which is not widely held. Aristotle's own high regard for the life of political virtue is apparent and his detailed account of its rewards makes it clear that he considers such a life genuinely fulfilling—if less fulfilling, in the end, than a life of thought, which is to be preferred to a career of political action for the same

reasons that explain why Aristotle rejects the equation of happiness with physical pleasure as a view unworthy of debate.

FAME

A virtuous man is one who "loves what is noble and feels disgust at what
is base."[1] He is temperamentally inclined to do the right thing. When he acts
properly, as he generally does, it is not by accident, or against the grain of his
inclinations. A virtuous man recognizes what is good, wants to pursue it, and
takes pleasure in hitting the mark—in living as his character inclines him to do.

A virtue is a disposition to act in certain ways—a power or potential that
is realized and hence fulfilled in the performance of the relevant actions. When
he is asleep, a courageous, just and generous man is only potentially these
things.[2] He becomes actually virtuous by fighting battles, exchanging goods
and making gifts. A man who possesses the habit of acting as virtue requires
will therefore seek out opportunities for doing so, since these offer the fulfillment he seeks.

A virtuous man may limit himself to the affairs of private life, defending
his city when called upon to do so, but devoting himself in the main to his
family and business relations. This is a perfectly honorable existence. But the
man who puts his virtue to work in making laws for his city (broadly understood to include the entire range of political activities) achieves something
greater. That is because law plays a foundational role in the establishment of
virtue itself.

A man cannot be persuaded by arguments alone to live a virtuous life. To
find such arguments convincing, he must already be habitually inclined to
act in a virtuous way.[3] The habits of a virtuous man are a product of his education. To have a virtuous character, one must receive "the right training for
virtue from youth up."[4] Whether a man receives such training depends on
many things (the sort of family into which he is born, his own intellectual
resources, and the like). But it depends, most fundamentally, on the laws of
the community in which he happens to live. These shape its political culture
by defining a conception of how one ought to live, and by establishing the
institutions that are needed to direct its citizens into a life that conforms to
this ideal.

To live a life of self-control and tenacity is not pleasant for most people,
especially for the young. Therefore, their upbringing and pursuits

must be regulated by laws; for once they have become familiar, they will no longer be painful. But it is perhaps not enough that they receive the right upbringing and attention only in their youth. Since they must carry on these pursuits and cultivate them by habit when they have grown up, we probably need laws for this, too, and for the whole of life in general.[5]

In order to know which laws are necessary to achieve this goal, one must both be virtuous and have an expert understanding of the nature of virtue itself. The second is not entailed by the first, nor does the first necessarily follow from the second. A man can be virtuous without having a reflective understanding of it, and it is possible (if unlikely) that a man possess a knowledge of virtue without himself being virtuous. Effective lawmaking demands both, since only those who know what virtue is can deliberately fashion laws to promote it, and only those with virtuous characters can be counted on to use their expert knowledge of virtue in a reliable way, and not to be distracted by self-indulgence, or corrupted by injustice, or blinded by poor judgment.

A virtuous man who devotes himself to the work of lawmaking is therefore distinguished from his private counterpart in two respects. First, he acts with a measure of self-awareness that the latter may but need not possess. Second, by enacting, improving and applying the laws of his city he helps to secure the continued existence of the framework of norms within which his own virtue and that of others is alone possible. We might say that his virtuous actions are deliberately aimed at preserving the space of virtue itself—the regime of laws on which even the privately virtuous man depends for his upbringing and support. In this sense, a virtuous lawmaker exercises his virtue not merely on a larger scale but at a more basic level than the just, generous and temperate man who confines himself to private affairs. His is the most active and therefore real existence that a life of virtue affords.

The greater reality of the lives of virtuous men who live for the sake of their cities is reflected in the greater durability of what they achieve. A man of private virtue may be remembered by those who knew him. But his celebrants and memorialists are fewer in number and lack the institutional resources that a city possesses to perpetuate the memory of those who have served it in word and deed. The memory of a virtuous man who lives his life in private often dies with his children or grandchildren. That of a man of public virtue is as long-lived as the city to which he belongs.

We call this more durable form of remembrance fame. It is the prize won by the greatest warriors, statesmen and public philanthropists. But fame is more than just the consequence of their actions. It is the prize they seek, for with it comes an individualized immortality that is unattainable within the realm of private life.

A famous man is renowned for his special achievements. He stands out from other, more ordinary men on account of his exceptional excellence. Through the perpetuation of his memory, a man famous for his excellence lives on, as an individual distinct from others, after the death of the body to which his character and virtues are joined. The only immortality that a life given over to physical pleasure offers is the immortality of the species—the anonymous immortality of the metabolic wheel to which the pursuit of pleasure, however refined, is permanently chained. Even those who live virtuously, but privately, are swallowed up in the anonymity of household life, where no one stands out because everyone's actions are organized around the blank and repetitive circle of need. The life of political virtue offers something more. It offers the chance of a life after death in the memory of one's community—not as a copy in one's offspring, but as oneself, as an individual who has said or done something remarkable that is worthy of being preserved.

The individual immortality that a man achieves in this way is less than perfect. It falls short of the individual immorality of the stars and other heavenly bodies. Unlike theirs, it is hostage to fate. And even a man of great public virtue who succeeds in becoming famous for his words or deeds, survives as an individual after death only in the memory of others, a shadowy thing by comparison with his flesh and blood existence while alive. *Yet still,* those who choose this life, and affirm its values, hope for a measure of individual immortality that others can never achieve. The knowledge that this goal is within their grasp, even in a limited way, is the source of the pride they take in themselves; of their sense of superiority to those who live virtuous but obscure lives in private; and of their lofty and contemptuous judgment that anyone who devotes his life to pleasure is completely lacking in shame.

CITY AND HIVE

Fame is a political phenomenon. It exists only within political communities. What is it about the nature of these communities that enables certain of their members to achieve an individualized life after death that has no counterpart in the anonymous circle of biological life?

Aristotle begins his account of politics with the famous observation that man is "by nature a political animal." To explain what he means, he contrasts a human city with a hive of bees.[6]

A city resembles a hive in two respects. First, both are marked by an internal division of labor. In each, some individuals perform certain tasks, others different ones. Relations among their members are in this regard like those among the various parts of an animal, except that the "parts" of both a city and a hive are separate individuals with independent lives of their own.

Second, a beehive, like a city, has a life that is potentially longer than that of any of its individual members. Bees are born and die but hives live on, just as a city survives the birth and death of its citizens. There is no natural built-in limit to the lives of cities or hives. In principle, both can survive forever, though none ever has.

But these similarities mask a deeper difference.

A beehive is organized in accordance with laws. A hive is not an anarchic, accidental conjunction but an orderly whole. A scientist who has studied bees understands these laws and can teach them to others. He can describe and explain the order that regulates the life of the hive, fixing the place that each bee occupies within it and determining the function it performs in the metabolic routines of the hive as a whole.

A human city is organized in accordance with laws too, and a scientist who studies it can describe these as well.[7] But the laws of a human city are the product of legislation, of a deliberate process of making (*poesis*) that resembles all such processes in its self-conscious orientation toward a goal the maker conceives in his mind before he realizes it in the shape of a finished product.[8]

A bed's maker sees the bed he is making in his mind's eye before he sees it completed in his workshop. He "thinks ahead" to the end of his productive work. In the same way, a legislator making laws for his city thinks ahead to the end he aims to achieve. He imagines what his city will look like when the laws he is making are in place. Like the bed maker's work, the lawmaker's is directed by his reflective attention to a goal he anticipates in advance of its realization.

The power that enables both the bed maker and the legislator to do this Aristotle calls "reason" (*logos*). Reason is the power of abstraction. It enables those who possess it to survey the movement of processes unfolding in time from a point of view outside these processes themselves. Without reason, neither a bed maker nor a legislator could abstract himself from the current of time that carries them and everything else in the world along. They could not consciously attend to a future that has not yet arrived. They would be trapped in the moment. All human making is a time-conscious activity.

Because the laws of a city are the result of a productive process that depends on the use of reason, the order they establish is a rational one, unlike that of a hive, whose order is strictly natural. Though the latter can be grasped by an inquiring mind, mind plays no role in its construction. The constitution of a human city, by contrast, is inherently rational, and the human beings who live in it may therefore be said to live not merely in a way that reason can comprehend, but in accordance with the self-imposed demands of reason itself.

As a work of reason, a city transcends the natural world of the hive. It "goes beyond" the boundaries of that world and creates a place for things that are impossible so long as human life remains within them. It creates a place for culture—for architecture and philosophy and all the other enduring works of man. Even man's metabolic interactions with the world are transformed in the process. A market is a deliberate and self-conscious way of organizing these interactions and stands in the same relation to the natural way of doing so as the deliberately wrought constitution of a city does to the laws of a hive. Every aspect of human life is "rationalized" in the mindfully organized space of the city, whose transcendence of the world of the hive affords human beings a freedom that among terrestrial animals they alone enjoy. As political animals, men do not cease to be animals. But everything about them, their animality included, is reshaped by the work of mind in the free realm a city establishes.

This helps to explain a further difference between city and hive that is essential to understanding why fame is a uniquely political phenomenon.

Hives and cities both outlast the lives of their members. But no hive has an individual identity of its own. The laws of bee life do not differ in any meaningful way from one hive to the next. Human cities, by contrast, possess distinctive identities. Athens has one identity and Sparta another. That is because their constitutions are the product of deliberation. The constitution of one city may resemble that of another, and nearly all address certain common concerns. But each has special features because each is the result of the judgments and decisions made by a particular group of human legislators in response to the problems that every city confronts.

In this respect, the life of a city resembles that of individual human beings. Men lead distinctive lives on account of the judgments and choices they make. A man is not merely an exemplar of his kind but an individual with a character and career. Hence his life—unlike that of a bee—is an appropriate subject of biography. The same is true of cities. They also have individual identities that can be described in biographical terms. (We call the biography of a city its history.) In both cases, the distinctiveness of a (city's or man's) character is the product of decisions that steer its life in one direction or another, and thus depends upon the liberating power of reason that is at work in all processes of production, including those of personal and civic self-production.

Memory plays a crucial role in this work. Only a being that remembers what it has been can project what it will be, and thereby distinguish itself from others of its kind through a deliberately planned career that connects its future and past. This is true of men and in an analogous way of cities too. A city carries its past forward in memory. It recalls its past and draws on it as it plans for the future. Its identity is the bridge between the two. Every city has distinctive traditions, ceremonies, memorials and laws that conserve its individual identity from one generation to the next, in contrast to a hive of bees, which has no memorials, and conserves nothing, and whose generations all begin their mindless life at the very same point, in a hive indistinguishable from every other.

The conserving traditions of political life are thus a condition of civic identity, which in turn is a condition of fame. A great warrior, statesman or philanthropist is remembered as a great Athenian or Spartan. He lives on, in the memory of those who follow him, as one who contributed in a special way to the work of making and sustaining the distinctive identity of his city. No hive has a memory. None has an individual identity. It is therefore impossible for a bee to achieve the kind of fame a man of political virtue desires. No bee can live beyond its mortal limits except by participating anonymously in the reproduction of its kind. The very possibility of fame, which is always individual, depends upon the individuating traditions of memory that make one city different from all others, and whose existence is the backward-looking counterpart of the same intelligence that displays itself in the forward-looking work of legislation.

A man of political virtue aspires to an honorable life after death in the memory of his fellow citizens. He longs for a kind of individual immortality within the sphere of political action. This is a goal that only human beings can pursue, since among the social animals, only they live rationally and therefore politically. The man who devotes himself to bodily pleasures can never reach this goal, no matter how much intelligence he applies to their satisfaction. The only kind of immortality he can hope to achieve is that of a bee or cow. By contrast, the man of political virtue strives to take advantage of the uniqueness of his nature as the earth's only political animal in order to partake of the eternal and divine while remaining an individual too—something no other animal can do. His is therefore a better life than that of bodily pleasure. It brings him closer to the goal that all things seek and the heavenly bodies achieve to a greater degree than anything else in the cosmos. It is therefore a serious candidate for the prize of the best life of all, though in the end Aristotle awards this prize to the life of thought instead, which is even closer to that of the stars, and assured of success in a way the life of political virtue is not.

THE FRAGILITY OF MEMORY

The man whose "main concern" is "to engender a certain character" in his fellow citizens by enacting laws that "make them good and well-disposed to perform noble actions"[9] longs to be remembered for his exceptional virtue. Of course, if he has to choose between virtue and fame—if he can secure the lasting recognition of his fellow citizens only by ignoble deeds—he will prefer a life of unnoticed virtue instead. But he wants both and if to keep the first must abandon the second, he is bound to feel frustrated and incomplete.

That this sometimes happens is a consequence of the fact that even the most virtuous man is hostage to the judgments of others so far as his fame is concerned. The opinions they form about him decide his reputation and though he can do a great deal to influence their views, he cannot eliminate the possibility that they will judge him wrongly or simply ignore him, so that he acquires an undeserved reputation or none, and therefore fails to achieve the special kind of immortality toward which his life is directed.

A tension therefore exists in the life of political virtue between self-control and immortality. A virtuous man may have great, even perfect, control over his own character. But the immortality he seeks is not within his power to achieve. It depends on the fickle and often mistaken judgments of others. The man who devotes himself to political virtue, and hopes to attain a kind of individual immortality through the fame of his noble actions, cannot escape the vulnerability to disappointment which his dependence on the judgments of others entails.

Nor is this the only way in which the achievement of his goal depends on others. Even if a man leads a life of the greatest possible virtue and is honored for doing so, the recollection of his life depends on the maintenance of those collective structures of memory without which it will be forgotten, and sink into the anonymity that is the fate of every other, nonpolitical animal. An outstanding statesman, a general who has saved his city from defeat, a public benefactor whose magnificent gifts have made his city durable and lovely: all these live on, as noble individuals, only as long as the fame of their deeds is preserved. When this fails, they die a second death that deprives them once and for all of the immortality they pursued in their lives.

Like everything else that man makes, a city needs to be kept in good repair. If it is not, it will begin to disintegrate, like a building left unattended for too long. Everything that is made by human beings, and therefore has a beginning in time, is subject to this requirement.

It is true that a city has no necessary end. A city is an artifact, like a statue or pot, and death is not built into its nature as it is into that of every plant and animal. But once established, a city must be constantly renovated to endure. The work of keeping it in working order can never end. There is no contradiction in supposing that this reparative work will go on forever. But everything we know about the frailties of human beings tells us that at some point, even the most glorious and beautiful city is bound to weaken and die, like the mortal individuals that compose it. Eventually, even the most long-lived cities disappear, and when they do, the conserving traditions of memory that sustained the fame of their greatest citizens disappear with them.

The man of political virtue wants to live on after death in these traditions. He relies on his successors to sustain them. But if he is at all self-reflective, he knows that he is doomed to fail to reach his goal, which can never be attained so long as it depends on the continued existence of a work that men have made. The life of political virtue has futility inscribed in its heart.

The actions of a man who chooses this life and perseveres in it, despite acknowledging its futility, have a special dignity and honor. They possess a distinctively human form of grandeur, which writers in all ages have recognized and admired. But the life of such a man does not become on that account the best a man can live.

The best life cannot be so self-defeating. Its pursuit of immortality must be more self-contained. Those living it must be able to reach the eternal and divine in their own lives and not merely those of their copies, which is the only way that irrational plants and animals can. And they must be less dependent on the fallible judgments and memories of others than the man who yearns for the individualized life after death of fame.

The best life is that of the philosopher. He is the happiest man alive because his experience of the eternal and divine is the least dependent and most complete of any a human being can have—yet still not wholly independent, or perfectly complete, since even a philosopher is able to partake of the eternal and divine only within the limits of his human nature, which it would be foolish to regard as shameful or embarrassing just because it bars him from an omnipotence that would be his if he had a different nature altogether.

CONTEMPLATION

Uniquely among all the animals on earth, human beings are able to comprehend the order of the world. The world has an intelligible structure and because we have minds we are able to grasp it—to articulate the world's order in speech. The life of every animal *has* an intelligible structure but only we have the power to *see and describe* the order that informs the movements of everything in the world, ourselves included.

Thought is the active exercise of this power. When we are thinking, we are actively at work articulating the order of the world. In doing this we go beyond merely living in an orderly way and make the order of the world a subject of reflection and study. Of course, we never leave life completely behind. Even as we study its laws, we remain subject to them. Our power to theorize does not exempt us from the requirements of life or abolish the limits to which, as living beings, we are subject. But it does enable us to step outside these requirements in our minds and words.

The world we study when we think is a vast complex of motions. Everything in it is moving in some fashion. The elements go up and down. The sun and stars go around in circles. Plants and animals move through their endlessly repeated cycles of life. These movements are intelligible to us only because they have an order. But the order that makes them intelligible is not itself something that moves. The order that gives structure and intelligibility to the countless changes we see in the world is itself changeless.

When we think, our minds are trained on this changeless order, and hence on the eternal. Indeed, they are part of this order. To that extent, when we think we are directly participating in the eternity of the world itself. Unlike the man of political virtue, whose connection to immortality depends on others and is compromised by the frailties of memory and the transience of human institutions, a man engaged in thought has an experience of eternity that is more independent and complete—the most complete available to us as rational animals.

An example may help.

Consider a marine biologist who spends his days exploring tide pools in an effort to understand the life of the small creatures that live in them. Aristotle himself spent several years on the island of Lesbos doing just this.[10] The biologist's investigations seem far removed from the lofty heights of a life of thought. But in truth they exemplify it, for his pursuit is not motivated by practical concerns. The biologist is moved by what Aristotle calls "wonder," and wants merely to understand what he is seeing.[11] His goal is simply to be able to give an account of what he sees—to explain it. According to Aristotle, this is the hallmark of all genuinely "thoughtful" pursuits and any man engaged in such an activity is living a life of thought.

Today we would call the biologist a "scientist" (from the Latin *scire,* "to know"). Aristotle called him a "theorist" (from the Greek *theoreo,* whose most primitive meaning is "to look" or "to gaze" at a spectacle of some sort with an "eye" to understanding it, in the way " theatergoers" do). "Contemplation" is a word that now carries too many other connotations to be entirely appropriate in this context. But it does at least suggest the kind of intensely active looking that, on Aristotle's view, all theorizing involves. If we understand the term in this way, we might say that the marine biologist, on his knees in a tide pool, staring with wonder and puzzlement at the snails and crabs he sees and straining to comprehend their movements, is engaged in contemplation in Aristotle's sense.

Still, it is likely to seem odd, to a modern reader at least, to say that the mind of the scientist *participates* in the order that he contemplates. The order of the lives of the animals he studies is one thing. It gives structure to their movements, crawling from one rock to the next in search of food, shelter and mates. The mind of the scientist studying this order is something else. It is not part of the order of the lives of snails and crabs at all. It exists apart from this order and investigates it as an "outsider." At most, we might say that the order of the world is "represented" in the mind of the scientist who studies it, as in a kind of mirror. This representation is, literally, a reproduction or reenactment in the scientist's mind (in his thinking and speaking) of an object that is something other than the mind that represents it. On this view, thinking always involves a relation between two things, between mind and world, whose separateness most modern readers take for granted. Those who do may find it odd to describe the first as "participating" in the second, as if these two were or could be the same.

Yet this is precisely Aristotle's view, and it provides the key to understanding why he believed that a life of thought offers human beings the most direct and fulfilling opportunity they have to share in the eternal and divine.

The scientist who looks at things does so in order to understand them. To understand something is to be able to give an explanation of it, to have an answer to the question of why it is as it is. This question does not always have a single answer. In most cases, there are different sorts of answers that can be given to it, each of which throws light on the subject in some way. Why, for example, does this snail move as it does? One answer is that its body permits it to move in certain ways but not others: the stuff of which it is made both creates and limits its possibilities of movement. A different kind of answer is that the snail moves as it does because it is searching for food or a place to deposit its eggs—that its movements are directed by metabolic needs peculiar to members of its kind.

In the second book of the *Physics,* Aristotle identifies four different kinds of answers that can be given to the question of why something is as it is.[12] These answers are all distinct in the sense that none can be reduced without loss to any of the others. Each has something special to contribute to our understanding. But though they are irreducible, they are not unconnected. In one way or another, all four answers make use of the idea of the *form* of the thing one is attempting to explain.

Even "materialist" explanations make use of this idea, since the capacity of different bits of stuff to move or be moved in certain ways cannot be explained except by reference to their form. Every answer to the question of why something is as it is, is in this sense "formalistic." A snail moves as it does because it has been set in motion by parents that have the same form it does. It moves as it does because it has the body of a snail whose organs and tissues are organized in accordance with a unique pattern or form. It moves as it does because its behavior, at any given moment, is conditioned by its form (or better, because its behavior *is* its form in action). It moves as it does because the same form that governs its behavior at a given moment also shapes and guides the snail's entire life cycle—its movement from immaturity to reproductive adulthood to death. All these answers have something distinctive to contribute to our explanation of the snail's movements. But all rest ultimately on an understanding of the snail's form, and it is this that a marine biologist grasps with his mind when, for example, he writes a monograph about the snail or explains its movements to his students.

The form he grasps is present in the snail. Its presence is what makes the snail's movements comprehensible. But the same form is also present in the biologist's mind. The snail, we might say, is "living" its form while the biologist is "thinking" it. There is an obvious and important difference in the way the form is present in each. But it is the same form in both cases, and the difference between these two ways of being present can better be understood as the difference between potentiality and realization, analogous to that between an immature snail and a grown one, than as the difference between a representation and its object.

A grown snail possesses a developed form that is already present in an immature snail as a power or potentiality. The latter is not completely formless. It has the potential to grow into a fully formed adult. This potential *is* the presence in the young snail of a specific form, though only as what might be called "a capacity with a direction." The form is the same in both cases, however. The difference between a grown snail and a juvenile one is not explained by the presence in them of two distinct forms. It is explained by the presence of the same form in both, though in two different ways—in the juvenile potentially, and in the adult actually.

The relation between the living presence of the snail's form in the snail itself and its thoughtful presence in the mind of the biologist who studies it can be understood in a similar way. The snail's form makes its movements intelligible, but only potentially so. Its movements first become actually intelligible in the mind of the biologist. The biologist's comprehension of the snail's form is the realization of its potential intelligibility. The form in his mind is the same as the form in the snail—only now its potential for being understood has been fulfilled, in the same way that a newly hatched snail's potential is fulfilled in the adult it can (and barring any accidents will) become.

To say that the biologist's conception of the snail's form is a "representation" of it is misleading for two reasons. First, it suggests that his understanding of the form and the form as it exists in the living snail belong to two different orders of reality, one outside the mind and the other in it, rather than constituting two different levels or grades within a single order of being (the potential and the actual). And second, it suggests that as between these two different orders of reality, the external and the mental, the second is inferior to the first because it is "only" an image or picture of it, and hence dependent

on the thing it represents, in the way that every image depends on its original, rather than being (as Aristotle thought) more fully real in the sense that
every actualized potentiality is always more real than the potentiality itself.[13]

The biologist's conception of the snail's form is not a representation of it.
It is that form itself: the potential intelligibility of the snail's movements made
actual in thought, the same form at a higher level of reality—a realization,
not a representation. And of course what is true of the snail is true of everything else in the world, from the elements to the stars. Everything moves
in an orderly way. Every movement is therefore potentially intelligible and
becomes actually so when its organizing form is grasped in thought. Thought
is the realization of the world's intelligibility. The intelligibility of the world
is present in it as an eternal possibility. It is always there, and never changes,
because the form of change, which alone makes the changing world intelligible, is itself unchanging. Thought is the fulfillment of this eternal potentiality. It raises to the level of actual existence the one thing in the world that
lasts forever: the eternal order that makes the movements of everything
within it potentially comprehensible. Thought is therefore not the representation of this eternal order. It *is* this eternal order itself, at its most real. So
long as he is engaged in thought, therefore, a man is a participant in this
order. He is not a spectator, looking at it from without, representing it on the
interior screen of his mind. His mind *is* the eternal intelligibility of the world
made actual by being understood. And to that extent, he partakes directly of
immortality in a way no other human activity allows. The marine biologist,
on his knees in a tide pool, *is* the eternity of the world realized in thought—
the minding of what is mindful in it.

The thinker engaged in what Aristotle calls "first philosophy," and we
by tradition call metaphysics, partakes of the eternal and divine in a still
higher way.

A biologist looks at a snail moving on the rocks and asks what it is. A philosopher asks what things are in general. What is it for something to be—
not this or that particular thing, but anything at all? In what does the being
of things consist? He answers that being may be spoken of in different ways.
It has multiple meanings. But among them one is preeminent. The being of
a thing consists, first and foremost, in the realization of its potential—in
the full being-at-work of its powers.[14] The movement toward this state is an
enlargement or enhancement of the thing's being, whatever kind of thing it
happens to be (whatever form it possesses, whether that of a snail or anything else).

What is true of the snail is true of the world as a whole. For the world has a potential too: the potential to be understood. This potential is realized in thought. Only in thinking is the world's potential intelligibility fully at work. Only in thinking is being as active as it can be. In the most fundamental sense, therefore, the being of the world consists in thought. The philosopher understands this. He understands the process of realization in which the biologist is engaged, just as the biologist understands the process in which the snail is engaged.

The snail does not understand its own movements. Only the biologist does. In a similar way, the biologist pays no attention to the movement that his own work represents toward the realization of the world's intelligibility. Of course, he may at any moment choose to attend in a philosophical way to the nature and meaning of the work in which he is engaged. Snails cannot become scientists, but scientists can and do become philosophers. And when one does, the mind's power to comprehend the way in which mind realizes the world's potential intelligibility, is itself fully at work—mind minding itself, the actualization of the mind's potential for understanding its own actualization of the world's potential to be understood. In philosophy, thinking therefore reaches a peak. Science is thinking and philosophy is thinking on thought, so that if the world is realized in thinking, thinking itself is realized in philosophy.

The snail participates indirectly in eternity by making another like itself. It participates in eternity at the level of its kind. The biologist participates directly in eternity by comprehending in thought the unmoving order that makes the snail's movements understandable. The philosopher also participates directly in eternity but at a still higher level—the highest that any being can attain—by comprehending in thought the potentially comprehensible movement of thought itself, a movement in which the biologist is engaged but that is not, for him, a subject of thoughtful attention. Philosophy therefore *is* eternity, and the more a man has of it in his life, the more fully he partakes of the eternal and divine. No other life offers such a direct and complete connection to immortality. That is why it is the happiest life of all.

GOD

While we philosophize we live a life that is "divine."[15] But even the most devoted philosopher cannot philosophize continuously. Even he needs to eat and sleep and must eventually die. Even our most complete participation in eternity, and hence our greatest happiness, is transient and fleeting.

Higher up in the cosmic order, there are other beings that are not subject to the same limitations. The deathless stars partake forever of the eternal and divine. Presumably, their participation in eternity is the same as ours when we philosophize. The stars are minds at work minding mind, except that their work never ceases. But even they are subject to a limit of sorts, though not one as restrictive as that imposed by our animal nature, for the stars are in motion too, so that their work is always being done from a different point of view. The circular movement of the stars is the least limiting kind of change we can imagine, but it confirms that even they, the best of all moving things, cannot be at rest in their work in every conceivable way.

Only a being that is perfectly motionless—or, what amounts to the same thing, that is perfectly real, since every motion, even circular, is a change from a potential state to an achieved one—can be at work philosophizing in an absolutely unqualified sense. In the tenth book of the *Metaphysics,* and briefly elsewhere in his writings, Aristotle describes the nature of such a being, whose existence he considered a necessity. He calls it "god," "intellect," "a substance which is eternal and immovable and separate from sensible things."[16]

Centuries of Christian readers have understood these phrases to be an intimation of their own God—a transcendent creator separated from the world by an absolute discontinuity in the order of being. The Christian faith, like the Jewish and Muslim ones, rests on the belief that God created the world from nothing. This is an idea that appears nowhere in Aristotle's writings. Indeed, he denies its intelligibility. It is also inconsistent with his repeated assertion that the world has neither a beginning nor an end in time. Still, many Christian readers have claimed that the God of Aristotle's *Metaphysics,* though not a creator, is at least *separate* from the world, and have seen in his idea of god the first step toward their own. They insist that Aristotle's god exists *beyond* the world of moving things and argue that the human aspiration to partake of the eternal and divine is a desire to mimic, so far as our nature allows, the condition of an *other*-worldly God who alone enjoys the eternal and fully realized existence that worldly beings, from the elements to the stars, experience in a more qualified way.

The highest state of actuality that any being can achieve is the exercise of the mind's power to comprehend its own capacity to grasp the mindfulness of the world—thought thinking thought. The life of Aristotle's god consists in the uninterrupted and endless exercise of this power. It is a life of philosophy, forever. On a Christian reading of Aristotle's theology, this life must be conceived as that of an otherworldly being who never eats or sleeps or dies, never moves from place to place, and the philosopher's longing for eternity as a desire to transcend the world, for the sake of a share in the life of this better being. Implicit in this interpretation is a devaluation of the world by comparison with something separate from and superior to it. That is why it is an interpretation that appeals to Christian readers, who see in this devaluation of the world a kind of proto-Christianity that needs only to be supplemented by the idea of divine creation to be made complete. But it is an interpretation that falsifies the authentic pagan spirit of Aristotle's philosophy, which knows only one world and thus rules out the possibility of its devaluation by comparison with anything else.

Aristotle's god is the best thing there is—but the best thing *in* the world. There is no gap separating it from the next best thing, like the chasm that separates the Christian God from the greatest of his creatures. The god of Aristotle's *Metaphysics* stands at the peak of the order of being. It is the culmination or fulfillment of that order. It is "separate" not in the sense of existing apart from the world but of possessing in a pure and unadulterated form the reality that other things possess only in a qualified fashion on account of their being in motion. Everything that has matter is moving in some way, and is therefore a blend of potentiality and achievement, though in proportions that vary from one kind of thing to another. Aristotle's motionless god is thus of necessity a being without matter. But this does not put it *beyond* the world. It makes it the upper limit *of* the world, which is bounded at the lower limit by prime matter—the perfectly shapeless stuff of which the elements are composed, a kind of pure potentiality that exists as a counterlimit to god's pure actuality.

The world is defined by these limits. They represent its asymptotes. But though they are bounding conditions, they are not boundaries beyond which one can go. The world is all that is the case. Within the world, a vast ensemble of beings pursue the eternal and divine in accordance with their diverse natures. Every one of these has matter—hence individuality, potency and motion—and because it does, falls short of the goal it strives to attain, to a greater or lesser degree. In the perfect and endless activity of mind minding mind, which has neither individuality nor motion and potency because it lacks the matter that is the source of all three, the goal of the striving of all material things is attained, but not by stepping beyond the world. It is reached by arriving at the completing limit of the world itself—the point at which the deepest desire of everything in it is finally fulfilled.

We might therefore say that Aristotle's world is self-fulfilling. It is sufficient for its own completion. Nothing outside it is required to reach the goal of immortality that everything within it strains to achieve. For Aristotle, eternity is not the special privilege, or unique possession, of some being beyond what Christians call the "temporal" realm. Aristotle's god is the fulfillment *of* the world, the actualization of its potential for immortality. It thus stands in the same internal relation to the world that a grown man does to a child, except, of course, that the pure activity of mind minding mind in which the world's potential for immortality is fully achieved has no individual existence, like that of the man in whom the child's potential is fulfilled. It is the eternity of the world as a whole, present in one way or another in every finite being, and fully active in any mind that grasps it, for however long it does.

The man who devotes himself to thinking experiences this nonindividuated state of pure activity, if only for brief periods of time. He experiences it directly and so is able, in his own life, to participate in the eternity that all moving things long to reach. To do this, he need not go beyond himself through reproduction, as other animals must. He need not expose himself to the frailties of judgment and memory that condition every effort to achieve immortality by means of political fame. He need not leave the world behind and through some mystical process of translation ascend to a higher level of reality. The eternity he experiences in thought is available to him, without risk or vulnerability, within the horizon of his own individual existence. It is not a gamble he must venture. It is not a heaven beyond the world that he must die to reach. It is the fulfillment of the one and only world there is— not something separate from the world, but the realized form of the world itself. The man who thinks partakes of it directly and free of the tragic limits that constrain his honorable companion, the man of political virtue.

For the philosopher, eternity is therefore not some otherworldly state he contemplates across a gulf he cannot cross. So long as he continues to think, he *is* eternal. Between him and eternity there is no gap, just as there is none between eternity and the world itself. A man who thinks *is* god, if only briefly—the greatest heresy imaginable to a Christian who accepts Augustine's explanation of the sinfulness of pride. That god is the internal fulfillment of the world and the life of thought a divine one that men are able to share on account of their reason: these are the twin premises of Aristotle's pagan theology, so remote on both counts from its Christian counterpart, which demands that we accept the insufficiency of the world to fulfill itself and acknowledge the abyss that separates the temporal order of creatures from its eternal, otherworldly creator, who brings the world into being by an act not of reason but will.

Aristotle believed that human beings can experience eternity in this life. He also believed that no man or woman lives forever. Christianity promises a personal immortality that Aristotle thought absurd, but only on the condition that God be separated from the world. It is a tempting bargain but a bad one, that has left us homeless in the wake of the death of the Christian God and less able to experience or express that gratitude for human things that Aristotle calls friendship—a thankfulness for the unearned love of parents and teachers and predecessors of all kinds that is fully compatible with his pagan conception of god, but shameful and confining when judged from the point of view of the omnipotence of the God of the religion of unrequited gratitude, whose divine powers we long to seize out of anger and envy.

CHAPTER 8

Friendship

GRATITUDE AND HUMAN FULFILLMENT

A great-souled man devotes his life to that of his city. He strives to distinguish himself by his outstanding deeds, displaying courage in war, wisdom in deliberation and magnificence in giving. He is proud of his superiority to others, who recognize and admire his greatness. After death, his fame lives on in the memory of his city, through which he achieves an individual immortality that men of more modest virtue, and those absorbed in private affairs, can never attain.

By contrast, a man devoted to philosophy withdraws from public life to the extent he can. He does his duty when called upon to serve, but what matters most to him is not honor and fame. He lives for those silent and invisible moments in which, undistracted by the business of politics and the everyday concerns of his fellow citizens, he is able to think, if only briefly. For a time at least, he becomes immortal, "so far as that is possible for human beings."[1] He stands at the summit of being, and for the supreme pleasure that accompanies this experience, "like the bloom of youth on those who are in their prime,"[2] some special name seems appropriate. Aristotle calls it *makarios,* which might be translated as "blessed" or "joyful."[3]

These two lives represent the most that one can hope to achieve in the realms of action and thought, respectively, and though they may, and perhaps generally do, overlap to some degree, they have different and even conflicting aims. One seeks happiness in the precincts of practical life and the other in the cosmic regions beyond it. In the Latin-speaking tradition that derives from Aristotle's account of these two lives, this distinction has come to be known as that between the *vita activa* and the *vita contemplativa*. Yet distinct as these lives are, the happiness of each shares something important in common with that of the other, for it consists in a measure of self-sufficiency that less active, and hence less real, men fail to achieve. Self-sufficiency is for Aristotle the common standard by which the highest forms of human activity, and the happiness they afford, are to be measured both in the realm of civic life and in the apolitical work of philosophy.

This is clear in the case of a great-souled man. In all his actions, a man of this sort shows that he cares for his independence before everything else. He is neither so attached to life that he will fail to sacrifice it for a worthy cause, nor so addicted to the applause and flattery of others that he is tempted to risk his life for something trivial. He is calm and self-possessed, and immune so far as any man can be to the demands of appetite and the vicissitudes of fortune. He is a giver, not a taker, and the scorn he feels for frightened and excitable and needy men is the contempt of one who knows that he possesses all he needs to live a magnificent and admirable life. He is justifiably "full of himself."

The life of thought is characterized by its self-sufficiency too.

What is usually called self-sufficiency will be found in the highest degree in the activity which is concerned with theoretical knowledge. Like a just man and any other virtuous man, a wise man requires the necessities of life; once these have been adequately provided, a just man still needs people toward whom and in company with whom to act justly, and the same is true of a self-controlled man, a courageous man, and all the rest. But a wise man is able to study even by himself and the wiser he is the more is he able to do it. Perhaps he could do it better if he had colleagues to work with, but he still is the most self-sufficient of all.[4]

The highest state that a man can reach in either politics or philosophy is thus one of self-containment. Those who reach it possess what others must look outside themselves to find. A man who relies on others for support; or is under their command; or fears death; or is addicted to bodily pleasure; or has no leisure because he must work for a living; or cannot free his mind from practical concerns, will never be able to experience either the pride of a great-souled man or the joy of a philosopher, and if, in the end, Aristotle judges the life of philosophy the happiest of all, it is only because it possesses, to an even greater degree, the self-sufficiency in which the happiness of both lives consists.

This explains why gratitude plays no role in Aristotle's account either of practical or theoretical virtue.

A great-souled man finds it uncomfortable to be even temporarily beholden to others. He looks down with a mixture of horror and contempt on those who are in such a position—on women, children, slaves, and the poor. All of these must rely on others for guidance and support, and have reason to be grateful when they receive it. Their gratitude reflects a lack of self-sufficiency, whose possession is the very thing on which the pride of a great-souled man is founded.

Gratitude is equally foreign to the experience of those engaged in thought. A man who thinks *is* God. His joy is not a gift *from* God. It is true that he cannot live a life of joy without interruption. But when he is thinking, he is in that state of active being that constitutes the fulfillment of the world. There is no distance between him and the world his thought completes. There is no God apart from the world to whom he owes his thanks for the joy of thinking. The very possibility of such thankfulness presupposes a separation between thinker and God, and between God and the world, that Aristotle's account of the blessedness of philosophy rules out.

That the world has the order it does and that it can be understood by those who possess the power of reason is a cause for wonder—for the amazement and curiosity with which all thinking starts. But it is not a cause for gratitude, which would be appropriate only in case the world were the gift of a God beyond it. Neither in the wonder from which thinking springs nor in the joy to which it leads, is there any room for what might be called a cosmic gratitude for the existence of the world as a whole. Gratitude of this kind makes sense only on the creationist premise of Christian belief. The joy of thinking, as Aristotle conceives it, is self-sufficient in a way that those who accept this premise, and humbly acknowledge their dependence on the otherworldly God to whom they believe they owe their thanks, can only regard with moral disgust.

Does Aristotle's account of these two lives leave no room, then, for thankfulness of any kind? Is there no one to whom and nothing for which a great-souled man has reason to be grateful? And is there no place for gratitude in a life of thought? The answer is that both sorts of lives, though defined by their self-sufficiency, not only leave room for love and gratitude, and the dependence these imply, but are founded on them. The dependence in question is the kind that is involved in relations of "friendship" (*philia*).

ANOTHER SELF

Aristotle devotes more pages of the *Ethics* to the subject of friendship than to any other. He analyzes the different forms of friendship with great care and assigns a high value to those of the best or "noblest" kind. Indeed, he says that without such friendships a man cannot be truly happy. But a friend is an "other." To need friends is therefore to be dependent on others. It is to be less than perfectly self-sufficient. And since the friendship of another person cannot be commanded or compelled without its ceasing to be what it is (in contrast to the justice of a trading partner), all friendship is a gift for which the appropriate response is one of thanks. In his account of friendship, Aristotle thus appears to recognize, even to celebrate, an attitude that greatness of soul and contemplative wisdom both devalue. How can this be?

Aristotle's concept of friendship is exceedingly broad. A father and his son, a trader and his partner, a donor and his beneficiary, the members of a club, fellow citizens and romantic lovers are all friends in Aristotle's encompassing sense.

These friendships differ in many ways. Some are relations between unequals, like that of parent and child; others, like the sort that exists among the members of a club, are relations of equality. Some are motivated by a desire for the pleasure or utility they bring. Others are based on the friends' admiration for each other's character. Some, like the romantic kind, tend to be exclusive, while others are open to a wider group. Some are typically short-lived, like the friendship of businessmen engaged in an exchange, whereas others are more lasting. Some are voluntary and others, like the friendship that siblings feel for one another, are strongly conditioned by fate.

But among all these different forms of friendship, there is one that Aristotle singles out for special attention. He calls it friendship of the "truest" sort,[5] friendship "in the primary and proper sense of the word."[6] Friendships of this kind are the benchmark by which every other must be judged.

True friendships have several related features. First, they are based on each friend's regard for the other's character and not on "incidental considerations,"[7] like physical appearance, age, or the ability to tell a witty story—things that can change without a person's character being altered. Second, they take time to develop because character is less obvious than more superficial attributes,[8] but also tend to last longer since character is more durable. Third, and most important, they are only possible among good men, since only a good man can be loved for who he is, whereas even a bad man may be valued for what he has (wealth, wit, good looks and the like). Friendships of the truest kind are therefore possible only among men who are equal with respect to the goodness of their characters—a form of equality that is compatible with differences of many other kinds.

"Because they are good men," friends of this sort "wish alike for one another's good."[9] They "wish for their friends' good for their friends' sake,"[10] and not, as those whose friendships are based on pleasure or utility do, for their own benefit instead. A friendship of the perfect kind is founded on a reciprocal and other-regarding affection, which only men equal in goodness can feel for one another. Those who are friends in this sense, but "are asleep or separated geographically,"[11] enjoy a friendship of the truest sort, but only potentially. To be "actively engaged in their friendship,"[12] they must be together and awake, "living in each other's company,"[13] which is what they yearn to do. Nothing, says Aristotle, is more characteristic of the best kind of friendship than this.

But in what does the good of such friendships consist? What contribution do they make to human happiness? And do even "supremely happy and self-sufficient people" need friends of this sort?[14]

The good of other, lesser kinds of friendship is easy to see. No man, not even one of perfect virtue or the greatest philosophical wisdom, has all the useful skills that a human being can possess. Even men of these sorts will therefore derive benefit and pleasure from their association with others who have the special gifts they lack—for preparing food, cutting hair, telling jokes, and the like. Even a perfectly good man has reason to befriend those who can do these things well. But his friendships with them will be instrumental and therefore limited. They will not be friendships based upon character, and hence not friendships in the truest sense. What need does a perfectly good man have for friendships of the latter kind?

The question is made particularly difficult by Aristotle's definition of goodness. A good man is one whose soul is in attunement. His passions are not at war with "the thinking part"[15] of his soul, but aligned with it. He knows what is best and does it with enjoyment. He "wishes for and does what is good for himself" and "does it for his own sake,"[16] for the sake of that part of his soul "that constitutes what he really is or constitutes it in a greater degree than anything else"[17]—even if this means that he must sacrifice some pleasure or other benefit so that the best in him may flourish. A good man is therefore a friend to himself. Indeed, he is "his own best friend."[18] "A good man has all [the feelings that one friend has toward another] in relation to himself."[19] The sign of this is that he "wishes to spend time with himself,"[20] to enjoy his own company in the way that friends of the best kind do—unlike bad men, who "avoid their own company" and seek to be with others so that they can "forget" who they are.[21]

In friendships of the best kind, each friend is a good man who wishes the other good for his own sake. But this is a wish that every good man already has for himself. His "friendly feelings" toward the other are therefore an "extension" of the "friendly feelings" he has toward what is best in his own soul. In this sense, his friend is "another self."[22] But what need does a good man have for *another* self, if he already has one that is good, with which he is on friendly terms? If a good man is his own best friend, and his happiness consists in being with himself, what contribution, if any, does the friendship of others make to his well-being? Aristotle's answer to this question marks the culmination of his long account of friendship, and explains why, on his view, even the most self-sufficient life can and indeed must have a place for gratitude in it.[23]

CARE

The life of a great-souled man and that of a philosopher are distinguished by their self-containment. It might therefore seem that the friendship such men feel toward themselves is all they require—that their souls are self-sufficient enough to free them from the need for other friends with whom to share their lives.

But Aristotle draws the opposite conclusion. "It would be strange," he says, "to make a supremely happy man live his life in isolation." "No one would choose to have all things all by himself." "Man is a social and political being and his natural condition is to live with others." A happy man therefore "needs friends"[24]—even a great-souled man whose independence is the hallmark of his pride, and a philosopher who lives a joyfully "divine" life so long as he is thinking. Even they need the companionship of true friends, which is always a gift when it comes because a friendship of this kind must be founded on love and unlike the one that a good man feels for himself, lies outside the orbit of what he can supply on his own.

One reason why friendship is essential to happiness in the sphere of practical life is that it gives an otherwise virtuous man the opportunity to be actively good. If a man is rich but ungenerous, he will not need friends to whom to make gifts. He will keep his money for himself. But if he is generous, he needs the "opportunity for good works," and "the works which deserve the highest praise are those that are done to one's friends."[25] More generally, "if the performance of good deeds is the mark of a good man and of excellence, and if it is nobler to do good to a friend than to a stranger, then a man of high moral standards will need people to whom he can do good."[26]

This is clearest in the case of virtues like generosity and justice. These consist in a certain way of relating to others and hence presuppose their presence, without which the relation in question cannot exist. But the same is true of other virtues, like courage. A courageous man is one who is prepared to give up his life for something worthy. If a man lives in isolation, there is nothing and no one for whom he can sacrifice his life. He may lose it, but he cannot give it up for the sake of something else. To do this, he needs other people for whose sake he is prepared to put his own life at risk. A man who does this for a stranger is reckless. Only a man who risks his life for a friend displays the virtue of courage. The most outstanding form of courage is that shown in defense of one's city in war. To demonstrate courage of this kind, a man needs fellow citizens bound to him by ties of loyalty. He needs civic friends, without whom he cannot be actively courageous on the field of battle, just as a generous man needs friends to display his generosity.

Even temperance, which seems to involve only a man's relation to himself and thus not to require the presence of other people, cannot be actively exercised except in the company of friends. No one can be temperate in isolation. Temperance consists in the regulation of appetite for the sake of something nobler, and all the noble things for whose sake a man might limit or suppress his appetite exist only in the sphere of civilized life whose existence is the result of a collaborative effort on the part of those committed to a common ideal of living. Those who share this ideal are bound to one another by a form of friendship. We might call them the "friends of civilization." To be actively temperate, a man needs friends of this kind.

If "happiness is some kind of activity,"[27] then a virtuous man can be happy only when he is actively exercising his virtues, and in each case this requires the presence of friends. But this way of putting things, though true enough, suggests that a good man needs friends only as an external condition for the realization of a power he already possesses—in the way that a man with exquisite taste in wine needs the presence of wine to activate his power of discrimination. But Aristotle recognizes that the need for friends is deeper than this, since one must have friends to acquire the power to be good in the first place, even before it is put to work.

To be potentially good, one needs a knowledge of right and wrong, virtue and vice, excellence and ordinary achievement. Knowledge of this kind cannot be gotten merely by inspecting one's own actions. To acquire it, we must observe the actions of others and listen to their judgments, "for we are better able to observe our neighbor than ourselves, and their actions better than our own."[28] Others are the mirror in which we learn to see ourselves. If the mirror is defective, then our self-understanding will be too. If their actions are ignoble and their judgments base then ours will be as well. Hence, even to have the right aspirations and standards of conduct—even to be potentially good—one needs other good people to look at and imitate.

It is not enough, moreover, that they merely be present for me to observe. They must also take an interest in my development. They have to be concerned that I acquire good judgments and habits, for if they are indifferent as to whether I do, or leave the process to chance, it is much less likely that I will ever become a virtuous man. To become a man who is habitually disposed to virtuous actions, whether or not the opportunity to perform them arises, I need other good men who care about my character. The activity of caring about the development of another person's character is what we call "training"[29] or education. Education is a process guided by the teacher's concern for his student's welfare for the student's own sake. To care for another in this way is an act of friendship. To be even potentially good, a man therefore needs teachers to befriend him. He needs their care to acquire the power of acting well, which he must possess before he can exercise it, just as an eye must be able to see before it looks.

Thus, though a great-souled man may be supremely independent of the wants and fears that hobble other men, he cannot achieve such independence, and the pride he feels because of it, on his own. No human being is born with the self-sufficiency that a man of virtue possesses, and none acquires it naturally, merely by growing up, in the way that birds learn to fly and human beings to stand on two feet. These are natural powers that birds and men come to possess without an education, and would enjoy even if they lived in isolation.

Virtue is the knowledge that some things are more important and valuable than others, together with the habit of treating them as such. A man is temperate, for example, if he knows that the reasoning part of his soul is more important than the appetitive part, and habitually subordinates the second to the first. He is courageous if he knows that the life of his city is more important than his own, and is disposed to risk his life for his city's, when circumstances require. He is prudent if he can distinguish between considerations of greater and lesser importance, and tends to weigh them in a calm and deliberate manner. In each case, a virtuous man is distinguished from an ordinary or bad one, and from the man who exhibits what Aristotle calls incontinence (*akrasia*),[30] by his possession of a sound knowledge about the rank order of better and worse, and his habitual inclination to act on this knowledge.

It is this knowledge and these habits that give a man of virtue the independence that distinguishes him from those who are self-indulgent, or cowardly or impetuous in deliberation. All these lack the self-sufficiency he possesses because they lack either his knowledge or habits or both. We are not, however, born with the knowledge of what is more and less valuable. Nor is the habit of acting on this knowledge inborn in us either. Indeed, it runs so sharply against the grain of other, more primitive and spontaneous inclinations that it might in one sense be called *un*natural. The habit of virtuous action is natural only in the sense that we all possess, by nature, the capacity to acquire it, and by acquiring it fulfill our distinctively human capacity for living lives of a higher and better sort than those of other animals.

It is for this reason that Aristotle calls the habit of acting on an understanding of the true order of values a "*second* nature" that completes and perfects our first.[31] This perfection can be achieved only through an education that is directed and supported by others. It is only because of their attention and care that a virtuous man receives the knowledge and acquires the habits he needs to be the man he is. Though his virtue manifests itself in his independence, he is dependent for his independence on those who took his education in hand and cared for him before he could care for himself. The friendship that a good man feels for himself is possible only because others befriended him first.

It is, of course, a piece of good luck to be born in a city whose laws provide for such an education. If a man who has become good on account of the laws of his city had been born in a regime with worse laws, and received a bad education, it is likely that his character would be worse as well. The fact that he was born where he was is just a stroke of good fortune, and however happy he may be to be an Athenian rather than a Persian, a good man has no reason to be grateful for the accident of his birth. There is no one and nothing to thank for it.

But unlike the advantage of being born in a city with good laws, the benefit of being educated as the citizen of one is not an accident in the same sense. It is the product of a deliberate effort on the part of teachers, parents and legislators to make their students, children and fellow citizens better and happier, not as compensation for some benefit received, but for their own good. It is a gift, not a piece of good luck—the gift that one generation of good and happy men makes to the next by giving it an education in virtue. It is an act of friendship of the truest kind, by means of which the opportunity to live an independent life is transmitted through time and saved from the forgetfulness and decay that threatens all human achievements. Without it, such a life would be unimaginable. Friendship is thus the condition under which mortal beings such as we are able to sustain, across long stretches of time, the independence in which virtue consists and to preserve the chance of attaining the fame a great-souled man hopes to achieve with his magnificent and memorable deeds.

Virtuous men thus have reason to be grateful to the friends who have given them their independence—to the teachers and parents and lawmakers whose concern for their well-being, in educational programs large and small, constitutes the indispensable gift on which their own independence depends. This is true even—indeed, especially—of a great-souled man. He also has reason to be thankful to his friends, and will want to express his gratitude in the best way that he can, by befriending others and conferring on them the gift of independence that he himself received from his predecessors in the civic enterprise to which he belongs, returning their care with a care as good and great. To this extent, even his supreme self-sufficiency, which is the greatest a man can achieve in the realm of political life, not only allows for but demands an ungrudging acceptance of the condition of dependence that gratitude for goodness received always assumes.

THE TRADITION OF THINKING

Something similar may be said about the life of a philosopher. When he is actively thinking, his life is no longer human. He has transcended (if only for a while) the sphere of human concerns, and partakes directly of the everlasting order of the world, at its highest level of reality. Yet even the most farseeing philosopher has not learned to think on his own. The unsurpassable self-sufficiency that he achieves in the realm of thought is the product of an education too.

A philosopher knows, what most men do not, that the most real thing in the world is mind minding mind. He is by habit inclined to devote every leisured moment to the investigation of this knowledge. But he has acquired both the knowledge and his love of it from others already engaged in and committed to a life of contemplation.

These include, most immediately, his teachers in the ordinary sense: those living human beings who first awakened in him a love of philosophy, and helped him to pursue it. But it includes many others as well, the dead along with the living, and men who live in cities other than his own, for philosophy is a cosmopolitan enterprise that knows no civic boundaries and whose history is not limited to that of any particular political community. From the long line of philosophers, stretching back as far as history records, the man who devotes his life to thought has valuable lessons to learn. These are his teachers too, and he therefore has reason to regard them as friends who have made him a gift of their ideas as well. If the generations of a city are joined by bonds of friendship born of their shared devotion to the city's good and to the education of each new generation in its distinctive laws and traditions, the generations of philosophers are joined by their devotion to the tradition of thinking. This is a species of friendship too, and gratitude the sentiment appropriate to one's dependence on it.

No philosopher has reason to be grateful for having been born a human being, with the ability to think, rather than a thoughtless sponge, any more than an Athenian has reason to be grateful for having been born there rather than somewhere else. Each is an accident of birth for which no thanks is due. Nor does a philosopher have reason to be grateful to a God beyond the world for the gift of the world and its intelligible order. There is no such God. There is only the world, eternal and divine, in whose ever-lasting reality the philosopher is fully competent to participate, for brief periods of time.

But just as a man of political virtue has reason to be grateful to the other human beings who have established and sustained the civic culture in which he has been educated, and grown to maturity and independence, a philosopher has reason to be grateful to his predecessors in the tradition of philosophy, who have kept open a place in the human world for the most useless and exalted of all activities, a space that every generation of thinkers clears and inhabits anew. He has reason to be thankful to his teachers in philosophy, and to honor their care for the activity he loves in the best way that a philosopher can, by scrutinizing their ideas in the light of the commitment to the eternal and divine that he and they share in common.

This is true not only of those who have gone before him in the tradition of philosophy, but of his contemporary coworkers in thinking as well. A philosopher may do his most important work alone—though the Socratic conception of philosophy, to which Aristotle was perhaps not entirely immune, suggests otherwise. But even if his greatest hours are his loneliest ones, a philosopher will want to share his wisdom with others and listen to their discoveries in turn. He will be encouraged and enlightened by their company, and grateful for it, since without their friendship it will be difficult if not impossible for even the most committed philosopher to continue in an activity which from the point of view of those with more worldly concerns is likely to seem either a harmless waste of time or a dangerous distraction, as the example of Socrates makes clear.

It is in keeping with this spirit of thankfulness for the humanly sustained tradition of philosophy that Aristotle generally begins his own lectures in a particular field of study with a careful review of the positions of his predecessors, generously searching for what in their views may be of lasting value and worth saving. And his lectures themselves, whose goal is to advance the study of the subject in question by educating others in it, represent an act of reciprocating friendship on Aristotle's part that honors the companionship of those that have thought about it before. Whether philosophy makes progress or moves around in a circle instead, the truth about things being discovered, and lost, and discovered again, it always depends on the gratitude that each generation of thinkers feel toward those that have gone before, on the selfless care they devote to the education of their successors, and on the spirit of comradeship that connects each philosopher to the others in his own generation who share his devotion to the impractical business of thinking. Thus even here, in the most sublimely self-sufficient of all human activities, there is not only room for gratitude but an essential role for it.

Yet like the gratitude that a great-souled man feels toward his teachers and friends, the kind a philosopher feels toward those who first awakened his passion for thinking and the others who now accompany him in its pursuit, is of a human sort too. It exists only on a human scale. It is the gratitude of one man toward others like himself, for their care of a way of life which, however divine, has a place in the human world only because there are a few individuals in each generation who love it and long to see it endure.

That we can share directly in the eternal and divine, within the limits of our individual lives, is a privilege no other animal on earth enjoys. For other animals, there is only the indirect participation in eternity that reproduction affords. But this special privilege is one we cannot exercise except under the conditions of mortality that we share with other animals. These are the source of our dependence on the love of others, without whom the enterprise of thinking could neither begin nor be sustained. If we had to depend on ourselves to clear a place in the world for thought, we could never do it. Life is too short and our needs too great. We are able to experience the divine self-sufficiency that among terrestrial beings we alone know briefly but firsthand, only because of the friendship of others, on whom we depend because we are mortal. That is our fate as rational animals. It is the distinguishing characteristic of our human nature, which enables us to enjoy, for a time, a divine existence, but only on account of the loving gifts of other human beings, for whose solicitude even the greatest philosopher has reason to be grateful.

But if a philosopher has reason to be grateful to his friends, there is no room in his life for gratitude on a cosmic scale. He has no grounds to be grateful to God for the existence of the world and our power to comprehend it. That is a marvelous thing, but it is not a gift. It is just the wonderful way things are, and the original provocation to philosophy. A gratitude to other men for their custodial care of the tradition that responds to this provocation, but none to the God of the world whose own eternal intelligibility is indistinguishable from the mind of the philosopher when he is thinking about it: that is Aristotle's pagan conception of gratitude, which Christianity turns upside down with its ideas of will and grace, demanding a new—and for Aristotle inconceivable—gratitude toward a transcendent creator that converts the philosopher's joy to the sin of pride and undermines the value of thankfulness on a horizontal human scale by insisting on a vertical gratitude to God that can never be requited, stirring in human beings the envious wish to take God's place and arousing in their hearts that contempt for their own finitude and for their dependence on the mortal love of others like themselves that animates our loveless world of rights.

CHAPTER 9

The First Cosmopolitan

PLATO'S DISCOVERY OF AN INVISIBLE SELF

When Aristotle died in 322 B.C.E., the world whose portrait he had painted in the *Nicomachean Ethics* was already slipping away. His most famous pupil had died the year before, leaving a string of conquered peoples that stretched all the way to India, over whom Alexander's generals immediately set to quarreling. The age of the independent city-state was over.[1] For the next seven centuries, the heirs of Greek philosophy would live and work in empires of one sort or another, first Hellenistic and then Roman, until the tradition of pagan thought came to an end, and its defenders were succeeded by Christian theologians who used their ideas but rejected their God with a kind of metaphysical horror.

Nothing, perhaps, more poignantly marks the transition from *polis* to empire than the abortive attempt of the citizens of Athens to reassert their independence in the confusion that followed Alexander's death and the suppression of their revolt by Alexander's general Antipater, himself a patron of philosophy who had funded the establishment of the Lyceum in which Aristotle taught. Athens would long continue to be a center of philosophical learning. Months before his death three centuries later, the Roman poet Virgil traveled from his beloved Italy to Athens to study philosophy, retracing the steps of countless pilgrims before him. But after Antipater, Athens ceased to be an independent political community of the sort whose existence had been the premise of Aristotle's account of practical virtue.

Aristotle's great-souled man acts within a particular setting, and the pride he takes in himself is inseparable from the city to which he belongs. He is not proud in the abstract. He is proud of himself as an Athenian, Spartan, or Corinthian—as a prominent member of a distinct political community to whose laws, traditions and citizens he is uniquely attached. He feels a special friendship for those whose care has enabled him to reach a peak of self-sufficiency in the nurturing space of the community they share, and reciprocates by working to sustain its laws and values so that others may reach this peak in turn. His city is not merely one among many in which he might lead an equally good life. It is the ground of his existence—the theater of his greatness as a human being. To be separated from it is to lose the possibility of living such a life at all. Beyond the walls of his city, there is nothing for whose sake he might display his courage and generosity, and no one to remember the deeds he performs—the highest form of immortality attainable in the sphere of political life and inferior only to the immortality of thought, which transcends the world of politics altogether.

The identity of Aristotle's great-souled man is thus bound to that of his city in an intimate way. When his city is submerged in a larger political order and subjected to laws that others have made from afar, the foundation of his pride is destroyed. His city may retain its social or cultural identity. It may continue to be a glittering center of art and philosophy. But it has lost the existential identity that a community possesses only so long as its members legislate for themselves and defend its boundaries with their lives. Aristotle's philosophy of pride presupposes this stronger form of civic identity. It assumes that a man's political orientation is fixed, and his friendships defined, by the particular city to which he belongs. By the time Aristotle was dead, in the year of the failed Athenian revolt, Alexander's armies had rendered this assumption obsolete. In the new world that was aborning, a different understanding of friendship and pride was required—one better adapted to the imperial conditions under which philosophy now had to proceed. The Stoics pointed the way.[2]

Beginning with Chrysippus in the third century B.C.E., the Stoics advocated the idea of a "cosmic" city to which all men everywhere belong, and reinterpreted the meaning of friendship in light of this idea. Their new cosmopolitanism, with its egalitarian implications, rested on the belief that every human being possesses a power of self-control that allows him to decide for himself whether he shall be happy or not.

The Stoic doctrine of self-control treats independence as a value of supreme importance. In this respect, it resembles Aristotle's account of greatness of soul. But it locates the source of our self-sufficiency at a deeper level.

For Aristotle, independence is a trait of character. It is the self-sufficiency of a man who has acquired the right habits through an education of the proper kind and possesses the resources he needs to live a noble and magnanimous life. It is the independence of a gentleman of means, whose actions display his self-sufficiency in a way that all can see.

For the Stoics, self-sufficiency is a function of the primal power that all men possess to affirm or deny the importance of what happens to them, and that they retain in every imaginable circumstance of life—in health and pain, wealth and want, liberty and bondage. Even an uneducated slave has and can use it. To possess this power, one need not be a member of a particular civic community with its distinctive laws and traditions, let alone of an educated and wealthy elite. On a Stoic view, one can be free anywhere and everywhere. Self-sufficiency is not the possession of a privileged few; in the most basic sense, it is not a political phenomenon at all.

The Stoic idea of a primitive power of assent, unaffected by our political status and worldly resources, opened a gap between the inner and outer lives of human beings that has no counterpart in Aristotle's *Ethics*. It supplied the basis for a new conception of self-sufficiency that no longer depends on one's civic identity. And it prepared the way for the entirely un-Aristotelian belief that all men can be friends—the inspiration for that most cosmopolitan of all ideas, the idea of natural law, whose original Aristotelian formulation the Stoics enlarged in ways that have shaped Western thought ever since.[3]

The Stoic doctrine of assent had a special appeal for the writers of the early church, who saw in it an anticipation of their own more radical concept of the will. Yet the Stoics remained within the orbit of Greek rationalism and never reached the idea of the will as Augustine defines it. The Stoic sage possesses an inner power of self-control that is untouched by events in the world, including the pleasures and pains of the body. He uses this power to liberate himself from suffering. But his ultimate aim is to comprehend the rational order of the world and to affirm its inherent goodness. His liberation is therefore a triumph of reason. By contrast, when Augustine gave the Christian idea of the will its first definitive formulation, near the end of the fourth century C.E., it was not to the tradition of Greek rationalism that he looked for the materials he needed to express this novel idea, but to Scripture instead.[4]

The moral universe of the Bible differs from the wisdom philosophies of pagan antiquity in two basic respects. First, it conceives God to be a transcendent creator who brings the world into being from nothing, and second, it assumes that the most fundamental relation between man and God is one of obedience, not understanding. In the biblical view, man's first responsibility is to obey God's commands, whether or not we comprehend them.

Augustine's concept of the will is inspired by these biblical beliefs, which are foreign to the whole of pagan philosophy, Stoicism included. A tremendous gulf therefore remains between the Christian idea of the will and the Stoics' highly interiorized yet still rationally oriented idea of assent. Stoicism goes as far as it is possible to go toward a biblical concept of freedom, within the limits of pagan rationalism. But the distinctive meaning of this concept only comes into view once these limits are surpassed. The Stoics built a bridge between the older idea of self-sufficiency that underlies Aristotle's understanding of greatness of soul, which remained tied to an ideal of civic life on whose ruins they undertook to construct a new and more cosmopolitan conception of pride, and the Christian idea of freedom that turned paganism on its head, making pride a sin and gratitude the greatest of virtues. To reach Augustine's more radical formulation of this idea, the bridge the Stoics built had to be crossed and burned.

AGAINST HOMER

The Stoics were not, however, the first to claim that human beings have an inner life that is completely independent of their outward circumstances, nor were they were the first to maintain that every man possesses an invisible power of assent that he takes with him wherever he goes, by means of which he can secure his happiness regardless of what happens to him in what we falsely call the "real" world. The Stoics were not the first cosmopolitans. That honor belongs to Plato.

Plato separated the soul from the body, and the true world from the apparent one, in a systematic and disciplined way. He taught that the soul inhabits the body as a temporary residence, whose destruction it survives. He argued for the metaphysical necessity of a timeless world of ideas, separate from the realm of becoming and change, and insisted that the second is merely an imperfect image of the first. Plato's doctrines prepared the way for the Stoic idea of self-control, and after that, for the theology of the Christian religion, whose architects found in Platonism what they took to be an adumbration of their own ideas of freedom, salvation and heaven.

The radical import of Plato's teachings as an inspiration for later thinkers is best grasped by recalling the depth and ferocity of his opposition to Homer, whose poems had served for centuries as an encyclopedia of Greek culture.

Early in the *Republic,* Socrates and his young companions set out to construct an educational regime for those who are being trained to rule their ideal "city in speech." If the rulers of a truly just city are to be properly brought up, Socrates says, their education needs to begin at an early date. Even as young children, they must be told the right kind of stories. Those that encourage bad habits and false beliefs should be avoided, since these are likely to corrupt the character of those who hear them. Socrates gives many examples of the tales his future guardians ought not to hear—stories about the terrors of death, the immorality of the gods, and the like. The majority of these are drawn from Homer's poems. Indeed, the whole of the educational program that Socrates sets out in the early books of the *Republic,* and the arguments he offers to support it, are deliberately and relentlessly anti-Homeric. The *Republic* is a sustained attack on Homer's metaphysics.[5]

Homer did not, of course, have a metaphysics in the sense that Plato did. He had no explicit philosophical system. But Homer's poems offer a picture of the world that implicitly rests on two basic assumptions that together constitute what might be called a philosophy of life. It is one that Plato emphatically rejects.

The first is that a man's soul has no meaningful existence apart from that of his body. Homer is attentive to the many, varied psychological phenomena of reflecting, choosing, feeling, loving, loathing and dreaming that characterize all human experience, and his heroes do have rich inner lives of a sort. But these are only weakly separated from their visible lives in the world of acts and events—from their gestures, reactions, triumphs and sufferings, which everyone can see.[6] Homer is insistent that a man's soul is not sufficiently separate from his body to survive the latter's death in any robust sense. After death, there is only darkness. To die is to fall out of the light in which men act and watch others act, into nothing. That is why the death of a hero in battle has the pathos it does.

A second assumption is that the world of the gods and that of men are not two worlds but one—a single continuous world with beings of different sorts, between whom there are no insuperable barriers to prevent their contact and communication. The gods on Olympus are immortal. They cannot experience the fear of dying and are therefore never driven by the passion for glory that moves Homer's heroes on account of their proximity to death (though his gods are surprisingly human in other ways). But despite this one all-important difference, the distance between the men and gods in Homer's poems is not absolute. It can be crossed, and often is, by gods who appear in the human world, meddle in the affairs of men, take human lovers and produce offspring that are half human, half divine. Olympus is not a world apart. It is just the peak (literally) of the one world that men and gods inhabit.[7]

The assumption that there is no soul detached from the body, and no other world of heavenly beings radically separate from this one, are the two premises of Homer's metaphysics. Without them, his poems make no sense. All the stories he tells about his gods and heroes depend for their terror and beauty on the finality of human death and the visible presence of the divine. But it is just these assumptions that Plato rejects, offering in their place a new, anti-Homeric metaphysics, and a revolutionary program of education adapted to it.

In this respect, Aristotle stands much closer to Homer than his teacher did. Against Plato, Aristotle maintains that the soul is not separate from the body but is merely its animating form, whose dissolution necessarily accompanies the death of the body. He also argues that ideas have only a notional existence apart from the individual things that exemplify or embody them, denying—what Plato affirmed—that ideas are more real than the impermanent particulars in which they are reflected. In both respects, Aristotle seeks to rejoin what had been together in Homer, but Plato broke apart. In a philosophy as abstract as Plato's own, he articulates and defends the metaphysical premises that underlie the picture of the world implicit in Homer's poems. The future belonged to Plato—to the Stoic and, later Christian, thinkers who would continue in Plato's line, deepening the separation of soul from body, and heaven from earth, until the gulf between them became absolute. But before Homer's world disappeared completely, it flared up one last time in the philosophy of Aristotle—Homer rendered in the language of being, the final and most self-conscious expression of pagan thought.

Nowhere is this more apparent than in Aristotle's account of greatness of soul. The pride that such a man takes in himself is a close relative of Homeric glory. It is less fierce, perhaps, and more attuned to politics than war, but like the glory of Achilles, is a kind of visible splendor that shines forth in the presence of admiring companions, joined in a venture of risk and inspired by a shared love of fame.[8] Simone Weil calls the *Iliad* a poem "of force."[9] It might

better be described as a poem of pride, for its central theme is the maintenance, display and loss of pride by Achilles, Agamemnon and others. In a
similar sense, the *Nicomachean Ethics* is a philosophy of pride that makes the
glorious greatness of a great-souled man the defining summit of human
achievement, within the realm of practical life.

The most striking feature of both is their association of greatness with
manifest splendor. In this respect, both Homer and Aristotle subscribe to a
metaphysics of presence. The first embraces it only implicitly, and the second
in a fully reflective way. But it is the common ground on which their otherwise different ideals of human excellence rest. Indeed, even in his account of
the invisible joy of thinking, which has no counterpart in Homer's poems,
Aristotle holds to the metaphysics of presence that he and the poet share, for
here too the philosopher's train of ideas, though supremely abstract, is guided
by a belief in the continuity of the human and divine that Homer presupposes as well, as he moves up and down the register of being, from the deathless gods who watch with such delight the battles that men fight to the mortal
combatants themselves.

To this metaphysics of presence, shared by the poet he sought to overthrow
and the philosopher who became his most searching critic, Plato opposes a
metaphysics of separation. He separates the soul from the body, and God
from the world, and by exploiting the gap his philosophy opens between
them, transfers the self-sufficiency that justifies a great man's pride in himself from the visible surface of things to the depths of the soul whose innermost
workings are now claimed to be unaffected by events and entirely hidden
from view.

GLAUCON'S CHALLENGE

At the beginning of the second book of the *Republic,* one of Socrates' interlocutors issues a challenge that sets the agenda for the long conversation
that follows.

Socrates and his friends have been discussing the nature of justice.
Thrasymachus has proposed "that justice is nothing other than the advantage of the stronger,"[10] belligerently insisting that a person will act justly only
when it suits his interest to do so (as it suits the interest of the weak to respect
the law only because their weakness prevents them from doing what they
please). Socrates has responded with a variety of arguments designed to show
that "justice is a soul's virtue,"[11] that a just man lives well, and that, in living

well, he is "blessed and happy"[12]—in contrast to the unjust man, whose life is necessarily wretched. His arguments have succeeded in quieting Thrasymachus but not in persuading him. "Let that be your banquet at the feast of Bendis," Thrasymachus sarcastically concedes.[13]

At this point, Glaucon enters the conversation and with "his characteristic courage" asks Socrates whether he "wants to seem" to have persuaded his listeners "that it is better in every way to be just than unjust," or "truly" to have convinced them of this.[14] Naturally, Socrates replies that he wants not merely to win a debater's victory, but really to convince his friends of the truth of what he is saying. To do this, Glaucon says, Socrates must persuade them that justice is good not only on account of its external advantages (a good reputation, and the like) but intrinsically as well. As a test, he suggests they consider a case where being just and having the external advantages that normally go with it are entirely distinct.

Glaucon proposes two such cases. The first is that of a man with a magical ring that gives him the power to make himself invisible and thus to do whatever he wants, without cost or punishment. The second involves a pair of men, one perfectly just, the other perfectly unjust, whose reputations and fortunes, both in this world and the next, are the exact opposite of their true characters, the first suffering all the punishments that an unjust man ought to incur, and the second receiving all the benefits that properly belong to a man with a just soul. Who would ever prefer the second life to the first? That is Glaucon's challenge. The rest of the *Republic* is Socrates' reply.

The key idea behind the challenge is that of invisibility. Everyone knows that things are not always as they seem. Our perceptions are often mistaken. From a distance, the tower appears square; on closer inspection, we see that it is round. Our neighbor seems to be acting benevolently; we learn more, and conclude that he was motivated by self-interest instead. That there is a distinction between how things appear, and how they truly are, is a familiar feature of human experience. Glaucon's challenge takes its start from this distinction and radicalizes it by postulating a *perfect and complete* disjunction between the world of appearances, on the one hand, and the true or real—but invisible—order of things on the other.

Homer, too, recognized that men make errors of perception and judgment—that things are sometimes other than they appear. But the notion of a perfectly invisible inner realm of real being that is completely detached from the world of appearances would have been incomprehensible to him. Glaucon's challenge depends on the intelligibility of this idea, and though

Socrates will in the end claim to have shown that men receive the punishments and rewards they deserve on account of their true characters, he accepts the assumption of an entirely invisible order of things and exploits it to frame his response.

SOCRATES' REPLY

Glaucon's imaginary case of the two men whose outward fates are the exact opposite of their true characters drives a wedge between the world and the soul. It separates them in a principled way. The result is that a man's worldly fortunes need no longer correspond *in any way at all* to the state of his soul. Given this possibility, Glaucon asks, who would not concentrate his energies on creating the right appearances—which affect his wealth, reputation and the like—rather than on the perfection of his true character, which is invisible, and may have no bearing on these things at all?

Socrates' response is long and subtle. But its guiding aim is simple. Socrates attempts to show that the radical separation of world and soul that Glaucon's challenge presupposes is a cause not of anguish but hope, since this very separation gives us reason to believe that we have the power to decide our own fates with an independence we could not possibly possess if our happiness were tied even in the smallest way to the world of appearances, over which we have at best modest control. What in Glaucon's example looks like grounds for despair—that even a perfectly just man may get the reverse of the treatment he deserves, because there is no necessary connection between appearance and reality—is thus converted, in Socrates' response, to a reason for optimism greater than any we can ever know so long as we continue to believe that our happiness is hostage to fortune. If our inner lives really are completely within our control, then assuming it can be shown that happiness consists in a certain condition of the soul, and in this alone, we may rest assured that our happiness is beyond the power of fortune to prevent or spoil. This is the conclusion to which Socrates' argument leads—a profoundly un-Homeric judgment that rests on the equally un-Homeric assumption of a perfect separation between the world of appearances, in which luck and fortune rule, and an invisible psychic realm where truth and reality reside.

Given this assumption, the task is to show that happiness consists in a certain right ordering of the soul, and that nothing else is needed to attain it. This is what the central books of the *Republic* are meant to prove.

The crucial premise of Socrates' argument is that there is a second realm of invisible things, which he calls "forms" or "ideas," that lie as far beyond the world of appearances in one direction as the invisible souls of men do in another. Socrates thus not only accepts Glaucon's hypothesis of a separation between body and soul, but *doubles* it by adding a second and equally radical separation in the opposite direction.

The world that we encounter in our everyday experience is characterized by transience and imperfection. Nothing in it lasts forever. The countless things we see about us are all constantly changing, coming into being and passing away, and every one of them is marred or blemished in some fashion. Nothing in the world of "sights and sounds,"[15] as Socrates calls it, is free of flaws, including that of impermanence, which is the greatest flaw of all.

To this world Socrates contrasts another—a world of eternal ideas that are reflected, in a distorted way, in the turbulence about us. Whatever limited order and intelligibility the changing things in the world of appearances possess, they have only on account of their relation to this other world of ideas, of which they are a blurred copy or image.

One can go further. Whatever limited *reality* the world of appearances has, it has only because it is the reflection of a world with more reality than it. The secondary and deficient kind of being that transient and imperfect things possess is thus entirely derivative from, and dependent upon, the unqualified being of the eternal ideas they reflect or represent. To the extent the world of appearances *is* at all, it is only through its relation to a world of ideas that *are* forever. The latter world is therefore not merely different from the former one. It is superior to it in every conceivable way, for the world of ideas is the source and ground of all that is intelligible and real in the world of sights and sounds from which human experience takes its start.

The world of ideas is not immediately present to us in our experience of the world of appearances. We do not see it in the way we see the mobile and impermanent things around us. But we do have an indirect access to it on account of our remarkable ability to see an image *as* an image. The ability to do this liberates us from the darkness in which we would otherwise be trapped by enabling us to conceive the endlessly changing things we encounter in experience as the appearances of other things that do not change. Thus, even though the world of ideas is available to us only mediately, through the exercise of our capacity to see the world of appearances as the reflection of another and more real one, we are imaginatively connected to it and not cut off from this other world completely, as we would be if we lacked the ecstatic power of seeing-as: the ability to "look" beyond the world of appearances and in that sense to transcend it.[16]

The power to look beyond appearances to the stable originals they represent is the precondition of all thought. Indeed, it is thinking itself, which might also be described as the power of abstraction. This power is most vividly displayed in mathematical reasoning even of the simplest sort—for Socrates, the paradigm of thought in general.

But there is more to the human soul than the power of thought. We are not only thinking beings, but appetitive and emotional ones too, and while thinking leads us away from appearances to ideas, our appetites and emotions tie us to the world of sights and sounds (appetite always, and emotion often), and thus block or impede the transcendence of thought.[17] If we are to reach that other, stabler world we must escape the gravitational field of the desires and feelings that chain us to this one. We must overcome the lust for changing things that can never bring us more than transient pleasures, and learn instead to love the changeless originals that are the source of all their beauty and being.

That this is something we can do, and are motivated to do, follows from assumptions that Plato shares with the entire Greek rationalist tradition, and with Aristotle in particular: that our deepest desire is the desire to be; that what is eternal possesses being in the highest degree; and that we have the power to reach the eternal in thought. It follows that if we do not act in a thoughtful way, subordinating the demands of appetite and emotion to those of reason, it is only because we are confused about the best way of fulfilling our deepest desire. It is only because we do not clearly understand what is in our own best interest and how to achieve it. Once we do, we will adjust our course and begin to live in a more self-controlled way. We will be more closely and steadily in touch with the world of ideas toward which all thinking is directed. We will be closer to what is most real and, as a result, more real ourselves. The man whose soul "turns around" from the world of appearances to that of ideas thus experiences an increase in being. He exists at a higher level of reality than the man who remains tied to appearances, which the lover of sights and sounds confusedly believes to be more real than the ideas they reflect.

The answer to the question of how a human soul should be ordered follows directly. A well-ordered soul is one in which reason controls the appetites and emotions, issuing commands to them from its superior point of view. A soul that is arranged in this way has the most reality a human soul can have. To put his soul in this condition, moreover, all a man needs is reason, for reason not only shows him what this arrangement is, and why it is best, but also supplies the motive and instrument to achieve it. Nothing more is required to reach this goal—in particular, nothing outside the soul, such as wealth, reputation and good fortune, over which a man has limited control. Even in the absence of these things, a man who possesses the power of reason has all he needs to arrange his soul in the way he must to live the most real, and hence happiest, life a human being can. And because he takes this power with him wherever he goes, he need not be anywhere in particular in order to live a life of this sort. One city is as good as another.

Of course, most men do not lead such lives. They race about instead, from one spectacle to the next, entranced by the play of appearances, lost in a world of nonbeing. Most men spend their lives in a cave, looking at shadows on a wall, mistaking them for reality, leading lives as unreal as the shadows they watch. This is the condition of the majority of humankind, few of whom ever free themselves from the chains of illusion.[18]

The principal cause of this is the power of social conventions. Most men lead slavish and ignorant lives because the conventional norms of their societies encourage them to do so, rewarding those who excel in the shadow play of appearances.[19] But to overcome the pull of convention, no matter how strong, a man need look no farther than himself. The faculty of reason that he contains in his own soul is powerful enough, if he will only use it, to enable him to escape from the cave of illusions and find his way up to the sunlit world of ideas.

THE SOUL UNCHAINED

The *Republic* addresses the question of what constitutes the best order for a soul. But it is also centrally concerned with the related question of what constitutes the best order for a city, and its main argument is organized around a famous analogy between these two kinds of order. Like a well-ordered soul, Socrates says, a well-ordered city is governed by reason. Hence if a city of this kind is ever to exist, it must be ruled by philosophers.[20] The city in speech that Socrates and his companions construct is based on this assumption. But the assumption is an impossible one, for the conjunction of wisdom and political power that it presupposes can never occur. The distance between them is too great. That is because it could be overcome only in case philosophers desired to rule and everyone else simultaneously desired for them to do so—a concurrence that runs against the grain of desire on both sides of the equation. For wisdom and power to be joined in the way that Socrates imagines, there would have to be a coincidence of passions so unlikely as to be inconceivable. The city in speech is a dream.

But the same is not true of the best sort of soul, which can come into existence even though the shadow-dwelling souls of most men are far removed from it. Individual human beings possess the power to properly order their own souls themselves. To do so, they need only exercise the reason they already possess, which can be done in bad cities (even those that put their philosophers to death) as well as good ones.

The existence of Socrates' city in speech is hostage to fortune. It is doomed by fate never to be. By contrast, the existence of a philosophical soul, though rare, is not impossible in the same way. It can and does happen, from time to time, that a man breaks free from the chains of illusion and the conventions that reinforce them, merely by exercising the reason he carries with him wherever he goes. If the political moral of the *Republic* is a bleak one—the best city can never exist except as a dream—the moral that it points for each of us, as individuals, is therefore the most heartening one imaginable. For whoever we are, wherever we live, whatever our outward circumstances, it is fully within our power to live a real and therefore happy life simply by listening to the voice of reason that leads us from the world of sights and sounds to the deathless realm of ideas.

LIFE IS A CHOICE

Glaucon's challenge opens a chasm between what appears and what is real. Socrates' reply exploits this opening by deepening the chasm in two directions, imagining behind the seen surface of things a thinking soul trained on ideas, the most real part of us attending to the most real objects of attention, in a concourse of invisible worlds. In this doubled invisibility of thought and idea, Socrates finds the metaphysics he needs to defend the claim, so outrageous from the standpoint of common sense, that it is better to be just than to appear so—that the life of the man whose soul is rightly ordered is more real and hence happier than that of the outwardly prosperous man whose soul is an unreal wreck. And he discovers the means to liberate human happiness from its dependence on the contingencies of life, including that of living in a particular city, which in Socrates' view no more constrains our prospects for happiness than the accident of being born with blue eyes.

Nowhere in Plato's writings is this ideal of independence expressed more vividly than in the myth with which the *Republic* concludes.

Socrates tells the tale of a young warrior named Er who dies in battle, but whose soul is returned to his body after a trip to "the world beyond"[21] so that he can report to others what he has seen. In a meadow, Er sees the souls of men resting after a thousand-year journey in which they have received the rewards or suffered the punishments for deeds in their last life. Eventually, they are taken to another place and instructed to choose their next life. Lachesis, the daughter of Necessity, speaks to them as follows. "Ephemeral souls, this is the beginning of another cycle that will end in death. Your daimon or guardian spirit will not be assigned to you by lot; you will choose him. The one who has the first lot will be the first to choose a life to which he will then be bound by necessity. Virtue knows no master; each will possess it to a greater or less degree, depending on whether he values or disdains it. The responsibility lies with the one who makes the choice; the god has none."[22]

Er watches in amazement as the souls choose their lives, some wisely, others foolishly, a few disastrously, even though they have all been told that "there is a satisfactory life rather than a bad one available even for the one who comes last, provided he chooses it rationally and lives it seriously."[23] After making their choices, the souls travel to "the Plain of Forgetfulness" and drink from the "River of Unheeding," then fall asleep and are carried "this way and that, up to their births, like shooting stars."[24]

The moral of the myth is that our lives are the product not of fate but choice. On the threshold of birth, we are free to choose the lives we shall live. We have the power to decide whether to live in accordance with reason or appetite and emotion instead. In the last lines of the *Republic,* Socrates urges his listeners to believe that we do not lose this power at birth but continue to possess it through the whole of our lives.

The *Republic* thus ends on a note of sublime hope: that the radical independence of the souls Er watches making their choices in the next world is ours as well—right here, in the midst of life itself. It is as if we stood, at every moment of our lives, at the point of the souls who are about to be reborn, and remain as free as they to decide what our lives shall be. The *Republic* is an invitation to think of ourselves in this way. For Socrates the invitation is real, not frivolous, because he believes that we possess an invisible power of thought that can liberate us from the world of appearances, whose seductive appeal is the cause of all our unhappiness and wrongdoing. This power is the key to the prison in which most men live their lives. It is perfectly portable and utterly immune to the vicissitudes of life. That we have this power, and can use it if we choose, is Socrates' declaration of independence. It is his reply to Glaucon's challenge, which separates the visible world from the invisible one but still ties happiness to fortune. Socrates accepts Glaucon's premise and radicalizes it, setting happiness free from the realm of contingency and change altogether.

This is the essence of Socrates' anti-Homeric program, introduced by the educational reforms with which he begins the construction of his city in speech and brought to a conclusion in the parable of the cave. For Homer's unbroken world of splendid appearances, of shining gods and prideful men, Socrates substitutes two worlds, divided by an ontological chasm—on the one side, a visible world of appearances, with no glory at all, and on the other an invisible realm of reason and ideas where all truth and beauty reside. Aristotle will put these two worlds together again, in a Homeric spirit, restoring glory to a place in the fleeting world of political action, and reuniting the eternal and divine with the realm of moving things, where it can be seen by those who know how to look. But the Stoics will follow Plato's lead and in their *cosmopolis* of free and equal souls set these worlds even farther apart than he did—as far apart as they can be set, within the limits of Greek thought, leaving it to the Christian thinkers who followed them to insist on a still more radical separation of heaven and earth that shattered these limits completely.

CHAPTER 10

῾Preparatio Evangelica

STOICISM ON THE WAY
TO CHRISTIAN THOUGHT

The Stoic tradition of philosophy was founded by Zeno of Cytium at the start of the third century B.C.E., fifty years or so after Aristotle's death. Its last great representative was the emperor-philosopher Marcus Aurelius, who composed his Stoic diaries six hundred years later. No group of thinkers had a greater influence on the intellectual and spiritual culture of the ancient world.[1]

There were differences, of course, from one period and place to another. Broadly speaking, the early Greek Stoics, and Chrysippus in particular, were especially interested in logical issues and technical problems of epistemology. Their Roman successors were preoccupied with the practical question of how a man can achieve peace in a life filled with suffering and shadowed by death. But despite these differences of emphasis and approach, many of the main themes of Stoic philosophy remained more or less constant from the start. The most important of these was the distinction between the things that are up to us and those that are not.

THE THINGS THAT ARE UP TO US

Chrysippus had already drawn this distinction and developed a psychology to support it three hundred years before Epictetus was born a slave in Rome, around the year 50 C.E. Epictetus was the most metaphysically inclined of the Roman Stoics. His best known work is the *Enchiridion,* or *Hand-book,* a collection of extracts from a larger set of writings composed after the philosopher's death by his pupil Flavius Arrianus.[2] The *Handbook* had a wide circulation in the ancient world and played an important role in the early modern revival of Stoic ideas.[3] Its very first sentence declares that "some things are up to us and some are not up to us,"[4] and the work as a whole may fairly be described as a meditation on the meaning of this distinction.

Among the things that are *not* up to us, Epictetus includes "our bodies," "our possessions," "our reputations," and "our public offices." It is obvious that none of these is up to us completely. No one has the ability to guarantee that he will be healthy, rich, or successful in public life. A person may take steps to secure these goods, and some actions are more likely than others to produce them. But each may be snatched away in an instant by forces beyond our control.

To tie one's well-being to advantages of this kind is therefore to make oneself a hostage to fortune. It is to turn oneself into a slave whose life is necessarily "thwarted" and unhappy. The remedy, Epictetus says, is to learn not to "care" about such things. It is to treat them as "indifferent"[5] and to dissociate one's true self from their good and bad effects. The truly free man is the one who is able to say of all the things that are not up to us, "some produce results that the majority of men equate with happiness, others results of an opposite kind, but none of them *is* me, and my own impregnable happiness consists in the knowledge that this is so."

From this point of view, the civically engaged life of Aristotle's great-souled man looks slavish, not self-sufficient.

Epictetus warns us to avoid seeking to be honored before others in the way that such a man does. Do not strive, he says, "to be a general or a magistrate or a consul."[6] Do not put your stock in gifts of "porticoes and baths."[7] Learn not to be disturbed by the suffering and death of your friends. Train yourself, in short, not to care about the very things that are at the center of the life of the magnanimous and politically active man whose proud career is the principal subject of the *Nicomachean Ethics,* for that is not a free life but its opposite. It is a life whose happiness is chained to what Epictetus calls "externals"[8]—one spent in the pursuit of contingent and evanescent goods that we may never attain and must always lose in the end.

Aristotle of course recognized the vulnerability of a life devoted to honor and pride, and understood that contemplation is more self-contained. But he did not dismiss the first on that account, or think it a servile existence unworthy of a man who cares for himself. Indeed, he considered the life of political virtue to be one of self-esteem.

Epictetus' view is the opposite. A man who really takes pride in himself will want, he says, to detach his affections from public affairs. To be sure, he will behave himself and avoid antagonizing others. He will observe the proprieties of civilized life. But his overriding goal will be to protect his true self by disengaging it from all those things that risk dragging him around like a hapless slave if he ties his identity and happiness to them—wealth, office, reputation, and eloquence included.[9]

Aristotle's magnificent man makes a spectacle of himself. He lives for the pleasure of being seen. Epictetus recommends a different course. He urges us to be "tolerant of being overlooked"[10]—to cultivate what is "inside"[11] us and not to be "carried away by appearances."[12] Like Socrates in the *Republic,* Epictetus withdraws all value and prestige from the uncontrollable goods of worldly life and transfers them to an invisible inner realm of perfect self-command where the true self, and real happiness, now exclusively reside.

This is the negative part of Epictetus' program. The positive part consists in his account of those things that *are* up to us, and of the radically different sort of pride that a man who cares only for such things is able to take in himself.

Epictetus initially lists "our opinions," "impulses," "desires," and "aversions" as things that are "our own doing."[13] But these are not immediately our own. They become such only on account of our "way of dealing"[14] with them. To begin with, our passions and beliefs are as little in our control as our bodies and possessions. This is clearest in the case of desires and aversions. We want certain things and fear others, either instinctively or conventionally, because others want and fear them. We experience these affective states as things that happen to us. We "can't help" fearing death and wanting fame. We are not the authors of these passions but their subjects, or rather, their victims. A life directed by them is in the custody of forces beyond our control.

The same is true of our opinions. These come to us from the outside as well. We take them in, uncritically, from those around us. We believe that certain foods are wholesome and others not, and that it is better to be beautiful than ugly, because others tell us these things. We accept their views and defer to them, much as we do to our own instinctive fears and desires.

Still, we are not condemned to remain their prisoners forever. For all the desires and aversions and opinions that we experience as something "other" than ourselves must appear before an internal tribunal of "judgment"[15] where "assent"[16] to them may either be given or withheld.

Before they are judged in this way, our beliefs and passions are mere "appearances," a term that for Epictetus includes emotional as well as cognitive states. We have no control over what appears to us. We can neither cause things to appear as they do, nor prevent them from appearing. But we can "work on"[17] appearances by choosing to assent to them or not.[18] No appearance necessitates our assent. However helpless we may be to prevent its occurrence, we remain free to say "yes" or "no" to it. Our independence in this regard enables us to "rule" appearances instead of being ruled by them. It thus constitutes, quite literally, the "ruling principle"[19] in us.

The things that befall us are therefore *not us*. Only our power to assent to them is. We may exercise this power poorly or well, but everyone has it and nothing can destroy it. Hence, every man has the power to take control of his life and on behalf of his true self to assert command over the external and uncontrollable things that do not really belong to him at all, though most men foolishly and unhappily identify with them.

THE CARE OF THE SELF

From others, we inherit the belief that death is an evil, honor a good, and many other things besides. But our power of judgment allows us to deny these beliefs if we choose.

This way of putting things suggests that the operations of judgment are logical or epistemological—that their function is to assign truth values to propositions of various sorts. Epictetus sometimes speaks of judgment in this way, as when he says that what is dreadful is not death "but the judgment about death that it is dreadful." But more often, and more characteristically, he defines judgment in affective rather than logical terms, as a power of caring or not caring. The power of assent enables us to adjust the truth values of our beliefs. But more importantly, it gives us the freedom to change the direction of our desires as well. Indeed, this is what really matters, since if we affirm that death is not an evil but continue to fear it, and to flee it at all costs, we have not made any meaningful progress toward the happiness we seek. Our main goal must therefore be to cause our desires to run in a direction opposite to the one they normally take.[20]

This is the reversal that leads to freedom and happiness. It is accomplished by an act of judgment understood as a rechanneling of feeling—a "therapy of desire."[21] Those who have undergone this therapy, or are committed to pursuing it, are the only ones who are justified in taking pride in themselves, for they alone have achieved the self-sufficiency that Epictetus, like Aristotle, makes the benchmark of a successful human life. By contrast, the great men of the world, who are proud of their status and reputation, have only an illusory pride, for even if they live lives of public virtue, their identity is tied to the wrong things. It is bound to what is external and therefore beyond their control, and must be unbound through a therapeutic reversal of desire that enables them to learn to care for their true selves instead.

But what exactly does it mean to care for one's true self?[22] The phrase suggests an inward orientation, away from the world of appearances toward a self that lies hidden behind it, and much of what Epictetus says about the self-destructive folly of those who live for the sake of appearances seems to imply such a view. But it is clear from the argument of the *Handbook* as a whole that this is not his view, which in an important sense is just the reverse, for the therapy of desire that he recommends leads not to a heightened preoccupation with the self, but to its disappearance instead.

According to Epictetus, the man who truly cares about himself will "wish to have happen only what does happen."[23] He will "not seek to have events happen as [he] wants them to, but instead want them to happen as they do happen."[24] He will not be "annoyed"[25] if things turn out differently than he expected or wished, but will work to bring his expectations and wishes into line with the way things actually are.

The man who cares most for himself will therefore be the one who cares least—who puts his own desires aside and counts them as nothing if they conflict with the actual state of the world. The therapy of desire, which at first seems to entail a redirection of care from the world to the self, thus in the end leads to the obliteration of a self distinct from the world and a boundless love for everything that is not up to us—the paradoxical result of the intensified experience of selfhood that lies in the discovery of a radically independent power of judgment before whose tribunal all that happens in the world must appear and be given its due.

The key to understanding this paradox is Epictetus' exaggerated commitment to the rationalist metaphysics that he shares with Plato and Aristotle.

Epictetus' world is a rational one. What happens in it happens for a reason. Indeed, this is true not just in general and for the most part. It is true in every respect. There is absolutely nothing in the world that happens for no reason at all.

Aristotle and Plato also believed that the world has a rational order, but left room for contingency or chance. Epictetus denies this. The rationality of the world, he says, is pervasive and complete. There are no real accidents in it, but only apparent ones that seem such on account of our meager powers of understanding. To assume otherwise is an insult to reason—an acceptance of limits on reason that cannot themselves be rationally explained or defended. Indeed, it is an impiety, if one equates the divinity of the world with its rationality, as Epictetus does.[26]

It follows that nothing in the world can ever be bad. If the world is perfectly rational, then it must be perfectly good as well. "Just as a target is not set up to missed, in the same way nothing bad by nature happens in the world."[27] Because we read this sentence against the background of two thousand years of Christian belief, it is hard not to think of the order and goodness of the world as a gift conferred upon it by a transcendent God who freely communicates his own eternal goodness to the world that he creates. But Epictetus knows no god of this kind. Like Aristotle's, his god is inseparable from the world itself. It is just the rationality of the world, from which its goodness immediately follows. The perfect goodness of the world is therefore also a part of its inherent nature, and if we do not always see this—if we sometimes think that what happens in the world is harmful or bad—that is only because of the shortsightedness that prevents us from comprehending its perfect rationality, for the two are at bottom the same.

Of course, we can never grasp the rationality of the world in all its detail. That is because we are limited in many ways. Our powers of reasoning are modest, and we are constantly being dragged about by desires that cause us to view the world from a selfish and distorted point of view. But though we cannot actually overcome our limits, we can discipline ourselves not to care about the things that seem important from a self-centered, and therefore necessarily mistaken, perspective. We can train ourselves to want only what happens—to love the idea, which for most of us remains only an idea, that the world is perfectly rational and therefore perfectly good. This is a difficult but attainable goal, and to reach it we must start by cultivating an intensified awareness of our independence *from* the world—of our freedom to judge appearances as we choose—for paradoxically, this alone is capable of producing in us that spirit of selfless resignation *to* the world in which true happiness consists.

By insisting that it is always up to us to give or withhold assent to our thoughts and desires—that we retain an impregnable autonomy of judgment even in the worst and most confining conditions—Epictetus carries the idea of an independent inner self beyond the point that even Socrates does in his response to Glaucon's challenge. Yet by claiming that the point of acknowledging our autonomy is to motivate a therapy of desire whose goal is the abandonment of the self to a world of exceptionless reason, Epictetus shows how deeply committed he remains to the fundamental rationalism of all pagan thought and to an idea of independence that is worlds away from the biblical understanding of human freedom, which Augustine interprets as a spontaneous power of creation and models on God's own.

Nothing, perhaps, is more indicative of the distance that still separates Epictetus from his Christian successors than his claim that a philosopher who has taught himself to love the idea that "nothing bad happens in the world" lives the life of a god and is "deservedly called"[28] divine (a claim that Aristotle would have endorsed). By learning to care only for the inherently rational and therefore necessarily good order of things, regardless of what it may bring, a man of this sort loses his human self and becomes divine in the process. Epictetus acknowledges that this is extremely hard to do. But from a Christian perspective, the struggle to become God is more than merely difficult. It is the first, and worst, of all sins.

Epictetus' extreme version of the rationalism he shares with every other pagan thinker thus puts him on one side of the metaphysical divide that separates the entire tradition of ancient philosophy from the theology of Augustine and his followers. Yet the very extremity of his rationalism presents a problem that only the latter theology can cure. That is because Epictetus' insistence that absolutely everything in the world has a reason, cannot be explained so long as one accepts the distinction between form and matter that he, like Plato and Aristotle before him, took for granted. In order for Epictetus' boundless extension of reason to be made metaphysically intelligible, this distinction must be abandoned, since it necessarily implies that the world is incompletely suffused with reason or mind. It is Christianity that first provides the means to do this. The idea of creation from nothing shatters the distinction between form and matter and thereby opens the way to a hyperrationalism of the sort that Epictetus taught but could not justify with the resources of pagan philosophy alone. It will be sixteen hundred years before anyone fully realizes the possibilities of such a metaphysics, and when Spinoza finally does, it will only be after having concluded that the theology of divine creation that prepares the way for it must be dismissed as an irrational myth.

A VIRTUE AS VAST AS LIFE ITSELF

Lucius Annaeus Seneca was born in Spain, a half century before Epicte-tus, to a family of wealth and privilege. As a young man, he studied rhetoric and philosophy in Rome and later served in the imperial household. At the age of sixty-five, on Nero's orders, he committed suicide for his alleged role in a plot against the emperor.

Seneca's essays constitute one of the largest bodies of Stoic writing to have come down to us from antiquity. The longest of these is entitled *De Beneficiis* (On Favors).

The subject of *De Beneficiis* is the giving and receiving of gifts. Seneca deals with the topic in considerable detail. To whom should one make gifts? On which occasions? How should gifts be acknowledged? When should a gift be refused? What, for example, "should a prisoner do if a male prostitute infa-mous for his oral activities offers the money for his ransom?"[29] Seneca calls this a "genuinely debatable" question and discusses the pros and cons at length.

It appears from Seneca's essay that the nature of gift-giving was a familiar topic of Stoic reflection. He refers several times to an earlier, now lost, trea-tise by Chrysippus on the subject.[30] But, according to Seneca, Chrysippus treated the matter in a superficial way. He failed to grasp the deepest truth about it—that the process of giving and receiving favors "more than anything else holds human society together."[31] This process is symbolically represented by the Three Graces, who are classically depicted "holding hands in a dance that goes back on itself."[32] What is "the point" of this image? "That there is a sequence of kindnesses, passing from one hand to another, which comes back nonetheless to the giver, and that the beauty of the whole is lost if the sequence is anywhere interrupted, while it is loveliest if it hangs together and the suc-cession is maintained."[33]

It is a virtue to maintain this sequence and a vice to disrupt it—indeed, the greatest vice of all, since what is broken are the bonds of human society itself. The name of this vice is ingratitude. "Among our numerous major vices," Seneca says, "none is more common than ingratitude."[34] It is something even worse that murder, robbery, adultery, and treason against the state, all of which "spring from ingratitude, without which no major crime comes to its full size."[35] Ingratitude is the "greatest of crimes"[36] and gratitude a virtue "as vast as life itself."[37]

In Aristotle's ethics of pride, gratitude occupies a marginal place. That is because it demands the acknowledgment of one's dependence on others—the admission of a lack of the self-sufficiency that every fully realized human being enjoys. A donor is more of a man than his recipient, and the gratitude the latter feels compelled to express reflects his relative lack of reality.

The human beings in Aristotle's world possess varying degrees of reality. They form a graduated chain of splendor and obscurity that is visible for all to see. Behind it, there is no other invisible realm in which all men stand on a par. The deepest longing of every human being is to move as far up the chain as his circumstances permit—to become as real as he can. The gratitude of the dependent man, who must look to others for support, is an expression of his failure to achieve the same degree of being as that of his donor, who stands higher in the chain.

Seneca reverses this order of values. He moves the slavish virtue of gratitude to a position of central importance and inflates its opposite into a crime of equal proportions. Aristotle's confident judgment that the grateful man is deficient in being, and his life less worthy as a result, is wholly missing from Seneca's essay. Indeed, it is not just missing, as if Seneca had lost his nerve and could no longer summon Aristotle's easy aristocratic disdain. Seneca's entire discussion is based on three assumptions that together undermine the metaphysical foundation of Aristotle's belief that gratitude is at best a servile necessity, and justify its conversion into a virtue of supreme importance instead.

Seneca insists, first, that dependence is a universal human condition, neither to be avoided nor disparaged; second, that those who inhabit this condition are all fundamentally equal, despite the superficial social distinctions that set them apart; and, third, that their equality is a consequence of their possession of an invisible power of assent that every man enjoys to the same degree—of the inner freedom that Epictetus identifies as the key to our release from the prison of appearances. Together, these three ideas support a picture of human society that Aristotle would neither have recognized nor approved. It is the cosmopolitan picture of human relations that underlies Seneca's radically un-Aristotelian philosophy of favors.

CAN A SLAVE DO HIS MASTER A FAVOR?

If men had to live as "isolated individuals," they would be "the prey of animals, their victims, the best and easiest blood for them to shed." Other animals are born to "wander and live apart." They possess enough strength for self-defense. But human beings lack "powerful claws or teeth" to protect themselves. Hence, if they "lived in isolation," they would be "no match for anything."

Yet man is in fact "the master of all things." He enjoys a "dominion over all animals," and is "lord even of the sea." He possesses these extraordinary powers not by virtue of his physical strength but on account of "reason and fellowship." It is man's capacity for fellowship that makes him the "strongest of all" animals—that "holds back the onslaught of disease, spies out supports for his old age, comforts him in pain." "Take away this fellowship and you tear apart the unity of mankind that sustains our life" and enables us to rule the world.[38]

But how is such fellowship possible? Seneca's answer is, through an "exchange of favors." "Our safety depends on the fact that we have mutual acts of kindness to help us."[39] The original source of all human power is the "sequence" of such acts, "passing from one hand to another," as represented by the round dance of the Graces. The social solidarity on which our strength depends begins, therefore, not with a formal agreement, motivated by individual self-interest, but with a series of gifts that circles back on itself, to the benefit of everyone involved. The most virtuous thing a person can do is to keep this circle moving. That is the function of gratitude. By contrast, "nothing so dissolves and disrupts the concord of mankind" as ingratitude. It is therefore "a thing to be shunned for itself," since it undermines the very possibility of the fellowship that is the ground of all civilized living.[40]

If the destructive effects of ingratitude are to be avoided, however, it is not enough that men be taught to be grateful for the sake of the benefits this brings. They must learn to be grateful on account of the intrinsic goodness of gratitude itself, for only an attitude of this sort gives the habit of gratitude the strength it needs to resist the pull of self-interest. There are "numerous people" who think they can "safely be ungrateful." If gratitude is tied too closely to their own well-being, they will be tempted to behave ungratefully when it appears to be in their self-interest to take favors without acknowledging them or making a suitable return. By doing this, however, they break the circle of gifts and lose the advantages of fellowship. If these are to be retained, the virtue of gratitude must be honored as a good in itself.

"[A] thing is only said to be 'chosen for its own sake' if any extra benefits which it may contain are set aside and removed and it still attracts. Yes, it pays to be grateful. But I will be grateful even if it harms me. . . . [A man] may well do everything that a good and dutiful friend should do. But if the idea of gain comes into his mind, he is simply fishing, sinking the hook. . . . A grateful mind is one that is captivated by the sheer goodness of its intentions."[41]

The circle of kindnesses on which our safety and comfort depend thus rests on a kind of paradox, for these can be secured only by means of a morality of gratitude that ignores them.

The naturally defenseless condition of men; their consequent need for fellowship; and the dependence of this fellowship on a spirit of gratitude that values the doing of favors and the acknowledgment of them as a good in itself, together constitute the universal circumstances that in Seneca's view shape the lives of men everywhere, regardless of their political or social condition. There is nothing peculiarly Athenian or Roman about them. The state of safe and civilized existence that gratitude alone makes possible is one that all men desire and seek to inhabit. It is not a *polis* but a *cosmopolis*. Outside of this *cosmopolis,* there is no human life of any kind at all, and within it no one is exempt from the duty to be grateful, which falls on every man with equal weight.

The equality of this duty is made particularly clear by Seneca's discussion of "the question of whether a slave can do his master a favor."[42] The question appears to have been a topic of discussion in earlier Stoic treatments of the subject, and Seneca clearly thought it quite important. His own answer is emphatic.

> [T]o deny that a slave may sometimes do his master a favor is to ignore his rights as a man. What matters is the state of mind, and not the status, of whoever bestows it. No one is barred from being good. Virtue is open to everyone, admits everyone, invites everyone— freeborn, freedman and slave, king and exile. It does not have to choose the great house or the great fortune; it is content with the naked man. What safety could there be against sudden changes, what grandeur could the mind promise itself, if its sure virtue were transformed by a change of fortune?[43]

A slave finds himself in his position by "fortune." It is his "lot"[44] to be a slave compelled to perform "menial services" for others. Yet the fact that their fortunes differ so dramatically should not obscure the deeper respect in which free men and slaves are alike.

To begin with, even the most powerful man sometimes finds himself in a situation where his safety and well-being depend on the favors of servants and slaves. Slaves owe their masters certain fixed duties. But "some [of a slave's] actions] are neither prescribed nor forbidden by law."[45] There is therefore always some discretionary room for a slave to do his master a favor, and it occasionally happens that his master's life depends on one. Seneca recounts several well-known examples.[46]

In fact, Seneca says, not even the greatest wealth and power can protect a man from the dangers to which all human beings are exposed on account of their natural vulnerabilities. So far as these are concerned, every man is in the same position. Nor does his lack of wealth and power deprive even a slave of all opportunities to do another a favor. Each human being is as vulnerable and dependent as the next one, and able to provide the gratuitous help that others sometimes require. In both respects, the human condition is one of equality, despite the superficial differences of status that set men apart.

The case of the slave who does his master a favor is important because it underscores their common humanity. It shows that master and slave are equals in the giving and receiving of favors. To insist that a slave cannot do his master a favor, merely on account of his position, is therefore "to ignore his rights as a man."

If a slave were unable to do his master a favor simply because of his status, he would be shut out from the circle of gift-giving on which all social life depends. He would be "barred from being good" and thus denied a share in the happiness that only participation in this virtuous circle can bring. And if that were true, no one could be protected against the danger of such unhappiness, since "sudden changes" of fortune may result in the loss of wealth, power, and juridical freedom. Seneca wants to reassure his readers that the mind can "promise itself" a life of "grandeur" and true "virtue" despite such reversals. But to do this he must detach the attainment of virtue from all the outward circumstances that determine a man's social position and material resources. He must *interiorize* it, just as Socrates does by insisting that no change of fortune in the world of appearances can ever touch the virtue and happiness of a soul in the right condition. Seneca explains his position in words that might have been Socrates' own.

> [I]t is a mistake to think that slavery penetrates the entire man. The better part of him is exempt. Bodies can be assigned to masters and be at their mercy. But the mind, at any rate, is its own master, so free in its movements that not even this prison which shuts it in can hold it back from following its own impulse, from setting mighty projects in motion, from faring forth into the infinite to consort with the stars. The body, therefore, is what fortune hands over to a master, what he buys and sells. That inner part can never come into anyone's possession. Whatever proceeds from it is free.[47]

Seneca's Socratic portrait of the relation between masters and slaves differs fundamentally from Aristotle's account of the matter.

According to Aristotle, some men are so lacking in the ability to direct their own lives that they must take direction from others. He calls such men slaves "by nature."[48] A natural slave is like a child, only permanently so. He is an immature human being whose potential has been incompletely realized. By comparison with a normally developed man, his humanity is not fully at work. He is a dim bulb whose glow is barely perceptible. Children are like this too, but generally brighten with time. They grow into the active exercise of their powers. Natural slaves never do. They are caught forever at a stage of arrested development.

Of course, Aristotle recognized that there are also slaves "by convention"— enslaved war captives and the like. But their condition has a practical explanation. That of natural slaves must be accounted for on metaphysical grounds. It can only be explained in terms of the distinction between potency and act that underlies Aristotle's theory of motion in general. These terms define a difference in the grades of being that different things and states of things possess, within a world of appearances that conceals no other, invisible realm behind it. Together they provide the backdrop for Aristotle's judgment that certain men are naturally fit to rule over others—a proposition he accepts with the same confidence that Homer had before him.

Given his belief in natural slavery, Aristotle would have been baffled by Seneca's claim that every slave has rights as a man and is the equal of his master because he can do him a favor. But he would have been even more puzzled by the metaphysical assumption on which this claim is founded—that behind the visible world of human striving, with its gradations of brightness and being, there is another, unseen realm in which all men stand on a common ground of equal freedom. Seneca shares the idea of such a realm with Plato and earlier Stoic writers. Indeed, it plays such a crucial role in his account of the phenomenon of gift-giving that one might fairly call it the principal theme of *De Beneficiis* as a whole.

TRANSACTIONS OF THE MIND

Every gift involves two persons, a donor and a recipient. What is essential to the relation on both sides, Seneca says, is the party's state of mind.

Consider the donor first. What is the nature of the favor he performs? A favor is "[a]n act of benevolence bestowing joy and deriving joy from bestowing it, with an inclination and spontaneous readiness to do so. Thus what matters is not the deed or the gift but the mentality behind them: the kindness lies not in the deed or gift but in the mind itself of the person responsible for the deed or gift."[49]

Seneca makes this point repeatedly. "A favor cannot possibly be touched by the hand; the transaction takes place in the mind. There is a great difference between its material and the favor itself. So it is not the gold or silver, or any of those things that are accepted as so important, that constitutes the favor, but rather the good will of whoever bestows it. The ignorant, however, take note only of what meets the eye, which can be handed over and held in possession, while attaching little value to what is dear and precious in itself."[50] "In doing a favor I am not grasping at profit, nor at pleasure, nor at glory. Content to please one person only, I shall give for the sole purpose of doing what ought to be done."[51]

Whether a benefit is a favor thus depends entirely on the donor's intentions, not its material value. Even a benefit of great value is not a favor if it is given with the wrong or no intention. If it is given, for example, in order to create a debt and with the expectation that it will be repaid, it is not a favor but a "business deal."[52] "There is no such thing as a favor with gain as its object. To 'give this and get that' is just a commercial transaction."[53] Similarly, if a benefit comes with no intention attached, if it is "granted unthinkingly," the recipient has "only himself" to thank for it.[54] The benefit "is not a favor but a windfall."[55] Only those benefits that are bestowed with the welfare of the recipient in mind, and nothing else, count as true favors. All others belong to the realms of entitlement or luck.

Intentions are just as decisive on the recipient's side. The gratitude with which he receives his gift is also an act of the mind or will, which Seneca treats indifferently. "Since we refer everything to the mind, a person acts only to the extent that he willed his action; and since piety, good faith, justice—in short, every virtue—is complete in itself, even if it is prevented from raising a finger, human gratitude, too, can be an act of will alone."[56] Accept a favor "with good will" and "you have already repaid it."[57]

In one sense, of course, to repay a favor the recipient must give something in return that is "similar to what was received." But circumstances may prevent him from doing this. He may have no resources with which to make a gift or no opportunity to do so. Still, even if he cannot give anything in return, he can be adequately grateful merely by accepting the gift in the right frame of mind. The gift is a favor because it is given with the proper intention, and "we have requited the [donor's] act of will with our own act of will" by "gladly accepting" his gift, though we have not yet made, and may be unable to make, a like gift in return.[58] Indeed, "just remembering [the gift]—and with no outlay at all—means that [the recipient is] grateful. It requires no effort, no resources, no luck; and failure to provide it has no excuse behind which to shelter."[59]

The utter interiority of gratitude; its complete independence of external conditions; and our power to decide, with perfect self-control, whether to be grateful or not, are all emphasized and their relations brought out in a remarkable passage that echoes Socrates' reply to Glaucon's challenge and anticipates Kant's description of the good will.[60]

> A grateful mind is one that is captivated by the sheer goodness of its intentions. . . . A person is called grateful if he has given something back in return for something received. Quite possibly, he can show off; he has something to boast about, to flaunt. But a person can also be called grateful if he receives with a cheerful mind and owes cheerfully. And that is a matter for his private knowledge. What advantage can come to him from his private feelings? And yet, even if he can do nothing further, he is showing gratitude. . . . The assessment of this as of any other virtue depends entirely on his mental attitude. If it is as it should be, anything missing will be the fault of fortune. . . . Indeed, I will go further and say that a person can be grateful while seeming to be ungrateful, having been misinterpreted and traduced by people's opinion. Such a man can only follow his conscience. Eclipsed though it be, it brings him joy, protesting against reputation and public opinion. Relying in itself for everything, when it sees a vast crowd on the other side and a verdict contrary to its own, it refuses to count the ballots but carries the day with its own one vote. If it sees loyalty subjected to the penalties of treason, it remains on its pinnacle, steadfastly surmounting the punishment. . . . "What use to me are my good intentions now?" [such a man may ask.] These have their use even on the rack, even in the flames. Though these be applied to one limb after another, though little by little they make their way round my living body, though my very heart in the fullness of its good conscience drips with blood, it will rejoice in the flames through which its loyalty shines forth.[61]

Both the giving of favors and gratitude for them thus consist in a state of mind that donor and recipient have the power to bring about if they choose and whose moral worth is unaffected by such outward circumstances as the donor's social status or the recipient's ability to offer a comparable gift in return. These make the external conditions of men unequal. They fix their positions in various hierarchies of wealth, honor and power. But none of them matter so far as the relation of donor and recipient is concerned. This relation is the universal basis of man's social existence, and wherever it exists the parties to it stand on an equal footing as persons whose true nature consists not in any of those things that make some men shine more brilliantly than others in the world of sights and sounds, but in their possession of an invisible power of self-direction that Seneca calls "conscience," which all men possess to an identical degree and that can neither be enhanced by greatness of a conventional sort nor lost even in slavery.

Hence, for Seneca there can be no such thing as a natural slave. Every man has the ability to decide for himself whether he shall be virtuous and happy, and nothing can deprive him of these things if he exercises his mind in the proper way. The invisible dignity of mind is superior to all the splendors of the world, which count for nothing by comparison with it. Human fulfillment lies in the confident possession of this dignity and not in an educated "second nature" that builds upon gifts men possess to different degrees and whose development depends on the good fortune of receiving the kind of training required to shape them into the virtues of courage, prudence and the like. It is therefore equally available to all.

These are the core teachings of Seneca's philosophy of gratitude, which devalues the world of appearances and exalts the unseen realm of mind or will. Together they define a cosmopolitan view of life that is universalist, egalitarian, and committed to the principled separation of dignity from glory. It is a philosophy well suited to the imperial circumstances in which Seneca framed it, and even more important, one that occupies a transitional position between an older pagan conception of the human condition and the Christian view of man and the world that eventually displaced it. For with its emphasis on the equal dignity of all men everywhere, as citizens of a *cosmopolis* founded on relations of gift-giving that require only their goodwill to establish and sustain, Seneca's promotion of gratitude to first place among the virtues simultaneously turns Aristotle's *polis*-based philosophy of pride on its head, and prepares the way for the Christian theology of grace: *preparatio evangelica,* an anticipation of the good news that we are all the beneficiaries of God's saving gifts, for which the only appropriate response is a gratitude beyond our human power to adequately express.

THANKS FOR THE WORLD

In one crucial respect, however, Seneca's view of gratitude remains far removed from the spirit and teachings of the Christian religion. That is because his philosophy, like that of Epictetus, is still guided by the rationalism that underlies all pagan metaphysics. Seneca's attempt to extend the principle of gratitude to the world as a whole brings this out with special clarity.

In a moving and heartfelt passage, Seneca enumerates the wonders that make human life possible and enjoyable: "the blood which holds in the warmth of life with its circulation"; "those delicacies that excite the palate with their rare flavors"; "trees in such number with their several ways of bearing fruit"; "living creatures in every kind"; "rivers that gird the plains in most delectable meanderings or offer a road to commerce as they proceed in their vast and navigable course," and so on.[62] These all contribute to our comfort and pleasure. They are not, however, mere accidents. They are the features of a world that has been arranged for our sake, as a human habitation. In this sense, they are favors.

"What leads heaven to complete its orderly changes? What leads the sun to lengthen and shorten the day? All these are favors. They are done to help us. It is the function of heaven to bring round the ordered cycle of things, of the sun to change the position of its rising and setting, and to do this for our well-being without recompense."[63] Seneca describes the whole world as a "huge residence"[64] that has been built for our use and enjoyment.

The architect of this residence is God, for whose many and magnificent gifts we have reason to be grateful. Indeed, our thankfulness to God should be greater than the gratitude we owe other men in the same proportion as his gifts exceed theirs. However much gratitude we owe our fellow human beings, we ought to be more grateful still to the God who made the world for our benefit, as a gift, with no demand for compensation.

But Seneca's own philosophy puts an obstacle in the way of this conclusion.

The extension of gratitude from the human to the cosmic level is natural enough. We are all struck from time to time by the fecundity and beauty of the world, and the thought that it has been arranged for our benefit is one that is likely to occur to most of us, at least occasionally. But Seneca insists that the order of the world is ordained by "fate."[65] Everything that happens in it does so on account of "a chain of connected causes" that unfolds in accordance with the dictates of reason. The world is shot through with reason.

Its processes are ordained by reason and could not possibly be other than they are without violating the requirements of reason itself, as Epictetus and other Stoics before him maintained. The many good things in the world of which we are the beneficiaries therefore exist by necessity, and while we certainly have reason to be happy that the world is arranged as it is, it is hard to see why we should be grateful for its rationally necessitated order, since what cannot be otherwise can never be a gift.

If another man does something that he is compelled by fate to do and I happen to be benefitted by his actions, my benefit, Seneca says, is a windfall, not a favor. It is merely a piece of good fortune for which I have no reason to be grateful. Similarly, if God or "nature" is constrained by reason to produce the results it does, it is difficult to see what gratitude is called for, however much these work to the benefit of human beings.

That the world is a comfortable home for men is just the wonderful way the compulsory power of reason causes things to be. The "spontaneous readiness" that Seneca insists lies at the root of all true benevolence is missing at this cosmic level, and without it, there can be no free intention of the sort that alone makes something a gift, according to Seneca's own definition of it. The recipient of a benefit has reason to be grateful to his donor only where a spontaneity of this sort exists. The gratitude of the one is therefore tied to the freedom of the other; if the latter disappears, the former does so as well.

Seneca's wish to enlarge the gratitude we feel toward other human beings into a thankfulness for the world as a whole may be a natural one, as he suggests, but his own intellectualist understanding of the world as a cosmos governed by reason makes this impossible. Seneca himself perhaps saw this, and any reader of *De Beneficiis,* reflecting on the tension between its author's insistence on the spontaneity of giving and gratitude, on the one hand, and his emphasis on the utter fatality of the world, on the other, is bound to notice it too.

What is needed to support a cosmic gratitude of this kind is a radically different idea of divinity, one that views God not as the inherent intelligibility of the world but its transcendent creator instead—the idea of God as a being apart from the world, possessed of a freedom so large that even reason cannot constrain it. This is the biblical idea of God as an omnipotent lord of creation, which not only allows but compels us to think of the world as a gift, and to reimagine the freedom of human beings in the image of God's own.

Seneca carries the idea of freedom as far as the tradition of classical rationalism allows. But he still accepts the pagan equation of God with reason and of both of these with the world, and thus lacks the metaphysical resources to justify a cosmic gratitude of the sort he seems to have wished to embrace. For that, the biblical understanding of freedom is required. In the biblical view, God is free because he has a will and man is free because God gave him one. Beginning with Augustine, the Christian philosophers who sought to give the idea of the will content and meaning construed it on the biblical model, as a power of creation from nothing. In part III, we shall examine this most unclassical of all ideas in more detail and explore the contradictions of the theology that rests upon it. Then we shall follow its unraveling to the end, until we arrive back where we began, in the homeless, loveless world of those who still embrace the metaphysics of the Christian religion but no longer have faith in its God, though with a better understanding of how we came to be here and brighter prospects for recognizing the other God in which we already believe.

PART THREE

Salvation

CHAPTER 11

❖━━━◆◦◦◆◦◦◆━━━❖

Creation

MAKING, BEGETTING AND CREATING

"Most glorious is the City of God: whether in this passing age, where she dwells by faith as a pilgrim among the ungodly, or in the security of that eternal home which she now patiently awaits until 'righteousness shall return unto judgment,' but which she will then possess perfectly, in final victory and perfect peace."[1]

So begins *The City of God,* Augustine's great panorama of Christian life.

Augustine began writing his book shortly after the sack of Rome in 410 C.E. He completed it in stages over the next fifteen years, amidst countless other duties and distractions. In a letter to a friend to whom he had sent the first installment in 413, Augustine famously describes the work as a "magnum opus et arduum." It is his greatest achievement and a cornerstone of Christian piety.

That we are wayfarers in the world; that the world will one day pass away; that our real home is elsewhere, with God, who is everlasting; that only those who have been saved by the grace of God from the wreckage of the world shall not perish with it but be resurrected at the end of days and live forever in his presence: these are Augustine's defining commitments.

Augustine believed that the greatest good a human being can achieve is salvation from the world as we know it. This world is a pandemonium of change—a pointless succession of birth and death, suffering and inevitable loss. There is no resting place within it that can ever satisfy our longing for eternity—no point of view from which the senseless motions of the world can be seen to have some permanent meaning and value. For that, we must look beyond the world to God, whose eternal life is our only hope for salvation. The beginning of wisdom is the knowledge that in this all-too-familiar world of love affairs and funerals, political quarrels and natural marvels, we can never be more than transients. The pathos of pilgrimage is the defining spirit of *The City of God*.

The idea that we are pilgrims in the world would have been incomprehensible to Aristotle. Aristotle recognized, of course, that we are mortal beings, and he acknowledged that our limits prevent us from engaging continuously in thought, the highest level of activity, and therefore of reality, that any human being can attain. But he also believed that we are able to reach this summit in our lives and that in reaching it we experience all the world has to offer—the one and only world there is. It would never have occurred to him to think that we must wait until we die to reach the peak of being. Aristotle believed that man is at home in the world, without denying that we have limits we can never surpass.

Both Aristotle and Augustine assume that what is motionless and therefore eternal has the highest degree of reality that anything can possess. Both further assume that everything that moves and exists in time is intelligible only in relation to what does not. And both agree that the yearning for eternity is our deepest desire. But to reach the motionless terminus of movement, Aristotle did not believe it necessary to leave the world behind. He did not think one has to be saved from the world. The very idea of salvation in this sense—Augustine's sense—is entirely foreign to Aristotle's thought.

For Aristotle, eternity is not something apart from the world. It is the intelligible form of the world itself, which has neither a beginning nor an end in time. Properly understood, eternity is just the enduring shape of time. This makes it possible to satisfy our desire for eternity in this world, by grasping its everlasting form with our minds. Aristotle's world is a home for man, as it is for every other being in the cosmos, all of whom are equipped to partake of its divinity in the manner their natures allow. To this conception of the world and our place in it, Augustine's portrait of man as a homeless pilgrim offers the sharpest possible contrast and marks the most momentous divide in Western thought.

HOMECOMING

Augustine was not the only thinker in late antiquity to maintain that the world is not our home. Homelessness is an important theme in the Neoplatonic tradition as well. Augustine had a good understanding of Neoplatonism and for a time at least, before his conversion to Christianity, enthusiastically embraced its main ideas.

Inspired by Plato's distinction between the fleeting world of appearances and the timeless world of ideas, Plotinus and his followers sought to explain how these two realms can be joined. This had been the main challenge for Platonism from the start. Plotinus met it by hypothesizing a graduated series of intermediate levels of being that link the highest and lowest orders of reality in a seamless continuum. The Neoplatonists taught that the material world in which we live, with its instabilities and imperfections, and the immaterial and immobile source of being from which it derives, are joined by a hierarchy of intervening "emanations," each the product of the exuberant unfolding of the (not fully containable) reality of the level immediately above it. According to Plotinus and his student Porphyry, the entire series forms a continuous and dynamic whole, moving from being to nothingness, intelligibility to ignorance, light to dark, in which the human soul occupies a middle position.

Those who took this teaching seriously were bound to feel a sense of remoteness from the source or ground of their own being. Plato had encouraged such feelings by describing the soul as a higher reality, immortal and pure, trapped in a polluting and impermanent body, from which it completely escapes only at death.[2] Neoplatonism intensified this feeling and provided a rigorous intellectual discipline by means of which the human soul, lost in a world of appearance and change, might climb up toward a reunion with God, in a process that Plotinus and his followers describe as one of homecoming.[3]

The followers of the third century Persian mystagogue Mani subscribed to a theocosmic philosophy that reflected a similar sense of man's homelessness in the world.[4] Augustine studied their teachings too and as a young man was strongly attracted to them.[5]

The Manicheans imagined the world to be a vast battlefield on which two great gods—one good, the other evil—fight for cosmic control. Neither is the product or descendent of the other. Each is an independent, aboriginal power, and everything in the world is caught in the struggle between them. Our souls are an especially important prize in their war for control. We are pawns on the field of battle, and experience this conflict within ourselves as the struggle between our good and bad instincts.

In the Manichean view of the world, the human soul is a fallen fragment of light. It belongs, by origin, to the kingdom of good, but now finds itself in the clutches of the power of evil, represented above all by the body. Its condition is like that of a soldier taken prisoner by an opposing army. All the soul's energies must therefore be bent toward a single goal—to escape captivity and return to its original home. The Manicheans taught that in this life we are prisoners of war, yearning for our day of release. They elaborated a complex theology to support this idea and developed highly refined intellectual and ritual techniques to help their followers implement it as a practical strategy for living.

Augustine's mature writings show the influence of Manichean as well as Neoplatonic ideas. His youthful engagement with their philosophical teachings continued to shape his thinking for the rest of his life. But Augustine's own Christian theology of suffering and salvation depicts man's homelessness in this world in a fundamentally different light. It portrays our present separation from God as a less remediable and therefore more anguishing condition. That is because Augustine rejects the rationalist premise on which these other theologies are based.[6]

Both the Neoplatonists and Manicheans acknowledged that our current condition is one of ignorance and vice. But they insisted with equal fervor that however far removed we may now be from our divine source, there is no radical discontinuity between our souls in their present state and the God we long to reach. In their view, we are connected to the ultimate ground of our being by an unbroken chain of increasingly intelligible levels of reality. Both Plotinus and Mani reassured their followers that they could ascend this chain to its very beginning if they used the minds they already possessed in a disciplined way.

This is something, they claimed, that we are able to do here and now. We may be distracted by appearances and misled by carnal desire. But we have the power to understand the divine reality that lies behind the world we see around us. This power may be dimmed and damaged but it cannot be destroyed. Moreover, the power in question is not merely aligned with the God it strives to apprehend. It is that God itself. It is the real if occluded residue of divinity in us. Through it we are able to escape the prisons of our lives and come home to God, like returning to like, in a reunion that we can achieve even in this world because the essential natures of what is reunited are exactly the same.

This is the hopeful promise of Plato's program for overcoming the vicissitudes of time. Plato separated the world from eternity with a rigor that Aristotle denied. In doing so, he made man homeless in the world, and encouraged the belief that the world is a condition from which we need to be saved (an idea that has no real counterpart in Aristotle's philosophy). But he also established a bridge of reason between the world and God that assured the possibility of salvation even in the midst of our cave-like existence. However far apart he set them, the world and God thus remained for Plato joined by an umbilical cord of mind that a thoughtful man, freed from the chains of opinion, might use to cross from one to the other. On Plato's view, our estrangement from God is therefore remediable here on earth, once we clear our minds of confusion.

Neoplatonism and Manicheanism followed the same basic pattern. They differed profoundly in other ways. The first was resolutely monistic; the second taught a cosmic dualism of warring gods. But both affirmed the intellectual continuity of the human soul with the source or ground of its own being and professed the possibility of a homecoming to God under the circumstances of human life as we know it.

Augustine emphatically denies this possibility. He insists that God's nature is radically different from ours, and that man's present distance from God is greater than any rationalist allows it to be. For Augustine, the gulf between creator and creature is absolute and incurable. There is no way to cross it, so long as we live in this world. Augustine's rejection of the rationalism on which both the Neoplatonists and Manicheans based their hopes for salvation in this life left man estranged from God in a new and more unsettling way, with no hope of escaping his homelessness through reason alone.

Augustine embraced this conclusion. Indeed, he celebrated it as an expression of Christian piety. That is because he defined God in a way that neither Plato nor any of his successors would have understood. For Augustine, God is a creator. He brought the world into being from nothing. This is God's most important characteristic, in both metaphysical and ethical terms. Yet it is one that the rationalist metaphysics of pagan antiquity is incompetent to explain.

GENESIS

"When God began to create the heaven and the earth, the earth was unformed and void, with darkness over the surface of the deep and a wind from God sweeping over the water. God said, 'let there be light'; and there was light."[7]

We cannot say for certain when these words were written, or by whom, or how they were understood by the person or persons who wrote them. We have only a limited knowledge of the other, earlier myths that lie behind them.[8] But we do know that they provided the inspiration for an utterly novel account of God's relation to the world that was first worked out in a philosophically rigorous way by the early Fathers of the Christian church.

The Church Fathers maintained that the opening words of the Hebrew Bible describe God's creation of the world from nothing. They emphasized that the idea of divine creation is unintelligible from the standpoint of Greek thought and stressed the differences between the pagan and biblical conceptions of God. But they were not the first to make this point. It had already been explored at length by Philo Judaeus, a philosophically educated Jew living and working in Hellenistic Alexandria during the years that Jesus was preaching in Palestine.[9]

In his voluminous writings, Philo sought to show that the wisest teachings of the Greek philosophers had all been anticipated by Hebrew Scripture, and that where conflicts exist, the scriptural view should be preferred. Among other things, Philo analyzed in detail the creation story in Plato's *Timaeus,* the best known philosophical account of the origin of the world to survive from Greek antiquity.[10] In his careful and nuanced treatment of the *Timaeus,* Philo emphasized the several ways in which Plato's account differs from that found in Genesis, noting in particular the absence from the former of anything resembling the idea of creation from nothing.

It is plausible to locate the beginning of philosophical reflection on this idea in Philo's discussion of Plato's *Timaeus.* But Philo's refined speculations had little immediate influence on other Jewish thinkers. In the centuries that followed, the intellectual energies of the Jews were deployed in a different direction. The great Jewish thinkers of the rabbinic period devoted themselves to the development of a body of laws and legal commentary that was intended to provide a biblically inspired framework for the regulation of life in all its details, so that the Jews might be able to continue to observe the commandments of God in the Diaspora in which it was now their fate to live. The Babylonian and Palestinian Talmuds are the culmination of this effort, and while there is much in them that might be called philosophical, their guiding spirit is not. They are the highest expression of a juridical civilization—one whose most representative and valued form of intellectual work is the kind in which lawyers and judges engage, reflecting on cases, testing general principles against the facts of particular relations and situations, seeking consistency of norms while providing useful solutions to real problems as these arise in the ordinary course of life. In the juristic world of rabbinic Judaism, Philo's philosophical reflections on Plato's *Timaeus* had little traction and no future.[11]

But they did have a future in the very different environment of early Christian thought. The Church Fathers were metaphysically inclined in ways their rabbinic counterparts were not. Many of them had been trained in philosophy before converting to Christianity, and were accustomed to using philosophical methods both to defend their beliefs against critics and to make them more attractive to converts. The milieu in which Christianity consolidated its teachings and defined its distinctive view of the world thus had a decidedly philosophical cast that made it more welcoming to Philo's speculations about the meaning of divine creation. It was in this philosophically charged environment that the idea of creation from nothing first began to be explored, and its implications probed, with an intellectual precision that had lasting consequences not only for Christian dogmatics but for the metaphysical and moral foundations of Western thought as a whole.

The sharpness with which patristic writers steeped in the culture of pagan philosophy eventually came to formulate the idea of creation from nothing was a result, in part, of their desire to distinguish it from two other ideas that pagan writers had long employed to explain the origin of the world.[12] These were the ideas of begetting and making. The philosophical concept of creation from nothing, which the Church Fathers read into the magnificent but obscure opening words of the Hebrew Bible, was defined in opposition to both.

BEGETTING AND MAKING

In book 7 of the *Metaphysics,* Aristotle takes up the subject of what he calls "comings-to-be."[13] This is a general category that includes any movement or change through which something comes to be what it is.

Aristotle is mainly interested in two kinds of coming-to-be, those that occur by nature (*phusis*) and those that are the product of art (*poesis*). The birth and growth of a human being is an example of the first, the construction of a house an example of the second. These are the paradigmatic forms of change to which Aristotle returns, again and again, in an effort to explain what it means for anything to become what it is.

There are of course important differences between natural and artificial
comings-to-be. One is that the builder who is the source or cause of the
coming-to-be of a house does not himself have the form of the house he makes.
He has the form of a man. He has the form of the house only in his mind,
not in himself. He does not "embody" the form of the house he builds but
merely "contemplates" it as a blueprint of the house he is making. By contrast,
in the case of the child, parent and progeny both possess the same form. The
child's father has the same kind of being as the child he begets. They are both
human beings and look fundamentally alike, whereas the builder and his
house do not resemble one another at all.

A second difference is that a child, once conceived, continues to grow on
its own. It has, as Aristotle says, a source of motion in itself. This may be deflected or extinguished by outside forces, but unless it is, continues to move
the child forward along its natural course of development. A house also continues to change once it has been built, but only through the effect on it of
external influences of one kind or another—of the weather, for example, and
of the natural tendency of its materials to decay (which is also something external to the house, understood as an artifact defined by the distinctive kind
of unity its maker has given it). Houses weather and decay but unlike human
beings, neither grow nor die.

These are important differences between productive and generative
comings-to-be. Yet both share something fundamental in common, for in neither case does the thing that comes to be—the child or the house—come to
be from nothing. In both, it comes to be from something. More precisely, it
comes to be from *two* things that precede it: from a preexisting form and an
already given reservoir of material stuff.

The form that exists beforehand has a different location in the two
cases. In one, it is present in the thoughts of the builder. In the other, it is
located in the father himself. But in both, the form of the thing that
comes to be already exists somewhere or other. And so does its matter,
which in the case of the house consists of the materials stored in the builder's shed, and in that of the child, of the bodies of its parents (or perhaps just
its mother).

The comings-to-be of the house and the child thus presuppose that their
form and matter are both present beforehand. In what, then, does their
coming-to-be consist? Aristotle gives the only answer he thought possible.
It consists in the joinder of these preexisting but separate components. For
Aristotle, there is no other way to explain any coming-to-be. It follows that a

true creation from nothing is inconceivable, for "it is impossible that anything should be produced if there were nothing before."[14]

In the *Metaphysics,* Aristotle is mainly concerned with the coming-to-be of individual things, whether living or artificial. But when the Greeks speculated about the origin of the world as a whole, they imagined its cosmic coming-to-be on the model of one or the other of the two processes that Aristotle describes.

The nameless authors of the Olympian myths, for example, explained the existence of the world as the result of a process of generation, of gods begetting gods, in a long and fractious line of descent. This is also how Hesiod describes the origin of the world in his later poetic reworking of these stories.[15]

In the *Timaeus,* Plato describes the coming-to-be of the world as a process of making in which a divine craftsman joins form and matter to fashion the world, like a builder constructing a house. Many of the details of Plato's account are obscure. But one thing is clear. In Plato's view, the cosmos is the outcome of a process of production whose overseer imposes a set of preexisting ideas (to which he looks as he goes about his work) on a body of already existing material (the relatively, but not completely, formless "receptacle" that he molds in accordance with the principles that constitute his plan).[16] Plato's demiurge works on a larger scale than other craftsmen, but in these fundamental respects his efforts are no different than theirs.

Whether in myth, poetry or philosophy, Greek speculation about the origin of the world thus followed one of the two basic schemes that Aristotle identified as the only ones for explaining any substantial coming-to-be, the productive and the reproductive. So long as one adheres to the belief that something cannot come from nothing, as Aristotle insisted must be the case, there is no other way to explain the origin of the world. And if no other explanation is conceivable, then no other origin is possible—the critical "if" of all Greek rationalism, however expressed.

EX NIHILO

Neither of these two patterns applies to the creation of the world as it is described in the opening chapters of the Hebrew Bible and philosophically glossed by the Church Fathers.

To begin with, it is absurd for anyone who accepts the creation story of Genesis to suppose that the world originated in an act of begetting. The very idea is obscene. It is an offense to God's dignity to imagine him engaged in such an act. More fundamentally, it is a mistake to assume, as this idea does, that there is a community of being between God and the world like that between parent and child. The latter are individually distinct, but identical in kind. By contrast, the God of the Bible differs essentially from all of his creatures who, unlike him, depend on something outside themselves to exist. The idea that God begot the world mocks his supremacy and reduces his infinite power of command to the large but still human power of a Roman *pater familias*. (How the Son of God can be one in substance with his father, yet a distinct person nonetheless, remained a thorny question for Christian theologians, but one they all agreed cannot be answered in terms of reproduction, on the biological model of human fathers and sons.[17])

Nor can the world-creating God of Genesis be understood as a kind of divine craftsman. Even the most powerful craftsman depends on preexisting materials and ideas. Every act of making has external preconditions and is to that extent constrained. This is true even if the materials and ideas a craftsman uses are themselves the product of earlier acts of making, for these must have had their own preconditions as well. But the God who made the world "in the beginning" is not dependent on anything outside of or prior to himself. It is a blasphemy to suppose that he is. We are therefore compelled to imagine that his construction of the world was wholly unconstrained. Whatever materials he used to make it, and whatever principles or laws or ideas he employed to shape it, must themselves have been brought into being from nothing. The coming-to-be of the world therefore cannot be conceived either as a production or a reproduction even of the most original kind. It must be thought of as a creation, a kind of coming-to-be that is completely unintelligible from the standpoint of Greek thought.

The technical term the Church Fathers invented to describe the origin of the world was *creatio ex nihilo*. From creation in this sense, they carefully distinguished both begetting and making. But this gave rise to a philosophical question that no Greek thinker had had to confront. How was the nature of the power that God exercises in creating the world to be understood and explained? A father has the power to generate a child and exercises it by imposing his own form on the mother's receptive material. A builder has the power to build a house and puts it to use by shaping materials in accordance with a design. But the power that God employs when he creates the world cannot be likened to either of these, for his creativity does not depend on any antecedent condition, unlike that of both fathers and builders. If the creation of the world is a process utterly different from any act of production or reproduction, then the power that God exercises in bringing the world into being from nothing must likewise differ from those employed in these other, more familiar comings-to-be. But what is this power? And is it possible to give an account of it?

Augustine inherited these questions, at the end of the fourth century of Christian belief. His theory of the will is the first philosophically rigorous attempt to answer them. And it is with Augustine's idea of the will that the Christian drama of man's homelessness in the world truly begins.

CHAPTER 12

Will

HUMAN FREEDOM AND THE
PROBLEM OF EVIL

Augustine's concept of "free choice" (*liberum arbitrium*) has no counterpart in pagan philosophy. It is as foreign to the world of pagan thought as the idea of creation from nothing, which provides both its motive and model. Augustine drew on classical sources to construct his idea of the will. But the idea itself is completely original.

The phenomenon of choice had been carefully studied by many pagan thinkers. Aristotle, for one, offers a detailed account of the process by which a person makes the choice to pursue one course of action rather than another. He calls this process "deliberation" (*boulesis*), and assigns it a central place in moral life. The good man, he says, is one who deliberates well.[1] There are passages in Augustine's writings that echo this view.[2]

The Stoic concept of "assent" (*sunkatathesis*)[3] seems even closer to Augustine's idea of the will. Stoic writers from Chrysippus to Epictetus insist that we have the power to affirm or deny the countless impressions that bombard us, and to treat with indifference the desires that lead most men about by the nose. We retain this power even in the most confining conditions. Its inextinguishable presence in us guarantees that a self-sufficient, hence free and happy, life is always within reach. This is just what Augustine says about the liberating power of the will.

But Aristotle's account of deliberation and the Stoic doctrine of assent both rest on an assumption that is incompatible with Augustine's view of man's relation to God. The premise of every pagan theory of choice is that human actions are always directed either by reason or desire. The freedom that men enjoy to disobey God's commands, and their sole responsibility for the evil that results when they do, cannot be explained on this assumption. To account for the boundlessness of the freedom men possess, without which their responsibility for evil cannot be absolute, we have to assume the existence in them of a power determined neither by reason nor desire.

The doctrine of creation from nothing forces us to make a similar assumption about God. God is not compelled by either reason or desire to bring the world into being. Like man's freedom to sin, God's freedom to create is absolute. The creation of the world therefore becomes conceivable only when God's power of choice is assigned to a faculty that is wholly independent of these two determining causes. Indeed, it is the attribution to God of a power of this kind that compels Augustine to assign a free will to human beings as well. Thus while the pagan understanding of choice leaves no room for the idea of the will, Augustine's theology and ethics both demand it.

DELIBERATION AND ASSENT

For Aristotle, deliberation is always among alternatives that can be ranked as better or worse, given the end one is pursuing. In this sense, deliberation is always about means. If a person deliberates about ends, it has to be against the background of still higher-order ends that he takes for granted. This is what all practical reasoning is like, on Aristotle's view of it.

One implication is that there can be no deliberation about ultimate ends. No one deliberates about whether to seek happiness.[4] Another is that when the best course of action has been identified through a process of deliberation, the decision to pursue it is a *fait accompli*. No further act of choice remains to be performed.

There are of course men who know what is best but act otherwise. Aristotle calls this familiar phenomenon *akrasia*, a term often misleadingly translated as "weakness of will."[5] *Akrasia* literally means "absence of power." According to Aristotle, it is a defect of character. It is a kind of bad habit—a lack of discipline that prevents reason from asserting control over desire when and as it properly should. *Akrasia* is a constitutional vulnerability to temptation that undermines reason, not a choice that overrides it, as its standard translation implies. For an infirmity of this kind, the only cure is more discipline and better training, though beyond a certain age these are unlikely to have much effect.

Aristotle recognized that some men are fully capable of understanding what reason requires but powerless to follow its lead because their desires are badly disordered. But he had no conception of a power separate from reason and desire, with control over both. For Aristotle, choice is always subject to the sovereignty of reason, hence always constrained by it, and where a man fails to act as reason instructs him to do, that can only be because the frailty of his character allows his reasoned judgments to be overwhelmed by his passions.

Neither aspect of Aristotle's account of choice is compatible with the idea of a God who creates the world from nothing. Augustine's God is free to create when and how he chooses, or not to create anything at all. His choices are constrained neither by reason, like those of a virtuous man, nor by desire, like the choices of a weak man whose bad habits leave him exposed to temptation. Aristotle's explanation of how men deliberate and why they sometimes fail to follow reason's commands thus lacks the one idea that is essential to account for the possibility of creation from nothing. This is the idea of a power of spontaneous initiation that lies beyond the causal influence of reason and desire alike. And because human willfulness, which manifests itself most dramatically in the puzzling phenomenon of sin, presupposes the presence in man of a similar power, it too cannot be explained using Aristotle's concepts of deliberation and choice.

The Stoic idea of assent is equally unavailable for these purposes. The sage who cultivates his independence from those things that are not up to him does so in order to accommodate himself to the necessity that rules the world. The freedom his detachment brings is for the sake of an apathetic resignation to the divine order of the cosmos. Nothing could be further from the freedom of Augustine's God, for whom there is no order apart from the one that he creates. Nor is anything more remote from the attitude of the pious Christian who knows that his own will is the source of all the evil in the world, against which he must struggle in a posture of heightened responsibility that is the very opposite of the diminished self-regard Epictetus recommends.

The Stoic understanding of assent extends the idea of independence beyond Aristotle's conception of self-sufficiency as a set of aristocratic habits, grounded in a shared way of life. But even the Stoic doctrine of freedom remains within the orbit of Greek rationalism, which in all its many versions, from Plato on, assumes that freedom consists in the subjection of one's mind and character to reason, and servility in the overpowering of reason by desire.

The great Stoic teachers shared a particularly exaggerated commitment to this view. Whatever similarity the Stoic doctrine of assent might appear to have to Augustine's idea of the will, the two are therefore fundamentally incompatible. To make sense of the idea of creation from nothing, we must assume that God possesses the power to begin something entirely new, on his own, without an external cause originating in either reason or desire. Likewise, to account for the existence of evil, as distinct from the wearily familiar phenomena of weakness and error, we have to ascribe to human beings a similar power of uncaused invention. The rationalist philosophies of pagan antiquity, Stoicism included, lack the resources to explain the nature, or even the possibility, of such a power.[6]

Consequently, when Augustine set himself the task of explaining divine creation and human sin in a conceptually rigorous way, there were no precedents in pagan philosophy to which he might look as a model. All the ideas that seem to bear some resemblance to the Christian philosophy he hoped to construct were conditioned by assumptions that leave no room for the power to innovate that Augustine had to presuppose in order to explain the two most basic axioms of his theology: that in the beginning God created the world from nothing, and that man brought evil into the world through his own uncaused refusal to obey God's commands. To elucidate the nature of this power, Augustine had to turn his back on the whole long tradition of Greek rationalism and strike off in a new direction.

A THEOLOGICAL PROBLEM

The name that Augustine gives to the power that God employs in creating the world, and man in sinning against him, is neither deliberation nor assent but "will" (*voluntas*), a word with Roman legal antecedents that Augustine puts to novel philosophical use.[7]

Augustine's first and most systematic attempt at a theory of the will is contained in a work he began in the spring of 388 C.E., at the age of thirty-four, shortly after his baptism in Milan, and completed three years later in the North African seaport of Hippo, where he had been appointed bishop and would serve for the rest of his life. Written in the form of a dialogue, *De libero arbitrio* betrays on every page Augustine's deep knowledge of classical culture and its rhetorical traditions. Yet it belongs emphatically to the new world of Christian piety whose philosophical foundations in the Latin West Augustine's essay helped to establish.[8]

The central subject of the essay is man's will, not God's. But what Augustine says about the first is essential to understanding his view of the second, and vice versa. The two are deeply entwined. In part, that is because man's likeness to God consists in his possession of a will, so that a proper understanding of our freedom provides a clue to the nature of God's. But most importantly, it is because the argument that leads Augustine to his concept of the human will is shaped at every step by the doctrine of creation from nothing.

The starting point of *De libero arbitrio* is a theological dilemma that anyone who accepts this doctrine must confront. "Please tell me," says Evodius, Augustine's interlocutor, "isn't God the cause of evil?"[9]

In the Manichean system to which Augustine subscribed as a youth, the answer is clear. There are two gods, one good and the other evil, and all the evil in the world is ultimately attributable to the latter god, even though some of it occurs through his human agents. But this answer is unavailable to a Christian like Augustine, who is required to assume that there is a single omnipotent lord of creation.

Nor, on this same assumption, can the existence of evil be explained as a result of the inherent recalcitrance of the uncreated matter from which the world is made. If God is all powerful, there cannot be anything outside him that limits his ability to create—neither another god, with opposing aims, nor some preexisting stuff whose natural tendency is to resist God's efforts to shape and direct it, like the knots in a board that deflect the carpenter's plane. "The truest beginning of piety is to think as highly of God as possible; and doing so means that one must believe that he is omnipotent, and not changeable in the smallest respect; that he is the creator of all good things, but is himself more excellent than all of them; that he is the supremely just ruler of everything that he created; and that he was not aided in creating by any other being, as if he were not sufficiently powerful by himself. It follows that he created all things from nothing."[10]

But if God is omnipotent in the way that Christian piety demands, an obvious problem arises. For if this world has no other source than God, it seems to follow that he is responsible for the suffering and evil in it along with everything else.

A believing Christian is therefore caught in a dilemma. Either he must give up God's omnipotence, which means abandoning the idea of creation from nothing, or he must deny God's beneficence, and attribute to God everything that is bad in the world together with all that is good. Augustine was unwilling to do either. *De libero arbitrio* is his explanation of how it possible to avoid both of these unacceptable options.

Part of Augustine's answer is the same as the one that Epictetus had given centuries before to the question of why evil exists. For Epictetus, the world is a thoroughly rational and hence beneficent place. The appearance of the existence of anything bad in the world can therefore only be an illusion created by the limitations of our human understanding. Augustine says something similar. Certain things appear to us to be evil because our finite minds cannot grasp what he calls the "nature and grandeur" of God's creation. The suffering of animals and small children is an example. These seem to us an evil, but that is an illusion. We would be cured of it if we could see things from God's point of view, which of course we can't. Whenever we see something we think is evil, we must therefore remind ourselves that its existence is likely to be a mirage.

This familiar line of argument, which is entirely compatible with the rationalism of pagan philosophy, saves God's omnipotence without compromising his beneficence, but only by denying the reality of what it seeks to explain. Augustine's Christian answer to the question of how there can be evil in a world created by a God whose power is absolute only really begins at the point at which he acknowledges that some, at least, of the evil in the world really and truly exists, and cannot be dismissed as an illusion that greater knowledge would dispel.

Augustine was unwilling to abandon the ordinary moral point of view from which the reality of evil is taken for granted and to embrace a wisdom philosophy that denies its very existence. But in conceding the reality of evil, he created a difficulty for himself that no pagan rationalist had to resolve, for if even a portion of the evil in the world is real, then it is hard to understand why the omnipotent God who made the world from nothing is not responsible for its evil parts too.

Augustine begins to work his way out of this dilemma by distinguishing two sorts of suffering. Some suffering is innocent—for example, that of small children. They have done nothing to deserve their pain.[11] If we could see things from God's point of view, we would understand that their suffering is for the good of the world, hence not really bad at all.

But other suffering is not innocent. It is a penalty for misbehavior. This kind of suffering cannot just appear to be bad. To be a penalty and not a mere misfortune, it must be bad in reality, which means, even when viewed within the context of the world as a whole.

But if the suffering involved in punishment is real, then who is responsible for it? It does not compromise God's goodness to say that he is responsible for innocent suffering. We know, in principle at least, that suffering of this kind is not really bad. But the suffering involved in punishment is a different matter. If God is responsible for this sort of suffering too, then he must be the author of something really (and not just seemingly) bad. So God cannot be responsible for the suffering of those whose suffer on account of their wrongdoing. They must be responsible for it themselves. They, not God, must be the authors of all the *real* evil in the world.

But how can anyone other than God be the author of anything in the world, so long as we assume that God created the world and everything in it from nothing? Either someone other than God is responsible for the crimes that justify the suffering that all true punishment involves, in which case God is not the cause of absolutely everything in the world, or God is the cause of everything in the world, including these crimes, in which case their criminality and the reality of the pain imposed as a penalty for them are as much illusions as the suffering of children and animals. Augustine's attempt to avoid both horns of this dilemma sets the stage for his theory of the will.

THE FREEDOM TO DISOBEY

Every part of God's creation is directed toward some end and contributes to a cosmic scheme whose purpose is too large for us to grasp. The specific end toward which a particular creature is directed is the "law" of that creature's being. It constitutes the creature's "nature." Every one of God's creatures has a law, or nature, in this sense.

To certain of his creatures, however, God has given not merely a law but the power to affirm or repudiate it as well. Only men and angels have this power. They alone are able to obey or disobey the law that God has assigned them—to rebel against their natures. A horse may act abnormally. But its actions are not acts of disobedience. The law of its existence is not, for a horse, a command it has the power to refuse to obey. It is only a behavioral regularity. Departures from this law are not crimes but mere anomalies. If we understood them better, we would see that they are a part of God's overall plan.

By contrast, some of the departures from the laws that God has ordained for men and angels *are* criminal acts. They are the result of a deliberate decision not to act as God has commanded. For men and angels, God's laws are more than ordering principles. They are orders that may be refused or obeyed. It follows that only a man or an angel can be evil, unlike a horse, which may be fast or lame, but never wicked.

Correlatively, only men and angels can be morally good since only they have the power to choose to do what God tells them they should. Why God created a world with creatures of this kind, rather than one populated entirely by law-governed beings without the supplementary power to obey or disobey the laws he has assigned them, is a question beyond our ability to answer. We can only infer that God judged it best to do so, since the world he created has more than mere anomalies in it. It includes criminals as well, both human and angelic, whose crimes are the defining events in the dramatic career of the world as a whole.

Still, even if we cannot comprehend *why* the world includes crimes, we can understand *what* a crime is. We can explain the nature of the wrong it involves.

One ancient explanation of wrongdoing is that it is the result of ignorance.[12] On Plato's view, for example, a criminal acts as he does because he does not understand what he should do. His fault lies in the inadequacy of his powers of reasoning. If these were better developed, or more actively employed, he would be cured of his ignorance. He would see what he should do, and do it.

Another explanation is that crime is the product of passion. The criminal knows what the law commands but is overcome by a desire that gets the best of his understanding—perhaps because he is an *akratic* man who has failed to develop the habits he needs to channel his desires in a more constructive direction, or, like Oedipus, is blinded by pride.

Those pagan philosophers who sought to account for human wrongdoing typically invoked one or the other of these explanations, or some combination of both. But Augustine insists that the crime of disobeying God's laws cannot be explained as a consequence either of ignorance or desire, since this would have the effect of reducing or eliminating the criminal's blameworthiness for his acts. For Augustine, the truly criminal nature of such disobedience, which alone warrants its punishment and therefore explains the existence of real evil in the world, only comes into view when we move beyond the pagan categories of reason and passion and conceive man's disobedience to God as the act of a rebellious will.

Augustine acknowledges the contribution that reason makes to obedience. But reason merely identifies the law one must obey. Obedience is a separate

act that follows the preparatory work of reason and thus cannot be identified with it. "By reason one becomes capable of receiving a commandment to
which one ought to be faithful." Reason "grasps the commandment" but "the
will is what obeys" it.[13]

Because reason is merely propaedeutic to obedience, a refusal to follow
God's laws cannot be explained as a defect of reason. Indeed, the more perfect a man's reason becomes, the clearer it is that the source of his failure to
do what reason commands lies outside the faculty of reason itself, in a power
that remains to be exercised after reason has done all that it can. The more
complete his understanding of God's laws, the greater a man's crime in refusing to obey them.

Augustine is also painfully aware of the power of desire to distract and
deform us. He emphasizes, in particular, the power of sexual passion to lead
us astray, in part, perhaps, because of his own experience with it. But Augustine insists that disobedience to God's law is never merely a matter of being
overwhelmed by desire. It always involves something more—namely, a *capitulation* to desire that desire by itself is powerless to effect. However strong a
man's desires become, it always remains for him to decide whether to give in
to them or not, just as it always remains for him to decide whether to follow the
instructions of reason. Disobedience is a kind of defeat. But it is a defeat the
will brings on itself. It is never the triumph over the will of a desire external
to it, for no desire is powerful enough to defeat the will in this way. Only
the will has such power. The downfall of the will is always and only its own
doing.

Augustine's motives for seeking to base the explanation of crime on something other than reason and desire were partly psychological. He was impressed, as Paul had been before him, by his own personal experience of a
power of disobedience distinct from both reason and passion. In his youth,
Augustine had done things he knew he shouldn't and with no desire for the
benefits they would bring.[14] The memory of these episodes haunted him all
his life. Among other things, Augustine's theory of the will is an attempt to
account for such purely malevolent acts, done for the sheer sake of breaking
the rules they violate, which his own youthful experience made seem painfully real.

But Augustine also had a powerful theological motive for assigning the
responsibility for wrongdoing to the wrongdoer's will.

In order to account for the existence of the real evil that some forms of
suffering entail, in a way that is compatible with the assumption of God's

limitless power, Augustine had to explain such suffering as a punishment inflicted by God on those of his creatures with the power to disobey his laws, for their crimes of disobedience. And to make the perpetrators of these crimes sufficiently responsible to justify their punishment, he had to deprive them of every excuse they might otherwise have, including their ignorance of God's laws and inability to resist the compulsory force of desire.

To explain wrongdoing as a consequence either of ignorance or irresistible desire makes the wrongdoer less responsible for his actions and his punishment less just. If the awful pains that an omnipotent God inflicts on his disobedient creatures for their violations of his commands are to be justified at all, the cause of their actions must therefore be located in a power of the soul that is undetermined by reason and desire. Augustine felt compelled to assume the existence of such a power on account of his profound love of God, for without the freedom the human will possesses, God's punishment of man—even for his largest crimes—is bound to seem unworthy of a deity who is able to arrange the world as he wishes.

CAUSE OF ITSELF

But if the will is determined neither by reason nor desire, what is it determined by? Augustine gives the only other answer he thinks possible. The will is determined by itself.

A man's will cannot be caused to act by anything outside it, since that would negate the responsibility for evil that Augustine's theology requires him to place on human shoulders. The will must therefore be its own cause. For "what could be the cause of the will before the will itself? Either it is the will itself, in which case the root of all evils is still the will, or else it is not the will, in which case there is no sin. So either the will is the first cause of sin, or no sin is the first cause of sin. And you cannot rightly assign responsibility for a sin to anyone but the sinner; therefore you cannot rightly assign responsibility except to someone who wills it."[15]

This is a difficult concept to grasp. That a man causes other things to happen with his will seems understandable enough. But how his will can cause itself to act is hard to comprehend. Among other things, it appears to involve an infinite regress. If the will causes itself to act, does it also cause itself to cause itself to act? Yet it is important that we try to understand the idea of the will as cause of itself, for it holds the key to the essence of willing. When his young companion expresses bewilderment at the idea, Augustine tells him not to "be surprised" that "even though we use other things by free will, we also use free will itself by means of free will"[16]—and then attempts to explain what he means.

Every man has intelligence, desire and will. The first two are set in motion by something outside themselves—by the objects of thought and desire. For this reason, their motions are not ones for which we are responsible. They therefore lack inherent moral value. They acquire such value only when they are affirmed or repudiated by the will, which sets itself in motion in an act (as later philosophers will call it) of self-determination. It is only when this happens that a man becomes responsible for his beliefs and appetites. Responsibility for one's actions, and the fairness of punishing those who act wrongly, therefore presupposes the existence in man of a power to move himself—to begin an entirely new causal chain. This is something that neither reason nor desire can do, since their movements are always determined by a cause external to them. The essence of the will, as contrasted with these other parts of the human soul, is that it is the cause of its own motions.

In the most general terms, the idea of a power that moves itself was known to pagan theology too. Aristotle considered the existence of such a power a metaphysical necessity. It is impossible, he said, that everything should be moved by something else. There must be at least one thing that moves on its own account. He called it the "first" mover. But Aristotle identified the uncaused cause of things with the everlasting mindedness of the world. His first mover is this mindedness itself, working at the highest level of activity—mind minding mind. In this sense, Aristotle's self-caused cause is what the world really is, not something apart from it.

Augustine's interpretation of the will as cause of itself points in a different direction. In his view, the will does not belong to the world at all, let alone constitute its essence. A man's desires belong to the world (to him as a worldly being). And even his mind belongs to the world, insofar as it is led and directed by the order of things, which he discovers by "turning his mind" to it. But his will transcends the world in a very specific sense. It is entirely separate from the orders of external causation to which both his thoughts and desires are subject. Between it and them there is an absolute break. As a being with a will, man is as distant from the world as the God in whose image he is made.

Everything in the world except human beings and angels moves only on account of something else. They alone have the power to move themselves. They may be in the world, but are not of it. The idea of self-causation, which

Aristotle and Augustine both accept, thus conceals the deepest metaphysical difference between them. Interpreted along Aristotelian lines, as energy or activity, this idea guarantees the reality of the world. But interpreted as will, it opens a gap between the world and the ground of its being that no pagan philosopher could have conceived—not even Plato, who placed the ideas at a distance from the world but maintained a bridge of reason between them.

Whatever similarity there may appear to be between Augustine's idea of the will as cause of itself and Aristotle's concept of a self-moved mover is therefore illusory. The same is true of its apparent similarity to the Stoic doctrine of assent.

The freedom of assent, to which Epictetus and others attach such importance, merely prepares the way for an acquiescence in truths that are external to the minds of those who grasp them. In accepting these truths, we become one with the world and God. This is the meaning of Epictetus' dictum that we should wish to have happen only what actually does. By contrast, the freedom of the will is the freedom to disobey these truths themselves. It is the freedom to repudiate reason, something that Epictetus would have thought insane but without which, on Augustine's view, the embrace of reason lacks all moral value. Unlike the freedom of the Stoic sage, which lies in his subordination to reason, the suprarational freedom that Augustine attributes to man, and makes the sole conceivable source of all genuine evil, is possible only because the human beings who possess it are not really of the world at all, but transcend it in the same way as the God who made them.

The difference between these two ideas—the Stoic and the Augustinian—is brought out with special clarity in a passage in book 1 of *De libero arbitrio* that at first glance seems to conflate them.

Augustine has asked Evodius whether he thinks he has a "good will." Evodius wants to know what this is. Augustine replies that a good will is one "by which we desire to live upright and honorable lives and to attain the highest wisdom." An exchange follows whose point is to establish that a good will is incomparably more valuable than anything else in the world—than "wealth or honors or physical pleasures, or even all of these together." Augustine concludes by emphasizing that this greatest of all goods is within everyone's grasp.

> Then I believe you realize it is up to our will whether we enjoy or lack such a great and true good. For what is so much in the power of the will as the will itself? To have a good will is to have something far more

valuable than all earthly kingdoms and pleasures; to lack it is to lack something that only the will itself can give, something that is better than all the goods not in our power. Some people consider themselves utterly miserable if they do not achieve a splendid reputation, great wealth, and various goods of the body. But don't you consider them utterly miserable, even if they have all these things, when they cleave to things that they can quite easily lose, things that they do not have simply in virtue of willing them, while they lack a good will, which is incomparably better than those things and yet, even though it is such a great good, can be theirs if only they will to have it?[17]

Epictetus likewise warns of the emptiness of wealth and reputation and other "earthly" goods, and urges us to detach ourselves from those things that are "not in our power." But for Epictetus, the purpose of ceasing to care about such things is to prepare the way for an acceptance of the benign order of the world, which is not in our power either. A man who trains himself to be disinterested in money and fame but fails to comprehend the necessity of everything that happens to him falls short of the wisdom that alone can set him free. For Epictetus, as for every rationalist, salvation comes with knowledge. It is in knowing the world that we are saved.

Augustine rejects this equation. He insists that even the wisest man in the world is not one step closer to salvation merely on account of his wisdom. He regards the rationalist's effort to understand the world as entirely futile, for he knows that understanding by itself cannot contribute to the repair of man's damaged relation with God, who demands not wisdom but contrition from his disobedient subjects. He knows that salvation comes with forgiveness rather than knowledge.

Yet this is not a cause of disappointment for Augustine, for he also knows that to win God's forgiveness, all one has to do is will the good without reservation. No human being ever fully achieves the good at which he aims. But in Augustine's view it is enough to *intend* to attain it. The life of a pious Christian rests on the belief that to be saved all he needs is a good will, and that to have such a will he requires only good intentions, which depend on nothing beyond the will itself. He knows that his salvation lies ready at hand so long as he wills with purity of heart to pursue it—something he possesses the power to do at every moment, no matter how dissolute his life has been to that point. This is the supremely good news that Augustine's idea of the will as cause of itself delivers to those who accept it.

Augustine drives the point home a few pages later. People are "happy," he says, when "they love their own good will." And that, he adds significantly, "in itself constitutes a good will." Loving one's own good will is what having a good will means!

A good will is one that wills to lead "a praiseworthy and happy life," and though many things may frustrate the attainment of this goal, nothing can ever prevent a man from intending to reach it. The will that does "loves and embraces" itself, and in that instant becomes the good will it aims to be—a "great," indeed supreme, good that we are able to secure "by the very act of willing to have it."[18]

In this respect, the act of acquiring a good will (or a bad one, for that matter) differs fundamentally from that of making a house or a child. To do either, a man needs something more than the intention to make one. He needs resources other than himself—lumber and nails in the case of a house, and the reproductive organs of another human being in that of a child. By contrast, a good will "makes" itself good merely by willing to be so. The act of willing is self-contained in a way these others are not. It is a making from nothing but itself. It is a making of the special kind that Augustine calls creation. When Augustine says that the will is cause of itself, and that it becomes good "by the very act of willing" to be such, he is therefore attributing to human beings a power analogous to the one that God exercises when he brings the world into being from nothing.

IN THE IMAGE OF MAN

To account for the existence of evil without either denying its reality, or blaming God for it, or attributing it to another divinity with whom God shares the rule of the world, Augustine is forced to assign the responsibility for the world's evil to certain of God's creatures, whose criminal wrongdoing brings it about. This is his only theological option. And to make this responsibility stick to those to whom he assigns it, so that it cannot rebound to their creator, Augustine is compelled to assume in them the existence of a capacity for spontaneous causation that is the image of the boundless freedom God employs when he brings the world into being from nothing.

The belief that God created the world from nothing thus gives rise to a theological dilemma that can be solved only by postulating the existence of a similar power of creation in his human subjects. But the image is better known to us than the original. We are acquainted, from firsthand experience, with the freedom we seem to possess in choosing to do what is wrong, despite knowing what is right and wishing to do it. We know (or think we know) what the will is because of the decisions we sometimes make to act badly, contrary to both reason and desire. We find (or seem to find) in ourselves a capacity for sinful disobedience that is something distinct from both ignorance and weakness of character. And because we do, we understand (or believe we understand) what a morality of good intentions requires, and how it differs from the morality of right reason that every pagan rationalist, from Plato to Epictetus, endorses in one form or another. All of this seems (relatively) obvious as we reflect on our own behavior, and in particular on those acts of purposeful wrongdoing that Augustine and Paul before him analyzed with such ruthless clarity.

By contrast, God's freedom is more obscure. Indeed, it is unintelligible. We cannot scrutinize or comprehend it. Why did God will to bring the world into being? When and how did he do so? These are not just hard questions. They are unanswerable ones. That is because a respect for God's freedom demands that we deny ourselves an understanding of it, and in particular that we not compare his creation of the world to the more familiar processes of making and begetting.

These are mostly intelligible. We can understand a great deal about them. They have a structure or form that allows us to explain how and why they occur. But the forms that make them comprehensible also limit the actions of those whose movements are directed and shaped by them. There are only so many ways one can make a pot or beget a child. To do either, one has to follow certain procedures and use specific materials. One cannot make a pot out of air, or produce a child by winking. The forms that give all such processes their intelligibility simultaneously confine them within limits that not even the most powerful craftsman or parent can exceed.

It is blasphemous to suggest that God's freedom is confined in a similar way. To honor it, we must therefore assume that his creation of the world is not a process with a structure or form, like that of shaping a pot or fertilizing an egg. But once we assume this, we deprive ourselves of every resource we would otherwise have to understand the act of creation itself. This now becomes incomprehensible in principle, and denying ourselves the power to understand it becomes an act of piety rather than a sign of defeat.

Still, we long to know something about God's freedom, and the experience we have of our own (or what we take to be such) tempts us to think that we can do so in a limited way.

Augustine's account of the experience of willing has considerable psychological force. Moreover, anyone who accepts his theology has the strongest possible reason for believing that human freedom is something real. It therefore seems reasonable to translate upward from our will to God's, from the image to the original. The power of creation in us, with which we believe we are acquainted firsthand, appears to provide a template of sorts from which to draw a picture of its divine counterpart. God's creation of the world can only be an act caused by itself, like the human act of intending to be good or evil. His will, like ours, must be purely spontaneous. To this extent, our human freedom seems to give us a modest but significant insight into the essence of God's own.

As a theological matter, of course, God's freedom is prior to ours. If he had not freely chosen to give us wills, we would not have them. Yet in attempting to form some idea of what God's will is like, we have no choice but to start with what we know, or think we know, about our own. In this sense, our reflections about man's relation to God move in a kind of circle. Our idea of human freedom is shaped by the need to insulate God from the consequences of acknowledging the reality of evil in a world he created from nothing. Our understanding of God's freedom is defined in turn by the nature of the power we must assume in ourselves to assure this result. It would be a terrible mistake, for Augustine at least, to say that our picture of God is merely a human projection. But even on his orthodox view of the relation between man and God, the definition of the freedom of each is tied to that of the other.

Beginning in the next chapter, we will see how on Augustine's view of this relation, divine and human freedom come apart, with important consequences for the tradition of Western Christian thought. Later in the book, we will explore what it means to deny the reality of both, as Spinoza does, by rejecting the idea of spontaneity that lies at the root of each. But for the moment it is enough to observe that for Augustine, who defined the will for the very first time, in terms that Kant still accepted fourteen hundred years later, the freedom of man and God are indissolubly joined.

CHAPTER 13

Grace

DIVINE OMNIPOTENCE AND THE AUGUSTINIAN DILEMMA

Augustine's definition of the will as cause of itself solves one theological problem but intensifies another.

If the responsibility for evil is to be ours, rather than God's, the will cannot be caused to act by anything outside itself. Yet God must have known what we would do with our wills before he gave them to us. And if he knew that we would disobey his commands, and chose to create us nonetheless, why is he not the one ultimately responsible for the evil in the world, and we merely his instruments or agents? Any other conclusion seems incompatible with God's omnipotence. At the end of book 1 of *De libero arbitrio*, Evodius raises this question directly. Augustine tells his young interlocutor that he is "knocking on the doors" of a "great and hidden" question, and asks for God's guidance in answering it.[1]

FREEDOM AND OMNIPOTENCE

The content of our choices is supplied by reason or desire. Neither is fully within our control. But the intentions we form regarding the dictates of reason and the promptings of desire are wholly up to us. They are our responsibility alone. We bring them into being spontaneously, in the same way that God creates the world. Human beings can be responsible for the evil in the world only on the assumption that they possess a power of this kind and form the intentions that give their choices whatever moral meaning they possess by an act of self-causation whose independence mimics God's own.

But if men create their own intentions, as Augustine's theodicy requires, then it follows that at least some of the things in the world are brought into being from nothing by men rather than God. God may create everything else in the world, but he cannot create our intentions, for if he did, we would not be responsible for them. God's own power of creation must therefore be shared with those of his creatures to whom he has given free wills. But this seems inconsistent with the assumption of divine omnipotence, which cannot be limited in any way without disappearing altogether.

There appears to be an obvious solution to this problem.

The will possesses the power to cause an intention to come into being merely by willing it. To have a good will, it is enough that I will to have one. But the will lacks the power to bring itself into being. It is the ground of what it wills, but not of its own power of willing. Viewed as the cause of its intentions, the will is perfectly self-contained. But God is the cause of the existence of the will, which in this respect is wholly dependent on a being outside it. So long as we keep this distinction in mind, man's power of creation from nothing poses no threat to God's omnipotence. Man wills freely, but it is God who causes man's free will to exist in the first place, along with everything else in the world.

This way of solving the problem depends on our ability to harmonize two very different views of human freedom.

The first is the one that men take of it themselves. It might be called the internal point of view. From this perspective, the freedom of the will seems undeniably real. The phenomenon of willful disobedience and the experience of moral obligation both support the belief that the will is the spontaneous cause of its own actions.

The second is God's view of human freedom. From God's perspective, the human will owes its being entirely to him. The same applies to all those acts whose existence is causally dependent on that of the will, including the intentions men form with it. What from the internal point of view looks like an uncaused cause thus appears from God's perspective to be the result of an especially complete kind of external causation.

It is essential to preserve both points of view. If the first is absorbed in the second, man's responsibility for evil vanishes. If the second is lost or forgotten, God's omnipotence is qualified and therefore destroyed. But it is not easy, or even possible, to reconcile these two points of view since each denies what the other affirms. Each contradicts the other's most basic assumptions. They are logically and psychologically at war.

I shall refer to this as the Augustinian dilemma. Augustine himself, of course, did not describe or even conceive it as such, but his philosophical account of the will as cause of itself sets the stage for the dilemma, and in the end, like many later Christian thinkers, he found he could resolve it only by grasping one of its two horns.

The first of these affirms the divine view of human freedom. It insists that God must have known exactly what his human creatures would do with their God-given powers, that he willed to create them with their subsequent choices in mind, and hence willed that these choices themselves exist. It maintains that men possess no real power of creation and that their experience of spontaneity is an illusion, since every causal chain of which they seem to be the authors has its real beginning in God. This preserves God's omnipotence but leaves no room for the idea of human freedom and the concept of responsibility associated with it.

The second horn of the dilemma adopts the internal view of human freedom. Its fundamental premise is that only what exists on account of the will's spontaneous acts possesses moral value. It is obvious that the will works on materials supplied from without. But from the internal point of view, these acquire moral value only through the will's intentions regarding their use or abuse. This applies in a straightforward way to beliefs and desires. But it also applies to the fact of the will's own existence, which (*arguendo*) God brings into being from nothing. What matters from the internal point of view is not this existential fact but one's response to it. No one can doubt that a man must have a will in order to act willfully. It is one of the conditions of moral responsibility. But in itself this condition has no more moral significance than any of the others under which human freedom is required to operate. It acquires such significance only when a man exercises his God-given will in a value-conferring act that has no cause but itself.

From the internal point of view, then, God's creation of the will is a fact without value, while from the external point of view the will's autonomy is a mirage. Each perspective swallows up the other and negates it by denying the very thing it seeks to establish: on the one hand, the reality of human freedom, and on the other, the omnipotence of God who, though he creates the human will from nothing, lacks the power to give its acts a moral value, which they can acquire only through the spontaneous choices of the men responsible for them.

It is therefore a mistake to think that human freedom and divine omnipotence can be harmonized merely by respecting the difference between these two perspectives. Each makes absolutist claims that cannot be reconciled with those of the other. One maintains that absolutely everything in the world, including man's will, owes its existence to God; the other, that no cause acting on the will from without can ever have any moral value of its own. Both claims cannot be sustained; one point of view must yield to the other. Either human freedom is real and God's power less than complete or he is omnipotent and man's freedom an illusion. The human and divine points of view that support these conflicting claims are mutually exclusive and any theologian who is determined to defend the premises of the Christian religion in a philosophically rigorous way must eventually choose between them.

ORIGINAL SIN

Augustine was the first Christian thinker in the West to offer a philosophical account of the two ideas around which these alternatives revolve, and between whose magnetically repellant poles the Western Christian understanding of man's relation to God has moved ever since. The first is the idea of the will. The second is that of grace.

Centuries before Augustine, Paul had made the ideas of human freedom and divine grace the organizing themes of his interpretation of sin and salvation. Paul's treatment of these ideas laid the foundation for all subsequent Christian thought. But Paul was not a philosopher, and neither he nor anyone else before Augustine worked out the implications of the concepts of freedom and grace in an intellectually disciplined fashion. This was Augustine's legacy to the Latin West, along with a deepening appreciation of the tension between these two ideas, which his more lucid account of them brought to the fore.

Written in the earliest days of his career as a Christian apologist, *De libero arbitrio* offers an interpretation of the will as cause of itself. Every later philosopher in the Christian tradition who has sought to defend the reality of human freedom has relied on Augustine's interpretation of it. Kant is the last and most influential representative of this point of view. In his rigorous formulation of the Augustinian concept of freedom, God's grace is reduced to what he calls a "postulate" of "practical reason"—a mere addendum to man's will.

But *De libero arbitrio* also includes a forceful statement of the concept of divine grace. The same idea plays an even more prominent role in the retrospective account of the essay that Augustine wrote decades later. Here (though not in the essay itself), Augustine associates God's grace with the terrifying doctrine of predestination, which he eventually came to see as its most perfect expression. In Augustine's later writings, the need to affirm God's limitless power becomes increasingly urgent, until man's freedom is completely eclipsed by it, in a theology of divine omnipotence that has served ever since as a model for those who have chosen to exalt God's power at the expense of human autonomy. From the antihumanistic perspective of Augustine's mature understanding of grace, which inspired Ockham, Luther, Maistre and others, the ambition to be the cause of one's own goodness—praised in *De libero arbitrio* as the very essence of a good will—becomes the worst desire a human being can possibly have.

Augustine's brilliant analysis of original sin illustrates the tension between these two ideas.[2]

Adam and Eve "began to be evil," Augustine says, on account of their "appetite for a perverse kind of elevation." "For it is a perverse kind of elevation indeed to forsake the foundation upon which the mind should rest, and to become and remain, as it were, one's own foundation." The devil was able to "lure man into the manifest and open sin of doing what God had prohibited" by promising Adam and Eve that they should be as gods themselves. "But Adam and Eve would have been better fitted to resemble gods if they had clung in obedience to the highest and true ground of their being, and not, in their pride, made themselves their own ground. For created gods are gods not in their own true nature, but by participation in the true God. By striving after more, man is diminished; when he takes delight in his own self-sufficiency, he falls away from the One who truly suffices him." The "first evil came . . . when man began to be pleased with himself, as if he were his own light."

In aspiring to make themselves their own "ground" or "foundation," Adam and Eve committed an ontological crime. They sought to reverse the "true" order of being. Augustine describes their act as the result of a perverse "appetite" or "striving." But he also calls it a "betrayal," and it is clear that he regards it as an act of will and not merely of desire. "For if the will had remained unshaken in its love of that higher and immutable Good by Which is bestowed upon it the light by which it can see and the fire by which it can love, it would not have turned aside from this Good to follow its own pleasure." Adam and Eve's assertion of their "own self-sufficiency" was therefore not the result of weakness or ignorance alone. It was a willful act—a free and deliberate choice—and thus a crime deserving to be punished. Any other explanation would diminish their guilt and turn original sin into something more like irresistible impulse or reckless incaution.

Augustine's account of original sin thus employs the ideas both of human freedom and divine omnipotence to explain the nature of Adam and Eve's crime. It uses the first to account for the wickedness of their state of mind, and the second to define the ontological presumption that constituted the substance of the crime they committed. But these ideas are in tension. Adam and Eve's desire to be self-sufficient is a crime only in case it is an act of will, and an act of will only if they already possess, in a certain respect at least, the self-sufficiency to which they aspire. That is because the will is either the ground of its own acts, even if it is not the ground of its own existence, or it is no will at all.

Hence either Adam and Eve have wills and therefore the power to bring something into being from nothing, in which case they are already "as gods themselves" so far as the exercise of this power is concerned. Or they lack wills, in which case their actions can never be criminal. Augustine's definition of the will as cause of itself, and of original sin as a striving for an independence that this definition assumes they already possess, therefore not only underscores Augustine's need for the ideas both of human freedom and divine omnipotence. It also reveals the tension between them. Augustine himself seems to have recognized this, for he goes to great lengths to explain how true perverseness of will, and the independence this assumes, can exist in a world created by an omnipotent God.

The "existence of the will as a nature is due," Augustine says, "to its creation by God." But then what accounts for the will's sinful presumption to self-sufficiency, through which it falls "away from its nature"? Is this also owing to God? Augustine attempts to avoid this conclusion by insisting that the will's falling away from God is a consequence of its creation from nothing. Like any "nature created out of nothing," man's will can be "perverted by a defect." The perversion of the will is to be explained by its creaturely nature.

But this explanation is unpersuasive. It elides the essential distinction between the will and other created natures. These, too, are brought into being from nothing and are therefore also necessarily defective. No creature can ever be perfect—neither a horse, nor a man, nor anything else. But only the will has the power to be perverse—evil, wicked, sinful—and therefore deserving of punishment. That is because only the will, though created by God, is the cause of its own actions.

No human being can cause things to be as he wishes merely by willing them to be so. Men are confined by the finitude of their condition, as God's other creatures are too. But within its range of operation, the human will possesses a power of spontaneous inauguration as great as God's own. It has the power to become the will it chooses to be. In Augustine's view, this is the sole ground of moral responsibility and the only way of avoiding the conclusion that God is responsible for the world's evil. By attributing the perversion of the will to its creaturely nature, Augustine eliminates the only conceivable source of human wickedness, which lies not in man's finitude but his godlike independence instead. His explanation of original sin as a consequence of the createdness of the will thus fails to answer the question of how it is possible for God to be omnipotent while sharing his power of creation with men. It merely avoids it.

But Augustine was a profoundly honest thinker whose philosophical scruples did not allow him to sidestep this question forever. He understood the tension between the ideas of human freedom and divine omnipotence more clearly, perhaps, than any Christian writer before him, and while his theology required both, the rationalism of the intellectual culture in which he had been trained as a youth made him sensitive to the difficulty of putting these ideas together in a coherent way. In the end, Augustine could not escape the need to make one the dominant pole of his theology. Compelled to choose between them, he chose the idea of grace. Having begun his theological career as a champion of human freedom, Augustine moved steadily toward an ever more extravagant defense of divine omnipotence until man's will was not merely displaced from the position it had once occupied in his thought but obliterated completely.

The doctrine of predestination, which belongs to the last phase of Augustine's career, completes this process. But his account of original sin points the way. By interpreting man's longing for self-sufficiency as his greatest crime against God, Augustine makes it clear how illusory man's freedom becomes when viewed from God's perspective, and lays the foundation for his teaching that all human wickedness since the Fall has consisted in the belief that men possess some measure of independence in the struggle to secure their happiness, whether on earth or in heaven. For the later Augustine, the presumption that human beings possess even a scintilla of such independence is the root of all evil and the key to understanding the sad record of man's biblical and postbiblical crimes.

THE CITIES OF MAN AND GOD

Augustine calls this presumption pride (*superbia*). The opposite of pride is humility (*humilitas*), the submissive acceptance of God's omnipotence and of man's complete dependence on God's free and unmerited grace.

Pride and humility are the master categories of Augustine's account of divine and secular history. They are the distinguishing marks of the two cities whose fates he traces from the beginning of historical time to the Day of Final Judgment—the city of man, populated by the children of pride, and the city of God, whose saintly members accept with gratitude their dependence on God's gifts here and in the world to come. It is no exaggeration to say that in Augustine's view every human failing that is recorded in the sacred histories of the Bible and in the chronicles of nations (especially those of Rome) represents an act of pride that reflects man's constitutional incapacity ever to be grateful enough to the God who gave him life and alone has the power to save him from history and time.

God gave Adam and Eve the gift of life without end in a paradise without labor or need. Like the recipients of any gift, they had reason to be grateful to their donor. But instead they sought to "make themselves their own ground." They attempted to liberate themselves from the very condition on which their duty to be grateful was based. Merely failing to give thanks where it is due is bad enough. It is the most familiar kind of ingratitude. But Adam and Eve's was something worse, for what they desired was the abolition of the condition of dependence that is the origin of man's obligation to give thanks to God in the first place. No greater ingratitude can be imagined, and no sanction that God imposed for it would have been unjust.

As a punishment, God changed the nature of the human beings he had created. He made them mortal; compelled them to work for a living; subjected them to ruinous desires over which they no longer had full control; and darkened their minds so that they could not see the meaning of the right and good as clearly as they had before. For the sin of attempting to become gods themselves, of delighting in their "own self-sufficiency," God condemned Adam and Eve to live the rest of their now mortal lives under these altered conditions, and to communicate their changed nature to their human descendants for the rest of time. Human history thus begins, on Augustine's

view, with a criminal act of ingratitude, and its signal events are all reenact-
ments of the primal, prehistorical crime for which the human condition as
we know it is God's penalty.[3]

The first historical wrong was Cain's murder of his brother Abel. The essence of Cain's crime was his lack of humility. Cain gave "himself to himself:
as do all who follow their own will and not the will of God." Cain acted from
"pride and envy." He could not stand the fact that God esteemed his brother's
sacrifice more than his own. He was filled with a "lust for mastery" and wished
to be first. But rather than submitting to God, he took matters into his own
hands and murdered Abel. He acted as if he, not God, were the master of life
and death—instead of gratefully acknowledging his dependence on God's inscrutable will. Cain thereby repeated his parents' original sin by seeking to
usurp God's "providence and omnipotence,"[4] which it was his duty humbly
to accept.

In Augustine's theologically inspired retelling of human history, Cain is
the founder of one city and his slain brother of another. The first is the earthly
city, or city of man, and the second the city of God, which Augustine calls
a "pilgrim" in this world. These are not actual cities. They do not correspond
to any existing communities, including the Church (many of whose nominal
members belong to the city of man). But the "allegory"[5] of their respective
careers provides the key to understanding all that has occurred in the world
since their founding by Cain and his innocent brother.

The difference between these "two orders" of men manifests itself in many
ways. Most fundamentally, though, it rests on the enduring opposition between pride and humility. Those who belong to the earthly city, in whatever
age, are driven by a "love of self extending even to contempt of God." By
contrast, those who belong to the city of God are motivated by a "love of
God extending to contempt of self." "The one, therefore, glories in itself, the
other in the Lord; the one seeks glory from men, the other finds its highest
glory in God, the Witness of our conscience. The one lifts up its head in its
own glory; the other says to its God, 'Thou art my glory, and the lifter up of
mine head.'"[6]

The members of the earthly city make self-sufficiency their highest value.
They rebel against the suggestion that they are wholly dependent on God. By
contrast, the inhabitants of the city of God dwell in a spirit of thankfulness.
They acknowledge that they owe everything to God, including above all their
chances for salvation from the corruptions of human life as we know it. The
careers of the two cities thus carry forward to the end of time the fundamen-

tal opposition between pride and gratitude that defines the nature of the original sin that inaugurates man's history on earth and grounds all our hopes
for redemption from it.

It is in the context of this opposition that Augustine locates the tradition
of authentic Christian belief and distinguishes it both from the teachings of
the pagan philosophers and the religion of the Jews.

Even the greatest pagan philosophers sinned in thinking that men can attain happiness through a disciplined effort of their own. Such a program
rests on the belief that the world has a rational order that the human mind
can grasp if properly trained. Every school of pagan philosophy shared this
assumption and drew the same conclusion from it—that human beings are
able to achieve a state of self-sufficiency, and hence of happiness, in this life,
whether or not another one follows it (as Plato supposed and Aristotle denied).
Any philosopher who holds this view is guilty of the presumptuous ambition
to be sufficient unto himself, and hence of the criminal ingratitude for which
God punished Adam and Eve.

> If, therefore, we are asked what response the City of God makes when
> questioned . . . [as to] what it believes concerning the Final Good
> and Evil, we shall reply as follows: that eternal life is the Supreme
> Good and eternal death the Supreme Evil, and that to achieve the
> one and avoid the other, we must live rightly. For this reason it is
> written, 'The just man lives by *faith*.' For we do not yet see our good,
> and hence we must seek it by believing. Moreover, we cannot live
> rightly unless, while we believe and pray, we are *helped* by Him who
> has *given* us the *faith to believe that we must be helped by Him*. The
> philosophers, however, have supposed that the Final Good and Evil
> are to be found in this life. They hold that the Supreme Good lies in
> the body, or in the soul, or in both (or, to state it more clearly, in
> pleasure, or in virtue, or in both). . . . With wondrous vanity, these
> philosophers have wished to be happy here and now, and to achieve
> blessedness by their own efforts.[7]

A few pages later, Augustine speaks with particular contempt of "the
shamelessness of the Stoics," who, with "amazing vanity" and "stiff-necked
pride," "believe that the Final Good is to be found in this life, and that they
can achieve happiness by their own efforts."[8] In his view, though, all the wisdom philosophies of the ancient world had this same defect. Some of these
endorsed an ascetic or contemplative way of life, others a hedonistic one. But

their shared assumption that the truth is accessible to the human mind and, once understood, provides all the guidance a man needs to live a happy and fulfilling life, made them equally guilty of the sin of pride. Their common lack of gratitude is the watershed that separates all the schools of ancient philosophy from the humble world of Christian faith.

Christians and Jews are divided for similar reasons.

The Jews are the children of Abraham too. Their sacred writings contain the stories of the creation and fall on which Augustine's own Christian theology is based. Moreover, the religion of the Jews not only affirms that the existence of the world is the gift of a God who transcends it, but places tremendous weight on the value of gratitude as well: for the world itself; for God's deliverance of his chosen people from slavery in Egypt; for the law he gave them at Sinai; and for God's loving patience in forgiving the Jews for their repeated shortcomings, from the sins of Sodom and Gomorrah to the crimes the prophets condemned.

In all these respects, Judaism and Christianity resemble one another and differ fundamentally from the rationalist philosophies of Greco-Roman antiquity. Both belong to the tradition of biblical voluntarism, which conceives the relation of man to God as one of subject to lordly commander, rather than of inquiring mind to intelligible order. Both make will, not reason, the pivot of human life—the power that determines whether a man is good or bad, obedient or rebellious, saved or condemned. But in Augustine's view, a profound difference remains between these two religions, for like the Stoics and other wise men of pagan antiquity, the Jews are prideful ingrates too.

The great failing of the Jews is their refusal to accept the gift of the Incarnation, proudly believing in the sufficiency of the law as an instrument of thanksgiving to God. However often they have failed to obey God's laws in the past, the Jews insist that it is only their own remediable vices that prevent them from doing so in the future. They recognize no absolute bar to the fulfillment of God's commands, and believe that once they have fulfilled them, their duties to God are complete.

The Jews believed this before the coming of Christ and continue to do so even after his death on the cross. Even after they have heard the good news of Christ's redemptive suffering, they stubbornly cling to their belief that it has no bearing on their capacity to act as God commands. They fail to recognize the significance of Christ's gift and its necessity to their salvation, conceiving their relation to God in narrowly legalistic terms and proudly affirming their ability to fulfill on their own the terms of the covenant they entered at Sinai.

The Jews fail to see their need for Christ because they underestimate the consequences of the sin that Adam and Eve committed and the magnitude of the penalty God imposed for it. Following Paul, Augustine interprets this sin philosophically. He treats it as an ontological revolt and views God's punishment as a change in human nature whose depth befits that of the crime. The Jews interpret the change superficially. They acknowledge that Adam and Eve's descendants are fated to die. But they refuse to concede that on account of their original sin we lost not only the endless, laborless life that Adam and Eve enjoyed, but also the capacity to obey God's law on our own.

For this, God's help is now required. Man has been punished for his presumption of independence by having his independent power to fulfill the law taken away. This is the most important consequence of original sin, since it removes even the possibility of salvation: a punishment of whose righteousness we have no standing to complain. The Jews fail to interpret the story of the Fall in an appropriately metaphysical way, and therefore do not comprehend the true meaning of the cross as a divine gift that restores to human beings the possibility of obedience to God's commands, and with that of salvation itself, which God had withdrawn on account of the first Adam's sin.

In Augustine's view, Adam's disobedience was an act of such monumental ingratitude that its consequences can be even partially repaired only by another divine gift—that of God's son, and thus of God himself, in redemption of the penalty that he rightfully imposed on his own prideful creatures for their wish to be gods themselves. The gift of Christ's suffering gives us the opportunity to make up for the ingratitude that is the cause of our fallen condition through the expression of an amplified gratitude that partly undoes its effects. For this gift, which affords us all a second chance we do not deserve, the only appropriate response is one of endless thanks.

If the Jews do not respond in this way, that is because they do not appreciate the magnitude of the change wrought by Adam's sin, or understand that our restoration to a state even of conditional hopefulness can now be brought about only by the unearned grace of the God who worked this change in the first place. The Jews' view of man's relation to God is based on a literal interpretation of the Fall that misses its philosophical meaning. Their ignorance of the depth of human sinfulness; their failure to be adequately thankful for the divine gift that alone can offset it; their insistence on their ability to fulfill God's law on their own; and their proud rejection of Christ, the universal savior of humankind, all reflect the philosophically primitive character of the religion of the Jews, whose sacred writings the Fathers of the Church were the first to interpret in a properly metaphysical light.

The essential vice of the Jews, like that of the Stoics and other pagan philosophers, is therefore one of ingratitude. But the Jews' ingratitude is something especially bad. A Jew at least believes in the divine creation of the world. He has received the law from God and been instructed to obey it. This brings him closer to God than any pagan philosopher can be. But just for that reason, his ingratitude for the gift of the Incarnation is a worse sin than the pride of the philosophers, to whom the truth of God's creation has not been revealed.

In Augustine's view, the sin of the Jews is therefore not ameliorated but aggravated by the law. That the Jews were singled out to receive the law should have made it especially clear to them that they needed God's help to fulfill it. It ought to have made them more receptive to God's grace instead of closing them off from it. The Jews' prideful rejection of Christ is thus an especially wicked sort of ingratitude, which explains why, though Augustine regards both philosophers and Jews as ingrates, he condemns the latter in particularly strong terms. It also explains why he reserves his harshest judgment for those fellow Christians who fail to grasp the immensity of their dependence on God's grace.

THE ENEMY WITHIN

Augustine spent the last fifteen years of his life attacking the British monk Pelagius and others who, though professing to be Christians, accorded man a freedom he believed incompatible with God's omnipotence.[9] Augustine's confrontation with Pelagius underscored the tension between the ideas of will and grace and made the choice between them the decisive test of Christian faith, as Luther would do again eleven hundred years later.

Much of the controversy revolved around seemingly technical matters, like the need for infant baptism. But Augustine fought his campaign against Pelagius with a passion unmatched in his long career as a polemicist because he recognized that something fundamental was at stake. The real issue, in Augustine's view, was the dignity of God himself. God's grandeur is impugned, he felt, by the suggestion that his power can be directed even in the smallest way by the free acts of human beings. This is a prideful view that strikes at the heart of Christian piety, as Augustine understood it, and he responded on behalf of his omnipotent God with all the energy he possessed.

In doing so, he had to address a nearly endless list of questions that Pelagius and his followers had answered in an appealingly modest way. Augustine's opposing views pushed him in an increasingly radical direction, toward a severe theology of grace from which the power of human initiative is wholly excluded.

Is Christ an inspiring teacher who shows us the path to righteousness, and leaves it to us to follow his example? No. The life of Christ is a gift that "assists" us through his redemptive suffering. The first view emphasizes our human capacity to act on our own, once we have been given proper instruction. The second stresses our incapacity to do anything that touches our spiritual fate without God's help. Those who take the first view are swollen with pride. Those who adopt the second humbly accept their complete dependence on God's unmerited love.[10]

Does Christ's gift consist only in the remission of past sins, leaving us free to live as God commands, if we now will to do so? No. To live as one should means more than abiding by the law. It requires a good will as well. But a good will comes only by the grace of God. It is a gift to the man who has it, as is his ability to persevere in willing the good once he starts.

Can a man be saved by good works? No. He must have faith too. Can he at least find the faith he needs on his own? No. We cannot acquire even this by ourselves. Faith comes to those who have it as a gift from God. Everyone, including Pelagius, acknowledges that man's capacity for freedom is God's gift. But what about its exercise and effectiveness—are these not up to us? No, and no. They depend on divine grace as well, as much as the capacity for freedom itself.

Can we at least be said to merit God's assistance by freely turning toward him, in an act of loving obedience? No, for even this turning is something we accomplish only with divine help. Is there anything, in short, that we can do to win our salvation? No. That is entirely in God's hands. He decides which of us shall be saved and which not. Indeed, he decided this before the world was created. We have no power to influence the outcome of that decision one way or another. There is absolutely nothing we can do to cause God to favor us even in the slightest degree. The freedom we think we possess to choose a good or bad life that will move God to reward or punish us is an illusion. Our choices are entirely the result of God's own. Any other view is an insult to God, whose power is adequately represented only by a doctrine of predestination that eliminates the very possibility of human freedom, as Augustine had conceived it in *De libero arbitrio*. All that is left of that earlier conception is the paradoxical belief that while our freedom is wholly illusory, we must act as if it were real, and accept this paradox as an article of faith, which means abandoning the search for a rationally intelligible theology that had been Augustine's ambition from his earliest days as a convert to Christian belief.

Augustine considered Pelagianism to be the most serious threat that Christianity had ever faced. That was because it arose within the Christian community itself, and drew support for its claim that man is able, in a limited way at least, to influence the judgment of God, from the quintessentially Christian idea of the will. As the inventor of that idea, Augustine understood its meaning better than anyone else and thus grasped with particular clarity the magnitude of the danger it posed to the competing idea of God's absolute power.

For Augustine, Pelagianism represented a failure of gratitude comparable to that of Adam and Eve. Like them, he said, the Pelagians commit the sin of affirming our human self-sufficiency by insisting that man's salvation springs "from no other source" than himself[11]—that men "have God not from God Himself, but from their own selves!"[12] This is the sin of pride, and it does not become one atom less evil just because those who embrace Pelagius' superficially reasonable teachings acknowledge their dependence on God in other ways. A professing Christian who gives any credence at all to the idea that he possesses a spontaneous power of free choice for whose self-caused actions he alone is responsible, and who affirms that these have a bearing, however slight, on his ultimate salvation, reenacts Adam and Eve's original sin and commits the greatest crime his religion knows. The rigid theology of grace that he constructed in the last years of his life in response to Pelagius' modest acknowledgment of human initiative was Augustine's final word on the matter.

In the end, there are only two consistent positions that Augustine's philosophically refined Christianity allows. The first puts an emphasis on dependence and gratitude and compels its adherents to condemn every assertion of human self-sufficiency as an act of pride. Its logical conclusion is the doctrine of predestination, which preserves God's power of spontaneous creation by abolishing man's.

The second acknowledges the reality of human freedom. By doing so it opens a crack in the wall of divine omnipotence that cannot be closed. It leads, with equal relentlessness, to the belief that God is a human construct—that he is "from" man, not the other way around. The triumph of this belief is both a cause and characteristic of the disenchanted world in which we live.

Augustine's early philosophy of the will provides the materials for the second of these ideas. It thus contains the seeds of the self-destruction of Christian belief. His late theology of grace provides the main weapons with which he and other Christian thinkers defended their religion against this existential threat—one that Augustine himself had helped to create. The contest between the theologies of will and grace is the key to the drama of Augustine's career, and to that of the tradition of Western Christian philosophy that, more than anyone else, he may be said to have founded.

But Augustine's concept of grace is of more than intellectual interest. It has tremendous psychological significance too. By converting every suggestion that there is anything we might ever do to make an adequate return to God for his gifts into yet another expression of human pride, it raises the demand that we be grateful to God to an unbearable pitch.

In Augustine's view, the only appropriate response to divine grace is one of perfect submission. A pious Christian acknowledges his complete incapacity ever to be grateful enough for God's gifts. He recognizes that even his submissiveness is itself a gift from God. The Christian doctrine of the Incarnation prepares the way for an exaggerated gratitude toward God, and Augustine's theology of grace converts this attitude into a philosophical system that makes the experience of the inadequacy of one's powers of thankfulness an ideal.

This ideal cannot be sustained. Gratitude in all its forms arouses the wish to make a return that adequately expresses one's thanks for the gifts one has received. The desire to do so is entirely and inescapably human. It is not the desire to repay a debt, but to reciprocate love with a love as good and great. Its frustration produces an anguish as deep as that of not being loved in the first place. To be forbidden the opportunity ever to be grateful enough to God is therefore bound to be a cause of immense suffering in those who long to love God in a way that is commensurate with his love for them.

Augustine's doctrine of grace blocks this desire. It does so not by accident, and incidentally, but directly and on purpose. It is therefore a source of profound human unhappiness, and gives rise to the wish to escape the crushing burden of a gratitude that can never be requited. The wish to do this is as inevitable as the unhappiness to which it responds. But it can be fulfilled only by reversing our relation to God, so that he is no longer the ground of our being but we of his: the Pelagian heresy. That the logic of Augustine's theology of grace, which is meant to fight this heresy, itself facilitates the reversal of man's relation to God and the satisfaction of the wish this represents, by requiring that God be placed at such a distance from us that nothing can any longer be thought or said about him, is an irony we shall explore in later chapters.

CHAPTER 14

"Not a Sparrow Falls"

THE ABOLITION OF THE DISTINCTION
BETWEEN FORM AND MATTER

The world is a beautiful, intelligible and morally exalted place. But for a Christian like Augustine, it is none of these things in itself. The world is not intrinsically knowable or lovely or anything else. It does not even have any reality of its own. The world exists only because a God apart from it freely chose to bring it into being. Its existence is not a natural fact. It is not a metaphysical necessity. It is the gift of a God beyond the world and therefore wholly contingent.

Only God is fully real. Only his being is self-contained. He alone exists necessarily and always. The existence of the world, by contrast, depends entirely on something (someone) other than itself. By transferring the ground of the being of the world to a God whose essence is defined by his separation from it, the Christian doctrine of creation drains the world of all inherent reality and value.

Even Plato, whose idealism Augustine found so congenial, assumes that the inchoate stuff on which his cosmic craftsman works is there before he starts to shape it. The "receptacle" into which the demiurge places his forms has a permanent and preexisting being of its own. To that extent, even Plato grants the world an independent reality that anyone who accepts the doctrine of creation must deny that it possesses.[1]

The contrast with Aristotle is even sharper. For Aristotle, there is only one world, the ordered cosmos of movements in which we and everything else has its place. This world contains all the being and value there is. The very idea of another one beyond it, of a "heaven" beyond the "earth," from which this world derives its existence and goodness, would have struck him as absurd. That the world we enter at birth and leave at death is inherently real and intrinsically good is the fundamental premise of his entire philosophy.

Because Aristotle accepted this as a self-evident truth, he also believed that the world is a home for man. He did not judge those who seek and find fulfillment in the world to be wicked or deluded. He did not regard them as blind or confused. They are just "doing what comes naturally." To Aristotle, the belief that the world in which we spend our lives is the only real one there is, seemed so obviously true that it never occurred to him to try to justify it with arguments of a less obvious kind.

All forms of worldliness, from the sensual to the philosophical, rest on this belief. To Augustine, it is more than a mistake. It is an expression of the original sin of pride—the assertion by God's human creatures of an independence and self-sufficiency that God alone possesses. This is the defining attitude of all who inhabit the city of man. Aristotle is their philosophical spokesman. He is the philosopher of pride. He takes the worldliness of the city of man as his premise and constructs a theology to support it.

Only those who understand that the world has no reality of its own, and acknowledge that its being depends on the grace of a God beyond it, escape the sin of pride. They are the saints of the city of God, pilgrims in an unreal world that for them can never be a home. They recoil with horror from the philosopher's belief that he is able to live the life of a god by means of thought alone, and condemn his false theology, which accords the world a reality it cannot possess.

Aristotle's philosopher knows that he is capable of understanding the order of the world, and further knows that when he has, he has grasped all that can be known about the most really real thing there is. His pride rests on a belief in his own intellectual competence and on the assumption that the world that is the object of his inquiries has an eternal being of its own.

The rejection of this latter assumption is the first step toward salvation. To begin to be saved, one must first believe that the world is nothing in itself. This belief is the antidote to the prideful ambitions of pagan philosophy. The hopes of the pilgrim-saints of the city of God thus all depend on the devaluation of the world, whose intrinsic intelligibility and goodness Aristotle took for granted.

PRIME MATTER

Aristotle recognized that we do not always perceive things to be as they are. Our senses often lead us astray. Ancient skeptics invoked the familiar experience of perceptual error to support their view that the truth of claims about the nature of things can never be proven conclusively. Yet even they never doubted that the world about which we make such claims possesses a reality of its own. They merely challenged our ability to acquire a demonstrably true knowledge of the world as it is in itself.

This was a serious challenge to the rationalist philosophies that were the skeptics' principal target, for these all assumed that the mind and the world are aligned in such a way that the first is able to discover and demonstrate the truth about the second. But when the doctrine of creation forced those who embraced it to acknowledge that the world that scientists study, and philosophers seek to explain, might be other than it is, or not exist at all, every form of philosophical rationalism had to confront a far more difficult problem.

For now, even on the assumption that we have correctly understood the order of the world, there is nothing to guarantee that our knowledge of it is either necessary or lasting. Like the world itself, what we know, or think we know, about it is wholly contingent. How to secure the validity of our reasoned judgments about the order of the world, under these conditions, is the question that Descartes confronts, and though he is able to answer it only by assuming a divine guarantor to whose help he is not, strictly speaking, entitled, the difference between his radical skepticism and the more benign variety espoused by ancient writers like Sextus Empiricus reflects the increased threat to any rationalist program of inquiry that the doctrine of creation from nothing presents.

The idea of creation thus raises a new and particularly formidable obstacle to all programs of this kind. But that is only half the story, for the same idea has equally large *positive* implications for philosophical rationalism as well. That is because, though it devalues the world by depriving it of all intrinsic reality, the Christian doctrine of creation also removes the barrier that stood in the way, for every pagan philosopher, of conceiving the world to be intelligible down to its smallest details. In this way, it sets the stage for a rationalism of an even more far reaching sort—for a *hyperrationalism* that refuses to concede, as all forms of pagan rationalism must, that the world contains a residual mindlessness that can never, even in principle, be understood or explained.

In later chapters, we will explore the ways in which this change of view manifests itself in every sphere of modern life. But first it is important to understand how such a change was possible at all—how a theology whose central teaching undermines the assumption of the world's inherent reality, on which pagan rationalism was based, could also, by virtue of the same idea, lay the foundation for a hyperrationalism inconceivable within the limits of ancient philosophy and science.

Aristotle's analysis of individual identity gives us a point of departure.

The question of what distinguishes one individual from another is among the fundamental problems of metaphysics. Aristotle discusses it at many places in his writings.[2] But he answers it in a way that makes the individuality of individuals ultimately unintelligible—a barrier beyond which no mind, human or divine, can ever go. That is because his answer turns on the distinction between form and matter. This distinction was for Aristotle, as for his teacher Plato, with whom he disagreed on many other issues, a metaphysical postulate of the most elementary kind. The doctrine of creation from nothing dissolves this distinction and thereby opens the way to a belief in the intelligibility of individuals as such, which Aristotle's metaphysics of form and matter rules out as a matter of principle.

Aristotle thought of individual things, including human beings, as composites of form and matter. He was influenced in this regard by his view of the process of making. Every maker joins a form that exists in his mind to some preexisting matter (the materials in his workshop). The thing he makes is the product of their joinder. This seems so obviously true in the case of artifacts (beds, poems and such), that Aristotle made it the model for his understanding of the process by which natural things, like frogs and men, come into being as well. In each case, he says, the thing that results from the process in question, whether productive or reproductive, is a combination of form and matter, whose common characteristics and unique identity must both be explained in these terms.

Any artificial or natural thing is the sort of thing it is (a bed as distinct from a chair, a frog as opposed to a man) on account of its form, which it shares with others of its kind. All beds and frogs possess their respective forms in common. But individual frogs and men do not share their matter. The matter of each is its alone. It is therefore the matter of a thing, Aristotle concluded, that makes it different from other members of its species. As his medieval commentators put it, matter is the principle of individuation in Aristotle's metaphysics.[3]

In the *Categories,* Aristotle offers an account of the order of the world that starts from the structure of language. The relation of things to their properties, he says, must be like that of subjects to the attributes we predicate of them. This leads Aristotle to ask, what are the most really real things in the world? What are the ultimate units of ontological account, from which more complex realities are constructed? His famous answer is that the most really real things are the composites (*sunholoi*) of form and matter of which individual things consist. Each such composite is a unique thing—what Aristotle calls a "this-such" (*tode tis*). It would seem to follow that the most real property of any thing is its individuality, and that every other feature we attribute to it—its color, shape, location, and the like—is by contrast a mere abstraction.

But when, in the *Metaphysics,* Aristotle focuses more carefully on the question of what it is about an individual that makes it real, he shifts ground decisively and identifies its reality in an increasingly emphatic way with its form alone: with one of the two elements of which it composed, rather than the composite itself. On this view, what is really real in a thing is not the union of form and matter that makes it a unique member of its kind, but the form that makes it one kind of thing rather than another.

That Aristotle was drawn in this direction is unsurprising, for like Plato he equated reality with intelligibility, and both of these with form. These equivalencies lie at the root of his entire philosophy. Anyone who accepts them is bound to conclude that only the form of a thing, which it shares with others of its kind, is knowable and real. By contrast, its individuality, which is attributable to the separate bit of matter in which its form resides, must be regarded as ultimately unknowable and unreal, and hence without that special sort of value that Plato and Aristotle assign to intelligibility alone.

This is not to say that the *parts* of a thing are unintelligible or unreal. Aristotle was deeply interested in the parts especially of living things, and studied them in detail.[4] But the same metaphysical pattern that exists at the level of an organism repeats itself in each of its constituent parts.

A frog, for example, is a composite of form and matter. Its matter consists of the frog's various organs (its legs, eyes, tongue, and the like), which the overall form of the frog organizes into an integrated, functioning whole. But each of its organs is itself a composite of form and matter (of bone, blood and tissue arranged in a particular way, for example, in the shape of an eye). And each of these latter components is in turn a composite of form and matter too (of earth, air, fire and water structured so as to make bone, blood or tissue).

At each of these levels, there is knowledge to be gained by investigating the composite in question. But all that can be known about it is its form. At each level, the intelligibility of the thing one is examining (organism, organ, organ components, basic elements) is limited to its general shape. The individuality of *this* frog, eye, bit of blood or drop of water—what later philosophers call its individuality "as such"—is literally incomprehensible, and hence unreal.

The point is driven home by Aristotle's account of what later philosophers termed "prime" matter.

If every thing or part of a thing is a composite whose individuality is due to its matter, but its matter is always a further composite of matter and form, then there must be some ultimate matter without form, for if there were not, it would be impossible to explain how any composite could ever be an individual thing, since the matter that individuates it can always be decomposed into a nonindividuating form embodied in a bit of matter of a lower-order kind—a process that cannot continue indefinitely without the very idea of matter (and hence of individuality) losing its meaning altogether. Hence, if there are to be any individuals at all, at any level of order, there must be a formless matter antecedent to them, from which the individuality of every individual, at every level, ultimately derives.

Aristotle accepts this conclusion. He describes the formless matter his metaphysics demands as a pure potentiality—pure because, unlike the potentiality of a tadpole or human embryo, it is not directed toward any specific end at all.

The best way to think of this is as the potential that each of the basic elements possesses to turn into any of the others. Water has a simple yet distinctive form, and so does air. They are two different kinds of things. But the potential of water to turn into air, and vice versa, exists prior to the distinguishing shapes they possess. The shapes of the elements are the most rudimentary of all. This prior potential must therefore be perfectly shapeless—a *pure* potential—and hence wholly unintelligible, since it is only the shape or form of a thing that makes it understandable at all.

The result is that while Aristotle's metaphysics requires the existence of a purely formless potentiality as the ultimate source of all individuation, his equation of form with intelligibility guarantees that the uniqueness of every individual, at each level of organization, must remain forever inscrutable. In this way, the concept of prime matter prevents the intelligibility of the world from going all the way down, to the very bottom of things. It blocks us from understanding why each individual is the one it is and not another—from accounting for what Leibniz terms the "identity of indiscernibles."[5] Prime matter represents the residual stupidity of the world. It is a cosmic principle of mindlessness whose existence necessarily rules out the possibility of our ever explaining everything in the world, since it makes the individuality of individuals inexplicable as a matter of principle.

Aristotle's interpretation of the dynamics of growth reflects a similar depreciation of individual uniqueness.

The growth of a frog or man from infancy to maturity is a movement toward a higher level of reality. In the process, the animal in question comes to *be* more and more completely. As it does, it exhibits the form of its kind with increasing clarity and energy. This is what realization means—an individual's ever-closer approximation to a state of activity in which the powers of its species are fully at work. Its fulfillment therefore has nothing to do with its individuality as such—with the achievement or expression of something unique—but consists in the attainment of a state of being-at-work that is no different for it than for any other member of its kind.

Of course, no individual reaches this state except as an individual. Every fulfilled frog or man is a particular frog or man, with characteristics, and a biography, uniquely its own. But these play no role in the definition of its fulfillment. So far as that is concerned, the individual's peculiarities are completely irrelevant. If anything, fulfillment is a movement away from individuality and toward species-being, from what is idiosyncratic toward what is general and shared.

In the end, therefore, the individuality of things is not only impenetrable even by the greatest and most active mind, which the philosopher himself becomes when he reaches the summit of metaphysical knowledge. It also has no connection to the state of realized being that everything in the world strives to attain. It has no share in the eternal and divine in which all things yearn to partake. The individuality of things is unrelated to God. If one equates intelligibility with being, and accepts the metaphysical ultimacy of the distinction between form and matter, no other conclusion is possible.

MIND ALL THE WAY DOWN

If, on the other hand, one assumes that God created the world from nothing, then everything in it must be suffused with mind. The world cannot have a residuum of unintelligibility, since anything that might serve as its source has itself, by assumption, been created by a being whose intellect is infinite. The Christian doctrine of creation demands that the intelligibility of the world go all the way down. To suggest otherwise is to impugn the omnipotence of its creator. It follows that the individuality of individuals must in principle be understandable too.

We human beings can never fully answer the question of why any individual thing has the unique characteristics it does, or exists at all. There will always be more for us to know about it. One might even define this "more," from a human point of view, as the individuality of the thing in question. But the doctrine of creation gives us grounds to be confident that, as we probe this unexplained residue, it will yield continuously to mind. So far as our finite minds are concerned, the world is a well whose bottom can never be reached. But the assumption that it is the creation of an all-powerful God whose divine mind is fully at work in every particle of it, gives us reason to believe that the world is as comprehensible as it is deep.

To the question, "Why is this individual the unique being it is?" Aristotle answered, "On account of its matter." This inevitably led him to the concept of prime matter, which rules out the possibility of any mind ever being able to answer the question that spurred it.

The doctrine of creation forces us to take a different tack. Jesus tells his followers that God numbers "even the hairs" on their heads. "Not a sparrow falls," he says, without God's will.[6] Aquinas makes the same point in more philosophical terms when he asserts that God knows not only the forms of things but their individual natures as well.[7]

For a Christian who believes that God created the world from nothing, it is an impiety to assert that the individuality of individuals is incomprehensible because the matter from which it derives has no form or intelligibility in it. The idea of creation makes the distinction between form and matter unsustainable as an ultimate metaphysical reality. To the extent it retains any meaning at all, it is only as a heuristic device that we with our finite minds must use to explain the limitlessly complex world of individual beings in which we exist. The claim that this distinction is embedded in the nature of things conflates our limited intelligence with God's boundless one, since from his divine perspective the intelligibility of the world must be as infinite as his own mind.

For Aristotle, the world is inherently but not infinitely intelligible. The Christian doctrine of creation destroys the intrinsic intelligibility of the world. But at the same time, it opens up the prospect of it's being infinitely knowable from a point of view beyond the world, and thereby prepares the way for a hyperrationalist science of nature defined by two beliefs that are incompatible with Aristotle's metaphysics of form and matter: first, that there is absolutely nothing in the world that cannot be understood; and second, that because our minds are finite, they must always fall short of that absolute knowledge to which we inevitably aspire as rational beings.[8]

For a hyperrationalist science of this sort to become a practical reality, all(!) that needs to happen is for men to come to believe that it is appropriate for them to strive to assume the position of the God to whom the doctrine of creation ascribes an infinite understanding of things, though without, of course, leaving their finitude behind. Christian orthodoxy resists this. It regards the wish to be God as the worst of all possible sins. But even the *idea* of such a science remains unthinkable so long as our human reason is hamstrung by the Aristotelian distinction between form and matter. The creationist metaphysics of the Christian religion dissolves this distinction. It erases the horizon that bounds every attempt to understand the world on its basis. And it thereby authorizes, potentially at least, a limitless increase in our knowledge of things, predicated on the assumption that the intelligibility of the world extends to the individuality of everything in it.

It also invites a similarly boundless expansion of our appreciation of the beauty and goodness of individual beings.

The goodness of the world as a whole follows from the beneficence of its creator. But the same applies to all the individuals in it, whose number and variety are infinite. God must have had a sufficient reason for creating them too—for making each the perfectly unique being it is. In each case, his reason can only have been to achieve something good, and because God is omnipotent, nothing could prevent him from doing so. It follows that the goodness of God's creation is manifest not only in the general order of things but in their individuality as well.

This too is something we can never fully grasp. We can no more exhaust the beauty and goodness of any individual than we can explain, in scientific terms, why it has the unique identity it does. There will always be more to be said about both. But the Christian doctrine of creation gives us grounds to believe that the goodness and beauty of each thing is as limitless as its intelligibility, and as endlessly explicable by us, though our powers of appreciation and sympathy remain within narrow bounds.

Plato, Aristotle and Plotinus all thought of the order of the world as an intelligible and therefore good scheme, embodied in a material medium that reason penetrates deeply but incompletely. As a consequence, they agreed that the world is not, and cannot be, perfectly good. Epictetus came closest to the idea of such a world with his teaching that fate arranges everything for the best. But even he accepted the distinction between form and matter, and thus had no way of explaining how the goodness of the world could include the uniqueness of individual beings. By converting matter to form without re-mainder, the Christian doctrine of creation provides the basis for an explana-tion of this kind and thus allows the pagan idea of fate to be extended beyond the limits within which the distinction between form and matter confined it. It transforms the idea of fate into the altogether different notion of providence, which for the first time provides the theological means to support the claim that the world is perfectly good.

When human beings take up the providential posture of the God for whom the goodness and beauty of every individual is directly apparent, and make his moral and aesthetic understanding their own regulative ideal, a path is opened to a conception of politics and art that Aristotle would have found as incomprehensible as the hyperrationalist science of nature which this same transgressive move allows. For Aristotle, the goodness and beauty of things resides in their form. The idea that anything, including a human being, can be beautiful or good on account of what makes it distinct from every other member of its kind, is one he would have thought naive or insane. To be good or beautiful is, for Aristotle, to conform to a form: the essence of classicism, in both politics and art. The equation of goodness and beauty with the indi-viduality of the individual is the counteressence of the anticlassicism that now rules in these domains. The regnant ideal in the political sphere today is that of diversity, in art those of genius and sublimity. Later we shall see how these ideals convey a belief in the infinite value of the individual, on whom Christian-ity's erasure of the distinction between form and matter confers a metaphysical dignity that cannot be explained so long as one remains within the frame-work of Aristotle's classicist account of political and aesthetic experience.

SACRED BODIES

On the whole, the Greeks and Romans appear to have had a more forgiv-ing attitude toward the body than did their Christian successors. In general, pagan writers do not disparage the body as something wicked or sinful. They tend to view its appetites as a fact of life, not evil in themselves though re-quiring discipline and control so as not to interfere with the pursuit of more important things, like wisdom and glory. Many even consider the measured satisfaction of bodily desire to be a component of human happiness. This is Aristotle's view, for example.

One finds, of course, expressions of a more hostile attitude toward the body. At the beginning of the *Republic,* Cephalus cheerfully announces his relief as an old man at finally being free of sexual longing, and Plato's view of the body is for the most part less accepting than Aristotle's (though there are passages that suggest otherwise).[9] But even Plato's most negative statements about the body portray its desires not as something morally wrong but merely bothersome—as an obstacle to happiness. And while a few pagan writers (philosophers mainly) view the passions of the body as a dangerous threat, there are others (Aristophanes, for example) who regard them as a source of amusement and comic relief.[10]

Pagan attitudes toward the variety of human sexuality also seem especially tolerant by Christian standards. The acceptance of certain forms of homoeroticism is well known.[11] In all these respects, the pagan view of the body, even at its most disparaging, seems far removed from that of Augustine, who reviles its movements and feelings—especially its sexual feelings—as the blameworthy badge of original sin, and attacks the body, with passionate loathing, not as something bothersome or bemusing but intrinsically evil. The Christian attitude toward the body appears harsher than that even of its harshest pagan detractors.

But in one sense, this puts things exactly backward, for the Christian attack on the body presupposes its investment with a value that no pagan philosopher, Plato included, could have imagined.

That is because even those, like Plato, who take a hostile view of the body regard it not as something wicked but merely stupid—a bit of matter that shares with all such bits a mindlessness that limits the expansion of reason so long as it remains tied to material things, the body included. The great mistake, from Plato's point of view, is to assign any meaning or value to the body at all—to treat it as if it had any reality. Plato and his followers urge us to do everything we can to escape the pull of bodily need because they view the body as the source of everything unreal in our lives, which becomes more real as we learn to conform our thoughts and feelings to the bodiless forms that alone truly exist. Even Epicurus, who advocates the pursuit of pleasure but defines it in strictly rational terms, sees things in this light.

A rationalist who accepts the metaphysics of form and matter can hardly view the body in any other way. From his perspective, it is bound to seem a drag on reason. Even Aristotle concedes as much when he says that it is the bodily needs of the philosopher that force him back down from the heights of contemplation, where he is able, briefly at least, to live the life of a god.[12] Plato's judgment is more severe. The body is a prison, he famously says, from which we escape only at death.[13] If, in the meantime, it is reasonable to take a somewhat more relaxed attitude toward the body and within limits indulge its appetites without shame, that is not because these have any intrinsic value of their own, whether positive or negative, but for precisely the opposite reason—because the body is a worthless thing whose movements are completely undeserving of serious concern, yet press on us with such insistence that they must be gratified, from time to time, merely in order to "put them out of mind."

The doctrine of creation upends this view by eliminating the distinction between form and matter, and with that, the negative side of the metaphysical ledger to which pagan rationalists of all sorts assigned bodily things. From a Christian point of view, the human body can no more be dismissed as a mindless, stupid thing than any other of God's creatures. My body is mine alone. It sets me apart from everyone else. It is the most vivid expression and dramatic reminder of my individuality, and like that of every other individual in the world, is the work of God too.

My body is therefore an appropriate object of spiritual concern. It is something I should care about for its own sake, and not just because its appetites must be quieted so that I can hear the voice of reason. Instead of devaluing the body as a thing of no account, the metaphysics of creation confers on it a previously unimaginable prestige. That the life of the body now becomes a theater of rebellion and sin, and acquires an unprecedented moral significance as a result, only confirms this new prestige, albeit in a negative way.[14]

The investment of the body with a spiritual value of this kind is dramatically illustrated by the doctrine of the resurrection, which, as Augustine recognized, made no sense to pagan philosophers.[15]

If the body is a tomb in which the spirit is trapped, why should anyone think that a restoration to bodily life on Judgment Day, for the saints who can now look forward to an eternity of embodied bliss at the feet of God, is preferable to release from the body with all its quirks and travails? Plato, certainly, held the opposite view, and even Aristotle characterizes the movement toward the eternal and divine as one of progressive dematerialization.

But for a Christian who believes in divine creation, the bodies that we have been given by God must like everything else in the world be valuable too. Their resurrection after death is therefore a supplement to the glory of salvation. It is a plus, not a minus, from God's point of view that his saints are rejoined to their bodies so that their ineffable joy can be experienced with all the concreteness and perspectival particularity of the unique physical selves he gave them when he brought them into being in the first place. And of course the same applies to the damned, whose eternal suffering must be physically particularized too if their pains are to have a concreteness comparable to that of the joys of the saints in heaven. It is only by means of the resurrection of the body that God's creative intentions can be fulfilled in the world to come with a specificity equal to that exhibited by the infinitely complex world of embodied beings in which we must live until then.

The pagan critics of Christianity ridiculed the idea of the resurrection of the body as a peculiarly irrational belief. From their perspective, it seemed ridiculous to assign any great value to the body in this life, let alone the next one. The philosophers of pagan antiquity generally agreed that we become real to the extent we shed our individuality. This requires us to detach ourselves, to the greatest possible degree, from the distractions and demands of the body. We are able to do this periodically in this life, when we think, or achieve that state of "careless" *apatheia* the Stoics defined as their ideal. It happens permanently when we die. That after death our liberated souls should be retethered to the mindless carcasses from which they have at last been freed was therefore bound to seem, from their point of view, an especially silly idea. It took the doctrine of creation from nothing, which for the first time conferred a moral and spiritual value on the individuality of individuals, and therefore on the bodies that individuate them, to put this metaphysical prejudice to rout.

The doctrine of the resurrection of the body brought the conflict between these two metaphysical systems into the open. But nothing did so more pointedly than the idea of the Incarnation, which became a lasting source of controversy between the philosophically minded champions of the Christian religion and their pagan opponents.

That a spiritual being can reside within a physical one was a familiar pagan idea. This is how Plato conceived the relationship between the soul and the body. The soul is *in* the body, he said, in the way a passenger is in the ship that carries him from place to place. But on Plato's view, the soul no more *is* the body that houses it than the passenger is the ship. Each is a transient resident, with an identity distinct from that of the conveyance in which he happens for the moment to be riding. This is the premise of Plato's doctrine of

metempsychosis, which he inherited from earlier sources.[16] It has its mythological origins in the stories of shape-shifting gods, who assume one human
or animal form after another, without ever ceasing to be the gods they are.

This is most emphatically *not* the relation that the son of God has to the
body in which he is incarnated during his time among men. Jesus is not a
divine being temporarily resident in a physical one. As John says, in a phrase
carefully chosen to distinguish his beliefs from those of his pagan contemporaries, "the word *became* flesh."[17] Jesus' divinity and corporeality are fused;
the one penetrates the other so completely that no distinction can be drawn
between them. The body of Christ therefore cannot be disparaged as "mere"
flesh. It is as holy as God himself.

Nor is John's statement merely a pious dictum without theological meaning. John himself made no attempt to unfold the implications of his statement in a systematic way. But others did, beginning with Paul, and the Church
Fathers who followed Paul's lead considered the unity of spirit and flesh in
Christ to be one of the dogmatic pillars of the Christian religion.

Unless Christ were wholly spirit, they argued, the agonies he suffered could
not have had the power to undo the effects of original sin. Only a divine act
of self-sacrifice possesses such redemptive authority; no human one does. On
the other hand, unless Christ were wholly flesh, his agonies must have been
less than fully real. For his sacrifice to have been as great as possible, his suffering has to have had the excruciating immediacy of bodily pain. The belief
that Christ was wholly spirit and wholly flesh, and that these two must therefore have been completely united in him, was a crucial premise of the theology of divine self-sacrifice that Paul outlined in his Letters. The need to provide
this belief with a secure conceptual foundation became the most urgent task
of the first three centuries of Christian theology, which were dominated by a
series of Christological disputes that tested it in one way or another.

These disputes were driven by the new religion's need to formulate a distinctive core of orthodox beliefs. But Christianity's emphasis on creedal
orthodoxy, which has no counterpart in the other Abrahamic religions, was
itself in part motivated by the encounter with pagan rationalism and its ancient demand for speculative coherence. The Church Fathers' preoccupation
with the idea of the Incarnation in particular was intensified by the especially
strong resistance this idea provoked among its pagan critics. Spirit may be *in*
the flesh, they said. Form may be *in* matter. But the union of the two is a
metaphysical impossibility. For John's claim that the spirit *became* flesh to be
intelligible at all, the metaphysics of form and matter had to be abandoned

and a new one, based on the radically different distinction between creator and creature, put in its place.

The perceived absurdity of the doctrine of the Incarnation, from a pagan point of view, compelled the first centuries of Christian philosophers to spend an extraordinary amount of time defending it, amidst hoots of educated derision. The elaborate theology they constructed to support it, though employing Greek categories of thought, brought out with increasing clarity the destructive implications of the metaphysics of creation for the distinction between form and matter, and with that, for the tradition of pagan rationalism as a whole.

One of these implications was that physical bodies possess a sacred value no ancient rationalist could conceive. In a Christian view of the world, every body has such value, as the doctrine of the resurrection of the body suggests. But it is preeminently the body of Christ, in whose fusion of spirit and flesh all our hopes for salvation reside, that possesses a value of this kind. The doctrine of the Incarnation is the supreme expression of the universal spiritualization of bodily life that follows from the destruction of the distinction between form and matter, and the investment of the individuality of individuals with a wholly unclassical value of its own. Among other things, it holds the key, as we shall see, to the meaning of modern art.

MORAL PERSONALITIES

All human beings possess bodies. But if the bodies of men are the work of God and not the product of some preexisting stuff, then their bodies cannot themselves be the source of the world's evil, as the Neoplatonists and Manicheans maintained. It was this line of thought that led Augustine to his concept of the will as a power of self-causation undetermined by the body. Evil comes into the world, Augustine says, not on account of the body, but because of what the will chooses to do with the appetites that spring from the body—because it turns away from God and indulges these appetites instead of obeying his command to keep them in check.

Every man possesses a will, as he does a body. But if the bodies of men make them different, don't their wills make them the same? Each man's body is unique. It gives him an individual identity. The will, by contrast, is a generic capacity, like reason. It is the same power in every man. If the will and not the body is the source of all the evil in the world, then the spiritually most significant attribute of human beings appears to be one they share in common. On the surface at least, this seems to conflict with the valorization of individuality that is entailed by the doctrine of creation from nothing and exemplified by Christianity's spiritualization of bodily life.

But the opposite is true. Though the will is a power possessed by all men, its exercise intensifies their distinctness rather than blurs it. The will is a source of further individuation beyond that attributable to the body (which human beings share with everything else in the world). To be an individual, in the special sense that only a will enables its possessor to be, is on Augustine's view the unique privilege of men and angels. The difference between reason and will makes this clear.

Reason is not an inherently individuating power. When two people are reasoning, their minds are numerically distinct, but the difference between them is an accident so far as their rationality is concerned. To *be* rational is to be active in a way that coincides with the similar activity of other rational beings. That is why Aristotle says, in his lectures on the *psyche* or soul, that active mind is *one* mind, in which every thinker participates when he is at work in the business of thinking.[18]

The will, by contrast, is necessarily individuating. Two men may exercise their wills in an identical manner, for example, by choosing to disobey the same law on the very same occasion. But what matters about the choices they make, so far as their responsibility for them is concerned, is not the content of their choices but the act of making them. This is an act no one can ever perform for anyone else. Others may think my thoughts, and in assessing their rationality, it is a matter of indifference whose thoughts they are. The fact that a thought is mine rather than yours has no bearing on its rationality; if anything, it is likely to be evidence of its irrationality. But where questions of responsibility are concerned, the reverse is true. Here, it is precisely the fact that *I* make a particular choice that explains my responsibility for it, which is neither increased nor decreased by its identity (in content or consequence) with the choices of others.

No one else can do my willing for me. No one's choices can be a substitute or surrogate for my own, consistent with my being a responsible person. What is least important from the standpoint of reason thus becomes all important from the standpoint of will. If the rationalism of pagan metaphysics inevitably depreciates the individuality of individuals, in the way that Aristotle's account of active mind does, then Augustine's theodicy of the will raises the worth of the individual to its highest possible pitch, and converts the goal of salvation from the deliberate suppression of individuality into its exact opposite: the cultivation of a sense of separate selfhood, grounded in the will, and the acceptance of a nontransferable responsibility associated with what Kant calls "moral personality."[19]

Each of God's creatures has a body and therefore a physical identity uniquely its own. But only beings with wills are also individuated by their responsibility for their acts, which no one else can possibly share with them. Between these two sorts of individuation there is, moreover, a crucial distinction. The second is one the individual creates for himself, while the first, even in the case of beings with wills, is received by them from God. To anticipate Kant's distinction, the individuality of the body is heteronomous, that of the will autonomous. And however precious the first may be from a Christian point of view, the same theology assigns an even greater value to the second.

It is true that no finite being can be an individual in the second sense without also being one in the first. There are no disembodied wills in God's creation. But only those creatures with wills are able to convert the physically unique location of their bodies into a spiritually unique one as well. In the fallen condition in which they are now condemned to live, they must do this by willing against the imperious demands of a body in rebellion. But whether the relation between body and will is one of conflict or harmony, the will alone has the power to create the special kind of "supernatural" individuality that Kant associates with our membership in the "kingdom of ends," a subject to which we shall return later on. And while the physical individuality of every being in God's creation is something that is intelligible and worthy of concern, the moral individuality of those embodied creatures who possess wills is even more so, for the self-caused motions by which they bring it into being exhibit the same autonomy that God possesses, and mimic his divine power of creation from nothing.

The moral individuality of creatures with wills is thus the image of God's own. It reproduces, within worldly constraints, the independence of the one perfectly free being who transcends the world altogether. In the whole of the created world, this special sort of individuality therefore possesses the greatest value any can. God's creation is pervasively mindful. Every individual in it matters. But the moral individuality of angels and men is supremely important, and provides the pivot of world history, whose drama of fall and redemption centers on the individual destinies that God's willful creatures fashion for themselves.

The learned pagans who viewed the Christian religion as a jumble of superstitious nonsense did not understand how the physical individuality of a thing could be valuable in its own right. The metaphysics of form and matter disallowed this. Nor, because they lacked the idea of the will, did they understand how certain beings could possess an even more important sort of individuality which they create for themselves. In both respects, pagan philosophy was limited by its rationalist presuppositions. The Christian teaching that the world was created from nothing by a God who transcends it, and that human beings, fashioned in God's image, possess a power of radical beginning as well, which they display in their rebellious but free acts of will, dissolved these limits once and for all, and laid the foundation for that hypervaluation of individuality, both physical and moral, that remains a cornerstone of scientific and ethical belief today.

HISTORY

The doctrine of creation gives individuality a value it can never possess in a rationalist metaphysics based on the distinction between form and matter. This applies, most obviously, to all the individuals *in* the world. But it also applies to the world *as a whole,* which must now be viewed as a unique individual too, with an utterly distinct character and career of its own. This is the meaning of the Christian interpretation of world history.

That it is possible to find a significance of some sort in the sequence of human events is an idea as old as Herodotus. Ancient historians from Thucydides to Tacitus took it for granted, and in their narratives sought to provide an interpretive explanation of the causes and consequences of what men had done and suffered in the past.

The events and personalities about which they wrote were of course unique. Thucydides' portrait of Alcibiades, and Tacitus' of Nero, delineate their subjects' peculiar traits with unforgettable precision. Still, the emphasis in both writers is on the enduring pattern of human events, which in contrast to the events themselves, is a feature of the world that never passes away. Lessons can be learned from the study of the past, but only because some things do not change. The human condition is always basically the same. The challenges that men face today are in essence no different from those of the past, and our response to them can be expected to follow the same pattern too. Human history is filled with novelties and wonders, but the distinctiveness of the events recorded in it must be set within a frame of changeless order that alone gives them meaning. Ultimately, it is only the everlasting order of the world that makes human history intelligible. In this respect, the fundamental premise of ancient history is the same as that of ancient philosophy. At a metaphysical level, Thucydides shares Plato's equation of reality with form, though as an intelligent lover of sights and sounds, his attention is riveted on the passing spectacle of appearances and not the changeless realm of ideas.

The Christian concept of history is altogether different. Augustine was the first to define it in a systematic way.

For Augustine, the whole of human history is a once-and-for-all event, whose meaning is to be found not in some larger pattern, endlessly repeated in a world without beginning or end, but in the uniqueness of the event itself. From the first point of view, the peculiarities that distinguish one personality and period from another are bound to be of less importance than the general form they display. Augustine's account of the drama of creation reverses this valuation. It makes the singularity of history's great events—of the Fall, Christ's passion, the final judgment and resurrection of the saints— the most important thing about them. It fastens our attention on their unrepeatable novelty, which reproduces, moment by moment, the originality of the whole of creation itself. To be sure, human beings repeatedly do what others have done in the past. In particular, they repeat, in countless ways, the original sin of Adam and Eve's prideful rebellion against God. But for Augustine, this pattern must be set against the background of the uniqueness of God's creation and interpreted in its light—an exact reversal of the interpretive approach on which all ancient history is based.

In this sense, one might say that human history is for Augustine novelistic. It takes the form of a once-told tale, whose chapters have the meaning they do not despite but because of their uniqueness in a temporal sequence that happens only once. The assignment of value to every individual body in creation, and the hypervaluation of the moral individuality of those creatures to whom God has given wills, is thus reflected, at a cosmic level, in Augustine's valuation of the uniqueness of the historical career of the world as a whole, indeed of time itself, which, for him, is something unique too—a linear movement from creation to final judgment, unfolding between two eternities, and never to happen again.

Aristotle saw time as the theater of eternity, displaying in its endless repetitions the everlasting forms of things, a world inherently divine. For Augustine, time is a realm apart from eternity, brought into being for a time(!) by an omnipotent God whose unchanging nature is infinitely remote from the transient world he creates. This world, and time itself, which is merely another name for the world, is an individual whose uniqueness is the key to understanding its own finite history and the meaning of all those repetitive movements within it that Aristotle wrongly believed to be eternal.

The idea of creation forces this conclusion upon us, and thereby brings about a reversal in every department of pagan thought. It opens new horizons in natural science, which is no longer constrained by the metaphysics of form and matter. It invites the belief that diversity is something good in itself. And it produces a revolution in historical thinking, which now for the first time finds the meaning of general patterns in the uniqueness of the world and time, rather than the other way around.

In the twilight of the ancient world, confronted with the growth of a religion whose most fundamental beliefs they considered absurd, the last champions of pagan rationalism declared the idea of creation irrational. From their perspective it certainly was, for at a stroke it dissolved the metaphysical foundations of every branch of ancient thought. But the idea of creation prevailed against its detractors, and in time supplied the basis for a new metaphysics that in contrast to the old one had the resources to explain why individuality matters—why it is something intelligible, beautiful and good in itself. In the process, it prepared the way for the family of beliefs that lie at the root of modern science, politics and art.

But the same doctrine that produced this unprecedented regard for the individuality of individuals, also brought about a far-reaching devaluation of the world, amidst whose distracting splendors no Christian can ever be at home. The radical separation of eternity and time, between which the doctrine of creation drives a wedge, deprives all that happens in the world of inherent value. It turns our lives on earth into a pilgrimage and makes the human condition one of homelessness, in which only a prideful and therefore sinful man or woman can find contentment. This view of the world, which contrasts in the sharpest possible way with Aristotle's philosophy of pride, lays the ground for other characteristically modern beliefs and experiences.

If the Christian doctrine of creation is the inspiration for the celebration of the individual that informs so many of our modern ideals, it is thus also the source of the experience of homelessness in the world to which even those who no longer believe in the Christian (or any) God have long been accustomed. The doctrine of creation from nothing—Christianity's greatest contribution to thought—is therefore at once the origin of our highest ideals and most distinctively modern forms of spiritual suffering, a blessing and a curse whose inseparability constitutes the peculiar fate of the West.

In later chapters, we will see how the dialectic of freedom and grace, unique to the Christian religion, has produced the disenchantment of Christianity itself, and why it leads to a world of despair and ingratitude: to our world, unbelieving, yet haunted by the ghosts of Christian belief, engorged with unprecedented powers, yet powerless to express in a public way the gratitude that every generation of human beings naturally feels toward its predecessors—a human gratitude which the anger and envy stirred by Christianity's demand for an unrequitable gratitude to God has put under a cloud of contempt. We will discover in a born-again paganism that restores eternity to time, while preserving the value of individuality in every domain, a way to be at home in the world again and joyfully grateful to the other human beings on whose love the endurance of our human place in the world always depends. And we will find in this combination of ideas—no longer either pagan or Christian—a better and more satisfying way to honor the most basic commitments of the science, art and politics that define the modern age, in which, amidst the emptiness of an outwardly confident but inwardly despairing secularism, our inextinguishable love of the eternal and divine waits to be reborn.

CHAPTER 15

The Contingency of the World

THAT WHOSE ESSENCE IS TO EXIST

Plato believed that the ordinary things we see about us owe their reality to something more real than they. The sights and sounds that fill the world are all, he claims, mere images or imitations of invisible forms that exist apart from them.[1] The latter are the source of whatever reality sensible things possess and of all the truth we can ever know about them. The question of how to conceive the relation between these unified and changeless forms and the many, moving things that imitate or embody them is the central question of Plato's metaphysics. Sometimes he describes this relation as one of reflection or representation; at other times, as one of participation.[2] But the separation of the forms from the worldly things that reflect or partake of them, and the ultimate unreality of these things themselves, are assumptions from which Plato never departed.

Aristotle attacks this view. He maintains that the forms of things that exist by nature are inseparable from the individual, sensible beings in which they are embodied, whose reality is something genuine and not an illusory veil through which we must look to see the really real order behind it.[3] The presumed reality of what he calls "this-suches" (this man here, that tree there) is the starting point for Aristotle's criticism of his teacher's metaphysics. All the most distinctive features of his own account of being follow from it.

Yet in pursuing the question of what makes a "this-such" real, Aristotle found himself driven back in Plato's direction. That is because, like Plato, he equates being with intelligibility, and both of these with form.

Every individual is a combination of form and matter. Its form makes it a "such" (a man, for example) and its matter a "this" (Socrates or Critias). But at whatever level we speak about the matter of a man—whether that of the whole man, or of his parts, or of the different sorts of material of which his parts are composed—it is only the form of the matter in question that we can understand and describe in speech. Only the form of any material object is intelligible and hence real. Its matter, as such, is neither.

The individuality of the individuals on whose reality Aristotle insists in his quarrel with Plato is therefore ultimately both unknowable and unreal, given the equation of form with being that both philosophers accepted. Aristotle's metaphysics thus ends in an *aporia*—a puzzle it can neither avoid nor resolve—for his rationalism compels him to deny the reality of the very things he claims, in opposition to his teacher, are the most real things of all.[4] Plato's metaphysics has other problems but not this one. His denial of the reality of worldly things is a consistent implication of the rationalism he shares with his student. Aristotle's insistence on the reality of individuals, coupled with his identification of being and form, leads him, by contrast, into an aporetic cul-de-sac from which there can be no escape within the bounds of pagan thought.

The idea of creation from nothing breaks this impasse. It dissolves the distinction between form and matter that Aristotle took for granted, and thereby makes the individuality of individuals both knowable and real (at least to the God who creates them). Every aspect of every creature that God brings into being, including its individuality, is necessarily endowed with reality and intelligibility, unlike the products of those processes of production and reproduction that Aristotle took to be the only sorts of coming-to-be and analyzed in terms of the distinction between form and matter, which guarantees that the reality and intelligibility of the world can never go all the way down.

The Christian doctrine of creation thus offers a way out of Aristotle's *aporia,* though it is not one that Aristotle himself could have grasped without repudiating the metaphysics of form and matter that shaped the outlook of every pagan philosopher, including Plato and his Neoplatonist successors, in whose idealistic rejection of the world the Church Fathers, and Augustine in particular, found encouragement for their own more radical form of other-worldliness. But if the idea of creation from nothing resolves a metaphysical paradox that Aristotle could not overcome, it also raises a question he had no reason to address, indeed, could not even have conceived. This is the question of how to explain the existence of the world as a whole. No question is further removed from the spirit of Aristotle's philosophy, or more central to the defining preoccupations of Christian thought.

CONTINGENCY

Every thing that exists in the realm beneath the moon is subject to generation and decay. Each comes into being and passes away—dogs and men, flowers and trees, bits of earth and drops of rain.

The existence of all such things is contingent in two ways. First, none owes its being to itself. Each depends upon something else for its existence. Second, each might not be at all. Socrates might never have been born or this particular lump of earth been formed by the other bits of matter that produced it. There is no contradiction in the thought of their nonexistence. It is easy to imagine the world without them.

All of this will be obvious even to a casual observer. The contingency of the existence of things in the sublunary world is one of their most striking characteristics. But what sort of characteristic is this? If a thing exists by necessity, its existence is explained by the nature of the thing itself. To know that it exists, and why, one need only know what kind of thing it is. But this is not true of Socrates or a lump of earth. Their existence cannot be deduced from their nature or essence. It is something distinct from it. What is this special property, "existence"? The question seems as obvious as the distinctiveness of the property itself. Yet it is not one that Aristotle treated independently of two others that he took to be fundamental. The first is the question of what makes each sublunary being a thing of a certain kind. The second is the question of what makes it a discrete member of the kind to which it belongs.

The first question concerns a thing's "suchness" and the second its "thisness." Aristotle answers the first by appealing to the concept of form. Socrates is a man, not a dog, because he has the form he does—one that all and only men possess. He answers the second in terms of the concept of matter. It is the matter in which his human form is embodied that makes Socrates not just any man but this one, different from all others. For Aristotle, the answer to both questions was thus to be found in the distinction between form and matter, which allows us, he believed, to account for the two dimensions of Socrates' composite being in the most elementary and rigorous way possible.

One can reasonably object to the completeness of Aristotle's account, however, by pointing out that any particular "this-such" might not exist—that its existence is something different from both its nature and its individuality, and therefore requires a separate explanation of its own.[5] Yet however obvious this difference may seem, Aristotle barely recognized it at all. That is because his reflections on the existence of things in the sublunary world were shaped by the assumption that everything in a thing that may truly be said to exist, is ultimately attributable to its form. The existence of such things appears to the untutored eye to be contingent in the two senses noted above. But a philosopher who thinks in a metaphysically accurate way knows that this is not really the case, since the existence of the forms that give them all the being they possess is not itself contingent in either respect.

Consider what it means, from Aristotle's point of view, to give an account of the fact that Socrates exists.

To give an account of anything means, for Aristotle, to assign a cause for it, in the broad sense in which he understands this idea. One thing is the cause of another if it is "responsible" for it in any of the several different ways that Aristotle identifies.[6] To ask what is the cause of Socrates' existence is therefore equivalent to asking what is responsible for each of the two dimensions of his composite nature as a "this-such" that on Aristotle's view constitute the totality of his being. Whichever aspect we isolate, there is only one possible answer. According to Aristotle, Socrates exists because another being with a specific form existed before him.

This is easiest to see in the case of Socrates' humanity. The cause of Socrates' existence as a man is his father, who had a human form and communicated it to his son through reproduction. But the same is true if we inquire about the cause of Socrates' individuality. It is his body that makes him an individual. And who or what is the cause of Socrates' body? Again, the only conceivable answer is, another being whose existence preceded his—in this case, Socrates' mother, in whose body the form of humanity sown by his father was nourished and grew and assumed a bodily shape of its own. But all that we can know about her body as the cause of his is ultimately reducible to its form. Socrates' mother's body was able to produce her son's because it had the uniquely human power to receive and nurture the form implanted in it by Socrates' father. Like any potential, this one possesses the reality it does only on account of its relation to the form it has the power to become. The very being of Socrates' mother's womb as a potentiality of a distinctively human kind is ultimately nothing but its receptivity to the form transmitted by his father's seed. Whether the question of why Socrates exists is interpreted as a question about his existence as a man, or as this particular man, it can therefore only be answered in "formalistic" terms.

The same is true if we ask about Socrates' parents. In general, no matter how far back we go in the chain of human generation, the existence of any of its members, either as a "this" or a "such," can only be accounted for in terms of the form of his or her predecessors in the chain. The existence of nonliving things follows the same pattern. The nature or "suchness" of a lump of earth is a function of its form. But so too is the individual shape and composition of the lump—its "thisness"—which is the result of other bits of elemental stuff interacting in accordance with their own distinctive tendencies to move in certain ways that are conceptually and ontologically derivative of the forms that shape and direct their movements.

The explanation of the existence of every sublunary being, considered either as a "this" or a "such," thus leads back to the forms of other beings that existed before it, and though beings of this kind last only for a time, the forms that alone explain both their nature and individual uniqueness do not themselves either come into being or pass away. Their existence is eternal and noncontingent. It depends on nothing other than themselves and the world is inconceivable without them.

Unlike those who live by the prejudices of ordinary experience, a philosopher will therefore understand that everything that really exists in the tumultuous realm beneath the moon exists by necessity. The idea that existence is something apart from necessity—from nature, form, essence—will strike him as naive. To think otherwise, he would have to believe that the existence of the forms that give each thing in the sublunary world every bit of being it possesses, is itself contingent, and hence in need of explanation, and anyone who believed that would be, in Aristotle's view, either a madman or a fool.

The Christian doctrine of creation turns this belief on its head. It asserts that the world and everything in it, including the forms that give it an intelligible order, has been brought into being from nothing by a transcendent God. On this assumption, even the forms of things have a contingent existence. Like everything else, they depend on something other than themselves, and might not be at all (since even on the strenuous assumption that any created world must have the order the existing one does, God might have chosen to abstain from creating altogether).

For anyone who adopts this Christian view of things, the most striking fact about the world will be its contingency, and the most pressing philosophical task that of explaining the sheer fact of its existence—an endeavor that Aristotle would have thought insane.

For a Christian, the entire world is covered by a pall of contingency. The idea that it *might not be* haunts all his thoughts and casts a shadow over every question he asks. In particular, it gives a new urgency to the question of what explains the existence of worldly things, since there is no longer anything *in* the world that is uninfected by contingency, at which the search for an answer might come to a stop.

Aristotle believed the order of the world to be eternal. By converting it into something contingent, the doctrine of creation forces us to separate the existence of things from their nature or form, in a way that Aristotle did not. And if it does this for the transient "this-suches" of the sublunary world, whose contingency seems so obvious to the philosophically naive, it is only because it does it for the world as a whole.

ESSENCE AND EXISTENCE

If the existence of the world is contingent, what explains it?

For those who believe in divine creation, there is only one possible answer. The world owes its existence to a God beyond it whose own existence is not contingent but necessary—whose essence is to exist, as Thomas Aquinas famously puts it in *De Ente et Essentia,* a short treatise written when he was still in his twenties.[7] Others had anticipated Aquinas' formulation, including the great Muslim philosopher Avicenna (d. 1037 C.E.), to whom Aquinas was deeply indebted.[8] But Aquinas' solution to the problem of the contingency of the world had a rigor and completeness that set it apart from earlier attempts, in the Latin West at least, and his formulation both of the problem and its solution eventually acquired a canonical status in the tradition of Christian philosophy.

Aquinas begins by observing that "a small error at the outset can lead to great errors in the final conclusions, as the Philosopher says in *De Caelo et Mundo.*"[9] The very first things "conceived" by the intellect, he says, are "being" and "essence." It is therefore especially important that anyone who wants to think clearly about the basic questions of metaphysics understand the proper meaning of these terms.

Aquinas' account of their meaning rests on a tripartite division among "various kinds of things," each of which has an essence of a distinctive sort. The first includes all those things that "are composed of matter and form." The second consists of "intelligences"—of souls that have individual identities and are many in number, but lack a material presence. The third category has only one member, the "first cause" of all the beings in the other two.

A human being like Socrates is an example of a composite substance. Every man has a distinctive form and a particular kind of body, one specially adapted to the form he possesses. It is in the "nature" of being human to possess both. We may think we can conceive of a man in an ox's body, or without any body at all, but in reality these are mere fantasies, for the essence of the kind of being we possess consists in a composition of form and matter, the second comprising a set of potentialities as uniquely human as the activities to which they correspond.

The same is true of all other earthly beings. The essence of each likewise consists in a union of form and matter, though a different one in each case. In general, every earthly species, including our own, has a composite nature that includes both elements, from which it follows that a man who lacks either is no longer human (a conclusion that presents special difficulties for the Christian belief in the survival of the human soul after death, and for the doctrine of the resurrection of the body, about both of which Aquinas has a great deal to say).[10]

Of course, Socrates is not just any man. He is this man, one among many. That is because he not only has a particular *kind* of body but the unique one that he does. Matter therefore plays a double role in his constitution. It is a component of his essence as a man, for without a body Socrates would not be a man at all. And it is the source of his individuality, since the body he has makes Socrates a unique member of the species to which he belongs. Matter plays the same two roles in the case of all composite substances. Only the first of these, however, is related to its essence. For while it is part of Socrates' essence to have a human body, it is not part of his essence to have a beard, or a snub nose, or any of the other features that distinguish him from Critias and Cebes.

Aquinas next considers the nature of "simple" substances, whose essence "is form alone." These further divide into two radically different types—those that Aquinas calls "intelligences," and God.

Aquinas begins his discussion of simple substances by observing that while "it is impossible that matter exist without a form," the reverse is not true. It is "not impossible that a form exist without matter, for a form, insofar as it is a form, is not dependent on matter." Some forms, to be sure, cannot exist without matter. This is true in the case of all composite substances. But that is because substances of this kind are relatively "distant" from God, who "is primary and pure act." Other substances are closer to God and need no matter to be what they are. I shall return to this idea in a moment.

By "intelligences," Aquinas has in mind a category of beings intermediate between God and composite substances. Like God, their essence lies in their form alone. Matter is not a part of the nature of such beings, nor of their definition, as it is of all composite substances. But unlike God, the intelligences are many. They are separate individuals, just as every composite substance is. Since they lack all matter, however, their separateness cannot be explained in the same way that we account for the individuality of men and dogs and elm trees. Each of the latter belongs to a species with an essence that includes matter as one of its elements, and is an individual member of its species on account of having the particular parcel of matter it does. It follows that if the intelligences are many rather than one, their individuality must be a constitutional feature of the very forms they possess, so that the familiar terrestrial distinction between species and member cannot be applied to them. Each of the intelligences must be a species unto itself. This is precisely the conclusion that Aquinas draws in the *Summa Theologiae*, appealing to Avicenna for support.[11]

In this regard, Aquinas' intelligences resemble Aristotle's planets and stars, each of which is also a species with a single member. Aristotle explains this peculiar conjunction of individuality and species-being by claiming that the heavenly bodies possess a special kind of matter that allows them to live forever, as individuals, in contrast to sublunary beings, whose material makeup is such that they are able to reach the immortality they seek only through their participation in the eternal lives of their species. Because his intelligences are immaterial beings, Aquinas cannot follow Aristotle's explanation of their special status.

But there is an even deeper difference between Aquinas' intelligences and Aristotle's celestial bodies. For what impressed Aquinas most deeply about the nature of the beings that populate his second category of substances is not that their essence is simple, that is, a function of form alone; nor that they are many; nor that each is, literally, one of a kind (a view he shared with Aristotle). The most striking characteristic of the intelligences, according to Aquinas, is the contingency of their existence—a notion that Aristotle would have found incomprehensible, given his assumption that the stars and planets are eternal.

Aquinas uses an Aristotelian distinction to make this radically un-Aristotelian point. The intelligences, he says, are "form alone," and hence "without matter." This makes them simple, in contrast to composite substances whose essence is a combination of form and matter. But the intelligences "are not in every way simple." Only that which is "pure act" (an Aristotelian idea) is perfectly simple. Everything that has "an admixture of potency" (another Aristotelian idea) falls short of such perfect simplicity. Hence, even if the intelligences are simple substances, they are not perfectly simple substances if there is *any* potency in them. And there is, according to Aquinas, for the essence of each lacks something that can only come "from beyond" its essence itself.

This additional something is the *existence* of the essence in question. There is nothing about the essence of any of the intelligences that tells us whether it exists. This is also true of the essences of composite substances. Each of these "can be understood without understanding anything about its existence: I can understand what a man is or what a phoenix is and nevertheless not know whether either has existence in reality."[12]

The essences of the intelligences and of composite substances, though they differ with regard to whether matter belongs to them as part of their definition, are alike in this crucial respect. Their existence is a "potency" that may or may not be realized. If it is to be realized, it can only be by the action of something that "comes" to the essence from "beyond" it and "makes a combination with the essence," joining a potentially existing essence to actual existence in a kind of metacomposition that even the simple intelligences must possess if they are to exist not merely as potential beings but real ones. "In the intelligences, therefore, there is existence beyond the form, and so we say that an intelligence is form *and* existence" (emphasis added).[13]

The difference between the essence of an intelligence and that of a composite substance is thus overshadowed by an even more fundamental similarity between them: the dependence of *all* substances of *both* sorts on something other than themselves for their existence. Their own essence does not and cannot secure this by itself. It is not of the essence of any thing of either sort to exist. The most that one can say is that, whatever their essence, such things may or may not be, that they have a potency for existence, whose realization is not guaranteed by the thing's essence alone. This is Aquinas' way of expressing the contingency of the existence of all worldly beings, celestial and terrestrial alike, using metaphysical terms of Aristotelian derivation to describe a distinction between form and being that Aristotle's metaphysics rules out.

THE BEING WHOSE ESSENCE IS TO EXIST

If we ask for the definition of a composite substance, we need only refer to its essence, which will always be some combination of matter and form. Similarly, if we ask for an account of what an intelligence is, we need not look beyond its essence, which consists of form alone. But if we ask *why* a substance of either sort *exists,* the answer necessarily lies outside its essence, in something else, which realizes the potential of the essence to exist. It follows that "everything the existence of which is other than its own nature has existence from another." But if the other from which it has existence itself only exists contingently (if it is not of *its* essence to exist), then its existence must in turn be explained by something else outside it, and so on.

We cannot, however, "go to infinity in causes." We cannot explain the contingent existence of one thing by appealing to another whose existence is equally contingent, hence equally in need of explanation by something other than itself, and so on *ad infinitum,* for if we proceed in this way we will never overcome the ultimate inexplicability of the existence of anything at all. To explain why anything exists, we must eventually come to what Aquinas calls "a first cause," one that "is the cause of existing in all things" because it "is existence only."

To avoid an infinite causal regress that would leave us without a satisfying answer to the question of why there is something rather than nothing, we must therefore assume the existence of a being whose essence is to exist. We must assume the existence of a being in whom essence and existence coincide. This is God, the third kind of substance that Aquinas identifies, and while God resembles the intelligences in being immaterial, he differs from them, and from all composite substances, in having an existence that is necessary rather than contingent.

Aristotle also recognized the need to avoid an explanatory regress of this sort by grounding the existence of everything in the world beneath the moon in something that never changes. All things of this kind are in motion. The movement of each, moreover, is caused by something outside it. Socrates is produced by his parents, lives for a time, and dies. Water rises with the heat of the sun, then falls again as rain. But the ultimate cause of all these motions lies in the forms of the things in question, and on Aristotle's view these are eternal and divine. The search for an explanation of the existence of sublunary beings comes to a satisfying stop here.

The same is true of celestial beings. The planets and stars are immortal individuals. But each is also in permanent motion, going round and round in a circle in the sky. Like the mortal motion of their earthly counterparts, the eternal motion of the heavenly bodies necessarily has its cause in something outside themselves that never moves at all. According to Aristotle, this is the motionless being-at-work of mind minding mind, a state of pure activity in which the planets and stars, like every other moving being, yearn to partake, but never can without qualification, given their material (ethereal) natures. This state is one of pure form, perfect *energeia,* everlasting and complete. For Aristotle, the explanation of the motion of the better beings we see above us in the sky, like that of all the things with which we share the earth, thus also comes to an end in the existence of something whose nonexistence is unthinkable—whose essence is to exist, to put it in Aquinas' terms.

Aristotle and Aquinas agree, therefore, that no finite being, on the earth or in the heavens, can be its own cause. Each must derive its being from something other than itself, and ultimately, from something that is the ground of its own existence. Yet this similarity masks a profound difference. In Aristotle's view, the divine source of all cosmic motion is an indwelling cosmic principle. It is the inherent intelligibility of the cosmos itself. The self-moved mover that is the uncaused cause of everything that moves on account of something else, from the elements to the stars, is for Aristotle just the eternality of the cosmos itself—of the one and only cosmos there is, a vast theater of diverse motions whose own internal, activating principles never move at all. For Aquinas, by contrast, the being whose essence is to exist necessarily exists beyond the world. That is because nothing in the world has an essence that entails its existence. Even the intelligences do not exist by virtue of their natures, but require something other than themselves, outside the world, to realize their potential for existence.

Aquinas inherited from Aristotle the idea of a hierarchy of worldly beings. He agreed that some of the things in the world are more real than others. That is because some are nearer to God. In particular, the intelligences are closer to God than composite substances like man. Indeed, they are the closest of all. "[A] form, insofar as it is a form, is not dependent on matter. When we find a form [like man] that cannot exist except in matter, this happens because such forms are distant from the first principle, which is primary and pure act. Hence, those forms that are nearest the first principle are subsisting forms essentially without matter."[14]

But even at the very top of this hierarchy, the distance between the matterless forms of the intelligences and God remains absolute, since the essence of the intelligences does not entail their existence in the way that God's does. Even the very best things in the world therefore exhibit the same contingency that lesser things do. Even they do not exist simply by virtue of being what they are. Even their existence is not necessary and eternal, as Aristotle supposed, but depends on something other than themselves for its actualization. And because they are the very best things in the world, this other can only be a being *beyond* the world—the one and only, necessarily otherworldly being whose essence is to exist.

In the most general terms, therefore, Aristotle and Aquinas give the same answer to the question, "why is there something rather than nothing?" Things exist because there is something whose essence is to exist. God is the only answer to the most fundamental question of metaphysics. But Aristotle's God, with whom all explanations end, is the everlasting mindedness of the world itself, while Aquinas' God is a being beyond the world whose necessary existence is the cause and ground of the contingent existence of the world as a whole and of everything in it, including the intelligences, the best of all creatures, whose essence consists in form alone. Aquinas employs Aristotle's distinction between potency and act to explain why the existence even of the intelligences depends on such a God. But the conclusion he draws from it would have baffled his pagan predecessor, who saw no need to look beyond the world for a God to ground its existence.

AN ONTOLOGICAL GAP

In Aristotle's cosmos, the hierarchy of beings is continuous and comprehensive. There are no radical breaks in it and nothing beyond it. The lowest things and the highest—those whose share in the eternal and divine is most fleeting and those, like the planets and stars, whose participation is most durable and complete—form the poles of a continuum that mark the antipodes of the world. To be sure, there are meaningful gradations of being within this continuum. We can observe and explain them. But the continuum includes all there is.

For Aquinas, by contrast, the most impressive ontological distinction is not that between one level or grade of being on this continuum and some other, however great the difference may be. It is the distinction between the continuum as a whole and the "first cause" that is responsible for its existence.

Nothing on the continuum of worldly beings has an essence that entails its existence. Only its "extrinsic" cause, which exists apart from the continuum, is "something whose quiddity is its very own existence." Between this extrinsic cause and every other being there is an ontological difference not merely of degree but kind—a chasm that cannot be bridged by imagining a series of intermediate beings that fills the gap between the countless substances that exist contingently through the action of something else, and their "first cause," the one and only substance whose essence is to exist. No such bridge is conceivable. The only possible connection between these two kinds of substances is *creation:* the uncaused communication of existence from the one being that possesses it of necessity to all those that do not, God's free gift of existence to the world.

At this point, of course, we are moving in a metaphysical circle. For what first makes the contingency of the world as a whole a puzzle to be explained is the doctrine of creation itself. Those who start by assuming that the world was created from nothing by God, cannot help being struck by the thought that the world might not be, and that its contingent existence therefore depends on something beyond it. The question then arises as to how the existence of the world is to be explained. The only possible answer is, by virtue of its relation to an otherworldly God whose essence is to exist. And what is the nature of this relation? Given the unbridgeable gap that separates God from the world, there is no way of conceiving the relation except as an act of creation, through which God freely and inexplicably confers existence on all those worldly beings whose essence does not entail it. So a belief in the divine creation of the world highlights the contingency of its existence, which can only be accounted for by equating God's essence with his existence, and by assuming that creation itself is the means that explains how existence is communicated from God, who possesses it necessarily, to a world that does not—by employing the idea of divine creation to solve the metaphysical problem it poses.

Because he equated being with intelligibility, and assumed the indwelling mindedness of the world to be eternal, Aristotle never got started in this circle. The contingency of the world never became a puzzle for him. As a result, he never distinguished (as Aquinas does) the existence of things from their essence and individuality, both of which he explains in terms of the everlasting forms that give all things whatever being they possess.

Aristotle acknowledged that things in the sublunary world are brought into being by others that precede them in time. And he assumed that every explanation of motion in the world, including even that of the heavenly bodies, must come to an end in a motionless God whose essence is to exist. But he saw no need to postulate a God beyond the world to meet this metaphysical need. For Aristotle, there is no gap between the world and its divine ground—between motion and motionlessness, time and eternity. The absence of this gap is the most striking feature of his metaphysics, and the one that distinguishes it most fundamentally from Aquinas' own, which though it draws on Aristotle's in many ways, is defined by its insistence on the impossibility (and impiety) of ever denying the awful gulf that separates the eternal and self-sufficient creator of the world from his changing, temporal creation.

That every being whose existence is not necessary depends ultimately on one whose is, is a conviction that Aristotle and Aquinas share in common. But for anyone who accepts the doctrine of creation, this necessary being cannot be found in the world. Only a God beyond the world is capable of supplying the necessity on which the contingent existence of the world depends. The result is a metaphysical devaluation of the world as a whole, from which a host of other devaluations—ethical, aesthetic and cognitive—follow.

Because Aristotle places the being whose essence is to exist within the world, his metaphysics leads not to the devaluation of the world but its divinization. Yet his world is incompletely divine. That is because, like Plato, he equates being with form. The nature of form—of activity or actuality—is for Aristotle defined by its opposition to matter or potentiality. At its most primitive level, the matter to which he assigns responsibility for the individuality of things is wholly lacking in form. It therefore cannot have the kind of being that form alone possesses. It is tempting to think it has some other. But Aristotle's metaphysics does not allow for this possibility. The forms of things, which are eternal and divine, give them all the being they have. Whatever completely lacks form thus has no being at all. It does not exist contingently. It doesn't exist at all. Everything in the world that truly has being therefore has it necessarily, but not everything in the world has being. God is in the world, but the world is not wholly divine.

The Christian doctrine of creation challenges this view in two respects.

First, if the world was created from nothing by an all-powerful God then everything in it must exist, and not merely those characteristics of things that can be accounted for in terms of their form. In particular, the individuality of individuals must be as real as their species-being. To suppose otherwise, one would have to assume that God's power to confer reality on the world is limited either by the resistance of some primordial stuff or the opposing power of another God. But neither assumption is compatible with the idea of creation. If the world was created by a single, omnipotent God, then it must be pervasively real. There can be no lacunae of being within it. Being must be coextensive with the world as a whole and attach to everything in it—in contrast to Aristotle's view that only form truly exists.

But second, if the world was created from nothing, then it and the things in it exist only contingently. Nothing exists by necessity except God himself. The world, by contrast, exists through God's grace alone. Unlike God, it might not be. This means that God, whose essence is to exist, cannot be found anywhere in the world—in contrast to Aristotle's belief that the world is inherently divine. The Christian world is pervasively, but only contingently, real.

The second of these ideas is the metaphysical warrant for the spirit of homelessness that Christianity holds up as a moral ideal. It is the justification for the devaluation of the world on which Christianity insists, and for the ever-renewed demand it makes on its adherents to be grateful to God in a measure they can never fulfill. It is the provocation for the philosophical and practical rebellion against God that has produced the disenchanted world of the post-Christian West.

But the first idea has survived the self-destruction of the Christian religion. Even those who no longer believe in a God beyond the world and reject the story of creation as a fable, still think of the world as pervasively real. They continue to believe that everything in the world, down to its last particle of particularity, has a share in reality, despite the demise of the religion that first made this belief metaphysically plausible. This in turn provides a justification for the closely related, indeed inseparable, belief that every individual, as such, possesses an intrinsic intelligibility, value and beauty of its own. That, too, is a Christian idea whose power has survived Christianity's loss of authority, and today occupies a position of unshakeable prestige in our scientific, political and aesthetic imagination.

To account for this idea in an adequate way we need a metaphysics that is neither Christian nor Greek—one that explains why the divinity of the world must be both intrinsic and complete. This is the central teaching of Spinoza's philosophy of joy, which recognizes the reality of all things and denies the crown of necessity to none. And it is the essence of his born-again paganism, whose God is the only one capable of reenchanting our world after the long and futile struggle of Christianity's greatest thinkers to remain faithful to their contradictory ideals of freedom and grace. In the remaining chapters of part III, we shall follow this struggle to its disenchanting end. And then, in part IV, we shall make a new beginning with the joyful metaphysics that gives us the God we need to understand the divinity that already inspires all our most modern beliefs.

CHAPTER 16

―◆―――◁∿❁∿▷――◆―

The Pagan Temptation

AQUINAS AND THE ARISTOTELIAN REVIVAL

Beginning in the middle of the twelfth century, and at an accelerating pace in the years that followed, Aristotle's writings on nature and metaphysics, newly translated into Latin, flooded the intellectual centers of the West, where they had not been seen since late antiquity. Six centuries before, the Christian philosopher Boethius had produced a Latin translation of Aristotle's *Organon,* the six treatises on logic and method that are meant to serve as a guide to clear thinking in every field of inquiry. Boethius had planned to translate the rest of Aristotle's works but never did. This was the last, lost chance these had to enter the canon of the Latin West, whose philosophical inheritance from the ancient world, for many centuries to come, would consist almost entirely of various Neoplatonic writings, some wrongly attributed to Aristotle, but all much closer to the spirit of Platonism, with its sharp distinction between sensible things and their otherworldly originals, than to Aristotle's idea of a cosmos naturally divine.[1]

That Aristotle's metaphysical writings never entered the curriculum of the monastic (and later cathedral) schools that became the principal carriers of Western Christian thought, was not wholly accidental. Plato's idealism opened a gap between the sensible world and its invisible ground. This fit comfortably with the even more radical breach between creator and creature on which the teachers of Christian doctrine insisted, and gave the works of Neoplatonic philosophy that survived from the first three centuries of the Christian era an advantage over their Aristotelian counterparts in the competition for Christian attention.

Aristotle's writings did not, of course, disappear entirely. They continued to be copied and read in the cities and universities of the Eastern Empire, and later of Byzantium, even after the last organized schools of pagan philosophy, which had been in continuous operation for the better part of a millennium, were closed by imperial degree.[2] In Alexandria and Antioch, then in Edessa in Mesopotamia and the Persian city of Nisibis, Aristotle's writings on the soul, on the heavens, on ethics, politics and metaphysics all remained in circulation, thanks in part to their continuing appeal to various groups of Christian thinkers (often, like the Nestorians, those later condemned as heretics) who were engaged in the fierce philosophical debates over the idea of a triune God, and of the unity of man and God in Christ, that dominated the more metaphysically adventurous life of the Eastern church during these centuries.

When the followers of Mohammed swept out of Arabia in the seventh century and conquered the Near East with its ancient centers of literacy and learning, they found themselves in possession of these Aristotelian texts. Along with other philosophical and scientific writings, Aristotle's treatises were translated from Greek, Persian and Syriac into Arabic in the ninth century as part of a deliberate campaign on the part of the Abbasid caliphate in Baghdad to capture the wisdom of the ancient world for Muslim advantage.[3] In Arabic, Aristotle's writings traveled to Spain, where they played a central role in that great Muslim-Jewish efflorescence known as al-Andalus.[4] And it was here, in the twelfth century, that these same writings were rendered into Latin, at Toledo and elsewhere, in organized programs of translation sponsored by the Catholic Church as part of its effort to exploit the intellectual riches of the far more advanced civilization it was in the process of "reconquering."

From Toledo, the "new" works of Aristotle, available for the first time in Latin, moved quickly from one center of European learning to the next, where they rejoined the "old," familiar Aristotle of the *Organon*. Soon after, translations of the newer writings were made directly from Greek into Latin, so that by the end of the twelfth century, the best thinkers of Europe once again had in their hands reliable translations of Aristotle's writings on everything from the stars to the parts of animals. It is hard to exaggerate the excitement the rediscovery of these forgotten texts caused, at Paris and elsewhere. It is equally hard to exaggerate the depth of the danger they posed to Christian belief.

THE RECOVERY OF THE WORLD

The most striking characteristic of Aristotle's philosophy is its worldliness. Whether he is investigating the behavior of living things, or inquiring about the best life a man can live, or exploring the principles of celestial motion, Aristotle always starts with the world we inhabit before we begin to philosophize about it—with what he calls "the phenomena." In his view, the goal of philosophy is not to detach us from this world or to teach us to see it as an illusion. It is to deepen our understanding and appreciation of the world without ever leaving it behind. In this sense, one might say that Aristotle's method is "phenomenological," and describe his basic principles of potency, motion, and being-at-work as the building blocks of a metaphysical phenomenology whose goal is to "save" the world of sensation and habit by grounding its reality in the eternal and divine—not, as Plato urges, to abolish the reality of this familiar world, which is our home on earth, by separating it from the invisible source of its being.

For the Christian readers of the newly recovered texts of Aristotle that began to circulate in the Latin West in the twelfth and thirteenth centuries, the worldliness of his philosophy was its most exciting feature. This was particularly true in the field of natural science.[5] Many causes contributed to the decline of the natural sciences in the West in the centuries between Augustine and Aquinas, but one was surely the otherworldliness of Augustinian theology itself, and of the Neoplatonism that supported it. The more seriously one took Augustine's injunction to think of ourselves as pilgrims passing through this world on our way to another, the less important it seemed to devote time and energy to the scientific investigation of this one. For those who were drawn in the latter direction, the rediscovery of Aristotle's natural philosophy offered guidance and encouragement, and a splendid example of how much might be learned from the disciplined study of natural phenomena, though of course it also raised the question of how to accommodate Aristotle's pagan science of nature within a framework of belief predicated on the assumption that the world is the creation of a God who transcends it.

This was important enough, but the worldliness of Aristotle's philosophy had a second, even deeper appeal.

The same theology of salvation that diminished the importance of natural science also encouraged an acute sense of homelessness in the world. This feeling had for centuries been the heart of Christian piety, cultivated in monasteries by virtuosi of homelessness, and celebrated in more routine ways by believers whose ability to sustain the feeling lay closer to the human norm. There were exceptions, of course, and in the reviving cities of Italy and northern Europe this-worldly attitudes had by the end of the twelfth century begun once more to flourish, in ways they had not since the collapse of the brilliant civic culture of pagan antiquity. But the dominant spirit of the intellectual milieu into which Aristotle's writings flooded in the second half of the twelfth century was one of alienation from the world, and among the pious Christians who read these writings there were some—including some of the most brilliant and philosophically gifted—who felt an open or secret thrill upon encountering a system of thought of such range and rigor that invited them to think of themselves as being once again at home in a world from which their entire tradition of belief taught them to feel estranged.

This invitation was a powerful temptation. It might be called the pagan temptation. For if one yielded to it, the result could only be a reunion of the worldly and divine. Aristotle had taken the divinity of the world for granted. It was the premise on which his pagan phenomenology of being at home in the world was based. But Aristotle's idea of a divinized world was one that every orthodox Christian had to reject, and in those who remained faithful to their beliefs, the temptation to follow his example, and rejoin God to the world, was bound to produce a metaphysical anxiety whose depth is difficult for us to grasp.

Some of Aristotle's thirteenth-century readers yielded to this temptation. Others, in the early years of the fourteenth century, recognizing the danger it posed to Christian belief, charted a new path in theology, motivated by their desire to preserve God's distance from the world against the appeal of a neo-pagan Christianity that threatened to abolish it. Among the theologians who led this counterrevolt, none took a more radical position than William of Ockham (d. 1347 C.E.). His spiritual descendants include Martin Luther and Immanuel Kant.

In the contest between freedom and grace, which Augustine had been the first to chart in a rigorous way, Kant and Luther defended opposing positions. But the roots of Kant's uncompromising morality of freedom, like those of Luther's equally uncompromising defense of grace, are both to be found in Ockham's insistence on the primacy of will over reason, and in the voluntarist theology that he constructed on the basis of this idea. Those whose views derive from Kant's, including the champions of the secularized ethic of human autonomy that has been the leading ideal in the West since the French Revolution, as well as their reactionary enemies, who have been motivated by the hatred of pride that animates every aspect of Luther's Reformation theology, are in this sense *all* the remote heirs of an intellectual movement that begins in the fourteenth century with the voluntarist revolt against the pagan temptation that Aristotelian metaphysics presented, and with the radicalized Augustinianism that Ockham and his followers offered as an antidote to it. Our disenchanted world is the legacy of this old theological quarrel.

In the next ten chapters, I shall trace these developments in more detail. But to understand the force of the reaction against this temptation, and the length to which those who led the resistance were prepared to go in order to protect their God against the supreme indignity of being assimilated to the intelligibility of the world he had created, it is necessary first to understand the power of the temptation itself, for the passion and ingenuity with which some fought against it only makes sense in light of the appeal it had for others.

In this regard, no one is a better barometer than Thomas Aquinas. Aquinas did not go as far as some in embracing the full implications of Aristotle's world-divinizing metaphysics (and even those who went farther typically couched their conclusions in terms that allowed them to disclaim a personal belief in the truth of what Aristotle had said).[6] Aquinas was an orthodox Christian who never doubted that God had created the world from nothing. He insisted that creator and creature are separated by an ontological gap for which Aristotle's *Metaphysics* leaves no room (except, perhaps, on a tendentious reading that violates its basic spirit). Indeed, it was Aquinas who, drawing on Muslim sources, constructed the philosophy of existence that gave the idea of such a gap its own rigorous metaphysical foundation. No one who has read Aquinas would ever think to suggest that he embraced the unity of God and world that lay at the heart of Aristotle's philosophy. Yet in the deepest reaches of his theology, Aquinas came dangerously close to this idea. Given the genuineness of his own Christian beliefs, the fact that he did reveals in a particularly pointed way the strength of the appeal that Aristotle's paganism had even for the most orthodox minds of the thirteenth century. Nowhere is this clearer than in Aquinas' account of the nature of God himself.

THE MIND OF GOD

That God exists, Aquinas says, is a "self-evident" proposition. "God" and "exists" are joined in an essential way, like "man" and "animal."[7] The predicate is "the same" as the subject. It is therefore as much a contradiction to suppose that God does not exist as to think that a man can live forever. Existence is part of God's nature in the way mortality is of ours.

Still, the *knowledge that* this is so is something we must work to acquire. The necessity of God's existence is not obvious from the start. We gain such knowledge only at the end of a long process of reflection that begins with things we do know and that reasons from them to an understanding of God's essence. Because the truth of "the proposition, God exists" is not immediately apparent, it "needs to be demonstrated by things that are more known to us, though less known in their nature, namely, by [God's] effects."[8] In the process, we discover that what we thought we knew is in fact only imperfectly intelligible, in comparison to the absolute transparency of our knowledge of God's existence, once we have secured it through reason. This is the first task of theology.

Aquinas is here following Aristotle's method of inquiry. In every philosophical investigation, Aristotle says, we must start with what is known to us and reason our way to what is knowable in itself.[9] Like Aristotle's theology, Aquinas' own therefore begins with ordinary experience. Each of his celebrated "five ways" to a knowledge of God's existence takes its point of departure from the familiar world of sights and sounds.[10] In this sense, one might say that Aquinas' theology is a phenomenological one too, though by describing the phenomena with which he starts as God's "effects," Aquinas makes it clear that his conception of the divine, unlike Aristotle's, already assumes a separation between God and those worldly beings through which we are able to gain some knowledge of him.

The implications of this assumption are most apparent in Aquinas' third proof of the existence of God—the only one that differs fundamentally from Aristotle's arguments for the necessity of what he calls a "first mover."[11] Aquinas' third proof reasons from the proposition that every thing that exists in the world "can not-be" (that is, exists contingently) to the claim that "everything [i.e., the totality of things] can not-be," and concludes that the contingent existence of the phenomenal world as a whole is explicable only on the assumption of a God beyond it who exists of necessity.

The doctrine of creation makes the contingency of the world imaginable in a way it was not for Aristotle. It also supplies the only possible answer to the question of how the existence of the world is to be explained, once its contingency is assumed. Though Aquinas' arguments for the necessity of the existence of God are all phenomenologically grounded, his inclusion of the contingency of the world among the phenomena to be explained thus inevitably leads him to a God that transcends the world and everything in it. The Christian God whose existence Aquinas proves in the third article of the second question of the *Summa Theologiae* is in this respect fundamentally different from the God that Aristotle derives in the twelfth book of the *Metaphysics*. Yet as he unfolds the nature of God's being in the articles that follow, the distance between Aquinas' conception of the eternal and divine and its Aristotelian counterpart shrinks dramatically.

That is because Aquinas assigns God's mind a decisive priority over his will. According to Aquinas, God's intellect is pure "act," a concept he interprets in the same intellectualist terms that Aristotle did, as the activity of mind minding mind. Nothing about this activity is contingent. It is necessary through and through. What God knows and how he knows it (which in the end are one and the same) cannot be other than they are. Of course, Aquinas' God is not merely a self-absorbed knower. He is a creator as well. He brings the world into being through an act of will. But on Aquinas' account of it, this act of divine creation proves to be, as we shall see, as necessary as the knowledge of the mind that directs it.

To anticipate: for Aquinas, there is no possibility of God's willing to do less, or other, than what his intellect knows to be true. To suppose that there could be a disjunction of this sort between God's mind and will is no more compatible with his nature than the supposition of his nonexistence. It follows that the world that God creates exists with the same necessity he does, and therefore partakes of his own divine being, whose essence is to exist. And if that is true, then the world is not separated from God by an ontological gap, but is *part* of him instead.

This is alarming enough from an orthodox point of view. But if one accepts Aquinas' interpretation of the relation between God's intellect and will, the Christian belief that absolutely everything in the world owes its existence to God, means that not only the general forms of things but their individuality as well shares in the necessity of God's existence. Aquinas himself never drew this conclusion. It would have seemed to him a blasphemy. Yet his account of God's nature compels it. Aquinas is in truth a closet Spinozist, whose rationalist theology takes us farther in the direction of a more complete fusion of God with the world than even Aristotle could have imagined. It is against the threat posed by this Christianized, and therefore radicalized, paganism that the great Franciscan thinkers of the next generation fought with such determination to save what seemed to them to be the truths of their religion.

I know that to describe Aquinas as a closet Spinozist risks giving offense, and will strike many who have studied his theology with care as deeply wrong-headed. To understand why Aquinas' account of the nature of God necessarily pushes him in this direction, we need to review in some detail his analysis of the divine intellect and its relation to God's will.

To begin with, we should note, as Aquinas does, that it is only a figure of speech to say that God has a mind distinct from his will. God's true nature is simple and undivided. Strictly speaking, he has no separate faculties or parts. But we human beings "can speak of simple things only as though they were like the composite things from which we derive our knowledge" of them.[12] We ourselves are composite beings, in whom intellect and will are distinct. The evidence for this is that we often fail to do what we know to be right—a phenomenon that both Plato and Aristotle recognized and sought to explain. Beginning from this familiar division in our own souls, we construct the idea of a God who possesses these two powers as well.

Aquinas calls this process of reasoning "analogical."[13] Through an analogy with the distinction between intellect and will that we discover in ourselves, we postulate a similar distinction in the divine nature and, building on this, arrive at a knowledge of God which, though imperfect, advances our understanding of his nature beyond the merely negative assertion that he is unlike us in every conceivable way.

To begin with, it is obvious that if we have minds, God must have one as well. That is because beings with minds are superior to those that lack them. A being without a mind has only its own form, but a "knowing being is naturally adapted to have also the form" of other things, which it acquires by thinking about them. A thinking being, Aquinas says (quoting Aristotle), "is in a sense all things."[14] To assume that God does not have a mind would therefore place him lower in the order of being than we are—a contradiction in terms.

It is therefore necessary that God have a mind. But it is also necessary that his mind be more perfect than ours. That is because, as composite beings, we have both minds and bodies. Our bodies constrain the work of our minds, whereas God's mind, being bodiless, is not limited in a similar way.

Our bodies confine our thinking because they possess a distinctive form that is different from that of other embodied beings. We can never "be" dogs or starfish. We can never be anything but human. Our bodies therefore give all our experience a specific, localized, character. Because we have minds, we are able to range over the whole of being and to acquire, in thought, the forms of other things. Our minds set us free from the local limits of our bodies and of the unique form of species-being materialized in them. But because we have bodies, our thoughts, however far ranging, always have a bodily character. Even when we are thinking, we are never entirely free of our bodies. We can only think by means of what Aquinas calls "phantasms"—images that supply a bridge between bodily sensation, on the one hand, and abstract reflection on the other.[15] It is thus our fate as embodied thinking beings to be able to be all things, but *only from* the point of view of the one distinctive sort of being our sensing bodies make us, whose perspective we can never overcome.

As a result, all our thinking has an element of passivity, for it depends on images whose origin lies in sensation. Every act of human thought has to rely on something it cannot supply for itself but must receive from without. Even when it is most energetically at work, the human mind is never fully self-contained.

Human thinking is always passive in a second way as well, for our bodies, which compel us to think with images, also condemn us to think in time. Thinking is a process of coming to know what one did not know before. Even the most advanced human thinker moves from a state of knowing something potentially, to actually grasping it with his mind. That is because the object of his thought is something outside him that can be apprehended only after a process of inquiry, either conceptual or empirical, in which the object is explored sequentially from different points of view. The same combination of perspective and transcendence that forces us to rely on images when we think thus also gives all human knowledge an essentially temporal character. What we know we learn through study and therefore comprehend only in time.

God's bodiless mind cannot be passive in either of these two ways, since that would be an imperfection in him. His thinking cannot depend on images that rely on sensations he receives from without. And it cannot depend on God's having the time to learn what he knows. Aquinas puts the point in Aristotelian terms. "God has nothing in Him of potentiality," he says, but is "pure act" instead.[16] If we are to grasp the nature of God's mind, we must therefore attempt to imagine our own human minds without those features that cause them to fall short of God's perfect activity.

The root cause of the passivity of our minds is the separation that exists between them and their objects. This separation is the source both of our dependence on sensory images and of the temporality that characterizes human thought. Hence, if God's mind is to be free from both sorts of passivity, there can be no separation of this sort. In every divine act of intellection, the mind that thinks and the object of its thought must be one and the same. Put differently, when God thinks, his thinking must always, and only, be of himself—mind minding mind, as Aristotle says—since any other assumption would introduce a distinction between the divine mind and its object, and with that, a passivity inconsistent with God's nature. "[T]he reason why we [human beings] actually feel or know a thing is because our intellect or sense is actually informed by the sensible or intelligible species. And because of this only, it follows that [our human] sense or intellect is distinct from the sensible or intelligible object, since both are in potentiality. Since therefore God has nothing in Him of potentiality, but is pure act, his intellect and its object must be altogether the same; so that He neither is without the intelligible species, as is the case with our intellect when it understands potentially, nor does the intelligible species differ from the substance of the divine intellect, as it differs in our intellect when it understands actually; but the intelligible species itself is the divine intellect itself, and thus God understands Himself through Himself."[17]

The mind of God thus *is* its own object. The unity of the two constitutes the uniquely active "substance of the divine intellect." This is the characteristic of God's mind that makes it the sort of mind it is. One can go further. The unity of the act of understanding and the object understood constitutes not merely the substance of God's intellect, as if that were a power or faculty distinct from his essential nature. It is God's substance *simpliciter,* the very essence of his being, since to assume otherwise would mean that there is something in God that is distinct from his mind, hence something the divine intellect can only know as other than itself—an inconceivable imperfection in the all-encompassing self-knowing that constitutes the very being of God's mind.

It is God's essence to exist. In him, nature and existence coincide. This distinguishes his necessary being from the contingent existence of the world and all it contains. The "form" of every creature, Aquinas says, is "something other" than its being.[18] Only God's form *is* his being. This is the divine essence that God knows when he knows himself—His "intelligible species," which, as the object of God's mind, is "entirely one and the same" with that mind itself.[19]

Hence, when God knows himself, *what* he knows *is that* it is his essence to exist. Indeed, even this is a misleading formulation, for the perfect activity of the divine mind *is* the perfection of God's being itself, which consists in the necessity of God's existence. Just as the being of every contingent thing is a merely potential kind of being, and to that extent imperfect, so our minds, which know their objects only potentially, are less perfect than God's for the very same reason. Aquinas' account of God's intellect thus joins Aristotle's pagan conception of the divinity of the world as mind minding mind, with the creationist definition of God as a world-transcending being whose nature is to exist. Or more accurately, it fuses these ideas, so that each becomes an expression of the other in a theology that defines the essence of God, as the one necessarily existing being, in intellectualist terms little different than those that Aristotle uses to describe the divine *energeia* that makes the world go round.

THE DIVINE WILL

But Aquinas' God is a creator as well as a mind. He brings the world into being from nothing by an act of divine will. The creative power that Aquinas attributes to God, and locates in his will, is the most distinctively Christian feature of his theology, and it is here that one naturally expects the distinction between Aristotle's conception of divinity and Aquinas' to be most sharply drawn. It is unsurprising that Aquinas' account of the divine mind should resemble Aristotle's as closely as it does. How else can one describe God's intellect except in intellectualist terms? What is more surprising (and disturbing, from a Christian point of view) is the extent to which Aquinas' description of God's will is informed by the same assumptions and leads, in the end, to a view of God's relation to the world that transforms his freedom of creation into something approaching the rational necessity of a geometrical proof.

Near the start of his account of the divine will, Aquinas emphatically affirms the freedom of God's creation. "We must hold," he says, "that the will of God is the cause of things, and that He acts by the will, and not, as some have supposed, by a necessity of His nature."[20] The existence of the world is an "effect" of God's will, which "causes" it to come into being.

When we human beings act so as to cause something to exist, we first conceive the "form of the thing to be done" with the intellectual part of our souls. But the form of a thing, insofar as "it is only in the intellect," is "not determined to exist or not to exist actually, except by the will."[21] As a mere "thought-thing," it does not yet exist in reality. The will confers reality on it by "executing the effect" first conceived in the mind. This is familiar to us from the countless executive decisions we make to do this or that—to take a walk, write a poem or eat a peach. First, we conceive the idea of doing something and then we resolve to do it. The decision is the cause of the existential reality of the thing we had it in mind to do.

According to Aquinas, God's creation of the world is like this. The world first exists in God's mind and then is realized by his will. It first exists as an idea and then as an actually existing thing outside the divine mind, in the way a finished bed exists outside the mind of its maker.

To be sure, God's will "follows" his intellect just as the realization of any human idea follows the idea itself.[22] But God's will is as free as that of a craftsman who, having conceived the idea of a particular piece of furniture, retains the liberty to make it or not as he chooses. By analogy, after conceiving the world, God could have chosen not to create it. There was no necessity in his doing so. The world, as an "effect" of God's will, "pre-exists in Him after the mode of intellect," but "His inclination to put in act [that is, to realize] what His intellect has conceived pertains to the will,"[23] and "since the goodness of God is perfect and can exist without other things [that is, without the world he creates], inasmuch as no perfection can accrue to Him from them, it follows that for Him to will things other than Himself is not absolutely necessary."[24] Moreover, God's perfection means that he has no needs of any kind whose requirements could conceivably compel him to create anything outside himself, unlike a human craftsman who needs to use or sell the bed he makes. God's creation of the world is therefore not merely *as* free as the craftsman's execution of his plan, but infinitely freer.

All of this is entirely orthodox from a Christian point of view. But Aquinas' distinction between God's mind and will is less sharp than these remarks suggest. Indeed, anyone who follows the labyrinthine path of his argument to its end is bound to wonder whether there is any difference between them at all.

After noting that, in the case of human beings, "the speculative intellect has nothing to say as to operation," and that the "power of the agent" to "execute the effect" conceived by the mind is a separate power that alone causes the effect to exist, Aquinas immediately adds that in God's case "these things are one." The analogy to human acts of making and doing, in which the powers of mind and will are divided, thus provides little help in understanding the act of divine creation to which Aquinas compares them. Aquinas was himself acutely aware of the limits of this analogy, and his appreciation of them led him in the direction of an ever more rationalist and necessitarian conception of the divine will itself. It is easiest to see this if we return to Aquinas' claim that God's will, like ours, "follows upon [the] intellect," and then note the qualifications he introduces as a result of his own reflections on the fact that these two cases are not really alike at all.

"Everything," according to Aquinas, has a "disposition toward its natural form." It is disposed to be the kind of thing it is. This is Aquinas' way of making the Aristotelian point that all things reach out toward that state of fulfillment that consists in their being fully what they are. When a thing attains this state, Aquinas says, "it is at rest therein." Being at rest in this state is the thing's good.

Most things—indeed, all created things—are not in this state automatically and forever. For them, it is a condition they must work to attain. This working toward its good is the most fundamental "tendency" of everything but God. In "things without knowledge" (those that lack the power of thought) this tendency takes the form of what Aquinas calls a "natural appetite." In "intellectual natures" that not only have a good but apprehend it "through an intelligible form"—that reach out toward an end they represent to themselves in their minds as an idea—this reaching out is not a natural appetite but something more deliberate and intentional. It is "will," a rational appetite that follows the intellect as a conscious "seeking to possess" the end the intellect sets up as an idea. Will follows intellect, therefore, not just in the sense that its executive power needs some goal to pursue if it is not to be literally pointless, but in the more consequential sense that will is a longing for the good the intellect specifies in beings with minds. "Hence," Aquinas concludes, "in every intellectual being there is *will,* just as in every sensible being there is *animal appetite.* And so there must be will in God, since there is intellect in Him."[25] (emphasis added).

But there is a problem with this conclusion that Aquinas notes, and attempts to resolve, in a characteristically thoughtful way. The problem is that will, so defined, can only be possessed by beings that lack the good toward which they strive. If the will of a thing is its rational appetite for the good that defines its end, then the existence of this appetite is only conceivable if the good in question has not yet been attained or, if it has been, if its retention is fragile and incomplete. Only in these cases does it make sense to think of a being with a mind striving to reach or to remain in the state of rest that constitutes its end.

Minded beings of this sort resemble natural beings without minds, for the latter also yearn for their fulfillment only because they do not already have it. Both sorts of beings strive toward something they do not yet possess. Both must therefore be distinguished from God, who cannot lack for anything.

God is always and already fulfilled, and it is unthinkable that he be vulner-able to having his fulfillment taken from him. In this respect, God differs fundamentally not only from mindless creatures, like dogs and starfish, but from human beings and even from the intelligences. It follows that if the pres-ence in us of the power that Aquinas calls the will can be explained only as a yearning for a good we understand but lack, then God, who understands his own good perfectly and possesses it completely and invulnerably, cannot have a will at all.

Aquinas' acknowledgment that this is so leads him to refine his concep-tion of God's will. "Will in us," he says, "belongs to the appetitive part, which, although named from appetite, has not for its only act to seek what it does not possess, but also to love and delight in what it does possess." When the human will has reached its goal, it thus still has work to do—to take delight in the possession of the goal it has attained. The will does not expire when its end is reached, but remains active even then. It remains joyfully at work in the enjoyment of its good. Of course, for us, the attainment of this good, and hence its present enjoyment, can never be complete so long as we remain on our way to God and have not yet been fully embraced by him. The delight we take in the progress we have made toward this end is always imperfect. It can never be more than an intimation of the delight that finally awaits us. But God "always" possesses "the good which is [his] object," and therefore takes perfect delight in its possession. Hence, only in this sense can will be "said to be in God," since any other view would require us to assume that God lacks what he wills to attain, which is absurd. But if God's will is noth-ing but the delight he takes in the possession of a good he cannot be without, then his will cannot "in essence [be] distinct from this good" but must be this good itself, conceived as a state of necessary and boundless self-appreciation, which of course is how Aquinas defines the mind of God, following Aristo-tle's lead.[26]

Still, it seems, God could delight in himself without ever choosing to cre-ate a world apart from him. He could remain within the pleasurable self-sufficiency of his own intellect and never take the further step of bringing anything else into existence. That God might exist without the creatures that depend upon him for their being seems perfectly conceivable. Indeed, the es-sential contingency of the existence of the world demands this possibility. And if that is true, then God's will must be something other than just the necessary enjoyment of his necessary goodness. It must be distinct from the mind of God. It must be a power that can be exercised or not, by means of which the world is brought into being from nothing. To assume the opposite, that God *must* create the world, violates the fundamental premise of Christian belief by closing the gap between the contingent existence of the world and God's own necessary being.

This conception of God's will is tenable, however, only in case God's will and intellect are distinguishable, the first taking its lead from the second yet acting independently of it, just as the human will follows the mind's lead but shows its independence by affirming or disaffirming the end the mind has brought to light. God's omnipotence leads Aquinas to conclude that his will, unlike ours, cannot be anything but a present delight in a good he necessarily possesses. The ontological gap between the world and its creator compels him to insist on the distinctiveness of the divine will as a power separate from God's mind, and on God's freedom to create the world or not as he chooses. Broadly speaking, the first line of thought is intellectualist and the second voluntarist. Aquinas' account of the divine will contains both. But at a crucial point, it tilts decisively in the former direction, though not without causing Aquinas himself some anxiety as an orthodox Christian.

To the question whether God wills something other than himself, Aquinas replies that he does, and explains his answer by appealing, once again, to the behavior of "natural things."[27] Things of this sort "have a natural inclination not only toward their own proper good, to acquire it if not possessed, and, if possessed, to rest therein; but also to *diffuse* their own good among others so far as possible. Hence we see that every agent, in so far as it is perfect and in act, produces its like. It pertains, therefore, to the nature of the will to communicate as far as possible to others the good possessed; and especially does this pertain to the divine will, from which all perfection is derived in some kind of likeness . . . . Thus, then, He wills both Himself to be, and other things to be, but Himself as the end, and other things as ordained to that end, inasmuch as it befits the divine goodness that other things should be partakers therein."[28]

Aquinas is thinking of the reproduction of plants and animals. Every living thing strives to "diffuse" its good by making another like itself. Once it has reached maturity and fulfilled its potential, one thing alone remains: to communicate to its offspring the actuality it has achieved in its own life and by doing so to participate in the endless life of its species. Natural things long to reach their end, and once they have reached it yearn to go outside themselves and convey (diffuse) their good to another.

A plant or animal may of course fail in either respect. It may not reach its end or succeed in reproducing. God cannot fail in either way. The analogy of God diffusing his goodness through the creation of the world to that of natural things diffusing theirs by reproduction is to this extent imperfect. But there is a further distinction of even greater importance. The reason that (non-reasoning) plants and animals long to reproduce is that this is the only way they can partake of the everlasting. They long to come as close to God as their natures allow, and reproduction is their only means to this end. For human beings, it is only one of the means, yet even those who strive to reach God in thought yearn for students who will keep the deathless enterprise of philosophy "alive." But God is already everlasting. He does not have to go out of himself to partake of the eternal and divine and hence cannot long to do so, in the way that all living things yearn to make another like themselves and even philosophers long for students to continue their work. If it is in the nature of God to diffuse his goodness as widely as possible, then it is unthinkable that he not do so, or that he try and fail, or even that he yearn to diffuse it before he has actually done so.

God's goodness, therefore, must of necessity be always and already diffused. If it is *possible* that there be finite beings that partake of God's infinite goodness in more limited ways, according to the restrictions their various natures allow, then these beings *must* exist with the same necessity as the infinite being whose goodness is the diffusive ground of their existence. To assume otherwise is to acknowledge the possibility that God either not diffuse his goodness at all, or do so incompletely, or with difficulty, or experience for however brief a time, a yearning to do something his nature demands but that he has not done already, in the way the nature of living things causes them to yearn to make a likeness of themselves before they have actually done so.

None of these possibilities is compatible with God's nature. If one of God's essential characteristics is to spread his own goodness as broadly as possible, then the likeness that God makes of himself—the world he brings into being—must share the necessity of God's own existence, though not of course his infinitude as well. To this extent, the world that God creates, through the diffusion of his goodness, cannot be thought of as existing outside the self-contained circle of God's own noncontingent existence. We must think of it instead as a cosmic panorama that expresses or enacts God's simple nature in an infinite array of finite but equally necessary beings. God's nature causes him to fill the space of all possible goodness. He would not be God if he didn't. The world is just this space filled out. The existence of the world, and of all that it contains, is therefore not contingent at all, but partakes of the necessity of the divine being whose own existence is necessarily diffused throughout it.

ABSOLUTE NECESSITY

Aquinas' own account of God's will appears to support this heterodox conclusion. But if the conclusion cannot be avoided, then the ontological gap between God and the world closes up, and the idea of the world as the creation of a God beyond it becomes unintelligible. This arouses a palpable anxiety on Aquinas' part. He deals with the danger by introducing a distinction between "two ways in which a thing is said to be necessary, namely, absolutely, and by supposition."[29]

Something is absolutely necessary "when the predicate forms part of the definition of the subject" or "when the subject forms part of the notion of the predicate." Thus, it is absolutely necessary that man is an animal, and that a number be either even or odd (Aquinas' examples).[30] By contrast, a thing is necessary by supposition if its necessity depends on our supposing some state of affairs to exist that might not. It is necessary that Socrates sits on the supposition that he is sitting and only so long as he does (again, Aquinas' example).

Applying this distinction to the case of God's will, Aquinas affirms "that He wills *something* of absolute necessity."[31] But the only thing God wills with absolute necessity is "the being of His own goodness." By contrast, God wills "things other than Himself" only "insofar as they are ordered to His own goodness as their end." Thus, God wills the world—he chooses to confer existence upon it—only in case doing so is a means to the end of his divine goodness.

In willing an end, however, "we do not necessarily will things that conduce to it, unless they are such that the end cannot be attained without them." Hence, even if God necessarily wills his own goodness, he cannot be said to will the existence of the world by a similar necessity unless the latter is indispensable to the former. And Aquinas insists it is not. "Since the goodness of God is perfect and can exist without other things, inasmuch as no perfection can accrue to Him from them, it follows that for Him to will things other than Himself is not absolutely necessary."

It is like the case of a man who wants to travel and chooses to do so with a horse (once again, Aquinas' example). He might travel without a horse. His choice of a horse as the means of traveling is not absolutely demanded by his end (which of course is not compelled by his nature as a human being either). Supposing he does choose a horse, it *is* necessary that he travel on horseback, but only by supposition. Similarly, if God chooses to create the world, it is necessary, by supposition, that the world exist. But it is not absolutely necessary, for God might have continued to will the one thing that it *is* absolutely necessary he will (namely, his own goodness) without willing the existence of the world as a means to it. It follows that the existence of the world is contingent and does not have the absolute necessity that characterizes the existence of God, whose essence is to exist.

But of course this makes sense only in case we ignore what Aquinas has said just a few paragraphs before—that "every agent, insofar as it is perfect and in act, produces its like"—a proposition that applies, on Aquinas' view, to God as well as natural things. For if this is true, then God's goodness necessarily *includes* the existence of a world that is his likeness, in which his goodness is diffused. The diffusion of God's goodness throughout the world is a *part* or *aspect* or *dimension* of his being, without which God would be incomplete and therefore imperfect. But that is impossible, since God is perfect in every imaginable way. Hence, if God wills his own goodness, as Aquinas insists he must, he must also will the existence of the world with the same degree of necessity.

The latter is not a *means* to the former that God might or might not choose to employ, in the way one might or might not choose to use a horse for locomotion. It is a *component* of the act by which God wills his own goodness. It is a predicate that belongs to that act by definition, in the same way that "animal" belongs to "man." The existence of the world is therefore necessary not merely by supposition, on the assumption that God brought it into being when he might have done otherwise (in the way that Socrates, who is sitting, might be standing instead), but absolutely necessary since the very nature of God's act of willing his own goodness implies it. If God is perfectly good by definition; if he wills (delights in) his own goodness by definition; and if by definition God's delight expresses itself in the maximal diffusion of his goodness, then the world must exist by definition—not contingently, or suppositionally, but with the same absolute necessity that God himself exists. Aquinas' distinction between absolute necessity and necessity by supposition cannot save him from this dangerously unorthodox conclusion.

In fact, from a Christian point of view, matters are even worse. For the logic of Aquinas' account of God's nature leads to the conclusion that even the smallest details of the world must exist with the same necessity he does. It leads to a necessitarianism that even Aristotle, who believed in the necessity of the existence of the general forms of things but considered their individuality to be unintelligible, would have rejected out of hand. It leads to a necessitarianism that is not merely rational but superrational on account of its insistence on the intelligibility of individuals as such, which the Christian doctrine of creation from nothing entails.

Aristotle assumed that our knowledge of the world extends only to a certain point and not beyond, even when it is most perfect or divine. The ultimate stupidity of matter prevents our minds from penetrating to the individuality of things. This built-in epistemic limit follows from the distinction between form and matter, and the equation of intelligibility with form.

The idea of creation from nothing dissolves this distinction and, with it, any barrier to God's knowledge of the world. Aquinas draws this conclusion explicitly. Some, he says, have claimed that God's understanding of "things other than Himself" is merely "general." But this is a mistake, for "to know a thing in general, and not in particular, is to have an imperfect knowledge of it. . . . If therefore the knowledge of God regarding things other than Himself were only universal and not particular, it would follow that His understanding would not be absolutely perfect; therefore neither would His being."[32]

We human beings have a capacity for knowledge. By exercising the "power" of our intellects, we are able to understand the forms of things—their "universal and immaterial" aspect. We apprehend their matter, however, and hence their individuality, by a separate power, that of perception. In us, these two powers are divided, and their division means that our knowledge of the individuality of things can never have the completeness or clarity that characterizes our intellectual grasp of their forms. In God's "simple intellect," by contrast, these two powers are joined. God therefore "knows singular things." He knows the matter of things, and hence their individuality, as perfectly as he knows their forms.

The reason for this is that God's "knowledge extends as far as His causality extends," and since the "active power of God" extends "not only to forms, which are the source of universality, but also to matter . . . the knowledge of God must extend to singular things, which are individuated by matter." The "same would apply," Aquinas revealingly adds, "to the knowledge of the artificer, if it were productive of the whole thing, and not only of the form." But of course human makers, and even Plato's world craftsman, do not cause the matter on which they work to come into being. They take it for granted, as something already there. Their causality, and hence their knowledge, extends only as far as the form they impose on this preexisting material.[33] But the God of the Christian religion is not a maker. He is an omnipotent creator, whose limitless causality is matched by a limitless knowledge of the world he causes to come into being—a knowledge that nothing in the world exceeds or escapes, including all the accidental properties of things and even "primary matter" itself, which is "created by the universal cause of things."[34]

God's knowledge of the world thus differs quantitatively from the knowledge a human artisan possesses of the product he makes. But it also differs qualitatively. An artisan has an idea of what he wants to make, and then uses various tools and techniques to make it. This is a process that takes time, and is governed by instrumental rationality ("this tool is a means to that end," etc.). The knowledge that is needed to complete such a process is experiential, which is why every human act of making is a *practical* art. Indeed, even the idea with which an artisan begins is derived from experience, for to have the idea, say, of a bed, one must first have had some experience of beds and derived an understanding of their characteristics from it.

The knowledge that God has of the world is altogether different. It is not experiential but conceptual. It is the kind of knowledge we have when we see "at the same glance" a "principle" and the "conclusion [that is] in the principle itself."[35] Knowledge of this sort does not derive its warrant from experience. It is theoretical, not practical. For us, such knowledge is attainable only within certain very limited domains, for example, those of logic and mathematics. By contrast, all of God's knowledge is of this kind. He understands all the effects he creates, whose totality constitutes the world, as being "in" their cause, that is, in himself, in the way the conclusion of a proof in geometry is "in" its premises.

No other assumption makes sense. God's knowledge is not acquired in time, nor is it fallible or incomplete, nor can the ground of its truth be in any way opaque to God. These are the defining marks of all experiential knowledge. We must therefore assume that God's knowledge not only extends to the individuality of every individual in the world, but that even in this limiting case, it is the sort of knowledge we possess only in geometry and similar disciplines. From God's point of view, the world's relation to himself must be one of logical entailment, down to its smallest details, and thus imbued with the especially strict sort of absolute necessity that distinguishes relations of this kind from the experience-based judgments of practical reason on which all human artisans rely.

When a human being forms the idea of something he wishes to make, his idea does not become a "principle of action" unless and until "there is added to it the inclination to an effect, which inclination is through the will."[36] The idea alone is not effective to make the thing. The maker of a bed must choose to turn his idea of a bed into an actual one, and there is no necessity that he do so. He might, for example, decide merely to contemplate his idea rather than give it material shape. And even if he sets out to make a bed, he may fail to achieve his goal in countless ways. None of this is conceivable in God's case. God's boundless and transparent knowledge of the world provides its own motive to realize the world he comprehends. It is unthinkable that God, knowing the world, might decline to cause it to exist, or that his causal powers might somehow prove inadequate to the task. God *necessarily* wills his own goodness. He therefore *necessarily* wills the existence of a world in which his goodness is diffused. And this *necessity* extends to the unique identity of every individual in the world, each of which stands in a relation of strict entailment to the infinite goodness of the being who is the causal ground of the world as a whole.

Human making is characterized by the absence of each of these necessities, God's creation by the presence of all three. When one puts them together, as Aquinas does, the result is a superrational necessitarianism born of the combination of Greek intellectualism with the limitless intelligibility of the world that follows from the Christian doctrine of creation.

Spinoza will unfold the metaphysical consequences of this born-again pagan theology in luxuriant detail. Aquinas himself never does so. Indeed, he recoils at the prospect. Time and again, his Christian scruples cause him to step back from the implications of his own account of God's nature and to affirm the fundamental articles of his faith, including, most importantly, the contingency of the world and the ontological gap that separates it from its divine creator. But despite Aquinas' caution in this regard, and his explicit repudiation of the most notorious pagan heresies of his time, others rightly saw in his theology a dangerous attraction to pagan ideas, and a proto-Spinozist tendency not merely to collapse the distance between God and the world but to endow the latter with the former's necessity, comprehensively and down to the smallest detail. Their condemnation of his rationalism and the voluntarist conception of God they offered in its place, set in motion the theological developments that produced the Reformation, the modern ideal of human freedom, the tradition of radical reaction that arose in response to this ideal, and the godless world in which we live.

ANTHROPOLOGY

Aquinas' theology so thoroughly subordinates God's will to his intellect that it threatens to eliminate the first as an independent principle of action. In the end, it is hard to resist the conclusion that, for Aquinas, the will of God is merely an aspect of his mind, whose own activity necessarily includes the existence of the world and everything in it. Aquinas' account of human nature has a similarly intellectualist bent.

Everything in the world strives "to become like unto God" insofar as it can. God "is the end of things as something to be obtained by each thing in its own way."[37] This universal striving is a longing for being. "Things give evidence that *they naturally desire to be;* so that if any are corruptible, they naturally resist corruptives, and tend to where they can be safeguarded, as the fire tends upwards and earth downwards. Now all things have being in so far as they are like God, who is self-subsistent being, since they are all beings only by participation. Therefore all things desire as their last end to be like God,"[38] just as Aristotle says in *De Anima* (emphasis in original). But while "all creatures," even mindless ones, "have some share of a likeness to God," those that possess intellects "attain to Him in a special way," namely, by "understanding." To understand God is "the end of [every] intellectual creature,"[39] including man. The fulfillment for which all human beings yearn is therefore a condition of intellectual bliss.

We can most fully achieve this state, here on earth, in the branch of speculative science called "first philosophy," or "divine science," which "is wholly directed to the knowledge of God as its last end." Every other theoretical inquiry, and *a fortiori,* every "practical science" is subordinate to this one and serves it by helping to supply the material conditions and preliminary sorts of knowledge that make this highest of all forms of knowing possible. Thus, according to Aquinas, all of human existence culminates in theology. Like Aristotle, Aquinas is endlessly curious about the other practices and disciplines that allow for the pursuit of this highest form of knowing, but also like Aristotle, he insists that theology constitutes the summit of human fulfillment by virtue of the proximity it allows those who pursue it to the divine object of their study.

Of course, we human beings are not disembodied intellects. We have bodies, appetites, and sensations as well as minds. We also have wills, which supply the motive power that moves us toward the ends we discern. It is not the job of the will to supply these ends. That is always done by the intellect,

a power extrinsic to the will. But once an end is set by the mind, it remains
for the person whose end it is to pursue it, and this requires a whole series of
instrumental calculations as well as a commitment to initiate the pursuit by
performing the action that constitutes the first link in the chain that leads
to the attainment of the end the intellect has discerned. This is the function
of the will, which Aquinas conceives in terms very similar to those that Aristotle uses to explain the phenomena of deliberation and choice.

Both Aquinas and Aristotle allow for the possibility that a person may
wrongly conclude that his highest happiness consists in something it does not
(for example, the accumulation of wealth). But both also insist that when a
man correctly grasps the nature of the end that brings the greatest fulfillment
(which for Aquinas, like Aristotle, consists in a state of knowing) he has no
choice but to pursue it. "[T]here are certain particular goods which have not
a necessary connection with happiness, because without them a man can be
happy; and to such the will does not adhere of necessity. But there are some
things which have a necessary connection with happiness, namely, those by
means of which man adheres to God, in Whom alone true happiness consists. Nevertheless, until through the certitude produced by seeing God the
necessity of such a connection be shown, the will does not adhere to God of
necessity, nor to those things which are of God. But the will of the man who
sees God in His essence of necessity adheres to God, just as now we desire of
necessity to be happy."[40]

The will is moved in every case by what it "apprehends" to be good and
fitting. Because we are "sensitive" as well as "intellectual" beings, we cannot
help but apprehend ourselves and the world under the influence of the passions.
As a result, we often misunderstand the nature of our own true good. But
when we do understand that our highest good consists in a state of unimpeded thinking about God, we not only grasp the necessity with which this
is our good but will, of necessity, *to be in* this state ourselves.

The definition of man's highest good in intellectual terms, the subordination of the human will to the human mind, and the necessitarian implications of Aquinas' account of the relation between these, provide an
anthropological parallel to his portrait of the divine nature itself. This is unsurprising, since the good of the one lies in its approach to, and ultimate
convergence with, the other. A similar parallel of course exists in Aristotle's
philosophy. According to Aristotle, a man is most completely active, hence
most fulfilled, when he is engaged in the business of thinking about the everlasting and divine, for then he is literally enacting the work of God, of mind

minding mind, the *energeia* from which everything in our kinetic cosmos derives its being and direction. But the parallelism is incomplete, for Aristotle assumes that one can attain such fulfillment in this life, while Aquinas insists we can achieve it only in a life beyond the grave.[41]

Aristotle's God is the eternal order of the world, and a human being can have as complete an understanding of this order as it is possible for any being to have. The knowledge that a man achieves through the study of metaphysics represents the peak of intellection, a level of understanding, and hence of reality, beyond which none is thinkable. Of course, a philosopher does not know everything. He does not know the individuality of individuals. But that is because this is inherently unintelligible. There is nothing to be known about it. Nor does his perfect knowledge last forever. It lasts only as long as he has it, and that cannot possibly be longer than his life. But while he lives, he *is* the God he studies, as completely as it is possible for any being to be. His mind and the eternal order it "theorizes" are one and the same. Moreover, in this active, if temporary, union of mind and God, the intellect of the philosopher is no more an individual being than the general form of the world it contemplates. The one is assimilated to the other and, *qua* intellect, loses all its individuality as well. The possibility of complete fulfillment in this life, and the loss of one's individuality in the process, thus both follow from the equation of being with form—the fundamental premise on which Aristotle's metaphysics is based.

The doctrine of creation from nothing unsettles both conclusions.

God knows the individuality of individuals because he has created them. If our fulfillment consists in a knowledge of God, and if such knowledge entails, as it does for both Aristotle and Aquinas, an assimilation of knower to known, then it must include the knowledge of individuals that God himself possesses. Anything short of this will be only an approximation to the divine being and therefore less perfect than it. In this life, however, we cannot hope to reach this goal. As embodied intellects, our minds have a "connatural relation to phantasms."[42] What we know, we first come to know only through the senses and imagination. This is true even of knowledge whose validity does not depend upon the senses (like that of mathematics). Moreover, all our knowledge—even the latter sort—is acquired in time. This remains our condition, so long as we live, and the result is that we can never have, while we are alive, a knowledge of individuals that is perfect and complete (as transparent, say, as our understanding of Euclid's proofs). The "phantasmic" nature of all mortal human knowing thus shuts us out from the divine knowledge that is our natural goal—the final happiness we seek. If that goal is to be achieved, it can only be beyond the limits of this life. But no natural goal is futile. (Aquinas says this over and over again.) The end of our yearning for perfect knowledge must therefore be attainable, but only in a life after this one.

In this life, all the practical arts and practical virtues serve the end of first philosophy. Knowledge of God is that for the sake of which we exercise these arts and practice these virtues. But this side of death, such knowledge remains incomplete, and the theological virtues (faith and hope especially) are needed to sustain us in our pursuit of that perfect state of knowing that constitutes our final good, in the life to come.[43] These virtues have no counterpart in Aristotle, nor is there any need for them, given his belief in the possibility of fulfillment in this life. But even the theological virtues all ultimately serve a supreme good that might be called hyper-Aristotelian in the sense that it not only defines this good as an intellectual experience, but includes within it a knowledge of things that Aristotle believed to be beyond the bounds of all possible understanding.

This experience, for which the faithful yearn, takes the form of a "vision" of God in which those who have it "enjoy the same blessedness as that which makes God happy" because they "see God as He sees Himself."[44] Their minds see God "through the divine essence itself; so that in that vision the divine essence is both the object and the medium of vision."[45] They know the individuality of individuals with the same immediate self-evidence that God does, and not, as they do in this life, only mediately through phantasms and the work of the imagination. And they have this vision not as disembodied minds, indistinguishable one from another, whose identity has been dissolved in a general act of intellection, but as minds whose resurrected bodies preserve the value of their own individuality, which is part of God's goodness too, and a condition of their having that perfect knowledge of individuals that is possible only when their powers of understanding and perception have been joined.

The postponement of human fulfillment to a life after this one is profoundly un-Aristotelian. But Aquinas' definition of man's supernatural end as an act of understanding not only preserves the heart of Aristotle's pagan philosophy, but radicalizes it by extending the scope of such understanding beyond anything Aristotle could have conceived. The blessed in heaven know what God knows, with the same transparency and down to the hairs on every man's head. The result is a superrationalism that mirrors, anthropologically, the intellectualism and necessitarianism that characterize Aquinas' account of the nature of God.

Here too, of course, Aquinas never abandons his orthodox faith. The distinction between this life and the next one remains as important to him as the ontological gap between God and the world. In this respect as well, Aquinas is a resolutely Christian thinker whose belief that God's goodness requires the possibility, at least, that our deepest longings will eventually be fulfilled, demands the existence of a life and world to come.

Once again, it is Spinoza who will draw the radical implications of Aquinas' teachings by making the endless refinement of our understanding of the necessity of things a collaborative human enterprise whose aspirational yet unattainable but wholly innerworldly goal is defined by the possession of that perfect knowledge of particulars in which, for Aquinas, the bliss of the saints consists. Spinoza will retrieve the end of human happiness from the next world and restore it to this one, where Aristotle had placed it, preserving Aquinas' expanded conception of happiness as absolute knowledge, while denying that it can ever be fully achieved by finite beings such as we, living in a world that is not only inherently but infinitely divine, without the prospect of an afterlife in which our yearning to see things as God does might at last come to rest.

Aquinas would have found Spinoza's views appalling and condemned him as a heretic, for the same reasons he condemned the more extreme followers of Averroes among his fellow faculty members at the University of Paris.[46] But in the eyes of some of his contemporaries, at least, Aquinas' own theology veered dangerously close to the rationalist and necessitarian metaphysics that represented the pagan temptation to which the Averroists succumbed.

Aquinas' critics rejected his emphasis on the primacy of mind over will and sought to restore God's dignity by reversing the relation between these. They aimed to put God back at a respectful distance from the world by stressing the incomprehensibility of his freedom to create and to save. But the movement of ideas they set in motion had the result of removing God to such a distance from the world that he ceased to have any practical or metaphysical meaning for his human subjects. In this way, they unwittingly provided a kind of logical relief from a God who had become psychologically unbearable on account of their own efforts to save him, which in the end produced an even more demanding version of the old Augustinian doctrine of grace and a mortifying piety that insisted, as Augustine himself had, on man's utter incapacity ever to be thankful enough for God's gifts—a God that man could love, as Luther says, only by hating himself.

The gospel of human freedom that Kant preached with unmatched power employed the voluntarist doctrine of the primacy of the will to restore man's independence *vis-à-vis* a God who threatened to destroy it completely, and had now been removed to an incomprehensible distance from the world on account of this doctrine itself. Kant's understanding of human autonomy was still tied to Christian beliefs. It remained linked to a vestigial conception of grace. But those who followed Kant and made man's freedom the basis of their wholly secular ideals cut this link completely. They set man loose from God once and for all. Their world—our world—is the antithesis of what the great modern champions of God, from Ockham to Luther, sought to preserve with their ever more demanding conception of grace. It represents what Luther's reactionary descendants called a "satanic" inversion of man's relation to God. And yet it rests on a belief in man's independence from God for which their own defense of God's grandeur provided both the logical opening and the psychological spur, by making God so distant and so great that human self-loathing was bound to become the essence of piety itself.

CHAPTER 17

God Unchained

OCKHAM'S DEFENSE OF DIVINE FREEDOM

On March 7, 1277, the Bishop of Paris issued a proclamation condemning 219 propositions of a philosophical and theological nature. The faculty of the University of Paris was thenceforth forbidden to affirm the truth of these propositions, on pain of excommunication. Even students listening to those who discussed them were subject to severe sanction.[1]

In the late thirteenth century, Paris was the liveliest center of philosophy in the Christian world. This was not the first time its freethinking faculty had aroused concern among the orthodox. Seven years before, a briefer list of propositions had been formally condemned as contrary to Christian belief. But the Condemnation of 1277 dwarfed this earlier attempt at doctrinal control in the number of errors it outlawed and the severity with which it did so.

The Condemnation of 1277 marks a turning point in Christian thought. It represents an unequivocal repudiation of the creeping paganism that many of his contemporaries detected even in the writings of Thomas Aquinas, who had died three years before to the day. There would, of course, be other Christian thinkers in the years and centuries ahead who would be tempted by pagan ideas. But after 1277, the future of Christian theology lay in a different direction. It belonged to those who fought these ideas in the name of a God whose incomprehensibly free will guaranteed that he would never again be confused with the immanent and necessary God of Aristotle's worldly philosophy. Those who took this path sought to rescue Christianity from what they perceived to be the most serious philosophical threat it had ever faced. The Condemnation of 1277 was their declaration of war, and the centuries-long campaign they fought to save their God from the divinized world of pagan philosophy has given us the godless world we inhabit today.

After receiving instructions from Pope John XXI to conduct a thorough review of the unorthodox ideas then in circulation at the University of Paris, Bishop Tempier assembled a group of distinguished theologians to help him assess the situation. That the list of propositions they condemned is as long as it is, as repetitive and even at points inconsistent, is perhaps best explained by the fact that it was the work of a committee. Yet despite the length and disorderliness of the list itself, most of the propositions on it can be gathered under a few discrete heads.

Many of the condemned beliefs affirm that the world is eternal and hence uncreated. Others maintain that it exists of necessity. A third set insist on the subordination of the will to the intellect, both in God and man. And a fourth claim that man's fulfillment consists in the exercise of intellectual powers which do not, in any meaningful sense, belong to the individual who has them, but collectively and inseparably to all who are engaged in the business of thinking—Aristotle's view, and Averroes' too, but one that has the unfortunate consequence, from a Christian perspective, of ruling out both the need for personal immortality and the possibility of attaining it.

All of these ideas fit comfortably within the framework of Aristotle's metaphysics. But each strikes at the heart of Christian piety. Believing Christians affirm that the world was freely created out of nothing by a God beyond it; that its existence as a whole is contingent; that man's will, like God's, is a power independent of the intellect and hence not compelled to follow it; and that in this life we can never be more than pilgrims whose true home lies elsewhere, in a heavenly life to which we shall be brought, by God's unfathomable grace, not as participants in some common cosmic mind but as individuals distinguished by the uniqueness of our souls and (resurrected) bodies.

Together, these beliefs form the core of Christian theology. The propositions on Bishop Tempier's list constitute the heart of Aristotle's countertheology. Some of these sound strange to modern ears, and their exact meaning is at points hard to grasp. But the overall aim of the list is clear. The Condemnation of 1277 sought to draw a line between paganism and Christianity. That line had become dangerously blurred. By redrawing it as comprehensively and emphatically as they did, the authors of the Condemnation defined a field of orthodoxy within which certain theological questions might continue to be debated, but whose boundaries were from that point on fixed by an unwavering commitment to the ideas of creation, will, salvation and grace that have no place in the pagan philosophy that lies on the other side of the line.

The theologians who played the leading role in this historic act of doctrinal demarcation drew inspiration from many sources, but none more important than the writings of Augustine. Augustine was the first Christian thinker in the Latin West to define the ideas of will and grace with philosophical precision. The thirteenth-century theologians who sought to reassert the authority of these ideas against the intellectualist and necessitarian beliefs of those who subscribed to the propositions condemned by Bishop Tempier's committee turned to Augustine for encouragement and support. They have therefore often been described as neo-Augustinians, and their movement as an Augustinian revolt against the pagan rationalism which the rediscovery of Aristotle's writings on nature and metaphysics had made so attractive to some.

Many of the leaders of this movement were members of the religious order founded earlier in the century by Francis of Assisi. The exemplary humility of Francis himself, institutionalized in the rules he established for his order, encouraged and reinforced the theology of humility which the great Franciscan philosophers of the late thirteenth and early fourteenth centuries all championed, in one form or another. The spirit of neo-Augustinianism thus found a natural home among the Franciscans, and their sometimes fierce opposition to the philosophy of St. Thomas, who in the eyes of his opponents threatened to bind God in chains of reason, assumed the form, in the years that followed, of a contest between the followers of St. Francis, on the one hand, and those of St. Dominic on the other, whose own order, also founded in the early thirteenth century, formally endorsed Aquinas' theology at a general chapter meeting in 1342.

Among the Franciscans who led the fight to rescue their God of will and grace from the pagan intellectualism of a theology more Aristotelian than Christian, three in particular stand out. One was Bonaventure, Aquinas' colleague at the University of Paris, and the first member of the Franciscan order to be authorized to teach theology there (as Aquinas had been the first Dominican). A second was John Duns Scotus, born a decade before the Condemnation, and the third was William of Ockham, born a decade after.

Ockham spent his entire life among the Franciscans, to whom his parents sent him as a boy of twelve or thirteen. He devoted the last twenty years of his life to the defense of his order's position in its complex struggle with the pope over the question of whether and how the Franciscans should be allowed to follow the example of Christ by living lives of poverty unencumbered by the ownership of things, as distinct from their physical use.[2] Ockham was a brilliant polemicist, and the leading role he played in the so-called "Franciscan poverty debate" of the 1320s and '30s led to his excommunication by the pope. (Earlier, he had been accused of heresy on account of certain of his philosophical views and in 1323 moved to Avignon to defend himself against these charges.) When Ockham died in 1347, he was still formally outside the church.

This, together with the controversy generated by the older charge of heresy, helps to explain why Ockham was regarded with a measure of caution by later theologians and why no school of followers devoted to the continuation of his work emerged in the years following his death—in contrast to Duns Scotus, whose views soon became the basis for organized programs of study at universities throughout western Europe. By comparison, Ockham remained something of an outcast. Yet despite this, his ideas proved more influential in the end than those of Bonaventure and Scotus, precisely because of their radical character, which made them disturbing to some but deeply appealing to others.

Ockham has been described as the father of Reformation theology, contractarian political theory, and modern natural science. He has even been called the inventor of modernity itself.[3] These are exaggerated claims and much has been written in the past twenty years to deflate them. But even those who have sought to put Ockham's contributions in a more modest light have been forced to acknowledge the core of truth in all these assertions.

The technical difficulty of Ockham's philosophical writings and their embeddedness in highly specific and now largely forgotten debates make it difficult to grasp the full range of his ideas. But there is one around which all his others revolve. This is the idea of God's boundlessly free will, submission to which is the ground of human morality and our only path to salvation. Among the Franciscan philosophers who championed this idea in the early years of the fourteenth century, none did so more vigorously or uncompromisingly than William of Ockham. His views carry to the limit the revolt against paganism that the Condemnation of 1277 declared. Centered on the idea of a God whose will has been unchained from the necessities of reason, and of a humanity perfectly submissive to his utterly free commands, Ockham's radical Augustinianism is the supreme intellectual expression of the

Condemnation itself, and from it flow—*pace* the qualifications that a generation of scholars have been eager to add—all the most distinctive features of the new theology, politics, and science of nature that in the centuries that followed together produced a world recognizably modern.

Ockham's theological writings are more fragmentary and scattered than those of Aquinas. There is nothing in them that compares with the vast and orderly architecture of the latter's two *summae*. But Ockham unfolds his own conception of God with as much precision as his Dominican rival. His theology, too, has an intellectual center, from which all of his beliefs about the nature of God and our relation to him radiate like the spokes of a wheel. The center of Ockham's theology is the distinction between God's "absolute" and "ordained" power.

Ockham was not the first to employ this distinction. Many others, including Aquinas, had used it before him. By the early years of the fourteenth century, the distinction between God's absolute and ordained power had become a staple of scholastic theology.[4] But Ockham interprets this distinction with unprecedented rigor and applies it across a wider range of problems than previous theologians had. His conception of God is founded upon it. His account of human morality is conditioned by it. Even his claim that general concepts have no extramental reality is motivated by an anxious desire to keep God at a distance from man by blocking all attempts to render him intelligible except on the contingent terms he has decreed—the principal aim of the distinction between God's absolute and ordained power, which Ockham inherited from his predecessors but extended in radical ways.

This is not a distinction between two separate powers that are divided in the way, for example, that the human power to walk is divided from our power to speak. God has only one power. No other view is compatible with his being *all* powerful. Furthermore, everything that God does, he ordains. God's ordained power is coextensive with his actions and therefore with the world he creates. There is nothing that exists that has not been ordained by God, and nothing he ordains that does not exist. The actual *is* the ordained.

But if the actual includes all that exists, and exists through God's ordained power, what remains for his absolute power to do? What is its field of action? Ockham's answer is that God's absolute power is not a separate power at all, with an independent jurisdiction of its own, but the reservoir of divine potency that can never be exhausted by anything God actually does.

All that God does, is, and all that is, he does. But there is no necessity that God do what he has done. Things might be otherwise. It is always *possible* that the *actual* world be different than it is. God has the power, absolutely, to create a world other than the one he has ordained, and retains this absolute power even after he has created it. Even if God ordains that the world shall go on in the familiar and law-like way it has to this point, there is no necessity that he continue to ordain *this*. No amount of ordaining can ever drain the reservoir of God's potential power.

Put differently, nothing can ever make the world other than contingent. Aquinas' theology compromises the contingency of the world by narrowing the gap between the necessity of God's existence and the nearly equal necessity of the world he "diffuses." Ockham's insistence on the importance of the distinction between God's ordained and absolute power is his way of underscoring the unqualified contingency of the world, and of preserving the ontological gap that separates it from its otherworldly creator.

To claim that God has an absolute power that cannot be exhausted by what he ordains is equivalent to saying that it is impossible for him to create a world that exists by necessity. According to Ockham, God's absolute power has only one limit. He cannot cause a contradiction to exist.[5] Because it would require us to affirm the contingency of the world and simultaneous to deny it, the assertion that God has the power to confer necessity on the world if he chooses is a contradiction and therefore false. It follows that God's absolute power is inalienable, for if he could irrevocably bind himself by his own decrees, the world would cease to be contingent and God to be free. The ontological gap between the world and God would be erased—something that God's own absolute power absolutely prevents him from doing.

The distinction between God's ordained and absolute power is therefore best understood as a device for preventing our contingent world from ever sharing in the necessity of God's nature. By ensuring that his freedom always exceeds what he actually does, it guarantees that our separation from God remains insurmountable and undermines the belief that human beings can comprehend, even if only in a limited way, the necessity of the operations of God's mind. It defeats, once and for all, the aspiration to construct a bridge of reason between the actual world and its divine ground. Ockham's insistence on the distinction between God's ordained and absolute power is meant to block this ambition completely.

The result is a conception of God in which the relation of will to reason is the reverse of the one Aquinas describes.

For Aquinas, will is a rational appetite. It follows the lead of the intellect and is therefore subordinate to it. This is true both in man's case and God's. Of course, the human mind is fallible and subject to distortion by the passions. The directions it provides the will are often mistaken. In this respect, there is an enormous gulf between the human intellect and its divine counterpart. But though one is finite and the other not, the reason that confusedly informs the human mind and perfectly animates God's, is not different in the two cases. Reason is the same for man and God, and therefore provides the means of acquiring at least an imperfect knowledge of him.

The situation is like that of two craftsmen who want to make the same thing. Each has a plan for doing so. The plan of the first is blurred and mutilated, that of the second detailed and complete. Both decide to put their plans into effect. Their decisions are distinct acts of will, since neither can exercise the other's will for him; that is something each must do for himself. But if the wills of the two are necessarily divergent, their plans are not. However much they differ in clarity and completeness, the plans of the two craftsmen have a common object. They are plans for the construction of the same thing. The divergence of their wills is therefore qualified by the convergence of their minds, and this establishes a commonality between them that is prior to the separate executive decisions that set them apart. That is because the will always follows the directions of the intellect, whether these are clear or confused.

God is of course a creator, not a craftsman. But for Aquinas, this only means that God's understanding is more perfect than ours. It does not undermine the dependence of will on mind, in God's case as well as ours, or negate the univocity of reason itself. It therefore does not cut us off from all knowledge of God. Quite the opposite. The general priority that Aquinas assigns mind over will guarantees that we remain on a common ground with our creator, despite our imperfections, and allows us, through the use of the reason we share with him, to reach a deeper understanding of his ways than Ockham thinks possible.

Ockham does not deny that the world has a comprehensible order. To the contrary, he insists that reason equips us to grasp the moral laws that tell us what to do, and the physical laws that govern the behavior of things in the natural world, both of which he describes in broadly Aristotelian terms. But the moral and physical order of the world is for Ockham just the order that

God has ordained. It is therefore as contingent as the existence of the world itself, and our understanding of it, no matter how complete, can never possibly give us the least insight into the mind of God, since we have no basis whatever for assuming that the order of his intellect is congruent with the ordained order we are able to discern through the use of our sensory and intellectual powers.

That assumption would be warranted only in case the operations of God's will were preceded by a rationally discernible order that directs and constrains it, in the way our human wills are constrained by the moral and physical order we discover in the world. But the distinction between God's ordained and absolute power rules this out. Whatever God does, there is always more and other he might do. Any rational plan we attribute to God's intellect, and treat as a constraint upon his will, therefore rests on a fallacious inference that ignores the precedence of the divine will over every possible (that is, noncontradictory) plan God might have chosen in creating the real but contingent world he has brought into being from nothing. In this way, Ockham's insistence on the distinction between God's ordained and absolute power turns Aquinas' understand of the relation between God's intellect and will on its head.

It is sometimes said that as a result, Ockham's theology leads to an arbitrary and despotic God, whose commands in both the natural and moral realms are binding only because he has commanded them. Defenders of Thomist rationalism in particular make this charge to underscore the comparative attractiveness of their God, whose perfectly rational mind we can at least glimpse in the world around us. By contrast, they say, Ockham's God is a tyrant whose laws compel only because he says so. To this conception of God, some have argued, we owe the positivist understanding of political authority that is expressed with matchless clarity, and remorseless brutality, in Hobbes' *Leviathan*.[6]

There is some truth in this characterization of Ockham's theology. But in one crucial respect it misses the point. A tyrant acts whimsically, even irrationally, for his own advantage. Ockham never once suggests that God acts out of any motive other than love or in an irrational manner. God regards his creatures—especially those he has created in his image—with unfathomable love, and everything he does for them he does for a reason. Nor does Ockham ever suggest that we ought to be skeptical about the reliability and goodness of the order that God has ordained. The order of the world is God's creation, and therefore necessarily good. In all these respects, Ockham's God is the familiar God of Christian piety, whose love and goodness make him utterly unlike the arbitrary tyrant he is sometimes said to be.

Ockham's distinction between God's absolute and ordained power is not meant to turn God into a selfish dictator, or to undermine our confidence in the goodness of the world, which we can discover through natural reason and the revelations of Scripture. But it *is* intended to rule out the possibility of our understanding the ways of God by reasoning back from the world he has ordained to the mind of God himself. Indeed, the very purpose of the distinction, as Ockham employs it, is to underscore our human incapacity to understand God, which we could do only in case there were laws of reason that bound him in the work of creation.

By converting any law that might bind God into the contingent product of his own free will, Ockham makes it impossible for the law in question to limit or constrain the divine will from which it proceeds. His insistence on the boundless reservoir of God's absolute power thus restores us to a position of humble ignorance regarding the nature of God. It cuts the inferential cord that would, if it existed, allow us to draw conclusions about the mind of God from the world he has created. It kills at the root the prideful temptation, to which Aquinas and others yielded, to disown our abysmal dependence on God by insisting that he too is subject to the laws of reason that direct all minds, his included.

In creating the world, God is therefore not bound to follow any rational order antecedent to creation itself. As a result, we have no hope of ever understanding the justificatory ground of the laws he has ordained in the moral and physical realms. If we could, the authority of these laws would be transferred from God to the directives of reason that he follows in ordaining them. And that would entail a tremendous depreciation in God's stature and commensurate increase in ours.

This is the very result that Ockham seeks to avoid.

By harnessing God's will to his intellect, Aquinas makes God beholden to reason, and thereby gives us a real, if imperfect, access to the inner workings of his mind. Ockham's reversal of this relationship sets God free and makes our ignorance of his nature incurable and complete. For Ockham, this adjustment in our conception of God, which puts the divine will first by insisting on the surplus of his absolute power over everything he ordains, is more than an intellectual quibble. It is an act of piety that is meant to restore God's sublime inaccessibility to man. Its purpose is to remind us of our utter dependence on his gifts, including that of law itself, which God has freely given his fallen human creatures out of a boundless love unconstrained even by reason. Ockham built his relentless voluntarism on a conceptual distinction familiar to every scholastic theologian. But its real importance lay in the new energy it gave to the original Augustinian concept of grace—the principal weapon that he and the other leaders of the fourteenth-century Franciscan revolt used in their campaign against pride.

WORLD AND MIND

In capsule histories of medieval thought, Ockham is often described as a "nominalist." This is meant to identify his position in a long-running debate among scholastic theologians regarding the ontological status of universals, such as "man," "equal" and "red." The classical roots of the problem lay in Aristotle's quarrel with Plato concerning the reality of the forms. On the one side were the "realists," who maintained that universals have a real existence in the world outside our minds. On the other were the nominalists, including Ockham, who insisted that universals are "mere" words or concepts that have no objective correlate of a comparably abstract kind. Those who took the latter view did not deny that universals figure prominently in human reasoning. They recognized, as anyone must, that without abstract concepts, we can neither think nor speak. They also acknowledged that the concepts we use refer to *something* outside the mind. But they were adamant that this cannot be a really existing, mind-independent universal like "humanity," "equality" or "redness." Much of their work was devoted to explaining what else it might be.

Theologians on both sides of the debate defended a range of nuanced positions whose complexities account, as much as anything else, for the enduring reputation of late scholastic thought as a wasteland of sterile distinctions. But the difference between realists and nominalists was an important one, and Ockham's own contribution to the nominalist cause had a lasting influence on later philosophical thought. It also helped to prepare the way for the new science of nature that would take shape over the next several centuries and culminate in the work of Galileo, by simultaneously freeing both the empirical investigation of the world and its mathematical description from the constraints of pagan metaphysics. But the principal motive for Ockham's nominalism was neither philosophic nor scientific. It was

theological. Like every other branch of his philosophy, Ockham's nominalism was driven by a desire to be faithful to the God whose ineffable majesty
realism impugns.

Though Ockham is often called a nominalist, the term, as applied to him,
is somewhat misleading, for it suggests that he believed that universals are
just names, with the implication that they are merely conventional and hence
arbitrary signs. Ockham's position is more complex.

The languages we speak and write are preceded, he says, by a language
we "think." This is a conceptual language that all human beings share. It is
natural, not conventional, and already employs universal concepts, which are
then "translated" into the conventional terms that different languages use to
express them. The words "man" and "l'homme," for example, refer to the same
class of beings. They are different terms for the concept from which both words
derive.

The languages we speak and write differ from one another in many
ways. But they all share certain logical features in common. They all operate according to certain basic rules for the combination of terms and the validation of truth claims. These shared logical properties constitute the grammar
not just of this language or that one, of English or French, but of thinking as
such. In his extensive writings on the logic of terms, Ockham sought to bring
this deep grammar to light by identifying the structure of the processes of
thought in which all human beings by nature engage before (conceptually,
if not temporally) they begin to express their thoughts in the conventional
language of a particular linguistic community. Some Ockham scholars
therefore insist that it is more accurate to call him a "conceptualist" than a
nominalist.[7]

According to Ockham, the primary units of the natural language of
thought are conceptual signs. Each of these points to something other than
itself. Some point to things in the world outside the mind, in the way the
concept "red" does. Others, like the concept "noun," point to other conceptual signs. But neither points to a particular thing. In this respect, all conceptual signs differ from proper names, like "Socrates" and "Critias," which
refer to one thing only. The concept "red," for example, points equally and
indifferently to all instances of the color, and the concept "noun" to all words
that perform a certain grammatical function. Thinking itself demands conceptual signs of this sort, for if every sign were a proper name, abstraction,
and hence reasoning, could never get a start.

But though we require abstract signs to think, Ockham insists that there is nothing in the world to which their abstractness corresponds. The world contains only individual substances and qualities—Socrates here, Critias there, the red of this particular vase and of that one across the room. (This is true of concepts that point to other concepts as well.) We must therefore avoid the temptation, to which every realist falls prey, of assuming that the ontological structure of the world matches the structure of our thoughts, so far as the reality of the abstractions we need to think is concerned. These do indeed refer to something real. They are not illusions. But what they refer to are not themselves abstractions, with an extramental being of their own, but always and only the individual things and qualities to which each conceptual sign indifferently points.

Ockham was led to this position in part because he considered the arguments in favor of the reality of universals philosophically untenable. His insistence on a principle of ontological parsimony that ruthlessly eliminates every kind of being reducible to some other (which later came to be known as Ockham's razor), also undoubtedly contributed to his rejection of realism, which assigns universals a being over and above that of the individuals to which they refer. But Ockham had in addition a powerful theological motive for endorsing the view he did.

However much we think we can learn about God by observing the order he has ordained, his absolute power guarantees that we can never comprehend the inner workings of his mind. If one understands God in these terms, as Ockham did, then the metaphysics of realism is bound to seem more than merely implausible. It has to appear impious too. That is because realism draws God too close to the world. It makes God's mind at least imperfectly accessible to human beings, and thereby gives encouragement to those who are tempted to seek to understand his ways. Ockham's nominalism rules this out completely. From a theological point of view, that is both its upshot and aim.

Once again, the contrast with Aquinas is instructive.

According to Aquinas, the forms of things are immediately apprehensible by us. Like other animals, we are directly connected to the world by means of perception. We are in contact with the things around us through sight, taste, smell, hearing and touch. But our perception of them is of more than their sensuous presence. We perceive their forms as well—what Aquinas calls their "intelligible species." This is something that every individual possesses in the same way and to the same degree as every other member of its kind. It is the

"suchness" that is present in it, along with the matter that makes it a "this."
Our perception of the thing includes a direct apprehension of this "suchness" itself. When we see a man, for example, we do not see just a hunk of
animated flesh. We see a *man,* a being of a certain kind with a distinctive
nature. We apprehend his species-being. For us and other rational beings, there
is no other kind of seeing.

The imagination plays a crucial role in Aquinas' account of how thought
arises from seeing things in this way. Our direct encounter with a thing gives
rise in the imagination to what he calls a "phantasm"—a mental state that
straddles the spheres of thought and perception and is therefore able to mediate between them. Thinking, for Aquinas, is the process of abstracting the
intelligible species of things from the phantasms that carry them across the
threshold from the world into the mind, where we are then able to reason
about them in a way that is no longer confined by perception. But on Aquinas' view, such abstraction is possible only because these forms have been there
from the start—because they are already present to us in our first sensory encounter with the world and are merely transferred by imagination to the realm
of thought.

We can therefore be confident that what we know about the world is part
of what is knowable in it. We cannot understand the world perfectly, of course.
That is because our perception of things, though partly intellectual, is not
completely so, in contrast to God's. We perceive more than we are able to
understand. Yet because we directly perceive the "intelligible species" of things,
we *are* able to understand at least the broad architecture of the world that God
has created, and to that extent to comprehend his mind. The forms of things
are really there, and we can really understand them, thanks to the partly intellectual nature of our immediate perception of the world and to the mediating work of the imagination. Even in this life, we are therefore able to
comprehend God's mind *directly* and *accurately* within the limits our finitude
permits.

Ockham's nominalism leads to exactly the opposite conclusion.

Ockham agrees that perception is the power that puts us in direct contact with the world. Through perception, we see that things exist. The perception of a thing in turn causes us to have what Ockham (following Scotus)
calls an "intuitive" cognition of its existence—to *know* that it exists as well as
to see that it does.[8] But neither the perception of a thing nor its intuitive cognition is mediated by concepts of any kind. Each is an awareness of existence
pure and simple.[9] The existence in question, moreover, is always and only that

of an individual substance or quality. Only individuals of these two sorts exist. Hence, only their individuality can be either perceived or intuitively cognized. Even after crossing the threshold that separates the world from the mind, the immediate cognition we have of things is of their individual existence alone.

In order to reason about individuals, however, we need general terms or universals. Ockham readily concedes this. The production of such terms is the work, he says, of "abstractive" (as distinct from "intuitive") cognition. But crucially, for Ockham, their production is not a distillation of something already present in perception. It is not a refinement of preexisting forms out of an experiential mass in which they are confusedly contained. Ockham's abstractive intellect is not a passive instrument, on which the intelligible species of things "impress" themselves. It is the author of these species themselves, which (unlike the individual substances and qualities that really exist in the world) have no being apart from the creative processes of abstractive cognition. The order we think we see in the world is therefore our own doing. It is something we spontaneously create. Abstractive cognition is not for Ockham, as it is for Aquinas, the deferential apprehension of an antecedent and independent order of some kind. It is not an act or operation of reason at all. It is an act of will—the creation of this very order, out of nothing but itself.

Ockham's nominalism, which explains the existence of universals as the creative work of abstractive cognition, thus affirms the priority of will over reason in human beings in a way that parallels his affirmation of the priority of will over reason in God. This marks an epochal shift in our understanding of the relation between man's mind and the world, and gives rise to a host of problems that no realist ever had to resolve. Chief among these is the challenge of explaining how our thoughts can be faithful representations of the extramental world they depict. By severing the link between perception and conception, whose continuity Aquinas assumes, Ockham makes the construction of any explanation of this kind problematic in a way it had not been before. Kant's later attempt to establish the authority of human reason by "transcendental" means represents a heroic effort to solve this problem, but it is worth noting that the problem arises for Kant, as it does for Ockham, precisely because Kant also attributes the existence of the abstractions we need to think to the work of an inventive power in the human soul whose very spontaneity makes it as "mysterious" and hence unintelligible as God's creation of the world.

Ockham's will-centered account of human cognition does more than merely parallel his voluntarist conception of God, however. There is an important motivational link between them as well, for Ockham's explanation of how we acquire the universals that human thinking requires is meant to ensure that our thoughts can never be even a partial and distorted version of God's own, but bear no discoverable relation to them at all.

The world that Ockham's God creates consists entirely of individuals. We human beings have an intuitive cognition of their existence, but can reason and speak about them only by using general concepts that we ourselves create. Yet precisely because these are our own creations, and thus correspond to nothing real in the world, it is impossible for us ever to have any reason to trust the naive but misguided belief that our understanding of the world, which depends on them, conforms to the world itself, let alone to God's knowledge of it. Given the complete disconnection between the abstractions we need to think, and the real world toward which our thoughts are directed, it is not merely difficult for us to gain some insight into the operation of God's mind. It is absolutely impossible. No matter how much we come to know about the world, or how clearly we think about it, we can never have the slightest degree of confidence that our knowledge corresponds to the world as it actually is, and mirrors, in a clouded but genuine way, the mind of its creator.

By contrast, Aquinas' realism allows for at least a measure of such confidence. What we know about the world, on Aquinas' view, is the order of the world itself—the very same order that God comprehends, though more perfectly than we. Ockham's nominalism destroys all such assurance by denying the worldly reality of the intelligible forms that provide a middle term between the human intellect and its divine counterpart. For all we know, the forms we need to think may be fantasies or illusions. The world may be completely other than we conceive it to be. Of course, that doesn't seem to be the case. What we understand about the order of the world appears to represent the true order of things. The laws of nature that we discover through observation and inquiry are as a rule confirmed by experience, leading us to believe that what we know about the world is really true. But if that is so, it is only because God has contingently ordained that we experience the world as a system of laws that conforms to our thoughts about it.

Hence, whatever confidence we *do* have about the connection between our minds and the world can itself only be God's contingent gift to us, and not, as Aquinas and others maintain, a rationally demonstrable truth. Without ren-

dering human reflection on the world pointless and vain, Ockham's nominalism guarantees that reason can never put us in touch with the world as
it really is, and thereby give us a stepping stone to the mind of God. The
very thing that Aquinas makes the final end of human striving, and understands to be the essence of beatitude, is thus converted into an illusion of
pride. In this way, even Ockham's highly technical contribution to the medieval debate regarding the status of universals serves to advance the theological goal that animates every branch of his thought by securing God's ineffable
transcendence against those pagan rationalists who would make his ways too
familiar to man.

One further consequence of Ockham's nominalism is worth noting. That
is its contribution to the intellectual development of modern science.

From a modern point of view, the science of Plato and Aristotle was limited in two respects. In the first place, the empiricism of Greek science was
severely constrained by the classical equation of being with form. To understand what an oyster is, it is necessary to observe oysters at work. Aristotle
understood this, and engaged in empirical research of this kind himself. But
on an Aristotelian view, there is a limit to how much research is required to
understand oysters or anything else, since only the form of a thing is intelligible, and this can be grasped completely after a finite number of observations. After that, there is nothing more to be learned from further empirical
study. True, no two oysters are exactly alike, but their individuality is not
worth investigating because, in the end, there is nothing intelligible about it.
Once one has made a few preliminary observations, the science of oysters can
be pursued by reasoning out the nature of their way of life through what we
today call "armchair" speculation.

Second, the use of mathematics as an instrument of explanation was limited by the same equation of being with form. For Plato especially, mathematics is the preeminent science of form and hence of reality. Mathematical
entities are not, in his view, mere abstractions. They are the building blocks
of the forms that constitute the order of the world. But Plato's mathematical
realism raised a barrier to the free development of mathematical ideas, for it
limited their range to the real order of things. Unreal forms, of the sort that
modern mathematics knows and uses in abundance, are a metaphysical impossibility for Plato. His mathematics is therefore more confined than ours,
for the same reason that Aristotle's empiricism is more limited too.

Ockham's nominalism dissolves both limits at once. To begin with, if the
world is completely contingent, we can discover its contents only by looking

to see what is there. It is not enough, moreover, to take a quick look and then retire to the armchair, deducing the rest by thought alone, for none of one's armchair speculations are necessarily true of the world. All of these must be verified by experience too.

On Ockham's view, this experience is always and only of individuals. If we want to understand what is really real in the world, we therefore have to try to grasp the individuality of the individuals we find when we look. Aristotle believed just the opposite, and because he did his empiricism stopped at an understanding of the general forms of things. By insisting that only individuals are real, Ockham tied our knowledge of the world to an empiricism without end. To be sure, all empirical knowledge depends on the use of universal concepts that are creations of the human mind. But the universals we employ when we think, which have no reality themselves, can never exhaust the intelligibility of the individuals we comprehend with their aid in a progressively more adequate way—through the grace of God, whose freely ordained conjunction of the orders of mind and world is the only possible source of whatever confidence we possess that our endlessly expanding empirical knowledge is true or right.

At the same time, Ockham's nominalism sets mathematics free from the realist limits within which it remained confined for Plato and his medieval followers. If the creations of abstractive cognition are not mental replicas of forms already present in the world, there are no restrictions, other than the law of noncontradiction, that limit the content of mathematical ideas or the development of notational systems expressing the relations among them. Ockham's attack on the metaphysics of realism dissolves the connection that yoked mathematics to the world and thus allows it to develop in its own independent fashion. Without such independence, neither algebra, which makes use of the un-Platonic idea of zero, as well as negative and unreal numbers, nor calculus, with its concept of the infinitesimal, could have acquired the philosophical legitimacy they did or been put to respectable use in the investigation of a world to which these ideas were no longer obliged to conform.

Strikingly, it is these unreal ideas that have proved most useful in our empirical study of the real world of individual things. Platonic mathematics never gets beyond the general forms of numbers and shapes. Individuality remains incomprehensible to it. Through the use of the infinitesimal and other devices, modern mathematics enables us to come closer to an understanding of individuality as such. Ockham's nominalism liberates mathematics from its Platonic straightjacket and thereby opens the way to the unreal ideas we need to render more intelligible the real individuals that our empirical investigation of the world discloses in ever greater detail (especially by means of those artificially contrived experiences we call "experiments").

The two most distinctive features of modern natural science are its boundless empiricism and commitment to the mathematization of all empirical data. Despite the apparent tension between them, these two characteristics belong together. The science of Plato and Aristotle lacked both. The new science that began to displace it in the fourteenth and fifteenth centuries, and that has developed in an unbroken line ever since, is defined by the seemingly paradoxical union of these two ideas, for which Ockham's theologically inspired nominalism provided the warrant. This now-regnant science of nature is, in the eyes of many, the most powerful antireligious force in the world today. Yet its metaphysical accreditation began not with an attack on religion, but with an interpretation of the relation between mind and world that was intended to protect the sublime dignity of God from those who would bind his will in chains of reason.

The same is true of ethics, as we shall now see.

THE MORAL ORDER

Ockham's writings contain hundreds of pages of ethical theory. Together these offer a complex but coherent answer to the question of which human acts are morally good and why. Ockham never gathered his ideas about morality into a single, organized treatise. As a result, there are points at which his views appear inconsistent. But there is an underlying consistency to everything he says about the nature and grounds of morality.

One's first impression is that Ockham's moral system is remarkably like that of Aristotle and his Thomistic followers. Ockham knew Aristotle's ethical writings well and drew on them heavily. Indeed, many of his views—those regarding the virtues, for example, and the role of habit in moral life—conform closely to Aristotle's own. On the surface, it can easily seem that in the realm of ethics, Ockham was an Aristotelian. But the appearance of similarity is an illusion. The difference between Ockham and Aristotle is as deep here as in the field of metaphysics, for in his ethical philosophy too Ockham's views are motivated by theological considerations that are entirely foreign to Aristotle's conception of the world and man's place in it.

According to Ockham, no external act is either good or bad in itself. External acts acquire moral value only through their relation to the will of the person performing them. Acts of will alone are "immediately" good or bad. External ones are only "mediately" so.

Thus, for example, the act of walking to church out of pride (in order to display one's piety) is mediately bad, and the prideful will to self-importance that lies behind it is bad in itself. By contrast, walking to church out of a love for God is mediately good, and the will to love God and to do as he commands inherently or immediately so. Ockham's ethics is one of intentions, not acts. In this respect, it resembles the ethics of Paul and Augustine and anticipates that of Kant.

But if only acts of will have inherent moral value, it does not follow that all such acts are morally good. It is a necessary but not sufficient condition for assessing the intrinsic morality of an act that it be an act of will. Once this has been established, it remains to be determined whether the act is good, bad or indifferent, and for that some further criterion is needed. In Ockham's view, this is the act's conformity to the dictates of what he calls "right reason."[10]

Ockham's insistence that only acts of will possess inherent moral value separates his ethics from Aristotle's in a profound way. His emphasis on the criterial role of right reason seems, however, to draw it back toward the naturalism of Aristotle's position. This is underscored by the fact that the *content* of the morality that right reason discloses is, for Ockham, largely congruent with Aristotle's own, with predictable exceptions for the theological virtues and other specifically Christian beliefs.

But what explains the status that right reason enjoys as a standard for judging the moral character of acts of the will? What gives reason the authority to serve as a moral criterion in this way? For Aristotle, that is no question at all. On his view, the dictates of reason are self-validating. Reason has the authority it does because it is what it is: a faculty for discerning the necessary order of things, including the moral order that shapes and directs the careers of human beings.

For Ockham, by contrast, the question of the source of the normative authority of right reason is an urgent one. That is because the Aristotelian belief that no answer is required makes sense only on the prideful assumption that reason is sufficient not merely to determine which human acts are good but to explain, in a deep and final way, *why* they are good as well: the very essence of the pagan morality that Ockham considers the antithesis of his own. A true Christian morality must ground the authority of reason as a criterion of moral judgment in something other than reason itself.

On Ockham's view, the norms that right reason discerns are authoritative because they have all been ordained by God. God has decreed that we use reason as a guide in deciding what to will. A person who refuses to do this is acting immorally. What makes his acts immoral, however, is not their irrationality *per se*. His acts are immoral because he has failed to do as God commands, namely, to conform his will to right reason.

The dictates of right reason supply the *content* of God's commands. They tell us what he demands: that we behave justly in our relations with others, refrain from murder, avoid adultery and the like. We are able to discover the substance of these requirements through the use of reason alone. But in addition to their diverse content, all the rules of right reason share a common *form*. Each is God's command, and this alone, according to Ockham, explains *why* we have a moral obligation to do *what* it says we should.

On Ockham's view, the normative authority of the dictates of right reason is thus due entirely to their form, from which it follows that if God were to issue a different set of commands, with a different or even contradictory content, we would be as fully obligated to conform our wills to them as we are to follow those that right reason discovers in the present order of things. That is because the form of God's new commands—their status as commands—would be the same as that of the ones he has actually issued. Though what God commands us to do would have changed, the reason why we should do it would not—a conclusion that Ockham enthusiastically embraces as an expression of the distinctively Christian character of his explanation of the authority of right reason, which is to be respected not on account of the inherent authority of reason but as a manifestation (ordination) of God's will.

Two important consequences follow. First, the ancient distinction between natural and revealed law ceases to be of fundamental importance. Some laws ("do not kill") are disclosed to us by the light of reason. These are laws that every human being can discover by means of reflection alone. Together, they constitute the natural law. Other norms ("make confession once a week") are not discoverable by reason. No amount of thinking, by itself, can ever bring them to light. We know that we have a duty to obey them only because others, speaking on behalf of God, have told us that we do—Moses, for example, or Jesus, or the pope in his capacity as leader of the church. These constitute the revealed law. (Human positive law, like God's revealed law, cannot be deduced by reason alone; it, too, must be declared to be known.)

But this is a distinction of a secondary sort. It marks a difference is the way we learn the content of the laws we are bound to observe. The *ground* of their authority, however, is the same in both cases. The authority of all moral laws, the natural as well as the revealed, derives from the fact that God commands us to obey them. This is equally true whether he has chosen to communicate their content to us through the voice of reason or that of a prophet. In this way, the entire realm of natural law, as traditionally conceived, is assimilated to that of revealed law and made a special subfield within it—the domain of those divine commands whose substance God discloses through the medium of reason alone.

Second, even those natural laws that reason discovers on its own are as contingent as the most arbitrary-seeming rules promulgated by God's agents (for example, the rule that the Christian Sabbath be celebrated on Sunday). The laws of nature appear necessary. It is as hard to imagine a world in which murder and theft are permitted, let alone required, as to imagine one in which pigs fly. But the appearance of necessity is an illusion. In deciding to issue one set of commands rather than another, God is not subject to any norm apart from himself. There are no rules, no obligations, no laws he is bound to respect, not even those he has previously ordained and graciously continues to observe, but remains free to disregard whenever he chooses. In this respect, God's situation is fundamentally different from ours, for we *are* bound by norms that exist independently of us. The very idea that God could be bound in this way is an insult to his glory. The most that we can ever say is that the norms of right reason obligate contingently in the actual world that God has ordained, but not necessarily in every possible (that is, noncontradictory) world he might.

Ockham drives this point home by insisting on the contingency even of the most fundamental laws of morality. He claims, for example, that God could mandate adultery if he chose.[11] There is no contradiction in a law commanding men to seduce other men's wives, and hence no impossibility in its enactment. It always remains within God's absolute power to enact a law of this kind, and if he did, we would sin if we refused to obey it. God himself would not sin by ordaining such a law, since sin is a failure to do as one ought and hence presupposes the existence of norms external to the sinner—something that is true in our case but impossible in God's. Indeed, even if God were to *cause us* to violate our moral duties—God is always a "partial" cause of our sinning but may, if he wills, be the "total" cause too—his causal agency would not itself be sinful, since there is no law outside of God to which he can be held accountable (though in this case we should have to say that our actions cannot be sinful either, since our freedom of will, which is a condition of any act being judged sinful, would by assumption have been taken away).

Of course, Ockham does not think that God would ever do any of these things. He has complete confidence in the goodness of God. His point is a logical one—that God *could* do them if he chose and that if he did, his commands would be as binding as the ones he has actually issued. Ockham makes this logical point in a spirit of piety. He believes that the best way of paying proper respect to God is to acknowledge the utter contingency of the moral order we take for granted in the world as it actually is, including those norms that seem to us most unassailably natural. Pointing out that God can, without sinning, command men to be adulterous, is thus for Ockham a way of honoring God, and reading his statements on the subject, one has the sense that he took a pious delight in insisting on what, from the point of view of our most deeply held moral beliefs, seems unimaginable.

This has led some, then and since, to accuse Ockham of making human morality a completely arbitrary affair. The laws that Ockham's God commands us to obey, his critics say, are binding only because God commands them. Our duties therefore rest on nothing solider than the pronouncements of a God unconstrained by reasons of any sort. This view, they claim, makes God look more like a tyrant with unchecked discretion than the wise and beneficent ruler he is, and cuts human morality adrift from any anchorage it might otherwise have in an intelligible order of things.

One way of putting this criticism is to say that for Ockham every moral obligation is conditional or (in Kant's terminology) "hypothetical." A law is binding *only if* God has commanded it, something he need not have done. If all our obligations were conditional in this sense, then none would be (again, to use Kant's term) "categorical"—that is, necessarily and not merely conditionally binding. Our duties are binding only in the actual world that God has ordained and only because he has ordained them. None is binding in every possible world, and therefore categorically in all. If this criticism were valid, the complaint that Ockham's account of morality makes it wholly arbitrary might be persuasive.

But it is not. Ockham strenuously insists that there is one obligation we have in every possible world regardless of whatever other obligations God imposes upon us. Conforming our wills to God's other commands is contingently virtuous because it depends upon the existence of norms whose nonexistence is perfectly conceivable. By contrast, the act of conforming our wills to the one obligation that exists in every possible world is "intrinsically" or necessarily virtuous since its moral goodness does not depend on a state of affairs that might not exist. According to Ockham, there must be at least one such act of intrinsic virtue, since otherwise all virtuous acts would be only conditionally so, producing a regress that makes even conditionally virtuous acts inconceivable. And for there to be at least one such *act,* there must be at least one *law* that binds necessarily, in every possible world.

This is the law, Ockham says, that commands us to love God unconditionally and to do as he says because he says it. A will that lovingly obeys this command is intrinsically virtuous. With the command to love God for his own sake, we reach the foundation needed to avoid a regress in morality and to dispel the charge that our duties are arbitrary all the way down.

That Ockham's morality requires this foundation is clear for the following reason. If we start with the proposition that only acts of will have immediate moral value, a criterion of some sort is needed to distinguish good acts of will from bad ones. According to Ockham, good acts are those that conform to right reason. But then we have to ask why the dictates of reason oblige. This cannot be because of their rationality. That would be paganism. The laws that reason brings to light oblige because God commands us to obey them, which he need not have done. But why should we obey God's commands? Hobbes' famous answer is that we are bound to obey them because God is omnipotent.[12] But that is no answer at all. God's omnipotence may explain why we are *forced* to do as he says. But it cannot explain why we have a duty to do so. If we have a duty to follow God's commands that can only be because we are already bound to obey him before he has told us what to do. To be bound to obey the laws that God has ordained, we must have a precedent obligation to conform our wills to his, regardless of the content of his decrees. This precedent obligation is the only one that has to exist in every world that God could possibly create. It is therefore our only necessary obligation, in contrast to all the contingent ones that God has imposed upon us in the world that he has actually chosen to bring into being, including those that reason discerns. This one necessary obligation alone explains why we have a duty to obey every other actual and hence contingent law. It is the obligation to love God with all our hearts and to do as he says for the sake of doing so alone.

Our other obligations are binding only on account of their form. Their content, which is contingent, merely specifies the duties we have. It is not itself a source of obligation. But for God's commands to be binding in every possible world solely because of their *form,* there must be at least one obligation that is binding in all such worlds on account of its *content,* since otherwise the regress that worries Ockham cannot be stopped.

Our obligation to love God in a spirit of perfect deference to his will plays this foundational role in Ockham's moral theory. Alone among our obligations, it is binding because of *what* it tells us to do. On it rests the obligatory force of the duties we have to obey all of God's other commands, which are binding merely because of their form, regardless of whether God has chosen to reveal their contingent content to us through reason or in some other way. The human being who wills to be and stay in this posture of boundless deference to God strives to do the only thing that is necessary from a moral point of view, and, if he succeeds, achieves the highest state of virtue a person can attain.

The logic of this argument helps us answer the much-discussed question of whether, on Ockham's view, God can command us to hate him. At one point, Ockham seems to acknowledge this possibility, but at another denies it. It is clear why he is moved to suggest that God has the power to issue such a command. If God can command murder and theft, why not hatred of himself? Suggesting that he can is a particularly forceful way of underscoring his absolute power. But it is also clear why Ockham should hesitate here. For though it is obvious that God can give our moral duties whatever content he chooses, it is less clear that he has the power to undermine the very foundation of our duty to do as he commands. Can God, without contradiction, issue a command commanding us to hate and therefore disobey him? If we have a duty to obey this command, it is only because we must love God and do as he says, so that if we fulfill the command in an obedient way we will be hating God out of a love for him—a logical, as well as psychological, contradiction.

All that one can say, perhaps, is that while God has the power to *issue* such a command, he lacks the power to *obligate* us to follow it. Ockham says repeatedly that God's absolute power is limited only by the law of noncontradiction. The one thing he cannot do is bring a contradictory state of affairs into being. God's incapacity to obligate us to hate him is the only material implication of this formal limitation in the whole of Ockham's moral theory. As such, it focuses our attention on the one law we have a duty to obey in every possible world—the law that commands us to subordinate our wills to God's out of gratitude for his free and unmerited grace. Of all our duties, this one alone binds us universally and necessarily, on account of what it commands and not merely because it commands it. To suggest that this duty too, is only contingently binding, assumes that God could, if he chose, abolish the grounds for our gratitude to him, which for Ockham would amount to his choosing not to be God. It is no more conceivable than that.

OCKHAM'S BEQUEST

The central tension in Christian ethics is that between man's will and God's grace.

The will possesses a power of creation akin to God's own. It is independent and free—the cause of itself. This alone gives its actions intrinsic moral worth. The autonomy of the will is therefore the premise of morality; one must assume it in order to explain why there is evil in the world and why man, not God, is responsible for it.

At the same time, man depends utterly on God's grace. Without it, he can do nothing at all. Those who acknowledge this are good; those who deny it, wicked and prideful. The result is an insurmountable paradox: a morality that makes the autonomy of the will the foundation of moral life, but views the will's assertion of independence, even in the smallest ways, as the root of all wrongdoing, and defines goodness or virtue as the will's unquestioning and unqualified subordination to the will of another—an especially stringent form of heteronomy.

The ideas of will and grace belong to the creationist metaphysics of Christian belief. Both are completely foreign to Aristotle's philosophy of pride. Those who follow Aristotle thus have no need to confront the paradox to which these two ideas give rise. But from a Christian perspective, that is only because they have not yet grasped, or worse, have learned and forgotten, the central truth of Christianity: that the world was created from nothing by an infinitely gracious God, against whose authority we human beings have been in a state of prideful rebellion since Adam.

The realist theologians of the thirteenth century were tempted by Aristotle's pagan metaphysics and had to be recalled to this Christian truth. That is what the voluntarists of the fourteenth century attempted to do. They sought to bring Christian theology back to its Augustinian roots. This meant restoring the ideas of will and grace to a dominant position in Christian theology—retrieving them from the shadow of reason in which they had been placed by pagan sympathizers like Aquinas, who of course accepted both ideas yet subjected them to limits that Ockham and others thought incompatible with the unknowable grandeur of God. But with the restoration of these ideas to the center of theology, the paradoxical relation between them returned as a challenge for Christian belief, in an even more self-conscious, hence radical, form.

Ockham's account of morality culminates in this paradox. On the one hand, he defends a strict morality of intentions that makes acts of will the only ones that have any direct moral value. The will alone possesses the autonomy that moral responsibility presupposes. On the other, he insists that the supreme principle of morality, by which all acts of will must be judged, is our duty to obey God's commands, whatever their content may be, out of love and gratitude alone—a principle of pure heteronomy that treats the will's subordination to the will of another as the only act that is necessarily good in itself.

Ockham's moral theory thus reproduces the paradox of freedom and grace that lies at the heart of Augustinian Christianity. Man is a moral being only because he has a will, and the human will is responsible only because it is free. Yet the only virtuous use we can make of our freedom is to give it away, by freely renouncing every ambition to self-sufficiency and embracing our complete dependence on God instead.

If we give up the idea that human beings possess the freedom to choose whether or not to follow God's laws, and the radical independence this implies, the whole domain of morality collapses. But if we fail to acknowledge our utter dependence on God's grace, both for the laws that guide us in this world and our salvation in the next, the result can only be a resurgence of pride, modest or satanic depending on the degree of independence one claims. For those who believe that God made us in his image, with our free but disobedient wills, autonomy is therefore at once the source and scourge of moral life.

There is nothing in Ockham's philosophy to help us resolve this dilemma. Ockham merely bequeaths it to his successors, as Augustine had done long before. To resolve the dilemma, a choice must be made between the ideas of freedom and grace. One must be subordinated to the other, which means, in effect, abandoned completely, since neither the grace of God nor the autonomy of man's will can be qualified or conditioned without ceasing to be what it is. Both are all-or-nothing ideas.

Luther resolves this paradox by making freedom disappear in the name of grace. Two centuries later, Kant provides the only other consistent solution by converting God's grace to a mere "postulate" of pure practical reason.

Today, Kant's argument for the priority of human freedom is accepted as a foundational principle of public morality throughout the secularized West.

It has triumphed over the Lutheran alternative, though not without a bitter struggle against the reactionary enemies of enlightenment who fought, one last time, to restore God's grace to the world. The acceptance of Kant's solution to the paradox of freedom and grace has contributed to the construction of a world freer and more prosperous than any that has ever existed before. This happy result is part of Ockham's bequest. Yet it has also produced a world that is spoiled by the depreciation of gratitude and haunted by the absence of the God whose paradoxical relation to man Kant finally resolved by putting man in God's place. This is Ockham's legacy too.

CHAPTER 18

◆────◆◇◆────◆

Theology of the Cross

THE LUTHERAN REFORMATION

Weeks before he posted his famous theses on indulgences to the door of the Castle Church in Wittenberg, Martin Luther offered another set of provocative assertions for debate. He called this earlier list a *Disputation against Scholastic Theology*. It was directed at the shortcomings of the tradition of theology in which Luther had been trained as a young monk in the Augustinian monastery at Erfurt.[1]

In 1517, Luther was thirty-four. He had been lecturing on biblical and philosophical subjects for nine years. During this time, his own theology, which he later called a "theology of the cross,"[2] had gradually taken shape. It was the result of deep reflection born of personal anguish.[3] The full implications of Luther's new theology would soon become apparent to the world at large, in the torrent of exhortatory and polemical writings that poured from his pen in the years immediately following his attack on the sale of indulgences. But the fundamental principles of his "reformation" (a word he himself did not use until much later) were already visible in Luther's broadside against scholastic theology.

Written in the specialized idiom of late medieval theology and intended for other teachers and students of the subject, Luther's ninety-seven theses on scholasticism never reached beyond a narrow audience. They were quickly overshadowed by his celebrated statements regarding the church's sale of indulgences, a subject of great importance to the mass of uneducated Christians to whom the church had for centuries preached that an indulgence is a short-cut to heaven. Yet despite its relative obscurity and lack of popular appeal, Luther's *Disputation* offers a better introduction to his general intellectual orientation than his more famous attack on indulgences. It defines, with great economy, the point of view from which he approached every other subject, practical as well as intellectual, throughout his thirty-year public career. Luther's revulsion at the sale of indulgences was not, for him, a starting point. It was not a premise but a conclusion. It was the corollary of a more fundamental belief concerning the nature and extent of God's grace, which Luther first presented as the inspiration for a revitalized Christianity in his attack on scholastic theology.

THE ENEMIES OF GRACE

Among the texts that Luther was assigned to teach at the University of Wittenberg when he joined its faculty in 1508[4] was Aristotle's *Ethics,* a work he later called "the worst of all books."[5] Luther knew it well. In *A Letter to the Christian Nobility of the German Nation,* he boasts that "I know my Aristotle as well as you or the likes of you. I have lectured on him, and been lectured on him, and I understand him better than St. Thomas or Duns Scotus did."[6] It is thus on the basis of a deep knowledge of the *Ethics* that Luther condemns it as an "enemy of grace" and maintains that "no one can become a theologian unless he becomes one without Aristotle."[7] "The whole [of] Aristotle," he insists, "is to theology as darkness is to light."[8]

According to Aristotle, a man becomes virtuous by acquiring certain habits. He learns these from his parents, teachers and friends. A good man therefore depends on others for his virtues, and even when he has acquired them is subject to the vagaries of chance, which may deprive him of the opportunities and resources he needs to exercise the virtues he possesses in a fulfilling way. The achievement of a virtuous life is therefore not fully within his control. But the acts whose repetition produces the habits in which his virtue consists, and those that later display it, *are* his own. Who else's could they be? In this sense, the happy life of a virtuous man is his own achievement. It is something of which he may be proud.

For Aristotle, the distinguishing mark of such a life is its self-sufficiency. Even in the midst of changing circumstances, a good man knows that he possesses the wisdom and strength to do the right thing. He knows that his virtue rests on an independent foundation that only immense misfortune can upset. This is especially clear in the case of a great-souled man, whose awareness of his exceptional independence is the sign and source of the nobility that sets him apart from ordinarily good men.

The life of a man who devotes himself to the study of philosophy possesses a still greater degree of self-sufficiency—as great as that of the God he becomes, for a time at least, in the activity of thinking, and even greater than that of the most virtuous man of affairs, whose independence is always tied to the exigencies of political life. In both the theoretical and practical realms, the cornerstone of Aristotle's account of human happiness is the value of self-sufficiency, whose inward and outward expression is that glowing self-assurance we commonly call pride.

Luther's *Disputation against Scholastic Theology* is a ferocious and sustained assault on human pride. "We do not become righteous," he says, "by doing righteous deeds but, having been made righteous, we do righteous deeds."[9] A man's virtue is therefore not his own achievement, even in the smallest degree. It is not something he acquires or displays on his own. Every particle of it is a gift from God, who graciously bestows righteousness on those he chooses, and by the same unfathomable grace enables them to perform righteous deeds.

To the Aristotelian gentleman who wears his self-sufficiency as a badge of pride, Luther opposes the humble Christian, who acknowledges that without God's help he can produce nothing that is not "perverse and evil" and concedes that even "doing all that one is able" is insufficient to "remove the obstacles to grace."[10] For Luther, the beginning of righteousness lies in the acknowledgment that we are completely powerless to take even the smallest step toward our own salvation from the depraved condition in which all men have lived since Adam, and in the "humiliating" knowledge that this acknowledgment itself comes only as an unearned gift from God.

Aristotle's ethics of pride rests on the assumption that all human beings long to share in the everlasting and divine. The clearest expression of this is the godlike life of the man of theoretical wisdom, which Aristotle holds up as the best life a man can live. In his view, the universal human desire to cross the line that separates the human from the divine is natural, admirable and attainable within the limits our condition permits.

Luther agrees that all human beings by nature wish to be God. But he regards this as a bad thing, not a good one. Indeed he considers it the source of the essential wickedness in man, who he calls "a bad tree."[11]

"Humans are by nature," Luther says, "unable to want God to be God. Indeed, they want to be God, and do not want God to be God."[12] This desire is the original sin from which all others spring.

So long as a man continues to believe that there are acts he can perform, laws he can obey, or virtues he can acquire, that by themselves have the power to advance him toward the goal of salvation, he is still the prisoner of the wish to possess the independence and self-sufficiency that is the defining characteristic of God's altogether different nature. He is still guilty of wishing to be God. To experience even the possibility of salvation—without, of course, ever being able to ensure that it will be forthcoming—a man must be released from the prison of this unholy desire, and for that to happen, he has to give up the last prideful shred of belief in his ability to achieve salvation on his own.

This is the dominant motif of Luther's attack on scholastic theology. It is Augustinian in substance and tone.

According to Augustine, man's original sin is his prideful ambition to be the ground of his own being.[13] This takes many different forms, all deserving of condemnation. Thus, the Stoics are to be censured for their prideful confidence in man's ability to grasp the eternal order of the world through reason alone. The Jews are to be blamed for their proud belief that obedience to the law is sufficient to win God's favor. And the followers of Pelagius—for whom Augustine reserves his most biting words—are to be branded as heretics for insisting that human beings are able to make even the smallest, voluntary contribution to their own salvation. It is in his polemical exchanges with this last group (and with Julian of Eclanum in particular) that Augustine states the implications of his theology of grace in their most uncompromising form.[14]

Luther's sharpest criticisms are likewise directed against his coreligionists. His fiercest attacks are aimed at those scholastic theologians who, like the Pelagians before them, affirmed doctrines that in Luther's view have the effect of reducing man's awful dependence on God and thus of encouraging our sinful wish to take his place. It is therefore unsurprising that Luther begins his *Disputation* by recalling Augustine's quarrel with the Pelagians. "To say that Augustine exaggerates in speaking against heretics is to say that Augustine tells lies almost everywhere." This "is the same as permitting Pelagians and all heretics to triumph, indeed, the same as conceding victory to them."[15]

Thus, for example, in "opposition" to the view held by "Scotus and Gabriel [Biel]," Luther insists that "it is false to state that the will can, by nature, conform to correct precept."[16] Scotus (a nominalist) and Aquinas (a realist) both taught that the human will possesses an independent power to choose the right course once it is known. Biel (who lectured at Erfurt a generation before Luther) held the same view. But to maintain that the will has a power of this kind is to assign human beings a meaningful degree of authorship, and hence responsibility, in matters pertaining to their own salvation. Luther refuses to allow even this much. The will, he says, is "innately and inevitably evil and corrupt."[17] Left to itself, it *always* chooses evil. When a man chooses good, therefore, his choice is due *entirely* to the grace of God; not a shred of human agency is involved.

"In opposition to Scotus and Gabriel," Luther insists that "the will is not free to strive toward whatever is declared good."[18] "In brief, a person by nature has neither correct precept nor good will."[19] He can neither discern the good on his own, nor will to do it without God's "prevenient grace."[20] Nor do our powers of reasoning, even at their highest pitch, give us the slightest insight into the nature of God. "In vain does one fashion a logic of faith. . . . No syllogistic form is valid when applied to divine terms. This in opposition to the Cardinal [Pierre d'Ailly, an important fourteenth-century theologian in the Ockhamist tradition]."[21] There is nothing, in short, that we can know of God as he is in himself, and nothing we can do to make ourselves acceptable to him. If a man is "justified" in the eyes of God, that is not because he has established his case, as a litigant might by putting proofs before a judge, but only because, despite his complete lack of desert, God has chosen to accept him in an incomprehensible act of "justifying grace."[22]

Luther makes this last point "in opposition to Ockham." For two centuries, Ockham and his followers had fought a continuing battle against those who would bring God close to man by making his mind intelligible to us and his will responsive to our acts. Luther's teacher at Erfurt was Bartholomaeus von Usingen, a student of Gabriel Biel's. Biel himself was a superrigorous follower of Ockham, who often disagreed with Ockham on Ockhamist grounds.[23] This is the theological tradition to which Luther himself belonged and, like his predecessors in it, his overriding objective was to rescue God from the rationalists and humanists who threatened to ensnare him in chains of reason and to make his actions dependent on man's. It might therefore seem puzzling that Luther's harshest criticisms in the *Disputation* are directed not at those, like Aquinas, who affirmed our rational affinity to God, but at the representatives of the voluntarist tradition from whom he may himself be said to have learned the meaning and magnitude of divine grace.

This is not a paradox, however, or even much of a mystery, if one assumes that Luther accepted his teachers' goals but believed they could be reached only by more radical means. Luther's challenge is not to their conception of God. It is to the inconsistency and incompleteness with which D'Ailly, Biel and others defended this conception in their writings. His criticism of their views is meant to show that in their war on pride even the most committed voluntarists *did not go far enough*.

Being so close to the truth, their backsliding was to Luther especially disturbing and he felt a particular need to correct their errors by demonstrating how complete the suppression of pride must be if man is to let God "be God." Even the great Augustinian theologians of the fourteenth and fifteenth centuries failed to reach this goal, against which our nature rebels. As their loyal heir, Luther sought to complete their work by anesthetizing pride at its root. This is the aim of his radicalized concept of grace, which teaches man's dependence on God at every turn and in all possible ways. Among other things, Luther was unafraid to draw the implications of this teaching for man's estimate of his own self-worth. There is a kind of "subtle evil," he declares, in the comforting "saying that the love of God may continue alongside an intense love of the creature." The sober truth—of which "Ockham, the Cardinal [and] Gabriel [Biel]" all fell short—is that "to love God is at the same time to hate oneself and to know nothing but God."[24]

Luther's first public statement of his new theology concludes with this terrifying remark.

WORKS, SACRIFICE AND PRIDE

For centuries, the church had sold indulgences on the premise that they possess the power to shorten the period of penance prescribed for the sins of those benefitted by them. Luther's attack on indulgences challenged the legitimacy of the practice in concrete terms. It stated a position that ordinary men and women could understand, and expressed with clarity and passion the rising resentment against a litany of church abuses. Written in Latin but quickly translated into German and printed in broadside form, Luther's ninety-five theses on indulgences became a *cause célèbre,* provoking a strong reaction from Rome and capturing the attention of the princes of Germany, whose own territorial ambitions soon became entangled with the movement for church reform.[25] The Reformation is conventionally said to have begun with their proclamation in October 1517.

Politically speaking, perhaps, this is true. But it would be a mistake to conclude that Luther's ideas about man and God were shaped by his views regarding indulgences. The relation is just the reverse. Luther's theology did not emerge from his attack on the church. It preceded and provoked it. Before he was a reformer of institutions, Luther was a critic of ideas, and his condemnation of indulgences—whose defenders he later mocked as the "filth" of a "vile smelling cloaca"—was merely one implication of his radical and uncompromising belief that every attempt to win God's favor by works of any kind is nothing but an expression of man's prideful wish to be God, who we can truly love only by despising ourselves.[26]

To maintain that the granting of an indulgence has the power to alter the consequences of sin, and by doing so to improve the beneficiary's relation to God, is to affirm in a particularly vulgar way that human beings are able to change how God treats them merely by performing certain acts. To be sure, the purchaser must be sincere. He has to buy the indulgence in a proper spirit of devotion. But his devotion alone is not enough to achieve the goal he seeks. For that, he must also *do something*. He must hand over the money the church asks in return for its favor, and this action is at least a necessary, and on some views a sufficient, cause of the spiritual benefit he receives in return.

The theological assumptions underlying the sale of indulgences were complex. It was sometimes said, for example, that the church was merely giving the purchaser, for a certain sum of money that was itself to be used for religious purposes, the right to employ on his own behalf a fixed amount of the good will the saints of the church had accumulated over time, and which the church maintains as a "working capital" for its members.[27]

But however one explains the origin of the power of an indulgence to shorten the period of penance owing for a particular sin, the assumption that it can accomplish this result presumes that human beings have the power to control God's actions by means of their own. On the theory most often offered to explain how this is possible, God's surplus of indebtedness to the saints for their supererogatory acts becomes a fund on which other, sinful human beings may draw for a good consideration. In this way, they become God's creditors, to whom he is obliged to convey the spiritual benefit they have rightfully purchased. Men thereby cease to be God's creatures and become his masters instead—the prideful reversal of roles that every man desires in his heart.

In the fall of 1520, three years after his first public statement on indulgences had made him an actor on the European stage, Luther published a much longer essay entitled *The Babylonian Captivity of the Church*. In it, he systematically reviews the main sacraments of the Roman Church (paying special attention to baptism, penance and "the sacrament of the bread"). His conclusion is that these are all abominations too, at least in the form then practiced by the church.[28]

In each case, Luther's objection is the same. It is that the church treats the act in question as "a good work and a sacrifice."[29]

Thus, the church teaches its members that their participation in the holy meal is a sacrificial act that wins them favor with God, who attaches positive value to its performance, in and of itself. Likewise with the sacrament of penance: the church regards the act of contrition (an essential element of penance) as a "merit" which the person performing the act can acquire on his own and "redeem" against God, who has no choice but to accept it. The same is true of baptism. Those who maintain that the mere act of immersion is itself capable of bringing one into the community of the church, under the protective eye of God, impliedly affirm the power of human beings to bend his will to theirs.

According to Luther, what gives these acts their value is the "faith" of the actor alone. (I shall return to Luther's concept of faith in the following chapter.) In itself, the act has no value of any kind. It possesses only the "pageantry of outward things."[30] A person who believes that he can advance his standing with God simply by going through the motions of the act is therefore guilty of the same kind of fetishistic thinking as one who purchases an indulgence in the belief that by doing so he can reduce the time that its beneficiary will have to spend in purgatory, paying down his debt to God.

Luther's assault on the church's understanding of the sacraments thus springs from the same basic principle as his earlier attack on indulgences. There is no work a man can do, in church or out, that can possibly increase his stature in God's eyes or add, even by a single atom, to his chances for salvation. These rest entirely with God, over whom we have no control at all. To believe that we do is pride. This is the evil at the heart of human nature. Instead of teaching humility and gratitude for God's gifts, the church therefore abets our human pride by affirming through its practices that we do in fact have the control over God for which we sinfully yearn.

To this extent, the church does something worse than merely fail to be a responsible steward of the Christian faith. It actively encourages an attitude that is the exact reverse of the one the Christian religion demands. The sacraments are not works we perform in order to improve our position in heaven.

They are gifts from God, which we ought to receive in a spirit of humility that is the opposite of the one the church instills in its followers. "When we ought to be grateful for benefits received, we come arrogantly to give that which we ought to take. With unheard-of perversity we mock the mercy of the giver by giving as a work the thing we receive as a gift, so that the testator, instead of being a dispenser of his own goods, becomes the recipient of ours. Woe to such sacrilege!"[31]

This amounts, in Luther's view, to a return to the Jewish understanding of man's relation to God. The Jews were given the law at Sinai, and believe that by obeying its commands they can win God's favor, as a nation in this world and individuals in the next. Theirs is a religion of works, or more exactly of sacrifice, for the belief that performing a certain work has the power to influence the mind or heart of God is the essence of every sacrificial religion.

The most telling symptom of this, according to Luther, is the prominent role that the rules of temple sacrifice played in ancient Judaism and that their rabbinic reformulations continue to play in the Jewish Diaspora. To say, as he does, that the church takes a sacrificial view of baptism and the other sacraments is therefore to accuse it of turning its back on the very event that separates the Jewish religion of "law" from the Christian religion of "grace"—the sacrifice by God of his own son for the sake of an unregenerate humanity.

The crucifixion was a work, to be sure, and a sacrifice of inconceivable power. But it was not *our* work or sacrifice. It was the work and sacrifice of God, done for us but not by us. This is the essence of the meaning of the cross, as Luther understands it. Christ is not Moses.[32] Moses is a "lawgiver," a "driver." He demands works of his followers. Christ demands no such works. He gives himself up for us, so that our death may be "swallowed up" in his. We are the passive recipients of Christ's gift, not its donors.

Paradoxically, Christ's active work takes the form of a pathos, or suffering. But his vulnerability on the cross is in fact the greatest imaginable sort of activity—a plenitude of life and being that we can never achieve on our own, and must accept as the gift of another. To receive this gift with an appreciation of one's total lack of power to do what it alone can accomplish, is the heart of the Christian religion and the attitude that separates it most fundamentally from Judaism, which in Luther's view reverses the relation of man to God by making us the active givers of gifts to him, rather than the other way around.

The Jews, who affirm the saving power of conduct in compliance with the law; the church, which takes a similar view of the sacraments; and even those sophisticated theologians who, while insisting on God's glory, leave room for the belief that human works can be at least a partial ground of justification, thus all make the same basic mistake.[33] They all deny the meaning of the cross. Instead, they add credibility and authority to the desire to do for ourselves what God alone can do and to be the source, in large ways or small ones, of our own salvation from the corruptions of original sin. This is the blasphemous wish to take God's place. It is the radical evil that Luther spied in all of the practices of the Roman Church of his day, and it explains why he argued, with such brilliant fury, for a reformation that would rescue the Christian faith from its Babylonian enslavement by those who love man more than God: the children of pride, who would seize the throne of their creator if they could, instead of falling on their knees before him in a posture of abject gratitude for the gift of the cross.

AGAINST THE ENTHUSIASTS

Certain of Luther's views seem to blunt the edge of this radical theology. They appear even to give it a conservative cast. Three in particular are worth noting.

The first concerns the proper interpretation of the sacraments.

Luther's insistence that the holy mass is not a work whose performance, by itself, is of value in God's eyes encouraged some to take the further step of arguing that it is not really a sacrament at all but merely an act of remembrance in which the celebrants do nothing but recall Christ's life and passion. On this view, which Zwingli and others defended, the Eucharist is just an occasion for reflection and prayer, a recollection of the Last Supper, whose reenactment has no inherent spiritual value of its own. Against Zwingli, Luther argued strenuously for the "real presence" of Christ in the bread and wine, and for the value of the Eucharist not as a mere memorial but a direct engagement with the cross, which requires that Christ really be there in the material objects the celebrants consume—a position that certain other reformers thought inconsistent with Luther's own attack on the fetishism of the Roman Church's theology of works.

In a similar way, Luther's claim that the physical act of immersing an infant in water while speaking certain traditional words of blessing over the child's head accomplishes nothing in itself, led other reform-minded thinkers to conclude that the practice of infant baptism should be abandoned completely, in favor of the baptism of born-again adults, since infants are incapable of the faith that alone gives the act its meaning. Again, Luther rejected their position, which might seem to follow from his own, and defended the baptism of infants instead. In the debates over the Eucharist and infant baptism (which had a ferocity unimaginable today), Luther thus appears to have taken a conservative stance against those whose views seem more consistent with the radical implications of his own theological principles.

A second conservative strain in Luther's thought concerns the continuing role of law in human affairs, even after its futility as a means of salvation has been acknowledged.

The law was given to Moses, Luther says, not so that the Jews could justify themselves to God by fulfilling it, but for precisely the opposite reason: to make it plain that no human being can possibly fulfill the law, which in addition to outward obedience demands a purity of heart we can never attain. Those who have learned this lesson understand that fulfilling the law does not take them one step further toward salvation, which depends on God's grace alone. From this, some of Luther's more zealous fellow reformers concluded that the law no longer has any importance for those who have grasped the true meaning of grace.[34]

Against these antinomians, Luther insists that even men and women of faith, who know that the law is not a path to salvation, remain bound by those of its prescriptions that either conform to "the natural law"[35] or have been enacted by a duly constituted political authority. He never wavered from this view. Until the end of his life, Luther remained a defender of the established legal order, despite his own relentless assault on those who argued for even the weakest link between law and salvation—a position that some regarded as hopelessly confused, and others condemned as a cowardly retreat from the consequences of his radical theology of grace, motivated, they said, by Luther's covetous desire to toady favor with the princely powers that supported his movement for reform.

Luther's doctrine of work in a calling represents a third conservative strain in his thought.

Luther insists that a man is justified not by works but faith. Yet those who have accepted God's grace are bound to be filled with gratitude for it, and to want to express the love they feel for their savior in their relations with other human beings. They will be moved to serve them in the way Christ served us all—through good works infused with the spirit of humility that defines the faithful Christian's response to the grace of God.[36] A true Christian is one whose understanding of the inefficacy of works thus leads him to a seemingly paradoxical emphasis on works as the best way to express his gratitude to God, which can never be requited directly and must therefore be deflected into one's social, familial and economic relations with others.

Of the many ways that a person may serve others, Luther emphasizes the importance of those appropriate to his or her station in life. Each of us has a vocation, or rather several. A vocation may be a profession (like that of doctor or businessman), or a status (for example, that of husband or wife). Each is a role that entails specific responsibilities. These are important, according to Luther, because they focus the otherwise indefinitely broad ambition to be a gift to others as Christ is to us all. They provide the definition and direction we need to pursue this ambition in a practically effective way. Luther's radical repudiation of works as a stepping stone to salvation thus leads him to endorse the value of innerworldly work in a calling as the best response of faith to grace—a position that seems oddly aligned with his own theological rejection of any possible connection between works and salvation.[37]

In various ways, then, Luther appears to take a surprisingly conservative position, given his insistence that no such connection exists. In each case he defends the view that works of one kind or another (the celebration of the Eucharist, obedience to the law, labor in a calling) do in fact have some spiritual value after all. But the explanation for his position is the same in all three cases, and rather than confirming that Luther is less principled than he seems, it underscores how consistently he holds to his rigorous conception of the opposition between pride and grace.

The key to Luther's stance with regard to all these matters is his abiding belief in the self-aggrandizing presumptuousness of human beings. From this perspective, it is not Luther but his adversaries who appear the real enemies of grace.

Those, for example, who would convert the Eucharist to a mere feast of remembrance ask too much of human beings. Even for a saint, faith is the hardest thing in the world to sustain. We all need help in this regard. The faithful thus require regular opportunities to act out their faith in the company of others, through rituals that give them the chance to reaffirm their belief that God is really present in their lives. Zwingli and the Anabaptists set their sights too high. A realistic appraisal of what men can achieve leads to a view of the sacraments more attuned to our natural sinfulness—one that accepts the need to maintain the rituals of the church more or less in their traditional form, as a sensuous aid to the preservation of faith, while simultaneously insisting that their meaning be preached from the standpoint of a theology that rejects any connection between works and salvation.

Luther's views regarding our duty to follow the law and to work within the limits of our stations in life, reflect a similarly realistic appraisal of the frailties of human nature.

It is true that obedience to the law cannot save us. But so long as we live "in flesh and blood," we need the law as a reminder and a restraint.[38] Even the saints need the law to remind them that they are incapable of meeting its requirements "otherwise than unwillingly." Human nature is such that we are unable to act with the purity of heart the law requires. In this respect, the law demands the "impossible" of us and thereby demonstrates, in a daily fashion, our dependence on God's grace for everything good. The best of men need the law to remind them of this and others, who are less good, need it to restrain their sinful appetites. The whole fearsome apparatus of the law is required to keep men in check and to maintain a minimum of civilized order. Those who think that human beings can live without the law are therefore hopelessly naive. They wrongly believe that most men are at least potentially good, and ignore the chastening role the law plays even in the lives of the very best.

The faithful know they cannot be saved by works. Yet they desire to work for the betterment of the world, moved by their superabundant love of God. They long to be a Christ to others. But unlike Christ, they must concentrate their energies in a disciplined way. Christ worked for the good of all, without limit. That is because he was divine. We, by contrast, are easily distracted from our work by temptation, curiosity and boredom. We do not really understand what the betterment of the world means or how to achieve it. We therefore require the constraints of a vocation to guide us in doing for others what our wish to imitate Christ moves us to do. These keep us on track, and ensure that our efforts are productive. Outside of them, we wander about, wasting our talents instead of using them in an effective way. The idea of good works outside a vocational framework is therefore as much a will-o'-the-wisp as that of an exemplary life outside the law, or faith outside the sacraments. All of these utopian ambitions ignore the irremediable sinfulness of our nature. They wish away the truth about us in favor of a rosier view. An honest assessment of the human condition leads to the conservative position that Luther defends in each of these debates, against the enthusiastic proponents of an idealized view of the sacraments, law and service to others.

As a political matter, Luther's conservatism left him in a middle position between those who shared his reformist aims but felt he had retreated from their implications, and the Roman Church, which remained resolutely attached to a prideful theology of works. From the one side, Luther appeared a destructive revolutionary; from the other, a hesitant and self-serving reactionary. But Luther's motive for resisting the enthusiasts to his left was at bottom the same as his motive for fighting the church on his right.

Luther attacked the church in the name of grace. He fought to restore an Augustinian appreciation of man's incapacity to be the ground of his own being. He underscored the nothingness of human beings. He insisted that we depend on God, utterly and completely, for our salvation from the world. This required a full-scale assault on all those teachings and practices of the church that encourage human pride by suggesting that our salvation is within our own power to achieve.

Luther's attack on his more radical fellow reformers had precisely the same goal. Each of these assumed that a reformed humanity can do without one or another of the aids we need in order to live up to the demands of faith. From Luther's point of view, this could only seem a reassertion of human self-sufficiency within the bowels of the Reformation itself—a return, under the guise of a more radical reformation, to the blasphemous ways of the church, hence not an advance but a retreat from the truly radical insight into man's powerlessness that constitutes the heart of Luther's theology of the cross. Seen in this light, it was not Luther but those who aspired to take his insights "farther," who were the real defectors from a theological position that is nearly impossible to sustain because it runs so strongly against the grain of our prideful nature. Luther's middle position between the church, on the one hand, and the advocates of a more radical-seeming reformation, on the other, is thus neither a compromise nor a conservative accommodation to the realities of worldly power. It is the only position that consistently refuses to yield to the claims of human pride, and therefore the most radical one of all.

After the publication of his ninety-five theses on indulgences, Luther found himself embroiled in a series of practical and institutional controversies that lasted for the rest of his life. He was forced to fight two wars at once, the first against the church, and the second against those whose efforts to extend the Reformation only tended, he believed, to encourage our natural tendency toward pride and self-reliance. In both campaigns, Luther took his point of departure from the concept of grace he first articulated in his *Disputation against Scholastic Theology* and reaffirmed a few months later, in the list of propositions he offered for debate with the brothers of the Augustinian order in Heidelberg.

"Arrogance cannot be avoided or true hope be present unless the judgment of condemnation is feared in every work." "The person who believes that he can obtain grace by doing what is in him adds sin to sin so that he becomes doubly guilty." "[O]ne should call the work of Christ an acting work and our work an accomplished work, and thus an accomplished work pleasing to God by the grace of the acting work." "To trust in works, which one ought to do in fear, is equivalent to giving oneself the honor and taking it from God. . . ." "It is impossible for a person not to be puffed up by his good works unless he has first been destroyed by suffering and evil until he knows that he is worthless and that his works are not his but God's." "[H]e who has not been brought low, reduced to nothing through the cross and suffering, takes credit for works and wisdom and does not give credit to God. He thus misuses and defiles the gifts of God."[39]

In these early statements, Luther defined the theology of grace that inspired everything he said and did until his death nearly thirty years later. Nothing ever caused him to doubt the truth of this theology, and even those polemical positions he later took that appear to represent concessions of one kind or another, only confirm how committed he remained to the man-hating metaphysics of the *Disputation*. That God is all and we are nothing; that everything good exists by God's grace alone; and that man's wish to be God is the source of every evil are axioms from which he never departed.

CHAPTER 19

The Hatred of Man

AUGUSTINE REDUX

"Works contribute nothing to justification."[1] There is nothing a man can do to save himself. What hope is there, then, of ever overcoming our alienation from God? Is there any path to the eternal life for which we yearn? Luther's famous answer is that man is saved by "faith" alone.

"Faith" and "works" are for Luther antithetical terms. He was led to this view by his meditation on the meaning of Paul's statement that "man is justified by faith apart from works of the law." It was this passage in Paul's Letter to the Romans that rescued Luther from the despair into which he had fallen as a young man on account of his conclusion that even an endless series of good works cannot by itself win God's saving grace.

In one respect, though, Luther takes Paul's message a step farther. For Paul, faith begins where the law leaves off, but it does not cancel or annul it. Law defines the outward propriety of our actions; faith is an inward state of belief. Faith and law thus belong to separate domains and those who seek salvation through faith in Jesus Christ must be careful to keep them apart. Yet they continue to exist side by side.

For Luther, faith is not merely separate from works. It is defined in opposition to them. Faith is the conscious rejection of the belief that works have any bearing on our salvation at all. Paul's Letter to the Romans perhaps already suggests this. But Luther's dialectical definition of faith carries Paul's suggestion to its logical limits.

The man who breaks through to faith, in Luther's sense, affirms the futility of works as a path to salvation. Yet precisely because he does, he alone is in a position to receive Christ's promise of salvation. To have faith in this promise, though, is the hardest thing in the world to achieve. "For our human weakness, conscious of its sins, finds nothing more difficult to believe than that it is saved; and yet, unless it does believe this, it cannot be saved, because it does not believe the truth of God that promises salvation."[2]

Those who do believe God's promise, despite their own contemptible unworthiness to receive it, are in the position, Luther says, of "ragged beggars" to whom a rich man makes a gift, without any need or duty to do so.[3] They know that their only appropriate response is one of gratitude, and shrink from the thought that their own thankfulness is itself a work that somehow "pays" for the gift they have received. True faith is constantly on the lookout for prideful temptations of this sort, and though none of us can achieve this state completely or sustain it continuously so long as we live in this world, the person who comes closest is the one who makes such ceaseless vigilance his goal and reaffirms it after each lapse or departure.

Outwardly, his life is a splendid example of service to others, motivated by the desire to express his overflowing gratitude to God through humble work in a vocation. But inwardly it is defined by his endless struggle to keep before his eyes the irrelevance of all his many fine and selfless deeds to the gift of salvation itself. It is marked by that invisible yet militant attunement to the utter gratuitousness of God's promise that is the essence of faith as Luther conceives it.

BONDAGE OF THE WILL

This raises an obvious question. If faith is a willingness to believe in God's promise, is such willingness itself something a man can achieve on his own? Once a man accepts that none of the deeds he performs contribute to his salvation, he must somehow move from this negative conclusion to a positive state of belief that God has indeed promised him the eternal life he desires. Is this movement, at least, the responsibility of the man who makes it, so that his faith may properly be said to be his own achievement?

Luther's emphatic answer is no. The faith that consists in an acceptance of God's gift of salvation is itself a gift. It is not earned by the works that precede it, nor is it itself a work of the man whose faith it is. "No one can give oneself faith."[4] A man's faith is the work of someone, to be sure. It is brought into being by a responsible agent. But like salvation itself, it is not the work of the man who benefits from it. It is the "divine work" of God—a gift that "changes us and makes us to be born anew of God."[5]

It is clear why Luther takes this position, for any other would undermine his theology completely. If a single particle of the faith that saves a man is held to be his own work, as opposed to something worked in him by another, then Luther's entire campaign against the theology of works falls to the ground. Let it be supposed that a man's outer works are good only because God allows them to be so, and do not count at all toward his salvation. And let it further be supposed that no amount of good works can prepare a man for faith, in the sense of making him better disposed to accept God's promise, if and when it comes. If, despite these concessions, we nevertheless affirm that a man's faith is even to a small degree his own achievement, we have once again yielded to the prideful temptation to believe in the self-sufficiency of human beings to save themselves from sin. We have merely transferred our power to do this from the realm of outer deeds to that of inner beliefs. Indeed, we have actually increased the power of pride, for by tying salvation to belief, which seems more completely under our control than the consequences of our actions, we have given the wish to be God an even more fertile field of operation. Luther's teaching that faith in God's gift of salvation is itself a gift is meant to block this danger.[6]

It follows that faith is not a "choice" we make. It is not a "decision" or "commitment" or act of "will." All of these expressions imply the presence in us of some power to spontaneously adjust our relationship to God in a way that improves our chances for salvation. But this is precisely what Luther wants to rule out, since the existence of such a power would be a fatal crack in the wall of grace. Even the smallest degree of human autonomy regarding our own salvation must be in derogation of God's omnipotence, which the doctrine of grace is meant to protect. Either divine grace or human autonomy: the two cannot coexist. Between them, there are no intermediate possibilities that combine the power of God and the freedom of man in different ratios. Either God has the absolute power his nature demands, in which case human freedom is an illusion; or human freedom is something real, and God an illusion. To grant that human beings possess the freedom to determine their own salvation by choosing or deciding or willing to have faith is therefore to confer on them a godlike power at just the point it matters most. Viewed in this light, the doctrine of the freedom of the will is bound to seem the supreme expression of human pride.

This is the position that Augustine took in his fight against Pelagius and his followers, the last great battle of his life. As the inventor of the idea of the will, Augustine understood its implications with special clarity. This perhaps helps to explains why he eventually repudiated it with such ferocity. But the very mildness of Pelagius' position also pushed Augustine to formulate his own view in ever more radical terms. Pelagius did not, after all, deny the operation of God's grace in most respects. He wanted only to preserve a brief moment of human freedom between the divine gift that prepares us to make the right choice and the grace that is required to implement it. But just because Pelagianism seemed such a reasonable resolution of the tension between freedom and grace, Augustine found it necessary to demonstrate that even the tiniest quantum of human freedom is an affront to God, so that the resoluteness of his attack on the concept of free will grew in proportion to the modesty of its defense.

The same is true in Luther's case. The conflict between divine grace and human freedom is, for Luther, absolute. And just as Augustine had been moved to state his view of this conflict most emphatically in his conflict with Pelagius, so Luther was provoked to do the same in his polemical exchange with a modern Pelagian who, like his ancient counterpart, sought to establish only a limited and reasonable place for human freedom within the framework of Christian belief.

Luther's adversary in this debate was Erasmus, the greatest humanist of the age, and a supporter (up to a point) of the reform movement that Luther had begun. In its earliest phase, he and Luther remained wary allies in the fight against what they both viewed as the moral and spiritual decay of the Roman Church. But after their famous public exchange on the question of free will, friendly relations between them could no longer be sustained, in large part because of the venom with which Luther attacked the moderate and conciliatory position of his opponent. It is important to understand just how moderate Erasmus' position is. He repeatedly concedes that even those who will to do what is good need God's "prevenient" grace to make such a commitment and his "free aid" to reach their goal.[7] Grace thus both precedes and follows a man's choice to pursue the good.

Still, Erasmus says, freedom of choice is not nothing. It is something real. While leaving a great deal of room for divine grace, he insists that human freedom be given a small but significant role as well. His view strives to accommodate both and this, he claims, is a point in its favor, for unlike Luther's "extravagant"[8] position, his own "mediates"[9] between those that attribute everything to either man or God.

Given the inherent obscurity of the subject, Erasmus argues, it is best to adopt a "moderate" position of this sort.[10] There are also theological advantages to doing so. According to Erasmus, his view avoids assigning the world's evils to God and simultaneously preserves the integrity of man's moral life, which becomes pointless if we give up the belief that human beings have at least some limited control over their choices. And finally, there are many passages in Scripture whose plain meaning favors Erasmus' position. How can any sensible person reject it? Erasmus implies that it would be irrational to do so. This is just what the Pelagians had said in their quarrel with Augustine more than a thousand years before, and the arguments that Erasmus offers in support of his balanced and reasonable view are the very ones they made in defense of theirs.

Luther's response is the same as Augustine's. The fundamental question, he says, is whether the will does "anything" or "nothing."[11] The "middle way"[12] that Erasmus recommends cannot be sustained. If we concede even "a tiny bit" to free choice—if we acknowledge that human beings possess even a "particle" of freedom to determine their own eternal fate—we make man the decisive agent in securing his salvation and effectively "deny grace altogether."[13] If they are to be consistent in their views, Luther insists, those who take this position must "attribute absolutely everything to free choice," just as the Pelagians were eventually forced to do. Their adversaries must "go all out" in the opposite direction "and completely deny free choice, referring everything to God."[14] According to Luther, these are the only logical possibilities.

Erasmus leaves ample room for grace, yet maintains that "if man does nothing, there is no room for merits" and thus for either "punishments or rewards."[15] But what does Erasmus' argument "prove" except "that *all* merit rests with free will?"[16] If a man's desert depends on the choices he makes, in the absence of which he cannot be said to deserve anything at all, then the "whole" of what he receives as a reward or punishment is due to his own efforts. "And in that case, what room will there be for grace?"[17] It is only a lack of clear thinking on Erasmus' part, Luther claims, that leads him to believe that his compromise solution is sustainable. In truth, there are two radically divergent alternatives and the only question is which of them is correct—Erasmus' view, which affirms that human freedom has some measure of reality, or Luther's, which maintains that it has none.

"On the authority of Erasmus," Luther writes, "free choice is a power of the will that is able of itself to will and unwill the word and work of God."[18] But "[t]his plainly means attributing divinity to free choice, since to will the law and the gospel, to unwill sin and to will death, belongs to divine power alone. . . ." In Luther's view, Erasmus' defense of free will thus entails the assignment to human beings of a divine power to create their own deservingness to be saved.[19]

Luther claims there is no conception of human freedom that does not have this result. To maintain that the human will is free is therefore to proclaim a doctrine whose effect is to put man in God's place by transferring the power of creation from the latter to the former, so far as our eternal destinies are concerned. It is to reverse the relation of man to God by making God beholden to man on account of the free choices that human beings make. This is "the old song of the Pelagians."[20] It is the siren song of pride, Luther says, and Erasmus is singing it again, with a seductive reasonableness that we must fight off like a deadly drug in order to grasp the blasphemous message it conceals. In Luther's view, the position that Erasmus is defending, under color of compromise and moderation, in reality amounts to a proposal to abolish God so that man may flourish in his stead.

For Erasmus, the human will "moves itself by its own power."[21] It has autonomy—the power to chart its own course. The claim that the will possesses such a power is the philosophical heart of Erasmus' argument, and he strives to establish it with a combination of logical arguments and scriptural quotations.

Luther's position is exactly the opposite. He denies that the human will has any independent power of self-direction. Whether a man "chooses" good or evil depends entirely on forces acting on his will from without. His will is a passive instrument, responding to external pressures of one kind or another. In Luther's famous image, the will is a "beast of burden," ridden either by God or the devil. "If God rides it, it wills and goes where God wills. . . . If Satan rides it, it wills and goes where Satan wills; nor can it choose to run to either of the two riders or to seek him out, but the riders themselves contend for the possession and control of it."[22] "[I]n matters pertaining to salvation and damnation, a man has no free choice, but is a captive, subject and slave either of the will of God or the will of Satan."[23] In neither case does the human will supply its own direction. It is always, and necessarily, directed by the will of another. In this sense, its condition is not one of autonomy, as Erasmus maintains, but of perfect heteronomy instead.

The recognition that this is so is the first step toward salvation. Those who claim that man possesses an autonomous will believe there is something he can do to be saved. Indeed, they regard this "something" as decisive. But even to be open to the possibility of salvation, one must renounce this prideful view.

> God has assuredly promised his grace to the humble, that is, to those who lament and despair of themselves. But no man can be thoroughly humbled until he knows that his salvation is utterly beyond his own powers, devices, endeavors, will, and works, and depends entirely on the choice, will, and work of another, namely, of God alone. For as long as he is persuaded that he himself can do even the least thing toward his salvation, he retains some self-confidence and does not altogether despair of himself, and therefore he is not humbled before God, but presumes that there is—or at least hopes or desires that there may be—some place, time, and work for him, by which he may at length attain to salvation. But when a man has no doubt that every-thing depends on the will of God, then he completely despairs of himself and chooses nothing for himself, but waits for God to work; then he has come close to grace and can be saved.[24]

Such despair is a preparation for faith. It sets the stage for the belief that despite one's own incompetence and lack of desert, one's salvation is assured, as Christ has promised. But this belief itself cannot be characterized in Eras-mian terms as the product of a free act of will—and hence as an autonomous achievement—without invaliding the entire process of humiliation that pre-pares the way for it. That would be to reenthrone human pride at the crucial moment and give it the victory it craves. There is only one other possibility: that even the faith the elect experience after having accepted that their sal-vation is not in their hands "comes about by no work of [theirs], but solely by the love and hate of God. . . ."[25]

Faith is therefore not made, let alone created, by those whose faith it is. For that to be possible, they would have to share God's spontaneous power of creation. They would have to be autonomous in a way that God alone can be. Since this is impossible, their faith must be something "received," not chosen or willed. It must be the gift of God, which he bestows on some and not on others. Many succumb to the temptations of pride. Others resist them, but wait in vain for the gift of faith. Theirs are lives of despair. A few are hum-bled by God and then infused with a saving faith, though not on account of any choice or decision or commitment of their own, but thanks entirely to the grace of God. They alone are his elect.

OUGHT IMPLIES CANNOT

And why does God elect to save some but not others? Why does he refuse his gift of faith to the prideful and despairing? This is not a question we can answer. It is not a question we even have any "business" asking. We can comprehend the "will of God as preached, revealed, offered and worshiped." We have a duty to follow the commandments of Scripture but know that doing so is no guarantee of salvation. This remains a gift whose distribution is a secret "hidden" in God's "inscrutable" will.[26] "It is enough to know *that there is* a certain inscrutable will in God," which decides the fates of human beings. But "as to what, why, and how far it wills, that is something we have no right whatever to inquire into, hanker after, care about, or meddle with, but only to fear and adore."[27]

God's revealed word is a guide to righteous conduct in this life. But his hidden will remains a mystery, until we arrive "there" and see him "with unveiled face."[28] Here on earth, the pious course is to renounce all attempts to comprehend the incomprehensible. We must accept that between God's revealed and hidden wills there is no connection the human mind can discern. "God hidden in his majesty" has "not bound himself by his word, but has kept himself free over all things."[29] Luther's words echo the distinction between God's absolute and ordained power that Ockham had used to beat back the pretensions of those who sought to make the ways of God intelligible to man, and remind us that his sixteenth-century Reformation was inspired by the same idea of an utterly free and unfathomably remote God that Ockham and his fourteenth-century followers had erected as a defense against the pagan temptation of pride.

All of this is an offense to what Luther calls "saucy reason."[30] Human reason cannot bear to be told that it is powerless to comprehend God's hidden will and must not even ask why God acts as he does. This is a prohibition that "Reason can neither grasp nor endure." It is "what has offended all those men of outstanding talent" who "demand that God should act according to human justice, and do what seems right to them, or else cease to be God." To them, "the secrets of [God's] majesty are no recommendation; let him give a reason why he is God, or why he wills or does what has no semblance of justice—much as you might summon a cobbler or girdle maker to appear in court."[31]

But God "is God," Luther retorts, and "for his will there is no cause or reason that can be laid down as a rule or measure." God's will "is itself the rule of all things. For if there were any rule or standard for it, either as cause or reason, it could no longer be the will of God. For it is not because he is or was obliged so to will that what he wills is right, but on the contrary, because he himself so wills, therefore what happens must be right. Cause and reason can be assigned for a creature's will, but not for the will of the Creator, unless you set up over Him another creator."[32]

To let God *be* God, reason must therefore renounce its desire to under-stand his hidden will—to know him as he is in himself. This is the humbling sacrifice that reason must make if our sinful wish to become God is not to destroy us. But just because it enjoys such ancient authority, this "reasonable" wish has to be fought with particular energy in order to protect the otherness of a God whose will so far transcends all possible standards of reason as to make his ways appear irrational to man.

To insist on the prerogatives of reason, as Erasmus does, and to condemn appeals to "the awful will" of God as a trick for reducing one's "opponent to silence whenever he becomes troublesome," is therefore in reality the subtlest device of human pride. In response to those who use it, Luther says, "it is most of all in place" to "exhort" them "to silence and reverence," so that they may be humbled and made ready for God's grace, which they will receive or be denied as God sees fit in accordance with a will hidden from the prying light of reason.[33]

In this respect, Luther's theology of faith is opposed not only to every doctrine of good works and to the concept of free will, but to the claims of reason as well. Reason by its nature strives to understand everything, in-cluding God. It is motivated by the same longing for self-sufficiency as the church's practice of selling indulgences and Erasmus' learned arguments for freedom of the will. Luther's attack on the pretensions of reason is therefore merely another branch of his comprehensive war against human pride.

One aspect of his exchange with Erasmus brings this out with special clar-ity and underscores what, from a modern point of view, can only seem the self-conscious irrationality of Luther's position.

Erasmus bolsters his argument for freedom of the will by appealing to the many passages in the Bible in which God is portrayed as commanding some-one to perform a certain act or to refrain from doing so. Why would God issue such commands, Erasmus asks, if those to whom he addresses them lacked the power to decide whether to obey them or not? Surely, God's in-junctions make sense only on the supposition that his human subjects possess such a power. The frequency with which such commands appear in the Bible is therefore compelling proof, Erasmus argues, that Scripture supports those who affirm the existence of free will. "Ought implies can," as Kant has taught us to say.

That Erasmus' argument today seems irrefutable is in fact due largely to Kant's influence. While conceding that the freedom of the will cannot be proved directly (since it lies beyond the bounds of all possible experience), Kant claims that it is nevertheless deducible as a "fact of reason" from the undeniable existence of moral imperatives that are intelligible only on the assumption that those to whom they are addressed have the power to obey or disobey them as they choose. In this way, he concludes, the freedom of the will can be established transcendentally by reflecting on the conditions necessary for the possibility of the commands that are constitutive of moral experience. By giving "ought implies can" a transcendental interpretation, Kant converts what for Erasmus is a merely reasonable proposition into one that appears refutable only on the condition that the reality of moral experience itself be denied. As a result, few propositions today seem more obvious. And yet the claim that "ought implies can" is the very one that Luther attacks with greatest ferocity in his exchange with Erasmus.

Luther acknowledges that God commands us to do many things. But the purpose of his commands, he says, is to make it plain that we lack the power to fulfill them without God's assistance. The function of God's laws is to humble us, by disclosing our incapacity to obey his commands on our own. God's injunctions therefore do not presuppose a power in us to obey them if we choose, as Erasmus claims. Quite the opposite: God issues them to demonstrate that we *lack* this very power and are completely dependent on his grace for our compliance, which is his work, not ours.

"Human Reason . . . thinks man is mocked by an impossible precept"— by a command that one has no power to obey. But against this entirely "reasonable" conclusion, Luther insists that man is "warned and aroused" by such precepts "to see his own impotence."[34] If for Erasmus "ought implies can," Luther's position is therefore exactly the reverse. In his view, "ought implies *cannot*." Indeed, the very purpose of God's commands is to demonstrate that this is so, for they "are given in order that blind, self-confident man may through them come to know his own diseased state of impotence if he attempts to do what is commanded."[35]

This is not merely a rejoinder to Erasmus' argument. It is an inversion of it. Luther turns Erasmus' scriptural defense of human freedom upside down, and uses the very passages that Erasmus quotes as a lever to dislodge the

presumption of freedom in favor of God's grace, which obliterates man's independence altogether. On Luther's interpretation of the passages in question,
which of course makes as much logical sense as Erasmus', the existence of the
divine commands to which a corrupted humanity is subject is therefore compelling proof not of man's autonomy, as Erasmus claims, but of his complete
heteronomy instead—of man's utter dependence on a being other than himself for the ability to live as he should. The deepest principles of Luther's theology of grace allow no other reading.

NEVER THANKFUL ENOUGH

Every real gift is an act of love. Gifts that are part of an exchange are motivated by self-interest, not love. They are gifts in appearance only. If God
gave the gift of salvation in exchange for good works, or as a reward to the
man who freely wills to obey him, his gift would be an apparent, not a true
one. God's love for the man he saves would be no different from the solicitude a creditor feels for his debtor.

But this is a blasphemy—on Luther's view, the most awful one conceivable. It reflects the demeaning view of God that underlies every theology of
good works and good will. God is not a creditor who can be satisfied by giving him something he demands. He is a loving benefactor whose promise of
salvation is unearned and undeserved by the sinful creatures to whom he freely
gives it.

Luther describes the nature of this gift in a striking passage in *The Babylonian Captivity of the Church*. After attacking those who view the celebration of the mass as a "sacrifice" (which makes sense only if one thinks of
it as an act of recompense in a *quid pro quo* exchange), Luther explains the
true meaning of Holy Communion. It is "as if" Christ were declaring to the
celebrants, "Behold, O sinful and condemned man, out of the pure and unmerited love with which I love you, and by the will of the Father of mercies,
apart from any merit or desire of yours, I promise you in these words the forgiveness of all your sins and life everlasting. And that you may be absolutely
certain of this irrevocable promise of mine, I give you my body and pour
out my blood, confirming this promise by my very death, and leaving you
my body and blood as a sign and memorial of this same promise."[36]

In response to this wholly unmerited gift, Luther says, those who have faith
in Christ's promise are bound to feel a "sweet stirring of the heart" and a reciprocating love for "that gracious and bounteous testator" whose own love

for man knows no bounds. For how, he asks, could anyone who experiences such unconditional love "help loving so great a benefactor, who of his own accord offers, promises and grants such great riches and this eternal inheritance to one who is unworthy and deserving of something far different?"[37]

The man who has grasped the full measure of God's gift feels his own "utter worthlessness"[38] and his incapacity ever to express his gratitude to God in an adequate way. The belief that one can be thankful enough for God's promise of salvation presumes that the power of the one who receives the promise is commensurate with that of "the benefactor" who gives it. But this is the essence of human pride. It is the *incommensurability* of gift and gratitude that defines God's relation to man, and only those who meditate their whole lives long on the unbridgeable gap between these may be said to live in the spirit that Christianity truly demands. Only they have the right kind of love for God. It is a love that by definition always falls short and is driven to ever more extreme expressions of its own inadequacy out of a desire to be faithful to itself.

It is in this spirit that men and women of faith strive to meet their vocational duties to others. Loving God more than they can say, they seek to be a Christ to their fellow human beings, serving them as Christ served man, within the confines of the specific roles they occupy as husband or wife, merchant or farmer, citizen or public official. This is the best way we can show our gratitude for God's incommensurable love—by acting toward others with a generosity that exceeds everything they owe us, always striving to go beyond what a mere equivalence of exchange would require, giving the other men and women with whom we interact a surplus of unmerited love as an expression of thanks for the divine love we have received.

In this way, a man's vertical gratitude toward God is enacted horizontally, on the plane of human relations—not, of course, in order to earn God's approval and increase his chances for salvation (that is out of the question) but to demonstrate in the sphere of worldly life, where it is possible to do some actual good, how grateful one is for the gift of God's promise of salvation from the world itself. Yet what a man of faith discovers, in attempting to be a Christ to others, is not only that the world puts obstacles in his way, but that every success he experiences is just one more illustration of how woefully short his human love falls of God's love for him. His effort to love other human beings as God loves us thus proves to be not a means to satisfy his longing to be grateful to God, but another occasion for recalling how futile, indeed sinful, the desire for such satisfaction is, and a further reminder that the only proper attitude toward God is one that starts by accepting the incommensurability between his gift of salvation and any gratitude we are able to express for it.

In chapter 3, I contrasted the gratitude that children feel toward their parents with the thankfulness that on a Christian view one ought to feel toward God. It is useful to recall this distinction here, because it underscores how remote Luther's conception of man's relation to God is from even the most powerful form of human love.

Like God's gift of salvation, the life a child receives from her parents is not part of an exchange the child completes by making a return of equal value. We may love our parents, and help them in old age. But nothing we do for them can ever equal what they have done for us. Our relation to our parents is asymmetrical, and no love we ever show them can adequately express our thankfulness for the gift of life they confer on us without merit or desert.

Yet we can love others in the way our parents loved us. This is most obviously true in the case of our children, to whom we give the gift of life, as our parents gave it to us. It is also true, in an extended sense, of all the other works we bring into existence through our own productive labor. By loving our children and the world as gratuitously as our parents loved us, we express our love for them in the best way we can. This is not a *quid pro quo,* the return of one benefit in exchange for another. It is not an exchange at all, but the expression of gratitude for love received, and it would not have the meaning it does if it were a bargained-for benefit instead of a gift. This looks like an analogue of the effort to express one's gratitude to God for his promise of salvation, by performing acts of loving kindness toward others that go beyond our obligations to them.

But the analogy is deceiving. To begin with, though we do not deserve our parents' gift of life, we have committed no crime that makes us unworthy to receive it. God's promise of eternal life is undeserved in this stronger sense. One who receives a gift, despite the fact that he merits the opposite treatment, has special reason to be grateful for it, since his donor's act is one not merely of benevolence but mercy as well.

But this is not the most important difference between our parents' gift of worldly life and God's promise of life everlasting.

No child is ever able to thank his parents enough, but he can do as much and as good for others as his parents have done for him. In this sense, there is no shortfall between the parental love he receives and the gratitude he shows and feels for it. The one is completely adequate to the other. It is therefore possible for human beings to fulfill their yearning to give thanks for the greatest gift they have received (which is not the wish to repay a debt but the long-ing to realize their own capacity for love) by participating in the ongoing work of care by means of which succeeding generations maintain the human home they share. This is the essence of Aristotle's concept of friendship. For Aristo-tle, the joy of inhabiting a world sustained by the loving care of others finds its most satisfying expression in those reciprocating acts of love by which this world is preserved and perfected so that one's successors in it may experience a similar joy in turn, partaking of the eternal and divine so far as their human nature allows.[39]

For Luther, this is a hateful idea. A Christian's gratitude for the chance to share in eternal life can never be adequately expressed in his relations with others, no matter how much love he bestows upon them. Indeed, if he is a pious man, his experience will be just the opposite. It will be one of inade-quacy instead. To suppose that we can ever be grateful enough for the op-portunity to partake of the eternal and divine, and to think that such gratitude could even possibly take the form of a reverence for the human world and the men and women who sustain it, represents, from Luther's point of view, the most perfect and therefore pernicious expression of pride—like everything else in Aristotle's *Ethics*.

Aristotle's conception of friendship affirms the inherent soundness of the human condition. It assumes that the love of God is compatible with the natu-ral goodness of our deepest desires, including the wish to give thanks for the gifts we receive from our parents, teachers and friends. It further assumes that this longing is not in vain, but that our human powers put its fulfillment within reach. Luther's theology forces us to the opposite conclusion. It com-pels us to deny the inherent goodness of man. It demands that we view even the best human friendships as reminders of our sinful incompetence ever to love God as we should. And it requires us to give up all hope of adequately expressing our gratitude to God in the sphere of human relations—not because this is difficult to do, but more fundamentally because the very idea repre-sents a blasphemous expression of the conceited belief that human beings find the highest fulfillment of which they are capable, here on earth, in the chain of friendships that keeps the world of politics, philosophy, science and art alive from one generation to the next.

This is the meaning of Luther's statement in his *Disputation against Scho-lastic Theology* that the love of God entails the hatred of man. With this dra-matic claim, he brings the tradition of late medieval voluntarism to a conclusion. Ockham and his followers had sought to distance man from God, out of a love for God. Luther carries their campaign to its logical limits. But Ockham's own defense of God's absolute power was itself merely a restatement of Augustine's doctrine of grace, which the neopaganism of Aquinas and others provoked him to reconstruct in a conceptually more rigorous and therefore more radical form. And Augustine's conception of grace was itself in turn a systematization and in that sense a radicalization, of the undeveloped theology of sacrifice and salvation implicit in Paul's Letter to the Romans.

All these thinkers belong in a line. They are fighting for a common ideal of God's incomprehensible distance from man and are motivated by the shared belief that human beings can never be thankful enough to God for the self-sacrifice he made so that they might be saved from the ruinous state into which they had fallen on account of their sinful desire to be the ground of their own being. Opponents to this belief have arisen in every age—Pharisees, Pelagians, Averroists, and Papists. Each of these has sought to narrow the gap between man and God in one way or another: by equating gratitude with obedience to the law; or by granting men the freedom to determine their own fate; or by subordinating God's will to his intellect; or by encouraging the belief that men can win favor with God by buying indulgences and going to mass. Against the threat these views pose to the sublimity and independence of their all-powerful God, the theologians who stand in the line that leads from Paul to Luther have insisted, over and over again, on God's remoteness from man and on our utter incapacity to be grateful to him in the measure his gifts demand. Luther's claim that the love of God implies the hatred of man expresses the spirit of this tradition with a succinctness that can never be surpassed.[40]

But if Luther's theology of the cross marks the end of one development, it represents the beginning of another.

Men find it impossible to live with the thought that in order to love God they must hate themselves. They cannot accept the frustration of being unable to give adequate thanks for the love that enables them to aspire to a reasonable measure of fulfillment in a world they experience as a good-enough home. The human world affords us all the joy of participating in the eternal order of things that our limited powers permit. The wish to give thanks for this is the deepest and best of our desires. At some point, its obstruction becomes unbearable. When it does, the natural reaction is to seek to free mankind from the burden of self-loathing that is entailed by an inhuman form of gratitude whose very inadequacy is claimed to be the ground of all true piety.

And the only way to do this is for man to seize God's place—the very sin against which the theologians of grace warn most loudly.

As part of their campaign to defend God from man, these same theologians insist, with increasing rigor and force, on the inscrutability of what Luther calls God's hidden will. But ironically this same idea helps prepare the way for the expropriation of God's powers by draining his divinity of all possible intelligibility, so that the conceptual barrier to man's attempt to assume God's role is relaxed and the wish to do so given the space it needs to expand.

The crucial transitional figure in the post-Lutheran revolt against the antihumanism of Luther's theology of grace is Immanuel Kant. In the next three chapters, we shall explore Kant's complex, and in the end unsustainable, effort to liberate man from God in the name of enlightenment and autonomy, while preserving a dependence on his inscrutable will that is consistent with Christian values. It will then remain to see how—after a long but failed reactionary campaign to save the God of grace, which begins with Joseph de Maistre and concludes with Martin Heidegger—the revolutionary expansion of the first of Kant's ambitions, and the abandonment of the second, has produced a disenchanted world in which the very success of the effort to free ourselves from our gratitude to God has left us as frustrated in our longing to give thanks for the human love that opens a way to the eternal and divine, as the Christian religion, now stripped of its authority, has long taught us we should be for the divine love that alone has the power to rescue us from the wickedness of the human condition.

CHAPTER 20

The Absolute Spontaneity of Freedom

KANT'S CHRISTIAN METAPHYSICS

Erasmus grants human freedom only a modest role in the drama of salvation. He concedes it is surrounded on all sides by divine grace, without which we can accomplish nothing at all. But the claim that human beings are free, even to a limited degree, is in Luther's eyes a blasphemy, and he repeatedly chides his adversary for failing to understand that no amount of human freedom can ever be compatible with the omnipotence of God.

The contest between freedom and grace is absolute. One must prevail to the complete exclusion of the other. Either God's grace is the cause of all things, and human freedom only the name of a prideful conceit, or freedom is a reality—in which case it is not just something, but everything, the sole source of all that is morally meaningful in the world. If Erasmus had the confidence of his convictions, Luther claims, he would embrace the latter position openly and honestly—which Luther knows that, as a confessing Christian, Erasmus can never do.

Luther's taunt expresses in a forceful way the contradiction between freedom and grace that Augustine bequeathed to Christian thought. Both of these ideas are essential to Augustine's defense of God—an omnipotent creator, yet one not responsible for the evil in the world he creates. By formulating the ideas of freedom and grace with such clarity and precision, Augustine brought out the unresolvable tension between them. He made them the horns of a dilemma, between which one must choose, absolutely and unconditionally.

In the end, Augustine chose grace over freedom. Luther did the same, and dared Erasmus—the Pelagius of Rotterdam—to declare his own commitment to freedom instead.

Many modern readers are no doubt prepared to accept Luther's challenge. Their response is to enthusiastically affirm what he rejects as an absurdity— that human freedom is the main if not exclusive source of all our most important public and private values. But if this view now seems so compelling, it is because we live in a world saturated by the ethic of freedom. The freedom to direct one's life, express one's views, and decide for oneself which positions to take in public and private matters is today regarded by many as the common moral touchstone of the practices and institutions to which they feel the deepest allegiance.

To be sure, not everyone shares this view. There are still those, in the West and outside it, who reject the ethic of freedom in the name of tradition, or fate, or a God whose commands it is heresy to disobey. But by modern standards, these are all outliers. The dominant theology of our age is the gospel of human freedom. Grace and God have no place in it, or more exactly, they have been expelled from it on principled grounds. Yet this theology too is a product of Christian belief, for even in its most aggressively secular form it derives its power and authority from the same metaphysics of creation on which Luther relies to defend his uncompromising rejection of human freedom in the name of divine omnipotence. It is the other side of the Augustinian coin—the radical alternative that Luther identified in his debate with Erasmus but was sure Erasmus himself lacked the courage to profess. It is Erasmus without embarrassment, a way of life defined by the veneration of human freedom and the conversion of Luther's hatred of man into its exact opposite—into what its critics call the idolatry of man: a world drained of that reverence for God's grace on which Luther knew he could still rely in his rhetorical jabs at his opponent.

There is, of course, an immense distance between Erasmus' idea of human freedom and ours. The expansion of this idea and the corresponding contraction of the concept of grace has been the work of centuries. Many forces, material and intellectual, have contributed to it. But one thinker, more than any other, has helped to give the idea of human freedom the moral, political and personal prestige it now enjoys.

In his writings on ethics and politics, Kant defends a radicalized conception of freedom that is the antithesis of Luther's theology of the cross. If Luther grasps one horn of Augustine's dilemma, Kant grasps the other by

expounding a philosophy as unyielding in its commitment to human autonomy as Luther's is to our complete dependence on God's grace. In this
sense, Kant is "our" philosopher. His morality of freedom articulates, with
unrivaled clarity, the basis of the system of values that now dominates life
in the West, and increasingly beyond it—the shared ideals to which the defenders of liberalism and libertarianism, capitalism and socialism, republican
constitutionalism and direct democracy all ultimately appeal.

But even Kant stands at some distance from contemporary belief. That is
because he continues to adhere to an attenuated version of the concept of grace.
Kant insists that belief in God's omnipotence is "morally necessary."[1] In this
respect, he remains a pious Christian. But Kant's philosophical idea of grace
is a mere shadow of the Lutheran conception of it. It is the final, vestigial version of what for Augustine and Luther had been a robust article of faith. And
the unconvincing arguments that Kant employs to preserve this idea in the
exquisitely rationalized form in which he is still prepared to accept it only
highlight the contradiction between the orthodox understanding of divine
grace and the idea of human freedom on which his practical philosophy rests.

Kant's failed defense of grace prepares the way for a Kantianism without
God, which is a good way of describing the moral outlook of our age. In the
movement from Erasmus, whose defense of freedom is still tempered by a
conventional Christian acceptance of divine omnipotence, to our world, in
which grace no longer plays any role at all, Kant is therefore a pivotal transitional figure, whose rationalization of the concept of grace makes God's saving power an intolerable anomaly that his own morality of freedom compels
us to reject. The road from Erasmus' qualified defense of freedom to our limitless endorsement of it leads through Kant and his diminished concept of
grace—the final, failed effort to preserve God in a world devoted to the principle of human autonomy, whose radical consequences Kant himself was unafraid to draw.

As to Kant's personal motives for taking the side of freedom against that
of grace, it is probably fruitless to speculate. But it may be worth noting that
Kant was raised and educated in the atmosphere of Pietism that dominated
the Lutheran Church in Germany during the late seventeenth and early eighteenth centuries. The Pietists were motivated by a desire to feel the reassuring
warmth of a direct and authentic inner connection with God. In part, their
movement was a response to the increasingly arid practices of orthodox Lutheranism. But more fundamentally, it was a reaction against the unbearable
distance between man and God on which Luther had insisted. The Pietists

sought to bring God into their hearts, and by doing so to achieve, even if only fleetingly, that rapprochement between human beings and their creator that Luther had forbidden once and for all.

As a grown man, Kant condemned every form of "religious enthusiasm" that mistakenly seeks to annul the intellectual and moral abyss that separates man from God.[2] In emotional terms, at least, this is what the Pietists sought to do. Yet Kant's own morality of freedom asserts the value and dignity of human beings far more directly than the Pietists themselves ever did, and in this sense may be said to advance their ambition of combating the man-hating consequences of Luther's doctrine of grace. Despite the fact that he came to regard the Pietism of his youth as philosophically and theologically misguided, it is therefore perhaps not too far-fetched to suppose that Kant found in the religion of his parents and teachers one of the sources of his personal commitment to carry forward their crusade to reinvest human experience with an intrinsic dignity and worth that orthodox Lutheranism denied it—to the point where his own rationalization of the doctrine of grace could no longer be sustained in the enlightened and godless world that his morality of freedom helped to create.

THE GROUNDS AND CIRCUMSTANCES OF MORALITY

Aristotle's *Ethics* begins with an account of human happiness that rests on his understanding of man's place in the world.

Man is one of the many kinds of animals that live in the realm beneath the moon. Each of these has a distinctive form of its own. At the start of its career, each member of a kind possesses the form appropriate to it, but only potentially. Later, if its life unfolds in a natural way, it possesses the same form actually. Human beings are no exception. We have a unique form too. Like other earthly animals, we are born, live for a time, and die. But men alone possess the power of reason, which manifests itself in the uniquely human activities of politics and contemplation. It is in these that man's distinctive potential is fulfilled, and hence in them that the highest and most authentic forms of human happiness consist. For happiness is just the active exercise of those powers that define the nature of a human being—a particularized version of a general cosmological principle that Aristotle's follows in his study of every kind of natural motion in the world.

Like other natural beings, men yearn to be all they are equipped to become. The specific content of this goal is fixed by their distinctive nature as reasoning animals. Its achievement is the supreme aim of human living, and hence the ultimate benchmark by which all subsidiary accomplishments must be judged. To understand how one ought to live, and what constitutes success in living, it is therefore necessary first to understand the kind of being man is, for this not only establishes the limits of human striving, but sets the end toward which it is directed. As the study of human happiness, ethics is therefore inseparably connected to the nature of the being whose happiness it seeks to define. That ethics is in this sense an anthropological subject would have seemed to Aristotle a proposition too obvious to defend.

Nothing distinguishes Kant's ethics from Aristotle's more fundamentally than this. To claim that an action is ethical because it promotes human happiness is, on Kant's view, the worst mistake one can make in practical philosophy, no matter how refined one's conception of happiness may be. Those who set human happiness up as a standard for judging the ultimate worth of a person's actions, and of his life as a whole, are guilty, Kant says, of perverting the very character of morality itself, not because the pursuit of happiness is necessarily "selfish" (it may or may not be), but because the idea of happiness is tied to that of human nature and cannot be made intelligible apart from it.

No conception of happiness is possible except in terms of our peculiar, hybrid nature as "finite rational" beings. On this, Aristotle and Kant agree. But while for Aristotle, happiness defines the only point of view from which any ethical inquiry can proceed, for Kant the very essence of ethics lies in the principled effort to transcend this point of view, and to see the question of how one ought to live and act, not from the perspective of happiness and human nature, but from a vantage point beyond it. The effort to do this is for Kant the heart and soul of morality, which demands that we repudiate the premise Aristotle took for granted as the natural, indeed inevitable, foundation for any meaningful study of the aims of human living.

In Kant's practical philosophy, therefore, the point of view one must adopt in order to explain the rightness of right living is not merely unanthropological. It is antianthropological. We may call this the *ground* of morality. It is defined by its conscious opposition to every ethical system that takes human nature as its standard. Yet even in Kant's view, the conditions in which the drama of morality unfolds—the *circumstances* of morality—must be understood in terms of our distinctive constitution as beings occupying a troubled position midway between the instinctive life of nonrational animals, on the one hand, and the perfect equanimity of God, on the other. Aristotle saw the human condition as an intermediate one too, and though Kant emphatically rejects the idea that our humanity can ever be the ground or measure of morality, he agrees with Aristotle that the problem of how to live an ethically meaningful life only arises within the special circumstances defined by our position between the unthinking animals below us and God above, in both of whose radically different natures we participate to some degree.

INSTINCT AND REASON

Why, Kant asks, has "nature," in "distributing her capacities," given us the power of reason at all?[3] Other animals do not possess it. They act by "instinct" alone. Would we perhaps be better off if we did so as well?

Instinct is the thoughtless pursuit of what one desires. In the *Critique of Practical Reason,* Kant defines *desire* as "a being's faculty to be by means of its representations the cause of the reality of the objects of these representations," and *life* as "the faculty of a being to act in accordance with laws of the faculty of desire."[4] A stone is not alive. It "represents" nothing at all. To the extent it contributes causally to the realization of any state of affairs (say, the motion of another stone with which it collides), it does so on account of its mass, motion and the like—that is, by virtue of its external properties alone. Stones cannot cause things to happen because of their desires, since they have none. Kant's definitions of desire and life thus mark the line between animate and inanimate matter, a distinction our modern understanding of nature takes for granted but one that Aristotle regarded as a subdivision within the larger category of natural beings, defined as those that pursue their own ends, in contrast to artifacts, whose function, goal, or purpose is set by something other than themselves.[5]

Like horses and sponges, human beings fall on the animate side of this line. We have desires that are the moving cause of the states of affairs they represent, in the way the desire for an apple is the cause of its being plucked and eaten. Even the least-developed living thing has causally efficacious desires of this kind. But we occupy a unique place in the world of plants and animals, and to understand why, we need to distinguish the concept of "representation," as Kant uses it in his definitions of desire and life, from that of thought or reason.

Here (though not consistently throughout his philosophical writings) Kant employs this concept in a broad way to include inner states of a prereflective kind—for example, the desire of a dog for its bone—as well as those that are shaped or conditioned by reason. If a desire of the former sort acts in a regular and predictable fashion, Kant calls it an "instinct." All living things, human beings included, have instincts in this sense—prerational desires of a routine and repetitive kind, like the desire for food or sexual gratification. But human beings have desires of a different sort as well. We also have rationally conditioned desires, whose content is, to some degree at least, the product of conscious reflection, and which we pursue by means of deliberately constructed plans of one kind or another. When Kant asks why nature has given us reason, he is asking what of value would be missing from the world if we had no desires of the latter kind but acted from instinct alone.

Kant's answer is that morality itself would be missing. That is because morality only arises with a question that animals whose lives are guided solely by instinct are never in a position to ask. This is the question of which of our desires we ought to indulge and which to reform or repress. All the varied phenomena of moral life spring from this question. Merely asking it makes one a participant in the world of moral action and judgment. But this is something that rational beings alone can do. Other living things, which have instincts but lack reason, are insufficiently detached from their desires to ask themselves what they ought to do with them. They cannot distinguish "is" from "ought," and so cannot hold themselves, or anyone else, accountable for their actions. They lack the power of reason that all such accountability, and hence the whole of moral experience, necessarily presupposes.

Still, one might think that the disappearance of morality might be a price worth paying for the gain in happiness that could be achieved by substituting instinct for reason. Reason is a source of error and illusion. It is plausible to suppose that if our actions were directed wholly by instinct, we might be happier than we are. But Kant's view is that no gain in happiness can ever compensate for the loss of the moral world. That is because the one thing he considers *absolutely* good cannot be pursued, let alone attained, outside this world. Kant calls this a "good will." It is the only thing, he says, "in the world, or even out of it, which can be regarded as good without qualification."[6]

The goodness of a good will is unqualified because it does not depend on that of anything else. Its goodness is freestanding and self-contained. Moreover, its absolute goodness is, for human beings at least, a necessary condition of the qualified goodness of every other good as well. In the absence of a good will, nothing else can be good for us at all. Hence, a good will is not just of greater value than other goods, like happiness, but of *incommensura-*

bly greater value, so that the loss of the possibility of achieving it, or even of being able to aspire to do so, can never be offset by a gain in happiness, no matter how great. But the substitution of instinct for reason would have exactly this result, since without reason there can be no such thing as a will of any kind at all, whether it be a good or bad one.

That is because the goodness or badness of a person's will is a function of the principle he adopts as a criterion for the evaluation of his actions. To decide whether a person's will is good or not, we must know what rule he has chosen to guide his conduct. We have to know how he has answered (or would answer) the question of which desires he ought to allow and which to reform or repress. The morality of an action is never, according to Kant, a function of its success. A good will may fail to achieve its goal and a bad one succeed. The moral character of an action, and of the person whose action it is, depend entirely on the "principle of volition"[7] that serves as a justification for the action in question. Only this can be good "without qualification." Every other good, including that of success, depends upon it. But the unqualified goodness of adopting the right principle of volition is only available to a being that possesses the capacity to conceive such principles in the first place and to orient itself to them in its actions. Kant calls this capacity "practical reason."

Animals that act by instinct alone lack practical reason. They are incapable of evaluating their own behavior from the standpoint of a principle of any sort, good or bad. They are therefore shut out from the realm of moral experience and do not have the chance even to fail to attain the one good that is good in itself. It is better, Kant believes, to have this opportunity and fail than not to have it at all, and no amount of happiness can ever make up for its loss.

If the existence of beings with practical reason has a purpose, it therefore cannot be the furtherance of their desires, since reason is at best a dubious means to this end. It can only be the establishment of a moral world, predicated on the presence in its members of a capacity for action in accordance "with the conception of laws, i.e., according to principles,"[8] because by exercising this capacity they are able at least to *pursue* a good of infinitely greater value than all the happiness they stand to gain by substituting instinct for reason. This is the only conceivable answer to the question of why such beings exist. The question has a teleological thrust. But even if one ignores this aspect of it, the concept of practical reason, on which Kant's answer relies, provides the cornerstone of his phenomenology of moral experience, whose very possibility depends, Kant says, upon the presence in the world of beings that possesses the power to frame laws and act on their basis.

But what exactly is this power?

ABSTRACTION

"Everything in nature works according to laws."[9] This is true of lifeless things, like stones, and of living ones like horses and sponges. The latter have desires, which stones lack, but their desires have laws of their own. The movements of all things in the world are lawful in the sense that they conform to rules of one kind or another. Indeed, for Kant, the very idea of their lawfulness is equivalent to that of nature itself. At the most elementary level, nature is *constituted* by its lawful regularity. It exists as nature, as a world, *only because* the motions of everything in it follow laws we can discover by means of observation.

But if the idea of nature implies that everything in it works according to laws, it does not follow that every natural being has the power "of determining itself to action in accordance with the representation of certain laws."[10] This is the unique privilege and responsibility of those beings whose behavior is governed not merely by laws, but by the *conception* of laws as well. Kant calls such beings "rational," on account of their capacity to act in this special, rule-oriented way—a power that has no place in the lawful, but thoughtless, actions of living beings that are moved by instinct alone.

At different points, Kant describes this power in different ways. It is the power, he says, of acting "according to principles,"[11] or of setting an end for oneself.[12] It is the power of "practical reason." It is reason itself, and "will," which "is a kind of causality belonging to living beings insofar as they are rational."[13] It is "freedom," the "property of this causality," which Kant also calls the "autonomy"[14] or "spontaneity" of the will.[15]

All these different notions—reason, freedom, will, autonomy, spontaneity—in the end come to the same thing. They are all descriptions of a single power, whose existence is the organizing premise of Kant's account both of the system of nature (the kingdom of "is") and of the realm of moral accountability (the kingdom of "ought"). Nothing plays a more important role in either branch of Kant's critical philosophy than the existence and operation of this power. Yet nothing is harder to define with precision than his own understanding of it and of the relationships among its various manifestations (as reason, freedom, spontaneity, and the like). Indeed, Kant himself concedes that there is something mysterious[16] about this power, whose own existence cannot be explained, despite the fact that it must be presumed in order to account for the possibility of both science and morality.

Consider the first of these.

Horses and sponges have no science because they have no "experience" of the world, in Kant's sense of the term. Things happen to them, of course, and they cause other things to happen (in part, on account of their desires). Like the actions and reactions of everything else in the world, those of horses and sponges have a place in the endless causal chain that constitutes the world itself. But neither they nor any other nonrational animal comprehends the world *as* a system of causes to which they themselves belong. Nonrational animals instinctively pursue things *in* the world, but the world itself is not for them an *object of attention,* nor are they such objects to themselves.

For us, the world is an object in this sense. We experience the world as an ordered whole, even though our encounter with it is at every moment partial and perspectival. Like other animals, we never "meet" more than a piece of the world at once. But behind every such encounter, there is, for us, another engagement with the world that shapes and conditions all the rest—our experience of it as an all-comprehending system of laws. The world, in this latter sense, is an object of consciousness for us. It is something we attend to (think and speak about) and only because we do are we able to seek to understand its laws through the discipline of science. We also attend to ourselves in a similar way. We are not merely conscious of the world but self-conscious too, and one of Kant's aims in the *Critique of Pure Reason* is to show that these two forms of attention are the coeval and reciprocally conditioned expressions of one primordial power, whose possession sets human beings apart from all nonrational animals.

Kant calls this power that of "synthesis according to rules."[17] It might also be called the power of abstraction.

To experience the world, as opposed to merely being in it, one must see the things that one encounters in experience as having some regular relation to one another. One must see them as being connected according to rules. In any particular case, the content of the rule may be unclear. But we must *see* things *as* connected according to some rule or other, if we are to have any experience *of* the world at all. Indeed, even this formulation is not quite right, since the capacity for seeing things as connected according to rules is, for Kant, not just a condition of any possible experience of the world, but equivalent to it. In Kant's view, these are complementary ways of describing the same elementary power, whose absence in the lives of nonrational animals accounts for the fact that they "have" no world at all.

Horses and sponges act according to rules, including those of desire, but they do not see their actions, or those of other things, as governed by rules. To do this, they would have to possess the concept of a rule, as something *distinct* from the actions it governs. But every such concept is an abstraction. It can be arrived at only by abstracting the rule in question from the actions it connects or "synthesizes." In one sense, the world is nothing but a vast constellation of individual things and events. To become a world in Kant's sense—the lawful totality to which we attend as the ever-present and all-encompassing background of individual things and events—these must be seen as acting in accordance with rules whose generality is not to be found anywhere in the world itself, but is only arrived at through a process of abstraction from it.

Even the idea of a thing is an abstraction. In reality, a thing is nothing but a series of discrete events, whose unity we provide by supposing behind or beneath them a durable object of some kind. In Kant's terminology, a thing is just a rule for the organization of a temporal series. But without this abstraction, which we ourselves supply, there could be no such thing as a thing, and without the complex system of abstractions that Kant analyzes in the *Critique of Pure Reason,* no world of things and no experience either of them or of ourselves. The power to form such abstractions is therefore the transcendental ground (again, to put it in Kant's terms) of that special kind of seeing-as that itself is the ground of all possible experience, though here too it would be more accurate to say that, on Kant's view, the first is not so much a condition of the second, and the second of the third, as that all three (abstraction; seeing things as governed by rules; the experience of the world and of ourselves as objects of attention) are variant descriptions of the same primal power, whose possession distinguishes the condition of human beings from that of every other animal on earth.

TIME-CONSCIOUSNESS

One other characterization of this power is worth emphasizing. This is Kant's description of it as the power of time-consciousness.

Time and space are what Kant calls "pure forms of intuition." They are the primitive organizing schemes that order the content (the "manifold") of intuition at its most basic level. The abstract forms of space and time supply the elementary building blocks that make possible all the further, higher-level sorts of ordering that Kant explores in the transcendental logic of the *Critique of Pure Reason,* where the abstractions of the categories of the understanding are joined to those of the pure forms of intuition by means of a "schematism" that is supplied by the imagination, whose transcendental function is to construct a bridge between them.

As between space and time, however, Kant assigns time a special role. That is because every experience of a thing in space is one that itself occurs at some moment in time, and hence has a temporal form, but not every experience is of a thing in space. (Musical experiences are an example.) Time is therefore the lowest common denominator of all possible experiences, including those that are of things that do not exist in space at all. (The priority of time over space is reflected in Kant's account of the schematizing work of the imagination, which enables the laws of the understanding to be applied to intuitions by recasting these laws as rules for fixing the relations among intuitions in time.)

Everything that we experience must therefore be represented as existing in time. But for this to be possible, the thing in question (a chair across the room, the tune of a popular song) must have a durability that survives the separate, evanescent moments of its existence—all the instantaneous "nows" through which it passes, for as long as it exists. Or rather, it has to be *seen as having* a durability of this kind, for otherwise there can be no *thing* that may be said to exist in time. To represent things as existing in time, we therefore have to see them as surviving from one instant to the next, and to do this we need to be able to remove ourselves from the ceaseless flow of time sufficiently to grasp the connection among the moments that constitute the existence of even the most short-lived thing. It is therefore possible to see a thing as existing in time only because we have the power to see time itself as an organized medium whose endless, instantaneous "nows" are bound together by a rule.

The power to form and apply such a rule is what we mean by time-consciousness—the awareness *of* time as distinct from mere existence *in* it. Everything in nature exists in time. But only those beings that possess a consciousness of time can represent themselves and other things as existing in time, and therefore have any experience of them at all (in Kant's sense), or of the world as an organized totality of things connected by rules.

The power of time-consciousness is thus, on Kant's view, a transcendental precondition of abstraction and hence of experience in general—or rather, it *is* the power of abstraction under a different description. That is because time-consciousness and abstraction are merely alternative ways of describing the most elementary and striking fact about us: our *release* from the prison in which nonrational animals are trapped (without, of course, knowing they are).

Our consciousness of time is a release from time, just as abstraction is a release from presence and particularity. The first frees us to see time *as* an organized medium, whose moments are connected by rules. The second frees us to see what is present in intuition *as* a system of things governed by laws. Both sorts of seeing are possible only because the one who sees has *escaped* the confining orbit of what he sees, and can see it from an independent point of view. We might describe this in more conventional, if equally elusive, terms as the *transcendence* of time and presence. But these are all metaphors, and it is less important to decide which is best than to recognize that each is an attempt to describe the liberating power that, by enabling us to see the world from a distance, allows us to experience both time and the things that are in it. To put it paradoxically, it is only on account of our power to transcend the world that we "have" a world at all.

Of course, we do not transcend the world completely. Our consciousness of time does not cancel the fact of our existence in it. We continue to live in time, despite our awareness that we do. Nor does our experience of the world as a system of rules cancel our dependence on the presence of things in intuition for any experience of them. Our escape from the world still leaves us trapped in it, carried along by time and dependent on intuition, in the company of all the other, worldly beings that surround us.

This is an excruciating position to be in. It inevitably gives rise to the wish to make our transcendence more complete. But we can neither repress nor fulfill this desire. The urgency of its demands and the necessity of its defeat constitute the incurable disease of the human condition, which Kant diagnoses with supreme wisdom in the "Dialectic" of the *Critique of Pure Reason.*

This disease is as unknown to nonrational animals as the world and time themselves. For the very same world-transcending power of abstraction that opens the world to us as an object of study and thereby makes possible the uniquely human enterprise of science, is also the one that allows us to grasp our own imprisonment in it, as beings whose knowledge of the world is doomed to remain incomplete—a tragic self-assessment that horses and sponges are spared. The agony of the human condition as well as its grandeur and glory, our peculiar defeats along with our singular successes, thus depend on that power of transcendence whose presence in us marks the line that divides the least of human beings from the cleverest of nonrational animals—

the lower boundary of man's intermediate estate between the beasts below and God above who, like us, transcends the world, but without limit.

SPONTANEITY

The world-transcending power of reason is thus the ground of all possible experience. Yet, in a very specific sense, it itself remains incomprehensible, for though we must assume its existence, we cannot explain how or why it exists. That is because the field of all possible explanations is only as wide as that of experience, and as the ground of experience, the power of reason is not something we *can possibly* encounter *in* it. Every experience already presupposes its prior existence, which therefore always outruns any attempt to explain it. This is why Kant describes the power of time-consciousness, by means of which we transcend the world and thereby encounter it as an object of attention, as an "art hidden in the depths of the human soul,"[18] of which no account can ever be given.

To account for anything, one must be able to point to something else as the reason for its being as it is. The most familiar explanations of this sort are causal. We explain the existence of one state of affairs by appealing to some other, antecedent state, which we call its determining ground. We may have no insight into the nature of the connection between these two states. But all causal explanations advance our understanding only by relating one thing, the *explanandum,* to another, the *explanans.* Even explanations of a noncausal kind—those, for example, that seek to explain the movements of an organism by bringing out the purposeful relations among its parts— exhibit the same general pattern.

If the existence of the power of reason is inexplicable (because its origin necessarily lies outside all possible experience, which always already presupposes it), then this power cannot conceivably be related to anything else as its determining ground, for if it could, it would be explicable after all. Hence, if we must assume that the power of reason exists (since it is only on this assumption that the possibility of experience itself can be explained) but cannot account for its own existence by appealing to anything else as its cause or ground, then we have no choice but to conceive the power in question as one that arises *spontaneously,* that is, as a power having the ground of its own being in itself—which of course is just another way of confessing that there is nothing we can ever know or say about what Aristotle would call its coming to be.

To describe something as spontaneous is to assert that it comes into being from nothing. Aristotle declared the very idea unintelligible. He thought it inconceivable that something could ever truly come from nothing (as opposed to arising from that conditional sort of reality he calls potentiality). His intellectualist metaphysics rules this out completely. By contrast, Augustine describes the freedom of the will in precisely these terms—as a power of self-causation analogous to the one that God exercises when he creates the world from nothing.

Augustine insists that only this view of the will is compatible with the belief that man, not God, is responsible for the evil in the world. But this forced him to concede that the freedom of the human will, like that of God's, is *necessarily inexplicable*, since any explanation of its actions would require us to treat the will as a natural power subject to nature's laws, and hence as something caused to act by an other, rather than acting spontaneously on its own. In this sense, every explanation of freedom, to the extent it succeeds, converts the thing it seeks to explain into a power that has its determining ground in something else, and thus into one that is no longer free. Augustine recognized this paradox, and accepted the fact that the freedom of the will, which he made the basis of his explanation of the whole of human morality, cannot itself be explained. In Augustine and his successors, the idea of the will as a creative power whose spontaneity is essential to the meaning of responsibility in all its forms, and yet simultaneously guarantees that its own existence must remain a mystery forever, became the cornerstone of a distinctively Christian ethics that differs most fundamentally from its Aristotelian counterpart precisely on account of the central place it assigns to the irrational idea of free will.

All the key conceptual terms in Kant's account of the system of nature— "world," "law," "rule," "synthesis," "reason"—rest on this same Christian idea. The laws that order the world, and in doing so make it a world for us, are arrived at by a process of abstraction that cannot itself be the result of other, antecedent laws derived by a similar process, for the assumption that they can would compel us to presuppose the existence of the world understood as a system of laws, and that is the very thing we are attempting to explain. Kant's transcendental method rules out any such assumption as a *petitio principi*. The only alternative is to assume that these world-constituting laws are themselves brought into being spontaneously through the exercise of a genuinely creative power.

The origin of the rules that give rise to the world we encounter in experience must therefore lie in a spontaneous act of creation that is as much our own free act as God's creation of the "given" manifold that we first experience as an object of attention on the basis of the world-constituting work these rules themselves perform. The ground of the being of these rules *as* rules thus has to be sought in our freedom, just as the ground of the being of the world we "receive" in intuition must be sought in that of God. Kant's account allows for no other conclusion.

The world-transcending power of abstraction that alone enables us to have a world at all can therefore only be conceived *as freedom itself,* and hence as a power whose own origin must be as inexplicable as that of any truly spontaneous act. When Kant claims that a being is free only to the extent (i.e., only because) it is rational, he is thus affirming the identity of reason not merely with time-consciousness and the power of synthesis according to rules. He is asserting its identity with freedom as well. Of the many names that Kant gives to the spontaneous transcendence of time and presence in which our encounter with the world first begins, freedom is perhaps the most basic of all.

GODLIKE

This power is the godlike element in us. It marks the divide, for Kant, between human beings and nonrational animals. In the theoretical realm, it is what separates men, who know they live in the world and time, from animals that lack this knowledge. In the practical realm, it is what distinguishes human beings, who are capable of living morally responsible lives on account of their capacity for action in accordance with the conception of a law, from animals that act by instinct alone. In both spheres, we occupy a unique position among all the living things on earth: in the first, as scientific observers of what "is," and in the second, as moral agents obligated to act as we "ought." In each case, the uniqueness of our position is due to the presence in us of a power of pure creativity that Kant calls the "absolute spontaneity" of freedom.[19] We share this power with God, who is a creator *par excellence,* and only because we do—only because we are free and rational beings whose transcendence of the world displays a spontaneous creativity resembling his own—are we able to form judgments of both a positive and normative kind that no other animal on earth can conceive.

But if the world-transcending creativity that lies at the root of both science and morals sets us apart from irrational animals, the limits that confine our creativity distinguish us from God. God's creative power is absolute; ours is not. In this respect, we are merely the "image" of God—a notion that combines the ideas of likeness and deficiency. Looking down in the order of being, we are justified in claiming for ourselves an elevated position, on account of our likeness to God. But looking up at God, it is our deficiencies that appear most striking. To be human is therefore to be incompletely divine. It is to resemble God in one way but fall short of him in another. Every aspect of human experience reflects this combination of resemblance and shortfall in some fashion.

Thus, all our knowledge of the world, though it arises only through the work of a power of abstraction that spontaneously creates the lawfulness of the world from nothing, is permanently dependent on intuition for its content, which it receives from without. The world comes to light for us only because we transcend it, but what we discover, when we "see" it, is that it is not of our own making. If the spontaneity of reason is a creative power whose existence cannot be explained by anything other than itself, the world it reveals to us is one we do not actively create but passively encounter.

That we are not the creators of the world is one of the great lessons of experience, which horses and sponges are incapable of learning. They are not its creators either but unlike us, they do not know this. We do, because our radical independence as rational beings gives us the detachment from the world we need in order to comprehend our own dependence on it. Kant calls this dependence "receptivity,"[20] our beholdenness to a world outside us for all our experience of it. To be beholden to something other than oneself is to be limited in the range of one's powers. This is the condition of all finite beings. We might therefore say that what human beings discover through the exercise of their divine power of reason (the condition of having a world at all) is their own finitude, or lack of divinity: the passive nature of all human experience, which can no more be overcome than our finitude itself, of which the receptivity of intuition is the defining mark in the kingdom of "is."

Because God is an infinite being, his creativity cannot be similarly constrained. Nothing can be "given to" God or passively received by him. The boundlessness of his creative powers rules this out. God must therefore be conceived as the spontaneous creator not only of the *order* of the world but of its very *existence,* which *we* have to accept as something given.

Kant expresses this idea by saying that God's intuition is not "sensible," like ours, but "intellectual"—that it causes the things it apprehends to exist through the very act of apprehending them, instead of encountering them, as we do, as objects of whose existence we are not ourselves the authors. The spontaneity of reason, by means of which we transcend the world, puts us in the company of God. But what it enables us to comprehend is the gulf between our finitude as sensuously dependent beings and his intellectual intuition. The godlike power that sets us apart from other terrestrial animals is therefore the very one that allows us to understand our own lowliness in relation to God, which they are too low even to grasp.

The consciousness *of* time that frees us *from* time thus reveals our condition to be that of finite beings *in* time, whose experience of the world is always temporal and receptive (for Kant these come to the same thing), in contrast to God, who relates to the world in a fashion that is neither. The knowledge of our distance from God is the highest sort of knowledge our godlike power of abstraction affords us, and though we are forever tempted to claim for ourselves powers that are fully divine, by seeking to know things "in themselves" and not merely the "appearances" of them that are given to us in intuition, the knowledge of our own deficiency in relation to God, from which all nonrational animals are shut out on account of their even greater deficiency, acts as a brake on the irrepressible but unattainable ambition to exchange our place, as finite rational beings, for his as a creator with infinite powers. This is the main lesson of the *Critique of Pure Reason*.

The same is true on the practical side, in the domain of moral experience.

Here, the question that absorbs us is not what "is" but what "ought" to be. This is not a question that arises for horses and sponges. They live their lives in accordance with the laws of desire, but lack the power to act on the basis of a conception of laws of any kind. They cannot make a rule the ground of their actions because they do not have the capacity to frame such a rule or to direct themselves toward it by adjusting their behavior to the rule as a justificatory norm. Like all nonrational living beings, they are prisoners of desire, and can no more escape the instincts that direct them than they can transcend the flow of time by taking notice of it.

To escape the life of desire, they would have to be able to ask themselves which of their desires they ought to allow and which to suppress or reshape. They would have to be able to take their desires as objects of reflection, and form rules regarding them (in the same way a time-conscious being takes time as an object and organizes its moments in accordance with various rules). And of course they cannot do this because they lack the spontaneous, world-transcending power of abstraction that enables human beings to escape the tyranny of their desires and time. The liberating power of reason, whose spontaneity is freedom itself, is thus the threshold of all moral experience, which nonrational animals cannot cross, just as they cannot cross that of cognition, on account of their lack of the very same power.

What we discover in the realm of morality, however, as in that of science, is that our transcendence of the world is incomplete. For though the power to take our desires as an object of reflection, and to judge them according to rules we freely devise, releases us from our desires in one way, it leaves us still subject to them in another. As finite beings, we can no more escape the pull of desire than we can that of time. We must accept the fact that we shall always have desires. We may be able to condition them, and perhaps even to do away with some altogether. But it is hopeless to strive to overcome desire completely—as hopeless as to aspire to know things in themselves.

Our desires supply the matter with which morality must work, just as intuition provides the material of all our knowledge of the world. The givenness of each is a consequence of our finitude. Because we are finite and do not create the world merely by intuiting it, our intuitions are passive or receptive. And because we are finite, and do not already possess all that we require to exist, we have needs for other things, and must spend our lives in pursuit of them. To be finite is to be dependent: in science, on a world that is already given to us, as something other than ourselves; and in morality, on the external objects of desire that we need in order to live and on our desire for them. This is the sad fact which the independence of reason brings to light.

We are thus faced in the moral realm with a paradox analogous to the one we confront in the sphere of cognition, for the godlike power that enables us to escape our desires by subjecting them to independent review, itself reveals our inability ever to do so completely. It discloses our incapacity ever to be happy. This is the comprehensive goal at which all our desires collectively aim, and its attainment would require that we either abolish or satisfy the needs to which we are permanently subject as living beings—a result equivalent to the abolition of the finitude that distinguishes our condition from God's.

The "oughts" we strive to live by, as moral agents, must therefore be pursued within a field of desire we can never escape. This means that morality is for us always a challenge. Just as in the realm of science, we are forever attempting to get closer to the nature of things in themselves, in morality we are continually striving to regulate our desires in accordance with a system of rules that specifies how we ought to treat them. But the urgency and intransigence and blind opacity of desire make this goal only imperfectly attainable, for the same reason that our finitude as sensuously intuitive beings forecloses the possibility of ever knowing things as they are independently of our experience of them.

In this sense, morality does not come to us "naturally." It is always something we must struggle to achieve, and no one ever overcomes the experience of resistance this struggle involves. Even the most upright men and women can never know, with perfect confidence, that their uprightness is not the product of a secret desire for happiness that makes the morality of their lives a sham. No finite rational being can ever eliminate such doubts altogether. The whole of our moral experience is clouded by an appreciation of the limits to which we are subject and by the awareness that morality remains for us, an "obligation" or "duty"—that is to say, something that is not part of our nature, and can never be fully achieved.

Because nonrational animals have no moral life at all, they are untroubled by this awareness, just as they are untroubled by a knowledge of the limits of their knowledge of the world. But we, who comprehend our finitude as needy beings, are also able to conceive a better being who, though rational like us, is as placidly unruffled by our moral struggles as he is by our epistemic frustrations. Unlike the animals below us, we know that we are limited. But the spontaneous power of reason that makes this knowledge possible also enables us to form the idea of an infinitely creative God, who stands as high above us in the moral realm as in the scientific, defining the upper limit of the middle ground we occupy in the kingdom of "ought," as well as that of "is."

In the realm of science, what distinguishes God from human beings is the intellectual nature of his intuition. In the moral sphere, it is the "holiness" of his will. God's will is not opposed by desires that he must struggle to shape and direct. There can be no tension, in God's case, between will and desire. God necessarily wills the good, and what he wills, he necessarily wants. Thus, one cannot say that there is anything God "ought" to do, or has a "duty" to do, for these ideas make sense only where the thing might not be done.

We, by contrast, have to work to do the right thing. That is because our desires always resist us to some degree. If we were all-powerful, nothing could oppose our wills. But we are not. We are finite beings with needs, and depend on things outside us to exist. God's being is self-contained. Hence, when God wills, he meets with no resistance, while our wills always confront independent and antecedent desires. God's "holy" will is therefore the moral equivalent of his intellectual intuition, for just as the latter creates its objects rather than receives them, his will is the cause of his desires, which have no independent existence of their own.

Kant expresses this idea by saying that God does the right thing by nature—by virtue of being who he is.[21] This is not true of us. Morality is always, for us, an (imperfect) achievement, like our knowledge of the world. Both must be wrung from the materials our finitude affords us. Indeed, the phenomenon of resistance and struggle is so central to our experience both of morality and science that, without it, one cannot conceive of either in its human form—of morality without obligation, or of science without a commitment to pursue the truth, which implies some imperfection in our possession of it.

Thus, though we are able to frame the idea of a God whose will and mind suffer no such (human) limitations, we cannot imagine him either as a moral agent or a scientist. Indeed, we cannot really imagine him at all, since to do so we would have to overstep the limits of all finite, hence human, thought. For Kant, the idea of God is therefore merely a notional term that sets an upper bound to the human kingdoms of morality and science, beyond which we cannot see, just as the notion of the purely instinctual lives of nonrational animals sets a lower bound that is equally unsurpassable in thought or imagination (since any attempt to comprehend what it is like to live the life of such an animal must make use of the very power of abstraction whose absence defines it).

THE DEPRECIATION OF MAN

The kingdoms of cognition and duty lie between these limits. They are the boundary stones of the human condition. They mark our intermediate place in the order of things, as finite rational beings whose spontaneity puts us at a transcendent distance from the world resembling that of our creator, but whose finitude chains us to the world, and confines the exercise of our godlike creativity within limits incompatible with the idea of God as an omnipotent being.

What follows from this peculiar combination of spontaneity and limitation, so far as our knowledge of the world is concerned? That is the central question of Kant's "speculative" philosophy. And what follows from it, with regard to our moral obligations? That is the central question of his practical writings. Both branches of Kant's critical philosophy thus take the in-betweenness of the human condition as the setting for the problems they

address, which in this sense may be said to arise only within an anthropological context.

But there is a fundamental difference in the attitude that Kant takes toward
our humanity in these two branches of his work. In the *Critique of Pure Reason,* Kant's account of the human condition serves as a reminder of the futility of all our efforts to comprehend God. The critical philosopher (Kant's wise
man) knows that the desire to do so, though irrepressible, can never be fulfilled. In this sense, one might describe the lesson of the *Critique of Pure Reason* as humanistic, for Kant wants us to measure our ambitions in the field of
cognition by expectations appropriate to the intermediateness of the human
condition.

By contrast, Kant's basic orientation in his practical writings is antihumanistic. Though he takes the combination of freedom and finitude that defines our human being as the necessary *setting* of morality, he insists that our
humanity itself can never be a *measure* of moral value, and fervently maintains that the only morally worthy aim is to strive with all our hearts to become as much like God as possible, by exclusively honoring that element in
our composite nature that alone resembles his—our spontaneity as free and
rational beings.

In this sense, Kant's practical philosophy stands at the furthest remove
from Aristotle's pagan ethics, which treats the human condition not merely
as the occasion for asking how one ought to live, but the standard by which
to judge the answers we give. Compared with Aristotle, one might therefore
say that Kant's morality *depreciates* our humanity.

And why is that? The short answer is, because he is a Christian, for whom
the worth of human actions, indeed of human beings themselves, must ultimately be judged in light of the idea of a God who exists apart from the world
and brings it into being from nothing, with the result that everything in the
world, including us and all we do, possesses whatever worth it does only
derivatively, through its relation to its world-transcending creator—an idea
whose distance from Aristotle's pagan philosophy of worldly fulfillment is well
captured by Kant's revealing characterization of all human desire as "pathological."[22]

To those who accept the Augustinian doctrine of creation, fall and salvation, this characterization will seem self-evident, for the depreciation of
man that it implies is a corollary of the grandeur of the God they worship.
Kant calls our desires pathological because he is a Christian in the Augustinian
line, who accepts the intrinsic worthlessness of the world and everything in

it, and his own relentlessly rational pursuit of this idea is the driving force behind his moral philosophy.

The next chapter explores the antihumanism of Kant's morality in more detail. Then, in the chapter that follows, we shall trace his attempt to preserve a connection between the central teachings of this morality, founded on the Christian idea of freedom, and the Christian doctrine of grace. This is the last such attempt in the epoch of Christian philosophy, which begins with Augustine and ends with Kant himself. Its failure has left us with the godless Kantianism that is the reigning morality of our age, in which the champions of reaction and the apostles of disenchantment fight their sterile war for the human soul, the one condemned to search for God in a direction he can no longer be found, and the other to proclaim their satisfaction with lives that have no meaningful connection to eternity at all—a hopeless and dispiriting condition for which the remedy, unnoticed, lies ready at hand in the born-again paganism that already inspires our deepest modern ideals.

CHAPTER 21

Our Better Selves

THE MORALITY OF AUTONOMY

All our actions are shaped by desire, from the noblest to the most debased. For us, there is no life outside its occasionally inspiring, often banal and sometimes deforming power.

But we also have the power to hold our desires to account—to judge their suitability and worth. We can do this because we are able to detach ourselves from our desires sufficiently to form the idea of a rule by which to judge them. The possession of this ability is the condition of admission to the kingdom of morality. Only the actions of those beings that possess it can be judged in moral terms. They alone can be either moral successes or failures.

But this merely establishes what Kant, who was fond of legal metaphors, calls the "jurisdiction" of morality.[1] It leaves open the question of what rule a being endowed with the capacity for action in accordance with the conception of a rule ought to adopt as a standard for judging the worthiness of his or her desires.

It is one thing to define the boundaries of the moral realm and another, it would seem, to identify the rule that defines the goodness of conduct within it. The latter question is the central topic of Kant's moral philosophy. Yet Kant's answer to it is already contained in his account of the jurisdiction of morality. In the end, for Kant, good conduct is nothing but fidelity to the power that enables us to be moral in the first place—the godlike power of reason by means of which we transcend the world, only to discover that

unlike God we can never do so completely. The most distinctive features of
Kant's moral philosophy all follow from this premise. These include his insistence on the priority of form over matter in the definition of moral value; his
celebrated suggestion that we test the worth of moral rules by their universalizability; and the principle of respect for persons, to which Kant attaches fundamental importance.

FORM AND MATTER

A rule that serves as a standard for the critical evaluation of behavior (one's
own or that of others) Kant calls a "maxim."[2] Every maxim is a rule, but not
every rule is a maxim. "Frogs live on a diet of insects" is a rule but not a
maxim. A frog that lives on something else is not to be blamed for failing to
follow the rule. This is true of all the rules that constitute the order of nature.

By contrast, the rule that "one ought to limit one's consumption of fattening foods" is a maxim. A person's failure to follow it is *prima facie* grounds
for criticizing his or her behavior. It is a reason for judging the person's behavior to be deficient or defective, pending an explanation that justifies it (for
example, that he has been advised by a doctor to adopt a high-fat diet for
medical reasons). Every maxim, from the lowest to the most exalted, is an
injunction or "imperative" to do or refrain from doing something. Comply-
ing with it is always at least a conditional basis for praise.

The laws of nature are not all on the same level. Some are broader than
others. The laws of vertebrate metabolism, for example, are more general than
those that describe the eating habits of frogs, and the former are narrower
than the laws of organic chemistry that govern metabolic processes of every
kind. The laws of nature form a hierarchy, with the most general ones at the
top, and more particular laws gathered under and governed by them.

The maxims of morality form a hierarchy too. The injunction not to eat
fattening foods is less general than the command to keep one's body in a
healthy state, which is less general than the imperative to live the best life that
one can. In the moral world as in the natural, we confront a system of laws,
arranged in order of ascending generality, the range and application of those
lower in the order being determined by laws higher up.

In our investigation of nature, Kant says, we are compelled to assume that
the hierarchy of laws culminates in a single law (or, what amounts to the same
thing, a set of laws whose relationship to one another follows a determinable
rule). We have to assume this in order to be able to conceive of nature as a

system, and we must do that, Kant claims, in order to be able to understand anything about the natural world at all. This assumption is in his view a transcendental presupposition that cannot be refuted merely by pointing out that we do not yet know—or indeed never shall—what the fundamental law of nature is.

The same is true in the moral domain. Maxims of limited generality are critical standards for the evaluation of behavior whose jurisdiction is fixed by laws of greater reach, which determine when, how, and under what conditions the specific maxims that fall under them ought to be applied. If morality is to be possible at all, Kant claims, disagreements about the rightness or wrongness of a person's behavior must in every case be resolvable in principle, whether or not they are resolved in fact, and for *this* to be possible, the hierarchy of maxims that constitutes the moral order must culminate in some single imperative that governs all the rest. In this respect, the natural and moral worlds resemble one another, though Kant insists that while the fundamental law of nature is bound to remain, even for the most sophisticated scientist, a "regulative ideal" that guides his study of the world without itself ever being fully understood, the basic law of morality is already implicit in the ordinary experience of uneducated human beings.

The most important challenge for any practical philosophy is therefore to identify this basic moral law. Until that has been done, no subsidiary ethical issue can be settled in a final and authoritative way. Every serious moral philosophy must have an answer to this question. But Kant claims that all moral philosophies other than his own are alike in one respect, which fatally compromises their attempt to define the basic law of morality.[3] To see what distinguishes Kant's answer from theirs, and to understand why he thought their answers all defective, we have to start by separating the two elements into which any maxim, or indeed any rule, may be analytically decomposed. These are its form and content.

The content of a rule defines its subject matter. It tells us what the rule is about. A rule that describes the diet of frogs is about frogs and what they eat. A maxim that enjoins the avoidance of fattening foods is about food. This is true no matter how high up in the hierarchy of maxims one goes. Higher-order imperatives, including even the fundamental law of morality itself, must have a content of some sort too, though a broader and more inclusive one than maxims lower down.

Every rule (and therefore every maxim) also has a form. The form of a rule is that feature or characteristic of it that makes it a rule rather than something else (for example, a statement of fact). Thus, if the content of the injunction to avoid fattening foods is food, its form is just the abstractness of the injunction itself: the generality of the command to avoid such foods in all cases to which the maxim applies. The specification of the jurisdiction of this maxim is the responsibility of some higher-order imperative, which has a different and more inclusive content (health as a whole, as opposed to food in particular), but whose form, as a maxim, is identical to that of the lower-order maxims it controls. Again, this will be true all the way up the hierarchy of imperatives. Even the basic law of morality must have a form that gives it the quality of "rulishness" that it shares with maxims of more restricted range.

The content of a maxim is therefore the differentiating element that distinguishes one moral rule from another. Yet the content of all maxims derives, Kant says, from a single source. This is desire. Every moral rule is *about* desire. It specifies whether a particular desire should be encouraged, repressed, refined or merely allowed to exist. This is easy to see in the case of a maxim proscribing the eating of certain foods. But it is also true of a rule enjoining one to be generous to others (to suppress the desire to exploit or ignore them); to vote in public elections (to check the wish to free ride on the participation of other voters); to treat animals with kindness (to take an interest in their well-being), and so on. Each of these is about desire too. In Kant's view, there is no other source from which the content of a maxim could possibly derive. Since even the most basic law of morality must have a content of some sort, it follows that it too has to be a rule about desire.

Desire can be defined more or less abstractly. The desire for fattening food is less general than the desire for food, which in turn is less general than the desire for health. Thus, while desire provides the content of every maxim at every level of generality, what distinguishes one level from another is the breadth with which the desire in question is defined. At the very top of the hierarchy of such maxims, the fundamental law of morality can only be a rule about desire in the broadest sense. Kant's term for this is "happiness"— the full and final satisfaction of all our desires, whatever they may be.[4]

But if the content of this law, like that of every maxim, derives from our desires (here, comprehensively defined), what is the source of its form? Kant's answer is that the form of the basic law of morality has its origin in the world-transcending power of abstraction that frees us from our desires sufficiently to allow us to take them as objects of reflection. This power is the source of the "rulishness" of every rule, including the fundamental law of morality.

The form and content of this law thus have their respective origins in the two components of our intermediate human being. The first has its source in reason, which we share with God, and the second in need or desire, which, as finite beings, we share with unreasoning animals. The combination of the two constitutes the setting or jurisdiction of morality. But in the case of any moral rule, including the very highest one, the normative stress may be placed on one component or the other. Either its content or form may be regarded as the "determining ground" of the maxim in question—as the reason for its authority. In this way, either side of our hybrid nature may be made the justificatory touchstone of moral judgment. It is the task of moral philosophy to decide which view is correct.

According to Kant, every moral philosophy (of which there are several) that takes the first approach and makes the content of the moral law its determining ground is flawed because it invites us to put our higher selves in service to our lower ones, employing the divine power of reason for the sake of desire. Only a moral philosophy that takes the second approach (of which, Kant claims, there is but a single version) properly honors the best part of our composite being, and is consistent with the very existence of morality itself, which only exists on account of the power of abstraction that makes it possible for us to ask what we ought to do with our desires.

The basic principle of morality in every moral system has to be *about* happiness, defined in general terms. It can have no other subject matter. Aristotle and Epicurus agree in this regard, though they differ in their understanding of what happiness means (the first defining it as the perfection of our natural powers, and the second equating it with pleasure). The same is true of modern utilitarians. Their highest principle is about happiness too, conceived as a property not of individuals but groups. Even Kant's basic principle of morality fits this general pattern. It also has to do with happiness. But the first three moral philosophies (perfectionism, hedonism and utilitarianism) are alike in one respect that distinguishes them all from Kant's. For the basic principle of each is not merely *about* happiness. Each also makes happiness the *determining ground* of morality—"that for the sake of which" one ought to act. Each treats happiness as the authorizing source of moral judgment and enjoins us to pursue certain goals *because* we have the desires we do.

Kant's morality does not. It makes the power of reason the sole determining ground of moral judgment. The regularity or "rulishness" of every rule, including the fundamental law of moral life, is the only component of it that is brought into being by the exercise of this power. By emphasizing the exclusive normative authority of reason, Kant therefore necessarily puts all the weight of moral justification on the form, rather than the content, of the rules we adopt as standards for the evaluation of our desires—so much so that their form becomes, for him, the only conceivable source of whatever moral value these rules possess.

Thus while Kant's highest moral principle is also about happiness, it does not make happiness the ground of morality, unlike the principles advanced by both pagan perfectionists and modern utilitarians. It instructs us to act in such a way that, whatever the *content* of the maxims we adopt as practical guides, we honor the divine part of ourselves that is the source of the form that every moral rule, however broad or narrow, necessarily displays. It commands us to judge the worth of our maxims by their *form alone,* for this is the only way, in Kant's view, that we can do justice to the world-transcending, godlike part of our being, rather than using it, as these other moralities do, to advance an end supplied by our worldly natures instead. From Kant's perspective, the use of reason for the latter purpose is more than a mistake. It is a perversion that reverses the proper relation between the higher and lower elements of our composite nature by putting the creative power we share with God in harness to needs that, however refined or distinctively human, all arise on account of the finitude we share with other creaturely beings.

UNIVERSALIZABILITY

Kant famously formulates the fundamental principle of morality as a test of universalizability. Act, he says, only according to that maxim "whereby you can at the same time will that it should become a universal law."[5]

Kant illustrates the operation of this principle with several examples, whose point is to show that some maxims cannot be universalized without contradicting themselves. Thus, if a man borrows money and promises to repay it, but secretly intends not to, he cannot will that everyone behave as he does, for that would undermine the practice of lending on which his own loan depends. In practical terms, the universalization of the rule he is implicitly following would contradict itself. Similarly, a man of means who is inclined to ignore the suffering of others cannot without contradiction will that everyone in such circumstances do the same, "inasmuch as cases might often arise in which one would have need of the love and sympathy of others and in which he would deprive himself, by such a law of nature springing from his own will, of all hope of the aid he wants for himself."[6]

Kant's universalizability test has often been criticized on the grounds that it is empty, and provides no real moral guidance of its own. Thus, in the two examples just considered, it is only because the conventional and natural worlds are arranged as they are, that one cannot coherently will to do something (defraud one's creditors, or ignore the suffering of others) and at the same time will that one's maxim be adopted as a rule by everyone else. But if the world were differently arranged, this might not be the case. If, for example, creditors were able to detect deceitful borrowers in the majority of cases, the fraud of one, or some, would be unlikely to bring the whole enterprise of lending down. A cheat could will that every borrower try to do what he himself is doing, hoping to succeed but knowing that the detection of most would-be cheats will leave the practice on which he depends intact. Likewise, if men were for the most part willing to forgo the help of others when it is needed (out of indifference or pride), it is hard to see what contradiction would be involved in a rule that excused one from helping others on the condition that they do the same. In both cases, whether the maxim in question is or is not universalizable depends on background factors that carry the real weight of the argument, whose outcome (Kant's critics argue) cannot be decided by the merely formal notion of universalizability itself.

Others have attempted to rescue the test by suggesting that its main function is to provide a barrier against what might be called "self-interested exceptionalism." The very essence of morality, they say, consists in not making an exception of oneself (unless, of course, one is prepared to do the same for others). Morality *means* treating oneself and others as having equal worth and rights, including the right, under certain circumstances, to assign one's own interests a special importance. On this view, the wrong of the fraudulent borrower consists in exempting himself from a rule he needs others to follow if his own fraud is to succeed. Similarly, the wrong of ignoring the pain of others lies in exempting oneself from a regime of mutual aid that others are expected to support, so that if a person is prepared to live with the consequences of his own misanthropy, he may not in fact be guilty of the kind of exceptionalism that, on this interpretation of Kant's test, it is meant to guard against.

The criticism of Kant's test as an empty formality and the defense of it as a way of policing against self-interested exceptionalism, are understandable in light of Kant's uneven and confusing exposition of the idea of universalizability itself. But both also miss the main point. The real purpose of the test is not to make the law of noncontradiction or the principle of equal treatment the fundamental basis of morality (however important these may be). It is to

compel the person applying the test to give exclusive weight in his moral judgments to the divine part of his being, which—as the source of the form of all
moral rules—alone possesses an intrinsic worth of its own.

Only the form of a maxim has inherent value because only it is attributable to the exercise of a power that is valuable in itself and not on account of
its relation to anything else. This is the godlike power of practical reason that
allows us to formulate rules for the government of our desires. In this respect,
our situation is like God's. There are many good things in the world that
God creates, but none of them is good in itself. The goodness of everything
good in the world derives from God's own intrinsic worth and exists only on
account of it. Our creative spontaneity is of course more limited than his. In
the cognitive sphere, it is constrained by the receptivity of our intuitions, and
in practical life by the givenness of our needs and desires. But just as only
God is intrinsically good in relation to the world he creates, the only thing that
can be good in itself in the realm of moral experience is the power of creativity that enables us to bring the form of the rules we frame for the regulation
of our desires, into being from nothing. All other moral goods are either
conditioned by or derived from this one. By focusing attention exclusively on
the form of the maxims we adopt—on their lawfulness *per se*—Kant's universalizability test thus forces us to put the entire weight of ethical judgment on
the divine side of our being and to disregard completely, so far as the moral
evaluation of our maxims is concerned, the creaturely side of human nature,
from which their content derives.

An example may help. A man is considering defrauding his creditor by
promising to repay a loan he has no intention of repaying. He asks himself
whether he can universalize the rule on which he proposes to act. Let us assume he concludes he cannot, for the reasons Kant suggests, and adopts a
maxim of honest dealing instead. Whether or not the borrower's desire to
cheat his creditor changes as a result makes no difference according to Kant.
The borrower may still *want* to do so, but this does not detract from the morality of his conduct, which depends entirely on his acceptance of the idea of
lawfulness in general as a standard of moral assessment.

By the same token, if his feelings undergo a revolution, and he ends up
wanting to be honest out of a benevolent regard for his creditor's interests,
that by itself adds nothing to the morality of his decision. If he adopts a rule
of honest dealing in order to increase his creditor's happiness (or his own, by
indulging his benevolent feelings), he makes the satisfaction of desire the
ground of his actions, and treats the rationality of the rule he adopts as a means

to it, rather than as something valuable in itself. In Kant's view, this deprives his maxim of any moral value it might have and perverts the enterprise of morality by placing the divine power of reason in the service of creaturely need.

In either case, the desires of the borrower are beside the point. They have no intrinsic moral salience. The only thing that has any moral value in itself is the form of the rule he adopts, and the reason why it alone has a value of this kind is that it is the only component of any maxim he might conceivably adopt that derives from the world-transcending "spontaneity of freedom" that puts him in the company of God.

This is even clearer, of course, in the case of a borrower who concludes that trying to cheat one's lenders is a maxim that *can* be universalized, on the assumption that few attempts of this sort are likely to succeed. His maxim is even more obviously bad. This is easier to see because the subjection of reason to desire is more apparent in this case than the last one. But however different they appear, Kant insists that from a moral point of view these two cases are essentially alike, for both subordinate the divine power of abstraction to something (infinitely) lower and incapable of ever possessing any intrinsic worth of its own. This is the mistake that Kant's universalizability test is meant to prevent by commanding us to focus on the form of our maxims alone.

There is one important complication worth noting. Because we are finite beings, we must attend to our needs in order to be able to exercise our godlike power of reason on anything like a significant scale. A life devoted to the satisfaction of basic needs leaves little room for either science or morality. It follows that we should do what we can to improve the material circumstances of human life, so that there will be more room for both. Indeed, Kant says we have a *duty* to do all we can to bring the world of finite existence into the closest possible alignment with our status as rational beings—to assure, so far as possible, that our "worthiness to be happy" coincides with happiness itself. Kant calls this coincidence "the highest good."[7] We shall examine its meaning more closely in the following chapter.

But it bears emphasizing that even though our duty to promote the highest good requires us to take an interest in the welfare of human beings (and therefore in their needs and desires), this interest is wholly derivative of our basic obligation to honor the divine side of our being. Far from implying that Kant believed the advancement of our creaturely interests could ever be of value in itself, it underscores his conviction that the only thing "in or out of

the world" that has an intrinsic value of its own is the power of practical reason which the fundamental principle of morality commands us to honor for
its own sake, albeit under the conditions of finite existence that constitute our
fate as human beings. Everything we do to make life in the world better for
men, we do for the sake of this power—the image or emblem of God's absolute will and, like it, not really of this world at all.

RESPECT

Kant proposes that we measure the authority of moral rules by their universalizability. This is not merely a logical test. It has a theological aim. It compels us to honor the divinity in our human being. Kant's second and third
formulations of the test make this clearer still.

The second states that we are always to act "as if" the maxim we adopt
"were to become through [our] will a universal law of nature."[8] In considering any maxim, we must ask ourselves how the world would look if the maxim
in question actually governed not only our behavior but that of everyone else.
Only those maxims whose adoption would produce a morally good result if
the behavior of every rational being in the world were in fact directed by them
pass this test.

Of course, we lack the power to bring about such a result on our own.
We cannot make the world be as we will. That is something only God can
do. God creates the world from nothing. We find or receive it as it is given to
us, in intuition and desire. But subject to these human limits, we too possess
a power of spontaneous creativity, and Kant's second formulation of the moral
law enjoins us to give this power an exclusive weight in evaluating the practical norms we might adopt by inviting us to imagine that we occupy God's
position as the creator of nature itself.

His third formulation reinforces the same theological ideal. The "supreme
practical principle" that ought to guide us in judging the moral worth of every
maxim rests, Kant says, on the belief that "rational nature exists as an end in
itself." It can therefore be expressed by the following imperative: "Act in such
a way that you treat humanity, whether in your own person or in the person
of another, always at the same time as an end and never simply as a means."[9]
Treating oneself and others in this way is what Kant calls "respect."[10]

Many "things" are useful to us as means, and there are no moral barriers
to our using them for whatever purpose we wish. By contrast, "persons" must
never be used solely as means. A person is a being who possesses the power of

reason. Through it, he or she transcends the world in thought and action. Every finite rational being is a person, as is God himself. The class of persons therefore consists of God, together with all those beings that resemble him on account of their (limited) power of creation—the source of the abstractness of the rules that in our case make both science and morality possible.

Because we are not God, and have needs, we are often compelled to use other persons as means. This regularly happens, for example, in contractual relationships. But in all our dealings with persons, ourselves included, we must remember that every finite rational being is the image of God and treat him or her accordingly. This imposes limits on the ways in which, and the purposes for which, a person may use himself or others. Kant explores the nature and contours of these limits in *The Metaphysics of Morals* and elsewhere. But all of Kant's writings on the subject are informed by his belief that a commitment to respect persons by honoring the godlike part of their being as the only one with any intrinsic value is the very essence of morality, from which we defect whenever we give precedence to the creaturely or finite side of our nature instead.

Thus, a man who resolves to kill himself if he becomes too unhappy employs his power of reason (which he uses to formulate this rule) in the service of his desire for happiness. He makes his happiness the ground of his maxim— "that for sake of which" he adopts it. In doing so, he turns the proper relation between his higher and lower selves upside down, and puts the God within him in chains to his worldly desires. He treats himself with disrespect.

A man who neglects to perfect his talents does the same. Through the perfection of our talents, we become better able to achieve the goal of treating all rational beings with respect—of honoring the divinity in them and us. That is because, as finite beings, we must pursue this goal under conditions that make its attainment difficult, and therefore have a duty to ease these where we can. This is clear in the case of material need, but the same applies to the obstacles created by ignorance, sloth and the like. We have a duty to relieve these as well, *so that* the respect we owe ourselves and others as godlike beings possessed of a world-transcending freedom may be easier to achieve and sustain. But if a person makes the perfection of his talents the *ground* of his actions—if he treats their perfection as something that has value in itself, for whose sake he does what he does—he acts with the same disrespect for himself as the man who neglects his talents, and indeed as the man contemplating suicide, for like them, he too subordinates his divine power of creativity to the refinement of his constitution as a natural being. He also assigns the givenness of his nature (which determines what talents he has) greater value than the power that enables him to transcend everything given in his makeup, like the would-be suicide who puts happiness before freedom.

Disrespect toward others is wrong for the same reason. A borrower who lies about his intention to repay his loan takes advantage of his lender's decision to trust him. Only a reasoning being can have this kind of trust. A dog will trust its owner if it has been well treated by him. The dog's trust is an acquired habit. The lender's trust, by contrast, is based, in part at least, on what the borrower tells him about his state of mind. The lender "takes the borrower's word for it." The borrower's past performance may augment the lender's trust. But this also rests on his reflective judgment that the borrower is telling him the truth. No irrational being is capable of making this judgment. To form the thought that something is true, one needs the power of abstraction that dogs and other irrational animals lack. The borrower's lie thus exploits the lender's reason to create a species of trust of which only rational beings are capable, *so that* the borrower's wish to be made happy by getting something for nothing can be fulfilled.

Here, as in the case of the man contemplating suicide and the one who lets his talents languish, reason is being used in a morally perverse fashion, as an instrument for the advancement of desire. Because it entails the subordination of the better part of human nature to an inferior one, the use of reason in this way is always self-abasing. The determination to avoid such self-abasement, and the revulsion one feels when it occurs, is what Kant means by respect.

As this last remark suggests, respect is for Kant not merely a principle but a feeling. He calls it a "moral" feeling, and acknowledges the paradox this implies. For how, Kant asks, can the belief that there is something in us that is better than all our interests, desires and feelings itself take the form of a feeling? How is it possible for us to desire to be moral, and to take an interest in having a good will? The claim that it *is* possible seems to presuppose the very link between desire and morality that is the mark of every philosophy (like Aristotle's) that makes human nature its standard. Kant was troubled by this question and devoted considerable effort to answering it. His fullest answer is to be found in the *Critique of Practical Reason,* where he describes respect as a feeling that arises out of the experience of "humiliation."[11]

According to Kant, the feeling of respect cannot precede the moral point of view or serve as its ground (which would be the case if moral actions were defined as those undertaken for the sake of satisfying the need this feeling arouses). Respect must rather follow upon the achievement of this point of view and be the result of reaching it, though once aroused it reinforces the commitment of the person whose feeling it is to act in a morally responsible way.

We come to feel respect for ourselves and other persons in the following manner.

Because we are finite beings with needs, various objects of "inclination" (of "hope" and "fear") force themselves upon us. The attainment of these is the earliest determining ground of our power of practical reason. It is "that for the sake of which" we employ this power. At the start, Kant says, our "pathologically determinable self" (the finite and therefore needy side of our being) strives to make its claims valid "as if it constituted our entire self."

But of course it does not. The use of reason itself makes this clear, even when it is employed in the service of need, for this is enough to demonstrate to a finite rational being that it is more than just need and desire. It is sufficient to show that it also possesses a power of abstraction that transcends all its desires and thereby provides an independent point of view from which their value may be judged. In this way, Kant says, the reason that is inherent in the human pursuit of desire "humiliates" the "self-conceit" that is implied in making our needy, pathological selves the ground of moral attention, and reminds us that we are something better than that.

A man who makes happiness (his own or that of others) the determining ground of his actions is conceited in this sense. He takes illegitimate "pride" in himself because he ignores the fact that happiness, in all its forms, is something we pursue only on account of our finitude as natural beings. He mistakenly regards the attainment of happiness as adequate to make our lives complete. In Kant's view, anyone who adopts happiness as his goal is therefore guilty of confusing a finite and conditional good with an infinite and unconditional one.

This is Kant's abstract version of the Christian sin of pride—the criminal longing for self-sufficiency with which the fall of man begins. Kant associates this longing with the pursuit of happiness as the highest good. Yet though the longing is universal, and cannot be escaped, the reason that is ingredient in every human action provides a built-in corrective to it by reminding us of what the pursuit of happiness always tempts us to forget: that there is something of greater value in us, which we must strive to honor by never allowing it to become the handmaid of creaturely need—as we do whenever we make happiness the ground of our actions.

This reminder is what Kant means by "humiliation." Humiliation is a negative feeling—an awareness that what one had thought worthy is not. But it has a positive aspect too: a reverence or respect for the world-transcending power of reason that allows, indeed compels, us to humiliate our finite selves in this way. Respect is a feeling of "self-approbation" that is "elevating" because it arises from the recognition of a power in ourselves that allows us to transcend the world, including our own selves insofar as we are finite beings within it, in the same way (though not to the same extent) that God does. It is an uplifting acknowledgment of one's likeness to God, and entails a corresponding devaluation of everything worldly in one's nature, which is drained of inherent value by the transfer of the source of all such value to a creative power beyond it. Respect recalls us to our true selves from the forgetfulness of our absorption in worldly things. It reminds us, as Augustine says, that our real home is not here but elsewhere, and we but pilgrims on the earth. And because respect is merely the positive side of humiliation, which reason delivers even to men of pride, it is a feeling that follows upon the experience that first gives rise to the moral point of view and does not precede it as its determining ground: Kant's autopoetic solution to the puzzle of how human beings can be motivated to be moral, without this motive being grounded in anything external to reason itself.

But if the feeling of respect is elevating in one way, it is belittling in another. The recollection of our likeness to God is at the same time a reminder of how far we are from him. We may aspire to "come into possession of holiness of will," and to be virtuous by nature, like God, who is "beyond all dependence." But we are finite beings in the world, and the effort fully to realize the godlike part of our being must be pursued under this condition. This remains for us a task that can never be fulfilled, even in a limitless period of time. In the meantime(!), we have no choice but to struggle to reach this unattainable goal, keeping before our eyes not only the infinite worth of the godlike power within us, but the shortfall between us and God, which compels us to work forever, in an earnest and dutiful way, to honor the better part of our selves.

Those who equate happiness with fulfillment thus not only demote the godlike part of their being to a position subordinate to that of their natural, desiring selves. They make the related mistake of affirming that such fulfillment is attainable in this world. They "fail to recognize" their "inferior position as creatures," and "deny from self-conceit the authority of the holy law." The truth is precisely the opposite. We are better than our natural selves, which means that the demand we impose on ourselves to honor our likeness to God can never be entirely met so long as we live in this world. Our moral condition is one of unfulfillment, not contingently but essentially. There can never be "world enough and time" for us to reach the goal to which the God within us calls. The recognition that this is so also belongs to the feeling of respect, which in this regard too is the antithesis of pride, whose puffed-up self-confidence is premised on the belief that we can be all that we are called to be, within the bounds of worldly life.

Kant contrasts those deformed by such self-confidence with the "humble common man"—an inspiring figure whose simplicity humiliates those filled with pride on account of their "superior position." There are also many extremely sophisticated philosophies of pride that make the human condition the touchstone of moral worth and affirm the possibility of reaching our highest goals here on earth. Kant calls these philosophies of "moral enthusiasm." The term is instructive. It implies a belief in the possibility of becoming divine. All the intellectualist philosophies of pagan antiquity affirmed this in one way or another. Aristotle's is a striking example.

Aristotle treats the human condition not merely as the setting of morality but its determining ground. He claims that happiness is the end of all human striving. It is that for the sake of which every man acts as he does. He insists, moreover, that human beings can be as happy in this world as it possible for them to be, and do not need to wait for another world and another life to be so. And he maintains that the highest happiness for human beings consists in their becoming, for a time at least, the divinity of the world they study as an object of contemplation. Kant condemns this whole complex of beliefs in the name of a moral philosophy that insists on the infinite gap between the human and divine—the inevitable result of a theology that starts with the idea of creation from nothing.

Our condition as finite rational beings, midway between the animals below and God above, is for Kant, as for Aristotle, the setting of morality. But the principle that on Kant's view defines how one ought to act within this realm makes respect for the divine part of our hybrid nature the exclusive ground of all goodness and virtue. And because Kant conceives this part of our being in the image of a God who transcends the world completely, our respect for it, so long as we live in the world, is bound to fall short in some way.

Aristotle's God does not transcend the world. It is just the intelligibility of the world itself, which we can comprehend completely, if only briefly, by turning our minds toward it. And because of this, it is possible for men, who like everything else in the world yearn to partake of the eternal and divine, to do so in a wholly fulfilling way during the period between birth and death, unless they are derailed by misfortune. Kant's rejection of our composite nature as the measure of morality; his claim that morality only begins with the repudiation of happiness as a final justification for the choice of any practical norm; and his ferocious insistence that our moral vocation cannot be fulfilled in this world, set his ethics apart from Aristotle's in the most radical way.

In the end, all these differences are due to a fundamental difference in their conception of the divine and our relationship to it. For Kant, God is a creator who brings the world into being from nothing. There is an unbridgeable chasm between him and us. For Aristotle, God is the everlasting mindedness of the world itself, whose being is wholly self-contained. We ourselves actualize it in thought. The ethical implications of this theological divide are already apparent in Augustine's *City of God*. Kant's great achievement is to have worked these out in a rigorously rational way, and thereby made them palatable to an enlightened age that demands that everything (God included) be justified before the tribunal of reason.[12]

Instead of a belief in the possibility of fulfillment in this life, Kant offers the prospect of endless movement, at the individual level, toward holiness of will, and at a social level toward a world reformed to facilitate the pursuit of this goal and the treatment of individuals in a manner commensurate with their attainment of it. This is the ideal of moral and material progress that to a large degree today still shapes the culture of Western civilization. Its theological underpinnings have now largely fallen away. But it is in origin and inspiration a Christian ideal that only makes sense against the background of the epochal shift in the conception of the eternal and divine that marks the divide between Aristotle's ethics and Kant's.

For us, the pursuit of this Christian ideal has become a human responsibility that no longer requires God's active involvement. It has become an innerworldly pursuit that we carry forward on our own, from one generation to the next, by means of science and law, without any need for that special form of divine assistance that Christians call grace, the humble acceptance of which was for both Augustine and Luther the soul of Christian piety. We live, today, in a graceless world, under the sign of a Christian ideal from which the God of Christianity has been exorcized like an unwelcome ghost.

In this respect, however, our situation is different from Kant's, who did so much to encourage the transformation of this ideal into an all-too-human value by insisting that the autonomy of human reason is the only truly divine part of our selves. Kant still believed in the necessity of grace. He thought that without God's help the project of individual and collective moral self-improvement is not merely more difficult but completely impossible. His brilliant attempt to explain the rational necessity of grace is the last such attempt before the concept loses all credibility among the proponents of enlightenment, and becomes the sole possession of those reactionary thinkers who have struggled, for two centuries, to stem the accelerating demands for human autonomy that Kant helped to unleash. The genius and failure of Kant's struggle to save a place for grace in his ethics of freedom is the subject of the following chapter.

CHAPTER 22

God Becomes a Postulate

REASON, FREEDOM AND KANT'S DEFENSE OF DIVINE GRACE

Human beings find the ground of the moral law in their own reason. The freedom they possess as rational beings defines the norm by which they ought to live and gives them the power to do so. Man's life as a moral being is in this sense self-contained. It is entirely autonomous. "Whatever does not originate from himself and his own freedom provides no remedy for a lack in his morality."[1]

In particular, human beings do not depend on God to tell them what to do or to give the moral law its binding force. They do not need God either to supply the content of the moral law or to sustain its authority. To suppose that men depend on God in either of these ways converts the moral law into a principle of heteronomy and thus deprives it of its only legitimate foundation.

Nor do men depend on God for their ability to do what the moral law requires. This is a power they already possess. There is never a moment at which it is not fully within the capacity of every mentally competent adult to make respect for himself and others as free and rational beings the determining ground of his actions. None of us can ever be sure that we have done this. There is always room for doubt about the purity of our motives for choosing the maxims we do.[2] But this is a cognitive, not a moral limitation. As rational beings, we do not depend on anyone other than ourselves for our ability to act as morality commands. The belief that only God can enable us to do so is completely incompatible with the idea of morality itself.

In this respect, Kant's morality is not merely free of theistic assumptions. It is incompatible with them. "[M]orality in no way needs religion (whether objectively, as regards willing, or subjectively, as regards capability) but is rather self-sufficient by virtue of pure practical reason."[3] Yet Kant *also* claims that morality "leads to religion," and does so not contingently or accidentally but "inevitably."[4] And he further claims that the religion to which morality leads is the Christian religion, properly understood. In the end, for Kant, a suitably purified Christianity is an essential adjunct to morality, and the grace of the Christian God a necessary "supplement"[5] in our endless struggle for moral perfection—propositions whose truth, he insists, can be demonstrated by reason alone.

How can a morality based on the autonomy of freedom be conditioned on the grace of God? For Kant, the answer lies in what he calls the "highest good in the world."

THE HIGHEST GOOD

Every maxim has both form and content. Its form is the product of reason. It is something we freely supply. The content of a maxim, by contrast, always derives from our desires and thus has its origin in our dependence or "receptivity." Happiness is the sum of all our desires. It constitutes our highest goal as finite beings. To make happiness the determining ground of our actions is therefore to give precedence to our finite or natural selves over the world-transcending, godlike power of reason in us. The moral law gives no weight to happiness at all.

The fact that morality cannot be based on happiness does not mean, of course, that I am never allowed to pursue it. Within a wide range, the moral law *permits* me to pursue my happiness as something not forbidden by it. There is nothing wrong with my satisfying my desire for food so long as I grow or purchase rather than steal it, though there is nothing inherently virtuous in my actions either.

It may even be true (though this is more debatable) that in certain cases the moral law *requires* me to take an interest in my happiness as an aid to the observance of this law itself. Extremes of pain or want make obedience to the moral law impossible except for the very strong. A person of ordinary powers therefore has a duty to avoid such extremes, so long as he can do so without violating the moral law itself. Of course, if I can meet my obligation to honor the divine part of my being only by completely ignoring my welfare, then that is what I must do. Yet short of this, morality often permits me to pursue my happiness as an allowable, if nonmoral, good, and may sometimes even require that I do so in order to equip myself for the rigors of moral duty itself.

Happiness is a good in these two limited and conditional ways. But for Kant it is a good in another, unconditional sense as well. For happiness, he claims, is a moral good in its own right, and hence one we have a *duty* to promote, *if* it is distributed on the basis of moral worth. Consider a world in which men are virtuous but unhappy. Kant insists that such a world is morally superior to one in which men are happy but lack virtue. But he regards a world of the first sort as morally inferior to one in which men are virtuous *and* happy in proportion to their virtue.

In general, for Kant, any world in which happiness and virtue are not aligned is less good, from a moral point of view, than one in which they are, and because of this, he concludes, morality itself demands that progress in virtue be accompanied by an increase in happiness that is keyed to the distribution of virtue itself. In the best of all possible worlds, all men will live, with a minimum of struggle, as the moral law requires and be as happy as their finitude allows. To reach this world, it is not enough that men be minimally happy—happy enough to be able to meet the demands of the moral law. They must enjoy a maximum of happiness, consistent with the degree of virtue they have achieved, and every human being, Kant says, has a moral duty to do what he or she can to help realize this state of affairs.

Kant calls this obligation a demand of "reason." Just as we are compelled as rational beings to acknowledge the supremacy of the moral law, so too, he says, we are forced by reason to conclude that a world in which the virtuous are as happy as their material circumstances allow is better than one in which they are less happy or not happy at all. This is not an empirical judgment but a requirement of reason alone, whose authority thus rests on the same foundation as the moral law itself.

In addition to our duty to obey the moral law, reason therefore imposes on us an obligation to promote "the highest good," which consists in a maximum of virtue accompanied by a maximum of happiness proportionate to it. Our duty to pursue this goal is both objective and universal. It is not conditioned on the particular needs we happen to have as individual men and women. It is not a hypothetical imperative that applies to some and not to others, whose violation represents at most a failure of prudence. It is a categorical imperative that applies to all finite rational beings and whose breach is a moral wrong—hence a duty that falls *within* the realm of moral obligation not outside it, in contrast to all those merely instrumental rules that instruct me to do this or that in order to satisfy my private, empirically contingent desires.

Kant's claim that we have a moral obligation to pursue the highest good raises an obvious question, given his account of the moral law. If this law has nothing whatsoever to do with happiness—indeed, is defined in opposition to it—how can it possibly be the case that we have a moral duty to promote human happiness, under any conditions at all? As finite beings, we cannot help but be interested in our happiness. But Kant repeatedly says that actions justified in terms of happiness lack all moral value, even if they outwardly conform to the requirements of the moral law (in which case they have legal but no moral worth). A person who wants to act morally must put his own happiness and that of others out of mind in choosing a fundamental principle by which to judge his maxims, and be prepared to stand by this principle even if he becomes unhappy as a consequence. This is a hard teaching, but only the person who is willing and able to endure great unhappiness for the sake of fidelity to the moral law may be said to be truly virtuous. How can it be, then, that Kant thinks we have a moral duty to promote the happiness of the virtuous?

Kant acknowledges the difficulty of the question and answers it with a distinction.

The concept of the highest good (the "*summum bonum*") contains, he says, "an ambiguity."[6] Highest "may mean either the supreme (*supremum*) or the perfect (*consummatum*)." The supreme good is the moral law. There is nothing that can take precedence over it. No amount of happiness can ever justify our suspending or violating the moral law. The duty it imposes is absolute. Virtue, which alone establishes our "worthiness to be happy," comes before everything else and we may not attend to our happiness, or that of others, until the requirements of the moral law have been fully met. Virtue is in this sense "the *supreme condition* of all . . . our pursuit of happiness and . . . is therefore the *supreme* good . . . ."[7]

"[I]t does not follow," however, that the attainment of virtue is "the whole and perfect good." There are goods other than this supreme one, and their attainment, though it can never be a reason for doing anything less than what virtue demands, adds to the good of virtue itself. It makes a whole greater than that even of its supreme part. This part enjoys a lexical priority in relation to the whole. Only when the good of virtue (of one's worthiness to be happy) has been secured may one go on to pursue other goods (all of which Kant gathers under the heading of happiness). But we are not merely free to pursue this more inclusive good once the requirements of the moral law have been met. We are morally obligated to do so, *on the condition that* the happiness we seek is correlated to virtue, that is, restricted to those (oneself included) who have first established their entitlement to it on account of their virtuous character.

If this condition is met, one has a positive duty to go beyond "mere" virtue, supremely important though it be, to a more complete and therefore perfect good that supplements the lexically first good of *worthiness* to be happy with *actual* happiness distributed on the basis of such worthiness, thereby curing the gap between virtue and happiness whose existence is such a striking feature of the world in which we live. A world in which this gap has been overcome Kant calls a "moral" world.[8] In it, the highest good has been fully achieved. Kant acknowledges that we can never reach this goal. But we are able, he says, to make steady progress toward it and have a moral obligation to go as far in this direction as we can, though in our efforts to do so we are not allowed to relax the rigors of the moral law by a single atom, or even, supposing that we ourselves are virtuous, to put our own happiness ahead of the achievement of a general distribution of happiness premised on virtue (whose attainment may require a sacrifice of individual happiness, in the same way that a devotion to the moral law often does).

By means of this distinction between perfect and supreme goods, Kant attempts to reconcile his resolutely anti-eudaemonistic account of the moral law with the claim that, under certain conditions, we have a duty to make the world a happier place. But one may still wonder why Kant thinks this a moral obligation rather than a counsel of self-interest. A man who has done all that morality requires will have an interest in being happy too. He will want to be happy and virtuous both. He will want other virtuous people to be happy as well. He will see the sum of virtue and happiness (theirs and his) as an inclusive good that is greater than the good of virtue alone, even if he grants that happiness, in the absence of virtue, is no good at all. But what justifies our saying that he has a *moral* duty to make the virtuous as happy as they can be? Why should we regard him as *morally* culpable if he fails to do so? Kant responds with a thought experiment.

> Assume a human being who honors the moral law, and who allows
> himself to think (as he can hardly avoid doing) what sort of world he

would *create,* were this in his power, under the guidance of practical reason—a world within which, moreover, he would place himself as a member. Now, not only would he choose a world precisely as the moral idea of the highest good requires, if the choice were entrusted to him alone, but he would also will the very existence of [such] a world, since the moral law wills that the highest good possible through us be actualized, even though, in following this idea, he might see himself in danger of forfeiting much in the way of personal happiness, for it is possible that he might not be adequate to what reason makes the condition for it. He would thus feel himself compelled by reason to acknowledge this judgment with complete impartiality, as if rendered by somebody else yet at the same time his own, and in this way the human being evinces the need, effected in him by morality, of adding to the thought of his duties a final end as well, as their consequence.[9]

"[T]o need happiness" (the condition of all finite beings), "to deserve it" (as all virtuous persons do), "and yet at the same time not to participate in it" (as is the case in any world, like ours, where virtue and happiness do not coincide) "cannot be consistent with the perfect volition of a rational being possessed at the same time of all power, if, for the sake of experiment, we conceive such a being."[10] No rational and all-powerful God would create a world in which virtue and happiness remain forever apart. He would have no reason for doing so and nothing to say to someone who questioned him about his choice. But God has a perfectly good explanation for creating a world in which virtue and happiness coincide (eventually, at least), since together these make a greater good than virtue alone. And because an omnipotent God can create any world he chooses, the world that God *has* created *must* be characterized by the eventual coincidence of these two things. Reason alone—which we share with God—makes this plain; and though we are not omnipotent, and must therefore struggle to do the right thing if we are to live in a way that honors the divinity in us, we have a duty to promote the coincidence of virtue and happiness that is the only rationally conceivable end of the world in which we actually live.

In Kant's thought experiment, three ideas come together. The first is that, like God, we too are rational beings. Kant sometimes expresses this idea by saying that both we and God are members of a kingdom of ends (we as subjects and he as sovereign).[11] The second is that the final coincidence of virtue and happiness is the only goal a world created by a rational and omnipotent

God could possibly have. And the third is that morality requires us to honor the godlike part of our being by doing all we can, as his fallible and finite creatures, to execute in time the purpose God must have had in creating the world in the first place—to work to achieve on earth that moral world whose realization constitutes the divine aim of creation itself.

Together, these three ideas explain why Kant thought the highest good a rational rather than an empirical concept. They explain why he believed that our pursuit of the highest good is a moral duty and not merely a prudent policy. And they bring to the fore the theological premise on which his account of this duty is based.

THE POSTULATES OF PURE PRACTICAL REASON

We have a duty to promote the highest good. This is something we ought to do. But "ought" implies "can." For Kant this is a fundamental axiom of morality. To demand that someone do something he cannot is, in Kant's view, wholly unintelligible.

In the case of the moral law, there is no question of our ability to do what we ought, however infrequently we do it and despite our irremediable lack of cognitive certainty as to whether we actually have. With regard to the highest good, however, things stand differently. Its realization is not a goal we can possibly achieve on our own. Yet we are morally obliged to pursue it. The only way that such an obligation can be rendered intelligible, therefore, is on the assumption that our inability to do what we ought to do will be made good by God, who alone can provide the (infinite) power needed to close the (infinite) gap that always remains between the moral command to achieve the highest good and our limited capacity to do so. This is Kant's argument, in summary form, for the rational necessity of what he calls the "postulates of pure practical reason"—for the rationality of belief in the immortality of the soul and the existence of God—through which religion is rejoined to morality as its indispensable complement.

Before we examine these postulates in more detail, it will be useful to recall where Kant's argument for them fits in the context of his critical philosophy as a whole.

Reason by its very nature demands that all our knowledge be "unconditioned," that is, perfect and complete. Knowledge that falls short of this can never satisfy the requirements that reason imposes on itself. In formal logic, for example, the derivation of a conclusion from certain assumptions (what we call a "proof") only leads to a demand for the proof of these assumptions themselves, and so on in an ascending hierarchy, until one arrives as a proposition whose truth depends on no assumptions and is therefore unconditioned.

The same is true, Kant says, in our investigation of the natural world. Here, too, reason compels us to ascend from our experience of particular things, each of which is preceded and therefore conditioned by other things in a series without end, to something that is not conditioned in this way and therefore cannot exist in time, as everything we encounter in experience does.

The experience we have of our own inner states follows the same pattern. We experience these one by one in a temporal sequence, but reason's demand for unconditional knowledge spurs us to seek a timeless ground for all of them—a "thinking nature" that "is self-sufficient and persisting through all possible changes of my state."[12]

Thus if in formal logic, reason of itself necessarily impels us ever higher in the chain of assumptions in search of a beginning that depends on nothing but itself, in the transcendental logic of experience, both outer and inner, it does the same. It drives us on until we arrive at the idea of an uncaused cause of the world and an eternal thinking substance underlying all my subjective states. These are the ideas of God and the soul. They are ideas that reason cannot help but propose to itself in its search for the unconditioned.

By the same token, however, the ideas of God and the soul can never have an experiential correlate. That is because the only experiences we can ever have either of external things or inner states are conditioned in some fashion. As receptive beings to whom these things and states are given in intuition, all our experience of them is limited in space and time. It is necessarily finite. We can therefore have no experience of the unconditioned, which by its very nature is spatially and temporally unlimited. In this respect, reason and understanding are fundamentally different, for the categories of the understanding not only have an experiential correlate, but must since they are themselves the organizing principles of experience itself. Hence, the awkward condition of human reason (in contrast to that of the understanding) is that in pursuit of its own self-imposed goals, it cannot help but form ideas of which there can in principle be no experience. The *Critique of Pure Reason* is an investigation of this awkwardness, which Kant poignantly describes in the first sentence of his preface to the first edition of it.[13]

Regarding the ideas of God and the soul, one may be either a "dogmatist" or a "skeptic." Dogmatists affirm the existence of both God and soul, and claim to possess some knowledge of their nature. In Kant's view, pagan metaphysics and Christian theology are equally dogmatic in this sense. But dogmatists make the mistake of thinking that these ideas, which reason unavoidably presents to itself, are representations whose correlates are available to us in experience and thus point to objects about which something can be known. The ideas of God and the soul have no experiential correlate, however, and there is therefore nothing we can ever know about them, in contrast to the operations of the natural world, which we are able to grasp precisely because they are constructed on the basis of rules we ourselves supply. Kant's demarcation of the limits of reason is meant to drain every species of dogmatism of the confidence with which it proceeds.

By the same token, however, Kant's argument deprives all skeptical philosophies of their confidence as well. A skeptic asserts that God and the soul can be shown not to exist. In this respect, he is a dogmatist in reverse, affirming the possibility of demonstrating the nonexistence of things whose existence the dogmatist claims to have proven. But the skeptic's dogmatism is no more warranted than the dogmatist's. We can know nothing about God or the soul—including whether it is true, as the skeptic claims, that they do not exist. The limits of human experience are such that both sorts of knowledge, the skeptic's as well as the dogmatist's, are forever beyond our reach.

As between dogmatism and skepticism, therefore, the debate must be left in a permanent state of indecision, not because the evidence is incomplete or inconclusive, but because the finitude of human beings, whose knowledge is always confined by intuition, makes them constitutively incompetent to judge the merits of these competing positions. The only coherent and responsible position, according to Kant, is the one he himself takes: the "critical" position that describes the dialectic created by reason's irrepressible demand for the unconditioned and the inevitable failure of this ambition in light of the unsurpassable finitude of the human condition.

Of course, the achievement of this critical position is itself an accomplishment of reason. It is the result of reason's self-critique. Though human reason lacks the resources to reach the goal of unconditioned knowledge that it sets for itself, it possesses all the powers it needs to assess its own limits and therefore to decide, unconditionally, whether there can be any speculative knowledge of God and the soul, either the positive sort the dogmatist claims or the negative knowledge of the skeptic. Reason's answer in both cases is "no." This answer can never be challenged, since the ideas of God and the soul are "merely creatures of reason"[14] whose availability as objects of experience reason needs nothing but itself to decide. This is the only absolute knowledge of God and the soul that we can ever attain, and though from one perspective it looks like a defeat, from another it represents a tremendous victory, the very pinnacle of human reason, the highest form of self-understanding available to us as finite rational beings, a knowledge won "by transcendental philosophy" that is both final and complete. In this respect, Kant believed his *Critique of Pure Reason* to be the last word on the subject.

But Kant also believed that when we abandon "the safe seat of critique,"[15] where as disinterested spectators we watch dogmatists and skeptics battle endlessly over the existence of God and the soul "in a play of merely speculative reason," and move to the challenges of practical life, where it is "a matter of doing or acting," we discover rational grounds for believing that both God and the soul exist, and thus find the warrant for a "hope" that speculative reason allows by proving the reality of these ideas to be undisprovable, but for which it itself provides no justification.

It is important, Kant says, for a "reflective and enquiring being" to devote part of his time to disengaged reflection, "withdrawing entirely from all partiality" (as Kant himself does in the *Critique of Pure Reason*).[16] But no one can maintain this posture of detachment forever. Eventually, we have to reenter the arena of practical life, where we are confronted with the question of what we ought to do. Sometimes this question has a merely technical character. ("Which of these tools should I use to drive nails, a screwdriver or a hammer?") But sometimes it is a moral question. ("Should I give my hand to a man in distress if I can do so only at some risk to myself?") Every thinking being confronts moral questions of this kind in the sphere of practical life and in answering them will inevitably be led, Kant says, to the idea of an obligation that is completely independent of happiness in all its forms.

This duty is expressed by the moral law, which commands us always to act with respect for ourselves and others as free and rational beings. The reality of this law, in the realm of "ought," is as indubitable as the reality of those experiences of the natural world that the *Critique of Pure Reason* takes as its phenomenal starting point in the realm of "is," and for which it seeks to provide a transcendental justification by explaining how these experiences are possible at all. In the practical realm the parallel transcendental problem is that of identifying the conditions necessary for the possibility of the moral law, whose existence can no more be denied than that of my experience of a world outside me in the domain of cognition. Kant solves this problem by concluding that the moral law is intelligible only on the assumption that we are free, for a law that commanded us to do something we were incapable of doing would in his view make no sense at all.

The reality of freedom is as unprovable by speculative reason as that of God and the soul. That is because the idea of freedom is also of something unconditioned. If a free act depends in any way on something other than itself, then it is by definition no longer free. A free act is therefore one that necessarily exists outside the whole series of conditions that determine relations among things and events in the world of experience. But this means there can be no confirmation, in experience, of the real existence of freedom—any more than of God or the soul.

In the practical realm, however, the idea of freedom has a direct and obvious reality these other ideas do not. If freedom were unreal, the very existence of this domain, which we have no choice but to take for granted in all our moral deliberations, would itself be incomprehensible. That we regard ourselves as bound by the moral law is a fact of practical life. It is the most important fact of this kind. And it allows us to infer, with transcendental certainty, that the reality of freedom is, for practical purposes, a fact as well. In the sphere of practical life, Kant says, freedom is a "fact of reason."[17] Among the three ideas of freedom, God and the soul, it is the only one that enjoys this status.

If we are to have rational grounds for the belief that from a moral point of view the latter two ideas possess as much reality as that of freedom, it is therefore necessary to show that they can be deduced from it with the same transcendental necessity as freedom itself can be derived from the existence of the moral law. Kant's deduction of the postulates of pure practical reason is an attempt to do precisely this. Using the practical reality of freedom as a springboard, he argues that the ideas of God and the soul must have the same kind of reality too. His conclusion is that all three ideas are transcendental conditions of the existence of a moral realm, which thereby becomes a religious realm, since the ideas of God and the soul, unlike that of freedom, carry us beyond the world of merely human things to the divine and everlasting.[18]

This, then, is the context of Kant's deduction of the postulates, which completes the project of his critical philosophy as a whole, whose aim Kant famously describes in the preface to the second edition of the *Critique of Pure Reason* as that of denying "*knowledge* in order to make room for *faith.*"[19] The key to Kant's deduction is the idea of the highest good, coupled with the principle that "ought" implies "can."

Compliance with the moral law establishes our worthiness to be happy. It is what makes a man virtuous. This is "within everyone's power at all times."[20] So far as virtue is concerned, therefore, we need no supplement to our power to achieve it. But virtue is merely the supreme component of a more perfect good that consists in virtue accompanied by happiness proportionate to it. This is the highest good, which we have a "duty" to strive "to produce and promote."[21]

But though it is conditioned on virtue, the happiness the highest good includes as one of its components is not within our own power to attain in the way that moral virtue is. This is strikingly obvious at an individual level. We are able to make ourselves virtuous merely by affirming the moral law. This requires fortitude and determination but is something we can do by ourselves. None of us, by contrast, has the power to assure that he or she will be happy. This depends on circumstances beyond our control, and no matter how much progress we make in securing the conditions of our happiness, we always remain vulnerable to disappointment.

The same is true at a social level. The conditions of human living may improve steadily, but there is no program of social betterment that can make us invulnerable to unhappiness. Moreover, there will always be an imaginable level of happiness greater than the one we presently enjoy. There will always be more happiness to be had.

Our permanent vulnerability to disappointment and the gap that always remains between how happy we are and how happy we might be are consequences of our limitations as natural beings. It is only in the godlike part of our being that these limits vanish. The moral law, standing by itself, commands us to pay attention to this part alone. But the highest good, which we also have a moral duty to pursue, requires that we join the worthiness to be happy with happiness itself. It demands that we bring the two parts of our being—the infinite and the finite—into a coordinated alignment. But this can only be done by increasing happiness to a maximum, and by conditioning its distribution perfectly on virtue, and *that* is *not* a state or condition we can ever achieve our own. Hence, if the realization of the highest good is to be a moral obligation for us, as finite rational beings, this shortfall in our power must somehow be overcome, for otherwise the "ought" of our duty to realize it will be rendered senseless by the fact that we cannot.

The deficit in our power to achieve the highest good can be repaired, Kant says, only on two conditions. The first is that we have an endless time in which to pursue it.

One of our disabilities, as finite beings, is the limited span of time we have to attain any of our goals. A human life is only so long. It is never long enough to achieve either that state of moral perfection in which the first component of the highest good consists, or to reform the world so as to produce a state of happiness commensurate with it (the second component). At the end even of a very long life that has been as virtuous and productive as a human life can be, there will still be a shortfall between aspiration and achievement in both respects.

If we were doomed to fail in this way, the command to realize the highest good would lose all meaning. We must therefore suppose that the time we have to pursue it is not limited to a single human lifetime, but is endlessly long, so that we are able to approach the goal to an ever greater degree and never have to resign ourselves to the disappointment of having gotten only so far. And this supposition is intelligible, Kant argues, only on the further assumption that the moral agent charged with the responsibility for achieving this goal itself endures, unchanging, through an endless stretch of time, and does not go out of existence at any moment in it (for example, at the moment of death). Thus, the first condition on which the intelligibility of the command to pursue the highest good depends is the immortality of the souls of those to whom the command is addressed.

But even this is not enough to make its attainment possible. The most that one can do, even in a limitless extent of time, is approach the goal more closely. To close the gap completely, one would have to have complete control over the world as a whole. Only then could the achievement of a maximum of happiness distributed on the basis of virtue be guaranteed. But no matter how great our powers over nature become, they will always be less than complete. Our ability to ensure that the virtuous are as happy as they can be must therefore remain incomplete, so long as we rely on our finite powers alone. To cure their inadequacy and reach the highest good that is the final end of all our striving, we must assume that if we do all we can to reach it, the gap that inevitably remains will be closed by an infinite power that offers itself in aid to our own.

This power, moreover, cannot be one *in* the world and time, for then it would be as conditioned and limited as ours. To have perfect control over the world, the power on whose supplemental help we depend to attain the highest good must be that of *the world's creator,* for only a being that has created the world from nothing can have infinite control over it and thus be in a position to give our finite powers the assistance they need to achieve the highest good. If we have a moral duty to reach this goal, and if ought implies can, then we are bound by reason to assume the existence of God, understood in the way the children of Abraham do. Together with the assumption of the immortality of the soul, that of God's existence (conceived in these terms) is therefore a second necessary condition for the possibility of our being under an obligation to reach an end that reason prescribes to us but which our finitude makes it impossible to attain on our own.

This is Kant's deduction of the two postulates of pure practical reason. *If* freedom is a "fact of reason" that the phenomenon of moral duty compels us to acknowledge; *if* reason itself forces us to conclude that our final and most comprehensive duty is the promotion of a moral world in which all are worthy to be happy and as happy as they are worthy to be; *if* the obligation to do this, like any obligation, is meaningful only in case we have the power to comply; *if* our power to achieve the highest good requires an endless stretch of time in which to pursue it *and* the supplemental help of an infinite power whose perfect control of the world is conceivable *only* on the assumption that he is its creator, *then* the immortality of the soul and the existence of God are themselves assumptions that are rationally required by morality itself. *Then,* starting from freedom as a fact of reason in the sphere of practical life, we can demonstrate the rational necessity, within this same sphere, of these other two ideas as well. *Then* we have rational grounds to hope that these ideas have objective correlates—a judgment that speculative reason must leave in suspension and gives us no grounds to affirm. *And then* we must concede the truth of Kant's claim—on the surface so surprising in light of his insistence on the link between morality and autonomy—that morality *inevitably* leads to religion.

FREEDOM AND GRACE

Aristotle believes that virtue is something that (in Kant's words) we acquire "little by little" through "long habituation" and a gradual "change of *mores*."[22] That is why a good character is only achieved slowly and also why it is generally slow to disintegrate or disappear. In Aristotle's view, the phenomenon of virtue is one that necessarily exists in time, like that of growth in general, which cannot be conceived apart from the time it takes to occur.

Kant's view is different. A man becomes virtuous, he says, only by freely affirming the moral law. This alone makes him "worthy" of respect, however much we may admire his other talents and gifts. To have any moral value at all, this act of affirmation must be completely spontaneous. But that means it cannot occur in time, for everything that does is conditioned by something else. From the standpoint of the endless succession of events in time, the act of will by means of which a man becomes morally virtuous can therefore only be conceived as occurring instantaneously, in a "revolution" of the soul as distinguished from the gradual process of "reform" through which, on Aristotle's view, one grows into the mature and settled habits that constitute a virtuous character.

The difference between Kant's conception of virtue and Aristotle's reflects the central role that Kant assigns the will in moral life. The idea of the will as a power of spontaneous creation has no place in Aristotle's philosophy. What first makes it plausible, and then compelling, is the doctrine of divine creation from nothing. More exactly, the concept of divine creation *is* the idea of will, which only needs to be transplanted to the field of human action in order to provide a new center for our understanding of ethical life. Kant's claim that virtue is founded on a revolutionary act of will, rather than the slow reform of mores, is a consequence of the shift in ethics that occurred when the Christian theology of creation displaced the older pagan identification of God with the world, and the conception of human fulfillment as a process of growth experienced and exhibited in time.

Kant himself describes this act in explicitly Christian terms. He calls it the putting on of "a new man."[23] When one freely and spontaneously affirms the moral law, he says, the sinful "old man" that one was immediately dies away. One's older self, whose identity was founded on its natural desires, ceases in an instant to exist and is replaced by a new self based on the moral law instead (on identification with the divine part of one's being). Like Saul's conversion to Paul, this transformation happens "in no time at all." The revolution that Paul experienced on the road to Damascus is Kant's model for every instantaneous act of will by which a man becomes worthy of respect.

The great challenge for Kant is to explain how the putting on of a new man, which is not an event in time, can be related to those acts and events that are. This is not a problem for Aristotle. In his view, virtue is temporal by nature. As a result, he never even recognizes conversion as an ethical phenomenon. Nor is it a problem for Kant, so far as mere *worthiness* is concerned. Whether or not I am worthy to be happy has nothing to do with the consequences of the spontaneous act of will through which I become a virtuous man. I can never know with certainty that my will is good, but for it to *be* good, nothing need happen in time as the result of my willing. The latter has a moral value that is wholly self-contained, like "a jewel shining in the night." Where the question is one of worthiness alone, I therefore have no reason to be troubled by the metaphysical difficulty of linking the worldless, timeless act of will in which such worthiness consists to events that take place in the world and time.

In the case of my duty to promote the highest good, however, these difficulties cannot be avoided. My resolution to do all I can to reach this goal may be an act of will outside of time. But the highest good itself includes two goals that can only be pursued in time and the worldly order constituted by it. My obligation to pursue the highest good is therefore meaningful only in case I am justified in assuming some positive connection between my will and the world, for otherwise the duty to pursue it establishes an "ought" without a demonstrable "can."

The first of these goals is the attainment of a maximum of happiness, distributed in proportion to virtue. This is a worldly state of affairs whose realization, though never fully complete, can only be approximated in time.

The second is the attainment of a maximum of virtue. In one sense, of course, a good will is always as good as it can be. This follows from the nature of the act that makes it good, namely, the spontaneous decision of an autonomous will that depends on nothing other than itself to do the right thing. But in another sense, it is possible to speak of making progress in virtue. Even the best finite will must struggle against inclination. It does not act virtuously by nature. Only God does that. To do the right thing by nature and not in response to a command is holiness of will. We can never attain perfect holiness of will, but we can train our natures to be less resistant to the demands of the moral law, and insofar as we succeed, we approach God's nature by increasing degrees.

Such training resembles the habituation in virtue that Aristotle describes, though with a crucial difference—that it is in service to a nontemporal power of spontaneous willing that has no place in Aristotle's philosophy. Still, keeping this difference in view, it is appropriate to speak of a person making progress toward holiness of will in Kant's sense by acquiring a sensuous nature that increasingly conforms to his super-natural status as a free and rational being. Like the progressive movement toward a maximum of happiness distributed in accordance with virtue, this one too takes place in time. In both these respects, therefore, the command to promote the highest good obliges us to undertake a campaign that can only be pursued *in* the world, though the commitment to do so is an act that occurs *outside* it. If this commitment is not to be rendered senseless by the fact that it can never be fulfilled, two related problems must be overcome.

The first is that things do not always go as I will. I will to reform my nature so that it better conforms to my dignity as a free and rational being, and to improve the world so that the distribution of happiness is aligned more closely to that of virtue. But I often fail in both respects. Indeed, there is no guarantee that I will *ever* succeed. My entire career may be nothing but a series of dismal failures, in which I never make the least progress toward either my moral betterment or the material improvement of the world. None of these worldly failures has any bearing on the worthiness of my will. This is determined solely by my timeless resolution to do the right thing. But in order for me to be able to respond in a meaningful way to my duty to promote the highest good, I must be able to assume that my timeless act of willing has some purchase on the temporal order of things.

The second problem is that even if I make uninterrupted progress toward the highest good, it cannot be reached in time. That is because it is defined by the final coincidence of the moral and natural orders as a whole—by the union of will and nature, God and man, eternity and time. The unsurpassable distinction between the infinite and the finite makes the attainment of this coincidence impossible. Hence, even if I am confident that I can make real progress toward the highest good, its final realization remains for me and other finite rational beings a hopeless assignment.

When I commit myself to the pursuit of this goal, what grounds do I therefore have to hope that I can reach it, in the world and time, where the shadow of failure hangs over me at every instant, and even a string of uninterrupted successes leaves the gap between what I have done and what I ought to do as great as it was before? By now, Kant's answer should be clear. If I am to be able to hope that my duty to promote the highest good is not a cruel impossibility, I must be able to count on help in overcoming these difficulties. No other finite being, or set of such beings, can provide the help I need. This must come from God, for he alone possesses the infinite power that is required to achieve the union of eternity and time that reason commands me to pursue.

Morality demands of us only what we are able do. Clearly, we have the ability to make a commitment to achieve the highest good. But our spontaneous and therefore timeless resolution to do so is bound to fail of effect in the realm of time, where the highest good must be pursued. Yet the inevitably of our failure need not leave us hopeless. That is because God, who sees the totality of time in an intuitive instant, takes as done what we in a spontaneous act of will commit ourselves to doing but lack the ability to achieve in any period of time. In this way, God supplements the comparative power-lessness of our good wills with the power we need to meet our obligation to achieve the highest good under the disabling conditions of time. From his vantage point outside of time, he closes, on our behalf, a gap we are commit-ted to closing but, as temporal beings, cannot.

God is able to do this because, as the creator of the world, his power knows no bounds. And we are entitled to hope that his help will be forthcoming because reason itself tells us this must be the case. Reason declares that we are entitled to hope for God's grace, so long as we freely will to pursue the high-est good, since a world in which we were obliged to do something we could not would be irrational (as anyone who considers what world *he* would create if he himself were God is bound to see).

In this way, grace is not merely assigned a place in Kant's moral philoso-phy. The principles of grace and freedom are made mutually supportive. The morally virtuous exercise of our freedom in affirming a commitment to the highest good becomes, in Kant's view, the warrant for the divine help we need in order to fulfill, in time, the task we set ourselves when we make this com-mitment. Human freedom ceases to be a threat to the grace of God (as Luther had insisted it must always be) and becomes the *sine qua non* of its dispen-sation instead. And most strikingly, perhaps, human reason, which Luther de-spised for its prideful pretensions, becomes the vehicle by which we are able to grasp and articulate this supportive relation between freedom to grace, and thus to supply an intelligible ground for the hope we demand in our moral lives but that speculative reason, though clearing the space for its possibility, can never provide.

THE CHURCH TRIUMPHANT

Each of us has a moral duty to promote the highest good. This is an obli-gation that falls on us as individual human beings, even though the end we are obliged to pursue is a state of the world that includes the virtue and hap-piness of others as well as our own. Still, in our individual efforts to reach this goal, it is essential that we act as a community of morally responsible per-sons. This is true for two reasons.

First, the highest good demands that our sensuous natures be brought into closer alignment with the requirements of the moral law. It also demands a steady improvement in our material well-being. The betterment of the world in both respects requires power. But the power we have as individuals is severely limited. By joining with others, we can increase our power exponentially. Every program of moral or material betterment, of any magnitude and durability, is a collective achievement that no individual can reproduce on his own, even though it is and remains his wholly individual responsibility to support it.

Second, "the propensity to evil in human nature"[24] dramatically increases in society. It is not rooted in our "raw," presocial inclinations. These are not bad in themselves, and morality does not consist in eliminating or suppressing them (as the Stoics wrongly believed). The only thing that can ever be morally bad in itself is the act of will by which a rational being makes his inclinations the determining ground of his actions. The responsibility for doing so is his alone. But the *temptations* to such an act of moral self-destruction are far greater in society. Indeed, Kant implies that they only arise when one enters the sphere of social life (an argument he borrows from Rousseau).[25]

> If he searches for the causes and the circumstances that draw him into this danger and keep him there, he can easily convince himself that they do not come his way from his own raw nature, so far as he exists in isolation, but rather from the human beings to whom he stands in relation or association. It is not the instigation of nature that arouses what should properly be called the *passions,* which wreak such great devastation in his originally good predisposition. His needs are but limited, and his state of mind in providing for them is moderate and tranquil. He is poor (or considers himself so) only to the extent that he is anxious that other human beings will consider him poor and despise him for it. Envy, addiction to power, avarice, and the malignant inclinations associated with these, assail his nature, which on its own is undemanding, *as soon as he is among human beings.* Nor is it necessary to assume that these are sunk into evil and are examples that lead him astray: it suffices that they are there, that they surround him, and that they are human beings, and they will mutually corrupt each other's moral disposition and make one another evil.[26]

Immorality is therefore a social disease that requires a social cure. It must be fought through the establishment of an "ethical community"[27] devoted to strengthening the "moral disposition" that society itself corrupts. Respect for the moral law can only be sustained in such a community. The same is true of our obligation to promote the highest good. The duty to do this falls on

our shoulders one by one. But we can only pursue it collectively and collaboratively as members of an ethical community striving to achieve the closest
possible approximation of each to God's holiness of will, accompanied by a
distribution of happiness based on the worthiness for it.

The ethical community whose establishment the moral law demands is
not a religious one. Nothing is required for it other than a belief in the dignity of all persons and a commitment to the principle of universal respect. By
contrast, if our duty to promote the highest good is even to be intelligible, we
have to assume that the soul is immortal and believe in the existence of an
author of the world whose grace makes up the difference between our power
to will the highest good and our inability ever fully to achieve it. The ethical
community that is required for *this* duty to be supported must therefore be a
religious one as well. It has to be a "church."[28] Only a church provides the
communal setting that human beings require in order to sustain the beliefs
on which our duty to pursue the highest good depends.

These beliefs have a rational foundation. Kant maintains that human beings nevertheless require their "grounds" to be represented in a form "that *the
senses can hold on to*."[29] This is a consequence of our finitude. Like all ideas of
reason, those of God and the soul can never be captured in an intuition. Yet,
as a practical matter, we must believe in their truth if we are to be able to
hope that we can do our duty to achieve the highest good. It is therefore essential that they be given a determinate shape of some sort that makes it possible for them to exert a practical influence in our lives. "[F]or the human
being," the postulates of practical reason need "to be represented through
something visible (sensible) . . . for the sake of praxis and, though intellectual,
made as it were an object of intuition (according to a certain analogy)."[30]

It follows that even a purely rational religion (i.e., one that endorses only
those beliefs whose necessity reason itself is able to show) must first take
the form of an "historical ecclesiastical faith"[31] based on specific experiences,
reports, traditions and ceremonial routines. It must first take the form of
a *revealed* religion which, like all religions of this sort, bases the truth of
its convictions not on reason alone but on a command or utterance from
"beyond"—one that, from the standpoint of reason, must always appear
irrational, since it claims authority regardless of what reason declares. Only in
this way can the postulates of practical reason become the basis of an actual
religious community and thereby enter the historical life of humankind.

There is an obvious tension, though, between the conditions under which
a rational religion is bound to emerge and its essential nature. The historical

revelation that is required to establish its existence as a church, and the liturgical traditions that evolve in response to it, will always be specific to a time, place and people. They will always form the basis of a particular religious community whose rituals and creed set it apart from other communities of this sort. But a religion of reason is not the sole possession of any particular group. It belongs to everyone. It is, by its very nature, a universal church since it is founded on principles that can be deduced by reason alone, hence ones that every rational being can discover for him- or herself. Nor can these principles be justified by appeal to a revelation of any kind. To do so contradicts the rational foundation on which their authority rests, and converts them into principles of heteronomy instead. It may be that a religion whose postulates are founded on reason alone can only come into being in the form of an ecclesiastical faith. But the specificity of such a faith, and its dependence on a revelation that is incompatible with the autonomy of reason, means that it is in conflict from the start with the rational religion it carries within it.

The "true church" will therefore be one that gradually works itself free of its peculiar historical origins and of the special revelation with which it begins. Its history will be one of liberation—of the ever more complete detachment of the universal, rational religious community it implicitly contains from the limits of its own original doctrines and routines.

> [H]istorical faith (which is based upon revelation as experience) has only particular validity, namely for those in contact with the history on which the faith rests, and, like all cognition based on experience, carries with it the consciousness not that the object believed in *must* be so and not otherwise but only that it *is* so; hence it carries at the same time the consciousness of its contingency. This faith can therefore indeed suffice as an ecclesiastical faith (of which there can be several); but only the pure faith of religion, based entirely on reason, can be recognized as necessary and hence as the one which exclusively marks out the *true* church.—Thus, even though (in accordance with the unavoidable limitation of human reason) a historical faith attaches itself to pure religion as its vehicle, yet, if there is consciousness that this faith is merely such and if, as the faith of a church, it carries a principle for continually coming closer to pure religious faith until finally we can dispense of that vehicle, the church in question can always be taken as the *true* one; but since conflict over historical dogmas can never be avoided, it can be named only the church *militant,* though

with the prospect at the end of flowering into the unchanging and all-unifying church *triumphant!*[32]

In Kant's view, only the ecclesiastical faith of the Christian church meets this requirement. It alone contains within itself "a principle" for its own purification—for the progressive liberation of its universal, rational message from the cultic orthodoxies that historically set it apart from other religious communities.

The essential "teachings" of Christ, according to Kant, are "pure doctrines of reason" that "carry their own proof." These include Christ's insistence "that not the observance of external civil or statutory ecclesiastical duties but only the pure moral disposition of the heart can make a human being well pleasing to God (Matthew 5.20–48); that sins in thought are regarded in the eyes of God as equivalent to deed (5.28) and that holiness is above all the goal for which the human being should strive (5.48); that an injustice brought upon a neighbor can be made good only through satisfaction rendered to the neighbor himself, not through acts of divine service," and so on.[33] In Kant's view, Christ taught a morality of "pure dispositions," though he also insisted that the purity of heart in which all true virtue consists "be demonstrated in *deeds* (5.16)," and thereby "rebuff[ed] the crafty hope of those who, through invocation and praise of the supreme lawgiver in the person of his envoy, would make up for their lack of deeds and ingratiate themselves into his favor (7.21)."[34]

In this way, Christ laid the foundation for a "universal religion of reason" based on principles that constitute "the supreme and indispensable condition of each and every religious faith."[35] The Christian church of course has its own distinctive dogmas and routines. But only here, Kant claims, do the universal principles of a strictly rational religion serve as the organizing premise of an ecclesiastical tradition, whose "statutes" and "forms and observances" must be evaluated from the point of view of the rational moral order they represent and call to mind.

Given the limitations of human beings, it was at first necessary to add these outward trappings as a "means for the establishment of a church founded upon those [universal] principles."[36] In this respect, Christianity is no different from any other religion. But among the historical faiths that human beings have followed, it alone rests on a morality of pure reason that gives its adherents the leverage they need to free themselves from the slavish belief that their religion is based on the specific practices and peculiar dogmas that set Christianity apart from other faiths.

The contrast with Judaism is particularly sharp. The Jews could not "conceive their obligation [to obey the moral law] except as directed to some *service* or other which they must perform for God—wherein what matters is not the intrinsic worth of their actions as much as, rather, that they are performed for God to please him through passive obedience, however morally indifferent the actions might be in themselves."[37] The attitude of the Jews, as Kant conceives it, was therefore precisely the opposite of the one demanded by Christ, who therefore cannot be regarded as a successor to the Jewish prophets and priests from whom, for the sake of accrediting his own mission in terms his followers would understand and accept, he initially claimed descent.

In Kant's retelling of the story, it was not the Jews who prepared the way for Christ but the "Greek sages," whose "moral doctrines on freedom" gradually "gained influence" among the Jews, inducing them to "reflection," thereby making them "ripe for a revolution" in their attitudes and beliefs. It was in this environment of increasingly rationalized moral reflection that Christ appeared, teaching an ethics of autonomy unknown to the Greeks but one for which their insistence on philosophical self-knowledge set the stage. In Kant's view, Christ's real predecessors were therefore not the Jewish kings of old, let alone the temple priests of his own day, but the Stoic philosophers of pagan antiquity, whose aspiration to establish a morality based on reason alone Christ finally achieves, by employing a biblical conception of freedom unattainable within the limits of Greek thought.

With Jesus Christ, therefore, an ecclesiastical faith appears for the first time in human history that is not only *capable* of outgrowing the peculiar circumstances of its origins, but that is *driven* to do exactly this by its own deepest principles, which base all religious obligations on a morality of pure reason. In the subsequent history of the Christian faith, many in the church have been tempted to return to the essentially pre-Christian belief that salvation consists in the performance of various acts of "divine service," regardless of the moral attitude that accompanies them. But those who take this view fall back into what Kant regards as a state of ethical confusion, taking the outward deed to be the thing that is of moral and religious worth, rather than viewing it as a mere "demonstration" of that inner state that alone possesses such value. Kant describes this confusion as a species of "fetishism"[38] that mistakenly identifies a visible object with the invisible source or ground of its value, and calls the religiously inspired service of those who make this mistake a "counterfeit" service,[39] in contrast to the genuine service of those who seek only to give a symbolic presence in the world to those other-worldly "dispositions" from which all true moral value flows.

But though this tendency to backsliding has never disappeared (and for long periods in the history of the church has been a dominant force), it runs, Kant says, against the grain of the animating core of Christian belief. The latter has always reasserted itself as a countertendency in favor of a purely rational religion based on moral principles "that human beings *could and ought to have* arrived at on their own through the mere use of their reason, even though they *would* not have come to it as early or as extensively as is required" if a "revelation" of these principles had not been given to mankind at a particular "time" and "place."[40] In Kant's view, this countertendency is the true destiny of the Christian religion which (to put it paradoxically) is *distinctive* among the religions of the world in the *universalizing* nature of its own deepest commitments, whose authority binds every human being, Christian and non-Christian alike, because it rests on reason alone, and not on any revelation purporting to disclose the commanding word of God, or on a system of rites and rituals that require us to serve God in any way other than by living a moral life according to the demands of reason itself.

From this, Kant draws a conclusion about the meaning of grace in particular.

It is of course wrong to suppose that in order to win the favor of God, one must perform certain sacramental or other acts. Such a belief is hostile to the true spirit of the Christian religion. It represents a form of fetishism and makes a counterfeit of the service to which Christ called his followers. In this respect, Kant and Luther are in agreement. They also agree that human beings cannot do all they are obliged to do without the help of God, and that God's grace is therefore a necessary supplement to morality. But Kant's conception of Christianity—as a rational religion contained within an ecclesiastical faith whose sensuous forms men need, at first, to help them grasp and follow the pure principles of reason that lie at the core of their faith but which, in time, they come to see as having no value in themselves—leads him to a view of grace that is an exaggerated version of the Erasmian position that Luther assaults with such fury. For on Kant's view, the only thing we need to do in order to secure the hope of God's assistance in our pursuit of the highest good is to live a morally honorable life, and that is a goal we always have the power to achieve since the morality of a person's life depends entirely on his inward commitment to act in accordance with the demands that reason itself generates through a process of independent reflection.

Thus, though Kant concedes that these demands cannot be fully met without divine assistance, the *hope* that such help will be forthcoming is not itself a gift of God. It is not God's grace that gives us hope. We establish the conditions of hope on our own, through an act of freedom that has value in God's eyes only because it is perfectly autonomous. The contrary view—that we can be put in a state of deservingness only by God—at once destroys the foundations of all morality and reduces human beings to "a state of groaning passivity." It converts God into an "idol."[41] The belief that faith is "itself imparted and inspired directly from heaven," that God "hath mercy on whom he will, and whom he will he *hardenth*," reduces "everything, the moral constitution of humankind included . . . to an unconditional decree of God." It is the "*salto mortale* of human reason."[42]

But this is just the view on which Luther insists in his exchange with Erasmus. Kant's claim that we ourselves are the authors of the hope that God will bestow his grace upon us, and that it would not be worth having if we were unable to supply the ground for hoping he shall, therefore represents the most profound challenge imaginable to the Lutheran view, for it not only establishes a place for human freedom but subordinates God's grace to it, putting religion in the service of morality rather than the other way around. This is the only intelligible interpretation of the gospel message, according to Kant. It reflects the true spirit of the Christian religion. From Kant's point of view, Luther's vehement defense of God's grace against the vanity and presumptuousness of Erasmus' modest argument on behalf of human freedom can therefore only be described as a *retrograde* position that must be overcome if Christianity is to fulfill its destiny as a religion of pure reason. In this respect, Kant does more than provide a metaphysical foundation for the Erasmian philosophy of freedom that Luther so scornfully rejects. He constructs an argument for thinking that it is the only philosophy a Christian loyal to his faith can accept.

The disagreement between Luther and Kant regarding the nature and scope of God's grace is at bottom a quarrel over the meaning of the legacy that Augustine bequeathed to his Christian successors.

If human freedom is a meaningful concept at all, then we must have the power to determine our own destinies in some fashion, however limited this power may be. But to suppose that we possess such a power, in even the slightest degree, is an affront to the dignity of God, whose majesty is impugned by assuming that anything that happens in the world, including the moral achievements and failures of its human inhabitants, is not within his power to control.

To this it is no answer to say that God gave man his freedom to use as he thought best, so that while God is the ground of our freedom, as of everything else, we are the ones responsible for its employment. Both of these ideas may be required to explain how a world created from nothing can possibly contain any sin, but they are irreconcilably at war, since the combination of divine omnipotence and perfect foresight (really, just an aspect of omnipotence itself) rules out the possibility of any real responsibility on the part of those to whom God gave a nominal freedom but knew they would use it in precisely the way they subsequently did. A choice must be made between these ideas, and those (like Augustine himself and Luther a millennium later) who elect to save the honor of God at man's expense will inevitably be driven to the freedom-destroying conception of grace that inspired Augustine's attack on Pelagius and Luther's on Erasmus.

Those who instead grasp the other horn of Augustine's dilemma, and affirm that human freedom is a real power of creation from nothing—the image of God's own—are bound to be led in the opposite direction. For them, grace must be contained so that freedom has the room it requires. But the only way to do this is to make grace dependent on freedom, as Kant does. If we need God's grace to achieve our highest goal (our "salvation"), then we must possess the power to win it on our own, for otherwise our freedom is useless for attaining the one thing that matters most. It is no longer a freedom worth having at all. In order to save the meaning of freedom, grace must be conditioned upon it. This is Kant's position. It is the opposite of the one at which Luther arrives and the only alternative to it, if one starts with the goal of reconciling the ideas of freedom and grace in a philosophically coherent way—an ambition the earliest Christian apologists inherited from the rationalist philosophies of the ancient world, and that has shaped the development of Christian theology in a way unique among the Abrahamic religions.

In one respect, however, Kant's position is not the mirror image of Luther's. Luther is prepared to completely abandon the claims of human freedom in order to preserve the glory of God. For Luther, the celebration of God entails the hatred of man. But Kant is unwilling to give up on the idea of grace in a parallel way. He insists that it can—indeed, must—be retained in a moral theology centered on the concept of freedom. No philosopher has ever given greater weight to this concept or developed its implications in a more rigorous fashion. Kant's attempt to save a place for the idea of grace in a philosophy built on that of freedom, must therefore decide whether this can be done. There are compelling reasons to judge his attempt a failure.

ENLIGHTENMENT

We have a duty not merely to work toward the achievement of the high-est good. We must do all we can to realize this state of affairs in the world and time. Its attainment is the historical aim of humankind. But no com-munity of human beings can ever reach this goal by itself. For that we need the help of God who, as the creator of the world, alone possesses the power to close the gap between obligation and achievement, so far as the highest good is concerned. That we have a duty to pursue the highest good *and that* God's grace is required to fulfill it are therefore both propositions whose truth can be demonstrated by reason alone.

In particular, their truth does not depend on a revelation from God himself. Instead of violating the autonomy of reason, the doctrine of the necessity of grace therefore presupposes it instead. Hence religion, which acknowledges our dependence on God's help, follows "inevitably" from morality, whose truths reason is competent to establish on its own. This is Kant's transcendental defense of Erasmus' claim that freedom and grace are compatible.

But there are two weak links in Kant's argument for the rational neces-sity of grace, and hence for the compatibility of morality and religion. At two points, his argument moves in a circle, presupposing the very thing it is meant to establish. Kant begs the question twice.

First, he assumes that reason itself leads to the idea of a highest good only on the further assumption that the world has a "purposive" order. For it to have such an order, Kant believes, the world must be the creation of a God beyond it. In Kant's view, the rationality of the idea of a highest good is there-fore unintelligible except in creationist terms. The assumption of God's sepa-ration from the world is already built into his interpretation of the meaning of this idea itself.

Second, Kant assumes that the intelligibility of our duty to pursue the highest good depends on our ability to reach it—something he claims we can-not do without divine assistance. But elsewhere Kant maintains that it is perfectly possible for us to pursue a goal in a meaningful way despite the fact that we can never attain it. This is the basis of his account of what he calls the "regulative ideals" that guide us in our scientific investigation of the natu-ral world. If, in the practical sphere, the pursuit of the highest good *must* be an endeavor that *can* be completed, that is only because Kant takes for granted the necessity of *actually closing* the gap between the finite and the infinite in this domain. And that is because he assumes that the world has a morally minded creator who demands such closure and possesses the absolute power to bring it about.

In both these respects, Kant's deduction of grace presupposes a Christian metaphysics of creation, rather than offering an argument for it. The rejection of creationism as an unsupported or inherently irrational doctrine therefore fatally undermines Kant's argument for the rational necessity of grace. It severs the transcendental connection that Kant sought to forge between morality and religion, and leads to a moral order that is still recognizably Kantian in many respects but without the religious backing Kant thought it requires. It leads to a system of moral values in which the pursuit of the highest good continues to be viewed as a duty derivable by reason alone, but whose meaning and value no longer depend on the possibility of its completion. This stripped-down version of Kant's Christian morality is *our* morality. It is the secular residue of his question-begging attempt to put the doctrine of grace on a strictly rational foundation—the last such attempt before Kant's own enlightened doctrine of freedom swept God's grace from the world.

Let us examine each of these circles more closely.

Because we are rational beings, we can see and judge the sensuous, temporal side of our makeup from a point of view outside it. The question of how we ought to treat our needs and desires only arises from this point of view, and the only answer to it that is consistent with the conditions that first bring this question to light is respect for the power that does. Both the question and the answer are therefore grounded in reason alone. We need only our reason to discover the moral law and to understand why we have a duty to obey it. This is a conclusion that Kant repeats over and over again.

Kant insists that our duty to promote the highest good is likewise derivable from reason alone. But his defense of this claim depends on an appeal to God in a way that his deduction of the moral law does not.

The highest good is a state of maximal virtue accompanied by happiness distributed in proportion to it. In the world in which we actually live, worthiness to be happy and happiness do not always coincide (to put it mildly). We can see, however, that reason demands their coincidence by imagining ourselves in the position of a world-creating God, and by thinking of the world as a "purposive" order that we have brought into being out of nothing with some end in view. It would be irrational, Kant says, for God to create any other world than one in which the highest good is finally achieved. There is no other purpose that God could rationally entertain. What Kant means is that, in considering the worlds he might create, a being with limitless power could never have any reason for creating a world except one with this final end.

In Kant's view, this thought experiment confirms two things. The first is that the goal of achieving the highest good is not random or arbitrary but dictated by reason itself. The second is that its actual achievement requires that the moral and natural orders, whose separation means that the worthy suffer and the vicious prosper, be "united under one sovereign"—that they be governed by a single omnipotent God who creates the world from nothing and therefore necessarily exists outside it, for only on this assumption can a kingdom of moral beings happy in proportion to their virtue ever "acquire true reality."[43]

But there is a problem with this argument. If it would be irrational for God to create a world with any other end than the realization of the highest good, that is because God himself is bound by what Leibniz calls the "principle of sufficient reason." Either God is bound by this principle or he is not. If not, then he is free to create a world that is offensive to reason, as certain radical voluntarists have always maintained.[44] In that case, Kant's thought experiment proves nothing. Or God is bound by the principle of sufficient reason, in which case we may reasonably infer that he would not create a world in which virtue and happiness remain forever apart, so long as he has the power to create one where they eventually coincide. And we may also infer that he would not choose to refrain from creating any world at all (on the assumption that being is rationally preferable to nothing). But this leads to the conclusion that the world that actually exists is the best of all possible worlds, and that it exists of necessity, in which case the need to think of it as a purposive order created by a God beyond the world no longer exists (a conclusion that Leibniz himself refused to draw, though his study of Spinoza perhaps led him to see that it cannot be avoided).[45]

Kant's thought experiment is meant to demonstrate that our duty to promote the highest good is founded on reason alone. But either it fails to establish what he claims it does (on the assumption that God is not bound by the principle of sufficient reason), or it does establish it, but in a way that makes the assumption that the world is a purposive order created by a God beyond it, otiose and unnecessary. If one accepts the principle of sufficient reason, as Kant must for his argument to succeed, it may very well be that the final harmonization of virtue and happiness is the only rationally intelligible end that humanity can have. But it does *not* follow that for this end to exist, it must first do so as a purpose in the mind of a God who stands outside of nature and time. One might also conclude, with as much or greater reason, that the end in question is inscribed in the nature of man himself, or in that of the world as a whole whose being is unintelligible except on the assumption that it is internally directed toward the realization of this end as its highest state of self-fulfillment (as both Aristotle and Spinoza assume).

One other possibility remains. Someone sympathetic to Kant's argument might perhaps concede that it is unnecessary to assume that the world is a purposive order, created by a transcendent God, in order to establish the rational necessity of our duty to promote the highest good, yet maintain that the power to *realize* this good, which human beings can never do on their own, requires this very assumption. This brings us to Kant's second circle.

Let us return for a moment to the *Critique of Pure Reason.*

The argument of the first critique has two basic aims. The first is to demonstrate that what knowledge we have of the world is objective. The second is to prove that this knowledge is necessarily limited, leaving room for faith.

The key to Kant's proof of the first proposition is his claim that the spontaneous work of the understanding is constitutive of our knowledge of the world, which is founded on, and extends only as far as, the organizing schemes supplied by the categories of the understanding. Since we "put" these "into" the world, our knowledge of them is invulnerable to skeptical challenge.

The knowledge they afford, however, is necessarily limited. The understanding can only work on intuitions that are not its own spontaneous creations but are "given" to it from "without." Human reason finds this limitation intolerable. It demands an "unconditioned" knowledge of the world. Such knowledge is unattainable, since the intuitive nature of all our knowledge keeps it forever within finite bounds. But though this demand of reason cannot be fulfilled, it can and does act, Kant says, as a salutary "rule"[46] for the direction of the understanding, which is impelled by reason continually to extend its efforts in an attempt to grasp the unconditioned ground of all its knowledge of the world. The knowledge of this ground itself, which can never be attained, thereby functions as a "regulative ideal" that motivates our endless pursuit of a more complete understanding of the structure and mechanisms of the world in which we live. However far we go toward such an understanding, a gap always remains between the knowledge we have and the knowledge we seek. The latter is an unattainable "asymptote,"[47] yet just because it is, spurs us on in our scientific endeavors. Thus despite the fact that its goal can never be reached, reason's own self-generated demand for the unconditioned plays an intelligible, indeed necessary, role in the speculative

pursuits of humankind by providing both motive and direction to our progressively deeper and cumulatively broader understanding of what "is."[48]

The same cannot be said of our obligation to promote the highest good.
This, too, is an unattainable goal for finite beings such as we. But the moral
necessity of our duty to pursue it depends, Kant says, on the assumption that
the gap between goal and aspiration can and will be closed for us by the grace
of God. If we do not assume this, he says, all hope is lost. Our moral commitment goes slack. The pursuit of the highest good ceases to have a point or
purpose—in contrast to our pursuit of an unconditioned knowledge of the
world, which remains fully intelligible, indeed irresistible, even though such
knowledge remains forever beyond our grasp.

There is thus a sharp discrepancy between Kant's account of our pursuit
of the infinite in the realm of speculative knowledge, on the one hand, and
in the field of practical life on the other. Kant's reasoning seems to be as
follows.

If the world is a purposive order, then its highest purpose must be found
in the existence of rational beings like ourselves, for a world that lacks such
beings is necessarily inferior to one with them. God would therefore only
create a world with rational beings in it. But if they are created, they are by
definition finite, hence needy in various ways. As rational beings, they have a
duty to live virtuously, that is, in a way that honors the best part of themselves. As finite beings, they are constantly seeking their happiness. The highest good of the best of all possible worlds must therefore consist in the union
of virtue and happiness. No God with the power to create whatever world he
chose would ever create one with any other end. But no God possessed of such
power would ever create a world whose purpose could not be fulfilled. In
order to honor the dignity of the world's creator, we are therefore *required* to
assume that the highest good *will in fact be achieved,* and since we cannot
achieve it on our own, we *must also* assume that God will make up the difference, through his grace alone.

Kant employs a similar line of reasoning in the *Critique of Judgment* to
explain how progress in our empirical knowledge of the world is possible (a
question left in suspension by the *Critique of Pure Reason*). The possibility of
such progress is explicable, Kant says, only on the assumption that the world
has a divinely authored order whose infinite intelligibility reveals itself, in ever
more refined ways, to the work of deliberative judgment on which all advances
in our empirical understanding of nature depend.[49] In the end, therefore, the
assumption that the world is the creation of a God beyond it grounds Kant's

account not only of our moral duty to pursue the highest good but of our speculative drive to achieve an unconditioned knowledge of the natural world as well.

But this assumption is not required to save the rationality of either. It is enough that the world be rational, however this is explained.

As rational beings, we cannot help but accept the principle of sufficient reason. For any unexplained state of affairs, a rational being will always ask, "Why?" and not be content until an answer is forthcoming. In the domain of speculative knowledge, this leads to the regress toward the unconditioned that Kant describes. So long as one assumes that the world is rational, whether its rationality is inherent in it or has been brought into being by God, this regress will be rewarded, though it can never be completed by any finite being.

The same is true in the practical realm. For a rational being, the discrepancy between virtue and happiness is bound to be a source of puzzlement and concern, and a motive to do what he or she can to repair it. But again, if one merely assumes that the world is rational, whatever the source of its rationality may be, one has grounds to hope that these efforts at repair will be effective and carry those that make them toward a final state that no community of finite beings can ever achieve.

In both cases, the incentive to do more and better is provided by reason alone, and the intelligibility of forward progress in both realms depends on no assumption other than that the world has a rational order. In particular, it does not depend on the assumption that the rationality of the world is *due to* its having been created by God with an antecedent purpose in mind. That is an additional assumption that reason neither needs nor warrants. It is an article of faith. In order to provide the kind of foundation that Kant seeks for our duty to pursue the highest good and for the possibility of progress in natural science, it is enough to assume that the world is rational and that we are finite rational beings, whose finitude prevents us from ever completely fulfilling the ambitions that reason itself puts before us. These are the only assumptions one requires, and if we restrict ourselves to them, Kant's argument for divine grace falls to the ground.

Put differently, Kant's argument rests on a Christian prejudice. It depends on the belief that the rationality of the world can only be explained in creationist terms. Unless we believe this, there is neither a God to dispense grace nor a motive for us to assume that he must. But from the standpoint of reason alone, this belief is completely gratuitous, as the rationalist but noncreationist metaphysics of Aristotle and Spinoza make clear. Moreover, Kant himself gives us two reasons to completely abandon the idea of God's grace.

The first is that it sits very uncomfortably with the principle of autonomy on which his account of the moral law is founded. Kant acknowledges that to accept "the concept of a supernatural intervention into our moral though deficient faculty" even as an "idea for a purely practical intent is very risky and hard to reconcile with reason."[50] That is because reason places the ground of moral conduct in the "pure spontaneity of freedom." An action that is the result of an intervention from without is heteronomous and therefore lacks all moral value. How the necessity of God's grace can be harmonized with this principle is mysterious. In a moral philosophy less committed than Kant's to the derivation of all aspects of morality from reason alone, this might be less of a problem. But Kant's insistence that even the link between morality and religion be rationally demonstrable makes the acknowledgment that grace is a mystery much harder to accept. It puts pressure on Kant's argument for divine grace and gives anyone who concludes that it is not really an argument at all, but a circle that assumes what it sets out to prove, reason to let the argument go and accept Kant's morality of autonomy cleansed of all reference to grace.

Second, Kant's own strenuous efforts to demonstrate that we can have no speculative knowledge of God make the affirmation of the necessity of divine grace, even for practical purposes, awkward at best. It is hard, if not impossible, to conceive of grace without attributing various characteristics to God—that of benevolence in particular. Yet it is just such attributes that Kant claims can never be either established or refuted by reason alone. In the *Critique of Pure Reason,* Kant seeks to quiet forever the "endless controversies" of metaphysics.[51] But the concept of grace is a metaphysical idea that cannot be rendered comprehensible except by specifying the nature of God in a way that Kant himself shows to be illegitimate.

More fundamentally, the concept of grace rests on the belief that the world has a purposive order—one created by a transcendent power with an aim or end in view—and this belief is not just another metaphysical idea, but the most basic premise of the Christian religion. It is the *one* metaphysical idea that Kant *must* save from critique in order to make his argument for grace rationally persuasive. But his critique itself gives us grounds to be as suspicious of this theology as of any other—except, perhaps, one that is based on the principle of sufficient reason alone, since this relies on nothing but reason to articulate and defend a conception of the everlasting and divine. Kant did more than anyone before him to validate and strengthen these suspicions. Their effect is to put a spotlight on the contestable metaphysics of his own argument for grace; accentuate its circularity; and give those who accept Kant's demand that the case for grace be made on the basis of reason not faith, good Kantian reasons to conclude that his argument fails.

Psychological factors encourage this conclusion as well.

Luther sought to put the dignity of God beyond the reach of human pride. He was the last, ruthless, champion of the tradition of radical voluntarism that was born in response to the theological crisis of the thirteenth century and the pagan temptation to close the gap between God and the world. The result of Luther's campaign to free God from our prideful human longing to understand and control him is a doctrine of divine grace that entails not merely the diminishment but the hatred of man. To love God properly, Luther says, we must learn to think of ourselves as *nothing whatsoever* in relation to him. Luther's theology demands this as a condition of genuine piety. But the demand is more than we can stand. It is psychologically unbearable. If Luther's theology of the cross is the inevitable conclusion of Augustine's doctrine of grace, the self-loathing it celebrates as a religious ideal must eventually provoke a revolt in the name of the Augustinian doctrine of freedom.

The Pietist movement in which Kant was raised as a youth encouraged this revolt, in a modest way, by teaching its followers that they were capable of an inward rapport with God of a sort that Luther had strictly forbidden. Spurred, perhaps, by the same longing to find a new dignity in human experience, Kant constructed a morality of freedom as radical as Luther's theology of grace. In Kant's philosophy, God becomes an adjunct to human morality and his grace a mere idea in service to human ends, reversing the relation of man to God as Luther conceived it. To God's rebellious creatures, chafing under the demand that they hate themselves as a condition of loving their creator, Kant's morality of autonomy offers a tremendous vindication of human experience against an unknowable and unbearable God. The pleasure of this vindication is the real source of the excitement behind his abstract, technical, but liberating claim that the existence of God is merely a practical postulate.

This excitement is hard to contain. It gives those readers who feel it a motive to complete Kant's house of reason by eliminating the last lingering traces of the doctrine of grace, which even in the rarified form he defends it, still makes man uncomfortably dependent on God. Kant was unwilling to let the idea of grace go. He tried to show that it can be justified on rational grounds.

But his defense is unconvincing, for reasons that Kant himself supplies. Given its implausibility, and the passion for human independence that Kant's own moral philosophy encourages to such an extraordinary degree, it is unsurprising that so many of his followers have abandoned the doctrine of grace entirely, in favor of an enlightened morality in which God no longer plays even the attenuated, transcendental role that Kant assigns him.

In the process, Kant's conception of the highest good becomes a wholly human ideal, now conceived in strictly secular terms. It becomes the asymptote of human history, toward which we move by fits and starts in an endless, collective and completely disenchanted campaign that retains its moral meaning despite the fact that God no longer plays any role in it at all. With this, the way is open to Hegel and Marx in the world of thought, and to the French Revolution in that of affairs.[52]

The path that leads to this world is marked by a massive shift of divine responsibilities to human ones—by the withering away of God's grace and a corresponding expansion of human sovereignty in every department of life. But not all have welcomed this development or even accepted it with passive dismay. Some have reacted with what can only be called a theological rage. They have seen in the gospel of freedom the final satanic assertion of human pride, and have fought against it, with every weapon available to them, on behalf of the party of God. Today, this sentiment is most strongly felt and openly expressed outside the West, in radical Islamist movements inspired by reactionary writers like Sayyid Qutb.[53] But for a century and a half, from the French Revolution to the Second World War, its principal spokesmen were a series of European thinkers, the latter-day descendants of the Catholic Counter-Reformation, who despite their often contemptuous attitude toward Protestantism were radicalized by the Augustinian doctrine of grace that inspired Luther's campaign for reform. Their names are Joseph de Maistre, Juan Donoso Cortes, Carl Schmitt and Martin Heidegger. The next three chapters trace the rise and fall of their self-consciously antimodern theology of reaction.

CHAPTER 23

Reaction

JOSEPH DE MAISTRE'S REVOLT
AGAINST PRIDE

The French Revolution had many enemies. The best known in the English-speaking world was Edmund Burke. Burke's *Reflections on the Revolution in France* was enormously influential in its own time and continues to be read and studied today. Even those who despise Burke's ideas concede his status as a thinker of the very first rank.

This has not been the fate of Joseph de Maistre, Burke's slightly younger contemporary, the Savoyard lawyer and diplomat whose ferocious assault on the French Revolution has sometimes been described as the continental counterpart of Burke's own. Unlike Burke's *Reflections,* Maistre's antirevolutionary writings are today barely known outside a small circle of readers. They are almost never viewed as works of comparable importance. Many have been out of print for long periods of time and are still unavailable in scholarly translations.

There are exceptions, of course. Isaiah Berlin's well-known study of Maistre has helped to reintroduce him to English-speaking readers.[1] But Maistre remains a figure far less well known than Burke and it is rare to see his works included on any list of influential texts in the field of modern political thought. Even in the Francophone world, Maistre is widely regarded as a marginal figure and his views dismissed as the extravagant ravings of a royalist fanatic devoted to a regime of privilege and hierarchy that even in his own day had already been swept from the stage.[2]

But the reasons for Maistre's relative obscurity are deeper than this dismissive view suggests. Maistre, like Burke, had supreme gifts as a stylist. He writes with a vigor and pungency equal to Burke's own, and many of his criticisms of the French Revolution are the very ones that Burke himself advances. All of this makes it puzzling that Maistre should today be as obscure as Burke is famous.

The reason that Maistre has been forgotten is that he interprets the French Revolution in terms that no longer make any sense to contemporary readers. Burke's criticisms of the revolution are wholly political. Maistre, by contrast, views it as a theocosmic event, unfolding within the framework of man's relation to God. For Maistre, the true meaning of the revolution can only be explained in the categories of providence, sin and redemption. Religious ideas of this sort play no role at all in Burke's attack on the revolution, which is as worldly in substance and tone as *The Prince* or *The Federalist Papers*.

According to Maistre, human affairs in general, and the French Revolution in particular, are incomprehensible except against the background of man's original sin. In this sense, his account of the revolution is a grandly metaphysical one, of the sort to which Burke was profoundly allergic, and if Maistre's writings have disappeared from the canon of modern political thought, it is because they are based on religious beliefs that, in the West at least, no longer command public respect.

The decline of Maistre's reputation and the general loss of interest in his work is a consequence of the disenchantment of the world—of the reduction of God to a postulate, and then to a personal "value."[3] Because Maistre affirms the primacy of providence over freedom and of God over man, his views have not survived this reduction. Burke's writings have endured because they rest on a strictly political conception of human affairs that is free of such religious commitments.

But if Maistre's theological orientation explains why he is no longer read or studied in our irreligious age, except by a handful of specialists, it also makes him, in one respect at least, a figure of greater historical interest than Burke, for it links him in a way that Burke's writings do not to the great drama of Western Christendom and to the radicalism of the Protestant Reformation in particular.

Maistre despised Protestantism. He regarded it as the source of the anti-authoritarian individualism that had done so much, in his view, to prepare the way for the French Revolution. Yet he remained close to Luther in one crucial respect. Like Luther, Maistre was a fierce apostle of grace. He insisted on the complete supremacy of God's power over man and on the utter folly of thinking that human beings can ever be truly free of divine direction, let alone capable of usurping God's role as a creator. At most, Maistre says, man is able to "cooperate" with God. By himself, he lacks the power to create anything at all. The only thing that human beings can do on their own is destroy; their power to innovate or initiate is wholly negative. In this sense, every human act, insofar as it strives for independence or autonomy, repeats Adam's original sin of pride. This is the essence of Luther's theology and of Maistre's as well.

Like Luther, Maistre was an opponent of human pride in all its forms. In Maistre's case, his opposition was sharpened by the growing authority of the ethic of freedom to which Kant had given supreme philosophical, and the French Revolution lasting political, expression. Whatever differences set them apart, Luther and Maistre were therefore both the champions of God against man, and if Maistre's formulations are even more extreme, it is because he wrote in an age in which the party of man had gained the upper hand.

Maistre is Europe's first great antirevolutionary thinker. His views are as radical in one way as those of Kant, Rousseau and Voltaire are in another. He hated their prideful endorsement of enlightenment and autonomy as much as Luther hated Erasmus' attempt to preserve even a modest place for human freedom in God's providential plan for the world, and for essentially the same reasons. In this respect, Maistre's views are as deeply shaped by the centuries-long struggle over the legacy of Augustine, as Luther's denial of the reality of freedom and Kant's transcendental deduction of it had been in an earlier time. His antirevolutionary writings thus link him to the deepest and most enduring tensions within the tradition of Christian thought, from which Burke's political conservatism is almost completely detached. In a longer perspective, therefore, Maistre may perhaps be regarded as the more important figure of the two, and if this seems implausible today, it is only because we no longer believe that our public values must be founded on the dogmas of the religion within whose bosom the spirit of disenchantment that now rules the West grew to explosive maturity.

Maistre's predecessors include Luther and the late medieval voluntarists who preached a radical version of the doctrine of grace. He has had influential successors as well. Isaiah Berlin stresses, in particular, Maistre's impact on later writers in the tradition of reactionary Catholic thought, including the Spanish diplomat and essayist Juan Donoso Cortes and twentieth-century fascists such as Leon Bloy and Charles Maurras.[4] But even Berlin underestimates Maistre's influence, for through Donoso, Maistre's Augustinianism was communicated to Carl Schmitt, a brilliantly original jurist and the best-known defender of the legality of the Nazi regime. Schmitt's criticism of parliamentary liberalism, his assault on what he calls the "neutralizations and depoliticizations" of the modern age, and his so-called "concept of the political" all derive from the same theological assumptions as Maistre's attack on the French Revolution.

Even Martin Heidegger, Schmitt's colleague at Freiburg University and fellow party member, must be counted as a descendent of Maistre, despite the fact that he left the Catholic Church in his late twenties and never refers to Maistre directly. At its core, Heidegger's complex and hermetic philosophy is a subtle reworking of Maistre's theology. Recast as an argument about the destiny of Western metaphysics and its fall from an original understanding of truth as "disclosure," Heidegger's attack on metaphysics, humanism and technology amounts to a learned restatement of Maistre's defense of God against man.

Donoso, Schmitt and Heidegger are all Maistre's children. Their ideas are driven by the same fierce revulsion at our freedom-loving age, with its prideful confidence in man's power to be the ground of his own being and that of the world as a whole. The theology that lies behind their radically antimodern beliefs is less explicit in Schmitt's writings than in those of Maistre and Donoso. In Heidegger's work, it is even further in the background. But Schmitt's attack on "technicity" and Heidegger's reconstruction of the history of the "forgetfulness" of being are both inspired by the equation of sin with pride, and by the belief that in setting himself up as the "lord of the earth,"[5] man has rebelliously cut himself off from that greater power on whose saving grace he shall always depend.

Carl Schmitt and Martin Heidegger were the two greatest thinkers to join the Nazi Party and to serve it in an official capacity. Both eventually claimed to have been disappointed by national socialism. Initially, however, they enthusiastically embraced it as a vehicle for their apocalyptic, antimodern hopes. Each was moved by other interests too, personal as well as professional. But at the deepest level, Schmitt's and Heidegger's attraction to the Nazi movement was motivated by their shared hostility to the rebellion against God that both men viewed as the defining characteristic of modern European civilization. Their positive view of Nazism reflected their wish to see man knocked off his impudent perch and made to serve a greater power again—the religiously inspired demand for the belittlement of man that Maistre did so much to install as a powerful force in nineteenth- and twentieth-century European thought.

The appeal of Nazism for both Schmitt and Heidegger lay in its open contempt for liberal humanistic values. From the standpoint of Maistre's theology of grace, humanism is more than a mistake. It is a crime of satanic proportions. Schmitt and Heidegger were drawn to the Nazi movement by their hatred of humanism, nurtured by the reactionary Catholic theology that both men absorbed in their youth.

Their endorsement of national socialism, however brief, can never be excused as a mere lapse of judgment.[6] But whether one is more interested in rescuing the reputations of Schmitt and Heidegger from the taint of Nazism, or in demonstrating that their ideas are stained to the roots by it,[7] their attraction to the Nazi movement, and willingness to serve it in word and deed, can only be understood in theological terms. It amounted to a *religious* reaction against the disenchantment of the world, embodied most powerfully in a liberal humanism that to their minds represented not just a flattening of experience or weakening of older values, but a sin of cosmic dimensions—the prideful reversal of man's relation to God, which the first great theologian of the Latin West long ago described as the cause of man's fall into history.

"REASON IS ALL WE REQUIRE"

Joseph de Maistre was born in Savoy in 1753. His family belonged to the upper middle class, though Maistre's father, a lawyer and state official, had been granted the hereditary title of count in recognition of his service to the Piedmontese government. Maistre was trained as a lawyer and his early career followed that of his father as a magistrate in Chambery. When the French invaded Savoy in 1792, Maistre fled with his family to Piedmont and then later to Switzerland.

By this time, Maistre had already acquired a reputation as a counterrevolutionary writer. The best known of his early essays, *Considérations sur la France,* was published anonymously in 1797. When Maistre's authorship of the work was revealed, his immediate chances for advancement in the Piedmontese government (which had allied itself with France) were stymied. Maistre spent the next two years in Turin and Venice without employment. From 1800 to 1803, he served as the highest judicial official on the island of Sardinia (a Piedmont possession), and in 1803 was appointed the representative of the Sardinian monarchy to the court of Alexander I in Saint Petersburg. Maistre spent the next fourteen years in the glittering salon world of the

Russian capital, surrounded by royalist émigrés from every corner of Europe, and it was here that he composed his masterpiece, *Les Soirées de Saint-Pétersbourg*. Maistre was recalled to Turin in 1817 and lived there until his death in 1821. *Les Soirées* was published a few months later.

Maistre read Burke's *Reflections* soon after its publication in 1790. In January of the following year, he wrote to a friend that Burke's book had strongly confirmed his own antirevolutionary beliefs. But despite his admiration for Burke, Maistre's attack on the revolution turned in a sharply different direction. To appreciate how different their views are, it is helpful to begin by recalling the main points of agreement between them.

Like Burke, Maistre rails against the idea that "a nation, that a *constitution,* that is to say, the totality of fundamental laws that are proper to a nation and that give it such-and-such a form of government, is an artifact like any other, requiring only intelligence, knowledge, and practice, that one can learn the *trade of constitution making,* and that any day they think about it, men may say to other men, *make us a government,* as they say to a workman, *make us a steam pump or a stocking frame.*"[8] In reality, "*no great human institution results from deliberation.*"[9] A "constitution is the work of circumstances whose number is infinite."[10] No amount of human "science and reasoning" can ever comprehend these circumstances, let alone reproduce them.[11]

It is therefore blind arrogance on the part of those who claim the power to construct a government from the ground up, according to principles that are clear and distinct and embodied in a writing that even the simplest person can grasp, to think they have the capacity to do what they pretend. The truth is just the opposite. According to Maistre, a government does not become better and stronger to the degree it approaches this ideal of reason. It grows weaker instead. In general, "human works are fragile in proportion to the number of men involved in their construction and to the degree to which science and reasoning have been employed a priori."[12] It follows that "[t]he weakness and fragility of a written constitution are actually in direct proportion to the number of written constitutional articles."[13] "Only when society discovers itself already constituted, not knowing how, can certain particular articles be made known or explained in writing."[14] In a society of this sort, however, the force of what is written depends entirely on what is not, which only confirms that the first can never replace the second or be the *ground* of political authority in the way the champions of constitution making insist it can and must be. In all this, Maistre and Burke see eye to eye.

They also agree in their skepticism about the value of political innovation. "[A]ll intelligent persons," Maistre writes, have an "innate aversion" to innovation. "The word *reform,* by itself and prior to any scrutiny, will always be suspect to wisdom, and the experience of every generation justifies this instinct."[15] What is great and lasting in human life has not been made. It has grown. It is the mature fruit of a natural process which by the time it ripens into something of value is always already *old.* Those who seek to substitute a new and artificial regime for an old and natural one are therefore bound to fail. "[A] man . . . would never imagine that he had the power to make a tree. How can he have imagined that he had the power to make a constitution?"[16]

In short, "nothing great has great beginnings,"[17] but grows by small and unnoticed steps from obscure origins into something visible and commanding, in the way a tree of great stature grows from a seed nourished by the darkness of the soil. Man's role in this process is at most that of a caretaker, whose job is to help preserve the results of a slow unfolding of natural powers that he may frustrate or destroy but can never reproduce on his own. In Maistre's view, the great innovators of the French Revolution made the mistake of confusing the proper custodial role of human beings with that of a true creator who claims the power to do in the realm of politics what all acknowledge no group of men can ever achieve outside it.

Maistre shares Burke's hostility toward political abstractions as well. He ridicules the revolutionaries' ambition to make a constitution "for man" with words that might have been Burke's own. "There is no such thing as man in the world," Maistre writes. "In my lifetime I have seen Frenchmen, Italians, Russians, etc.; thanks to Montesquieu, I even know that *one can be a Persian.* But as for *man,* I declare that I have never in my life met him; if he exists, he is unknown to me."[18]

The idea of man "is a pure abstraction," a "hypothetical ideal," and though the makers of a constitution fashioned in accordance with this ideal insist it is "made for all nations," in truth it "is made for none."[19] It lacks the rooted specificity that every constitution requires in order to grow over time, as the political life of a people adapts to its peculiar character and situation. A constitution "which treats only of man" is a *"school composition,"*[20] a barren exercise without practical meaning, and those who put their trust in it show they have no understanding either of history or politics.

In all these respects, Maistre is deeply doubtful about the competence of human reason, and in particular about the ability of men to establish a political sovereign on their own. "Man cannot create a sovereign."[21] The belief

that he can is the most extravagant presumption of reason. Against this arrogant belief, one needs to insist on the value of what has been inherited, as
opposed to invented, and on the essential opacity of all authority, which must
be protected by a "magic wall" of political piety that accepts without asking
why.[22] Once this wall is breached, the "charm" that authority needs to survive
"is broken"[23] and the scramble of men to reconstruct it on a strictly rational
basis is doomed.

The great rule of human history is that a people must always "accept" its
masters and can never "choose" them. It is therefore "essential that the origin
of sovereignty should show itself to be beyond the sphere of human power."
If, as a result, the ground of sovereignty seems "obscure," that is only because
it is concealed in the depths of "time," which the abstractions of reason can
never comprehend and all the ingenious innovations of man can never replace
or even improve.[24]

In these and countless other passages, Maistre endorses a prescriptive
view of authority nearly identical to Burke's own—one motivated by an
hostility to what both men considered the insane claims made on behalf of
the absurdly rationalist conception of politics advanced by the leaders of the
French Revolution.

"AN INSURRECTION AGAINST GOD"

Yet, despite these similarities, Maistre's attack on the French Revolution is
inspired by wholly different concerns.

For Burke, the reckless and destructive rationalism of the revolutionaries
represented a failure of perception and judgment. In his view, the revolutionaries showed an appalling ignorance of certain basic political facts—that
authority only grows slowly; that old institutions, even with their faults, generally embody more wisdom than can be expressed in a set of formal rules or
fully comprehended by the human mind; and that an abstraction like "the
rights of man" only acquires meaning in the context of a particular people's
own unique historical experience. Those who think otherwise, Burke says, are
fools. Their eyes are closed to the essential nature of political life. But their
foolishness is not a sin. It does harm to other men but not to God. For Burke,
the wickedness of the French revolutionaries lay in the injustices they committed against their fellow citizens and the lasting damage they did to the
institutions they had inherited from the past. He considered these great political crimes but not an assault against God himself.

For Maistre, by contrast, the French Revolution was above all a rebellion against divine authority, and those responsible for it not merely foolish but wicked. He viewed the revolution as the climactic event in an immense theological drama. He saw it as the reenactment on a world historical scale of the original sin of pride, for which the whole of the eighteenth century had prepared the way with its spirit of "philosophism,"[25] and that was bound to produce in reaction a divine punishment of even greater proportions, through which the regeneration of a fallen humanity would finally be achieved.

Maistre placed the whole of the French Revolution in a cosmic frame of reference. He located it within the Christian story of fall and salvation, and insisted that its real meaning can only be grasped in these terms. This is the master theme of Maistre's writings. It has no counterpart in Burke's *Reflections,* whose ferocious condemnation of the revolutionaries' destructive naivete remains anchored in a set of strictly political values and the worldly outlook these reflect.

Maistre calls the eighteenth century an age of "theophobia."[26] Its most characteristic movements all rest, he says, on the belief that men possess the power to construct schemes of moral, political and intellectual order on their own, without the help of God. "The unsuspecting, overweening self-confidence of the eighteenth century balked at nothing, and I do not believe it produced a single stripling of any talent who did not make three things when he left school: an educational system, a constitution, and a world."[27] Certain thinkers even dreamed of creating a new language on their own—a "philosophic language"[28] of perfect clarity and precision, that would be free of all the ambiguities of every existing, historically evolved tradition of speech. In all these various endeavors Maistre discerns a common spirit of "unconquerable pride," goading those whose souls it has inflamed "incessantly to overthrow everything not made by themselves."[29] He calls this "philosophism" or "science," which he repeatedly contrasts with "religion," whose defining attitude is one of humility and gratitude instead.

Looking back at the eighteenth century from the early years of the nineteenth, Maistre saw the prideful spirit of science gaining ground everywhere, sweeping away centuries of tradition and piety as if these were cobwebs or clutter, and replacing them with a new ideal of world and self-mastery based on a boundless confidence in the autonomy of human reason. Everywhere, Maistre says, the great thinkers of the eighteenth century sought to substitute independence for reverence; control for subservience; knowledge and science for prayer. They sought to put man in the place of God. The effort to do this, with a brazenness unparalleled in human history, reaches its apotheosis in the French Revolution.

To say that the prideful optimism of the eighteenth century was foolish or mistaken is on Maistre's view true enough. But it does not begin to capture the depth of his loathing for it, and for the French Revolution in particular. The philosophism of the eighteenth century is for Maistre something *radically* bad because it rests upon a belief that is the *exact opposite* of the truth. It turns the truth upside down. In reality, man's power to make things is not merely limited, as many will be prepared to concede. It is *nonexistent.* Without God's help, man has absolutely no power to create anything at all. At most, he is able to refrain from destroying what God has created. Even this is supremely difficult. Man is by nature a destroyer, not a creator. Left to himself all man can do is destroy God's works, including the other human beings with whom he shares the earth. In this sense, the prideful dogmas of the eighteenth century, which affirm man's power to create without divine assistance, are the *mirror image* of the real truth that without God man lacks the power to create a single atom of political or intellectual value.

It is religion that teaches this truth and urges man to his knees in prayerful thanks for God's creative goodness. Science is by contrast something diabolical. It seduces human beings to acts of ever-increasing destructiveness in the belief that they are creators like God, just as the serpent seduced Adam and Eve to a primal act of destruction with the promise that by eating the forbidden fruit they would become gods themselves. Modern science is therefore not the greatest good, liberating man from centuries of superstition and oppression, as its eighteenth-century champions insisted. It is the greatest evil—a hypertrophic expression of pride, whose inevitable consequence is not to elevate and improve human beings but brutalize and degrade them instead, through the spiraling acts of destruction it invites once men are loosed from the pious acknowledgment of their complete dependence on God and invited to think of themselves as beings endowed with the power and wisdom to re-create the world according to their own enlightened ideals.

Man fell into his present condition through an act of pride. Adam and Eve's prideful wish to be God was the original sin that inaugurated the history of human beings on earth. History began with their fall, and its narrative is nothing but a chronicle of repeated acts of pride like the first. To whatever period of human events one turns, the spectacle is always the same. For Maistre, like Augustine, the whole of human history is one unrelieved record of prideful self-assertion, of attempted usurpations of God's creative powers, which will end only when history itself does, with the resurrection and final judgment.

In this respect, the eighteenth century is no different than any of those that preceded it. Yet in the scope, ferocity and openness of their pride, the apostles of enlightenment have reached, Maistre says, a previously unattained peak of godlessness. And *this* is something new in human history, for "[a]lthough impious men have always existed, there never was before the eighteenth century, and in the heart of Christendom, *an insurrection against God*."[30] The culmination of this insurrection is the French Revolution, which is therefore an event of world-historical significance (something its defenders, blinded as they are by their delusions of human self-importance, are in general happy to concede). The French Revolution is the greatest and most self-destructive act of pride in a drama that began with Adam and Eve's revolt against God and that the revolutionaries bring to a close by rebelling against the creator of the world with a shamelessness that can only presage a break in the human condition as fundamental as man's original fall into history.

BLOOD

In Maistre's view, the French Revolution is doomed to fail. Given man's innate incapacity for self-control, the attempt to supplant authority and prescription with freedom and self-legislation is bound to collapse and to be succeeded by a new regime of dictatorial command, as Napoleon's rise to power had already confirmed to Maistre and his royalist allies. The first lesson of the French Revolution is that man's attempt to seize God's place and exercise his powers can never succeed.

But there is a second and more important lesson to be learned from the revolution. It is that pride is a sin that must be punished before the sinner can be rejoined to God, from whom his own rebellious self-assertion has estranged him. We cannot conceive that God would ever finally and completely abandon man to sin. His infinite goodness forbids this. But it is equally inconceivable, according to Maistre, that man can be reunited with God without paying the price for his pride. Sin demands punishment as a condition of salvation. This is the most fundamental truth about man's relation to God and the deepest law of human history, which the French Revolution brings to light with unprecedented clarity by offering us a spectacle of human suffering on a scale commensurate with the pride of the revolutionaries themselves—whose own criminal acts, through a divinely arranged symmetry, at once merit and cause this suffering.

We see this first in the escalating bloodshed of the Terror, but even more clearly in the endless, spreading violence of the Napoleonic Wars. Some of those who lose their heads to the guillotine or die on the field of battle are of course criminals themselves. They are guilty of outrageous acts of pride. But many of the men and women caught up in the maelstrom of revolution and war are as innocent as it is possible for human beings to be (which is never completely innocent, since each of us bears the weight of original sin and is therefore guilty of a crime for which no punishment can be too severe). What the French Revolution illustrates, therefore, is a corollary to the law than salvation demands suffering. It establishes, beyond all doubt, that the greatest human crimes demand payment on a scale that the guilty alone can never provide. Forgiveness for the greatest crimes demands that others who are innocent must suffer as well. The French Revolution teaches us that the path to salvation lies through the spilling of innocent blood, and that there is no other way for man to restore his connection to the God on whom he has turned his back—just as the story of the Fall instructs us that we who have lived under the shadow of death ever since must suffer on account of our parents' abysmal crime.

Maistre recognized, of course, that human beings have no monopoly on suffering. Indeed, he regarded the whole of the nonhuman world as an immense theater of suffering too—a kingdom of bloodshed and violence. "In the vast realm of living things, there reigns an obvious violence, a kind of prescribed rage that arms all creatures to their common doom. As soon as you leave the inanimate kingdom, you find the decree of violent death written on the very frontiers of life. You feel it already in the vegetable kingdom: from the immense catalpa to the humblest herb, how many plants *die,* and how many are *killed!* As soon as you enter the animal kingdom, the law suddenly becomes frighteningly obvious. . . . There is no instant of time when some living thing is not being devoured by another."[31] Why this is so, we cannot know. We must simply assume that it is for the best, though God's reasons for making the lives of plants and animals so savage and painful are beyond our power to fathom.

We *can* understand, however, why this reign of violence is tremendously amplified in the sphere of human life—why men kill one another with a cruelty that even the most brutal animals never inflict on their fellows. The explanation is that human beings are criminals. They are guilty of a willful disobedience to God, and the extraordinary suffering they experience at each other's hands in the mayhem of civilian life and in the sanctified killing of war is the penalty for a disobedience of which catalpa and herb, eagle and mouse, can never be guilty since they lack the freedom that crime presupposes.

The suffering of innocent human beings is to be explained in a similar way. First we must remember that no human being is truly innocent. To one degree or another, we all harbor the wish to be God. Some deny it, or repress it, or work hard to keep it under control. But no human being can escape it completely. To be human is to have this desire. That is the meaning of original sin, and anyone who claims, as many eighteenth-century thinkers did, that man is either good by nature or can be made good, is a foolish optimist who cannot see that the human condition is in its essence morally degraded and that no human being therefore ever has grounds to complain that whatever suffering he experiences is undeserved.

Second, to the extent there is a disproportion between degrees of innocence (among the essentially guilty) and degrees of suffering, this too can be explained by man's criminal nature. The crime of disobeying God is so great that it cannot possibly be expiated except by means of innocent blood. No matter how much we are punished for the sinful yearning to be God that is inscribed in the soul of each of us, there will always be a debt that remains. There will always be a surplus of suffering due. To pay this debt down, human beings naturally look for the most valuable currency in which to do so, and this, Maistre says, is the blood of the (relatively) innocent.

The blood of an innocent human being is the most valuable thing on earth and hence the most precious currency in which to pay off our debt to God. The disproportion between guilt and suffering in human life, which otherwise seems so inexplicable, thus becomes perfectly understandable once one grasps the basic principle that governs the spiritual economy of man's relation to God. In truth, the *more* innocent a person is, the *larger* the payment he can make on behalf of his guiltier neighbor through the sacrifice of his own innocent blood. Maistre calls this "the dogma of substitution"—the belief "*that the innocent can pay for the guilty.*"[32] Human beings have always subscribed to this belief, he says, even in pre-Christian times.

The Christian religion embraces this dogma wholeheartedly. Indeed, it takes the principle of substitution to its logical limit by postulating the sacrificial bloodletting of a *perfectly* innocent man as the *only conceivable* means to man's redemption from sin. In the figure of Christ on the cross, the "universal idea"[33] that human beings can be redeemed by the sacrifice of innocent blood thus achieves its highest and final expression. Knowing this, Maistre says, we should welcome the rivers of "innocent blood covering the scaffolds that covered France"[34] as a salutary reminder of the law of vicarious sacrifice that runs through the whole of human history and that reaches its culmination in the defining beliefs of the Christian religion.

PROVIDENCE

In Maistre's view, the eighteenth century represents an extreme both of sinfulness and suffering. On the one hand, its science and philosophy extend the reach of human pride beyond all previously known limits. On the other, its wars and revolutions prepare a sacrifice of innocent blood commensurate with the unprecedented crimes of the age. In fact, Maistre says, the eighteenth century reaches a limit on both sides of this equation that cannot be exceeded. That is because man's age-old rebellion against God now begins for the first time in human history *to take pride in pride itself.*

Every human being since Adam has harbored the criminal wish to seize God's place. But in the past, this wish has always been accompanied by a sense of shame. Now for the first time, Maistre claims, human beings have begun to exult in their own pridefulness and instead of asking to be forgiven for the wicked desire to supplant God, openly celebrate it as the highest measure of moral and political value. No greater blasphemy can be imagined. The French Revolution is therefore not merely another crime in the long record of human impudence and ingratitude. It is "an event *unique* in history"; "it is the *highest* degree of corruption ever known; it is *pure* impurity."[35]

In this sense, the age of the French Revolution marks a theological limit beyond which men cannot go. It must therefore be the *last* age in man's conniving and sinful campaign to steal God's powers. And this means it has to be followed by a *new* age in which God's promise to save us from sin is finally fulfilled despite our utter lack of desert. Even if the spirit of the French Revolution continues to dominate the lives of human beings for centuries to come, it cannot last forever. It must be a *preparation* for something else. It must be a prelude to the *restoration* of humility and prayerful subjection on a scale as global as that of the antithetical ideals of the revolution itself. No other result is conceivable. That is because no other outcome is compatible with the promise of salvation that alone allows us to make sense of human history as a whole.

None of this, of course, is an accident. "Nothing happens by chance in this world."[36] Everything in creation fulfills the role that God assigns it and is guided by his providential care. This is true even—especially!—of the French Revolution, which on its surface appears to represent the fulfillment of man's wish to free himself from God's control and assume dominion of the earth. Precisely here, where human autonomy seems greatest, the truth that history "leads men more than men lead it" has "never been more striking."[37] Paradoxically, Maistre says, it is just at the point that men believe they have finally broken the shackles of religion that God's providence is most powerfully at work. The French revolutionaries believe they are in control of their destiny, and that henceforth human beings shall decide how everything in the world will be ordered. They think they are "the masters of the earth."[38] But in reality they are not the directors and engineers of history. They are only "the instruments of a force" that "knows more than they do."[39] God "employs" them as a "passive instrument" for his own ends.[40] He "makes sport of human plans," and above all of the human pretension to independence and control. Viewed in this light, the proud and powerful men of the age are revealed to be a "nullity" instead.[41]

For those who have eyes to see, therefore, the meaning of the French Revolution is precisely the opposite of what its defenders claim. It represents not the triumph of man, as they insist, but the most "palpable" expression in all of human history of God's "Providence,"[42] though which he uses "the vilest instruments" to bring about the sacrifice of innocent blood that alone can lead to man's "regeneration."[43] Flushed with pride, the leaders of the revolution and the philosophers and scientists of the eighteenth century who prepared the way for them thus unwittingly act the part that God has assigned them in the great drama of salvation, and despite their own ambitions, help to hasten a new, counterrevolutionary age of piety and prayer.

All the "parties" in the French Revolution have "wanted" one thing. That is "the debasement, even the destruction, of the universal Church and the monarchy, *from which it follows*," Maistre says, "that all their efforts will culminate in the glorification of Christianity and the monarchy" instead.[44] For Maistre, this is not merely a probability but a certainty. *"Evil is the schism of being; it is not true."*[45] Because it is radically evil, the French Revolution marks a maximum of untruth. It represents the most complete "schism of being" imaginable, and therefore can only be explained as a prelude to an age of truth and closure, in which man's separation from God is finally healed. It is not merely incompatible with God's nature that he would let schism and untruth prevail, but inconceivable that he would *even let it happen in the first place* with any other goal than the final redemption of goodness from evil, truth from falsity, unity from division. This is the salvific end to which the revolution directs all who are caught in its net, the innocent and guilty alike—unknowingly, remorselessly, providentially. Only those who are blinded by the eighteenth century's mania of pride are unable to see the real world-historical meaning of the revolution, which cannot be grasped except from the standpoint of the divine plan to which it belongs.

How long will it be before the tide turns and a new age of counterrevolution begins? And can anything be done to hasten its arrival? At times, Maistre writes as if a new age were already at hand. But more often he acknowledges that it may be a long time coming, and insists that it is fruitless to speculate about when and how it will start.[46] To think that one can predict the counterrevolution with certainty, he says, is to presume to know the mind of God. That is the same mistake the revolutionaries make. In the meantime, all we can do is "wait."[47]

The right attitude is one of alert passivity. "[W]e must hold ourselves ready for an immense event in the divine order, toward which we are moving with an increased speed that must strike every observer."[48] We have to be prepared to receive God's saving grace when it comes. But in addition to "awaiting something extraordinary," as every "truly religious man in Europe" now does, we must fight the "eternal sickness" of attempting "to penetrate the future," of seeking to decipher God's plan, and instead allow ourselves to be carried along by his will as it manifests itself in worldly events. We must cultivate a spirit of thankful passivity that is the exact opposite of the attitude preached by the apostles of the French Revolution, with their criminal pretension to human autonomy and self-control. The name for the latter is "science." The name for the former is "prayer."[49] As we await the coming of God, we must pray for his forgiveness, which has been promised to us by an incomprehensible act of grace that is repugnant to all who seek to render the natural world transparent to human intelligence, and insist on their right to rebuild the arrangements under which men live on the basis of reason alone.

LUTHER'S HEIRS

Maistre believed that the Protestant Reformation had prepared the way for the eighteenth century's antiauthoritarianism in both intellectual and political matters. In particular, he calls the attack on indulgences "one of the greatest crimes men have ever committed against God,"[50] and defends the practice by appealing to the same principle of vicarious sacrifice that Christ's own suffering exemplifies. According to the reformers, "*The Man-God paid for us; therefore we have no need of other merits;* but one must say: *Therefore the merits of the innocent can be of use to the guilty. As redemption is only a great indulgence,* an indulgence, in its turn, is only a *reduced redemption.* Undoubtedly the disproportion is immense, but the principle is the same, and the analogy uncontestable."[51]

Because they failed to grasp this principle, Maistre says, Luther and his followers expanded their attack on indulgences into a full-scale assault on the church and the institution of the papacy in particular. The universal authority of the church was damaged as a result, and the pope put on the defensive.[52] This encouraged a new spirit of independence in religious life. The national Protestant churches declared their independence from the church of Rome, and each Protestant believer now felt justified in establishing his or her own relation to God, without the mediating authority of traditions and priests.

This led to "the foolish and yet fundamental doctrine of Protestantism, *private interpretation.*"[53] Maistre condemns the idea of private interpretation as an expression of the belief that human beings are competent to work out their salvation by themselves, without the coercive discipline of established institutions whose authority they ought to accept. He sees it as a precursor to the far more radical attack on established authorities of all kinds that gathered momentum in the eighteenth century. In Maistre's view, the Lutheran Reformation was a movement inspired by the same longing for independence that lay at the root of the French Revolution, and like it belonged to the world-historical eruption of human pride that makes the whole of modern European civilization something "radically bad."

All this seems to put Maistre and Luther at a great distance from one another. In particular, Luther would have been baffled by Maistre's claim that the Reformation had the effect of freeing man from God's authority since Luther's aim was just the opposite. Still, there is a fundamental connection between the two, for Maistre's belief that human beings are inherently wicked, that pride is the source of all evil, and that everything good in the world happens by God's incomprehensible grace alone, was Luther's deepest conviction as well.

Luther sought to restore an Augustinian conception of man in a culture of religious complacency that had grown used to the idea that human beings can influence God's decisions in various ways. To do this, he was forced to express himself with an uncompromising rigor that led him in his exchange with Erasmus to deny the reality of human freedom altogether. Here and elsewhere in his writings, Luther did more than merely defend Augustine's idea of grace. He gave it a *radical* interpretation that left no room for human initiative at all.

In this respect, Maistre is more Luther's heir than his opponent. Maistre had different enemies, of course. His adversaries were not the worldly prelates of a church grown soft, but hardened revolutionaries who challenged every form of prescriptive authority in the name of human freedom. He believed, moreover, that Protestantism itself had contributed in important ways to the creation of the culture of individualism that encouraged the revolutionaries' brazen presumptions. But like Luther, Maistre viewed his enemies as the proponents of a Babylonian ethic of pride, and fought them with an Augustinian theology defined by its unsparing insistence on the impotence of human beings and their abject dependence on God's mysterious and unearnable grace.

Wherever Maistre looks he sees, as Luther had before him, the symptoms of original sin. It is from this point of view in particular that he defends the established authority of the Roman Church. The premise of Maistre's defense is not the genial and accommodating thought that men need the comfort of the church's rituals and routines, which provide them with a welcoming home on earth, adapted to their mix of strengths and limitations. It is the fierce belief that outside the discipline of the church, men can only do evil. Left to themselves, human beings are hopelessly bad. The office of the church is to chain and restrain them. In this respect, Maistre's *defense* of papal authority is motivated by the same Augustinian theology of grace that three centuries before had provoked Luther to *attack* the church on account of its concessions to human pride.

Among the Catholics who rallied to the defense of the church against its Protestant critics there were some who did so on the grounds that men need comfort and solace in this world, and that it is the function of the church to provide it. They defended the church in an essentially Thomistic spirit, as a component of God's beneficent and fulfilling plan for humankind, whose outlines reason can discern.

But there were others who sought to justify the authority of the church in a wholly different way. In their eyes, Protestantism itself was just another expression of the longing for human independence that Luther had identified as the real evil in the sale of indulgences. They defended the church on the

Augustinian grounds that Luther had attacked it, and turned the tables on his Reformation theology by using its insistence on the ubiquity of pride to construct an authoritarian conception of religious rule as a barrier against the antiauthoritarianism they rightly or wrongly associated with Protestantism itself.

Some among this latter group of Counter-Reformation theologians eventually came to see the science and politics of the eighteenth century as the supreme expression of Protestant beliefs. When they did, the fundamental principles of their own radical theology of grace enabled them to construct an interpretation of the previous three centuries of European life that defined this entire period, from the Reformation to the Napoleonic Wars, as a single event in the history of man's relation to God. And with this they laid the foundation for a new, counterrevolutionary movement that conceded the world-historical importance of the French Revolution, but assigned it a meaning that was precisely the opposite of the one ascribed to it by the revolutionaries themselves.

These were Luther's true heirs, using the same Augustinian ideas of grace and original sin that Luther had employed in his attack on the church, to fight the deformities of a world swollen with pride whose existence they blamed in part on Protestantism itself. Joseph de Maistre was the first and greatest among them, and if one looks for the authentic spirit of Lutheranism in the age of revolutions it will not be found in the writings of Luther's comparatively moderate Protestant followers, let alone in the humanistic philosophy of Kant, but in the works of reactionary Catholics like Maistre, who viewed the entire modern world as a vast "satanic"[54] revolt leading inevitably to a new order of things.

Maistre and his successors are Luther's real descendants. Their hatred of the modern world, with its commitment to the principle of autonomy that Kant defended with such passion and care, is rooted in the same theology of grace as Luther's hatred of man, and their attack on Kant's ideal of human freedom is as uncompromising as that ideal itself, in whose countless moral, political and cultural manifestations they saw something not merely mistaken or unwise, but the work of the devil himself. Recast in secular terms, this is the view that Carl Schmitt and Martin Heidegger will carry into the storms of the twentieth century.

CHAPTER 24

·>——◄I◇◖◍◗◞◦I——<·

"Fantastic and Satanic"

THE ILLIBERAL THEOLOGY OF DONOSO CORTES
AND CARL SCHMITT

Carl Schmitt's concept of politics was inspired by the writings of the Spanish parliamentarian and diplomat Juan Donoso Cortes, the Marques de Valdegamas. Schmitt calls Donoso a "prophet" of our times. When in 1922 Schmitt offered his own account of the climactic conflicts of modern European civilization, it was to Donoso's earlier diagnosis that he looked back.[1]

More than any other writer of the nineteenth century, Donoso helped to sustain the tradition of reactionary thought that Joseph de Maistre had inaugurated, and to communicate Maistre's theology of sin and grace to a later generation of thinkers, including many, like Schmitt, who played a pivotal role in the fascist counterrevolution of the twentieth century. If Maistre belongs to the first generation of counterrevolutionary thinkers, and Schmitt to the third, then Donoso is the central figure in the second. His rabid attack on rationalism and liberalism provides a bridge between the other two.[2]

Like Maistre before him, Donoso viewed all the most characteristic features of the modern world as an expression of man's sinful rebellion against God. He believed this had brought about an unprecedented rupture in man's relation to God, but was also convinced that events were moving toward a cataclysmic conclusion in which God's supremacy would be restored. His interpretation of the meaning of the modern age and visceral hatred for it arose from the same complex of religious beliefs as Maistre's attack on the French Revolution.

Carl Schmitt's later assault on our "age of neutralizations and depoliticizations"[3] belongs to the tradition of Catholic reaction as well. Along with Donoso and Maistre, Schmitt also judged the modern world from the standpoint of the theology of original sin that he learned as a child and then, as an adult philosopher, made the "anthropological" premise of his radical attack on liberal ideals, guided by the Spanish thinker whose prescience he claimed to profoundly admire.

"PHILOSOPHIC CIVILIZATION"

Juan Donoso Cortes was born in 1809, the year that Maistre completed *Considérations sur la France* and began work on *Les Soirées de Saint-Pétersbourg.* Donoso's father was a provincial lawyer whose social standing straddled the line between the upper bourgeoisie and lower nobility. Like Maistre, Donoso also followed his father into the practice of law. As a young man, he taught and published widely on a variety of political subjects. His early views were vaguely liberal and romantic, but the revolutions of 1848 pushed him sharply to the right. Donoso expressed his increasingly rigid beliefs with clarity and passion in a series of speeches in the Spanish Parliament in 1849 and 1850, and more systematically in a collection of essays, published shortly before his death in 1853 in Paris, where Donoso served as the Spanish ambassador to France for the last two years of his life.

For Donoso, as for Maistre, the first challenge of any philosophy is that of explaining the existence of wickedness and suffering in the world. The fundamental tenet of "Catholic civilization"[4] is that the world's evil is due to man's sinful attempt to free himself from dependence on God, and to the penalty that God imposed on Adam for his primal act of disobedience. God's punishment altered Adam's "constitution,"[5] and with it, that of all his children to the end of time. From the debased condition in which human beings have lived since the Fall, no chance of salvation existed until God assumed a human shape and died in "the bloody tragedy of the cross,"[6] an act of unfathomable love that carries the pagan idea of blood sacrifice to its ultimate limit (a subject that Donoso, like Maistre, discusses at considerable length).[7]

If Adam's disobedience is the archetype of human pride, Christ's sacrifice is the supreme expression of God's grace.[8] The penalty incurred by the first is one we all must bear. But the hope of salvation restored by the second is a "universal"[9] inheritance too. This is God's providential scheme: to endow us with the freedom to sin, knowing full well that we will, but knowing at the same time that a redeemer will come who will take man's sins on himself and thereby give us back the hope of restoring our relation to God—not the relation of intimacy that Adam once enjoyed, for nothing can bring that back, but a renewed relation of obedience and love to be consummated in the life to come.

One may ask why God has arranged things in this fashion, rather than simply ensuring that Adam not sin in the first place. The only answer our fallible minds can conceive is that no other arrangement could possibly manifest God's justice and mercy as fully or well as this one.[10] To suppose otherwise, one must either deny that man is free, which would have the inconvenient result of placing the blame for the world's evil on God's shoulders (a favorite theme of Augustine's, about whom Donoso speaks with reverence as "the most beautiful of geniuses and the greatest of doctors"),[11] or one must believe that having punished man for his sin, God turned away from the "masterpiece"[12] of his creation with a justifiable but coldhearted contempt—an equally unacceptable conclusion because it denies the boundlessness of God's love. Only the drama of fall *and* redemption avoids both these results. Only the "subtle harmony and consonance" of Catholic theology, the "dogma of the transmission of sin and of penalty, and that of the purifying action of the latter when freely accepted,"[13] is capable of explaining the existence of evil in a way that neither elevates man nor debases God. Moreover, only Catholic dogma provides an adequate foundation for "the organic laws of humanity."[14] It alone is able to secure, in a lasting way, the various forms of "solidarity,"[15] familial, social and political, that a well-ordered human society always displays, and without which it becomes a mere "casino,"[16] unable to last more than a day.

In contrast to "Catholic civilization," which "teaches that the nature of man is wounded and fallen," "philosophic civilization teaches that the nature of man is radically whole and healthy in its essence and in the elements which comprise it."[17] No difference of outlook could be deeper or more consequential.

From the denial of man's sinful nature, many things follow.[18] Life on earth ceases to be "a vale of tears."[19] It becomes an infinitely perfectible source of ever increasing enjoyment, which we no longer have reason to fear as a temptation but can now embrace with a clear conscience. And because human reason, like every other power we possess, is not "crippled" by sin but essentially "sound," there is "no truth it cannot reach."[20] On the "philosophic" view, human beings are able to better themselves and their societies through the exercise of their own innate capacities, reasoning and reforming their way to a heaven on earth.

This leads to "a vast naturalistic system" premised on "the immaculate conception of man,"[21] who now is able "to pursue the good without the supernatural aid of grace."[22] The philosophic view thus represents the triumph of "pride," for it says to its followers that man "has no flaws and does not need God."[23] It is characterized by a "satanic audacity," whose real god is "Lucifer," the "god of pride."[24]

Donoso blames the Reformation of the sixteenth century for having loosed the god of pride.[25] Since then, he says, the philosophic conception of man has been gaining ground. It has undermined established hierarchies of authority by encouraging the belief that human beings need no governors but themselves. It has weakened social mores by popularizing the idea that pain is an evil (rather than a chastisement) and pleasure a good (instead of a temptation). And it has transformed the relation between rich and poor into a class struggle, marked by an absence of charity on one side and of patience on the other.[26] In all these respects, the conflict between the philosophic conception of man and its Catholic counterpart could not be sharper.

The revolutions of the eighteenth and nineteenth centuries—"the iron century of philosophic civilization"[27]—have widened this conflict until it has become the organizing principle of our "apocalyptic times,"[28] which are marked, Donoso says, by a "gigantic struggle between good and evil, or in Saint Augustine's words, between the City of God and the city of the world."[29]

On the one side are the Catholics, the last defenders of the doctrine of sin and redemption, and on the other, the philosophers and revolutionaries, the apostles of human self-sufficiency and pride. Between these no accommodation is possible. One must triumph and the other be vanquished in a final "catastrophe" that the laws of history make inevitable.[30] This is the greatest of Donoso's "black prophecies,"[31] though he declines to predict how or when the catastrophe will come.[32] But come it must, if God's providential design for the world is to be fulfilled, with the penitent returning to God through an acceptance of his grace, and the champions of pride being punished for their rebellion against him, as every such rebel, from Lucifer to Proudhon, must eventually be.[33]

THE HALFHEARTED LIBERAL

Among the apostates of the nineteenth century, Donoso distinguishes two sorts, the liberal and the socialist. Both start from the dogma of human innocence and perfectibility, and place the blame for the world's evils on something other than man. Both are therefore guilty of the sin of pride. But Donoso regards socialism as the more dangerous of the two. In the end, he says, it is destined to sweep the halfhearted and contradictory spirit of liberal parliamentarianism from the stage and prepare the way for a final confrontation between heresy and faith. In socialism, Catholic civilization thus finds an enemy worthy of itself, whose self-conscious antitheology makes it an adversary of appropriately grand ambition in the drama of fall and redemption.

By contrast, Donoso mocks liberalism for its inconsistencies and lack of nerve.[34]

> The Liberal and Rationalist school denies family solidarity, inasmuch as it proclaims the principle of the legal aptitude of all men to attain all public offices and all the dignities of the State, which is a denial of the action of ancestors on descendants, and the communication of the qualities of the former to the latter, by hereditary transmission. *But* at the very time it denies that transmission, it acknowledges it in two different ways—first, by proclaiming the perpetual identity of nations; and second, by proclaiming the hereditary principle in monarchy. The principle of national identity either signifies nothing, or it means there is a community of merits and demerits, of glories and disasters, of talents and aptitude between past generations and the present, the present and the future; and this community is totally inexplicable, unless considered as the result of hereditary transmission. *On the other hand,* hereditary monarchy, considered as the fundamental institution of the State, is a contradictory and absurd institution whenever the principle of the virtue of transmission by blood, which is the constitutive principle of all historical aristocracies, is denied. *Finally,* the Liberal and Rationalist school, in its repugnant materialism, gives to riches communicated the virtue it denies to transmission of blood! The rule of the millionaires appears to it more legitimate than the rule of the nobles![35]

The chief fault of liberalism, according to Donoso, is that it lacks the courage to be faithful to its own guiding principles, and thus ends in a morass of contradictory commitments that cannot withstand the searching criticism of those who are prepared to embrace the sweeping reforms these principles entail, including the abolition of family, monarchy and private property.[36] Unlike the socialists, who know that "man was born to act"[37] and are unafraid to use political power in whatever way is needed to advance their ends, the wishy-washy liberals for whom Cortes expresses such contempt attach fundamental importance to freedom of the press and the principle of "discussion." The liberal school "never says, *I affirm,* or, *I deny,*" but always "*I distinguish.*" Its "supreme interest" is in "preventing the arrival of the day of radical negations or of sovereign affirmations; and that it may not arrive, it confounds by means of discussion all notions, and propagates skepticism, knowing as it does, that a people which hears in the mouth of its sophists the *pro* and the *contra* of everything, ends by not knowing which side to take."[38]

The most basic commitment of liberalism is to "the dissolvent principle of discussion," which rests on the assumption that the truth of any matter can be discerned so long as the discussion of it is permitted to continue without end. But in reality, Donoso says, this principle does not promote the discovery of the truth. It obscures it instead, dissolving the bonds of ancestry, conviction and faith that join the members of every political community. The "reign" of the principle of discussion is therefore bound to be "ephemeral" and "transitory."[39] The supremacy of liberal ideas must eventually yield to stronger thinkers who are unafraid to affirm in an unqualified way the fundamental premise of liberalism's meliorist philosophy, and are prepared to suppress the freedom of the press, to override the "sovereignty of deliberative assemblies,"[40] and to cut short the endless debate of principles and policies in order to achieve their own ideals.

According to Donoso, every political philosophy is founded on a theology.[41] That is because none can avoid taking a stand on the most basic theological question of all—whether man is sinful or good by nature. Liberalism claims to be nontheological. It declares itself free of those divisive beliefs about God that from time out of mind have set the partisans of different religions at each other's throats. Indeed, many liberals regard this as their greatest achievement: to have finally overcome the religious quarrels that have always divided the universal community of man into warring camps of heretics and believers. But this is an illusion, Donoso says, for by affirming the inherent goodness of man, liberalism in fact endorses a theology, though in a muddy and contradictory way that gives the false appearance of having no theology at all. What liberalism lacks, he claims, is not a theological premise but the courage to affirm the one it has in an honest and forthright way.

In this respect too, "socialists grasp the nettle that liberals are afraid to touch." Starting from the same premise of innate human goodness, they shamelessly unfold its consequences to the last detail. The result is a theology that represents the polar opposite of Catholic dogma, which rests on a belief in original sin. In this way, socialism makes manifest the theological divide that still lies hidden in the conflict between Catholics and liberals. It brings to light for all to see the gulf that separates those who accept their dependence on God and attribute all the evil in the world to man's sinful disobedience of his commands, from those who insist that man is the master of his fate and the inventor of the idea of God, which he is now mature enough to discard as a child's fable.

> The Socialistic schools, prescinding from the barbarous multitudes which follow them, and considered in their doctors and masters, are far superior to the Liberal school, just because they go straight to all the great problems and questions, and because they always propose a peremptory and decisive solution. Socialism is strong, only because it is a theology; and it is destructive only because it is a satanic theology. The Socialistic schools, inasmuch as they are theological, will prevail over the Liberal school, inasmuch as it is anti-theological and skeptical; and inasmuch as they are satanic, they will succumb before the Catholic school, which is at once theological and divine. . . .
>
> When Socialism says the nature of man is sound and society unhealthy; when it places the former at open war with the latter, to extirpate the evil which is in *it,* through the good which is in the other; when it convokes and calls on all men to rise up in rebellion against all social institutions, there is no doubt that in this way of proposing and solving the question, though there is much that is false, there is something gigantic and grand, worthy of the terrible majesty of the subject; but when Liberalism explains the evil and the good, order and disorder, by the various forms of government, all ephemeral and transitory; when, prescinding, on one side, from all social, and, on the other, from all religious, problems, it brings into discussion its political problems as the only ones worthy by their elevation of occupying the statesman, there are no words in any language capable of describing the profound incapacity and radical impotence of this school, not only to solve, but even to enunciate these awful questions. The Liberal school, enemy at once of the darkness and of the light, has selected I know not what twilight between the luminous and dark regions, between the eternal shades and the divine aurora. Placed in this nameless region, it has aimed at governing without a people and without a God. Extravagant and impossible enterprise! Its days are numbered;

for on one side of the horizon appears God, and on the other, the people. No one will be able to say where it is on the tremendous day of battle, when the plain shall be covered with the Catholic and Socialistic phalanxes.[42]

Socialism thus openly negates what Catholicism affirms. "The fundamental negation of Socialism is the negation of sin, that grand affirmation which is, as it were, the center of the Catholic affirmations."[43] This leads to "nihilism."[44] By denying the reality of sin, socialism undermines all personal responsibility. It converts wrongdoing into a problem whose solution requires therapy rather than punishment. It turns the criminal into a patient. Then, "individual responsibility being denied, responsibility in common must be denied" as well.[45] This in turn "annihilates" the basis of solidarity in all human institutions, from the family to the state. Lacking the "unity" which only the acknowledgment of responsibility can supply, none of these any longer is "one." Each becomes a multitude without order.

A similar process of disintegration takes place at the individual level. Without a sense of responsibility, there is nothing to guarantee that "in different moments of his life [a man] is one and the same person." There is "no bond of union" between his past, present and future. A man without responsibility "only exists in the present moment." His existence is therefore "more phenomenal than real." He has only "the speculative existence of a mathematical point."[46] In this way, the denial of sin leads inevitably to the dissolution of human beings and of all the traditions, practices and institutions that sustain and order their lives.

The coming battle between Catholicism and socialism is therefore a war between the forces of being and nothingness. It is a war between God and those "future Nihilists" who will be unafraid to press their rebellious campaign against God to its limits. But their rebellion is itself a part of God's plan for the world and therefore doomed to fail. The nihilists must eventually be beaten into retreat. On that day, God will once again draw "good" from "sin and penalty,"[47] as he has done in the past. This is the cleansing and sanctifying "catastrophe," the "supreme crisis,"[48] the "hurricane,"[49] the "cataclysm,"[50] toward which all the forces of Europe are hurtling. It is a fate prepared by God, one that brings the "tree of error" to "providential maturity" in the "satanic audacity" with which the heresy of human goodness is affirmed.[51] Donoso demurs from predicting when this crisis will arrive. But he insists that "God has made gangrene for putrid flesh and cauterization for gangrenous flesh."[52] And he takes comfort in the knowledge that God's "exterminating angels"[53] will come to the aid of those obedient Catholics who, though dispirited by the prideful and rationalistic age in which it is their fate to live, can only "give thanks to God"[54] for the privilege of being able to fight on his side in this world historical "struggle"—a battle which, with the "grace" of God, they are bound to pursue to "victory."[55]

On none of these points does Donoso hesitate or waver. His convictions are as unyielding as Maistre's. That is because both men view the modern world from the standpoint of a theology that events in the world can never disturb. What happens here on earth always only confirms God's plan for the world, especially when it seems not to.

Maistre thought that the modern age had come to a climax in the French Revolution. Donoso was convinced that the worst is yet to come, in the form of a nihilistic revolt against all established order. But both believed that the modern age is defined by its addiction to pride and that the order of providence, which decrees that pride be punished, cannot be reversed by man. That man is by nature sinful; that his worst sin is the wish to be God; that the wars and revolutions of the nineteenth century have unchained this wish from all previous inhibitions and constraints; and that the result can only be a divinely ordained sacrifice of blood commensurate with the crime that man has committed: on all these matters, Maistre and Donoso agreed. They are the twin apostles of a theology of reaction that even into the middle years of the twentieth century continued to attract some of Europe's best minds.

THE CONCEPT OF THE POLITICAL

One of these was Carl Schmitt, an original thinker whose works are still read and admired today, despite his active support of the Nazi movement in the early 1930s. Though scarred by his association with Nazism, Schmitt's reputation has survived largely intact. He now has followers on the left as well as the right, and many would say that he deserves to be included among the greatest European thinkers of the twentieth century.[56]

Carl Schmitt was born in 1888, to a family of Franco-German origin. He was raised as an orthodox Catholic, in an environment in which German Catholics, especially in the western part of the state, felt increasingly alienated by the program of laicization aggressively pursued by Bismarck's predominantly Protestant empire. The result was a long and fiercely fought *Kulturkampf* between Protestants and Catholics. Schmitt's own beliefs about a range of social and political matters were shaped by his passionate attachment to the Catholic cause in this "war."

As a young man, Schmitt studied law and then taught it, from 1922 to 1929, at the University of Bonn. In 1922, he published two books, *Roman Catholicism and Political Form* and *Political Theology*. The second of these permanently established Schmitt's reputation as a thinker whose ideas were of interest to many beyond the narrow circle of Catholic apologists. His most famous work, *The Concept of the Political,* appeared as a journal article in 1927, and his essay *Dictatorship* was published the following year.

Consistent with the argument of the latter essay, Schmitt publicly defended the legitimacy of the so-called "emergency clause" of the Weimar Constitution, through which the Nazis came to power in 1933. He officially joined the Nazi Party in May of that year and for the next three years supported a number of Nazi initiatives, including the Nuremberg Laws of 1935. By the late 1930s, Schmitt had fallen out of favor with the party on account of his insufficiently "Aryan" beliefs (despite the openly anti-Semitic remarks he made on a number of occasions). Schmitt's actions were watched by the SS, but he was allowed to continue teaching and writing until the end of the war.

After the war, Schmitt was detained by the Allies for more than a year and interrogated as a possible war criminal. In the end, it was decided not to prosecute him, though because he refused to acknowledge the wrongfulness of his actions during the Nazi years, Schmitt was never formally de-Nazified and could not return to university teaching in any official capacity. For the rest of his long life, he lived an essentially private existence. Schmitt nevertheless remained a visible and controversial figure on the European scene until his death in 1985.

Carl Schmitt is best known for his definition of the "concept" of the political. What, he asks, are the features that distinguish political from other sorts of communities?

Schmitt begins by observing that human beings organize themselves into groups of many different sorts with varying aims and values. There are religious, economic, aesthetic and cultural communities. Each of these is organized around a fundamental distinction of one kind or another—in the case of religious communities, between the holy and profane; in economic communities, between partnership and competition; and in aesthetic communities, between beauty and ugliness (or beauty and mediocrity). The life of each rests on a specific interpretation of the meaning of the distinction that defines communities of its kind.

These interpretations not only differ; they are incompatible. Conflict among them is therefore inevitable. The conflict may be mild but always has the potential to escalate to the level of a life or death struggle. An ecclesiastical community, for example, may find itself confronted by heretics within or missionaries without who are determined to destroy or transform it. When this happens, the existence of the community is placed in doubt. From its point of view, threats of this sort are "existential," for unless they can be successfully resisted, the community must eventually disappear or—what amounts to the same thing—be merged into another community organized around a different interpretation of the distinction that lies at its core.

For those who belong to any such community—economic, religious, whatever—its destruction may entail a material or spiritual loss sufficiently great to move them, as individuals, to fight to the death for its preservation. Whether any given individual chooses to do this will depend on the magnitude of his investment (economic, salvific, etc.) in the beleaguered community.[57] For some, the threat to the community may be experienced as an existential threat to them personally. It may present a challenge to their interests or identity worth risking their lives to defeat. For others, it may not. How an individual assesses the nature of a particular threat will determine his or her response to it.

For a community to be a *political* association, however, it is not enough that it have enemies, even ones who hope to destroy it. This is a necessary but not sufficient condition for its being or becoming political. A sports club, for example, may have rivals who want to force it to disband. By itself, however, this does not make the club a political association. A more telling example is that of the Diaspora Jews, who were hated by many but remained an essentially nonpolitical people. Nor does a community become a political association in Schmitt's sense just because it has members—even many members—who are prepared to kill and die in order to preserve it, so long as the decision to do so is left up to them as individuals.

It is an axiom of liberalism, according to Schmitt, that no one has a right to tell anyone else what is worth killing and dying for. Every truly consistent liberal philosophy delegates this decision to the individual—but just for that reason, Schmitt says, groups based on this philosophy lack a political character. In Schmitt's view, a community whose substantive norms may be defined in religious or economic or any other terms becomes a political community only when it acquires the power to command its members to give up their lives for the sake of its own preservation. This power may have many different sources, both psychological and material. In most cases, it is likely to rest, in important part, on a shared conception of legitimate authority. But whatever its source, a community is a political association, in Schmitt's sense, only in case its members have ceded to the community as a whole (under compulsion or otherwise) the right to decide whether to kill and die in order to defend it against threats to its existence—a decision that henceforth lies with the leaders and representatives of the community, and not its individual members.

THE EXTREME CASE

Whether a community *is* a political association can therefore only be determined by looking to see how its members behave in such a crisis. If they act on the assumption that each has the right to decide for himself whether to fight to the death, it is not yet a political community, regardless of how many choose to fight. If, on the other hand, the members of the community (a sufficient number of them, at least) show by their actions that they are prepared to subordinate their own right to decide this mortal question to whatever decision the leaders and representatives of the community make on its behalf, we may properly speak of a community that has attained a political status, regardless of the nature of the material or spiritual interests that bind its members together. What Schmitt calls "the extreme case"[58] is thus the *only* one in which it is possible to determine whether a community that calls itself political really is.

Schmitt's discussion of the extreme case reveals the philosophical gap that separates him from the leading neo-Kantians of his generation.[59] According to Schmitt, the crucial question in any purported emergency, where the threat to a community is arguably existential, is whether in fact the situation *is* an emergency calling for the mobilization of the community's physical forces or the employment of other strongly self-protective measures (sanctions, diplomacy and the like). Schmitt insists that no system of rules and procedures, however detailed, can ever *by itself* decide this question. That is because whatever answer the system produces can always be challenged on the grounds that the situation in question is not one for which the rules provide, and that the choice of a response must therefore be made on some other basis.

The rules by which a political community orders its affairs apply in "normal" circumstances. But they can never decide whether they themselves should be suspended in order to secure the survival of the community itself.[60] This is not a practical truth, according to Schmitt, but a logical one that no amount of tinkering with the rules can ever refute. It is always possible that the rules that order the life of a community must be put aside, for a time at least, so that the community may survive, and the mere existence of this possibility means that the rules themselves are logically incapable of adjudicating the truth or falsity of the claim that such a situation actually exists.

Schmitt concludes that the only truly political situation is one of lawlessness. In sharp contrast to Hans Kelsen and others, who define the legitimacy of the state in terms of its conformity to law (*Rechtsstaat*), Schmitt insists that politics only begins where the law ends, since it is only in extreme cases that one can decide whether a particular association is political or not, and all such controversies, he claims, necessarily lie beyond the power of the law to decide.

The leaders of a constitutional *Rechtsstaat* may refuse to abandon their commitment to the rule of law even when the community's survival is at stake. But all this shows, Schmitt says, is that their outlook is not a political one after all. The leader who refuses to compromise the principle of legality, even in the face of an existential threat to his community, may be a man of great moral or religious principle. He may deserve to be regarded as an ethical hero or saint. But by virtue of his refusal to suspend this principle, he forfeits his claim to be a leader in the *political* sense. From *this* point of view he is a failure or, more exactly, nothing at all.

Because the law is unable to decide what ought to be done in a genuine crisis, it follows that the choice of a response can have no ground but itself. A response cannot be justified by appealing to the law or, more generally, to norms of truth and reason. Political leaders do make appeals of this sort, but that is for rhetorical purposes only. If it were really the case that reason required a response of a particular kind, the apparent emergency would be governed by rules after all. It would not be the exception it appears to be, but an event whose meaning can be assessed according to general laws.

For a neo-Kantian like Kelsen, the legitimacy, indeed the very intelligibility, of any political decision depends on the possibility of its subsumption under rules. For Schmitt, by contrast, the genuinely political nature of a decision is a consequence of the impossibility of doing precisely this. Schmitt's concept of the political is therefore not merely lawless but irrational. The response that every truly political situation demands is one that can never be validated by appealing to an order of reasons that precedes and governs it. It must be *self*-validating instead. It must rest on the (often unexpressed) claim, "This is the right course to follow because I declare it to be such. It is not the right course because the established law of the state or some higher law of nature or reason demands it. The rightness of the course I now prescribe is a function of my prescription of it and nothing else." Every claim of this sort involves tremendous risks. But for Schmitt these are simply the risks of politics itself, and the one who succeeds in establishing his claim to determine the existential fate of his community by prescription alone, is the only one to whom, he says, the term "sovereign" properly applies.[61]

In opposition to those who believe that sovereignty is a legal concept whose meaning is defined by the role it plays within a rationally derived system of rules, Schmitt associates himself with the view expressed in Hobbes' famous dictum, *"auctoritas, non veritas facit legem."*[62] According to Hobbes, the law is not binding because of its conformity to some transcendent set of norms that reason can discern. It is not binding because of its "truthfulness." The law is binding, on Hobbes' view, because the sovereign has commanded obedience to it.

To be sure, the mere fact that one person commands others to behave in a certain way does not mean they are bound to do so. Only the commands of the sovereign are binding in this manner. The question is why. Thinkers in the natural law tradition answer that the commands of the sovereign are binding to the extent they are true, that is, in alignment with preexisting norms embedded in the order of things. Hobbes emphatically rejects this whole tradition of thought, and insists instead that the commands of the sovereign are binding only because he has the power to impose his will on those to whom his commands are addressed. For Hobbes, sovereignty is defined by the possession of this power itself.

On the Hobbesian view, which Schmitt endorses, law is therefore founded not on reason but will. As a result, the question of whose will "makes" the law becomes a factual rather than a normative one. The answer to it depends entirely on the actual distribution of power among those involved. One of the sources of power may be the belief that certain individuals have the authority to issue commands. But this increases their power only as a matter of (psychological) fact, and not because the belief is true.

Even the laws of nature that bind men before they enter civil society must be understood in these terms.[63] In the state of nature, men are under a duty to seek peace. To do this, they must agree with others to establish a sovereign with the power to command them all. But the duty in question is binding only because it has been commanded by God, whose power is boundless— just as the duty they will soon be under to obey the commands of their civil master binds them solely because he has the power to compel their obedience. In this sense, the prepolitical or "natural" duty to seek peace also rests upon a self-validating act of will (in this case, God's will), whose authority, like that of the sovereign, is a function not of the conformity of his commands to preexisting norms of truth or justice, but of the power of the person who issues them, which in God's case is absolute. Hobbes' equation of authority with will and of will with power thus applies both to God and man. In it, Schmitt finds the inspiration for his view that "[s]overeign is he who decides on the exception."[64]

POLITICAL THEOLOGY

As these last remarks suggest, the conception of authority that Schmitt discerns in Hobbes' political writings has deep theological roots. It is inspired by the view of those who claim that God's commands are binding simply because they are his commands, and who insist that to inquire after their rationale, or to measure their validity against some independent norm of truth, is to seek to bind God's will in chains of reason. This is the error that every voluntarist from Ockham to Luther sought to correct. Whatever his own views about religion may have been, Hobbes is the intellectual heir of their centuries-long campaign to free God from the prideful ambitions of human reason. He belongs, Schmitt says, to the voluntarist tradition in Christian theology.

By contrast, the theorists of the *Rechtsstaat* draw inspiration from the competing tradition of "deism," which maintains that the laws of nature are not changeable even by the God who created them.[65] In its strongest form, deism asserts that these laws are deducible from reason alone, and that God had no choice but to adopt them in the first place. According to Schmitt, the clearest expression of this view is found in the philosophy of Leibniz.[66] He claims that Kelsen and the other defenders of the *Rechtsstaat* assign the same rational necessity to the laws of the state as deists like Leibniz do to those of the natural world.

Schmitt associates his own political philosophy with "theism" instead. He sides with those who insist on "the personal sovereignty of God" and locate the source of his authority in an "absolute decision created out of nothingness."[67] The spirit of theism animates the Franciscan scholastic tradition that culminates in Luther and the Protestant Reformation. In Schmitt's view,

Hobbes belongs to this tradition as well, despite his attraction to natural-scientific forms of thought.[68] The Catholic counterrevolutionaries of the nineteenth century are even more outspoken defenders of theism in Schmitt's sense of the term.

The God of all these thinkers transcends the world and remains radically free in relation to it. On their view, the very existence of the world is a "miracle," since it cannot be accounted for on rational grounds.[69] The deists of the eighteenth and nineteenth centuries tended, by contrast, to identify their God ever more closely with the rational order of the world itself, which, they claimed, can be grasped through an "impersonal scientism." This attitude is represented in juristic thought by Kelsen's neo-Kantian philosophy of law, and in social science generally, by the positivism of Auguste Comte. The inevitable result, Schmitt says, is an "immanence pantheism" of which Hegel is the "greatest systematic architect."[70] In Hegel's philosophy, as in that of Kelsen and Comte, the distinction between God and the world disappears. The world *becomes* God, and therefore no longer needs a transcendent creator to guarantee either its existence or intelligibility. The Marxists and anarchists of the late nineteenth and early twentieth centuries are the last representatives of this tradition, whose essential goal, Schmitt claims, is revealed by their demand that "mankind" be "substituted for God."[71]

Against this, the defenders of theism have fought to save God from man and the world. They have battled to reclaim the boundlessness of God's freedom and to compel men to once again acknowledge their complete dependence on him. Their campaign has been, quite literally, a struggle *for God,* whose transcendence is obscured or denied by every facet of modern rationalism, as exemplified by the natural and social sciences alike.

Among those who have led this reactionary fight Schmitt singles out Donoso Cortes as a figure of special importance. He calls Donoso "one of the foremost representatives of decisionist thinking,"[72] and associates his own views on sovereignty and dictatorship with those of the Spanish writer.[73]

Like Donoso, Schmitt sees twentieth-century Europe as a vast battlefield on which two opposing theological parties are engaged in a fight to the death. One of these seeks to exile God and the other to save him. Schmitt characterizes his own voluntarist definition of the concept of the political as a purely scholarly exercise undertaken for the sake of intellectual clarification alone.[74] But there can be no doubt that it rests on Schmitt's own commitment to the party of God in the struggle for the soul of European civilization.

THE DEPOLITICIZATION OF THE WORLD

This is the first way in which Schmitt's concept of politics is linked to the reactionary Catholicism of Donoso and Maistre, who were, as Schmitt observes, more Protestant than Catholic in the fervor and unrelentingness of their Augustinianism.[75] But there is a second and deeper connection between his political philosophy and the theology of sin and grace that Donoso espoused. This comes out most clearly in Schmitt's famous critique of liberal parliamentarianism and of what he calls the "depoliticization" of the world.[76]

Democracy and liberalism are importantly different. The first is essentially a voluntarist ideal: the will of the people shall control. The second is thoroughly rationalist. Liberal parliamentarianism rests on the principle that political action ought to be governed by what is "rationally correct" and assumes that this can be discovered by means of an open "discussion" among "disinterested" participants—open both in the sense of having no restrictions as to content and no conclusion other than the discovery of the truth itself.[77]

Schmitt concedes that democracy tends in a rationalist direction on account of the need to determine which of the many possible ways of representing the people's will is the "true" one, so that what is originally a voluntarist ideal eventually becomes a rationalist one instead. This leads him to remark that democracy may be "fated to destroy itself."[78] Still, for the time being at least, democracy and liberalism remain discrete political values. The first of these is age-old. The idea that government is an expression of the will of the people is one the ancient Greeks already understood. By contrast, liberalism is a distinctively modern phenomenon. It is a product of the triumph of the deist theology that insists that everything in the world is transparent to reason and that human beings possess the capacity to direct their own affairs in a strictly rational fashion. Liberalism is the most important expression, in the political sphere, of the victory of deism over its theistic opponent.

Yet paradoxically, Schmitt says, the ascendancy of liberalism as a political ideal signals the end of politics itself. That is because it is in principle incapable of acknowledging what he calls "the concept of the foreign."

Every democracy draws a distinction between those who belong to or are allied with it (its "friends") and those who threaten its existence in some fashion (its "enemies").[79] This means that democracies face the same possibility of extinction as other political regimes and have the same need to command the lives of their citizens in an extreme situation where a decision must be made either to capitulate or to fight for the survival of the regime itself. In this respect, democracies are no different from monarchies or republics.

Liberalism, by contrast, is essentially un- or antipolitical. The rationalist ideal of open and endless discussion directed toward the eventual discovery of the truth does not itself allow for the recognition of a distinction between friends and enemies, since there is nothing in this ideal that justifies excluding some men, who are rational beings too, from participating in the truth-seeking conversation that liberalism sets up as the benchmark of legitimate authority. Nor does liberalism, considered in its own terms, acknowledge the possibility of an extreme case in which its existence must be defended in a fight to the death, for there can never be a *liberal* reason to terminate discussion or to respond to those who would do so with anything other than a renewed commitment to persuade them of the error of their ways. As a consequence, a liberal regime that remains faithful to its own ideals can never find itself at a fateful moment of decision, in an existential struggle with enemies who stand outside the universal community these ideals themselves assume. If it does, that is because it has subordinated its commitment to liberalism to *something else*—the promotion of economic interests, the protection of territory, the vindication of the will of the people, and so on.

The goal toward which the logic of liberalism carries its defenders is therefore the establishment of a world-state—a community encompassing the whole of mankind in which every political question is simply a problem of "management"[80] to be resolved by means of discussion alone. But such a community is no longer, Schmitt says, a political one at all. It is only the possibility of an existential fight against one's enemies, in which some command others to sacrifice themselves so that their community may survive, that gives any community of human beings its political character. The innermost tendency of all liberal thinking is to eliminate this possibility once and for all. According to Schmitt, the triumph of liberalism would therefore mean not the vindication of a political ideal but the complete elimination of politics itself. It would mean the "depoliticization" of the world as a whole.

It is reasonable to ask what is undesirable about this. If the existence of politics is tied to the friend-enemy distinction, and with that to the ever-present possibility of war, then the abolition of politics would seem to mean the end of war, with all its horror and suffering. In place of the bellicose posturing of states, we might look forward to the peaceable solution of practical problems in the discursive and rational way that liberalism recommends.

Fighting issues would become problems of administration to be settled on the basis of universal goals and neutral techniques, rather than the parochial loyalties of statesmen and warriors.

There is much to be said for this ideal, especially against the background of the endless fighting that has marked man's political life on earth so far. Yet Schmitt recoils from it with horror. There is nothing he hates as much as the prospective depoliticization of the world, and though he pretends at times to regard its inevitability as a mere historical fact, the withering away of politics is something Schmitt contemplates with fear and disgust. Why? Schmitt gives three answers.

The first is that a world-state would possess terrifying power. No other state would exist to block or limit its dominion over human beings. Today, as in the past, men live in a political "pluriverse" of separate states. In a world-state, all power would be concentrated in the hands of a single administrative apparatus. No greater threat to individual freedom is imaginable. This might be called Schmitt's libertarian objection to liberalism.[81]

His second objection shares a certain affinity with Nietzsche's critique of modernity. In the world that liberalism holds up as an ideal, there would be nothing for the state to do but manage the flow of traffic, in Schmitt's derisive phrase.[82] To be sure, the careful management of resources might expand human opportunities enormously. It is not unreasonable to think that in such a world, men would be freer than ever before. But "[f]or what would they be free?" Schmitt asks.[83] The lives of human beings would be peaceful and comfortable, but "riskless" and therefore without meaning.[84]

More precisely, the inhabitants of a liberal utopia would face no *political* risks. Presumably, they would still face the risks of disease, unemployment and the like, but these would all be problems of management to be dealt with administratively. In addition, of course, they would confront the challenge of deciding how to live their lives—of determining what their defining loyalties should be. But given the peaceable values of their world and its insistence on the discursive resolution of all issues, no matter how pressing, they would be discouraged from carrying these loyalties to a suicidal extreme, instead of living to argue for another day. And in any event, even if some decided to give up their lives for the sake of their deepest commitments, that would be a purely personal decision. No one could command them to do it. That is possible only in politics. No matter how intense, the loyalties of the citizens of a liberal world-state can therefore never be anything more that *personal* values, whose subjectivity renders them forever vulnerable to self-doubt and puts their meaningfulness under a cloud of insecurity from which no one can ever escape.

In a world-state that realizes the liberal ideal, life must therefore either be spent in the pursuit of meaningless trivialities that lack all dignity and glory—a warm bed, an evening's entertainment and vacations from time to time—or in the pursuit of an identity whose foundations rest on attachments of a wholly personal kind, and thus can never possess the unshakeable objectivity of the identity one has as the member of a political community with the power and authority to command its members to die. In a liberal world-state, life would be comfortable and free but pointless. Schmitt's characterization of the essential emptiness of such an existence echoes Nietzsche's description of what he calls Europe's "last man."[85]

It is Schmitt's third criticism of liberalism, however, that betrays most clearly his allegiance to the tradition of Catholic reaction represented by his hero Donoso.

Immediately after asking whether the freedom of human beings in a world-state would have the value liberals suppose, Schmitt says that the answer to this question ultimately turns on the answer to another—whether man is by nature good. This is the "anthropological" question to which one finally comes in assessing the merits of liberal ideals.[86]

On the one side are those who believe in man's inherent goodness and regard the evil that men do as a consequence of the material and other constraints from which, in a posthistorical liberal world-state, they would at last be freed. When this happens, the goodness that is latent in men will flourish and ramify in endless ways. Eventually, after this process has gone far enough, there will no longer be a need for government to keep men in check through the threat of coercive violence, though the complexity of human relations will always require administrative oversight and organization.

On the other side are those who deny that human beings are by nature good. Some, like Machiavelli and Hobbes, do so because their observation of human behavior has led them to conclude that men are always selfish and cruel. This is for them an empirical not a theological judgment. In Hobbes' case, it is one of the factual premises of his argument for the necessity of an authoritarian state. Schmitt admired Hobbes' authoritarianism but mistrusted the rationalizing spirit in which Hobbes proceeds to construct a science of politics on the basis of his bleak assessment of human nature. In Schmitt's view, this prepared the way for further rationalizations, which when joined to the utopian conception of human nature embraced by those who answer the anthropological question in the affirmative, produces the modern, liberal technocratic state whose culture and ideals Schmitt despises.

Schmitt himself identifies with another group of thinkers who like Hobbes give a negative answer to this question, but for essentially religious reasons. This group includes Maistre and Donoso and others in the tradition of reactionary Catholic thought. Their political theory starts with the assumption that men are not merely selfish but sinful, and that since their sin is "original" and cannot be removed, it must be kept in bounds by force. This is the anthropological premise that underlies Augustine's defense of political authority in *The City of God*. In the view of those who accept Augustine's premise, politics is at once the most basic expression of, and the best defense against, the sinfulness that lies at the heart of human nature. Schmitt's own conception of politics rests on this assumption. It provides the key to understanding his interpretation of the meaning of the friend-enemy distinction.

According to Schmitt, human beings cannot help dividing the world into friends and enemies. This is a characteristic of human nature that no amount of education will ever expunge. "Enmity" is therefore always a "real possibility."[87] Men will always have enemies and be prepared to kill them for the sake of their friends.

The first significant human act after the fall was Cain's murder of Abel. In killing his brother, Cain showed the world and God the wickedness in his heart—a preview of the evil that has corrupted human history ever since. But Cain's murder of Abel was a private act. It was not political in nature. It was a crime, not an act of war. The political killing that is done in war, when the members of one community slaughter those of another because they have been ordered to do so, is vastly greater in magnitude than all private killings taken together, and more sinful because of the permission to kill that has been granted those who do it, on account of which they feel discharged from personal responsibility for their murderous acts. In this sense, politics is the *most striking expression* of the ineradicable sinfulness of human beings. To assume, as liberals do, that the world can be depoliticized is therefore to believe that men can be cured of the homicidal lust that has been our condition since Eden. For those, like Schmitt, who accept the idea of original sin, this is an insane aspiration.

It is a dangerous one as well. The fantastic view of human nature that underlies the liberal ideal of a world-state cannot make the sinfulness in human nature disappear. All it can do is conceal it, under the utopian pretense that men are essentially good. And when the reality of sin is denied, and thereby hidden from view, it is bound to fester and eventually erupt in even more extravagant forms. If a world-state were ever to come into being, it would therefore not be the peaceful kingdom liberals imagine. It would be a killing field of unprecedented proportions, since the wickedness of men, now backed by limitless power, would be completely unconstrained and given license by the state's authority to treat every criminal as a traitor to humankind.

The best defense we have against the sin in our souls is to recognize its presence openly and accept the inevitability of the political pluriverse that is both its most visible expression and most reliable (if still imperfect) remedy. This is the only realistic position and the safest one too, for the humble acceptance of our broken condition and of the political enmities it entails is far more likely to keep sin in check than the prideful pursuit of a world beyond politics—which in the severe Augustinian anthropology that Maistre and Donoso and Schmitt all accept, could only be an imaginary world beyond man.

TECHNICITY

Ultimately, for Schmitt, the denial of man's sinful nature is more than a dangerous error. It is an offense against God himself. It is itself a sin of the gravest kind.

Liberalism assumes that every problem in the world is amenable to a technical solution. It rests on a belief in man's "unlimited power and the dominion of man over nature, even human nature; the belief in the unlimited 'receding of natural boundaries.'"[88] This may not seem to be a religious dogma. Indeed, its defenders generally insist that their beliefs are merely technical in nature. But in fact, Schmitt says, the gospel of "technicity" is a religious doctrine that takes a clear stand on matters of ultimate concern. It is a gospel of salvation—one that teaches that man is able to achieve his own salvation, without any help from God. In this sense, the religion of technicity is an "anti-religion,"[89] for its central teaching is the precise opposite of the one that lies at the heart of the Christian religion whose values form the spiritual bedrock of European civilization.

Christianity teaches that God, not man, is the master of the world; that man is broken, humiliated, sinful and dependent; that no human being can achieve salvation except through the grace of God; and that men today are tempted, just as Adam was, to usurp the place of God, claiming for themselves the right and power to supply the ground of their own being—a

monstrous presumption. In the Christian view, this has always been the satanic temptation, and the anti-religion of technicity on which liberalism is
founded represents, for Schmitt, the world historical culmination of satan-
ism in twentieth-century Europe.

The developments of the previous four centuries have prepared the way
for this epiphany of pride and its confrontation with the Christian view of
life. The "most consequential shift"[90] occurred when "the concepts and arguments of Christian theology" were displaced by a natural-scientific metaphysics that transformed our understanding of nature and man.[91] Of special
importance in this regard was Descartes' mechanization of the human body,
which in turn influenced Hobbes' conception of the state as a vast, artificial
machine (an imaginative shift that, despite Hobbes' own authoritarian view
of political authority, laid the ground for the rationalization of law and administration on which the modern *Rechtsstaat* is founded).[92]

In the process, religion (which before had been identified with the state)
was transformed into a private phenomenon, beyond the power of the state
to control. Schmitt blames Spinoza for this development. He suggests that it
was Spinoza's "Jewish" detachment from the state that motivated his desire
to privatize religion and thereby convert it into a purely subjective set of beliefs that the law cannot reach.[93] The result was a weakening of religion and
the eventual disappearance of God from the public world. Among other
things, this led to the displacement of the Christian doctrine of grace by the
morality of autonomy that Kant sought to put on an impeccably rational
foundation.

In this new and godless world, ruled by Cartesian mechanics and Kantian ethics, hitherto unimaginable human ambitions became routine. Everywhere, natural-scientific thinking took hold, with its optimism about the
perfectibility of human beings and confidence in their powers to improve their
own condition without limit. Schmitt cites Condorcet's assertion that man
can attain "a kind of worldly eternity" by pushing death farther and farther
back, as a characteristic expression of such thinking.[94] In this and countless
other ways, the Europe of the eighteenth and nineteenth centuries assumed
the form of an ever more aggressive civilization of pride, based on a repudiation of the age-old Christian understanding of life as a pilgrimage to another
world, and of death as the badge of original sin—rather than an inconvenience
to be overcome by technical means.

Our age, the age of technicity, is the historical product of all these developments. Its spirit, Schmitt says, is "fantastic and satanic,"[95] for today the am-

bition to convert every problem of human living into one of administration is motivated more openly than ever before by the shameless wish to be God and to transform the world into a paradise of our own making. The natural-scientific, liberal view of politics expresses this ideal in a particularly bold way. It sneers at the doctrine of original sin. It mocks those who claim our salvation depends upon God. It exults in the spirit of human autonomy. With the teachings of modern liberalism, we thus reach the end of a centuries-long process of "neutralization" that from Descartes to Kelsen has been animated by what Schmitt calls the "anti-religion" of technicity.

On the other side stand the knights of grace, more resolute than ever in their belief that man is born to sin and can be saved only by God. The confrontation between these two religious ideals is an event of immense political importance. It is bound to affect the future of politics in Europe and beyond. But for Schmitt, it has an even larger significance. It is a theological struggle whose meaning transcends the ordinary world of political conflict because it touches the nerve of man's relation to God. It is a battle of cosmic proportions, like the one that Maistre saw in the French Revolution and Donoso in the contest between Catholic and "philosophic" civilizations. The conflict between technicity and its enemies is Carl Schmitt's version of Augustine's war between the cities of man and God.

In 1922, writing as an historian of European civilization, Schmitt calls the confrontation between the secular ideal of human freedom and Donoso's belief in man's irremediable wickedness "a great alternative," a "big either/or."[96] Seven years later, in the midst of the constitutional crisis that led to the downfall of the Weimar Republic and the ascension of Hitler and the Nazi Party, Schmitt describes this same confrontation as a "decisive moment," a "decisive event," an "enormous climax."[97] Things are quickly coming to a head, he says, and one must choose sides in the struggle—between the ideology of technicity, represented by the Bolshevists and Americans (brutally in the first case, more genially in the second),[98] and the politics of authority, which insists that man's destiny lies in hands other than his own.

Carl Schmitt was a brilliant and educated man who understood the history of modern Europe with a depth and refinement few could match. He must have found the stupid thuggishness of the Nazi leadership revolting. But for a time, at least, he cast his fortunes with the Nazis because he saw in their movement the last best chance of victory against the spirit of pride that liberalism represents. Schmitt had other, more specific and opportunistic reasons for supporting the Nazis, and the majority of those who did so were moved not by theological concerns but economic ones and the crudest kind of racial hatred. But the deepest source of Schmitt's own Nazism was, if one may be permitted the phrase, more refined. For it sprang from the tradition of reactionary Catholicism that Schmitt inherited from Donoso and Maistre— itself the final stage in the voluntarist revolt against the rationalization of God that began in the fourteenth century.

Within a few years, Schmitt's theologically inspired commitment to Nazism was overwhelmed by a movement that openly reviled the Christian religion and sought to replace it with a barbaric ethic of folk and race. When this happened, Schmitt's star went into decline. He came under suspicion on account of being insufficiently anti-Semitic. But before this happened, he was an enthusiastic supporter of the Nazi Party, and if one asks how a man of such learning and intelligence could even for a time have endorsed a political movement whose inhumanity was clear from the start, the answer lies in Schmitt's religiously grounded hatred of man—in his lifelong belief in the theology of grace that was the central tenet of the tradition of reactionary Catholicism he absorbed as a child. The metaphysics of pride and grace, subtilized and reworked yet still endowed with philosophical grandeur, was the lens through which Schmitt conceived the nature of political action and judged the ultimate meaning of the events of his time. Only a theological frame so profound, so responsive to our deepest human concerns, could have deluded, even for a moment, an otherwise sharp observer of people and events into thinking that he might find redemption from the spirit of technicity in the murderous company of Hitler and Göring.[99]

CHAPTER 25

The Oblivion of Being

MARTIN HEIDEGGER'S RECONSTRUCTION
OF WESTERN PHILOSOPHY

In 1967, one of the greatest poets of the twentieth century went for a walk with one of the century's most famous philosophers. The poet was Paul Celan, a Romanian Jew who had lost most of his family in the Holocaust. The philosopher was Martin Heidegger. Celan admired Heidegger's writings, and Heidegger Celan's. At the philosopher's invitation, Celan made a visit to Heidegger's hut in the Black Forest, and the two took a stroll together.

In the 1930s, Heidegger had been a member of the Nazi Party and for a time was active in the movement. Many felt he never adequately apologized for his actions. It seems that Celan went hoping for a word of contrition that would allow him to establish a deeper human relation with the philosopher— something more than Heidegger's shocking remark, in an essay written years after the war, that the Nazi death camps had been offensive in the same way and to the same degree as factory farming. The word never came. Celan records his disappointment in his poem "Todtnauberg."[1]

If he had really understood Heidegger's philosophy, Celan ought not to have been disappointed. Nor should anyone be shocked by Heidegger's comparison of Auschwitz with a mechanized farm, for the comparison reflects the inner core of all his thinking from 1930 on. In Heidegger's view, the camp and the farm are both manifestations of man's will to be lord of the earth. They are equally evil because both are driven by a common ambition of such cosmic impudence that differences in its expression are mere matters of degree.

Like Carl Schmitt's political theology, Martin Heidegger's philosophy of being has its roots in the Augustinian theology of grace he was taught as a child. It also culminates in a religiously inspired hatred of technology. And, as in Schmitt's case, Heidegger's loathing for the blasphemous excesses of the modern world explains his brief but heartfelt commitment to Nazism. To expect Heidegger to apologize for this would have been to demand that he repudiate everything he most deeply believed.

Heidegger's so-called "later" philosophy is organized around the meaning of the idea of metaphysics, as this has been understood in the tradition of Western philosophy from Plato to Nietzsche. Most of the works that Heidegger discusses in explaining and criticizing this idea are philosophical texts outside the field of dogmatic theology—the writings of Plato, Aristotle, Descartes, Kant and others. This makes it difficult for those not on the lookout to grasp the central role that Augustine's theology of fall and redemption plays in Heidegger's thought. But its influence is pervasive and shapes every branch of his work, which in reality is no mere exercise in "thinking," or attempt at a new philosophy of being but the last systematic theology of reaction in the line that descends from Joseph de Maistre.

THROWNNESS AND SURRENDER

Martin Heidegger was born in 1889 in the small South German town of Messkirch. Like Carl Schmitt, he was raised in an ardently antimodernist Catholic milieu shaped by an unrelenting theology of sin and grace.[2] At the age of twenty, Heidegger entered a Jesuit seminary but left after three semesters. The following winter, he enrolled at the University of Freiburg, with the ambition of studying the natural sciences in order to equip himself to make a distinctive contribution to "the religious and cultural development" of the Catholic Church.[3] He soon became absorbed in logical and philosophical questions instead. These occupied his attention for the next four years. During this time, he continued to write for various reactionary Catholic journals.

After completing a doctorate on the logic of propositions (influenced by his close study of Edmund Husserl's *Logical Investigations*), Heidegger wrote a second dissertation on a technical topic in fourteenth-century scholastic philosophy ("Dun Scotus' Doctrine of Categories and Meaning"). In 1918, he began his academic career as an assistant to Husserl. Shortly after, Heidegger formally broke with the Catholic Church. It was a difficult decision, arrived at only after much soul-searching. He nevertheless remained deeply interested in the nature of religious experience and continued to show a personal sympathy for it, as his lectures on religion in 1920–21 make apparent.[4]

In 1923, Heidegger was appointed to a professorship at Marburg and within a few years had begun to attract wide attention. By the time he moved to Freiburg in 1928, as Husserl's successor, he was regarded by many as the most daring and brilliant philosopher in Germany, principally on account of the publication of *Being and Time* the year before. In 1933, Heidegger joined the Nazi Party and for a year served as the rector of Freiburg, working actively in this capacity to advance the party's program in the sphere of higher education. Heidegger continued to teach and write until the end of the Second World War, after which he was banned for a time from university teaching on account of his association with the Nazis.

Several of Heidegger's most influential works were either written or first published after the war. During these years, his reputation continued to grow. When he died in 1976, many shared the view of his student Hannah Arendt, who declared that her teacher belonged in the company of Plato and Kant, and should be forgiven his brief involvement with the Nazi Party. Others considered this an inexcusable failing, but Arendt and those who shared her view saw it as the understandable lapse of a great thinker unused to the complexities and treacheries of political life.[5] No question about Heidegger's philosophy remains more controversial than that of its connection to Nazi ideas.[6]

During his first two years at Freiburg, Heidegger's attention was still focused on what he calls the nature of *Dasein,* literally the "being-there" that defines our distinctively human way of existing—what others more simply call the human condition. This had been the principal subject of *Being and Time.* Already, there, Heidegger had announced that his fundamental preoccupation was not with man but being. But man is the only being for whom being itself is a question. In the metaphorical sense that the word *Dasein* invites, man is the "place" where the question of being arises. An investigation of the human condition is therefore a necessary prelude to an inquiry into the nature of being itself.[7]

"On the Essence of Ground" (1929) reflects Heidegger's continuing engagement with the preliminary question of the condition or situation of *Dasein*.[8] He begins the lecture by returning to one of the main themes of *Being and Time.*

Human beings do not merely exist among other beings. We "are pervasively attuned to them." We exist "ecstatically," reaching out toward a "world" that lies beyond us. Heidegger calls this reaching out "transcendence." Through it, we "surpass" all other beings—not in the sense that we are better than they, but that our being, unlike theirs, is not self-contained. We are the beings whose being is to "go beyond" ourselves. This going beyond is an "irruption." It is the "primordial movement that freedom accomplishes with us ourselves," and it brings to light, for men alone, the "world" conceived as a totality of beings, or cosmos. Even the cleverest animals are merely "in" the world. They do not "have" one.[9] This is our unique privilege, for only we possess the freedom that makes possible "a world-projective surpassing of beings."

Our freedom and attunement to the world, as opposed to mere presence in it, are thus, for Heidegger, correlative ideas. Together, they constitute the essential condition of *Dasein*—that of an ecstatic being for whom the world exists, as a world, on account of the freedom that releases us from the circle of worldless immanence in which all other beings are trapped. The key to grasping the uniqueness of this condition is to be found in certain distinctively human moods, such as anxiety and boredom, whose very nature reveals that we are attuned to the world as a whole, and not merely, as other animals are, to particular objects of fear and desire.[10]

But for Heidegger, this is only half the story. The other half concerns the origin of the freedom that constitutes our transcendent being-in-the-world. Where does this freedom come from? Are we the authors of it? Most certainly not. "The fact that" we exist as free, ecstatic beings "does not lie in the power of this freedom itself." We find ourselves in possession of freedom, but without the power to give it to ourselves. Freedom is, for us, a condition into which we are "thrown"—one whose source lies beyond us and which we therefore cannot secure on our own. Our freedom is not an achievement but a gift, and its "thrownness" reflects our "impotence," a condition of receptivity or passivity that is "the essence of finitude in Dasein."[11]

Through the gift of freedom, we encounter the world as a whole, though always at a "distance," as a totality of beings we discover but do not create. Anyone who pauses to reflect on this must be filled with wonder in Aristotle's sense. Most of the time, however, we do not wonder at all about our paradoxical constitution as beings thrown into transcendence, free and finite at once. We "lose sight" of who we really are amidst all the noisy distractions of everyday life.[12] Indeed, we *want* to lose sight of this because there is something unnerving about it. In 1929, Heidegger stills calls this kind of deliberate inattention "inauthenticity," the name he gives it in *Being and Time*. Those who live inauthentically are like the prisoners in Plato's cave. They do not

THE OBLIVION OF BEING 517

know who or where they are because they have chosen not to know out of fear of being overwhelmed by the uncanniness of their condition.

To live authentically, one must learn to "listen into the distance" that our thrown transcendence opens for us. (Other animals cannot do this, since they have no distance from the world at all.[13]) Soon, Heidegger will reinterpret the meaning of such listening in terms of man's relation to being, the announced but as-yet-unexplored topic of *Being and Time* and the main focus of his work from 1930 on. But in the two or three years immediately following the publication of *Being and Time,* he continues to construe the aim of listening, as he does there, principally as a way of orienting oneself toward other human beings.

Attentive, ardent listening into the distance "awakens Dasein to the response of the other Dasein in whose company it can surrender its I-ness so as to attain itself as an authentic self." As "creature[s] of distance," our condition is one of essential loneliness. We strive to forget this by losing ourselves in mere busyness and chatter. Indeed, few of us can bear, for long, to recall how lonely we are. To save myself from this state of anxious forgetfulness, in which most men live their lives, I must surrender my solitary self to another human being, coming *to* my self by *giving it up* in the selfless care for another who is haunted by anxiety too (a form of care as far removed from its everyday imitations as true self-knowledge is from the ignorance of the chattering crowd in Plato's cave).

Even at this stage, the idea of surrender is intimately connected in Heidegger's thought to that of salvation. To be saved, one must give oneself up to something or someone else. Heidegger's understanding of the meaning of surrender will change in the years ahead, as his attention shifts from the nature of *Dasein*—the one who inquires after being—to being itself. But the idea of surrender will remain at the center of his thought to the end of his career and be linked with growing urgency to a doctrine of salvation that echoes Augustine's theology of grace at every step along the way.

TRUTH AND ERRANCY

Heidegger's 1930 lecture, "On the Essence of Truth," is an important transitional work in this regard.

Heidegger begins, once again, by characterizing freedom as transcendence, and transcendence as the place where the world comes to light as a world. It is only in freedom that the world is disclosed. The achievement of freedom is therefore that of "letting beings be." From this, Heidegger now draws a further conclusion regarding the nature of truth. In the most basic sense, truth is "disclosure." "The fulfillment and consummation of the essence of truth" lies in "the disclosure of beings." All other conceptions (most importantly, that of truth as the accuracy or correctness of our representations) presuppose this one, for it is only through their antecedent disclosure that beings appear to us and become representable at all, whether correctly or otherwise.

We do many things to and with the beings that our freedom brings to light. We shape them for practical ends, and investigate them for scientific purposes. Human beings are constantly "working on the world" in these and other ways. But the primal disclosure of the world, on which all these activities depend, is no more our doing than freedom itself. The "disclosure of beings"—truth in the most primitive sense—is a gift, in the same way that our freedom is. Indeed, they are the same gift, for no matter how hard we strain to comprehend the world our freedom discloses, and to map and commemorate it in speech, all our efforts depend upon the world already being there for us on account of an antecedent revelation we receive from a source beyond the freedom in which our *Dasein* consists.

Heidegger calls this primal revelation a "mystery." It is not something for which we can account. That is because in order to account for it, we would have to be its authors ourselves. But we are not the authors of this revelation, any more than of the freedom through which it comes to light. Quite the opposite. No amount of human activity can ever overcome the mysterious dependence implied by our original possession of the power of sight that alone makes possible all the countless things we see and do with it. The deepest truth about the "essence" of truth is that we are its beneficiaries not its creators.

This suggests what might be called an "ethic" of truthfulness, though Heidegger himself does not use the term.

One who is mindful of the mystery of freedom will strive to remain "resolutely open" to it. To do this, he must "let beings be." "Letting" of this kind is hard work. It requires concentration and effort. Indeed, there is no harder work on earth. But it is work undertaken in service to a gift one has received. The thinker or artist or statesman who employs his freedom in this spirit "remembers" that he is the beneficiary of an unaccountable gift and strives to honor the world that has been disclosed to him through a revelation of which he is not the author but merely (to use an image that will figure prominently in Heidegger's later writing) the caretaker or custodian. Such remembering is the mark of all authentic work, whether of a philosophical or any other kind.

This is not, however, the only possible response to the mystery. Our freedom always contains within itself another possibility—that instead of letting beings be, we will strive to subordinate them to ourselves in a self-aggrandizing fashion. When this happens, beings are "covered up and distorted." The mystery that first brings them to light is "forgotten." In the mysteryless world that remains, man "replenishes" what he finds "on the basis of his latest needs and aims, and fills out that world by means of planning and proposing." Human beings now take their "standards" from their own plans and from "the most readily available beings," that is, those that are the most understandable in human terms and hence the least mysterious. This leads to an "inordinate forgetfulness," which "persists in securing itself by means of what is readily available and always accessible." In this way, man "is turned away from the mystery." "The human being's flight from the mystery toward what is readily available, onward from one current thing to the next, passing the mystery by—this is *erring*."

Erring does not merely happen from time to time. "Human beings are always astray in errancy." Errancy is therefore something deeper than the tendency to make mistakes. It is "the open site and ground" of this tendency.

In this sense, errancy is built into our nature. If the essence of man is freedom—the power to let beings be—errancy is "the essential counteressence to the originary essence of truth." It is the turning away from the mystery of truth as disclosure toward a conception of truth that is comforting because it is one that man takes from himself.

In turning away, man makes himself the measure of all things, as if human beings "were open of and in themselves." The belief that they are themselves the ground of freedom and truth is the deepest "forgetfulness," the darkest oblivion, into which human beings can fall. Yet their very nature prescribes that they are constantly falling into it, because in their innermost being men wish to live without mystery and without thankfulness for a gift they have not created and therefore can never understand.

It would be a mistake, however, to think that our willful refusal to let beings be, and to accept the mystery that brings them to light, is entirely our own doing. We *are* responsible for our acts of refusal, philosophical and other, but the condition of errancy from which all such acts arise is no more our creation than the freedom we exercise when we err. It, too, is something we simply receive—a condition into which we are "thrown." Thus, both the power of disclosure *and* that of concealment—the ability of human beings to honor the mystery and their longing to turn away from it, toward self-sufficiency and self-control—are granted to us as beings of the kind we are.

Among other things, this means that just as we can never succeed in re-creating for ourselves the gift of our own freedom, we can never decide on our own whether the mystery of this gift will reappear to those who disavow it "in and for forgetfulness." Man freely cooperates in such forgetfulness. But he is no more its ground than he is of the mystery it conceals. Even in the darkest recesses of forgetfulness, therefore, the possibility always remains that the mystery will once again make itself manifest in a way that moves men to let it be. There is always room to hope that a god will appear and "save us" (as Heidegger says in a later essay) from the prideful delusion on which the tendency to errancy rests: the belief that we are the authors of the being of beings, and create it from nothing rather than receiving it through a mysterious revelation from which our own yearning for self-sufficiency moves us to turn away.

Recast in traditional theological terms, Heidegger's position in "The Essence of Truth" might be restated as follows.

Among all the creatures in the world, human beings are the only ones who are free. (The essence of *Dasein* is transcendence.) Man's freedom is a gift. (Men are not "open of and in themselves.") Because they are free, human beings are able to avow or disavow the gift they have received. (Both truth and errancy are for them primordial possibilities.) But man rebels against acknowledging the gift on which his freedom depends. (Men set up their own plans and standards as the measure of truth.) In their pride, human beings repudiate the one who gave them the gift in the first place. (They turn away from the "mystery.") The longing to be God is the original sin that stains our human nature. (We are "always astray" in errancy.)

Still, the possibility of acknowledging God's grace is also always present. (The mystery may be "forgotten" but can never be abolished.) Those who do so will be saved from their worldliness (recalled from forgetfulness) and humbled in their pride. (They will see that in order to live in the truth they must give up the attempt to reconstruct the world "by means of their own resources," and resolve instead to let beings be in gratefulness for the gift of disclosure.)

Heidegger's 1930 lecture contains this theology *in nuce*. He expresses it in novel philosophical terms, but behind his strikingly original formulations, it is not hard to discern the outlines of the older theology of grace and sin that

Augustine had defended long before. Over the next two decades, in an idiom all his own, Heidegger will reinterpret the history of Western philosophy from the vantage point of this theology, and on its basis construct a reactionary critique of the modern world as sweeping as Joseph de Maistre's.

FALL

In Heidegger's retelling of the story, the tradition of Western thought begins with an act of forgetfulness in which an earlier understanding of truth as disclosure and thinking as reverence is displaced by a new conception of truth as "correctness" and philosophy as "metaphysics." This occurs already in Plato, whose Parable of the Cave still contains traces of the older understanding it displaces.[14]

In Plato's parable, the "sun" is that which "enables everything that 'comes to be' to go forth into the visibility of its stable duration." It "makes whatever appears be accessible in its visible form (*eidos*)." It "grants" the "appearing of the visible form in which whatever is present has its stability." This granting is a "saving." The sun "saves" the being of beings. It is the "salvation" of the world. Conceived in this way, Plato's image of the sun preserves the pre-Socratic understanding of truth as disclosure (*aletheia*).

At the same time, the Parable of the Cave subtly yet decisively pushes this older conception of truth to the margin, and replaces it with a different one based on the notion that truth consists in the accuracy or correctness of the mind's grasp of the form or *idea* a thing displays. Within the parable itself, Heidegger says, "*aletheia* comes under the yoke of *idea*." This is "the unspoken event whereby *idea* gains dominance over *aletheia*." As a result, the understanding of truth as the disclosure that precedes all seeing and knowing is displaced by a conception of truth as the "alignment" or "agreement" of seeing and knowing with the *idea* of what is seen or known.

In the parable itself, there is an "ambiguity" regarding these two conceptions of truth. The ambiguity is captured in Plato's use of the image of the sun to describe *both* the light that first discloses the realm of beings as a whole and is therefore necessarily prior to it (is "beyond being," as Plato says),[15] *and* the greatest (the brightest and most visible) being within this realm itself. Plato's own philosophy resolves this ambiguity in favor of the latter conception. The movement from error to truth, which the Parable of the Cave illustrates and explains, comes to be conceived as "the process whereby the gaze becomes more correct." "Truth becomes *orthotes*." With this shift in the understanding

of truth, thinking becomes metaphysics—the discipline that seeks to comprehend the being of beings, that is, their most general property or "essence."
What Heidegger calls the "ontological difference" between being and beings
is thereby lost from view, for the ideal of truth as correctness "loses sight" of
the fact that there is something antecedent to the essence of beings, namely,
the act or "event" by which their being is first disclosed.

After Plato, all of Western philosophy proceeds on the assumption that
truth is correctness and that "[t]he assertion of a judgment made by the intellect is the place of truth and falsehood and of the difference between them."
Philosophy becomes "metaphysics" and its twin discipline "logic." These are
not the neutral sciences their practitioners claim but *interpretations* that rest
on the forgetfulness of being. They are born of an amnesia that no longer recalls the gift of the light in which human beings dwell. They have ceased to
be inspired by the reverential awe this gift once awakened, before Plato, in
the first great age of Greek thought. One can still detect this spirit of reverence in the mysterious fragments of Parmenides and Heraclitus, if one knows
how to read them. But today that is nearly impossible.[16]

With Plato, Western man begins his descent into oblivion, driven by the
desire to comprehend and thereby master the world. The doctrine of truth as
correctness is the first, fatal step in this direction. It liberates the desire for
intellectual and practical control by providing the indispensable means for
it. After Plato, Western thought moves farther and farther away from anything that might remotely be described as an attitude of thankfulness for the
gift of being. It is caught in a widening spiral of pride. The origin of metaphysics in Plato's conception of truth as correctness marks the moment of
Western humanity's fall from grace.

Whatever other differences there may be between them, Plato and Aristotle are in this respect the same.

An "echo" of the pre-Socratic understanding of truth as disclosure may
also still be heard in Aristotle's writings too. But here, as in Plato's philosophy of ideas, a new conception of truth moves to the fore.[17] This becomes clear
if we examine carefully the concept of *phusis* in Aristotle's *Physics,* "the hidden and therefore never adequately studied foundational book of Western
philosophy."

According to Heidegger, *phusis* originally means "presencing," the process
whereby something comes forth on its own, out of darkness and concealment,
into the realm of the visible. This is the defining characteristic of "*phusei*-
beings," which "blossom forth" and "show themselves" to be what they are

in an unforced display. These are the sorts of things that "grow" by themselves, in contrast to artifacts which lack the same power of self-display.

The form (*morphe*) of things that blossom in this way must be understood, in the first place, not as an independently subsisting reality but a process or act: "the act of standing or placing itself" into appearance. So conceived, the form of a thing is not distinct from its appearance. It is just the power of "making an appearance" that stays "for a while," and that "preserves the 'while' (the presencing) of this appearance, and by preserving the appearance, stands forth in it and out of it."

The form of a thing is the power that grants it its moment in the sun and "saves" it there for a time. Such granting is a gift to which human beings, who alone have "the word," properly respond by "collecting" and "gathering" what appears in this way in a manner that lets the form of each *phusei*-being "be seen, from the being itself, what and how the being is." This is the original office of speech, which is an "act of revealing." "Unconcealment" is the power by which all *phusei*-beings come into the open out of the dark, and speech is the "place" where this power is acknowledged in thought, poetry, architecture and statecraft.

Yet in Aristotle's *Physics* too, as in Plato's Parable of the Cave, a new conception of form and of its relation to speech is already beginning to eclipse this older one. For Aristotle, form is not only the power of disclosure. It is also the most durable "aspect" of that which is disclosed. It is the "most real" aspect of *phusei*-beings, and, by extension, of beings of other sorts as well (especially those that result from a process of making, or *poesis*). In this sense, form is at once the "brightening" through which beings come to light *and* the brightest feature of them. It is disclosure *and* that which is most clearly disclosed, in the same way that the sun in Plato's parable is the light and that which is most brightly lit.

Understood in the second way, form is the "target" of mind. It is that which the mind aims to grasp by means of "logical" thinking. The being of beings is their form, and truth the accurate depiction of it.

This understanding of the being of beings, which is already gaining ground in Aristotle's *Physics,* eventually displaces the other completely. The interpretation of *morphe* as *substance,* and of *phusis* as *nature,* on which the tradition of philosophy in the Latin-speaking West henceforth depends, completes the process, covering in oblivion the understanding of *phusei*-being as unconcealment and of language as the reverential act of letting the blossoming forth of things be seen as the unforced gift it is. Aristotle gives this tradition the concepts on which its metaphysical understanding of being and truth is based. The philosophers who come after him work in ever-deepening forgetfulness of what the thinker on whom they rely still distantly heard as "the last echo" of the "great beginning of Greek philosophy."

BEING AS BEING-CREATED

With this shift, a change also takes place in the understanding of the divine. God is reinterpreted in metaphysical terms as well. The divine is no longer something beyond the realm of being. It is the *highest being within* this realm, like Plato's sun. As such, it is the "object" of the most profound sort of knowledge. This knowledge too is premised on the assumption that truth is correctness. To know the divine (like anything else) is to accurately represent its "nature." Knowledge of this kind is the highest one can possess. It is correct knowledge of the highest possible object of knowledge, which by definition is the highest being within the realm of beings. According to Heidegger, book lambda of Aristotle's *Metaphysics* already expresses this idea in a canonical form.

Christian theology likewise starts with the metaphysical assumption that God is the highest being, though one who exists beyond the world of created beings. The distinction between creator and creature is basic to Christian thought. But even the creator of the world is not beyond being. He is a being too. He is the most real being—the one that has more being than any other. Even in the epoch of Christian philosophy, therefore, the goal of thinking remains what it had been for Aristotle, namely, the correct apprehension of God. Different as they are in other ways, Aristotle's pagan conception of the eternal and divine and its Christian successor thus both belong, in Heidegger's view, to the tradition of metaphysics that starts with the obliteration of the ontological distinction between being and beings and the consequent reduction of being to the best of beings, as both Aristotle and Aquinas maintain.

Still, despite this essential continuity, an important shift occurs with the movement from pagan to Christian theology. Aristotle claimed that the being of beings resides in their form—in what came to be known as their nature or substance. He thought of God as the being with the most form or reality. This remains true for every Christian theologian as well. Being is substance, and God the most substantial being of all. But Christian doctrine teaches that God's essence lies in his will, an idea unknown to Greek philosophy. God therefore has the most substance because he has the greatest will.

Indeed, God's will (and hence his being or substance) is infinite because, as the will of one who brings all other beings into being from nothing, there is nothing to oppose it.

To have a will is to be a "subject." Christians express this idea by saying that God is a "person." Hence, in the Christian tradition, though God continues to be understood as the highest of all beings, his infinite substantiality now comes to be equated with his infinite subjectivity. Substance becomes subject, and the way is prepared for the modern philosophy of subjectivity that in Heidegger's account of the tradition of Western thought comes to a conclusion in Nietzsche.[18]

The possibility of this happening depends on two further developments, both of which Christianity itself sets in motion. The first is the reduction of the distance between man and God, and the second the establishment of a powerful motive for man to assume God's place.

Because God is merely the highest being there is, he belongs to the same realm as man. Both are beings within the realm of beings, some higher and some lower. The same is true, of course, of every other being as well. Horses and sponges belong to the realm of beings too. But as the being whose substance is subjectivity, God shares something in common with man that he does with no other creature. Among God's creatures (angels to the side), man is the only one who possesses a will. He is the only subject—the only being made in God's image. This establishes a special rapport between man and God and brings him close to God in a way no other creature can be.

Yet the reinterpretation of substance as subject, on which this special relation depends, raises a challenge for Christian metaphysics that its Aristotelian predecessor did not have to face. Both rest upon a conception of truth as correctness. But for Aristotle, things themselves are the ultimate guarantor of the correctness of our judgments about them. We see and say what is true about a thing by grasping its form, and we do this simply by looking at it. Truth and error are grounded in the visible order of the world, which requires no further guarantee of its own. The Christian doctrine of creation makes Aristotle's naive appeal to the truth of things impossible. That is because the world is nothing in itself. It is entirely the result of God's creative will. How then can the world by itself guarantee the truth of what we know about it? It cannot. It is God who must now play this role. God guarantees the truth of things because he has created them. Most importantly, he guarantees the truth of the moral and spiritual requirements that men must satisfy in order to be saved. The pursuit of salvation depends on rules and principles whose truth

God alone can assure. The validity of science and the meaning of human existence thus both rest at every moment on the freely given word of God.

When this guarantee is called into question, therefore, the entire enterprise of metaphysics loses its foundation and man's salvation is placed in doubt. By the time this happens, in the later Middle Ages, it is too late to abandon metaphysics and return to the way of thinking that preceded it.

Moreover, under the influence of the soteriological message of Christian belief, Western man has long counted on being saved from the world. He has grown used to the idea that he is a mere pilgrim in the world and can never be fully at home here. He demands assurance that he is connected to a higher order of things. No amount of Aristotelian confidence in the truth of the visible world can possibly provide such assurance. It is much too late for that. Only the revealed will of God can supply the assurance that men seek, so that when our knowledge of God's will is called into doubt—when men lose confidence in their ability to discover it on their own—the result is a spiritual crisis of the deepest and most compelling sort. Men cast about anxiously for a new guarantor of the truth of things that might be able to perform the epistemic and salvific role that God once did but no longer can. And what being other than God could conceivably play this role? Only man himself, for he alone, among all the creatures in the world, is a subject like God, endowed with the power to create something from nothing.

In Platonic, Aristotelian and Christian philosophy, truth is conceived as "correctness" or "certainty," and defined by the "adequation" of thinking to "what presences unthought in its presence,"[19] that is, by the conformity of mind to the world. In the case of Christian theology, this conformity is guaranteed by a creator God unknown to the intellectualist metaphysics of pagan antiquity. But in Heidegger's view, this is a minor detail. The really fundamental thing is the conception of truth as certainty that rules in all three schemes, and though the loss of faith in "the truth of Christian revelation and the doctrines of the Church"[20] undermines the possibility of guaranteeing the certainty of our beliefs through their fidelity to the *world,* it leaves the conception of truth as certainty intact and intensifies the demand for some such guarantee, which can now be satisfied only by reversing the direction of adequation and demonstrating that truth consists in the conformity of the world to *our representations of it,* rather than the other way around.

Descartes is the first philosopher to accomplish this reversal in a systematic way. In doing so, he refounds the enterprise of metaphysics on subjective grounds. With Descartes, the certainty of subjectivity becomes the basis for the certainty of all our ideas about things. Beings exist only insofar as we can clearly and distinctly represent them. In this way, the being of beings, which before was understood to lie in their substance or reality (whether created or not) is transferred to the subjectivity of the subject, which now becomes an even more reliable guarantor of the truth of our representations.

In Descartes, the certainty of subjectivity still functions as a path back to God, who remains the ultimate ground of the correctness of all our ideas. The metaphysical reversal that Descartes initiates therefore remains incomplete. Kant carries it a step farther.

In Kant's view, the objectivity of the object is *constituted* by our representation of it. There is *nothing to* the world (nothing, in any case, about which we can speak) other than the system of concepts spontaneously produced by the transcendental subject.[21] Indeed, Kant's philosophy rules out even the possibility of our ever attaining an independent point of view from which the correctness of our representations might be challenged. Man thereby assumes the position that God had previously occupied as the indubitable guarantor of the correctness of his own representations. He becomes the creator of all things—the being to whom all others owe theirs.

It is true that for Kant man remains a finite being who receives the material of his representations from "without," as something "given" in intuition. But the form of these representations, which exhausts all that can be known and said about them, is man's creative work alone—his spontaneous invention. "[S]elf-liberating man," who has unchained himself from God and assumed the creative powers that before belonged to God, thus "establishes himself" in Kant's critical philosophy "as the measure of all measures with which whatever can count as certain, i.e., as true, i.e., in being, is measured off and measured out."[22]

"Christianity reinterprets the Being of beings as Being-created."[23] Kant accepts this equation and shifts the locus of creation from God to man. The result is an explanation of how it is possible for our representations to be correct that is more persuasive than any that depends on faith in a God beyond the world, or on the naive belief that the "forms" of things are directly apprehensible to their human observers. Kant's radicalized subjectivism, which assumes the Christian identification of being with being-created and simultaneously transfers God's creative powers to man, thereby gives the conception of truth as correctness an indubitability that neither the intellectualist wisdom philosophies of antiquity nor their medieval successors could possibly attain.

Kant describes all these earlier philosophies as "metaphysical." He conceives his own task to be that of explaining the truth of our representations in a way that no longer depends on the controversial and unprovable assumptions that underlie every metaphysical scheme. But in Heidegger's view, Kant's very obsession with this task places him within the tradition of Western metaphysics, not beyond it. Kant's solution to the problem of how to account for the certainty of our representations does not "overcome" metaphysics, Heidegger says, but furthers it instead, for by making our representations constitutive of experience, Kant frees their adequation from dependence on any standard apart from these representations themselves, and thereby solves the deepest difficulty that all previous metaphysical thinkers had faced. With Kant, the metaphysical understanding of truth as correctness that defines Western thought from Plato on is not abolished but enters a decisive new stage, marked by growing confidence among thinkers of all sorts that this conception of truth has at last been given the secure foundation it demands in the world-constituting spontaneity of the transcendental subject.

VALUES

The most remarkable feature of Heidegger's reconstruction of the history of Western thought is its relative indifference to the philosophical distinctions that are usually taken to be of greatest importance in explaining it. In Heidegger's account, these all appear as variants on a single theme. The distinction between Platonic idealism and Aristotelian realism; between the pagan belief in the eternality of the world and Christian creationism; and between the ancient doctrine of substance and the modern concept of the subject are for Heidegger of far less importance than the commitment these all share to the conception of truth as correctness. Every one of these philosophies starts, he claims, from this same conception. Each is therefore conditioned by forgetfulness of the ontological distinction between being (the event of disclosure that precedes our apprehension of a realm of beings) and the beings that occupy this realm themselves. Forgetfulness of this distinction is for Heidegger the essence of metaphysics itself.

In Heidegger's view, the whole of Western thought is metaphysical in this sense—and to be condemned as such. That is because the forgetfulness with which it starts, and entrenches in ever more assertive ways, amounts to a denial of the gift that precedes all thought. Its effect is to transform man from the wonderstruck and grateful recipient of this gift into the conniving master of the world, whose powers of control are underwritten by the concept of truth as correctness. Understood in these terms, the history of metaphysics represents one long unbroken fall from grace, in which all the greatest thinkers from Plato to Kant are complicit.

The only real challenge, therefore, is that of overcoming this tradition altogether, and restoring man to the humility and gratitude that ought to define his proper role as the thankful custodian of being. But this is a supremely difficult task. Just how difficult is made clear by Heidegger's interpretation of Nietzsche, to whose work he devoted much of his time in the 1930s and '40s.

Nietzsche's stated goal is the abolition of metaphysics. Yet in Heidegger's view, Nietzsche's attempt is a failure. His "revaluation of all values" leads not to a philosophy "beyond" metaphysics but to the most extreme possible expression of the metaphysical attitude itself. Many consider Nietzsche the "most modern" of all thinkers, a smasher of idols, a genealogist who discredits metaphysical pretensions by sniffing out the human passions behind them. In reality, Heidegger says, Nietzsche is the last and most daring metaphysician and his philosophy the end or goal of Western thought, for it valorizes more explicitly than ever before the very desire for control that has been the tradition's driving ambition from the start.

Nietzsche declares that God is dead. By this he means that all supersensory values have lost their authority. Plato first established their authority with his theory of ideas. The ideas, which are not of this world, are the source of the being and truth of everything that is. Christianity replaces Plato's ideas with God. The creator of the world, who stands beyond it, now possesses the moral and epistemic authority that Plato's ideas once did. When God loses his authority, his vacant place is taken by "conscience," "reason," and values of various sorts, for example, those of "historical progress" and "civilization." But these are all just "variations of the Christian-ecclesiastical and theological interpretation of the world," which in turn was based on an *ordo* first established by Plato.

Today, Nietzsche says, the very idea of a realm of supersensory values—Platonic, Christian, modern, whatever—has been completely "ruined." It no longer has the power to command. It has lost the ability to serve as a ground of being or truth. One interpretation of the supersensory (for example, as reason) may perhaps replace or "annihilate" another (e.g., as God). But all such annihilations and substitutions are impermanent, for they are themselves vulnerable to annihilation in turn. The acknowledgment that the supersensory in all its manifestations has forever lost the authority it once possessed, Nietzsche calls "nihilism." Many people still subscribe in a superficial and uncomprehending way to one supersensory ideal or another. But Nietzsche insists that the deepest truth about our present condition is the triumph of nihilism, and our greatest challenge that of overcoming it.

Heidegger accepts Nietzsche's diagnosis of nihilism. He also regards it as the fulfillment of a tradition of thought that begins with Plato. But Heidegger rejects Nietzsche's proposed cure for it. Nietzsche presents this most fully in his late, unpublished notebooks. Here he expands the idea expressed by his earlier dictum that "there are absolutely no moral phenomena, only a moral interpretation of the phenomena,"[24] into a cosmological system organized around the concept of what he calls the "will to power." According to Heidegger, this is Nietzsche's last and highest idea. But Heidegger claims that instead of offering a genuine alternative to the tradition of Western metaphysics, which culminates in the nihilistic devaluation of all values, Nietzsche's doctrine of the will to power merely carries the prideful premise of this tradition to its final conclusion.

For Heidegger, Nietzsche is a fellow spirit. He is the only philosopher before Heidegger to have glimpsed the magnitude of the loss entailed by the devaluation of all values. Nietzsche describes this as the loss of the "earth." Heidegger calls it the "oblivion" of being. Yet in the end, Heidegger says, Nietzsche could not resist the pull of the metaphysical way of thinking that reaches a new peak of human self-promotion in the subjectivist philosophies of Descartes and Kant. Indeed, in Heidegger's view, Nietzsche's concept of the will to power represents not merely a capitulation to this way of thinking but its very highest stage—the supreme expression of man's drive to subdue the beings that he finds around him by means of various techniques of manipulation that rest on a forgetfulness of the gift that grants their appearance to men in the first place. For Heidegger, the greatness of Nietzsche's philosophy thus lies not in the originality of the solution it offers to the problem of nihilism (which Heidegger equates with that of metaphysics), but in the extravagant way it reproduces this problem itself, and thereby underscores the depth of the oblivion into which we have been falling since Plato.

Nietzsche maintains that values "are not something in themselves." This is true even of supersensory values, whose worth, as values, appears to be entirely self-contained. Values are what they are only because they have been "posited" as such. "Value *is* value provided it is valid. It is valid provided it is *posited as* what matters."[25] The world exists for us only to the extent it has value (for example, as the "real object" of our representations, and hence as the guarantor of "truth"). It therefore exists only because it has been evaluated, that is, invested with value by one who posits that the world possesses it.

Nietzsche reinterprets the history of Western thought in light of this principle. Even the most independent-seeming values, whose authority derives from their apparent objectivity, prove on closer inspection to be evaluations whose being depends entirely on the "evaluators" that posit them. Their very objectivity turns out to be nothing more than a value that "matters" to an especially high degree. In this way, the idea of objectivity itself is reconstituted as a subjective value.

Kant's transcendental deduction transforms the object, insofar as it is knowable, into the spontaneous work of a subject, but leaves intact the idea of the object as a thing-in-itself, unknowable yet real, the objective horizon that bounds our creative powers. Nietzsche's interpretation of being as value, and of value as evaluation, erases even this boundary and converts the thing-in-itself into something that exists for us only because it "matters." In this sense, Nietzsche's equation of being with value represents a further extension of the principle of subjectivity that already guides the philosophies of Descartes and Kant—indeed, the furthest extension possible, since anything that might be set up as a limit or barrier to it (God, world, the thing-in-itself) must immediately be reconceived as *just another value* that someone has posited for one reason or another.

But what reason can there be to posit anything as a value? If there are reasons to do so, then there is something that is prior to all values and hence not itself a value. In that case, there is something that has the independence once (illegitimately) claimed for supersensory values that can serve as the ground of the evaluations from which such values derive. According to Heidegger, Nietzsche interprets the nature of this ground in light of the phenomenon of "life."[26]

The act of positing a value should be thought of as a kind of "seeing," hence a "representing," and this in turn as a "striving" undertaken from a point of view or "perspective." The perspective is that of a being that wants to extend its range of control—to master its environment in one way or another. This is the essence of life. Every living thing strives not merely to preserve itself but to expand its dominion. Nietzsche calls this the will to power. Like other living things, human beings share this ambition. They too strive to dominate the world, and the values they posit are merely one expression of this striving.

We might say that this is the "reason" they posit the values they do, except that the striving in question is not itself something rational. It is the prerational ground from which all reasons spring.

In Nietzsche's philosophy, two ideas that lie at the heart of modern thought thus come together. The first is the idea that the ground of being lies in the subject—that the being of beings consists in their being evaluated. The second is that the being of the subject who posits the values that constitute the being of beings is itself nothing but a striving for power. Descartes and Kant enshrine the principle of the subjectivity of being, and do so in order to extend and perfect the program of world mastery that has been the aim of Western thought from its beginning. But their philosophies constrain the principle of subjectivity (with the idea of God or the thing-in-itself) and thus conceal the extent to which this principle is grounded in a desire for world domination.

Nietzsche liberates the principle of subjectivity from its last remaining limits and thereby brings to light the desire for control that is its true but previously unrecognized ground. Indeed, he elevates this very desire to a position of supreme metaphysical importance by treating the will to power as the essence of the being of beings. As a result, the drive for control ceases to be merely an anthropological "fact" and becomes instead the source or ground of the being of all that is.

In his unpublished notebooks, Nietzsche proposes that we think of everything in the world, animate and inanimate alike, not merely as having its being for us in its being posited as a value, but also as an evaluator in its own right, striving, as are we, to expand its dominion over the countless other beings around it—as a being whose own being *is nothing but* this striving itself. With this thought, Heidegger says, Nietzsche reaches the limits of Western philosophy, for by defining the being of beings as the prideful will to dominate that constitutes the essence of metaphysics, he converts this very ambition into a metaphysical principle and thereby brings to a climax the whole project of metaphysics, whose aim is "achieved for the first time knowingly" in Nietzsche's philosophy.[27]

When Zarathustra steps from his cave and exclaims, "You great star! What would your happiness be if you had not those for whom you shine?"[28] it might seem that Nietzsche is proposing the most profound reversal of Platonic values imaginable. But according to Heidegger, what matters here is not the superficial (!) distinction between Plato's concept of ideas and Nietzsche's characterization of value as a "posit." The essential thing, in Heidegger's view, is the *continuity* between these two, which are linked by the spirit of pride that suffuses the entire tradition of Western thought.

From its beginnings in the great metaphysical systems of Plato and Aristotle, the philosophy of the West has sought to secure, in ever more compelling ways, the certainty of human experience, *so that* man will no longer need to depend on anything other than himself for his knowledge and mastery of beings. This has required the forgetfulness of the gift on which the original disclosure of beings depends—or rather, the *determined repression* of the memory of this gift, which haunts the human pursuit of independence and control so long as it has not been pushed entirely from mind. It has demanded the oblivion of being. Worse, it has demanded that this oblivion itself be forgotten. It has "masked the occurrence of this denial."[29] With Nietzsche's philosophy, we reach the last stage in this process.

"When the being of beings is stamped as value and its essence is thereby sealed, then within this metaphysics . . . every path toward the experience of Being itself is obliterated."[30] "The horizon no longer illuminates of itself." Being can no longer be recognized as that which gives the light that reveals a realm of visible beings. Being is just the being of beings, the most essential trait of all the things that are, and *this* is now understood as the state of being a point of view "set in the disposition of value of the will to power."[31] To be is to be a "viewpoint" that strives to direct and dominate the world by representing it. With this formulation, the prideful spirit of usurpation that has driven Western philosophy from Plato on is itself raised to the level of a metaphysical axiom. For Nietzsche, to be means to be proud. No more extreme expression of the longing for independence, and of the forgetfulness of the gift of being on which this longing depends, can be imagined.

Nietzsche himself conceived the metaphysical equation of being and pride in terms of the idea of art. An artist is one who strives to dominate through representation—to impress his values, perceptions and judgments on the world. Every being is, for Nietzsche, an artist in this sense. Thus the artist, who for Plato remains a figure remote from being,[32] comes in Nietzsche's philosophy to constitute its very essence. Yet in Heidegger's view, this is only an apparent inversion that in reality paradoxically fulfills the longing for mastery that Plato's doctrine of ideas (which is the basis of his attack on the unreality of art) already expresses.

Heidegger emphatically rejects Nietzsche's association of the will to power with art. Just as Nietzsche fails to see that his equation of being with evaluation, which is meant to undermine the ambitions of all previous metaphysical systems, fulfills these ambitions instead, he likewise fails to see that it is not art but technology that expresses the will to mastery he identifies as the being of beings. The real complement and counterpart to Nietzsche's idea of the will to power is not the music of Wagner or the old master paintings that he admired. It is the modern hydroelectric plant. And it is only in art, Heidegger says, that one may still hope to find a refuge of thankfulness and devotion in a world now ruled by technology—by the practical triumph of the philosophical idea that Nietzsche offers as the last answer to the first question of metaphysics.

TECHNOLOGY

From the 1930s on, Heidegger was preoccupied with the meaning of technology.[33] To grasp its real significance, he says, we must begin by rejecting two conventional beliefs about it.

The first is that technology is a mere instrument—a tool that may be put to different purposes but has no meaning of its own. On this view, technology is something neutral. Whatever meaning it has derives from the ends to which it is put. These may be good or bad, beautiful or ugly, constructive or destructive. But in itself, technology is indifferent. Quite literally, it is *nothing*.

The second is that technology is an antihumanistic force. Those who hold this view see technology as the enemy of the values that humanism promotes. From their perspective, the challenge that technology presents is that of preserving these values in a world increasingly dominated by impersonal and mechanical ones instead.

We can begin to comprehend the true meaning of technology, Heidegger says, only when we see how fundamentally mistaken these two beliefs are.

Our age is dominated by the ideals of research science, whose results manifest themselves in technology. Modern science "founds and differentiates itself in the projection of particular object domains" or disciplines. This is true even of philosophy. In each of these domains, beings are "summoned" or "called to account" with "regard to the way in which, and the extent to which, they can be placed at the disposal of representation." Beings that cannot be represented do not exist; they do not "count as in being." In this way, all beings become "objects of explanatory representation" and thereby subject to "calculation."

The goal of this process of scientific objectification is to "be sure" or "certain" about beings, so that they may be grasped, ordered, moved about and, ultimately, placed at our disposal. Today, we take all of this for granted. For this reason, Heidegger calls ours the "age of the world picture." He does not mean by this that our age rests upon a picture of the world (*Weltanschauung*) in the way that every age does. He means that our age is defined by its understanding of the being of beings as that which can be pictured. This is the Platonic understanding of truth as correctness—"the presupposition which— long prevailing only mediately, in concealment and long in advance— predestined the world's having to become picture." What distinguishes modern science is only the thoroughgoing way it carries out the program of "the mastery of beings as a whole" that is implicit in this understanding.[34]

Technology is the most pervasive and commanding expression of this program. It is therefore anything but neutral, for it too rests on the metaphysics of representation that underlies all modern science. Indeed, to the extent that this is not just one metaphysics alongside others, but the essence of metaphysics as such, the meaning of technology lies in its being the supreme practical embodiment of all metaphysical thought, for the same reason that Nietzsche's doctrine of the will to power is its highest philosophical expression.

What is unique about both is not their endorsement of man's striving for control. Men have always sought to control the world around them. Nor is the concept of representation, which underlies and facilitates such striving, peculiar to them either. This concept is as old as Plato. What distinguishes Nietzsche's philosophy from its predecessors is the completeness and finality with which it carries through the West's age-old program of control by conceiving representation as evaluation and evaluation as will to power. Similarly, what sets modern technology apart from every premodern technique of control is the "ruthlessness"[35] with which it pursues man's mastery of the world to its furthest possible limit.

Technology is "a challenging which puts to nature the unreasonable demand that it supply energy that can be extracted and stored as such."[36] From a technological point of view, the entire world *is nothing but* a storehouse of forces to be unlocked and "stockpiled" for human use, "on call, ready to deliver" what we need when we need it, "driving on to the maximum yield at the minimum expense." Technologically conceived, beings therefore *have no being* other than as knowable and controllable forces. To be sure, we do not yet know everything about them and therefore cannot control them completely. But *to that extent* they do not yet exist. From the standpoint of technology, to say that something *is* means *only* that it is calculable (knowable) and disposable (capable of being moved from one place to another and stored indefinitely for future consumption).

"Nature" thereby becomes what Heidegger calls a "standing reserve"—something that is "ordered to stand by." When this happens, that which is ordered to stand by "no longer stands over against us as object." It ceases to offer any resistance. It becomes something whose existence is defined by its being at our disposal. Beyond that, there is nothing at all. For those who think technologically, the being of beings thus *consists in* their being available to and for us. Modern technology thereby obliterates, with unprecedented thoroughness and self-approval, the original gift of disclosure on which the appearance of the world depends. Like Nietzsche's philosophy of the will to power, it does this in the most extreme way possible. It takes the *last* step that *can* be taken toward the elimination of everything that might conceivably resist the expansion of human pride into the organizing principle of the world as such.

This explains why Heidegger regards humanism not as the enemy of technology but its natural companion.[37]

In all its various guises, humanism asserts that "being is the product of the human being." It maintains that human beings decide whether and how God and history and nature come into being and depart from it. Humanism makes man the lord of creation, the one who gives the gift of being to other beings, "the entity through which being is first fashioned."[38] In this sense, Descartes' *cogito* is a humanistic invention, along with Kant's transcendental subject, Nietzsche's concept of value, and Sartre's teaching that in man existence precedes essence.

From Heidegger's point of view, these all belong to the humanistic tradition that conceives man to be the "Subject" whose subjectivity constitutes the "substance of beings," and sets him up as the "tyrant of being" who "deign[s] to release the beingness of beings into an all too loudly glorified 'objectivity.' "[39] In this sense, humanism does more than merely assign a special dignity to man, as one being among others. It does more than remind us of the beauty and greatness of human beings. It makes man the ground of the being of beings—the one *through whom* every other being has its being, in precisely the way that technology converts nature into a storehouse of forces whose being is *nothing but* their availability for human use.

Humanism and technology are therefore both the late, ripe fruit of the forgetfulness of being that has shaped the course of Western thought from its start. They are twins in whom a "thoughtful" man who has managed to free himself from the dominance of the scientific spirit of our age may discern the final stage of the rejection of the gift of being that begins with Plato's doctrine of truth as correctness.

In them, man's drive to grasp and measure, and ultimately to ground, the being of beings reaches an acme of pride. If Plato's doctrine marks the moment of fall from a pre-Socratic state of grace in which human beings still regarded themselves as the reverent servants of being whose task is to gather and preserve the gift of disclosure that precedes all measurement and calculation, then our age represents the final, satanic expression of Plato's original sin. The modern age, the age of technology and humanism, is an age of unembarrassed human pride, freed from the last residue of guilt that once constrained it and now deliberately installed as the ground of the being of beings instead—the most perfect expression of the blasphemy toward which the civilization of the West has been hurtling for centuries.

THE FATE OF THE EARTH

Like Maistre and Donoso Cortes, Heidegger conceives the modern age in apocalyptic terms, as the culmination of a theocosmic drama defined by man's rebellious refusal to acknowledge the gift on which his own ecstatic being depends, and by the prideful attempt to supplant this gift with powers of his own invention. In Maistre and Donoso, this drama is still cast in Augustinian terms. It is the Christian story of divine grace and human pride. In Heidegger's writings, these familiar theological categories are no longer explicit. They have disappeared behind a dazzling array of philosophical abstractions like "disclosure" and "oblivion." But the outline of the story is the same.

Instead of gratefully accepting that he has been " 'thrown' by Being itself into the truth of Being, so that ex-sisting in this fashion he might guard the truth of Being" as its caring "shepherd,"[40] man has sought instead to reverse this relation of dependence by making himself the one who grants and denies the being of beings. It is through man's transcendence alone that the world comes to light. In this sense, man is the "clearing" of being. But he is not the ground of the ecstatic "projection" that constitutes this clearing. Men do not construct or create this "projection" themselves. "What throws in such projection is not the human being but Being itself, which *sends* the human being into the ek-sistence of Da-sein that is his essence. This destiny *propriates* as the clearing of Being—which it is. The clearing *grants* nearness to Being," a blessing that men cannot secure for themselves.[41]

If man is the clearing of being, the fact that he finds himself cast in this role is not something he can account for let alone bring about on his own. It is a gift we could explain only in case we were able to throw ourselves into transcendence—which of course we are not. The recognition that this is so naturally expresses itself in thankfulness. Gratitude is the only appropriate—indeed, the only possible—response to the gift we human beings *are.*

By contrast, the refusal to acknowledge this gift is the greatest act of ingratitude imaginable. It is an ontological form of pride (the kind that Augustine equated with original sin) for it amounts to the denial that human beings depend on anything other than themselves for their own being. Western thought has long been driven by this denial, which culminates in the world of technology and "values," the most ungrateful world that men have ever made.

The world today is characterized above all by homelessness and unholiness. Man is the "Da," the place or "clearing," of being. He is the "dispensation of Being itself."[42] This is his "home." But to be "at home," he must acknowledge with gratitude the "dispensation" by virtue of which he is who he is—the gift that brings being "near." The human being who denies this and pridefully asserts that he depends on nothing but himself lives "away from" home. His condition is one of "homelessness," which is "coming to be the destiny of the world."[43]

By means of science and technology, and the metaphysics that supports them, we seem to have made the world our home, to have domesticated its powers and transformed the world into a comfortable dwelling for man. But just the opposite is true. All our vast powers of control—the conceptual and technical mastery of nature and its conversion to a storehouse of forces "standing by" for our use—have only served to carry us farther and farther away from home, into a wilderness of our own construction.

Here, we are well-fed and warm. We are in touch with other human beings around the world. Everything that happens anywhere on earth comes to our attention at once. Never have so many men been so close to one another. Yet in our closeness, we are lonely, and amidst our countless comforts we are without a home. Like Adam's pride, which opened a new and immense distance between himself and God, and led to the condition of exile that has characterized human life on earth ever since, the spirit of pride that infuses every aspect of modern life, the practical along with the philosophical, has produced a world of exiles too, deluded by the comfort of their circumstances into thinking that they are where they belong—the most extreme form of homelessness imaginable. This is the condition of Nietzsche's "last man," who haunts every page of Heidegger's writings, from his dissection of "everydayness" in *Being and Time* to his fierce polemic against Jean-Paul Sartre more than twenty years later.

In our homelessness, we remain closed off from "the dimension of the holy."[44] We have forgotten the gift of the "clearing" by virtue of which we encounter a world at all. The mystery of our human being has been lost from view. In our rush to comprehend the world and reshape it to our ends, we have lost sight of what is inexplicable in our condition—of the "dispensation" that grants us a world in the first place. This is a gift, for which gratitude is the only appropriate response. The man who understands this, and devotes himself to the work of thanking—which is harder, even, than that of science— alone "dwells" in the region of the holy.

For the rest of us, Heidegger says, this region "remains closed." Its closure defines the modern era. "Perhaps what is distinctive about this world-epoch consists in the closure of the dimension of the hale [*das Heilen*]. Perhaps that is the sole malignancy [*Unheil*]." To reopen it, man must regain "the essential poverty of the shepherd, whose dignity consists in being called by Being itself into the preservation of Being's truth. The call comes as the throw from which the thrownness of Dasein derives."[45]

Those who hear the call and respond to it with gratitude for the gift of the freedom that lights the world in transcendence, instead of abusively using their freedom to master the world in thought and action, dwell once more in the home that being has prepared for them. They have come out of the wilderness of human conceit and are near, again, to that which "grants" the light. Their nearness *is* their thankfulness, just as their distance was their pride, and in such nearness they recover the holiness that can never be destroyed (for how could human beings do that?) but which the modern world has covered in oblivion to a nearly unfathomable depth.

This world is one of darkness, though it claims to be a world of light—of "enlightenment" in all things. "[O]n the earth, all over it, a darkening of the world is happening. The essential happenings of this darkening are: the flight of the gods, the destruction of the earth, the reduction of human beings to a mass, the preeminence of the mediocre."[46] Today, the darkening of the world is accelerated by humanism and technology. These elevate man to the position of lord of creation and carry him farther than he has ever been from home and the holy.

In 1935, Heidegger called this darkening the "fate of Europe"—the destiny that is being prepared by the forces of enlightenment that have erased the last limits on human pride and dissolved the lingering vestiges of a world in which the name of God, at least, still retained some power to terrify and inspire. And because these same forces, though grown to maturity in the West alone, have a universal reach and appeal, the fate of Europe, Heidegger claimed, is today "the fate of the earth." Everywhere on earth, the light is failing. Everywhere, "the wilderness grows."[47]

There are a few points of light in our darkening world. These are the works that remind us of the gift from which the world arises in transcendence. Reminding us of this is the task of all true works of art—of painting, architecture and poetry, insofar as they pursue their real goal, and not some kitschy simulacrum of it. A genuine work of art, Heidegger says, brings us back to the original "happening" of disclosure and invites us, helps us, to dwell in it instead of hurrying away to pursue some task or other. Its achievement is just this remembrance, and the gratitude that goes with it.

This is a supremely difficult undertaking, given our inclination to rush to "put the world back in place," to restore the comprehensibility of things, to cut and measure, order and plan, direct and control, *so that* the uncanniness that accompanies every encounter with the gift of being will cease to disturb or distract us from the sober business of "making a living." Only in the greatest works of art are we able to sustain a gratitude for this gift even for a moment.

At the beginning of Greek philosophy, before Plato transformed it into metaphysics, this was the goal of thinking as well. But with the forgetfulness of truth as disclosure, thinking has declined into mere "knowing" and art alone remains, for us, an avenue to the recollection of what has been lost in the tradition of metaphysics that begins with Plato and ends with Nietzsche. Art is today the only way we can experience, for however brief a time, the holiness of a homecoming out of the "monstrousness that reigns here"—where the being of beings is defined by their being available for technological employment—into the space of our true belonging, where the poet's song of thanksgiving celebrates the gift of the light.

In the homecoming that art prepares there is therefore room for "hope."[48] In art, we still find a "saving power"—the only one we have left. Art is the only cord that still connects us to the mystery of being, in a world whose organizing principle is the dissipation of all mysteries through enlightened understanding. Among the works of man, art alone now possesses this salvific power.[49] But if the poetry of Hölderlin and Rilke, with its pious spirit of "service,"[50] offers the most extreme counterpoint imaginable to the spirit of technology, on account of which "the impression comes to prevail that everything man encounters exists only insofar as it is his construct . . . [so that] it seems as though man everywhere and always encounters only himself,"[51] it is not poetry but technology that today defines the fate of the earth.

It is important to be clear about the meaning of this "fate." Heidegger is emphatic that technology is not a fate in the sense that things could not possibly be otherwise—a "fate that compels."[52] It is not a fate in the sense, for example, that developing into a frog might be said to be the fate of a tadpole. Technology is the result, in part, of a free human response to the disclosure of the world that we alone experience.

But technology is a fate in three other senses. First, and most obviously, its interlocking systems of equipment and the power grids that support them cannot simply be dismantled or avoided. Even those, like Heidegger, who have grasped the inner meaning of technology are condemned to live among its works, in a civilization dominated by its spirit.

Second, technology completes the history of Western thought by bringing the guiding aim of metaphysics into the open and making it the basis not just of a few esoteric systems of philosophy but of an entire material world. Technology is a fate in the sense of being "that toward which" the West has tended from the start—its *telos* or target.

Third, and most important, technology is a fate in the sense that even the forgetfulness of being from which it springs is not itself wholly the work of man. To suppose this would be to repeat the error of technology itself. For being to be forgotten, human beings must cooperate in its concealment. But the *disposition to forget* is no more a human creation than the transcendence it presupposes. It also comes to man from out of being itself. It comes as a "challenging" that "sets upon man" and "calls [him] forth" to order the world technologically. Heidegger calls this challenging "Enframing."[53] All "technological activity" is a free response "to the challenge of Enframing, but it never comprises Enframing itself or brings it about."[54]

Man alone hears the call of being. Only he is challenged by it. The call is "an exhortation or address"[55] to man whose transcendence uniquely equips him both to receive it and to fashion a response. The call is an invitation to "share in revealing." It is only through man that revealing "comes to pass." Being "needs" man as the only place where revealing can happen, and invites him into "the innermost indestructible belongingness"[56] of his role as the caretaker of being.

But to this invitation, which no one can avoid, there are two fundamentally different responses, and man's freedom means that he is never "simply constrained" to give either. One is refusal: the repudiation of the call to "belongingness" and the prideful assertion of radical independence instead. The other is devotion: a pious dedication to the task of honoring the gift we have been given as "safekeepers" of the light. The first is the technological response, the second the poetic, and while one now dominates every aspect of human life on earth, the other is always an open possibility.

This is not to say, however, that the call comes to all men at all times in precisely the same way. Today, it comes as "Enframing"—as an exhortation to arrange the world in "the ordering of the standing reserve."[57] It comes as an invitation to remake the world along technological lines. With few exceptions, this is the only way that human beings are now *able to hear* the call of being, and the fact that this is so is not itself a wholly human achievement, as if we had control not only over our response to the call but to the way in which, and the terms on which, it comes to us in the first place.

To assume that we have such control would be the pinnacle of human pride. It "would mean, after all, that man is the master of Being."[58] The truth, according to Heidegger, is exactly the reverse: That today men everywhere can only hear the call of being as a "challenging-forth into [the] ordering [of technology]"[59] is a "destining"[59] of being itself, hence a "fate" not of our own devising. It is the destiny that being thrusts upon us, casting (throwing) us into a world in which the invitation to service, to gratitude, to the humble spirit of guardianship, to the piety of art, is all but inaudible. That invitation can never be destroyed, nor can our freedom to take it up. But today, the destiny of "Enframing," which "among Being's modes of coming to presence" now rules the world as the fulfillment of all the West has striven to attain, makes it almost impossibly difficult to hear the invitation and harder still to summon the courage to respond with a grateful "yes."

THE NAZI AND THE QUIET OLD MAN

This is the modern, reactionary Catholic drama of redemption in thin disguise.

Man is made in the image of God. (Man alone exists ecstatically. He alone transcends.) Human beings are therefore the only creatures who can hear

God's commands. (Only they are able to hear the call of being). Because of this, man alone is capable of disobedience. (Only man can fall into oblivion.) Human beings sin by cutting themselves off from the ground of their being and seeking to be self-sufficient instead. (Man forgets that his transcendence is a gift, something "thrown," and seeks to master the world through metaphysics and technology.)

Sin begins with an original act of disobedience. (Western metaphysics starts with Plato's doctrine of truth as correctness and the concealment of the pre-Socratic understanding of truth as disclosure.) The subsequent history of the world is nothing but sin. (The inner meaning of Western metaphysics from Plato to Nietzsche is the forgetfulness of being.)

The modern world is the most sinful of all. (In it, metaphysics reaches its furthest limit and the ambition to put being in thrall to man triumphs on a planetary scale.) The modern world therefore stands at the greatest possible distance from God. It is something satanic. (A darkness now spreads over the world. Ours is the age of the "greatest malignancy.") That this has happened is itself the work of God. It is part of God's redemptive plan for the world. ("Enframing" is a "destining" of being.)

But it is inconceivable that God, having tried and tested man, should abandon the most beloved of his creatures forever. The modern age, lost in its prideful delusions, will be followed by a new, counterrevolutionary age of gratitude and humility, though we cannot know how or when this will happen. When it does, it will be by the grace of God. (The overcoming of metaphysics will initiate a "return" from "oblivion" to "safekeeping." This remains, for us today, "a favor as yet ungranted." But if and when it comes it will be on account of "the saving power of Being."[60]) In the meantime, all we can do is wait. (The "essence [of man] is to be the one who waits, the one who attends upon the coming to presence of Being in that in thinking he guards it. Only when man, as the shepherd of Being, attends upon the truth of Being can he expect an arrival of a destining of Being and not sink to the level of a mere wanting to know."[61])

For Maistre, who gave the tradition of reactionary Catholicism its start, the idea that we must wait for God to bring the counterrevolution was obvious. Man is no more able to achieve this on his own than he is to do anything else. To suppose otherwise is to accept the prideful assumption of the revolutionaries who assert that man is the master of his own fate. In truth, we are merely actors in a drama directed by God. Waiting for God is all we can do.

Yet though he denied that we can know when and by what means the counterrevolution will come, Maistre's writings are suffused with apocalyptic expectation. The day of divine reckoning is near. All Europe trembles with anticipation. The oceans of innocent blood that have already been spilled in Europe's wars and revolutions presage God's arrival. Events are moving rapidly to a climax. The last act in God's drama is about to be performed. We have reason to think we will live to see it. A half century later, Donoso Cortes said the same, and Carl Schmitt echoed their views fifty years after that, when he declared that Europe was confronting an immense "either/or."

By 1935, Heidegger was already moving in a more quietist direction. That we must wait patiently for "the arrival of another destining"[62] of being, which alone can rescue us from the oblivion of "Enframing"; that we cannot know when or how a new destining will come, or indeed even whether it will; that in the meantime, we must learn to wait, "for a lifetime" if necessary; that in "an age for which the actual is only whatever goes fast," we need "the right endurance" to wait for "the right moment;"[63] and that all we can do is pray that the "bright open space of the world" be lit once again by a sudden "flash" that shows man to himself in his true character as the caretaker of being: these are all propositions on which Heidegger insists with growing urgency after the war, but that are anticipated in his writings two decades before, when he still wore a Nazi uniform. Even then, one might conclude, there was an immense distance between Maistre's millenarian fervor and Heidegger's philosophical quietism, however close in spirit their understanding of man's relation to God may have been.

What we know now, of course, is that for a brief time at least Heidegger also shared Maistre's apocalyptic hopefulness, and believed that the end of the age of metaphysics was at hand.

Today—Heidegger told his students in 1935, speaking with the passion of a prophet—the earth is in "spiritual decline." Everywhere on earth life is characterized by the "hopeless frenzy of unchained technology." Only "new, historically *spiritual* forces" can resist this. These must come from Europe, which is caught in "the center" of a "pincers" represented by America, on the one hand, and the Soviet Union on the other, both equally dominated by technological thinking and the metaphysics that underlies it. And among the Europeans, only the Germans—"our people," placed at the center of Europe as Europe is at the center of the world—have the spiritual resources for a resistance movement of this kind.

Only the Germans, Heidegger declared, are still capable of "retrieving" the question, "how does it stand with Being?" Only they have the strength to call Europe and the world back to the pre-Platonic understanding of truth as disclosure, out of the oblivion of self-conceit that rules the liberal West and communist East alike. Only they possess the resolve to challenge the whole tradition of metaphysics that today poisons everything we think and do. Only the Germans have poets like Hölderlin whose words remind us of the gift that precedes all our ridiculous bustle and industry, calling us home to a truth we have been busily forgetting since Plato.

The salvation of the world thus lies in the hands of the Germans. They are the shock troops in the battle to restore everything Western civilization has buried for millennia. What battle could be more important? What role in it more exalted? Those who understand this must be filled with martial valor, Heidegger told his students in 1935. To be sure, the ultimate outcome is in doubt. But those who see things in this light cannot help but view the fight to which they have been summoned as the grandest one conceivable, a war of cosmic proportions, waged against an enemy of satanic dimensions, in which no sacrifice is too small.

Two years later, Heidegger had already begun to retreat from this apocalyptic vision of Germany's role as an instrument of salvation. Disappointed by events, he came to see the German ambition to save the world as *just one more* expression of the pridefulness of technology itself, and therefore no better, in essence, than its declared enemies. He gave up the idea that Germany or any nation can be a vehicle for the recovery of the question of being and concluded that every form of nationalism is merely the "egoism" of a "people," hence corrupted by the same presumptuous humanism as metaphysics itself. He came to regard national socialism as part of the problem rather than a solution to it. But for a while, at least, Heidegger entertained the same apocalyptic fantasy as Maistre and Donoso, and like them, was prepared to see blood spilled in its name, inspired by a führer in whom he thought he saw the Napoleon of being.

Much has been made of the brevity of Heidegger's apocalyptic endorsement of Nazism; of his cloistered innocence and lack of political experience; and of the distance between the rector of Freiburg—the impassioned leader of torchlight rallies and inspirational retreats—and the gentle old philosopher resigned to waiting quietly for the call of being, which he knows may never come.

But however much importance one attaches to the temperamental distance between these attitudes, they spring from the same theology. Heidegger's disillusionment with Nazism was certainly real. But it reflects not even the smallest adjustment in his understanding of modernity or judgment upon it. Until the end of his life, Heidegger continued to view the modern world as an episode "within the history of Being," whose deepest meaning cannot be grasped except in terms of the drama of disclosure and oblivion that technology brings to its satanic finale.

Heidegger gave up the idea that it is possible to resist modernity in an organized, public way. He resigned himself to the thought that all one can do in the face of the immensity of the malignancy of metaphysics, humanism and technology—the interlocking and reinforcing expressions of man's insane wish to be God—is quietly prepare oneself inwardly for the "flash" that lights the world and invites us to look "out toward the divine."[64] This might seem to mark an important shift in belief. But Heidegger's resignation only confirms his unaltered sense of how bad the modern world really is—so bad, in fact, that nothing can be done about it at all.

In this respect, Heidegger's later quietism represents a reaffirmation rather than a renunciation of the philosophical theology to which he subscribed from 1930 on. Its elements are already outlined in his lecture, "On the Essence of Truth." The roots of this theology lie in the reactionary Catholicism that Heidegger continued to espouse until he was nearly thirty years old. His brilliant if eccentric restatement of it supplies the connecting thread that joins every phase of his career. By comparison, the shift from the activist and apocalyptic demand that sacrifices be made for the sake of recovering the question of being, to the quietist acceptance that nothing can be done to force human beings out of their delusional paroxysms of pride, reflects only a superficial adjustment of mood—one that, if anything, underscores Heidegger's unwavering commitment to the Augustinian theology of sin and grace that inspired his view of man and the world from the time he was a child.

It is in this context that one must understand Heidegger's morally insane remark that Auschwitz was as bad as (and therefore no worse than) modern factory farming.

In the end, for Heidegger, the problem with Auschwitz was not the murders committed in its camps and crematoria, but the technological spirit in which these were carried out. The sin of Auschwitz was the sin of pride—the conceited belief that man is the master of death, as of everything else on earth, including the "forces of growth" in whose "keeping" the peasant of old placed his "seed," unlike today's agribusinessman, who seeks to bring these forces under control and to convert them to a "standing-reserve" of power for his own use.[65] By comparison with the great, historic disaster of modernity itself—of man's prideful revolt against being, from whose call we have all turned away in deafness and frenzied self-importance, the Germans along with their Russian and American enemies—the fact that so many were murdered at Auschwitz, and the civilization of European Jewry destroyed is of secondary importance. To think that the real meaning of Auschwitz lies here is, for Heidegger, to confuse a symptom with a disease. The disease is pride, for which the only cure is grace: the coming of a new God, whose arrival we cannot hasten, let alone compel, and for which we must therefore wait patiently, for a lifetime or more if need be, meditating on how far the desolation wrought by our forgetfulness of the gift of being has spread.

It is in this mood of pious resignation that Heidegger reviews the results of the war and his own brief endorsement of Nazism, from the perspective of the peace that followed. Some have seen in this the wisdom of a philosopher ill-equipped for political life who in old age has returned to the quiet precincts of his beloved thinkers and poets, to Parmenides and Hölderlin, and renounced, implicitly at least, the youthful radicalism that gripped him for a moment, as it did so many other cultured Germans of his generation who, wounded by the disgrace of national defeat, longed for their country to be restored to a place of honor in European life, and amidst the cultural confusions of the 1920s and '30s were briefly tempted to see in national socialism a kind of salvation. But to view Heidegger's quietism in this light is to miss the radicalism that continues to pulse through all his words to the end of his life. It is to miss the depth and intensity of his hostility to the modern world, which Heidegger continued to regard as an event whose essential awfulness can only be grasped in theological terms.

To judge the modern world from this perspective is to see it as something radically evil—a world as dark and corrupting as its champions claim is enlightened and free. The French revolutionaries radicalized the latter idea, and gave it an unprecedented authority in public life. Maistre and those who followed him radicalized the opposition to it. They were the last to defend, with ruthless consistency, the gospel of grace that Augustine bequeathed to the West, against the gospel of human freedom, which was Augustine's legacy too—one grown, in the eyes of its enemies, to an inconceivable monstrousness of pride that proclaimed the death of God himself. In this respect, they were Ockham's successors, and Luther's as well, and the reaction they mounted against the forces of freedom was the last before this battle was settled, once and for all, in Europe at least, in freedom's favor. It is to this tradition of radical reaction that Martin Heidegger belongs. The quietism of his old age is at once the final, anguished statement of Maistre's theology of grace and the despairing acknowledgment that its day is done.

CHAPTER 26

The Disenchantment of the World

MAX WEBER AND THE PROBLEM OF NIHILISM

In November 1917, Max Weber gave a famous speech to an overflow crowd at the University of Munich. The atmosphere was charged. The high hopes with which Germany had entered the war no longer seemed secure. In Germany itself, revolutionary movements on both the left and right were gaining ground. In a year, the First World War would be over. Germany's defeat would be complete—then made worse by the humiliations of Versailles. Though an early supporter of the war, Weber had become a vocal critic of Germany's methods and goals and an advocate of democratic constitutional reform. Many viewed his actions as a betrayal. He had come to Munich at the invitation of the Free Students Union. What would he say to those gathered in the hall at this expectant and volatile moment?

In 1917, Weber was fifty-four. For fifteen years, he had pursued his monumental researches as a private scholar, after a nervous collapse that made it impossible for him to continue his teaching career. Yet despite his self-imposed exile from the academic world, Weber's reputation had grown to near mythic proportions. No one since Hegel had offered such a sweeping view of the whole of Western civilization or possessed the learning to back it up. Because of this, some saw Weber as a prophet, and though he disavowed all prophetic powers and sharply criticized those academics who claimed to possess them, an aura of hope and expectation surrounded the great man as he entered the lecture hall to address the students who had invited him to speak. What truths might he bring, out of the depths of his wisdom and learning, to comfort and guide them in an hour of need? For those who had come hoping to be reassured, it is hard to imagine a more dispiriting message than the one that Weber delivered.

Weber chose as the title of his lecture, "Wissenschaft als Beruf" ("Science as a Calling"). The choice of a word with such heavy religious connotations was deliberate. After some preliminary remarks on the material obstacles that any young person must overcome if he wishes to pursue a career in academic research, Weber came to the heart of the matter. Is it possible, he asked, to find salvation in science?

About the political issues of the day, Weber had nothing to say. He had come to Munich to address a spiritual question instead. For those who choose an academic career, Weber told his audience, their work offers no prospect of salvation—nor, for that matter, does any other discipline or activity in a world from which the gods have fled once and for all. Our age, he said, is characterized by "rationalization" and "disenchantment." We must now find our way to God—if we can—on our own, in a spiritual wasteland that allows us the freedom to pursue our religious beliefs in private, but provides no organized, public support for the longing to be saved, whether in science or any other domain of life. Only those who have the courage to face this sober truth and are able to persevere in their commitment to scholarship nonetheless have a true calling for science. No other spiritually honest attitude remains for those whose "fate" it is to live in a "godless and prophetless time."[1] Weber's message of renunciation and tragic despair must have struck his young listeners with the force of a thunderclap. We can still hear its echo today.

THE DISENCHANTING RELIGION

In "Science as a Calling," Weber uses "rationalization" and "disenchantment" as roughly equivalent terms. Elsewhere, though, he distinguishes several different senses of rationality, not all of which are synonymous with disenchantment.[2] A theologian, for example, may be said to "rationalize" his beliefs by arranging them in a comprehensive and orderly scheme. In this general sense, reason can serve religious as well as nonreligious goals. When Weber equates rationalization with disenchantment, and treats the first as the cause or complement of the second, he has a particular kind of rationality in mind. Broadly speaking, he is thinking of what he calls "instrumental" reason—the sort that is involved in the adaption of means to ends.

This is the type of rationality that modern capitalism and bureaucratic administration both exhibit to a uniquely high degree. Each is a vast, organized system of instrumental reason, distinguished from other, premodern methods of production and administration by its immensely greater efficiency and speed. As a consequence, each allows for an unprecedented increase in man's control over himself and the natural world.

For this power to reach its maximum, however, instrumental reason must be freed from the limits that constrain it so long as the ends men set for themselves are not freely revisable in whatever way they think best. This is the case in all religious systems of belief and in every regime based on the sanctity of tradition. These rest on different conceptions of authority and cosmic order. But the basic norms of each must be accepted as something given, not made, and hence as postulates that keep the human reasoning employed on their behalf within fixed bounds. The starting points of a normative order cease to be confining only when human beings assert the right to define them on their own. For instrumental reason to have the widest possible field of employment, whether in the economic, administrative or any other sphere, men must claim this right against both God and the dead hand of tradition.

This is the premise of what Weber calls "legal rational" authority.[3] Among the various types of authority that men have accepted at different times and places, this one alone is capable of fully liberating the calculative powers of instrumental reason. Hence, only it leads to the disenchantment of the world that is brought about by the hypertrophic expansion of these powers. In this sense, disenchantment is a consequence of the acceptance of the principle of legal rational authority. But at a deeper level, it is the very meaning of this principle itself, which already enshrines the substitution of human for divine authority.

According to Weber, the dominance of legal rational authority is a uniquely occidental phenomenon. Only in the modern West has the idea that man himself is the source of the legitimacy of the normative order he inhabits gained a decisive ascendancy over all other forms of authority. Only here, as a result, has technical reason escaped the bounds set by every conception of authority that locates its ground in some extrahuman scheme or command. The question—to which Weber devoted a lifetime of thought and research—is why. Why in the West, and there alone, has this "humanistic" conception of authority displaced the other, "deferential" ones that from time out of mind instructed human beings to look for the source of their deepest and most cherished values not in themselves but God, or in the "eternal yesterday" of a tradition that is as much a part of the natural world as the life cycle it orders and frames?[4]

Weber identifies a bewildering variety of factors that have contributed to this development. None of them, he says, is solely accountable for it. At the end of his famous monograph on the Protestant ethic and the spirit of capitalism, Weber pointedly observes that his description of the role that certain religious beliefs played in the growth of early modern capitalism is only half the story, and that a complete account would have to include a number of material and political factors as well.[5] This statement and others like it give the impression that Weber remained agnostic about the relative importance of the many causes of modern Western rationalism, and in particular about the weight to be given those of an ideal as opposed to a material kind.

But this impression is misleading. Weber had a profound appreciation of the diversity of factors that have helped to produce the disenchanted world of the modern West. Yet he assigned a privileged place to one. Weber believed that religion, and more specifically the Christian religion, has played a uniquely important role in this process—not by itself, of course, but as a cultural force conditioning the direction of all the rest.

Up to the end of the European Middle Ages, the great civilizations of Asia and that of China in particular enjoyed a decisive material and technical advantage over the Latin-speaking West.[6] For centuries, moreover, the intellectual resources of Mediterranean antiquity eclipsed those of western Europe. Yet neither in Asia nor in ancient Greece did the belief that human beings have the power to confer legitimacy on their social and political norms merely by affirming them, ever acquire anything remotely like the prestige it came to enjoy in the early modern West.

It seems reasonable to suppose that the explanation for this has something to do with the one feature of European civilization that distinguishes it most sharply from all these others. Uniquely among the great civilizations of the world, that of the West evolved within the Latinate tradition of Christian belief on which Augustine placed his stamp at the start of the fifth century of the Common Era. As a working hypothesis, it therefore seems plausible to assume that occidental Christianity is connected in some distinctive way to the modern Western conception of man as the author of the norms that bind him and to the process of disenchantment unleashed by this idea—whose results are today, of course, no longer the special possession of the West in any meaningful sense at all. Weber never states this conclusion in such simple and unqualified terms. But his writings on religion all point toward it.

During the decade before his Munich lecture, Weber devoted an immense amount of time and energy to the study of the world religions. He was a scrupulous scholar, and no summary of his writings on religion can possibly do justice to their scope and complexity. But Weber's sociology of religion is more than a collection of discrete parts. It is an organized whole, unified by a common theme. According to Weber, whatever other differences exist among them, the religions of Asia and the cults of the ancient Mediterranean world are *all* distinguished from the Abrahamic religions by the latter's conception of God as a creator endowed with an omnipotent will, and by the radical separation of God from the world that this conception entails.[7] It is this distinction, he claims, that explains the fateful connection between the religion that has shaped the development of Western civilization and its disenchantment today.

The roots of this conception of God are to be found, Weber says, in ancient Judaism, though for reasons he explores at length, the Jews themselves never developed its intellectual implications in a thoroughly rigorous way.[8] Instead, especially in the Postexilic Period, Judaism became an orthopractical religion based on precepts sanctified by tradition and glossed by generations of juristically minded rabbis. Weber never undertook a comparably detailed study of Islam, but his few remarks on the subject suggest that he believed that something similar had happened there as well.[9] Only in the Christian religion have the philosophical implications of the Abrahamic conception of God been drawn in a systematic and uncompromising fashion. Above all, Weber suggests, this is true of Protestant Christianity, which radicalizes the teachings of the Christian religion in the same way that Christianity radicalizes those of Abrahamism in general, by insisting on the most rigorous interpretation possible of the idea of a creator God, inconceivably distant from the world, who brings it into being from nothing through an inscrutable act of will.

According to Weber, every religion responds to the human demand that the world be a meaningful place. It seeks to meet the need to believe that the blessings and sufferings of men are not random or senseless. This is a spiritual demand we can never repress or abolish.[10] For more than a millennium and a half, the main elements of Western civilization—political, economic and artistic—have all been conditioned by the particular solution to this universal theodicy problem that is embodied in the teachings of the Christian religion and those of Augustine in particular. Hence, if there is an *internal* connection between these teachings and the disenchantment of the West—if the second did not merely displace the first but emerged from it in a dialectical fashion—that must be because this theodicy, uniquely among those associated with the world religions, leads to its own demise, and does so more quickly the more rigorously its own commitments are construed. It must be because the Christian doctrine of salvation from the threat of meaninglessness that men everywhere seek to escape disenchants itself in a way no other doctrine of this kind does. It is impossible to study Weber's sociology of religion without concluding that this was in fact his view.

Weber was of course not the first to hold it. Kant, for one, insists that Christianity is the only religion in the world that is driven by its own principles to cleanse itself of the superstitions that accompanied its birth, though he sees this process of self-disenchantment from a standpoint still shaped by the philosophically refined remnants of the Christian ideas of salvation and grace. Later writers including Hegel affirm a similar view, from a secular perspective free of any lingering attachment to Christian belief.[11] Nietzsche is a particularly violent proponent of the idea that the godlessness of the modern world is a by-product of Christian faith.

Weber therefore had distinguished predecessors in claiming that the Christian religion is responsible for its own disenchantment. He frames this claim in terms of the theory of authority that represents his own most distinctive contribution to political thought. According to Weber, the disenchantment of the world is a consequence of the acceptance of a principle of authority that ascribes to human beings the right and power to create the norms that bind them, which frees instrumental reason from all preestablished limits, both natural and divine. Weber locates the origins of this principle in the "positivistic" idea of divine will that the Jews invented and their Christian successors refined. In his view, the modern conception of legal rational authority is the result of a transfer to human beings of a power of lawmaking that once belonged exclusively to God as the creator of the world.

This last claim is the crucial link in Weber's attempt to connect the distinctive features of the creationist theodicy that the Christian religion expounds in its purest form, with the disenchantment of modern Western civilization. But why did this transfer occur? That is a question Weber never answers. But having followed the course of Christian thought from Augustine to Kant and beyond, we are now in a position to provide one on Weber's behalf and to explain, from the inside as it were, why the Christian religion disenchants itself and with it, the civilization shaped by its contradictory ideals.

A CONFLICT OF WILLS

Augustine was the first to analyze the will as a power of creation from nothing. This is not because the great philosophers of antiquity simply failed to notice something that to Augustine and Paul seemed so obvious. Their blindness was metaphysically induced. The metaphysics of both Plato and Aristotle rests on the rationalist premise that to be is to be intelligible. If the actions of the will are to be intelligible, they must conform to a law of some kind, either mechanical or teleological. But the will is free precisely because it has the power to obey or disobey every law. This is what Augustine means when he says that the will is cause of itself. It follows that the will is essentially antinomian and therefore incomprehensible. There is no place for it within the intellectualist framework of pagan thought.

It is true that Aristotle also believed in something he describes as the cause of itself. But in contrast to Augustine's will, whose freedom makes it unintelligible in principle, Aristotle's unmoved mover is nothing but the intelligibility of the cosmic order as a whole—"mind minding mind," as he puts it. It is necessity itself—hence, the very opposite of the freedom to which Augustine is referring when he speaks of the will as a power of spontaneous beginning (of miraculous intervention, as later writers will say). Aristotle and Augustine agree that the being of finite things depends on their relation to the eternal and divine. But when Augustine undertook to rethink this relation in terms of the idea of the will, he embarked on a task that from a pagan point of view was bound to fail, since he sought to explain it by appealing to a power whose very essence lies in its inexplicability.

For a pagan rationalist like Aristotle, or a modern one like Spinoza, any philosophy that is based on the idea of the will is therefore more than implausible. It is self-contradictory, since it affirms the possibility of making sense of things by referring them to what, in the end, cannot be made sense of at all. In addition to this general problem, however, Augustine faced another (and from his perspective more urgent) one as well. This second problem arises on account of the contradictory demands imposed by the theodicy that provides the motive for Augustine's insistence on the existence of the will in the first place.

Augustine's God is an all-powerful creator. He brings the world into being from nothing. His freedom is absolute. But to avoid the unacceptable conclusion that God is responsible for the world's evil along with its good, human beings must also possess wills as free (though not as powerful) as his. Augustine's faith requires that the incomprehensible power he calls the will be in two places at once—in God, and in the human beings he creates in his image.

Few Christians, perhaps, see a tension, let alone a contradiction, in this assumption. In practical terms, most are prepared to live with the belief that God has a will and man does so too. But this seemingly plausible belief cannot withstand philosophical scrutiny.

Early in its history, the Christian religion was pressed in a more self-consciously philosophical direction by the challenges it faced in its mission to the gentiles and by the disappointment of its eschatological hopes. As a result, it quickly became a philosophical religion, in contrast to the ortho-practical religion of the Jews. But this meant that any serious Christian theologian had to confront the conceptual tension implicit in the assumption of two wills, one human and the other divine, and to resolve it in some fashion.

The tension can be described as follows. If God is all-powerful, then everything that happens in the world, including what happens through the agency of human beings, is his doing. But this leaves no room for human freedom. God's omnipotence does not allow for the existence of a separate, independent power of beginning, whether in man or anything else. If, on the other hand, man is really free, then God's power must be less than complete. Human beings must have the power to decide for themselves how to respond to God's ordinances. In this sense, they, not God, are the final arbiters of the rule of divine law on earth.

There are only two philosophically consistent ways of resolving this tension. Each takes one pole of the relation between man and God and assigns it priority, reducing the other to a position of secondary importance and eventually abolishing it altogether.

One can start, for example, by emphasizing the reality of human freedom, while still assigning a large role to God as the enabler of man's will (as both Pelagius and Erasmus do). But the more one insists on giving man's freedom its due, the less compatible it is likely to seem with any deference to God's will at all. In the end, such deference is bound to seem only another form of "heteronomy," and therefore incompatible with the "autonomy" of the human will. If the idea of God survives at all in such a view, it is merely as a notional aid to man's freedom—as what Kant calls a "postulate" of practical reason. Kant's philosophy of autonomy is the final, systematic expression of Augustine's claim that human beings possess true freedom of will. For Kant, man's freedom is still tethered to the concept of God. But his own arguments give those who accept them compelling reasons to cut the cord completely, and after Kant, his wholly secular successors embrace this way of resolving the tension between man's will and God's without any reference to God at all.

The alternative, of course, is to magnify God's freedom at the expense of man's until the latter disappears completely. Again, at first, human freedom may still play a modest role. But the more rigorously this view is developed, the more difficult it becomes to reconcile any role of this sort with the fact of divine omnipotence. This is the theology of the late Augustine, who in reaction to the challenge of Pelagianism stressed with mounting fervor the completeness of God's freedom, and the illusoriness of man's. It is the theology of the Franciscan voluntarists who recoiled at the prospect of a God whose freedom Aquinas and others had trapped in chains of reason; of their Protestant descendants, including Luther especially; and of those nineteenth- and twentieth-century reactionary Catholics who viewed the French Revolution and the liberal reforms inspired by it as a single vast spectacle of pride, arranged by God himself to remind his human creatures of their complete dependence on divine grace.

These two theologies represent the only intellectually consistent solutions to the problem created by Augustine's doubling of the will—on the one hand, a disenchanted philosophy of human autonomy, whose advocates cheerfully embrace the conclusion that God no longer exists, and on the other, its radical opposite, an uncompromising theology of grace, which discerns in our widening culture of human freedom an unintended proof of God's limitless power. The first puts freedom wholly in man, the second wholly in God. Intermediate positions and compromises are of course possible, and practically appealing, but none are philosophically sustainable. None comes to grips with the fact that divine omnipotence and human freedom are both absolutes, neither of which can be accommodated to the other without ceasing to be what it is. Either God is everything and man nothing at all, or man is the master of the earth and God a fantasy he has finally outgrown. These are the only two possibilities that a rigorous interpretation of the Augustinian understanding of man's relation to God allows. They are the only answers that a civilization shaped by the theodicy of the Christian religion can offer to the question of why men suffer and prosper as they do.

HUNGRY HEART

Neither view is more consistent than the other. Neither has a greater degree of intellectual coherence. From the standpoint of philosophical rigor alone, there is nothing to recommend one over the other. It might therefore seem that between them one must simply choose. But if there is no philosophical justification for preferring the doctrine of human autonomy to the gospel of God's grace, there is a compelling psychological reason for doing so.

Men long to be thankful to God. The more rigorously the doctrine of grace is expounded, however, the clearer it becomes that they can never be thankful enough. The human condition becomes one of permanently—indeed, deliberately—frustrated love. But this is humanly unbearable. Men cannot help but want to escape it, and in the end will do so in the only way they can—by abolishing the God for whose gifts they can never be adequately grateful, substituting their will for his and assuming God's powers on earth.

A rigorous theology of grace makes gratitude the supreme virtue and condemns pride as the root of all vice. Augustine takes this conclusion to its limit. Pride is, for him, more than a weakness or flaw. It is an ontological crime—the ambition, as he puts it, to be the ground of one's own being. It represents the most awful repudiation imaginable of man's dependence on God's gifts. Augustine's demonization of pride as the radical antithesis of gratitude turns the pagan valuation of pride upside down and celebrates the deliberate belittlement of man.

For Aristotle, pride is a virtue of commanding importance. A man who reaches the peak of human living is properly "full of himself." His life is one of exceptional independence.

Men may debate whether the best life is that of a statesman or a philosopher. But both are characterized by their outstanding self-sufficiency, and a man who succeeds in living either may be proud of what he has achieved, for he has fulfilled, in a uniquely human way, the longing to partake of the eternal and divine that men share with everything else in the world. He has gotten as much of God into himself as his human nature allows. The God that such a man becomes, for a time at least, either in the stillness of thought or the memorable splendor of great deeds, is for Aristotle the eternality of the world itself, which human beings alone, among the animals on earth, are equipped to partake of in more than one way. This is the theological premise of Aristotle's pagan philosophy of pride.

Aristotle recognized, of course, that human beings are finite. We all depend on other things to live and even the most fortunate among us grows old and dies. It follows that no man can ever be permanently and perfectly self-sufficient. This means that our participation in the everlasting is always temporary and in that respect (but only that) incomplete. Even if a philosopher becomes God for a moment, that moment never lasts. He soon grows tired and needs to rest. A statesman's powers are limited in even more obvious ways.

In particular, our finitude makes us dependent on the love of others for our ability to share in the divine. This is true in both politics and philosophy. It is only on account of the care of our parents, teachers, and the generations of citizens who have gone before us that families, cities and traditions of thought exist at all. These are the indispensable conditions of man's most rewarding attempts to reach the God of the world. We therefore have reason to be grateful for the love of those who have secured these conditions, and are naturally moved to want to return their love with our own, by caring for those who come after us so that they may flourish too. We feel a similar kind of love toward those of our contemporaries with whom we are engaged in the work of thought and action, and want to see them prosper for their own sake as well. Their well-being is not merely a condition but a component of our own. All these relations of affection, within and across the generations, Aristotle gathers under the name of friendship. Friendship is, in his view, an essential part of human happiness and the basis for a form of gratitude which, like every other, is rooted in the experience of being loved and the longing to love in return.

But the gratitude that Aristotle celebrates in his account of friendship differs from its Christian counterpart in two crucial respects. First, it is supported by the same theology that undergirds every other aspect of Aristotle's philosophy of pride. This assumes a continuity between the human and divine that from a Christian point of view is as blasphemous as man's wish to be God.

Second, it locates the love from which gratitude springs within the horizontal relations that men have with one another. Gratitude is appropriate, indeed necessary, here. But for Aristotle, it has no place at all in man's relation to the eternal intelligibility and beauty of the world as a whole. That is because this is not anyone's gift—certainly not that of a God beyond the world. It is just the way things are.

Christianity stands this conception of gratitude on its head. It teaches that the world *is* God's gift and demands a thankfulness for it that exceeds anything that could ever be required, or expressed, in our relations with other human beings. It demands a gratitude that transcends the human world altogether.

This shift in the understanding of the nature of gratitude has important psychological consequences.

From a Christian point of view, my gratitude to God must always fall short. The recognition that this is so is the soul of Christian piety, which insists in a principled way on the acknowledgment of our incompetence ever to be adequately grateful for the gifts that God bestows upon us.

But this frustrates the deepest longing of every human heart. Even if we are only moderately fortunate, we come into a world prepared for us by others, who look after us until we are able to care for ourselves. We long to reciprocate their love by loving others in return. That is not because we feel burdened by a debt we must discharge—love and debt are altogether different things. It is because love is a fulfillment. It is in loving others with a love as good and great as the one we have received that we discover what it is possible for us to be at our best. We reach a state of relatively selfless affection that is the largest consolation any of us can ever know for the sentence of death to which we have all been condemned.

Where the love we long to return is that of other human beings, this fulfillment is within reach. So long as we remain within the plane of our horizontal relations with others like ourselves, it is possible to love them with a love as imperfectly grand as the one we have received as a gift from our parents, teachers and friends. But when the love that matters most is the vertical love of a God whose love for us we can never adequately reciprocate—when the shortfall in our ability to love him as well as we should is made the very essence of our humanity—the longing to love is not given a wider expression but blocked at its root. The yearning to be as loving as we are loved is denied as a matter of principle. Its suppression becomes a theological requirement. And when this happens, the love of God eventually turns into its poisonous opposite. It becomes an envious hatred of the one who bars the way to fulfillment in love.

This inevitably produces a wish to turn the tables on God—to make him our dependent, rather than the other way around. The gospel of grace intensifies the frustration that gives rise to this wish. The morality of human autonomy fulfills it instead. Each resolves, in an equally consistent fashion, the philosophical tension created by a theology that affirms both God's omnipotence and man's freedom. But the latter does so in a way that satisfies the human longing to be adequate in love and therefore enjoys a decisive psychological advantage over the doctrine of grace, which deliberately stymies this longing at every turn.

It is Kant who first expresses the ideal of human autonomy with perfect clarity. In Kant's philosophy, God is demoted to the position of a postulate of practical reason—a mere aid to human morality. This reverses man's relation to God.

The doctrine of grace supplies the motive for this reversal. But it also facilitates it conceptually. It prepares the way for its humanistic rival by stressing the unintelligibility of God as a way of honoring his freedom and power. By insisting on God's incomprehensibility, his fiercest defenders make it easier for the champions of human freedom to argue that, in both practical and conceptual terms, God is nothing to man. Kant has nearly arrived at this position, though his account of what human beings can know and ought to do, is still joined by a vestigial link to the Christian idea of God as the creator of the world. After Kant, this link is broken once and for all. The idea of human freedom, based on the Christian concept of the will, is unchained from Christian doctrine altogether. It becomes a wholly secular ideal, whose vindication not only permits but demands the expulsion of God from the world.

Man thereby liberates himself from his dependence on God. But he does something more. He claims God's powers as his own. Human beings can of course never actually be omnipotent. But the endless expansion of our technical and other powers allows us to move in this direction without limit, and always to aspire to go farther. In this way, the now discredited idea of divine omnipotence becomes the standard by which to judge all human achievements, whose meaning and value is to be measured by their approximation to the works of a God in whom men no longer believe. Men grow used to the idea that it is their right and duty to strive to annul whatever distance remains between their finite human powers and that of a God who is able to summon the world into being from nothing. The principle of legal rational authority expresses this aspiration in a particularly clear way. It states that whatever values have authority in human life do so *only because* men declare them to be authoritative. This is the triumph of pride, anathematized by the Christian religion as the greatest of all sins, yet spurred by Christianity's own demand for a gratitude beyond measure, and facilitated, paradoxically, by the logical separation of God from the world on which the enemies of pride themselves have always insisted. It is the disenchantment of the world.

This has not happened without a fight. In the West, the counterrevolutionary movement that began with Joseph de Maistre and ended with Carl Schmitt and Martin Heidegger fought a long and ferocious campaign against the ethic of human pride, in the name of divine providence. Its spokesmen were driven by a theologically motivated hatred of the ideal of autonomy that in the late eighteenth century began to transform every department of European life. Heidegger and Schmitt were attracted to the Nazi Party because they saw in it the beginnings of the longed-for counterrevolt against the spirit of technicity that both regarded, in cosmic terms, as a satanic rebellion against God. In the 1930s, the reactionary antimodernism that inspired them remained a powerful force in European culture and politics, as it had been since the French Revolution. But if their books are still read, and their ideas discussed, in academic circles at least, the tradition of religiously motivated antihumanism to which Schmitt and Heidegger belonged has many fewer supporters in the West today.

Pockets of reaction remain, of course, but these are mainly nationalistic in character and, in Europe at least, are largely driven by the loss of local identities in a cultural and political environment increasingly governed by universal liberal ideals. Some of these identities have a religious component. But even where they do, the parties of reaction in Europe for the most part now draw their appeal from the wish not to be lost in a melting pot where one's distinctive practices and traditions, including religious traditions, are submerged in a civilization defined by abstract and colorless norms. This is something very different from a religiously inspired rejection of modernity as such. The latter is a theocosmic ideal, as universal in its outlook and aims as the civilization it opposes. Today, this ideal no longer plays a significant role in European politics. Indeed, to the extent that religion remains a political force of any importance, it tends to press in the opposite direction—toward the veneration of what is local, rooted, and therefore nonuniversal instead.

Increasingly, it is not a force at all. For the past forty years, religion has been dying out in Europe. Today, the secular principle of respect for persons rules from the Atlantic to the Urals, in theory and more unevenly in practice. The idea that human beings are the authors of their own destiny, which they are free to fashion as they choose through democratic processes constrained by liberal rights, is widely if not universally accepted. The battles that continue to be fought over political and economic integration, immigration, and the scope of human rights, are all waged within the framework of this system of beliefs. Those who see this entire system as the work of the devil and long for man to be humiliated by the God of grace, against whom he has been in rebellion since Adam, are few in number and, in Europe at least, their theological hatred of modernity no longer commands any significant measure of public respect.

When Max Weber told his audience in 1917 that they lived in a "godless and prophetless time," he could not have foreseen the horror of the last apocalyptic movement to inspire hope among some that the prideful pretensions of what Donoso Cortes calls "philosophic" civilization would at last be beaten back. Nor could he have foretold the completeness and finality with which his diagnosis of the disenchantment of the world would be vindicated by the peaceable, rights-respecting, godless Europe that emerged from the battlefields and crematoria of the Second World War. But this is precisely what has happened.

In Europe today, the gospel of grace survives only, as Weber says, *in pianissimo*. It has become a "preference" or "value" that individuals remain free to affirm as a matter of private belief, but that is rigorously excluded from public life as a doctrine antithetical to the humanistic premises on which all forms of political legitimation now rest. It is only outside of Europe, in the Muslim world especially, that belief in man's dependence on God retains its public authority. The widespread demand for the restoration of Shari'a, even in countries that have shown some attraction to Western ideas, is one expression of this belief. The radical Islamists whose antimodern campaign of terror has caused immense suffering and fear are another. At its heart, the battle that the terrorists hope to force with the West is not a fight over oil or independence or cultural respect, though these are not inconsequential factors. It is a fight over God. They want to see God restored to the world—or rather, the world restored to God. They refuse to accept the spreading humanism which, born in the West and made attractive by its material success, threatens to elevate man to a position of supreme authority and to reduce God to the status of a preference or value. In their view, this is more than a political danger or cultural threat. It is the demonism of modernity itself, represented above all by the European and North American states that have capitulated to it so completely.

Against this spirit, they say, the fight must be waged without quarter. That is because absolute values are at stake, and nothing short of an all-out war can possibly be accepted by those who understand the conflict in its proper perspective, as a battle between Satan and God. Whether their Western enemies see it in these terms is for the terrorists themselves, a matter of indifference. Those in the West may wish to view the struggle as an innerworldly contest for political and economic power. But in the minds of the jihadists who seek to force the issue, it cannot be contained in this way. It cannot be domesticated or reduced to the level of politics as usual. In their eyes, it is a struggle to vindicate a demand that transcends the world and everything in it—one that God Almighty makes on his human subjects, whether they hear him or not.

The Muslim terrorists that today hide in the caves of Afghanistan and scatter themselves throughout the cities of the world and aspire to establish a new caliphate in the heartland of the old one are in this sense the planet's last heirs to the tradition of Christian reaction that in its final, apocalyptic incarnation brought ruin to the whole of Europe before vanishing as a force of any consequence in European life itself. They have already spilled blood in God's name, and will spill more. But there is reason to think (and in this respect, of course, to hope) that the godless wasteland Weber describes will continue to spread—that the spirit of disenchantment, which grew on European soil, nourished by the contradictory and ultimately unbearable demands of the Christian religion, will in time blanket the rest of the world, as have the irresistible rationalizations of economy and administration made possible by man's expropriation of God's powers, which these very demands themselves have fueled. If Weber were alive today, I suspect that he would find nothing in any of these developments to cause him to revise, in a fundamental way, his claim that we live in a godless time, and much, perhaps, to confirm it.

LOVELESS

For the most part, "Science as a Calling" is written with a cool dispassion that suggests that Weber is merely reporting objective facts in the "value-free" spirit he made famous in his essays on scientific method.[12] But those who heard Weber's lecture in 1917, or read it today, cannot miss the tone of despair that runs through it. The disenchantment of the world may be an irreversible fact. But for Weber it also represents a spiritual loss of unprecedented proportions.

Many, of course, do not share Weber's despair. The disenchantment of the world seems to them an entirely positive development. They see its good side—a dramatic improvement in the material conditions of life even for the disadvantaged; a widening commitment to the ideal of human rights; and increased freedom from superstitions of all sorts. They either do not see, or see but discount sharply, the spiritual loss that Weber regarded as the necessary complement of these developments.

Even Weber himself would never have been tempted to follow a prophet who promised to repair this loss by putting us in thrall to God again—assuming that were possible. He valued the freedoms and achievements of our godless age too highly to feel the least sympathy for a reactionary program of this kind.[13] Yet at the same time Weber insists that we acknowledge the magnitude of the loss we have sustained. Our world is freer and more prosperous than any that men have ever known before. But it is also hostile to the deepest longings of the human spirit. Their frustration makes our disenchanted world as unbearable as it is preferable to any other we might substitute for it. It is the combination of these ideas that gives Weber's lecture its tragic tone.

The spiritual barrenness of the modern world has three principal manifestations. It is reflected in the lovelessness of public life, the pointlessness of science, and the groundlessness of our personal values. But it is crucial to understand that none of these is a result merely of the belief that man is now authorized to seize God's powers, or of the disenchantment that follows from our appropriation of them. Each arises only when this belief is accompanied by the conviction that the God to whose powers we lay claim has to be conceived as a world-transcending deity of the sort in whom we no longer have faith. Taken together, these two beliefs are a recipe for self-defeat. Those who accept both can neither go back to God nor forward to fulfillment. They are haunted by the shadow of the otherworldly God they have rejected, who still rules them from the grave by defining their understanding of divinity in such a way that they are shut out from any possibility of ever reaching it, no matter how large their worldly powers become.

Nietzsche was the first to diagnose this spiritual predicament. He called it "nihilism." According to Nietzsche, nihilism is a uniquely European disease. It is, he believed, the defining condition of the modern West, which is post-Christian in the double sense of having repudiated the Christian faith while remaining attached to the metaphysical principle on which it depends. This is the principle that the value of the world can only come to it from a source beyond the world. Today, this would require that we be able to fill the place left vacant by the now dead God of the Christian religion. Since we cannot, those trapped in this double bind have no choice but to acknowledge that the world has no value or meaning at all. The despair of "Science as a Calling" rests on a similar diagnosis, though unlike Nietzsche, Weber believed the disease to be incurable. He saw no way out of, and nothing beyond, the self-defeating nihilism of our post-Christian age. He considered it a terminal condition and not, as Nietzsche did, the prelude to joy.

The lovelessness of modern public life is one manifestation of this dilemma.

Each of us depends on the love of others, without which we could not exist or flourish. Our dependence on their love is especially deep since there is nothing we can ever say to "justify" our "claim" to it—in contrast to the demands we make on others to respect our rights. The gratitude we feel for the gift of love is inseparable from this uniquely deep dependence; it is at once an expression and acceptance of it.

It follows that a person who is completely independent can never have any occasion to feel gratitude toward anyone else. This is God's condition. His creatures depend on him for all they have and are. The gratitude they feel toward him therefore exceeds any they might feel toward the other human beings on whose love they depend in more limited ways. But God has no reason to feel the least shred of gratitude toward any of his creatures since he does not depend on their love in even the smallest degree. Thus, on one side of the relation between man and God there is gratitude without limit and on the other none at all.

The wish to escape the unhappiness of this lopsided relation drives men to want to take God's place. It finds satisfaction in the ideal of human autonomy and in the principle of legal rational authority, which expresses this ideal as a political norm. Those who invoke this principle insist that man is the sole source of the authority of the rules by which his public life is governed. In a regime based on this principle, love plays no role at all.

This contrasts sharply with regimes that rest either on tradition or the declared word of God. The first acknowledges the sanctity of one's ancestors as a reason for obedience to the norms they have bequeathed to their descendants. Those who accept the authority of tradition act out of a love for those who have gone before. The second recognizes the love of God as a reason to obey the laws he has revealed.

By contrast, legal rational authority drives love from public life. It drains it of the power to justify the laws by which men live and the actions of those who administer them. It makes impersonality a virtue and demands that administrators perform their duties in a strictly dispassionate manner—"*sine ira et studio*," as Weber says. And it does this not accidentally but deliberately and systematically because the principle of legal rational authority is rooted in an ideal of human self-sufficiency that is modeled on God's own, from whose perspective dependence on anything, including love, is a threat that must be minimized and devalued.

The triumph of this principle as a source of public authority is characterized by the transformation of all norms into entitlements, whose possession and exercise must henceforth be justified in a "discursive" community of human beings who view themselves as the equally independent authors of the only laws by which their relations may legitimately be governed. The idea that any member of such a community should ever view the rights that he or she possesses as a gift motivated by the love of others is offensive from the standpoint of the conception of legitimacy that determines the meaning of all public values in a community of this sort.

Of course, we can never overcome our dependence on love and the gratitude that goes with it. That would be possible only in case we actually were the God we wish to be. But though love cannot be abolished, it can be devalued. This is what happens in a regime based on the principle of legal rational authority. In such a regime, love endures as a positive value in the realm of private relations only. Even here, however, it lives under the shadow cast by its public depreciation. At best, this means that our dependence on the love of others becomes something we must struggle to affirm without the support of anything beyond our private and isolated experience of it. At worse, it means that love seems, at times, a liability we would shed if we could.

The gratitude for love received, in whose expression we experience the deepest fulfillment of our longing to be adequately loving toward others and the world, is thus made harder to sustain, even in our most intimate relations, on account of the dominant public norms of the age, which encourage us to evaluate ourselves from the standpoint of a being who is free of the need for love altogether. From this perspective, love is an embarrassment, and the gratitude with which men and women respond to it is a symptom of weakness rather than strength. In this respect, the system of public values that we impose upon ourselves in an effort to usurp the place of the omnipotent God whose love for us is more than we can bear ends by making us ashamed to be who we are, like Adam and Eve when they first saw their nakedness from God's censorious point of view—though unlike our parents in that enchanted garden, the inhabitants of our industrial civilization continue to condemn themselves despite the fact that God is dead.

Wherever the principle of legal rational authority is accepted, the laws by which men are bound cease to be viewed as commands issued by a God beyond the world. They come to be regarded as human inventions instead, fashioned and administered by men, who now claim the right to determine for themselves what is and is not law.

For those who assert this right, God no longer exists as a source of public value. Yet the authority they claim for themselves is constructed in the image of the one he once possessed. When human beings still recognized and deferred to God's authority, they did so because they assumed that whatever

God wills is binding on his human subjects. If men now have the right to rule themselves, it is for a parallel reason. It is because they too possess wills and hence have the power to bring laws into being from nothing and make them binding by *fiat* alone. This is the originally theological, now wholly secularized, premise on which every regime of legal rational authority is based.

But love is always a threat to this conception of authority. That is because love is a condition of dependence and therefore incompatible with the will's power of self-determination, which on this view alone qualifies it to be an author of binding norms. This is already clearly stated by Kant, who regarded love as something "pathological" from the standpoint of his ethics of autonomy. The principle of legal rational authority rests on the same ideal. From its perspective, too, love can therefore only be a heteronomous feeling that compromises the independence of the will and hence its capacity to be a source of values of any kind at all.

The devaluation of love in a world based on the principle of legal rational authority thus illustrates the double bind of nihilism, for it arises from the assumption by human beings of a position of innerworldly authority that is justified by their asserted possession of the power that defined the being of the otherworldly God in whom they no longer believe. It depends upon the continuing acceptance of the Christian doctrine of creation from nothing, which Augustine correctly understood to be the essence of willing, even after the death of the Christian God. This guarantees that the public world becomes a loveless place, drained of the love of a God who has ceased to exist, and at the same time made hostile to human love by the equation of our autonomy with the unconditioned freedom of a nonexistent deity in the image of whose self-sufficiency we now interpret the meaning of our own.

Understood in these terms, nihilism is at war with our humanity. Every ideal opens a gap between who we are and aspire to be. But nihilism, which is an ideal too, and not, as many think, the denial of all ideals, puts us at odds with ourselves in a peculiarly self-destructive way by devaluing the love through which we give thanks for being at home in the world, and strengthening the authority of a loveless regime from which there is no escape, except into the isolation of private life.

Those who experience the fulfillment of love have the best chance of being reconciled to the reality of death without suppressing their human longing to partake of the eternal and divine. By contrast, those who find it hard to hold onto this experience, because they live in a world whose public norms aggressively devalue love, are more likely to see their finitude as a senseless, even hateful thing, when measured by the conception of God that the men and women of our godless age still use to judge themselves and their desires. That is why Nietzsche regarded nihilism as a radically destructive ideal, and believed the age of its domination to be the most inhuman of all. Weber's judgment is even more despairing, for while he shares Nietzsche's view that the triumph of man has made him homeless in an inhuman world, he sees no path out of the spiritual desert in which the disenchantment of the world has stranded us—unless and until, he says, "new prophets" arise, and bring the word of God back to a world that has lost the power to hear it.

POINTLESS

Today, our knowledge of the world expands without limit. It never concludes; it never "comes to a point." There is always more of it than there was the day before. As a result, no scientist can ever grasp the whole of things or reach a final resting place in his research. His contributions are all quickly superseded by those of others. His achievements are transient and incomplete. Indeed, if he is a true scientist, this is his avowed aim. He hopes that his discoveries will be replaced by new ones, the sooner the better. The very idea of the everlasting is therefore out of place in modern science, with its endless, restless pursuit of higher forms of knowledge. In this respect, Weber says, the situation of those who adhere to its ideals is diametrically opposed to that of a "peasant of old" who, after a long life of hard work, could die secure in the knowledge that the world lasts forever, and that he had experienced all it has to offer to mortals like himself.

The peasant of old lived in a world saturated with eternity. He worked in the immediate presence of the everlasting and divine. He encountered it every day, on his way to the fields, under the constellations that mark the seasons of sowing and reaping. By contrast, the work of the modern scientist cuts him off from eternity. It leaves him adrift in time. His research has no terminus or goal. It never circles back on itself, like the work of the peasant. And because of this it is pointless in a very specific sense, for no matter how far he and his colleagues progress in their understanding of the world, all their discoveries are merely stepping stones to their own supersession, and leave those who make them as distant from God as they were when they began.

The realm of science is today entirely godless. The eternal and divine, which the peasant saw face-to-face, is nowhere to be found in its disenchanted precincts. One who looks for salvation in science is therefore a fool. This must be found, if it can be at all, in private experiences that fall outside the realm of science altogether.

It is a sign of maturity to recognize and accept this. A young person who feels called to science must summon the courage to acknowledge that he can never reach the everlasting in or through it. Only then has he shown that he really understands the responsibilities entailed by a commitment to research. Everything else is wishful thinking. This is the sober message that Weber came to Munich in 1917 to deliver to the students who had invited him to speak.

The mood of resignation that colors Weber's account of the spiritual emptiness of modern science has its roots in a combination of ideas whose nihilistic implications might be described as a kind of Kantianism without God.

To understand something, according to Kant, is to bring it under a law. Science is the discipline of constructing or discovering laws. At the deepest level, it rests on the primitive work of rule making carried out by the transcendental understanding. This provides the foundation for every science, regardless of its subject matter. On the basis of these primitive rules, which give the world its elementary order, the various sciences seek to identify more particular laws of an empirical kind that govern one domain or another. This is true both of the "spiritual" and "natural" sciences, which study what Kant calls "inner" and "outer" experience, respectively.

The search for the laws that govern a particular domain of experience always proceeds in two directions at once. On the one hand, it moves downward, toward laws of ever greater specificity. Any given law is a generalization that requires further refinement. On the other hand, it moves upward, toward laws of continually greater abstraction. Viewed from the first perspective, every law is a generality requiring additional specification. Viewed from the second, it is a specific rule that must be anchored in a higher-order law if its own application to a limited range of phenomena is to be explained and not merely accepted as a brute fact.

This twofold process is characteristic of every scientific discipline. But it has a terminus in neither direction. However detailed the laws of a discipline become they can always be analyzed into laws of a still more specific kind. And however far the scientists in a particular field have gone in identifying the broad, covering laws of their subject, these will always need to be grounded in still broader laws that provide a warrant for them. The work of science proceeds, in both directions, toward an unattainable ideal—in one direction, toward a specification so complete that the laws of science coincide with the actuality of the world, and in the other, toward laws of such comprehensiveness and generality that there could not possibly be any higher-order laws that condition or ground them (toward what Kant calls the "unconditioned"). The imperative to proceed endlessly in both directions, despite the unattainability of the goal at which one aims in each, is the "regulative ideal" that today governs all scientific research.

The distinctively Christian character of this conception of science stands out when we compare it with its Aristotelian counterpart.

According to Aristotle, we understand a thing by grasping its form. The form of a thing is what it shares in common with others of its kind. It is the "law" of the thing in question.

The forms of things are arranged in a hierarchy. To fully understand any particular form, it is necessary to appreciate its place in this hierarchy. The form of an organ, for example, can only be understood by seeing how it fits into the form of the organism to which it belongs; the form of an organism becomes intelligible when we see how it exemplifies that of ensouled beings in general; and we understand the form of ensouled beings by identifying their position in the great chain of being that stretches from prime matter at one end to the prime mover at the other.

But this hierarchy of forms has a terminus in both directions, unlike the nested system of laws whose endless articulation is for Kant the goal of all scientific research. With prime matter, form runs out, and with the prime mover it achieves an absolute fulfillment, beyond which nothing can be conceived. The former brings science to a halt. It marks a final frontier of utter mindlessness that represents the downward limit of all understanding. The latter brings science to an end in a different way, for though Aristotle, like Kant, believed that a true and perfect understanding of anything demands a knowledge of the unconditioned, he also believed that such knowledge is available to us in this life, notwithstanding our finite nature.

This last assumption explains Aristotle's confidence that a scientist can reach the everlasting in his work. God is just the form of the world, which the mind of man is able to grasp completely, for a time at least, so long as one pays close attention to it. The doctrine of creation destroys this confidence in two ways.

First, because the God who creates the world creates it from nothing, the distinction between form and matter disappears. There can be no lower limit to the "en-formedness" of the world. There will always be more mind in the world than we have grasped so far.

Second, because on a Christian view the unconditioned ground of the world lies beyond it rather than in it, as Aristotle supposed, our understanding of the world, however complete, can never reach its ground. The unconditioned will always be beyond our grasp.

In a science shaped by Christian beliefs, both the upward search for the unconditioned and the downward search for laws of greater specificity must therefore go on forever. But this means that one can never reach God in science, for to do so it would have to be possible to comprehend the mindedness of the world down to its last atom of particularity, and up to the unconditioned being of God himself. Our finitude prevents us from doing either. Once we separate God from the world, and reconceive the relation between them as one of creation, the finitude of human beings becomes an absolute bar to their ever understanding God by means of science, rather than merely a barrier to their retaining that understanding for more than a limited period of time.

For Aristotle, science has a point because it comes to a point. The possibility of arriving at a complete knowledge of God, which anchors everything else we know in a final way, guarantees the spiritual value of scientific research. It assures that those who devote themselves to science are on a path that leads to the eternal and divine, which they can reach unless they are prevented from doing so by accidental factors. But once science becomes the endless process it must be on a Christian view of the world, this guarantee disappears and another must be found if the fact that it never comes to a point is not to render it pointless in the sense of being unconnected to God.

Kant acknowledges this problem and solves it by saying that all our scientific inquiries depend for their intelligibility on the assumption that the world whose laws we strive to unfold with ever-greater specificity in one direction and ever-greater generality in another has an "author," whose unity of purpose guarantees the unity of these laws themselves. We may never be able to comprehend this unity but must assume it if our efforts to define the laws of creation are to be meaningful despite their necessary incompleteness.[14] The meaningfulness of science thus depends, for Kant, on the assumption of an omnipotent God beyond the world, who brings it into being from nothing. This assumption destroys the ground of Aristotle's confidence that God can be reached in science, but simultaneously provides a new ground for the belief that although science cannot reach God, it at least points toward him, which is enough to ensure that the connection between our human efforts to understand the world, on the one hand, and eternity on the other, is not broken completely.

The disenchanted science that Weber describes with such spiritual pathos no longer proceeds on Kant's assumption that the world has an author. Any scientist may, of course, continue to believe that it does. But Weber insists that this belief is merely a personal conviction. Perhaps it gives comfort and assurance to the person whose belief it is, but it no longer has any necessary connection to the work of science itself. Kant still thought it did. But the disenchantment of the world has converted what was for Kant a transcendental presupposition of scientific research into a private value that one is free to adopt or reject as one chooses, and that has no more authority, as an objective matter, than any other religious belief. In this way, science is cut adrift from the assumption that kept it anchored to God, once God was separated from the world.

Yet because our conception of the everlasting has been so deeply shaped by the Christian idea of God as the author of the world, it is now impossible for the work of science to be reconnected to the eternal and divine through any other conception of it—for example, the Aristotelian idea of God as the indwelling mindedness of the world. So long as our understanding of God continues to be conditioned by Christian beliefs in whose objective validity we have lost all confidence, we are therefore caught in a double bind. We can neither resurrect these beliefs nor, since they still define, even *in absentia,* our conception of the divine, find our way forward to a different notion of it. And this means that, so far as science is concerned, all its endless, marvelous discoveries can be connected neither to the now-dead God of the Christian religion, nor to a new God whose emergence is blocked by our continuing attachment to the shape of the place the Christian God left behind in our minds when he died.

GROUNDLESS

Weber insists that science has no value in itself. Neither does anything else. Art, politics, and erotic love are all inherently valueless too. These things acquire value for those who pursue them only by being valued.

A valuation is an act of will. It may assign an intrinsic value to some feature of the world or interest we take in it. But before it is valued, nothing has any value in itself.

The acts of will that bestow value on the world have the power to do this because they are free. It is their freedom that gives them this power. Only what is free has value in itself and is therefore capable of conferring it indirectly on anything else. A person's will sets him apart from every other individual because only he can exercise it (in contrast to the power of reason, which one person may exercise on behalf of another). It follows that the values that result from the acts of will that create them must be individual too, however much they overlap in content.

This is the essence of Weber's account of the nature of value. It is easy to recognize the influence on it of Kant.[15]

Like Kant's ethics, Weber's own is rigorously formalistic. The content of our value-creating decisions is fantastically diverse. But what makes their objects valuable is in every case the same. It is the act of choosing, committing or deciding that defines the common form of all our valuations, whatever their substance may be.

For Kant, this formal conception of value leads to a universalistic ethics based on the principle of equal respect for persons. For Weber, it leads to an anomic existentialism that denies the possibility of ever judging anyone else's values except from the standpoint of one's own. The assumption, which Weber shares with Kant, that every value has its source in an act of will, thus leads him to the radically un-Kantian conclusion that even the most "objective" values can never have more than a "subjective" warrant. Weber believed that any honest person must eventually come to this conclusion, and insisted that those who do are bound to feel an intensified sense of personal responsibility for the values they choose—in Weber's view, the highest form of ethical accountability.

No orthodox Kantian will accept this conclusion. Like Weber, Kant assumes that the will alone has intrinsic value and that other things acquire value only in relation to it. But Kant attempts to demonstrate that this assumption entails an objective principle for assessing the moral soundness of the choices we make, not Weber's subjective "polytheism of values."[16] Weber was led in the latter direction on account of his acceptance of what might be called a radicalized version of the Kantian idea of free choice. According to this view, even the assertion that there is an objective ground for moral judgment is itself just another act of valuation, for which no antecedent ground exists. For Weber, choice goes all the way down. To suppose that there are objective laws of any kind that determine the worth or value or propriety of the choices we make is, in Weber's view, to abandon the fundamental principle that all values, including especially the most "objective" ones, exist only because we freely assign a value to them. Weber seems to have been influenced in this regard less by the neo-Kantian philosophers of his day, who continued to defend a broadly orthodox interpretation of Kant's ethics, than by Nietzsche's more radical understanding of the nature of value (though Weber himself never overcame the nihilism that Nietzsche describes as the terminal illness of modern European civilization).

By adopting Kant's formalistic conception of value, while extending the idea of valuation to include Kant's own claim that ethics has an objective foundation, Weber aggravated a difficulty that already exists for Kant, but which, as a believing Christian, Kant still had the resources to meet. This is the problem of explaining how any judgment that assigns an *intrinsic* value to the world can possibly be true.

Standing on its own, Kant's ethics makes this hard to do. That is because it assumes that the only thing that is valuable *in itself* is not "of" the world at all. But Kant's ethics is backstopped by a theology that justifies the conclusion that the world does have inherent value, independent of whatever value we human beings assign it. Weber's loss of belief in the objective truth of this theology leaves him with no way of supporting the idea that the world has any value of its own and forces him to conclude that it has none.

So long as one believes, as Kant did, that there is an author of the world, the problem of explaining how it can possess value in its own right has an otherworldly solution. The disenchantment of the world takes Kant's solution away. If one insists, therefore, on the irreversibility of the process of disenchantment, while continuing to affirm, as Weber does, that the will is the only conceivable source of value, the attribution of inherent value to the world becomes utterly senseless in a way it was not for Kant, despite the formalism of his own practical philosophy. By embracing an even more radical understanding of the will than Kant did, while simultaneously repudiating the God who for Kant still secured the inherent value of the world, Weber puts himself in the same nihilistic dilemma we have now met twice before.

This becomes particularly clear if we focus on the value of diversity.

The diversity of human values is for Weber an important theme. He was impressed by the range of different—even contradictory—values around which human beings arrange their lives. But the diversity of human experience was for Weber more than just a fact. He admired it and assigned a value to it. One cannot read Weber's heroically sensitive survey of the diverse range of human types and ways of life without concluding that he believed diversity to be of value in itself. Yet his own theory of value rules this out. For if what makes any value a value is the will that wills it and nothing else, why should it make any difference at all—aesthetically, ethically or otherwise—whether what people will is the same or different? For that to be the case diversity would have to possess a value *of its own* (as Weber often appears to assume), but this is just what his radicalized version of Kant's formalistic theory of value denies as a matter of principle.

The problem is even more serious. It is not merely that of explaining how we can assign an inherent value to human diversity in general, but to the distinctiveness of our individual lives as well.

That I am the author (in some sense) of the values that shape my life is a condition of these being values for me at all. Values that are imposed on me by others are not my values but theirs. Still, the value of my life is not, for me, wholly a function of my willing or choosing the commitments that guide it. It is also a function of the particular shape my life has on account of the substance of these commitments themselves. My life is valuable, to me at least, because it is different from the lives of others, just as their lives are valuable, to them, on account of their distinctiveness too. In this sense, diversity is not just a third-personal value. It is a first-personal one as well. If the value of my life could be fully accounted for by the fact that I have chosen the values that shape it—in which respect I am no different from anyone else—then the most valuable thing about my life, certainly for me and perhaps for others too, would have been stripped away. This can be avoided only if the distinctiveness of my life is seen to be something valuable in itself. But that is impossible, so long as one accepts the view that the will is the only thing "in or out of the world" with a value of its own.

For Kant, the idea of God provides a way out of this dilemma. From God's point of view, the diversity of individuals is something objectively valuable. This follows from the idea of creation, which dissolves the distinction between form and matter and thereby confers being and beauty on the individuality of every individual thing. This is most obviously true of human beings. God's world would be incomplete without us. We are the chef d'oeuvre of creation. And while the sameness of persons (which consists in their being endowed with practical reason) has special value from God's point of view, their uniqueness as finite rational beings does so as well. Why else would he have created so many such beings and given them the motive and material to exercise their wills in such diverse ways? God's infinite power and goodness compel us to assume that, from his perspective, the diversity of human beings must have value in its own right, over and above the value they possess as rational beings with a capacity for action in accordance with the conception of a rule.

If God is to guarantee the objective value of diversity, however, he cannot himself be a personal value whose status depends entirely on the will of the person endorsing it. If that is the case, then the belief that God is the author of the world is no different than the belief that science, or erotic love, or anything else, possesses the highest possible value. The assignment of value to God now stands on the same level as these and all other innerworldly valuations. Religion becomes a matter of human choice too, and even if those who continue to believe in God find personal strength in their faith, they have no objective basis for declaring their belief superior to that of a man who affirms the ultimate value of science or painting or sex.

Kant's conception of God as a postulate prepares the way for this reduction of God to a value. The former remains within the horizon of an objectively grounded faith, but only tenuously so. When the truth of this faith ceases to be regarded as something that is rationally demonstrable, as Kant still believed it to be, the most familiar consequence is a godless ethics that remains tied to the Christian idea of the will. This is the post-Christian ethics on which Weber's theory of value is based. It is nihilistic in Nietzsche's sense of the term.

For Weber, the value of God, like that of everything else, owes its existence to the will of the person who affirms it. But this means that God can no longer ensure the objective value of the diversity of the human world in general, or of the distinctiveness of my life in particular. To do that, God must stand above all the acts of willing that produce the values that human beings endorse, for it is only from a point of view outside the totality of all such acts that God, as the author of the world, is able to knit them together into a single scheme endowed with objective purpose and value. Once God is assimilated to the field of human willing—once he becomes just another value that certain human beings endorse, and by endorsing cause to be a value—he can no longer perform this integrative function and thereby underwrite the belief that any feature of the world, including the diversity of the human beings who live, love and work in it, has a value of its own.

The assumption that God is merely a personal value thus renders the belief that our lives have value on account of their uniqueness objectively groundless. Most of us share this belief. Indeed, it is hard to go forward except on the assumption that the value of what we do in and with our lives is a function, in part at least, of what makes them distinctive. We recoil at the thought that their value is due entirely to our status as indistinguishable members of a universal kingdom of ends. But Weber's nihilistic ethics cuts the ground out from under this belief. It deprives us of the otherworldly resources on which Kant was still able to draw to defend this belief from a standpoint other than that of subjective choice.

We must find the strength, Weber says, to go on living despite our knowledge that no such standpoint exists. This is a counsel of despair, like his stern advice that those who feel called to science must accept the pointlessness of everything they can conceivably accomplish in it. And like the latter judgment, this one too is the result of a continuing adherence to the Christian idea of creation, expressed in the form of an ethics that refers all values to the will, *coupled with* a resolute acceptance of the death of the Christian God who once had the power to guarantee the objective value of the diverse lives men and women choose for themselves by willing one thing or another.

BEYOND THE SHADOW OF A WORLD BEYOND

In the fall of 1917, amidst the dislocations of war and revolution, Max Weber gave a lecture on the modest-seeming question of how to prepare for a career as a scholar. But his real subject was broader. What is the meaning, he asked, of the modern world as a whole? He answered with two words, "disenchantment" and "rationalization."

The disenchantment of the world has allowed the societies of the West to achieve an unprecedented level of wealth and well-being, and given human beings a degree of control over themselves and the natural order never before attained or even imagined. And yet, Weber told his audience, there is a spiritual emptiness at the heart of this rich and powerful civilization. Men have lost their connection to the eternal and divine. The spirit of God, which coursed through the cities of the ancient world and dwelt in the churches and cathedrals of Europe, today survives only *in pianissimo*, as a private "value"; for many, it has disappeared completely. But without a connection to God, human life becomes pointless. Its meaning slips away. So ours is at once the age of greatest prosperity and maximum meaninglessness. These are the two faces of disenchantment, welded together, Weber believed, with an iron necessity.

Today, nothing fundamental has changed. After a century of wars hot and cold, and an orgy of purposefully orchestrated bloodletting on a scale never before seen in human history, the modern West remains a land of plenty, by comparison with earlier civilizations. Never have so many lived so well or had so much control over their lives—even those at the bottom of the ladder. Injustices remain. Many, even in the West, are still underfed and ill-housed. We are only beginning to address the environmental damage that has been an unaccounted cost of economic progress. The shadow of nuclear destruction, which has hung over the West for sixty years, remains ominously long. The terror campaigns of radical Islamists represent a new and unexpected source of insecurity. *And yet,* despite it all, the rationalization of the world proceeds, and with it the hope that the lives of those in West—already better provisioned and more secure than those of human beings at any other moment in history—will become steadily more so, and that the blessings of peace and prosperity they enjoy will one day be the common possession of humankind.

Nothing has happened in the century since Weber's Munich speech to upset this hopeful expectation in a basic way. Of course, the world might end tomorrow. And there is certainly no guarantee that we will produce enough food to feed everyone, even in the West, while repairing the environment, controlling the nuclear risk, and blunting the appeal of religious extremism. But the same expanding powers of rational control that have produced the civilization of the modern West give us confidence to believe that we can continue to make progress in this direction, and support the conviction that there is no other responsible, or even conceivable, course for us to follow. Indeed, to an ever-increasing degree, this is now the conviction of sensible people everywhere—as if the diverse forces that we gather under the rubric of "globalization" had accelerated to prove the truth of Weber's claim that the rationalization of the world, which began in the West, and has gone farther there than anywhere else, is today the fate of the earth.

But then if Weber is right, the spiritual emptiness that comes with rationalization is our fate as well. This manifests itself in different ways. The pointlessness of science, the groundlessness of the personal values that give our lives their individual meaning, and the expulsion of love and gratitude from the world of public authority are all expressions of it. Yet different as these are, there is a deep connection among them, for each is a consequence of the same nihilistic combination of beliefs. Each is a result of the *abandonment* of belief in the existence of a God beyond the world, coupled with the *survival* of the belief that for the world and human life to possess any meaning or value, they would have to be related to a now nonexistent God of just this kind, whose shoes we shall never be able to fill. Whether any of these dispiriting results can be avoided depends, therefore, on the availability of a way out of the spiritual cul-de-sac into which we are led by this self-destructive pair of beliefs.

Weber himself sees no way out. He offers no alternative. Instead, he recommends a posture of noble resignation in the face of a spiritual dilemma to which he believes there is no solution. His own charisma as a tragic prophet of modernity is based on the resoluteness with which he refuses either to deny the gravity of our predicament or to accept the easiest and most common response to it.

That, of course, is, as he says, to return to the church—to affirm again, in one confessional tradition or another, the existence of the otherworldly God on whom the being and worth of the world depends.[17] This is always an option, and those who exercise it are no longer in the nihilistic bind created by an adherence to the ghost of Christian belief.

But a personal decision to return to God requires what Weber calls a "sacrifice of the intellect." It demands that one refuse to follow the requirements of reason beyond a certain point. This puts the man or woman who takes this path at odds with the whole of modern occidental culture. The commitment never to give up on reason is the ruling principle of our age. It underlies all our most cherished public ideals. Between it and the faith of those who choose to return to the church and be born again in God's grace, no reconciliation or accommodation is possible, for the first rests on the presumed sufficiency of reason to solve, in the long run at least, every problem that can be stated intelligibly—which is precisely what the second denies.

For those who make this choice, their salvation from the spiritual emptiness of the modern world can thus never be anything but a purely personal decision. It can never have an anchor in the world of public values, which today are explicitly divorced from any reliance on the God to whom they pray. In this respect, they are like children, who naively believe that wishing can make it so. They simply refuse to concede, what any grown-up can see, that the inexorability of the rationalization process, though it leaves us plenty of room to indulge our private religious beliefs, has once and for all made God a fairy tale that no thoughtful adult can ever take seriously again.

Weber had respect for those who are prepared to make the intellectual sacrifice that a belief in this fairy tale requires. But he thought they lack the maturity to confront the magnitude of their desolate fate. The fact that maturity of this kind is rare, and that multitudes still find solace in the arms of the church, does not change things fundamentally. So long as the rationalization of the world proceeds apace, belief in a God beyond it, on whose inscrutable grace we depend for our salvation, can never be more than a childish fantasy that is belied by our growing mastery of the world, which at once draws inspiration from, and at every step confirms, the truth of the belief that in the fullness of time reason brings all things to light.

If some seek to avoid despair by returning to the church, others do so by adopting the opposite strategy—by denying their need for any connection to God at all. For them, the idea that life has meaning and value only through its connection to eternity seems the height of childishness itself. Why is it not enough, they ask, to live and work for a time, have relations with others that last for a while, and then to disappear from the world, having enjoyed some transient satisfactions (perhaps even of an elevated kind) without ever once experiencing a connection to anything that lasts forever—because of course nothing does?

This is the gospel of those who have given up not only on the God of Abraham, but on the need for a replacement. Theirs is a teaching of good cheer: of contentment with impermanence, loss, nothingness even—an affirmation of the value of life in a world where everything passes away. This is harder to achieve than may seem. The prejudices that chain us to the belief that we cannot live without eternity are strong. But those who have managed to free themselves from these prejudices appear, in their own eyes at least, the most mature ones of all, and feel that they have outgrown Weber's adolescent despair by cutting their ties to eternity altogether.

Yet this position is no more sustainable than that of those who make the necessary sacrifice of intellect and seek peace in the dogmas of the church. The latter are at war with the rationality of our civilization. But their bemused critics, who claim that we can live without any connection to eternity at all, are at war with our humanity. They ignore the ways in which the defining human experiences of truth, beauty and love all depend upon a connection of this kind. Weber believed that the disenchantment of the world rules out the possibility of ever establishing such a connection again. But he also believed that a fully human life demands it. In this respect, he took for granted what Plato, Aristotle, Aquinas, Kant and Nietzsche all assumed as well. The conviction that truth, beauty and love cannot be understood except in connection to the eternal and divine is one that nearly all the great philosophers of the West share in common.

Every limited truth, if it is to count as a truth at all, must be warranted by less restricted ones, and these, in turn, by truths of a still more basic kind. But this process cannot go on forever without every truth losing its warrant.

If any truth is to be valid across its restricted range, there must therefore be at least one truth whose validity is, as Kant says, unconditioned, and therefore not subject to restrictions of time and place. For truth to be possible at all, some truths—indeed, truth itself—must be everlasting. The belief that this is so Kant calls a requirement of "reason."[18] With the possible exception of Hume, no philosopher before or since would have disagreed. Even Wittgenstein and the other twentieth-century philosophers who advocate an antifoundationalist conception of truth assume the unconditionality of their own characterization of it.

Nor would any philosopher in the Western tradition who has studied the nature of love have disagreed that it is distinguished from bodily appetite by the longing for permanence that is such a striking feature of it. Our needs and desires are as transient as the use we make of things and people to satisfy them. Love is distinguished from these by its aspiration to go on, without end. It is true that love, too, comes to an end. But this does not mean that it aims at something temporary or limited. Love is a boundless affection. It longs to endure not just for a time but forever, so that when this longing ceases to exist, love disappears or turns into something else. Love is therefore connected to eternity in an essential way. Plato believed this, and so did Aristotle, Augustine, Aquinas, Leibniz, Spinoza, Kant, Hegel and even Nietzsche. Each of these conceived the everlasting in a distinctive fashion, but all agreed that love by its very nature strives to reach it, even in the shadow of the knowledge of assured disappointment.

The same is true of beauty. Only human beings experience the world as a beautiful place, and strive to make beautiful things. A useful thing meets a temporary need. It is always useful for a limited purpose and a limited period of time. But nothing can ever be beautiful except under the aspect of eternity. There is an essential uselessness to beauty, which can never be accounted for by its relation to any finite end, and therefore by its relation to something else in time. When we attempt to explain our judgment that a thing is beautiful and not merely useful, we discover how difficult it is to establish its connection to values that transcend the order of time. We can never fully succeed in this attempt. There will always be others who disagree with our judgments, and we often change our own views about what is beautiful and what is not. But the experience of beauty itself, without which human life would no longer be human at all, is inseparable from the conviction that for a thing to be beautiful, it must partake of the eternal and divine. We cannot help but think of beauty as the face of God. When we cease to do so, it becomes something else. A beautiful thing becomes a merely useful one, which no matter how intensely we desire it, can no longer be regarded with the disinterestedness that is the mark of the uniquely human experience of being in the presence of something whose loveliness exceeds all our finite needs and desires.[19]

Truth, beauty and love are essential to the human condition. Only human beings know and value these things, each of which presupposes a longing to reach a goal beyond time. Because we are finite beings, we can never satisfy this longing completely. But neither can we give it up, without obliterating all the distinctively human attachments that assume it. Those who seek to escape the dilemma that Weber describes by insisting that life can have meaning and value even without a connection to eternity thus deny our humanity and would destroy it if they succeeded. Even if we can make do without the God of Christianity, we cannot survive, as human beings, without the longing for eternity that drives the search for truth in science, beauty in art, and love in one other's arms. To think that we can is as futile and destructive as the wish to no longer be human.

If Weber's nihilistic dilemma is created by a disbelief in the God of the Christian religion, coupled with the continuing belief that only a God beyond the world can give it the connection to eternity that human beings require, then *neither* those who return to the church, in the hope of restoring their faith in such a God, *nor* those who claim to have reconciled themselves to life in a world without any connection to eternity at all, offer a way out of this dilemma that can possibly satisfy anyone who wants to live an honest *and* human life in our disenchanted age. Is Weber right, then, to insist that we cannot escape it?

He is not. There is another alternative. Nietzsche already grasped it. The alternative is a born-again paganism based on the belief that God and the world are the same. This was the premise of Aristotle's philosophy of pride, which his Abrahamic critics attacked so ferociously in the name of their other-worldly God. The restoration of this belief to metaphysical plausibility is the key to reestablishing our connection to the eternal and divine in a world from which the God of Abraham has been banished forever. Weber accepted Nietzsche's diagnosis of modernity as the rule of nihilism. But he failed to see that it is possible to get beyond nihilism by going back behind the lingering metaphysics of divine creation on which the double bind of nihilism itself depends, to an older metaphysics whose truth seemed so obvious and attractive to the philosophers of pagan antiquity, until its intellectual, aesthetic and moral appeal was shattered by Augustine's critique.

Of course, one cannot go back to pagan philosophy, just like that. It is impossible to resuscitate Aristotle's metaphysics as if nothing had happened in the intervening twenty-five centuries. For one thing, Aristotle's science is hopelessly bad by modern standards. It is insufficiently empirical, inadequately mathematical, and hobbled by beliefs that today strike us as absurd (for example, that the planets and stars are eternal living beings whose motions are essentially different from those of things in the realm beneath the moon). For another, his politics is fundamentally undemocratic, since it presumes that some human beings (women and those he calls "natural slaves") are disqualified by nature from participation in the work of their political communities. No modern state can possibly endorse such a view. And finally, his aesthetics has no place for artistic genius, and is unable to explain the most characteristic forms of modern art. In all these respects, Aristotle's philosophy is badly out of date and cannot be made to serve our needs today without a whole series of basic reforms.

But all these deficiencies spring from a single source and can be corrected with a single adjustment. Each is rooted in the distinction between form and matter that provides the foundation for Aristotle's philosophy as a whole. One consequence of this distinction is the equation of intelligibility, and therefore of being, with the general properties of things—the forms they share with others of their kind. This eliminates the possibility that individuals can ever be intelligible, beautiful, or valuable *as such*. It forces us to view their individuality as something that at bottom lacks reality. But the assumption that the individuality of individuals is real, valuable and beautiful is a fundamental premise of modern science, politics and art. It is the key to understanding the aims of research science, the appeal of diversity as a political ideal, and the beauty of the portrait and the novel as forms of artistic expression. It is the shared assumption that makes all these activities, achievements and values distinctively modern, and thus connects them in an elementary way. None, therefore, can be understood or explained without modifying Aristotle's metaphysics of form and matter so as to allow for the reality of the individuality of individuals—which in the end cannot be done without abolishing the distinction between form and matter itself.

This is precisely what the doctrine of creation does. In a created world, the uniqueness of individuals must be as knowable, beautiful, and worthy as their general forms (from God's point of view, at least). The value of the individual is an Abrahamic discovery.

It does not follow, however, that to unseat the distinction between form and matter, as a first principle of metaphysics, one must accept the idea that the world was brought into being from nothing by a God beyond it. This idea opens the way to a new appreciation of the reality and worth of individuals but is not metaphysically required for it.

For most of its history, Western philosophy has been organized around one of two beliefs. The first is the pagan belief that the world is divine, but the individuality of individuals ultimately unreal. The second is the Christian belief that the world is not divine, but the individuality of the individuals in it as real as every other created thing (which is only derivatively and dependently real). There is, however, a third possibility. One can combine the first element of paganism with the second of Abrahamism. One can affirm that the world is both inherently *and* infinitely divine. This third metaphysics I call born-again paganism, because it returns us to the divinized world of pagan thought, but with our eyes opened by a baptism in Abrahamic belief, and thus able to see what Plato and Aristotle could not.

There is no contradiction in the ideas this metaphysics joins. It is therefore a real philosophical option. But it is more than that. It is a better metaphysics than either of the other two, for it is at once free of the limits of pagan philosophy and uncompromised by the inherent irrationality of the doctrine of divine creation. It is also immune to the psychologically self-destructive implications of this doctrine, with its crippling demand for an unrequitable gratitude that leaves those subject to it feeling inadequate in their love of the world and of those whose care has helped to make it a home. It is the best metaphysics of all.

Most surprisingly, perhaps, it is the one we already have. It is the metaphysics that implicitly informs the work of scientists, politicians and artists today. We therefore do not need to strain to invent it, but merely to acknowledge and accept it. To grasp this is to understand the way in which all our most characteristically modern beliefs, and therefore the modern world itself, already share in the eternal and divine, not through their connection to a God beyond the world, in whom we no longer believe, but to the God that is the intelligibility and splendor of the world itself, down to its last particle of particularity. The acknowledgment of the real presence of this God in our world is the solution to the spiritual dilemma from which Weber believed there could be no escape.

Nietzsche found his way to a version of this metaphysics. His doctrine of the eternal return is an expression of it. But he was neither the first nor the most systematic thinker to do so. That honor belongs to Spinoza.

Spinoza was born into a world in which the process of disenchantment was already well advanced, and he saw farther into its essence than any of his contemporaries, whose philosophical imagination was still constrained by Abrahamic beliefs. Indeed, Spinoza was not merely an acute observer of the disenchantment of the world. He was an enthusiastic supporter of it. He was a champion of modern science and the liberal politics that goes along with it.

Weber saw in these a spreading soullessness that cuts us off from the eternal and divine. That is because he judged them from a nihilistic point of view still tethered to the Christian belief that the world and man can only be saved by an otherworldly God who no longer exists. Because of this, the rationalization process could only be, for him, a cause of despair.

For Spinoza, who judged these same things from the standpoint of a metaphysics that recognizes no other God than the world itself—*deus sive natura*—the widening authority of reason was a source not of despair but joy. Spinoza viewed the modern world not as the enemy of the eternal and divine but its ever more complete expression, and on the basis of his joyful, born-again paganism prepared the way for a revival of the ancient ideal of love and gratitude that Aristotle had defended under the name of friendship, now adjusted to fit the political and intellectual circumstances of our post-Christian age.

It is to these topics that we turn—at last—in part IV.

PART FOUR

Joy

CHAPTER 27

—•———◄••◗◆◊•—————•—

The Worm in the Blood

SPINOZA'S CONCEPTION OF SCIENCE

In 1665, Benedict Spinoza was living in the town of Voorburg, in the Netherlands, forty miles from Amsterdam. He was thirty-three years old. For nine years he had been living, quite contentedly it seems, as an outcast from the Jewish community in Amsterdam that had expelled him at the age of twenty-three for "abominable" but unspecified heresies.[1]

On November 20 of that year, Spinoza sent a letter to an Englishman named Henry Oldenburg. The two had been in correspondence for some time. A month before, Oldenburg had written to Spinoza asking for a fuller account of the philosopher's views "as to how each part of Nature accords with its whole, and the manner of its coherence with other parts."[2] The original of Spinoza's reply survives, along with a copy he made for himself.

Oldenburg was the secretary of the Royal Society of London. The society had been informally established a quarter century before by a group of "natural philosophers" that included Robert Hooke, Robert Boyle and later Isaac Newton. In 1662, the society received its first royal charter from King Charles II, who spoke of his desire to "extend not only the boundaries of the Empire, but also the very arts and sciences," and to "encourage philosophical studies, especially those which by actual experiments attempt either to shape out a new philosophy or to perfect the old."

The members of the Royal Society were experimenters and theorists devoted to the advancement of the new science of nature represented on the continent by Galileo, Descartes, Huygens and others. Like their continental counterparts, they shared two fundamental beliefs. The first was that the workings of the natural order are best explained in mechanical terms, as the product of external forces acting on material objects defined by their size, shape and density alone, and without any reference to the mysterious inner strivings that play such a central role in Aristotle's explanation of natural phenomena. The second was the belief that the laws governing the behavior of things in the natural world can most easily be discovered and confirmed by means of those unnatural contrivances we call experiments.

This new science of nature, mechanical in theory and experimental in practice, was, as Spinoza's correspondence with Oldenburg reminds us, a European phenomenon. It had proponents and practitioners in every city and university in Europe. Through Oldenburg, for example, Spinoza kept himself informed of Boyle's efforts to determine the chemical composition of potassium nitrate, or saltpeter, and of other inquiries in which the English scientist was engaged. In return, Spinoza described his own experiments with saltpeter, and the different conclusions he drew from them.[3] His letters to Oldenburg reveal Spinoza to have been an enthusiastic supporter of—even an active, if marginal, participant in—the new experimental physics that by the middle years of the seventeenth century had already transformed man's understanding of the natural world, and of himself as a part of it, in a recognizably modern direction.

But Spinoza's correspondence with Oldenburg underscores another feature of seventeenth-century science that is more remote from modern belief. This is the conviction, which both men shared, that physics and metaphysics belong to a common enterprise—that the first raises questions which the second must resolve if the science of nature is to be put on a foundation secure enough to fulfill its own aspirations for completeness and rigor. The charter of the Royal Society implies a connection of this sort between scientific and philosophical studies, and like many of their contemporaries, Oldenburg and Spinoza simply took it for granted.

Thus, when Oldenburg writes to Spinoza, in October of 1665, to report that he and "Mr. Boyle" join in urging Spinoza to pursue his "philosophizing with energy and rigor," and then proceeds to ask if the philosopher has "any light to cast on the difficult question" of how the parts of nature "accord" with the whole of it, he is raising a metaphysical question to which Spinoza replies in his next letter back. Modern readers are likely to find this part of their exchange puzzling and quaint, not because of the actual content of Spinoza's response, but more fundamentally because of the writer's unspoken assumption that metaphysics has something important to contribute to the study of the natural world. Among professional scientists, and the rest of us who live in the world their discoveries have made, the prevailing view today is the opposite—that the theoretical and practical successes of natural science depend upon the renunciation of the habits of metaphysical thinking, especially the nonempirical and abstract kind exemplified by Spinoza's philosophy.[4]

How implausible it must seem, therefore, to suggest that Spinoza's own peculiar metaphysics, which was eccentric even by seventeenth-century standards, is not only relevant to modern physics but holds the key to understanding its deepest ambitions. Physics today claims to be the sovereign science of the natural world. Its authority rests, in important part, on its abjuration of the sort of metaphysical speculation in which Spinoza engaged, with its theological pretensions and lingering air of medieval conceptualism. In what sense, then, can Spinozism be said to provide a useful, let alone necessary, adjunct to modern physics? Many will answer, "None." But the truth is precisely the opposite. Our physics not only needs a metaphysics. It needs the one that Spinoza provides. It needs Spinoza's God.

Einstein said something similar on a number of occasions.[5] He claimed that Spinoza's God was his own. It is hard to know how seriously he meant this. But whatever his own intentions may have been, Einstein's judgment is essentially correct—more so, perhaps, than even he surmised. For Spinoza's theology is the foundation on which not only Einstein's physics but the whole of modern natural science is built.

To support this claim is a doubly difficult task—first, because it requires some familiarity with the fundamental principles of Spinoza's theology, which are set out most fully in the *Ethics,* a work of daunting obscurity; and second, because it demands that his theology be brought into alignment not only with the physics of Spinoza's own time, but with developments since, including the theory of relativity and quantum mechanics. These matters are the subject of this chapter and the next. Before beginning to address them in detail, however, it will be helpful to sketch Spinoza's attitude toward the enterprise of science in general. Broadly speaking, what did he believe its powers and limits to be? Spinoza's response to Oldenburg's request for a clarification of the relation between the whole of nature and its parts gives us a place to start.

A PARABLE

Spinoza begins by asserting "that each part of Nature accords with the whole" and "coheres" with all its other parts, but disavows any knowledge of the "actual manner of this coherence." That is "beyond" his comprehension, he says, for such knowledge would require an understanding of "the whole of nature and all its parts," a subject of "infinite" scope and complexity.

Spinoza's answer to Oldenburg's question thus combines a breathtaking optimism regarding the orderliness and intelligibility of the world as a whole, with a sober appreciation of how little we understand of it. On the one hand, he writes, "the laws or nature of one part [of the world] adapts itself to the laws or nature of another part in such wise that there is the least possible opposition between them." Everything in the world fits together in a lawful and intelligible way. On the other hand, precisely because each part of nature "adapts itself" to every other, our understanding of the laws of any one of them is bound to be provisional and incomplete, since to grasp it fully we would have to comprehend all the others as well.

This helps to explain Spinoza's otherwise puzzling remark, a little further on in the letter, that the infinite lawfulness of nature provides no justification for the judgment that the world is "beautiful" or "well-ordered." These are human judgments, delivered from the standpoint of what he calls "our imagination," the image-making power of perception that renders every bit of experience acquired through it perspectival and therefore one-sided. Even to say that nature is "well-ordered" is improperly (if understandably) anthropocentric, since it presumes that we, with our finite minds, are capable of comprehending the order of the world sufficiently to pass judgment on it. Spinoza's emphasis on the interconnectedness of all the parts of the world, and of their separate laws, is an invitation to the continual refinement of our understanding of these laws through an ever more expansive appreciation of the connections among them. But his stern warning that one must not "attribute to Nature beauty, ugliness, order or confusion" is a reminder of the limits within which the pursuit of such understanding is, for us, forever confined.

There is a deeper metaphysical point behind this warning. In an important sense, the very idea of a "part" is an artifact of the imagination. A part is an identifiable element of some more inclusive whole. But a thing that is a part in one respect may be a whole in another. For example, when we focus our attention on the ways in which the different particles in the blood "adapt themselves to one another in accordance with size and shape so as to be fully in agreement with one another and to form all together one single fluid," we regard them "as parts of the blood." But if we ignore these adaptive relations among the particles, and treat each as something "different" from the others, "to that extent we regard them each as a whole, not a part." The relation between part and whole is adjustable. Every whole may be viewed as a part of some larger whole, up to the "nature of the universe," whose parts are infinite in number and variety, but which is not itself a part of anything else.

We are able to move up this ladder in our investigation of the world, to ever-higher levels of inclusiveness, gaining at each step a deeper understanding of the ways in which the parts of the world "adapt themselves" to one another. As we do, our notion of what constitutes an individual changes. What at a lower level appear to be separate individuals with parts arranged in a specific "ratio of motion and rest" become, at a higher level, elements in some larger system with a determinate ratio of its own. This process continues all the way up to the universe as a whole. This is an individual too, Spinoza says, whose parts are also always moving and resting, but in a ratio that never changes, unlike that of all the individuals it contains.

The acquisition or loss of such a ratio is for Spinoza the equivalent of what Aristotle calls "substantial change"—the coming into being or passing away of an individual thing, or more exactly, its mutation into something of a different kind (for example, the decomposition of a plant or animal after it dies). In Spinoza's view, every individual part of the world eventually undergoes such change because its ratio of motion and rest cannot be sustained forever. Only the world as a whole does not change in this way. It alone is eternal.

To adequately account for any part of the world, however small or fleeting, one must be able to define and explain the ratio of motion and rest that gives it its temporary identity. But because this ratio is itself intelligible only as an element of some larger whole, and ultimately of the entire world, to fully explain even the least thing in it one must comprehend its relation to the infinitely complex and eternal ratio that defines the being of the world as a whole. This is for us, of course, an impossible task.

In this respect, Spinoza says, our position is like that of "a tiny worm living in the blood." Imagine that such a worm were able to distinguish by sight "the particles of the blood" and to observe "how each particle, on colliding with another, either rebounds or communicates some degree of its motion, and so forth." A creature of this kind "would regard each individual particle of the blood as a whole, not a part, and it could have no idea as to how all the parts are controlled by the overall nature of the blood and compelled to mutual adaption as the overall nature of the blood requires, so as to agree with one another in a definite way." We may be amused by the image, and smile condescendingly at the worm's ignorance. But we should not laugh, Spinoza says, because "that worm would be living in the blood as we are living in our part of the universe."[6]

How small the worm's world is! Yet ours is just as small and we must train ourselves to think of it as such. We must recognize that "our part of the universe," like the blood in which the worm is living, is but a part of an infinite whole, "surrounded" by other parts and "reciprocally determined" by them "to act in a fixed and determinate" way. This will never allow us to escape the finitude of our condition. But it can strengthen the conviction that as our view of the world expands, we will be able to grasp more and more of that limitlessly complex system of reciprocal determinations in which the "infinite potency" of the world as a whole resides.

The world is infinitely intelligible. Even if we had an endless stretch of time, we could never comprehend more than the smallest portion of it. But so long as we do not mistake the part we understand for the whole, the prospect of a continual movement toward an ever more complete comprehension of things remains open and inviting—indeed, irresistibly so, given the desire we share with all finite beings to persevere in existence, a goal we pursue by striving to expand our knowledge and power without limit.

Spinoza's parable of the worm in the blood thus teaches two lessons. The first is that there are no limits to how far we can go in our efforts to understand the world. The second is that the world as a whole always remains beyond our grasp—that we are forever confined, as the worm is, to a part or neighborhood of it. But this "beyond" is not something other than the world or outside it. It is just the world as a whole, or more precisely, its infinite intelligibility, which our finitude prevents us from ever exhausting. Together these ideas define a radically ambitious yet supremely modest conception of scientific inquiry, and set the stage for Spinoza's own theology of natural science, which differs fundamentally from the Christian conception of God that Spinoza viewed as an insuperable barrier to the further development of the new physics that Christianity itself had helped to inspire.

THE CONDEMNATION OF 1277, AGAIN

Spinoza was the only great thinker of the seventeenth century to openly repudiate the doctrine of divine creation, which he considered a piece of superstitious nonsense. There were others among his contemporaries who also believed that Christianity is a superstitious religion. Hobbes, in particular, seems to have held such a view, though he never expressed it openly.[7] But Spinoza's boldness in attacking the Abrahamic idea of God set him apart from everyone else and made him a uniquely disturbing figure, then and later, to all whose faith compelled them to regard his principled assault on creationism as the worst heresy imaginable.[8]

Spinoza's God is not separate from the world, and unlike the God of Abraham, who possesses an omnipotent will, has none at all. Indeed, for Spinoza, there is no such thing as the will, human or divine. The world and everything in it exists by necessity. It follows that the world is intelligible down to the smallest detail. Every part of it (every "mode," in Spinoza's vocabulary) is in principle a perfectly explicable expression of the one, eternal and all-powerful god that is identical with the world as a whole.

This is the essence of Spinoza's theology, about which I shall have more to say in due course. But at the outset it is important to note the features that set it apart most fundamentally from its Aristotelian and Abrahamic counterparts.

In Spinoza's theology, as in Aristotle's, there is no gap between God and the world. For Aristotle, the divinity of the world is identical to its activity; for Spinoza, to its intelligibility. In both cases, the world is eternally self-sustaining. It depends on nothing outside itself. This belief lies at the heart of the pagan theology that Augustine attacked with such ferocity.

But Spinoza's conception of God also differs from that of Aristotle in a fundamental respect. For Aristotle, the world has divinity in it, but not everything in the world is divine. Some things are just mindless; they cannot be understood or explained. This is true, most importantly, of the individuality of individuals. For Spinoza, by contrast, the intelligibility and hence divinity of the world has no limit. There is nothing in the world that in principle cannot be understood.

The idea of a God that is not merely eternal but infinite, is an Abrahamic invention. It follows from the concept of creation from nothing, which erases the distinction between form and matter. Because Spinoza's theology joins this idea to the belief that God and the world are the same, it can no more be called a pagan theology than an Abrahamic one. It represents what I have called a born-again paganism, whose combination of ideas offers a distinctive alternative to the other two theologies that have shaped Western thought from the start.

Spinoza claims that his hyperrationalist theology holds the key to understanding the nature of human happiness and the way to obtain it.[9] The question of how to do this is the central subject of the *Ethics*. Like Aristotle, whose
own lectures on ethics are devoted to the same question, Spinoza insists that
it can ultimately be answered only in theological terms. The happiest life, he
says, is one closest to God—a life suffused with what he calls the "intellectual love" of God, "the very love of God by which God loves himself" (a phrase
that Aristotle would have recognized and approved).[10] Spinoza's principal aim
in the *Ethics* is to develop the theology that is needed to make this ideal compelling and to show that the Christian conception of God, to which he contrasts it, is incapable of providing a solid foundation for the happiness that
all men desire.

"Most people," Spinoza says, "are induced to live" according to the precepts of morality only by their hope of a reward, or fear of punishment, after
they die. "If men did not have this hope and fear, but believed instead that
minds die with the body, and that the wretched, exhausted with the burden of
morality, cannot look forward to a life to come, they would return to their natural disposition, and would prefer to govern all their actions according to lust,
and to obey fortune rather than themselves." But this conclusion is "no less
absurd" than the belief that just because "the mind is not eternal" one "should
prefer to be mindless, and to live without reason."[11] Because the dogmas of the
Christian religion support this irrational view, they are a stumbling block to
what Spinoza calls true "blessedness."[12] To understand what such blessedness is,
and how we can obtain it, we must reject this ignorant and fearful theology in
favor of one that accords with reason instead. Only a theology of the latter sort
can provide the foundation for a genuinely happy life. This is the theology that
Spinoza outlines in part 1 of the *Ethics*. He concedes that only a few are likely to
have the strength of mind to discover and embrace it. But they alone, Spinoza
says, will ever find the path that leads to "true peace of mind."[13]

This is the heart of Spinoza's ethics. It is also the foundation of what might
be called his philosophy of science.

Science is the name we give to our ongoing, collective effort to comprehend the infinitely complex order of the world. According to Spinoza, the same
conception of God that holds the key to a correct understanding of human
happiness is essential to the advancement of science as well. Having the right
theology is crucial to both pursuits. Indeed, for Spinoza, these are not, in the
end, two different pursuits at all. The knowledge that science strives to secure
is the essence of the happiness we seek.

To many today, this is likely to seem a puzzling, even incomprehensible view. That is because we tend to draw a sharp distinction between science and ethics. We associate the first with facts and the second with values, and place an unbridgeable chasm between them. But the distinction between facts and values is itself a consequence of our lingering attachment to the Christian metaphysics that Spinoza rejects. In his view, our power and activity, and hence our reality, increase with our understanding of the world. As we come to know it better, we become more real, and that is what we desire most of all (another proposition that Aristotle would have approved). Science is therefore the highway to happiness, or rather it is happiness itself, which for Spinoza consists in the joyful movement from a lower level of reality to a higher one. It is an inherently ethical enterprise.

By assigning a pivotal role to the will, Christian theology obscures the internal relation between knowledge and happiness and thereby drains science of all intrinsic value. But it does more than this. It also blocks the growth of science itself by raising a permanent barrier to the extension of our knowledge of things. Spinoza understood this too, and knew that only his God could support the ambitions of the new mechanical science of nature to which he enthusiastically subscribed.

The reason why Spinoza believed Christianity to be an obstacle to the progress of science is easily stated. The Christian doctrine of creation assumes that something can come from nothing. Indeed, it assumes that the whole world has been brought into being from nothing. But every scientific explanation depends upon our ability to relate the thing to be explained to something else, which is either logically or temporally prior to it. Where this is not possible, the thing to be explained must remain inexplicable. Because the idea of creation from nothing rules out explanations of either sort, it compels those who accept it to acknowledge that in the search for explanations they must eventually come to a fact that cannot be explained.

Christian apologists of course reject this argument. They say that the existence of the world and all the things it contains can be explained in a perfectly satisfying way—through their relation to the God who brought them into being. To the question, "why does the world exist?" the answer is obvious. It exists because God created it.

But this answer is an illusion. The doctrine of creation requires those who embrace it to affirm that God's act of creation itself cannot be explained. That is because, if it could, God would no longer be God. The idea of divine creation therefore raises more than an empirical and hence contingent roadblock to the advancement of science. It erects a principled one instead. To the inquiring scientist, it holds up a sign that says, "No explanations permitted beyond this point!"

The theology of the Christian religion is therefore incompatible with the aspirations of modern science, whose drive to explain the world cannot tolerate a self-imposed limit of this kind. Spinoza puts the point succinctly in part 1 of the *Ethics*. Anyone who believes that God has a will, he says, endorses a view that those who "reflect on the matter" will see is not only "futile" but "a great obstacle to science."[14] Creationism and science are fundamentally at war. Among the great philosophers and scientists of the seventeenth century—including Descartes, Leibniz and Newton—Spinoza was the only one to see and say this.

Yet if Spinoza was correct to insist that the Christian belief in an omnipotent creator is a barrier to the advancement of our knowledge of the natural world, he failed to appreciate the role this same belief had played in preparing the way for the rise of modern science, and of modern physics in particular. For centuries after Aristotle's writings on nature were reintroduced into the Latin-speaking world, his physical and cosmological ideas continued to dominate the theory and practice of Western science. Modern physics begins with the dismantling of these ideas. This was a long and gradual process. But the first, decisive step took place in the thirteenth century, with the recognition that the Aristotelian worldview is hopelessly incompatible with the Christian idea of an all-powerful God who brings the world into being from nothing. The defining event was the Condemnation of 1277.

The Condemnation sought to suppress the Aristotelian naturalism then flourishing at the University of Paris and elsewhere. Aristotle's philosophy teaches that the world is inherently divine and governed by laws whose nonexistence is as unthinkable as that of the world itself. The necessaritarianism of Aristotle's metaphysics represents a direct threat to the freedom and omnipotence of the Christian God. If God is free, how can the world he creates and its laws be said to exist by necessity? The answer, of course, is that they cannot. This is the principal point that the authors of the Condemnation reiterate again and again.

We have already explored some of its consequences in the fields of religion and ethics. In part III, we traced the effects of the voluntarist reaction sparked by the Condemnation on man's understanding of his relation to God, and on the meaning of human salvation, which Ockham and later Luther made wholly dependent on God's inscrutable will. But the Condemnation of

1277 had implications for the study of the natural world as well. By insisting on the boundlessness of God's creative power, it undercut the premises of Aristotle's physics and opened the way to a new understanding of motion, place, and time. This in turn prepared the ground for the scientific revolution that is conventionally said to have begun in 1543 with the publication of Copernicus' *De Revolutionibus*, and been brought to a close a little more than a century later with Newton's *Principia*. In this respect, as Pierre Duhem famously remarked, the Condemnation of 1277 is "the birth certificate of modern physics."[15]

In Duhem's exhaustively researched account, the crucial transition from Aristotelian to modern physics did not occur suddenly, in the sixteenth century. It began in the early fourteenth, in the age of Ockham, and was completed over the next three hundred years. The main stimulus to this development was neither better observation nor more aggressive experimentation, though these certainly played a supporting role, and by Galileo's time had become defining features of the new science that was rapidly sweeping the old one from view. According to Duhem, the key to this long, and in the end complete, revolution in man's understanding of the natural world was an *idea* instead: the Christian idea of God as an omnipotent creator, which Spinoza rightly viewed as a barrier to the further growth of the very science it had spawned.

A few details from Duhem's magisterial study will help to illustrate the point.

The world we see about us is one of ceaseless motion. Everything in it is moving. In his lectures on physics, Aristotle seeks to explain these natural movements. More precisely, he seeks to explain how they are explicable. Two principles guide his account. The first is that, among the motions we observe, movement in a circle occupies a privileged place. The second is that all motion, even of a circular sort, is intelligible only in relation to something that does not move at all.

Aristotle recognized, of course, that some movements proceed in a straight line. Even the life of a human being may be described as a kind of linear movement whose beginning and end are not the same. But the linear career of every individual plant and animal is merely an episode in the larger, circular routine of the species to which it belongs, and can only be understood in that context. In a similar way, individual bits of elemental stuff are sometimes jarred out of place, and sent moving in a straight line. This happens, for example, when water evaporates in the heat of the sun, or a rock is thrown in the air. But these violent, rectilinear motions all eventually come to an end. The thing that has been torn loose from the place to which it belongs returns to its natural position in a circular movement that encompasses and therefore explains its temporary movement in a straight line. Taken in isolation from the larger circles to which they belong, movements of the latter sort are incomplete and unnatural, and therefore incomprehensible on Aristotle's view of them.

Every motion we observe in the natural world thus belongs to a circle of some kind. This is what makes it intelligible to the inquiring naturalist. But each of these circular motions is itself relative to something motionless, apart from which it cannot be conceived. This follows from the logical and ontological priority of being to becoming. Hence, all the circling movements that make our world understandable must have some fixed point of reference. This cannot, however, be a point beyond the world, for the world is all there is. In a *metaphysical* sense, the unmoving point to which these motions refer is the eternal, and hence motionless, actuality of the world as a whole, which everything in the world strives to partake of as fully as it can. Aristotle calls this the "unmoved mover"—that "for the sake of which" every moving thing moves. But the circular movements of the natural world require a motionless point of reference in a *physical* sense as well. They must all revolve around some one stationary object. Aristotle assumes this to be the earth, whose unmoving axis forms the pole or spindle around which everything else in the cosmos revolves, including the planets and stars.

This revolving world is eternal but not infinite. It has a definite place. That is because the place of a thing is, for Aristotle, just the inner surface of the thing that contains it. The place of the ball in my hand, for example, is the inner surface of my palm. The fixed stars contain the world in this way. But because there is nothing beyond them to contain the stars themselves, they have no place in Aristotle's sense. Strictly speaking, they are "nowhere." and beyond them there is nothing, not even empty space.

Nor is there any time apart from their motions. For Aristotle, time is merely the measure of motion; it has no independent existence of its own. The movement of the stars, which is the most regular of all, serves as the measure of time in the most perfect and complete sense. If the stars were to cease to move, which of course is inconceivable, given the eternality of the world, time would therefore stop as well. Hence, beyond the moving stars, whose eternal paths we trace in the sky, there is neither space nor time, which exist only within the eternal but finite world whose endless, circling motions, above and beneath the moon, all have the earth as their fixed center.

This is a remarkably consistent and comprehensive picture of the world. It also explains a great deal of our ordinary experience of it. But from a Christian point of view, the most striking thing about this picture is not its coherence or descriptive power. It is the assumption that the world must be as it is. Aristotle's world does not just happen to have the shape it does, which we discover by observation. It exists by necessity. No other world is possible, nor can the nonexistence of this one be conceived. But this strikes at the heart of Christian belief, which insists that God could have made the world differently, or not at all, if he had chosen to do so. In the theological reaction against the necessitarianism of Aristotle's physics, a new physics was born.

Can God, for example, move the world as a whole to a different place? To say that he cannot because, on Aristotle's "container" view of place, there is no place outside the world to which it can be moved, is an offense to God's power. To preserve God's omnipotence, the Aristotelian conception of place must be abandoned.

But if God can move the sphere of the fixed stars to a different place, then anything's place, including that of the world as a whole, must now be defined as its position in a space that extends infinitely in all directions (since to assume that space has any limits constrains God's power to place things as he chooses). At a stroke, we shift, in Alexander Koyre's famous phrase, from a "closed world" to an "infinite universe."[16] On this new view, it continued to be assumed that for motion to be intelligible, it must be referred to something unmoving. But in place of a motionless earth, which in principle is as subject to God's power of dislocation as anything else, the immobile frame of infinite space now became the only theologically permissible reference of this kind.

In this endless, directionless space, it is of course possible for God to move any object in a straight line forever. There is no limit to the length of the line he can draw, and nothing to compel him to round it in a circle. Indeed, in God's infinite space, the most elementary ("natural") motion is rectilinear, not circular. What now needs to be explained, therefore, are deviations from movement in a straight line. For Aristotle, circular motion is the primitive form; it is rectilinear movement that must be explained as a component of, or violent departure from, some more basic circular motion. Now that relation is reversed, and it is movement in a circle that demands explanation.

Indeed, even the priority of rest over motion that is a bedrock premise of the metaphysics that underlies Aristotle's account of natural movement requires a radical reinterpretation. If God can equally well choose to move the world or allow it to remain at rest, then neither of these states can any longer be regarded as a natural default. The same is obviously true of every thing *in* the world, including the earth, which moves or rests in endless space depending upon whether the world as a whole does. Consequently, neither motion nor rest may be said to be prior to the other by nature. Neither can be explained in terms of the other, but only as the result of something else—of a "force" that, by acting on the world and the things in it, causes them to be in one state or another.

This outside force is of course the will of God, which is the cause, and hence the explanatory ground, of both motion and rest. The only thing that by its very nature rests—that is eternally and necessarily unmoving—is God himself. In this way, the fulcrum of motionlessness that every movement requires in order to be intelligible at all, is transferred from the world, where Aristotle placed it, to a position outside it.

The assumption of God's omnipotence demands a similar adjustment in our understanding of time. Just as God can move the heavens from one place to another, he can cause their movement to stop altogether, as he is reported to have done during the Battle of Jericho.[17] If time were nothing but the measure of motion, and perfect time merely the measure of the most perfect motion, then God's decision to arrest the movement of the heavens could not be an act *in* time. But God has the power to act at whatever moment he chooses. The framework of the temporal order he establishes at creation must therefore be as wide as the spatial one in which God has the "room" to move the world wherever he wishes. It must be infinite too, just as space is. Of course, God might have chosen not to create either space or time. Neither exists by necessity. But only a universe in which space extends infinitely in all directions, and time exists in an absolute form that is prior to the movement of all things, even the most perfect, is one that is sufficiently expansive to give God's power the boundless scope of intervention it demands.

These adjustments in the understanding of space and time destroy the doctrine of proper place. This is the most fundamental principle of Aristotle's physics. According to Aristotle, every thing has a natural home in the world, and when separated from it, strives to return. For Aristotle, this is not merely a plausible hypothesis. It is a metaphysical necessity. To be is to be active. Activity is the exercise of the powers one possesses as a being of a certain kind. Different things have different powers; these define their positions in the order of things. When a thing is exercising its distinctive powers in the most complete and expressive way it can, it is where it belongs. It is as real as it is possible for it to be. Hence, when it is dislocated from its proper place, it always seeks to return to it, for every thing yearns to be as fully as its powers permit.

The belief in a God whose omnipotence allows him to put his creatures wherever he chooses deprives this entire system of identities, and with it the doctrine of proper place, of its metaphysical necessity. The idea of multiple worlds brings this out with special clarity.

If space is infinite, then the world in which we live (the earth and the heavens above it) occupies but a portion of space. There is always "room" for worlds other than our own. That being so, there is nothing to prevent God from creating other worlds, with stars and planets and an earth just like ours. The Condemnation of 1277 explicitly anathematizes the teaching that our world is the only one there can be.[18]

But if there is another earth, in another world, with the same four elements as ours, then these will presumably arrange themselves in relation to that earth just as the elements in our world do. This would mean, however, that the elements in one part of the universe have one proper place, and those in another a different one. Each would have as many different proper places as there are different worlds, whose number is, potentially at least, as infinite as the space in which God puts them. But to say that a thing can have more than one proper place, let alone an infinite number, is equivalent to saying it has none. The very possibility of multiple worlds, which Christian piety demands, thus undermines Aristotle's belief that the motions of things in the natural world are to be explained by their longing to be in the one and only place they belong.

The same applies, in a particularly unsettling way, to the human beings who live on the surface of the earth. For Aristotle, the earth is man's home. It is where he belongs in the cosmic order of things. Human beings can exist nowhere else—not because conditions on the moon, say, would be inhospitable to them, but more fundamentally because man is an "earthly" being. His deepest biological, political and philosophical longings are all determined by the position he occupies as the one thinking animal at the center of the only possible world. Once we assume that it lies within God's power to create other worlds with other centers of this sort, the very idea of a center loses its meaning. As a result, man can no longer be said to have a unique home in the universe, on one earth rather than another. For all we know, there may be other earths with human inhabitants too. Indeed, even the other planets and stars in our "local" neighborhood may be populated with men and women like us, since God is free to place on them whatever creatures he chooses.[19]

The radical voluntarism of the Condemnation of 1277 thus destroys at a stroke all the basic principles of Aristotle's physics. It forces a reconception of space and time. It reverses the priority of rectilinear and circular motion. It challenges the claim that a true "void" is impossible, for how could it be beyond God's power to create one? It undermines the contention, which Aristotle defends at length, that infinitely small things are not actually real, and infinitely large ones not even potentially so, by putting it in God's power to create both. And most importantly, it upends the doctrine of proper place—the cornerstone of Aristotle's account of natural motion.

Still, Aristotle's key concepts continued for centuries to provide most of the working assumptions on which the investigation of the natural world was based. The old physics died slowly, and by degrees. This is less puzzling than it seems, however, for what the Condemnation challenged was not the claim that God has *actually* created a world that conforms to the principles of Aristotle's physics, with one earth at its center, and everything else arranged around it in its proper place, but the very different proposition that our world is the only one that God *could possibly* have made. This is the familiar distinction between God's absolute and ordained power, whose consequences for theology and ethics we explored in chapter 17. Its implications for natural science were equally great.

Ockham, for example, argues that while the boundless reservoir of God's absolute power allows him to divide any thing into infinitesimally small parts, or to increase it to infinite size, he has elected not to do so, but has created a world of finite bodies instead, whose size has both a lower and upper limit. Similarly, Ockham says, though God has the power to "detach" time from every conceivable motion and to create an absolute temporal frame that is independent of all the motions within it, he has chosen to exemplify this "absolute clock" by the motion of the fixed stars, so that we can reliably treat their movement as a perfect measure of time, just as Aristotle maintains. But Ockham stresses that God's choice of the stars as a timekeeping device to make visible this absolute clock is a purely contingent one—a *de facto* decision that must not be confused with his *de jure* power. God could, after all, have chosen the motion of any other body for this purpose instead. It would therefore be a theological mistake to assume that the movement of the stars defines time by a natural necessity.

In this way, the distinction between God's absolute and ordained power abolishes the metaphysical necessity of Aristotle's science of nature, while preserving a secondary but wholly contingent validity for his ideas that allows those engaged in the study of the natural world to continue to employ them in good faith. At the same time, it opens an intellectual space, compatible with Christian belief, for thought experiments that suspend one or another of the doctrines that in Aristotle's physics are assumed to follow from the nature of being itself. Some of the experimenters were bolder than others, and several carried their speculations beyond the point the church was prepared to allow. But their venture was inspired, at the deepest level, by the liberating power of the idea of God's omnipotent will.

The authors of the Condemnation of 1277 insisted on this idea as a conservative antidote to the irreverent rationalism of the Latin Averroists and their followers. But their conservatism gave theological legitimacy to an intellectual movement that in time produced the most radical revision in man's understanding of nature since the Greeks first began to speculate about it in an organized way. By displacing the earth from the center of things (as the sun, the solar system and our galaxy would eventually be displaced in turn), Copernicus merely expounded, in a manner better adapted to astronomical observation and prediction, the decentering implications of the theological assault on Aristotle's physics that two and a half centuries before had already made it a heresy to maintain that the earth, or anything else for that matter, must *necessarily* be at the center of God's infinite creation. And when more than a century after Copernicus, Newton codified the results of the new physics in a mathematized mechanics that invites us to imagine the movement and interaction of bodies within a framework of absolute space and time, where rectilinear movement is the default, and rest has no principled priority over motion, he drew with lines that remained indelible for two hundred years, a picture of the world whose outlines one can already discern, as a theological possibility at least, in the proscriptions that Bishop Tempier and his committee issued in honor of their infinitely powerful God.

DESCARTES' DIVINE PHYSICS

Spinoza's metaphysics has two principal sources. The first is the tradition of medieval Aristotelianism that he studied as a youth, in the writings of Maimonides and others.[20] The second is the work of Descartes.

To say that Descartes was a champion of the new mechanical physics that Galileo had pioneered a generation before is an understatement. Descartes not only made a substantial contribution of his own to the study of the laws of motion (and of optics as well). He sought to put the discipline of physics as a whole on a new and more solid foundation.

Descartes' *Meditations* is today viewed as a freestanding work. We think of it as a response to the perennial challenge of philosophical skepticism and assess it in these terms. But in Descartes' own mind, it had a more specific aim. The goal of the *Meditations* is to expose and defend the ground on which the growing edifice of modern physics is based, so that those engaged in it may proceed with confidence that their deepest assumptions about the nature of the world are well founded.[21] In this sense, even Descartes' metaphysics is subordinated to the advancement of the new science of nature he so enthusiastically embraced. To the end of his life, this remained his principal aim.

Spinoza was an attentive and admiring reader of Descartes. His first published work (the only one published in his lifetime under his own name) was a commentary on the first two parts of Descartes' *Principles of Philosophy*, presented in what Spinoza calls "the geometric manner."[22] At the beginning of his commentary, Spinoza reminds the reader that Descartes' ambition was to lay "the solid foundations of the sciences," and that his method of radical doubt is merely a means to this end. He then goes on to explain the basic principles of Cartesian metaphysics—the nature of God, mind, body, truth and error—and in light of these to outline and elucidate Descartes' account of the laws that govern the movement and interaction of bodies in the physical world.

Spinoza's friend, Lodewijk Meyer, wrote a preface to the *Principles of Cartesian Philosophy* in which he cautions the reader to "note" that Spinoza's commentary is an attempt to give a strictly accurate account of Descartes' teachings, and that "no one should conclude that he [Spinoza] here teaches either his own views or only those of which he approves. For although he holds some of [Descartes'] doctrines to be true, and admits that some are his own additions, there are many he rejects as false, holding a very different opinion."[23]

Indeed one might go further and say that all the most distinctive features of Spinoza's metaphysics emerge from his criticism of Descartes. This is shaped by two related ideas that he inherited from the veiled paganism of certain of the Jewish writers he studied as a boy. The first is that God and the world are the same. The second is that the order of being is continuous and graded, not radically disjunct, as it must be in every metaphysics that assumes the world to have been created by a God beyond it.

Together, these ideas mark a difference of outlook as profound as one can imagine. Yet despite the gulf that separates his metaphysics from that of Descartes, Spinoza shares the latter's view that the work of science cannot be firmly grounded except on the basis of a correct understanding of the relation of God to the world. In this sense, both philosophers accept the dependence of science on theology. But in contrast to Descartes, who assigns the creator God of the Christian religion a crucial role in his account of the laws of motion, Spinoza regards the idea of such a God as an absolute bar to the progress of science, which depends, he thinks, on the adoption of his own radically different theology instead.

The Christian God is at work everywhere in Descartes' philosophy. That is because Descartes is constantly encountering difficulties that he believes can be resolved only through the agency of a God beyond the world. These difficulties themselves are the result of Descartes' violent rejection of the late medieval Aristotelianism whose explanation of the natural world he thought hopelessly confused on account of its failure to distinguish bodies from minds.

Within the framework of scholastic physics, to be a thing of a particular kind (a stone, for example, or a man) meant to have a yearning of a certain sort—an inclination toward a specific goal or proper place. In this sense, scholasticism conceived all bodily things to be "minded." But this picture of the world leads nowhere, Descartes says, or only to a tautological account of the phenomenon of motion, the most ubiquitous feature of the natural world and the one most in need of explanation.

To make progress in this regard, he insists, we first have to separate minds and bodies in a rigorous way. Each must be defined as a separate, freestanding substance, neither of which is a property or mode of the other. Once we do this, however, a problem arises. For surely there is some sort of communication between bodies and minds. When my arm is pinched, I feel pain; when I choose to move it, it goes up. How is this possible? Only, Descartes says, through the will of God, a substance even more perfect than these other two (because *entirely* freestanding, in contrast to all finite beings, both physical and psychical, which depend on something other than themselves for their existence). In the end, Descartes cannot conceive of any way in which the divide between bodies and minds can be crossed except through a divine intervention that itself is inexplicable and therefore, strictly speaking, miraculous. That he saw the need for such a miracle to put them back in touch was a consequence of the completeness with which he felt compelled to separate bodies and minds in the first place, for the sake of a deeper and more disciplined account of natural motion.

This is not the only point in his philosophy where Descartes turns to God's miraculous agency to solve an otherwise intractable problem. The most famous example is his invocation of God as the guarantor of the truth of our clear and distinct ideas (including that of God himself)—something that Descartes is forced to do in order to end the process of corrosive doubt that he uses to clear a path to a new and indubitable foundation for physical science. But what is most relevant to an understanding of the implications of Spinoza's critique of Descartes' philosophy for the work of natural science is the role that God plays in Descartes' detailed account of the laws of motion.

The wedge that Descartes drives between the realms of body and mind denudes the former of all the spiritual or psychical characteristics it possesses in Aristotle's physics and prepares the way for a stripped-down analysis of a strictly quantitative kind. According to Descartes, the individual bodies that occupy this realm all share one and only one property in common. This is the attribute of extension, without which their bodily nature cannot be understood or explained. Descartes regards extension as the essence, or definition, of bodily being. All other physical characteristics (size, shape, hardness, and the like) are modifications or modes of this one.

Descartes' reduction of the essence of body to extension is accompanied by a reduction of motion to locomotion, the movement of a thing from one place to another—the other, qualitative forms of motion that Aristotle includes under the heading of *kinesis* (such as growth and decay) either disappearing or being redefined in terms of local motion only. In Descartes' view, this one basic form of motion holds the key to understanding all the actions and interactions of bodily beings, which move and are moved locally by means of external contact only—other sorts of attraction and repulsion having been expelled from the world of material reality as illegitimate residues of the confused, "psychical" conception of physical motion that plays a foundational role in Aristotle's science of nature.

Descartes' account of the motion of bodies is further distinguished from Aristotle's by the absence of two related priorities that the latter takes for granted: that of rest over motion, and of circular movement over the rectilinear kind. In Descartes' physics, rest and motion are always equally appropriate starting points from which to begin. Neither enjoys a privileged position on account of "the nature of things." In every case, the challenge is to explain the fact that a body moves from one state to the other (or accelerates, a special case of movement from a fixed rate of motion conceived as a state of rest). The elementary form of all such movements is endless, "pointless" motion in a straight line. Circular movement now becomes the exception, which has to be explained in terms of the more basic rectilinear kind. Among the movements that must be explained in this way are the circling paths of the planets and stars.

The rectilinear motion to which the latter must be reduced, moreover, is the same as that of bodies on earth. In Descartes' new bare-bones physics of extension and locomotion, the qualitative distinction between celestial and terrestrial motion, which Aristotle believed to be a fundamental feature of the cosmos itself, thus disappears completely. The physical world that remains is uniform and soulless throughout. It might appear to be godless as well. But nothing could be further from Descartes' view.

The reduction of motion to local motion vastly expands our power to explain the behavior of bodies both on earth and in the heavens. It increases our ability to measure their movements in a mathematically precise way. But fundamental questions remain. How did the movement of bodies begin? What set them in motion in the first place? What "conserves" the total amount of their motion (something Descartes believed to be an unvarying sum)? And what explains the existence of the particular laws of motion that govern the interactions of bodies (for example, those having to do with their direction and speed following a collision)? To all these questions, Descartes' answer is God.

If one body causes the motion of another by giving it an "efficient" push, it is God who sets the entire world in motion with a divine shove of his own, and God who ensures that the movements of bodies in the world follow laws that are intelligible to us by establishing these through an act of creation as well. The existence both of moving bodies and of the laws that govern their motions is thus due, on Descartes' view, to the agency of a God beyond the world who brings them into being from nothing. Beyond and before the disenchanted world of bodies without souls whose law-abiding and calculable movements are the subject of Cartesian physics, we are therefore compelled to imagine a world-transcending spirit whose omnipotence alone explains how such a world is possible at all.

But this entails an enormous sacrifice of explanatory rationalism—the very thing that Descartes' despiritualized physics is meant to advance. The latter dramatically extends our ability to account for the motion of things in the world. Yet the actions of the God on whom the possibility of such a physics depends put a stop to its advance. That is because God's actions are not merely difficult to grasp, as would be the case, for example, if they were like our own, only more complex. God's actions are *in principle* unintelligible because they are absolutely unconstrained. There are no laws or rules or principles that God must obey in exercising his primal power of creation. The mere suggestion that there *could* be, contradicts the idea of God himself. Hence, there is nothing we can ever say—are ever *allowed* to say—to explain the fact that he has chosen to exercise this power one way rather than another.

As a matter of fact, the world that God has created is wonderfully intelligible (far more so than the Aristotelians, with their confused beliefs about substantial forms, were able to conceive). But the intelligibility of the world is merely contingent, for it owes its existence to the incomprehensibly free act of a God whose creative decisions are not themselves understandable in light of some further principle or law. To suppose otherwise is to impugn the grandeur of God. Hence, backstopping the tremendous encouragement that Descartes' physics gives those who seek to understand the world is a God whose inscrutable will guarantees that the rationalization of the study of bodies can be carried only so far, because it rests on an assumption that by definition must remain inaccessible to reason.

In this sense, the whole of Descartes' physics is informed by the distinction between God's absolute and ordained power, which he presumably learned as a student at La Fleche, where he was educated in the decaying scholasticism of the late sixteenth century.

That this was a distinction of great importance to Descartes cannot be doubted. He employs it, for example, to explain both his opposition to atomism and his denial of the existence of vacua in nature (positions that were later rejected by those who took their lead from Newton instead). As to the first, Descartes reasons that we cannot conceive a least, irreducible atom; hence, there cannot be such things, since God's absolute power allows him to do only what is conceivable, and he would not deceive us by "pretending" to ordain an arrangement incompatible with the extent of his power. Regarding the second, Descartes claims (in response to his critics) that a vacuum is not strictly inconceivable, and that God therefore has the absolute power to create one, but as a matter of fact has chosen not to do so. In Descartes' view, God's ordained laws include the rule, "no vacua in nature," though this law, unlike the one "ruling out" the existence of atoms, is merely contingent.

These arguments have been challenged, of course, and their consistency is doubtful. But what they demonstrate is the importance to Descartes of the distinction between God's inexhaustible and utterly inexplicable reservoir of absolute power, on the one hand, and the wonderfully explicable world he has chosen to ordain on the other. With this distinction, which Ockham put to such good use in reconciling God's omnipotence with the dictates of "right reason," Descartes is able to promote the rationalization of the science of nature while honoring the glory of God, whose dignity is infringed the moment one suggests that the laws he has decreed for the world exist by a kind of natural necessity.

This accommodation of science to theology comes at a considerable price, however, for as Spinoza recognized, it makes the very existence of physics itself a brute fact that cannot be explained. This remains true no matter how much we learn about the behavior of bodies, whose analysis in terms of extension, locomotion, and efficient causation alone allows for an unprecedented increase in our understanding of the natural world. So long as this achievement rests on the assumption that the laws that make it possible are themselves divinely ordained by an omnipotent God whose creation of the world must remain absolutely incomprehensible to us, Descartes' announced ambition to place science on a foundation secure enough to sustain it is bound to fall short of its goal. Only an explanation of the explanatory power of science itself can supply such a foundation—one that is capable of supporting what is built on it by being transparently intelligible too. The Christian doctrine of creation, which provided a tremendous impetus to the development of the modern, mechanical physics that Descartes embraced and sought to ground in a rigorous way, thus emerges with special clarity in Descartes own metaphysics as an obstacle to the further rationalization of physics itself, and to the completion of the task that Descartes sets himself at the beginning of the *Meditations*.

The relevance for modern science of Spinoza's critique of Descartes begins at this point.

GOD, TWO WAYS

Part 1 of Spinoza's *Ethics* is entitled "Of God." Some balk at the word because the God Spinoza describes has no will, creates nothing, and is indistinguishable from nature itself. In short, it lacks precisely those characteristics that define the God of Abraham, whose claim to the title has for centuries had such a monopoly on the Western philosophical imagination that to many any other conception of God is likely to seem unworthy of the name.

Spinoza's God nevertheless shares two essential features in common with the God of Abraham. Like the latter, it is both eternal and all-powerful. In these respects, it is different from every other being in the world. Spinoza calls these less-than-eternal beings "modes," a term he borrows from Descartes. A mode is a modification of something else. In Spinoza's theology, this is and can only be God, the one eternal and infinitely powerful being, for which Spinoza reserves the ancient philosophical term "substance," also of crucial importance to Descartes.

In Descartes' metaphysics, the distinction between God, who is eternal and omnipotent, and all those beings that are not, is understood and explained as the difference between creator and creature. Spinoza recasts this as the distinction between substance and mode. Unlike the one eternal and omnipotent being they modify or express, Spinoza's modes are neither everlasting nor all-powerful. But in contrast to God's creatures in the orthodox Christian scheme, they are not summoned into being from nothing, and as features rather than creatures of God they participate directly, albeit incompletely, in the necessity, eternity and omnipotence of God's own being.

It is hard to imagine a more fundamental philosophical revision. Yet because Spinoza insists, along with Descartes, that every finite being must have its ground in something everlasting and divine, his metaphysics may properly be called a theology too. Indeed, it is the most powerful reminder in modern philosophy (before Hegel, at least) that Christian theology is merely one variant of it, and that long before the study of God came to be identified with the grateful worship of a divine creator beyond the world, it meant something else—the joyful contemplation of the eternal divinity of the world itself, which Aristotle considered the supreme topic of all human thought. This is the pagan theology that Spinoza revives in part 1 of the *Ethics,* albeit in a radicalized form that shows the impress of the Christian theology he emphatically rejects.

Like Descartes, Spinoza insists that there is only one being that is not dependent on any other. There is only one, as he puts it, that is the cause of itself.[24] Spinoza further argues that there cannot be more than one such being, and that it cannot *not* be. With all this, Descartes of course agrees. For Descartes too, there is only one necessary and self-sufficient being. This is the God who brings the world into being from nothing. He alone exists on account of who or what he is—"by definition," one might say. Everything else in Descartes' world exists by the sufferance of God, hence through the causal agency of a being other than itself.

Descartes is often viewed as a dualist twice over: first, on account of his distinction between God and the things he creates, and second, because of the divide between bodies and minds, which he describes as separate substances too. But it is perhaps more accurate to call him an "independence monist," for his metaphysics, like that of every Christian philosopher, permits one and only one being whose existence is both necessary and self-contained. In this respect, Spinoza follows Descartes strictly. The break between them comes in their characterization of the relation between this one, truly independent being, and everything else in the world.

In Descartes' view, this relation is volitional. God wills all other things into being. For Spinoza, the relation is modal. Every finite being is an expression of the one being whose existence is necessary and self-caused. Put differently, Spinoza views finite beings as adjectival qualifications of God or substance, or nature as a whole. For him, they all inhere "in" God in a way that no Christian, Jew or Muslim can accept without repudiating the orthodoxy of God's separation from the world.

The "in" relation of modes to God is both causal and conceptual. Spinoza's God is at once the causal ground of the finite beings that express it and the concept that contains them, in the way that any concept may be said to contain the propositions entailed by it. Indeed, for Spinoza, these two relations are ultimately the same. This is bound to seem odd, if not absurd. Entailment, after all, is a logical relationship. Where it exists, it does so by necessity, in contrast to causal relations, which exist only contingently, as a matter of fact. Yet Spinoza insists on the coincidence of these seemingly different relations. We shall return to this point in the following chapter. But to anticipate, it might be put in the following way. For Spinoza, every causal account of the relations among finite modes, and of these to the infinite substance in which they inhere, is an explication, under the conditions of time, of relations that exist *sub specie aeternitatis* and possess the logical necessity that all such relations do. We asymptotically approach an understanding of these conceptual relationships through an ever more "adequate" grasp of the infinitely complex web of causal relations that we discover in the temporal succession of things.

Spinoza's characterization of the relation between the one truly independent being and its infinitely many modes as one of inherence rather than creation reflects his unwavering commitment to explanatory rationalism.

About every finite being one can ask, "Why does it exist in the way and at the time it does?" "Why is it the thing it is?" The assumption that there is in principle an answer to every question of this sort, whether we are able to supply it or not, Leibniz christened the principle of sufficient reason. No philosopher—Leibniz included—has ever been more devoted to it than Spinoza. His rejection of Descartes' volitional theology in favor of his own modal account of the relation of God to the world is motivated by Spinoza's desire to honor this principle in the only way that is fully consistent with its own demands.

Because we are finite beings, we can never fully account for the existence of any finite thing, ourselves included. To do so would require that we be able to relate it to its cause, that cause to an earlier one, and so on *ad infinitum*. It would also require that we be able to account for the necessity of the infinite series of finite causes to which the particular thing in question belongs. If the series itself is contingent, we cannot give a *full* account either of it or of any of its members. To do that, we must explain why this series and no other exists, and that requires, in principle at least, an explanation of the necessity of the one eternal, all-powerful being in whose own necessity the infinite series of finite causes participates by way of inherence. This is asking a lot, to put it mildly. But Spinoza thought it rationally indefensible to demand anything less, and his reinterpretation of the relation between God and the world of finite beings as one of inherence rather than creation is meant to secure the intelligibility of this demand.

The radicalism with which Spinoza embraces the principle of sufficient reason is matched by the modesty of his expectations regarding our ability to make progress toward achieving what it assumes to be possible. We are hemmed in on all sides by ignorance and passion. As a result, most human beings make little headway in understanding the world. Indeed, they barely know even themselves. That is why, Spinoza says, they remain for the most part unhappy. But the difficulty of making such progress never caused Spinoza to doubt the soundness of the principle of sufficient reason itself—unlike many other philosophers, who have been prepared to give up on the principle rather than accept its boundless demands.

Most important, Spinoza's acceptance of these demands is not, for him, a mere act of faith. One cannot simply choose to affirm or deny them. That is because, in his view, even the most limited use of reason already entails a commitment to the principle that every question has an answer, whether one knows it or not.[25]

If a thing is partly intelligible to us—and of course many are—we can always ask why it isn't intelligible to a greater degree. Why aren't we able to understand more about it than we do? If we assume this question has no answer, then our knowledge of the thing, however incomplete, is just an inexplicable fact. But to accept that it is amounts to an abandonment of reason itself, whose most primitive requirement is that we be able to account for the truth of what we understand, if it is to count as understanding at all.[26] Alternatively, if we assume, as Spinoza believed even the most modest commitment to reason compels us to do, that the question has an answer, then whatever it is and however difficult it may be to find, the answer will inevitably carry us beyond the limits it purports to explain—a process that repeats itself endlessly, at every level of understanding.

We are thus faced with two alternatives. Either the best current knowledge we have of the world is an inexplicable fact, and hence no knowledge at all, in which case all the knowledge that depends on it is a fact of this sort too, and hence no knowledge either; or we have reason to believe that the limits within which our knowledge is presently confined (whatever these may be) can eventually be explained, and hence overcome, in a process of ever-deepening comprehension that continues forever. The first of these is incompatible with the ambitions of reason even in their most limited form. To know anything at all, we must know how and why we know it. From this point of view, to say that we know something about the world, but that our knowledge of it is a fact we cannot explain, is a contradiction in terms. To escape it, we have no choice but to assume that the world itself is at least partly intelligible, and once we do we are forced to concede that we have no reason to think that its intelligibility must stop here or anywhere else. Indeed, reason itself compels the opposite conclusion: that our understanding of the world *cannot* stop at any particular point, but must go on increasing forever, which is equivalent to saying that the world is intelligible not merely in certain ways, or within certain limits, but infinitely so, however little of it we understand at any given moment. This is an extravagant conclusion, but it follows, in Spinoza's view, from the least claim to knowledge. There is no way to avoid its radical implications if one claims to know anything at all.

The modern science of nature accepts this radical view. It refuses to acknowledge that there are any built-in limits to our understanding of the world. It demands that every explanation be probed and tested until a better one is found that explains its predecessor's limits, and by doing so transcends them, in a process without end. In this sense, modern physics is committed to the

principle of sufficient reason, and to the proposition, which this principle implies, that the world is infinitely intelligible, while conceding, as anyone
must, that our finitude prevents us from ever exhausting its intelligibility completely.

This commitment is incompatible with the creationist theology that underlies Descartes' metaphysics. That is because the rationalist ambitions of
modern science cannot be reconciled with the belief that the world is intelligible only up to a point. If physics is to be put on a metaphysical foundation
of the sort that Descartes and Spinoza agree it requires, then Descartes' God
must be abandoned. This does not mean, however, that it can do without God
altogether. Modern physics needs a conception of an eternal and necessary
being, just as Aristotelian and scholastic and Cartesian physics did, for without some such conception, its commitment to the sufficiency of reason lacks
the anchor it must have to be coherent at all. But it needs a God that supports
rather than frustrates this commitment, and Descartes' God is debarred from
playing this role.

According to Descartes, the mechanical laws of nature structure the
motion of bodies in a way that makes them intelligible to us—far more so,
he believed, than Aristotle's jumbled psychophysics. But to the question "Why
these laws?" there is no answer. Indeed, it is impudent even to ask. Their
existence is a brute fact—the inexplicable creation of a God beyond the
world. With the fact of creation, we come to the limit of all possible human
knowledge—one that is inherent in the nature of the world itself as a *crea-
tum.* So long as the will is defined as the power to bring something into being from nothing, any view of God's relation to the world that conceives it in
voluntarist terms inevitably imposes a limit of this sort on our understanding
of things and forces us to renounce the ambition to extend our knowledge
beyond a certain, immutably fixed point.

The only alternative to the Abrahamic belief that the intelligibility of the
world is the incomprehensible gift of a God beyond it is the rationalist view
that the world is inherently intelligible—that its being is *to be* intelligible. This
is Spinoza's position, formulaically expressed in his equation of God with the
world. It is also Aristotle's view. For Aristotle, too, the being of the world and
of all the things in it is constituted by their mindedness. The idea that the
intelligibility of the world is the gift of an otherworldly God whose will
we cannot fathom would have seemed as absurd to Aristotle, who lived before this idea had taken possession of Western thought, as it did to Spinoza,
who lived in a civilization deeply shaped by it.

But Spinoza's uncompromising commitment to the principle of sufficient reason, which leads him to reject Descartes' creationist theology as a rationally indefensible barrier to the endless expansion of our knowledge of the world, sets his theology apart from Aristotle's in a fundamental way too. For Aristotle, the world is inherently but not wholly divine. It is divine to the extent it can be comprehended, but not everything in the world is comprehensible. This follows from the distinction between form and matter, and the identification of intelligibility with form alone.

That a dog has certain general features and behaves in the way dogs generally do is for Aristotle a consequence of its possessing a particular form. Its form makes these features and behaviors intelligible. Indeed, in Aristotle's view, their intelligibility is *nothing but* the form of the dog itself.

But a dog not only has certain general features. It also always has distinctive ones as well—ears that tilt at a peculiar angle, spots in a particular place, and the like. Each dog is one of a kind. These distinctive traits are due to the matter in which the dog's form is embodied, and though the dog's material being (its body) is intelligible insofar as it is composed of parts that have subsidiary forms of their own, at some point in our analysis of the body of any thing, Aristotle says, we come to matter without form, and here all understanding ceases.

The existence of this "prime" matter must be assumed in order to explain the potential of the simplest elements to exchange one form for another—as water does when it evaporates and turns into air. Its pure potency is the ultimate source of the most basic alterations in the world, and therefore of all others, which depend on these. It is the source of the motions of all things. It is also the ultimate source of their individuality, for the uniqueness of the members of each particular kind is due to the formless matter that distinguishes even their most basic parts from the similar parts of others like them. Prime matter therefore plays a central explanatory role in Aristotle's metaphysics. But because it lacks all form, it itself cannot be explained. Its existence is a brute fact we must acknowledge but can never comprehend. In this respect, it represents a barrier to understanding that is built into the very structure of the world itself and therefore keeps our efforts to "mind" it within limits that are permanently fixed.

Within these limits, we are able to know everything in the world that is knowable. Our finitude is no bar to that, though it does prevent us from holding onto such knowledge forever. But beyond these limits, there is nothing to be known—only the incomprehensible fact of formless matter. The existence of these limits is decreed by the pagan distinction between form and matter, which sets bounds to the principle of sufficient reason as unalterable as those entailed, in a different way, by the Christian doctrine of creation.

The doctrine of creation requires that we think of the world as having been brought into being from nothing, unlike the house a builder constructs from wood and other materials. It thereby erases the barrier to our understanding that flows from the distinction between form and matter. At the same time, however, it erects a new one, which does not exist in Aristotle's metaphysics. It does this by removing God from the world and reconceiving the relation between them as one of will. The doctrine of creation thus substitutes one barrier to the intelligibility of the world for another and blocks the extension of the principle of sufficient reason with equal finality, though from a different direction.

The only way to overcome this second obstacle is to abandon the creationist understanding of God's relation to the world on which Descartes' physics is based, and to replace it with one that defines this relation in modal rather than volitional terms. The intelligibility of the world must be reconceived as its own indwelling nature, inherent in—indeed identical to—the being of the world itself, and not as the free (and hence inscrutable) gift of a God beyond it. This is Spinoza's response to Descartes. It is his protest against the limits the doctrine of creation irrationally imposes on the boundless expansion of reason itself.

Spinoza's affirmation of the identity of God and the world makes his metaphysics essentially pagan. But it represents no mere return to Aristotle's theology. Though Spinoza's conception of God is defined in opposition to that of Descartes, it carries over the abolition of the distinction between form and matter that follows from the latter's Christian faith in the doctrine of creation, without this doctrine itself. The result is a new metaphysics, neither Christian nor pagan, that acknowledges, as any must, the finitude of our human powers and the consequent incompleteness of whatever understanding of the world we are able to achieve, yet affirms the infinitude of the world's intelligibility, and the endlessness of the progress we can make toward comprehending it—one that denies *both* the pagan dogma of form and matter, which permanently limits the first, *and* the Christian doctrine of creation, which establishes an insuperable barrier to the second. The God of this new metaphysics is the principle of sufficient reason, blocked in different ways by classical and Christian theology alike. Spinoza's God is the boundlessness of reason's own demands. He defines these in a philosophical vocabulary that has the same scholastic roots as Descartes' own. But Spinoza's God succeeds in doing what Descartes' cannot. It provides a foundation for the modern physics that Descartes did so much to advance and hoped to put on lastingly secure metaphysical grounds, but could not because of his own antirational Christian beliefs.

Most people find it hard to affirm the intelligibility of the world as unreservedly as Spinoza did. They find it difficult to deny the existence of certain brute facts. But the assumption that the world is infinitely intelligible and that the only limits we ever meet in seeking to comprehend it are those that derive from the inadequacy of our own powers of understanding is the premise of the new science of nature that acquired unprecedented authority in the seventeenth century, spurred by the idea of God's omnipotence yet at the same time fatefully constrained by it. Neither Descartes' God nor Aristotle's accords with this assumption. Only Spinoza's does. Spinoza's God is the God of modern science. It is the divinity of a world whose inherent and boundless intelligibility is at once the inspiration for and confirmation of all that modern science seeks to grasp in its endless, restless endeavors, today as in the past.

CHAPTER 28

The God of Sufficient Reason

PHYSICS AFTER SPINOZA

Descartes was for Spinoza a hero of reason. But Spinoza saw that Descartes' rationalism is incomplete.

So long as the study of nature is yoked to the idea of divine creation, its achievements rest on sand. Their explanatory power cannot be explained. A confident and secure science of nature is possible only on the basis of a different theology, one that rejects the Christian doctrine of creation and equates God with the infinite intelligibility of the world instead. This is the essence of Spinoza's born-again paganism, which is better suited to the new physics that Descartes and later Newton did so much to advance, than the Ockhamist theology that both thinkers embraced.[1]

Yet there is something implausible about the suggestion that Spinoza's hyperrationalist theology, to which the atmosphere of medieval scholasticism still seems to cling so tightly, is more congenial to modern physics than the Christianity of those who built it. In fact, Spinoza's metaphysics seems out of touch with the practice and presuppositions of modern science in a number of ways.

Four are particularly striking.

First, Spinoza seems little interested in facts. It is true that he followed Boyle's experiments and conducted a few of his own. He also appears to have had a detailed knowledge of lens making, which implies at least some curiosity about the way things in the world actually work. But the whole tenor of his philosophy is remorselessly conceptual. Factual inquiry seems to play little or no role in the pursuit of what he calls "adequate" ideas. What relation can an intellectualist metaphysics of this sort have to a science of nature that insists on empirical observation as a condition for the formulation and verification of every scientific hypothesis? Where in Spinoza is there even a faint hint of Galileo's experimentalism, or of Tycho Brahe's devotion to the meticulous recording of facts, on which Kepler and Newton built their astrophysical laws?

Second, Spinoza appears to have less confidence than any of these others in the power of mathematical explanation. Galileo famously remarked that the book of nature is written in the language of mathematics.[2] For Descartes, the realm of extension is geometry "made real." Spinoza, by contrast, regards mathematical knowledge as inferior to another sort that he calls "intuitive." His doubts about the ultimacy of mathematical understanding seem, in a curious way, to reflect an attitude that is the opposite of his disinterest in factual inquiry, and to put Spinoza out of touch with the other great principle of seventeenth-century science, which was as committed to the mathematization of the world as to its empirical investigation.

Third, Spinoza has little to say about the laws of physics themselves. His only extended treatment of the subject (apart from his commentary on Descartes' *Principles of Philosophy*) is contained in a brief digression in part 2 of the *Ethics*. This makes things difficult enough for anyone seeking to establish a connection between Spinoza's theology and his understanding of natural science. What makes matters worse is that Spinoza's physics appears strikingly different from that of Descartes and especially of Newton. Newton's physics is one of mass points moving or at rest in an absolute spatial and temporal frame from which they are themselves distinct. By contrast, for Spinoza, an extended thing is a mode *of* space, not some thing *in* it. His physics rests on what some have called a "field" conception of the modal nature of bodies.[3] In this respect, it seems incompatible with the very different view of discrete objects in space and time that underlies the classical mechanics of Newton and his followers, down to the quantum mechanical revolution of the twentieth century. Furthermore, Spinoza's idea of *conatus*—his claim that all things by their nature strive to persevere in being—appears to conflict, in a basic way, with the principle of inertia, as both Descartes and Newton understand it.

Fourth, and finally, Spinoza's principal aim is ethical, not scientific. He seeks a happiness "whose discovery and acquisition would afford [one] a continuous and supreme joy to all eternity."[4] Scientists rarely use ethically charged words like "happiness" and "joy" to describe their work. Most of course, concede that ethical questions are important. But they assign these to a different sphere of inquiry and concern. By contrast, Spinoza insists that science itself is a spiritual quest. It is, he claims, an inherently ethical enterprise. Can anything be further from the disenchanted culture of modern science?

In the remainder of this chapter, I address the first three questions. The last is the subject of chapter 31.

EMPIRICAL KNOWLEDGE

For Spinoza, the most perfect form of knowledge is conceptual. We know something conceptually when we understand that it is true by definition. In this sense, all conceptual knowledge is self-contained. The rules of geometry are an example.[5] That the interior angles of a triangle always equal two right angles is a truth contained within the concept of triangularity itself. This is not obvious at first glance. Some effort is required to see it. But only when a student understands that the rule in question is true "by definition" may he be said to possess what Spinoza calls an "adequate" idea of it.[6] If, after measuring the angles of a number of triangles, he concludes that the rule is true, but only as a matter of fact, his knowledge is imperfect.

Every philosopher from Plato to Kant recognizes that there are at least some truths of this kind. But Spinoza's view of the realm of conceptual truth is exceptionally wide. That is because he rejects two widely held assumptions that limit its range.

First, he rejects the belief that the ultimate premises of those conceptual truths we acknowledge, like the truths of geometry, are mere stipulations or "posits" that must be accepted as brute facts. For Spinoza, a "positivist" view of this sort is incompatible with the demands of reason itself, as expressed by the principle of sufficient reason. If the premises of these truths are themselves arbitrary posits, we have no reason to adopt them, and hence only a weak, conditional reason to endorse their implications, whose own rationality can never be greater than that of the assumptions on which they are based.

In Spinoza's view, the first premises of all conceptual truths must therefore be true by definition as well. They must be necessarily, and not merely positively, or accidentally, true. These basic premises include the propositions that God exists, is one, and has an infinite number of modes. The main aim of part 1 of the *Ethics* is to demonstrate that the existence, unity and modal diversity of God are truths of the same self-contained kind as the rule that the interior angles of a triangle equal two right angles. This is the real meaning of Spinoza's famous use of the method of geometry to unfold his meta-physical ideas.

Second, Spinoza rejects the view that conceptual truths are different in kind from the empirical ones that we discover by means of experience, through the use of what he calls "imagination" (the truth, for example, that water boils at one hundred degrees centigrade).[7] With the exception of Leibniz, who also rejects this distinction, all the great rationalist philosophers of the seventeenth and eighteenth centuries, up to and including Kant, assumed that conceptual and empirical truths belong to different domains. All the great empiricists, up to and including Hume, accepted the existence of this divide as well; their goal was merely to limit what might be placed on the conceptual side of it. In contrast to both, Spinoza denies that there is, in reality, any such divide at all. In his view, every empirical truth is an inadequately conceptual one, whose necessity we imperfectly grasp. In principle, such truths are always capable of being converted into more adequate ones, though our finitude prevents us from ever grasping their truth, as Spinoza puts it, under the aspect of eternity, as we do those of geometry.[8] For Spinoza, the distinction between empirical and conceptual truth is thus one of degree only, like that between an ignorant and a wise man, or between a human being and God, to which, as we shall see, it bears an important resemblance.

This appears to create a point of tension between Spinoza's metaphysics and the modern science of nature. The claim that empirical and conceptual truths belong to a continuum and are separated not by kind but degree might seem to imply a belief in the unimportance of experimental research, as opposed to the kind of strictly conceptual analysis that Spinoza employs in the *Ethics*. But a closer look at what he means by the "adequacy" of our ideas suggests a different conclusion.

All truths of experience are bound to be inadequate, when measured against the standard set by those of mathematics. That is because every experience is a representation of one's body, insofar as it is acted upon, and hence modified by, a body or bodies external to it.[9] Indeed, for Spinoza, an experience is nothing but the idea of one's body insofar as it is caused to see, feel, record or remember something on account of the action on it of a body other than itself. To understand any experience (for example, my perception of a chair across the room, or the cold I feel when I touch a piece of ice) I must therefore know what caused it. I must know what other body, acting on mine, brought the experience about. All experiential knowledge is causal in this sense.

But the cause of my body's being disposed in a certain way, which lies outside my body, always has an external cause of its own, and so on *ad infinitum.* It follows that the understanding I gain of any particular experience will always be imperfect and incomplete. This is a consequence of the relation between causation and time.

Every causal explanation of an experience assumes that its cause precedes it in time. This is true even where two events are reciprocally determined, for the existence of such a relation is itself explicable only on the assumption that, considered as a whole, it has an antecedent cause of its own. Every bit of experiential knowledge therefore falls under the aspect of time.

But the temporally ordered series of causes that accounts for my experience of the world itself has no beginning in time. For each link in the causal chain, there is always an earlier one that explains it. To fully (adequately) understand an experience, I would therefore have to possess a knowledge of this endless series of causes. But the finite, modal nature of my being makes this impossible. I am myself an essentially temporal being; I live in time, and for a time. This does not prevent me from acquiring an adequate knowledge of certain truths (like mathematical ones) that are founded on relations that exist independently of time. It does, however, bar me from ever fully understanding anything whose explanation itself depends on the temporal relation of cause and effect, for that would require that I comprehend time itself as a whole—from the outside, so to speak.

But though empirical knowledge is necessarily imperfect, it can always be improved. No matter how much I know about the causes of my bodily states, I can always learn more. Sometimes I do this in an informal way, merely by paying closer attention to the experiences that befall me. But I can also increase the understanding I have of my experiences in a more deliberate fashion, by means of a carefully thought-out program of study and research. This is the aim of all scientific experimentation.

As my knowledge of causes expands and becomes more secure, I am able to give a better account of why I have the experiences I do. I can see with greater clarity that my experiences are dictated by their antecedent causes—that they follow from them with necessity. The necessity I discern in the relation between my experiences and their causes approaches by degrees the conceptual necessity that is characteristic of mathematics, and would be identical to it if I could grasp the infinite chain of causes that precedes every given experience. Were I able to attain a knowledge of this sort, I would see that my experiences are entailed by—contained "in"—their causes with the same necessity that the proposition that the angles of a triangle always equal two right angles is contained "in" the idea of triangularity.

My finitude precludes me from ever fully acquiring such knowledge, but not from coming closer to it than I am at any moment. As I do, the experiences I seek to understand gradually lose their appearance of contingency, just as the rule regarding the internal angles of a triangle ceases to be a mere fact and becomes a conceptual necessity once I grasp its relation to the idea from which it derives. In this way, my empirical knowledge approximates ever more closely, under the conditions of time that inform all causal understanding, the self-contained conceptual knowledge of relations *sub specie aeternitatis* that is for Spinoza the benchmark of true understanding. And though it must always fall short of this mark, our empirical knowledge of causes is in one respect superior to it, for unlike mathematics, which is necessarily abstract, the science of nature that emerges from a disciplined study of causes yields an increasingly adequate knowledge of reality, making physics more edifying than mathematics, to which, as we shall see, Spinoza insists it cannot be reduced.

Another way of describing Spinoza's conception of empirical knowledge is the following.

I understand an experience when I grasp the causal connection between it and some antecedent state of affairs. This connection is expressed in the form of a law, which implies a relation of necessity: given a particular antecedent state, a certain experience must follow.

My understanding of this relation is always incomplete in two respects, however. First, because the law in question is cast in general terms (as every law must be) it inevitably suppresses some of the complexity involved in the relation. To fully (adequately) understand this relation, the law I have framed must continually be refined. Second, so long as the antecedent state that is the purported cause of my experience is merely taken for granted, and not itself explained, my understanding of the experience is less than comprehensive. To remedy its incompleteness, I must attempt to explain, in causal terms, this antecedent state as well, and so on, without limit.

The expansion of my understanding of the world, which I come to know only in experience, thus proceeds endlessly in both directions. It increases through an ever more detailed refinement of the causal laws that govern the relations among events, and a widening comprehension of the antecedent conditions that every causal explanation assumes as its minor premise. The further this twofold process of expansion proceeds, the more our empirical understanding of the world enables us to see the necessity with which all things happen as they do, and thus steadily to approach, without ever reaching, a perfectly adequate knowledge of the whole of reality—which, were we able to attain it, would be characterized by the transformation of every empirical truth into a conceptual one.

To maintain that these two sorts of truth are fundamentally different implies that in their empirical investigation of the world, scientists must reach a point beyond which they are compelled simply to take certain things for granted. It implies that there are facts that can never be explained. Spinoza rejects this conclusion. Though their inquiries remain forever incomplete, the scientists who undertake them have no reason to think that these must be broken off at any point. Indeed, the principle of sufficient reason compels the opposite conclusion. It affirms that a further step can always be taken, even if it requires centuries to do so. This makes sense only on the assumption that empirical truths differ from conceptual ones in degree rather than kind. Spinoza's seemingly peculiar view of the relation between these two sorts of truth is therefore the only one compatible with a commitment to the principle of sufficient reason, on which the unending campaign to extend our knowledge of causes is founded.

This is the defining commitment of modern natural science. It bears a resemblance to Aristotle's belief that the world is inherently intelligible but differs from it in a fundamental way. Aristotle thought it obvious that the necessity of the order of things must be apparent to anyone who truly understands it. Yet because he believed that the world is intelligible and therefore necessary only up to a point, he also thought that a true understanding of it is both limited and complete. The principle of sufficient reason disallows the concession and blocks the conclusion. It presumes that the world is intelligible all the way down, and that there is therefore no end either to its necessity or our labor to comprehend it. Modern experimental empiricism, in contrast to the casual, armchair sort that Aristotle practiced, rests on this assumption.

Those who embrace the principle of sufficient reason thus have no choice but to reject Aristotle's theology of form, which confines the intelligibility of the world to one part of it only. Nor can they accept the God of the Christian religion, whose incomprehensible will represents an insurmountable barrier to our understanding of natural causes. For these conceptions of divinity they must substitute another—that of an inherently and infinitely intelligible world, whose own reality is both necessary and self-caused, as that of any God must be.

This hyperrational theology in turn compels us to abandon the belief that empirical truths are essentially, and irrevocably, different from conceptual ones. In a world that is inherently and infinitely divine, the only possible explanation for the apparent contingency of truths of the former kind is our incompetence, as finite beings, to fully explain them. This may seem like a retreat to an older form of conceptualism hostile to experiment and research. But the truth is just the opposite. For along with the Spinozist conception of God from which it derives, the characterization of the distinction between these two sorts of truth as one of degree only is needed to make sense of the endless, restless ambitions of modern empirical science, which is distinguished from its ancient and medieval counterparts by its refusal to acknowledge that there are any limits to what a scientist may rationally seek to know.

MATHEMATICS

These considerations throw light on what appears to be a second point of conflict between Spinoza's metaphysics and the new science of nature that Galileo sketched, Descartes refined and Newton brought to completion.

All three insist that mathematics holds the key to understanding the behavior of objects in the physical world. Indeed, so close is the connection between the mathematics they use to describe the motion of bodies in nature, and these motions themselves, that the first came to be viewed not merely as an accurate description of the natural world but its constitutive essence—as the source of whatever reality bodies and motions possess. In this sense, seventeenth-century physics promoted the mathematization of nature itself.

This required a new mathematics. Ancient mathematics was essentially static. It described the motionless forms of things. Like Descartes two millennia later, Plato identified the real with number and shape, but was able to do this only by denying the reality of movement and change. For Descartes and his contemporaries, living and working in a culture shaped by the Christian belief in the reality of all things, including the movement of bodies, the Platonic identification of the real with the mathematical could be preserved only on the condition that a method be devised for the representation and analysis of motion itself, whose unreality was for Plato a consequence of the metaphysical equation of being with form. Because motion is a temporal concept, this necessitated a technique for the mathematization of time—something that Greek mathematics ruled out as a matter of principle.

Using algebraic techniques foreign to the Platonic conception of number and shape, Descartes took the first great step toward the mathematization of motion in his new, "analytic" geometry, which treats time as a numerically representable variable. But to the extent that the *continuity* of motion still could not be represented in numerical terms, even in Descartes' new graphical geometry, its essential temporal character remained beyond the reach of mathematical analysis. The calculus of Leibniz and Newton made this possible for the first time, and with it, that distinctively modern identification of reality with mathematics which (in contrast to Plato's) includes motion and change within the scope of the real. This is one important source of the optimism that has characterized the discipline of physics since the pioneering work of Galileo. The mathematization of motion that these new methods allowed encouraged the belief that the *entire* reality of the natural world, dynamic as well as static, might now be captured in mathematical terms, making the whole of things, and not merely their unchanging forms, comprehensible in the language of number and shape.

Spinoza disagrees with this widely shared assumption. It is a mistake, he says, to confuse mathematics and reality. "Number, Measure [and] Time" are "merely aids to the imagination."[10] They help us understand our experience of the world, but are not themselves ultimately real. Only those who are ignorant "of the true nature of reality" would confuse "these three concepts" with it. This seems flatly inconsistent with Descartes' conviction that extended things are nothing but "geometry made real."[11] It also seems to conflict with Spinoza's own use of mathematics, and of geometry in particular, as a standard by which to measure the adequacy of our ideas. The self-evidence of the truths of mathematics is, for Spinoza, a model of all true understanding. Yet he insists that the mathematics we employ to understand the world is only a crutch that we must carefully distinguish from the reality we seek to comprehend by means of it. Can these views be reconciled, and squared with the aspirations of modern physics generally?

Yes, if we keep the basic principles of Spinoza's metaphysics in mind.

The goal of natural science is to understand the world in causal terms. But a truly adequate understanding of anything is conceptual. It conceives the relation between the thing to be explained and its explanatory ground as one of entailment, and not of causation viewed as a relation in time. Mathematical understanding is conceptual in this sense. To the extent that we can reconstruct the relations among the things we encounter in experience in mathematical terms, we thus acquire a more conceptual, and hence adequate, knowledge of them. This is what physics aims to do. It seeks to reformulate causal relations as numerical or geometrical ones, and to the extent it succeeds, endows what before was a contingent or brute fact with the necessity that is characteristic of all mathematical relations.

But this process of reformulation is bound to fall short of the completely adequate knowledge we seek. That is because mathematical relations are always general ones that apply to a class or category of things or events. Number, measure and time are abstractions. This is precisely what gives them their immense explanatory power. Yet their abstractness also guarantees that they can never completely capture the individuality of things and events in their explanatory net. There will always be more to be explained than any system of mathematical ideas can comprehend, no matter how refined it becomes. There will always be a residue of inexplicable particularity that is left out of account.

Because reality, which we encounter in experience (through "imagination," as Spinoza puts it), always outstrips our mathematical powers, it would therefore be a mistake to equate one with the other. This is the meaning of Spinoza's claim that number, measure and time are not themselves ultimately real. But it would be as great a mistake, in Spinoza's view, to maintain that our mathematical understanding of the world is limited because there are certain brute facts that no amount of mathematics can ever explain. In Spinoza's metaphysics, there are no such brute facts. Everything is explicable, though never fully explained, and mathematics is the most powerful tool we possess in our ongoing effort to close the gap between concept and percept—between the knowable and the known.

Putting these thoughts together, Spinoza's position might be described as follows.

Science converts our empirical understanding of the world into an increasingly conceptual knowledge whose hallmark is the transformation of contingent relations into necessary ones—of brute facts into events whose connection to their cause is intellectually transparent. Mathematics is at once the most familiar example of such transparency and the best instrument we have to reduce the opacity of the causal relations we discover in experience.

But it would be an error to confuse the world we seek to understand with the mathematics we employ to do so. The abstractness of mathematics is itself a permanent bar to an adequate understanding of the individuality of things and events. Their individuality is real and fully intelligible. Mathematics, by contrast, requires us to aggregate individuals into groups or classes or sets—to "cut" the world, which in reality is an undivided whole, into discrete units or parts. In this respect, mathematics is as distorting as it is indispensable. And while we must recognize that the distortion cannot be avoided, we need also to accept that the only weapon we have to fight it is *more* mathematics—not the abandonment of the one, necessarily limited but truly conceptual, form of understanding we possess, for some other nonmathematical sort.

On the one hand, to equate number, measure and time with reality is to affirm that a transparent knowledge of the world is fully attainable. On the other, to maintain that mathematics can take us only so far and that its explanatory power must at some point be exhausted is to affirm the existence of brute facts impenetrable to our, or any, understanding. Both are inconsistent with the aims of modern science, whose reliance on mathematics reflects the belief that all truth is ultimately conceptual, but whose open-endedness rules out the possibility that the full truth about the world can ever be known by finite beings such as we. Our finitude condemns us to use the abstractions of mathematics as our key to the book of nature. They are the surest, perhaps the only, key we possess. Yet these same abstractions, precisely because they *are* abstractions, ensure that we shall never read the book completely. Hence, neither those who refuse to recognize the power of mathematics, nor those who, thinking too highly of it, equate its methods and discoveries with reality itself, strike the right balance between the boundless confidence of modern science, on the one hand, and its constraining modesty on the other, that Spinoza seeks to capture with his image of the worm in the blood.

THE PHYSICAL DIGRESSION

This brings us to the details of Spinoza's own account of the physical world, or as he puts it, of "substance" conceived under the "attribute" of "extension."

A few inferences regarding his conception of physical reality may be drawn from scattered remarks in Spinoza's letters and from his reconstruction, in geometrical form, of the second part of Descartes' *Principles of Philosophy.* But the most explicit presentation of anything that might be called a "physics" is contained in the series of Axioms and Lemmas that Spinoza appends to Proposition 13 of part 2 of the *Ethics,* the so-called "physical digression."

The propositions that precede and follow this one deal not with the nature of bodies but minds. According to Spinoza, the mind of a man (or anything else) is a collection of ideas with a distinct but transient unity of its own. In

Spinoza's view, ideas are representations, and every first-order idea is the representation of a body—most importantly, though not exclusively, the body of the being whose mind it is. (I say "first-order" because Spinoza acknowledges that complex minds have ideas of ideas, but these reflective chains all end in an idea that represents one or more bodies.) Because Spinoza defines minds as collections of ideas, and the most basic sort of idea as the representation of a body, some understanding of the nature of bodies is required to grasp that of minds. This is why he finds it necessary to interrupt his account of minds with an abbreviated physics that outlines a few of the basic principles governing the nature and movement of bodies.

The physics that Spinoza sketches in the digression is shaped throughout by his deepest metaphysical convictions.

The first of these is that bodies and minds are not different kinds of "things." They are merely modifications of the one and only "thing" there is. Bodies and minds have a modal, not a substantive reality. Moreover, though there is a *representational* relation between them, these two different sorts of modes are not, and cannot be, *causally* connected. That is because there is no way to explain how a mental event could ever be caused by a physical one, or vice versa. The assertion of a causal link between events of one kind and those of another would therefore put the person asserting it in conflict with the principle of sufficient reason. The existence of every idea can be fully explained, in principle at least, as can that of every body, but only by locating it in the infinite causal chain appropriate to it.

Indeed, for Spinoza the existence of a body or mind, on the one hand, and its location within the causal chain to which it belongs on the other, are more intimately linked than what I have just said may suggest. That is because bodies and minds do not exist independently of the frameworks within which we seek to explain them. Spinoza calls these frameworks "attributes"—the causal schemes under which substance is "conceived" (accounted for or explained). There are, he says, an infinite number of such schemes, but we possess only two, those of thought and extension. For Spinoza, the claim that something *is* a mind is equivalent to the assertion that it can be accounted for under the attribute of thought. The mind whose existence we postulate has no being before we locate it within the explanatory matrix of the laws of thinking. The same is true of bodies. To say that something *is* a body amounts to the claim that it can be conceived under the attribute of extension. Because the attributes of thought and extension are as wide as the world, there is nothing that cannot be accounted for from each of their distinct points of view. In particular, there is nothing in the world that physics is in principle unable to explain.

These assumptions guide Spinoza's account of the nature of bodily being. It is strikingly different from the one offered by Descartes and Newton.

The latter two did not, of course, see eye to eye in all respects. They disagreed, famously, on two issues in particular—the infinite divisibility of matter and the existence of empty space. Descartes denied the possibility of indivisible quanta of extended stuff, and of space with nothing in it. In each case, his reasons were theological. Newton, by contrast, assumed the existence of both particle points and vacua. His assumptions carried the day. Descartes and Newton nevertheless shared two other beliefs that sharply distinguish their physics from that of Spinoza.

First, both conceived bodies to be distinct from the space they occupy. Bodies are *in* space. They move *through* space, from one place to another, maintaining their identity as they do. This follows from the assumption that bodies have a substantial being of their own, which they maintain at rest and in motion, whether this be conceived as movement through an empty void or a plenum packed with bodies.

Second, both Descartes and Newton agreed that bodies have no natural tendency to be either in motion or at rest. Whichever state it is in, they said, a body will persevere in that state, unless and until it is affected in some fashion by an *other* body. If bodies have any tendency of their own, it is the merely negative one of persisting in whatever state of motion or rest they happen to be in at the moment. All change from that state (from motion to rest, rest to motion, or, in the case of acceleration, from one state of motion to another) must therefore be explained by a cause *outside* the changing body—by a "force," external to the body, that explains why it has changed from its previous state to a different one. This is what came to be known, somewhat misleadingly, as the principle of "inertia."[12]

Spinoza's metaphysics entails a view of the material world that differs from that of Descartes and Newton precisely with respect to these two basic points. For Spinoza, bodies are not and cannot be independent of the space they "fill." They also necessarily possess a positive internal force that, in additional to those pressing on them from without, directs them toward a particular end or goal.

Let us consider these two differences in turn.

In Spinoza's metaphysics, there is only one substance. It may be accounted for under different explanatory schemes, but in each case is identical to the world as a whole. Nothing exists outside it, nor can—least of all, a God apart from the world of the sort that Descartes and Newton assume.

When it is conceived under the attribute of extension, this one, undivided, all-inclusive and everlasting substance appears as an extended space or field. An infinite number of bodies occupy positions within it. These cannot, however, be substances in their own right (as they are for Descartes and Newton), since that would offend the principle that, conceived under any attribute, substance is necessarily both boundless and one.

There is only one other metaphysical option. That is to understand the relation between a body and the space it fills in modal terms. Viewed in this way, a body is nothing but a modification of space. It is not distinct from the space it occupies, but just the way that space is modified, "here" rather than "there"—place terms that have no meaning apart from the modifications that define them, and which therefore cannot be understood, as they are in classical physics, as points on an abstract grid that organizes the layout of space prior to, and independently of, the bodies that fill it.[13]

Conceived in these terms, the relation of a body to the space it occupies is like that of a blush to the face it reddens. The latter relation is "adjectival," and so too, on Spinoza's view, is that of bodies to the space they "qualify." This is hard for us to grasp, given our tendency to think of bodies as having a substantial existence of their own—a habit that Cartesian and Newtonian physics strongly reinforce. But to be consistent with the most basic principles of Spinoza's metaphysics, any attempt to account for motion and change, and the other phenomena that a science of nature seeks to explain, must start from the unnatural-seeming premise that bodies are not *in* space at all, but constitute its infinitely diverse modifications instead, like those of a face (Spinoza calls it the "face of the whole universe"[14]) that is blushing here, wrinkled there, and so on.

In a Spinozistic physics, then, what can be meant by saying that a body has "moved" from one place to another? If bodies are substantive things, their movement is easy to picture and explain. But if a body is just the way that space is organized at a particular point, then the movement of a body "in" space has to be visualized as a successive series of restructurings of adjacent "patches" of space, each assuming, for an instant, the modal organization that constitutes the body in question, then relinquishing it, and reassuming the shape it had before.

This is an awkwardly abstract way of describing something as apparently simple as the movement of a body in space. But if we think again of a blushing face, it is perhaps not such a bad description after all. The movement of a blush from throat to cheek is nothing but a series of qualitative changes in neighboring bits of skin, as each in sequence turns from white to red and back to white again. A wave passing across the surface of the sea is another example. Each "bit" of water across which the wave is moving is momentarily re-formed by it, and then, when the wave has passed, resumes its previous, "quiescent" state. If the hardest body in the world is not a substance in its own right, distinct from the space it fills, but merely a mode of space itself, then its movement too must be conceived on the model of that of a blush or wave, substituting for the face and water through which these move, the extended universe as a whole.

In addition to the difficulties it raises regarding their movement, Spinoza's modal conception of bodies presents an even more basic question. What can it mean, on his view, to say that this body is one, and that another—that they are two distinct bodies with separate identities of their own? Again, on the conventional view that bodies are substances in their own right, the question seems more tractable. But if every body in the world is merely a mode of one extended substance, it is harder to see what might account for their individual distinctness. The explanation that Spinoza offers in the physical digression is suggestive, but obscure, and underscores a second fundamental difference between his physics and that of his Christian contemporaries. In this case the difference has to do with their contrasting understanding of the meaning of the concept of inertia.

According to Spinoza, every body is constituted by a certain "ratio" of motion and rest. He calls this rule or law an "immediate infinite" mode of extension. What he means is that the truth of this law follows *directly* from the concept of extension itself, unlike other, equally universal but "mediate" laws, whose derivation requires additional concepts or rules. (Descartes' laws governing the collision of bodies are an example.)

Spinoza does not define "ratio" and it is unclear what he means by it. We almost certainly should not interpret it in a strictly numerical sense, for if we do, it is difficult to explain how a body can remain the same during a period of acceleration. So perhaps it is best to define the idea more loosely, as an "ordered pattern" of motion and rest that in some but not all cases may be expressed in numerical terms.[15]

In this general sense, a body is a (relatively) stable arrangement of movings and restings, no finite body ever being wholly one or the other. Most important, a body does not merely *have* such an arrangement. It *is* one, so that when a body's ratio of motion and rest changes, *it* changes in a fundamental way. It undergoes what Aristotle calls a "substantial" change (in Spinoza's metaphysics, a modal change), in contrast to other sorts of alteration (of place, for example, or the kind involved in growth) that are compatible with the maintenance of a (relatively) constant ratio of motion and rest.

Among these ratios or patterns Spinoza distinguishes two basically different kinds—the homogeneous and the heterogeneous. Patterns, and therefore bodies, of the first kind are uniform throughout. Spinoza calls such bodies the "simplest" ones, not on account of their size (as atomic theories do) but because of the homogeneity of their constitutive patterns of motion and rest.

Bodies of the second kind resemble complex quilts. They have an overall pattern made up of different patterns, each of which constitutes an identifiable part of the body in question. Indeed, such parts themselves are often constituted by a heterogeneous "pattern of patterns," down to the level of the simplest bodies, which though finite and hence destructible, are uniformly patterned and therefore have no parts. Moving up this chain of increasing complexity, we come to bodies whose patterns incorporate ever greater degrees of heterogeneity, until we arrive at the whole of reality, which Spinoza regards as an individual too, but an infinitely complex one whose own eternal pattern of motion and rest incorporates all the transient ones that constitute the individual modifications—the "separate" bodies—of nature or God conceived under the attribute of extension.

On this view, the parts of a cell—its mitochondria, for example—are bodies. So are cells, and organs, and organisms, and even organized groups of organisms, such as hives or packs. Each of these has its own pattern of motion and rest and therefore counts as an individual body. The same is true of atomic nuclei, of atoms, of molecules and the materials formed of them. Every one of these has an individual identity too, though its individuality is also an element within that of some more complex body. The concept of individuality thus does not belong exclusively to any one of these levels. A cell is as much an individual as a human being, a molecule of water as the hydrogen and oxygen atoms of which it is composed.

Is there anything, then, in Spinoza's view, that distinguishes one body from another, and makes it the individual it is, apart from the relative complexity of its pattern of motion and rest? Spinoza's answer is important because it underscores the heterodox nature of his understanding of the principle of inertia.

According to Spinoza, every body not only exhibits a more or less complex pattern of motion and rest. It also "strives" to "persevere" in the pattern in question. This striving is the deepest source of its individuality. It is what makes it the individual it is. Spinoza's assumption of the universal existence of such a drive, to which he gives the Latin name *conatus,* requires a fundamental revision in the strictly externalist account of the movement of bodies that both Descartes and Newton present.

In some cases, greater complexity goes hand in hand with greater perseverance. Consider, for example, a multicelled organism. Not only is its body constituted by a more complex pattern of motion and rest than that of its individual cells; the organism's pattern is more resilient too. When a cell loses its pattern, it ceases to exist. But the organism to which it belongs survives, for a time at least, despite the loss of its cells, which are constantly "dying" and being replaced by new ones. Its distinctive pattern persists through these replacements. Indeed, the organism might be said to *be* the pattern of this persistence itself. In a similar way, the ocean survives the destruction and reconstitution of numberless individual molecules of water every day. This reaches a limit in the case of the universe as a whole, whose infinite complexity perseveres forever.

To be sure, greater complexity is not always accompanied by an increase in durability. There are chemical compounds which, though more complex than the ingredients of which they are composed, are more volatile too, and quickly disintegrate into their stabler parts. But even in these cases, there is something that binds the elements of the compound together, however briefly. Wherever this binding force is present, we are justified in saying that what is held together by it are the parts of a higher-order whole with an individual identity of its own. The weaker this force becomes, the less the "parts" in question may be considered the parts of anything at all. The more they must be viewed as mere items in a "heap."

Thus, while everyone would concede that the rocks in a pile are individual bodies, the pile itself is one only in an attenuated sense. The pile looks more like a heap. That is because a pile of rocks, though it has a pattern of sorts, is less able to persevere in it than the rocks are in their own. Atoms, molecules, organisms, forests, weather formations and galaxies all possess an obvious and measurable power of this kind. If one objects that even a pile of rocks has such a power—just one too weak for us to detect—that only means that the pile ought to be regarded as an individual too, though one with a *lesser degree* of individuality. Metaphysically speaking, the important point is that the individuality of *every* body, however simple or complex, stable or short-lived, is defined by the presence of a power of variable strength to maintain *some* pattern of motion and rest against the external forces that threaten to disrupt it and always eventually do.

Spinoza calls this power *conatus*. The best English translation is "endeavor," the word that Thomas Hobbes uses to describe the phenomenon of mental and physical striving.[16] Spinoza may have borrowed the term from Hobbes, but gives it a more metaphysical interpretation. For Spinoza, the endeavor of a body to maintain its ratio of motion and rest constitutes its very being. (The same is true of minds, as we shall see in chapter 30.) *Conatus* therefore cannot be a force impinging on bodies from without. If it were, it could not play the role that Spinoza assigns it as a *principium individuationis*. It must be an internal force instead—one that preserves, from within, the integrity of the body that possesses it, against the unremitting assault of external forces to which every body in the world is exposed. In this respect, Spinoza's concept of *conatus* differs fundamentally from the Cartesian and Newtonian idea of inertia.

"Inertia" is often described as a "tendency" that bodies "have," namely, to remain in whatever condition they are in until acted upon by outside forces. But this is misleading, for what the principle of inertia really means is that bodies *have no* tendencies of their own at all—none that incline them, by themselves, in one direction or another.

According to both Descartes and Newton, each of the forces that act upon a body has a distinctive vector of its own. It comes from a particular direction, and causes the body it affects to move one way rather than another (by colliding with it, exerting a gravitational "pull" upon it, etc.). The direction the body takes as a result is the sum of the vectors of these external forces. Inertia is not a separate vector in this sense, to be added to that of other forces. To say that a body acts "inertially" is equivalent to saying that the *only* forces that explain its movements are ones that originate outside it. Understood in these terms, inertia is not a force in its own right but a condition of unresisting accommodation to others.

The central place of the principle of inertia in the new mechanical physics of the seventeenth century reflects the thoroughness with which Descartes, Newton and others sought to expel from the physical world every last vestige of the belief that natural bodies, as distinct from artificial ones, possess a built-in tendency to move in a certain direction, unless impeded by external forces. This had been the fundamental premise of Aristotle's science of nature. Their new physics rejects the notion completely. Spinoza's highly unconventional account of the physical world revives it in a modified form.

For Spinoza, every finite body consists in a more or less complex pattern of motion and rest. When this pattern is destroyed, the body ceases to exist. It becomes something else, another body or bodies. For a finite body, retaining its pattern and losing it thus represents the difference between being and not being. But no finite body is "indifferent" between these two states. Every body of this sort is "prejudiced" in favor of being. It endeavors to be for as long as it can—to come as close as it is able to the condition of the one infinite and everlasting body, that of the world as a whole.

This "striving to be"—what Aristotle calls *phusis* and Spinoza *conatus*—is a kind of ontological glue. It is the force that holds bodies together, and makes them, for a time, the individuals they are, in the presence of all the other forces that continually batter them from without. In this sense, it is a positive and directed striving, and hence a vectorial force in its own right, that must be included in the full array of such forces, both internal and external, that are needed to explain, in causal terms, the behavior of bodies under the attribute of extension.

Like *phusis, conatus* is thus a positive inclination in favor of being. It is the internal drive toward reality that for Aristotle is the hallmark of every natural thing. Descartes and Newton had nothing but scorn for this idea, and Spinoza's acceptance of it, in however modified a form, was bound to seem, by seventeenth-century standards, a step back toward a more primitive, magical view of the world—one that had already, in his own time, become a historical curiosity.

But the charge that Spinoza's idea of *conatus* marks a return to an older, discredited view of the natural world is mistaken. It ignores a basic difference between Spinoza's interpretation of the striving to be and the one that Aristotle gives it. We shall explore this difference in more detail in the chapters that follow. But a few preliminary words of explanation may be helpful.

For Spinoza, the striving to be is interminable. No finite being can ever reach the goal it seeks, since every conceivable increase in its power still leaves it exposed to more powerful external forces of one kind or another. This is clear to us from our own experience. But all finite beings are in essentially the same condition.

In Aristotle's view, by contrast, there is a natural coincidence between striving and goal. Nothing, including man, strives for what it cannot reach. This distinguishes *conatus* from *phusis* in a crucial respect. The distinction is due to the difference between the Aristotelian and Spinozist conceptions of God—more specifically, to the influence on Spinoza's conception of the doctrine of divine creation, which prepares the way for his view that the world is infinitely intelligible and therefore real. This opens a gulf between Spinoza's and Aristotle's interpretations of the striving to be, and converts it from a finite to an infinite endeavor. Any suggestion that Spinoza's idea of *conatus* represents a straightforward revival of Aristotelian thinking is to that extent fundamentally wrong.

The result, however, is not to bring Spinoza's physics back into closer alignment with seventeenth-century science. Together with his modal interpretation of the relation of bodies to space, Spinoza's resurrection of the ancient belief that all things are moved by the desire to be and his identification of this desire with individuality as such, as distinct from the general forms of things, had the effect of widening the gap between his understanding of bodily motion and the soulless physics that came to dominate our understanding of the natural world.

Yet unorthodox as it was by contemporary standards, Spinoza's view of the nature of physical reality, and the metaphysics on which it is based, may in fact be better equipped than Newton's to withstand the revolutionary developments that in the past hundred years have relegated Newtonian physics itself to the status of a special case, yielding reliably good results within certain parameters of size and speed, but presenting an essentially false picture of the world.

What are the grounds for believing this to be true?

RELATIVITY, QUANTUM MECHANICS AND QUARKS

Any answer must be speculative. Spinoza's own physics is too sketchy, and developments in the discipline since too complex, to allow for more. Moreover, the strongest grounds for an affirmative answer lie not in the details of Spinoza's account of the physical world, but in his unswerving commitment to the principle of sufficient reason. Still, it is worth considering a few of the ways in which Spinoza's view of material reality seems to fit better with certain of the most striking, and conceptually challenging, ideas of modern physics, than the Newtonian picture of the world, which these same ideas have reduced to the status of a useful illusion.

I will mention three. The first is the theory of general relativity.

Einstein's theory of special relativity (1905) upends the Newtonian conception of absolute space and time. In order to preserve the constancy of the speed of light, and with that the validity of the laws of electromagnetism across inertial frameworks whose point of origin is defined by objects in motion relative to one another, Einstein found it necessary to "relativize" time and space to these frameworks themselves. As a result, time and space could no longer be conceived in Newtonian terms, as absolutely fixed frames encompassing all conceivable motions and providing a uniform benchmark by which to measure their distance and duration (which the "additive" approach that Galileo had taken to the measurement of relative motion also implicitly assumed). Nor could space and time still be thought of as magnitudes or dimensions independent of one another. In the theory of special relativity, these become functionally interdependent. The length, for example, that one observer assigns to an object—a bar of steel, say—as compared to the length assigned to it by another moving relative to him, must differ according to the meaning of simultaneity in their two inertial frames. Length (a spatial concept) thus has no meaning apart from simultaneity (a temporal one). In Einstein's special theory of relativity, space and time are therefore not only relativized but fused into a single concept, that of space-time.

These represent important adjustments to the Newtonian picture of the world. But the special theory of relativity remains faithful to this picture in two important respects. First, as Einstein never tired of pointing out in his popular writings on the subject, he found himself compelled to relativize space and time in order to save the uniformity of the most basic laws of nature. His reinterpretation of the meaning of Lorenz's famous equations was meant to secure the constancy of the laws of electrodynamics across all inertial frames. In this sense, Einstein was not a relativist but an absolutist. Second, though objects in steady, rectilinear motion relative to one another exist in different space-times, Newton's fundamental assumption that objects are *in* space remains unaffected by the special theory, as does the assumption that the space they are in has a shape well described by the principles of Euclidean geometry.

It is this last assumption in particular that the general theory of relativity (1915) compels us to abandon. Einstein's formulation of the general theory was motivated by his desire to extend the results of the special theory to the case of acceleration. This led him to the principle of equivalence, which identifies the effects of acceleration with those of gravity, to the identification of gravity with the structure of space, and to the analysis of this structure in non-Euclidean terms.

In the general theory, gravity becomes the shape of a region of space, and to the extent that an object *is* the attractive force it exerts on others, objects may be said to become such regions themselves. On this view, it is no longer correct to say that objects are *in* space. They are the space they occupy, or more exactly, modifications of it. But if an object is just the bending of space in a region, the metaphysical distinction between object and space, which Newton takes for granted, is no longer sustainable. The only metaphysics that makes sense of such a view is a modal one like Spinoza's. Of the two branches of Einstein's theory of relativity, the special and the general, the latter challenges the assumptions of Newtonian physics at a more fundamental level, and it is precisely here that Spinoza's physics, with its eccentric view of bodies as modes of substance, begins to look more attractive.

The same may be said about certain features of quantum mechanics.

Quantum mechanics differs from its Newtonian predecessor in a number of striking (and to those brought up on Newtonian physics, baffling) ways. One is its characterization of things as waves, and of waves as probability distributions. In Newton's world, every individual body occupies a determinate place. It is somewhere or other, and when we inquire as to its whereabouts, we are looking to see where it is. No body, moreover, can be in two places at once; this follows from the determinateness of its location, which follows from its individual identity, as *this* body rather than *that* one.

Quantum mechanics upsets all these assumptions. In quantum mechanical terms, a body, strictly speaking, is not at a point in space, but is spread through the whole of space, though not with the same probability. On this view, it is wrong to say that a body is here, not there. What one should say instead is that it is here, with some probability, and there with some probability. When we look to see where it is, these probabilities are "converted to" an actuality. They "collapse" and become something definite—a body in a place. But before we fix the body's location with one measuring tool or another, it is, strictly speaking, everywhere, though not with the same probability.

This is counterintuitive, of course, and perhaps incomprehensible. But it begins to make some sense if we think of bodies not in terms of particle points, in the way that Newton did, but as waves instead. A wave is spread out in space. It can be at two places at once. Indeed, it can be at an infinite number of places at the same time. Physical waves are all, of course, in a medium or field of some sort—water, air, the electromagnetic field through which a current "pulses." If bodies are waves, one wonders, what is the medium in which they exist? The answer, from a quantum mechanical perspective, is probability itself, an abstract idea that is made somewhat more intuitive by the fact that a probability distribution can be mapped or represented by a wave, with a definite frequency and amplitude.

This is admittedly difficult to picture (some physicists say we should not even try), but one thing at least is clear. A quantum mechanical interpretation of the meaning of such simple statements as, "body B is at location x," cannot be reconciled with the Newtonian assumption that bodies have a substantive being of their own, independent of the space they occupy, for if that were true, no body, before it is observed, could with some probability be at every point in space, as quantum mechanics insists. It makes more sense, on this latter view, to think of individual bodies as adjectival (here, probabilistic) modifications of the whole of space, as waves or complex sets of waves whose patterns of "interference" we mistake for substances in their own right on account of our finite powers of observation. Once again, as in the case of Einstein's general theory of relativity, there is arguably a better fit between this aspect of quantum mechanics and Spinoza's modal metaphysics, than there is between quantum mechanics and Newton's "corpuscular" view of bodies in space.

A third example comes from the field of modern particle physics.

In Newton's world, bodies move or rest in absolute space and time. They are caused to do what they do by forces acting on them. These forces are of two sorts. The first is the kind that one body exerts on another when the two come into contact or collide. The possible results of such a collision are many, depending on the mass of the bodies, their relative speeds, the direction of the impact, and so on. The second is the attractive force of gravity. Every body exerts a gravitational "pull" on every other, though the pull in most cases is too weak to be detected. These two forces are different, of course. The first is "local," acting only by direct "touching," while the second acts "at a distance" (something that physicists have always found hard to explain). But both are external to the body on which they act. The body itself is "inert." It is entirely "at the whim" of the forces acting on it from without and exerts no positive counterforce of its own.

In the eighteenth century, this picture of the world was mathematically refined through the work of Lagrange and others. Then, in the nineteenth, it was modified in two important respects. First, a new force was added to those that Newton had identified. This was the electromagnetic force, which Faraday demonstrated to be a single force, and whose laws Maxwell described in his famous equations. Second, the revival of the ancient atomic theory of matter, and its subsequent refinement, led to a reconceptualization of the nature of the abstract mass points assumed by Newtonian physics. These were now to be thought of as atoms, the elementary units of material stuff of which all larger aggregations are formed, though these units themselves were soon "decomposed" into more elementary parts when even the simplest atoms were discovered to have an internal structure of their own—a discovery that touched off the search for ever more basic "particles" that by the second half of the twentieth century had produced an agreed-upon list that came to be known as the "standard model" of atomic physics.

Neither the discovery of electromagnetism, however, nor the triumph of atomism, by itself required a revision of the Newtonian principle of inertia, which along with the conception of bodies as substances rather than modes, remained a metaphysical premise of physical science. With the former, it is true, a crucial new idea was added to the repertoire of physics, namely, that of a field. The electromagnetic force is a wave passing through a field, defined on analogy to the physical media through which waves of sound and water pass. But this wavelike force is one that acts on bodies from without, just like gravity and the force that bodies communicate when they collide. In this respect, the supposition that one body is attracted to another if their electromagnetic charges are opposed but repelled if they are the same, left Newton's assumption that the motions of a body are wholly determined by forces external to it undisturbed.

Nor did atomism at first challenge this assumption. The atomic view of nature, which is as old as philosophic speculation, is essentially substantive. It conceives the elementary building blocks of the world, however small these may be, to be separate substances exerting a force on one another from the outside, like tiny billiard balls or planets. But just as the quantum mechanical description of these smallest units of bodily stuff as probability waves spread over a region of space challenges the view of them as substantial "things" and arguably supports a modal interpretation of their nature instead, the relentless decomposition of the atom puts pressure on the Newtonian principle of inertia and perhaps points in the direction of something like Spinoza's idea of *conatus*.

That is because the "breakup" of the atom into electrons, protons and neutrons, and then into the even smaller units called "quarks" (which themselves come in many different varieties), makes the question of what holds these units together increasingly urgent. If an atom is a tiny ensemble of quarks, why do they remain, even for an instant, in a pattern of some sort? Why do they persevere, however briefly, in an atomic form? Put in more old-fashioned terms, what gives an atom its identity?

This question has led physicists to postulate the existence of the so-called "strong" and "weak" nuclear forces, which unlike those acting on atoms from without, act from within to give and keep them in the "shape" that they possess. These internal forces are not quite Spinoza's *conatus,* for it is possible to view them as external to the most elementary substances of all, and therefore not constitutive of their own "quark-being." But those who accept the existence of these forces seem to be moving closer to the view that atoms and everything composed of them are patterns of motion and rest, held together by a weaker or stronger inclination to persevere in being, without which the very idea of an atom with even a temporary identity of its own is impossible to conceive.

This cohesive force, however strong, is never strong enough to withstand forever the forces that press on atoms from without and cause them to change their form from one pattern to another. But these external forces are insufficient by themselves to explain the behavior of atoms in the terms that modern particle physics requires. Something like Spinoza's *conatus* is needed too: an internal force with the power to preserve, for a time at least, the patterned relations among the elementary particles of which atoms are composed.

Even a hydrogen atom, the simplest in the periodic table, is constituted by a complex set of such relations, and though it can be "smashed" by external forces, something within the atom itself is required to explain how it is able to resist such smashing at all. The idea that every organized pattern of motion and rest—beginning with the simplest—has a built-in tendency to persevere in being thus seems a useful and perhaps necessary supplement to the Newtonian view that bodies are essentially inert. By assigning the strong and weak nuclear forces a role in accounting for the behavior of quarks, modern particle physics acknowledges the existence of such a tendency and weaves it into the organization of the physical world at its most elementary level.

"THE OLD ONE"

These are speculative judgments. It would be foolish to insist that Spinoza's ideas about the structure of the physical world are demonstrably superior to those of Descartes and Newton, when it comes to making metaphysical sense of relativity theory, quantum mechanics and particle physics. Spinoza's reflections are too sketchy and the conceptual challenges posed by modern physics too great to support a claim of this kind. All one can reasonably say is that the most distinctive features of Spinoza's short but suggestive discussion of the nature of extended substance offer some possible solutions to a few of the metaphysical difficulties posed by the twentieth-century revolution in physical science, while Newton's more careful and systematic analysis, with its view of bodies as inert substances occupying an absolute space separate from them, is the source of many of these difficulties instead.

There is, however, a much stronger basis for the claim that Spinoza's metaphysics better supports the aspirations of physicists today than the more familiar, and in many ways more intuitively plausible, metaphysics of the great scientist-philosophers of the seventeenth century. Modern physics rests on a commitment to the principle of sufficient reason. The doctrine of creation is incompatible with this commitment. Among the metaphysical systems that were constructed in the formative period of early modern science to provide a foundation for it, only Spinoza's removes the barrier this doctrine presents.

The new, mechanical physics of the seventeenth century was the product of a theologically inspired reaction against Aristotle's view of the natural world, and though it was ultimately imprisoned by the very theology that provoked it, the physics of Descartes and Newton represents a tremendous advance over its Aristotelian predecessor, from the standpoint of the principle of sufficient reason. Newton's unification of the laws of motion illustrates the point.

For Aristotle, the difference between the circular movement of the planets and stars, on the one hand, and the rectilinear motion of rain falling from the sky, on the other, is explained by a difference in the nature of these things themselves. The stars and planets move one way, and the sublunar elements another, because they have qualitatively different natures. All the motions in the cosmos thus divide into two heterogeneous groups, the terrestrial and the celestial. The explanation of this distinction comes to an end, in Aristotle's physics, with the difference in the nature of the beings that belong to these two realms. *That* they have the different natures they do is simply a brute fact about the world in which we live.

Newton's physics dissolves the distinction between celestial and terrestrial motion. An apple falling to the ground obeys the same laws as the moon circling in the sky, and the fact that their motions are different can be explained in terms of these cosmically uniform laws, without appealing to some inexplicable distinction in their natures.

Indeed, for Newton, the natures of the apple and the moon are the same, just like the laws that govern their motions. Both are bodies and nothing more. This is of course a more abstract way of thinking about them than the view that they possess qualitatively different natures. But it allows for a unified account of every motion in the universe as a whole, and thus permits us to dispense with the ultimately inexplicable fact that things in the sky just happen to have a different nature from those on earth. In this sense, Newton's physics depends on fewer brute facts than Aristotle's, and therefore offers a superior account of the world from the standpoint of the principle of sufficient reason.

In important respects, of course, Newtonian physics is also based on the acceptance of certain brute facts that we must simply accept. The most obvious of these is the fact that every body attracts every other. The assumption of a universal force of this kind enables us to explain the motions of all moving bodies with a single set of laws and to measure the magnitude of their movements with mathematical precision. But what is this force? And why does it exist? Newton declines to answer these questions.[17] The existence of the force we call "gravity" is a real but inexplicable feature of the world that God has created, and it is no more reasonable to inquire into the reasons for its existence than it is to ask why God created the world in the first place.

The divinely created framework of absolute space and time is another brute fact we must take for granted.

According to Newton, the presumed existence of a framework of this kind is required to make scientific sense of motion itself. He believed that to do this, we must be able to fix the position of every body in space and time "objectively," that is, in a manner all observers will agree is the correct one, whether they are moving relative to the body or not. Without an all-encompassing, uniform, nonrelative frame in which every body is placed, Newton thought, such agreement becomes impossible and the hopes for a rigorous science of nature fall to the ground.

But though it depends on the assumption of such a frame, Newtonian physics does not purport to explain its existence. Indeed, Newton denied that it can be explained. Absolute space is, in his celebrated phrase, the "sensorium" of God, a physical manifestation of God himself, and therefore, in the final analysis, as inexplicable as any other feature of the world that God has ordained in the exercise of his unfathomable power. The same is true of the "world clock" that measures all movements in time with perfect uniformity, without which there could be no such thing as an objective explanation of bodily motion. Like the other features of the world that make it comprehensible to us, this one too is an incomprehensible gift of the God who brought the world into being from nothing.

In these and other ways, Newton's physics remains dependent on brute facts that limit its explanatory power. All of these derive, in the end, from his acceptance of the dogma of creation, which raises an insurmountable barrier to the extension of reason beyond the point fixed by the *fiat* of God's ordained order. Newton succeeded in formulating a universal theory of motion that no longer relied on the unaccountable fact that different things have different natures. He was thereby able to explain what Aristotle had taken for granted. But his own creationist theology set a limit to the explanatory power of the new physics he constructed on the ruins of the old peripatetic system.

Newton's successors refined and extended his physics in three different ways: first, by supplementing his catalogue of basic forces with two new ones, those of electricity and magnetism, which they invoked to account for a range of previously unexplained phenomena; second, by carrying Newtonian mechanics beyond the world of visible bodies into the invisible realm of atoms; third, and most importantly, by seeking to preserve the explanatory power of this expanded version of Newtonian physics without reliance on the brute fact of absolute space and time, or a conception of gravity that treats it as an inscrutable force whose existence we must simply assume.

All of these developments, which culminate in Einstein's theory of relativity, extend the power of physics to account for the natural world. But each extension only strengthens the demand for an even deeper account. The more that physics explains, the less its practitioners are prepared to accept the inexplicability of what they cannot. In this way, reason feeds on itself. Each triumph becomes the occasion for a still more intensive campaign. As a result, the authority of the principle of sufficient reason steadily increases. And this in turn puts growing pressure on those who accept the principle to abandon Newton's theology in favor of one that honors its demands instead—as Einstein implicitly acknowledged when he said that his God was that of Spinoza and not the otherworldly creator on whom Newton relied.

Important steps along the way include: Lagrange's refinements of the calculus and rigorous restatement of the principles of Newtonian mechanics in precise mathematical terms (1788); Michael Faraday's experiments with electricity, which confirmed that electricity and magnetism are different aspects of a single force (1821); Maxwell's formulation of the laws of electromagnetism, which provided the basis for a unified understanding of electricity, magnetism and light as waves traveling through a common field at a single, constant speed (1865); and the same physicist's use of statistical methods to describe the movement of atoms in gases—too many and fast to be tracked one by one, unlike the visible objects on which Galileo and Newton had focused their attention, but still presumptively subject to Newton's universal laws of motion (1866).

Together, these developments brought the phenomena of nature within an increasingly comprehensive and rigorous scheme. They extended the reach of Newtonian physics. As a result of these refinements and syntheses, the neo-classical physics of the late nineteenth century was able to account for more of the natural world than had ever been possible before. Never, in the history of science, had the principle of sufficient reason had such wide application. Still, certain features of the world continued to be regarded as brute facts—the existence of absolute space and time; of corpuscular bodies (now conceived as atoms) within a single, all-encompassing frame; and of gravity defined as a universal but incomprehensible force. For someone like Maxwell, who was a deeply religious man and still thought in explicitly theological terms, these inexplicable "givens" were a consequence of the fact that the world has been brought into being by a transcendent God whose reasons we shall never be able to grasp. In this respect, Maxwell's physics remained tethered to the same God as Newton's, and confined within boundaries eternally fixed by his incomprehensible will.

By "relativizing" space and time, Einstein freed physics from the need to assume their existence in absolute form. In this respect, he made the laws of physics "background independent." Put differently, he brought space and time themselves *within* a framework of explanatory rationalism and made them part of what physics explains rather than what it assumes. This represented a significant extension of the range of the principle of sufficient reason beyond the limits fixed by the assumptions of classical physics.

In the general theory of relativity, Einstein extended the principle still farther by demonstrating that the laws of physics remain constant across the "space-times" of bodies that are accelerating (or rotating) relative to one another, thereby dispensing with the need to assume, as the special theory had done, the constancy of their relative motion; and by giving an account of gravity, which Einstein explains, first, in terms of its "equivalence" with acceleration, and second, as a modal property of space itself (its "shape," according to one or another of the non-Euclidean geometries that Einstein uses to expound the general theory).

In the general theory, gravity thus shifts its role from that of *explanans* to *explanandum*. Its existence ceases to be a fact that must be assumed to explain the behavior of bodies, but that cannot itself be explained. It is now one of the things for which physics is able to give an account. Even more important, the general theory is able to explain the apparent truth of the laws of Newtonian physics as a special case that holds when the speed of bodies accelerating relative to one another is relatively small. Within certain parameters, Newton's seemingly true laws turn out to be a good approximation of the really true ones established by the theory of relativity, which thereby grounds and explains the explanatory power of the Newtonian system in a way that Newton himself could not, given his view that the truth of the laws he had discovered is a brute fact about the world that God has made.

In each of these respects, Einstein's theory of relativity represents a powerful affirmation of the belief that everything is in principle explicable; that nothing lies beyond the power of reason to comprehend; and that only the finitude of our powers of understanding prevents us from ever exhausting the infinite intelligibility of the world. When, in what he called a "religious" mood, Einstein reflected on the grounds of this conviction, he confessed his belief in the only theology he deemed compatible with his own deep devotion to reason itself.

For Einstein, God (or the "old one," as he calls it) is just the inherent intelligibility of the world itself, unfathomably deep, yet yielding at every step to the human minds that continually probe it, in the search for a better account of the world than the one they already possess. The world has more reality than any theory of it can encompass. But from Einstein's point of view, this is equivalent to saying that the world is more intelligible than we will ever understand, though through the slow and patient work of science we are able, by degrees, to bring its intelligibility more fully to light. Indeed, these are the same. The reality of the world *is* its intelligibility, which is infinite, unlike the theories we devise to explain it, using concepts that are inevitably limited because they are necessarily abstract.

Descartes was right to think that science cannot do without some conception of the eternal and divine. Only this can ground its own explanatory aims. Without a theological foundation of some sort, these aims themselves remain inexplicable. But the doctrine of creation fixes a point beyond which it is inappropriate for scientists to inquire. It is therefore incompatible with the spirit of modern science, which refuses to recognize any principled limits of this kind. The only theology that *is* compatible with it, and able to provide a foundation for it, is Spinoza's hyperrational, born-again paganism, which in contrast to the theology that every physicist from Descartes to Maxwell embraced, equates God with the inherent and boundless intelligibility of the world itself.

Einstein understood this but chose to downplay the Spinozistic nature of his God, to avoid antagonizing those with more conventional religious beliefs. But there can be no doubt that in Einstein's view, the only God capable of supporting the rationalizing ambitions of modern physics is Spinoza's God, and the only attitude appropriate to a serious physicist, the combination of radical optimism and profound modesty that Spinoza defends in his letter to Henry Oldenburg in 1665. Einstein's theory of relativity, and his reflections on the nature of the immortal God of the world that anchors its truth, represent the high-water mark of Spinozism in twentieth-century physics.

Much has happened since, of course, to cast doubt on Einstein's conviction that the world is intelligible all the way down. To many physicists, that conviction now seems either dubious or naive—a piece of metaphysical confidence that can no longer be justified in light of more recent discoveries. These appear to put Spinozism itself in doubt, and make it harder to believe that Einstein's God is still the God of modern physics.

Two developments are of special importance in this regard. One concerns what some call "absolutely small" things—the subject of quantum mechanics. The other has to do with absolutely large ones—with our understanding of the universe as a whole, whose origin and destiny is the subject of cosmology. Developments in both fields seem to some to compel a retreat from Einstein's theology. Whether or not they do remains to be seen.

REASON IN RETREAT?

Einstein was famously worried about the troubling implications of quantum mechanics, for which he himself helped lay the foundation with his 1905 paper on the photoelectric effect.[18]

The quantum mechanical view of the nature and behavior of bodies at the subatomic level was first proposed by Max Planck in 1900 as an arbitrary stopgap to help explain certain experimental results that could not be accounted for in a more conventional way. Only later was it fully theorized, by Werner Heisenberg and Niels Bohr, and organized into a picture of the world at the most basic level of physical reality. The picture it presented was, and remains, deeply disturbing from the standpoint of Newtonian mechanics.

First, there is the idea that electrons, photons and the like (the elementary units of which the material world is composed) can only occupy discrete states, each representing a specific quantum of energy, but none of the states in between, and that in passing from one to the next they "jump" across the interval without ever actually occupying it *in transitu*. This contradicts the Newtonian assumption that bodily motion is always continuous. On a Newtonian view, for a body to get from one place to another, it must pass through all the points in between. Quantum mechanics denies this.

More fundamentally, it challenges the very idea of bodily reality that is presupposed by classical physics. Before it is measured or observed, a body, on a quantum mechanical view, is spread through a region of space. The probability of its being found, when observed, at one point rather than another is variable. It is not the same for every point in the region, but is distributed unevenly throughout it. This distribution can be represented as a wave, or "wave function"—a probability curve. When we look to see where in this probability space the body actually is, we find it to be at a particular point, in the same way that, when we flip a coin that has an even chance of landing on either side, we always find it to be on one side or the other. But before we "determine" its location, the body has none, or rather, it has them all, with varying degrees of probability.

This is disturbing enough. What makes it even more unsettling is a crucial difference between quantum mechanical probabilities, on the one hand, and those that govern coin tosses, on the other. The latter are designed to help us overcome our ignorance of the world. When a coin is flipped, its uneven distribution of mass, the angle of the flip, and the like, determine how it will land. But these factors are too complex to measure, toss by toss. So, as a second best, we settle for a probabilistic prediction of how, over many tosses, the coin is likely to land.

By contrast, the probabilistic distribution of bodies in space, on a quantum mechanical view of the world, is generally interpreted as a feature of the world itself, and not a way of expressing our ignorance about it. On this view, an electron *really is* everywhere in the relevant region, with some probability. It *is not* at a particular point, which our methods of measurement are simply too crude to determine. Conceived as a probability wave function, an electron thus resembles a physical wave which likewise occupies a whole region of space at once. Upon measurement, this probability becomes a reality. The electron's possible presence at many points becomes its actual presence at one. But the measurement of its location is not the observation of an antecedent state. It is the cause of the electron's conversion to a fixedness of place that did not exist before.

This conversion is not lawless. Quantum mechanics does not require that we abandon the belief that the world operates according to laws that can be formulated in a rigorous way. Nor does it challenge the idea that these laws express a system of causal relations among physical states.[19] What it *does* call into question is the assumption that every state of the world is fixed in advance, down to its smallest details, and that only our finitude prevents us from grasping the causal relations that produce it. At its very deepest level, on a quantum mechanical view, the world has a built-in indeterminacy that nothing can ever dispel. It is *constitutionally* indeterminate, and because of this the age-old hope that ever more exact methods of measurement will bring us closer and closer to an understanding of the antecedently fixed order of things must be abandoned once and for all. The best-known expression of this is Heisenberg's famous "uncertainty principle" which demonstrates why, on the view of reality proposed by quantum mechanics, greater precision of measurement in one direction necessarily entails the loss of precision in another, so that a comprehensive *and* precise account of the world is ruled out as a matter of principle.

Nor is this all. There is also the disturbing question of "entanglement." It was first suggested, more than seventy years ago, that the measurement of certain subatomic states (the direction of an electron's "spin," for example), which before being measured are indeterminate in the way that quantum mechanics presumes, might cause the same states of other particles that were originally associated with them but a few nanoseconds later have gone their own way, to assume, upon measurement, a reciprocal, determinate value of their own. This suggestion has since been experimentally confirmed. How the measurement of a probabilistic state can cause it to take on a determinacy it did not already possess is puzzling enough. How the determination of one such state can simultaneously cause the determination of another, at a distance from it, is even harder to comprehend. The claim that it does seems to offend the principle of "locality"—the assumption that one thing can have a causal effect on another only when the two are "in touch." To assume otherwise one must suppose that it is possible for one thing to act on another from which it is spatially distant, in no time at all. It was just this that made Newton's universal law of attraction so troubling to many, including Einstein, whose "spatialization" of gravity brought it into line with the principle of locality. The quantum mechanical idea of entanglement—which Einstein found incomprehensible for the same reason, and fought a sustained but ultimately unsuccessful battle to refute—raises the specter of instantaneous action at a distance in an equally disturbing way.

Quantum leaps across untraversed intervals of energy and space; the probabilistic nature of reality itself; the "spooky" (Einstein's word) entanglement of quantum states: these profoundly counterintuitive ideas are said by the champions of the new quantum mechanics to hold the key to understanding the nature of the world as its most fundamental level. From this point of view, the old Newtonian world becomes a parochial case, as it does in relativity theory—one whose laws hold only because the larger objects to which they apply are relatively unaffected by our measurement of them and thus appear to have a determinate reality that quantum mechanics teaches us their atomic components, and thus ultimately these objects themselves, do not truly possess. Within a restricted range, Newton's laws remain a good approximation of the truth. They work well enough in the world of sense experience. But if we want to understand the way the world really is, we must conceive it in the strange light of quantum mechanics, which unlike that of relativity theory, seems to compel us to accept a series of beliefs that are openly at war with the idea that the world remains rationally explicable however far down we go in an effort to grasp its constitutive order.

Over the past century, the quantum mechanical view of reality has been repeatedly confirmed by experiments of one kind or another. Whenever it has been possible to test the accuracy of its descriptions against those of Newtonian physics, the quantum mechanical view has prevailed. Even its most ardent defenders concede, of course, that quantum mechanics is more than a little baffling. What can it mean to say that a thing is everywhere before it is measured, and that its measurement causes its probability distribution to "collapse" to a determinate value? And what is meant by the claim that the measurement of one value not only causes it to become determinate, but simultaneously causes another, at a distance, to become so as well? These are mysterious ideas by anyone's lights. Still, they neither compromise the mathematics of quantum mechanics nor refute the experimental data that confirm it. The tight fit between the math and the data has been validated over and over again, despite the puzzling picture of the world that quantum mechanics forces upon us. Perhaps, some have said, we must simply learn to accept that the world is the way it is, though we cannot understand or explain why—a small price to pay, Richard Feynman maintained, for the increase in rigor and predictive power that quantum mechanics brings with it.[20]

In this sense, the mysteries of quantum mechanics constitute a new set of brute facts that explain much but cannot themselves be explained—ones we should perhaps not even aspire to explain. If that is so, then quantum mechanics entails something more than an acknowledgment of our inability to live up to the demands of the principle of sufficient reason. It amounts to a repudiation of the principle itself.

The principle of sufficient reason equates being with intelligibility. That is its metaphysical meaning. If quantum mechanics is interpreted as implying that the world is incomprehensible in its innermost being, then it represents a direct challenge to the metaphysics underlying the principle of sufficient reason itself. That is why Einstein fought it with such passion. His opposition to quantum mechanics was in essence a theological quarrel.

The same may be said of his initial reluctance to accept the discovery that the universe is expanding.

Today, all serious cosmologists agree that it is. But Einstein at first found the idea deeply disturbing. That the earth, and the solar system, and the galaxy to which it belongs are all moving were facts that Einstein was happy to accept. But the claim that the universe as a whole is expanding raised, in his mind, a far more troubling question—one that strikes at the very heart of physics itself.

If the universe is expanding (indeed, as many cosmologists now believe, at an accelerating rate), then it must have been smaller in the past than it is now. Following this process back in time, we eventually come to its beginning, before which there was no universe at all. This conclusion appears unavoidable if we assume that the observed expansion of the universe did not mysteriously start from some earlier "steady state," but has been a constant feature of the universe at every moment of its existence, like the laws of thermodynamics.

The expansion of the universe is intimately related to the second of these laws, which postulates that ordered states tend to become less ordered, so that if two states with differing degrees of organization are compared, we can confidently affirm that the more ordered precedes the less ordered in time. The essential asymmetry of time—the fact that it moves in one direction only—follows directly from the thermodynamical concept of entropy. Indeed, the law of entropy is just another way of expressing the unidirectional nature of time. The expansion of the universe—its movement from a more highly ordered "before" to a less ordered "now"—may therefore be thought of as time itself. If this process had a beginning, and tends toward a state of perfect entropy (of maximum disorder) that cannot be reversed, then it seems to follow that like everything *in* time, time as a whole is a transient phenomenon that begins, continues for a while, and eventually comes to an end.

A physicist naturally wants an explanation of this process. To explain something, one must identify its cause. This means relating it to an antecedent state of some sort, in accordance with a law. But if that is so, then it might appear that there can be no explanation of time, and hence of the existence of the universe, since there is nothing antecedent to them that might serve as their causal ground. The notion of antecedence implies a relation in time—the very thing to be explained—and every causal explanation presupposes the existence of laws governing this relation, which by assumption cannot exist before time itself does.

Creationists have always had a way of dealing with this difficulty. "Before" the world and time there was God, worldless and timeless. A creator outside the world and time is the source or ground of both. He brings them into being from nothing, out of the self-sufficiency of his own eternal nature. This was Augustine's solution to the problem of the origin of time.[21]

Einstein viewed creationist explanations of this sort as superstitious nonsense. He did not consider them explanations at all, but an abandonment of the effort to find one. Still, the creationist account of the existence of time has one feature that Einstein strongly approved. He agreed that time must be grounded in eternity if it is ever to be explained in a scientifically adequate way.

Things and events in the world can be explained only in causal, hence temporal terms. But if time itself is inexplicable, then every explanation that science offers is merely a way of holding the unintelligibility of the world at bay. Those who accept this conclusion are bound to view the whole of science as resting on a kind of quicksand, unless and until they can give an account of the nature of time.

Creationists do this by appealing to an eternal God who brings the world into being by an inscrutable act of will. But if one rejects creationism as a defection from the ambitions of science and a repression of man's boundless desire to know, only one metaphysical option remains. That is to place the eternal ground of time in the world itself and not outside it.

This is why Einstein fought so hard to preserve the eternity of the world in the face of the discovery that it is expanding, through the introduction of a "cosmological constant" he later conceded to be an arbitrary device. But though he gave up on this particular notion, and came to accept that the universe has grown larger with time, he continued to believe that in order to understand and explain this process we must assume the existence of an eternal lawfulness that is intrinsic to the world and constitutes its very nature or being. The only alternative, as Einstein saw it, is a creationist theology that dissolves the metaphysical identity of nature and God on which the indefeasible rationalism of modern physics depends.

In different ways, then, and from different directions, both quantum mechanics and modern astrophysics put pressure on the principle of sufficient reason and the Spinozist theology that supports it.

The path of modern physics from Newton to Einstein reflects a growing confidence in the power of reason to explain the natural world within the framework of an ever more unified set of laws whose own background conditions are increasingly subject to explanation themselves. Quantum mechanics challenges this confidence by forcing us to accept a view of the world for whose most elementary features we can no longer account. It enables us to better explain phenomena explicable only in an incomplete and faulty way within the framework of classical physics, beginning with the effects of "black box" radiation that prompted Planck to introduce his constant as an ad hoc device. But this increase in explanatory power is conditioned on an acceptance of the inexplicable nature of quantum behavior itself—of the collapse of probability waves when measured or observed, entanglement at a distance, and the like. That we must give up the effort to explain these in order to construct a physics that is able to account for so much else has seemed to many an acceptable bargain, especially in light of the experimentally demonstrated superiority of quantum mechanics' highly refined calculations. But from the standpoint of the principle of sufficient reason, any compromise of this sort looks like a defeat, and to that extent a retreat from the boundless rationalism of Einstein's theology.

A cosmology founded on the assumption that the universe is expanding from a point in time and space that even our most ambitious theories can never quite reach represents a compromise of a similar kind. So much more can be explained on this assumption. Yet once the eternality of the universe is renounced, its existence as a whole becomes a brute fact we cannot explain. We may be able to push our understanding of the universe farther and farther back, to within a few nanoseconds of its beginning, but beyond this point no human science can see, not because our powers of insight are limited, but because once the origin of the universe is conceived as a coming into being from nothing, it becomes as incomprehensible *in principle* as the act of divine creation to which orthodox Christians sometimes compare it.

A cosmology of this kind forces us to accept that there are limits to our knowledge that arise on account of the nature of reality itself, as opposed to the finitude of our capacity to explain it. Like quantum mechanics, it demands a "sacrifice of the intellect" by compelling us to concede that the world by its very nature puts certain matters beyond the scope of all possible understanding. This conflicts with the belief that the world is infinitely intelligible. From a Spinozist perspective, this is the fundamental premise of scientific inquiry, which goes slack once certain features of the world are declared to be permanently off-limits to rational explanation. Because he shared this view, Einstein fought against the implications of modern cosmology, which threaten to make the existence of the world an inexplicable fact, as strenuously as he did against the foundational ideas of quantum mechanics, whose unintelligibility many of his contemporaries embraced with a gleeful enthusiasm that Einstein saw as a stumbling block to the rationalist aspirations of physics itself.

Einstein lost both campaigns. Since the publication of the theory of general relativity in 1915, theoretical physics has been dominated by three developments: the consolidation and refinement of the new quantum mechanics; the detailed mapping of the world of subatomic particles; and the rise to a position of undisputed authority of the "expansionary" cosmology first put on solid empirical ground by Edwin Hubble's observations in the late 1920s. These are the product of novel discoveries and breathtaking progress in the mathematical and experimental techniques of physical science. Yet in the same period the entire enterprise of physics has come increasingly to rest on a picture of the world that appears to guarantee the frustration of reason's ambition to grasp the true order of things, in contrast to its Newtonian predecessor, which was perfectly adapted to reward this ambition within the unsurpassable limits set by the theology of divine creation.

The tremendous advances of twentieth-century physics have thus demanded as their price a retreat from the high-water mark of explanatory rationalism represented by Einstein's theory of relativity, which brought to a close the epoch that Newton had opened and whose long prehistory reaches back to the Condemnation of 1277. If Spinoza's metaphysics is the one best suited to the hyperrationalism of a physics that assumes there is nothing in the world that is inherently inexplicable, then the rise of quantum mechanics and the acceptance of a cosmology that drains the universe of its eternal necessity seem to carry us away from Spinozism, toward some other metaphysics more accepting of mystery, contingency and freedom.

In recent years, however, the tide has begun to turn back. In certain respects, contemporary physics reflects a more Spinozistic view of the world.
But this is unsurprising because the acceptance of mystery, contingency and
freedom is ultimately incompatible with the enterprise of science itself, which
ceases to be what it is once the principle of sufficient reason is abandoned.

Physics today is in an unsettled state. Still, it has a distinctive spirit or
mood. This is best exemplified by the exotic new theories that are currently
being given serious consideration by many in the field—string theory, loop
quantum gravity and the like. The proponents of these theories differ among
themselves. But they share a common ambition, for all seek, in one way or
another, to *explain* features of the world that quantum mechanics and modern astrophysics place beyond the explanatory reach of physical science.

Each of these diverse and competing lines of thought attempts to account
for some aspect of the world whose unaccountability has been a premise of
the most advanced and enlightening work in physics for most of the past
century. In this sense, each is characterized by a more radical commitment
to the principle of sufficient reason than has been in favor in physics for some
time now—in a word, by the spirit of Einstein, whose own aspirations seemed
to many physicists hopelessly outdated just forty years ago. This is the real
meaning of the ferment in physics today.

I am not competent to judge the relative strengths of these competing theories, or their prospects for success. These are questions on which even the
best-trained physicists disagree. Some are especially enthusiastic. They see
great hope in one particular approach, or in the combination of several. Others
are more doubtful. They warn against the dangers of speculative theorizing
unmoored from empirically testable claims. It may be some time before a new
consensus develops around a particular view—one of the alternative versions
of string theory, perhaps—or around the conclusion that none of the competitors presently in the field is likely to carry the day. These disagreements
and uncertainties are significant. But they are of secondary importance. The
most striking fact about the discipline of physics today is the growing conviction among many in the field that the status quo will no longer do—that
the accepted versions of quantum mechanics and astrophysics leave too many
fundamental questions unanswered, and that the most pressing task of this
and the next generation is to answer them.

Physicists can no longer accept being told that elementary particles
behave in the probabilistic way that quantum mechanics predicts—don't
ask why! They cannot accept that decoherence and entanglement are real

phenomena—don't ask what explains them! They cannot take the existence of a primal "inflaton field" from which our universe grew in the first few seconds of "life" as an agreed-upon fact—don't ask how such a field could have come into being in the first place, and the arrow of time shot on its way! They cannot simply acknowledge the existence of "singularities" (of "black holes" and "big bangs") where the standard laws of physics all fail—don't ask how such things are possible or what revisions of these laws they entail!

Each of these "don't asks" has become intolerable. Together, they are the provocation to that luxuriant flowering of speculative proposals that reflects the hyperrationalist spirit of physics today. Many, perhaps all, of these will fail. They may all prove to be internally incoherent, or mathematically intractable, or incapable of empirical disconfirmation. But nothing is going to deter those who are looking for a grand synthesis of quantum mechanics, astrophysics and general relativity theory that is capable of solving the puzzles these present in isolation. The physicists of the twenty-first century have inherited these puzzles from their predecessors in the last, and no amount of frustration or disappointment will bring their search for answers to an end. That is because it is driven by the belief that physics is the most demanding of all the natural sciences and *just for this reason* is the one least able to accept the existence of brute facts, except as a temporary resting place from which to launch a more aggressive inquiry into the reasons for them.

Today, there is no other way forward in physics, however long it takes to find it. If "business as usual" means accepting the mysteries of quantum behavior and the unidirectionality of time, and proceeding from there, then the business of physics is no longer usual. Disagreements about how best to explain these mysteries are abundant and deep. But the demand for an explanation is deeper still. At the very deepest level, it represents a renaissance of the spirit of radical rationalism that quantum mechanics and modern astrophysics have appeared, for a time at least, to stymie. In the long run, the period that begins with Planck's constant and ends with the renewed search for a unifying theory of the sort that Einstein sought but failed to find is likely to seem a kind of intermission, marked by a temporary weakening of the principle of sufficient reason that has been the defining characteristic of physics since Newton, and followed by an even stronger commitment to it.

To declare, as quantum mechanics does, that there are certain inexplicable facts we must simply accept is an offense to the spirit of science. Creationism is an older and more familiar offense of this kind. The only assumption a scientist is permitted to make, if she honors the aims of her calling, is that everything eventually yields to mind, though an unexplained residue always remains. And the only metaphysics that supports this assumption is one that equates the whole of reality, including all that seems most fleeting in it, with intelligibility itself, for as soon as we allow even the least discrepancy between these, the possibility arises that the world may be incompletely understood not on account of the limitations of our powers of cognition but because (as Aristotle thought) there is an element of ineliminable mindlessness in the constitution of the world itself. The belief that there is makes the scientist's optimism more foolish than inspiring. There is no room for this belief in science, and if one says, "Well, yes, but surely there is room for it outside of science," that is not a conciliatory proposal to which any scientist can agree. For from a scientific point of view, there is no "outside" of this sort. There is nothing that lies beyond the power of science to explain, hence nothing that could possibly contradict the equation of being with intelligibility on which the limitless optimism of science is based.

This is a Spinozist—or, if one prefers, Einsteinian—way of thinking. No other is compatible with the aspirations of science itself. The excitement and confusion of physics today is an expression of these aspirations, which may be cabined or suppressed for a time, but always revive, on a grander scale, after every period of dormancy and despair, demanding answers to questions that have been deemed unanswerable by those who went before. And when this happens, the clearer it must eventually be to the men and women making these demands that the only picture of the world that fits their aspirations is the one that Spinoza presents in the *Ethics*.

The *Ethics* is not a widely read book. Its language is forbidding and obscure. It has very little to say about physics as such. But its theology provides the best foundation for our conviction that man's endless attempt to comprehend the world under what Spinoza calls the "attribute" of "extension" is something more than a fool's errand. Many Christian readers, then and since, have been appalled by Spinoza's theology. But Einstein grasped its necessary connection to the aims of modern science, and physics today tends, on the whole, to confirm it.

CHAPTER 29

"Endless Forms Most Beautiful"

DARWIN'S DIVINE BIOLOGY

In the seventeenth century, Aristotle's closed world became an infinite universe of absolute space and time in which the motion of inert bodies with no natural place could be measured with mathematical precision. But Newton's universe remained tied to the doctrine of creation that had prepared the way for it. Its order can only be explained, Newton claimed, by reference to the mind of the God who made it. In the end, though, this is no explanation at all since we are forbidden even to try to grasp the purpose of God's plan. Beyond a certain point, the doctrine of creation blocks the explanatory progress of modern science. To honor the second, the first must be abandoned. Neither Descartes nor Newton, nor even Leibniz, had the nerve to do this. Only Spinoza understood that it cannot be avoided.

The war between creationism and science continues to this day. Three and a half centuries after the manuscript of Spinoza's *Ethics* had to be smuggled to a publisher in Amsterdam to avoid religious censorship, some still maintain that modern science not only leaves room for Newton's God but cannot do without him. There are cosmologists, for example, who insist that the expansion of the universe only makes sense on the assumption that God brought the world and time into being from nothing. But the discipline in which the conflict between the rationalizing spirit of modern science and the theology of creation remains most intense is not physics or astrophysics. It is the field of biology, or more precisely, of evolutionary biology, which began its career as a separate science with the publication in 1859 of Darwin's epochal book, *On the Origin of Species.*

This conflict has spilled into the realm of politics and law, where the question of whether Darwinism is compatible with the doctrine of creation continues to be debated and litigated.[1] Many still believe that it is not, and few politicians have the courage to say otherwise.[2] For their part, the champions of evolution respond by attacking creationism with reciprocal zeal. A number are outspoken atheists, proud of their freedom from religious ideas of every kind and eager to persuade others to join the party of nonbelief.[3] But in their eagerness to beat back what they rightly judge to be the irrationality of Christian theology, Darwin's defenders overlook the possibility that their own view of life depends on another conception of the eternal and divine.

On the Origin of Species is a relentlessly anticreationist work. With unflagging energy and a wealth of supporting detail, Darwin attacks the appeal to divine creation on nearly every page of his book. He emphatically rejects it as an explanation of any aspect of what he calls the "entangled bank" of life.[4] At the same time, Darwin's biology is ferociously anti-Aristotelian. One of the chief results of the theory of natural selection is the dissolution of everything that Aristotle thought eternal in the world of living things. There is no more room in Darwin's theory of evolution for the God of Aristotle than for that of Abraham.

But it would be wrong to conclude that Darwinism is a godless science. Darwin's biology has a theology too. It is the one whose lineaments Spinoza sketches in the first part of the *Ethics,* though unlike Einstein, Darwin seems to have been unaware that he was following in Spinoza's footsteps.

Many are likely to challenge my claim that modern physics rests on Spinozist assumptions. But the suggestion of an essential link between Spinoza's theology and Darwin's biology is bound to seem even less plausible. Spinoza at least has something to say about physics, brief and obscure though it is. He says almost nothing about the phenomenon of life. In what sense, then, can Spinoza's *Ethics,* which has no biology, be said to supply the God presupposed by Darwin's—whose defenders generally locate the greatness of his theory of evolution in its ability to explain the world of living things without any theology at all? The proposition seems doubly dubious.

We must begin by putting the idea of life in a larger perspective.

LIFE

"Life" as such is not a separate category for Spinoza. The physical digression in part 2 of the *Ethics* deals with bodies in general. Living ones are not singled out for special treatment. As bodies, they are subject to the same laws as every other. In this respect, they are indistinguishable from those lifeless objects that seem, in our experience of them, so different from the plants and animals to which we ascribe the wonderful power of life. Did Spinoza then have no concept of life? The answer is that he did. Indeed, he had an exceptionally broad one. Like many other features of his philosophy, it combines ancient and modern ideas in a strikingly original fashion. To see how it does, we need to start by recalling Aristotle's views on the subject.

Aristotle lectured and wrote on a number of specifically biological topics. But in a broader sense, he took his general philosophical bearings from the phenomenon of life, whose characteristics shaped his understanding of reality as such.[5]

For Aristotle, the clearest example of a freestanding substance is a living organism. Its combination of form and matter, and growth from a state of potency to one of activity and power, provide the key to his understanding of the meaning of these concepts in general. In this respect, one might say that Aristotle was first and foremost a biologist, and that his metaphysics was biologically inspired, just as one might say that Plato was above all a mathematician, whose metaphysics takes its start from the phenomenon of geometrical proof, which brings to light with startling force the mind's power of abstraction from the world of sense and motion.[6]

Both Plato and Aristotle accepted the equation of form with intelligibility. This gives their philosophies a common intellectualist cast. But while for Plato the form that exemplifies every other in a paradigmatic way is that of the invisible triangle whose image we recognize in the figure drawn in the dirt, for Aristotle the form we need to keep in mind as we attempt to make sense of the concept of being is the emergent shape of a plant or animal as it grows to maturity and comes into possession of the powers that living things of its kind possess.

Aristotle did not, however, equate life with the whole of reality. He carefully circumscribed the domain of living things with a pair of basic distinctions. The first is that between artificial and natural beings. The second is the distinction between things with "souls" and those that lack them.

An artifact like a bed does nothing on its own (except decay). It "moves" from one state to another—from a pile of materials to a finished piece of furniture—only through a power external to it. By contrast, natural things, though they may at first be set in motion by something outside them, in the way that water is when evaporated by the sun, or a puppy when conceived by its parents, do move on their own account, toward the place where they belong—unlike a bed, which has no self-directed motion and no fixed position in the natural order.

Not every natural thing has a soul, however. A drop of water, for example, does not. Only those that in addition to possessing an internal source of motion preserve their integrity through a self-stabilizing interaction among their parts and with the environment as a whole may be said to have souls.

The most fundamental features of this interaction are metabolism and growth. Every living being possesses these two attributes. They distinguish it from a natural but inanimate heap or pool (of water, for example), whose unity is not the result of an active process of self-stabilization. Other, more complex powers (of sensation, perception and movement) are built up from these elementary ones but the latter mark, in the most basic way, the line that separates all that is alive in the natural world from everything that is not.

To see where Spinoza's conception of life resembles Aristotle's and where it differs from it, an intermediate step is required. We have first to contrast the Aristotelian view of life with that of Descartes. All the most basic features of Spinoza's philosophy are the result of his critical reflection on Descartes'. This is true of his understanding of life as well. Spinoza's idea of life is deeply anti-Cartesian. But the latter is just as deeply anti-Aristotelian. In rejecting Descartes' view of life, Spinoza is in an important sense returning to Aristotle's earlier one, though (as we shall see) in a radically altered form.

I say "Descartes' view of life," but that is misleading, for Descartes has no idea of life at all. Strictly speaking, the phenomenon of life disappears in Descartes' metaphysics. It ceases to have any independent reality of its own. For Descartes, the phenomenon of life is a mirage. Various things may appear to be alive, but their liveliness is explained by the laws of a mechanical science that account for the motions of living and lifeless bodies in exactly the same way—as a result of the pressure of external forces on extended substances that have no inherent drive or direction of their own. This idea is most vividly expressed in Descartes' famous description of animals as complex machines.[7] Many readers have been shocked by his description, but it follows directly from the creationist presuppositions of Descartes' philosophy as a whole.

For Descartes, God's creatures are substances of two different kinds. Some are minds or "thinking things" and others are bodies. God is of course a substance too—indeed, the only perfect one, since he alone fully satisfies the definition of a substance as a being with an independent existence of its own.

Clearly, God is a substance of the thinking kind. Bodily being implies limitations of dimension, place and the like that are incompatible with God's infinite reality. Hence, only those created substances that are minds resemble their creator, though because they are created, and in every case attached to a body, they lack God's independence and necessarily fall short of his perfection.

Man alone is a creature of this godlike sort. Only he has been created in God's image. Every other creature is just a body without a soul. That is because Descartes understands "soul" in Christian rather than Aristotelian terms— as a capacity for voluntary self-direction that resembles God's power of creation and since Augustine has been known as the "will."

Only men have souls in this sense. To be sure, every man also has a body, separate from his soul. This raises the difficult (Spinoza thought unanswerable) question of how two such fundamentally different sorts of substances can interact. But the important point, for present purposes, is not that Descartes' Christian metaphysics gives rise to a "mind-body" problem. It is that it squeezes life from the world.

On the one hand, God has created a limitless number of bodies without souls. These include plants and animals as well as bits of inanimate stuff. None of these bear any resemblance to God at all. That is because they all lack the power to freely (willfully) set a course for themselves. Only those beings that possess this power have any inner life at all. The apparently self-directed movement of plants and animals is therefore an illusion that must be explained in strictly external terms identical to those we use to account for the movement of one ball when it collides with another. Other than man, therefore, none of God's creatures can be said to be alive in Aristotle's sense.

But of course neither can man.

Conceived in strictly physical terms, as an extended substance, a man is no more alive than any other body. Like those complex machines we call horses and dogs, his own body is a lifeless puppet on a string. It is moved entirely from the outside, by other bodies and minds including that of God, who gives everything in the world the initial "push" it needs in order to move at all.

Yet conceived as a mind, or soul, a man is not alive either. That is because his soul is eternal. It is destined to survive the destruction of his body. This means that it is more real than his body, but not that it is alive, for nothing that is deathless is alive.

Thus, whether we regard man as a body or a soul, the concept of life has no application to him. Nor can the relation between these two substances (hard as it is to conceive) be viewed as some third thing that might be said to be alive. There is no "psychophysical" unity constituted by the interaction of body and soul that has, so to speak, "a life of its own." In Descartes' view, the principal vice of the old Aristotelian physics was precisely its assumption of the existence of such psychophysical beings. For science to advance, Descartes believed, this unity must be dissolved into separate bodies and souls, neither of which can be a bearer of life in Aristotle's sense. The price of the advance of science is therefore the elimination of life from the world.

For Aristotle, then, only some things are alive, though these have special importance because of what they reveal about the nature of being as such. For Descartes, nothing in the world is alive. This follows from his division of created substances into bodies and minds, and his interpretation of the latter as immortal souls with wills that resemble God's own. Spinoza's view, succinctly stated, is that everything is alive. The most basic axioms of his metaphysics compel this conclusion.

According to Spinoza, there is and can only be one substance. Everything else is a modification of it. Finite beings are therefore not separate substances in their own right, as they are for Descartes, but modes of the one and only genuinely freestanding thing there is.

It follows that the distinction between minds and bodies cannot be a real difference between two kinds of things whose substantive natures or "essences" set them apart. It is only a difference of "attribution" that arises as a result of our effort to explain any given mode within the framework of one of two distinct systems of laws that "conceive" the explanatory relations among modes in physical and hermeneutical terms, respectively. Every mode can be investigated from either point of view. When we say that a mode *is* a body or a mind, we are merely indicating which system of laws we are employing to explain it.

This dissolves the substantive difference between minds and bodies but raises the question of what makes any finite being distinct from any other. Spinoza's monistic view of substance presents this question in an especially challenging way that Descartes' belief in the existence of infinitely many created substances enables him to avoid.

Spinoza's answer is that the individuality of every mode is defined by its striving to persevere. This is what makes it the individual it is and not another, so that wherever such striving exists, we may properly speak of *a* body or mind, depending upon the explanatory framework within which its relation to other individuals is conceived. Among other things, this view allows for grades or degrees of individuality, depending upon the strength of the striving involved, and for the existence of higher-order individuals composed of lower-order ones, as in the case, for example, of bodies made of cells, and religious communities composed of believers.

At higher levels of strength and organization, the universal striving to persevere in being, which constitutes the individuality of every mode, whether conceived under the attribute of thought or extension, expresses itself in the processes of metabolism and growth that Aristotle identifies with living things alone. From a Spinozist perspective, however, these processes cannot be radically discontinuous phenomena that spring into being from nothing. They must be the outgrowth, literally, of more primitive versions of themselves. That is because this is the only way to explain them. Any other view requires us to assume a gap between living and "dead" bodies that can only be bridged by a miracle, and that is as great an offense to the principle of sufficient reason as the doctrine of creation itself.

In order to account for the phenomena of metabolism and growth, reason therefore compels us to view these as highly developed expressions of a drive that is already present in the world of seemingly lifeless things, whose individuality is defined by their own low-level striving to persevere.[8] Life merely brings this to light in a way that our limited powers of understanding permit us to grasp. In reality, it has to have been there from the start.

Every body must therefore be alive in the sense that it is actively fighting against the forces that threaten to destroy it, rather than waiting, inertly, to be moved about by external pushes and pulls. Eating, growth and reproduction are only the most visible manifestations of this universal striving in the world of extended reality (of substance conceived under the attribute of extension).

The same is true of minds. Their individuality is also constituted by their striving to persevere. At higher levels of complexity and power, they do this by means of mimesis, an intellectual process that promotes the growth and survival of ideas in the same way that metabolism promotes that of bodies.[9] And just as metabolism is prefigured by the less active forms of *conatus* that exist at lower levels of physical organization, the mimetic activities of complex minds such as ours must somehow be anticipated by the mental lives of stones and drops of water—a challenging, but impeccably Spinozist, conclusion.

Thus, if Spinoza has no biology, it is because his entire metaphysics is biological. Physics and psychology are for Spinoza separate disciplines only because each deals with the world under a self-contained explanatory rubric of one sort or another. By contrast, the striving to persevere, which manifests itself in the metabolic and mimetic actions of certain particularly powerful bodies and minds, is a characteristic of *all* finite beings, conceived under *either* scheme, every one of which may therefore be said to be alive in the deepest sense of the term.

From the standpoint of ordinary experience, of course, this is bound to seem implausible. The commonsensical position is Aristotle's—that some things are alive but others not. Neither the Cartesian view that nothing is alive, nor the Spinozist view that all things are, fits our familiar experience of the world.

Yet of these three conceptions, Darwin's is closest to Spinoza's. That is because he explains the phenomenon of life in terms that can and indeed must be extended to the whole of reality, though Darwin himself never does.

The theory of natural selection rests on the assumption that plants and animals are striving to achieve an eternal existence through the replication of their own finite selves under conditions of scarcity that allow some to succeed for a time but none to do so forever. This is Darwin's law of life. He uses it to explain the behavior and history of living things. But properly understood, it expresses a metaphysical principle that applies with equal validity to every finite being—to crystals and ideas as much as organisms and genes. Darwin's theory of natural selection has a universal reach that others have since recognized and exploited. But that is only because it is implicitly based on the Spinozist principle that every individual, of whatever sort, including those we conventionally call inanimate, is striving for an immortality that no finite being can ever fully attain.

Spinoza was driven to this conclusion by his relentless rationalism. If the phenomenon of life is not to be regarded as an inexplicable fact, then it must have emerged from something that was already alive, albeit in a more primitive fashion. By contrast, the Aristotelian view of life depends on the acceptance of a "natural" distinction between living and nonliving beings that cannot meet the demands of the principle of sufficient reason. Nor, even more obviously, can the Cartesian view, which relies on the miraculous agency of a God beyond the world. Those who accept Darwin's view of life must come to the same conclusion, odd as it seems from the standpoint of common sense, for it alone is capable of satisfying the remorseless demand for explanation that is the defining characteristic of Darwin's biology too.

SPECIES

Darwin was endlessly curious about the natural world. He was puzzled by features of it that others had either failed to notice or regarded as mysteries we cannot explain. He was also a rationalist who believed that our understanding of these phenomena is constantly increasing, and though always limited, never reaches a point beyond which further inquiry is fruitless or misguided. The doctrine of creation erects an explanatory barrier of this kind. It brings the search for answers to a halt and dignifies the decision to stop by insisting that it is impious to go on. Darwin loathed such obstructionism with every scientific bone in his body.

Why, to take just one of the dozens of questions that Darwin discusses, do the same species sometimes occupy geographically distant regions but not the areas in between? Those who say that the appearance of the species in each of its separate habitats is a "special" creation—a small, retail "miracle" that replicates on a more modest scale that of the creation of the world as a whole— offer no explanation at all.[10] They are just throwing up their hands and declaring that they have given up the effort to find one—or worse, believe it wrong even to try. To Darwin this represented the abandonment of reason itself. He considered the doctrine of creation the enemy of scientific naturalism and fought it at every turn.

Darwin was anxious to avoid antagonizing those with more orthodox beliefs and sought to minimize the hostile reaction he knew his book would provoke. For the most part, he worded his arguments judiciously and left their religious implications unstated. But no reader can miss the real depth of his contempt for the idea of creation. Darwin mentions it countless times, as a purported explanation of some feature of plant or animal life, only to underscore that divine creation explains nothing at all—in contrast to the theory of natural selection, which increases our understanding of the phenomenon in question and makes it less of a brute fact.[11]

Why, for example, do the "blind cave animals" of different continents show a greater affinity to "the other inhabitants" of their respective territories than to one another? Why, when a particular part or organ of a plant or animal is developed to "a remarkable degree" is it "eminently liable to variation"? Why do we observe the phenomenon of "reversion"—the "reappearance of very ancient characters"—in the cross-breeding of "equine species" (horses and zebras)? Why do the "habits" of some animals not agree with their "structure"? Why are "the parts and organs of many independent beings . . . invariably linked by graduated steps?" Why are plants and animals appropriately, *but not perfectly,* adapted to their circumstances? Why is it that, on oceanic islands, "though the number of kinds of inhabitants is scanty, the proportion of endemic species (i.e., those found nowhere else in the world) is often extremely large"? Why do "low and slowly-changing organisms [range] more widely than the high"? Why are "similar bones" in the same creature ("the wing and leg of a bat," for example) used "for such totally different purposes"? Why are there "rudimentary organs," such as "teeth in the upper jaws of whales," that can be "detected in the embryo, but afterwards entirely disappear"? Why does the "tree of life" have the shape it does?[12]

These questions give some sense of the range of Darwin's curiosity. But they also underscore the depth of his hostility to the doctrine of creation, for in each case he explicitly (and sometimes mockingly) rejects the view that an appeal to the doctrine throws any light on the puzzle at hand. The problem with the doctrine of creation is its principled resistance to reason—its implication that there are some things we ought not even attempt to explain. By contrast, the theory of natural selection honors the principle of sufficient reason by constantly pushing our search for answers beyond the point that creationism allows.

This is not to say that the answers it provides are definitive or complete. Darwin repeatedly reminds us of how little we know about the natural world. It is "infinitely" complex, he says, and we never grasp more than a tiny fragment of it. But no part or aspect of the world is permanently off-limits so far as the mind of the inquiring naturalist is concerned. Everything in the "tangled bank" of life is intelligible, including that part we call human life, which is not a separate kingdom miraculously governed by laws of its own, but a branch of the tree of life explicable in the same terms as every other.

We can therefore always understand more about plants and animals than we do at present, though what we grasp will always be limited by the ignorance that remains. This counsels modesty regarding our achievements. We must never forget how small and provisional our existing knowledge is. Still, we should have confidence in the power of reason to bring the world of life ever more fully to light. The doctrine of creation makes such confidence a sin. It puts a wall in the path of understanding, and instructs us to revere it.

The doctrine of natural selection clears the path instead. It brings everything in the world of living things within the range of intelligibility, though as we grope our way forward in this now endlessly knowable world, we must be careful to remember that, like explorers in a cave, we proceed step by step with a light that never reaches to the end.

This is the deepest point of contact between Spinoza and Darwin. Both are committed to the principle of sufficient reason, which presumes that the world is intelligible down to the distribution of finches on the Galapagos Islands. Both also acknowledge that as finite beings we can never fully comprehend the infinite intelligibility of the world as a whole. In these respects, Darwin's great book exemplifies the spirit of Spinoza's parable of the worm in the blood. But there are other, more substantive features of Darwin's biology that further underscore its relation to Spinoza's metaphysics. The first of these is brought out by Darwin's attack on the idea of natural kinds.

Aristotle takes the permanent existence of such kinds for granted. This is a consequence of the metaphysics of form and matter that underlies his account of living things. On Aristotle's view, every plant or animal is a composite of form and matter. But only the form that it shares with others of its kind is real and intelligible. Its matter, which is uniquely its own, is merely perceptible, not knowable, and in the deepest metaphysical sense, not really real at all.

We call the forms of living things their "species." This is a usage that persists to this day. The Latin term "species" is a translation of the Greek word *eidos,* which in Aristotle's philosophy signifies the shape or look or form of a thing. Because he equates being with intelligibility and both of these with form, Aristotle not only regards the species of living things ("horse," "dog," "maple" and the like) as something real, but more real that the individuality of the individuals that belong to them. For Aristotle, the only thing that is ultimately real about a plant or animal is its species-being, which it preserves through growth and transmits by means of reproduction. Everything else in its makeup is idiosyncratic and accidental. Only the kind or type to which a plant or animal belongs is part of its definition and hence both necessary and eternal, since what exists by definition cannot "be other than it is."

Darwin turns this judgment on its head. Our division of the world into species is not, he says, a natural but an artificial one. It is a "classification" we make for the sake of intellectual and practical convenience. The term species is one we "arbitrarily" assign to "a set of individuals closely resembling each other."[13] It does not correspond to anything real. In reality, the species into which we divide the world of plants and animals are composed of subspecies, these of types or "varieties," and so on. There is no one "essence" that the members of a species possess.[14] A species is an invented group that consists of individuals in an infinitely graduated spectrum of similarities and differences. It is the individuality of individuals and not their species-being that is the really real thing about them.

This may be true within those groups that we conventionally define as species. But what about the distinctions among species themselves? Surely, the differences that separate the various kinds of things that live in reproductive isolation from one another are natural or essential differences. Darwin denies this too. The separate species we see about us in the world are also connected by a series of individual gradations, just as their own members are, though in the first case the connections, which are spread out over unimaginably large periods of time, have disappeared from view and can only be glimpsed in the spotty fossil record from which we are able to infer their existence.

Darwin does not describe the processes through which reproductive isolation occurs. In this sense, as has often been remarked, *On the Origin of Species* is inaptly titled, since it fails to explain how such isolation "originates."[15] But in principle, Darwinism no more allows for gaps between species than within them. For Darwin, neither species nor their subdivisions are irreducibly real. Only individuals are. His biology rests on a nominalist metaphysics that puts individuals first and treats species as unreal abstractions, reversing the Aristotelian view of the relation between them.

Moreover, every group that we declare to be a species, even of the most seemingly distinct and isolated kind, is itself, in Darwin's view, a fluid and transient entity, with a mortal career of its own. In this respect, it is no different from the individuals of which it is composed. Even the artificial concept of a species thus comes, in Darwin's theory of natural selection, to share the defining characteristics of individual existence.

This has important implications for our understanding of the meaning of reproduction.

According to Aristotle, every living being strives to make a "copy" of itself. But what it copies is only its form. In this sense, its reproductive striving is "for the sake of" the species to which it belongs. The individual is an agent of its species. It is a vehicle for the preservation of the immortal species-being of its kind, which is the only really real thing in its hybrid constitution.

In Darwin's biology, this relation is also reversed. Species do not reproduce. Only individuals do, and from the individual's point of view, it is the species that serves as a vehicle for reproduction, not the other way around. For a long time, a species may serve this function well. But when it ceases to do so, as a result of environmental pressures of one kind or another, a new species gradually takes its place, through a process of natural selection. Like Aristotle, Darwin believed that the drive to reproduce is a fundamental characteristic of all living beings. But he locates this drive at the individual level, and uses this assumption to explain why species themselves evolve—something that Aristotle's biology rules out on metaphysical grounds.[16]

The individuals that Darwin has in mind are organisms. They are whole plants and animals. Modern biology locates the drive to reproduce at the level of the gene instead. This represents the most important refinement to Darwin's theory of natural selection since he first presented it a century and a half ago. But even the discovery of the genetic basis of the replication of organic traits, which Darwin assumed but could not explain, does not fundamentally alter the fact that the units of striving in evolutionary biology are individuals not kinds.

From the gene's point of view, the organism to which it belongs is merely a vessel for its reproductive ambitions. It is just the gene's way, as Richard Dawkins says, of making the journey across the divide that separates one instantiation of itself from another—the trip across the generations.[17] The fate of the gene may be yoked to that of the organism, but the latter is, in essence, an instrument for the attainment of a goal the former sets.

Indeed, the connection between genes and the striving to reproduce is even more intimate than this, for such striving is not merely an attribute that already-formed genes possess, but the ground of their identity *as* the fundamental units of reproduction themselves. When it comes to defining which bits of chromosomal material count as genes from the point of view of modern evolutionary biology, the answer is, those on which the process of natural selection operates in a meaningful way. Put differently, something *is* a gene just in case it can succeed or fail to replicate itself. This answer is circular, of course, but the important point is that it only makes sense on the assumption that the unit of material we have chosen to call a gene for evolutionary purposes is striving to make another like itself. To *be* a unit of evolution— one that is capable of evolving in response to the pressures of natural selection—is thus to strive to reproduce. This striving is what constitutes its being as a unit of this sort, and every such unit, large or small, is a single individual, not a category or kind, so that the relocation of the striving from the level of the organism, where Darwin placed it, to that of the gene, does not alter things in a metaphysically significant way.

One might object that nothing is more uniform and therefore less individual that a gene. Genes typically exist in a vast and homogeneous population. There are often unimaginably many organisms with precisely the same gene, encoded countless times, in exactly the same form, in the cells of the bodies of each of them. The location of the striving to reproduce at the genetic level may thus seem to represent a dramatic move away from Darwin's view that, in contrast to Aristotle, it is individuals not kinds that are the real units of such striving.

But it would be a mistake to draw this conclusion, for what strives to reproduce, even on the modern genetic reinterpretation of Darwin's theory, is not a population as such, but always this or that particular gene, from whose point of view other copies of the same gene are merely the allies or instruments of its own replication, just like the organism that serves as a vessel for its voyage to the next generation.

If it sometimes happens that one copy of a gene sacrifices itself for the sake of another, this therefore cannot be explained as an act of genuine altruism, which would make sense only in case the survival of the gene had meaning or value from a collective point of view that presupposes that kinds or types (in this case of genes) strive to reproduce in their own right. The often manic inventiveness with which evolutionary biologists construct "selfish" explanations of seemingly altruistic behavior to avoid this "collectivist" conclusion underscores their commitment to the metaphysical principle that the striving to reproduce is always and everywhere that of an individual, whether organism or gene or allele or molecule, and indeed *must be* since it is constitutive of individuality as such—Darwin's nominalism preserved and transposed to other levels of striving.[18]

In this connection, it is important to note an important distinction whose neglect has been a source of much fruitless debate.

Darwin is frequently accused of being a reductionist—of reducing man's social and cultural life to something cruder and less complex. In the eyes of his critics, Darwin is guilty of treating the brutal struggle for survival as the only true reality, and the rest of human experience as an illusory superstructure built on its uniquely solid foundation. His modern successors are frequently charged with reductionism too—with dissolving the reality of love and politics and poetry and replacing these with genes that now hold the exclusive title to being really real.

But neither of these criticisms is compelling because there is nothing in the metaphysics of Darwinism that compels a reduction of this sort. What Darwinism does require is that the striving to reproduce always be that of an individual. No group or kind or type, as such, ever strives to reproduce. But individuals can be more or less *complex*.

For example, an individual gene typically belongs to an individual organism, and each is an independent center of reproductive striving. By "independent" I mean that the reproductive goal of one is not wholly definable in terms of the other. The goal of the organism is always that of an individual plant or animal with genes that have reproductive aims of their own, and though these are tightly interlocked (since in most cases, the reproduction of the organism's genes is dependent upon that of the organism itself), they are nevertheless distinct. This comes to light most clearly in cases of conflict, where the reproductive ambitions of the organism and those of its genes diverge, as they do when an organism's "selfish" drive to reproduce reduces the chances of its genes' reproduction, which would be better served by more self-sacrificing behavior on the organism's part. That human beings strive to outlive their reproductive powers, and by doing so to leave a more lasting impression of themselves as individuals in the memory of the communities to which they belong, is an expression, within the human world, of the conflict that can arise between the drive to reproduce at different levels of individual identity.

What is true of genes and organisms is true of organisms and groups too. A group can also have an individual identity, formed and reinforced through mimetic patterns of one kind or another, and the survival of its memes—and hence of the group—can conflict in many ways with that of its individual members. For example, a man may seek to keep his individual identity alive, after he is dead, through works and deeds whose notoriety depends on their mimetic opposition to the prevailing norms of his community, fighting, as it were, a war on two fronts, against both his genes and his group, each of whose prospects for survival are damaged by his selfish pursuit of posthumous fame. Of course, the man's survival and his group's are also intertwined, just as the survival of his genes is with that of his body (at least through reproductive maturity). At every level up and down this hierarchy, there are linked dependencies of the most complex sort imaginable. But every level also represents a meaningfully distinct grade of individuation, occupied by individual genes, organisms and groups that not only compete with one another, but with other individuals at other levels too. Nothing in Darwinism rules out the recognition of a graduated scale of this kind, or requires its adherents to deny the reality of the individuals that exist at every level but one. Some followers of Darwin are reductionists in this sense, but Darwin himself was not, and there is nothing in the theory of natural selection that forces one to be such. All that Darwinism demands is that at every level of reality, the striving to reproduce be that of an individual whose individuality is constituted by this very striving itself. In a Darwinian view of life, the struggle to survive—or more exactly, to make a copy of oneself—is the *principium individuationis* that explains why each gene, organism and group is the one it is and not another. It is true, therefore, that Darwin offers a radically individualist account of life but false that his account is reductionist in a way that would diminish the subtlety and range of its explanatory power.

The connection to Spinoza is clear.

For Spinoza, the striving to persevere in being functions as a principle of individuation too. In Spinoza's metaphysics, striving and individuality are extensionally and intentionally equivalent. Spinoza also recognizes the existence of individuals at varying levels of compositional complexity, down to the simplest bodies that have the least complex patterns of motion and rest and up to the world as a whole—an individual of infinite complexity. At all these levels, individuals struggle to survive in an environment of external forces, which consist of other individuals striving to do the same, with some of whom some measure of cooperation may be possible at times but whose ambitions inevitably conflict. The forms of cooperation and conflict are endless, so that we can never grasp more than a minute fraction of them. But they are all fully intelligible, and further study will always enable us to comprehend them in greater detail. That is because the world is everywhere governed by the same laws, beginning with the law of *conatus* itself.

These metaphysical principles provide support for Darwin's belief that only individuals are real because they alone struggle to survive, and for his confidence that in the study of the natural world we never encounter a fact that in principle cannot be explained. But a profound difference still seems to remain between Spinoza and Darwin. It concerns their attitude toward the eternity of the world.

Darwin's world is one of endless comings and goings. Nothing in it endures. The transience that Aristotle recognized in the lives of individual plants and animals comes in Darwinism to infect their species-being as well. For Aristotle, the everlastingness of the forms of plants and animals is a manifestation of the eternity of the cosmos as a whole. Where in Darwin's universe can one find even a shred of the divinity that Aristotle ascribed to it? This is what Darwin's religious critics have always found most disturbing about his views—that he abolishes the God beyond the world, and offers no other, worldly god to replace him, leaving us entirely cut off from the eternal and divine.

The contrast with Spinoza seems obvious. Spinoza's conception of nature is in important ways anti-Aristotelian, and his idea of God is certainly heretical from an Abrahamic point of view. But Spinoza's world is saturated with eternity—unlike Darwin's, which seems drained of it by the principle of natural selection itself.

This is an understandable but mistaken conclusion. There is more God in Darwin's world than might appear. Indeed, God is *essential* to Darwinism—not in the superficial sense that a creator God could have made a world that operates according to the principles of evolution if he chose (the old Ockhamist distinction between God's absolute and ordained power), but in the different, and fundamentally Spinozist, sense that the struggle for life that is the engine of natural selection and the cause of the endless pageant of ever-changing forms we discern in the geological record of life on earth, *is itself* a striving for eternity, driven by what pagans and Christians alike call the love of God.

The equation of the struggle for life with the love of God will of course seem especially far-fetched to those who are used to thinking of Darwinism as a godless science. But Darwin's account of life only makes sense on this supposition. Thus, just where the difference between the Darwinian and Spinozist views of the world appears widest, the connection between them proves closest.

ETERNITY

The struggle for existence in which all living things are engaged is always that of an individual. It is the struggle of this organism or that one, of this particular bit of genetic material or some other. But the struggle is not for the sake of the individual's own life, except in a secondary way.

Organisms and the genes that "ride" them from one generation to the next strive to live longer before dying, as all of them eventually must. But this is not their deepest ambition, on a Darwinian view of life. The fundamental drive of every living thing, whether it be an organism or gene, is not to live on as the individual it is, but to make a copy of itself, and thereby live on in another. To the extent it strives to preserve its own life by fending off enemies and other hostile powers, it does so for the sake of replication—so that it will have the time and resources it needs to make a copy of itself before expiring. There are many different strategies for doing this. But the common aim of all of them is to escape the bonds that confine every living being within the limits of its own mortality. Death can be postponed but never avoided. The only resource that plants and animals and genes have against it is their power to reproduce.

Like Aristotle, Darwin thus assumes that what living things desire most is to leave an image of themselves behind. Indeed, without this assumption, the process of natural selection makes no sense at all. What this process selects among are competing attempts to reproduce. Unless this is taken as the shared goal of the parties involved there is nothing for them to compete about, and no measure by which to judge their success.

Aristotle interprets the drive to reproduce as a striving for immortality. He assumes, moreover, that living things can actually achieve this goal by means of reproduction, since the copies they make of themselves replicate the eternal forms of their species or kinds. No living thing, on earth at least, lives forever, but every one of them is equipped through reproduction to share in the everlasting and divine. Its longing to be part of the divine order of things is one whose fulfillment this very order assures in the ordinary course of events.

Darwinism rules this out. That is because, on Darwin's view, no species lasts forever. No matter how long-lived, it is bound to fall short of the everlastingness that Aristotle assumed to be the defining mark of all natural kinds. Darwin's nominalism entails that species are individuals too and therefore finite. None is able to withstand forever the forces against which it must struggle to survive—any more than an individual organism or gene can. All species die, and because they do, their members' desire to reach the everlasting by making copies of themselves is doomed to fail.

For Aristotle, this is inconceivable. Nature does nothing in vain. The idea of a natural striving that cannot be fulfilled is, from his point of view, a contradiction in terms.[19] By contrast, those who follow Darwin have no way of avoiding this conclusion. That is because they can neither deny that the struggle to reproduce is a striving for immortality nor admit that it can be fulfilled. The latter is obvious, given Darwin's demolition of the belief that species are immortal. But the former is a fundamental feature of Darwinism too, for even on Darwin's view of life, reproduction can have no other aim than life without end.

If plants and animals could not reproduce, they would still strive to live for another day and another after that. Death cuts this process short, but doesn't change its basic goal. That is to live on, however long one has lived already. The same is true of reproduction. Instead of struggling to survive "in their own skins," which is something they can do in any case only for a while, organisms and genes reproduce in order to live on in their descendants for an indefinitely longer time. But here too, no limited extension of life is ever enough. No finite number of descendants is sufficient to satisfy the longing that drives the reproductive process. It may be impossible to imagine the line of one's descendants beyond the first few generations. Who can conceive of his or her great-great-great-great-great-great-great-grandchildren—and that's only ten generations? But if asked whether one would prefer to have the line end there, or farther down, the answer will always be, "farther down."

Individual organisms cannot live forever. Aristotle acknowledges this, but insists that plants and animals are able to fulfill their yearning for immortality indirectly, through the offspring they produce. Darwin forces us to accept that this is impossible too. Yet the drive to reproduce, which he places at the center of the drama of natural selection, cannot be conceived except as a longing to live forever, since no finite success in the competition for life can ever fully satisfy the ambitions of those involved. There is no end to the number of descendants they desire, though their yearning for an endless existence is doomed to disappointment by the finitude of everything in the world, species included. This is the source of the pathos that colors the Darwinian view of life.

From an Aristotelian perspective, this view is bound to seem profoundly dispiriting. The deepest longing of plants and animals and men and stars, even of lumps of earth and drops of water, is to share in the eternal and divine, which for Aristotle is synonymous with reality itself. Human beings pursue this goal in different ways—biologically, politically and philosophically. The first of these is the most common. It is a path open to all, including those shut out from politics and philosophy on account of their gender or status. Even a man who is a slave by nature can share in eternity by having children. Darwinism cuts this route off, while leaving the longing intact.

None of this is discouraging if one believes in a transcendent God who possesses the eternity that Darwinism eliminates from this world and who offers men the hope of reaching it in the next. But Darwin blocks this path to eternity as well. The world whose intelligibility he discovers wherever he looks owes its being to nothing but itself. On Darwin's view, the desire for life without end that sets the stage for the competition that drives the evolutionary process can therefore be satisfied neither in this world, as Aristotle thought, nor beyond it, as Augustine supposed.

On the Origin of Species is not, however, a dispirited or discouraging book. Quite the opposite: it is suffused with excitement and joy. One senses Darwin's own immense pleasure as one puzzle after another is resolved in an intellectually satisfying way. This is particularly true with regard to the question of the life and death of species. For Aristotle, it is simply a fact that the world contains the kinds of living things it does. Why are there frogs and bats and spiders and pine trees? This is not a question that Aristotle could even have conceived. There have always been such things and always will be; the existence of these and other natural kinds is just a feature of the world, as necessary as the existence of the world itself. By contrast, Darwin not only asks why these kinds exist but gives a rigorous answer that avoids relying on the claim that they exist because God chose to create them. The theory of natural selection dissolves all that to Aristotle seemed immortal in the lives of living things. It converts even the most long-lasting features of life on earth into transient episodes that open and close, without God's intervention, in a rationally explicable way. From either an Aristotelian or Christian perspective, this may seem an inconsolable loss. But it is offset by an incomparable gain in the intelligibility of life itself, which the theory of natural selection renders understandable to a degree that is unthinkable from either of these other points of view.

In this way, Darwinism restores the world's eternity, though in a form that is neither Aristotelian nor Christian. It is true that the events his theory seeks to explain, including the origin and extinction of species, all belong to the moving stream of time. But it aims to explain these from the vantage point of principles that never change. It strives to account for the ever-changing spectacle of life *sub specie aeternitatis*. This is true not only of the most basic principles of evolutionary biology but of all the more detailed laws that follow from them—for example, that in processes of sexual reproduction the behavior of the participants varies according to the relative size and number of their gametes.[20] This law applies only under certain conditions. It therefore has a more limited scope than the theory of natural selection itself. But within its range, it is timelessly valid too because like every law, it states a necessary relation of cause and effect (which may of course be proven false by further research, though any law that is offered as a replacement must aspire to state such a relation as well).

The more we understand the infinitely complex phenomenon of life, the further we bring it under the aegis of law and hence under the sign of eternity. The greater our ability to do this, the more "adequately" we conceive the world in Spinoza's sense, without either affirming Aristotle's doctrine of natural kinds or embracing the irrational dogma of creation. Darwin drains the world of the eternity that Aristotle assumed to be present in it and severs its connection to an eternal God beyond the world. But the explanatory rationalism that guides his account of the history and diversity of life dramatically extends the foothold in eternity that every scientific advance affords us.

The infinite complexity of the world guarantees that this foothold can never grow into full possession. But a foothold is still something. It is a real connection to eternity and the only one that remains after the gods of Aristotle and Augustine have been vanquished. To some, it may seem modest by comparison. But it has the inestimable advantage of not requiring us to accept anything as an inexplicable fact, which we cannot do without violating the spirit of reason itself. Darwin believed that the theory of natural selection gives us such a foothold on terms that reason can embrace. This belief is the source of the joy that pervades his work—an affect that Spinoza defines as the feeling that accompanies every increase in understanding and power, spurred by what he calls our "intellectual love" of God.

EVOLUTION UNBOUND

Two implications of the theory of natural selection are of special importance in this regard. The first is that the drive to reproduce leads necessarily to the pursuit of greater power. The second is that the theory not only can but must be applied outside the realm of life as well as within it. Each strengthens the connection between the principle of natural selection, on the one hand, and the idea of eternity, on the other, and brings Darwin's biology into even closer alignment with Spinoza's metaphysics, whose austere geometry gives it a static appearance that seems, on the surface at least, so remote from the dynamism of evolution itself.

One of the best known images in *On the Origin of Species* is that of the "tree of life."[21] Darwin uses it to illustrate two points. The first is that the kinds of plants and animals that exist at any given moment are the descendants of other kinds that existed before. The second is that life tends to "branch out," to assume a greater diversity of forms, spreading (to follow the image) from a single trunk into ever-smaller offshoots.

This process may be stalled or interrupted, perhaps for long periods of time. But the theory of natural selection implies that there is a built-in tendency toward diversification in the world of living things. That is because there will always be *some* advantage to further specialization. Other things equal (which of course they never are) it will always improve the survival chances of an organism or a gene to acquire the power to eat what its competitors can't or live where they don't. As a result, the powers of plants and animals tend to become more diverse over time, by virtue of the process of natural selection itself. This may be thought of as a process of qualitative expansion that can be blocked or even reversed by environmental changes, but always exerts a pressure in the direction of greater variety.

To this there corresponds another, quantitative expansion—that of living things from less to more control over their environment and thus to greater degrees of power. Darwin does not emphasize this aspect of natural selection. He is eager to avoid any suggestion that later, more powerful plants and animals are a goal their predecessors are striving to reach, with the implication that the whole process has been designed to achieve this result. Darwin's anticreationism caused him to be profoundly suspicious of teleological explanations of this kind. (I shall return to the idea of teleology in the final section of the chapter.) But even if one rules out such explanations, the competition that drives the process of natural selection inevitably tends to produce living things with ever-greater quanta of power.

The reason is that the competition takes the form of what evolutionary biologists like to compare to an "arms race."[22]

The fundamental premise of Darwin's theory of natural selection is that competition within and between species arises because the pursuit of reproductive advantage always outstrips the available resources. This is the Malthusian state that Darwin insists is a condition of life as such.[23] If resources were infinite, or competition limited to those that exist, it would slacken and perhaps disappear. But the first, at least, can never happen, and the second is impossible too, for as long as resources are finite, any plant or animal that "accepted" such a limitation would diminish its chances of successfully copying itself and thus reaching the goal of life without end that all living things strive to achieve.

In the struggle that results, it sometimes happens, often for long periods of time, that a condition of stability arises among the competing parties. When and why this happens are questions of special interest to evolutionary biologists.[24] But such stability can never be more than a local and temporary phenomenon. It is always vulnerable to disruption from the outside, by the intrusion of a domineering power, or from the inside, if one of the participants acquires a power that allows it to disregard the existing equilibrium and to appropriate a larger share of the available resources for itself.

The process of natural selection will always favor such increases of power, and thus will also always favor defensive strategies that protect against them, which represent an increase of power as well. The result is that even the most stable environment is only a tense standoff that may be upset at any moment, and that tends toward a "balance of powers" at ever-higher levels, as the plants and animals in it jockey for advantage, offensively and defensively. Again, this process may be disrupted or even reversed (by a change in the climate, for example, or an asteroid crashing into the earth) but the tendency is always toward organisms and genes that are not merely different from their predecessors but more powerful too. Viewed in this light, the evolutionary emergence of human beings with the power of speech and foresight and the capacity to understand and eventually control the pace and direction of evolution itself is a natural phenomenon to be explained in the same terms as the emergence of eukaryotes and organisms with more than one cell.[25]

More power means the ability to do more things in more ways. But no living thing has unlimited power. None, therefore, can ever be assured of having enough power to withstand the forces that threaten its existence. The most striking evidence of this is that many very powerful species, which existed in the past, no longer do. Man is the most powerful being yet to emerge from this process, but his powers too are finite. Hence, there is no guarantee that even he will last forever. Like every other plant and animal, even man, with all his suppleness and strength, is confronted by forces greater than any he can ever possess and is therefore always vulnerable to destruction by them.

For Darwin, there is only one thing that may be said to escape this fate— to be all-powerful and therefore eternal. This is the process of evolution itself. More precisely, it is the intelligibility of this process. Only the mindedness of the world can never be destroyed by a power greater than its own. This is the immortal God of Darwin's biology, which resembles that of Aristotle who also identified the divinity of the world with its intelligibility.

But there is a crucial difference between their Gods, for on Darwin's view, no finite mind can ever fully comprehend the infinite complexity of relations that a perfect understanding of the process of evolution would require. A gap therefore always remains between even the most powerful animal and the eternal mindedness of the world as a whole. Still, the *increase* in power which the process of evolution itself tends to produce represents a movement in the *direction* of God, so understood. And science too, which emerges only at a late stage in this process, strives to reach God in this sense as well, by doing all it can to grasp the laws that govern, or rather constitute, the infinite and eternal power of the world, as these laws manifest themselves in the incomprehensibly complex parade of what Darwin calls "endless forms most beautiful."

This is the Spinozist theology on which the principle of natural selection is based. But the principle cannot be restricted to the sphere of life alone. Darwin's own commitment to explanatory rationalism demands that it be applied to the whole of reality. Darwin himself was reluctant to take this step; he had battles enough to fight. But for those who embrace his theory, there is no good reason to stop at any point. Beginning with the question of how to explain the emergence of life, Darwin's followers have been emboldened by the relentless rationalism of the principle of natural selection to apply it on an ever widening scale, up to the level of the basic laws of physics themselves.

On the Origin of Species is a consistently anticreationist work, except in one respect. Only with regard to the first appearance of life does Darwin soften his position and allow that its emergence out of a world of otherwise dead matter is a mystery that one may (and perhaps must) describe in the language of creation.

It is difficult to tell, from the text itself, whether Darwin really believed the origin of life to be a mystery of this kind, or refrained from attempting to explain it in evolutionary terms for fear of further antagonizing his Christian readers, and of making the other applications of his theory seem less plausible by carrying it a step too far. But whatever his own motives may have been, Darwin chose to draw a line at life itself and to treat its existence as a brute fact that must be explained as the work of the God who "first breathed" life into "some one primordial form," from which all the others in the world are descended.[26]

Once this primordial form exists, there is no need to invoke a subsequent series of *special* creations to explain its articulation into the tree of life. This is just what Darwin's book is meant to establish. But for the theory of natural selection to have anything on which to work at all, we must assume the existence of life, and this, Darwin suggests, is an assumption the theory itself is incompetent to explain.

But this is an exception that threatens to wreck the theory completely. In the first place, to acknowledge a mysterious coming into being from nothing at the threshold of life, which one explains by appeal to the idea of creation, is shockingly inconsistent with the resolute rejection of all such explanations within the realm of life itself. Second, the acceptance of an inexplicable gap between the living and nonliving violates a fundamental principle of evolutionary biology: that apparent gaps in the record of life are really only gaps in our knowledge, which were it more complete would demonstrate that even those forms that emerge most quickly (as the result, perhaps, of some catastrophic event) do so from antecedent forms by an evolutionary path that we can understand and explain. Third, and most important, if one concedes that God created the first living form from nothing, then one can just as easily insist that all the subsequent elaborations of this form were built into its original creation—that they were part of the divinely conceived design of the first living thing. But that restores to the doctrine of creation the ubiquity Darwin found so offensive to reason. To every question, "Why does this plant or animal look and behave as it does?" the answer can now be given, "Because its evolution was already inscribed in the being of the first living thing that God created." In this way, the one exception to the theory of evolution that Darwin seems to have been prepared to allow swallows the theory as a whole and makes its explanatory power dependent upon an act that in principle cannot be explained.

The only alternative, of course, is to save the theory by using it to explain its own presuppositions—in this case, the existence of life on earth. Every explanation must of course take something for granted, but only in a temporary and provisional way, as a "base of operations" for purposes of answering the question at hand. If one is interested in explaining how and why single-celled organisms evolved into multicellular ones, it is perfectly appropriate to take the existence of the former for granted. But only provisionally: there is all the difference in the world between saying, "For the sake of *this* argument, we must take certain things for granted," and insisting that these same things, whatever they are, lie forever beyond our power to explain.

Darwinism cannot tolerate the latter view at any point in the chain of explanation, without weakening, if not dissolving, the entire chain. The chain must therefore be endless. Every link we add to it can only be an invitation to further explanation. If we allow it to be cut at any point by an appeal to the mystery of creation, the chain loses all its explanatory power. It unravels and becomes merely a more elaborate statement of this mystery itself.

This applies in particular to the question of the origin of life.

To avoid making a fatal concession to their creationist opponents, the defenders of Darwin's theory of natural selection have therefore felt compelled to pursue the search for an evolutionary explanation of the emergence of what we conventionally call living beings (those that metabolize and reproduce, by fission or otherwise) out of nonliving ones—for example, complex molecular structures that display patterns of appropriation and growth that resemble these organic functions. Only an explanation of this sort can close the gap between living and nonliving things by providing an evolutionary bridge that explains the metabolism and reproduction of the simplest viruses as a more successful strategy for achieving the goal of replication that even certain crystals appear to be pursuing. No explanation has yet been proposed that enjoys anything like the degree of assent that similar ones do within the field of biology. But that is not the important point. What matters is the felt urgency of finding such an explanation, for to abandon the search as hopeless would be more than a small defeat. It would bring the whole of Darwinism crashing to the ground. If "Darwin's dangerous idea," as it has been called, is to be honored on its own terms, the existence of life on earth cannot be regarded as a mysterious exception to it. It has to be treated as just one more thing to be explained.[27]

Nor can anyone who accepts the principle of natural selection stop here. Any explanation of the emergence of life presupposes the existence of the physical laws that govern the interaction of bodies in the universe in which we live. Is the existence of these laws, then, a brute fact at which explanation must come to an end? That is an unacceptable conclusion as well.

It may be, as some have claimed, that our world (and therefore, *a fortiori,* the existence of life) is possible only because gravity is not stronger than it is or absolute zero colder. It seems, in fact, that the range of variables within which our world could have come into existence at all is tightly constrained. Is this just an accident, then, or perhaps evidence of God's plan? Those who accept Darwin's idea have to reject both conclusions. There must be an explanation as to why the laws of nature themselves exist in the form they do and it can only be that these laws too have evolved through an intelligible process of natural selection—perhaps one involving a competition among universes with different laws, all struggling to survive (difficult as that is to conceive).[28]

This is all highly speculative, of course, but it suggests the direction in which the science of nature must evolve (!) to avoid defecting from the rationalism of Darwin's biology. The principle of natural selection loses *all* its explanatory power if one acknowledges the existence of a *single* fact it cannot explain. For the theory of evolution to survive (!), it must therefore be carried up into the realm of astrophysics and extended laterally into the field of psychology as well, for there can be no exceptions here either. The phenomena of memory, foresight, and consciousness must also be explained as emergent properties that grow seamlessly out of an appetite for survival that we conventionally regard as pre- or unconscious, in order to avoid another sort of miraculous gap that would undermine Darwinism completely.

As a consequence, the whole of natural science, including the disciplines of physics and psychology, comes under the sway of Darwinian biology. This cannot be avoided. If the theory of evolution is to be saved from a self-defeating appeal to brute facts, the principle of natural selection must be extended to what a metaphysician would call "being as such." This is possible only on the assumption that all things—molecules and crystals and physical laws as much as organisms and genes—are striving to persevere in a competition that compels them to grow in power in order to survive. To explain what happens in the seemingly narrow realm of life, one is therefore forced to assume that all things are alive in Spinoza's sense—that their very being is constituted by a longing for immortality which by definition they cannot fulfill. Nothing could be further from Descartes' world of lifeless bodies and bodiless souls to certain of whom God has promised an afterlife without end.

CHANCE

Spinoza denies that anything ever happens by chance. Of course, we don't always know why things happen as they do. In fact, we never have a truly adequate knowledge of the reasons for their occurrence. But that is a consequence of our limitations, not of a contingency inscribed in the nature of things. There is no such contingency. Indeed, there cannot be, so long as one accepts the fundamental premise of Spinoza's metaphysics—that to be is to be intelligible.

By contrast, chance seems to play an essential role in Darwin's theory of evolution. In each generation, fresh differences appear, seemingly from nowhere, among the individuals who are the raw material on which the process of natural selection works. Some of these differences confer an advantage on their possessors, others a liability, so far as their reproductive prospects are concerned. Many are neutral, neither increasing nor decreasing the likelihood that their possessors will do better in the race to reproduce. The latter explain the phenomenon of "genetic drift," but the former determine the direction of evolution.[29] They do so only slowly, over immense stretches of time; to have a meaningful effect, they need not be large differences at first. Darwin takes such variability as a given, as indeed he must, for without it, there would be nothing for the process of natural selection to select. If the members of succeeding generations were exactly the same in all respects, no evolution could occur. A change in conditions might cause all individuals with certain characteristics to increase, or to dwindle and disappear, but in the absence of variation from one generation to the next, there could be no evolutionary adaptation in response to such a change. Darwin's theory of evolution presupposes the existence of variations of this kind.

It would be a mistake, however, to regard such variations as chance events, in the way the expression "random mutation" suggests. It is true that Darwin himself was unable to explain how and why they occur. He had no theory of variation—no account of the mechanism that produces the differences that arise among individuals in the course of reproduction itself. That is because he lacked an understanding of the genetic basis of reproduction. Today, we have a better understanding of why genes sometimes fail to produce exact copies of themselves, as the result of "transcription errors" and the like.[30] This means that we are better able to account for a phenomenon whose existence Darwin was compelled to assume but could not explain, and therefore sometimes describes in a way that makes it sound like a kind of arbitrariness in nature itself, which randomly produces in each generation enough variability to give the process of natural selection alternatives among which to "choose."[31]

To conclude that this is Darwin's considered view, however, violates the basic spirit of Darwinism itself. For Darwin to have conceded that the variability his theory presupposes is the unaccountable product of chance would have been no more consistent with the theory itself than an admission that even one of the phenomena it purports to explain is the result of an act of divine creation. The only position that a Darwinist can consistently adopt is that this presupposition of the theory too, like all its others, must in principle be fully explicable—another example of the theory swallowing its own tail.

This is the danger in Darwin's dangerous idea, but it cannot be avoided except by capitulating to an obscurantist belief in creation or chance. For those who refuse to make the intellectual sacrifice this involves, as all true Darwinists must, only one alternative remains. That to insist that every variation, however small, is never a chance event, but is always caused by an intelligible chain of previous events, while conceding that the complexity of the world prevents us from ever fully understanding precisely why it occurs when it does.

The debate over Stephen Jay Gould's revisionist account of the theory of natural selection illustrates the point.

Gould maintains that the process of evolution has not been smooth or continuous, but punctuated by contingent events that have produced dramatically new environments in which chance mutations of one kind or another have flourished in wholly unexpected ways. He calls the latter "hopeful monsters."[32]

Gould stresses the role of contingency in the evolutionary process in order to combat all forms of teleological thinking. He insists that the process might have taken any one of a number of different directions and that there is no necessity to the path it has actually followed, or to the emergence of the particular forms of life (including man) to which it has given rise. To suppose otherwise, he claims, is to reintroduce into the process of evolution the guiding hand that Darwin worked so hard to eliminate—in Gould's view, a crime against Darwinism itself.

Gould's critics respond that his emphasis on the contingency of the process is the real crime. They concede that the pace and direction of evolution may have been affected by rapid environmental changes on a large, perhaps even planetary, scale, but insist on two further points: first, that the cause of these changes can itself be explained (in astrophysical or other terms); and second, that the tendency of the process of evolution is necessarily toward greater diversity and power, and though it may be slowed or interrupted, always eventually resumes, and when it does, tends in the same direction as before—without the guiding hand of a designer who has built it in accordance with a plan. By insisting on the role of contingency in evolution, Gould's critics say, he has restored on a smaller scale, and in nontheistic terms, the central tenet of Abrahamism itself, which maintains that the world as a whole is contingent. And from their point of view, this represents an abandonment of the science of evolutionary biology, which can no more allow for contingency on Gould's more modest terms than on the cosmic ones of the theologians that both he and his critics oppose.

The theory of evolution is necessitarian. It cannot accept that anything happens by chance, for once it does, it acknowledges the existence of phenomena it cannot explain and gives the creationists who oppose it the opening they need to defend their God against the rationalizing ambitions of the theory itself. Not even the most philosophically self-conscious champions of the theory have drawn this conclusion in an explicit way. Perhaps they are concerned not to appear too extreme, or worried about the ethical and political implications of such a view. But there is no way to take Darwinism only so far and limit its ambitions in the way that Gould urges us to do. Either one rejects it or follows it to the end, to a world as necessary as it is intelligible, where Darwinism and Spinozism converge.

TELEOLOGY

Darwin was a naturalist, not a metaphysician. Yet his theory of natural selection rests, as any comprehensive theory of life must, on unstated philosophical assumptions. These cannot be the ones that underlie either the Aristotelian or Christian view of life, for Darwin's own theory differs fundamentally from both. One might even say that it is defined in opposition to them. The result is a biology of a third and distinctive kind whose implicit metaphysics is as unique as the conception of life it supports.

I have identified several ways in which this metaphysics resembles that of Spinoza. But one further point of contact remains to be explored. This is their shared opposition to all forms of explanation that are commonly described as "teleological."

"Nature," Spinoza says, "has no end set before it."[33] There is no "final cause" for the sake of which it acts. The belief that nature acts "on account of an end" arose when men transposed their own experiences to the things they saw around them, and eventually to the world as a whole.

Men "act always on account of an end, namely, on account of their advantage, which they want," and not knowing why other things act as they do, suppose that they too act in order to attain a goal of some sort. They ascribe to them purposes like the ones they discover in themselves. From this arises the idea of nature as a purposive order. But this is just an anthropomorphic mistake. It is a superstition from which many other false beliefs follow—for example, that certain natural events ("storms, earthquakes, diseases, and the like") occur "because the gods (whom they judge to be of the same nature as themselves) are angry on account of wrongs done to them by men, *or* on account of sins committed in their worship."[34]

According to Spinoza, all religions begin with this mistaken inference. In truth, nothing in the world happens in accordance with a plan. The order of the world is explicable but unplanned. We can account for it, but not because it has been brought about by a designing mind.

Spinoza's insistence on the purposelessness of events in the natural world was consistent with the spirit of the new mechanical physics, which sought to expunge every residue of the Aristotelian doctrine of final causes from the study of bodily motion. But Spinoza extended this view in a radically heterodox fashion by insisting that it ruled out the idea of divine creation as well. If the belief that things in the world move on account of purposes internal to them is a groundless superstition, then so too is the belief that the existence of the world as a whole can be explained by the purposive *fiat* of a God beyond it.

This is Darwin's view as well. His assault on the doctrine of special creation is a sustained attack on teleological explanations of precisely the sort that Spinoza said we must give up if we want to make progress in our understanding of the natural world. Some find it unsettling to think that there is no plan of which the world is the result, and that events do not unfold in accordance with a preconceived design. The discomfort this causes is a principal source of the continuing hostility to Darwinism today. But Spinoza and Darwin are resolute in their agreement that this discomfort is the price of all true science, and outweighed by the joy of greater understanding, which is conditioned on the rejection of the doctrine of intelligent design.

But what exactly does this mean? What is implied by the claim that nature does not act in accordance with a plan, yet is nonetheless wholly intelligible? And how can this claim be reconciled with the belief (to which both Spinoza and Darwin subscribe) that every thing in the world is striving to preserve itself in being, and in that sense acting for the sake of an end—which certainly sounds like the kind of purposive explanation they otherwise so emphatically reject? To answer these questions, we need to return, for a moment at least, to Aristotle's concept of nature, where the idea of action for the sake of an end plays a central role.

The clearest case of purposive action is what Aristotle calls "making" (*poesis*). The maker of a bed or poem or constitution first forms an idea of it in his mind and then "executes" his plan by "realizing" the thing he has thought of in advance. If we look at the finished product and ask, "How did this come to be? What explains its existence?" one answer—in many ways, the most obvious one—is that it is the result of actions purposefully undertaken in accordance with a plan whose aim or goal was conceived in advance and which existed in the maker's mind before it existed in reality.

Aristotle begins his account of nature by distinguishing between the ways in which natural and artificial things come into being and move. The latter "take shape" on account of a plan in the mind of their maker. They therefore have the cause or ground of their movement outside themselves. Natural things, by contrast, move "on their own account." The source of their motion is internal to them. This is the fundamental difference, for example, between the growth of a plant (a natural becoming), and the emergence of a statue from a block of stone (a making, or artificial becoming).

Aristotle was first and foremost a biologist, in the sense that he took the phenomenon of life to be not merely a fundamental feature of the world but the one in terms of which all its other characteristics are best understood, including the dynamic duality of potency and act that holds the key to understanding the very nature of being itself. For Aristotle, the whole world is thus to be approached from the standpoint of those processes of growth and maturation that he distinguishes in a principled way from all artificial comings-to-be.

And yet, when he constructs his own account of natural movement (*phusis*), Aristotle interprets it on the model of making. He does so most explicitly in the case of those movements that he considered a paradigm of the whole realm of becomings-by-nature, namely, the growth of plants and animals. The result is that the phenomenon of life, to which Aristotle assigns a central place in his overall view of the world, is analyzed by analogy to the process of planning in terms of which we explain the existence and movement of artificial things whose defining characteristic is precisely that they are *not* alive— that is, do not move by themselves.

The idea that links these otherwise disparate phenomena is that of action for the sake of an end. When a craftsman makes a bed, the bed comes about as a result of his actions, and these are "for the sake" of the plan in which the bed is represented in advance in the craftsman's mind.

In an analogous way, the growth of plants and animals is "for the sake" of an end as well. We observe that the career of all living things follows a similar pattern. It begins in a state of immaturity, then grows into one of greater competence, and finally declines in power and dies. It moves from less power to more to none, in a parabolic arc that describes the natural shape of the life of every living being. Of the points on this parabola, however, one is of special importance. This is its highest point, at which a plant or animal is actively exercising to the fullest extent the powers that things of its kind possess. This is the end of its life, not in the sense of a termination but a goal. It is that "for the sake of which" everything that precedes it occurs.

Thus if we ask, "Why do plants and animals grow?" Aristotle's answer is, "So that they may reach the peak of power available to them." It would make no sense to reverse things and define growth as the end for the sake of which

maturity exists—any more than to say that maturity exists for the sake of decline and death, which ends life but cannot reasonably be considered its end
(a view as absurd as the claim that the eventual decay of the bed is the end at
which the bedmaker aims). The movements that take place, both in the
craftsman's shop and in the growing body of a young plant or animal, can
therefore meaningfully be explained, among other ways, as movements toward
an end "for the sake of which" these movements themselves occur. In Aristotle's view, this is a common characteristic of phenomena belonging to the
distinct domains of *poesis* and *phusis*.

But if that is so, what is the analogue in the domain of living things of
the plan in the mind of the maker that is presupposed by every explanation
of "poetic" movement as something that occurs "for the sake" of an end?

For Aristotle, only one answer makes sense. Immature plants and animals
have a tendency to grow in a certain direction. They incline toward the mature states that things of their kind are equipped to achieve. This tendency is
more than a mere possibility. It is a kind of default. Unless blocked by external forces, it will carry the organism whose tendency it is in one direction
only. It is what Aristotle calls "potential" (*dunamis*). Potential is the analogue,
in living things, of a maker's plan. The maker's plan guides his actions, as
he gathers materials and fastens them together in order to make a bed. In a
similar way, a plant or animal's potential to become a fully developed member of its kind shapes in advance the developmental pathway it follows to
this end.

Both plan and potential are therefore characterized by what we might call
"anticipatory orientation toward an end." In the case of artifacts, the orientation is supplied from without. It is not "in" the artifact itself. By contrast, living things are themselves the source of this orientation. It is their own potential
that supplies it, and if we are to understand how this is possible, Aristotle
says, we must think of the potential of a plant or animal as analogous to the
plan of a maker who is working on himself—who is at once the source *and*
subject of the direction that gives the arc of his life an intelligible shape.

The clearest case of making is one in which the maker makes something
other than himself (a bed, for example). But a maker can "operate" on his own
mind or body too, in the way that a physical trainer does when he follows the
regimen he prescribes for others. According to Aristotle, this is precisely what
the natural movement of living things is like. "Nature," he says, "is like a doctor doctoring himself."[35] Nothing reveals more clearly the degree to which his
understanding of *phusis* rests on a "poetic" model.

But the analogy is inexact. When a doctor works on a patient, or even on himself, he conceives beforehand the therapeutic result he hopes to achieve. It is there, finished and complete, as an idea in the doctor's mind before he sets to work, and during the course of the work functions as an inspiration, guide and check. The cure that "emerges" from the doctor's work is fully present beforehand in the shape of an idea, and only emerges on account of this idea, which both motivates and directs the process that produces it (or at least aims to, since the doctor's efforts sometime fail). By contrast, the growth of a tadpole into a frog is not a process directed by a "preconception" of this sort. Neither the tadpole nor anything else has an idea of what it should be, or guides and checks the development of the maturing frog by reference to it, in the way a doctor checks his patient's progress against the diagnosis he makes at the start.

In a sense, the whole frog is present in the tadpole in the form of its potential. But this whole only becomes visible as it emerges in the course of the tadpole's growth, unlike the doctor's diagnosis which brings the end of his treatment to view before the doctor begins. The doctor (and anyone to whom he explains what he is doing) can "see" the result of his work in advance, and it is precisely the doctor's "vision" that causes him to act as he does, and therefore explains the course of treatment he prescribes.

In the case of the tadpole, the frog that exists when its growth is complete (the analogue of the patient's health) can be seen only at the end of the process. This process has a discernible direction. But it is not directed in the way the doctor's ministrations are—by a picture of the result that "envisions" it as if it were already finished. The tadpole itself has no such picture in mind. Neither do its parents, which "make" the tadpole by a process of reproduction that is as mindless as the growth of the tadpole itself. Wherever we look in the world of natural comings-to-be, we find movements that can be explained (among other ways) as processes of growth, which are intelligible only in case we distinguish between potency and act. But none of these—in contrast to every "poetic" coming-to-be—is the product of a plan. There is no mind whose reflective guidance is required to account for the phenomena of natural growth. In this sense, nature is fundamentally unlike a doctor doctoring himself. It is, to borrow a distinction of Kant's, a "purposive" order, but one that neither exhibits nor assumes an underlying "purpose" of any kind at all.[36]

The shift from Aristotle's pagan metaphysics to a Christian conception of the world obliterates the distinction between natural and artificial comings-

to-be and requires that the first now be explained, like the second, as the outcome of a plan.

On a Christian view, the world as a whole and everything in it is set in
motion by a transcendent God whose mind contains in advance the idea of
all their subsequent movements. Everything that happens in time God takes
in "at a glance" at the moment of creation. It follows that everything in the
world is explained by his plan for it, in the same way the progress of a patient
is explained by the treatment his doctor conceives for him at the start. Unlike a human doctor, of course, God is not hampered by any preexisting imperfections in the material on which he works. God is a creator, not a maker
in Aristotle's sense. We mark this difference by saying that God's plan is *providential:* there is nothing that falls outside its scope, or frustrates its execution. Still, these two processes are alike in one crucial respect, for in both there
is a supervising intelligence that comprehends the process as a whole before
the process has begun, and whose comprehension is essential to the explanation of what follows.

In the case of a human act of making, both the conception of the plan
and its implementation are events that occur in time. The entire process, from
conception to completion, is a temporal one. To have a view of it, its maker
need not stand outside of time. God's creation is different. If God creates the
world as a whole, and time with it, his plan must be conceived from a standpoint beyond the world and time. This allows for a tremendous increase in
explanatory power, for the "poetic" mode of explanation now becomes ap-
plicable to absolutely everything in the world, and to natural processes in particular, which need no longer merely be analogized to artificial ones, since
they are actually artificial through and through.

But this increase in explanatory power is an illusion. The value of the "poetic" explanations that Aristotle offers depends on our being able to put ourselves imaginatively in the position of the human maker whose plan accounts
for the particular process we are trying to grasp—that of a doctor, for example, whose prescription explains why his patient is no longer feverish. But we
cannot do this in God's case. We cannot put ourselves, imaginatively or otherwise, in God's position. The difference between him and us is not just great.
It is infinitely great. As a consequence, we can never comprehend his plan for
the world. All that we are able to say is that there must be one. But what it is,
and how it works, necessarily exceed our powers of understanding.

This means that if the world is to be explained as the product of God's
plan, there is nothing in it that we can explain. The radical extension of

"poetic" explanation to cover the world as a whole, coupled with the equally radical separation of man's mind from God's, leaves the world wholly incomprehensible in "poetic" terms, and prepares the way for the explanation of all worldly phenomena through a strictly mechanical science from which all reference to purposes has been systematically excluded.

Spinoza rejects the idea of creation. To suppose that the world was brought into being by a God beyond it violates the principle of sufficient reason. This is where Spinoza parts company with Descartes and every other seventeenth-century thinker. But the fact that the world is not the product of a plan does not mean it is devoid of the directed striving that in Aristotle's view is a property of all natural beings. Indeed, in Spinoza's metaphysics, such striving is conceived even more broadly than in Aristotle's account of natural motion. For Spinoza, the striving to persevere belongs to every being as such. In its higher reaches, it takes the form of planning. A man who devises a plan of study in order to gain a more adequate understanding of the world is striving to increase his power in a "planful" way. At lower levels, however, this striving is less planful or not planful at all, in the sense that it is not guided by a preconception of the end to be attained. A plant, reaching up to the sun, is striving to persevere, but not according to a plan. A dog searching for a bone falls somewhere in between.

In sum: Spinoza's world, unlike Descartes', is not the product of a plan. But also unlike Descartes', it contains infinitely many beings whose movements cannot be explained except in terms of the idea of striving toward a goal. His acknowledgment of the reality of such striving brings Spinoza's metaphysics closer to Aristotle's. Yet three important differences remain.

First, *conatus* is a property of every being, including artificial ones. The striving to persevere is not restricted, as it is for Aristotle, to a separate realm of nature. For Spinoza, all beings are natural—even the pan in the sink.[37] Second, the distinction between planning and growing, between *poesis* and *phusis,* is for Spinoza a difference of degree rather than kind. Planning is just growing of a particularly advanced and well-organized sort. By contrast, for Aristotle the distinction between these marks a fundamental divide.

Third, and most important, the striving that Aristotle attributes to natural beings is in every case for something determinate. Its goal is the development and expression of the powers that belong to each being as a member of its kind. It is therefore a striving that can be fulfilled. Spinoza's world is by contrast a scene of universal disappointment, for the striving that constitutes the being of every thing in it is for a state or condition that no finite being can ever attain—one of infinite power, which belongs only to the world as a whole.

This last point helps to explain why, though certain beings of a highly developed sort engage in the kind of making that allows and indeed requires us to explain their actions as the result of a preconceived plan, the same sort of explanation cannot be used to account for the existence and order of the world itself.

Only a being that sees things from a point of view is able to form a plan. A plan gathers things together in a perspectival fashion. It may organize a great deal in this way. But however much it includes within its scope, it always arranges its materials in accordance with some determinate set of interests and ambitions. Otherwise, it is not even recognizable as a plan.

All human planning is like this. Whenever we plan, we always do so from a particular point of view. But it is only because we are finite that we see the world in this way. It is our finitude that both enables *and* compels us to plan. For the whole world to be the product of a plan, it would have to be conceived all at once, from the "outside," so to speak, and only an infinite mind, beyond space and time, could do this. But an infinite mind does not see things from a point of view. It is therefore a contradiction to assume, as creationists do, that a mind of this sort could engage in any planning at all. Creationism thus rests on the illicit extension of the phenomenon of planning, which we know firsthand from our own experience and is explicable only because of the finitude of our cognitive and other powers, to the imagined case of a being free from these limits, who just for that reason is unbound by the constraints on which all planning depends. This is the essence of the bad anthropomorphism to which Spinoza attributes the belief in gods with intentions and desires generally, and faith in a creator God specifically.

In Spinoza's metaphysics, the infinite mind of the transcendent God of the Abrahamic religions disappears, and is replaced by the infinite intelligibility of the world itself, which is unplanned yet wholly explicable, as it must be, in Spinoza's view, if *anything* in it is ever to be explained at all. Yet despite the disappearance of planning at this "cosmic" level, the unplanned world that remains has room in it for beings like us, who do plan, and whose "poetic" endeavors represent a peculiarly refined expression of the universal, if unfulfillable, pursuit of infinite power that every finite being strives to achieve—purposively, though for the most part with no purpose "in mind."

Darwin's view is not far off.

His account of the process of natural selection begins with a long discussion of animal breeding—the purposeful selection by human beings of animal and plant types especially adapted to their breeders' uses. Breeding is a "poetic" activity. It is motivated and guided by a plan in the mind of the breeder who knows in advance what he wants and pursues it in a deliberate way, checking at each step to see how well he is doing. Neither the result of his efforts, nor these efforts themselves, can be explained except by reference to the plan the breeder conceives before he begins.

But then Darwin shifts from the farm to the wild, to the natural world that lies outside the relatively small area of human cultivation, and draws an analogy reminiscent of Aristotle's description of nature as a doctor doctoring himself. For here, too, Darwin says, we see a process of selection at work that resembles the one that occurs under the supervisory control of the breeder—a process of "natural" selection that produces "fitter" individuals, better adapted to their environment with greater chances of success in the struggle for existence. The fact that such results can be produced in a "poetic" way by human making, where the process of selection is vividly apparent (in part because of the relatively short time in which it occurs and in part because we all have some firsthand experience of making, and so can place ourselves imaginatively in the breeders' position), makes it easier to believe that similar results can be achieved in the natural world, where the analogous process is too long and slow for the human eye to take in at a glance.

But the analogy, as Darwin points out, is inapt in two ways. First, the breeding of plants and animals is not ultimately for their own advantage. It may increase their longevity, reproductive success and the like, but only because these redound to the benefit of their breeders. The interests of the organisms being bred is entirely subordinate to that of the human beings who do the breeding, so much so that it sometimes produces characteristics that limit the mobility and flexibility of the organisms in question. The process of natural selection, by contrast, selects only those advantages that are useful to their possessor, except in cases of complex interdependency where the evolutionary fates of two different kinds of plants or animals have become entwined. (Darwin was particularly interested in such cases and devotes several fascinating pages to what he calls the "slave-making instinct" in certain species of ant.[38])

Second, and more important, the process of natural selection is not really a "poetic" one at all. It is not directed by a plan, either one constructed by those who undergo it, or by anyone else outside the process, supervising it from "above," in the way a farmer supervises the breeding of his sheep. To explain its results, we do not need to assume that what happens in the wild runs according to a script that has been thought out in advance. This assumption is entirely appropriate, indeed unavoidable, in the realm of animal husbandry, where Darwin begins his account of the ideas of selection and fitness. But we can employ these same ideas in the vastly wider sphere of natural selection without making the same assumption. Indeed, this is the chief advantage of Darwin's theory of natural selection—that it allows us to explain a process that weeds out and selects, and tends over time to produce better-adapted plants and animals, without ever appealing to a plan of any kind, either human or divine. All we need to assume is scarcity and competition, driven by the universal desire to exist (which really means, as we have seen, to live on without end). Nothing more is required to account for the enormous diversity of life that has emerged on earth, during eons of time, through the unplanned workings of natural selection. In particular, there is no need to assume the existence of a mind in which the results of this process have been envisioned in advance, in the way a breeder sees, before starting out, the goal of his efforts and the means by which to reach it.

To be able to do without this assumption in our attempt to explain the phenomena of life represents a tremendous victory for the principle of sufficient reason. That is because only a mind beyond the world could take in all these phenomena at once and arrange them in accordance with a plan, and since any mind of this sort must remain inaccessible to us, relying on it as a principle of explanation brings the search for understanding to an end. One particularly dramatic illustration of this is the difficulty of explaining, on the basis of God's plan for the world, the many features of plant and animal life that appear useless or counterproductive.[39]

Still, if Darwin's explanation of the process of natural selection has no need for the idea of a plan, it cannot do without the concept of purposeful striving. The competition that drives the process arises because the competitors are struggling to reproduce in a world of scarce resources. Competition among them is therefore inevitable. But it would not even exist unless those engaged in it were striving to increase their strength and presence in the world, though not (except at higher levels) in accordance with a plan. Thus, if Darwinism undermines the idea that the world works according to a plan, it also requires us to assume that every living being is motivated, indeed constituted, by the kind of directed longing that Aristotle invoked to explain the growth of plants and animals and Spinoza attributes to all beings as such.

To the question, "Why does life on earth look the way it does?" Darwin believed that an answer can in principle be given, though we shall never be done with the work of providing it. His confidence depended on the rejection of every appeal to creation, which he considered a roadblock in the way of understanding. To know why life looks as it does, we must give up the belief that the world is the product of a plan. But we need not, indeed cannot, abandon the idea that every living thing in the world is striving to reach a goal—and not just any goal, but life everlasting, the eternal and divine, *deus sive natura*—for without this its career and that of the species to which it belongs would be wholly unintelligible.

The world of life can thus in principle be entirely understood but only if we abandon the creationist fantasy that it has been created in accordance with a plan, *and* simultaneously affirm that everything that happens in it does so for the sake of an end. This combination of ideas is certainly not Christian. But neither is it Aristotelian, for its hyperrationalist ambitions cannot be satisfied by the metaphysics of form and matter on which Aristotle's philosophy rests.

There is only one metaphysics that joins these two ideas in the way the theory of natural selection demands. This is the born-again paganism of Spinoza. For Spinoza, like Darwin, the world is unplanned yet despite that wholly explicable precisely because every thing in it yearns to have as lasting a share in the infinite power of the world as it can. This is the view that shocked Spinoza's readers and many of Darwin's too. To their critics, it seemed a godless philosophy, and from either a pagan or Christian perspective it certainly is. But there is another theology, distinct from either of these, that suffuses the work of both. For despite their disbelief in an eternal God beyond the world and shared insistence on the transience of every thing in it, both Spinoza and Darwin joyfully affirm the existence of one thing, at least, that lasts forever, and of which we can partake, though never as fully as we desire. That is the intelligibility of the world itself, which is as deep and enduring as its reality, because at bottom these are the same.

We might call this their shared faith, except that "faith" connotes a groundless belief. For Spinoza, at least, any purported divergence between reality and intelligibility would itself have to be explained and anyone who attempts to do this, rather than remaining mute, thereby demonstrates (grudgingly, perhaps, like Socrates' interlocutors) his own allegiance to the principle of sufficient reason, which is a shorthand expression for the metaphysical principle that to be is to be intelligible.

In a similar way, the demand that the theory of natural selection account for its own presuppositions—which its creationist critics advance in order to deflate the theory, but its most thoughtful defenders embrace—reflects the view that outside the circle of reason, which Darwin did so much to extend, there is nothing at all. Those who pray to a God beyond the world are likely to regard this idea as a sin. But to those who follow Darwin in spirit as well as word, his boundless commitment to reason must seem the best way to understand the meaning of the eternal and divine in a world whose highest ideals are today expressed in scientific terms that rule out the idea of a creator God once and for all.

CHAPTER 30

The Navel of the Dream

FREUD AND THE SCIENCE OF THE MIND

Spinoza's God is one, eternal, uncreated, and modified in endless ways. Because our minds are finite, we can apprehend it only to a limited degree. We do so under two distinct explanatory schemes. Spinoza calls these "attributes." They are the self-contained and separate (hence partial and incomplete) systems of observation, inference and law within which we attempt to account for the "absolutely infinite" reality of what Spinoza variously terms "substance," "nature" or "God."

One of these explains the modal order of the world under the rubric of "extension." It imagines the world to be a system of bodies and forces acting on one another from without, in ever-shifting constellations of motion and rest. Spinoza gives us a brief sketch of what such a science might look like in the "physical digression" that follows Proposition 13 of part 2 of the *Ethics*.

The other views the world as a system of minds. A mind is an idea or set of ideas, and an idea is a representation.[1] There are higher-order ideas that represent other ideas, but the most basic ones represent or depict bodies. They have bodies as their intentional objects. Still, even the simplest idea differs from the body it represents. It has what we might call an "inner" reality—an intentionality that no body conceived merely as an extended being possesses. Viewed under the attribute of thought, the world appears to us to be an infinitely complex order of this inward, or psychological, kind.

Spinoza's own interests drew him more in the direction of psychology than physics. With the exception of the physical digression, four of the five parts of the *Ethics* are devoted to the study of the mind—first, in part 2, of the mind in general, and then in the remaining three parts, of the human mind and its passions.

Four basic principles guide Spinoza's psychology.

The first is that every psychical event, like every physical one, is in principle perfectly intelligible, though we shall never be able to account for it completely.

Second, psychological explanation, like its physical counterpart, is causal in nature. We explain an idea by placing it in a chain of ideas whose predecessors cause it. If our knowledge of the chain were complete, we could explain every link in it. From the fact that we cannot, we wrongly infer that the psychical chain is broken at points by chance or spontaneity, which we conventionally call "freedom." But that is as much a mistake in psychology as in physics. Both sciences are deterministic. To the extent they are sciences at all, neither can allow for the existence of freedom, which is just the name we give the shortfall between the intelligibility of the world and our understanding of it.

Third, though we explain ideas by placing them in a presumptively determined causal chain, the principles that govern this chain necessarily differ from those that structure the one by means of which we explain the behavior of bodies. Ideas are representations. To explain the existence of an idea, we must therefore insert it into a chain of ideas whose causal relations to one another are themselves representational in nature. Thus, one idea can cause another by association, repression and the like, but not, as bodies do, through impact, gravity, or the interference of electromagnetic waves.

The causal laws of psychology are *sui generis,* as are those of physics. It is thus an error to suppose that an event conceived under the attribute of extension can ever be explained by appealing to an antecedent idea, and equally erroneous to think that the same event, conceived as an occurrence in the order of ideas, can be accounted for by a prior physical state. This is Spinoza's famous doctrine of the explanatory independence of the attributes of extension and thought. He offers it as a solution to the otherwise insoluble problem that Descartes' metaphysics presents of how to conceive the relation of bodies to minds. While Spinoza insists that every mode is in principle perfectly explicable, whether we view it as a being of a physical or psychical kind, these two forms of explanation run along parallel tracks that never meet.

Fourth, and finally, though the laws of psychology may be applied to the study of any mind, we have a special interest in understanding one in particular. That is the human mind. We are most immediately and intimately interested in the structure of our own thoughts and ideas. In this sense, we are all peculiarly self-regarding. Such self-regard is not, moreover, an accidental trait like having blue eyes or a deep voice. It is the essence of the striving to persevere in being that makes each of us the individual he or she is.

In human beings, this takes the form of a striving to know. It is through knowledge that our power and therefore activity and reality grow. As we come to know more and more, our ideas, which are always partly cloudy and partly clear, partly dependent and partly self-contained, partly passive and partly active, move in the latter direction. We come closer to the state of perfect self-sufficiency that only the world as a whole enjoys. Every sort of knowledge contributes to our growth in this regard. But one kind is especially important. This is the knowledge a reflective man or woman gains of his or her own mind, for it alone helps one to see why knowledge of any sort is worth pursuing and has the power to free us from the chains in which our ignorance confines us, like the prisoners in Plato's cave.

One may come to understand this in general terms, by gaining a deeper understanding of the liberating potential that all knowledge possesses for those imprisoned in what we call the human condition. But the most valuable knowledge of this kind is first-personal in nature. It is a knowledge of the darkness in one's own mind, and of the power of understanding to brighten it. The general laws of psychology that Spinoza unfolds in books 2 through 5 of the *Ethics* are all meant to bring the reader to an individualized self-understanding of this sort, and with it, to a level of activity that is as close to that of God as a human being may aspire to reach. In this sense, Spinoza's science of the mind is more than merely instructive. It is therapeutic as well. It is at once a psychology and an ethics. For those habituated to the belief that "is" must be separated from "ought," Spinoza's conflation of psychology and ethics is bound to seem a mistake. But that judgment itself is shaped, as we shall see in the following chapter, by the lingering authority of the creationist metaphysics that Spinoza sought to overthrow.

PSYCHOLOGY AND PSYCHOANALYSIS

Many, of course, have followed Spinoza's lead in attempting to construct a rigorous science of the human mind. The whole of modern psychology might be described as an effort of this kind. But one psychologist in particular stands out on account of the affinity between his ideas and those of Spinoza. I am referring to Sigmund Freud.

Others have noted the Spinozist cast of many of Freud's central beliefs and late in his life he made some admiring remarks about the philosopher, whose work he had read as a student.[2] But there is no evidence that Freud ever consciously drew upon Spinoza's philosophy in framing his own ideas. Indeed, he repeatedly denied being motivated by philosophical concerns of any kind at all. Freud preferred to portray himself as an empiricist, guided by his attention to the facts alone. Yet despite his protestations, Freud's theory of the mind clearly belongs to the long tradition of philosophical reflection on the nature of the human condition, and is marked by its resemblance, in several respects, to Spinoza's account of our place in the order of things.

To begin with, Freud is as resolute a rationalist as Spinoza himself. His commitment to the principle of sufficient reason is equally deep. This may seem like an odd thing to say. After all, isn't Freud the thinker who, more than any other, drew attention to the pervasive irrationality of our mental lives—to the presence in them of the dark and disturbing forces that Aeneas summons from below in the passage that Freud chose as the epigram for *The Interpretation of Dreams?*

This common view of Freud's psychology rests on a mistake.

Freud insists, of course, that many mental activities defy, or at least appear to defy, the laws of logic. This is particularly true of those primitive forms of mentation he calls "primary" processes. It is also true of the phenomenon of "ambivalence"—the simultaneous embrace and repudiation of one and the same object (what we conventionally call "love-hate" relations).[3] But it is precisely these seemingly illogical aspects of our mental life that Freud seeks to render intelligible. He does so mainly by means of a theory of intrapsychic conflict that views the mind as a community of partly cooperative, partly warring agencies that sometimes "want" opposite things.

Later, we shall explore in more detail the theory Freud employs to rationalize these various phenomena, which others before him attributed to demons or disease or gave up trying to explain altogether. What I want to emphasize now is something more basic. That is Freud's conviction that nothing in the realm of mental life is in principle inexplicable. Freud is not merely a rationalist but a hyperrationalist like Spinoza, who believes that the intelligibility of our mental lives extends to every thought, feeling, image, or fantasy, however absurd or mindless it seems—the doctrine of sufficient reason applied to the universe of psychic events, or what Spinoza calls the world conceived under the attribute of thought.

Nowhere is Freud's rationalism more apparent than in *The Interpretation of Dreams.*[4] Over and over again, Freud follows a seemingly meaningless dream, or fragment of a dream, into an expanding web of associations that by degrees renders it more intelligible in the context of the dreamer's mental life as a whole. The confidence with which he pursues this rationalizing inquiry into the darkest corners of the most obscure dreams, is as impressive as Spinoza's.

Yet like Spinoza, Freud tempers his confidence with the sober recognition that our success in this venture can never be complete. "There is often a passage in even the most thoroughly interpreted dream," he writes, "which has to be left obscure." Freud calls this the "dream's navel, the spot where it reaches down into the unknown."

"[F]rom the nature of things," he concludes, the interpretation of any dream is therefore an endless endeavor. It can never come to a "definite" close. It is "bound to branch out in every direction into the intricate network of our world of thought."[5] We may continue on, for as long as we are able, confident that our inquiries will continue to throw further light on the dream in question. But at some point, we must stop, not because the dream, or the world, forbids us to proceed, or blocks us from taking a further step, but because our powers are exhausted and we have done enough for the purposes at hand. Freud's image of the dream's navel is his version of Spinoza's worm in the blood, and conveys the same confidence in the power of reason, chastened by an awareness of our inability to comprehend more than a fragment of the infinitely complex "tangle" of the mental life of the one whose dream it is. This is the first point of contact between them.

A second is their understanding of what it means to explain anything at all, and psychic events in particular. To explain a mental event, Freud says, we must insert it in the chain of ideas and feelings to which it belongs. This chain stretches back to our birth and continues uninterrupted until we die. There are no gaps or breaks in it. Even apparent lacunae—moments of forgetfulness, for example, or those brief episodes in which we seem to have nothing on our minds at all—are links in the chain. (It was the appearance of such lacunae that first drove Freud to postulate the existence of the unconscious, whose role in his theory of mind may therefore be said to derive from his prior commitment to the principle of sufficient reason.)

Each link, moreover, is determined by the ones that went before. Given its predecessors, no other thought or feeling is possible. The appearance of spontaneity in our mental life is therefore an illusion. In reality, there is no such thing. The experience of spontaneity is either a wish (to be explained by its antecedent causes) or ignorance of these causes themselves. In this respect, Freud is as uncompromising a determinist as Spinoza. This is reflected in the fact that in his several different "maps" of the mind—his so-called "topologies" of mental functioning—Freud never once assigns a place to the will, though he makes many other refinements to accommodate his increasingly complex picture of psychic determination.

Early in his psychoanalytic career, Freud conflated psychic and physical determination, inspired, no doubt, by the wish to give his new science a stature comparable to the one already enjoyed by certain of the more advanced medical sciences most proximate to it (neurology in particular). He later abandoned this approach in favor of one that emphasizes the explanatory independence of the psychological laws that determine the chain of mental events, and settled on a view that more closely resembles Spinoza's account of the causal parallelism of events conceived under the attributes of thought and extension.[6]

The general laws of mental life that Freud evolved in the course of his research (the early processes of ego formation, the stages of infantile sexuality, the mechanisms of repression, the dynamics of the oedipal situation, etc.) thus all employ, in one form or another, the concept of representation (as desire, wish, image, projection and the like). Each takes into account the interiority, or intentionality, that distinguishes every idea from all strictly physical states. And while Freud was happy to concede that states of the body and states of the mind may run in parallel order, the independent explanatory power of his psychology is inevitably lost in any attempt to reduce it to a physics of electrical discharges or biochemical reactions from which the idea of representation has been purged.

Freud's unwavering rationalism; his unflinching determinism; his belief in the representational nature of the causal relations among psychic as opposed to bodily states; and his acknowledgment of the limits to which the explanation of any item in the chain of mental events is permanently subject are important Spinozist themes in his work. But there is another that is more important still. This is the conviction, which both men share, that understanding oneself is the key to living the healthiest, freest, and most powerful life one can.

Like Spinoza, Freud sought to construct a general theory of the human mind. He continued to revise his theory from the mid-1890s on. Freud's theory changed in important ways from one phase of his career to the next. Statements of the theory may be found in chapter 7 of *The Interpretation of Dreams* (1900); *Three Essays on the Theory of Sexuality* (1905); "Narcissism" (1914); the series of papers that Freud describes as essays in metapsychology (1915–17); "Mourning and Melancholia" (1917); *Beyond the Pleasure Principle* (1920); *The Ego and the Id* (1923), and elsewhere.

But Freud did more than expound a general psychology. He sought to apply it to the study of individual patients with the help of techniques whose goal is the understanding of this or that particular mind. Psychoanalysis differs from psychology in its focus on the individual and only makes sense on the assumption that each patient's unique history and experience of the world is in principle as accessible to reason as the development and operation of the human mind in general. This is the assumption that underlies Freud's account of the otherwise baffling symptoms of Elizabeth von R. (1895), Dora (1905), the Rat Man (1909) and other patients whose treatment he describes in his various case studies.

The aim of psychoanalysis, however, in contrast to that of psychology, is not merely cognitive. It is therapeutic as well. Like Spinoza, Freud believed that of all the individuals in the world, we are each especially interested in the one we happen to be. He was also convinced that psychoanalysis has the potential to enable the analysand to live a relatively more active life—one less hostage to forces that must otherwise be suffered in an unknowing and therefore unhappy way. Freud's account of how and why the self-knowledge that psychoanalysis affords can produce even a partial liberation of this kind changed significantly over the course of his career. He also became increasingly doubtful about the ease and speed and permanence with which it can be secured. But despite these doubts, he never wavered in his conviction that such knowledge possesses a curative power. To the end of his life, Freud continued to believe that psychoanalysis is at once a science *and* an ethics—a method of self-understanding *and* a technique for living well or at least better than one otherwise might. In this respect, psychoanalysis rests on the same fusion of "is" and "ought" as Spinoza's philosophy (which is one reason it now seems so dubious to many). This is the deepest point of connection between them.

Today, psychoanalysis is on the defensive. Its authority as a science and effectiveness as a therapy have both been called into question. From a position of intellectual prestige, which reached its peak in the middle years of the twentieth century, the practical and theoretical stature of psychoanalysis has declined sharply. In this regard, Freud's fate as a thinker has been strikingly different from that of Darwin and even of Einstein, whose search for a unifying account of physical reality capable of harmonizing quantum mechanics with general relativity theory is once again increasingly fashionable, after having been dismissed by many for the past fifty years. Freud's situation is different. From the science he claimed it to be, psychoanalysis has been demoted to the position of a literary technique or wisdom philosophy, akin to that taught by certain ancient philosophers who also insisted on the ethical value of self-knowledge.[7]

Some of the critics of psychoanalysis say that it is too expensive for any but a few to afford. They claim that other forms of psychotherapy, including those that rely heavily on drugs, are cheaper and more effective. They offer clinical data to support their view.[8]

Philosophers of science attack psychoanalysis from a different direction. Some, like Karl Popper, dispute its ability to produce falsifiable claims.[9] Others, like Adolph Grunbaum, concede that psychoanalysis makes such claims, but deny that they have yet been tested in a rigorous way, and challenge what they take to be Freud's unproven assumption that the truth of an interpretation is validated by its positive effect on the patient's well-being.[10] They criticize those, like Jürgen Habermas and Paul Ricoeur, who attempt to save the dignity of psychoanalysis by construing it as a "hermeneutic," or interpretive, activity concerned with meaning rather than causation—correctly observing that Freud himself was preoccupied with questions of causation, and, more generally, that meaning and causation cannot be separated in any scientific inquiry, whether it be concerned with bodies or minds. Along with growing doubts about its pragmatic effectiveness, these philosophical objections to the status of psychoanalysis as a science have damaged Freud's standing in our culture generally—partly because of our impatience with therapies that take too long or cost too much, and partly because of the widespread belief that science is only instrumentally, and not inherently, connected to well-being: the dogma of the separation of "is" and "ought."

Whether the Freudian science of psychoanalysis will ever be restored to the prominence it once enjoyed is impossible to say. But it should be emphasized that the criticisms most often brought against it leave its aspirations untouched.

The claim, for example, that other therapies work better and faster assumes a benchmark of well-being that psychoanalysis does not. To accept this contention at face value is thus to beg the question it is meant to settle. That lesser sorts of improvement can be obtained more cheaply in other ways does not disprove the claim that psychoanalysis aspires to something better, if at greater cost. What Spinoza said remains true even in our age of accelerating expectations: "everything excellent is difficult and rare."

Moreover, the fact that a person's moods change with the biochemical states of his body and that these can be manipulated by drugs of one kind or another does not decide the question of whether the latter *cause* the former or *run in parallel* to them. The successes of modern psychopharmacology do not resolve the metaphysical dispute between Descartes and Spinoza. And as to the claim that Freud was wrong to tie the truth of the analyst's interpretation to an improvement in his patient's condition, this also begs the question in a crucial respect, for it leans heavily on a view of science that sees its relation to ethics as an external rather than internal one, which however obvious it seems to many, is a view that psychoanalysis rejects.

Still, however one adjudicates these issues, it is striking that both the critics and defenders of psychoanalysis today largely agree that it is no science at all. This is a judgment they share, though they draw different conclusions from it. But despite their agreement on this basic point, there is one respect in which Freud's theory of the human mind may be said to exhibit the spirit of modern science to an exemplary degree. This is its uniquely strong commitment to the principle of sufficient reason.

The same commitment led Einstein to believe that the seemingly insoluble questions posed by quantum mechanics and by the evidence that our universe began with an event that defies the laws of physics in their present form must one day yield to the mind's persistent efforts to answer them. Darwin accepted the principle of sufficient reason too. It is the premise of his belief that all the most puzzling features of life on earth can in the end be explained by the theory of natural selection, and of his relentless campaign against creationism, which he viewed as an abdication from reason.

Freud's theory of the human mind starts from a similar premise, but his confidence in the power of reason is arguably even greater than that of Einstein and Darwin. In part, this is because he insists that reason has the power to illuminate not only the most obscure corners of the mind but also those that have always been viewed as essentially irrational (that is, directed against the use of reason itself). More fundamentally, it is because, in contrast to these other two, Freud extends the principle of sufficient reason to the analysis of individual cases.

In physics and biology, individuals are important because of their evidentiary role in supporting or challenging competing theoretical claims. They serve as examples and test cases. In psychoanalysis, this relation is reversed. The focus is on the individual herself. The ultimate *explanandum* of all psychoanalytic inquiry is the individuality of this or that mind. Freud's general psychology is an aid in this endeavor, but only that.

This makes Freud's rationalism especially robust, for it is precisely the individuality of individuals that has always seemed to lie beyond the reach of understanding, on account of the generality of reason itself. That we can make progress in understanding who we are not only as human beings in general, but as individuals with a unique identity, forged in the course of our own distinct life experiences, is the hyperrationalist premise on which the enterprise of psychoanalysis rests. This is the boldest conceivable expression of the Spinozism that underlies the whole of modern science. It is a particularly powerful example of its deepest commitments and not, as the critics of psychoanalysis claim, an abandonment of them. It is also, as we shall see, despite Freud's own professed antipathy to religion, a strikingly clear manifestation of the born-again paganism that constitutes the implicit theology of modern science in general—its affirmation that the world is not only inherently intelligible, as Aristotle claimed, but infinitely so, as the self-negating religion of unrequited gratitude first taught us to understand.

"OUT OF THE CRADLE, ENDLESSLY ROCKING"

Freud's psychological account of human development is cast in general terms. Still, it is centrally concerned with the question of how one becomes an individual, and in this way linked to the psychoanalytic effort to make sense of a single life. This point has been emphasized, in particular, by Hans Loewald, a philosophically oriented analyst who as a young man studied with Martin Heidegger.[11]

Loewald puts the search for an individual identity at the very center of Freud's theory of the human mind. This aspect of Freud's theory is brought

out, Loewald says, by his concept of "repetition." According to Freud, the relations we have with others as adults "repeat" those formed in earlier stages of
our lives. They follow lines of expectation and anxiety laid down in early childhood, or before. But each repetition has something novel about it. It does not
merely reenact but reshapes or reformulates inherited patterns of thought and
feeling. In this sense, we are constantly becoming something new and different than we were before. Our individuality is a lifelong work in progress, and
the movement toward an ever-richer, more inclusive, more complex or "structured" individuality defines, in Loewald's view, the arc of a fulfilling human
life, as Freud conceives it.

This conception, Loewald says, contrasts fundamentally with the "primitive" idea of repetition, as Mircea Eliade and others have described it. On
a primitive view of the world, according to Eliade, to repeat an experience
(to make a sacrifice before a hunt, or participate in a totemic feast) is to
return to the same unchanging "place" one occupied before and that others
occupied in the more distant past—a place that is in fact no past at all, but
an eternal, motionless present, where novelty and individuality do not exist. The meaning and value of repetition, so conceived, lie not in the originality and uniqueness of the event but its recurrence and sameness instead.

Loewald might also have contrasted the Freudian theory of human development with Aristotle's more philosophical account of it, for on Aristotle's
view too every human life is a repetition in this same primitive sense.

According to Aristotle, a human being is born and, if things go reasonably
well, grows to adulthood and into the full possession of his powers. These are
powers that all men share. They constitute one's humanity—the form of
one's being as a man, as distinct from one's matter, which make each human
being an individual member of the species to which he belongs. As a man
matures, the formal side of his being emerges more clearly. He "comes into
his own" as a man. In Aristotle's view, this represents a movement in the direction of greater reality, which for all things, including human beings, resides in their form alone. What makes a grown man real, therefore, has nothing
to do with his individuality. It is entirely a function of his species-being. In
the endless wheel of reproduction, by means of which the human species, like
every other kind of plant and animal on earth, imitates, in a moving way, the
motionless eternity of the mindedness of the cosmos as a whole, each generation arrives back at the same peak of fulfillment that its predecessors had occupied in the past—one defined by the unchanging form that human beings
will always possess, from which every trace of novelty and individuality are

absent. For Aristotle, too, there is nothing new under the sun, and his conception of repetition reflects this.

Freud, by contrast, interprets the phenomenon of repetition against the background of a view of human life that places immense weight on what might be called the vicissitudes of individuation: the struggle to be or become an individual, and above all, to come to terms with the fact that one is an individual with a life uniquely one's own. Indeed, Freud does more than merely place weight on this struggle. It is, for him, the organizing premise of his psychology—of his account of childhood love and loss, of the peculiarly idealistic nature of human sexuality, and of the illnesses that we, the only neurotic animals on earth—impose on ourselves in an understandable if self-defeating effort to defend against the vulnerabilities to which every individual is exposed. For Freud, the meaning and value of human life lie in the poignancies and partial successes of this struggle.

At the start of life, of course, we are not individuals at all. We are not "subjects," confronting the "world." Language fails us in our attempt to describe this condition. The grammar of our language presupposes distinctions (of subject and object, for example) that do not yet exist. The best we can do is try to express this pregrammatical state of oneness with the world in metaphorical terms. Loewald, for example, describes the mental life of a newborn as wholly engulfed in an undifferentiated "force field," which he calls the "mother-child dyad." Strictly speaking, it is not the mental life *of* the child, because that as yet has no separate reality of its own. Nor can the child at this stage be said, even in the most rudimentary way, to feel love for its mother or anything else, since love is always relational—it is always of or for something other than the one who feels it, hence the expression of an experience of separateness that presupposes the distinction of subject and object whose absence is the hallmark of the preindividuated state from which we all emerge.

How does this emergence take place? How is it even possible? Freud offers only hints. But he has some suggestive things to say, and later analysts have built on his suggestions.

According to Freud, the infant's unity with the world is first disrupted by the experience of hunger.[12] To be hungry is to want something one lacks, hence to be separated from it. Hunger is typically followed by satiety, in which the unity that hunger has disrupted is restored. For the infant, this experience is (literally) fulfilling. It is a cause of pleasure, just as hunger is a cause of unpleasure. From the very beginning of our lives, therefore, pleasure is associated with the restoration of wholeness following an experience of separation from what one longs for and needs. It is the birthplace of love.

Freud says that when the infant becomes hungry again, it "remembers" the satiety that followed its hunger before, and begins, slowly, to pursue it in an increasingly purposeful (though still unconscious) way.[13] But this early step in our development, which Freud crosses in a hurry, raises a host of difficulties. How does the infant remember anything at all? How can it distinguish its present from its past, or direct itself toward a future that has not yet arrived? All these things presuppose at least a rudimentary form of time consciousness, and the experience of individual separateness associated with it, that Freud is attempting to explain.

Loewald offers the following gloss.[14] In the periods of quiescence that follow feeding and fullness, the infant is not psychically inert. It remains active—attentive and attuned. Typically, during these receptive moments, the child's mother is talking to it. To the child, the mother's words are merely a soothing sound—part of the pleasurable experience of satiety itself. For the mother, by contrast, her words have meaning. They convey thoughts and feelings. That is because the mother exists at a more advanced stage of individuation than the child. She has long been accustomed to her own separation from the world (though in her dyadic relation with the child, she experiences again, glancingly at least, her lost rapport with it). To the child who will emerge, in Walt Whitman's phrase, "out of the cradle, endlessly rocking," the mother communicates an intimation of her own more advanced self-awareness by "teaching" the child to hear in her words something more than mere sounds. She causes to begin reverberating in the child's undifferentiated mental field a first, nearly inaudible echo of her own time-conscious mind.

This could not happen, of course, if the child did not already have the potential to develop along these lines—if it were not equipped to receive the communication its mother sends with her words. In this sense, even Freud cannot avoid the Aristotelian assumption that our human development is explicable only because we are potentially human from the start. But in Freud's case, this development is one that leads toward a deepening appreciation of one's uniqueness as an individual and not (as it does for Aristotle) toward a pinnacle of species-being—the consummating exhibition of one's common human form. In Loewald's view, this development begins with the emergence of the child as a separate psychic unit with a memory and mind of its own, out of the unity of the mother-child dyad, spurred by the mother's encouraging words. All the later stages of individuation, and the attempt to understand

and make something of them, up to and including the child's eventual awareness that its own individuality must one day disappear from the world, are
built on this foundation.

The infant's emergent psychic separateness prepares the way for its first
experience of love. Love always has an object. It is of something the lover is
not, or does not fully possess. It therefore presupposes the separation of lover
and love object, and the experience, on the part of the first, of an emptiness
that can be repaired only by possession of the second.

In a broad sense, all animals feel love. But we generally reserve the word
for human beings because of the unique intensity with which we feel it. We
are more acutely aware of our separation from the world than other animals
are. Our longing to be reconnected to it is therefore keener as well. This makes
human love especially intense. It also assures that we are bound to be disappointed in love in a way no other animal is. Beginning with the infant in the
cradle, every human lover longs for a state of wholeness that remains unattainable for more than the briefest moments. Each of his love objects, starting
with his mother, is only a part of the world, and thus limited and imperfect,
as any part must be. It can never be the world as a whole, no matter how desperately the lover longs to find the whole world in it. All human love is thus
characterized by what Freud calls "overvaluation."[15] It invests more in its
object than the object can possibly return. The knowledge that this is so
grows with time. It is the price that we must pay for the development of an
increasingly refined sense of our own individuality, tempered, perhaps, by
the knowledge that it cannot be otherwise for any human being.

The special character of human sexuality is related to this.

In all living things, the sex drive represents an immense concentration
of otherwise free-flowing energy—of what might, for lack of a better word,
be called vitality itself. Sex concentrates this energy in one particular set of
sensations, localized, in more advanced forms of life, in one set of bodily
organs, and channels its expenditure in a particular direction. The localizing
and canalizing (Freud calls it "cathecting")[16] of vitality is characteristic of sex
in general.

Human sexuality is distinguished by its tendency to move in the opposite
direction as well: to shift this concentrated energy to other times and places
and acts. Sex, for us, is peculiarly labile. Without losing its intensity, it can
change focus in all sorts of ways. Human sexuality is inherently restless; it
tends to overflow whatever limits are imposed by the demands of reproduction itself. In Freud's terms, it is inherently "perverse."[17] The reason is that we

are always looking for something in sex that no single act, or organ or sensation can possibly contain. We are always looking for love, whose true object
is boundless.

Despite what many believe, there is no such thing as loveless human sex.
The unsatisfiable longing to be at one with the world, which we experience
with unique intensity, infects and transforms all our most basic desires, sex
included. The so-called "perversions" (sadism, masochism, fetishism, and the
like) reveal this most clearly, for their very "unnaturalness" exposes the impossible demands that love makes on sex, causing it to spill over every natural limit, in the restless pursuit of a satisfaction that can never be found. That
sex, which is the principal means by which living things transcend their separateness from one another and the world, should be an especially urgent site
in our insatiable search for love, which is born of the distinctive human pathos of separation itself, is a cornerstone of Freud's account of the early life
experiences that set the pattern for what our later experiences of sex and love
shall be.

At the beginning of life, of course, the process of individuation, without
which there can be no subject that loves an object distinct from itself, or feels
sexually drawn to it, has only just begun (inaugurated, perhaps, as Loewald
proposes, by the mother's interactions with her child). According to Freud,
the almost complete lack of separation that marks this first stage of human
development is reflected by the absence in the mental life of the infant of any
distinction between its own psychical states and the actual presence of what
a philosopher would call their intentional object—first, and most urgently,
the mother's breast.

To form an image of its mother's breast—to represent it—is, for the infant, indistinguishable from causing the breast to appear in reality. The lack
of such a distinction is the mark of an hallucination. Thus, even if the infant
is already sufficiently detached from the world to take something in it as an
object, his detachment is still so rudimentary that the relation between himself and the object he desires—his first love object—is one he experiences as
an *intrapsychic* relation: imagining it makes it real. To that extent, he and the
world remain the same. This is the essence of all "magical thinking," of what
Freud calls the "primary processes" of mental life, which are characterized by
the absence of a more "realistic" appraisal of the separation of subject from
object. At the start of life, the infant's entire psychical being consists of processes of this kind, and though these are later supplemented by other processes of a realistic and logical sort, which rest on a sharper and more focused

appreciation of the distinction between self and world, they never disappear completely but spring back to life every night when we dream, though in a form barely recognizable on account of the complex distortions of the dream work itself.[18]

The infant's hallucination of the breast represents its first, primitive effort to overcome the gap that has opened between its mind and the world. Like every hallucination, it is self-fulfilling. It creates the object of its representation by representing it. In this respect, it resembles—though at the opposite end of the range of mental powers—the intellectual intuition that Kant attributes to the mind of God, whose intuitions, unlike ours, bring their objects into being from nothing.[19]

Put differently, the infant's hallucinations are self-contained. They require nothing but themselves to achieve their aim. This is in fact the source of the pleasure they afford, for through their self-containedness they restore, as an intrapsychic second-best, the original unity that has been disrupted by the infant's emergent distinctness from its mother and the world. The hallucinatory mind of the infant—a cauldron of primary processes, free-flowing and without logic or form, much like our fluid planet before it cooled and formed a crust—anticipates in this regard all the later strategies of self-containment that at higher stages of psychical development seek to make the thing one loves a part of the lover himself, and thus no longer separate and unavailable (a strategy that repeats itself over and over again in the course of human development, from the autoeroticism of thumb-sucking to the later formation of a beloved internal ideal, or "super-ego," all of which represent variant expressions of what Freud terms "secondary narcissism," the attempt to overcome the liabilities that always accompany the love of an object by loving oneself instead).[20]

The problem with the infant's hallucinatory solution to the challenge of separateness, of course, is that it cannot work. Reality inevitably intrudes. The infant may dream that its mother's breast is present, but that is no guarantee it will be. Freud calls this the "reality principle," which is the name he gives to the fact of finitude itself—our vulnerability to powers greater than our own, over which we have at most limited control.[21]

The infant quickly learns that this is so, and that in order to find the fulfillment he seeks, must pursue it by a roundabout path that gradually relinquishes the ineffective self-pleasuring of hallucination in favor of a strategy that accepts the infant's separation from the world and looks, in increasingly "deliberate" ways, for means to overcome it. In essence, a decision has been made—or rather, forced upon the infant by the world itself—to seek a solution to its predicament in the opposite direction, by strengthening its resources and becoming a more independent being rather than a less independent one. This is the point at which, Freud says, an organized "ego" begins to develop, from whose primitive nucleus will eventually grow the adult's advanced powers of reflection and planning, and, with these, which depend on an awareness of time, the dawning knowledge that none of its plans can save it from death.

Still, if the ego is set on a course of ever-greater individuation, its aim remains what the infant sought with its hallucinations, namely, a reunion with the world, though one that is now to be achieved through the strengthening of its independent powers, that is, by means of the development and deepening of its individuality itself. The fact that this enterprise is doomed to fail and that the process of individuation leads to an acknowledgment of its own futility, does not alter the essential nature of its aim, or entirely remove the infantile urgency that drives it, no matter how wise we become.

The developing ego now finds itself engaged in a war on two fronts. It must grapple with reality, of course, by constantly devising new methods to avoid or exploit the powers of the external world. At the same time, it has to contend with the old, hallucinatory demands for immediate self-gratification that dominate the first stage of life. These must be suspended or suppressed if the ego is to get anything done, and the energy that would otherwise be at their disposal co-opted for the ego's own projects. Naturally, the infant in oneself resists. It wants what it wants when it wants it. The resulting tension is the source of a deep intrapsychic conflict that remains with us the whole of our lives. It is the origin of the phenomenon of repression—of the active effort by one psychical power to check or control another, or deny it recognition altogether by driving it out of the field of what we are able even to acknowledge in ourselves, into the domain of what Freud calls the "unconscious."

Freud (who had a fondness for topological metaphors) locates these warring powers in two distinct compartments of the mind, the "ego" and the "id." But this is just a metaphor, and we must not let it obscure the three most important features of Freud's account of the unconscious reservoir of mental life in which our infantile longings, and the primary processes of mentation associated with them, are confined by the ego in its twofold campaign for control.

The first is that we can never have conscious access to these longings and modes of experience. At most, we are able to infer their existence from other things that *can* enter conscious life. Of some things (at any moment, many things) we are not consciously aware. Our power of attention is limited. The field of consciousness is like a brightly lit but delimited field into which only a few things can enter at once. But the unconscious cannot be brought into this field by directing our attention toward it. (This is what distinguishes the unconscious from the preconscious, in Freud's metapsychology.) In this sense, we are more than merely ignorant of the unconscious. It lies beyond the limits of our powers of conscious representation, and that is because—this is the second feature of Freud's account of the unconscious—we have ourselves placed it there, as a necessary condition of maintaining the individual identity that is the work product of the ego. So long as the ego remains even modestly intact, everything consigned by it to the domain of the unconscious must therefore continue to be not accidentally (as in the case of things about which we are merely ignorant) but essentially unknowable. This is the heart of the difference between ignorance and ordinary forgetfulness, on the one hand, and the deeper sort of forgetfulness that is actively sustained by the ego itself on the other, to which Freud gives the name of "repression."

But—and this is Freud's third point—what is repressed does not disappear. It lives on, its vitality confined but undiminished, and remains for our whole lives a generative source of need and anxiety, and a fund of energy on which the ego continues to draw for its own purposes. Nothing in our mental life, Freud says, ever vanishes. All the stages we have lived through continue to exist, one on top of the other, and no amount of education or refinement or self-awareness can ever cause the child in us to disappear. It is as if, Freud says in a remarkable passage in *Civilization and Its Discontents*, one were able, looking at the ruins in the Roman Forum, to see all the buildings that had been constructed in every era of Rome's rule, superimposed on one another, yet still in their original condition.[22] Along with his insistence on the active nature of repression, Freud's belief in the survival in the mental life of even reasonably normal adults of the most primitive forms of experience and representation, and his recognition of the depth of suffering this can cause, gives his account of intrapsychic conflict a richness that Spinoza's own subtle but more conventional explanation of such conflict does not possess.

These general considerations set the stage for the next great act in life's drama—roughly, the one that spans the period from early childhood to adolescence and reproductive maturity. Freud organized his views about this period in human development around the concept of what he calls the "oedipal" complex.[23] He has been criticized for giving it too much weight and for basing his views on a historically contingent form of family life—roughly, the modern bourgeois family with its peculiar arrangements for ordering the intimate (especially sexual) relations of its members.[24] But Freud's theory of the oedipal complex can, I think, be stated in a sufficiently general way to avoid most of the criticisms directed against it.

The starting point of the theory is a biological fact. Unlike nearly all other animals, human beings reach sexual maturity only after a long delay, which Freud calls the "latency" period. During this time, the developing individual remains psychically active, of course, but is able neither to reproduce nor fully to care for himself. If he is to survive at all, therefore, he must be cared for by others, older and more powerful than he. For this care to be provided in an adequate way, moreover, it must be consistent and durable, and this requires that a relatively stable framework of some sort be established for its provision. This is what we mean by a "family," a general structure that historically has assumed many different forms.

As the child grows, it experiences its separateness from the world with increasing clarity, and with that, an increasing anxiety about the precariousness of its position as an individual, exposed to dangers of all sorts. It learns that it cannot meet these dangers on its own, in the hallucinatory and narcissistic way it once did, but must instead look outside itself for the resources to do so. These become its first love objects—the first things in the world through whose appropriation and incorporation the child hopes to overcome, now in a roundabout way, the vicissitudes of its individual existence. Among these resources, none is more important than the child's parents, using that term in the broadest sense to mean those larger and more potent human beings who, within the framework of its family, regularly provide the child with the nourishment and shelter it needs.

The child's first love objects will therefore be its parents. Like all human love, this one too is bound to have a sexual character—to exhibit the focal concentration of free-flowing Eros that is the essence of sex in all its forms, though not (as yet) the specifically genital focus that becomes characteristic of sex only later, under what Freud calls "the sway of the reproductive function."[25] Put differently, the child will love its parents with a sexual passion, and when, in the latter part of the latency period, it begins to approach reproductive maturity and this passion takes the special form that we (mistakenly) equate with sex in general, the way is prepared for a new and tumultuous set of conflicts with its parents, whose own, adult sexual relations with one another constitute, for the child, a field of opportunity and danger.

In the meantime, however, the child enjoys a reprieve. It is temporarily freed from the urgent demands of reproduction—the need to find a mate, fend off rivals, and the like. It has time to grow and develop in other directions. The human child, Freud says, possesses a natural curiosity about the world, and during the latency period, conducts ever-wider researches into the nature and origin of things (including the origin of children themselves). These bolster its developing powers of reason, and give its growing ego greater strength.

It also begins to develop what we might call a moral personality—a sense of how it ought to behave. To begin with, these "oughts" appear in the form of external commands, which the child naturally associates with the grown-ups who issue them. The child loves his parents, and wants to be as close to them as he can. If he could somehow get his parents inside himself, he would never have to worry about being separated from them again. This is the same old longing for self-containment that characterizes the newborn's hallucinatory world. It continues to operate even at this more advanced level of development and leads, Freud says, to the "introjection" in the child's psychical life of certain adult characteristics—namely, the approval of the child's parents, for which he so eagerly longs but is always in danger of losing (the fate of any object one loves). By becoming his own "board of approval," the child converts a vital but vulnerable object-love into a form of self-love instead.

To escape the vulnerability that arises with birth has been the child's ambition from the start. The internalization of its parents' approval, in the shape of what we commonly call a conscience and Freud terms the super-ego, is another expression of this same desire. Like all the earlier ones, however, this one too is doomed to disappointment. That is because the voice of authority that the child has now made a part of his own makeup continues to speak with a censoriousness that is hard for the child to quiet—harder even than its parents' voices had been. The child finds himself struggling to hold onto a new and even more elusive love object whose demands present a third challenge to its ego or individual self, so that in addition to campaigning against the forces of reality and its own, never fully repressible id, the ego must now do constant battle with the super-ego as well. In this threefold struggle, the individual identity of the maturing child assumes an ever-clearer shape, and he experiences with increasing self-awareness the distinctive pathos of human life, which arises from our excruciating consciousness of individuality itself.

As the child nears reproductive maturity, he reaches a point of crisis in his life. The fixation of sexual energy on the genitals and copulation brings the child, in his own mind at least, into a dangerous field of competition. So long as the child's sexuality remained channeled in other directions, it presented no threat to the adult sexual relations already existing among the grown-ups in its family. These are charged with the feelings of anxiety and jealousy that sexual relations among adults always possess. But now the child—so he thinks—is an intruder in them because—so he believes—he has become a competitor for the sexual attention of his mother (or father as the case may be).

From the earliest days of his infancy, the child has longed to be united with his mother, who for the infant embodies the world. Now, as his experience of love and sex come to be conditioned ever more imperiously by the demands of the reproductive function, this longing takes a less "innocent" form in the child's unconscious mental life. That the child is not conscious of his wish to take his father's place as his mother's sexual partner—let alone never acts on this wish—is unimportant. The wish itself, which is but another, more recognizably adult expression of the child's primal longing to be reunited with the world, is the decisive thing. For the child himself it presents a grave risk, since it brings him, potentially at least, into conflict with his vastly more powerful father.

It is a wish he must therefore repress, or gratify in a way that avoids an open confrontation with his father. Earlier in his life, the infant's developing ego required the repression of the hallucinatory forms of experience that stood in the way of a more productive adjustment to reality, which threatened to destroy him unless he put his infantile hallucinations away. On the cusp of sexual maturity, the child must now do the same with the dangerous wish that exposes him to death or mutilation at the hands of his father (or so he imagines). Through a second, immense effort of repression, he must force this wish, too, out of his conscious life. He must keep it buried in the charnel house of the id, and because, like every other dangerous wish imprisoned there, it continues to live on and to make its savage demands—which from the standpoint of the ego, threaten ruin—he must also devise alternative satisfactions that give the wish enough of what it wants, in a concealed and therefore less threatening form, to entice it to accept, however grudgingly, its permanent state of house arrest.

From this stormy period in our lives, and the psychic compromises it produces, emerge, Freud says, those general patterns of longing and frustration that shape our experience of love and sex from then on. What, as adults, we long for and fear in the love of others, and what form our sexual desires assume—what objects we choose, and how we relate to them—are decisively conditioned, in Freud's view, by the arrangements the ego makes with the id during the exceptionally volatile passage, toward the end of the latency period, from the still-enchanted world of childhood to the realm of adult relations and responsibilities. These arrangements form the prism though which we encounter the vicissitudes of adult sexual life, which is formed and deformed by them in ways the relatively "carefree" sex life of other animals is not.

Some, who are otherwise sympathetic to Freud's theory of human development, insist that he puts too much weight on this particular phase of it. But whether or not Freud overemphasizes the oedipal complex, or views it from a gender-biased perspective, he interprets the meaning of this phase of our psychic career in essentially the same terms as he does all the earlier ones. Each represents a stage in our lifelong struggle to accommodate ourselves to our finitude as individual beings, in the world but separate from it. Each repeats, under different conditions, the crisis of the human condition and results in a new adjustment to it, layered on top of those we have already made, which like the strata in a geological deposit, remain part of the record of the individual existence we spend our lives constructing.

The oedipal complex is merely one such episode—a particularly potent one, perhaps—but in essence no different from the other "complexes" that precede and follow it. Every one of these is a crisis through which we pass in our effort to come to terms with the question of how it is possible to bear being an individual at all. For Aristotle, who believed that the individuality of individuals is at bottom nothing real, and viewed the repetitive nature of human life as a return to the unvarying form of our species-being, this question never arises. By contrast, Freud places it at the very center of his account of the human condition.

But Freud does more than merely organize his psychology around our sequential attempts to meet the challenge of being or becoming an individual. He insists that there are better and worse ways of doing so. His theory of human development as a process of individuation is an ethics as well.

Freud's central ethical commitment can be put in the following way.

From the moment we are born, we face dangers on all sides. Many of these come from without. Others, however, come from within. External dangers can sometimes be avoided by flight. Internal dangers, by contrast, are always with us. We cannot run away from them in the same way. We can, though, isolate them and contain the risks they pose. We can put them in a kind of quarantine where their power to do harm is confined. Freud's general term for this is repression. It is already present in the mental life of the infant, whose struggle to be "more realistic," to become a shrewd observer of opportunities and an architect of strategies to exploit them, requires the repression of the tempting but empty hallucinatory satisfactions of its earliest days. The same basic process is at work, at a later stage of life, when the child begins to round the corner to adulthood and enters the zone of oedipal dangers. To avoid these, he must repress the internal thoughts and feelings that put him in danger, and take into his own mind the most threatening of the external powers he faces, where, in the form of his conscience, they become a new, internal source of danger to his fragile and inadequate self.

At every stage of life, therefore, repression is essential to survival. Its effects, moreover, are cumulative. The intrapsychic compromises we make with ourselves as infants and children and adolescents become the template we apply to the challenges of adulthood and old age. In this sense, repression is the key to understanding why a person has the particular traits he or she does.

Yet though it is an essential feature of the human condition, and thus cannot be avoided, there are better and worse forms of repression. Those that are worse keep us from living lives that are as fulfilling as they might otherwise be. They shut us out, to varying degrees, from the human good as Freud conceives it. We approach this good to the extent we are able to overcome them.

Freud sometimes expresses the distinction between better and worse sorts of repression in economic terms. Repression is always a compromise, a bargain of sorts between the ego, whose survival is at stake, and the internal wishes and desires that threaten its existence. These cannot be made to disappear; nothing in our mental life ever does. They can, however, be offered substitute gratifications of one kind or another as an inducement to keep their silence. They can be bought off in a variety of ways. But in some cases, the price we pay is higher than it needs to be.

Dreaming, for example, is a universal and relatively innocuous way of allowing our repressed wishes to vent themselves in an artfully altered form that disguises their true character and so makes them less shameful or shocking. Compulsions, phobias and other neurotic behaviors are more costly forms of compromise. They interfere with waking life in a way dreams generally do not, and to a degree that is often unnecessary. Without repression, we would be powerless to defend ourselves against the forces that assault us, from within as well as without. Up to a point, therefore, repression is a means for the increase of power. But it can be carried too far, and when it is, it becomes an obstacle to power instead. It prevents us from living as powerfully as we might.

At this point, repression becomes self-defeating. Born of the need to enhance our strength, it begins to drain it away. That no price is too great to pay for the repression of a wish—even one that demands a crippling substitute in exchange—may seem, at the time the bargain is struck, the only reasonable view, given the gravity of the threat posed by the wish itself. But this judgment is conditioned by fears born of ignorance and by feelings of vulnerability that, however appropriate to one's circumstances at the time, in retrospect appear exaggerated. By this time, of course, the pattern fixed by the repression has become entrenched in one's life, and merely seeing that it represents a bad bargain does not mean the pattern will change. (How such change is possible at all is the subject of the following section.) But by whatever path knowledge leads to cure, the fact is that some repressions are more costly than they need be, and reducing their effect in our lives converts a state of relative helplessness or passivity, under the dominion of a bad bargain we have imposed on ourselves, into one of greater activity less hostage to the ghosts of the past.

This is an ideal of human living. It grows naturally out of Freud's account of human development. It is the ethics *of* his psychology, not a judgment tacked onto it from some independent point of view.

If one wants a single word to summarize this ideal, "maturity" would be a good choice. Maturity does not mean the abolition of anxiety. That comes with the human condition. The mature person recognizes this and finds no comfort in the thought of ecstatic transcendence. She is suspicious of those who say it is possible to be transported to an "oceanic" state in which one's individuality is submerged in the wholeness of being, and pain at last disappears. She regards such claims as the expression of a familiar, unattainable, wish, one she recognizes in her own life, as far back as she can see. She also understands the inevitable disappointment in love, which is a yearning for transcendence that no love object can grant as completely or unreservedly as we wish. In this sense, she has put childish things away.

But Freud's mature human being is not a recluse or misanthrope or skeptic. He is what one might call a sober enthusiast of life. He knows that no love can be complete or lasting, yet seeks—longs—to love on terms that are amplified and deepened, not diminished, by the knowledge that this is so. Between loving childishly and not at all, he sets his sights on grown-up love, which, in its highest and most poignant moments, draws its passion from the lovers' acceptance of their inability to be everything the other wants, or even all they wish themselves to be. In a similar way, he strives to be a mature individual: one who does not run in fearfulness from the condition of vulnerability and need that is the fate of every human being; nor who seeks to escape it through ecstatic transports of one kind or another; nor who repudiates the wish to overcome it (which ceases only with death), but who strives, within the limits of his own finite existence, to take in as much as he can of the world from which he has been separated since birth, and, since birth, has longed to rejoin.

We "take the world in" first and most basically by eating parts of it. Where it involves the penetration of one body by another, sex also has an incorporative dimension. Nothing can compare with these for their immediacy and sensory power. But the only way to take in a wider swath of the world is through knowledge. To the extent we understand the world, we get it "inside" our minds. We get it inside ourselves. In the act of knowing, the mind becomes the world, as Aristotle says.[26]

Because he equated reality with form, Aristotle believed that we can get the whole of reality inside us. For a hyperrationalist like Freud, this is impossible. The infinite intelligibility of the world—even of a single human life—means that no finite mind can ever get itself around the whole of it. But it is possible to make progress in this direction—to come to understand more and more about the world, and in particular about oneself. As this happens, one's individuality expands to encompass more. It grows richer. It assumes, in Hans Loewald's words, greater "structure" and "complexity." Within the limits of his temporal existence, the individual whose knowledge of himself is increasing in this way becomes, by degrees, a more comprehensive witness to the world, and though this can never bring the transcendence that was his earliest, and remains his deepest, wish, it represents a movement toward it: the only satisfaction of this wish that we human beings are allowed.

This is Freud's ideal of maturity—of the grown-up who, without relinquishing his or her longing for wholeness (which in any case cannot be done), or allowing it to be diverted into the childish cul-de-sac of an individual or collective neurosis, has come to understand how this unattainable goal may nonetheless be approached by the path of knowledge and resolves to stay on it for as long as he or she can. That is because the mature person knows that this path alone points in the direction of a greater reality, of an expanded existence that takes in more of the world, and is more active in it, than the relatively shrunken lives of those who have turned off it into a self-imposed prison of ignorance, on account of an old and exaggerated fear of themselves.

This is Spinoza's ethical ideal too.

Freud's psychology is in certain respects more complex than Spinoza's. The active role the mind plays in constructing its own "bondage," to use Spinoza's term; the continued existence in our minds of childish wishes we never completely outgrow; and the entanglement of sex and love from infancy on are all essential features of Freud's psychology that have no exact parallel in Spinoza's. But despite these differences, the two share an ideal of human fulfillment that is approximately the same. It is one that views the condition of individuality itself (of what Spinoza calls our "modal" being) as the source of our deepest desire; that defines this desire as a longing for transcendence; that acknowledges the impossibility of ever satisfying it completely, but affirms the possibility, and value, of doing so to an increasing degree; that conceives the state of a person who succeeds in this respect as one of relatively greater activity, and hence happiness; that emphasizes the crucial role that knowledge plays in the achievement of such progress—indeed, that identifies knowledge with activity and happiness themselves; and that assigns a central role to the mechanisms of self-defeat through which we deny ourselves as large a measure of happiness as we might otherwise hope to attain.

Like Spinoza's description of the human mind, Freud's own thus simultaneously answers the normative question of how we ought to live, and does so in roughly similar terms. Yet to the further question, "How can I best learn to live as I should?" they give divergent replies. Spinoza's is that of a philosopher. He encourages us to study his psychology and the metaphysics on which it is based. He assumes that contemplation will set us free. Freud's response is different. To live as actively and happily as one can, it is not enough to study the theory of the mind. This may lead to a better understanding of the human condition in general, but to gain a deeper knowledge of one's own self, it is necessary to make it a separate object of study. This is the task not of psychology but psychoanalysis.

Freud's account of the psychoanalytic relation between doctor and patient and of the program of self-study it facilitates is completely original. It has no counterpart in Spinoza's philosophy. Yet even here, as we shall see, a connection exists, for the Freudian theory of psychoanalysis rests on a commitment to the principle of sufficient reason that in one respect at least is even more radical than Spinoza's because it carries the philosopher's desire for knowledge into the depths of his or her own unique but poorly understood life.

THE GHOSTS TASTE THE BLOOD

Why does a person enter psychoanalysis? Some do so, perhaps, merely because they are curious about themselves. But this is rarely their only motive. It is almost always accompanied by a longing to be well.

The patient feels unwell. His life has gotten off track.[27] He has encountered difficulties of one kind or another, and kept their dangers at bay, but at significant cost to his own freedom and flexibility. He feels that he has become less mobile—that he is stuck, frozen in place, held captive by past longings and fears that continue to rule his life and keep him from moving forward to a fulfillment he dimly conceives but cannot reach, especially in his most intimate relations with others.

He believes, moreover, that to break free of these self-imposed chains, he must revisit his past, in the company of an experienced guide who can help him understand it. He hopes that by doing so he will be able to resume the process of growth that has become stalled in his life. He wants a life that is richer, fuller, more inclusive and accepting of what it now rejects. He feels he is the prisoner of an imaginary world, and longs to be in closer touch with the real one. He believes this will make him happier, though he doesn't know how. Perhaps all he feels, at the start of his analysis, is the inarticulate confidence that somehow, if he pursues it long enough, it will yield a deeper understanding of his life that sets him free in a way no general knowledge of human psychology can do.

This confidence is shared by the analyst who treats him. Indeed, it is the most fundamental premise of the psychoanalytic process itself. How such confidence is to be justified is therefore *the* crucial question for the theory of psychoanalysis. It bothered Freud from the beginning of his career, and his answer to it changed over time.

Before we examine Freud's mature explanation of the curative power of psychoanalysis, however, we need to inquire by what gate the patient and his guide enter the land of the dead. The patient hopes and his analyst believes that their work together will lead to a larger life—one whose reality has increased with the patient's power to understand, and thus actively take in, more of what before he passively experienced as the dead hand of an unintelligible past. But what is their thread through the minotaur's cave—the device the patient and his analyst use to find their way to the ghosts of the patient's past and then back to his present again? Freud's answer is, "free association." He calls it the "fundamental rule" of psychoanalysis and the key to what he rightly claims is an entirely new form of human friendship.

When a patient begins an analysis, she is told that she should report whatever comes to mind, just as it does, without censorship or alteration. This is what Freud means by free association. In one sense, of course, free association is never really free at all, since the mental states the patient reports—assuming she follows the rule, which no patient ever does—belong to a stream of psychic events, each of which is fully determined by those that precede it. Every thought, fantasy, feeling or mood, no matter how arbitrary and disconnected it seems from the rest of the patient's mental life, belongs to a series of representations that are linked to one another in an endless causal chain. This alone makes them intelligible. A thought may appear to be arbitrary, but this appearance itself is a part of the thought that can be explained by inserting it into the psychical series to which it belongs. Freud embraced the principle of sufficient reason and the strict determinism it implies. Far from contradicting this principle, the rule of free association is the most emphatic expression of it in the whole of Freud's thought.

Nor is free association mere recollection, the patient's thoughts and feelings about things that happened in the past. Recollection is an essential part of free association, but by no means the whole of it. Many of a patient's reported mental states will be directed toward, or suggested by, his present situation, that is, by his relation to the doctor to whom he is now describing his mental life as it unfolds. Indeed, even when the patient's mind is focused on the past, and he is expressing thoughts and feelings aroused by the memory of something he experienced long before, his choice of words, sequence of moods, and (generally unconscious) deletion of certain elements from his report will always be shaped, to some degree, by his present relation to the doctor, sitting there behind him, listening as he speaks. In this sense, there is no such thing as an "uncontaminated" free association, if one means by that a report whose meaning can be assessed entirely apart from the immediate circumstances in which it is made—from the patient's wish to please his doctor, for example, or anger at him, or boredom with the analysis itself. Indeed, it is precisely their contamination by the patient's feelings toward his doctor that holds the key to understanding the potential curative power of his free associations to persons and events outside the analytic situation.

If free association is not mere recollection, and is never really free, what then makes it special? What sets it apart from the ordinary flow of mental life, in which representations follow one another in a determined sequence,

whatever we are doing, awake or asleep? Aren't we free associating every minute we are alive?

The answer, of course, is that we are, but generally pay little conscious attention to the sequence of our thoughts and feelings, except when we are
deliberating in a purposeful manner, and even then, much about the sequence
itself escapes our notice (or we deliberately put it out of mind). The doctor's
injunction to the patient simply to report what comes to mind requires the
patient to pay conscious attention to everything that happens in his mental
life, at the very moment it is happening, while keeping this heightened
scrutiny from interfering with the psychical flow on which it is trained (for
example, by failing to report a certain thought because it is too trivial or
embarrassing). Free association thus combines two contrary attitudes: a rigorous attention toward oneself, more disciplined and detailed than anything
we ever experience outside of psychoanalysis (one that indeed is incompatible
with the demands of practical life), coupled with an equally rigorous abstention from any active involvement in the reported stream of thoughts and
feelings, which, the patient is told, must remain uncorrupted by his own
judgments of relevance, shamefulness, and the like. The patient must be perfectly alert to this stream as its unfolds, yet wholly disengaged from it at the
same time. He must report it, as accurately and honestly as he can, but simply let it flow.

The result is that the purposiveness of our "ordinary" thought processes,
which are often tightly constrained by their conscious orientation toward a
goal, and trimmed and shaped with this in mind, is relaxed, and a new, unnoticed purposiveness emerges in its place—one guided by unconscious fears
and desires that we are generally too busy or anxious to see. Free association
is intended to bring these fears and desires to light. But this is supremely difficult to do, for the combination of rigorous attention to one's own mental
life, and perfect abstention from any censorious involvement in it, is one that
few of us, if any, can sustain for very long. The more we notice about our
minds, the harder it becomes not to push some of what we are thinking and
feeling back into the dark. The fundamental rule of psychoanalysis in effect
requires the patient to take a perfectly scientific attitude toward himself, which
is hard if not impossible, since the would-be scientist in this case has the most
passionate relation imaginable to the subject of his study. But this is what the
patient must strive to do, and the success of his psychoanalysis depends on
how well he is able to follow the rule.

To the extent he does, he and his analyst become scientific collaborators in a common enterprise, for the analyst also is striving to pay attention, alert but disengaged, to the unfolding stream of psychical events the patient reports. The analyst must also be on his guard to avoid censorious distortions of his own. That is impossible in his case as well, but the analyst has more practice at it, and is better equipped by his experience and training to discern the unnoticed purposiveness that guides the patient's associations. His superior ability to do this is especially evident at certain moments in the analysis—when the patient falls silent, for example, or reveals his feelings about the analyst in some form other than words. At these moments, the analyst's role as the senior investigator on the team becomes apparent, though the point of the inquiry, one might say, is to bring the analyst and patient into greater parity in this respect. This is one meaning, at least, of Freud's statement that psychoanalysis is founded on a shared love of the truth.[28]

If he succeeds, even fitfully, in following the fundamental rule of analysis, the patient gradually learns more about himself, with the help of his senior colleague. He discovers that his mind is a complex thing with many parts, some of which he knows only on account of the distorting gravitational pull they exert on other, more observable parts. He comes to understand that certain of his wishes and desires are at war with others, and that some have been not merely forgotten but actively repressed in his struggle to protect what meager power he possesses as an individual beset by threatening forces from within and without. And he learns that those wishes and desires he has repressed in order to survive (in light of what now seems to him a rather childish view of the world), are still alive in his mind—that he is still a child at heart, who is ruled more than he needs to be by ancient wishes and fears.

If things in his analysis go well, the patient learns all this about himself. But how can such knowledge cure him of the illness that induced him to enter psychoanalysis in the first place?

Early on, Freud believed that if the analyst, who has a superior understanding of the workings of the human mind, merely communicated to his patient the truth about the origin of the latter's phobias and compulsions, these would disappear or at least become less disabling. For an analysis to have these curative effects, it should be enough, Freud thought, for the patient to learn the truth about him- or herself, much in the way an attentive student learns the truth about any subject of study.[29] That patients sometimes refused to accept the truth, or professed to accept it without their neuroses changing in any fundamental or lasting way, was a source of puzzlement and frustration to Freud, who was compelled by these experiences to rethink the question of how a deeper knowledge of oneself can ever lead to a happier life.

Freud's mature answer to this question can be pieced together from his papers on the phenomenon of "transference," which contain his most profound reflections on the nature of the psychoanalytic relation.[30]

Long before the time he begins his analysis, the patient has developed what Freud calls a "stereotype" for intimate personal relations.[31] Rooted in his childhood experiences, this stereotype defines the frame within which he approaches such relations later in life—the hopes and expectations, fears and longings, conditions of object and self-love—that form the ground rules of his relations with others. In this sense, all his later, intimate relations are repetitions of earlier ones. This is true of the patient's relation with his analyst at well.

These ground rules are at once cognitive and affective. Together they comprise a system of beliefs and feelings, each of whose elements is at once a thought and an emotion. For Freud, there are no emotionless thoughts. Even the most abstract idea has what might be called an affective "tone"—the feeling, for example, of competence and mastery that a scientific understanding of any aspect of the world arouses in those who possess it. And even the most primitive feeling of anger or lust has a cognitive component—a representational element—that distinguishes it from mere animal passion (that gives it, so to speak, a "fantastic" dimension). The stereotype that shapes the patient's relation with his analyst is thus a fusion of thoughts and feelings, of ideas and fantasies, that conditions both what the patient is able to learn from the analyst and how he reacts to the special form of intimacy that psychoanalysis offers.

This stereotype is shaped by the patient's past, but in the psychoanalytic relation it is immediately alive. It belongs to the patient's present, and determines what he is now experiencing, lying on the couch, attempting to obey the fundamental rule of psychoanalysis, in the presence of the analyst who is sitting unseen behind his head. It directs the flow of his associations as these unfold in real time.

The patient does not see this, however. For him, the frame through which he receives the analyst's words, and experiences his feelings toward him, is like a window through which one has been looking for so long that its existence is forgotten. Though actively at work in the patient's present-tense relation with the analyst, the stereotype that conditions his experience of it is not itself an object of attention. It is not noticed, let alone studied, but merely "acted out," here as in the patient's other intimate relations.

One of the aims of psychoanalysis is to help the patient see how this stereotype is at work in his cognitive and emotional interactions with the analyst. To do this, the patient must come to understand that what he is thinking and feeling now, in this relation, is a repetition or reenactment of what he thought and felt in other earlier ones, whose memory he has repressed, but which established the now-entrenched pattern of hopes and fears that continue to structure the patient's experience of intimacy in the psychoanalytic setting and elsewhere. This requires that two things happen at once. The patient's present, which is very much alive, must be reexperienced in the light of a distant and dead past, and his past must be brought back to life as a contemporary force that is still actively at work in the patient's relation with the analyst. It must be restored to vitality, and made present again, through its connection to the immediate cognitive and emotional demands of the psychoanalytic relation.

By means of this two-way transaction between present and past, the past is made present and the present past. The patient's life becomes less disjointed as a whole. Its parts come into a better-understood relation with one another. They become more integrated. To a greater degree than before, the patient is no longer mindlessly acting out a stereotype inherited from the past, sleepwalking through life. He recollects the past *in* his present and thereby achieves a higher degree of wakefulness with regard to the small but potentially influential part of his life that he has committed to psychoanalysis.

Hans Loewald explains the meaning of this two-way transaction between present and past by elaborating on a classical allusion that Freud invokes to make a related point in *The Interpretation of Dreams*.[32]

To find his way home, Odysseus is told that he must visit the underworld and speak with the prophet Tiresias, who will tell him how his return to Ithaca and Penelope can be accomplished. But ghosts are mute, and to get them to speak Odysseus must first give them a taste of life—of blood from a sacrificed animal. Only when he does this, the enchantress Circe tells him, will the speechless shades of the underworld recover their voices and tell Odysseus what he needs to know.

This is what happens in psychoanalysis too, Loewald says. The patient's relation with the analyst gives his past warmth and vitality—an immediacy that restores the ghosts of his past to life. It is the blood that allows them to find their voices and speak: Loewald calls it "the blood of recognition." When they do, they tell the patient something he didn't know about his present circumstances, a secret he has hidden from himself. They point the way toward a reunion of past and present in the patient's soul, and having been "released from their ghost life," where they are "compelled to haunt" the patient's intimate relations, in the form of stereotypes that he unwittingly acts out over and over again, "they are laid and led to rest as ancestors whose power is taken over and transformed in the newer intensity of present life."[33]

Two questions remain, however. The first is how the psychoanalytic relationship itself helps the patient achieve a reunion of this kind, and the second is why the deepened knowledge of himself that he acquires as a result has any therapeutic value at all.

To answer the first, it is important to stress the uniqueness of the relation between patient and analyst. The two see each other regularly, but only at prescribed times and within sharply defined limits. The one pays the other a fee for his services. In these ways, the analytic relation is segregated from the rest of the patient's life in the most exacting manner. It is thus unlike other forms of friendship, which spill out over wider areas of involvement and concern, and generally cannot be bought. Yet within its prescribed limits, the relation of the patient to his analyst is the most intimate he will ever experience. That is because it is premised on absolute transparency.

Everything the patient thinks and feels—including, most importantly, everything he thinks and feels about the analyst himself—must be put into words. No other relation demands this from those involved in it, or could withstand such candor. Only the limited nature of the psychoanalytic relation makes even the aspiration to achieve it possible. But to the extent it is achieved, the analytic hour becomes, in Freud's words, a "playground" of fantasy, where the deepest, oldest, most embarrassing thoughts and feelings are permitted to come forward, hesitantly at first, with their faces covered in shame, into what Loewald calls the "daylight of analysis."

The carefully staged detachment of the patient's relation with his analyst is meant to create a space in which the patient will find it easier to say what comes to mind. Yet even so, nothing is harder to do, for what comes to mind often seems terrible and shocking to the battle-worn self that has emerged, scarred but victorious, from the past wars it has had to fight to keep its own destructive impulses under control. The patient's thoughts and feelings about the analyst himself are likely to be especially difficult to put into words, for social etiquette and the fear of a reprisal make it hard for the patient to share his associations with the very person to whom they are addressed. To play in the playground that analysis affords thus takes a special form of courage. To summon and sustain it, the patient needs something more than an expert who can help him see the unnoticed stereotypes by which he lives. He needs a friend, who without offering forgiveness or consolation, which are cheap and have no lasting effect, bears the patient a discernible goodwill, and cares for his welfare for the patient's own sake—who wants to see the patient advance to a more mature existence, and live more actively than his neurosis now permits him to do, for no reason other than the happiness of the patient himself.

In this respect, the analyst is like a parent of a uniquely disinterested kind, whose disinterest is essential to the advancement the patient hopes to make, through self-understanding, toward an individuality that takes in more of what is real in himself and the world. The patient can be guided in this venture by the analyst, whose greater experience and more advanced maturity allow him to make connections between the patient's past and present that the patient himself cannot see. But if the patient is to take the analyst's words to heart, these must be delivered in a spirit of friendship that the patient recognizes as such. His recognition that the analyst is a friend of a singular kind—one who is prepared to hear everything, without praise or blame, who offers companionship and insight but neither absolution nor hope of salvation from the vicissitudes of the human condition, a playmate in the artificially confined fantasy world that psychoanalysis clears in the middle of life—is a crucial step toward the acknowledgment, in a similar spirit of friendship, of those parts of himself that the patient has disowned on account of the threat they pose to his battle-scarred ego.

In all his other intimate relations, the patient is acting out ancient stereotypes too. But it is hard if not impossible for him to make them an object of reflective attention in these relations themselves, for that requires a kind of self-absorption that is incompatible with love and friendship in all their common forms. The one exception is the psychoanalytic relation. For though this, too, is a species of friendship, its only goal is to help the patient understand the pattern he is repeating in it—to convert repetition to remembrance, or as Freud famously said, id to ego.[34]

The psychoanalytic relation is a species of friendship because the analyst cares for his patient. He is more than just a technical specialist with an advanced knowledge of human psychology. He is a companion willing to accompany the patient, for years if need be, in the patient's completely self-centered exploration of his own life, which is of greater importance to the

patient than it can possibly be to anyone else in the world, the analyst included. The patient knows this. He sees the analyst, of course, through the
window of old wounds and longings. The analyst is in this sense a fantasy.
But he is also a real presence, not a dream, and the friendship he shows by
giving himself up—for an hour a day!—to wander free-associatively through
the labyrinth of the patient's own mind, is a potential source of strength for
the patient, and one that may, if things go well, give him the courage he
needs to engage in the two-way transaction between present and past that
alone can lead to the enlargement of self at which psychoanalysis aims: to
what Aristotle describes as the friendship a man feels toward himself when
he knows his own worth.[35]

If this transaction is even partly successful, it produces what Loewald calls
"an extra piece of mental freedom." The patient now knows that he is reen-
acting an old routine, and even if the routine itself remains mostly intact, the
patient's knowledge of it changes his relation to the routine, and to himself,
in a basic way. His symptoms may persist—in some form, they always do—
and even the most successful psychoanalysis yields only a small gain in
self-knowledge. Freud's own expectations in this regard grew steadily more
modest over the course of his career. Yet still there is a difference between
going round and round in a circle, and not knowing you are, and being sufficiently detached to see this.

Detachment itself is a form of liberation. It is always limited, of course,
and may or may not touch the habits it allows one to see. But the life of a
person who has achieved it, in whatever measure, is more expansive than the
life of one who has not. When he surveys himself, his glance takes in more
than it did before. He is able, as it were, to keep more of himself in mind.
More of what before he merely suffered, he now comprehends—as a necessity,
perhaps, but one his mind grasps and to that extent transcends, in the way the
mind of a physicist grasps the necessity of the laws of motion, except that
the necessity here is one that governs the patient's own individual life.

From passivity and suffering, the patient thus moves to a higher level of
activity by virtue of an increase in self-understanding. This is not the same as
an increase in happiness, as that term is commonly understood. Putting aside
the fact that the patient's symptoms may persist, self-understanding itself can
be a source of new frustrations that did not exist before. But in most cases
most people prefer to know rather than be kept in the dark. That is because
they want to be as active as they can, and because every increase in understanding, which brings more of what is real in the world within its scope, rep-

resents an increase in the activity and reality of the one who achieves it. This is the mark of a successful analysis. The patient who completes such an analysis leaves it more active and real than he was at the start. In this sense—but only in this sense—he leaves it happier than before, and if he is asked whether he would trade this happiness for a more conventional kind, on the condition that he again repress into unconsciousness everything he has learned about himself, it is almost the definition of a successfully analyzed patient that he would decline to do so. This is the tremendously optimistic yet modest ideal of mental health on which Freud's account of the talking cure is based.

In broad terms, it is an ideal Freud shares with Spinoza, though the latter's version of it might perhaps more accurately be called a "thinking" cure—the release from a self-imposed bondage of superstition, fear and baseless hope by means of ever more "adequate" ideas, beginning with the idea of God or substance itself.

The parallels are striking. Both view the human condition as one of vulnerability and weakness. Much happens to us that we cannot control. In this respect, we are essentially passive or suffering beings. Both also conceive our deepest longing to be the desire for greater control, whose limit is omnipotence, though neither think this limit can be reached. Still, both insist that a human being can have more or less control over himself and the world and that progress in this regard can only be made through understanding, by means of which we become more active in our lives, less the victims of incomprehensible powers, both within us and without, and therefore more happy, though always less happy than we wish to be. To recognize that such progress is possible, and to pursue it with all one's heart, while accepting the limits within which it is permanently confined, is for both Spinoza and Freud the mark of a wise or mature human being.

Still, an important difference remains. For Spinoza, the process of maturation is a largely solitary one. Freud, by contrast, emphasizes the potential that a special form of friendship holds for moral or spiritual growth, and conceives this friendship in exquisitely personal terms. Spinoza does say that "nothing is more useful to man than man." He even calls man "a god to man."[36] These words suggest a theory of friendship whose implications for modern science in general are the subject of the following chapter. But there is no inkling in the *Ethics* of anything like Freud's account of the unique sort of friendship that exists between analyst and patient, and of its possibilities as a venue of empowerment.

Spinoza's conception of the process by which one becomes more active and free has as its model the philosopher alone in his study. This represents a lingering Cartesian bias in a metaphysics otherwise built on anti-Cartesian ideas. To Freud's other great discoveries—the reality of infantile sexuality, the eroticized vicissitudes of family life, the continued existence in the mind of the adult of ancient childish desires, the phenomenon of repression as distinct from mere forgetfulness—must therefore be added, as perhaps the greatest of all, his discovery of a species of human friendship that opens the way to a knowledge of oneself more personal than anything Spinoza imagined.

Even this last discovery, though, underscores the most important point of contact between Spinoza and Freud. The premise of Freud's theory of psychoanalysis, as distinct from his metapsychology, is that the lives of human beings, with all their quirks and absurdities, with all their seemingly mindless and self-destructive passions, are intelligible not merely in general but one by one, down to the smallest details. The purpose of psychoanalysis, from the patient's point of view, is not to learn something about humankind, but about himself—about his own unique experience of life and the patterns of longing and apprehension he has formed as a result. In the process, of course, the patient becomes better acquainted with the human condition in general. But that is not his goal. His aim is to know himself, not as a representative of mankind, but as the unique individual he is, and this ambition is intelligible only on the assumption that even the most idiosyncratic features of his mind are accessible to understanding, though he shall never reach the navel of the dream.

Put differently, Freud's conception of the psychoanalytic relation, original though it is, makes sense only in light of his commitment to the principle of sufficient reason, which he shares with Spinoza. The hyperrationalism this implies, coupled with an acknowledgment of how little we shall ever know of our infinitely intelligible world, our individual selves included, is the deepest bond between them, and one that is brought out, with special clarity, in Freud's account of psychoanalysis, whose fundamental rule of free association might be called the principle of sufficient reason in action.

There is one way, however, in which Freud's conception of the human condition seems to conflict sharply with a rationalist view of it, and to distinguish his own view quite fundamentally from that of Spinoza. I have in mind Freud's postulation of what he calls a "death wish" or "death drive." Is there room for such a drive in Freud's otherwise hyperrationalist psychology?

A DEATH WISH?

Freud came to believe, though with reservations he never abandoned, that human beings not only die but wish to die as well. This death wish, he claims, exists alongside the equally primitive wish to live, grow and prosper. The first is the root of all irreducibly self-destructive behavior and of certain other-directed forms of aggression, whose real aim, Freud says, is the destruction of the order and beauty of the world, and its reduction to a blank nothingness instead. In opposition to this impulse of annihilation, he sets the desire to increase one's own order and reality, and that of the world as a whole.

In an essay written late in his life, Freud describes these opposing drives in metaphysical terms as cosmic forces whose eternal interaction is the cause of the world's endless oscillation between order and disorder, and compared his own view to that of the pre-Socratic philosopher Empedocles, who had sought to explain the constancy of movement in the world as the product of a timeless war between "love" and "strife."[37] Empedocles was a dualist, and Freud insists that he is so as well. Indeed, looking back over his career from a point near its end, he claims to have been a dualist from the start, though even in his last and most far-reaching statement of it, he remains careful to qualify his dualism by describing it as an unproven hypothesis intended merely to advance research.

Freud felt compelled to postulate the existence of a separate death drive in order to explain certain psychic phenomena that cannot, he claimed, be explained in any other way. Foremost among these are the self-hurting behaviors conventionally gathered under the name of "masochism."

Early in his career—before, in fact, he became the dualist he later claimed to have been all along—Freud viewed masochism as a form of sadism redirected toward oneself, against an easy victim, one might say.[38] On this view, the sadistic wish to hurt others, which is a way of magnifying one's power at their expense, is the primary drive, which is deflected inward when it proves too dangerous to pursue in the realm of external relations. Even in this self-directed form, however, sadism retains its original character as an instrument of aggrandizement—a means for increasing one's power (however misguided the assumptions on which its use depends may be) and not a technique for abolishing such power instead.

For reasons that are not entirely clear, Freud later reversed his position and concluded that the self-destructive character of most masochistic behavior derives, in part at least, from a separate and freestanding wish to abolish oneself—a wish to die that cannot be derived, in a roundabout way, from a more fundamental wish to live, of which it is only the perverse (Spinoza would say foolish or ignorant) expression.[39] Having introduced the idea of an independent death wish for limited explanatory purposes in order to account for certain specific human behaviors, Freud then extended the idea to the whole of life, suggesting that the existence of a death drive in human beings is best explained on the assumption that it arises as a result of the travails of life itself, to which every organism is exposed from the start of its mortal career. Freud's late, Empedoclean characterization of the death drive as a cosmic force coextensive with reality as such is his final metaphysical—though still conjectural—formulation of this idea.

Yet even as a conjecture, Freud's postulation of a death drive sits uneasily with the rationalism of his psychology. Like Spinoza, Freud was committed to the principle of sufficient reason. But Spinoza maintains that this principle rules out the possibility that any thing can ever directly desire its own destruction.[40] He acknowledges, of course, that every finite mode is eventually overwhelmed by other modes with powers greater than its own. This is a fundamental axiom of his metaphysics. But considered strictly in itself, Spinoza claims, no mode ever longs to disappear or die. Even suicide is a consequence of being overcome by forces outside the core of one's own modal being—by affections that one suffers, as distinct from actions one performs. The same is true of masochism and related phenomena. Spinoza concedes that human beings are often overwhelmed by passion and do self-destructive things as a result. Indeed, this is a central premise of his entire investigation of human psychology. But he characterizes such behavior as ignorant or unenlightened, and insists that only ignorance, which is a form of powerlessness, can explain why any finite being, whose very existence is constituted by the drive to persevere that all such beings share, acts in a self-defeating way. To Spinoza, the postulation of a second, independent drive that seeks the very opposite of perseverance would have seemed an offense to reason itself.

There are two reasons (!) why this is so. The first is that the idea of a death drive is irrational in itself.

Reason is power. The more one understands, the less one experiences the world as a brute fact—as something that just happens, and must be passively suffered as a result. No finite being can ever be perfectly active. All suffer to some extent. That is the meaning of finitude itself. But if finitude imposes a limit on our power in general, and on the power of reason in particular, even this limit is not a brute fact that reason must simply accept. That is because the existence of finite beings can itself be explained, in metaphysical terms, on the grounds that their nonexistence would result in an overall diminution of the world's reality, and that an ontologically poorer world is always inferior, from the standpoint of reason, to one that is relatively richer.

About the world, one can always ask, "Why is it not either more or less real?" The principle of sufficient reason assumes that this question is a meaningful one and therefore deserves an answer. But once the question is posed, it may be asked over and over again, until at last one arrives at one of two polar conclusions: that the world is either as real or unreal as it is possible for it to be. But the latter conclusion is unintelligible because it rules out the existence of reason itself, along with everything else, and thereby denies the premise of the reflective inquiry that leads to it. In this sense, it is self-contradictory. Only the first conclusion makes sense. The only rational world is a maximally real one, hence one composed of an infinite number of finite beings, each in principle perfectly intelligible, yet limited in its power to maintain itself in existence.

That we must die is therefore not irrational in itself. Indeed, the necessity of the death of every finite being is rationally defensible. By contrast, the suggestion that we *long* to die, and *strive* to do so, is inherently irrational, for there is no way to explain the existence of a deliberately antirational drive, as distinct from the existence of a limitation on a rational one. A true death drive would aim at the extinction of order, being, and reason itself. How could that be accounted for in rational terms? Unlike the phenomenon of finitude, which limits what reason can do, but is explicable in metaphysical terms, the existence of a death wish—in human beings, let alone in living organisms generally—would have to be accepted as a brute fact, and thus as a different and deeper sort of defeat for reason than the one entailed by mere ignorance. The Spinozist explanation of self-defeating behavior as the result of ignorance on the part of a being that strives only to exist is thus inherently better suited to the hyperrationalism that he and Freud share than Freud's explanation of the same behavior as the product of a separate wish to die.

The second reason why Freud's explanation is inconsistent with his otherwise sweeping commitment to reason is a consequence of the dualist metaphysics it leads him to embrace, for any dualism, including Freud's own, rules out the possibility that everything in the world can in principle be explained.

If there are two coeval drives that press or pull us in opposite directions—toward order and life, on the one hand, and blankness and death on the other—the question arises as to whether the conflict between them can be

explained. By "explained" I mean accounted for in a way that makes it intelligible why one drive prevails over the other at any given moment, and how
the balance between them in general is struck. This question is intelligible,
however, only on the assumption that there is a supervening principle that
regulates the interaction of these drives, in which case their duality is not really
fundamental after all, but merely the manifestation of a subsidiary conflict
within a higher-order monism of some kind.

Of course, one may insist that no such principle exists—that the dualism
of the life and death drives is an ultimate reality. But that amounts to denying the intelligibility of the question of how to explain their interaction. It
represents a repudiation of the principle of sufficient reason at the deepest level
of cosmic order. To embrace this principle at all, one must embrace it without limit. The only metaphysics that is compatible with the boundless commitment to explanation that the principle of sufficient reason entails is therefore
necessarily monist in nature. Spinoza understood this. Indeed, in part 1 of
the *Ethics* he attempts to prove it. What makes Freud's postulation of an independent death drive, and his claim that this implies an irreducible duality
of cosmic powers, so puzzling, is his otherwise unwavering commitment to
reason and science in the study of the human mind. Freud appears not to have
fully grasped the corrosive effect that any dualism must have on the ambitions of science itself.

To preserve Freud's rationalism, which is not merely compromised but undone by the Empedoclean metaphysics he somewhat playfully endorses
toward the end of his life, it is therefore necessary to give up his speculative
claim that there are two fundamental and opposing drives in the human soul,
and substitute for it the idea that there is only one, which always seeks greater
power, order and life, yet necessarily falls short of its goal on account of the
finitude of the being whose drive it is.

In fact, this is not difficult to do. Consider the case of masochism, whose
reexamination prompted Freud to abandon his original, monistic account of
the phenomenon in favor of one that presumes the existence of an independent death drive instead.

There is obviously something puzzling about masochism. How can a being that longs for power and life, deliberately hurt itself and derive pleasure
from doing so? A good explanation—suggested by Freud's own theory of
human development—is the following.

As children, we long for the love of our mothers. To begin with, this longing is an undifferentiated desire for reunion with the world. In time, it be-

comes more focused and eventually assumes a sexualized form. This brings the child into an area of danger, where it risks destruction if it acts on its desires. To avoid this, the child anticipates the punishment it fears by punishing itself. It preempts the wrath of the offended parent (mother or father) by inflicting a survivable wound on itself first.

This serves two purposes. First, it substitutes a lesser hurt for a greater one, and thereby pays a more affordable price for its actions (which of course are really only its desires). Second, it makes itself more loveable in the eyes of its parents. It makes itself a model child, who knows enough to punish itself before its parents do—and wins their affection as a result. Where such behavior, which is undoubtedly widespread, cuts a groove into which the child's intensifying genital energy flows, the result is the kind of adult masochism that in its most extreme form marks certain men and women as "perverts" by comparison with the rest of humanity, in whom masochistic tendencies also exist, though to a lesser degree.

Understood in these terms, masochism is explicable as the result of a longing for power and life, pursued under conditions of scarcity, which includes the limits of one's ability to know or control the sources of parental affection. It is the solution to an economic problem. Finitude plays a crucial role in this as in every economic problem. But there is no need to account for such behavior by presuming a freestanding death drive, which rather than advancing the cause of explanation arrests it instead.

The same applies to the wide range of compulsions and phobias that Freud studied in such detail. These, too, can be understood in economic terms, for each is a way of pursuing power under certain constraints—for example, the danger of being hurt if one seeks it more directly. A compulsion or phobia is a device for obtaining as much power as one can, at the very best price, as determined by one's estimate of the cost of alternative means of procuring it, which in turn is based on one's (often if not always) ignorant and fearful beliefs. Even the most self-defeating symptoms thus need not lead us to presume the existence of a death drive, as distinct from a longing for life and power, coupled with the scarcity of resources available for attaining them.

Those outward forms of aggression that seek the destruction of something or someone other than oneself can be explained in a similar fashion.

Every human being acts aggressively. Some do so in especially pronounced ways. But to explain such behavior, it is not necessary to assume, as Freud occasionally does, that we are motivated by a longing to destroy the world that is locked in eternal combat with the loving wish to see it flourish. It is enough that the aggressor be motivated by a desire to expand his power. Aggression is not driven by the nihilistic wish to make the world disappear. Its goal is to capture or command new resources, especially the bodies and minds of other human beings. Even the cruelest and most wasteful assaults fit this pattern by gratifying the wish to be the master of others through terror and intimidation.

As a matter of fact, aggression often has self-destructive results. But that is only because the aggressor does not fully understand the consequences of his actions or is blinded by a passion that prevents him from seeing these as clearly as he might. In the whole field of human aggression, there is nothing that cannot be explained on the assumption that men desire only greater power, but are compromised in their pursuit of it by cognitive and affective limitations that are as universal as this desire itself. Even Satan's cosmic spirit of negation is best explained by his envious desire for omnipotence, fueled by a rage that blinds him to the fact that his war against God is bound to end in defeat.[41]

Masochism, neurosis and aggression can thus all be explained without invoking the idea of a separate death drive, which undermines the rationalism that is fundamental to Freud's account of the human mind. But his most extensive argument for the existence of a death drive is not based on anything specifically human. It rests instead on a philosophical interpretation of the conditions of life in general. In a speculative passage in his 1920 essay, *Beyond the Pleasure Principle,* Freud suggests that even the simplest organism yearns to die. He claims that the desire for death is coeval with life itself. To this extent, Freud's postulation of a death drive is more than a psychological axiom. It is a hypothesis regarding the entire realm of animate being, if not, as his later invocation of Empedocles implies, that of being as such.

Every living thing is subject to stimulation. Some of the stimuli it experiences come from without, others from within. This experience, Freud says, is essentially painful. Stimulation, as such, is a source of unhappiness to the living beings that feel it. In response, they seek to eliminate or reduce it. They do this in various ways—by fleeing or consuming the external objects that are a cause of stimulation, and by quieting, as best they can, the internal drives that disturb them with their insistent demands. Freud calls the desire to be free of all stimulation the "Nirvana principle."[42] The whole organic world, he claims, is subject to its demands.

But why is stimulation *per se* a cause of pain? Ordinarily, we say that some stimuli are pleasurable and others painful. We pursue the former and avoid the latter. Freud's view (to which he did not adhere with perfect consistency) that all stimulation is painful rests on an unstated philosophical assumption that can be put in the following way.

To be stimulated by anything is to be on the receiving end of a power that lies outside one's sphere of control. This may be the power of an object (a falling stone), or of another person (an angry neighbor or a sexually attractive one). It may be lodged in one's own gut (in the form, for example, of hunger). Each of these is a stimulus, and though we generally view some as painful and others not, all impinge on the being that receives them and challenge its ability to preserve its identity in the face of forces, external and internal, that threaten to overwhelm or dissolve it.

In the case of human beings, these threats give rise to a struggle on the part of the ego to preserve itself against the assaults of the id and those of the world, and eventually against the punishing attacks of the super-ego as well. The stimuli that come from these various sources all remind the ego of its exposure and vulnerability. This is the experience of finitude itself—of what Kant calls "receptivity."[43] It is inseparable from the condition of individual existence, and made present to every organism in the world by the ceaseless stream of stimuli that bombard it from the moment it begins to live on its own. Human beings have an especially keen appreciation of their finitude on account of their reflective awareness of time. But to one degree or another, all plants and animals feel it.

Hence, the only basis for claiming, as Freud does, that stimulation is painful as such, is the assumption that the condition of finitude that every stimulation entails is itself a cause of suffering to those that experience it. Against such suffering, living things have only two weapons.

The first is to increase their power, so that more of the world and of themselves is subject to their control—is "in" them, not outside them, as Spinoza says. This strategy can never be more than partly successful. No finite being can ever master more than a fragment of the world, itself included.

The second is to eliminate the condition that gives rise to the suffering in the first place. In simple terms, this means destroying one's existence as an individual, for as soon as one ceases to be an individual, finitude and the suffering that accompanies it vanish as well. This second strategy is always guaranteed to be completely successful.

Freud associates the first strategy with love. It is motivated by the desire for ever more inclusive order and the mastery that comes with it. It seeks the integration of a widening circle of complexities within a unifying framework of a progressively subtler sort. Modern physics is one manifestation of this strategy. Darwinian biology is another. Psychoanalysis is a third.

The second strategy leads in the opposite direction. It seeks not mastery but relief. Its goal is the emptiness of nonexistence, which is no order at all. Its aim is death, and the desire that drives it is a longing for oblivion itself.

According to Freud, every living thing is drawn in both directions. A war begins in its breast the moment it is born. On the one side is Eros, contending for order and power. On the other is Thanatos, calling for victory through death. Each is a powerful force and knows how to co-opt its enemy. Creative love finds ways to harness and incorporate the impulse to destroy. Every great work of art, every lasting political achievement, every love affair worthy of the name, is built on the ruins of its competitors and predecessors. For its part, the desire to hurt and abolish enlists Eros in its service, so that the most generative power on earth becomes an added source of pleasure in acts that attack this power itself.

But if Freud is right, a question remains that is hard to answer on the assumption that these two strategies and the drives associated with them are equal in their originality and power. For how is it possible that life endure even for a moment, let alone develop into highly complex forms, if its emergence is accompanied by a longing to return to the unstimulated condition of inorganic matter that can be gratified at once and completely? What stands in the way of the first, primitive organism simply lapsing back into the world of inanimate things, and so relieving itself of the unhappiness that its rudimentary, but real, experience of finitude brings? The question is especially puzzling in light of the fact that, as between the two strategies that living things have for dealing with the suffering this experience entails, the pursuit of death is the only one guaranteed to eliminate it completely, whereas the pursuit of life—of power, order, and an increasingly rich individuality that includes more and more of the world within it—is doomed to fail.

That life, once it emerges, endures and unfolds in ever more complex ways, can be explained only on the assumption that Eros has more power than Thanatos—that there is an asymmetry in their relation, so that the power of love, though never complete, is always superior to that of the death drive. If the love of life enjoys an advantage over the longing for death from the start, that is because living things strive to maintain their place in the world, with varying degrees of success, rather than turn back from the world of life, at the entrance to it, in horror at the agitation and suffering that lies ahead, preferring instead the realm of the dead, with its eternal quiet.

But why should this asymmetry exist? To answer *that* question, one needs a principle superior to both these drives that explains the relation between them. Once such a principle is introduced, Freud's alleged dualism dissolves into a higher-order monism. To be consistent with the rest of his psychology, the monism that is needed must be constructed along Spinozist lines.

That living things possess a higher degree of order than those we conventionally call dead; that every thing, living or dead, strives not only to maintain but expand the quantum of power it possesses; that living things therefore strive to live, and indeed to live ever more fully, but that even the most advanced is subject to powers greater than its own, and so must eventually be overcome by them, are all best explained on Spinoza's assumption that the individuality of every finite being is constituted by its *conatus*. Freud's postulation of a separate death drive cannot explain these things, or explain them as well. It is a superfluous assumption and one that enervates the rationalist spirit of his psychology as a whole. More important, it undermines the ethical ideal of psychoanalysis.

This ideal rests on the assumption that to be an individual is to suffer—to be separated from a world that has what one needs and threatens to keep or take it away. All our lives we are looking for ways to overcome the anguish this causes. To varying degrees, we remain prisoners of the strategies we devise as infants and children to relieve ourselves of such suffering. These are based on hopes and fears we later repress. In psychoanalysis, one comes to have a somewhat greater understanding of their genesis. Under the right circumstances, this can have a therapeutic effect. It has the potential to relax, to some extent, the self-imposed shackles that limit our movement as adults, and thereby to increase our power.

This increase may be described in the way Hans Loewald does, as a movement toward a more inclusive individuality that knowingly embraces what before it faced as foreign powers, converting the not-I to I, id to ego, suffering to mastery. It can also be described in the ancient metaphysical vocabulary that Spinoza employs, as a movement in the direction of reality, toward a higher stage of being.

Mature men and women, who have been helped to a deeper understanding of the childish superstitions that to some extent still rule their lives, know this about themselves. They know they desire to be as real as they can, for as long as they live, and affirm their striving toward reality, while soberly acknowledging its inevitable defeat, without yielding to the equally childish temptation to believe that defeat can be avoided in this life or the next. They know that death will cut their progress short and realize that at some point they will lose the strength to persevere—that it is their destiny, like that of every individual, eventually to return to the world from which they were separated at birth. But this knowledge is merely the recognition of death, not a longing for it. So long as they are not defeated by forces outside them, they move from each stage in their development as individuals to the next higher one with the joy that Spinoza defines as the experience of moving up the ladder of being.

Even the most successfully analyzed patient is still the prisoner, partly at least, of his childish wishes and of those aggressive feelings that are woven into the most loving human relations. He still lives to some degree, as every human being does, under the shadow of the fear of death, which represents the sum of the forces he longs to control. But though even a mature man can never entirely rid himself of the fear of dying, he does not wish to die. He wishes to live. He wants to have as much power as his circumstances permit. Inevitably, at some point, he will be worn down by the world. When this happens, he may "give up" and allow himself to die. He may even play an active part in arranging his death. But this is not the manifestation of a death wish. It is the expression of a desire to maintain a maximum of control within a rapidly shrinking world of possibilities—to die on terms of one's own choosing. It is the expression of a desire to live as well as one can, tempered by the knowledge that no one lives forever. A wise man is not tempted by the fantasy of life everlasting. But neither does he yearn for death for its own sake. As long as he lives, he wants only to live. His life is, as Spinoza says, "a meditation of life."[44] No phrase better captures Freud's ideal of how a human being should live.

This is the picture of human happiness that emerges from Freud's psychoanalytic writings. His musings on the death drive do not fit this picture. In fact, they render it unintelligible. Given the tension between his postulation of a death drive, on the one hand, and the ethical ideal of psychoanalysis, on the other, it seems best to dismiss the first as a speculative proposition that cannot be sustained, and to regard Freud's own attraction to it as a misguided expression of his sound belief that though we all love life, we generally pursue it in blindingly ignorant ways. The results are often self-defeating, and in this sense look—but only look—suicidal. To explain them, however, no death drive is required: only the *conatus* constrained by inadequate ideas that forms the basis of Spinoza's account of the trajectory of all finite being. It is Spinoza's metaphysics, and not the Empedoclean one that Freud himself tentatively proposes, that best fits Freud's own most fundamental convictions about the role of reason in the world and his account of the sort of happiness we may reasonably hope to attain. His postulation of a death drive is a metaphysical mistake.

"OUR GOD LOGOS"

The first part of Spinoza's *Ethics* is called, "Of God." His conception of God is not, of course, one that any Christian, Jew or Muslim would accept. Spinoza's God, like Aristotle's, is indistinguishable from the eternal intelligibility of the world itself. Without a God of this sort, he insists, nothing in the world can be or be understood. The theology of part 1 of the *Ethics* is the foundation of Spinoza's entire philosophical system, including, in particular, his examination of the question of how it is best for human beings to live.

Though Freud's answer to this question is strikingly similar to Spinoza's, it seems not to be based on anything that might remotely be called a theology. Freud was famously skeptical about religion. He was fascinated by it as a phenomenon and devoted three books to the subject, but claimed to have no religious feelings himself.[45] He was suspicious of those who said they had experienced a release, even if only for a moment, from the limits of thought and feeling that Freud believed to be our inescapable fate. He viewed such claims with the skeptical eye of one who has come to accept the childishness of all human behavior, yet continues to insist that greater maturity is always possible.

This view is not far off from Spinoza's. Yet for Spinoza the first step toward genuine maturity is an understanding of the nature of God. For Freud, by contrast, the path to adulthood leads to an acceptance of the disenchantment of the world and the rejection of everything that traditionally has gone under the name of religion. To Spinoza's "god-saturated" metaphysics, Freud's godless science of psychoanalysis seems to stand in the sharpest possible contrast.

The difference between them is smaller than it appears, however. It is true that Spinoza and Freud differ temperamentally so far as their approach to questions of theology is concerned. The fact that Spinoza's philosophy grew out of his own religious training and his reflections on its shortcomings, whereas the theory of psychoanalysis emerged in the course of Freud's work as a doctor and scientist, surely has something to do with the latter's greater discomfort with theological subjects. But the difference in their attitude toward God diminishes—indeed, I think, it vanishes—when one takes two things into account. The first is that the childish God Freud says we have outgrown is the same primitive conception of divinity that Spinoza ridicules in the appendix to part I of the *Ethics* and elsewhere in his writings. The second is that the mature God of Spinoza's metaphysics is the one that near the end of *The Future of an Illusion* Freud twice refers to as "our god Logos," the presiding spirit of modern science, in whose divinity Freud believed as deeply as Spinoza.[46]

According to both Spinoza and Freud, the creator God of the Abrahamic religions is the last and most powerful expression of the superstitious belief that there are superior beings who take an interest in human affairs and have the power to affect it in ways no human being can. The gods are pleased by some of the things men do and displeased by others. They must therefore be placated; if not, they become angry and punish those who fail to do as they wish. Sickness, famine, infertility, and natural catastrophes of all kinds are among the punishments they inflict on their inattentive and disobedient subjects.

These beliefs are as old as human life itself. They inevitably encourage the idea of more and more powerful gods. As the power of the gods increases, more of human suffering becomes explicable, and the antidote to it grows in strength as well. This leads to the idea of a single all-powerful God, and then to that of an omnipotent lord of creation, whose separation from the world, and ability to bring it into being from nothing, represents the ultimate peak of divine power. Judaism, and then in an even starker and more principled form, the Christian religion, make the idea of such a world-transcending God the pivot of religious belief, which has its beginnings in man's first primitive attempts to explain and control the world by postulating the existence of divine beings more powerful than himself.

To this general account, which he shares with Spinoza, Freud adds a novel detail. The invention of such beings has its roots, he claims, in the travails of the oedipal situation. The first watchful and avenging god is a hypertrophic expression of the angry tribal father, murdered, Freud says, by his rebellious sons who have conspired to destroy his monopoly over the females of the tribe. The murdered father now takes revenge, from beyond the grave, in the form of a god with the power to punish his sons for their primal misdeed, and all subsequent acts of disobedience to the system of rules they have erected to prevent its recurrence. There is no parallel in Spinoza's explanation of the origins of human religion. But Freud's speculative reconstruction follows the same general pattern, for it too traces the belief in gods—and eventually, in a single, all-powerful God—to the experience of human weakness and the need for beings with superior powers to control what men cannot, in this case the wish to kill their father and seize the women he wants to keep to himself.

It is characteristic of Freud's account that he locates the danger that makes human beings feel weak and in need of a guardian god, not in the external world, as Spinoza does, but in the internal demands of the id instead. Still, the strategy for dealing with the danger is the same. It calls for the invention of a god with the power to provide protection against a danger that human beings are powerless to avoid—here, the threat to social order posed by the transgressive appetites of the id. Moreover, like Spinoza, Freud believes this primitive strategy is rationally explicable, but only if we view it as the result of ignorance and fear. He regards all the more sophisticated versions of it as similarly confused. In Freud's view, the whole of human religion, from the totemic practices of the primal horde to the theology of the God on the cross, represents a childish attempt to solve a real problem by magical means—an abdication of reason in favor of fantasy, whose persistence into adult life can only be called a neurosis. Spinoza did not know the word, but his judgment is the same.

To religion in this sense, Freud opposes science. Through "scientific work" we "gain some knowledge about the reality of the world, by means of which we can increase our power and in accordance with which we can arrange our life." This is true, for example, of the work of physics, which studies the behavior of bodies. But psychoanalysis, Freud claims, is a science too, whose task is to help us understand the origin and function of the self-imposed neuroses that are the result of our own childish fears.

This is true for individuals and also for humanity as a whole, whose infancy is dominated by the "collective" neurosis of religion. In an individual psychoanalysis, the first step toward a freer and more powerful existence is an understanding of how one came to be neurotic in the first place. Similarly, in the analysis of man's religious life, which has been an intimate part of his experience from the start, the first step toward a form of social existence no longer hobbled by the ignorance and fear on which all religion rests, is an understanding of the phenomenon of religion itself as a response to the experience of frailty in the face of powerful drives, against which men feel the need for protectors with more strength than their own. As in an individual analysis, such understanding brings a real increase in power, never complete to be sure, but greater than the illusory power that men enjoyed so long as they believed, in a childish and dreamlike way, that they were in the protective custody of stern but caring beings of a superhuman kind.

To those who object that men will always need a god who protects and consoles them, Freud responds that such "infantilism is destined to be sur-mounted."[47] The yearning for power and control is a permanent feature of human existence. Eventually, however, men must learn that the old religions, on which they have been brought up since the dawn of humankind, give them less power than the discoveries they make with their own minds—less power and less reality too, for the illusory world of religion stands in the same rela-tion to the disenchanted world of science as dreams do to waking life. The long historical movement from the first to the second represents a process of maturation, the analogue of the one that takes place on the analyst's couch as the patient slowly discovers the origins and dimensions of the prison he has built for himself. At the end of the penultimate chapter of *The Future of an Illusion,* Freud expresses his confidence in the inevitability of this movement, citing in support a fragment of a poem by Heine, to whom Freud refers as "one of our fellow unbelievers," a term that Heine himself applies to Spinoza.[48]

The psychoanalytic ideal of maturity combines the joy of moving from one grade of power to a higher one, with the recognition that such progress inevitably remains hostage to the childish fears and desires that even the wis-est man or woman can never wholly escape. Freud's ideal of civilizational pro-gress is the same. Science, in the broadest sense, represents the collective maturation of humankind and is likewise a source of continuing joy—the experience of movement to ever-higher levels of power and reality as our ideas about the world become increasingly adequate, though never perfectly so.

The fewer the brute facts these ideas must assume, the more they explain. The more adequate and hence powerful they become. In every branch of science—psychoanalysis as much as physics—contingency is therefore a sign of inadequacy and immaturity. The aim of science in all its depart-ments is to convert accident to necessity, or what amounts to the same thing, the inexplicable to the explained. The more one succeeds in this en-deavor, the closer one comes to seeing the world *sub specie aeternitatis,* for this is what eternity means: the timelessness of what, in Aristotle's phrase, cannot be other than it is.[49]

All those who are engaged in the work of science are drawn forward by their love of eternity in this sense. They have a God too, though not one defined by the transcendence of reason, as the God of Abraham is. Their God is the eternal necessity of reason itself. It is what Freud calls the "god Logos." Unlike the God of Abraham, whose inexplicable creation of the world raises a permanent barrier to the expansion of reason, Freud's God is not only compatible with the aspirations of modern science but defines its innermost spirit, and the joy experienced by those, like Freud, who succeed in pressing back the frontiers of contingency that limit our knowledge of the world.

This experience of joy must be distinguished from the "oceanic feelings" of the religious devotee. The latter succeeds in escaping the bonds of finite existence. He briefly inhabits a realm beyond the world and time. A scientist like Freud recognizes that no escape of this kind is possible. He knows that his limited understanding of things rules this out forever, and that he can never reach the end that draws him on: the worm in the blood, the navel of the dream. This is a disappointment, but one he is prepared to accept, just as the successfully analyzed patient is prepared to accept that he shall never find the all-embracing love he has been seeking since he first emerged from his mother's womb. Maturity as an individual and a civilization means accepting these limits, without relapsing into the gratifying, but infantile fantasy of a final union with God.

Yet it also means embracing the God without which science itself is inconceivable. Though we can never fully understand the world, the science by means of which we seek to do so is premised on the conviction that the world is intelligible all the way down—that what seems accidental and therefore inexplicable is so only because we have so far failed to grasp its necessity. No scientist has ever been more committed to this idea than Sigmund Freud, or carried the scientist's program of enlightenment farther into the once-dark world of childish longings and grown-up neuroses. If Freud remained detached from the "oceanic feelings" of religious life, the joy of science, tempered by the wisdom that its work is never done, is evident on every page he wrote, and inseparable from the modern scientist's conception of the everlasting and divine: of the necessity of all that happens in our infinitely intelligible world, without which human life, inevitably disappointing as it is, would be mindless and vain.

From the very beginning of his career, Freud insisted that psychoanalysis is a genuine science. Many have dismissed or ridiculed this claim, on the grounds that Freud's conception of science was naïve and shaped by now discredited theories of the nervous system and the like. But at bottom Freud felt that it was urgent to defend the scientific status of psychoanalysis because he embraced the theology on which the whole of modern science is based, as backward as the neurology and biochemistry of his time appear from the perspective of ours.

If the prestige of psychoanalysis has declined relative to these other fields, however, it is not mainly because its science now seems out of date. It is because psychoanalysis is openly ethical, both in theory and practice. Most scientists today claim to start from a principled distinction between facts and values. But that is a metaphysical prejudice founded on the decaying remnants of Christian belief. It is inspired by a theology that modern science no longer accepts. That science is an inherently ethical enterprise is a truth they fail to grasp, but one that both Spinoza and Freud understood. In this respect, the beleaguered science of psychoanalysis comes closer to the truth about science in general than those who insist on the distinction between facts and values are able to see. In the next chapter, I pursue this question further and explore the implications of the ethics of modern science for our understanding of human friendship generally, and for the meaning of gratitude in a world no longer haunted by the attempt to thank a God to whom we can never be grateful enough.

CHAPTER 31

"Man Is a God to Man"

THE MODERN RESEARCH IDEAL

Spinoza's chief concern is with the ancient philosophical question of how to live a happy life. It is the same question that Aristotle asks at the beginning of the *Nicomachean Ethics*. Spinoza gives his own answer in part 5 of the book he chose to call an *Ethics* too. There he describes a life of "joy," devoted to the pursuit of an ever more adequate knowledge of oneself and the world.

This is preceded by an account in part 4 of why most men live unhappily or, as he says, in "bondage." But to understand what bondage means, we first need to study the passions, for it is these that both keep us in chains and hold the key to our liberation from them. The passions are the subject of part 3.

Before we can grasp the nature of the passions, however, we must understand that of the mind. A passion is a cloudy or inadequate idea that represents the world from a limited point of view.[1] Each mind is a collection of such ideas. Spinoza explains the nature of the mind in part 2 of the *Ethics*.

But the explanation he gives of the mind cannot stand on its own. It presupposes an understanding of the world our minds depict. In part 1, Spinoza seeks to prove the unity, necessity and infinite diversity of what he calls "nature" or "God" and to demonstrate its identity with the world as a whole. This is where the *Ethics* begins. It is the most difficult and demanding part of the work. But the theology of part 1 is merely the first step in an argument whose final goal is ethical and humanistic in the sense that its subject is the happiness of human beings.

This goal seems incompatible with the aims of modern science as these are now widely understood. Many today—scientists and laypersons alike—insist that there is no inner connection between science and ethics. Scientific discoveries may of course be used to promote the welfare of human beings but science itself, they claim, has no ethical aims of its own. It declares nothing to be good or bad. It merely reports the facts and explains them, leaving it to us to decide their ethical value on independent grounds that may be morally or politically compelling but have no scientific authority. Max Weber strongly defended this position, whose roots lie in the Christian metaphysics of the will and in the positivist conception of value associated with it.

Spinoza's understanding of the relation between science and ethics is fundamentally different. In his view, science is inherently ethical. It is the path to happiness, or rather, it is happiness itself.

Spinoza's equation of knowledge and happiness was a premise of the ancient ethical systems on which he models his own, though his identification of both with the endless, collaborative work of scientific research distinguishes his ethics from the wisdom philosophies of pagan antiquity in a fundamental way. Spinoza's philosophy conflicts even more sharply, however, with the reigning spirit of modern science, whose commitment to the separation of facts and values is as hostile to the idea that scientific inquiry is an inherently ethical enterprise as its contempt for metaphysics is to Spinoza's belief that the study of nature must be founded on a metaphysically rigorous conception of God if it is to be a science at all.

Those who maintain that God has no place in science generally have the God of Abraham in mind. To the extent they do, they are right. The doctrine of creation is incompatible with the principle of sufficient reason on which the enterprise of science is based. But another conception of God is needed to make sense of this principle itself.

Those who claim that ethics can be joined to science only from without, by a free act of will, adopt a similarly narrow point of view. Their conception of ethical value is likewise shaped by Christian beliefs, even if they purport to reject the theology on which these are based. But just as there is another theology that underwrites rather than anathematizes the boundless rationalism of modern science, there is another ethics that supports the view that the human good is the inner meaning of science itself, and not a separate value fastened to it by a judgment for which there can be no scientific warrant.

Many scientists report an experience of joy that resembles the one Spinoza defines as the essence of ethical progress.[2] But their acceptance of the dogma of value-free science prevents them from being able to explain why they are happy. To do this, they must make a fresh start. They must abandon their conception of the relation of science to ethics, which is still covertly shaped by the theology of creation, and begin instead with the born-again paganism of Spinoza's *Ethics,* whose metaphysics alone has the resources to explain why the endless adventure of modern science is by its very nature a spiritual quest marked, above all, by joy.

BEING, ETERNITY AND POWER

For Spinoza as for Aristotle, the most important ethical question is how to achieve as much happiness as one can. In this respect, his ethics begins at a very different point than Kant's.

For Kant, the basic challenge of ethical life is to live in a way that is respectful of one's autonomy and that of other rational beings. Everything else follows from this elementary requirement. It is dictated by our possession of a capacity for self-direction that resembles God's own. Unlike God, we lack the power to bring the objects of our willing into being from nothing. But the act of willing is itself wholly within our control. We create our intentions— we choose our maxims—just as God creates the world. Respect for this god-like autonomy, in ourselves and other persons, is the meaning of the moral law. The starting point of Kant's ethics is the Christian idea of creation—what he rather blandly calls "spontaneity." Spinoza dismisses this idea as unintelligible and rejects the view that it is possible (let alone necessary) to found an ethics upon it.

This is not to say that Kant's moral principles have no place in Spinoza's ethical system. Spinoza affirms the importance of respect and toleration and endorses a version of the principle of equality. He also insists that only the establishment of a political society with centralized powers of control can cure the vicissitudes of what he too calls a "state of nature."[3] But Spinoza's defense of these ideas, in sharp contrast to Kant's, is nested within a metaphysics that rests not on the Christian idea of the will, and the separation of facts and values this implies, but on the pagan equation of nature and god that lies at the root of Aristotle's eudaemonistic ethics as well as his own.

Aristotle's cosmos contains a multitude of different kinds of things. Each has a distinctive nature of its own. Each, moreover, has only a limited degree of power. The best evidence of this is that all of them move. Nothing remains in that state of perfect, ceaseless activity that is the defining trait of the everlasting and divine. Only the cosmos as a whole does. By contrast, the finite things that fill it can do no more than strive to partake of the divinity the world as a whole alone possesses.

This is true of human beings too, though man's reason sets him apart from other terrestrial beings by enabling him to participate reflectively in the eternal order of the world. The lives of human beings are governed by this order. But with the exception of the planets and stars, which Aristotle believed to be thinking things as well, only men are able to comprehend the order of the world in thought—to see and understand it, and express it in speech. This gives them a power other sublunary beings lack.

Not every human being realizes this power. In most it remains underdeveloped, and is employed only for practical ends. But a few pursue it for its own sake, seeking to grasp the order of the world as fully as they can. Their pursuit culminates in philosophy, and more specifically in that branch of philosophy known as metaphysics. In the life of the metaphysician, the distinctively human power of reason reaches a peak. His is the most powerful life a man can lead. Indeed, it is not merely more powerful than other lives. The activity of contemplation affords those who experience it a divine degree of power—an absolute maximum, as much as it is possible to possess—though because, like other men, even the greatest metaphysician has needs of various kinds, he cannot hold onto such power except for brief periods of time.

With every aspect of this pagan theology of science, except the last, Spinoza is in basic agreement. He, too, believes that the world possesses an intelligibility of its own; that this is not the gift of a God beyond it, but the very being of the world itself; that men strive to participate in the immortal reality of the world as fully as they can; and that science is the best and most satisfying way they have of doing this—hence, the most powerful of all human activities.[4] Spinoza's understanding of the aims of science, like Aristotle's, is thus shaped by the identification of God with the world, and by the equation of being, eternity and power. It is only with Aristotle's claim that in contemplation a man actually becomes, however briefly, the God of the world, that Spinoza fundamentally disagrees.

According to Spinoza, every finite being is a mode of God. It is one of an infinite number of unique expressions of the world as a whole. As such, it strives to persevere in being. In this respect, its condition is unlike that of God. The world or God has all the being there is, and always will. There is therefore nothing for it to strive to attain. By contrast, each of its modes has only a limited quantum of power, or what amounts to the same thing, a limited quantum of being. This is not nothing. Even the simplest and most evanescent mode has some reality and power. But none has so much that there is not another with more. This means that every mode is vulnerable to forces outside it, and must work to avoid being destroyed by them, though its destruction is inevitable and can therefore only be postponed. Its condition is thus an essentially temporal one, unlike that of the world as a whole, which can no more be said to exist in time than the truths of mathematics that serve as an imperfect model for the infinite set of factual truths whose necessity we would comprehend with equal transparency were we able to grasp the order of events in time *sub specie aeternitatis.*

The human intellect conceives the world under the attributes of thought and extension. These are the only two explanatory frameworks we possess. They are logically independent in the sense that an event in one can never be the explanation of an event in the other. Yet despite the conceptual gulf between them, in one respect the world looks the same from both points of view. Whether we conceive it under the attribute of thought or extension, the world appears to us to be a hierarchy of increasingly complex individuals, each striving to preserve its identity against insurmountable odds. As we move up this hierarchy, we encounter individuals whose power is greater—that can do more, and are more effective in resisting the forces that threaten to destroy them. But no individual is all-powerful. Hence, none ever ceases striving to hold onto whatever degree of reality it possesses.

This state of striving is one that all modes share. But it is also what gives each its individual identity, unique in all the world and time. Thus, in one sense, every mode is striving for the same thing—for reality and power. But in another, each is working for itself alone. It is striving to preserve its own reality, not that of any other thing. The striving for reality that in Spinoza's metaphysics is the hallmark of every finite being thus simultaneously anchors all of them in a common world and individuates each from the others, so that it functions both as a principle of cosmic integration and infinite differentiation, uniting the world as a whole with the individuality of each of its endlessly diverse modifications.

Spinoza calls this striving for reality the "love of God."[5] It is a phrase he uses to describe the intellectual ambitions of human beings, but strictly speaking it applies to all finite beings, below as well as above the threshold of conscious attention. Every one of these is moved by its love of God in a metaphysical sense. Each aspires to hold onto its share of being, which only the world or God possesses without limit, and none gives up its share without a fight. That is because every thing in the world feels the attractive pull of being, and strives to partake of the world's infinite reality and power for as long as its circumstances allow.

This is not a striving to reach or thank a God beyond the world, who has created it from nothing. There is no such God; the very idea of one is unintelligible. But Spinoza is not an atheist. He insists that even the most short-lived event cannot be conceived except by reference to the everlasting and divine. Yet like Aristotle, he regards this as a property of the world itself, not of a God beyond it. In Spinoza's view, there is nothing outside the world on which it depends either to be or to be intelligible. Indeed, for Spinoza, the eternal intelligibility of the world as a whole follows from the very definition of it. In this respect, Spinoza and Aristotle share a *worldly* conception of God, and agree that every finite being longs to reach and be a part of it.

Importantly, though, they assign the universal longing for immortality to different levels of reality. In Aristotle's view, the love that draws all things toward God is anchored in their species-being. It is as members of their kind that plants and animals and the four simple substances strive for immortality and achieve it. Spinoza, by contrast, locates this striving at the individual level (as do Darwin and Freud). More precisely, he treats it as the ground or explanation of individuality itself, which Aristotle declares to be unintelligible as such. This is a crucial difference with large implications for their respective views of human science and bears directly on the question of whether (as Aristotle supposed) our search for knowledge and power can ever reach a definitive end.

Aristotle's view of contemplation as an end of this sort rests on his species-based interpretation of the immortality that philosophers achieve in thought. This in turn is dictated by his acceptance of the metaphysical distinction between form and matter. The doctrine of creation destroys this distinction and compels the conclusion that the world is "minded" all the way down. Spinoza rejects the theology that forced Augustine and Aquinas to embrace this conclusion, but accepts the conclusion itself. In combination with his pagan belief in the inherent divinity of the world, this leads him to the idea of a natural order that is not merely intelligible in itself, but infinitely so. To comprehend this order therefore necessarily becomes, for finite beings such as we, an endless collaborative task whose aims and methods can only be conceived in terms radically different from those associated with Aristotle's contemplative ideal.

To get a better understanding of Spinoza's view of these matters, and of his grounds for believing that the modern science of nature, with its endless program of research, possesses an inherent spiritual value of its own, we need to consider more closely his account of the form the love of God takes in the case of man.

PERSEVERANCE AND PROGRESS

Like everything in the world, men strive to persevere in being. "Persevere" has a conservative ring. It suggests the maintenance of a given *status quo*. But in the case of human beings, at least, it has an expansionary meaning. The way that we protect whatever power we possess is by seeking more. We do not strive merely to hold our own against the world, in a static way, but to increase our existing quantum of power, whatever this happens to be. This is not an occasional or accidental feature of human striving. It is constitutive of it at all levels.

That this is so is due, Spinoza says, repeating an argument of Hobbes', to the human ability to anticipate the future—to look ahead in time, and thus prepare for possible but not yet present dangers.[6] Only a being that is aware of its existence in time can do this. An awareness of this sort implies a recognition of the distinction between existing in time and existing outside of it, and hence between time and eternity. This seems to be a peculiarly human insight. It might appear to follow that the striving of other finite beings is not similarly expansive. Whether this was Spinoza's own view is uncertain. But it cannot be doubted that, in the case of human beings, he believed that the striving to persevere in being necessarily takes the form of a pursuit of ever-greater power.

This striving can never come to an end. No matter how much power a man or woman has, the world always has more. The most urgent sign of this is our mortality. But it does not follow, just because we are mortal, that there is no point in striving to increase our power. More power is always better than less, for the more power one has, the more one's desire to be is fulfilled. The more real one becomes. Greater power is therefore always a good thing, and worth striving to achieve, even if any increase in it falls short of the absolute power that only God or nature possesses.

This view resembles Aristotle's in one way. It equates power with being, and assumes there is a graded hierarchy of both. It further assumes that we can move up this hierarchy to higher levels of reality and power. In another way, though, Spinoza's view differs from Aristotle's, for unlike the latter he denies that it is possible for us ever to reach the end toward which we strive. At the same time, Spinoza's position also differs from that of Hobbes. Despite his belief that man's striving for power is interminable, Spinoza affirms its intelligibility and value—in contrast to Hobbes, who concludes from the endlessness of our striving that it must be pointless too. In different ways, then, Spinoza's view of the human condition is distinct from that of both these other philosophers. Like his metaphysics as a whole, it is defined by Spinoza's unique combination of ancient and modern ideas.

The human striving for greater power takes many different forms. Some, of course, are common and crude. Many people, for example, seek to increase their power through possessions and wealth. Others do so by acquiring social status and political authority. But these forms of power leave their possessors vulnerable in familiar ways. Their power can be destroyed in a twinkling. The knowledge that this is so is sometimes expressed by the saying that all such power is "hostage to fortune."

More secure than these, Spinoza says, is the power that comes from knowledge or understanding. This can never be absolute either, but is more durable than any other kind. Here too, Spinoza and Aristotle agree, though once again, not in every way. For while Aristotle assumes that it is possible for a wise man to comprehend, briefly at least, all that is comprehensible in the world, Spinoza denies this, and insists that progress in knowledge, as in every other dimension of power, is always limited and must therefore continue without end.

Spinoza's interpretation of the distinction between conceptual and empirical truth as one of degree rather than kind reflects this general metaphysical outlook.

We possess a small number of conceptual truths. These are distinguished from other truths by their self-evidence. A conceptual truth is transparently obvious to those who comprehend it and, once understood, cannot be refuted by further experience. The truths of mathematics are truths of this kind.

Traditionally, this idea has been expressed by saying that such truths are eternally valid. They are not qualified or conditioned by the point of view of the being who grasps them. They are true from every point of view or, what amounts to the same thing, from none. In Spinoza's terminology, when I fully comprehend a mathematical or other conceptual truth—when I can demonstrate and explain it—it is *in* me, in the sense that its truthfulness can no longer be dislodged by anything that happens *to* me. With respect to this truth, at least, I possess a divine self-sufficiency. I am, with regard to it, all-powerful, because there is nothing outside me that can cause its truth to disappear (though I may, of course, forget that it is true, or lose the ability to explain why, but that is a different matter).

This is tremendously good news. But unless one writes off all other, experiential knowledge as essentially illusory (in the way that Plato did), it is tempered by the dispiriting realization that, in the realm of understanding, we are able to establish only a tiny beachhead of truly divine wisdom, which is characterized by its formality or abstractness, and hence by its distance from the infinitely complex and vivid world we encounter in experience.

What Spinoza calls imaginative knowledge can never be perfectly independent or self-contained in the way such fragments of divine knowledge are. To begin with, all experience is perspectival and depends on the existence of beings other than the one who has it. In this sense, it is always "in their power." When I see a ball drop from a tower, for example, I see it from a point of view, and my seeing depends on the external presence of the tower and ball which, so to speak, make an "impression" on me.

Because I see these things from a particular perspective, my understanding of what is happening when the ball drops is always liable to error and distortion, and since the ball and tower must be present for me to have any experience of them at all, whatever knowledge I derive from the experience is hostage to their presence. This remains true no matter how abstract such knowledge becomes. Knowledge of this kind can therefore never be as independent as my understanding of the Pythagorean theorem. It can never be entirely *in* me in the same way.

Knowledge that is fully self-contained Spinoza calls "adequate." Knowledge that is not he terms "inadequate" or "confused." All our experiential knowledge of the world is therefore, by definition, confused in Spinoza's sense. But though the limits within which such knowledge is contained can never be entirely erased, they can, in Spinoza's view, be made progressively less confining. Doing so is the work of science, which seeks to narrow the gap between conceptual truths, on the one hand, and those of experience on the other, by constructing a system of ever more complete and refined causal laws.

The science of nature works by means of such laws. It is possible, for example, to formulate a law that describes the motion of a falling ball and to test it experimentally, as Galileo is reputed to have done.[7] A law is a generalization, and so, if valid at all, must apply not just to one ball but to others, indeed to every falling object. Moreover, the very idea of a law implies that of necessity.[8] If it is a law that an object, when dropped from a height, falls at a fixed rate of acceleration, then it is necessarily true that one state (acceleration) follows from another (the release of the object from a constrained and stationary position). To say that there is a lawful connection between these is just another way of describing the necessity that joins them. Hence, to the extent that we are able to place an experience within a system of laws, and to explain it by doing so, our understanding of the experience becomes at once more general and less conditional. It comes a step closer to the absolute universality and perfect necessity that every conceptual truth possesses.

Of course, a gap still remains—or rather, two gaps. The first is the one between percept and concept. We may think of it as a gap in the "downward" direction.

To stay with the falling ball for a moment, even supposing we have formulated a law that accurately describes its acceleration, in every particular case there will always be some deviation from the behavior the law predicts. The law is an idealization. It abstracts from the full particularity of any given situation. As a consequence, there always remains something in the behavior of a falling object that is not explained by the law and which can be accounted for only by modifying or qualifying it in some fashion, for example, to include the effects of friction. These modifications must themselves be laws, of course, to have any explanatory power. If they possess such power, they help to narrow the explanatory gap left by the first, relatively undiscriminating law, though they too inevitably leave something about the behavior of any individual falling object unexplained. While the residue of inexplicability is decreased by adding such refinements, the process of adding them can never reach the unattainable goal of a system of laws whose subtlety and discrimination reaches all the way down to the individuality of the behavior in question, entirely eliminating the gap between percept and concept.

The second gap that science can never completely close lies in an "upward" direction.

To explain the action of a falling ball by appeal to the law of acceleration immediately raises a further question. Why do falling objects accelerate? We may say, "On account of gravity." But that is just a word, and until we can give an account of the nature of the force that causes them to accelerate, our explanation remains incomplete. It leaves something—indeed, the most important thing—unexplained. Whatever necessity the law of acceleration may appear to possess thus proves to be dependent on a brute fact which, precisely because it cannot be explained, compromises the law's necessity in a manner foreign to the nature of conceptual truth. The challenge is to explain this brute fact too, by demonstrating its necessity in light of some higher-order law, and so on forever, in an ascending, if unending, process of ever-wider explanatory schemes, that seeks to close the gap between the actual and the necessary in an upward direction.

This double-ended program of research generates a web of laws increasingly wide and fine. If the process could be carried to its limit, the web would be as wide as the world and so fine that nothing could possibly fall through it. Every individual event in the world would be explained and its explanation tied to an ascending set of laws that eventually linked it to the order of the world as a whole, whose own necessity would be transparent because dependent on nothing but itself.

The laws that form this web are causal in nature. They explain events by relating them to others that are prior in time. Normally, of course, we distinguish causation from mere antecedence. We regard the second as a necessary but not sufficient condition of the first. But this distinction is also an artifact of our finitude. In reality, the whole of the world at any given moment is the cause of the world at the next. This is Laplace's famous formulation, which is sometimes viewed as an objectionably strong expression of scientific determinism.[9] Yet rightly understood, it merely states one of the most basic assumptions underlying all empirical research.

If something is inexplicable to us, that is because we are insufficiently knowledgeable about its causes, and though our effort to gain a greater understanding of these may be blocked or thwarted for a time, the work of research depends on the assumption that there is no absolute bar to our making ever-greater progress toward that perfect specification of each temporal state of the world which, were we able to provide it, would explain everything about the state that follows.

At that point, the distinction between antecedence and causation would vanish, as would the distinction between causal explanations, which presuppose the existence of time, and conceptual ones, whose necessity is a consequence of the timelessness of the relations they describe. Our finitude prevents us from reaching this point but not from making continual progress toward it—toward an unconditioned understanding of the limitless intelligibility of the world whose secrets science is able to capture in its net of laws because they are not really secrets at all.

With every step in this direction, our power grows. Our understanding of the world is less dependent on brute facts we cannot explain. It is more self-contained, and would be wholly so if we could reach the point at which all our causal explanations had been converted to conceptual ones. The explanation of everything in the world would then be "in" us, in the way that mathematical explanations are. The latter give us a taste of what such understanding would be like. This lies beyond our reach. We are modes, and therefore essentially, not contingently, finite. But like everything else in Spinoza's metaphysics, finitude comes in degrees. We can be more or less self-contained, and therefore more or less divine. By increasing our self-containedness, science brings us closer to God.

There is nothing mystical about our efforts to do this or the goal we seek to reach. Both are wholly rational because identical with explanation itself. God is just the eternal intelligibility of the world and science our striving to partake ever more fully of it. The other ways in which human beings strive for greater power—by means of wealth and fame—have the same objective. They too are paths to God. But by comparison with the path of understanding, they are pathetically weak. Only science and philosophy, whose task is to explain the aims and methods of science, bring us measurably closer to that participation in the eternity of the world for which every finite being yearns—though because the intelligibility of the world is infinitely deep, the effort to reach it must be endlessly long.

RESEARCH

For Aristotle, natural science culminates in philosophy, which in turn culminates in metaphysics. These are continuous activities or disciplines. The movement from one to the next is motivated by the same desire to know, which remains unfulfilled at lower levels of inquiry. With metaphysics, however, the search for understanding comes to an end. The desire to know is satisfied at last. There is no form of wisdom that lies beyond it, and nothing intelligible about the world that one who possesses such wisdom fails to comprehend.

That this is so is explained by the distinction between form and matter.

The fundamental question of metaphysics is, what is the being of beings?[10] In his lectures on the subject, Aristotle considers a number of possible answers. Several are plausible, and contribute something to our understanding. But one is decisive—that the being of a thing consists in its active realization of the form that distinguishes it as a being of a certain kind. This is all the being any thing possesses. It is there to be seen, on the surface of things, for those who have the curiosity and patience to look.[11]

Of course, not every aspect of a thing's behavior is explained by its form. Some of its movements and characteristics are idiosyncratic. But beyond a certain point, these are unintelligible. There is nothing that can be understood about them. That is because they are due not to the thing's form but its matter, whose ultimate formlessness guarantees its unintelligibility.

The student of metaphysics understands that the being of a thing consists in its form. He acts on this philosophical principle by looking at the appearances of things to see what forms they possess. If he succeeds, he acquires not only the *highest* knowledge but *all* there is to be had. At this point, the desire to know that drives all human inquiry, from the simplest, least articulate expressions of wonder, to the rarified heights of philosophy, is completely fulfilled. It would be the sign of a fool to ask for more. To be sure, no human being can maintain this posture forever. His concentration is bound eventually to flag, and though it can be renewed, so long as his mind remains strong, old age and death destroy it completely. This is a limit that no amount of human wisdom can surpass. But it is not a limit on the amount or degree or extent of the wisdom a human being can acquire. His wisdom may not last forever, yet while it does, it is perfect and complete.

To attain this point of timeless understanding is the highest goal a human being can pursue. No man is able to do it on his own, however. He needs friends to help him. He needs teachers to prepare the way for him, and companions with whom to study. The space he enters when he contemplates the order of the world must have been prepared and kept open by others before him. His predecessors in the venture of philosophy, even those long dead, are his friends in this extended sense. That he needs such friends to reach, even for a time, the state of divine self-sufficiency that contemplative wisdom brings, is a consequence of his dependence on many things, his friends included. For their help, he has the most obvious reason to be grateful, but his gratitude toward his friends is the horizontal thankfulness that one human being feels for others like himself, and which he can therefore reciprocate in an adequate way by doing as much and as good for those who come after him in the same human venture.

In one sense, Spinoza's view of science, and of the friendship it assumes and invites, is the same. In another, it is fundamentally different.

For Spinoza, too, science and philosophy are continuous. Both are motivated by the striving to persevere, which in the case of human beings takes the form of an endless pursuit of "power after power."[12] What we seek at every stage of this pursuit is a deeper understanding of things, for the more we can explain, the more the world, which we initially encounter as a bewildering kaleidoscope of external objects and forces, is "in" us instead.

This search for explanations culminates in the knowledge that the eternal substance of which every individual mind and body is a mode, the being of their being, is intelligibility itself. The knowledge that this is so provides the foundation for a movement back down from the heights of theology to the concrete investigation of the physical and psychological world, just as Aristotle's metaphysics provides the foundation for all the specialized branches of natural science.

But no matter how long and carefully we study the world, we shall never possess the detailed understanding of it that Spinoza's metaphysics assures us is possible. That is because the intelligibility of the world is not exhausted, for Spinoza, by the forms of things alone, but encompasses their particularity too.

Spinoza's radical extension of the idea, which Aristotle accepts in a more circumscribed version, that the very being of things consists in their intelligibility—in their openness, as Aristotle puts it, to an "accounting"—presupposes the destruction of the distinction between form and matter whose erasure is the chief result of the doctrine of creation. This is the defining principle of philosophy in the epoch of Christian belief. With its destruction, the work of science becomes endless, and the achievements of any individual scientist subject to a limit other than the obvious ones that Aristotle acknowledges.

Aristotle observes that no human scientist lives forever, or is able to maintain an uninterrupted state of alertness so long as he does. That is certainly true, but a Spinozist is bound to add: even at the pinnacle of his or her career, the most active and attentive scientist in the world never comprehends more than an infinitesimal sliver of it. The notion that, even for a moment, a philosopher or scientist might know all there is to know, is undermined completely once the equation of being and intelligibility, which Spinoza enthusiastically accepts, is radicalized under the influence of the doctrine of creation, which Spinoza emphatically rejects, but whose metaphysical implications decisively shape his born-again paganism and the conception of science it implies.

As a result, the idea that science makes progress from one generation to the next, and is in this sense a historical enterprise, becomes unavoidable. The scientists of each generation must of course understand what their predecessors have done. They have to be "brought up to speed." But the point of their education is not to return them to the same position of timeless wisdom that those who went before had already achieved. It is to enable them to go farther. On a Spinozist view, science necessarily becomes a collaborative enterprise in a deeper sense than it was for Aristotle, since its work now requires not merely the transmission from one generation to the next of a body of unsurpassable wisdom, but a multigenerational program of research in which each new cohort of scientists makes its own individual contribution to a growing stockpile of knowledge that has no natural limit, unlike the activity of contemplation which, on Aristotle's view, marks the terminus of man's longing to be.

That there can be no end to our striving to comprehend the world, is a consequence of the gap that always remains between our modal being and the infinite intelligibility of the world we long to know. But this is not the same as the gap that exists between the God of Abraham and his children. That gap cannot be narrowed by an inch, and the suggestion that we ought to strive to do so is the heresy of pride. By contrast, the gap that exists in Spinoza's metaphysics between substance and mode can always be further reduced, and the endless effort to bridge it—to become God—is more than merely legitimate: it is man's noblest work. This is neither an Aristotelian nor a Christian conception of science. It rests on a metaphysics different from both, and invites a view of friendship that is equally distinct.

Spinoza understood the importance of friendship. Nothing, he says, is more helpful to a man than other men. We do not seek to understand the world on our own, in isolation from others, nor could we. The pursuit of such understanding is a collective activity. We engage in it with others, living and dead, and depend on them to educate, guide, correct and improve us. However great the accomplishments of any individual philosopher or scientist, her achievements are the work of many hands, and for the help of others—teachers, colleagues and students—she has reason to be grateful. They are her indispensable companions in the shared pursuit of a common good.

This companionship, and the gratitude one feels for it, is a horizontal relation among human beings. It is the thankfulness that one human being feels for the presence and assistance of others like him- or herself, all of whom are striving to increase their power and reality, within the limits their finitude imposes on them. It is therefore a gratitude that can be adequately reciprocated because the gifts that one receives are commensurate with those that one is capable of making in return. There is no residue of unrequited gratitude that a horizontal, human friendship of this kind imposes on its beneficiaries, in contrast to the thankfulness one owes to God on the supposition that he created us from nothing. For Spinoza, "man is a god to man."¹³

This idea of friendship closely resembles the one that Aristotle discusses at length in the *Nicomachean Ethics*. Both philosophers insist on our need for the help of others; conceive this help in strictly human terms; and assume that we are able to give as much and as good in return. Hence, neither's view of gratitude is burdened by the spiritual and psychological liabilities that attend the radically asymmetrical gift implied by the doctrine of creation. In this respect, their horizontal conception of friendship and gratitude differs fundamentally from the vertical theology of grace. But here again, Spinoza's post-Christian ideas show the impress of this theology in a way that Aristotle's do not, and bring his understanding of friendship and gratitude into alignment with modern ideas of honor, affection and love.

Spinoza concludes the *Ethics* with a famously encouraging observation. The path to wisdom and true happiness is difficult to find, he says, but others have found it in the past, and so can we if we search for it in the right way.¹⁴ This seems to imply that in the search for wisdom, the point at which one arrives is always the same. But that cannot be true, on a Spinozist view of God. A wise man knows that the eternal order of the world is not confined (as Aristotle believed) to the forms of things. It extends infinitely to the whole of reality. Hence, if wisdom consists in an actual and not merely abstract knowledge of the everlasting and divine, it can never be complete for any finite being.

Still, though our knowledge of the world must remain unfinished, it is also always increasing. Collectively, at least, it grows from year to year. This is the work of science. And because science is a progressive endeavor, every contribution to it represents something new, unknown or unheard of before, whose originality possesses a value of its own. In this sense, its individuality matters.

The scientist who makes such a contribution may modestly disclaim credit for it. She may say that the important thing is the discovery itself, not the identity of the man or woman who makes it. Disclaimers of this kind are common, if hard to believe. But even when they are sincere, the originality and hence uniqueness of the contribution is something we have reason to value for its own sake.

If it were possible to have a perfect knowledge of the world, as Aristotle supposed, it would be absurd to think it could be increased or improved. Once such knowledge is attained, it can only be lost, and found again. Those who rediscover it return to the very same place. Their wisdom is entirely impersonal. It is no different than that of anyone who possessed it before, or may do so again in the future. They have reason to be grateful to their teachers, of course, who helped them reach this point, but not on account of the originality of what their teachers have done. If anything, their gratitude is for their teachers' fidelity to what is old and unchanging. In order for the originality of a discovery to matter *as such,* our knowledge of the world must be endlessly cumulative. The individuality of a scientist's accomplishments can possess an intrinsic worth only in case the enterprise to which she contributes is a permanently open-ended one, without a fixed and attainable goal. And for that to be true, the world must be minded all the way down. The classical distinction between form and matter rules this out. Spinoza's metaphysics of substance and mode compels it.

This is the premise of the modern research ideal, and of the special form of friendship associated with it. The gratitude that one scientist feels toward her predecessors and collaborators is today colored, in every branch of study, by an appreciation of the originality of their achievements. She thanks them, actually or implicitly, on account of their individual contributions to their common work, which is animated by the belief that the world is "numbered"— calculable, ordered, intelligible—down to the hairs on our heads. This is the teaching of the Gospels, shorn of the dogma of creation in whose soil the idea that the world is infinitely intelligible first took root. In Spinoza's metaphysics, this idea is transposed to a born-again paganism that reunites God with the world, while preserving the infinite intelligibility of the one eternal substance that may be called by either name. Among the consequences of this transposition is a new and distinctive conception of friendship which, though still cast in wholly human terms, as a horizontal relation among men, values the individuality of individuals in a way that Aristotle's metaphysics cannot explain.

ROMANCE

We have been following these consequences in the realm of science, where they find expression in the ideal of an endlessly cumulative program of research to which each scientist rightfully aspires to make an original contribution of his or her own. But they also help us to understand the modern ideal of love, seemingly so distant from the impersonal ethos of science. In the

final chapter of the book, we shall explore the relation of this ideal to that of
liberal democracy, from which love also seems remote. But it will be useful
to say a few preliminary words about the nature of human love, as it appears
from a Spinozist perspective, and to note its surprising resemblance to the
spirit of friendship that informs the modern research ideal.

Socrates tells his companions in the *Symposium* that a priestess named
Diotima once told him the truth about love.[15] According to Diotima, love is
always of the everlasting. Whatever form it takes, its true object is eternity.
This is true even in the case of the love that one human being feels for another. One's beloved is of course a mortal being like oneself, but what one
truly loves in him, Diotima says, is the immortal form of beauty exemplified
by his physique, movements and speech.

On this view, it is not the unique physical and spiritual traits of the beloved to which the lover is attracted. Quite the opposite. There is nothing loveable in these at all. What one loves—all one loves—in the beloved is the
general form of beauty that remains once every idiosyncrasy has been stripped
away. That alone is everlasting. If lovers appear sometimes, even to themselves,
to love these idiosyncrasies—the mole on the beloved's cheek, the sound of
his laugh, his unique personal history—that is because, like all lovers of sights
and sounds, they regularly confuse the eternal forms that are the only real
source of being and value with their ephemeral embodiments, which have no
reality or worth of their own.

The wisest lovers are those who understand this. They are the philosophers
who have weaned themselves from the nearly universal, but pathetic, human
habit of confusing the eternal forms with their transient and imperfect images, and whose love is steadily directed toward the former alone. By comparison, the man who loves another man (or woman) and believes his beloved
to be unique in all the world, and loveable on that account, is living in a cave
of superstition or error. On this view, the singular devotion that lovers feel to
each other is a metaphysical mistake.

The Christian idea of love, which has shaped our modern attitude toward
it, resembles the Platonic in one way. On a Christian view, what makes another human being worthy of being loved is the fact that he or she is a creature of the one eternal God. Apart from their connection to God, human
beings have no inherent worth of their own. Like everything else in God's
creation, what value they possess is entirely derivative from that of their creator. He alone is intrinsically good, beautiful, and the like. Their creaturely

share in these same qualities (transient and imperfect by comparison) is God's free gift to them, and loveable solely on that account.

A man who loves another for his or her sake alone, who sees a beauty in his beloved that has no source but itself, therefore commits a terrible sin. It is characteristic of the Christian view of love that it condemns such love as a species of wickedness—a failure of the will—while Plato conceives it to be a form of ignorance instead. But both identify the object of any love worthy of the name with the everlasting and divine, to which the particular human beings with whom we fall in love are joined either by their participation in the immortal forms that Diotima describes or the part they play in the drama of creation, staged by a God beyond the world and time.

There is, however, a fundamental difference between these two conceptions of love. For Plato, the peculiarities of the beloved are completely unloveable. They have no connection at all to the true, timeless object of love. They are dross, pure and simple, a distraction we must train ourselves to ignore. On a Christian view of love, these same peculiarities *are* loveable, not in themselves to be sure, but as an expression of God's infinite goodness, which is manifest everywhere in his creation, high and low. Though Christians are required by their faith to deny that the faces and smiles and voices and histories of those they love possess an intrinsic value of their own, they are also required, by this same faith, to assign a derivative value to these things, as to every other unique feature of the world they inhabit—something that is literally unthinkable from a Platonic point of view.

Like his Platonic and Christian counterparts, the modern lover is also looking for a connection to the everlasting and divine. He too believes that love endures because it is of something durable, in contrast, most dramatically, to sexual appetite. As a result, his yearning can never be fully satisfied by anything that lasts only for a time, even if it is a lifetime. For those who are most deeply in love, a lifetime is never enough. To concede that some period (fifty years? a hundred? a thousand?) would be enough, and that, at the end, they would be happy to go their separate ways, would be for them to confess that their love is incomplete—which all human love is, of course, though its incompleteness is shadowed by a longing for something beyond the reach of time. This is the old passion for eternity, which Plato calls the love of the forms and Christians the love of God. Its tragic and comic consequences are as absorbing today as in the past. No subject has a more familiar place in both our high art and popular culture.

The other great theme in all modern depictions of love is the uniqueness of the beloved.

The lover may be looking for eternity but hopes, indeed needs, to find it in an other whose looks and style and spirit are unique in the whole of time. Love shades off from this into the more generalized affection we feel for family and friends. But the focal case, the one that defines what love truly is, is the kind we call "romantic"—the love of another man or woman in whose singular qualities we find the "one and only" human being capable of satisfying our longing for love without end. This is the secular residue of the anti-Platonic, Christian belief in the loveableness of individual things, stripped of the belief that what makes them loveable is their creation by God. The love of a single man or woman, unlike any other, with whom one can establish a connection indefeasible by time, not through an eternal God beyond the world, but an eternity that is present, awkwardly yet potently, in human love itself: this is the romantic ideal of love in which many today find their deepest source of solace and hope.

Platonic and Christian love both have their own metaphysics. The first relies on the distinction between form and matter. The second depends on the idea of creation. The modern, romantic conception of love has a metaphysics too. It is the born-again paganism of Spinoza's *Ethics,* which fuses in a wholly natural way the elements of timelessness and singularity that the ideal of romantic love joins as well.

Each of us is a mode of God—one of the infinitely many ways in which the intelligibility and power of the world manifests itself. Of course the same is true of every individual. But we are drawn with a special curiosity and passion to those that look and act as we do. From time to time, we "fall in love" with one of them. This is something different from admiring another person's talents, or finding her interesting, or being sexually attracted to him. Falling in love is more than any of these things. It is a glimpse, which may last for a week or a lifetime, into the infinite depth of another human being.

The Christian religion ascribes such depth to each of us too, but only because we are all the creatures of God. On a Spinozist view, we possess a depth of this kind because each of us *is* God, modally conceived. Each of us *is* an absolutely unique exhibition of the infinite intelligibility and power that constitutes the being of the world as a whole. This is what the romantic lover "sees." His love of God, which every human being feels, comes to be fastened on a particular other, so that the first is fused with the second, not through an act of divine creation, but because the other's particularity is already "in" the divinity of the world, and essential to its completion.

There is more. Falling in love is something that happens to us. We don't do it deliberately. Love is a passion in Spinoza's sense. It is therefore an expression of our finitude. The idea of God falling in love is absurd. Nor is it possible for us to fall in love with everyone. Everyone may be loveable, but our limited powers of attention and affection prevent us from ever loving more than a few. This is a consequence of our finitude too. Far from allowing us to escape the bounds of our finite existence, love reminds us of them in an excruciatingly poignant way.

And yet, though love is not a remedy for finitude, it is a kind of consolation, for it helps us see that we do really partake of the everlasting and divine, if only in a transient and imperfect way. Love helps us understand and accept this. Neither of the alternatives is preferable or in the end even bearable.

The first is to give up on the idea of God and reconcile oneself to a life that has no connection to eternity at all. This is to give up on love, as it is both commonly and philosophically understood. The second is to pursue eternity in the belief that one can attain it, in this world or the next. But that is to deny the essential pathos of the human condition.

In contrast to the advocates of both of these other views, the Spinozist maintains that every human being *is* God, though only incompletely. The acknowledgment that this is so is the inspiration for a form of humanistic self-regard that asks neither too little nor too much of oneself. Nothing is more helpful to achieving and sustaining a humanism of this kind than the love of another human being. Lovers cannot release each other from their mortal chains. But their love is a reminder, each to the other, of the infinite worthiness of their lives, however brief and blemished these may be. This is not salvation, in the Christian sense, but its value is such that it justifies us in thinking that for most human beings, and perhaps for all, the kind of passionate, fallible love that unites us, for a time at least, to a few, unique, other men and women out of all those in the world is the greatest good we can experience.

The modern research ideal springs from a similar root. It is driven by a cooler passion than that of personal love. Yet it offers a related form of inspiration and consolation to those who embrace it.

No scientist can ever grasp more than a vanishingly small portion of the world. He may make an individual contribution to the storehouse of knowledge, but this is bound to be as fleeting as the loveliness of body and spirit we discern in those we love. A dedicated scientist recognizes, perhaps, that he is helping to uncover the eternal mindedness of the world, step by patient step; perhaps he is cheered by this thought. But the awareness that his finitude shuts him out from the experience, which Aristotle still thought possible, of a perfect, if short-lived, knowledge of everything that is knowable about the world may be a source of discouragement, perhaps even despair.

Against this, he has only one protection. That is the experience of membership in a community of collaborators, living, dead, and yet to be born, each of whom is only a mortal human being, but whose shared devotion to the endless task of understanding the world offers the best possible (because the only available) affirmation of the connection of those involved to the eternal and divine. This is the analogue, in the large and impersonal community of scientific research, to the encouragement the lover gives his beloved in the intensely personal community to which they alone belong. It is cooler and more diffuse, and like the personal love it resembles, falls short of the salvation the Abrahamic religions all promise. But it offers consolation of a meaningful kind, and in a form that acknowledges rather than ignores the finitude of those who seek it. The modern ideal of scientific research seems so different from that of romantic love. Yet each reflects, in an intimate way, the spirit of our age, and is best explained by a theology that affirms the identity of God and the world with a completeness that only a disenchanted child of Abraham can conceive.

There is one more implication of this theology for both science and love that is worth noting.

It is possible to fail in each. Indeed, it seems impossible not to. What scientist makes no mistakes? What lover loves as wholeheartedly and unwaveringly as he or she aspires to do? The question is not whether we fail but why. Why are we not better scientists and lovers than we are? Why do we constantly fall short in both?

Descartes explains our scientific failures in characteristically Christian terms. These are not attributable, he says, to a defect in our powers of perception or understanding. They are due entirely to the will, which outstrips sensation and reason by affirming the truth of propositions for which neither provides an adequate ground.[16] When we err in science, we do so "willfully." Error is thus a kind of presumption, or pridefulness, rooted in our power to say "yes" to whatever we choose, including things for which we have no warrant. It is therefore a species of sin.

The Christian explanation of failure in love runs along similar lines. We know what we must do to be loving spouses, parents, and friends. If we fail, it is because our wills rebel and refuse to follow the path that duty prescribes. We are prideful creatures, jealously striving to unseat the God who made us. The faithlessness we show the other human beings we love less well than we should is just the smaller emblem of our greater faithlessness to him. It is a sin, and morally blameworthy as such.

Neither of these answers is available from a Spinozistic point of view. For Spinoza, the will is as much a superstition as the doctrine of creation. Indeed, they are the same superstition, for both rest on the unintelligible belief that something can come from nothing. There must therefore be another explanation of why we fall short in science and love. The only alternative is an explanation that starts from the modal nature of our being.

We make mistakes in science, and are faithless in love, because we are finite. We are not fully in control of ourselves, but subject to passions of all sorts. We are constantly led—and often *mis*led—by forces that are "external" to us in Spinoza's sense. These pull us hither and yon, blurring our vision and causing us to behave badly toward others. This is regrettable, of course, and we should do what we can to reduce the role that ignorance plays in our lives. It is especially important that we establish social and political structures that help us do this. But the failure in question is one of understanding, not will, and though a scientist who falsifies the results of her research, or a lover who abuses his beloved, may, on Spinoza's view, be considered stupid or foolish, she or he cannot be called sinful or wicked. There is no metaphysical justification for that. If we do, in fact, use the language of Christian morality to describe such behavior, and employ elaborate institutional schemes to punish people for acts we explain in the vocabulary of will and repentance, it is because this vocabulary, and the arrangements that enforce it, serve as a convenient shorthand for a rationalism that expresses the real truth of things, but which our limited knowledge and lack of self-control prevent us from applying, undiluted, in the rush and confusion of human affairs.

I shall return to this last topic in chapter 37, where I defend the claim that Spinozism provides the only coherent foundation for our modern democratic ideals. But first it is important to see that the most characteristic forms of modern art rest on the same theology and to explore the ways in which they do.

Art provides a link between our deepest values in the realms of science, politics and personal love. The endless perfection of our knowledge of the world, the kaleidoscopic diversity of democratic societies and the joy and suffering of romantic love are all aesthetic values, or at least lend themselves to aesthetic representation. Art is therefore able to play an integrative role in what often seems our increasingly fragmented civilization. But that is only because the art that today moves us most deeply is inspired by the same idea of divinity that lies at the root of all these other values as well. Nietzsche calls this the idea of "Dionysus reborn" and contrasts it with the Christian idea of God on the cross. This characteristically extravagant expression is his name for the born-again paganism that Spinoza was the first to define in a metaphysically rigorous way. What did Nietzsche—who has so much more to teach us about art than Spinoza did—mean by this and what light do his own theological reflections throw on the aspirations of artists today?

It is to these questions that we turn next.

CHAPTER 32

The World as an Aesthetic Phenomenon

ART, TRUTH AND MORALITY
IN NIETZSCHE'S PHILOSOPHY

The doctrine of creation dissolves the distinction between form and matter on which Aristotle's theology rests and opens the way to a hyperrationalism whose fundamental tenet is that everything in the world can be explained, though our explanations are bound to remain provisional and incomplete. At the same time, the Christian religion raises a special barrier to the advancement of reason by declaring the pursuit of absolute knowledge to be an act of pride and therefore a sin. In this way, it converts the acceptance of our finitude, which is merely a necessity, into a moral requirement, imposed by the law of God.[1] This puts a cloud over the work of science and burdens it with an inhibition that has no justification from the standpoint of science itself.

Two tendencies converge to dissolve this inhibition. One is an increasing awareness on the part of those engaged in scientific research that the doctrine of creation is hostile to their own rationalist aims. Spinoza understood this with particular clarity and many others have done so as well, including Einstein, Darwin and Freud.

The other is the tendency of Christian theology to undermine its own authority. The Christian idea of God requires that he be placed at an ever-greater distance from the world in order to preserve his dignity. As a consequence, God's relation to man attenuates; he becomes a less salient presence in the moral and intellectual lives of human beings. This creates the logical space for God's children to assume his place, which they are motivated to do

by the psychologically unbearable demand that they accept their own humiliating inadequacy ever to be adequately thankful for God's grace as the condition of salvation itself.

Thus, both on account of the internal demands of the hyperrationalist science to which it gives rise, and the self-destructive consequences of its own
conception of man's relation to God, the Christian religion comes under increasing pressure in every branch of scientific inquiry, until it is finally forced
to withdraw altogether. When this happens, the creationist theology that gave
birth to modern science is replaced by a freestanding rationalism that equates
the reality of the world with its infinite intelligibility, which we seek to grasp
by means of an endless program of research and experimentation.

This is the born-again paganism on which modern science is based. Its
signs are evident everywhere.

The entire course of modern physics, for example, represents a continuous campaign of rationalization that at each stage seeks to explain what before had been accepted as a brute fact. Newton's construction of a uniform
theory of motion that no longer relies on an inexplicable distinction between
the movement of things on earth and that of those in the heavens; Einstein's
attempt to account for the nature of gravity, whose existence Newton felt compelled to accept as one of the mysteries of God's creation; and the present
search for a unified theory that aims to solve the puzzles of quantum mechanics
and general relativity by using each to answer the most important questions
the other cannot are all expressions of this hyperrationalist program. For
centuries, its goal has been associated with Galileo's famous dictum that the
text of the world is written in the language of mathematics.[2] The identification of the real with the mathematical expresses the essential spirit of modern
physics, so different in this respect from that of Aristotle, who considered the
idea of a mathematical physics a contradiction in terms—but only if we add
that although the world yields to mathematical analysis at every stage of our
increasingly subtle understanding of it, the abstractions of mathematics can
never be more than an approximation of its infinite intelligibility, or what
amounts to the same thing, that the distinction between conceptual and empirical truths is one of degree only.

Further evidence may be found in the field of evolutionary biology, whose
expanding program likewise depends on a born-again paganism from whose
perspective the doctrine of creation is bound to seem a defection from reason
itself. Even in the discipline of psychoanalysis, which to many, perhaps, appears remote from the ethos of modern science, the same hyperrationalist con-

viction is at work, for the psychoanalytic investigation of the human mind only makes sense on the assumption that the intelligibility of our mental lives extends to their darkest corners.

This conviction expresses a view of the relation between time and eternity. Theology is the branch of philosophy that attempts to explain this relation. Plato, Aristotle, Augustine and Kant all have theologies in this sense. So do the practitioners of modern science. Their work rests on a theology too. Those who deny this do so only because they equate the everlasting and divine with a God beyond the world. But that is an Abrahamic prejudice. Neither Aristotle nor Spinoza knows a God of this kind. Yet each affirms the existence of a timeless and perfect being whose eternal reality is the conceptual and metaphysical ground of everything that falls short of it.

The God of both Aristotle and Spinoza is the eternal intelligibility of the world itself. But Spinoza's god includes the individuality of things as well as their general forms (which are only the shorthand devices we use to explain what we perceive). His world is therefore saturated with eternity, down to its smallest details. This is the secularized deposit of Christian belief. It is what distinguishes Spinoza's theology from that of every pagan rationalist.

This difference is related to another. Aristotle claims that a man who studies nature closely enough can, for a moment at least, become the God of the world. Some Christian mystics believe this too, though they view the union of man and God in emotional rather than intellectual terms. Spinoza's born-again paganism rules out the possibility of any union of this kind. No other conclusion is conceivable if one assumes, as he does, that we are finite beings in an infinitely intelligible world, who through a collaborative, accumulative, and interminable program of study are able to understand it ever more fully, but can never close the gap that always remains between ourselves and its eternal reality. This is the theology of modern science, which today shapes our experience of the world more deeply and pervasively than any other cultural force.

From the standpoint of Christian belief, modern science means disenchantment. That is because its progress depends on the ruthless elimination from every explanation of the world of any reference to divine creation. Those who claim that modern science cuts us off from the eternal and divine and therefore empties the world of all meaning thus continue to judge our scientific civilization from a Christian point of view—even if, like Max Weber, they have given up on the idea of a God beyond the world. This is nihilism. It cannot be combated by attempting to resurrect the God of Abraham in any form. That is no longer a serious option. The only viable alternative is Spinozism, which ascribes to those committed to the work of modern science the conception of God they must accept if they merely pay attention to their own aspirations.

The same is true of modern art.

The most characteristic forms of modern art are not the despairing expression of a nihilism that assumes the world could have aesthetic value only in case it were the creation of a God who no longer exists. The real source of their spiritual power is the theology that Proust announces at the end of his long novel—one that declares the world to be infinitely beautiful, and even the least things in it, down to the taste of a biscuit, imbued with an eternal presence that art strives to remember and save. This is the born-again pagan theology of modern art—an affirmation of the inherent divinity of the world, deepened by the long middle passage of Christian belief, through which art has passed on its way from Aristotle's classical aesthetics of form to the numinous individual whose boundless beauty is the unattainable object of every modern artist's attempt to depict it.

This is an extravagant claim. It will take time to explain and defend. But it is encouraging to note at the start that something very close to it is the central theme of the most comprehensive and compelling study of Western literature that anyone has attempted in the past hundred years. I am referring to Erich Auerbach's *Mimesis*.[3]

Auerbach's subject is what he calls "the representation of reality in Western literature." He approaches this grand topic through a series of brilliant case studies. Any attempt to summarize these here is out of the question. But his nuanced account of the two dozen or so works of poetry, drama and fiction that he analyzes in such splendid detail are held together by a single idea that can be stated rather simply.

According to Auerbach, the story of Western literature has three defining moments. It is the story of how the literature of classical antiquity, which knew no God beyond the world and accepted the rank order of men within it, was first Christianized and then became pagan again, but in a more radical way that reflects the aftereffects of the otherworldly theology from which it is now completely detached.

In the famous first chapter of his book, Auerbach contrasts the conception of reality implicit in Homer's account of the moment when Odysseus' aged nurse Eurycleia recognizes her long-absent master by the scar on his thigh, with the strikingly different conception presupposed by the biblical story of the binding of Isaac.

The Homeric world has no hidden or mysterious backdrop. It is entirely present for the poet to see. Of course, it cannot all be seen at once. As the poet brings one feature of the world to the foreground, others recede; then his attention shifts, and something else comes to light. But nothing transcends the world or the poet's power to represent it.

By contrast, the world of the biblical writers is defined by what lies outside of or beyond its visible borders. This is true in two respects. Inwardly, the story of the binding is marked by a depth of feeling that no writer can reach. Abraham's thoughts, as he leads Isaac up Mount Moriah, remain inscrutable to us. Outwardly, it is characterized by the mysterious involvement in the world of a God we cannot see, whose mind lies beyond our power to comprehend. How can we possibly understand a God who commands his first and most loyal subject to sacrifice his own son as a show of obedience? In the pious and awestruck view of the biblical writers, the worldly signs of what lies beyond the world are its most important characteristics. Nothing could be further from the serene confidence of the pagan poet who knows that his vision reaches all that can be seen.[4]

This distinction is accompanied by another. Homer's attention is fastened on the great deeds of great men. These alone are worthy of serious representation. Others—the lowly and insignificant—may be the subject of literature too, but their depiction belongs to a wholly different genre, to comedy or farce, which may entertain but can never achieve the dignity or stature of epic poetry and later of tragedy. The latter are concerned with the splendor and suffering of those whose greatness sets them apart from the rest of humanity on account of their superior status. This means, first and most obviously, their higher social and political position, but also, more fundamentally, their greater reality—that intensified presence and concentration of power that distinguishes Achilles, Odysseus, Hector, Philoctetes, Orestes, Antigone and Oedipus from ordinary human beings.

The distinction between greatness and banality, and the forms of literary representation appropriate to them, came eventually to be codified by Horace in his *Ars Poetica* and in the classical doctrine of the "separation of styles."[5] Horace recognizes the existence of certain "mixed" styles but assumes, as do all the writers of Greece and Rome, that the great majority of human beings are unworthy of the most elevated and serious artistic regard because there is not enough to them to justify such an effort. They are nullities that may perhaps be worth a laugh, but our interest in them is as fleeting as the laughter their actions and passions provoke.[6]

The moral and spiritual universe of the biblical writers is shaped by the contrary assumption. Already in the stories of the patriarchs and matriarchs, ordinary men and women figure as the protagonists in a narrative of the most exalted kind. The story of Christ's passion carries this tendency to an extreme. A provincial rabbi, who is scorned by the ruling powers and spends his time with whores and tax farmers, suffers the most disgraceful death imaginable—which proves, in the telling of the Gospelists and especially of Paul, to be no ordinary death but the pivotal event in a theocosmic drama directed by God himself. A man who according to classical values could never be a subject of serious poetry or drama is placed at the center of the greatest story ever told.[7] It is as if the bedraggled figure of Thersites, whose challenge to Agamemnon in the second book of the *Iliad* moves Odysseus to strike him with a stick, causing the assembled warriors to convulse with laughter at the spectacle of his shame, had been made the hero of the poem instead.

Such a radical "blending" of styles is utterly unthinkable from a classical point of view. How is it conceivable at all? The most fundamental article of Christian faith provides the answer.

The God of the Bible is the lord of all creation. Even the least of his creatures has been created in his image. There is therefore no human being, however insignificant or even wicked, who God does not watch with a love that surpasses all understanding. God's love is distributed equally among those who stand high and low in the judgment of the world. In his eyes, every human being is infinitely precious.[8] It is therefore possible to discover the materials for a literary representation of God's relation to man in the life of any man or woman whatsoever. For the poets and dramatists who later worked within the system of values fixed by the biblical writers, this meant that the separation of styles no longer had any meaning at all.

So long as the Christian theology that gave birth to this radical revaluation of the lives of ordinary human beings continued to be accepted as the background of every artistic attempt to represent the nature and meaning of human experience, the literature of the West retained an otherworldly orientation. But beginning in the late Middle Ages, the framework of belief that had for centuries anchored these efforts began to unravel. As a result, interest gradually shifted from the suffering and salvation of human beings viewed as prototypes of mankind in general, acting their symbolic parts in a morality play written and directed by God, to the uniqueness of their experience it-self. This represented a profound reorientation of curiosity and concern. Yet when it happened, the infinite value that Christianity had conferred upon the life of every individual was not lost in the process. It was preserved and its significance heightened, though in terms that no longer depended upon a God beyond the world to explain or ratify it.

Auerbach claims that Dante was the one mainly responsible for this shift. Although the characters of his *Comedy* all have their place in a divinely ar-ranged scheme, Dante's portrait of them is so compelling that the reader often forgets about God and is riveted on the idiosyncrasies of their human personalities instead. The poet sketches these with such lucidity and compas-sion that they come to possess an interest of their own that distracts the reader from the theological story that Dante purports to be using them to tell.[9] This marks the beginning, in Auerbach's view, of a new humanism that unlike the literature of the classical world regards every aspect of human experience as invested with inexhaustible meaning, yet in contrast to the religiously inspired literature of the early Middle Ages has detached this meaning from the tra-ditional Christian theology of divine creation and love.

Rabelais, Montaigne and Shakespeare are important representatives of this new humanistic point of view. With fits and starts and occasional backslid-ing in the direction of orthodox Christian belief, it eventually comes to dom-inate all forms of literary representation, and reaches full maturity in the modern novel. The novelist, Auerbach says, seeks to represent some fragment of the endless meaning that resides in common things, through which we glimpse the infinite reality of a world whose being is wholly self-contained, like that of the once regnant Christian God who has now disappeared from sight. He illustrates the point in his concluding chapter with a masterful ac-count of an episode in Virginia Woolf's novel *To the Lighthouse,* in which the prosaic work of knitting a stocking opens a window, brief and opaque as it is, onto a landscape of passions, yearnings, frustrations and accommodations that give the reader the experience of having touched, for a moment at least, the heart of Mrs. Ramsey's tangled and all-too-human existence.

This is the theological premise of the modern novel, which assigns a bound-less and eternal value to the unique experience of every human being, with-out the otherworldly God whose omnipotence first made it necessary to do so.[10] It is the same theology that underlies the science of Einstein, Darwin and Freud. In this respect, Auerbach's narrative parallels the Spinozist in-terpretation of modern science that I have offered in the preceding five chapters. His reconstruction of the course of Western literature from Homer's pagan world of visible gods to the born-again paganism of Woolf, Proust and Joyce, via the orthodoxy of the God on the cross, reflects a similar understanding of the shifting conceptions of divinity that have shaped our modern aesthetic as well as scientific ideals.

But this is only a suggestive comparison. To make it plausible, a more systematic account of the theological foundations of modern art is required. Auerbach himself does not provide one. He has no interest in doing so. He is a literary critic, not a philosopher like Spinoza. We must therefore look elsewhere to find an account of the sort we need.

Not, however, to Spinoza. In the whole of the *Ethics,* there is only one passage that might be said to deal with art, however tangentially. I am thinking of Spinoza's offhand remark that a wise man will permit himself to enjoy in moderation the pleasures of the theater and similar entertainments, as well as those of plants and perfumes and the other adornments of civilized life.[11] Beyond this there is nothing—certainly no explicit recognition of the value of art or account of its relation to the theology of the first part of the book. It is true that the *Ethics* has been a source of inspiration to many writers and other artists.[12] But a philosophy of art cannot be drawn from its pages.

Where then might we look to find a philosophy of this sort that is compatible with Spinoza's conception of God? My suggestion is, to the writings of Friedrich Nietzsche.

To say that these are unsystematic is an understatement. Nietzsche never attempts to present his views in a comprehensive and organized way. Yet he does in fact have a theology—one that in many ways resembles the far more systematic theology of the seventeenth-century philosopher he describes in a late letter to his friend Franz Overbeck as a "predecessor."[13] Nietzsche is a born-again pagan too, and his idea of "the world as a work of art giving birth to itself" is the key to understanding the God of Virginia Woolf's novel.[14]

There are two reasons to be skeptical about my suggestion.

First, Nietzsche was famously hostile to metaphysics. He includes those who pursue it among "the teachers of the purpose of existence," an enterprise he reviles.[15] Second, though Nietzsche occasionally expresses a positive view of Spinoza—most enthusiastically, in his letter to Overbeck—the majority of his remarks about him are extremely hostile. It is hard, moreover, to imagine two men temperamentally less alike.[16]

Given all this, it may seem implausible if not frivolous to describe Nietzsche's philosophy as a metaphysics of art that expresses the same idea of God

as Spinoza's *Ethics.* Only a detailed consideration of Nietzsche's views can overcome these reasonable doubts.

THE JUSTIFICATION OF THE WORLD

The Birth of Tragedy was Nietzsche's first book. He wrote it when he was
twenty-eight and still a professor of philology at Basel. The book is divided
into twenty-five sections and covers a wide range of topics, among which
Nietzsche moves in a loose, sometimes rambling fashion. He states the book's
main theme in section 4. "[O]nly as an *aesthetic phenomenon*," Nietzsche declares, "is existence and the world eternally *justified*."[17] He returns to this
idea ten years later in *The Gay Science.* "As an aesthetic phenomenon existence
is still *bearable* to us, and art furnishes us with the eye and hand and above
all the good conscience to be *able* to make such a phenomenon of ourselves."[18]
It would not be far-fetched to say that the whole of Nietzsche's philosophy is
an attempt to expound this one idea, expressions of which may be found in
all his writings, including the unpublished notebooks that contain his last sane
thoughts.

Nietzsche's claim that "existence and the world" can be justified only as
an aesthetic phenomenon has both a negative and positive meaning.

Beginning with *The Birth of Tragedy,* and more aggressively in later works,
Nietzsche interprets a wide range of human endeavors that by their own terms
are hostile to art—more notably, those of science and morality—as aesthetic
phenomena, whose true significance, he insists, has remained opaque to the
philosophers, scientists and religious thinkers that have been their principal
advocates. Late in his career, he generalizes these interpretations by describing the entire tradition of Western thought as a series of attempts to freeze
the fluidity of what he calls the eternal "becoming" of existence in one or
another conception of "being," each of which is an illusion that falsifies the
world in a basic way. To grasp the real meaning of these illusions, Nietzsche says, we must see them as what they are—as works of art whose aim is
to order, explain, evaluate and therefore justify the world. This is the negative
side of his claim.

The positive side is Nietzsche's own attempt to answer the most basic of
all metaphysical questions in aesthetic terms. According to Aristotle, the first
question of metaphysics is, "What is the being of beings?" Nietzsche's answer
is that the being of beings is art, understood not from the spectator's point
of view but the artist's. On the basis of his reversed understanding of the

meaning of art, Nietzsche constructs a view of the world that culminates in an account of the essence of being. It is one that assigns to being the eternity that has always been identified with it, while avoiding what Nietzsche considers the fundamental error of every prior metaphysical scheme, namely, the denigration of becoming as something that "falls short" of being and should therefore be valued less highly or not at all. Nietzsche faults all the great systems of Western philosophy on these grounds. In opposition, he offers a metaphysics that seeks to restore what he repeatedly calls "the innocence of becoming."[19] Its crucial premise is the presumed ubiquity of the drive that he identifies in *The Birth of Tragedy* as the essence of art. This is the positive side of his youthful claim that the world can only be justified as an aesthetic phenomenon.

To understand both the negative and positive dimensions of this claim and the relation between them requires a great deal of patience. Nietzsche's philosophy is a thicket of ideas, of brilliant *aperçus* and snatches of argument whose connections are often unclear. Indeed, Nietzsche himself sometimes seems determined to keep them from becoming too clear. One way to enter the thicket is to begin by reflecting on the meaning of the two most important words that Nietzsche uses to state the central idea of *The Birth of Tragedy*. One of these is "justified." The other, of course, is "aesthetic."

The demand that something *in* the world be justified is familiar enough. So is the way of meeting it. Broadly speaking, we justify one thing by pointing out its relation to another, which belongs to the world as well. We say, for example, that the decision of a judge is justified by the law that establishes his authority to render it. But the demand that the world *as a whole* be justified is of another order altogether. It is essentially theological in nature.

The demand for a justification of this kind is irrepressibly human. Man is a "venerating animal" who can never overcome his longing for a theodicy of some sort.[20] Every religious and philosophical system is an attempt to provide one. The Christian religion offers one such theodicy and modern science another. Both seek to justify the world as a whole by explaining the suffering and confusion that seem so deeply woven into its fabric. The first does this by appealing to a beneficent creator. The second does it, according to Nietzsche, by invoking an ideal of objectivity that ever since Plato has been thought of as something separate from the chaos of appearances, which have no meaning or value except in relation to it.

Each of these theodicies attempts to justify the world, with its ceaseless, senseless motions, by relating it to a changeless order of reality that some call

God and others truth. Nietzsche is a fierce critic of all such justifications, which manifest what he calls an "ill will" toward the world by assuming that it can be made intelligible and acceptable only in terms of an otherworldly standard or goal.

It does not follow, however, that Nietzsche rejects the demand for a theodicy altogether. On the contrary, his claim that the world can only be justified as an aesthetic phenomenon is an attempt to provide one—to meet this demand in a way that avoids the hatred of the world implied by both the Christian and Platonic justifications of it. Moreover, though he opposes the separation of being and becoming these other theodicies entail, Nietzsche assumes, as the proponent of every theodicy must, that the demand for a justification of the world as a whole cannot be met except by connecting it to the eternal and divine. The challenge of establishing such a connection without separating the world of becoming and time from the God that alone can justify it, is one that Nietzsche is already struggling to meet in *The Birth of Tragedy*.

Other philosophers and moralists teach that appearances are not to be trusted. This causes them to be hostile to art, which employs the very techniques they most strongly condemn—above all, the creative use of illusion. From their point of view, art is in essence a kind of "lying."[21] Nietzsche's theodicy is founded on an aesthetic conception of reality instead.

Nietzsche insists that art alone has the power to justify the world precisely because it manifests what he calls a "good will toward appearance."[22] This turns Plato's judgment on art upside down. According to Plato, art leads us away from the truth and spoils our chances of reaching what is timeless and therefore real.[23] Against Plato and his scientific successors; against the dreamy otherworldliness of Jesus and his reverence for the artless honesty of children; and against Paul's theology of sacrifice and salvation, which expresses a contempt for worldly things, Nietzsche teaches that eternity lies not beyond the realm of becoming but in it, and constructs his justification of the world on the basis of art's beautiful lies.

Our first task, therefore, is to clarify Nietzsche's understanding of the meaning of art. Aristotle's *Poetics* gives us a useful place to begin.

The *Poetics* is the first attempt at a scientific treatment of art. In it, Aristotle examines the conditions for success in the making of poems and plays, and analyzes the effects that such works have on those who hear or see them. His discussion is dominated by the craftsman model that guides his account of every kind of making—those that aim at producing literary objects as much as houses and beds. In each case, the maker imposes an antecedently given form on certain material (wood and stone in the case of a house, words and meter in that of a poem). Aristotle's account of literary works focuses on their structural properties as combinations of form and matter, and the only psychological effects he considers are those that pertain to their audience—most famously, the power he ascribes to tragic drama to purge its viewers of the horror its representations arouse, through the artful use of pity and fear.[24]

Aristotle barely notices the psychology of the poet or playwright himself. That is because there is less of psychological interest in the work of a craftsman than in that of an artist, as we understand the term today. A craftsman produces artifacts according to the fixed rules of his discipline. These specify how the pregiven form and matter with which he works are to be joined. His success in doing so is measured by the formal perfection of the object he makes, and this is best judged not from the vantage point of its maker but the disinterested perspective of a consumer or critic instead. Nietzsche calls this way of thinking about the meaning of art the view of the "spectator."[25] (Plato is a more complicated case. His attack on poetry in book 10 of the *Republic* is launched from the spectator's point of view too. There, poetry is said to be bad for the souls of those who hear it on account of its being even further removed from reality than the things it represents. The craftsman model governs this discussion of art as well. Indeed, Plato employs it to justify a much harsher verdict on the value of art than the one Aristotle renders in the *Poetics,* where the craft of poetry is portrayed as a kind of medicinal technique.[26] But in the *Phaedrus* Plato's attention shifts from the psychological effects of art to its motives—from the spectator's point of view to that of the artist, who is moved to write, he says, by a kind of divine madness.[27] Whether Nietzsche fully appreciated the significance of this shift is unclear.)

Kant's account of beauty differs fundamentally from Aristotle's—most obviously, perhaps, in its conception of beauty as a judgment about things rather than a structural property of them. Yet it too remains wedded to the spectator's view of art. According to Kant, the judgment that something is beautiful is in essence a disinterested report, on the part of the one making it, of a subjective state that he predicts others will share if they place themselves before the thing in the same way he has. Here too the emphasis is on the psychology of the person who sees, reads or hears the object in question— though Kant conceives the relevant state in transcendental terms, as the experience of the free play of the imagination, through whose mediation the perceptive and cognitive powers of the viewer's mind are brought into a harmonious relation with one another. Even his account of genius stresses the novelty of the work and its effect on others, rather than the needs and interests of the artist. Kant's interpretation of aesthetic phenomena is no longer conditioned by the distinction between form and matter or the craftsman model associated with it. It highlights the subjectivity of the experience of the viewer in a way that Aristotle would have found incomprehensible. But it remains as firmly tied to the spectator's point of view as Aristotle's classical account. The psychology of the artist plays no important role in it either.

Nietzsche turns this approach on its head. To understand what art means, he says, we must begin with the artist, not the spectator—with the artist's needs and drives rather than the emotional or intellectual state his work arouses in the one who views it. The whole of *The Birth of Tragedy* is colored by this reversal of outlook. Nietzsche acknowledges that he was inspired to make it by Schopenhauer's interpretation of art,[28] though he eventually rejects Schopenhauer's own metaphysics on the grounds that it represents a form of nihilism that is still tied to Christian values despite its rejection of orthodox Christian belief.[29] Still, the assumption that we "must take the artist himself and his psychology" as our interpretive guide in the analysis of aesthetic phenomena is one that Nietzsche continues to accept for the rest of his life.[30]

If we look at art from this point of view, the important question is not, "What is the effect of a work of art on its viewer?" but "What drove the artist to make it in the first place?" In *The Birth of Tragedy,* Nietzsche offers an answer that he later refines but never abandons. According to Nietzsche, the artist is under a compulsion to "delineate." He is driven by the need to construct images that shape and arrange the world and his experience of it—to put things "in their place" so as to make them meaningful and therefore bearable. This is the essential aim of every work of art.

In the epic poetry of Homer, these images are self-contained. Each is complete in itself. Even the most brutal is serene. By contrast, the plays of the early tragedians (those of Aeschylus in particular) are centered on characters whose delineation is uneasy or unstable. That is because the playwright's depiction of them is haunted by the knowledge that however much effort he pours into his work of image making, it will never be enough to tame a world that at its heart is contradictory and self-destructive.

The world is a senseless place, and no image can ever fully succeed in making sense of it. The artist's work is therefore doomed to fail. In the tragedies of Aeschylus and Sophocles, this insight becomes the substance of the play itself, which is divided between the meaning-giving figures on the stage and the commentary of the chorus, whose words remind both the characters themselves and the audience in the theater of the futility of every attempt to make sense of the world by means of art.[31] This is what Nietzsche calls the "Dionysian" wisdom of the tragic poet: his understanding that man cannot help but strive to render the world bearable by ordering or shaping it; that all his efforts in this regard are doomed to disappointment; and finally, that both this striving and its inevitable defeat have their roots in the world itself, which acts out its own self-contradictory nature in this endless series of failed artistic attempts—something the world "requires," Nietzsche says, for its "continuous salvation."[32]

As this last remark suggests, Nietzsche's reversed understanding of the meaning of art holds the key not only to his interpretation of tragic poetry but to his theology as well. Nietzsche's justification of the world as an aesthetic phenomenon seeks to preserve the wisdom of the tragic poets in a more general and self-conscious form. He calls his theology a "joyful science" that neither aims to save the world from a vantage point beyond it, nor despairingly accepts the impossibility of doing so on the self-defeating supposition that the world could only be justified from a now-unattainable perspective of this sort.

The Birth of Tragedy is the prelude to Nietzsche's joyful science. He will spend the next fifteen years attempting to construct it. But the crucial first step is the one he takes here, by redirecting attention from the effect that art has on its viewers to the drive that propels those who make it. From *The Birth of Tragedy* on, Nietzsche's artist-centered aesthetics remains the point of departure for all his attempts at a joyful "redemption" of the world conceived as the "sole author and spectator of this comedy of art," through which being "prepares a perpetual entertainment" for itself.[33]

In the next chapter, we shall explore in more detail the constructive side of Nietzsche's interpretation of the meaning and value of art. This leads him to a view of the relation between time and eternity that is similar in many ways to that of Spinoza. But first we need to consider the negative use that Nietzsche makes of his view of art to explain the leading scientific and moral ideals of modern Western civilization.

These are fundamentally opposed to the imperatives of art. Yet both, Nietzsche claims, are intelligible only in aesthetic terms, as expressions of the compulsion to master the world through depiction. Their ideals are therefore themselves works of art. They are the product of an artistic drive that is even more basic than the antiaesthetic, and therefore self-deluding, ideals to which it gives rise. This turns the judgment that science and morality pronounce on art upside down and gives us a first rough sense of the philosophical significance of the new understanding of art that guides Nietzsche's reinterpretation of the meaning of ancient Greek tragedy.

"AESTHETIC SOCRATISM"

According to Nietzsche, the Dionysian wisdom of the tragic poets vanishes with the rise of another and eventually dominant attitude that he calls "aesthetic Socratism." Much of the *Birth of Tragedy* is devoted to its analysis.[34] This new attitude is already evident in the plays of Euripides, which by contrast to those of Aeschylus and Sophocles are marked by their "daring intelligibility."[35] But its greatest champion is the man for whom it is named.

The "supreme law of [aesthetic Socratism] reads about as follows: 'to be beautiful everything must be intelligible.'" A second and closely related axiom is that "'only the knowing one is virtuous.'"[36] For Socrates, "intelligible" means accountable. To know something is to measure it or count it out. The "mission" of such an accounting is "to make existence appear to be comprehensible, and therefore to be justified."[37]

Every artist is a surveyor who separates things and draws boundaries between them. Nietzsche associates the artistic work of measurement with the god Apollo. Apollo is the god of lines and limits and hence the inspiration for every attempt to carve the world up into discrete elements or regions. Conceived in the broadest terms, Apollo represents the "principle of individuation"[38] that every work of art employs in its attempt to justify the world.

The plays of Aeschylus and Sophocles remind us that all such attempts fall short of their goal. This is the deeper wisdom of the tragic chorus, which is lost or forgotten by Socrates and his successors. "[I]n every unveiling of truth," Nietzsche says, the tragic artist "cleaves with raptured eyes only to that which still remains veiled after the unveiling." By contrast, "the theoretical man," inspired by the fundamental law of Socratism, "finds the consummation of his pleasure in the process of a continuously successful unveiling through his own unaided efforts."[39]

Socrates is therefore "the opponent of Dionysus."[40] He is the champion of a countertheodicy. For those who share it, the "unveiling" of truth is more than merely useful. It is the only way to secure the meaning of the world as a whole.[41] This is the antitragic theodicy whose confidence in the accessibility and value of truth defines the triumphant spirit of modern science, under whose dominion we live today.

The meaning of Socratism is a subject to which Nietzsche returns often in later writings. He does so at greatest length in one of his last books, *Twilight of the Idols* (1889). Nietzsche devotes an entire section of the book to what he calls "the problem of Socrates."[42] His diagnosis of the "problem" is subtle and compressed, but its main lines are as follows.

Nietzsche portrays Socrates as a reactive figure who fights against the established aristocratic milieu of his day. The prevailing culture is dominated by aesthetic judgments that equate the good with what is visibly beautiful, strong and the like. These are the late and highly refined, though weaker and less self-assured, expression of an older, rougher, heroic ideal based on the value of glory or splendor. Into the decaying aristocratic culture of fifth-century Athens, Socrates enters with a consuming desire for the very thing this culture values most—for strength, power and the authority to command. But he lacks the wealth and social standing and good looks that are the conventional sources of such authority. So, Nietzsche says, he must find a way to win what he is after by altering the terms on which power and authority are distributed and deference to them based.

He does this by devaluing everything the old aristocracy reveres. He demotes its visible emblems of authority to mere appearances and transfers the source of their true worth to an unseen realm of ideas that is apprehensible only by minds that are as invisible as these ideas themselves. For Socrates' devaluation to succeed, of course, he must persuade at least some of his aristocratic listeners to follow him against their own class ideals, and this cannot be by reason alone, since it is precisely the primacy of reason that is in question. Socrates needs to draw on forces that are older and deeper than reason to achieve his goal. He can succeed only through seduction, which is why Nietzsche calls him "a great *erotic*," who despite his "awe-inspiring ugliness," was able to attract some of Athens' most beautiful young men, including Plato, the greatest of his conquests.[43]

How did Socrates accomplish this seduction? Nietzsche's answer is, by offering his young interlocutors a new source of power that appealed to their aristocratic taste for command. This was the Socratic ideal of truth. Those who embrace it acquire a lever by which to move the entire world of appearances—a standard for weighing and judging everything that happens in it. By comparison, the world itself becomes a realm of dreams and shadows.

The things we see about us seem so shining and splendid. But their beauty is an illusion. Indeed, it is the enemy of all true beauty, which now resides in the mind and its ideas alone. For some, at least, among Socrates' youthful and highborn followers, who felt the traditional bases of their aristocratic authority slipping away, this new and relentlessly antiaristocratic ideal of truth promised to restore the power they sensed themselves to be on the verge of losing. This was the source of its erotic appeal, and many of his most gifted listeners succumbed to it, betraying their own class ideals of worldly splendor for the sake of an austere conception of truth that required them, among other things, to explicitly repudiate the countercharms of art, which Socrates twice attacks in the *Republic*.

Socrates' attack on art underscores the ascetic nature of his teaching, which demands that we reject as lying and deceptive the senses through which we discover the beauty of the world. It compels us to submit their judgments to the tribunal of reason.[44] Yet despite its antiaesthetic content, the motive for Socrates' teaching is the same as the one that drives all artists to create. Like every work of art, Socratism is a response to the Apollonian demand for order that is our only antidote to the contradictoriness of existence and the powerlessness we feel in its presence—in Socrates' case, the powerlessness that results from his lack of those qualities that give the strong and well-born their worldly authority. In this sense, Socrates is as much an artist as the tragic poets he attacks with such ferocity in book 9 of the *Republic*. The only difference between them—and it is an immense one—is that Socrates pursues his artistic goal by means of an ideal of truth that draws its power as a remedy against the chaos of existence from its unyielding antagonism to the world itself, whose terrible beauty the tragic poet affirms not despite but because it eventually destroys every attempt to render it safe for understanding.

Notwithstanding its hostility to the splendor of appearances, Socratism is therefore itself an aesthetic program, or rather the beginning of one. To complete it, a new metaphysics had to be constructed on the basis of Socrates' equation of beauty with intelligibility. Plato's doctrine of the forms represents a first step in this direction.

Behind the kaleidoscopic world of appearances, where nothing stays put for a second, we must assume the existence, Plato says, of another world of enduring forms that remain forever the same. These alone allow us to stabilize our experience of the world so that it becomes comprehensible to us.

Plato's distinction between appearances and the forms in which they participate, is the source of our concept of a "thing." This becomes fundamental for the entire tradition of Western philosophy and science, even up to Kant, who in contrast to Plato denies that the object of our study of the world of appearances can ever be directly grasped by the mind, but preserves the idea of a "thing" as the organizing, if unattainable, target of human experience, without which it would have no coherence at all.

A second essential component of aesthetic Socratism is the idea of a "cause."

To assert that one thing causes another is equivalent to saying that the latter can be explained. The claim that the things whose stability anchors the flux of appearances are causally related amounts, therefore, to an affirmation of their intelligibility, and provides the logical foundation for our pursuit of a true knowledge of the world, which since Plato and Aristotle has been defined as the knowledge of causes. Again, Kant carries this idea to its limit. Cause is not, for Kant, a real relation among things that we grasp with our minds but the transcendental precondition of any possible experience whatsoever. Yet even in his rarefied interpretation of it—indeed, here, as never before—the idea of a cause helps to secure the basic aim of Socratism, whose equation of beauty with intelligibility is meant to dominate and replace the older identification of beauty with worldly appearances, amidst whose contradictory and transient brilliance nothing of lasting truth or value can ever be found.

Socratism has been stupendously successful. Its "supreme law" is the premise of the scientific culture that now dominates all aspects of human experience. The ruling spirit of this culture manifests itself in a particular type of human being—that of the "specialist," who Nietzsche describes as a "hunchback" or "dwarf."[45]

Unlike Socrates himself, the millions of specialists who today live and work within the picture of the world that he and his successors created have no artistic greatness at all. They are small and industrious workers who never notice the immense artistry that was required to invent the world they inhabit, with its guiding ideas of "thing" and "cause" and principled distinction between truth and appearance. They never feel even a twinge of the urgency that drove Socrates and Plato to labor to build a home in which they could be safe from the world of sights and sounds, whose pointlessness they lacked the strength to embrace more directly, as Aeschylus had done. In this sense, the condition of the specialist is one of supreme forgetfulness.

Only a distant echo of the artistic drive that motivated Socrates' original revaluation of aristocratic norms can still be heard in the specialized culture of science today. Scientists often speak of the "elegance" of a theory; in modern physics, the principle of "symmetry" is said to be fundamental.[46] But these familiar expressions belie the essentially antiaesthetic spirit of science as a whole, which is characterized by the same mistrust of the senses, and skepticism toward appearances, that Socrates exploited to seduce his listeners to a new view of the world.

The work of today's specialist only makes sense on the assumption that there are two worlds between which he must maintain a rigorous separation at all times. One is that of deceptive appearances and the other of true but invisible realities, best represented in mathematical terms that alone provide the standard by which to measure and judge the world of sensory experience. But whereas Socrates was keenly aware of the quarrel, as he put it, between philosophy and poetry, his small-minded heirs have forgotten that their ideals were forged in a struggle against the power of worldly beauty, and certainly do not see that their own research program is itself an "artistic projection"[47] motivated by the longing for salvation from the measurelessness of the world by means of mensuration—the essence of the Apollonian art of depiction. They do not see that even modern science rests on a picture of the world that seeks like every other to tame its wild heart with distinctions and delineations that establish "boundaries" in "the midst of the sea," and fix a "due proportion" among things whose separateness is not the premise but result of the artistry that first sets them apart.[48]

This way of putting things reverses the relation between science and art. It implies that beauty is not to be judged from the viewpoint of science— as conformity to the truth—but truth from the viewpoint of art. It follows that science cannot be adequately understood from within its own horizon of values. A genuine understanding of science requires that its antiaesthetic ideals be aesthetically appraised. Only by interpreting the Socratic equation of beauty and intelligibility as an aesthetic phenomenon can its true meaning be grasped.

This of course raises the specter of circularity. Why isn't Nietzsche's explanation of the Socratic conception of truth as a work of art itself just another work of this sort, and his answer to the "problem of Socrates" vulnerable to the objection that it implies that there can be no standard of truth by which its own superiority may be defended? For how can there be such a standard if we accept Nietzsche's contention that the idea of truth is only an artistic projection? I shall return to this question in the following chapter.

THE SLAVE REVOLT IN MORALITY

In *The Birth of Tragedy*, Nietzsche contrasts the Dionysian wisdom of the tragic poets and aesthetic Socratism in the sharpest possible terms. He describes the latter, with its "unprecedented esteem of knowledge and insight,"[49] as a "murderous" assault on the tragedians' more courageous acknowledgment of "the absurdity of existence."[50] But Nietzsche has almost nothing to say in his first book about a related subject that will occupy him to an even greater extent in later works. This is the question of the origin and meaning of the Judeo-Christian morality that together with the scientific ideals of Socratism has played such a decisive role in the development of modern European civilization.

Nietzsche's account of this morality and his criticisms of it start from the same conception of art that he first presents in *The Birth of Tragedy*. According to Nietzsche, the moral values that have been the inspiration for the West's most cherished ethical and political ideals can also only be understood from the point of view of the artist and his needs. They too have been created as an antidote to the experience of helplessness that motivates the construction of every work of art—though as in the case of Socratism, the need that lies behind their invention is concealed by a picture of the world and human life that is ruthlessly antiaesthetic.

Nietzsche gives several different accounts of the origin and later development of Western moral values. In *Beyond Good and Evil*, for example, he offers an especially lucid explanation of the first primitive formulation, subsequent refinement, and eventual "self-overcoming" of what he calls the moral point of view.[51] But Nietzsche presents his most sustained analysis of the phenomenon of morality in general, and of Judeo-Christian morality in particular, in *On the Genealogy of Morality* (1887) and supplements his argument there with an extended historical discussion of ancient Judaism and early Christianity in *The Anti-Christ*, published the following year.

Nietzsche begins his genealogy with the premoral world of Achilles, Beowulf and Arjuna. This is a fiercely judgmental world. In it, men judge and are judged quickly, often with immediate life and death consequences. Their judgments are aesthetic in nature. They are based on appearances and reflect the relative grandeur or obscurity, beauty or deformity, strength or weakness of the men who make their presence known to one another through their deeds in a sunlit world.

Those who stand out on account of the forcefulness of their personalities and the brilliance of their actions are "good"—bright, clean, to be listened to and followed. Those who lack these qualities are "bad"—weak, blemished, with no authority or prestige. The first are the truthful ones. Their splendor is more reliable than anything that cannot be seen. The second are unsteady, unreliable, deceptive and deceiving. That is because there is so little to them. Everyone can see how insubstantial they are. They are fit only to follow and serve those stronger than themselves. They are slaves by nature—an echo of this archaic judgment can still be heard in Aristotle's defense of natural slavery—and have to accept their position in the hierarchical order to which they belong regardless of the suffering this entails, just as the little lamb must vis-à-vis the eagle.[52] In a world organized on the basis of strength, beauty, health and the like, the weak must accept their fate as obscure nonentities who barely make an appearance at all. And this is what they always did—until the slave revolt in morality.

It was the Jews, Nietzsche says, who began this revolt, which turned the values of the warrior world upside down, for both good and ill. Today, its effects can be felt in every sphere of life. The success of the slave revolt in morality is the fundamental fact of European civilization. The Reformation, the French Revolution, the triumph of modern democratic ideals—all these are in Nietzsche's view merely repercussions of the assault the Jews first successfully launched on "the unconditional rule of aristocratic values, Roman values," which like those of Homer's heroes, whose outlook they preserved in a more polished form, equated authority with worldly presence and power.[53]

Nietzsche's account of the slave revolt in morality takes the form of a story that goes roughly as follows.

To begin with, the Israelites were a war confederacy, a political community with territorial aims and enemies against whom they were constantly battling. Their God was a war God, to whom they prayed for support. In this respect, he was like other gods, only stronger (in the eyes of his followers at least). The Israelites' belief in the exceptional strength of their God was vindicated by their triumph over their political foes, and the establishment of a territorial state centered on a temple devoted to his worship under the supervision of a closed class of priests.

The Israelite state was short-lived. It was soon overwhelmed by the great empires that bordered it on all sides. But instead of taking this as a reason to abandon the God who had been unable to secure their political existence, the Israelites construed their defeat as a sign of the strength of their divine protector instead. They interpreted the meaning of their defeat as an expression of God's displeasure with them—of his anger at their failure to abide by the terms of the covenant the Israelites (now the Jews) had sworn to keep.

This new interpretation of the Jews' relation to their God was invented by the prophets, who stood outside the class of temple priests and blamed them, along with others, for the disastrous results of their lack of fidelity to the promise their ancestors had made at Sinai. In the view of the world that this prophetic reinterpretation installed, once and for all, as the organizing narrative of Jewish experience, the Jews remained the special object of God's solicitude despite his disappointment with them. Their loss of worldly power became a confirmation of their unique place in God's affections, and of their continuing possession of a stature infinitely greater than that of their imperial neighbors, who were now demoted to the status of mere instruments for the chastisement of the Jews.[54]

Like countless other peoples that have lost their place in the world, the Jews might have abandoned the God who let them down, or chosen another in his place, and melted away as a distinct community. But they took the opposite course and converted their loss of worldly strength into an immensely durable power of a different kind—so successfully, that among all the nations of the ancient world, they alone survive today. That the Jews refused to capitulate to their political fate and used it as a springboard for the preservation and accumulation of authority instead, can only be explained on the assumption that they were motivated by an implacable desire for power—one as insatiable as the longing that drove Socrates to demand the acceptance of philosophy as the standard of authority in an aristocratic milieu by whose lights he was a bothersome nobody.

Socrates increased his power by attacking the world of sights and sounds and inventing a realm of ideas that no one can see. In the Jewish narrative, the surface of the world is similarly devalued. Everything that transpires there has meaning and value only through its connection to a God beyond the world, and to acts of obedience and disobedience, promise making and promise breaking that are no more visible than the God to whom they are directed.

On this view, all that happens in the world is merely a sign of events occurring outside it, in one of the two invisible realms that transcend the world in opposing directions. This doubling of invisibilities parallels the one on which Socrates insists, though in his case the relation of the soul to God is intellectual in nature, whereas the Jews and their Christian successors conceive it in moral or legal terms instead, as the obedience men owe to the commands of an omnipotent sovereign. But the effect is the same, for on the Jewish interpretation as much as the Socratic the splendor of the world—its pomp and beauty and the authority that attends all worldly success—becomes the mere symptom of acts, human and divine, whose origins cannot be seen, and that are now declared to be the only source of everything that may properly be called worthy, valuable, and true.

This opens up the possibility that the value of worldly things is precisely the opposite of what it seems—that the strength of their enemies is proof not of the weakness of the Jews but of their inestimable importance in the eyes of God, who continues to be concerned above all else with the welfare of his chosen people, despite their disobedience and backsliding. This turns every worldly ethic upside down, in the same way that Socrates' response to Glaucon does. Indeed, in one respect, the Jewish devaluation of worldly power is even more radical. For Socrates, the glory of the world is a distraction to be ignored. In the theodicy of the Jews, it is the means by which God demonstrates that he will keep his promise to them. The splendor of the world is thereby transformed from a mere illusion into the instrument of its own destruction—a dialectical refinement that allows the prophetic reinterpretation of Jewish suffering to drive a wedge between the visible world and its hidden ground that is even sharper than the Socratic version of this same distinction.

The Jews themselves never draw the full consequences of their own reinterpretation of the meaning of worldly values. Even after the original political disaster that spurred its invention in the age of the prophets, the Jewish theodicy of loss and redemption remains tied to quasi-political ideas. Following the destruction of the Second Temple, their earlier Babylonian exile becomes a permanent diaspora. Yet over the centuries, the Jews maintain their separateness, amidst the kingdoms of the world, as a shadow-polity of their own, and continue to look forward to an eventual day of homecoming. They remain a people apart, held together by the natural bonds of kinship and cultural practice, but most fundamentally by the law, which they carry with them wherever they go—an orthopractical scheme detailed enough to regulate every aspect of human behavior, yet unaccompanied by the instruments of conventional political power, hence one that can be preserved only by teaching and tradition. In this way, the Jews retain their status as a special people whose unique juridical life still bears the shadowy impress of the political condition from which it distantly derives.

In Nietzsche's narrative, the loosening of the Jewish revaluation of values from all political constraints is the achievement of the Hellenistic Jewish sect that became the nursery bed of the Christian religion. It is Christianity that transforms the Jews' theodicy of suffering into a universal theology in which all differences among peoples vanish in the general concept of man.

The crucial figure here is not Jesus but Paul. Nietzsche views Jesus as a kind of Buddhist, who teaches that peace can be attained by following his own sublime example of loving kindness. For Jesus, salvation lies not in correct belief or rigorous obedience to the ritual requirements of the law, but the performance of selfless acts of generosity and forgiveness instead. Jesus himself continues to honor the law of his ancestors. In this respect, he remains within the world of law-abiding Jews. But for the ethic of obedience to the commands of the Torah, he substitutes one of boundless love for Jews and gentiles alike.[55]

This is beautiful and moving but hard to emulate. Paul offers a more manageable version of Jesus' teachings. He reinterprets these in orthodoxical terms. After Paul, to be a Christian means to believe that certain things are true.[56] From Paul on, disputes among Christians take the form of disagreements about the truth of various propositions and, however fierce these become, there is agreement on a few—that God created the world from nothing, and man in his image; that through man's prideful disobedience to God, he has fallen into a state of sin; that Jesus gave his life for us, so that we might be saved from ourselves and restored to the hope of a life everlasting; and that the long and turbulent history of the world will one day come to a close with a final judgment in which our eternal fates are settled once and for all.

These propositions remain the backbone of Christian belief in all its variant forms. They represent the core of Christian orthodoxy, whose most striking characteristics are, first, its aspiration to universality, and second, its insistence that true belief is at least a necessary, and perhaps sufficient, condition for salvation. Intensified by the proselytizing ambitions of its earliest proponents, these orthodoxical commitments drove the church in a more philosophical direction than the orthopractical Judaism from which it emerged, and eventually toward the nihilism that in Nietzsche's view represents the last stage of Christian belief—one the Jews could never reach on account of the intellectual and practical restrictions that were built into their theodicy from the start.

This is the barest sketch of Nietzsche's brilliant and arresting account of the slave revolt in morality. Many of the details are controversial. But to appreciate its significance for his philosophy as a whole, it is less important to resolve these controversies than to see how his account is guided by the conception of art he first presents in *The Birth of Tragedy*. For on this view, Nietzsche says, the morality inspired by the Jews' revaluation of worldly power must be counted among the greatest artistic achievements in all of human history, despite its own professed hostility to aesthetic values.

Like Socrates, the Jews find themselves is a position of weakness. Their God has been vanquished, their kingdom destroyed. Another people might have accepted its fate. But the Jews longed to escape their weakness and vulnerability and did so by the only means still available to them—through the artistry of an interpretation of worldly success that drains it of all real value.

According to the Jews, the meaning of their experience must now be found outside the world, in the omnipotent but invisible God to whom they pray and in the hearts of his faithful followers. In this new picture of things, to be good no longer means to be politically powerful or rich or highborn. The good are now the righteous and morally pure—those who remain steadfastly obedient to the word of God. And the wicked are the "great ones of the world" whose devotion to earthly goods shows that they are nothing in God's judgment, which trumps any merely human assessment of the meaning of glory and suffering in the political realm.

Two features of this reinterpretation of the meaning of worldly values explain its astounding success. The first is its simplicity. Instead of adding refinements to the age-old ethic of aristocratic honor, it merely substitutes a negative sign for a positive one, and vice versa. At a stroke, it converts every aspect of this ancient ethic to its exact opposite.

The second is its hermetic character. For those who accept the Jews' reinterpretation of sanctity, hope and reward, every attack on it is further confirmation of its truth. This was an important part of its seductive appeal both for the Jews and then later for the Christian missionaries who carried their revaluation of values to the gentile world.[57]

Jews and Christians of course understand the triumph of their view of human experience in moral terms. To them, it represents the victory of righteousness over evil, of the city of God over that of man. But Nietzsche understands its success in aesthetic terms instead—as the slow, then accelerating and finally irresistible acceptance of a picture of the world invented, as all such pictures are, to provide an antidote to suffering, whose remedial power depends on its own illusionistic charms. Together with the Socratic interpretation of the world, and the concepts of "cause," "thing" and "knowledge" it employs, the morality of the Jews, refined and strengthened by their Christian and post-Christian successors, constitutes, in Nietzsche's view, one of the two pillars of the unnoticed aesthetics of modernity itself.

This it is hard for us to see because our morality, like our science, is so hostile to aesthetic valuations of all kinds. It encourages us to be suspicious about the beauty of appearances, with their lurid colors and erotic charms, and warns us not to assign them an inherent value of their own. At most we are permitted to enjoy the beauty of the world indirectly, as the visible gift of an invisible God, who we may be helped to worship by the splendors of nature and the arts of man, but always at the risk of an idolatrous confusion about the source and nature of their value.

All Christian art rests on this premise and presents this danger. Even its most beautiful works exert their pull in the shadow of a theology that regards the power of worldly beauty with something between caution and contempt. This tension manifests itself with special clarity in the iconoclastic attacks on image making of all kinds that have punctuated the history of Judeo-Christian morality, beginning with the destruction of the golden calf at Sinai.[58] And while the doctrine of the Incarnation has provided a warrant for centuries of Christian painting and sculpture that have no counterpart in the Jewish tradition, whose iconoclasm is stricter in this regard, the Christian conception of moral value is even more emphatically antiaesthetic than its Jewish predecessor in another respect, for its principled insistence on the abstract equality of all human beings undermines in a particularly sweeping way the worth of those distinctions on which all judgments of beauty depend.

Beauty stands out. It is by definition an exception. For something to be beautiful, it must rise above what is coarse or common. But in the eyes of God, every man and woman is of equal worth. The least are as valuable as the greatest. This means that from God's point of view, none of the distinctions that underlie our earthly rankings of human beauty really matter at all. The only one that does is the distinction between righteousness and sin, and since we are all equally endowed with the freedom to pursue the first and avoid the second, the sole difference that has any meaning from God's point of view offers no room for the sort of aesthetic discriminations we make when we rank human beings as striking or ordinary on the basis of their relative power to dazzle and awe us. We still draw such distinctions, of course. The power of beauty strikes us with irresistible force. But the democratic outlook the Christian religion forces upon us by demanding that we evaluate the world from the otherworldly point of view of its creator places all such judgments under a cloud of disrepute, and requires us to be perpetually suspicious of them. It demands that we be on our guard against beauty.

The leveling of human distinctions in the presence of God is a premise of the Jewish theodicy too, which lowers the standing of those with earthly glory and raises that of the dispossessed, to the point where the first become an instrument for the moral reproof of the second. But the Jews' account of their role in God's drama still preserves the inherent value of one worldly difference—that between his chosen people and everyone else. By abolishing this distinction and carrying the good news of God's saving grace to the nations of the world, Paul completes the program of equalization begun by the prophetic reinterpretation of the disasters that had overwhelmed the kingdom of David, and points his followers in a different direction from that of the rabbis who taught the Jews how, through observance of the law, they might remain a people apart even in diaspora. Paul's radicalization of the leveling of worldly values thus attacks in still more far-reaching terms the intrinsic worth of those distinctions on which all appraisals of beauty depend, and carries to an extreme the antiaestheticism that Judaism implies from the start. According to Nietzsche, this attitude reaches a limit of sorts in the gospel of democracy and equal rights on which the moral culture of our nominally post-Christian age is founded.

Nietzsche gives us a portrait of the type he considers the outstanding representative of our age in his withering description of what he calls the "last human being."[59]

Everything about the last human being is small. There is no greatness in him. He seeks only a modest and comfortable existence, in whose pursuit he is protected by laws that guarantee him the same rights as everyone else. Wherever he looks, he sees others like himself—some rich and others poor, a few with great official power and many with none, but all identical in status and value, as these are defined by a morality that assigns no intrinsic weight to worldly differences of beauty, rank and power, but acknowledges the equal rights of every man and woman regardless of their insignificance or grandeur. Jesus tells his followers that the meek shall inherit the earth. The last human being is the fulfillment of this promise. His morality is the final, because most radical, expression of Christianity's insistence on our equality before a majestic God in whom the last human being, with his plebian conception of happiness, no longer has much interest at all.

The world of the last human being is suffused with moral judgments. Every one of its institutions and practices, and all of its governing ideals are shaped by the thought, "I'm just as good as you are—as worthy, valuable, and deserving of respect." And precisely because its deepest norms rest on a relentless egalitarianism of this kind, it is a world that has no place for beauty, which can exist, Nietzsche says, only where distinctions of power are acknowledged as possessing an inherent value of their own. That museums exist in large numbers and are visited each weekend by crowds; that novels are published by the thousands and read by millions; that the beauty of film stars and other celebrities is a subject of obsessive attention is no evidence to the contrary, for none of these are more than entertaining diversions for the equally worthy citizens of a morally leveled and therefore artless world. For art to possess real power, the distinction that every work of art claims for itself as an exception to what is banal and common would have to be accepted on its own terms. This cannot happen, Nietzsche insists, so long as the hostility to beauty that underlies the moral judgments of the last human being continues to inform our cultural and political attitudes at their deepest level.

Yet despite—or rather, because of—its antagonism to the inequality that art always assumes, the "herd morality" of the last human being must itself be understood as an aesthetic phenomenon in Nietzsche's sense. That is because its depiction of what is real and valuable in the world (the pure heart, the modest man, the equality of persons, the identification of happiness with comfort) is motivated by the same longing for metaphysical solace that inspires the creation of every work of art, up to and including the system of antiaesthetic ideals that makes its first appearance in the world with the slave revolt in morality.

It is hard to see this longing at work today, in the world of the last human being, whose most striking characteristic is his lack of creative drive. To grasp its urgency and power, we need to return to the original event from which our modern ideals derive. But even the artistry of the Jews, who Nietzsche ranks among the most creative human beings the world has ever known, conceals its artfulness in a theodicy that denigrates more worldly expressions of beauty and power. This very concealment is the secret of the Jews' success, and of the still greater triumph of their Christian successors, in popularizing a picture of the world whose artistry is hidden behind a theology that eliminates the very conditions on which any affirmation of the value of beauty depends. The slave revolt in morality succeeds by hiding its own character as an aesthetic phenomenon. In time, this deepens into a full blown forgetfulness of the value of art and an anesthetization of the drive to create. But even this can only be understood, Nietzsche says, as an immensely successful artistic creation, in the sense required by his reversed interpretation of the meaning of art.

ASCETIC IDEALS

Socratism and Judaism are the principal elements of the worldview that shapes the whole of modern Western civilization. Nietzsche interprets both as works of art that are defined by their hatred of art. Each is the product of a drive to gain power over the world of appearances by transferring the source of its meaning and value to an unseen ground beyond it. In both cases, the artistic motive for this revaluation of worldly beauty has been repressed and forgotten.

But Socratism and Judaism are merely local expressions of an even more general phenomenon whose effects can be seen outside the West as well, for example, in the tradition of Buddhist thought that emerges from the highly intellectualized milieu of the priestly stratum in the classical Hindu caste system. Nietzsche was deeply interested in Buddhism and drew frequent comparisons between it and the nihilism of the post-Christian West, which he calls a form of "Buddhism for Europeans."[60] In his view, these belong to a class of phenomena that includes not only Western science and ethics but the metaphysical systems of the Indian philosophers and the world-denying beliefs of the Buddhist sages as well.

Nietzsche's term for the common principle that unites this diverse collection of attitudes and practices is "the ascetic ideal."[61] It is the most ubiquitous of all human ideals, and has assumed an immense variety of forms under different cultural and historical conditions. But it is an aesthetic phenomenon too, and wherever its effects appear on earth these must be interpreted as works of art. The full breadth of Nietzsche's claim that the world can only be justified as an aesthetic phenomenon is revealed most clearly by his account of ascetic ideals, which in turn prepares the way for that "daring bound into a metaphysics of Art" that he declares himself ready to take in the next to last section of *The Birth of Tragedy*.[62]

The ascetic is one who turns against life. We think first, of course, of the "saint," of the Christian anchorite or Hindu gymnosophist who disciplines his body in order to achieve a state of sanctity or enlightenment. Through abstinence from food and sex, deliberately imposed states of sleeplessness and withdrawal from social life, the ascetic seeks to detach himself from the demands of the flesh so that those of the spirit may be fulfilled. He longs to be free from the noisy and distracting requirements of life for the sake of his soul, which yearns to escape the prison of bodily need. To achieve his goal, the ascetic develops a system of self-mortification—an armory of techniques for the suppression of physical needs that can be taught and practiced in a methodical way. The highly structured routines of work and prayer practiced by monastic communities of all sorts are a familiar example. Another is the dietary and gymnastic regimens that most ancient schools of philosophy required adherents to follow as an essential complement to their intellectual teachings, whose liberating potential could be achieved, it was believed, only if the student's body were first properly trained.[63]

These familiar types of asceticism share an open antipathy to the body, and more generally to life. But a similar hostility can also be detected in the highly refined systems of thought constructed by the greatest philosophers of India and Greece. All of these reflect what Nietzsche calls a "contemplative" attitude toward life—one that judges it to be less true than something else that is more stable and enduring. He terms this "peculiarly withdrawn attitude" toward life "the *philosophical attitude as such*"[64] and describes it as another species of self-mortification, subtler perhaps but in essence the same as that of the flagellant who seeks to get beyond life through a routine of self-inflicted pain whose message is, "the body means nothing to me."

In this respect, philosophy is an ascetic discipline too. So is the culture of specialized science that is inspired by the contemplative ambition to discover the truth behind the bodily surface of things, from whose beauty the scientist must train himself to look away by means of various methods of abstraction (of which the experiment is a leading example). These are the equivalent of the anchorite's refusal to be taken in by the charms of the world. And of course the same is true of the moralist who preaches the wickedness of instinct and appetite, and the irrelevance of all superficial forms of beauty; who pleads with us to reject these for the sake of purity, righteousness and the like; and who insists that we view life as a threat to be contained in the name of some moral ideal that instructs us when and on what terms we may yield to its demands. To have discovered the ascetic, life-denying impulse that connects these different phenomena—the Indian yogi in his twisted pose, the Christian hermit, the polished Athenian philosopher, the scientist at his workbench, the politician preaching the gospel of equality—is one of Nietzsche's greatest insights.

A second and even deeper one is that "the situation" in all these cases is "the precise opposite" of what "the worshippers of [the ascetic] ideal imagine it to be." Asceticism opposes and condemns life. Yet in reality, Nietzsche says, it is "a trick for the *preservation* of life."[65] The "ascetic priest" (a term that includes philosophers, scientists and moralists as well as religious saints) is the "apparent enemy of life." But "this *negating one,*—he actually belongs to the really great *conserving* and *yes-creating* forces in life."[66]

Behind this startling judgment is Nietzsche's assumption that "[e]very animal, including the *bête philosophe*, instinctively strives for an optimum of favorable conditions in which fully to release his power and achieve his maximum of power-sensation. . . ."[67] This instinct is shared by all living things. Indeed, it is that by virtue of which they may be said to be alive in the first place. For some, the path to its expression is direct and uninhibited—as in the case of those blond beasts that roam the warrior world of Achilles and Beowulf and impose their power on ordinary men, to whom they are a fate, coming down "like night," as Apollo does on the hapless Greeks at the beginning of the *Iliad*.[68] But wherever this path is blocked, another will be found to its goal. The goal itself is irrepressible. Everyone alive is driven by an instinctive longing for power, and if the most direct route to its fulfillment is stopped up by opposing forces of one kind or another, a new and more roundabout channel will be carved to the same end.

It is on the basis of this universal psychological principle that Nietzsche interprets the meaning of asceticism in its crudest and most refined forms. The ascetic, too, desires "an optimum of favorable conditions" for the "release" of power, but stymied by the prevailing norms of an aristocratic culture that stamp him as a weakling (Socrates) or by worldly powers great enough to force him into political submission (the Jewish prophets) or by a neurasthenic constitution that is otherwise unable to withstand the pull of physical desire (religious ascetics of all kinds), he seeks to fulfill his longing for power—the essence of life—by turning against it and condemning life in order to achieve a greater mastery of it. The means by which he does this is an interpretation of the world that puts life in its place, draining it of its power to hurt or confine him by assigning life a negative value—the last instrument of power that remains to those who have otherwise lost it, and the most powerful by far that human beings have yet discovered to satisfy their longing for command.

It is in the phenomenon of asceticism, seemingly so hostile to life, that Nietzsche thus finds the most compelling evidence of its universal dominion. "[T]he ascetic ideal," he writes, "*springs from the protective and healing instincts of a degenerating life* which uses every means to maintain itself and struggles for its existence."[69] Its chief means is the interpretation of life as something bad and hence to be overcome. But this picture is merely an inverted expression of the striving that is life itself—the same striving that in *The Birth of Tragedy* Nietzsche identifies with the creative drive that moves every artist to measure and form the world in order to render it beautiful: the essence of art as he sees it. Putting these two thoughts together, one might say that for Nietzsche life is art, and that the key to their identity is to be found, paradoxically, in those intellectual, religious, moral and scientific movements that are united by a common hostility to the value of aesthetic experience, yet can themselves only be understood as aesthetic phenomena, and hence within a wider frame than they themselves provide.

This brings Nietzsche to a "seductive riddle" that he poses in the course of his account of the meaning of ascetic ideals. Nothing, he says, has been more valuable to the advancement of the species, and to its becoming the most interesting form of life on earth, than these ideals themselves. "Read from a distant planet," the earth appears to be "the ascetic planet *par excellence.*" Everywhere one looks one sees the triumph of the ascetic ideal, in one form or another, and with it, the triumph of humankind—not just quantitatively, but qualitatively too, in the cities and works and cultures of man, all of which are the product of ascetic discipline and order. But how is this possible? Nietzsche wonders. "It must be a necessity of the first rank which makes this species continually grow and prosper when it is *hostile to life,—life itself must have an interest* in preserving such a self-contradictory type."[70]

This is Nietzsche's mature formulation of an idea that he announces for the first time in *The Birth of Tragedy*—that the world process, the all-inclusive One, the ground of being itself, throws off for its own eternal delight an endless stream of individuals who, tormented by their finitude and inability ever to close the gap between themselves and the world, salve the pathos of their condition by means of art, the only, if inevitably inadequate, means of salvation available to them. With this, we stand at the threshold of Nietzsche's metaphysics of art, similar in so many ways to Spinoza's theology—a born-again paganism that redivinizes the world absolutely, but in contrast to that of Spinoza, which is silent on the subject, puts art at the very center of things and helps us grasp the God that animates its most characteristically modern expressions. To cross this threshold, only one more step is required. That is to equate art not merely with life but being itself.

CHAPTER 33

The Spider in the Moonlight

NIETZSCHE'S INTERPRETATION OF THE WILL
TO POWER AS ART

Nietzsche's writings contain many suggestive remarks about the relation of being to becoming and other metaphysical topics. But he never develops these in a disciplined way. Indeed, he repeatedly expresses his hostility to the whole enterprise of metaphysics, which he regards as a symptom of the very disease he is fighting. Those who speculate about a realm of being generally do so in order to denigrate that of motion and time. They separate being from becoming so as to drain the latter of meaning and value. Like all ascetics, they lack the strength to affirm life on its own terms, with the Dionysian confidence of the tragic poets. This perhaps helps to explain why Nietzsche remained reluctant even in his unpublished writings to defend his metaphysical ideas in the straightforward way that every philosopher from Plato to Schopenhauer had done.

But his reluctance to state these ideas more explicitly should not be confused with the lack of a metaphysics. From *The Birth of Tragedy* on, Nietzsche was unable to let his highly original interpretations of particular persons and events stand on their own. He felt the philosopher's compulsion to embed these in a general account of reality. Indeed, he felt the need to construct a metaphysics of an especially far-reaching kind that would not only support his own interpretation of philosophy as an ascetic discipline, but also explain the fundamental error that every philosopher before him had made.

811

Nietzsche never presents his metaphysics as an organized whole. The very attempt to do so would have been temperamentally alien to him. But many of his most arresting ideas only make sense in the context of his rich if unsystematized account of being and becoming.[1] These include the will to power, perspectivism, *amor fati,* the eternal return, nihilism, nobility, and the religion of Dionysus reborn. It is therefore important that we make the effort, on Nietzsche's behalf, to assemble and arrange the elements of his metaphysics in a more explicit way than he did.

When we have done so, its resemblance to Spinoza's will be clear. Each expresses, in its own distinctive idiom, their shared conception of the world as both inherently and infinitely divine. This is the born-again paganism to which both thinkers subscribe. I have tried to show that Spinoza's version of it gives us the God that modern science needs to account for its aspirations. Nietzsche's does the same for modern art. It provides the theology that is required to explain the deepest ambitions of art as we now understand it. It gives us the God we need to make sense of the relation between time and eternity as this is portrayed in Virginia Woolf's description of the simple act of knitting a stocking.

DRIVE

The basic unit of account in Nietzsche's metaphysics is what he calls the "will to power."[2] The will to power is the essence of every being, however simple or complex. It is that by virtue of which it may be said to be at all.

The term has had a notorious history[3] and in one important respect poorly expresses Nietzsche's central idea, for the "will," he says, is an illusory concept, like "thing" and "cause" and "I," that human beings have invented to help them extend their control over the world. In reality, there is no such thing at all.[4] There is no power of autonomous self-affection, as Kant understands the idea. Put differently, the will is not a genuine *causa sui.*[5] The belief that it is, is merely an "afterthought" that summarizes in a metaphysically misleading way a whole series of movements, sensations and actions, and expresses the feeling of growing command.[6] If we are to understand what Nietzsche means by the will to power we must therefore give up the idea of will as autonomy—as a power of self-determination independent of the series of heteronomous causes that constitutes the natural order of things—which the greatest Christian philosophers, from Augustine to Kant, have made so familiar and plausible.

The right way to think of the will to power is not as will in the Christian sense but as force or drive instead—or rather, as "forcing" or "driving," since on Nietzsche's view the elemental drive that he denominates with this term is not a thing but a process.

This reverses the standard view of the relation between things and drives. On the standard view, things come first. We begin with things that have drives that move them in a particular direction, bringing them into conflict with other things that have opposing drives of their own. For Nietzsche, the process of "driving" is the primordial phenomenon and things only temporary consolidations of it. A thing is an expression of this process—a way or mode of driving, and not its substantive premise.[7] Driving is fluid and dynamic, and everything that appears fixed or stable—that looks like a thing with enduring characteristics—is merely the transient precipitate of a drive, or many drives, that have reached a temporary "truce" and come to be arranged, for a time at least, in accordance with the demands of one of them.

This reversed conception of the relation between drive and thing is as fundamental to Nietzsche's metaphysics as his emphasis on the needs of the artist, as opposed to the effects of the artwork, is to his aesthetics. Indeed, they are essentially the same and lead to the same basic question.

If drives precede things, rather than the other way around, what is it that makes one drive different from another? In metaphysical terms, what is the principle of individuation that sets them apart? And how can this question be answered without assuming that different drives have a separate substantive being of their own—are things, in precisely the sense that Nietzsche emphatically insists they are not? We shall return to this question later in the chapter. To prepare the way, it will help first to consider Nietzsche's argument against the commonsensical view that individuals are distinguished from one another by their bodies.

Following what he calls "the thread of the body,"[8] Nietzsche observes that in the case of living things (his paradigm example), bodies are not individuals with an independent being of their own, but complex collections of drives that have been "masterfully" gathered into a hierarchical community of leading and slaving forces. In this sense, the individuality of the body of a plant or animal is not a primitive fact but a hard won achievement—the result of the dominion of some of its parts over others.

The same is even more obviously true at the level of "political bodies." These have their separate identities too, but not because they are real things whose existence is the ground of that of their members. A political body is also a community of forces, some commanding and others obeying, in one of those temporary accommodations we call a structure of authority.

If instead of moving "up" from organisms to polities, we move "down" to the parts of which plants and animals are composed, the pattern is repeated. Organs, too, are not self-subsisting things but constellations of drives (now conceived, perhaps, as arising at the cellular or subcellular level) whose collective identity is also the result of a process of struggle and consolidation.

Beginning with the organism and moving up and down the ladder, to more and less complex sorts of bodies, we thus find that none is qualified to serve as a principle of individuation. No body is fundamental in the way that such a principle requires—not even, Nietzsche says, the atoms of which modern science is so fond.[9]

The same is true of minds, which are also just fleeting compacts among warring drives. Nietzsche devotes a great deal of effort to showing that human minds are not individual things. Neither are those more complex forms of mentality we sometimes describe as cultural worldviews. There are no psychical atoms, just as there are no physical ones. On the one side as the other, there is only an endless play of drives whose interaction produces transient constellations great and small, like the waves on the surface of a turbulent sea, which for the sake of navigation we call individuals and fictively treat as if they were the source of these interactions rather than the other way around.

But then—to state the question again—how are we to account for the multiplicity of these drives themselves? Even if they are not individual bodies or minds, they must be plural and diverse, since otherwise they could neither compete nor join together in more complex aggregations. The challenge that Nietzsche faces in this regard is the same as the one that Spinoza confronts in accounting for the existence of an infinite diversity of modes under the attributes of thought and extension. His solution is strikingly similar. For Nietzsche too, there is only one real individual, namely the world as a whole, and every drive is a feature or attribute of it—in his terminology, a portrait of the world from a point of view or perspective—and this one infinite individual necessarily expresses itself in a maximum of finite depictions. This is a difficult concept to grasp. It involves three of the most basic terms in Nietzsche's metaphysics—"world," "perspective" and "drive." To see how these fit together, we may start by noting the ways in which Nietzsche's idea of a drive both resembles and differs from its Aristotelian predecessor.

DOMINATION

The defining feature of every drive is that it is *toward* or *for* something. It is a movement with a goal. Insofar as a motion is a drive, it therefore cannot be explained by the action on it of forces from without. It exhibits the power of self-movement that Aristotle calls *phusis*, which Descartes sought to expunge from the world with a strictly inertial account of motion based on the assumption that nothing moves on its own account except God.

For Aristotle, only some beings possess this power. Artifacts that come into existence as the result of a process of making do not. Still, Aristotle's concept of *phusis* is broad enough to include not only all living things but some inanimate ones as well (the four elements, or simple substances, and the "bits" into which they are always dispersed). The motion of these too, he claims, cannot be fully explained except in terms of their internal tendency to move toward an end or goal of some sort.

Nietzsche's doctrine of drive radicalizes Aristotle's by extending it to the motion of all beings as such. To the extent that anything *is* at all, he says, its being is that of a movement toward a goal. Nietzsche's metaphysics thus not only rests on an assumption antithetical to the inertial science of motion that Descartes made canonical for our understanding of the natural world. It extends to its furthest conceivable limit the more restricted Aristotelian idea of *phusis* that Descartes saw as the chief obstacle to the advancement of science.

The radicalism of Nietzsche's concept of drive manifests itself, among other ways, in his refusal to limit its application to the realm of what we conventionally call living beings. That plants and animals move on their own seemed obvious to Aristotle and will to anyone who accepts the reality of the phenomenon of life (which Descartes of course denied). What is striking about Nietzsche's view of life is that he extends it to inorganic beings as well—to crystals and the like.[10] These too, he claims, are units or centers of drive, not inert things moving only in accordance with the impact on them of external forces of various kinds. In this sense, Nietzsche's world is alive throughout—even in the seemingly dead domain of inanimate things. His definition of the being of beings as will to power, and interpretation of the latter as drive, thus entails a hylozoism that folds the whole of existence into the realm of living beings. Nietzsche enthusiastically embraces this conclusion and even offers it as a clue to the proper understanding of his metaphysics, which compels us, he says, to view the entire world from the "inside"—including those parts of it that seem to have only a soulless external existence.[11]

It is a conclusion, moreover, that Nietzsche believes reason itself requires us to accept. In his view, the acknowledgment of a gap or jump between animate and inanimate things is intellectually indefensible. A metaphysics that aspires to coherence cannot simply assume as a brute fact that some things lack drives and others possess them.[12] For anyone who accepts this view, there are only two possibilities: a world that is entirely dead or one that is wholly alive. The first is Descartes' position, the second Spinoza's and Nietzsche's.

Nietzsche's defense of hylozoism thus rests on his acceptance of a version of the principle of sufficient reason. An implicit commitment to the same principle also underlies his attack on the idea of the will, which he rejects on the grounds that it assumes the existence of an unaccountable break in the causal order of things. And it informs his relentless effort to naturalize all human phenomena by reinserting them into a world in which man is not, in Spinoza's famous phrase, a "kingdom within a kingdom," but a being that plays by the same rules as everything else.[13] In all these respects, Nietzsche may more accurately be described as a hyperrationalist than the irrationalist he is sometimes said to be.

That Nietzsche himself understood this is suggested by his frequent and favorable references to Leibniz, whose "monadology" is a form of hylozoism constructed in accordance with the principle of sufficient reason.[14] In one very basic respect, however, Nietzsche's comparison of his own views to those of Leibniz is misplaced. Leibniz was a Christian philosopher whose belief in the doctrine of creation compelled him to deny that the units of drive he calls monads, of which the world is composed, have a true life of their own, since their internal careers must be set in motion by a divine cause external to the world as a whole.[15] Leibniz's employment of the principle of sufficient reason and his hylozoist metaphysics are both constrained by a Christian dogma that Nietzsche fiercely rejects, and explains in the same naturalistic terms that he does every other human idea of a God beyond the world. The closer parallel, which Nietzsche at times recognizes but at others resists, is between his own conception of the being of beings as will to power and Spinoza's idea of *conatus*.

Spinoza defines *conatus* as a striving to "persevere" in existence. It is the essence, he says, of every finite being. In the case of human beings, it takes the form of a striving for ever-greater power. But there is no reason to assume that the same is not true of other beings as well. Spinoza suggests as much and his own commitment to the principle of sufficient reason supports this conclusion. Nietzsche is more explicit. The being of beings is drive, he says, and the aim of every drive, human or not, is an expansion of whatever power or control it possesses. The essential goal of every drive is always *more*.[16]

Nietzsche characterizes this process of expansion as one of appropriation or incorporation.[17] Of course, it is not effortless or unimpeded. As one being struggles to expand its range, it encounters others that are doing the same. They resist its expansion and strive to incorporate or appropriate its powers into their own. The result is a contest in which some drives are forced to yield to others. The losers become aspects, features or elements of the drive that prevails. For the losers, yielding to a stronger drive is their best way of achieving a maximum of power under the prevailing conditions, since by doing so they are able to have at least a subordinate share in the other's dominion.

Nietzsche calls the outcome a regime of "enslavement" and describes it in terms reminiscent of those that Aristotle uses in book 1 of the *Politics* to define the relation between a master and his natural slave.[18] But Nietzsche again interprets this phenomenon more radically than Aristotle by maintaining that the existence of *all* bodies and minds, even those of the most masterful and free human beings, is the product of a contest in which certain powers have been subdued and enslaved by others. The process of enslavement is ubiquitous at the social level too. In Nietzsche's view, every social and political scheme, including even those that by their own terms are most hostile to the idea of enslavement, is a product of the triumph of one power over another and of the latter's slavish deference to the first. (His interpretation of our modern egalitarian ideals as a product of the slave revolt in morality is a case in point.)

In short, for Nietzsche the phenomenon of domination is as wide as the realm of being itself. It arises of necessity at every level of individuation, from that of the body, or even the cell, to the most complex formations of social life. One can put the point even more strongly. In Nietzsche's view, the identity of every individual is *nothing but* the hierarchical order that exists among the drives this order gathers into a structure of command and obedience— one that satisfies, for a time at least, the longing for greater power that all drives share (in the case of the master drive, by extending its control over weaker ones, and in theirs by allowing them to participate derivatively in a coordinated expansion of power *vis-à-vis* the rest of the world).

This view guides Nietzsche's account of structures as diverse as the human body and the Roman Empire. Its premise is that every individual is a complex of drives; that the aim of every drive is greater power; that power is control; and that control is the result of a process of ordering—one drive gaining control over another when it succeeds in ordering (shaping, directing, defining) the latter's position (its function or value) within an arrangement the former projects (within its "project").

It is natural to think of such ordering in a relatively crude way, on the model of the commands a drill sergeant barks to his recruits. But though the projection of power can seem as artless as this, it is important to remember that even the sergeant's commands have the force they do only because they are backed up by a scheme of authority that represents a picture of the world of great complexity and refinement. In these respects, it resembles a work of art, and that is precisely how Nietzsche regards it. Indeed, even the most brutal expressions of power must in his view be understood in aesthetic terms. The work of ordering, of command and deference, in which every localized center of individual being consists, from the eukaryotic cells that first successfully incorporated other living bodies into themselves, to the Roman people who digested countless others by arms and law, is in every case, according to Nietzsche, an expression of the Apollonian drive to delineate the world that he defines in *The Birth of Tragedy* as the essence of art.

ART

The artist measures and arranges things. He separates and relates them, bringing order to what would otherwise be a chaos of indistinct forces. In this way, he gains control over the endless, senseless, self-destructive swirl that threatens to render everything that happens in the world pointless and absurd. Art is a means of fighting back. It is a response to the demand that the world be an orderly and hence meaningful place.

Art meets this demand by depicting the world in a way that makes sense. It is an antidote to the weakness and vulnerability which the lack of such a picture entails. But the longing for greater power that art seeks to gratify is not unique to those exceptional human beings we normally call artists—to poets, painters and the like. Ordinary men and women experience it too. Nor is it even limited to human beings. The striving to enhance its power is constitutive of every being as such. Each, moreover, pursues this goal in the same way that the greatest poets and painters do. Every being, human or not, strives to enlarge its power by ordering others to "fall in line" with its project and fit into its picture of the world—to have the place and therefore the value this picture assigns it, as something positive or negative, supportive or adversarial, similar or strange and the like.

Success in this regard means drafting others into one's program. It means enslaving them in Nietzsche's sense—forcing them (physically, or by subtler means) to abide by the rules that order the world in accordance with one's project. The projection of such an order is art, the compulsive assignment of structure and meaning to things. For the most part, it proceeds without those special qualities of attention that we associate with its human expression and mistakenly treat as part of the definition of art. In reality, Nietzsche insists, *every* drive, however simple or complex, lowly or refined, is an artistic endeavor, and *every* individual—every transient association of competing drives, arranged in a hierarchical scheme of command—is a work of art in his sense. For Nietzsche, the being of beings is art, a proposition that merely elevates to a level of metaphysical generality an idea already contained in his early account of the Apollonian passion for the redeeming power of form.

In Nietzsche's view, the human body is a work of art, and so are the Laws of Manu,[19] as much as the Medici Palace. Even a flea is a work of art. With the exception of the Medici Palace, none of these has been fashioned by an artist separate from the work itself. This therefore cannot be what makes them works of this sort. For Nietzsche, their defining characteristic as works of art is simply their form. Each is an ordered whole whose form is a structure of domination that expresses in a concrete and congealed way the triumph of one drive over others in a struggle to determine what the rule of their relations shall be. Nietzsche calls this an artistic achievement. It is the result, he says, of one drive's success in imposing on others in its neighborhood a "masterful" conception of order, analogous to the success of the poet who finds the words to command the attention of his audience by fitting their experience of the world into his picture of it, so that afterward, for a time at least, they can only see things as he does.

This imposed order is not the result of the conscious efforts of an artist who stands apart from his finished work, as opposed to being an element of it (again, with the exception of the Medici Palace). But this is irrelevant to Nietzsche's basic point, which neither assumes that the creation of art is a deliberate and self-conscious process, nor that the artist and his artwork are distinct from one another. Indeed, his repeated description of the ordered structures of domination that emerge from the universal war among drives, as the outcome of a struggle to incorporate or digest one another, suggests the very opposite, for the process of digestion requires no reflection and results in a single whole to which both victor and vanquished belong.

From this point of view, the conscious sort of artistry that results in a separate and freestanding work (such as Medici Palace) is an exception to a more comprehensive process of arranging, subordinating, shaping and the like that has neither of these characteristics—to what might be called the unconscious Apollonian striving, the artist's *conatus,* that is the source and explanation of every fragment of order the world contains. And in fact the exception is only apparent, for if one wants to understand what the Medici Palace really means, it and its architect Michelozzo must be placed within that larger scheme of patronage and domination that we call Medici Florence, whose order was the result of one family's campaign, driven by a need deeper than any of the conscious strategies its members devised to fulfill it, to digest their beloved city by making it part of a whole of which they would be the leading component.

Because Nietzsche's metaphysics makes drive the basic unit of account and defines its essence in terms of what Wallace Stevens calls the artist's "blessed rage for order,"[20] it reverses the direction of the process of sublimation, as we normally conceive it. The word implies the concealment of something low by giving it a different and better appearance—one that makes it "sublime." What becomes sublime in this way is not so to begin with. It is rough, ill-conceived, even obscene. When we speak, for example, of the sublimation of sex in the higher forms of love and poetry, this is what we have in mind—a process that leads from below to above.

By carrying the artist's compulsion to order down into the bowels of being, where we see it at work in the least of things—in the peristalsis of a monkey's stomach—Nietzsche's conception of the being of beings as art endows the entire world, even its smallest and dirtiest corners, with the sublimity of the greatest artworks we know. The monkey is a Homer of sorts too, less powerful of course, but only explicable as a structured arrangement of organs and movements that grows from the same drive as the one that connects the poet to his poem. The result is that every last bit of reality acquires something of the beauty, dignity and value that we conventionally reserve for those extraordinary works of art that go as far as any product of human effort can toward satisfying our demand that the world have a comprehensive and permanent meaning. This demand achieves a clarity in human life that it has nowhere else, but wherever the drive for order exists the longing for a theodicy is present in a nascent form. Our human art is merely the highest-order expression of this longing—the most far-reaching expression of the passion for control that constitutes the essence of even the least complex being. The whole of the world, as Nietzsche sees it, is thus suffused with the sublimity of art, and with the longing for eternity that every human artist strives to palliate in one way or another.

Yet if even the least things share in this sublimity, they also share in the essential disappointment that is the fate of the highest ones too. That is because there is no resting place at which the drive to master the world through the projection of order can come to a stop. However much it achieves, it will always want more. In this respect, the artist's striving for order resembles the endless pursuit of power that Hobbes defines as the motive of all human action, and the struggle for reproductive advantage that Darwin views as the fundamental characteristic of life (though Nietzsche fails to see the similarity between his own view and Darwin's).[21]

The endlessness of the artistic striving that Nietzsche conceives in the broadest possible terms as the being of beings distinguishes it in a fundamental way from Aristotle's idea of *phusis*. The latter is always a movement toward an attainable goal and hence one that in principle is capable of fulfillment. This is the heart of Aristotle's doctrine of proper place. By contrast, the drive that Nietzsche calls will to power always and necessarily falls short of the mark. It is in every case the drive of a *finite* being toward an *infinite* goal. Only the mastery of the world as a whole could satisfy this drive; anything less leaves room for a further expansion of power. Aristotle believed that such mastery is possible. His world is eternal and divine, despite the ceaseless motion of everything in it. Yet because its divinity is limited to its form, a finite human being can master it completely. Nietzsche's world is divine too, but infinitely so. Its eternality is not limited to its form, but shared, as we shall see, by the fleeting particularity of all the individuals that exist within it, each a singular work of art among a countless, diverse many. The goal of mastering the world is therefore not just a difficult but manageable task, as Aristotle thought. It is one that no finite being can ever complete.

Of course, if one believes in a God beyond the world with whom one will be reunited in a life to come, the striving for eternity, though doomed to frustration here on earth, may yet reach its goal. But this belief, Nietzsche says, is just another work of art, invented by finite beings to satisfy their longing for total control. In truth, the only eternity is that of the world itself, beyond which there is nothing at all. And because the eternity of the world extends to every crack and crevice of it, the longing to depict it completely can never be fulfilled. In this world, every being is an artist of limited power seeking to extend its control by constructing an ever more compelling picture of the world that always remains incomplete.

This is the same dialectic of sadness and joy that Spinoza expresses in terms of the idea of *conatus.* Every mode strives to persevere in being. This impels it toward an eternity it can never attain. Spinoza conceives this striving in intellectualist terms, as a desire for knowledge or science. Nietzsche describes it in the language of aesthetics instead. But both view the striving and its inevitable disappointment as the essential condition of all finite beings in a world at once inherently and infinitely divine. Consistent with his interpretation of the world as an aesthetic phenomenon, Nietzsche defines the pathos of this condition in terms of the idea of perspective.

PERSPECTIVE

Poets, painters and architects seek to gather as much of the world as they can into an ordered and meaningful whole. They do this by selecting certain objects or states and assigning a pivotal meaning to them, around which others are made to revolve.[22] Though every artist aims to say or show something of "long lasting" value, his work is therefore necessarily "one-sided."[23] It always shows the selectivity of the artist's preferences and prejudices. These include his culture, class and much else besides. Taken together, they distinguish each artist's point of view from that of every other. They define his particular "perspective," a term that Nietzsche uses to summarize the countless factors that determine the finitude of all artistic striving. Though every artist aims at a result that is no longer hostage to the limits of the perspective from which he departs, even his most comprehensive and durable achievements inevitably show the traces of these limits themselves—of a perspectivity that no artist can escape, any more than he can jump over his shadow.

Nietzsche's metaphysics extends this feature of human art to reality in general. The world that he shows us in his "mirror"[24] is an immense complex of drives, all striving to increase their power. At every level of organization, from the simplest and least durable to the most complex and long lived, power is the product of order. Indeed, it *is* order itself and the drive to produce it is art—the longing to master the world by assigning other forces their position and value. Hence if the work of every human artist betrays the marks of its perspectival origin, the same must be true of the being of all beings, defined as a drive for order, or compulsion to depict. If every individual (cell, body, society, etc.) is a work of art in Nietzsche's sense, then it must display—it must *be*—the point of view or perspective of the dominant drive in whose picture of the world other drives have been made to fit, and must exhibit the partiality of this perspective, no matter how successfully it is concealed by an order whose apparent goal is the good of some larger whole (that of the body, for example, or of the Roman people, or of God or the world, which poets and philosophers depict in a way that hides the birthmarks of their own one-sided needs and beliefs).

In Nietzsche's conception, the world is therefore a totality of competing perspectives. He expresses this thought with characteristic compression in his famous remark that "there are absolutely no moral phenomena, only the interpretation of moral phenomena." Taken in isolation from the rest of his metaphysics, this phrase has sometimes been misinterpreted to imply a shallow relativism that is more a symptom of the nihilism Nietzsche sought to combat than an expression of the constructive goal of his philosophy, which he describes as the "redivinization" of the world.[25] To understand how Nietzsche thought this might be done, it is important to keep in mind both sides of the dialectic of finitude and infinitude that his perspectivism implies.

It is true that every drive orders the world from a point of view. But the world it seeks to depict is eternal and divine, indeed infinitely so, since there is nothing in it that is not eternal too. It follows that no finite drive can ever fully capture the divinity of the world in its portrait of it. Still, one drive can come closer than another (this is the essence, as we shall see, of Nietzsche's conception of truth) and no drive—no perspective—lacks all power to represent the world that each strives to portray. Hence, if the world is nothing but a clashing multitude of perspectives, even those that are most quickly integrated into some other point of view or erased altogether express a tiny fraction of the everlasting and divine. None *is* God, but every one of them *depicts* God from a certain angle. In this sense, Nietzsche's perspectivism leads not to a world from which eternity has been banished altogether, but to one in which it has been diffused throughout, so that even the meanest perspective captures it in a limited way.

The contrast between Nietzsche and Plato is particularly instructive in this regard.[26]

Plato acknowledges that our ordinary way of encountering the world is perspectival. We see the things about us from different points of view. One person says, "This is how it looks to me." Another disagrees and says, "I see it differently." The result is a clash of opinions. The fundamental question of Plato's philosophy is whether and how we can escape from the realm of opinion and achieve a true knowledge of things.

For Plato, such knowledge must be nonperspectival. It cannot be from a point of view. The person who possesses it sees things as they truly are, alone and by themselves, in contrast to their images, which give us only a shifting glimpse of the forms they represent in one-sided and incomplete ways. To escape from the cave in which we live means leaving all perspectival seeing and judging behind. It means grasping the world with a directness that is no longer compromised by the deformities that distort every attempt to understand and explain it from an "opinionated" point of view.

Plato is supremely confident that we can do this. He identifies perspective and opinion with the body and true knowledge with the soul. If the soul takes command of the body, and judges the latter's experiences in the light of reason, the path is open to a knowledge of things that is no longer hostage to the perspectivity inherent in bodily sensations of every kind. Mathematics (arithmetic and geometry) provide the key to the rationalization of sensation, and with that to our release from perspectival judgment. That we are able to grasp and use this key is explained by our possession of the liberating power of abstraction—of seeing images *as* images—without which we would be trapped forever in our separate perspectives.

Of course, so long as we are alive and have bodies, we are condemned to seeing things from a point of view. But even in this life, Plato believed, it is possible to learn to understand the world from "nowhere," in accordance with the requirements of reason or thought, and afterward, when we are finally rid of our bodies, to enjoy this kind of understanding directly and without interruption. Plato thus affirms the possibility of overcoming the limits of perspectival knowledge and judgment in a way that Nietzsche rules out. He maintains that human beings are driven by a love of the divine and insists that the gap between our finitude and the divinity of the object we long to reach can be closed completely, in this life or the next.[27]

With this conclusion Aristotle is in fundamental agreement. The anti-Platonic worldliness of his philosophy fuses Plato's ideas and images more closely than Plato's metaphysics allows and leaves no room for a life after this one. Yet even so, Aristotle's account of contemplation reflects the same confidence as Plato's story of the cave that we can overcome the gap between the human and divine, though his resolute focus on this life leads him to conclude that even the greatest philosopher cannot do this except for brief intervals of time.

Nietzsche's metaphysics assures that this gap can never be closed. For Nietzsche, there is only one world and every being in it is straining toward a goal that its perspectivity puts forever beyond reach. Its being is therefore to-be-disappointed. Plato and Aristotle would have rejected this conclusion as absurd, but it follows inexorably from Nietzsche's conception of the world as an eternal and self-contained system of drives defined as will to power.

Each of these is striving to depict the divinity of the world from a point of view it can never transcend. This is an enterprise that is doomed to fail, except on the assumption, which Nietzsche rejects, that there is some other world in which the narrowness inherent in every perspectival rendering of this one will at last be overcome. The result is an omnipresent yearning without end. This is the pathos of Nietzsche's metaphysics and of Western art, once it freed itself from its dependence on a Christian theology that assumes, as Plato had much earlier, that the gap between man and God can be closed, and began to explore the implications of attempting to portray the everlasting and divine from within the horizon of a perspectival vision of the world that aims at a comprehensiveness and objectivity no such portrait can ever attain.[28]

TRUTH

The world is a totality of drives. Each seeks to order the world from a point of view and necessarily falls short of its goal. But what is this totality itself? What is the world as Nietzsche conceives it?

I have already said that Nietzsche's world is eternal. It is also necessary rather than contingent, and without any guiding purpose or goal. Nietzsche's world is a single, all-embracing purposeless whole, whose parts are bound to one another in a web of rising and falling powers, even the most trivial and transient aspects of which could not possibly be other than they are and share in the eternality of the world as a whole.

This is the world as it appears in Nietzsche's mirror. It is a remarkable portrait. But before we examine it in more detail, we need to address a threshold question. We encountered it in the last chapter but set it aside. It may be put in the following way.

Nietzsche claims that every philosophy is the expression of a drive that seeks to increase its power by offering a true account of the world. But the truth is never what it claims to be. It is always just a perspectival view of things dressed up as something better. In this sense, all philosophies are falsifications. But then Nietzsche's own must be as well, for how can it escape the charge he levels against the ideas of other thinkers? Either Nietzsche is not claiming that the world as it appears in his mirror is the true one, or he is making such a claim, in which case it is self-refuting, since it is impossible that Nietzsche's conception of the truth escape the perspectivity to which, on his view, every other conception is hostage. By building the idea of perspectivity into his account of the being of beings as deeply as he does, Nietzsche deprives himself of the right to claim that his portrait of the world is more truthful than any other. We are therefore entitled to treat it as an aesthetic diversion rather than a serious philosophical position.

Is there a conception of truth that is compatible with Nietzsche's perspectivism which supports the claim that his account of the world is the true one?

We can begin by noting that this question arises because of the way in which Nietzsche's perspectivism undermines the conception of truth that has been the dominant one in Western metaphysics from Plato on. This is the conception of truth as adequation. An idea or theory is true, on this view, when it adequately represents, or corresponds to, its object.

No philosopher can deny that we see and think about things from different points of view. So long as our sensations and thoughts are conditioned in this way, any claim that we make for their truth must be qualified or restricted. It can never rise higher than the claim that what we see and think is true is merely what appears to be true from our point of view. This is a conclusion that Sextus Empiricus long ago drew with ruthless clarity. For a philosopher who assumes that truth is correspondence, there is therefore only one way to demonstrate that we can grasp the truth without qualification, and that is to show that we are able to escape the perspectivity of our initial encounter with the world.

Plato believed this to be possible, and tried to show how it can be done. Aristotle followed suit. Kant gave up on the idea that we can have any knowledge of things in themselves. He sought to show that the perspectivity of our experience cannot be overcome. Still, he subscribed to the principle of truth as correspondence, and sought to save the idea of an unqualified truth by arguing that the very possibility of our perspectival experience of the world depends upon a universal and necessary scheme of ordering concepts.

Nietzsche radicalizes Kant's position. Like Kant, he insists that we have no way of relating to the world except from a perspective, but unlike Kant denies that the perspectives from which we experience the world are structured in some unavoidably uniform way. In Nietzsche's view, our perspectives are diverse and competing. They have nothing in common other than their perspectivity. (Expressed formulaically, Nietzsche "historicizes" Kant's transcendental analytic.) So long as one holds onto the idea of truth as correspondence, the result of Nietzsche's radicalization can therefore only be a thoroughgoing subjectivism in which any claim to truth becomes merely the expression of an interested point of view with the same status as every other claim of this kind—that of a mask or disguise behind which the partiality of the perspective of the claimant is hidden, even if this happens to be Nietzsche himself. For truth to be anything more, a different conception of it is required.

Nietzsche's metaphysical interpretation of perspective as the unsurpassable horizon of a boundless striving gives us the starting point from which to construct the alternative conception he needs.

Every drive seeks endlessly greater power by arranging more and more of the world from its own point of view. If it were able to order the entire world in this way, the gap between its perspective and the world would disappear. But this can never be done. A shortfall always remains, and with it, the impossibility of satisfying the requirement imposed by the concept of truth as correspondence. Still, one drive can achieve more power than another. It does this when it forces a competitor (and all other drives are competitors from its point of view) to live within the frame of the picture it projects. Though no drive can ever be all-powerful, different drives may therefore possess different degrees of power. Indeed, they *must,* for if every individual, at whatever level, is a hierarchically organized complex of drives, without such differences there could be no domination of the sort that Nietzsche thinks is required for such complexes to exist at all. The gradation of drives according to their relative degrees of power is therefore a condition of the being of any being whatsoever. It is a metaphysical necessity, and implies a conception of truth very different from the traditional one of truth as correspondence.

A remark that Nietzsche makes in *On the Genealogy of Morality* helps us understand why.[29]

The world before the slave revolt in morality was one of lords and underlings. Those who exercised command were the shining, clean and strong ones; their inferiors were "dark," weak, unclean and obscure. This distinction was expressed in another way as well. The masters who ruled called themselves the "truthful" ones. They considered those of low status "deceitful." To the masters "truthful" meant trustworthy—a man whose actions reveal no gap between appearance and reality, one who is what he appears to be. The lives of lesser men, who are always hiding from danger and afraid to show themselves too openly, are defined by just such a gap. They are cunning and deceptive; their motives are generally concealed from view. As a result they can never be trusted. They are essentially crooked, not straight (*orthotes*—right or true).

Implicit in this series of contrasts is the equation of truth with reality. Those who are more truthful are so because they are more real. The master stands higher than other men in the order of being. But his greater reality is not just something that enables him to be more truthful. It is truthfulness itself. It is the display of things as they really are—the absence of that gap between appearance and reality from which all error, illusion and deceit arise. The master's posture coincides with the world to a degree the slave's does not. His attitude is therefore not merely an opinion or viewpoint or value judgment that others might contest. It is the most impressive manifestation of the world as it is, and if others defer to him it is not just because he has physical force on his side but truth as well.

For the blond beasts that roam the world of Homer's poems, and the Spear-Danes that feast in the mead hall, reality equals truth and both of these are identical to power—to their command of other, weaker, less truthful human beings. But this series of equations does not hold for them alone. It continues to apply even—especially!—in the world of inverted values brought about by the triumph of Judaism and Socratism.

The Jews fight for power by reinterpreting their situation. But their fight is for reality and truth as well. The Jews want to be the ones that really matter and to demote their enemies to the role of instruments in God's plan for his chosen people. They long to be the truth of the history of the world. Socrates fights for power by means of a reinterpretation too. What the lovers of sights and sounds adore, he says, is not worthy of human concern. But his fight is also for truth and reality. He wants to save these for the kingdom of ideas. This means detaching them from the world of appearances. In fact, these are all just different ways of describing the same struggle, which aims to secure power, truth and reality at once. This is the meaning of the phrase that Nietzsche uses to describe the triumph of the attitude that Socrates' most famous pupil installed at the heart of Western philosophy: "I, Plato, am the truth."[30]

But are truth and power not distinct? Equating them implies that might is right. Is this equation even coherent? We often judge the truth to be on one side of a contest and power on the other. How could we make such judgments if power and truth were the same?

The best way to answer this question is to begin by turning the formula around.

Truth is always power, of a limited kind at least, and if its power is incomplete that is because there are competing powers with the strength to determine the direction of people's attitudes, commitments and beliefs. Consider the Christian martyrs who died in the Coliseum. They did so for the sake of the truth. They were opposed by a pagan establishment that had a different and (at the time) more powerful view of what is valuable and lasting in the world, hence of what is real or true. But the martyrs' understanding of truth eventually displaced its pagan opponent. It became *the* truth, and what had once seemed so was demoted to the status of an illusion.

Christians of course describe this as the triumph of truth over superstition, as if the truth were one thing and its victory another. But that is a partisan description. In Nietzsche's view, it is more honest and accurate to say that one system of command was unseated by another, and in the process lost the privilege it had previously enjoyed of fixing the distinction between truth and error, which now passed to its successor as the very essence of its newly acquired power. The Christian struggle of truth against power was a battle to determine where the line shall be drawn between the world as it really is, and how it wrongly appears to be in the mistaken opinion of the losers. It was a contest between competing truths and not between the truth and something else (illusion, prejudice, raw power, etc.). The latter is the victor's after-the-fact view of things, which always falsifies the situation as it appeared beforehand from the vantage point of the defeated party. One might even say (this would be Nietzsche's way of putting it) that what the parties fight for in contests of this kind is the power to make such falsifications. According to Nietzsche, this power is not a mere consequence or corollary of the truth, and hence conceptually distinguishable from it. It is the essence of truth itself. His interpretation of the will to power as art provides the metaphysical foundation for this claim.

Every drive seeks mastery through order. It aims to control its environment by compelling other drives to fit into its picture of the world. This picture is in every case one-sided; it portrays the world from the point of view of the drive that projects it. But if the picture could speak it would not say, "This is how things look to me; mine is only one perspective among a countless many; nevertheless, I demand that you accept your place within it." It would say, "This is how things really are; the world is as I see it; others see it differently, but their views are incomplete or mistaken; mine is the highest and most comprehensive—the truest—perspective; it is the truth itself; this is what I demand you accept when I order you to arrange your affairs from my point of view."

In this respect, the order that every drive projects onto the world makes a claim on its own behalf that transcends its perspectivity. To succeed in enslaving other drives, this claim must be accepted by them. A drive becomes dominant when its conception of the truth is acknowledged to be authoritative. This is the key to its success. In this sense, truth is power. It is success in compelling others to take their place in one's picture of the world, so that nothing that contradicts this picture or is opposed to it can any longer seriously claim to have truth on its side. It is the victory of one truth over another, which now falls outside the truth as something incomplete, mistaken, "opinionated" or the like.

The statement that one view is truer than another is therefore equivalent to saying that the first is more powerful. Power of this sort is not acquired by brute force—by putting a gun to the head of one's adversary and demanding that he concede that his idea of the truth is mistaken. One conception of the truth gains dominance over others by a process of "incorporation," to use Nietzsche's term. Incorporation means that competing conceptions are "taken into" the dominant one by having the error of their assumptions, judgments and arguments accounted for from the latter's point of view. An idea of the truth that is simply dismissed without being explained in this way retains its potency, in exile as it were, and can return to disrupt the view that displaced it. Only when it has been pacified by having the roots of its appeal exposed and "explained away" does it cease to be a threat and become enslaved to the picture of the world that has incorporated it. Only then are those who before accepted it compelled to acknowledge the authority of the dominant picture, though the process is rarely a simple or easy one and often takes a great deal of time.

This gives Nietzsche a measure by which to rank the comparative truthfulness of different portraits of the world without presuming that there is any absolute vantage point from which their correspondence to the world as it really is might be judged. The more that an ordering takes in the truer it is. What it takes in are other points of view. Since the world is the totality of all such points of view, a rank order among them may therefore be fixed according to how much of the world they incorporate, without assuming that there is any way to make this judgment from outside the horizon of any perspective at all, in the way the definition of truth as correspondence requires.

It follows that truth is always relative—it is the power of a view whose strength can only be measured in relation to that of others. It also follows that truth is never complete. Since every perspective is finite, its power is necessarily inadequate to incorporate the world as a whole. The possibility always remains that even the most powerful point of view will be incorporated into one with a wider reach—that a new and more comprehensive understanding of the truth will enslave and displace it. This process could come to an end only with an absolute truth that closed the gap between perspective and world, and that would require (what is metaphysically impossible) that the finitude that defines the essence of every perspective were finally overcome.

But to say that every conception of the truth is relative and that none is absolute is not the same as saying that we have no way judging among them just because each depicts the world from a point of view. This is the relativist—one might say democratic—conclusion that some wrongly assume follows from Nietzsche's claim that all such conceptions are perspectival in nature. In fact, Nietzsche's equation of truth with power leads to precisely the opposite view—to an aristocratic insistence on the rank order of truths depending on their relative power to incorporate or enslave one another.

Nietzsche defends this rank order with virulent passion. It is the key, as we shall see, to his conception of the new nobility that he claims must arise from the ruins of our leveled world, in which all values have been put on a par by the nihilism that represents the last stage of Christian belief. In tone, at least, it is hard to imagine a teaching more remote from Spinoza's philosophy. Yet the metaphysical premises from which they start are remarkably similar, for Spinoza also equates truth with power, and ranks finite beings according to their truthfulness, which in his view too is always relative and less than absolute.

In Spinoza's vocabulary, every mode has some power, but none has an infinite amount. There is always another with more. What power a mode possesses can be described as a balance of passivity and activity. To the extent that it is passive, it is determined by other things. It "belongs" to them, not to itself. Insofar as it is active, its relation to other modes is the reverse. They belong to it. They are part of its being, which when conceived under the attribute of thought means that they are understood or accounted for by it.

The more a mode takes into itself, either physically or intellectually, the more power it acquires, though some residue of passivity always remains. Viewed under the attribute of thought, this represents an increase in the truthfulness of a mode's depiction of the world as a whole. The more it is able to explain things—to "digest" them intellectually—the less the world confronts it as a brute fact. The more the mode in question may be said to represent things as they truly are, since the being of the world is nothing but reason itself. The more truth there is in or to it.

In this sense, a mode's growing power and truthfulness are just different ways of describing the same phenomenon, and though the longing to persevere in being that drives this process forward can never reach its end, it is possible to make progress toward it. The result is a hierarchy of achievements, some further along toward their shared goal than others. Those that are higher up, Spinoza says, are closer to God. They are nobler, to use Nietzsche's term. For both, the equation of truth with power, and of these with the degree of divinity or nobility a being possesses, is a metaphysical axiom.

It is against the background of this equation that we need to evaluate Nietzsche's claim that his own picture of the world is truer than that of his philosophical rivals, and consider whether this claim might be justified not despite but because of the perspectivism that on the surface appears to refute it.

One philosophical interpretation gains in power *vis-à-vis* another when it incorporates the latter into its own scheme as an explicable error or exception. This is a familiar process in the development of scientific theories. Something like it happens in theology too, when one view achieves the status of orthodoxy by successfully explaining others as heresies that attach an improper meaning to a particular dogma or doctrine.

Nietzsche's picture of the world may be thought of on this model. According to Nietzsche, every philosophy is an expression of the drive for control. It is a work of art. But its proponents do not see this, or at least they do not acknowledge it. They claim for their philosophy the absolute privilege of truth. In this respect, however, they remain blind to a greater truth, namely, that their account of the world depicts it from a point of view. Nietzsche's own philosophy is founded on the recognition of the perspectivity of all such accounts, and therefore expresses a higher-order truth that other philosophies not only fail to see but deliberately (though often unconsciously) suppress.

More important, Nietzsche's concept of will to power is able to explain this blindness in other philosophies as an optical illusion that is rooted in the perspectival striving for domination itself, and thereby to incorporate their own shortsightedness into a more encompassing picture of the world with greater explanatory power. If it is objected that Nietzsche's account is just another perspective too, instead of weakening the authority of his account, the objection strengthens it by demonstrating that it is impossible to construct a wider picture of the world into which his may be fit.

In this sense, Nietzsche's metaphysics has a reach no other can match. It has a boundless power to digest all other points of view by characterizing their pretensions to truth as the necessarily one-sided expressions of finite and competing drives. *This* truth—Nietzsche's truth—is one whose power can in principle never be surpassed, and any attempt to do so by arguing that it suffers from the same partiality as every other point of view confirms rather than undermines it. Nietzsche's metaphysics is a work of art that no other can enframe and thereby put in its place. It is a painting without borders.

Of course, if Nietzsche merely said that every philosophy is an expression of the drive for control and left it at that, this all-embracing truth might seem rather thin. But he is far more interested in the application of this idea to specific cases than in its abstract restatement and defense. Nietzsche's primary concern is to show how particular conceptions of truth—Plato's, Paul's, Descartes', Kant's, Mill's—are pictures of the world that aim to bring it under greater control. His writings mostly consist of a brilliant series of such interpretations, and it is these that give substance and credibility to the abstract claim that every philosophical account of the truth is an attempt to master the world from a finite and interested point of view. This idea comes alive in Nietzsche's historical and psychological sketches. These are themselves great works of art that give color to his borderless canvas and make it something more than a blank sheet.

Nietzsche's sketches consistently display his uncanny ability to place himself inside an attitude or system of belief—to grasp its motives with an immediacy that only those who share them generally can—while simultaneously holding these same motives at arm's length as he dissects their genealogy with clinical sangfroid. It is extremely difficult to do both things at once, to see the values and ideas of others from the inside and the outside in this way, for it requires a nearly contradictory combination of passion and dispassion. It is easier either to embrace them uncritically, as if they were the truth itself, or to dismiss them out of hand, as errors or illusions, with no appreciation for the pathos that lies behind their creation as works of art. The third attitude, which Nietzsche adopts, is harder by far, yet alone points the way to a richer understanding of the truth as he conceives it. He calls it the path of "honesty."[31] It might be described as a form of connoisseurship whose aim is the inward appreciation of as many diverse points of view as possible in a spirit that is hostage to none.

Nietzsche repeatedly says that his own goal is to be as honest as he can—to go as far in understanding the world as a connoisseur of this sort might if his powers of sympathy and insight were boundless. He also says (what amounts to the same thing) that his aim is to see how much truth he can stand.[32] Every triumph of connoisseurship—of honesty in Nietzsche's sense—adds a bit of local color to his picture of the world and therefore further validates the abstract claim that his portrait is the most truthful one imaginable, because it possesses the power to digest all the rival ones that other philosophers have drawn. Nietzsche's picture has no borders and can therefore never be complete. But every genealogical sketch adds to its truth, which remains a standard by which different works may be judged and placed in a rank order of excellence, despite the collapse of the correspondence theory of truth into a perspectivism that rules out the possibility of ever establishing the correspondence this theory requires.

WORLD

For Plato, Augustine and Kant the true world is one that exists apart from the realm of appearance and change. Nietzsche denies this emphatically. There is, he says, no sphere of intelligible forms or blessed saints or things in themselves separate from that of motion and time. In this sense he is a monist, not a dualist.

This brings his idea of the world closer to that of Aristotle. Like Nietzsche, Aristotle views the world as an all-embracing whole with neither a beginning nor end in time. But not every aspect of Aristotle's cosmos shares in its eternal reality. Certain features of it belong to the realm of becoming, not being. The individuality of every individual and the movement of every motion, as distinct from the form that defines the first and guides the second, must be placed on this side of the ledger. To this extent, Aristotle's metaphysics is shaped by the same dualist distinction that defines Plato's as well. Nietzsche's metaphysics represents a more radical form of monism, for it wholly annuls the distinction between being and becoming and treats it as a necessary illusion. According to Nietzsche, one may just as well say that the world is nothing but being and nothing but becoming since these are in reality one and the same, contrary to what every philosopher and theologian since Plato has taught.

Nietzsche's radical monism has no antecedent in Western philosophy other than Spinoza's. Like Spinoza's, it follows from his identification of eternity and time—from the claim that every moment in time can and must be viewed *sub specie aeternitatis.* Nietzsche asserts this most directly in his famous statement of the doctrine of eternal return. This is the cornerstone of his metaphysical picture of the world. It is the deepest expression of his born-again paganism and the most important point of contact between Nietzsche's philosophy and Spinoza's. I shall return to it in a moment. But first we ought to note two other ways in which their views of the world are alike.

According to Nietzsche, the world is a totality of drives, all seeking to extend their range of control. Each does this by striving to put the world into order. The process of ordering is one of gathering parts into a whole. But first the parts must be marked off or defined, and this requires that distinctions be made: "here is one thing, there another." One particularly forceful expression of this is the idea of "the sovereign individual" who stands apart from other things and passes judgment on them by an independent act of will.[33]

But the existence of separate individuals, including this supremely independent one, is an artistic illusion. In reality, the world is the only individual that truly exists. It is a "continuum"[34] with no real parts, and the different drives that belong to it are merely—to borrow Spinoza's term—modes of the one and only individual that possesses—to borrow another—any substantial being of its own. They are aspects or expressions of a single individual and therefore interconnected, so that a change in any one of them entails a change in every other.

As the power of one grows, that of all the others must therefore diminish. This is so not merely because they are competing for external resources. They are also internally yoked by their conflicting ambitions. Each is striving to reduce every other to order—to determine its place in its own self-aggrandizing portrait of the world. The repercussions of even the smallest success are thus bound to be felt, *in pianissimo,* throughout the world as a whole. In this sense, the competition among drives is a vast, artistic zero-sum game—a constantly shifting rearrangement of priorities among the countless moods or attitudes that a single individual can assume, comparable, one might say, to the shifting expressions on what Spinoza calls the "face of the universe."[35]

Nietzsche is therefore not only a monist for whom there is only one world, but a holist, who believes that each part of the world is connected to every other. Nothing in the world is in reality separate from anything else. Each of its seemingly separate components is just a local upsurge or decline in a single hydraulic system, whose total pressure, rising here and falling there, remains forever the same. The closest analogue is Spinoza's conception of modes as transient expressions of the one being whose ratio of motion and rest never changes. To the question of how many individuals *really* exist, Nietzsche's answer is therefore the same as Spinoza's. There is only one real individual and that is the world as a whole. Everything else that appears to be an individual is merely a feature of this one, dynamically linked to every other but lacking the kind of freestanding existence that for both philosophers is the mark of individuality in the only true sense.

This last judgment rests on the assumption that whatever is finite must have its being "in" another, infinite one and thus cannot be an individual in its own right. Spinoza makes this assumption explicitly. It is for him a fundamental metaphysical principle. Nietzsche is less explicit, but his holistic monism requires some such assumption as well. Yet if the idea that finite beings can only be conceived as aspects or modes of an infinite one answers the question of how many individuals really exist, it raises another. Why are there finite modes or drives at all? Why isn't the face of the world a blank sheet instead of the diverse and mobile spectacle it is? This question remains even if all the seemingly independent individuals *in* the world are conceived to be facets *of* it, and the world itself judged to be the only individual that truly exists.

We have encountered a version of this question before and it may be enough to recall what was said then.

The most promising answer is one that combines a version of the principle of plenitude with the claim that the principle of sufficient reason compels it. The latter asserts that for each thing there is a reason why it is what it is and not something else. Its application therefore assumes the existence of beings that are distinct and hence finite. But no reason can be given for limiting the number of such beings in a way that leaves a blank space in the world that might otherwise be filled—and in particular for leaving the whole world blank, since then the assumption on which the possibility of asking for such a reason depends would itself (by assumption!) be denied. The principle of sufficient reason can therefore only be coherently stated if finite beings exist, and once their existence is granted this principle itself provides a justification of a negative kind for the conclusion that there must be as many such beings as possible. If it is objected that the principle is not self-evident but requires a justification of its own, a good reply is that this objection employs the very principle it seeks to unseat by assuming that there must be a reason why the principle is either binding or not.

This argument leaves much to be desired. It would have to be considerably filled out to be persuasive or perhaps even plausible. Yet some argument along these lines seems required to connect the idea that the world is one in-dividual to the claim that its manifestations are necessarily diverse, let alone as diverse as possible. Spinoza comes closer than Nietzsche to providing an argument of this sort. But the fact that Nietzsche's holistic solution to the problem of individuation makes the need for one clear, underscores how sim-ilar their metaphysics are in this respect.

They are similar in another way too, for both insist that everything that happens in the world does so of necessity. For Spinoza, this follows from a commitment to reason itself. This commitment cannot be halfhearted. It is an all-or-nothing affair. It leaves no room for the idea that any event in the world, or the existence of the world as a whole, could be other than it is, for then it would be inexplicable in principle, as opposed to being merely unex-plained, given our current state of knowledge. Nietzsche's view is not far off. He repeatedly insists that everything is fated to happen just as it does.[36] He even makes the acceptance of this idea a test of sorts for determining how much truth one can stand. He calls it the doctrine of *amor fati*.[37]

There is of course a Christian analogue to this idea. On Augustine's view, and Luther's too, a Christian ought to love the world not despite but because everything that happens in it has been predestined by God. It is a sign of pride to wish or even think that we possess the power to cause things to be other than they are. Nietzsche's doctrine of *amor fati* teaches that even the smallest event in the world is ruled by an iron necessity too, though one that has its foundation in the world itself and not a God beyond it. It may therefore be thought of as a version of the Christian doctrine of predestination without the Christian God.

The worldly necessitarianism of Nietzsche's doctrine is a consequence of his rejection of every idea of the will, human or divine. The will, he says, is just a word we give to states of increasing power in ourselves and others. In reality, these are always the completely determined result of prior states, and thus have their origin and explanation in something other than themselves. Their existence is by its very nature heteronomous. The idea of an autono-mous human power of self-determination is in fact wholly unintelligible, as is the idea of divine creation from which it derives. Whether we assign it to man or God, the existence of such a power is a fiction—a helpful (because power-enhancing) summary of a whole series of prior states whose relation to one another we do not fully grasp. But no such power exists, and therefore nothing that happens in the world is truly "contingent" (another term that merely describes our ignorance of causes). Nor can the world as a whole be said to be contingent either, since such a claim only makes sense only on the assumption that it was brought into being from nothing by a creator who might have chosen to make a different world for no reason at all. The idea of a causal lacuna between events in the world, or between the possibility of the world and its actual existence, that must be filled up with a creative agency that by definition cannot be understood or even described, is an idea that Nietzsche dismisses with the same contemptuousness that Spinoza ridicules the childish belief in a providential God that guides human affairs.

At any given moment, Nietzsche says, the world as a whole is an immense complex of reciprocal expansions and contractions, the power of some drives increasing as that of others declines, so that it is impossible to give an adequate account of even the smallest feature of the world in isolation from the entire system of relations in which it is enmeshed. This is how the world looks if we take an instantaneous snapshot of it. If we view it diachronically, as a succession of such moments, we see that each is determined down to its smallest details with an equally rigid necessity by those that went before. The career of the world could not be other than it is, whether because of God's unfathomable freedom or a cosmic accident of some kind. The result is a necessitarianism as thoroughgoing as Spinoza's. Only those who have the strength to affirm it, Nietzsche insists, will ever know the joy of the Dionysian metaphysics he offers as an antidote to the illusory freedom taught by the religion of the God on the cross and its secular descendants.

To Nietzsche's picture of the world as a single individual with numberless manifestations, each in constant motion and linked to all the rest by a necessity that rules their actions and reactions so completely that none could possibly be other than it is, we must now add one more feature. It is the most important of all.

According to Nietzsche the world is eternal, not merely in certain respects as Aristotle believed, but exhaustively so.[38] Its eternality extends to everything in it, including the individuality of individual beings (of those temporary constellations of drives that give the appearance, for a time, of having a substantive reality of their own). This is the heart of Nietzsche's solution to the ancient problem of the relation of being to becoming. The key to understanding it is his doctrine of eternal return. Nietzsche calls this his "highest" idea.[39] It is also the most obscure.

The idea of eternity is as old as philosophy itself. But every philosopher before him, Nietzsche says, has used it to demote the prestige of time and becoming. On the one side they place eternity. It is necessary and unchanging. It alone deserves to be called real. On the other they put motion and change and the realm of time in which these occur. These lack the necessity and reality of the eternal. In truth, they *are not*. Parmenides gives the first and most forceful statement of this view, and with it sets the agenda for Western philosophy.

The question that Parmenides bequeaths to his successors is how motion, change and time can have any reality of all, even if it is deficient by comparison with that of the everlasting and divine. Plato's theory of the one and the many, and of the relation of participation that connects them, is his attempt to answer this question without departing from the Parmenidean premise that only the eternal is perfectly real.

Aristotle is a Parmenidean too. He takes the distinction between being and becoming for granted, and assigns complete reality to the first alone. Guided by this distinction, he seeks to make the phenomenon of natural movement intelligible. For Aristotle, as for Plato, this means finding what is eternal in it. The key terms in Aristotle's solution to the Parmenidean challenge are potency, movement and activity (*dunamis, kinesis* and *energeia*). In Aristotle's view, movement is intelligible but only because of the presence in it of something that never moves. Its reality is entirely dependent on the motionless forms that guide and shape it; in itself, movement is nothing. Like Plato, Aristotle concedes (what Parmenides does not) that becoming has some kind of reality and is intelligible to a limited degree. But for him too it is a reality of a derivative sort that depends on the relation of becoming to being, which he continues to identify with what is beyond time and change.

Christianity carries this assumption forward in an altered form. The God who creates the world is eternal but the world itself is not. It has a history and becomes. By insisting that the whole world has a temporal career of its own, Christian metaphysics widens the realm of becoming as Aristotle conceived it, but saves it from nothingness in the same way that he did—by relating it to what does not become but is timeless and therefore supremely real. On this view, becoming still stands condemned of unreality, as it had been in the great systems of pagan philosophy, and once the God who created the world, which has now been suffused with becoming to an unprecedented degree, ceases to be a credible guarantor of its derivative being, the result is a world *wholly* stripped of reality—the universal nothingness that is the inevitable result of continuing to believe that only such a now-discredited God could give the world an anchor in eternity. Nietzsche calls this nihilism. It is the very opposite of Parmenides' philosophy, which denies that nothingness is anything real at all. But it shares with its opposite the belief that the world is real only insofar as it is eternal or related to something eternal beyond it—a requirement the nihilist accepts, while denying that there is anything in or outside the world that can fulfill it.

It is against this background that Nietzsche's idea of eternal return should be interpreted. He presents it in the form of a parable. Its first statement appears at the very end of the first edition of *The Gay Science* (1882), a year before the publication of the first two parts of *Thus Spoke Zarathustra*.[40] Nietzsche calls his parable "the heaviest weight."

Suppose, he says, "a demon were to steal into your loneliest loneliness and say to you: 'This life as now you live it and have lived it you will have to live once again and innumerable times again; and there will be nothing new in it, but every pain and every joy and every thought and sigh and everything unspeakably small or great in your life must return to you, all in the same succession and sequence—even this spider and this moonlight between the trees, and even this moment and I myself.'"

The demon's supposition is a test. How one responds to it reveals the deepest and least-acknowledged premise of one's view of the world and place within it. For many, the demon's thought experiment will be unbearable. They will "gnash" their teeth and "curse" him. There is so much in life that is trivially, ridiculously, "unspeakably" small. It is enough that these things happen once, and disappear. That they should happen again and again in an endless wheel is a thought that makes one dizzy, even nauseous. Who wouldn't prefer, under these circumstances, to escape the wheel altogether, as the Buddhist sages sought to do in one way and the modern European nihilist does in another, by denying that the absurd happenings to which human beings attach so much importance have any connection to eternity at all—let alone are suffused with it, down to their smallest details?

But for a few, Nietzsche says, who are "well disposed" toward life and themselves, the demon's teaching will not be a crushing burden but a liberation instead. For them it will be what he calls an "ultimate eternal confirmation and seal" and a source of immeasurable joy. These few are the noble ones whose greatness of soul sets them apart from the countless mediocrities who live suspended between the narcotized forgetfulness of small comforts and a nihilistic rejection of the world whose ceaseless, pointless movements have no meaning or value since there is nothing in them that is immune to the ravages of time. But however few they are, Nietzsche insists, the future of humanity belongs to them to shape, and one day the joyful metaphysics of the eternal return, which holds the key to their liberation, will supplant the nihilism that stalks the modern world as the still unburied ghost of Christian belief.

But what exactly is this metaphysics? It is easiest to say what it is not. It is not Plato's, which rests on the distinction between being and becoming—between this world of change and a changeless heaven of ideas. Nor is it Aristotle's, which restores eternity to the world but excludes the individuality of things and ultimately, in the deepest sense, their movements too, from any share in it. Nor, even more obviously, is it a Christian metaphysics that saves becoming by placing its ground in an eternal God wholly separate from the world he creates. Nor, finally, is it a form of nihilism that asserts there is nothing that has the power to redeem becoming in the way that Plato, Aristotle and Augustine all sought to do—a philosophy defined by its rejection of every conception of eternity, whose characteristic mood wavers between superficial cheerfulness and despair.

The metaphysics of the doctrine of eternal return differs from all these. To begin with, it affirms the *identity* of being and becoming without denying the reality of either. Eternity is real and so are time and movement—contrary to what Parmenides and the modern nihilists who invert his metaphysics maintain. Moreover, each is just as real as the other. Being and becoming are *equally* and therefore both *completely* real, that is, coextensive with all that is—a view opposed to Plato's teaching that what becomes has only a defective reality by comparison with that of the ideas.

But perhaps the most striking implication of the doctrine of eternal return is its insistence that the identity of being and becoming extends to the least of things—to the smallest and most evanescent features of the world, which have nothing of the grandeur of eternity in them. If I am to take the doctrine seriously, Nietzsche says, I must accept that even the least consequential and most fleeting episodes in my life and not just its greatest moments, return endlessly—that the spider in the moonlight, which belongs to the unnoticed background of things, is invested with the same eternal being as everything else.

The doctrine of eternal return endows the transience of the world with the dignity of the everlasting not, as Aristotle's metaphysics does, by separating individuality and movement into two components, the formal and material, and then by ascribing eternity to the unmoving forms of things alone. On the contrary, Nietzsche's doctrine locates the eternity of the world in movement and particularity themselves, so that the distinction, which

Aristotle took for granted, between being and becoming is erased and the whole world covered with the veil of divinity, which now extends to the individuality of individuals and hence to their "temporality"—another word for the uniqueness of every finite being.

When Nietzsche says that his aim is to "restore the innocence of becoming" and thereby to "redivinize" the world, this is what he means. The restoration he has in mind is not a return to Aristotle's cosmos, whose divinity was inherent but incomplete. It is the affirmation of a world in which eternity is present throughout, down to its seemingly least lasting details—in which, as the Gospelist says, the "last" shall be "first," though without the idea of a creator God that first made it necessary to assume that the individuality of things is connected with eternity too (a metaphysical conclusion most strikingly expressed by the doctrine of personal immortality).

According to Aristotle, motion is change—the movement from one state to another. It is therefore defined by a difference between its points of departure and arrival, and hence by disappearance or nonbeing. Where or what a thing was to begin with is left behind in the course of its movement. It ceases to be a property of the thing, and is replaced by another, defined by the place or state at which it arrives.

But if movement—and time, which Aristotle defines as the form of motion—is a process whose essence is one of disappearance, where should we look for something eternal in it? In one sense, the answer is obvious. Every motion follows a law of some kind. This is equally true of the kind of movement that takes place when a stone thrown in the air falls to the ground, and the sort that occurs when a kitten grows into a cat. The law that the movement in question follows remains the same throughout. It is the changelessness in change, the being in becoming that alone enables us to understand anything at all about the movement with our minds.

Is there, though, a form of change that itself mimics or exemplifies the changelessness of the law that renders it intelligible—a moving image, to borrow Plato's expression, of being in the realm of becoming? To this question, Aristotle and Plato both give the same answer. The only kind of movement that mimics the motionlessness of being is the sort that goes around in a circle, thereby restoring permanence and presence to a process of becoming that is marked by difference and disappearance if we look only at a linear segment of it. Circular motion alone is capable of exhibiting the eternity of being in the realm of becoming, as a form of change or movement itself rather than something separate from it, like the laws we "abstract" from motion and use to explain it. Aristotle and Plato concur in this view, and Nietzsche joins them as well. He does so, however, with a crucial modification that reflects the distance between their pagan metaphysics and his born-again version of it.

Consider, for example, Aristotle's account of the circular life of an animal species. Individual members are born, reproduce and die; then others like them take their place. In this way, the life of the species goes around forever in an eternal wheel. The circularity of the reproductive process is a moving image of eternity, in which each individual participates by making another like itself. But it is only as a member of its kind—as a being with a certain form—that it does so. Its individuality is lost or consumed in the process. The form of the species returns with every new generation, but the matter that makes one individual "numerically" distinct from another is, as it were, "boiled off" in the movement from parent to child, whose individual identities last only as long as their lives, and disappear when they do, never to return. In Aristotle's metaphysics, the individuality of plants and animals, including men, is thus excluded from participation in the circular motion that directly displays the eternality of being in the realm of becoming and hence from reality itself. (Fame, which disappears, and wisdom, which is impersonal, confirm rather than contradict this conclusion. Only the heavenly bodies might be regarded as an exception to it.)

By contrast, the endless circle that Nietzsche imagines includes the individuality of beings within it. Their uniqueness is not vaporized in the process of becoming, but preserved forever. Indeed, this is Nietzsche's main point. The very thing that Aristotle's metaphysics excludes from a share in the eternal wheel of being now belongs to it too; along with everything else in the world, the quickly vanishing identities of individual human beings return again and again in a circular movement that imbues their temporality with a permanence that Aristotle reserved for the forms of things. In this sense, Nietzsche's doctrine of eternal return might be described as the Christian idea of personal immortality brought down to earth. Like the latter, it asserts that individuals live forever, as individuals, but unlike it maintains that their eternal life is not in a heaven beyond the world, where they shall at last be free from corruption and change, but in the realm of mortality itself, and thus forever subject to the limits of time and death, from which Nietzsche's radical fusion of being and becoming allows no escape.

For Platonists, Aristotelians, Christians and Buddhists this is an intolerable idea—the "heaviest weight." They all look for an escape from these limits. The nihilist relieves himself in a different way, by insisting that there is nothing to which one might escape. In contrast to all these, the eternal circle that Nietzsche envisions invites us to affirm the transience and particularity of things—including, especially, that of our own lives—with a seriousness that is possible only if we give up the belief that there is something eternal beyond the world that we can reach by means of contemplation or prayer, *and simultaneously* view all that becomes, changes and dies as completely suffused with the timelessness of being.

In Aristotle's metaphysics, it is still possible to distinguish between being and becoming in the eternal circle of worldly motion. Being is what endures in the movement of things; becoming is what passes away. Nietzsche's doctrine of eternal return obliterates this distinction. Nothing in any movement ever passes away. Everything about it returns, exactly and endlessly, just as it was before. But how then are we to understand the distinction between being and becoming, if Nietzsche's metaphysics joins them so completely that every aspect of every event in the world is both at once?

On the traditional view of it, this distinction now no longer makes sense. That is because being has always been defined as what becoming is not, and vice versa. Nietzsche's fusion of the two is therefore not an intervention in the age-old debate that Parmenides bequeathed to his successors about the proper way of understanding the difference between them. It is not an attempt to say what the first is by contrast with the second. It is an effort to step outside this debate altogether. The doctrine of eternal return denies the premise on which the debate has proceeded and thereby renders it moot.

But if Nietzsche's doctrine erases the metaphysical distinction between being and becoming, he still treats them as if they were two different things. His writings consist mostly of genealogical reflections on the origin of various beliefs and their modification over time—of what moves and changes, as opposed to remaining the same. Even if there is no metaphysical difference between being and becoming, Nietzsche's historical analyses proceed as if there were. This requires an explanation of some kind.

His idea of perspective provides one. Seen from a perspective, the world always appears to be a wilderness of movement and change. To gain even the smallest degree of control over it, we have to stabilize its movements by projecting into or beyond them some fixed point of reference. In this way, a distinction arises between being and becoming. But this distinction is an artifact of perspectivity itself. It is what we might call a necessary illusion. If we could see the world from outside the limits that are inherent in every point of view, we would understand both the necessity and unreality of this distinction.

The inescapable finitude of our projective encounter with the world makes this impossible. The notion of a perspectiveless comprehension of things is therefore bound to remain a thought experiment. The doctrine of eternal return, which teaches the identity of being and becoming, is an experiment of this kind. We can never be wholly successful in entertaining it, but the struggle to do so serves as a constant reminder that the distinction between being and becoming is only an artistic device that our finitude compels us to employ in our endless campaign to master the world. Were this campaign to reach its goal, we would no longer require the distinction. But then we would be the world itself, and not a view upon it. This is an unattainable objective. Still, we can make progress toward it, and our (always limited) capacity to do without the distinction between being and becoming, as Nietzsche's doctrine encourages us to do, is a measure of how powerful we have become—of what he calls our "quantum" of being.[41]

Here too, Nietzsche's position is close to Spinoza's. Every mode, Spinoza says, is an unstable ratio of motion and rest. It is constantly moving and must eventually disappear. Its essence as a mode is that of becoming, not being. Yet every mode is *in* substance, whose essence is the timeless intelligibility of the world and all it contains. This means that every mode is perfectly intelligible too, and would be fully understood if the infinite web of relations in which it exists could be comprehended all at once (which no finite mind can do). It follows that every mode is as timeless as the world as a whole because it belongs to or is part of or is conceptually derivable from (is "in") the world, whose being is to be intelligible, and because every bit of genuine understanding conceives its object *sub specie aeternitatis.*

In Spinoza's metaphysics, the distinction between being and becoming is therefore not a real one either, any more than it is in Nietzsche's, but an illusion inseparable from the modal nature of every finite being. Spinoza's theology helps us think our way beyond this distinction, but only by means of an ideal conception of truth—the truth as we would know it if we saw everything under the aspect of eternity. This is something we could do only in case everything were *in* us, that is, only if we were the God of the world, and not a mere mode of it. In this respect, Spinoza's austere proofs arrive at the same conclusion as Nietzsche's poetic parable of the eternal return, whose central teaching, like that of Spinoza's *Ethics,* is that even the most infinitesimal scrap of becoming is suffused with the eternality of being.

One last similarity is worth noting.

For both Nietzsche and Spinoza, the identification of being and becoming means that the world as a whole cannot be judged either good or beautiful. Any judgment of this sort presupposes a vantage point beyond the world from which it might be found either satisfactory or wanting. Because no such vantage point exists, no judgment of this kind is possible. That the world is eternal, down to its smallest details, is just the way things are. It is a fact and not a value. In particular, it is a fact that cannot be converted to a value by imagining that the world has some point or purpose toward whose fulfillment it is directed. Spinoza insists that no view of this sort is even intelligible, and Nietzsche's attack on those he calls the "teachers of the purpose of existence" expresses a similar thought.

Spinoza and Nietzsche therefore agree that the world as a whole has no goal. But they also agree that finite beings do, indeed, are essentially goal-directed. Every being of this sort is a locus of striving that Spinoza calls *conatus* and Nietzsche the will to power. This striving always has the same unattainable end. It always seeks an increase of power, and thus could come to rest only with the mastery of the world as a whole. Human beings are no different in this respect. They desire ever greater power too, and in their pursuit of this goal construct ethical and aesthetic ideals, which they project onto the world, calling it "good" and "beautiful" and claiming that these give the world a purpose or point. All such judgments are therefore paradoxical in a way, for should any of them be vindicated, its triumph would not mean that it had finally established the truth of its claim to have discovered the point of existence, but transcended the perspectival limits that alone give such claims their intelligibility in the first place, and become the world itself, whose being is eternal and pointless.

To those who insist that the world must have a point to be meaningful and therefore bearable, this conclusion will seem more than a paradox. It will be a cause for despair. To relieve their unhappiness, they may attempt to resurrect one or another of those otherworldly ideals that in the past gave the world purpose and value. But if they are unable to do this because all such ideals have been revealed to be mere human projections, and yet continue to insist that existence would be bearable only in case such an ideal could be found, their situation is bound to be one of irremediable anguish, which they may accept with a kind of stoic resolve, as Weber did, but can never overcome. Nietzsche's metaphysics is intended to provide a way out of this nihilistic impasse, though not, of course, by inventing yet another God beyond the world with the power to redeem it.

Nietzsche insists that no finite drive can ever express the world except from a point of view. But he also maintains that some do this more powerfully than others. Some perspectives include more of the world in themselves. They are further along toward the unreachable goal that all drives share of mastering the world as a whole. In this sense, they are more real than their competitors, and more truthful, though like all drives, incompletely so.

Many who achieve such a position of relative dominance attribute their power to the goodness or beauty of their picture of the world. But so long as they imagine that the world can be judged according to some standard they project, the world as they conceive it falls short of the world as it truly is (is less inclusive on account of postulating something other than the world by which its worth may be measured). To hold onto this illusion is a species of powerlessness because it confines the one whose illusion it is within the limits of his perspectival and self-serving view of the world.

The nihilist who claims to have seen through all such illusions but has not given up his belief that the worth of the world could only be measured in terms of some standard of this kind is still hostage to what might be called their illusory logic. To achieve the maximum of power that it is possible for a human being to attain—greater than that of those who claim to have a standard by which to judge the world, and greater even than that of the nihilist who mocks such claims but still adheres to their logic—one must attempt to hold onto the following two ideas: first, that the world is eternal and pointless, and second, that everything that happens in it, however purposeful it seems from a finite point of view, is endowed with the same eternality as the world as a whole, which has no purpose at all. Those with the strength to sustain these thoughts neither affirm the value of the world from a point of view beyond it, nor despair because no such point of view exists, but strive instead to see the eternality of its self-contained and pointless being in the spectacle of becoming instead. They come as close as any finite being can to closing the gap that always remains between themselves and the world.

No one can do this continuously. We are always being drawn back into our perspectives, from whose vantage point it is impossible to escape the temptation to judge the world on the basis of our portrait of it. But the man or woman who goes farthest toward accepting the pointlessness of the world and the eternality of everything in it becomes the strongest and truest human being he or she can—stronger and truer by far than the nihilist who is still tethered to the distinction between being and becoming, even as he insists that the first has no meaning at all.

Nietzsche's doctrine of eternal return is an exercise for developing such strength. It is a gymnastic for the soul, and those who use it properly have a greater chance of being able to do what the nihilist cannot: of saying "yes" to the identity of being and becoming in all things large and small, and of accepting the world as it is, rather than praising or condemning it, while continuing to strive, as all finite beings must, to extend their power by insisting that the world be seen and judged from a certain point of view.[42] Those who can sustain this attitude, even for the briefest time, are to that extent freed from nihilistic despair. They experience what Nietzsche calls "joy"—the highest prize of his "gay" science.[43] Their god is not the "crucified one," whose sacrifice and never-to-be-repeated return from the dead stands for the view that the world is passing away and must be judged from an eternal standpoint beyond it, but Dionysus, the god of tragedy and comedy, who is destroyed and returns each year in a ceremony that reminds its participants of the all-encompassing and self-sustaining circle of existence, in which they and everything else go round and round forever, with a motion no less real but no more purposeful than the eternality of the world as a whole.

MODERNITY

I have stressed the similarities between Nietzsche's metaphysics and Spinoza's. But in one respect their views seem fundamentally opposed. I am thinking of their differing attitudes toward modern values.

Spinoza is a champion of the modern science of nature and the liberal ideal of toleration, which he defends with energy in his *Theological-Political Treatise*. He is entirely at home in the modern world and welcomes the growing authority of its scientific and political practices. Nietzsche, by contrast, often writes as an enemy of modernity. He loathes the very things that Spinoza reveres—the triumph of scientific thought, the amelioration of human suffering that science makes possible, the spread of liberal democracy with its commitment to the equal worth of human beings, and everything else that we generally include under the idea of modern enlightenment.

More fundamentally, Nietzsche regards our age as one of transition—as a period that both concludes and points ahead. For millennia, Nietzsche says, God was a living presence in the lives of men. Today he is dead and nihilism reigns. But nihilism itself shall be surpassed. To Nietzsche, the modern world is a bridge between epochs. It is in its essence an in-between age, and he himself a prophet of the world to come who writes for readers not yet born.[44] There is nothing like this in Spinoza.

Yet the difference between them is perhaps less extreme than it seems. Like Nietzsche, Spinoza also regards his situation as one marked by an incomplete detachment from Christian belief. The Christian idea of God has prepared the way for the new science of nature that Spinoza endorses, but remains an obstacle to its further development. It has laid the ground for the political ideal of toleration, but hampers its extension by limiting the freedom to speak and teach to views broadly compatible with Christian doctrine.[45] In both respects, Spinoza sees his age as a transitional one too, suspended between orthodoxy and reason. He is cautious about the prospects of persuading most people to abandon their belief in a providential God who takes an interest in human affairs. But he hopes that the influence of this belief will gradually weaken, and equates the power of the few who in a tolerant regime will be permitted to study the truth in quiet, with the joyful embrace of the wholly un-Christian god sketched in the first part of the *Ethics*. Both Nietzsche and Spinoza view the lingering effects of the Christian religion as an obstacle to the advancement of their born-again paganism, whether this takes the form of an esoteric wisdom philosophy cultivated by a small number of virtuosi, or the starting point for the reorganization of all human life on earth, as Nietzsche sometimes grandly suggests.

Still, Nietzsche's interpretation of the modern world has one striking feature that Spinoza's entirely lacks. This is his account of why the Christian religion and the nihilist metaphysics that represents its final, half-decayed product, necessarily devalue themselves. According to Nietzsche, Christianity collapses not because of external forces but on account of the efforts of its followers to be faithful to their own deepest beliefs. Among the great religions of the world, Christianity is unique in this respect, and the same dialectical self-destructiveness that sets its theology apart from that of other religions also undermines the nihilism to which it gives rise.

There is nothing comparable in Spinoza's philosophy. Spinoza simply assumes that most people will always be hostage to superstition, which in the West means Christian belief. He regards this as a permanent liability of the human condition. Nietzsche, by contrast, gives us reasons to think that Christianity and the nihilism it produces must break down under the weight of their own ideals and yield to a Dionysian metaphysics that after millennia of devaluing the world, affirms its divinity instead.[46] In this respect, though perhaps only in this, Nietzsche's analysis of modernity is even more rational than Spinoza's, for it ascribes the attenuation of Christian belief and the emergence of a new "sacred yes-saying" to something other than chance and the goodwill of human beings.

Nietzsche's explanation of the self-destructiveness of the Christian religion begins with its founder, Paul of Tarsus.

Paul defines Christianity as a creedal religion. To be a follower of Jesus means, in Paul's view, to hold certain beliefs—to subscribe to a creed. This not only set Paul apart from Jesus but from his Jewish peers, who placed the emphasis not on what one believes (the fundamental statement of Jewish belief is brief and exceedingly broad) but on practice instead—on obedience to the law, as this had first been specified in the Torah and then elaborated by the temple priests into a comprehensive set of requirements for living.

Paul's creedal orientation made it supremely important for the members of the earliest Christian communities to settle the question of what, in fact, one must believe in order to be saved. This gave rise to many controversies that were not easily or quickly resolved. The history of the early church, in both the East and West, was one of continuing doctrinal disputes, whose aim was to settle in an authoritative way the question of which beliefs about God, Jesus and the world are true and which are false.

But this meant that Christianity was committed from the start to the ideal of truthfulness in a way that Judaism is not. The question of whether one is a Jew is settled, according to the law, by descent and behavior. The question of whether one is a Christian turns on what one believes—more specifically, on whether what one believes is true, for if it is false, then one is a heretic and not, as we say, a *true* believer. (Islam also differs from Christianity in this respect. It is true that Islam has a creedal core, but its defining beliefs, like those of Judaism, are few and simply stated. Here too, the emphasis is on the lawfulness of one's conduct.[47] Among the reasons why Islam and Judaism never became creedal religions to the degree that Christianity did, is the mystery of the Incarnation, which stands as a special challenge to reason and thus serves as a permanent stimulus to clarifying which beliefs about this most incomprehensible of all events are true and which are not.)

The demand for truthfulness that distinguishes Christianity from the other Abrahamic religions is part of the meaning of Nietzsche's famous remark that Christianity is "Platonism for the people." This same demand is the defining characteristic of Plato's philosophy too. In Plato's case, however, there is no tension between this demand and its object. This is because, according to Plato, there is a necessary alignment between our minds, which long to discover the truth, and the truth itself. But this alignment is disrupted if one assumes that the object of our truth-seeking by its very nature lies beyond the range of truth and error, so that any attempt to grasp it is bound to fail.

This assumption is foreign to the spirit of Platonism and of ancient philosophy in general. But it is the fundamental premise of the Christian religion. Christianity locates the divinity of God not in his reasonableness but in the freedom of his will. If God's will were intelligible, it would no longer be what it is. It is therefore impossible to form any true beliefs about God's essence or being, as Christians understand this.

Coupled with the demand for creedal clarity, the conception of God as an omnipotent creator thus places the would-be true believer in a predicament, which can be postponed but not resolved by maintaining that the only true belief about God is that he is inconceivably remote from the world. Each time the demand for clarification is renewed, intellectual honesty demands that God be put at an even greater distance from those who want above all to know which beliefs about him are true. The end result is a God about whom nothing can be known or said—one that is "dead" for all practical and theoretical purposes.

But the demand outlives its disappointment. The true believers for whom God no longer exists continue to insist that only the truth about him, which has now become as empty as the idea of God himself, could save them and the world from the spiritual desolation that the death of God leaves behind. Their conflicted condition is the one that Nietzsche calls nihilism, the terminal phase in the Christian pursuit of the truth about a necessarily incomprehensible God, and the defining characteristic of modern European civilization.

But nihilism is not a cul-de-sac from which there can be no escape. It, too, devalues itself. Like the earlier stages of Christian belief, it also undergoes an internal transformation on account of the commitments of those who subscribe to it—one that brings them to the threshold of a new theology no longer founded on Christian metaphysics at all (even in the shadowy form this still assumes in the post-Christian milieu of European nihilism) but on the religion of Dionysus instead, whose central teaching is the parable of eternal return.

This is bound to happen, Nietzsche claims, because the adherents of nihilism are as devoted to the truth as the orthodox believers they mock. They claim, in fact, to possess the highest truth, namely, that God is dead. But this truth brings to light another and still deeper one that those who proclaim the death of God fail to see.

This deeper truth is that man cannot live without willing, even if what he wills is nothing—the nonexistence of the God who before gave the world its being and meaning.[48] The Christian God may not exist, but what *does* is the drive to invent him. The nonexistence of a God beyond the world is the negative truth of nihilism. Its positive truth is the equally undeniable existence of the striving for being and immunity to time which the nihilist accepts even as he denies the possibility of its fulfillment—of what in *The Birth of Tragedy* Nietzsche calls the Apollonian drive to measure and order and later describes in more general terms as the will to power, the constitutive principle of all beings as such.

Nietzsche's metaphysics of joy begins with the reversal that occurs when we turn from inquiring into the effects of the artist's work and ask about the needs of the artist himself. Nihilism does not make this turn. But it invites it by bringing the irrepressibility of man's theodicical needs to light with a clarity that only the frustration of their previously highest expression allows. Nihilism compels those who share its commitment to truth to ask where these needs come from and what, despite their frustration, they mean.

This is the point at which Nietzsche's own metaphysics begins. It starts with a reflection on the positive truth that the negative message of nihilism contains. Those who make this turn with Nietzsche discover that nihilism is not the dead end it is sometimes thought to be—a terminal state that one must either accept with resignation or attempt to escape with some renewed form of Christian belief. They come to see it as a transitional phase that points toward a truer conception of being, best expressed by the idea of eternal return. And having made the turn, they find themselves in a world that is divine once again, indeed infinitely so, a world whose eternity extends to every vanishing instant of change, death and decay—the antithesis of the world as the nihilist sees it, from which the everlasting and divine has been wholly expunged.

If we define modernity as a state of nihilistic disenchantment, then with the passage from nihilism to the metaphysics of eternal return, the world becomes postmodern, or more accurately post-Christian in a way that even nihilism is not. That Nietzsche saw in nihilism the dialectical makings of its own self-destruction and transformation into a theology of a radically different sort is the deepest source of the confidence implied by the many passages in which he intimates—even as he catalogues the desolations of modern life—

that the day *must* come when his books find the audience for which they are written.

Moreover, though modern nihilism is to begin with a Christian and therefore European phenomenon, Nietzsche sometimes describes it as a universal destiny—as what he calls the "fate" of the "earth."[49] It follows that the self-overcoming of nihilism must be a destiny of the same kind as well.

There have been other forms of nihilism in the past, of course. Nietzsche places special emphasis on the Buddhist version. These too grew from a relentless commitment to the truth. But only a few could understand their esoteric philosophical teachings. Doing so required great effort and talent. The Christian religion begins by carrying its glad tidings to everyone. Its central doctrines are easy to grasp, and those who believed them sought from the start to persuade all men of their truth. The nihilism to which the Christian commitment to truth necessarily leads therefore shares the universality of the religion from which it springs. It is similarly cosmopolitan in nature. It is a nihilism for everyone and not just a few spiritual adepts.

In its peculiarly Christian form, nihilism has a tendency to spread to every corner of life and to become the dominant attitude of an entire civilization—as it has in modern Europe. But its sprawl cannot be contained there. Its gospel of meaninglessness is bound to be heard around the planet. This takes time but nothing can stop it. None of the old gods are able to compete with the truth that God is dead; they must all eventually give way before it. This process is hastened by the growing authority of modern science and the technologies of comfort it spawns (which are also of European provenance). These spread with the nihilism that follows in the wake of the death of Europe's God and make it easier to accept. The result is the global ascendancy, wherever human beings live in even modest comfort, of the pointless satiety of Nietzsche's last man.

Yet if it is the destiny of European nihilism to widen its grip until every man and woman on earth is held tight by it, the revaluation of its own ideals that nihilism invites must be a global event as well. The redivinization of the world that Nietzsche announces as his goal is therefore more than a private philosophical program. It is more even than the future of Europe. It is the fate of the earth, whose coming Nietzsche at times prophesizes with a passion that borders on madness.[50]

In these passages, the distance between Nietzsche and Spinoza seems greatest. Their apocalyptic tone is remote from the cerebral serenity of the *Ethics*. More important, Nietzsche's dialectical argument in support of the claim that modern nihilism is inherently unstable and undermines its own repudiation of the eternal and divine, has no parallel in Spinoza's philosophy. Yet Nietzsche's conception of the redivinized world to which nihilism's self-defeat leads resembles Spinoza's account of the world as substance or God, and both insist that the truth of this conception is one to which, at first at least, only a few will find their way.

The *Ethics* concludes by remarking on the rarity and excellence of those who do. They are the noble human beings to whom Spinoza addresses his proofs. In a similar way, Nietzsche declares that his teachings are meant for a new kind of nobility. The test for admission is whether one can embrace the idea of eternal return. On occasion, Nietzsche expresses his hope that those who can will one day become the architects of a new world order. But whether or not they succeed in this regard, his born-again free spirits are separated from other men by the pathos of distance that has always stood between what is noble and common. Spinoza's wise man is separated from the ignorant crowd by a similar gap, and the supreme practical aim of his philosophy, as of Nietzsche's, is to answer the question of how to live nobly in a world where most do not. Both, moreover, answer this question in a similar way. The noble human being is one who possesses a greater quantum of power.

Still, their paradigms of nobility are not the same. For Spinoza, the greatness of those with rare and powerful souls manifests itself above all in their enlarged understanding of the world, which they achieve through the study of causes. The hero of the *Ethics* is a scientist. Nietzsche's noble man is an artist. On whatever scale he works, he strives to depict the world in a way that captures as much of its resident divinity as he can. His nobility is a manifestation of the metaphysics of the will to power—of the interpretation of the being of beings as art. Or rather, it is an enactment of this interpretation itself, and as such displays with special clarity the essential if not always well-understood theology of modern art, just as the wisdom of those who follow Spinoza's lead in their endless study of natural causes exemplifies and elucidates the god of modern science.

NOBILITY

Nietzsche is an enthusiastic admirer of noble individuals and cultures. He celebrates the values and achievements of ancient Rome[51] and Renaissance Florence.[52] He writes approvingly of the Indian caste system, the constitution of Venice and the Catholic Church, whose aristocratic culture was undone, he says, by the plebian spirit of the Reformation.[53] His heroes include the proud and contemptuous warriors of Homer's poems, who cared more for glory than life, and he repeatedly praises Napoleon for his hard resolve and strength to mold whole masses of men in accordance with his vision of Europe.[54]

This is a historically diverse set of examples. But one theme connects them all. In each case what Nietzsche admires is the successful expression of the drive to order or command. This takes hard work and a long time. Nietzsche is hostile to the idea that anything great can be accomplished by mere inspiration, or brought to completion quickly. He regards the modern idea of genius as a romantic conceit,[55] and considers the bourgeois view of marriage shallow by comparison with the dynastic conception to which all aristocratic classes subscribe.[56] Success in mastering even the smallest part of the world requires immense discipline, hence the development of severe and unyielding habits, above all that of self-sacrifice. That is why, Nietzsche says, every genuine creator feels himself to be not the master but slave of his gift.[57] When, as is often the case, this discipline takes generations to achieve, it assumes the form of "breeding" and the cultivation of "style" or "taste."[58] But wherever it reaches its goal, the result is always the same—the establishment of a "rank order"[59] of men based on the premise that some are more real, worthy, and true than others: the essence of every aristocratic culture, whatever its distinctive values may be. It is their greater quantum of being that Nietzsche admires in those who succeed in creating an order of this kind, from whose highest rung they survey, with bemusement, indifference or contempt, the mass of less notable human beings that occupy positions of relative inconsequence beneath them.

The very idea of such a ranking is antithetical to the ruling values of our age, which are fiercely egalitarian. We of course accept great differences of wealth and power and enjoy the ever-changing spectacle of celebrity in all its forms. But at the same time we insist that these distinctions do not touch the core of a person's being, and our laws and cultural norms enforce the expectation that no one should be shut out from any of these privileges on account of who he or she is (which is precisely what every aristocratic regime assumes and expects). Our morality is that of the "herd,"[60] the secularized expression of the relentlessly leveling morality of the Christian religion, which demotes the significance of all differences among human beings relative to the one, all-important distinction between them and God.

From this point of view, the grades of brilliance and power that set some men apart from others are worldly vanities that mean nothing at all. To regard them as having a value of their own is pride. This judgment survives the death of the God who initially underwrites it. It remains an anchoring principle of the nihilistic world that represents the last stage of Christian belief. Indeed, its truth becomes even more obvious. The nihilistic conviction that all values must be judged from the now-vacant point of view of a God beyond the world converts them to merely personal beliefs of equal significance, or rather insignificance. Nihilism only reverses the sign of their meaning, from positive to negative, while preserving the equality among them. In this sense, modern European nihilism is the most profoundly antiaristocratic ethic the world has ever known, and its eventual displacement by the born-again innocence of Dionysus means, among other things, the restoration of the idea of a rank order of men to the respectability it enjoyed in every noble culture of the past.

But what form will this new nobility take? Nietzsche sometimes writes in a way that suggests a particularly brutal answer.[61]

New masters will arise, he says, and others shall be their slaves. Their dominion will be universal; they will be the lords of the earth. The masses are being prepared for this even today. They are growing more docile and complacent. They will be the unresisting material on which their masters work, kneading and shaping them to meet the requirements of their farseeing plans. A new age of mass enslavement is about to begin, for which the easy suggestibility of the last man, who attaches no importance to anything but comfort, and the powers of modern technology, which have made our lives so comfortable, are together easing the way.

It is not always clear how seriously to take these statements. At times Nietzsche seems to write mainly to shock his readers out of what today we would call the stupor of political correctness. There are also many other passages in which Nietzsche ridicules the stupidity and clumsiness of modern power politics—especially the German variety.[62] No one, moreover, has ever understood more deeply than Nietzsche the impossibility of bringing the old blond beasts back to life. Too much has happened in the meantime. The slave revolt in morality has made man deep and interesting—it has given him an interior life he lacked before—and any new nobility must be founded on these post-Abrahamic conditions, not those of Homer's vanished world. Still, it would be implausible to insist that Nietzsche meant his prophecies of world enslavement merely as a provocation to reflection or a subtle metaphor for something else. One cannot escape the conclusion that Nietzsche was, to some degree at least, in earnest, though it is impossible to believe that he would have found anything in common with the monsters that later took him at his word and put his words into effect.

The difficulty of deciding how seriously to take Nietzsche's most brutal statements about the meaning of greatness today is not the end of the matter, however. There is another and better way of understanding his conception of the new nobility that must eventually rise from the leveling culture of modern nihilism. This alternative ideal has its roots in Nietzsche's own conception of the truth and in the metaphysics that underlies it. To the question, "What does it mean to be noble today?" it offers an answer that is grounded in Nietzsche's philosophy as a whole and that supports its other elements like the keystone in an arch. In the past, the noble human being was a warrior or philosopher or priest or titled lord. Today, Nietzsche says, he is an artist, and his life a work of art.

There is a sense, of course, in which every person's life is a work of art, as Nietzsche understands it. Even the least distinguished human being constructs a picture of the world in order to protect himself from hostile powers and extend his own. Metaphysically speaking, his existence is nothing but this picture itself. But the idea of nobility implies a hierarchy among these pictures themselves. It assumes that some are more compelling than others. To explain this, a criterion for ranking them is required and Nietzsche's conception of truth provides one.

One picture of the world is truer than another if it incorporates more within its interpretive frame. The more an interpretation illuminates and explains, the greater its truth or power, which for Nietzsche are the same. Nietzsche's perspectivism, for example, has more truth than metaphysical schemes that assume a distinction between being and becoming, because it can account for their origin and limits in a way they themselves cannot. Similarly, the interpretation of his life at which a person arrives at the end of a successful psychoanalysis has more truth or power than the one with which he began. And a novelist who interprets the experience of a single human being, or even a fragment of such experience, in a way that begins to expose the limitless web of relations in which the subject of her novel is caught, and the inexhaustible meaning these have for the subject and others, produces an interpretation that is richer and more comprehensive than those we construct for ourselves in the ordinary course of living. Her novel comes closer to the truth than our everyday, nonliterary interpretations do. It has greater splendor and stands higher in the rank order of power in the same way and for the same reason that the self-interpretation of a successfully analyzed patient does. It possesses a nobility that less observant interpretations lack.

The example of the novelist is especially instructive. It reminds us that while a truer interpretation is always one that covers more ground, this can be understood intensively as well as extensively. Even the least of things has a depth of meaning that can never be plumbed. Every passing moment possesses an eternal significance that no interpretation can exhaust. This is the central meaning of the doctrine of eternal return. Those who today aspire to live nobly will therefore find the materials for doing so ready to hand, in the ordinary circumstances of life, whether their own or that of others. To succeed, of course, they must do something outstanding with the materials they find. They must arrange them in a picture that carries one further toward what Freud calls the navel of the dream—the unattainable fullness of meaning that every speck of existence contains. That is as rare an achievement as the materials it employs are common. Nothing, perhaps, displays this combination of revelation and familiarity more dramatically than a novel like Virginia Woolf's *To the Lighthouse.*

In this respect, the greatest of our modern novels give us a benchmark for measuring the meaning of nobility in a world redivinized by the fusion of being and becoming that Nietzsche's anti-nihilistic metaphysics proclaims. They define a standard of excellence that we can aspire to reach in our own lives by understanding ourselves as deeply as the novelist understands the characters in her book. In the one case as the other, there will always be more work to be done. Yet the *relative* truth of a person's interpretation of himself or others (*vis-à-vis* his own neurotic self-deceptions or the more obscure understanding that the characters in a novel have of themselves) is a measurable achievement and the criterion by which nobility today must be judged.

Erich Auerbach defines the modern novel as an exploration of the infinite value of ordinary things, without the God beyond the world that first endowed them with it. In his view, Woolf's novel and others like it rest on a theological premise that is neither classical nor Christian, but a peculiar hybrid of the two. This is Nietzsche's theology too. He develops its metaphysical premises more elaborately than Auerbach has any interest in doing. But the modern novel is perhaps the best and certainly the most public example of what it means, for both writers, to live as fully as one can in a world that is infinitely divine, whether as an artist of one's own life or of the imagined lives of others.

This is a cheerier conception of nobility than the Napoleonic vision of world domination and mass enslavement that Nietzsche sometimes proclaims. It is also one that seems, on the surface at least, less distant from at least certain of our modern political values, in particular our reverence for diversity, though any ideal that ranks the lives of human beings according to their relative splendor and power conflicts in an obvious way with the egalitarianism that nearly all liberal democratic communities today accept as a norm. Whether it is possible to reconcile this norm with any idea of nobility is a question to which we shall return in chapter 37.

But even if this conflict were intractable (I shall try to show that it is not) the idea that nobility consists in living with a novelist's attention to the inexhaustible reservoir of meaning contained in ordinary things is not only a kinder and gentler idea than the Napoleonic alternative. It fits better with Nietzsche's metaphysics in general. It is a natural expression of his belief that things vary in their degree of reality; that the quantum of being a thing possesses is a function of the power of the interpretation it projects onto the world from its point of view; that a strong interpretation is one that goes farther toward satisfying the demand, which is the essence of the being of beings, that the world be an ordered and meaningful place; and that an inexhaustible supply of material for the strongest interpretation that any human being can ever construct lies ready to hand in the banal rubbish of life, as every great novelist knows.[63]

These are the guiding principles of Nietzsche's metaphysics. Anyone who accepts them has reason to make the novelist's ambition his own, and to regard his success in achieving it as the basis for determining his place in the rank order of human beings. This seems, in fact, to have been Nietzsche's view of his own life, whose goal, he said, was to see how much he could stand— how far he could go in exploring the underworld of human values, and in retrieving from its depths an unseen treasure of meaning, in the way a novelist or psychoanalyst does. Not his blustering remarks about the class of iron-willed overlords who will one day rule the rest of us as slaves, but the way he chose to live his own life offers the best clue to Nietzsche's idea of nobility in a born-again pagan world.

Understood in these terms, nobility means something very different than it did for Aristotle, or for anyone who still accepts the premises of Christian belief.

Aristotle's noble man attains his goal in this life. His nobility consists in living in accordance with a pattern that human beings are by nature equipped to achieve, though a measure of good fortune is always required as well. He is serene and self-contained. There is no disappointment in him. That is why we call him noble.

The Christian who lives nobly is one who keeps the disappointment of the world constantly before his eyes. He knows that there is nothing in the world that can fulfill him. Though he lives in the world, he is not of it. His attention is fastened on heaven and God, on his true home beyond the world, to which, God willing, he shall return at the end of days. Christian nobility is the capacity to sustain this attitude through all the ups and downs of life.

The novelist lives for this world. She knows there is no other. In this respect, she is a pagan too. But she also knows that her achievements can never be final. She may open up vast regions of meaning, but will never do more than scratch the surface of a world whose significance is infinite because every atom of it is divine. She accepts disappointment as her fate, as do the psychoanalyst and his patient. But disappointment is not defeat. If the drive to master the world cannot be fulfilled, neither can it be annulled. Even the Buddhist who strives to overcome it is caught in its grip. To see this and accept it, and yet to strain at every moment for a further increment of meaning, is the novelist's nobility. It is not that of Aristotle's great-souled man or the Christian saint. It is the nobility of a born-again pagan, which Nietzsche describes with characteristic *Sturm und Drang* and Spinoza expresses more quietly by observing that just because we do not live forever is no reason to forbear from striving, while we do, to come as close to the God of the world as we can.

This is the nobility of modern science. It is the nobility of modern art too. Spinoza's philosophy of substance and mode is the key to understanding the first. Nietzsche's metaphysics of perspective and power is the key to the second. In the next two chapters, we shall pursue the latter claim in more detail by examining, first, the theology of the novel as a species of literary representation, and then the spiritual ideals that have shaped the course of Western painting from the Renaissance on.

CHAPTER 34

"The Gift of Transmigration"

THE THEOLOGY OF THE MODERN NOVEL

For the 1908 New York Edition of *The Portrait of a Lady,* Henry James wrote a new preface in which he described the inspiration for the book and offered some general thoughts on the nature and purpose of novels in general. These are harder to define than one might suspect.

The novel is an endlessly plastic species. Its members are bound together neither by a set of stylistic conventions nor an agreed-upon subject matter. There are novels of narration and introspection; tragic novels and comic ones; novels that sprawl over immense regions of space and time and those that concentrate on a pinpoint of action or experience; novels that reinforce social habits and ones that fiercely attack them; realistic novels (like *Bleak House*) and surreal ones (like *The Trial*) as well as many (like *The Magic Mountain*) that fall somewhere in between. In contrast to all the classical forms of literary representation, each of which has its own relatively fixed rules of construction and more or less well-defined subject matter, the novel seems hopelessly promiscuous in both respects. It is therefore easy to despair of the attempt to say what a novel *is.* But to give up would be a singular defeat, for as many have suggested, the novel is the preeminently modern form of literary representation and crucial to understanding the culture and thought—and ultimately, the theology too—of the age to which it belongs. So we must make the attempt, and James' observations in his preface to *The Portrait of a Lady* give us a good place to start.

What James says is likely to seem unsurprising to a modern reader. He draws a distinction that is as old as Aristotle's *Poetics* between the story line or "plot" of a novel and the "character" of the individuals who play a part in it. As between these two, he claims, the second is by far the more important. To put it in Aristotelian terms, one might say that for James the characters in a novel are "that for the sake of which" the plot exists. There must be a plot of some sort if the characters are to have anything to do. But the plot is merely an enabling device—a kind of required armature. It must be there if the characters are to act and thereby show us who they are. The point of their acting, however, is not to advance the plot. Rather, the point of the plot is to provide occasions for the characters to say and do things that will bring their distinctive identities to light.

In James' view, the novelist's attention ought to be focused entirely on the latter goal. A novel that has more "architecture" than is required for this purpose is defective for that reason. So is one that employs its characters to promote a moral or political agenda. James dismisses novels of both sorts as mere "fables" and claims that *The Portrait of a Lady* is a work in which neither plot nor moral judgment has been allowed to overwhelm the principal objective of exploring "the character and aspect of a particular engaging young woman."[1] Some critics (F. R. Leavis among them) have complained that in his later novels, James dilutes the element of plot beyond the minimum required to hold his readers' attention and fails to give his characters enough to do to reveal their states of mind to those who are attempting to understand them. This may or may not be a fair criticism. But James' insistence that the plot of a novel exists for the sake of its characters, not the other way around, represents a view so widely held by novelists and critics alike that it might be called the orthodox position.

One further feature of James' view is worth noting. He claims that a novel (a good one, at least) is not moralistic in the sense that its characters are deployed to make an ethical point. Is there then no "ethics" of novel writing? Or is the activity of writing and reading such works merely a form of entertainment—a purely aesthetic diversion, to put it more grandly?

This is not what James thinks. A novelist, he says, strives to reach "all the varieties of outlook on life, of disposition to reflect and project, created by conditions that are never the same from man to man (or, so far as that goes, from man to woman)," and his work succeeds "in proportion as it strains, or tends to burst, with a latent extravagance, its mould."[2] This is an unattainable goal. A character in a novel can never be more than an approximation of an individual human being, whose particularity of outlook is always more complex than any depiction of it. But a novelist can illuminate this outlook to a greater or lesser degree. How far he is able to do so depends on the "enveloping air of the artist's humanity"—on "the kind and degree of the artist's prime sensibility, which is the soil out of which his subject springs." Where this sensibility is a "rich and magnificent medium"—one that is able to encompass the widest possible diversity of human lives, each with its peculiar longings and vulnerabilities, and to represent them in a way that makes them accessible to others—we may speak of a kind of greatness of soul (to borrow from Aristotle once again). The cultivation of such greatness and its exercise in the work of writing novels is for James more than entertaining. It is more than a form of aesthetic refinement. It is an ethical achievement: the attainment of a uniquely important human good and the source of the "worth" of the work that displays it—the key to what James calls "the 'moral' sense of a work of art," putting the word in quote marks to indicate his own special understanding of it.[3]

In this respect too, James' view is unexceptional. Other writers have defined the moral spirit of the modern novel in similar terms. One particularly interesting example is the Spanish philosopher Miguel de Unamuno, whose reflections on the nature and ambitions of the novel echo James' own. In a brilliant essay on the subject, Unamuno at one point exclaims, "Sublime and beneficent the power of this sovereign modern art that multiplies our existence, freeing us from our own self and generously bestowing upon us the gift of transmigration!"[4] It is hard to imagine a more fitting paean to the art of the novel as James conceives it (though Unamuno's statement has a vaguely religious tone that is missing from James' account—a point to which we shall return).

Like James, Unamuno insists that the focus of the novel is character rather than "action." In its essence, a novel is not a "story," though some measure of storytelling is required to achieve its primary purpose. As we move forward from *Don Quixote,* he says, the element of storytelling recedes in importance relative to that of character, until finally, in Proust, it disappears almost completely (a feature of the work that Unamuno censures, rightly or wrongly, for the same reason that Leavis criticizes the absence of plot in James' later novels).

From this basic assumption, which he shares with James, Unamuno develops several further characteristics of the novel as a literary genre. These all follow from its central focus on the exposition of the attitudes, experiences, challenges and choices that make every human life a unique event.

One of these is what Unamuno calls the characteristic "density" of the novel (which is not the same as its length). In order to represent the individuality of a character, an accumulation of details is required. A novel may be short, but it cannot be thin. (*Mrs. Dalloway* and *Barabbas* come to mind.) Many of course are both long and thick but only the latter is an essential consequence of the preoccupation with individual perspectivity that sets the novel apart from the epics of Homer, Virgil, Dante and Milton.

A second feature of the novel, according to Unamuno, is its tempo. Novels are "slow moving," in contrast, for example, to the *Iliad* and *Aeneid* which move at a brisker pace. That is because the latter attach a greater intrinsic value to the unfolding of their stories. A novel tells a story but only for the sake of its characters, whose individuality is best revealed, Unamuno says, not in those "extraordinary" moments to which epic and drama give such weight but in what he calls the "wonders of the simple, unhaloed hour"—a phrase reminiscent of Erich Auerbach's description of the novel's characteristic attention to ordinary things, whose meaning can be excavated only if we take the time to look at them in a sufficiently leisurely way.

In the third place, every successful novel creates a world unto itself. Readers who enter it forget that there is any world outside the one its characters inhabit. Unamuno calls this the "imperviousness" of the novel, by which he means its self-contained and self-sealing nature. The experience of losing oneself in a book is of course not limited to novels alone. But the invitation to suspend one's own preoccupations not merely for the sake of a good story but in order to replace them with those of another individual whose needs, fears, dreams and disappointments are as commanding as one's own, and to reimagine the entire world from an equally unique but entirely foreign point of view, intensifies the experience of self-loss to an unprecedented degree. In Unamuno's view, this is the source not only of the special pleasure of reading a great novel but its moral value as well: the novelist's "sublime and beneficent" gift of an increased freedom from oneself, the attainment of what James calls a more generous view of "life," onto which, as he puts it, "the house of fiction" looks with "not one window but a million—a number of possible windows not to be reckoned, rather."[5]

At its deepest level, this conception of the novel assumes that the individuality of individuals is something worthy of representation in its own right—that it possesses a value of its own and hence is of importance to the novelist not merely as a means for illustrating some general feature of human experience (though it may of course do that as well). This is an assumption that will seem so uncontroversial to the readers of modern novels as to appear hardly worth stating. But it is newer and more surprising than its obviousness may suggest and reflects the emergence of an outlook in aesthetics, and in literary taste specifically, that just a few short centuries ago did not exist at all.

In *The Rise of the Novel,* Ian Watt offers a classic account of the social and economic changes that first encouraged the belief that the distinctiveness of individuals is a subject worthy of serious literary representation and thereby created an audience for the novelist's art. Watt's historical analysis is richly detailed and no simple summary can do it justice. It will be useful, though, to recall a few of his most important conclusions.

According to Watt, the rise of the novel as a literary genre required a reading public that was both equipped to read such works and interested in their subject matter. The first was the result of a dramatic increase in literacy, especially among women. The second only became possible, he claims, with the emergence of a new social and economic order that placed an unprecedented value on the actions and attitudes of individuals and accelerated their diversification in ways that made the members of an increasingly heterogeneous culture more closely dependent on and curious about one another.[6]

Watt associates these developments with Protestantism in the sphere of religion and capitalism in that of material life. Together, these produced a new civilization, composed of individuals at once more valuable in themselves and more isolated than ever before, yet bound by ties of dependency whose complexity could no longer be fathomed. The characteristic experience of those living in this civilization, Watt writes, was one of alienation, to which the novel, with its gift of transmigration, offered an antidote of sorts.[7] It was the experience of Robinson Crusoe, whose insular existence was the subject of the first English novel and in a general way a model for the lives of all the characters in the later novels of Dafoe, Richardson and Fielding.

The longing to find a satisfying connection to another in the realm of personal love—to be loved for one's own sake and have the opportunity to offer a symmetrically unique love in return—became a theme of special importance in this regard. One might even call it *the* theme of the modern novel (particularly its English branch) which in this respect reflects not only a change in social values and economic relations but in the understanding of love and marriage as well. Jane Austen's novels are an obvious example, but *Middlemarch, Ulysses* and even *Lolita* (about each of which I shall have more to say in due course) might be cited as well.

Watt makes many other brilliant observations. One is that in contrast to earlier genres of representation, the novel puts a special value on the phenomenon of time.[8] No work of literature ignores the passage of time. Even the *Iliad* marks events by the rising and setting of the sun. But the novel attaches an unprecedented significance to time itself. It treats temporality as something of value in its own right, rather than the mere shadow of an eternal order that lies beyond it. This is closely connected to its emphasis on the value of individuality. Indeed, these are merely different ways of describing the same outlook, since the individuality of the individual is precisely what is transient (or seemingly so) about him or her, in contrast to the enduring generalities that define the common categories of human action. Reflection on the meaning of time as a subject of literary representation, and its relation to the eternity from which every classical dramatist and poet distinguished it in a fundamental way, reaches a culmination in Proust's novel, which Watt discusses, though only very briefly, at the end of his essay.

A second observation, of particular importance to our concerns here, bears on the relation between the rise of the novel and changes in the background of philosophical thought. Watt draws a parallel between the novel's emphasis on the reality of individual experience and the empiricism of Locke in particular, whose epistemology is ruthlessly hostile to the idea that anything other than individual sense data can ever be called real in an ultimate sense.[9] Though Watt himself does not develop the point, the roots of Locke's empiricism lie in the nominalist revolt against Aristotelian realism that began in the early fourteenth century, and that was motivated by a desire to save the dignity of God from a radicalizing rationalism that threatened to do away with the notion of divine freedom altogether. The rise of the novel is thus closely linked to the theological struggle that produced, first, the voluntarism of Ockham, then the Reformation of Luther, and finally the death of the God of the Christian religion. It belongs to an age of disenchantment. But this puts the point in a misleadingly negative way, for the modern novel also expresses a positive spiritual ideal. Erich Auerbach (who Watt cites with approval) makes this point more explicitly. But even Auerbach fails to grasp the full meaning of the post-Christian theology that underlies the modern novel and explains its distinctive emphasis on character rather than plot.

In the remainder of this chapter we shall explore this theology in more detail by examining five novels in particular. The choice of these five reflects my own interests and taste. I have chosen them because I love them, but also because they offer, I think, particularly useful lines of approach to my principal subject. Before we turn to the first of these, though, we need to take a long step back and recall certain of the central ideas in Aristotle's *Poetics,* the first work of literary analysis in the Western tradition, for the theological significance of James' claim that the plot of a novel exists for the sake of its characters only begins to become clear when we examine Aristotle's reasons for adopting exactly the opposite view.

THE IMITATION OF ACTION

Neither a poem like the *Iliad* nor a play like *Oedipus Rex* exists by nature. Neither has what Aristotle calls a "principle" or "source" or "beginning" of motion in itself. Both belong on the other side of the basic distinction that he draws in book 2 of the *Physics* between natural beings (those with such a principle) and artificial ones (things that have their source of movement outside themselves). What we today would call literary works thus belong to the larger class of works generally—of things that exist and move only on account of the efforts of those who make them. In this respect, a poem or play is no different from a pot or lyre.

Within the general class of works, however, those of a literary sort are distinguished by what Aristotle calls their representative or mimetic function. A pot has a use, but it is not to depict or imitate something other than itself. It serves its purpose by being what it is. A poem or play, on the other hand, is *essentially* imitative. Its defining purpose is to represent something else, and if it fails to do this well, it is not a good poem or play.

Before Aristotle, Plato had also defined works of this special sort by their imitative function, but this was enough, he thought, to condemn them in a wholesale fashion. Any imitation, Plato claims, is deficient in reality by comparison with the thing it represents, and therefore farther from the truth. Its attractions are thus a danger to be avoided. Aristotle, by contrast, argues that imitative works have an important role to play in helping human beings attain their highest good. He therefore takes more seriously than Plato the question of what makes such works successful. This is the question to which the *Poetics* is addressed.

Aristotle starts by observing that although poems and plays are essentially imitative, they do not represent just anything at all, in the way a mirror indiscriminately depicts whatever it happens to capture in its reflection. The proper function (*ergon*) of a poem or play is to imitate one thing in particular. This is human "action" (*praxis*).

Human beings of course have a nature or *phusis* in Aristotle's sense. They move on their own account. But in contrast to other natural beings, in the sublunary realm at least, men alone are capable of a special sort of self-directed movement. We might describe this as movement in accordance with a plan—one the actor conceives in his mind before he begins to move and that guides his subsequent behavior. All movements of this sort contain a conceptual component, in contrast to those that are motivated by desire or appetite alone. To some degree, motives of the latter kind invariably condition these planned movements as well. But the execution of a plan includes an additional element of thoughtfulness. According to Aristotle, this is a uniquely human phenomenon (putting celestial souls to one side). It is therefore at least partly definitive of what we today would call the human condition.

Every movement guided by a plan has a purposive arc. This starts with the plan itself, moves through its execution, and concludes with the end the plan projects (which the person who has made the plan may or may not succeed in reaching). Consider the case of a potter. He first conceives a plan of the pot he intends to make and then puts it into effect. In the case of the potter, however, the end that guides his movements (putting clay on the wheel and glaze on the pot) is the construction of something separate from himself, whereas in other cases, like that of a student reading a book, the goal of the movements his plan requires (moving his eyes from line to line, taking notes as he reads) is the improvement of his own character or constitution. Aristotle uses the term "action" in a special, technical sense to denote self-informing planful movements of the latter kind.

The work of a poem or play is to imitate human action in this sense—to depict men and women forming plans to make themselves better or better off and then either reaching or missing the goals they have set. We know from the *Ethics* that every plan of this sort is ultimately directed toward a single, overarching end that Aristotle calls "happiness" or "well-being."[10] In the simplest terms, therefore, the special class of artifacts that Aristotle calls "mimetic" is devoted to the representation of human beings engaged in the pursuit of happiness and to the depiction of their success or failure in attaining it. Imitative works do this by means of a narrative with a beginning, middle and end whose own coherence reproduces the unifying purposive arc that every human action possesses on account of the final end toward which it is directed—the state of happiness for the sake of which every actor does what he does.

According to Aristotle, the unity or integrity of a poem or play is secured by its "plot" (*muthos*). This is what gives it its coherence. To be sure, a plot never exists by itself. It is not a freestanding abstraction. It is always the story *of* someone or other—of Agamemnon and Clytemnestra, for example, or Antigone and Cleon. Every work that imitates an action must therefore have both a plot and characters. These may be thought of as its form and matter respectively. The plot of a play, for example, is what makes it a tragedy rather than a comedy. If it has the required moments of recognition and reversal, and concerns the fortunes of "serious" human beings, it is a work of the former kind. At the same time, Aeschylus' play is the tragedy of Agamemnon rather than Antigone because it tells the story of one human being instead of another. In this respect, the relation of plot to character is analogous to that between the form and matter of an individual like Socrates. Socrates is a human being by virtue of his form. He is also one human being in particular (Socrates rather than Critias) because the form he shares with others of his kind is "embodied" in a discrete portion of matter.

Aristotle identifies other "parts" (*meroi*) that mimetic works typically or for the most part possess, but plot and character are of special importance because together they allow us to answer the two questions that we always have reason to ask about any thing at all, whether natural or artificial. First, what kind of being is it? A man or a dog? A lyre or an *aulos*? And second, which one of its kind is it? Socrates or Critias? The lyre that Simmias built or the one made by Glaucon? In every branch of his philosophy, Aristotle invokes the related concepts of form and matter to answer these two questions. The *Poetics* is no exception.

More important, the metaphysical priority that he assigns form over matter elsewhere in his writings is manifest here too. As between plot and character, the first, Aristotle says, takes precedence over the second. The plot of a poem or play is "the most important" of its parts. It is that for the sake of which its characters act as they do.[11] True, characters are needed to give a story flesh and blood, but the point of their actions is to bring the story to life for those listening to it or watching it unfold on the stage. The audience's attention is directed in a fundamental way not to the characters, who give the work its individuality, but to the plot that determines its general form as a work of a certain kind. This is what Aristotle means when he says that the plot of a tragedy is its "origin" (*arche*)[12] and declares it to be the "end" (*telos*) for whose sake all its other parts, including that of character, are arranged as they are.[13]

This judgment reflects the intellectualist prejudice that underlies the whole of Aristotle's philosophy (and of Plato's too)—the identification of the real with the intelligible, and of the latter with the general forms of things. According to Aristotle, we can only grasp these forms in their embodied states. They nevertheless contain all that can be known, and hence everything that is real, in the individuals that give them a material presence in the world. In the end, for Aristotle, the individuality of individuals is wholly unintelligible— the product of a pure potentiality whose formlessness guarantees that nothing can be known about it at all. This basic metaphysical assumption underlies Aristotle's inquiries into the movement of natural beings and the production of artificial ones, including the special kind whose function is to imitate human action. His insistence on the priority of plot over character, in mimetic works of art, is merely one expression of it.

The significance of this priority is brought out by a curious remark that Aristotle makes about the superiority of such works to those of historians like Herodotus.[14] A historian is concerned with what actually happened at a particular time and place, for example, at the Battle of Salamis. He is therefore essentially and not merely incidentally concerned with the individuals involved and their specific actions—the ones that produced the event in question. Historians are of course generally interested in larger themes as well. But these merely provide the scaffolding for their account of the actual events on which their attention is principally focused. A historian employs his story line as a frame to highlight the individuality of those involved in an occurrence that really took place at an earlier moment in time.

The historian is primarily interested in recording the singularity of this occurrence and the human beings responsible for it. Though his work, like that of a mimetic artist, combines elements of character and plot, their relative importance is therefore reversed. This follows from the historian's preoccupation with *actual* events, for these have a uniqueness which those represented in a poem or play lack—the particularity that distinguishes each moment from every other in the irreversible stream of time. Poets and playwrights, by contrast, do not need to be concerned with the historical actuality of their characters and can make do, as Aristotle says, with a repertoire of stock characters "constructed around a few households"[15] that belong to the eternal realm of myth rather the endless before-and-after of historical time.

Given his equation of being with form, it is therefore unsurprising that Aristotle judges the work of the historian to be further removed from reality than that of poets and playwrights. The historian's fascination with particular people and actual events restricts him to a sphere whose reality is deficient by comparison with the timeless order that gives the cosmos and its contents all the being they possess. "Poetry tends to speak of universals, history of particulars." The priority of plot over character in mimetic works reflects this difference and makes it clear, in Aristotle's words, that "poetry is a more philosophical and serious thing than history."

Of course, if poetry is more philosophical and serious than history, philosophy is more philosophical and serious than poetry. Aristotle never says this explicitly in the *Poetics*. But there can be no doubt that he believed the work of mimetic art to fall in a middle range between that of history on the one hand and of philosophy on the other, the latter being the highest and most fulfilling activity in which it is possible for human beings to engage.

This naturally raises the question of what good is served by the mimetic works that belong to this middle position. What are such works for? To give the question a more modern formulation, what is the "value" of listening to the *Iliad* or of going to a performance of *Oedipus Rex?* Aristotle does not give us an answer that is nearly as clear or succinct as his account of the value of philosophy in book 10 of the *Nicomachean Ethics*. We must reconstruct it from a few scattered hints. Aristotle's basic contention is that the good of mimetic works consists in their use of the uniquely human power of representation to promote the highest good that human beings are able to achieve within the limits of their humanity, as distinct from the even higher good the philosopher attains, for a time at least, by leaving his humanity behind. The key to understanding this claim is Aristotle's famous idea of *catharis,* which he mentions in the *Poetics* but never explains in detail.[16] It is also the key to appreciating the distance between the theology that shapes his account of mimetic art and the one that underlies the modern novel, which turns Aristotle's insistence on the priority of plot over character upside down.

The arts that Aristotle calls imitative in the narrow sense are those whose products perform their function by representing something other than themselves. A pot performs a function too. It holds water or wine. But the work of a pot is not by its nature representative; there is no need for it to point to anything else in order to do its job. If mimetic works in the narrow sense advance the good of human beings, this must therefore be because the activity of representation itself is somehow connected to this good, so that poems and plays help to perfect our humanity by means of the very characteristic that sets them apart from other made but nonmimetic works.

That this is so is suggested by a remark Aristotle makes near the beginning of the *Poetics*. "Representation," he says, "is natural to human beings from childhood. They differ from the other animals in this: man tends most toward representation and learns his first lessons through representation. Also everyone delights in representations. An indication of this is what happens in fact: we delight in looking at the most proficient images of things which in themselves we see with pain, e.g., the shapes of the most despised wild animals and of corpses. The cause of this is that learning is most pleasant, not only for philosophers but for others likewise (because they share in it to a small extent)."[17]

Like other animals, human beings make copies of themselves. Every plant and animal participates in the eternal and divine through reproduction. But a reproduction is not a representation. The first is a duplicate whose nature is no more to depict something other than itself than that of the original from which it has been copied. The second is essentially depictive. Its nature consists in pointing elsewhere, to the thing it represents.[18] According to Aristotle, men alone "tend toward representation" and "learn" through it. We are the only mimetic animals on earth. It is also the means by which we are able to achieve a higher and more complete relation to the god of the world than the one we experience through reproduction. To see why, it is important to note the parallel between imitation and reason, which first manifests itself in the phenomenon of wonder—in the questioning attitude that asks why things are as they are and stops to search for an answer.[19]

Only a being that already has some distance from the world is capable of wonder. Other animals are so thoroughly engaged in their routines that they lack the requisite detachment. Among terrestrial beings, we alone transcend the world sufficiently to inquire about it. Reason (*nous*) is the name for this transcendence. It is the power that lies at the root of all science and philosophy. It is also a prerequisite of every act of making. Even a potter must anticipate in his mind's eye the pot he means to make. This presupposes a form of time-consciousness unavailable to any being that is merely carried along by the stream of time with no awareness of it. But in that special sort of making that Aristotle calls mimetic, the transcendence that every kind requires, is itself made an object of attention and becomes the source of the unique delight that representative works afford.

When we view an imitation of something *as* an imitation (and not, say, as a copy) our perception of it as the sort of thing it is is constituted by an appreciation of its reference to something it is not—to the thing it imitates, which transcends the imitation in the sense that it always exists outside of or beyond the imitation itself. To take pleasure in an imitation *as* an imitation (in the picture of a wild animal, for example) is thus to enjoy for its own sake the experience of transcendence that imitations not only presuppose, in the general way that all artifacts do, but draw to our attention in a deliberate and self-conscious fashion.

According to Plato, the capacity to see an image *as* an image is the rudimentary power that releases us from bondage in the cave that no other animal ever escapes.[20] In Aristotle's account of mimesis, when we listen to a poem or view a play, we take delight in the playful exercise of this power for its own sake, detached from the pursuit of every objective end, like the making of a pot or design of a constitution. Our humanity is at work in these latter activities too. No other animal makes utensils or laws. But in the theater the power of transcendence that sets us apart from every other animal on earth is enjoyed for its own sake, so that here, one might say, our humanity is not merely at work but is the very thing on display, made manifest by means of a representation that draws the audience's attention in a conscious and particularly pleasurable way to the power of transcendence that the play they are watching employs (as every uniquely human activity does).

Aristotle's word for this special pleasure is *catharis*. It is a term with medical overtones and means something like "purging" or "cleansing." To get a better sense of what Aristotle has in mind, and to understand why the mimetically induced experience of *catharis* is a benefit to those who undergo it, we need to recall certain basic features of his conception of the human good.[21]

Every animal has a good. This consists in the active exercise of the powers peculiar to it. Other animals pursue their good directly. They do not need to be taught what it is or how to achieve it. They move toward the good appropriate to them by just doing what comes naturally. In the case of human beings, however, reflection is essential to their identification of the end in which their good consists and to their attainment of it.

Putting philosophy to the side, the most fulfilling life a human being can lead is one of active virtue accompanied by good fortune. Each of the virtues (courage, justice, prudence and the like) has reason as one of its elements. It

cannot be defined if reason is left out of account. Moreover, virtue in the complete sense presupposes a coincidence of aim and desire. A truly virtuous
man not only knows what courage is but wants to act courageously. This coincidence does not exist by nature, however. It can only be achieved through
a process of education by means of which a young person is gradually trained
to enjoy the exercise of virtue and becomes habitually disposed to do so.
This process must be overseen by teachers who understand its goal and
guide their students toward it. Reason is thus required both to define the
human good and to equip the young to reach it. In this sense, their attainment of the good appropriate to them in not assured by nature, but represents what Aristotle calls a "second" nature in order to mark the twofold role
that reason plays in it.

This gives us the background we need to understand the relation between
catharsis and the human good. To a person (especially a young person) bent
on living a life of virtue—acting courageously, justly, generously, and the
like—in a civic community of the kind that constitutes the necessary setting
for the exercise of all the virtues, there are two familiar experiences that are
bound to seem especially discouraging. The first is the ever-present risk of accidents, including catastrophic ones that can derail even the happiest of lives,
as happened to King Priam.[22] The cultivation of the habitual attitudes and
feelings in which virtue consists can never eliminate this risk altogether. The
second, which might perhaps be viewed as a species of accident too, is the
ever-present danger of mistake (*hamartia*). A virtuous man, properly proud
of his outstanding character, may make an important mistake about his situation, and acting on it, do himself and others terrible damage. In cases of
this kind, the pride that is normally the crowning expression of virtue becomes a destructive accelerant instead, with especially awful results. Even
the most determinedly virtuous man cannot protect himself from the danger
of mistake either.

"Serious" works of poetry and drama help those who long to lead virtuous lives grapple with the discouraging fact that all their success in acquiring
the traits of character that constitute the sum of human virtue, and hence
the key to human happiness, offers no immunity against accident and error.
Works of this sort imitate the actions of great and noble human beings, in
contrast to comedic plays and poems, which depict the experiences of those
who are foolish or ridiculous.[23] A virtuous man will therefore find it easy
to identify with the protagonists of such works since they are aiming at the
same target as he. But because it is *only* a poem or play, the identification is

incomplete. The virtuous man who listens to or sees it is thus able to live through the action it represents and simultaneously to preserve his detachment from it—to be at once "in" the action and "outside" it, a participant and spectator both.

It is the imitative nature of the work that allows for such a doubling of experience. Unlike a copy, an imitation deliberately announces that it is something other than the thing it represents. A play reminds those in the theater that it *is not* the actions it depicts, even if they momentarily forget this. The theatergoers are thereby helped to put themselves in the place of the human beings the play portrays without really doing so. This makes it easier for a serious man attending a serious play or listening to a serious poem to undergo the devastations of Oedipus and Priam, which are the result of misfortune and error, without doing so in fact. He is able to feel pity (*eleos*) and terror (*phobos*) on account of his identification with them, and yet to experience a great surge of relief (*catharsis*) because he has not really done or suffered what they did but only been moved by an imitation of it.

The entire experience does not, however, leave the one who has undergone it just where he was before. Having endured, if only in what we might call a "playful" way, the terrors that Oedipus and Priam actually underwent, he is likely to be just a little more hardened against the dangers of accident and mistake that forever haunt the pursuit of human virtue. He is likely to be just a little less discouraged by the effects of the less consequential misfortunes and mistakes that befall every human being and therefore marginally more inclined to persevere in his pursuit of excellence and happiness despite them. Viewed in this light, serious imitative works, like the *Iliad* and *Oedipus Rex,* contribute to the affective training that constitutes an important part—if not, indeed, the core—of ethical education. It is therefore good for a young man, who is still undergoing such a process of training, to be exposed to such works, and for a mature man, who despite the resilience of his character remains exposed to the dangers of accident and error, to continue to "enjoy" them for the sake of the *catharsis* that acts, like a regularly prescribed medicine, to reinforce his resolve to act nobly, whatever life may bring.

Serious imitative works thus play an important role in helping those for whom they are composed to live as well as they can. This is the ethical good of literature, as Aristotle conceives it. But this way of expressing the idea that lies behind his notion of *catharsis* immediately reminds us of how far removed Aristotle's conception of the human good is from ours.

For Aristotle, the human good consists in a way of living that is only superficially affected by the differences in culture and convention that distinguish one city from another. The best life a man can live, regardless of where he happens to be born, is one of courage, generosity, wisdom and the like, and these can all be defined, broadly at least, in universal terms. (The same is even more obviously true if the best life is defined to include the activity of contemplation as well.) There is only one good for man. Imitative works make a distinctive contribution to the attainment of this good as part of an educational program whose overall goal is the attunement of human reason and desire. This is something we must work to achieve as a "second" nature. To the extent we succeed, we make reason effective in our lives and therefore become not only happier but more real. Or rather, we become happier *because* we become more real, the reality of a man being measured by the degree to which he develops the power of reason whose exercise puts him in touch with the eternal intelligibility of the world that constitutes its inherent divinity.

The philosopher, who has left human things behind, temporarily at least, has an even greater share in this divinity. His is the most active life of all. But among those who remain in the world of human affairs, the man of virtue comes closest to this goal by living as rationally as one can in a realm roiled by desire and forever subject to misfortune and mistake. He comes as close to living a divine life as it is possible to do in the sphere of practical activity. Insofar as the rational powers that define the general form of his humanity predominate in his life, and everything that is peculiar or idiosyncratic in his makeup as an individual is subordinated to them, he achieves the happiness at which all men aim, more completely than anyone except a philosopher, whose individuality vanishes altogether in the activity of thought. That this is so follows from the equation of being with intelligibility, and of the latter with form, that underlies every aspect of Aristotle's philosophy, including his account of the good of *mimesis*.

This is the metaphysical premise of Aristotle's inquiry into the nature and ethical value of those works whose special function is to imitate human action, and in particular of his judgment that in all works of this kind plot (or form) enjoys a necessary priority over character (or matter). Henry James offers the opposite judgment in his account of the art of the novel. One therefore cannot explain James' understanding of what he calls the "'moral' sense" of the novel on the basis of Aristotle's theology. Does this mean, perhaps, that the priority of character over plot, to which he attaches such significance, rests on no theology at all?

James himself does not address this question in his preface to *The Portrait of a Lady*. But he does refer in especially positive terms to another novelist for whom the question was of great importance. It may be that James mentions George Eliot and singles her out for particular praise because her novel *Daniel Deronda* was in certain respects a model for his own.[24] But whatever James' debt to Eliot may have been, she was a far more philosophically inclined writer than he, and if we want to understand the radically non-Aristotelian theology on which James' conception of the art of the novel depends, her masterpiece *Middlemarch* gives us a good place to start.

"THAT ROAR WHICH LIES ON THE OTHER SIDE OF SILENCE"

Middlemarch begins with a "Prelude" and ends with a "Finale" that help to define the theological question that George Eliot's story of her provincial heroine is meant to answer.

The "Prelude" invites us to reflect "on the life of Saint Theresa."[25] Even as a child, the Spanish saint sought to live "an epic life." She achieved her goal and is remembered to this day as one of the great figures of her age. In her pursuit of greatness, St. Theresa was helped by the fact that she was born into a "coherent social faith and order" that gave her the epic theme or "epos" she required. Two facts about the life of St. Theresa are therefore of special importance. The first is that it was an exceptional life easily distinguished from the insignificant and forgotten ones of most of her contemporaries. The second is that its greatness was tied to the existence of a religious worldview that provided the social, indeed cosmic backdrop to her actions—a grand narrative of meaning on which St. Theresa was able to draw in an effort to give her own life meaning as well.

By contrast, the life of Dorothea Brooke cannot be called an "epic" or memorable one in a similar sense. Dorothea is a woman of modest wealth and appealing character, but her life is limited by its provincial circumstances. However much a reader may admire Dorothea, it is impossible to view her as a hero on a world-historical scale.[26] "Her finely touched spirit had still its fine issues, though they were not widely visible. Her full nature, like that river of which Cyrus broke the strength, spent itself in channels which had no great name on the earth." Dorothea's acts are "un-historic" and her life but one of the countless many that "rest in unvisited tombs."[27]

Neither is Dorothea's world shaped by the same encompassing spiritual narrative as that of St. Theresa. *Middlemarch* has its share of real and professed believers, but the Christian religion no longer provides even for them a universally accepted framework of belief like the one to whose promise of salvation St. Theresa could confidently attach her yearning for transcendence. In this sense, Dorothea lives in a godless world. At the start of the novel, she is still an enthusiastic Christian. She is moved by a longing for martyrdom, not unlike that of St. Theresa. This draws her into her disastrous marriage with Causabon. But as she comes to understand the nature of their relation and to despair of ever finding the salvation she sought in it, Dorothea's "religious faith" begins to fade and the circumstances of her life are "disenchanted."[28] Despite great suffering, she retains a saintlike quality, but it becomes further and further removed from the naive Christian piety she proudly displays in the opening scenes of the novel. By the end, the reader sees that neither Dorothea nor anyone else can be saved in the manner the Christian teaching concerning this life and the next both allows and requires.

Dorothea is therefore distinguished from St. Theresa in two respects. She is an ordinary person, not a world-historical hero, and she lives in an age in which the Christian religion has lost its saving power. Together these define the theological question to which the novel is addressed. Is it possible for the actions of ordinary human beings, like Dorothea Brooke, to possess a spiritual grandeur that can never be lost or corrupted by the passage of time, even in an age in which this is no longer guaranteed by the connection of the world to an eternal God beyond it?

George Eliot's answer is yes. In this sense, she is neither a romantic nor a nihilist. She knows that the enchanted world of St. Theresa can never be brought back to life, yet refuses to accept that the disappearance of Christian faith means the loss of any link that human beings might have to an order of values impervious to time. *Middlemarch* steers a path between these opposing but related views. It is not a Christian work and most decidedly not a nihilistic one. Eliot affirms the value of the life of the spirit in a secular world in which "the medium" that St. Theresa could rely on to give her "ardent deeds" their "shape" is "forever gone."[29] Her affirmation amounts to a theology whose basic principles she puts in the mouth of Dorothea herself.

Even after Dorothea has abandoned the Christian mysticism that at first makes her look so much like a Protestant version of St. Theresa, she continues to insist on a moral creed with a strong religious tone. When Dorothea returns from her honeymoon with Casaubon in Rome and settles into her new life at Lowick, Will Ladislaw calls her existence there "a dreadful imprisonment." Dorothea tells him he is wrong. "I have a belief of my own," she says, "and it comforts me." And "what is that?" Ladislaw asks. "That by desiring what is perfectly good, even when we don't quite know what it is and cannot do what we would, we are part of the Divine power against evil—widening the skirts of light and making the struggle with darkness narrower." Ladislaw calls this "a beautiful mysticism," but Dorothea urges him not to put a "name" to it. It is just "my life," she replies, though it is a life clearly still inspired by a religious calling of some kind.

Dorothea acknowledges that she has "been finding out [her] religion since [she] was a little girl." The religion of her childhood was based on prayer. It assumed a fabric of conventional Christian belief. But now at Lowick, Dorothea says, "I hardly ever pray." She has lost her faith in a providential God who controls the fates of human beings from a seat beyond the world. Yet she has not slipped into a mood of blank despair, or adopted the irreligious belief that Ladislaw defines as the foundation of his own romantic aestheticism—"to love what is good and beautiful when I see it" (a creed whose amorality Ladislaw's friend in Rome, the painter Peter Naumann, affirms with a relish that reminds one of the young aesthete in Kierkegaard's *Either/Or*.)[30]

One of the cornerstones of Dorothea's mature religion is her belief "that people are almost always better than their neighbors think they are." She makes this remark late in the novel to explain her exceptionally generous attitude toward Tertius Lydgate, a man shunned by his neighbors on account of their belief that he has taken a bribe.[31] In Dorothea's view, we are all bound to do the most we can to see the better selves of those around us—to judge their character and actions in a charitable light. This requires that we put our selfish interests aside to the extent that we are able. "We are all of us born in moral stupidity," Eliot writes, "taking the world as an udder to feed our supreme selves." She offers this observation at the very moment her main character begins to "emerge" from her own "stupidity" and to feel "the waking of a presentiment that there might be a sad consciousness in [Casaubon's] life which made as great a need on his side as on her own."[32]

Eliot's interjection implies a conception of the relation between self and world that she elaborates with an extended "parable" suggested by "an eminent philosopher."

The "events" of the world are like the scratches "going everywhere impartially" on a reflecting surface such as a piece of "polished steel," and the "egoism" of each individual resembles a "candle" that makes of these scratches "the flattering illusion of a concentric arrangement" falling "round that little sun."[33] Each of us illuminates the whole of reality from a particular point of view and organizes the world according to the needs and interests that define our peculiar position within it.

But if one takes the reflection for the truth of things the result is a form of imprisonment. The assumption that he exists at the center of the world, whose order can only be glimpsed from the vantage point of the light he throws upon it, confines him within an unrealistically narrow view of reality. The overriding goal of life should therefore be to escape the limits of our egoistic prisons for the sake of an expanded and more generous conception of things. Above all this means a deeper appreciation of the longings and sufferings of other human beings.

Even the most generous among us can never do this completely. We all remain tethered to the deformities of our individual points of view and would have to overcome our finitude altogether in order to see the world fully in the light of others' candles. "If we had a keen vision and feeling of all ordinary human life, it would be like hearing the grass grow and the squirrel's heart beat, and we should die of that roar which lies on the other side of silence. As it is, the quickest of us walk about well wadded with stupidity."[34] But the attempt to overcome our natal incapacity to see the world except from a single point of view can succeed to varying degrees, and it is always possible to gain more of the selfless understanding that with increasing clarity Dorothea strives to attain as the novel moves toward its conclusion.[35]

On its surface, Dorothea's ethics of generosity bears a strong resemblance to the Christian doctrine of good works. "What do we live for," she famously asks, "if it is not to make life less difficult for others?"[36] Eliot underscores the point in the concluding paragraphs of the "Finale." There is "no creature," she writes, "whose inward being is so strong that it is not greatly determined by what lies outside it." We each possess only limited power and therefore depend on others for help. That "things are not so ill with you and me as they might have been" is a consequence of others' "un-historic acts" of generosity, which though small and unremembered are "incalculably diffusive" and contribute to "the growing good of the world."[37] All of this might have come from a standard Christian manual on social ethics. What makes Dorothea's creed distinctive is the central value it assigns to generosity on behalf of others in the absence of a judging God who gives such acts their warrant and reward.

To the question, "Why ought we to serve others?" the Christian answer is, "because God commands it," or perhaps more elaborately, "because we should respect their humanity, that is, their resemblance to the divine Author of the world" (a Kantian formulation). Dorothea's answer is different. Generosity to others is good because it has an enlarging effect on those it serves. "The presence of a noble nature, generous in its wishes, ardent in its charity, changes the lights for us: we begin to see things again in their larger, quieter masses and to believe that we too can be seen and judged in the wholeness of our character."[38]

The result is an increase in the breadth of the vision, understanding and power of the one who is the beneficiary of such generosity. Eliot calls this "the divine efficacy of rescue that may lie in a self-subduing act of fellowship."[39] She stresses that the effect is reciprocal. The person who strives to see the better selves of others, and to encourage their growth, herself becomes more powerful in the process. To the extent that she succeeds, she escapes the "moral stupidity" of her own egoism and is able to take in more of the world as others see it. Her understanding of the world increases. Her soul becomes less partial and on that account more active. "I wish to exert myself," Dorothea says to her uncle after Casaubon's death.[40] She yearns to be as active as she can, and by the end of the novel knows that the most active life available to her is one that embraces the dreams and accepts the failings of others with a maximum of generosity. In this way she attains what Eliot calls "the least partial good"—the widest view of things and the greatest quantum of activity or power, which for Dorothea remains a good worth pursuing even in a disenchanted world where human ethics can no longer be founded on the promise of an eternal life beyond it.

Recasting the highest human good in these terms compels one to acknowledge that its attainment can never be complete. A Christian saint like Theresa expects to finish her journey, if not here on earth then in heaven. At the beginning of the novel, Dorothea seems to have an expectation of this sort. By the end, however, she has come to terms with her limits, among other ways by accepting her love for Ladislaw, which in contrast to her otherworldly love for Casaubon, springs from Dorothea's all-too-human passion for a vital, exciting and imperfect young man. She sees that her limits cannot be transcended so long as she is living and no longer hopes that they will be when she dies. Yet the impossibility of overcoming these limits, in life or death, does not cause her to revise her ethical beliefs or shake the serene confidence of

the spiritual outlook at which she arrives. The fundamental vice, as Dorothea sees it, is selfishness or egoism and the fundamental virtue the expansion of self—the substitution of activity for weakness in oneself and others
alike. This is the essence of Dorothea's religion of generosity whose authority
is untouched, for her at least, by the impossibility of ever reaching the goal it
prescribes. The good it affirms is what remains of the Christian idea of salvation when sainthood is no longer available and all that remains to human beings is the possibility of continually enlarging their minds, though never to
the point of taking everything in.

No reader of *Middlemarch* can doubt that George Eliot embraces this religion herself. She frequently endorses its values directly and the reader's affection for Dorothea is a consequence of the fact that among the characters
in the novel, she is the one that comes closest to embodying the author's point
of view. Broadly speaking, it is the same point of view—the same religion—
that Spinoza expounds in the last two parts of the *Ethics*.

We should always act, Spinoza says, in a way that allows us to grasp more
of the world in a manner less distorted by our passions. In his terminology,
we should strive to comprehend the world *sub specie aeternitatis*. To the extent we succeed, we become more powerful and therefore real—the goal
toward which every being moves on account of the striving to persevere in
existence that constitutes its identity as the finite mode it is—though the finitude of every mode ensures that this goal can never be reached. Recast in less
philosophical terms, this is the ethic of empowerment through generosity that
George Eliot puts in the mouth of her central character, and if it seems a stretch
to compare the theology it represents to that of Spinoza, it is important to
recall that shortly before the publication of her first work of fiction George
Eliot translated the *Ethics* into English.[41]

Still, if Dorothea is the character in *Middlemarch* who most self-consciously
expresses its author's Spinozism, some readers, at least, may find the development of her character less rich and satisfying than that of many others in the
novel. By comparison with its other leading figures, Dorothea seems rather
two-dimensional. She is admirable, of course, and we are clearly meant to ap-
prove her words and deeds, especially after her profoundly unwise choice of
Casaubon as a husband. But on the whole she remains more an idea than a
character—less a human individual with a unique balance of virtue and vice,
of selflessness and destructive egoism, than the representative of a philosophical ideal.

Even given Dorothea's evangelical pietism, for example, it is difficult to understand how she cannot see what Sir James Chettam and her sister Celia and nearly everyone else does—that Casaubon is a dreadfully inappropriate match. Granted that Dorothea is presented to us, in the opening chapter of the novel, as a young woman who resembles "the blessed Virgin" and is so preoccupied with the "eternal consequences" of her actions that she is "likely to seek martyrdom" in one way or another, still, the reader wonders, how could she make such a monumental mistake?

Others in the novel commit equally grievous errors of judgment, but their mistakes almost always seem easier to comprehend because the psychologies that lie behind them have been more fully developed. The reader has a deeper understanding of the complex mix of selfishness and generosity from which their judgments spring. A similar mix of course exists in Dorothea's case as well. Her longing for martyrdom has an element of selfishness in it. But it is harder to appreciate the nuances of her character than those, say, of Lydgate, Rosamond, Casaubon and even Bulstrode. Dorothea never ceases to be too good to be true. By comparison with the novel's other richly drawn and all-too-human figures, Dorothea remains throughout something of a stick figure, an icon of almost saintly powers, in the world but never wholly of it. Even her passion for Ladislaw has a sacrificial quality. She gives up her fortune for his sake, and the lion's share of her energy too—just as she had sacrificed herself for Casaubon not all that long before. This makes it hard for us to follow her example. Dorothea may be the most perfect expression in the book of Eliot's theology, but the relative lack of realism with which her character is drawn makes this theology seem less credible, or at least less available, to ordinary human readers who, having rejected romantic aestheticism and nihilism alike, are drawn to Eliot's conception of salvation in a world without God, yet find her religion difficult to embrace if this means modeling one's own life on that of Dorothea.

But to the question, "What does it mean to take this religion seriously and to strive to live according to its dictates?" *Middlemarch* offers another, better answer. That is to live not as Dorothea does but in the spirit of the novel itself: to strive to view the larger world, so far as one is able, with an attention to the complexities of the men and women in it similar to that displayed by the author of the book with regard to the individuals in the smaller, fictional world she has created. It is not Dorothea's life but George Eliot's own sympathetic excavation of the dreams and failures of the novel's other leading characters that give its readers the best illustration of what her theology demands of those who take it to heart.

Casaubon, for example, is a supremely selfish man. He is superficially solicitous of Dorothea's interests, but at bottom only engaged by his own. He is consumed by his project, to which Dorothea is merely a helpful adjunct. He loves her solely for what she can contribute to his comfort and to the success of his work. Even the work itself is motivated by a selfish desire. Casaubon professes to care nobly about the advancement of knowledge, but in fact is consumed by the wish to refute his detractors' low opinion of him. And finally, of course, the cruelty of his decision to humiliate Dorothea even after he is dead and cannot possibly benefit from her suffering, is an act of jealous egoism that represents the very opposite of the expansive generosity the author of *Middlemarch* affirms. And yet, despite all this, she manages to engage the reader's sympathies on Casaubon's behalf and helps us see the poignancy of his failure. Instead of mocking it, as others do, she invites us to view the world from his perspective without, of course, denying how pinched and powerless it is.

> [I]f Mr. Casaubon, speaking for himself, has rather a chilling rhetoric, it is not therefore certain that there is no good work or fine feeling in him. Did not an immortal physicist and interpreter of hieroglyphs write detestable verses? Has the theory of the solar system been advanced by graceful manners and conversational tact? Suppose we turn from outside estimates of a man to wonder, with keener interest, what is the report of his own consciousness about his doings or capacity: with what hindrances he is carrying on his daily labors; what fading of hopes or what deeper fixity of self-delusion the years are marking off within him; and with what spirit he wrestles against universal pressure, which one day will be too heavy for him and bring his heart to its final pause. Doubtless his lot is important in his own eyes; and the chief reason that we think he asks too large a place in our consideration must be our want of room for him, since we refer him to the Divine regard with perfect confidence; nay, it is ever held sublime for our neighbor to expect the utmost there, however little he may have got from us. Mr. Casaubon, too, was the center of his own world; if he was liable to think that others were providentially made for him, and especially likely to consider them in the light of their fitness for the author

of a *Key to All Mythologies,* this trait is not quite alien to us, and like the other mendicant hopes of mortals, claims some of our pity.[42]

Lydgate has a more direct claim on our sympathies. We are attracted by his vitality and reformist ideals. We admire his ambition to make a fundamental contribution to the science of medicine. His gentrified connections add to his appeal. In the provincial world of *Middlemarch,* Lydgate represents a breath of fresh air—a welcome cosmopolitanism that together with his charm and passion and devotion to public health makes him attractive to many others in the novel, and above all to Rosamond Vincy. But Lydgate is an egotist too. There is more sexual energy in his attraction to Rosamond than in Casaubon's to Dorothea, but at bottom Lydgate also wants a wife who will be an adjunct and ornament. Like Casaubon, what Lydgate desires most of all is to be allowed to pursue his professional ambitions. He wants a comfortable home and attentive wife who will look after his needs and makes sure he is sufficiently refreshed from his labors. Lydgate talks "fervidly to Rosamond of his hopes as to the highest uses of his life" and finds it "delightful to be listened to by a creature" who will "bring him the sweet furtherance of satisfying affection—beauty—repose—such help as our thoughts get from the summer sky and the flower-fringed meadows."[43] Indeed, Lydgate enjoys more than a mere sufficiency of such help. He likes living beyond his means, so long as he doesn't have to worry about the economic details. This is a form of selfishness too. Like a child absorbed in his own interests, Lydgate is unable or unwilling to take a wider view of things. In this respect, he and Casaubon are similarly compromised, despite the differences in age and energy that set them apart.

Moreover, Lydgate's selfishness is perfectly adjusted to his wife's. If Lydgate values Rosamond because she fits the picture of happiness he has constructed from his own point of view, Rosamond values Lydgate for a similar reason. Rosamond is a romantic. She wants a life of glamour and prestige like that of the heroines in the novels she reads, though her conception of happiness is provincial and small-minded.[44] Rosamond loves Lydgate not for his own sake but because he suits this imagined ideal. She is unable to understand why he can't adjust his career to ensure that she has the money she needs to pay for the refinements she feels she deserves. This leads her to disregard her husband's instructions and to act in a way that he (though not she) views as a betrayal of their marriage.[45] Yet Rosamond's egoism is merely the reflex of

Lydgate's. Each is a prisoner of the other's imagination, consigned to a role circumscribed by the other's self-centered view of the world. This is a recipe for a bad marriage, which leads to a loss of power on both sides—to the diminishment of what each is able to do and be—and though they find a way to survive, it is not a happy survival, nor as the "Finale" reveals, a very long one either.[46]

Still, Eliot engages our sympathies on behalf of both of the parties to this reciprocally destructive relation. This is easiest to see in Lydgate's case. Lydgate's weakness first becomes apparent when he fails to resist Bulstrode's manipulations regarding the appointment of a new minister at the hospital. But Lydgate's inattention to the matter seems understandable, given his preoccupation with larger and more important matters. And who can blame him, at first at least, for paying less attention than he should to his household finances, in part because it delights him to see Rosamond so happy? Lydgate may be weak and selfish, but his dream to do something great with his life is thrilling. "[I]n the multitude of middle-aged men who go about their vocations in a daily course determined for them much in the same way as the tie of their cravats, there is always a good number who once meant to shape their own deeds and alter the world a little." Most of course never do. "Lydgate did not mean to be one of those failures."[47] The reader is on Lydgate's side. Even the moral agony that he experiences when Bulstrode's saving gift appears in retrospect to perhaps have been a bribe, strengthens our sympathy for Lydgate just as his life is unraveling.

It would be a misjudgment, though, to say that our sympathies for Lydgate are bought at Rosamond's expense. She is a weak and superficial person—not a grown-up woman, but a selfish and spoiled child, given to tears and sulking when she doesn't get her way. But Eliot warns us to "think no unfair evil of her," since Rosamond "had no wicked plots, nothing sordid or mercenary" and "never thought of money except as something necessary which other people would always provide." Moreover, "she was not in the habit of devising falsehoods, and if her statements were no direct clue to fact, why they were not intended in that light—they were among her elegant accomplishments, intended to please."[48]

This is said of Rosamond early in the novel, before impending bankruptcy has driven her to something that looks more like deliberate deceit. But even here the simpleminded way in which she conceives her predicament and the best solution to it, draws the sting of censure and leaves the reader feeling she is no more to be blamed than a child. And when, near the end of the novel,

Rosamond is "taken hold of by an emotion stronger than her own" and tells Dorothea that what she is thinking about Ladislaw "is not true," the singular selflessness of her act, when measured against the unrelieved egoism of everything she has done to that point, reminds us that even a spoiled child can on occasion take a more generous view of things. When she hears Rosamond's words, Dorothea's "immediate consciousness" is "one of immense sympathy without check," and it seems clear that the author of the novel means for that to be the reader's reaction as well.[49]

Even Bulstrode invites a measure of sympathy. He is the darkest figure in the book, haughty and demanding, the holier-than-thou apostle of an unbending Calvinism that makes him indifferent to the human sufferings of those around him, a man with a disgraceful and concealed past, and in the end a murderer. Yet Eliot helps us to see the world even from Bulstrode's point of view. At crucial moments in the book, and especially toward the end, the reader is made to experience the pathos of the tortured and ultimately doomed project of self-improvement that defines the egoistic vantage point from which he views and uses every other character in *Middlemarch*.

Bulstrode has done awful things to make his fortune, but the remainder of his life amounts to a kind of atonement. He may be unfeeling in his human relations, but he is struggling to correct the balance of good and evil in his life as a whole—even before John Raffles appears to undo his carefully constructed concealments. However selfish Bulstrode's efforts may seem, like those of Casaubon and Lydgate they are motivated by a professed devotion to a selfless ideal. There is hypocrisy in this, of course, but his determination to lead an exemplarily pious life and to do all he can to save the souls of others is not a complete lie. There is a measure of genuine conviction in it. And when Bulstrode is wrestling with his conscience about whether to let Raffles die through planned inadvertence and engages in a kind of moral casuistry that displays his commitment to morality along with his selfish preparedness to set it aside, who among the novel's readers has not done the same, in a situation where the stakes were lower?[50] We know that Bulstrode acts wrongly. But our complete lack of sympathy for Raffles makes it easier to imagine reaching the decision he does. (Raffles is the only character in *Middlemarch* who lacks the psychological complexity required to enable us to see the world from his point of view. He is a caricature, a *deus ex machina,* more at home in the milieu of *David Copperfield* or *Oliver Twist*.) When Bulstrode is unmasked and his world falls apart in humiliation and shame, Eliot's readers are torn between feelings of righteous approval and a more sympathetic attitude toward him, represented by his silent and long-suffering wife, who is an appealing figure precisely because it is hard not to share her view of Bulstrode, in a limited way at least.[51]

What the reader discovers in Bulstrode's case is true of every other character in the novel as well: there is more to the person than one initially suspects. Like the characters themselves, the reader tends at first to arrange his impressions of them into neat "concentric circles" organized around the reader's own sense of right and wrong. But the novel itself fights against the "moral stupidity" of this tendency. It compels the reader to acknowledge that Casaubon's project is both foolish and grand; that Lydgate is a weak but noble man; that despite her selfishness and venality, Rosamond remains capable of what for her represents a remarkable act of self-sacrifice; and that even in the darkest hour of his life, Bulstrode retains an agonizing measure of moral self-awareness that makes him something more than the monster we wish him to be.

In each case, the reader of *Middlemarch* is helped to enact Dorothea's ethic of generosity. The result is that the small world of Eliot's novel—what Jane Austen famously called the "little bit" of ivory on which she wrought her art—becomes steadily more real.[52] Perspectives multiply. The number of candles in whose light we see the world increases. Gradually the reader is loosened from his or her own egoistic presumptions and offered an experience of life less compromised by them (though progress in this respect is always relative). One comes to see that the world is made up of individuals whose complexity no scheme of egoistic judgments can exhaust, and with this knowledge becomes more real oneself, for reality is merely the measure of the extent to which a finite being is able to take in the infinitely complex world that lies outside it—the very thing our prejudices prevent us from doing.

The modern novel offers its readers "the gift of transmigration" as an antidote to their "moral stupidity." Its effect may therefore also be described as a kind of *catharsis*. But the treatment it offers differs in a fundamental way from the one that Aristotle attributes to imitative art of the serious sort.

The latter presupposes a single human good fixed by the common form that all men share and a conception of happiness founded on an intellectualist theology that denies the intelligibility and therefore reality of individuals as such. The novelist's gift of transmigration rests on a different theology. It assumes that the individuality of individuals is something real too and therefore assigns the world an infinite as opposed to merely finite reality.

The idea of such a world is a Christian discovery. But the cathartic gift that novels like *Middlemarch* offer their readers is not that of a God beyond the world to his human creatures. The modern novel emerges as belief in such a God falls away. As a form of literary representation, it belongs to an age of disenchantment and whatever saving power it possesses increases as that of the Christian God declines. The novelist's work is the gift of one human being to another. It is founded on a collaborative act of friendship motivated by the longing, which reader and writer share, to move toward the unattainable God of the world, so far as strength and time allow. This is the same longing that lies, as we have seen, at the root of the modern research ideal, seemingly so remote from the imaginative milieu of the novel, yet joined to it, as Eliot's masterpiece suggests, by a born-again paganism that is neither Christian nor Aristotelian but theologically distinct from both. Its clearest philosophical statement is that of Spinoza's *Ethics,* a book Eliot knew and loved.

THE SPINOZA OF ECCLES STREET

James Joyce's *Ulysses* violates three of the requirements that Aristotle establishes for imitative works of a serious sort.

First, Joyce's novel barely has a plot of any kind at all. Many things happen in it but they do not have the dramatic unity of an "action" in Aristotle's sense—of a purposeful endeavor whose internal coherence is imitated by a story with a beginning, middle and end. Henry James' dictum that the modern novel subordinates plot to character, rather than the other way around, is illustrated in a particularly extreme way by Joyce's nearly actionless epic, whose story line, in the conventional sense, might be summarized as follows. An unhappily married middle-aged man wanders about the city of Dublin while his wife entertains her lover at home. An unhappy younger man has a number of separate experiences of his own. That evening, the two meet and eventually return together to the older man's home. There is the promise of a friendship between them that may be of benefit to both. The novel concludes with some silent reflections on the part of the wife that weakly suggest a possible rapprochement with her husband as well. That a summary of this sort so completely misses the depth and grandeur of Joyce's novel is an indication of how completely it upends the Aristotelian conception of the relation of character to plot.

Second, the unity of *Ulysses* is not one of action but time. The events it records are bound together by their contemporaneity. There are complex causal and psychological relations among these, of course. Various characters enter the thoughts, feelings and dreams of others. But at the deepest level, what gives the novel its coherence is the fact that everything that happens in it takes place on a single day. Aristotle claims that contemporaneity can never be more than an accidental relation. Things that happen at the same time do not have an intelligible relation to one another solely on that account. In order to have such a relation, they must be part of a single, purposeful scheme. *Ulysses* turns this judgment upside down as well. It multiplies perspectives and styles of presentation in order to force the reader to accept that the unity of the novel is a merely "coincidental" one instead.

Indeed, it does something even more radical. It encourages the reader to believe that the temporal unity of what happens on this single day is not only real but infinitely so, in contrast to the formal and therefore finite reality that a plot of the classical sort possesses. The progressive unfolding of this reality requires the ever more elaborate reconstruction of the novel's relations of simultaneity as ones of causation and intention instead. This process of conversion has no determinate end. The story of June 16, 1904, can never be fully captured by an explanatory scheme of either kind. But Joyce's novel holds the promise of a limitless intelligibility that can be progressively redeemed by converting this single fragment of time from a merely contingent concatenation of events into an intelligible web of physical and psychological interactions. As one moves in this direction the "order of the day" increases and the accident of contemporaneity is steadily transformed into the necessity of understanding. None of this is metaphysically conceivable from an Aristotelian point of view. For Aristotle, the idea of boundless order is a contradiction in terms and the equation of necessity with time a metaphysical mistake. To make sense of these ideas, a different metaphysics is required. The one that best fits Joyce's novel is Nietzsche's. Bloomsday is the artistic representation of Nietzsche's doctrine of eternal return. However many times one reads *Ulysses,* it is always the same day with its infinite tangle of meanings, a transient and forgettable moment yet one that is infused down to its smallest details with a timeless order that reflects the real if never fully transparent identity of eternity and time.

Third, the central figure in the novel is not the sort of person that Aristotle considers an appropriate subject of serious art. Leopold Bloom is an ordinary man, indeed something of a buffoon. When we first meet him, he is engaged in the simple business of fixing breakfast and moving his bowels. Later, we see him masturbate in his pants; fantasize about watching Molly have sex with Blazes Boylan in their marital bed; and then ejaculate on her rear end when he finally joins her in that same bed at the end of a very long day. At moments, he seems more like a woman than a man. Yet at other moments—in his confrontation with The Citizen, for example, and his protectiveness of Stephen—Bloom possesses an admirable largeness of feeling that sets him apart from everyone else in the novel: so much so that at times he seems the most magnificent human being in all of Dublin, even, as Bloom himself imagines, a figure of Christlike proportions (and of course, throughout, a latter-day Odysseus). From an Aristotelian perspective, this mixture of characteristics makes him as unsuitable to comedy or lampoon as to the serious kind of imitation that alone possesses the morally educative power of *catharsis*. But if Bloom's neurotic grandeur is an offense against the separation of styles for which Aristotle's *Poetics* provides the original warrant, it is the key to understanding the role he plays as the divine yet all-too-human hero of *Ulysses*—the Spinoza of Eccles Street—and to appreciating the very non-Aristotelian theology that lies behind it.[53]

What kind of man is Leopold Bloom?

To begin with, he is a naturalist in Spinoza's sense. He is curious about the way things work and inclined to explain them in scientific terms. Why, for example, is the penis of a hanged man erect? What are the advantages of a proper diet and regular exercise? How does the plumbing system of Dublin work? What happens to a body after it is buried? Bloom's view of these matters is entirely free of awe and superstition. He answers each question with the same dry scientific precision. Indeed, he relishes being a man of science, unlike most of his fellow Dubliners whose beliefs have been distorted by myths and fables of one kind or another.

Bloom's rationalism applies equally to natural events and to human phenomena. Like Spinoza, he refuses to concede that man "is a kingdom within a kingdom." One set of rules applies to everything in Bloom's world. His ubiquitous rationalism is particularly pronounced in his attitude toward religion. When he enters the Church of All Hallows, for example, and finds a Communion service in progress, Bloom is prompted to a series of reflections on the social and psychological utility of what he himself considers "a rum idea: eating bits of a corpse why the cannibals cotton to it."[54] His graveside thoughts about the service for Paddy Dignam are in a similar vein. Throughout the day, Bloom remains a scientific observer of the Catholic world that surrounds him.

In one obvious sense, of course, Bloom's detachment from this world is a consequence of his being Jewish. He thinks of himself as a Jew and others do as well. This makes him an outsider in the city and country to which he nevertheless feels a profound loyalty. In his confrontation with The Citizen, the perception of Bloom as an outsider boils over into overt anti-Semitism. But Bloom is not a Jew in the religious sense. To begin with, he is not even technically Jewish because his mother Ellen wasn't. More important, though he has some knowledge of Jewish law, he shows no allegiance to it. He begins his day with a pork kidney for breakfast. Bloom's Judaism is entirely sentimental. It gives him a connection to his father Rudolf and his own dead son Rudy, but entails no beliefs or ritual practices. In fact, Bloom has never even been circumcised. He is a convert to Roman Catholicism and has been baptized three times. Still, his self-identification as a Jew remains intact. In reality, therefore, Bloom belongs neither to the world of rabbinic Judaism, on the one hand, nor that of orthodox Catholicism on the other. This helps explain the detached view he takes of both and his inclination to subject their dogmas to rational scrutiny—in particular, beliefs about the soul, sin, the afterlife and the doctrine of creation. Bloom's musings on these topics reflect his naturalist attitude toward the world in general.

It would be a terrible mistake, though, to conclude that Bloom has no religious feelings at all. In the first place, he is deeply interested in theosophical speculations of an exotic (that is to say, non-Abrahamic) kind. This is a theme that is introduced in his first exchange with Molly (and the last, until he goes to bed by her side at the end of the day). Molly asks about the meaning of the word "metempsychosis," which she has encountered in one of her semipornographic novels. Bloom's knowledgeable answer suggests a basic acquaintance with some elements of pagan metaphysics as well as an interest in them, which Molly of course wholly lacks. We return to the same theme in Molly's concluding soliloquy, when she recalls how bored she was listening to Bloom talk about Spinoza and the soul. This is the third time the philosopher is mentioned. The first is when Bloom cites him as an example of Jewish achievement in his reply to The Citizen, and the second when a summary of Spinoza's philosophy is reported as being among Bloom's books in one of the exhaustive catalogues of the penultimate episode of the novel. Detached as he may be from the traditional beliefs of Jews and Catholics, and despite his calmly scientific dissection of them as baseless superstitions, Leopold Bloom is clearly a man with spiritual interests and a curiosity about the divinity of things, regarding which he hopes, it seems, to find enlightenment in the speculative philosophies of ancient and modern writers outside the Judeo-Christian tradition.

Second, and more important, the spiritual side of Bloom's character is manifest not only in his intellectual interest in theosophy but in the manner of observation that defines many of his encounters with people and objects during the course of the day. Bloom is filled with an immediate wonder at things. His explanations are relentlessly materialistic. But his urge to explain is rooted in an ardent state of wonder that no one else in the novel possesses to a remotely similar degree—with the important exception of Stephen, whose sense of wonder has turned against itself and become a self-destructive nihilism.

Unlike Stephen, who is tormented by his loss of belief, unbelieving Bloom is free to be amazed at everything that crosses his path, beginning with the cat that does so twice, once early and once late. And what an astounding world it is, seen through the eyes of Leopold Bloom: how inexhaustibly rich in people, animals, and even inanimate things that have the power to stop an observant human being in his tracks and cause him to ask why they act as they do! Even the question of what the cat's meow means is enough to occupy one for a lifetime. Bloom sees the extraordinary in the ordinary. He is struck by what might be called the resident divinity of things. He glimpses the God of the world wherever he turns, unlike Stephen, who no longer sees God anywhere at all, and the other characters in the novel, for whom God has been confined to a narrow corner of practice and belief. In this sense, Bloom is a pantheist, though of the rationalist and scientific (which is to say, Spinozist) variety.

That he is able to see God in the least of things does not, of course, insulate Bloom against ordinary human feelings of melancholy and regret. He remembers with sadness how he and Molly once felt, years before on Howth Hill, and experiences an overwhelming sense of the pointlessness of the metabolic wheel of life after watching a room full of men stuff themselves with lunch. More fundamentally, his entire day is shadowed by the depressing knowledge of his wife's infidelity and the neurotic disturbance that has deeply deformed his marriage. Yet these episodes of depression and the mood of unhappiness that shapes his life more generally are offset by recurrent moments of joy—not of ecstasy, for Bloom's wonder at things never carries him beyond the realm of human experience, but the steadier sort that is aroused by a wakeful attention to the endless mystery of the world and the endless enlightenment to which its rational investigation leads.

Moments of such joyful attention punctuate Bloom's day and reach a steady crescendo in the catechism that concludes it, in which the contents of

Bloom's world, mental and physical, are surveyed with a lyrical rigor that represents the intellectual counterpart of Molly's final "Yes." Sitting with Stephen in his kitchen, drinking a cup of "Epps' soluble cocoa," Bloom is happier than he has been all day. The rapturous naturalism with which the whole scene is described, from its humblest features to its most sublime ones, from the operations of Bloom's stove to "the heaventree of stars hung with humid night-blue fruit," expresses perfectly the combination of exuberant wonder at the infinite complexity of the world and boundless confidence in its rational explicability that constitutes the heart of Bloom's unorthodox religion.

It is in this light that we should understand Bloom's characteristic posture as a disinterested yet sympathetic observer of others.

Bloom watches those around him from a distance. He views their actions with a measure of clinical detachment. He is therefore able to diagnose the causes of their suffering with greater objectivity. This is strikingly true of his relation with Stephen. But a similar spirit of objectivity characterizes many of Bloom's other interactions: with the congregants in All Hallows; the mourners in the cab on the way to Paddy Dignam's burial; the diners at Burton's; the young men drinking and joking at the lying-in hospital; and the denizens of Nighttown. In each case Bloom sees what others don't or can't. He is a panopticon among men, the one vantage point from which the whole of Dublin may be seen. His perspective seems at times no perspective at all but a comprehensive point of view from which others are shut out on account of the prejudices that limit their range of understanding.

Yet the detachment that allows Bloom to grasp the fears and foibles of his fellow Dubliners with an objectivity their own passions obscure, does not produce, as one might expect, a cool disregard for human suffering. Quite the opposite: Bloom's judgments are rarely harsh but reflect instead a tendency to sympathize with everyone and everything he observes. He buys cakes for the pigeons, pities the blind piano tuner, empathizes with the cattle in the slaughterhouse, and finds himself in the bar where The Citizen is holding court because he has come there to inquire about the insurance for Paddy Dignam's widow.

What distinguishes Bloom is his capacity to see things from the outside and at the same time to feel them from within: to comprehend the world as a whole with an objectivity that is possible only if one is free of the passions that define each particular perspective on it, and yet able to understand these passions and the distortions to which they give rise in the way that only a fellow sufferer can. A man who could see all things all the time in both of these two ways would no longer be a human being but a divine one. He would be the God of the world, and if Bloom at moments seems to take on a semi-divine status it is because he comes closer to this approachable if unattainable condition than any other character in the novel.

But Leopold Bloom is no God. He is a neurotic human being, anxious and lonely, and all his powers of observation and sympathy cannot save him from the unhappiness that arises from a deep disturbance in the most important relation in his life.

If Bloom has more power than anyone else in *Ulysses* on account of his superior capacity for objectivity and fellow feeling, the same detachment that is the source of his strength is a cause of passivity and weakness as well. Bloom is supremely watchful. This allows him to see beyond the narrow horizons of others' points of view. But it also shuts him out from the intimacy that every human being craves. It makes him the wisest figure in the novel but the loneliest one too, for the watchfulness that gives Bloom his Archimedean leverage on the world is at the same time the isolation of a man without a friend. It is the masturbatory voyeurism of a timid man who prefers the safety of his private world of dreams to the riskier one of real friendship with others.

Exchanging looks with Gerty MacDowell at the beach while he fantasizes about her (and she about him) until his "Roman candle" bursts; reading the letter that his secret correspondent Martha has sent to her "naughty boy" Henry; exclaiming "Show! Hide! Show! Plough her! More! Shoot!" as he "clasps himself," watching Molly and Boylan in the phantasmagoric dream world of Bella Cohen's brothel (confirming that Bloom has been an active conspirator in facilitating their adulterous union and perhaps enjoys it as much as they): at these moments, Bloom seems pitiably incapable of establishing real contact with a woman. Every real relation between human beings threatens its participants with a loss of self-control. This is most painfully clear where sex is concerned. To Bloom it seems better to avoid this danger by satisfying his longings on his own. It seems better, in short, to be a voyeur than a vulnerable participant in the drama of (sexual) life. But this is an ersatz form of control. It is the illusion of power, not its reality. If Bloom possesses a godlike watchfulness that makes him the most rational and therefore powerful figure in the novel, his voyeurism, which is the other, poignantly human side of his watchfulness, makes him the weakest, and reminds us that the pursuit of divinity is an enterprise in which we need the company of friends.

It is not wrong to strive to become the God of the world. One could not even renounce the effort if he chose. But it is wrong to think that we must undertake it on our own. The limits of what Spinoza calls our "modal" nature guarantee that the longing for omnipotence can never be fulfilled. But these same limits supply the motive and provide the means for the myriad forms of friendship that are the greatest and most distinctively human resource we possess in our struggle to reach this irrepressible goal, and the deepest consolation that any man or woman ever knows for the failure to achieve it.

The attempt to master the world on one's own is therefore not a sign of maturity or the wisdom of a philosophical sage. It is an infantile disorder—the wish to substitute a false omnipotence for the real but unreachable one that attracts not only us but every finite being. It is a neurosis for which friendship alone is a cure. If Leopold Bloom may be called a Spinozist on account of the naturalistic spirit of wonder that defines his encounter with everything in our infinitely intelligible world, he is a neurotic Spinozist whose anxieties have led him in middle age to an isolation that makes him less powerful than he would be if he were able to share his life with a friend or two. The plot of *Ulysses,* to the extent it has one, is the story of how Bloom finds the friends he needs, or by the end of the novel appears at least to be poised to find them, and they him, since real friendship is always a two-way street.

Bloom's two friends are of course Stephen and Molly. Let us briefly consider his relation with each.

Unlike Bloom, Stephen Daedalus is by temperament a metaphysician. Bloom does have some speculative curiosity and his attitude toward life in general has a spiritual coloration. But Stephen is obsessed with theological arguments to a degree that from the perspective of Bloom's more naturalistic approach to life is bound to seem extreme.

Yet for all of Stephen's theology, his faith has fallen away—in contrast to Bloom, who may be lonely and at times even melancholic, but displays a steady confidence in the meaning and value of the world around him. Stephen is in fact in a state of crisis, heightened by his mother's recent death. Deeply knowledgeable about the Catholic doctrines he was taught as a child, he now regards them as fables. Yet he still lives agonizingly in the shadow of his abandoned faith. Stephen seems to have concluded that if the Catholic conception of God is not true, then none can be. His predicament is that of the nihilist who simultaneously rejects the dogma of divine creation and holds onto the idea that the only God who could save us from the pointlessness of human existence is one who stands apart from the world in the way the Christian God does. Stephen's nihilism has led him to flirt with a sterile aestheticism (evidenced, among other ways, by his frivolous theory of *Hamlet*). But instead of helping to resolve his crisis of faith, Stephen's empty playfulness has only deepened it. His friends, moreover, are not real companions and Stephen's relation with his father has reached a dead end. Like Bloom, he is a lonely man too.

Their needs are indeed symmetrical. Bloom has lost a son and wants one. He wants to be able to care for a man younger than himself, just as Stephen, who has lost his way and is at risk of squandering his gifts, needs an older, wiser man to take the place of his self-absorbed and negligent father. Each, moreover, longs for a genuine intellectual companion. Stephen engages in a great deal of agile repartee with Buck Mulligan and others, but none of it is serious. He is flashy, quick and full of esoteric ideas, but shows no commitment to anything he says. His displays of wit are a mere simulacrum of real conversation, separated by long stretches of moody loneliness that make it clear that even when Stephen is talking most brilliantly he remains within a solitary shell. Bloom is not isolated from others in a similar way, yet in his daylong wanderings he has not found a single person with whom he can speak in anything more than superficially conventional terms. He longs to have a friendly conversation that touches on matters of philosophical, scientific and moral importance in the thoughtful terms these deserve. Alone with Stephen in the cab stand and then later in his kitchen, Bloom at last finds the conversational partner for whom he has been searching, and the directness of Stephen's replies suggests that for the first time since the day began he is in earnest too. One has the sense that when Stephen leaves the house on Eccles Street shortly before dawn, his conversation with Bloom has only begun, and that the two men will meet again and their nascent friendship ripen into something like the father-son relation for which both hunger so deeply.

A philosophically inclined reader may even be tempted to imagine that as they continue to talk, Stephen will find the antidote he needs to his own post-Christian nihilism in Bloom's more joyful God of the world, and that with Stephen's help Bloom's inarticulate Spinozism will gradually become more explicit and the book on his library shelf (*Thoughts from Spinoza*) evolve into something like a conscious philosophy of living that the two men share, each in his own way. This is a fantasy, of course, but the fact that Stephen Daedalus grew up to become the author of the novel whose hero is Leopold Bloom gives one perhaps some modest warrant to indulge it.

Even more important than Bloom's relation to Stephen is his complicated and unhappy marriage to Molly. It is here that we feel Bloom's loneliness most acutely. Again, the loneliness is reciprocal. If Bloom has retreated from the marriage into a masturbatory isolation, she has retreated into a series of adulterous relations that (judging from her afternoon tryst with Blazes Boylan, who is merely the latest in a long line of lovers) appear to have left her as lonely as before—a condition she blames on her sexually inattentive husband. It is not entirely clear why their sexual relationship has broken down so completely. The death of their son Rudy seems to have had something to do with it. But whatever the cause, Poldy and Molly have now given up on penetrative sex, and so far as their relation is concerned, are capable only of self-induced and parallel orgasms, each in mental and physical isolation from the other.

Can this relation be repaired? More fundamentally, is there any reason why it should be? After all, the two share very little in common. Molly is coarse and silly. Her thoughts never get much beyond the surface of things. She doesn't have a philosophical bone in her body. Unlike Stephen, she is a wholly unsuitable intellectual partner for her husband. Indeed, from her point of view, he seems a bit ridiculous. But there is an undercurrent of respect for Bloom in Molly's soliloquy and an appreciation of how much each now shares with no one else in the world. Even after reviewing her earlier lovers, in the romantic glow of her girlhood on Gibraltar, and briefly entertaining a fantasy about a possible future relation with Stephen, Molly comes back to Bloom and endorses her choice of him with a qualified but resonant "Yes." For his part, Bloom still cares about Molly. He remains solicitous of her needs. He brings her breakfast in bed, orders the perfume she wants, even arranges to be away for the day so she can entertain her lover at home. He also seems still to be aroused by the fleshy beauty that attracted him to her in the first place. All things considered, there seems to be enough on both sides to draw them closer together. But again, why should that matter at all? Why do Poldy and Molly need to do more than share a bed in which nothing happens between them?

Sexual intimacy is a uniquely intimidating and rewarding kind of friendship. Nowhere else are we as vulnerable. Our fears and longings are on display here with a directness that elsewhere is more muted and often not visible at all. We are immediately confronted in our sex lives with what we are least able to control, and experience the deepest form of passivity that most people ever know. Sexual intimacy thus poses a peculiarly intense threat to our longing for control and provides an especially strong incentive to avoid it. No human being ever lives without some strategies of avoidance. But their pathological exaggeration produces a false experience of power, which in reality is a form of weakness in disguise that deprives the one who seeks safety in it of the consoling love we all need to bear the fact that none of us ever achieves more than a vanishingly small degree of control over the world we inhabit for such a short time. The loneliness of Bloom's voyeurism is a weakness of this kind. To combat it, he needs an intimate partner to whom he can trust his deepest vulnerabilities. These include the vulnerabilities of love and loss as well as of sexual desire. There is only one person in the entire world who offers Bloom a friendship of this sort. That is why he must find a way to re-enter his marriage and, literally, his wife.

Will this happen? It is impossible to say with confidence. The novel ends on a joyous but ambiguous note. Perhaps if they are able to talk with greater honesty about some of the things that are troubling them and about the loss of their son in particular, Poldy and Molly may be able to draw close again. There is still a residue of affection on each side and enough sexual energy to transform this into physical desire—the kind that overcame them the day their son Rudy was conceived. This may never happen, but the reader cannot help but hope it will since the renewal of intimacy between husband and wife seems the best hope they have of escaping the loneliness that in early middle age now imprisons both.

If we allow ourselves to imagine what might become of their relationship, the following hopeful fantasy occurs. Poldy and Molly have no intellectual interests in common. He reads Spinoza and her favorite author is Paul de Kock. Yet each has a capacity for wonder and joy—his speculative, serious and scientific; hers intuitive, aesthetic and mocking—that is equally remote from orthodox Christian belief and Stephen's nihilistic despair. Each thinks traditional religion rather foolish. But both are occasionally moved by the sense that even ordinary things are surrounded by an inexhaustible aura of meaning and beauty (a cat's meow, the memory of "those handsome Moors all in white and turbans like kings"). Each at moments seems to glimpse the divinity of the world. Their experience is never ecstatic and is punctuated by feelings of weakness and isolation. But though qualified and intermittent, it constitutes a spiritual bond between husband and wife. The capacity of both to see the world from time to time as an infinitely wonderful place without the need to secure its worth by appealing to the idea of a God beyond it, gives them a basis on which to build a friendship that is deeper even than the intellectual one than Bloom and Stephen may develop, and richer than the spiritless sex to which each has turned as their marriage has fallen apart. This is the happy thought to which Molly's final, joyful "Yes" gives some modest encouragement. It is a satisfying conclusion to the story of a day in the life of a neurotic

Spinozist who, at home at last in his bed, has the chance, at least, of overcoming the worst effects of his illness by reviving a friendship of the most
intimate and healing kind that any human being can ever experience.

THE METAPHYSICS OF THE MADELEINE

As *In Search of Lost Time* nears its end, Marcel Proust's Narrator is back
in Paris after a lengthy stay in a sanitarium. He is on his way to an afternoon
party at the home of Mme de Guermantes, an important figure in the Narrator's real and fantasy life. He wonders who will be at the party. He expects
to see many old acquaintances and worries that they may expect him to slip
back into the role he occupied at an earlier time in his life. This concerns him
because he is hoping at last to begin his career as a writer. He has felt called
to write since his childhood days at Combray. Will he ever do so? the Narrator wonders. Time is running out; it's now or never. If he allows himself to be
drawn back into the glittering world of the Guermantes, he may never get to
the serious business of writing, on which, he senses, his personal fate depends.

But a deeper obstacle stands in the way. The Narrator wants to be a writer
but as yet has nothing to write about. Since the day he wrote his first short
sketch on "the twin steeples of Martinville," he has been searching for "a
philosophic theme for some great literary work."[55] Now back from the sanitarium, on the threshold of middle age and about to enter Mme de Guermantes' salon, he still has not found it. But at just this moment, the Narrator
has an experience that gives him what he has sought for so long. He finds the
theme for his life work and is saved from the despair into which he might
have fallen if, at this crucial turning point, he had failed to discover the subject of the book he now knows that he must write.

The Narrator does not so much discover as literally stumble upon it. En-
tering "the courtyard of the Guermantes mansion," he trips "against the uneven paving-stones in front of the coach-house." This calls up a "dazzling and
indistinct vision" that he soon recognizes to be the memory of "two uneven
stones in the baptistery of St. Mark's," which he had visited for the first time
as an adult after having dreamt about making such a visit since he was a child.[56]
In its richness and evocative power, the Narrator's memory of Venice, triggered by the accident of stumbling on the stones, reminds him of another,
the most famous in the novel, aroused by "the flavor of a madeleine dipped
in tea" that years before had recalled to the Narrator the lost world of his childhood in Combray.[57]

But this second memory (the one of Venice) not only reminds the Narrator of the earlier one (aroused by the taste and smell of the madeleine). It moves him to stop and reflect on the nature of such memories in general and to ask why the earlier one possessed the power it did. This leads to an extended reverie on the meaning of memory, reality, time, eternity and art that provides the philosophical foundation for the novel as a whole—the metaphysics of the madeleine. Standing in the courtyard of the Guermantes mansion, the narrator remains lost in thought, until by the time he enters the house and joins those already there, he has found his "philosophical theme." As he walks into the party and is confronted once again by the glittering social world of his youth, now disfigured by the passage of time, the Narrator is filled with resolve to begin. Proust's novel contains many epiphanies, but the greatest, perhaps, is the knowledge that the book the reader holds in her hands is the fulfillment of this resolution itself.

To unravel the metaphysics of the madeleine, we can begin by reflecting on the Narrator's observation that his memory of the stones in St. Mark's filled him with a "joy" that made "death a matter of indifference."[58]

Every human being dies and everything we make eventually vanishes. "Eternal duration is promised no more to men's works than to men."[59] Still, the Narrator claims to have glimpsed an eternity of some kind and however fragmentary and "fugitive" his "contemplation" of it, his vision produces a feeling of joy that is infinitely more precious than the "social pleasures" to which he has devoted his life so far.[60] In this respect, his experience resembles that of the Christian saint who finds salvation by disengaging himself from the temporal world and living for the sake of God instead. But there is an elementary distinction between them. For the saint, eternity is opposed to time. It exists apart from and by contrast with it. For the Narrator, on the other hand, the eternity he glimpses in the memory triggered by the stones in the Guermantes' courtyard belongs to the transient moment recorded by the memory itself. Indeed, it is that very moment conceived in a certain way. Every fragment of time, the Narrator concludes, is already eternal. It has eternity in it, though only potentially, and if we fail to see this that is only because we have not yet grasped its "essence," which lies "outside of time."[61] The Narrator's eternity is thus not a realm distinct from that of time, as it is for the Christian saint, but an aspect or modality of it.

Because he locates eternity in time and not outside it, the Narrator's conception of what he calls the "extra-temporal" might be thought to be closer to Aristotle's instead. But here too the difference is fundamental. Aristotle's sage not only comprehends the immanent and changeless form of everything that moves and therefore exists in time. He is able to do this completely. All that is eternal in every moment is fully intelligible to him. For the Narrator, by contrast, the timeless essence that each moment contains—or rather *is,* when seen in a certain light—can never be adequately expressed. There are two reasons why this is so.

The first is that "the slightest word" and "most insignificant action" is interwoven with countless others in a web of infinite complexity. To comprehend its timeless essence one would therefore have to understand that of the world as a whole.[62]

The second is that the experience of time is necessarily "subjective."[63] Indeed, time *is* subjectivity. Their identity is the essence of human finitude. We are incapable of seeing the world except from a point of view or of experiencing it outside the framework of time. These are merely different ways of describing the same phenomenon. Together they account for the fact that "the world appears to each one of us" in an utterly unique fashion. Were it not for the gift of transmigration wrought by works of art, this appearance "would remain forever the secret of every individual."[64] Yet because it is unique, no individual's experience of the world can ever be exhaustively conveyed to others even by the greatest works of this sort. To some degree it must always remain opaque.

The eternal "essence" of each moment therefore lies beyond our power fully to comprehend, unlike the one that Aristotle's philosopher takes into his mind when he devotes his attention to it. The metaphysics that underlies the Narrator's idea of eternity thus resembles that neither of Augustine nor Aristotle, but is closest to Nietzsche's, which not only equates time and eternity but extends the latter to the most trivial and transient events in a way that ensures that no finite being is ever able to see to the bottom of the eternal reality of a world that appears (but only appears) to be continuously passing away.

Still, if one can never completely grasp the timeless essence of any passing moment, it is possible to do so to a greater or lesser degree. Most people live with no appreciation of the eternity that at every instant encompasses the world as a whole. In this sense, they are not only lost *in* time; time is lost *to* them as well, for it lacks the meaning and value that only what is "extratemporal" can confer upon it. To recover or save time, one must therefore attempt to see and express the eternal in it. The task of doing this can never be completed. But one may at least begin and those who do experience the only—limited but real—form of salvation available in a world in which neither Augustine's conception of eternity nor Aristotle's still has the power to compel belief.

According to the Narrator, it is not philosophy or science but art that bears the principal responsibility for undertaking this task. He calls the works of artists "the most real of all things"—more real than any "public event" or even than the profound but always disappointing experiments in love that absorb the Narrator's attention (principally, Swann's affair with Odette and his own infatuations with Gilberte and Albertine).[65] "True art" enables us "to rediscover, to reapprehend, to make ourselves fully aware of that reality, remote from our daily preoccupations, from which we separate ourselves by an ever greater gulf as the conventional knowledge which we substitute for it grows thicker and more impermeable, that reality which it is very easy for us to die without ever having known and which is, quite simply, our life."[66] Art alone has the power to save time by recalling what is eternal and therefore real in it. It is therefore the only path to salvation that remains open to us today.

The time that art saves is preeminently *past* time, to whose eternality the Narrator finds the key in the phenomenon of involuntary memory.[67]

The present and future are filled with tasks. These demand that we adopt a purposeful attitude toward our surroundings and ourselves. We must be selective in what we attend to and are compelled to organize our thoughts and feelings on the basis of various structured and therefore limiting plans of action. This makes it impossible to see the "reality" that is "our life." At most, we catch a glimpse of it. The past gives us at least the chance of concentrating our attention on this reality more directly. That is because there is nothing to be done in the past. All we can do is regard it. The attitude we take toward the past is necessarily contemplative.

Most of the time, of course, our view of the past is a limited one too. We tend to be just as purposeful and selective in remembering as in planning. We recall certain things and forget others in order to protect some cherished image of ourselves, so that in the end our memories become anecdotes that limit the reality of our past lives as much as our plans do that of the lives we are now leading. Sometimes, however, a particular memory disrupts this effort to confine the past within a selective scheme of meaning. What the Narrator calls "voluntary" memories can never do this because they necessarily impose a purposive structure on the past. This is clearest in the case of conscious voluntary memories but the same is true of unconscious ones as well. Our unthinking recollection of the past is almost always tendentious too. Yet once in a while we have a memory that is accompanied by an inchoate sense of the fullness of a past experience that cannot be contained within any of the anecdotal structures we devise to organize and pacify the past.

Most of the time, of course, we quickly pass by this sensation. It gives us nothing more than a curious but momentary feeling that our voluntary memories of the past are somehow incomplete. It is always possible, however, to stop and dwell on this feeling instead. The exigencies of life compel us to plan our present and future actions but nothing imposes a similar compulsion on the field of memory. There we are uniquely free merely to attend to what presents itself as something that no longer exists. We almost always fail to do this, under the powerful but avoidable compulsion to see our past in a self-serving light. Yet the opportunity is there, and those special memories that are surrounded by an aura of boundless reality that no anecdotal schema can contain (like that of Aunt Leonie's bedroom on Sunday mornings in Combray) are a standing invitation to seize this opportunity and to explore, as far as we are able, the infinite essence of things to which such memories point—much in the way that a patient in psychoanalysis who has been temporarily freed from the purposeful requirements of his present life by the practice of free association, is invited by the memories that come to light to investigate his real (as opposed to anecdotal) past up to the limits of understanding represented by what Freud calls "the navel of the dream."

This investigation is the task of "art" as the Narrator conceives it. The artist strives to render comprehensible as much as possible of the experience of infinite reality that is aroused by certain particularly potent memories. Our "abstract intelligence" has "long been at work" constructing a fictional past. The artist attempts to undo this work of self-deception by first heeding the feeling of unfathomable reality aroused by memories like that of Aunt Leonie's bedroom and by paying attention to everything our habitual abstractions leave out of account. He allows himself to be guided by this feeling as he looks in a spirit of acquiescence to see where it might lead. But then a crucial second step is required. Whatever the feeling reveals must be carefully thought through, for until its contents have been brought "within range of the intellect one does not know what they represent. Then only, when the intellect has shed light upon them, has intellectualized them, does one distinguish, and with what difficulty, the lineaments of what one felt."

A work of art is therefore one of both feeling and thinking. More precisely, its "work" is that of converting the first to the second. Feeling takes the lead by pointing the way toward a greater reality than our voluntary memories suggest. Then the intellect follows up by transforming this reality into something we can understand and communicate to others—by turning the passivity of feeling into the activity of thought, as Spinoza says. The result is an enlargement of self. The process can never be complete but through the conversion of the infinite reality of his own past to something he and others comprehend, the artist becomes progressively more real himself and the experience fills him with joy, for every step in this direction brings him closer to his "true life"—to the timeless essence that is there to be discovered in every moment of his past.[68]

This is an introspective and solitary undertaking. The artist must find the materials he needs for it "within" himself.[69] No one else's past can be a substitute for his own. On the Narrator's view, art is therefore a necessarily first-personal project. It follows that the salvation it offers has no counterpart in the realm of interpersonal relations and that to seek it there is a distraction if not a delusion.

This explains the spirit of loneliness that haunts the whole of Proust's novel. But there is one consoling note of friendship that offsets it.

Near the end of his reflections on the nature of art and eternity, the Narrator exclaims that a life "worth living," one "restored to its true pristine shape" from the deceptions that always deform it, can only be lived "within the confines of a book." Nothing expresses more poignantly the Narrator's self-absorbed idea of salvation. But he then declares that the "long" book he intends to write (whose last pages the reader is now reading) may perhaps serve as a model and inspiration for others to discover "their own selves." "My book," the Narrator says, is meant to be "merely a sort of magnifying glass like those which the optician at Combray used to offer his customers." It will "furnish" its readers with "the means of reading what [lies] within themselves."[70] In this sense, author and reader, artist and public, are collaborators in a venture of self-realization and though we must each experience for ourselves the joy of discovering that time is eternal and everything in the world infinitely real, the artist is a friend and guide motivated by an affection for his readers that has its roots in his recognition of the human condition they share as finite beings joined in ways we rarely notice to the one God of the world. Not everyone can be a great novelist, of course. But the books that novelists write are gifts that help the rest of us to find the path to God in an age in which "the everlasting and divine" can only be understood in the terms that Spinoza and Nietzsche provide. We shall return to this theme in chapter 37 when we consider the place of the poet in a modern democratic society.

"LISTENING TO DYING"

The modern novel pays serious attention to common things. It treats their particularity as a fund from which meaning may be drawn without limit in the way "the whole of Combray" emerges from the Narrator's cup of tea. In these respects, it violates Aristotle's dictum that imitative art of a serious sort must be about extraordinary actions, like the murder of Agamemnon, and contradicts his claim that there is nothing of mimetic interest in the peculiar traits of individual characters as distinct from the formal role they play in the plot. This reversal of aesthetic values presupposes a wholly un-Aristotelian sanctification of the individuality of people and events, yet without the Christian God that first demands it. The Narrator's reflections in the court-yard of the Guermantes' mansion at the end of Proust's long novel make this new theology explicit.

Hermann Broch's *The Death of Virgil* carries these reflections a step fur-ther. In it, Broch tells the story of the poet's final hours, from the moment of his arrival in the port of Brundisium with "death's signet . . . graved upon his brow," to "the word beyond speech" that carries him into the sea of eter-nity, "steel-blue and light," like the one over which he has traveled home to Italy from Athens, "the city of Plato," where "shelter had been denied him" by "fate."[71] The story is told almost entirely from Virgil's point of view. With the exception of one long conversation with his friends Plotius Tucca and Lucius Varius and the emperor Augustus, *The Death of Virgil* takes the form of an internal monologue that follows the feverish wanderings of the poet's mind as he approaches the threshold of death, narrated in a third-person voice whose grandeur at times seems jarringly inconsistent with the supremely private subject matter of the story.

The protagonist of Broch's novel is of course no ordinary man. He is the greatest poet of the Roman world. Nor does the style in which the novel is written seem naturally suited to common experiences. The heroic tone of Broch's narrative reminds one more of the *Aeneid* than of modern novels like *Middlemarch* and *Ulysses*. Yet both the extraordinary fame of the man whose experience the novel records, and the epic style in which it does so, serve only to underscore both the ordinariness of the experience and its utterly individ-ual nature.

In one sense, of course, nothing is more common than dying. It is hap-pening to others all the time and we know it must one day happen to us too. Indeed, if dying is not just the terminal phase of the process of leaving the world, but the whole of it, then we are all dying from the moment we are born, and death is not something different from life but life itself. What can be more ordinary and familiar than that?

Yet the common thing that we call dying is also the most intensely personal experience imaginable. Early in Broch's novel, Virgil calls it "the last loneliness," meaning not just the one that comes last in a sequence of events (though it is that too) but last because nothing can possibly be lonelier than it. Death is something we must each experience for ourselves. No one can take our place as the one to whom death has been assigned. Of course, the same may be said of our lives. The lifelong encounter with death is merely the other side of the experience of the separateness of one's life from that of every other. Broch's novel shows us that even the greatest Roman poet was not exempt from the isolation of this most common of all experiences. It focuses on the last phase of dying in a way that brings out the essential individuality of everything we do and experience during our brief time on earth and thereby carries to a limit of sorts the conception of the novel as a work in which character is prior to plot. With a masterful sense of historical irony, Broch uses an extraordinary figure from the ancient world and an epic style appropriate to the actions of famous men to express an idea that is likely to seem intuitive to most modern readers but that cannot be fit within the aesthetics that Virgil inherited from the Greek writers whose work he so admired.

For the poet who is dying in a guest room in the emperor's palace, death is no longer a mere fact of life. It has ceased to be one of those general features of the world that we take for granted without thinking about it too much. It has become instead the essential fact of *his* life, which the dying man now struggles to comprehend. Looking back, Virgil feels that he has merely inhabited his life without ever understanding its meaning. He senses that the question of its meaning has hovered in the background and that he has heard it from time to time, but only to put it aside. Now, just as his life is about to end, he recognizes the overwhelming mystery of what he has experienced. The extraordinariness of his own death, which he alone can experience, has at last brought the uniqueness of his life into view and Virgil realizes that to the extent he has had intimations of the wonder of being one mortal among many, he has been "listening to dying" all along.[72]

Now at last he is rigidly alert, straining to hear what death has to say. The poet's strength is failing and his mind is clouded by fever. But his reflections possess a lucidity they have never had before. For the first time in his life—and of course the last—Virgil sees himself and his relation to the world as they truly are. And to what conclusion does he come? Astonishingly, that the *Aeneid* is a failure.

At one level, his judgment is based on an estimate of the poem's originality and its relation to the authentic spirit of Rome. On his deathbed, Virgil concludes that his greatest work is a mere imitation of Greek forms, artful to be sure, but lacking the vitality of the original—civilized, elegant and highly refined yet, unlike Homer's poems, without a real soul. Virgil resolves to burn the manuscript of the *Aeneid,* which he has kept close by in a chest.[73]

Augustus hears that the poet intends to destroy the manuscript and comes to persuade him to turn it over for safekeeping. The emperor makes a powerful appeal. The poem no longer belongs to Virgil, he says, but to the Roman people. It is *their* poem, not his; he has no right to burn it. Virgil eventually capitulates to the emperor's request, but before he does, offers a forceful reply, one that reflects a view that other Roman writers sometimes defended as well.[74]

The genius of the Roman people, Virgil tells Augustus, is not expressed by their literature and philosophy, which can never be more than a second-rate reproduction of what the Greeks achieved in these fields. It lies instead in the art of government—in the system of laws and forms of administration—that the Romans have brought to unprecedented heights. By comparison with these genuinely Roman achievements, Virgil insists, the *Aeneid* is a work of decoration only, a frivolous bit of entertainment that has no lasting value by comparison with the Romans' legal and political inventions. It is inauthentic and thus deserves to be destroyed by the man who has wasted so many years on it. At the end of his life, the poet has come to regard his greatest work as a monumental mistake. He begs Augustus to allow him to burn it (which the emperor of course refuses to do) because in the feverish but enlightened clarity of dying this appears to Virgil to be the one form of redemption that remains.

Behind this plea lies a philosophical vision of the nature of individual existence and of the responsibilities it entails. As Virgil listens to dying, the vision takes shape. Its central theme is the relation of human finitude to the boundlessness of the world, and of time to the immortality of the ground from which our human encounter with the world originally springs.

Life is an "interrealm."[75] Its essential nature is that of something in between. We come into life out of the world and return to the world when we die. Time exists only in this interrealm. The world by contrast is timeless and infinite. Its parts form a single "divine" whole—a word the poet uses to express the eternal and boundless nature of the world, whose essence differs fundamentally from ours in both respects.

In the interrealm of human being we thus confront the world as something radically different from ourselves. But unlike other animals, we recognize the divinity of the world and are moved to express it as best we can. In this sense, the "fearful glory of the human lot" is to reach "beyond itself." Our condition is essentially "ecstatic."[76] We wonder at the world and attempt to grasp it in speech. Other animals live mutely. They have not yet crossed the threshold of wonder. And the world itself, because it is eternally self-sufficient, has no need of speech, which is always the sign both of a power and a lack. Between the infinite god of the world and the speechless realm of brutes lies the uniquely human sphere of "the word."

With speech comes responsibility. Human beings are summoned by the world they encounter in speech to honor the "inscrutable divinity in the universe, in the world, in the soul of one's fellow-man."[77] This is the highest duty men have. It is the inspiration for every other. No one can ever fulfill it completely, of course, but those who fail to "pledge" themselves to try, or who make the pledge and break it, are worse than animals because they are guilty of a "dereliction" that no animal can ever commit.[78] They are guilty of an offense against God.

One way that men have of honoring the divinity of the world is art. Art aims at the creation of beauty. Virgil calls beauty "the infinite in the realm of the finite."[79] A successful work of art employs forms (which are always limited) to intimate the limitlessness of the world. Among the arts, poetry occupies a special position because it works with words, the medium in which every human experience, poetic or prosaic, silent or spoken, takes place. It is therefore connected to "the human event" in a particularly intimate way.[80] "No vocation [measures] up to poetry" because it is "the only one dedicated to the knowledge of death," that is, to the experience of finitude in a world without end.[81] As a consequence, the poet is under a special duty to honor the God of the world that is revealed to all human beings—mortals "in the midst of immortality"—by the power of the word they possess in common.[82] The neglect of this duty on the part of a poet is thus a uniquely serious shortcoming. It amounts to a form of "perjury"[83]—something far worse than merely failing to do an adequate job, which of course no poet can do.

Virgil recognizes that he is unable to bring his poem to an end.[84] For that he can perhaps forgive himself. What is unforgiveable is his "fall" into mere "literarity," his preoccupation with "the embellishment of things long since conceived," and therefore with a kind of self-promotion, as opposed to the advancement of beauty and truth and through these, genuine service to the god of the world.[85]

The poet is about to leave the world, or rather to become it once again, and from the vantage point of death he judges his life's work to have been a "betrayal of the divine as well as of art," motivated by "self-idolatry" and "self-gratification," a violation of the "pledge" he made as a poet to push "on toward that ultimate spark of the divine, that secret, which, ready to be disclosed and to be awakened, could be found everywhere, even in the soul of the most degraded."[86] Instead, he has settled for "a worthless, wretched, literary life, not a whit better than that of a Bavius or a Mavius or others of their sort whom he had despised as mere phrase-makers"[87]—a life blind to the "deathlessness" of the world that is revealed to men in the ecstatic shadow of death and that he himself once glimpsed as a child.[88]

Virgil concludes that he has betrayed his calling as a poet. But this is more than a personal failing. It is a failure of love, which he tells his friends Plotius and Lucius is "the reality," though they interpret his exclamation in a "trivial" and "literary" way.[89]

Most human beings "drowse on, forgetting reality."[90] They have lost sight of the eternity that surrounds them. Their condition is one of forgetfulness, like that of the prisoners in Plato's cave. Together, they form a great "mob . . . groveling, sneaking, swarming though the streets, having staggered so long that it had forgotten how to walk, upheld by no law and upholding none, the re-scattered herd, its former wisdom forfeited, unwilling to have knowledge, submitting like the animal, like something less than the animal, to every chance, and at last to a chance extinction without memory, without hope, without immortality. . . ."[91]

We hear this mob shouting its "vilifications" as Virgil is carried on his litter up from the harbor to the palace, along that "hellish alley-gorge" the poet calls "Misery Street."[92] Nothing could be further removed from the civilized world of wit and polish that Virgil shares with his friends. Yet in the end he comes to see that he is one of them, essentially no better than they. He realizes that a poet who turns his back on the vulgar and forgetful crowd and indulges his own refined tastes fails to be the leader he is called upon to be. Such a poet may be famous and live well but his life is lonely and loveless. It lacks the spirit of selflessness that comes with the recognition that the poet's service to the god of the world can and must be a light to others, who though less gifted than he, less wonderstruck at the immensity in which even the most debased human being dwells, possess to some degree at least the power to respond to the poet's evocation of "life's immeasurable meaning" which comes "only from the fullness of meaning revealed by death," to the knowledge of which the poet alone is devoted.

This reverses Plato's judgment in a fundamental way. For Plato, poetry is the enemy of wakefulness. It is like a narcotic that causes those who consume it to dream on, lost in the forgetfulness that only the philosopher escapes. The few who do escape realize that death is nothing real, and that one should strive to live as if he were already dead as opposed to merely dying. Behind this judgment lies Plato's most fundamental metaphysical conviction—that what changes and passes away has no or at most a deficient kind of reality, that mortality and finitude are therefore essentially unreal, and that the experience of being an individual separated from others by the loneliness of dying is an illusion we must train ourselves to regard as such. By contrast, for the poet of Broch's novel the separateness of dying is part of reality—not the whole of it, to be sure, but not an illusion either—and the calling of poetry is to give voice to this aspect of reality in relation to the immortal whole of which it forms a part. This assumes that mortality itself, and hence the individuality of the human being who experiences it as the basic condition of his life, belongs within the circle of being and not outside it, as Plato supposed.

But if mortality is real, it is not the most real thing there is. It is not the ground of reality.[93] The lives of human beings, who do not merely die but experience death as the boundary of their encounter with a world that is immortal and divine, arise from and are summoned toward "the unity of an enduring meaning . . . by which life was and is maintained as creation, eternally to be remembered as such." Poetry cannot create this unity. It is founded on it and draws its power from it. But it can convey the meaning of the human place within it, and to the extent it succeeds, helps to fight the twofold forgetfulness to which all human beings are prey: that of our mortality, on the one hand, and of the immortality that surrounds us on the other, which is there to be seen if we merely open our eyes and look.[94]

Only the poet who strives to convey the uniquely human experience of transience in a timeless world may be said to be a friend to those who pass their lives without knowing what it means to be a human being. They live in a state of alienation. The poet helps to restore them to their true selves. No greater act of love can be imagined.[95] The result is the establishment of a community between the poet and his audience based on the solidarity of their humanity. Though the poet leads the way and others follow, he is as much a beneficiary of this community as they, and if he turns aside instead and allows himself to be distracted by the egotistic pleasures of skill and fame, he becomes even further lost in the loneliness of dying. The poet's art offers the only remedy that men possess for the "thicket of separateness" that death imposes on us.[96] Virgil's judgment that he has failed to show the way out of this thicket leaves him feeling more alone in his life than the fact that it is coming to an end can explain.

Virgil's failure also reflects a larger historical fact. There are men in every age who hear the call to serve the immortal god of the world even in the midst of life, which is to say, the midst of dying. But the response that seems the most exalted varies from one epoch to the next.[97] In the great age of the Greeks, it took the form of art and philosophy. These had their "ground" in the immediacy of "perception." The work of those who struggled to respond to this perception—of Homer, Aeschylus and Plato—was "surrounded" by "the gods of yore."[98] The gods not only called to but sustained them. They gave poets and philosophers the help they need to find the words to express the immensity disclosed to men alone. But in our age, Virgil tells his friend and patron Augustus, the roots of philosophy and poetry have dried up. These are no longer nourished by an original perception of the sort that gave the Greeks their inspiration and direction. They no longer enjoy the favor of the gods. As a result, they have declined into the sterile imitation of something that once had life but is now "a mere sham-artistic, decorative adornment of life," the pursuit of which is not a form of divine service but an act of "perjury" instead.[99]

In the age of Augustus, the greatest art is that of "ruling," the "art of state-regulation and peace," by comparison with which "all other arts, not only the alas so ravishing one of artistic dalliance, are pale."[100] The only exception is architecture, which "like the state" seeks to establish "a similitude of order in space."[101] It is here, in the monumental enterprise of state building, in the construction of roads and temples and the enactment of laws that the real artists of the Roman people may be found. Like their Greek predecessors, they also are responding to the primal human longing to express the everlasting in a form that gives it a presence among men. Yet because every form is a boundary that limits and confines, even Augustus' work can never reach its goal. In the end the Roman Empire must therefore be a disappointment too and lose the creative spirit that drove the centuries-long effort to construct it, just as the poetry and philosophy of Greece has lost its spirit in the age of Rome and become an empty sort of *belles-lettres*.

Yet so long as Roman attitudes prevail, the work of poetry will lack the divine support it once enjoyed among the Greeks, and without the help of the gods no poet can frame an authentic response to their call. "Aeschylus was able to produce works valid for eternity because by means of them he fulfilled the task of his era, and therefore his art was the equivalent of perception . . . the time determines the direction in which the task lies, and he who goes contrary to it must collapse . . . an art that is consummated outside these limits, evading the real task, is neither perception nor help—in short it is not art and cannot endure."[102] Virgil is therefore a poet out of season and the *Aeneid,* which seeks to express "the Roman spirit" in a work modeled on those of Homer, is a contradiction in terms.

Virgil sees his dilemma as that of a poet who stands "between two epochs." He looks back to the age of the Greeks which is "no longer" and ahead to an age that is "not yet," when poetry shall flourish again because it once more receives the divine summons to "the deed of truth."[103] For this to happen, the age of Rome must come to an end, as that of the Greeks did before it. Yet as he lies dying in the palace of the emperor, Virgil is suffused with an ecstatic confidence that this will happen and tells his host that though their own time is "impervious to poetry," divine help is on the way to revive the poet's calling. He describes his mood as one of "expectancy, not emptiness." "Fulfillment on the way," he says, "is almost fulfillment," and those "who are blessed to wait and watch" embody "the tension [that] lies in waiting"; they remain "ready for [the] fulfillment" that must one day arrive.[104]

Virgil's words now rise to prophetic intensity. The new god will come from the East. His arrival will be announced by a slave. The kingdom he establishes will be one of freedom for all, "the kingdom of man and his humanity" as opposed to "a state of citizens."[105] His appearance will be a "miracle" and his task that of a savior. He will be a "world-redeemer" who makes a "real sacrifice," not like the superficial ones of those whose blood is spilled "on the sands of the arena." His sacrifice "will be the ultimate and decisive form of perception on earth." "The bringer of salvation," whose "star" will "rise on the eastern firmament," will "bring himself to the sacrifice out of love for men and mankind, transforming himself by his own death into the deed of truth, the deed which he casts to the universe, so that from this supreme and symbolic reality of helpful service creation may again unfold."[106]

"Some day," Virgil tells Augustus, who accuses him of speaking in riddles, "there will come one who will again live in perception; in his being the world will be redeemed to truth."[107] In his life and death, the redeemer will prepare the way "for the divine renewal of the world" and "call out the eternal in men who wish to be saved."[108] The Roman state with its far-reaching laws has "leveled the ground" and prepared the way for this renewal. But the intimacy with which the savior speaks even to slaves and the universality of his appeal to all men will surpass the limits of the world that Rome has built and create a "new kingdom" in its place—one where it is possible to experience again, in a direct and authentic way, "the divine perception" that gives poetry in every age whatever real power it possesses.[109]

This perception is "not yet." But it is bound to come and when it does, it will not repeat or reenact the Greek understanding of the relation between mortality and immortality. The sacrificial death of the redeemer whose star shall appear in the East will fuse the loneliness of dying with the knowledge of eternity. It will join the experience of being an individual separated from others by the isolation of death, to the "divine perception" that even in this "last loneliness" one belongs to "the pledge-protecting god" who saves men from the pointlessness of dying all alone with no glimpse of anything beyond the realm of time in which they pass their lives.[110] It will offer a new perception of the "eternal in man."

The "savior" who is coming will "conquer death" through a self-sacrificing act that erases the distance between individuality, on the one hand, and divinity on the other. The Greek encounter with the God of the world ruled out such an erasure. For the Greeks, the pathos of mortality unfolded in a realm untouched by the everlasting and divine, which might be glimpsed by mortal men but had always to be distinguished from the essence of their mortality itself. This was a premise both of Homer's poems and Plato's philosophy (and of Aristotle's as well). Nowhere in the Greek perception of "reality" is there room for the idea that eternity is *in* the individuality of individuals rather than outside of or beyond it. This is the saving truth the "bringer of salvation" will reveal by "his life and his death," which together constitute "one single deed of perception."[111] It is a message for everyone and not only the wise and cultured few. The isolation of individual existence, which the dying poet is now experiencing as if for the first time in his life, is the common condition of all human beings. To put eternity here, in the heart of time, where its absence seems most striking, is thus to offer the prospect of a meaningful death, and with that of a meaningful life, to "everyone" whose fate it is to die—even, Virgil says, to "me."[112]

This wholly un-Greek message prepares the way for a radically new understanding of the calling of art. If art is to be more than a "decorative adornment," if it is to touch the eternal reality of things, it must draw its inspiration from a perception of the divine. The perception that is coming, though Virgil does "not yet" have the eyes to see it, will abolish the distinction between individual and God in a way no Greek poet or thinker could conceive, and provide the revelatory impetus for wholly new forms of art, as different from their Greek predecessors as the God on the cross is from Homer's all-too-human gods and the serenely intellectualized God of Plato and Aristotle.

Beyond the range of Virgil's vision, and the pages of Broch's book, the reader sees the coming pageant of Christian art which will struggle to express the truth of the Incarnation—that a dying man and God are in some mysterious way one and the same. The attempt to do this will for centuries remain confined within the dogmatic boundaries of Christian belief until, as Eric Auerbach suggests, the idea that every individual is infinitely valuable and hence a worthy subject even for the greatest work of art, comes to stand on its own, without the need for a God beyond the world to support it.

This is the "perception" of divinity to which the drama of Christian art eventually leads. One of its principal expressions is the modern novel, whose claim to be a serious form of literary representation rests on this post-Christian theology. *The Death of Virgil* takes us back to a time just before the good news that first opened the way to the genre of literature to which Broch's novel itself belongs. In the loneliness of the dying poet who still remembers the "miracle of immortality" despite his many failings, it anticipates the passion of Christ, whose death reveals the divinity of the individual to be a universal law for humankind. When the Christian religion eventually lost its power to sustain this law, it became the vocation of others to do so, including novelists like Broch, whose art seeks to save the immeasurable meaning of death, which is both the commonest of all experiences and the source of everything unique in our lives.

"AUROCHS AND ANGELS"

One cannot call Humbert Humbert the "hero" of *Lolita* in any conventional sense. The word implies a measure of sympathy and admiration that no reader of Nabokov's novel can possibly feel for its main character. Unlike Leopold Bloom, who remains a hero despite the ordinariness of his life and the neurosis that disfigures it, Humbert ruins the life of a young girl for the sake of a pedophilic passion that puts him outside the range of ordinary human experience. How can one even understand a man of this sort, let alone feel the slightest sympathy for him?

And yet one does. A reader of *Lolita* has the uncanny experience not only of finding Humbert vastly more attractive than the utterly banal Americans among whom he has come to live (including Dolores Haze herself) but more disturbingly, of siding with him in his plot to seduce a twelve-year-old girl. When Humbert's wife dies in an automobile accident shortly after having discovered his secret passion for her daughter, it is hard not to be relieved that she is out of the way so that his plan can proceed. Later, as events move toward the consummation of his carefully prepared scheme, the reader shares Humbert's exasperation with the other fools at the hotel; hopes the purple pills will do their job; feels his anxiety as the moment approaches and then—afterward—experiences a kind of moral relief that it is *she* who initiates the act of intercourse itself. This is the most disquieting aspect of the novel. To find oneself rooting for a criminal psychopath is unsettling, to put it mildly.

The modern novel reverses the Aristotelian hierarchy of character and plot by putting the individual first. It finds infinite richness in each person's experience of the world and seeks to expand the reader's sympathies with "the gift of transmigration." The novelist does this by means of an art whose function is to immortalize the transient froth of life.[113] In a word, the subject of the novel is individuality; its ethic that of sympathy; and its goal the revelation through art of an eternity that is present in time, not beyond it.

Lolita appears to violate this tradition in all three respects. The individuality of its protagonist is defined by a madness we cannot comprehend. The sympathy its author arouses on Humbert's behalf seems a perversion of the ethic of the novel, not an extension of it. And in the character of Humbert himself, art is portrayed as a form of aestheticized solipsism that, far from saving anything from the isolation of our separateness as mortal beings, only intensifies it instead. Yet Nabokov's supremely clever novel gives us reason to question each of these judgments.

On the surface, Humbert Humbert is an eminently sociable human being. He is well educated and well mannered—a refined representative of an advanced stage of civilization. This is how he impresses the residents of Ramsdale and especially Mrs. Haze, who is seduced by his cosmopolitan flair. But Humbert's superficial polish conceals a life more remote from that of the reader than the lives of any of the characters in the novels we have considered so far.

Casaubon, Lydgate and Bulstrode are ordinarily complex human beings. Each is moved by hopes and fears that every reader of *Middlemarch* is sure to know firsthand, if not perhaps in the exact form they assume in the lives of these particular characters. This makes it relatively easy to see their struggles from the inside—to sympathize with their ambitions and to experience the pain of their defeat.

The same is true of Leopold Bloom. His sexual quirks may strike some readers as odder than anything in the pages of George Eliot's novel, but the combination of loneliness, fear and desire that lies behind them, and the complexities of his relation with Molly, will hardly be unknown to any middle-age reader of *Ulysses* who has had some experience of the travails of intimate life.

The world of Combray and Balbec, of Swann and the Guermantes, is remote from that of nearly all of Proust's readers today. Yet the humbleness of the experiences from which he sets out to save the lost time of his past, and the universality of the moods whose evanescence he seeks to immortalize through art, give credibility to the Narrator's invitation to the readers of the novel to do the same thing for themselves. And as regards the experience of dying, every reader may not only look forward to it but is having it already, so that nothing can be less unfamiliar than the loneliness of the hero of Broch's book.

The modern novel seeks to convey some understanding of the uniqueness of human experience. But the four we have considered are helped in this regard by commonalities of attitude and feeling that make the books' protagonists more or less familiar even before the story begins. Nabokov goes to great lengths to ensure that Humbert Humbert never becomes familiar in this way. He uses the culture of his protagonist and his manic facility with words to encourage an illusion of familiarity on the part of the reader, who is likely to be pleased that he shares so many of Humbert's recondite jokes. But this only underscores how distant Humbert's mad perspective is from that of any normal human being. Humbert is not just tortured, as Casaubon is, by an unattainable though perfectly acceptable ambition. He is more than neurotically unhappy, like Leopold Bloom. He is in the grip of a sexual compulsion that has overtaken the whole of his life. Nothing that he says or does, however conventional it seems, is untouched by its distorting demands. Whatever its aetiology (about which we are given only Humbert's self-serving account) the obsession that engulfs his life makes it stranger and less accessible than that of these other two characters. They are merely idiosyncratic. Humbert is completely crazy and his craziness entails an extreme of solitude that presents a

special challenge to the reader who wishes to understand it. Nabokov's protagonist is of course not the only character in modern fiction that sees the
world in a crazy way. But the seamlessness of his obsession makes Humbert's
madness peculiarly resistant to entry from without. In this sense, it represents
a form of individual experience whose inaccessibility might be thought to
mark the limit of the novelist's art.

The greatness of Nabokov's achievement is that he helps the reader over
even this apparent limit. First, he slyly encourages the reader to suspend any
immediate feelings of revulsion that stand in the way of taking Humbert's
life seriously. Humbert is irresistibly charming. We enjoy his company too
much to be put off by the fact that he happens to be a pedophile. And then
we discover that it all makes sense, that everything in Humbert's life has purpose and value in relation to the passion that directs it. We even come to see
the *point* of pedophilia—the beauty of what has not yet been scribbled over
by life; the room its blankness affords to a mature imagination; the thrill of
mastery and control, both sexual and pedagogical; and so on.

The reader is first seduced by Humbert's wit, then grows to appreciate the
supreme orderliness of his life, and finally is convinced to adopt, in a qualified fashion at least, the erotic outlook that defines it. At some point in the
course of reading the novel, most readers are likely to be shocked by these
experiences, especially the last (though no one who has enjoyed Plato's *Symposium* should be). Having and then recoiling against them is an important
part of the pleasure of the book, which carries the reader over the threshold
of madness into a world one might have thought wholly impenetrable. In this
respect, *Lolita* achieves a result similar to that of Freud's novelistic case study
of the "Rat Man" whose outwardly conventional but inwardly delusional life
Freud succeeds in making both engaging and intelligible to the reader.[114] If
the aim of the modern novel is to uncover and articulate the particularity of
individual experience, then Nabokov, like Freud, may be said to carry this
effort beyond the point that even Joyce and Proust reached before him.

This brings us to the question of sympathy. Nabokov helps the reader understand the mind of his protagonist. But does he mean for us to sympathize
with him?

There is an obvious stumbling block in the way. The "Rat Man" suffers from
an obsession that harms only himself. He does no injury to anyone else. One
pities his suffering and hopes he gets well. Humbert, by contrast, is not only
crazy. He is guilty of rape and murder and should be sent to prison or confined in a mental institution. How can a reader avoid this judgment? Nabokov

draws the reader into Humbert's world and makes his passion for nymphets plausible in disturbing ways. But surely a sane reader will recoil from this experience, regain his balance, and condemn Humbert from a distance safely beyond the seductive appeal of his own exculpatory narrative.

But if Humbert doesn't deserve our sympathy, who does? Lolita? Yes, of course, like the victim of any crime. The problem is that Nabokov presents her in a way that gives the reader very little with which to sympathize. Lolita herself (as distinct from the artistically embellished nymphet of Humbert's mad obsession) is a coarse American teenager with bad habits and a limited imagination. There is little or nothing to like or admire about her. Every glimpse of Lolita's true character only makes the reader prefer Humbert's exotically elaborated version of it.

Perhaps the person with whom the reader can most comfortably identify is "John Ray, Jr., Ph.D.," the author of the "Foreword" that presents Humbert's "Confession" as a "case history" with "scientific," "literary" and "ethical" value.[115] Ray is an interested but clinically detached observer, as the reader wishes to be—absorbed by Humbert's story yet sufficiently sure of his own sanity not to be swept away by it. Yet Nabokov makes it impossible to sympathize with him as well.

Ray professes to recognize that Humbert's memoir is "a great work of art" whose literary worth "transcends its expiatory aspects." But his dominant attitude is moralistic. He concludes his "Foreword" with the shallow proclamation that "'Lolita' should make all of us—parents, social workers, educators—apply ourselves with still greater vigilance and vision to the task of bringing up a better generation in a safer world."[116] Ray is a pompous fool that no "serious reader" (his phrase) can take seriously. Indeed, the effect of his moralizing, like that of Lolita's coarseness, is to drive the reader back toward Humbert's refined aestheticism, which however criminal its consequences, has real greatness in it, in contrast to the flat and banal points of view of these other two. But if Humbert's criminality in the end prevents us from sympathizing with him either, then it seems that Nabokov's novel leaves the reader in a state of frustrated suspension and rather than strengthening our powers of sympathy mocks the effort to deploy them with a playful irony that contradicts the ethical seriousness of the genre to which it belongs.

Yet despite its wit and ferocious mockery of our conventional ideals, Lolita is an ethically, or rather spiritually, serious work. To see why, we have to assess Humbert's life from a perspective different from those considered so far. This is the point of view of Nabokov himself. From the vantage point of the artist who made the novel of which Humbert is the protagonist, Humbert's life must be judged a failure but not in conventional terms (as Lolita's victimization invites us to do and John Ray explicitly urges). Humbert's life is an aesthetic failure. It is a failed work of art. That it is becomes clear only when we measure his life against the standard set by a more successful, nobler work of art. This is *Lolita* itself, and it is with Nabokov's view of life—not Humbert's, or Lolita's or John Ray's—that the reader is ultimately meant to sympathize. The triumph of its author's point of view is the true "moral apotheosis" toward which the novel "unswervingly" tends—not the vindication of our ordinary moral beliefs which, as Nabokov knows, need no vindication at all.

Humbert Humbert has the domineering eye of a compulsive artist. Everything he sees becomes material for his mordant wit and erotic aims. This is most obviously true of Lolita herself. She is a blank sheet on which Humbert can inscribe his fantastic imaginings nearly without limit. He can make of her what he wishes—the nymphet of his dreams. The same is true of the other characters in the novel. They offer no resistance to Humbert's artistic drive. Even the vast emptiness of the landscape through which he and Lolita travel on their way from one unremarkable motel to another, is merely more material for Humbert's relentless attempt to transform an ordinary American girl and soulless American places into a work of art.

Humbert's passion for Lolita is the sexualized expression of a more general passion for beauty. This is what sets him apart most fundamentally from the others in Ramsdale. He is an artist among philistines. In contrast to them, his attitude toward the world is essentially active. They are passive by nature—the victims of life. Humbert strives to be the master of life, though the artistry by which he does so has to be concealed. It is too dangerous to be displayed and no one would understand it if it were. Only to the reader does Humbert reveal his art. This is the real source of his appeal, for one cannot help but be carried away by the brio and cleverness—the sheer will to power—with which he proceeds to convert everything in his otherwise banal surroundings into something ecstatic and sublime. By comparison with Mrs. Haze, the Chatfields, the Farlows, Dr. Quilty and all the other impotent bores that populate his world, Humbert alone possesses the power to weave their lives into a work of art that dominates its material by compelling one to see and value it from the artist's point of view.

Nietzsche's word for such artistic command is "nobility." Noble human beings and cultures are those that succeed in drafting others into their interpretive schemes. Every further success in this regard represents a step up what

Nietzsche calls the rank order of being. A picture of the world that organizes a larger area of it in accordance with its own principle of interpretation is more powerful and therefore real than the viewpoints it incorporates within itself. Understood in these terms, Humbert Humbert is the noblest human being in Nabokov's novel.

Yet even his nobility is limited. The nobility of a work of art is a function of how much of the world it takes in. Some are more comprehensive and hence nobler than others. But the success, indeed the very existence, of any work of art depends on the partiality of what Nietzsche calls its "perspective." This is his way of describing the finitude of every artistic endeavor, whatever its position in the rank order of being. Thus even if Humbert's art is more powerful than that of any other character in *Lolita,* it is bound to have limits as well. The most obvious of these is its failure to include within its program of beautification any meaningful representation of Lolita's own perspective on things.

Humbert himself comes to see this at the end. He remembers a conversation between Lolita and her childhood friend Eva Rosen. Eva had remarked that it would be better to die "than hear Milton Pinski, some local schoolboy she knew, talk about music," and Lolita replies "so very serenely and seriously," that "what's so dreadful about dying is that you are completely on your own." At that moment, Humbert says,

it struck me, as my automaton knees went up and down, that I simply did not know a thing about my darling's mind and that quite possibly, behind the awful juvenile clichés, there was in her a garden and a twilight, and a palace gate—dim and adorable regions which happened to be lucidly and absolutely forbidden to me, in my polluted rags and miserable convulsions; for I often noticed that living as we did, she and I, in a world of total evil, we would become strangely embarrassed whenever I tried to discuss something she and an older friend, she and a parent, she and a real healthy sweetheart, I and Annabel, Lolita and sublime, purified, analyzed, deified Harold Haze might have discussed—an abstract idea, a painting, stippled Hopkins or shorn Baudelaire, God or Shakespeare, anything of a genuine kind. Good will! She would mail her vulnerability in trite brashness and boredom, whereas I, using for my desperately detached comments an artificial tone of voice that set my own last teeth on edge, provoked my audience to such outbursts of rudeness as made any further conversation impossible, oh my poor, bruised child.[117]

A reader may wonder how honest Humbert is being at this point. Every-thing else he has said has been self-serving. Perhaps this recollection is too. But looking back he seems, at least, to glimpse the limits of his art. In any case, the reader surely does. Humbert's relentless campaign to transform the world into a work of art fails to reach the reality of the child that lies at its heart. His art-fully constructed version of Lolita remains a superficial fiction that in the end convinces no one, not even Humbert himself. It falls short of the truth and to that extent lacks the authority and hence power at which every artist aims.

Many readers are likely to view the limits of Humbert's art as a conse-quence of his pathology and to judge them in medical or moral terms. If Hum-bert leaves the reality of his nymphet out of account, that is because he is in the grip of an obsession that compels him to ignore everything except his own perverse pleasure—an exaggerated selfishness that must be quarantined or punished. Humbert's limitations are either the symptom of a disease or man-ifestation of a wicked heart. But to take this view of things is to side with John Ray, Jr., Ph.D., whose opinions are made to seem ridiculous even before Humbert's story begins.

There is another possibility. To judge Humbert a sick man or a bad one is to assess him in conventional terms. One can also diagnose his failings as an artist from the point of view of art itself. Humbert's "Confession" is a failed work of art because it leaves Lolita out. So much else that is common and unlovely is made beautiful, funny, worthy of note, a subject of serious aes-thetic attention, by Humbert's witty musings—*except* the real life of the com-mon and unlovely child around whom these all revolve. Seeing this, a reader may be moved to condemn Nabokov's protagonist on nonaesthetic grounds. But one can also say, "Yes, it is true, Humbert is the only artist in the novel, the only noble human being, by comparison with whom everyone else seems dull and passive; but his art is incomplete; he is not the artist he aspires to be; his will to beauty and power reaches only so far; at a crucial point, it loses steam; one must therefore assess his failure not from the standpoint of medi-cine or morality, which is external to that of art, but from the point of view of Humbert's own artistic ambitions, and look to see if there is a superior art that incorporates the limits of his within its own larger picture of the world and thereby goes farther toward making everything, including the barely com-prehensible madness of a compulsive pedophile, as beautiful as it can be."

The reader who looks for this superior work will of course find it. It is Nabokov's novel itself, of which Humbert's "Confession" is merely a part. We do not see Lolita except from Humbert's point of view, but Nabokov's artistry (as distinct from Humbert's) illuminates the limits of his protagonist's peculiar perspective on the world. Dimly at least, we hear the "roar" of the life that "lies on the other side" of Humbert's "silence" and in this way attain a more comprehensive vision of things than Humbert is capable of providing, though one that preserves a place for the logic of Humbert's isolating obsession. By Nietzsche's standards, *Lolita* itself is the wider work of art that provides the measure we need to judge the artistry of the lesser work on which it purports to be based. It follows that if Humbert is the noblest character *in* the novel, the nobility of its author is greater still.

Humbert has instructed that his "Confession" not be published until both he and Lolita are dead. The reader knows from John Ray's "Foreword" that this is in fact the case. Lolita has "died in childbed, giving birth to a stillborn girl on Christmas day 1952," and Humbert of a heart attack a few weeks before.[118] Though the memoir he has written is addressed to the "ladies and gentlemen of the jury," it therefore cannot possibly have been intended for use at Humbert's trial. The "jury" is composed of the readers who now hold the work in their hands and though he sometimes suggests that its purpose is to excuse him in their eyes, Humbert makes it clear, in the very last sentence of his report, that its real aim is not moral but aesthetic. By writing it, Humbert says, he hopes to give himself and the "poor, bruised child" whose life he has consumed a kind of "immortality"—the incomplete but still meaningful sort that art alone confers. Addressing Lolita herself, he tells her not to "pity C. Q.," who Humbert has murdered a short time before. "One had to choose between him and H. H., and one wanted H. H. to exist at least a couple of months longer, so as to have him make you live in the minds of later generations. I am thinking of aurochs and angels, the secret of durable pigments, prophetic sonnets, the refuge of art. And this is the only immortality you and I may share, my Lolita."[119]

Like Proust's Narrator, Humbert is therefore engaged in an attempt to salvage something lasting—everlasting—from the wreckage of time. He hopes to immortalize a young American girl of no particular distinction whose life will otherwise pass without notice and end in an "unvisited" tomb. Of course, Humbert succeeds only because Nabokov does. His lesser work of art achieves its aim because it too is saved by the larger, nobler work of which it forms a part. If Lolita is remembered by "later generations," as Humbert hopes she will be, that is because the author of *Lolita* has preserved her place as a girl with a life of her own, or more precisely as the *idea* of a girl with a life of her own. The interpretation of her life is not within the power of Humbert's narrower art, whose limits Nabokov's greater one exposes. Yet if the art of the novelist transcends that of his protagonist, when Humbert defines the aim of art as the immortalization of "*this* Lolita, pale and polluted, and big with another's child," he speaks for Nabokov too.[120]

Only once in the novel does Humbert reflect on his situation in what might be called a theological spirit. On his way to kill Quilty, he recalls a visit to a "French-speaking confessor" to whom he had turned for "an old-fashioned popish cure" for his "drab atheism." "I had hoped," Humbert says, "to deduce from my sense of sin the existence of a supreme Being." So far as Lolita is concerned, the cure doesn't work. Humbert is "unable to transcend the simple human fact that whatever spiritual solace [he] might find" in the idea of such a Being, "nothing could make . . . Lolita forget the foul lust" he has inflicted on her. There is no God beyond the world to whom Humbert can look for redemption or repair.

He then considers the nihilistic alternative. Perhaps "in the infinite run it does not matter a jot that a North American girl-child named Dolores Haze has been deprived of her childhood by a maniac." But this would have to be "proven" and "if it can, then life is a joke." There is no order of everlasting truths, of "lithophanic eternities," apart from that of time. Yet if time is just an "infinite run" in which nothing lasts forever, then everything in it must be pointless, including the life of Lolita. If these are the only alternatives, Humbert's "misery" is incurable.

But there is a third possibility. Humbert concludes his theological musings by observing that he sees "nothing for the treatment" of his unhappiness "but the melancholy and very local palliative of articulate art."[121] This is of course the one he employs. His "Confession" is a work of art that aims to give the events it records an eternity of sorts despite their insignificance in the endless run of time. It seeks to endow them with at least a measure of the meaning they would have if there were a God beyond the world who saw and judged them. The fact that any human work of art can do this only to an infinitesimally small degree means that the saving power of such a work can never be more than "very local" and is always tinged by "melancholy" on account of the shortfall between its aspiration and achievement. Yet even so, Humbert's theology is founded on the conviction that nothing is too odd or insignificant to be beyond the power of "articulate art" to rescue from the waste and forgetfulness of time.

That this is possible at all depends on the identification of time and eternity that Nietzsche joyously affirms. This is Humbert Humbert's metaphysics too, though he does not express it in philosophical terms. And it is also that of his creator, whose nobler art rests on the Nietzschean belief that beyond the Christian understanding of salvation and the all-too-Christian nihilism that is commonly opposed to it, lies a third path to the divine and everlasting—not one, like those of Aristotle and Augustine, that can ever reach its goal, either in this life or the next, yet is inspired by the knowledge that the artist who pursues it approaches the eternity that sanctifies the least of things, even the madness of the pedophile and the "dim and adorable" mind of the unremarkable child he ruins. This is the born-again paganism of *Lolita* and of the modern novel in general, whose aspirations rest on a theology that inverts the one that underlies Aristotle's judgment that in every imitative work of a serious sort character exists for the sake of plot.

CHAPTER 35

Genius and Sublimity

PAINTING SINCE THE RENAISSANCE

For the nineteenth-century Swiss historian Jacob Burckhardt, the Italian Renaissance was characterized above all by a new impulse toward what he calls "the highest individual development."[1] "In the Middle Ages," he writes, "man was conscious of himself only as a member of a race, party, people, family or corporation—only through some general category." Beginning in Italy, in the thirteenth century, "this veil first melted into air" and "man became a spiritual *individual*." By the end of that century, Italy "began to swarm with individuality; the ban laid upon human personality was dissolved; and a thousand figures meet us each in its own special shape and dress."[2]

This sweeping claim is the organizing theme of Burckhardt's panoramic survey of the political, religious and artistic dimensions of what he calls the "civilization" of the Renaissance. Many of his judgments have since been corrected or refined by other historians. But Burckhardt's association of the Italian Renaissance with a heightened appreciation of individual experience and achievement continues to be so widely accepted that it seems less controversial than clichéd.[3]

Among the many expressions of the spirit of individualism that shaped every branch of Renaissance life, Burckhardt mentions in particular the new genre of biographical writing "which no longer found it necessary, like Anastasius, Agnellus, and their successors, or like the biographers of the Venetian doges, to adhere to a dynastic or ecclesiastical succession," but instead emphasized the personal quirks and peculiar traits that set the lives they recorded apart from those of everyone else—that portrayed their subjects, in Burckhardt's words, as "remarkable" individuals.[4] As an example he cities Giorgio Vasari's famous sixteenth-century biographies of the artists who had pioneered the new tradition to which Vasari himself belonged, beginning with Cimabue three centuries before. Without Vasari's "all-important work," Burckhardt declares, "we should perhaps to this day have no history of Northern [Italian] art, or of the art of modern Europe at all."

In Vasari's case too, scholars have discovered gaps and errors in his work, though the search to find them has been made more difficult by the fact that in many cases he is the sole source of the information he reports. Yet even today, *The Lives of the Artists* retains its fascination for us. It promises, despite its acknowledged flaws, to put us in touch with the personalities of the artists who produced the masterworks of Renaissance art, and one still sometimes sees tourists walking the streets of Florence, with Vasari's book in hand, hoping through his eyes to catch a glimpse of the artist at work, and to understand in more human terms what the museum guides mean when they say that modern art began, as Vasari says it did, with Cimabue and those who followed in his steps.

VASARI'S BOOK OF PORTRAITS

As Burckhardt notes, Vasari may fairly be credited with having inaugurated the historical study of Western art. Vasari was the first to divide the whole of Western art into three distinct periods, the ancient, medieval and modern; to associate the last of these with the recovery of techniques and ideals that had flourished in the first but been lost in the second; and to conceive the third period itself in historical terms, as a process marked by the progressive refinement of artistic methods and goals. Even today most introductory courses in the history of Western art accept Vasari's three-part scheme, though the development they trace in the third or modern period ends not with the Mannerist art of the mid-sixteenth century but Picasso, Pollack and Warhol instead.

The most strikingly modern aspect of Vasari's book, however, is its emphasis on the individual personalities of the artists whose lives it relates. Many of these—Brunelleschi is an example—began their careers as artisanal craftsmen. Their emergence as creative artists with unique styles of their own, out of the anonymity of the craft traditions in which the makers of many the most beautiful works of the Middle Ages are submerged without a trace, coincided with the growing acceptance of the idea of a separate realm of "fine" art comprised of works that are valued for their uniqueness, like their creators themselves.

Today, the idea that a work of art is valuable, in part at least, on account of something the artist contributes to it as an individual with a distinctive temperament of his or her own, seems so obvious as to be hardly worth stating. The word that best expresses this idea is "genius." The genius of an artist cannot be duplicated or transferred. Others may admire it and be inspired by it but the attempt to copy it is bound to fail since an artist's genius cannot be detached from the bundle of experiences, thoughts and attitudes that together constitute his or her unique perspective on the world. Vasari's biographies put great stress on the idea of genius as a way of understanding both the nature of a work of fine art and the distinctive sort of value it possesses. We have grown so used to this idea, however, that it is hard for us to see how radical it once was. To appreciate the novelty of Vasari's conception of artistic creativity, we must begin by returning, as we have so many times before, to the philosophy of Aristotle, for the idea of genius has no place, and indeed could have none, in his account of what he calls "making" (*poesis*).

For Aristotle, the distinction between fine art and craft does not exist. There is no fundamental difference, in his view, between the process by which a sculptor shapes a statue and the one by which a potter molds a cup. The sculptor who wishes, let us say, to make a statue of a man must first observe some number of human beings. These differ, of course, on account of the matter in which their common form is embodied, but the form itself never changes. The sculptor "abstracts" this form from the human beings in whom he sees it. An idea of it takes shape in his mind. This idea is the mental representation of the form—more exactly, it is the form itself with the matter stripped away. The sculptor then copies this form in stone. Having abstracted it from one sort of body, he restores it to another. A good sculptor is one who is skilled both at seeing the forms of things and at transferring them from the material in which they originally exist to matter of a different kind.

In the case of a statue, the material to which the form is transferred lacks the dynamic potency of the flesh in which the humanity of living human beings is embodied. This is an important difference, but even it can only be understood in relation to the form in question, which is the sole source of everything that is real and hence valuable in the work the sculptor produces. Because every embodied form is compromised by the ultimate unreality of the material in which it resides, the sculptor's work can no more be a perfect expression of the form he seeks to copy than the bodies of the human beings in which he first discerns it. This dooms every artifact to imperfection. But still a sculptor can aspire to make his work as perfect as possible. This means ridding it of everything that is extraneous to the form itself—including the sculptor's own peculiarities as an individual human being, which on this view constitute a hindrance he must strive to overcome like the intractable particularity of the material on which he works. In this sense, the sculptor *aims at* anonymity. This explains why the conception of the artist as a genius whose individuality is essential to the meaning and value of his art is incomprehensible from Aristotle's point of view, which in this respect, as in every other, is shaped by the metaphysical equation of being with form.

It also explains why Aristotle ranks philosophers above makers, including those we now call artists. Like the sculptor, the philosopher looks at the world and seeks to abstract from the things he sees the forms that give them their reality. And he too may be said to copy these forms with his mind, though the medium in which he does so is reason or speech (*logos*) rather than stone or wood. This is the only perfect copy that is possible. That is because the conflict between the intelligibility of form and the unintelligibility of matter no longer exists when the matter in which the form is embodied is reason itself. No maker can ever produce such a copy. The business of thinking therefore occupies the highest position in the hierarchy of human activities, higher, as we have seen, than that of the man of practical virtue, and higher too than the activity of every maker, including those whose works we now regard as masterpieces of fine art and praise on account of their genius.

Vasari's easy acceptance of the idea of genius underscores the distance between his conception of art and Aristotle's. But his book reminds us of the gulf between them in another way as well. *The Lives of the Artists* is a series of portraits in prose. It belongs, as Burckhardt suggests, to the broader tradition of Renaissance portraiture and shares its basic aim. This might be described as the representation of the individuality of the portrait's subject. No painter or biographer can ever do this completely. There will always be more to his subject than even the greatest artist can convey. The idea that a portrait, or any work of art for that matter, should strive to capture the uniqueness of a particular individual therefore sets a goal that cannot be attained. Yet despite this it retains its authority even today, along with the idea of genius to which it is closely related.

What these two ideas share in common is the value they assign to individuality as such—on the one side that of the artist, and on the other, that of
the person he is striving to portray. From the fifteenth century on, the tradition of Renaissance portraiture was shaped by the latter objective. In this respect, it differed fundamentally from its ancient counterpart, which manifests
the same indifference to individuality that Aristotle expresses in more philosophical terms.

Broadly speaking, ancient portraits served two functions, one private and
the other public. Private portraits were commissioned by wealthy families to
memorialize a family member who had died, or soon would. As Pliny reports,
these portraits were fashioned mainly for "use at family burials," where they
would be brought out and carried in the procession, so that the person who
had died could be "accompanied" by his or her ancestors.[5] To perform their
intended function, the portraits in question had to bear some resemblance to
the individuals they represented. They had to be reasonable likenesses. But
their purpose was not to capture the peculiar identity of those they depicted.
They were meant to serve as good-enough reminders so that the subjects of the
portraits could participate in the communal solidarity of their family, into
whose collective identity their own distinctive ones were dissolved.

Public portraits functioned as a form of publicity. A political ruler could
not be present everywhere at once. To strengthen his authority, he had images of himself set up in places he rarely visited. Again, this required that the
image be a reasonable likeness, but here too the important thing was not to
convey a sense of the ruler's idiosyncrasies but of his virtues instead—of his
conformity to a general type of human being, defined by the possession of
qualities like justice and generosity. In the same way that the individuality of
the subject of a family portrait was "lost" in the life of his family, that of the
ruler disappeared in the archetypal representation of the virtues he had to possess in order to be, quite literally, an authority figure. In neither case was the
portrait maker's primary aim to convey an appreciation of the unique qualities that distinguished his subject from everyone else. If the picture he made
or bust he carved did this to some degree (as it could hardly help from doing),
this was the unavoidable by-product of a work conceived for other ends.

Like their ancient counterparts, many of the portraits that were made in
northern Italy in the fifteenth and sixteenth centuries were commissioned
either as family memorials or as emblems of public authority. Here, too, general qualities were stressed and aspects of the subject's physical appearance
often suppressed in order to create a more pleasing likeness. Ghirlandaio's por-

trait of Giovanna degli Albizzi Tournaboni, which was commissioned by her husband to commemorate his wife's early death, has been described as an expression of "the canonical formula for the representation of feminine virtue and beauty," and Pietro di Spagna's remarkable painting of Federigo da Montefeltro, the Duke of Urbino, with his son Guidobaldo, not only conveys a reassuring sense of succession—always a crucial element of political authority—but hides from view the disfiguring wound to the duke's right eye that a frontal portrait would have revealed.[6] Yet anyone looking at these paintings is bound to feel that the painter has sought to convey some sense of what his subject was like not merely as the representative of a type but as an individual with an identity uniquely his or her own.

For Ghirlandaio and Di Spagna, the formulae of virtue and authority are devices for representing the individuality of their subjects, not the other way around. Ancient painters and sculptors used their subjects' idiosyncrasies as a vehicle for depicting them as the occupants of a role. The astonishing revival of the art of portraiture in Renaissance Italy starts from the opposite premise: that the aim of the artist is to capture, as best he can, the unique personality of his subject, using conventional forms, which are always general in nature, as a means to this end.

The curators of the exhibition of Renaissance portraits that was organized by the Staatliche Museen zu Berlin and the Metropolitan Museum of Art in New York in 2011–12 must have had this reversal in mind when they chose Ghirlandaio's *Portrait of an Old Man and a Boy* for the cover of the exhibition catalogue. The picture shows an elderly man holding a young boy. They are looking at each other lovingly. But there is something that upsets what might otherwise be taken for a general, if not platitudinous, depiction of the power and dignity of love across the generations. The old man's nose is deformed by rhinophyma, which gives his otherwise serene expression a clownish appearance. But he is most certainly no clown. The old man retains his dignity despite his deformity. Indeed, his deformity is *part* of his dignity, along with everything else that makes him an individual whose identity can never be fully expressed by any set of conventional tropes (those of loving grandfather, thoughtful patriarch and the like).

As we look at Ghirlandaio's portrait, our interest is focused on *this* man. What was *he* thinking and feeling? How did the world look though *his* eyes, cast down, over his nose and whatever it must have meant to *him*, toward the boy whose own feelings appear to be unaffected by it? We are drawn toward the uniqueness of the man and of the moment the painter has sought to express, and because any formal categories we employ to help us comprehend its meaning always leave something out that remains beyond reach, we feel we must return to the painting again and again, not as an act of veneration but one of discovery instead. Expressed in the language of perspective (to which we shall turn in a moment), one might say that the individuality of the subject of Ghirlandaio's portrait is the vanishing point toward which the viewer's eye is irresistibly drawn—the real subject of interest in Renaissance portraits generally, in contrast to the ancient ones that often served as their models but for whose makers the phenomenon of individuality, though it could hardly be overlooked, was of less interest and perhaps none at all.

There are two ways, then, in which Vasari's *Lives* illustrates Burckhardt's claim that the spirit of the Renaissance lay in its reverence for the individual. First, like Ghirlandaio, Vasari drew his portraits in order to capture, as best he could, the uniqueness of his subjects, and second, he attributed the value of their own work to the artists' distinctive qualities of temperament and imagination. For the latter idea, we have the familiar word "genius." For the former, I shall use the term "sublimity." I will have more to say about the concept of sublimity, which has a long philosophical history. But a first approximation would be the following: what invites and always rewards further study, yet remains forever beyond our power to comprehend, both delighting and disappointing us on account of what it simultaneously reveals and conceals, is sublime. Sublimity, in this sense, is to be contrasted with beauty as the pagan philosophers understood it, and only becomes an aesthetic value when the individuality of individuals comes to be regarded as something that is valuable in its own right (a proposition that Plato and Aristotle would have thought absurd). This is the common root from which the ideas of genius and sublimity both spring.

But where is this root to be found? What was the inspiration for the ideas of genius and sublimity that reflect, in different ways, the ideal of individuality that Burckhardt identifies as the spiritual center of Renaissance civilization? Burckhardt fails to answer this question. More specifically, he fails to see that the answer lies in the theological revolution that separates the Renaissance from the classical world its artists sometimes seemed to wish to emulate in a slavish fashion.

The rebirth of classicism in Italy in the fifteenth and sixteenth centuries was accomplished through the midwifery of Christian belief. In the process, every ancient aesthetic ideal received a wholly new meaning. This is above all true of the pagan ideas of imitation and beauty. Under the influence of the doctrine of divine creation, which for the first time demands that individuals be considered real and valuable as such, these ideas were transformed into those of genius and sublimity instead.

Before we explore their theological roots, however, we must pause to consider the Christian provenance of another idea that is often associated with Renaissance art, and with the inventive spirit of Renaissance painting in particular. I am referring to the idea of perspective.

The technique of perspective painting was known to the artists of the ancient world but lost to their Christian successors, whose paintings were characterized by an absence of depth and the reduction of three-dimensional space to the two dimensions of a plane. One may therefore be forgiven for assuming that the recovery of perspective, beginning in the fourteenth century, depended on a *repudiation* of Christian beliefs in favor of an older, pagan view of the world. But the truth is more nearly the opposite. In Erwin Panofsky's words, the "perspective interpretation of space which, originating with Giotto and Duccio, began to be accepted everywhere from 1330–40," represents the "most characteristic" artistic expression of the nominalist tradition in late medieval theology, which placed unprecedented weight on the value of the individual as such.[7] The Renaissance idea of perspective, as distinct from the ancient conception of it, is therefore a Christian invention as well. It reflects the endorsement, not the rejection, of Christian beliefs. To see why, we need to take a brief look at the book that gave the modern understanding of perspective its first, definitive formulation.

A SCIENCE OF PERSPECTIVE

When Leon Battista Alberti sat down to write his short treatise on the art of painting, more than a century before Vasari completed his *Lives,* the technique of perspective painting was already far advanced. But Alberti was the first to offer a theoretical account of the methods on which it is based. Indeed, he was the first modern writer to offer a theory of painting in general, and perhaps the first ever, in the West at least, for the ancient writings on the subject that have survived lack the rigor that set Alberti's book apart.[8]

Alberti's aim is to provide the foundations for a science of perspective and then to offer some practical help to painters who want to make use of his scientific discoveries. This is a more daring project than may seem. To appreciate its originality, we need to begin by contrasting Alberti's conception of painting, and of perspective in particular, with that of Plato, who thought more deeply about the relation between perspective and truth than any other ancient philosopher.[9]

So long as our souls remain imprisoned in our bodies, Plato says, we cannot help but see things in a perspectival fashion. Our embodied state condemns us to always being at one place rather than another, and hence to seeing the world from the particular vantage point this place affords, which changes the moment we move somewhere else. The same applies to the temporal point of view that is ours at any given time—today rather than yesterday or tomorrow. The temporal perspectivity of our experience is rooted in the body too. We are mortal because we have bodies, and experience the world in an ever-changing sequence of times as well as places only because we are mortal beings.

But on Plato's view, the worst mistake that one can make is to confuse the way the world looks from a spatial or temporal perspective—the way it looks *here* and *now*—with the true nature of the world itself. This is the mistake made by all those Socrates calls the "lovers of sights and sounds."[10] To correct and overcome it one must practice being dead, as Socrates tells his listeners in the *Phaedo*.[11] One must learn to see things from no perspective at all. Correcting one's perspectival judgments by comparing them with one another is a necessary step toward this end.[12] But a true knowledge of the world is available only to those who have not merely corrected or improved their judgments in this way, but overcome the habit of perspectival thinking altogether. They alone possess the kind of knowledge that is worthy of being called a "science." It follows that for Plato the very idea of a "science of perspective" is bound to seem a hopeless contradiction since real science, as he understands it, begins only when one leaves all perspectives behind.

On Plato's view, the person who continues to believe that there is any truth at all in the particularity of things as they appear from his spatially and temporally mobile point of view remains a prisoner of illusion. He cannot grasp the omnipresent and everlasting forms that give the always changing panorama of the world whatever reality it possesses. In his struggle to free himself, he has no greater aid than the discipline of mathematics, which teaches human beings to think in nonperspectival terms. And he has no greater enemy than art, which exploits the naive pleasure we take in illusions and thereby fastens the soul even more strongly to the untruth of perspective. Plato directs his ferocious criticism of art mainly against poetry, but the plastic arts are guilty of the same purposeful confusion of perspective and truth, and among these painting is surely the most guilty of all, for the two-dimensional representation of three-dimensional objects relies upon illusions that even the sculptor is able to do without.

Alberti's view of painting differs from Plato's in the sharpest possible way. To begin with, he assigns painting a high value on the same grounds that a Platonist is bound to assign it a low one. According to Alberti, painting is not the least worthy of the arts because it makes a particularly extravagant use of illusion, but the greatest *for precisely this reason*. Painters are more ingenious than sculptors and architects in creating the illusion of viewing the world from a particular place, as if one were actually standing there, and are to be congratulated for their masterful manipulation of the illusions of perspectivity rather than condemned for dragging the soul of the viewer down into a cave of intellectual and spiritual depravity.

Even more strikingly, Alberti claims that mathematics can be used to represent the truth that lies in each perspective. In his view, mathematics is an instrument for the rationalization of perspectival experience, not the means by which we transcend it. For Alberti, mathematics is *in service to* perspectivity—a view of their relation that to a Platonist will seem a perversion of the noblest art we possess.

In this respect, one can draw a parallel between Alberti's program for the mathematization of perspective painting and Galileo's geometrical analysis of the movement of falling bodies. By employing the truths of mathematics to rationalize the illusions of motion rather than to help us escape them, Galileo's new science of nature turns Plato's view of the relation between truth and mathematics on its head. Alberti's use of geometry as a tool for making the illusions of perspective amenable to understanding, rather than as a springboard to help us overcome their destructive grip, entails a similar reversal of the Platonic conception of the relation between mathematics and the realm of bodily life, to which the truthless illusions of motion and perspective are tied.

This is enough to make it clear that Alberti's science of perspective is no mere revival of a classical preference for order and form, or of an ancient technique suppressed by centuries of two-dimensional Christian art. In fact, Alberti's use of geometry to solve the problem of how to construct a perspectival representation of the world in such a way that it will be immediately apprehensible to others as an accurate depiction of the world from that point of view, is conditioned by Christian beliefs. This is true in two respects. The first, as Panofsky notes, concerns the understanding of the nature of space that Alberti presupposes.[13]

For theological reasons, the voluntarists of the thirteenth century strongly encouraged the idea that space is infinite and homogeneous. The acceptance of this idea ruled out the possibility of a qualitatively differentiated space of the sort that Aristotle's doctrine of proper place requires. It also undermined the ancient conception of space as a closed container and extended space without limit uniformly in every direction.

A corollary of this new idea of space is what might be called the "indifference" of perspective. In an infinite and homogeneous space, there are a limitless number of positions. Each of these represents a unique point of view on the world as a whole. But while each differs from every other in one respect, the infinity of space means that in another they are all the same, since none enjoys a special place by virtue of its location in a world with definite size and shape, in the way, for example, that an organ occupies a special place in the body to which it belongs. In one sense, therefore, in an infinite space the world appears the same from every point of view—as the infinitely distant vanishing point where parallel lines meet. Their sameness in this respect makes it possible to compare or "commensurate" different perspectives by means of mathematics, which abstracts from the features peculiar to each and treats them as mere points whose relation to all others can be represented in identical terms and thereby displayed in a fashion that renders them equally accessible to anyone who adopts the point of view in question. Alberti's anti-Platonic claim that the art of perspective painting can be put on a scientific basis by means of mathematics assumes an indifference of perspective that rests on a novel conception of space which itself was the result of the voluntarists' revolt against the rationalism of Aquinas and the Latin Averroists.

The second way in which Alberti's science of perspective is shaped by Christian beliefs is even more important.

Being an individual and having a perspective on the world are different ways of describing the same thing. In the pagan metaphysics of Plato and Aristotle, individuality, and hence perspectivity, is a function of the mindless matter in which the forms of things are embodied. It follows that we can learn nothing about the world by studying the individuality of things as such. But if God created the world from nothing, then the quiddity of every individual will not only be intelligible. It will also express in a unique way the goodness of its creator, and though no individual can ever adequately represent God's infinite being, it nevertheless makes an irreplaceable contribution to the glory of his creation as a whole. We therefore learn something new about God every time we assume the perspective of one of his creatures. The only nonperspectival position is that of God himself. But this is not available to us, here on earth at least, as Plato believed the truth is if we practice being dead. Our access to God is exclusively through the finite perspectives of the countless individuals with whom he has filled the world. A faith in God's infinite power and goodness compels us to assume that each perspective adds in some distinctive way to the value of the world as a whole, even if we cannot see how it does.

That perspectivity has positive worth rather than the negative one Plato assigned it is a consequence of the doctrine of creation, which dissolves the distinction between form and matter on which all pagan metaphysics is based. By validating the intelligibility and value of individuality as such, Christian theology confers an inherent dignity on the perspective nature of experience that no Greek thinker could accord it. It encourages the search for a method of representation that will enable artists to render, and viewers to see, the truth *in* perspective, instead of rejecting the very idea as an oxymoron. Alberti's treatise *On Painting* assumes the legitimacy of this program and seeks to carry it out by using geometry to organize the way the world appears from an individual point of view in such a way that the uniqueness of the appearance is rationalized and made intelligible to others, *without being lost in the process*—something Plato thought impossible on metaphysical grounds.[14]

For Alberti, the manifold of perspectives remains anchored in an objective reality whose existence he takes for granted. They are all perspectives on a common world. He also insists that although we always see things from a particular point of view, the world itself has an inherent order that can be discerned by careful observation. He urges painters to study nature so as to understand this order and be able to reproduce it in their work. Moreover, in his writings on sculpture and architecture, and in his work as a practicing architect, Alberti shows a reverence for classical forms and the perfectionist ideals of harmony and order associated with them.[15] In all these respects, Alberti was more Greek than Christian and despite his insistence on the value of perspective, which is always individual, and his search for a method to find and depict the truth in it, the most important implications of the Christian religion for the modern understanding of art are missing from his treatise on painting.

These are the ideas of genius and sublimity, both of which also start from the Christian belief that individuality has a value of its own and is therefore essential to our judgment of the value of a work of art, whether we consider it, from the artist's side, as the expression of an individual temperament, or evaluate it in terms of its representational content, as an attempt to capture the individuality of a particular person, place or experience. Alberti's theory of perspective gives us a first preliminary glimpse of the extent to which the tradition of modern art has been conditioned by Christian beliefs. But to understand the Christian roots of the ideas of genius and sublimity, which have shaped our experience of art for the past half millennium, we need to take a large step back and explore in more detail the theological background against which the extraordinary event that we call the Renaissance took place, and that made it something more than a mere recovery of classical ideals.

SACRED IMAGES

In the course of the fifteenth century, painters on both sides of the Alps became increasingly proficient in the use of perspective. Following the example of Giotto, Masaccio led the way in the south. Van Eyck and Van der Weyden did the same in the north. By the end of the century, the works of Ghirlandaio, Botticelli, Memling, Van der Goes and others all exhibit a mastery of the techniques of perspectival realism that today any competent artist may be assumed to possess. A growing fluency in the use of these techniques is one of the defining characteristics of early Renaissance painting.

Another is that the pictures in question are of human beings. Many portray religious figures, though some, like Botticelli's *Primavera,* are inspired by classical sources and others (most portraits, for example) have strictly secular subjects. But in all these otherwise diverse paintings, the landscapes and still-life arrangements that will later become the subject of works devoted exclusively to them are mere compositional elements, subordinated to the representation of the human form, in one guise or another. The depiction of the human figure is so central to Renaissance painting that we hardly notice its ubiquitous position.

Yet the Christian religion, like Judaism before it and Islam after, originally prohibited the making of images. With some important exceptions, this prohibition has permanently discouraged the representation of human beings in the art inspired by these other religions. One is therefore bound to ask how and why this obstacle was overcome so completely in the art of the West, which like Western philosophy and science, matured in the crucible of Christian belief.

The answer is complex. But in one crucial respect it is theological. Christianity is distinguished from Judaism and Islam by the doctrine of the Incarnation. In contrast to both, it teaches that God became man. This opens the way to the idea that artistic images of the man-God are not only permitted but share in the sacrality of the embodied divinity they represent—that they too partake in the mystery of the word become flesh. And once this idea is established, it eventually becomes possible to claim that the representation of any of God's human creatures, indeed of any created being, shares in this sacred mystery too. The result is a sacralization of the image as such—a spur to the development of Western painting from the Renaissance on, and one of the sources of the ideas of genius and sublimity that still dominate our view of art even in an age of disenchantment.

The expression "sacred image" is for Plato as much a contradiction as the phrase "science of perspective." An image may serve as an aid to the recollection of the divine, as it does for the slave boy in the *Meno* who is helped to remember the Pythagorean theorem by means of a figure drawn in the dirt. But the image itself has no divinity in it. It is useful only if one learns to look through and beyond it. The image is what it is—namely, an image and not the original it dimly represents—on account of its body, and once this is removed in thought, it ceases to be an image at all. For an image *as such* to have divine meaning, the body that makes it an image must possess some intrinsic divinity of its own, and this is just what Plato's metaphysics rules out as a matter of principle.

The creationist metaphysics of Genesis is distinguished from Plato's in a radical way. The world of the biblical writers is not made, as Plato's is, by a divine artisan who shapes it in accordance with eternally preexisting forms. It is brought into being out of nothing by a God whose freedom is absolute. Philo stresses this distinction. Yet he also observes that in one respect at least Platonism and Judaism are alike, for both maintain that nothing *in* the world of visible things can ever adequately represent the nature of the invisible divinity *beyond* it. This is the source of the Jewish prohibition on image making, a practice that Plato characteristically regards as a sign of ignorance, and the writers of the Hebrew Bible, equally characteristically, as the violation of a divine command.

This last distinction had important consequences. The Jews' conception of the relation between the human and divine as one of obedience rather than understanding, early on led to the treatment of the text in which God's commandments are inscribed as itself a cultic object of sorts. When the ancient Israelites went into battle, they carried their sacred book in a wagon. Today, the Torah is still housed in an ark that is opened to display the text inside it on every Sabbath in every synagogue in the world. If it were merely a work of philosophy, attaching such significance to the book itself would make little sense. It would be a form of fetishism, of the sort that Socrates warns against in the *Phaedrus* when he speaks of the dangers of writing.[16] But the Torah is not a work of philosophy. It is more akin to a contract, and as with all contracts, it is important to preserve the Torah in its original written form so as to be able to refer to its exact language.

Despite the incommensurability between the human and divine on which both Jews and Platonists insist, Jews therefore assign a sacred importance to at least one object in the world and do so, in part at least, on account of its physical presence—because of what we might call its "thingly" nature. The fact that the disfigurement of the Torah, or even its deterioration though use, is viewed as an offense demanding redress is one expression of this profoundly un-Platonic attitude.

But the Torah is not a golden calf. The God whose commandments the Torah memorializes is not present in the text in the same way that the gods of the Canaanites were present in the objects they revered. In the latter case, god and cultic object were fused with such completeness that one could not say where the matter of the object ended and the god's divinity began. The god and its embodiment (in a statue, for example, or in the flesh of a sacrificial animal) were so closely identified as to be, for all practical purposes, one and the same. This is just what the Israelites found abominable. Even if their holy book acquired a cultlike status, the fact that it was a *book* or collection of *signs* served as a constant reminder that the God to whom they prayed was not in the work itself, but elsewhere, beyond the book, beyond the world, in an invisible place to which the signs of the book pointed by means of the invisible relation of signification.

The cult objects of the worshippers of Baal and Astarte resembled the gods they embodied. They looked like them and this made their identification easier. But a word need not look like the thing it represents. Even in pictographic systems, the gap between the appearance of words and that of their referents tends to widen over time. For the worshippers of Yahweh, it was essential that the book that bound them to him do so not by means of resemblance, which is always concrete and therefore capable of being seen, but by means of signification, which is necessarily abstract and must be grasped by the mind, since only this latter mode of representation is compatible with the essential nature of God himself, as a world-transcending deity who lies beyond the furthest horizon of sight.

In certain respects, the Christian religion stresses the transcendence of God even more rigorously than the orthopractical Judaism from which it emerged. For Jews, man's relation to God is mediated by a system of laws that penetrate every aspect of daily life and endow all worldly activities with a religious meaning that compels those who observe them to recognize the presence of their lord in the routines of eating and bathing as well as at the altar of the temple. Distant as he is from the world in one sense, the God of the Jews is spread throughout it in another. He is omnipresent in the lives of his chosen people by virtue of the law he has given to them alone. When Paul and his followers rejected the law as the key to salvation, and challenged the exceptionalism of those who affirm its authority, they did so in the name of a God whose distance from the world is so great that his grandeur cannot possibly be confused with anything as trivial as the question of whether or not one is permitted to eat the meat of animals with cloven hooves.

But in another respect, of course, Paul's Christianity insists upon a connection between God and the world that is more intimate than anything Judaism allows. For the broad but comparatively thin presence of God in the law, it substitutes his intense but localized presence in Christ. One might say that it condenses the former into the latter with such force that in Christ God achieves a *visible presence* as contrasted with his *invisible omnipresence* as the unseen giver of the laws that for observant Jews direct every action they take.

In Judaism, the relation between the law and God remains one of signification. The Torah is the word of God; the law is the Torah in action; and like the book in which it is recorded, the law points to God in the way a word signifies its referent. The relation of Christ to God is fundamentally different. Christ is the word *become flesh*. What this formula means is that God is present in the body of Christ in such a way that our bodily eyes can see him there, not the invisible way in which the referent of a sign is "in" the sign that points to it. The second kind of presence requires no resemblance between the sign and what it signifies. Indeed, the weaker the resemblance, the more clearly this abstract form of presence appears to the eye of the mind. But the first kind—the way that God is present in Christ—is only possible if there is a resemblance between the two. If we can actually see God in Christ that is because Christ *looks like* him in some respect.

It is essential to add the qualification, "in some respect," for otherwise the presence of God in Christ might be confused with the divinity of the golden calf and mistaken for a form of pagan idolatry.

The relation of the calf to the god it represents is more than one of re-semblance, as distinct from signification. The resemblance is so close as to be one of identity. Calf and god are merged with such completeness that no remainder of divinity is left behind. This is bound to appear blasphe-mous to those that worship a God who is defined by his transcendence of all worldly things. The Christian God is therefore both visible and invisi-ble. Indeed, he is at once the most *and* least visible deity imaginable. On the one hand, he transcends the world so completely that even the Jews failed to grasp his ineffable grandeur. And yet, on the other, he assumed a visible physical form and entered into the depths of bodily suffering even "unto death."

This radicalized conjunction of transcendence and visibility, of remote-ness and resemblance, is the meaning of the central dogma of the Christian religion. For an orthodox Christian, the Incarnation is a mystery that must be accepted on faith. For a philosopher, it is an affront to reason. As a reli-gion of orthodoxy, rather than orthopraxy, Christianity itself has done much to strengthen the philosophical demand for a rational account of its own creedal premises, including this one in particular. In previous chapters, we have seen how this demand leads to the self-disenchantment of Christian the-ology and its devolution into the nihilism that represents the last, attenuated stage of Christian belief in the civilization of the modern West. Now we must briefly trace the way in which the mystery of the Incarnation, which para-doxically spurred the philosophical rationalization of the Christian religion, also helped to free Christian art from the iconoclastic prejudice that all three Abrahamic religions share, and by promoting the sacralization of the image determined the peculiar direction that Western art has followed for the past eight centuries.

No one has developed these themes more persuasively than Hans Belting in his masterwork, *Likeness and Presence*.[17]

According to Belting, the doctrine of the Incarnation played a crucial role in legitimating the practice of image making in the Christian world—first the eastern half, then the western—and in conferring upon it a spiritual value that enabled it to withstand the attack of iconoclasts who appealed to the orig-inal biblical injunction against the making of images.[18] There were of course other nontheological factors that encouraged this practice in areas where the church established its authority in the early centuries of the Common Era. One was the proliferation of cults devoted to local saints, who as Peter Brown and others have observed, met the all-too-human need for intercessors to mediate between an incomprehensibly remote God and his anxious followers.[19] Wherever such cults were established, the ancient practice of painting portraits as a means of memorializing the dead and of preserving the continuity of the families to which they belonged was easily adapted to the new purpose of insuring that the spiritual powers of a saint were not lost when he or she died but embodied in the image that served as a lasting substitute to which the prayers of the faithful might be addressed.[20]

A second factor was the merger of political and religious authority following Constantine's conversion to Christianity. The use of paintings to ensure that an image of the emperor was present wherever he could not be, antedated the fusion of these two authorities and served as another ancient precedent for the similar use of suitably Christianized images after the emperor's authority had come to be seen as dependent, even if only symbolically, on that of the church.[21]

But though these developments encouraged the practice of image making for important institutional reasons, in order to overcome the explicit iconoclasm of the biblical text itself, a theological justification for the practice had to be found. Belting contends that it was the theologians of the Eastern Orthodox Church who first constructed such a justification, during the Iconoclastic Wars of the eighth and ninth centuries.

The theological defense of image making hinged on the idea of the Incarnation. Jesus is not, it was claimed, merely a sign of God (as the symbol of the cross is). He is God's visible image instead—the way God looked when he walked among men. The iconoclastic claim that any image of God is a blasphemy because it implicitly conflates his invisible grandeur with something that can be seen is therefore incompatible with the most basic teaching of the Christian religion itself.

The Incarnation thus serves as a warrant for the general proposition that an image can be sacred—that it does not lose its divinity merely on account of its status as an image. This is the first crucial step and once it has been taken, others follow more easily. If the image of God that is Christ is inherently sacred, then it seems reasonable to assume that its sacrality can "rub off" on the other bodies that touched his, and even that a picture of him painted by one of Christ's disciples might share, at one remove, in the sacredness of its subject. In these and other ways, the legitimacy that the doctrine of the Incarnation conferred on the idea of a sacred image gradually widened until the practice of painting pictures of Christ and of the main events in his life, and then of the other human beings who played a role in it, came to be accepted not merely as something that Christian doctrine permits but as a sanctified extension of its most distinctive theological commitment.

Once the legitimacy of image making had been secured on religious grounds, various writers in the East began to speculate on the aesthetic effects of painting and to compare these with those that poetry has on its listeners. So long as the iconoclastic contempt for image making retained widespread support, the freedom for such speculations hardly existed. But with the suppression of iconoclasm, a new and specifically Christian aesthetics of painting began to emerge. Its central premise was that the purpose of a painting that represents a scene from the life of Jesus or that of his family (especially his mother) is to arouse a devotional attitude in the viewer by engaging his or her feelings in a personal way. A corollary was that the picture should express the equally intimate feelings of the painter. A painting that neither expresses such feelings on the painter's side, nor arouses them on the viewer's, is a lifeless object without spiritual value. Paintings that possess such value do so, it was claimed, because they provide an objective medium through which two souls—the painter's and the viewer's—are able to communicate their innermost spiritual longings to one another. When the icon painters of the East carried their art to western Europe in the eleventh and twelfth centuries, they took this new aesthetics with them. One can see its effects in the soulful *Maestà* of Cimabue that now hangs in the Uffizi in Florence.

This new aesthetics could emerge only after the basic question of the legitimacy of image making had been settled. But once it was established, it altered the way the sacred image itself was viewed and accelerated its transformation from a holy object into what Belting calls a "work of art."

Jesus neither points to God in the abstract way a sign denotes its referent, nor depicts him as a portrait does its subject. Jesus *is* God, even if he is not the whole of God but only one of the three persons that constitute God's divinity in its entirety. The relation of Jesus to God is one of embodiment. If it is theologically permissible to make an image of Jesus because the image may plausibly be viewed as an extension of his own incarnate divinity, then the image too must be treated as an embodiment of the divine. It must be regarded as possessing a resident holiness of its own—one that inheres in the image, just as Jesus' holiness inhered in the body that was nailed to the cross, not in something else to which his body merely pointed. This follows from the argument that was used to defend the legitimacy of image making during the Iconoclastic Wars. So long as it was accepted, the images that were made with its warrant continued to be venerated as holy objects.

But as it came to be assumed that the value of a painting lies in its power to express the religious feelings of its creator and to awaken those of its viewers, this older conception of the image as a holy object lost its theological foundation. A painting could no longer be regarded as an embodiment of the divine. It had to be viewed as a representation of it instead—as the purposeful depiction of a sacred scene, fashioned by human hands with the aim of conveying a particular inner state and of arousing one in others. It had, in short, to be viewed as a work of art, as we still understand that term.

This epochal shift in the conception of the nature and value of a painting is one aspect of a wider process of disenchantment, which drained the entire world of its inherent value and transferred it to valuing subjects instead. In the field of art this resulted, on the viewer's side, in an increasing emphasis on the personal and therefore private nature of the experience of looking at a painting, which now no longer functioned as a cult object to be used in public processions and the like, but as a stimulus to pious reflections and feelings that had value only insofar as they were the viewer's own.

On the artist's side, this same shift encouraged a parallel process of personalization. It became more and more important that the artist bare *his* soul in creating the work, just as the viewer bares his or hers in responding to it. Indeed, these quickly came to be seen as interdependent: for a viewer to be moved by a painting, its creator had to put as much authentic feeling into it as he demanded from his audience in return. This led inexorably, Belting argues, to "the cult of genius in a new religion of art."[22]

The importance that the Christian religion attaches to personal salvation further reinforced the association of the value of a painting with the individuality of the artist who makes it. Everything else is mere craftsmanship—or worse, inauthentic imitation, what today we would call kitsch. In the centuries since the sacred image was transformed from a holy object into a work of art, the religious background that still conditioned the idea of artistic genius at the end of the Renaissance has fallen away. But the concept of genius, which survived this sea change in the spiritual life of the West, continues to be invested with the aura of sacrality that it acquired when the holiness of the sacred image was transferred from the image itself to the individual soul of its human creator.

The idea of the sublime, which like that of genius has no counterpart in classical aesthetics, owes its existence to the sanctification of the image as well, and thus ultimately to the Christian doctrine of the Incarnation that provided a justification for it.

For Plato, an image always has less reality than the original. The being of the original is self-contained. It does not need the image in order to be what it is. The being of the image, by contrast, is wholly dependent on that of the original, and this dependency means that its stands lower in the ontological hierarchy of things. In this respect, the reflection of an object in a mirror exemplifies the status of images generally.

The doctrine of the Incarnation upends this view completely. Jesus makes God visible to men. But his relation to God is altogether different from that of a triangle drawn in the dirt to the idea of triangularity. To use one of Plato's favorite metaphors, the drawn triangle "reflects" the original. It "participates" in it by way of representation. By contrast, Jesus looks like God because he *is* God in the flesh. The relation between them is not one of representation. It is the vastly more intimate one of embodiment. For centuries, the greatest thinkers of the early church struggled to find a language to describe this relationship and to distinguish it from the very different one that in Plato's philosophy connects the visible world of sights and sounds to the ideal realm of the forms. That they had to use the vocabulary of pagan metaphysics to do this made their task more difficult if not impossible. But whether one judges their efforts to have been successful or not, the often-tortured formulations of the Church Fathers reflect their shared understanding that the presence of God in Jesus makes his status as a visible image of the divine radically different from that of any image as Plato understood it.

One consequence of this is that God's own incomprehensibility is transferred to his son, who can no more be fully understood by the human mind than his divine father. God's reality is greater than any finite being can grasp. It overflows all our attempts to conceive and describe it. If the body of Jesus is more than a mere representation of God, if it is God himself become flesh, then the same gap between the boundlessness of God's reality and our limited powers of comprehension must exist with respect to this particular body as well, despite its visibility.

This unsettles the Platonic view of images in two respects. First, according to Plato, the idea one sees represented in an image, like that of a triangle drawn in the dirt, is fully comprehensible. There is nothing about it that the mind is unable to grasp. This follows from the very being of the idea itself, which is its intelligibility. Second, insofar as an image *is* an image, on Plato's view it lacks all reality and therefore all intelligibility. Qua image, it is altogether bereft of being. By contrast, the God to whom Christians pray, unlike a Platonic idea, is defined by the excess of his being over and above whatever we can comprehend with our limited categories of understanding. And insofar as God is present in the visible body of his son, not by way of signification or depiction but embodiment instead, we are bound to experience the same incomprehensibility when contemplating this image of God as we do when reflecting on the divine nature itself. The result is that rather than being drained of reality, as all images are in Plato's philosophy, this particular image is filled up with so much reality that no human mind can ever fully grasp it—though it is right there to be seen.

This is the origin of the idea of sublimity, which is something more than mere grandeur. The sublime is what we know to be greater than we can comprehend, and admire just for that reason. There is no room for this idea in pagan metaphysics. Despite its enthusiastic reception by later thinkers, Longinus' famous essay on the subject has nothing to do with sublimity understood in these terms, but belongs, as we shall see, to a pre-Christian world of thought. The very first thing in the world of visible bodies that may properly be called sublime—though certainly not beautiful in a classical sense, for its bruised and bloody figure invites an altogether different reaction than the serenity of a Greek statue—is the body of Christ. When the theologians of Byzantium later justified the making of images on the grounds that they are visible manifestations of divinity too, and therefore in principle authorized by the Incarnation, which establishes the legitimacy of the claim that God can be seen, the sublimity of this one divine body was extended to human pictures of it and survived their transformation from holy objects into works of art. Later, this process of transference was further extended by another Christian belief: that even though Christ is unique in being an embodiment or "person" of God and not one of his creatures, every created being is endowed with a measure of value that no human being can fully fathom and therefore also shares in a reality greater than any pagan philosopher could conceive. The museumgoer who today stands in front of a painting of some wholly secular scene, at once thrilled and disappointed by the knowledge that its depths can never be plumbed, is the disenchanted heir of the aesthetics of sublimity to which the doctrine of the Incarnation first gave life.

IMAGINATION TAKES THE LEAD

The Italian Renaissance was no mere resurrection of classical ideals. These were seen through the prism of Christian belief and transformed as a result. This is notably true of the eclectic form of Platonism that was championed by Alberti's contemporary, Marcilio Ficino. Ficino's hybrid metaphysics relies on a concept of the imagination that has no counterpart in Plato's philosophy but was the product of a reinterpretation of certain Platonic motifs from the standpoint of Christian theology. In contrast to Plato's own metaphysics, which was deeply hostile to art, Ficino's Christianized Neoplatonism, and his understanding of the role of the imagination in particular, inspired a more favorable view of artistic creativity and helped to further legitimate the ideas of genius and sublimity that mark the watershed between classical and modern aesthetics. No one has offered a better account of these developments than Erwin Panofsky.[23]

According to Panofsky, the late Roman world saw the rise of what he calls a new "art metaphysics." This appears to have coincided with an increase in the social prestige of artists themselves. Platonism was ill-equipped to account for this phenomenon. For Plato, art can never be more than a copy of a copy. It is therefore always ontologically inferior to the things it imitates, which are themselves inferior to the ideas they mimic in a blurred and transient way. Panofsky detects the beginnings of a more favorable view of art in the writings of Plotinus.[24] According to Plotinus, the artist looks at an object and by exercising his imagination, forms an image of it in his mind that is *closer* to the ideal archetype of the object than the object itself. In this way, the artist's imagination enables him to draw *nearer* to what is really real rather than carrying him in the opposite direction, toward nothingness or nonbeing instead.[25] On this view, the artist ceases to be a slavish copyist whose work must by definition be inferior to the thing that he copies. He becomes, for the first time, an artist as distinct from a craftsman, and the art he fashions with the aid of his imagination is transformed from a hindrance to a help in the soul's struggle to reach the divine.

Though more receptive to the value of art than Plato's metaphysics had been, Plotinus' view of the artist as an "idealist" whose imaginative reworking of everyday reality represents an ontological improvement upon it nevertheless remained tied to the intellectualist assumptions of pagan metaphysics generally. For Plotinus and his followers, matter continued to be regarded as a source or principle of cosmic stupidity that keeps the world from being wholly transparent to reason and thus acts as a drag on the soul in its upward flight toward being. Despite his imaginative transcendence of the world of ordinary things, the artist's attempt to embody what he has imagined in a material medium of some sort is therefore doomed to fail. An artist may not be the mere copyist Plato supposed him to be. But he is still inferior to the philosopher who grasps the truth not with his imagination, which is a hybrid of thought and sensation, but with the purer faculty of reason that alone is able to apprehend the everlasting and divine in a direct and undistorted way.

For Plato and Aristotle, the imagination is best thought of as an aid to reason. It assists the human mind in its effort to grasp the mindedness in things, either by enabling us to see the form of a sensible object as the "image" of an invisible original (Plato), or by producing the "phantasms" that supply a needed bridge between the form that gives a thing its "looks" and the mental representation of this form in the mind of the one who is looking at it (Aristotle).[26] In both cases, the role of the imagination is subordinate to that of reason and confined by it. The imagination may be useful and productive, even necessary, but it is not genuinely creative. At most, it makes what is thinkable visible, in the shape of those quasi-visible images that constitute its special stock-in-trade. But the imagination cannot enlarge the boundaries of reason. It enables our thinking but adds nothing new to what can be thought. The Neoplatonic suggestion that the artist is an idealist who imagines more than the forms of visible things reveal opens the way to a conception of the imagination as an innovative rather than merely implementing power, but for Plotinus and his followers the implications of this view were constrained by their pagan equation of matter with mindlessness and of eternity with the simplicity of form.

The doctrine of creation upset this equation and compelled those Christian thinkers who were attracted to the teachings of the Neoplatonists to redefine the ground of being as a willful God rather than a cosmic force that unfolds with strict necessity. It also invited a new conception of the imagination as a faculty that leads instead of follows, on whose inspiration reason depends, and thereby provided the theological justification for a view of art that assigns it a radically more important role than Plotinus' "art metaphysics" allows.

From a Christian perspective, the forms that Plato describes as the source of all reality, and whose basic ontological position the Neoplatonists preserved, can no longer be regarded as the ruling principles of an independent natural order. The only way to conceive them is as ideas in the mind of God. Christian theology requires that Plato's forms be converted into divine representations. Augustine already expresses this new view quite clearly.[27]

But God's representations differ from ours in a crucial respect. Our ideas are abstractions. They structure and arrange material that as Kant says we "receive" from without.[28] By contrast, God's ideas are not abstract at all. He is the author of everything in them; there is nothing in God's ideas that comes to him from some other source; and for every individual in creation, God has a completely self-generated idea that is just as concrete as it is. The distinction between form and matter that characterizes all human cognition thus has no counterpart in God's mind. Kant expresses this thought by saying that God's ideas, unlike ours, are "intellectual intuitions."[29] Each *simultaneously* possesses the transparency of the clearest thought and the intuitive density of an immediate perception. We experience each of these, but only separately. From an epistemological point of view, this is the most striking consequence of our finitude as created beings.

But if we, unlike God, must relate to the world by means of abstractions that can never have the fullness of perception, it is nevertheless possible for us to approach God's intellectual intuitions more closely with the help of the imagination. The imagination not only supplies schemata for our existing ideas and thus makes them more concrete. It also *anticipates* forms of order, harmony and the like that our ideas are not yet able to express, and through their imaginative prevision reaches out beyond the present limits of our intellectual understanding. In this respect, the imagination is an innovative and liberating force that makes it possible for us steadily, if never completely, to loosen the constraints on our understanding that result from the division between intuition and cognition that characterizes all human experience, and gradually to approach the mind of God, whose ideas are defined by the absence of this very division.

In this way, the doctrine of creation provides a foundation for the idea—which no intellectualist metaphysics can wholly explain—that the human imagination is a creative power with the capacity to *expand* our understanding of things and to bring us progressively closer to God. Potentially at least, this enhances the prestige of the artist in a way that neither Plato nor Plotinus could allow. For if the imagination does not merely implement the requirements of an already competent reason, but through its inventions expands the territory of reason itself, then the stature and importance of the artist, whose imagination exceeds his power of articulate thought, is at least equal and perhaps superior to that of the philosopher—a radical inversion of the original Platonic conception of their relative worth.

Despite his professed devotion to Plato, Ficino describes the role of the imagination in terms that suggest an inversion of precisely this sort. Ficino himself appears to have had little direct interest in art. But the function he assigns the imagination in his philosophy generally has the effect of putting the artist in a leading position *vis-à -vis* that of the thinker, or at least of merging them in a novel way.

According to Ficino, it is by means of the imagination that we ascend from our earthly station to the neighborhood of God. We cannot climb the ladder of being by means of reason alone. No matter how high we fly, we depend on the inventions of the imagination to narrow the gap that always remains between our human ideas and God's intellectual intuitions. The creative imagination (as distinct from the strictly facilitative one that Plato and Aristotle recognize) in fact plays the leading role in Ficino's account of the soul's upward journey to God—a view that remains unthinkable, or at least unsupportable, so long as the pagan distinction between form and matter retains its authority. By dissolving this distinction, the doctrine of creation invites a new view of the artist as a guide to the divinity of the world who extends the limits of what we know by means of what he imagines. It thereby prepares the way for the ideas of genius and sublimity that have been central to our conception of the value of art ever since.

This is clearest in the case of genius. The work of a genius cannot be reduced to rules. If it could, others would be able to produce the same things themselves with proper training. A genius sees and expresses things in a distinctive way on account of the creativity of his imagination, which does not follow rules but extends, or rather invents, them instead.

The idea of sublimity also draws support from Ficino's view of the salvific role of the creative imagination.

According to Plato, the greatest form is that of the good. It is the source of the reality of all the rest. For Aristotle, the prime mover is the highest conceivable being—that for the sake of which every other moves as it does. But neither Plato nor Aristotle recognizes the existence of an unbridgeable gap between the greatest being the mind can conceive and the mind that strives to grasp it. Both assume that, with sufficient study, the mind is in principle capable of understanding all that can be understood. By contrast, for those who believe that the world was created from nothing by an omnipotent God, this gap can never be closed, in this life at least. The acknowledgment that this is so, coupled with a reverential wonder for the attunement of mind to world that allows us to progressively narrow the gap despite the impossibility of ever closing it completely, is the essence of the experience of sublimity as distinct from that of beauty, on the classical conception of it.

The creative imagination is the seat of this experience, for it both gives us an inkling of what it would be like to have God's intellectual intuition of the world, and reminds us that we never shall. This is a kind of defeat. But it is not only that. It is also an occasion for recalling the transcendent nature of the God who brought the world into being from nothing, and for expressing our gratitude to him for endowing us with the capacity to comprehend his creation in ever more adequate ways. Thanks to its creative power, the imagination offers us an intimation of a closure we can never attain. Orthodox Christians call this the experience of grace. Its spiritual value remains when the reason-transcending power of the imagination ceases to be seen as the gift of God and comes to be viewed in strictly human terms instead, as the genius that enables a few rare individuals to glimpse realities the rest of us do not yet comprehend, and to convey a sense of the sublimity of the world through works even they cannot explain.

"NEVER SEEN BEFORE NOR THOUGHT OF BY ANY OTHER MAN"

A craftsman abstracts the form from his model and applies it to other material. His imagination allows him to do this. But the imagination a craftsman exercises is wholly subordinate to the power of thought by means of which he grasps the principle or rule that gives both his model and the copy he makes of it their order and intelligibility. By contrast, a genius sees what those who proceed merely by rules cannot. The power that enables him or her to do this is also the imagination. But the imagination of a genius, unlike that of a craftsman, is a source of new ideas. It is innovative and creative. The work of a genius is defined by its originality and possesses value on this account. Originality has no meaning or value in Aristotle's metaphysics of making, which emphasizes imitation instead. In this respect, a genius resembles neither the maker of Aristotle's *Poetics* nor the demiurge of Plato's *Timaeus* but the God of the Christian religion, whose creation sets the standard for the originality of all human endeavors.

It follows that the work of a genius possesses value not despite but because of its personal character. The work of a creative artist is valuable insofar as it manages to convey the peculiar outlook, sensibility and mood of the one who creates it. The idea of genius is therefore connected to that of perspective. A work that succeeds in expressing the genius of its author has value precisely because it manifests a point of view that is distinguishable from every other. The equation of genius with perspective and the assignment of value to both springs from the belief, for which the doctrine of creation first provides a metaphysical warrant, that individuality as such possesses a reality and truth of its own—one that provides the indispensable starting point of every human being's attempt to grasp the infinite reality of the world by means of those imaginative inventions that alone enable us to narrow the gap between intuition and understanding (between perspective and objectivity).

The idea of genius implies something else as well. A genius does not merely see things in an original way. He has the ability to convey to others an appreciation of his unique experience of the world—of the way it looks from his perspective. An artist who cannot do this lacks the talent that sets a genius apart from the rest of us, who all see the world from an individual point of view too.

This is the aspect of genius that is hardest to understand. The reason is obvious. Communication between artist and audience presupposes that they share a common ground. If this ground is truly common, it cannot belong to either alone. In this sense, the forms of expression or representation that make such communication possible are necessarily abstract. But if what a creative artist sees and hopes to communicate belongs to him or her alone, how is he or she able to convey it by means of forms whose abstractness by definition can never fully capture the individuality of what the artist seeks to express?

This question does not arise for Aristotle. On his view, the maker of an artifact and its viewer both abstract the same form from the material in which it is embodied. The form they both see establishes a common ground between them. By contrast, the idea of genius presents this question in an especially pointed way, and the only answer that is possible, so long as one continues to accept the legitimacy of the idea itself, is that a genius uses the common forms of communication to indicate something that lies beyond their range, on both the artist's side and that of his viewer.

A genius employs these forms in such a way as to avoid the implication that they capture or exhaust all he means to convey. Yet at the same time he must use them to establish a common ground of appreciation and enjoyment that is capable of serving as what might be called a "springboard" for the imagination of artist and viewer alike. Without this, a genius has nothing to say or show. Indeed, he cannot be called a genius at all, for an essential part of what we mean by the term is the ability to find those forms that are capable of serving the double purpose of both pleasing on account of their intelligibility and pointing beyond the pleasure they afford to something that, as yet, can only be imagined but not understood. If the pleasure we take in form is what we mean by beauty, and the experience of the inadequacy of this very pleasure to reach the full reality of things is the essence of the sublime, then genius may be defined as the ability to exploit beauty for the sake of sublimity. Any aesthetics that seeks to account for the value of genius must therefore reinterpret the first in light of the second, as Kant in fact does.

All of these ideas are already present in a highly articulate form in the work and writings of Albrecht Dürer. Half a century before Vasari, Dürer succinctly states the principle on which the modern concept of artistic genius is based. The true artist, Dürer says, apprehends things "never seen before nor thought of by any other man."[30] His work is therefore original by definition. This is tied to the uniqueness of his perspective on the world, which a genius is able to make accessible to others, unlike those of lesser talent.

Dürer's concept of the artist as a creator of original works is most famously expressed by his portrait of himself, at the age of twenty-eight, in the guise of Christ the Savior. Joseph Koerner has explored the meaning of this painting in great detail.[31] There are precedents for it, but none as daring. The viewer is meant to think that the painter, like Christ himself, has brought something entirely new into the world. The painting also suggests, even more boldly, that the artist's work possesses a salvific power. A great artist helps his viewers to a deeper understanding of a particular point of view—one that is part of God's creation and therefore essential to an adequate knowledge of it. No general formula can fully capture its meaning. Using his imagination, the artist brings more of its meaning to light and thereby draws the viewer nearer to the all-comprehending mind of God. The result is a "glorification of the artist" that is completely unimaginable within the horizon of pagan thought.[32]

Originality, individuality and perspective acquire a value of their own only with the dissolution of the distinction between form and matter that ancient metaphysics presumes. For Dürer, their value is still tied to the theology that first brought this revolution about. It is characteristic of Dürer's orthodoxy that he regards the artist's genius as a gift from God. Even the most original artist must therefore avoid the sin of regarding himself as the author of his own creative powers. Genius is a temptation to pride against which the artist must be on his guard. If he exults in his originality, the genius needs to humble himself by recalling his dependence on God, and by reflecting on the shortfall between aspiration and ability that he knows better than other, less talented men. Dürer's study *Melancholia* (1514) and his late portrait of himself as the *Man of Sorrows* (1522) are meditations on this aspect of genius, which in exact proportion to the heights it allows him to reach, reminds the artist of the immeasurable distance that always remains between him and God.

Most important, the inventiveness of the artist, as Dürer understands it, continues to be anchored to a world of objective realities whose existence God guarantees. This means that the artist must use his gifts to depict the world as it really is. His paintings and drawings are not mere fantasies. They are not the arbitrary products of the artist's feelings and thoughts but (to borrow Alberti's celebrated image) windows on a world that is there for all to see, with the help of the artist's inventions, which are not substitutes for reality but aids to its appreciation instead. A genius has a unique perspective on the world but he is not the author of it. It would be blasphemous to think otherwise. Piety therefore demands that he employ his creativity in service to the greater genius who created the world and gave it a reality that transcends all perspectival judgments, including his own.

Dürer's theology thus compels him to acknowledge the distinction between the subjectivity of the artist, on the one hand, and the objectivity of the world on the other. Anyone who accepts this distinction will be compelled to ask how reality and genius can be joined. Dürer himself was fascinated with two methods for doing so. One was the art of perspective and the other the theory of proportion. His last and largest work of art theory is devoted to the latter topic.[33]

As exemplified by the work of Vitruvius and others, the classical theory of proportion sought to define the general lineaments of bodies and objects— the structure or shape that gathers their parts into a harmonious order. It disregarded individual anomalies in order to describe the common forms that underlie them. In this sense, it was necessarily idealizing. Dürer appropriates this classical tradition but puts it to a radically nonclassical use. In Dürer's hands, the science of proportion becomes a means of displaying the individuality of things rather than of effacing it. For Dürer, the universality of proportional relations, which can always be expressed in mathematical terms, ultimately converges with the unique shape of each body and may be used by an artist of genius as a guide to representing its distinctive identity. Dürer's conception of proportion is therefore not opposed to individuality, as it was on the classical view, but constructively related to it.

For the ancients, proportion meant beauty. It signified the symmetry of regular forms. Its use helped to create a space of ordered shapes in which individuals could meet and communicate precisely because their individuality was suppressed by the regularity of the shapes in question. For a Christian like Dürer, individuality possesses value as such. An artist strives to communicate his unique experience of some individual object or scene, and to arouse in his viewer an experience of a similar kind. Each corner of this three-cornered relation among artist, object and viewer is defined by its individuality. Yet the very possibility of such a relation presupposes some sort of common ground, and like his ancient predecessors, Dürer uses proportion to measure it out.

Looking at Dürer's drawings, woodcuts and paintings, one's impression is always of something beautifully rendered, whatever the subject happens to be. But unlike the artists of antiquity, Dürer makes things beautiful not for the sake of washing their defects away but in order to help the viewer see the loveliness that resides in each of God's creatures, including those that are ugly in a conventional sense, or have been deformed by the effects of passion. In Dürer's work, beauty thus becomes a means for communicating something that goes beyond beauty, since the individuality of a person or object can only be approximated by the use of proportion (for the same reason that the individuality of an event in a causal chain can never be exhaustively described in mathematical terms).

One might express this relation by saying that, for Dürer, beauty is a vehicle for sublimity. Without beauty, there can be no communication between artist and viewer. Yet what it communicates lies beyond the power of either to reach. Ernst Gombrich makes a similar point when he says that the general forms or "schemata" employed by "post-medieval" artists (by which he means everyone from Cimabue on) help the artist "probe reality" and "wrestle with the particular" by providing a set of endlessly revisable rules (including those of proportion) to guide the artist toward the right expression of the "unique and unrepeatable experience" he "wishes to seize and hold."[34]

In Kant's philosophical analysis of genius, the theology that plays such a prominent role in Dürer's discussion of it has receded into the background. Kant seeks to explain the meaning of genius without any explicit reference to God. In this respect, his account of genius resembles his defense of the authority of the moral law, which likewise stands on its own with no need for divine validation. But just as a highly rationalized version of the Christian conception of God is eventually required to weld all the elements of Kant's moral philosophy into an organized whole, something similar is needed to support his conception of genius as well. Despite appearances, Kant's interpretation of the nature and value of genius remains tied to the theology from which it arises and that is still explicit in Dürer's aesthetics, though the connection between them has now become so refined as to be nearly invisible.

Kant presents his account of genius in the context of a larger inquiry into the grounds of aesthetic judgment. An aesthetic judgment is one that attributes beauty either to a natural object or a work of art. According to Kant, it is wrong to view such judgments either as reports of subjective pleasure or as reactions to an objectively determinable order that is present in the thing to which beauty is ascribed. The first view reduces the experience of beauty to something trivial. The second falsifies what for Kant is one of the defining characteristics of the experience itself. Kant insists that there is more to the beauty of a flower, or the painting of a flower, than we can ever adequately explain. If beauty consisted (as the perfectionist aesthetics of the ancient philosophers assumes it does) in an intelligible order that the mind can grasp and express in speech, there would be nothing in the experience of beauty that exceeds our power of understanding and nothing to prevent us from persuading others of the truth of our aesthetic judgments, except their ignorance or own lack of insight. But Kant insists that this is not the case. He refuses to concede that an aesthetic judgment is just an emphatic way of declaring one's personal preferences, and yet maintains that such judgments can never be validated by a concept or rule or idea—by an abstraction of the sort that on the ancient view of beauty guarantees its objectivity and communicability. The central question of the first part of the *Critique of Judgment* is how, in the case of aesthetic judgments, a measure of objectivity and communicability is nevertheless possible despite the inadequacy of all abstractions to explain and justify them.

Simplifying drastically, Kant's answer is as follows. Despite the fact that aesthetic judgments attribute beauty to something other than the person making them, they should properly be understood as statements about the judging subject himself, though not about his feelings of pleasure in the ordinary sense, which differ from one individual to the next. Certain objects stimulate what Kant calls the "free play" of the imagination. They prompt the imagination to an inventive exploration of possibilities, unconstrained by the rules of the understanding. In such cases, the imagination takes the lead rather than following the understanding, as it does when it serves it, in a subordinate role, by providing the images that are required to visualize its abstractions.[35] Yet though the relation of imagination and understanding is reversed in the presence of those objects that provoke the first to play freely with them, the second is not disconnected from the process, like a gear that has been disengaged from the machine to which it belongs. Indeed, the most striking thing about such experiences, according to Kant, is the harmonious adaptation of these two powers, though here it is the understanding that adapts to the imagination rather than the other way around.

To be sure, the understanding can never "catch up" with the inventive creations of the imagination. It always lags behind. But it is not incompetent to express them, even if only incompletely, in the abstract terms that all thought and communication employ. This is the wonderful thing about an experience of beauty as Kant conceives it. For in every such experience, we encounter the "surplus" reality of the world, which always exceeds our power of comprehension; discover that the imagination, which reaches out beyond thought and speech, is competent to lead us forward in an endlessly richer engagement with the world; and find that the understanding is able to follow the trail the imagination has blazed, up to a point at least, and to put into words some of what, in the experience of beauty, necessarily goes beyond their jurisdiction. The wonder of the experience of beauty, conceived in these terms, is thus something more than a merely subjective pleasure. It is the wonder of the human condition, which all men and women share, and therefore something that, in principle at least, is universally communicable rather than essentially private, like the pleasure, Kant says, one person takes in a wine that another finds distasteful.

This same conception of the relation between the imagination as a creative guide, and the understanding as a patient if pedestrian follower, also underlies Kant's explanation of the possibility of empirical natural science (as distinct from that of experience in general) and his account of the wonder that every scientist is bound to feel when reflecting on the endless expansion of our factual knowledge of the world. It thus provides the hinge that joins the two parts of the *Critique of Judgment*. It also sets the stage for Kant's reflections on the nature of genius.

In the first part of the *Critique,* Kant's principal concern is with the nature of aesthetic appreciation—with the experience of the spectator in the presence of something he judges to be beautiful. His leading examples are all drawn from the realm of nature. Indeed, so far as the appreciation of beauty is concerned, Kant often appears to assign the natural kind a principled priority over the sort possessed by artificial works like poems and paintings.[36] His account of genius is therefore anomalous in two respects, for it is concerned with the creation rather than the appreciation of beauty, and is necessarily limited to the sphere of fine art. Yet the same relationship between imagination and understanding that underlies the spectator's judgment of natural beauty and justifies his claim to its universality validity, also explains the genius' creation of artificial beauty as well.

In creating the work he does, a genius follows no rule, unlike the "academician" who adheres to a strict formula that has been established in advance. The latter resembles Aristotle's craftsman. He has a blueprint in mind before he begins and proceeds to implement it. A genius cannot explain his actions in a similar way. He cannot point to a plan and say, "My aim is to realize the idea this plan sets forth and to the extent the finished work deviates from it, it is a failure." Nor even after the work is complete, can he point to it and say, "The meaning and value of what I have done is explained by the idea I had in mind while I was doing it." Neither before nor after its creation is a work of genius explicable in these terms. There is always more to the work than the genius can say. That is because it is a product of his creative imagination, whose power to invent new forms outstrips that of the understanding to articulate them, so that the latter is forever struggling to comprehend, in its slow-moving vocabulary of thoughts, principles and the like, what the former has "seen" in a flash. In this respect, the experience of the genius is analogous to that of the ordinary observer of beauty, whose judgment that something is beautiful also always signifies an excess of imaginative insight over what can be discursively explained.

But if the genius is inspired by an imaginative intuition that can no more be reduced to a rule than the spectator's judgment of the beauty of a flower or painting, it is not wholly unintelligible and incommunicable on that account. In each case, there is the implied possibility that what the imagination has glimpsed can be progressively, if never fully, translated into the language of thought. This assumes that the creation of beauty rests on the same harmonious adjustment between imagination and understanding as its appreciation does, for unless we assume that such a harmony exists, the work of a genius must be dismissed as the expression of a purely subjective state too.

According to Kant, this falsifies the meaning of genius as much as it does that of aesthetic judgment. The genius is "onto something," though even he cannot explain how. Yet if his inspirations did not have a latent intelligibility, they would be mere whims or fancies whose value for others was arbitrary and accidental. They would be unable to arouse and then sustain in others the harmonious interplay of creative imagination and sober understanding that for Kant constitutes the essence of aesthetic experience.

One important indication of this is Kant's claim that while a genius follows no rule, he must first master the rules of his art, which provide the necessary springboard for his work. A genius gets beyond these rules in the way a mere academician does not. But in doing so, he does not leave the realm of intelligibility altogether and enter one of subjective fantasy instead. It is more accurate to say that a genius shows the way to a new conception of what his art can do by means of an imaginative leap that cannot be deduced from concepts of any kind—a leap for which the existing rules of the art provide a point of departure, and that critics afterward help everyone (even, perhaps, the genius himself) to better understand by translating his achievement into the language of ideas.

But what guarantees the possibility of such a convergence between imagination and understanding in the work of the genius? What underwrites his confidence that he has seen something new in the order of things? What gives the artist grounds to hope, at least, that his imaginative creations are more than a private conceit or the expression of a personal preference that others may or may not share? (One might ask the same question, on the spectator's side, regarding the grounds of his confidence in the universal validity of his judgments of beauty.) For Dürer, God provides this guarantee. It is God who assures that the genius, seeing what no one has seen before, nevertheless grasps a world of objective realities. In Dürer's aesthetics, it is God who provides the link between the artist's unique perspective on the world and the world as it is "in itself." Where in the *Critique of Judgment* does Kant offer an answer to the question of how these can be joined?

The answer is not to be found in his analysis of aesthetic judgment. Here, the question is raised but not answered. To find it, we must turn to Kant's account of teleological judgment, which addresses the seemingly different question of how an empirical science of nature is possible.

There can be no such science, Kant claims, except on the assumption that the imaginative hunches that guide empirical research will eventually be proven or disproven in a way that leads to an ever-deeper understanding of the workings of the natural order, not in the formal sense contemplated by the *Critique of Pure Reason,* but in material detail. This assumption in turn, he argues, makes sense only on the further supposition that the order of nature is a *purposive* one—that it can only be explained as the effect of an idea, which by definition must be the idea of a being that is not itself a part of this order, that is, of an omnipotent God who necessarily transcends the world and everything in it.

In the establishment of the system of nature in general, the understanding plays the leading role. The imagination is a subordinate power whose function is to provide the schemata that make possible the application of the categories of the understanding to the manifold of intuition. In empirical science, the relation is reversed, as it is in aesthetic judgment. Here imagination leads the way and understanding follows. But for the two to work in harmony—or more precisely, for us to be able to assume that they work in harmony—it is necessary to suppose that their harmonization is guaranteed by a God who created us and the world in such a way that our imaginative explorations of it lead to a widening comprehension which, if it could be extended without limit, would in the end coincide with the understanding that God himself has of the world as a whole. This supposition is the counterpart, in the realm of theoretical understanding, of the one that guarantees the intelligibility, in the moral sphere, of our duty to advance what Kant calls the "highest good." Kant makes the parallel between these explicit in the concluding sections of the second part of the *Critique of Judgment*.

The analogue in the case of aesthetic judgment—which is required to explain the possibility of the harmonization of imagination and understanding that underlies Kant's account both of the creation and appreciation of beauty—is the supposition that what the imagination creatively intuits is amenable to understanding because the beauty of the world is as great as its intelligibility: infinitely great in fact, and therefore beyond our power to adequately cognize, yet accessible to us on account of the ability of the imagination to transcend what the understanding can explain, and the adaptability of the latter to the former, so that even for finite rational beings such as we, the boundless beauty of the world can be brought more and more within the range of explanation and communication. That the world and our powers are arranged in this way is a precondition necessary for the possibility both of genius and aesthetic judgment, and because it is not within *our* power to so arrange it, we have no choice but to assign the arrangement in question to an omnipotent creator who stands outside the world altogether.

Of course for Kant, the existence of such a God is merely a supposition. We can have no knowledge of his existence or attributes. This is one of the most basic implications of Kant's transcendental philosophy. But the existence of such a God, and of the grace by which he bestows on us the gift of a connection between the subjectivity of our experience and the objectivity of the world that both the genius who creates art and the person of taste who judges it must assume, is a *necessary* supposition without which the experience of neither would be comprehensible at all. In Kant's account of aesthetic judgment, and of genius more specifically, Dürer's theology, which for him was a metaphysical truth, is thus reduced to the status of a transcendental one, just as it is in Kant's moral philosophy, preserving, if only in an attenuated form, the doctrines of creation and grace that for an orthodox Christian like Dürer remain articles of faith. In this sense, Kant's account of genius is continuous with Dürer's, though it extends the theology through which the idea of genius came into the Western understanding of art to a breaking point beyond which the only alternatives are nihilism, on the one hand, and the born-again paganism of Nietzsche's justification of the world as an aesthetic phenomenon on the other.

For Nietzsche, genius designates a grade of power—a position in the rank order of being. Every being is an artist, striving to impose its perspectival picture of the world on the other beings in it. This is a universal drive; it is the essence of the being of beings. But some are more successful in their artistic campaigns. They achieve a wider and more lasting dominion. Others are compelled, sometimes by brutal and sometimes by subtle means, to assume a place within the framework defined by the ambitions of a superior power. From their perspective, the dominant power to whose interpretation of the world they must bow always appears to be a source of irresistible values that constitute a kind of "fate."

In the broadest sense, this is the meaning of genius in Nietzsche's metaphysical interpretation of art as the being of beings. A genius is merely one to whom others defer as a superior artist—as the author or conservator of the values that constitute the shape of the world as lesser powers find it. Any organized center of power may be said to possess a measure of genius in this sense, whose magnitude depends on its ability to force or seduce others to accept its view of the world. Even if we conventionally reserve the term for individual human beings, like Napoleon, the concept of genius applies equally to forms of domination both above and below this particular level of individuation, to those exercised, for example, by dominant organs and peoples. The brain is a genius too, *vis-à-vis* the intestine, and so are the Romans and the Jews in relation to those they conquered with their arms and ideas.

Several things follow from this way of understanding the meaning of genius. First, genius is always relative. It is merely a way of describing the superiority of one power over another. Second, it is never absolute. Even the greatest genius is a perspectival and therefore finite being, whose interpretive conquest of the world always leaves something out of the picture. There is no power, however great, that cannot be overshadowed by a greater one.[37] Third, genius denotes a position *in* the world, not a state that approximates the intellectual intuition of a God *beyond* it. There is no such God. The world is all there is, and a genius is merely a being who has more of the world "in" it, as Spinoza would say.[38]

This means, of course, that just as no being can ever possess an absolute degree of genius, none ever lacks it altogether, since there will always be powers below as well as above it in the rank order of being. Hence, when we describe a work as one of genius, and single it out on that account, the only way to understand this claim is in *dynamical* terms—as expressing an *increase* in power, or a movement up the ladder of being, which has neither a top nor bottom nor end beyond itself, unlike the "great chain of being" of which Christian writers speak, whose end lies in the world-transcending God that created it from nothing.[39] Understood in this way, genius is identical to truth, for truth means only a dynamical increase in power and not the correspondence of an interpretation of the world to the world as it is in itself.

On this view, the problem of coordinating the imaginative creativity of the genius with the real order of things, which Dürer solved by appealing to God and Kant by appealing to the transcendental necessity of the idea of God, no longer exists. Genius is just another name for the growth in power that occurs when other perspectives are incorporated into one's own. When the attempt to do this fails, no subjective residue of creativity remains behind. And when the attempt succeeds, the genius of the one whose interpretation triumphs over those of others becomes, for them, a fact of life whose objectivity requires no further guarantee. Those who complain that the equation of genius with power, and of both with truth, makes genius and truth alike "merely" relativistic ideas are implicitly still measuring these ideas against a standard that is not "of this world," by comparison with which everything in the world necessarily falls short, as the word "merely" implies. But once all standards of this sort are understood to be mere slogans that various worldly powers use in their struggle for domination, the shortfall disappears and one is left with the phenomenon of rank alone, which defines the direction of increasing power that constitutes the objective meaning of genius itself.

This represents a radical departure from Dürer's conception of genius, with its specifically Christian ideals. In one respect, however, even Nietzsche's born-again pagan metaphysics of art bears a resemblance to Dürer's, for though Nietzsche rejoins time and eternity in a way that no Christian can accept, like Dürer he interprets beauty, not as the ancients did, as an adequate expression of what is enduringly real, but as the only means a finite being possesses for representing a reality that transcends all possible forms.

For Dürer (and Kant), this transcendent reality is the creator God of the Christian religion. He alone is sublime and beauty is our best, indeed only, way to depict him. Nietzsche preserves the Christian distinction between beauty and sublimity but reconceives it in wholly non-Christian terms as the distinction between Apollo and Dionysius. The endless competition for power in which all finite beings are engaged is, for Nietzsche, a struggle among incompatible interpretations of reality. Each of these is a "picture" of the world drawn, as all pictures are, with the Apollonian techniques of delineation and demarcation whose aim is to impose upon the world a form of one kind or another. These forms beautify the world. Every picture that employs them is a work of art. But no form, and therefore nothing beautiful, can ever capture or contain the whole of the reality of what, as Nietzsche puts it in *The Birth of Tragedy,* every finite being is a mere manifestation. The excess of the world's reality over the beauty of any portrait of it is what Nietzsche means by the infinitude of the Dionysian world process and later defines, in more metaphysical terms, as the eternity that is present in the least lasting of things. This is Nietzsche's reconception of the sublime—the infinite and eternal being of the God of the Christian religion restored to the world itself, whose divinity exceeds the beautifying frame of even the greatest picture of it. On this view, genius is the power to approach the sublimity of the world more closely by means of art.

To this conception of genius another may be opposed. Though not Christian in the orthodox sense, it nevertheless represents an extension of Christian belief, for while those who hold it assume that there is no God beyond the world, they also insist that we could place an objective value on what happens in the world only in case such a God existed. This is what Nietzsche calls nihilism, and describes as the last stage of Christian theology on account of its continuing adherence, if only in a negative form, to the religion's most fundamental principle of valuation.

One of the implications of this nihilistic metaphysics is that there is no way of distinguishing among the many works of art that are praised as achievements of genius. For Dürer and Kant, God is the ultimate arbiter of all such claims. For Nietzsche, the question is settled by the rank order of power. For the nihilist, neither of these solutions is available. The only position he can coherently defend is that there is no objective measure for determining who is a genius, and that every artist has an equal right to be considered one if he or she expresses an original view of some sort, regardless of how shallow and fleeting it happens to be. On this conception of genius, all that matters is that the artist has *valued* the world, even if the valuation has no intrinsic *value*.

Indeed, for the nihilist the question of intrinsic value disappears completely. There is nothing to be said about it, just as there is nothing to be said about the relative worth of the commitments that different people make to live one way or another, on the value-free conception of personal choice that Max Weber defends in his nihilistic speculations regarding the source of moral and political authority in the modern age. The view that artistic genius consists in the expression of a value judgment, whatever it happens to be, is the aesthetic equivalent of Weber's decisionist ethics. Between this nihilistic conception of genius, on the one hand, and Nietzsche's born-again paganism on the other, there is an immense metaphysical gap, for whereas Nietzsche identifies eternity with the world, the nihilist claims that it can be found neither here nor anywhere else. In the realm of literature, it is Nietzsche's view that has prevailed. But in the plastic arts, and in the field of painting in particular, the reigning metaphysics has a more nihilistic cast.

The modern art museum has become a "temple to genius."[40] Visitors come to worship the genius of the artists whose works hang on its walls. Yet what makes a work one of genius is something that few are able to say, beyond observing, perhaps, that it expresses the artist's values, which often seems enough to settle the matter.

Many works of contemporary art produce a strong visual and emotional response. Their colors and shapes command the viewer's attention, whether or not these have any representational meaning. Some viewers may be tempted to explain the power of these works in Nietzschean terms. But others are likely to fall back on the all-too-Christian explanation that the works in question are great because they express in an honest way the freedom of the artist to affirm whatever values he or she chooses—because they are "authentic." Yet even the most thoughtful defenders of this view, like Meyer Schapiro, are compelled to concede that in the end it is no explanation at all, since the freedom to which it appeals is shared by lesser artists as well, and therefore cannot by itself account for the greatness of certain works as compared to others.[41] Some theorists rush into the vacuum and attempt to explain the greatness of a work on the grounds that those who control the decisions of museums and galleries have decided in its favor.[42] There is truth in this view, but it is a weak echo of Nietzsche's metaphysics of power, without which it degenerates into a conventionalism of the most pedestrian sort, as a backstop to the nihilism whose deficiencies it is meant to repair. I shall return to these themes in the concluding section of the chapter.

Classical aesthetics has no more room for the idea of sublimity than it does for that of genius. Its master principle is the concept of beauty. For Plato and Aristotle, to be is to possess a particular form, which consists in an ordering of elements or parts. This ordering is a kind of harmony, and harmony is beauty. A being that exhibits the form appropriate to it in an especially perspicuous way is perfect. In the aesthetics of the classical philosophers, beauty, being, goodness and perfection are all ultimately one and the same.

The Christian doctrine of creation overturns the metaphysics on which this aesthetics depends. For those who believe that God created the world from nothing, the being of beings can no longer be equated with their possession of a form that is visible to the mind and reproducible by a craftsman who abstracts it from the mindless matter in which it is embodied. Every form delimits. It draws a boundary that rules some things in and others out. But each of God's creatures has more reality than any delimitation can contain. Its existence depends wholly on that of its creator, but its intelligibility and value exceed what the forms we use to represent it are able to express. This is not a contingent fact. It is a necessary consequence of the gap between God's infinite power and our finite ability to comprehend and portray even the least of his creatures.

Yet despite this gap, we possess an intimation of what lies beyond the capacity of the forms of human representation, and are not wholly unequipped to grope our way toward it with the use of these forms themselves. This is the condition of human art as well as science.

Both artists and scientists strive to discover and express the reality of things, but so long as they accept the metaphysical premises of the Christian religion (which they need not be Christians to do) their experience is bound to be one of simultaneous exultation and defeat. The artist who accepts these premises appreciates that there is always more to the world than he can see or say, and the intimation that this is so is for him the source of a special kind of joy from which his pagan predecessor was excluded. It is also the source of a peculiar form of disappointment. Neither the joy nor the disappointment he experiences is conceivable within the framework of the classical aesthetics of beauty. To express the meaning and value of this experience, a concept other than that of beauty is required. Since the eighteenth century, the idea of the sublime has played this role.

Burke and later Kant contrast sublimity and beauty in a pointed way. Kant, in particular, gives the idea of the sublime a rigorous philosophical definition. Of course, there were others before Burke who sought to define it too, generally in psychological terms. Shaftesbury made an especially important contribution in this regard.[43] He and other early modern writers on the subject refer back even further to a treatise on the sublime that is sometimes attributed to the third-century rhetorician Longinus.[44] But Longinus' text belongs to an intellectual milieu dominated by pagan categories of thought, in particular by the equation of sublimity (*hupsos*) with greatness of soul and the correspondingly high-minded style of writing that is appropriate to its expression. Though routinely cited as the *locus classicus* for later discussions of it, Longinus' account of the sublime is in truth remote from the world of Christian belief that formed the background for the attempts of various eighteenth-century writers to define the concept with precision, culminating in Kant's *Critique of Judgment*.

Kant's conception of sublimity might seem to be the opposite of his idea of genius rather than its correlate. The genius is one whose imagination outstrips his capacity for explanation (and ours as well). His images delight and inspire us in ways that no rule can capture or enable others to reproduce. The crucial distinction here is between the power of the creative imagination, on the one hand, and the understanding on the other—the faculty of rules, as Kant describes it. By contrast, the experience of sublimity (which Kant divides into two sorts, the "mathematical" and "dynamical") is defined by the discovery of the incapacity of the imagination to represent an idea that we are able to think by means of the faculty of reason. Here, the contrast is between imagination and reason, not understanding, and the shortfall is on the side of the imagination. But though reason and understanding are for Kant powers of very different sorts, the phenomena of genius and sublimity, as he describes them, share two crucial characteristics in common.

First, each manifests our appreciation of a reality that we cannot see and think at the same time—in the case of genius, by enabling us to see what cannot be thought, and in the case of the sublime, to think what cannot be seen. In this sense, both genius and sublimity give us a hint of God's intellectual intuition of the world.

Second, both are reminders of the disappointment that a finite being is bound to experience in striving to understand the infinite reality its imagination allows it to glimpse in advance or, alternatively, to imagine the infinite reality its reason permits it to think as the idea of what Kant calls the "unconditioned."[45] Hence, whether one emphasizes the transcendence of the imagination and the inadequacy of the understanding relative to it, or the transcendence of reason and the inadequacy of the imagination to represent its ideas, the result is a combination of joy and disappointment. This constitutes the essence of sublimity, as distinct from that of beauty as the ancients understood it (which is not, of course, how Kant does, since his own account of beauty depends on a similar combination of affects or attitudes and to that extent may be said to derive from his understanding of the sublime, despite the seemingly secondary place the latter occupies in his analysis of aesthetic judgment).

Kant illustrates the idea of sublimity with examples drawn exclusively from the realm of nature (towering mountains, stormy seas and the like) as opposed to that of art. But for centuries before he sought to give the idea a precise philosophical formulation, the values associated with it had shaped the efforts of Western artists to express the ineffable reality of a world that had become infinitely deep, thanks to the Christian theology of creation.

Many of the works of High Renaissance art whose self-containment and composure appear to exemplify a classical ideal of beauty already anticipate the aesthetics of sublimity that becomes more explicit in the Mannerist and Baroque periods that followed. This is particularly true of portrait painting, where beginning at an early date the artists of the Renaissance reversed the approach of their ancient predecessors, and instead of using individual traits to depict general ones like courage and magnanimity, employed the conventions of status and role to suggest their subjects' unique personalities. This can never be fully captured by any representation and therefore remains ineffable even, or rather especially, in the greatest of portraits. The most famous example is Leonardo's *Mona Lisa*—a painting of great beauty, but one whose lasting appeal as a work of art can only be explained by its intimation of what lies beyond the artist's ability to depict it, at the point where every finite perspective on the subject vanishes in the unfathomable mystery of a personality that even the greatest artist in the world can make only partly visible to us. It is not the beauty of Leonardo's painting that explains its aesthetic value but the sublimity its beauty reveals.

In the century between Leonardo's completion of the *Mona Lisa* and the death of Caravaggio, the aesthetics of sublimity came to dominate every branch of southern Renaissance art. Heinrich Wolfflin famously describes this development as the movement from a "linear" to a "painterly" style.[46] Since its beginnings in the late eighteenth century, the field of art history has been centrally preoccupied with the study of the various phenomena that can be gathered under the rubric of "style," and no theoretical scheme has had a greater influence on the subject than Wolfflin's.[47]

Wolfflin himself understood his distinction in explicitly philosophical terms, modeled on those that Nietzsche employs to distinguish between what he calls the Apollonian and Dionysian conceptions of art. The influence of Nietzsche is evident on every page of Wolfflin's art historical writings. Nietzsche's own distinction, moreover, is a reformulation of Kant's earlier one between beauty and sublimity, detached from the theology that first inspired it and joined to a radically different metaphysics instead. But because Wolfflin adopts Nietzsche's distinction without the anti-Christian metaphysics that supports it, the concepts of the linear and painterly, as he employs them, have an ahistorical character that obscures the connection between Christian theology, on the one hand, and the aesthetics of sublimity that in the course of the sixteenth century transformed the look of Italian art, on the other.[48]

Nowhere is this connection clearer than in the work of Caravaggio. Like his predecessors, Caravaggio devoted his greatest efforts to religious subjects. In *The Calling of St. Matthew*, *The Beheading of John the Baptist*, and *The Supper at Emmaus* (which he painted twice), Caravaggio depicts homely scenes of ordinary places that are nonetheless alive with a sacred meaning that transcends everything the visible world contains. One can look at these paintings forever and still be moved by their beauty. And yet the most striking thing about them is not their beauty. Each points beyond its margins, in the way all "painterly" art does, and derives its power, as Wolfflin says, from its own manifest incompetence to represent what is in essence unrepresentable.

This is the aesthetics of sublimity. It is the only aesthetics appropriate to a Christian artist who, in contrast to his pagan counterpart, is required to assume that the individuality of every one of God's creatures possesses a reality that transcends our finite powers of understanding. The doctrine of the Incarnation is the first and most powerful expression of this idea. Caravaggio's religious paintings extend the metaphysics of the Incarnation to the world at large. They depict scenes of a prosaic sort in such a way that we are able to glimpse in them a measure of the same unmeasurable holiness that to begin with belongs to Christ alone. In this way they provide a bridge of sorts between the devotional works of earlier Christian painters like Fra Angelico and the later disenchantment of the aesthetics of sublimity in the genre paintings of northern artists like De Hooch, Ter Borch and Vermeer.

The painters of the north were not the only ones to draw their subjects from ordinary life. In Italy, the Carracci brothers and others painted pictures of common people engaged in the simple business of eating, working and playing. But southern painting continued to be dominated by religious and classical motifs remote from the scenes of everyday human existence that beginning with Brueghel in the sixteenth century became a staple of Dutch painting in the seventeenth. The courtyards and parlor interiors; the urban streetscapes; the tavern scenes and rustic celebrations—all the most characteristic Dutch paintings of the period—how distant these seem from the grandiose works of the Italian Baroque! Some, of course, are caricatures. They are meant to mock and demean. Others have a moralizing tone. They teach lessons of virtue and vice. But the greatest Dutch paintings of the seventeenth century neither poke fun nor preach. They portray the furniture of the world (literally, in many cases) in such a way that its familiarity is both preserved and endowed with a new reality that makes it unaccountably strange.[49]

A painting of Vermeer's in the Frick Collection in New York may serve as an example. It is conventionally titled *Officer and Laughing Girl*. A young woman sits at a table talking to a man in an officer's uniform. We assume that he is young too, though his face is mostly hidden from view. They seem engaged in some trivial banter. A window between them is open, and light falls through it onto the wall behind the smiling woman. The light at first seems just the light on a parlor wall. But it is more than that. It is the enlightenment that befalls those who now for the first time see the aura that surrounds this banal and fleeting scene, so simple and so quick to disappear yet invested with a splendor that no viewer can possibly fathom. There is a map on the wall behind the young woman. It is only a decoration, a simple household furnishing. But it points to a larger world, beyond the picture's frame—beyond the frame of any picture the artist could paint. It reminds the viewer that there are immense spaces beyond this one—that the room in which the woman and her gentleman friend sit is but the smallest corner of the world "at large." And yet the viewer could spend every day of his life exploring the world the map depicts and never find a greater surplus of reality than the one in this small room, or anything more lasting than the fleeting smile on the face of the woman who looks out at us from the painting. Here is one of those moments of lost time of which Proust's Narrator speaks, whose meaning, he claims, art alone has the power to save—with words, as the Narrator aspires to do, or with canvas and colors, like his favorite painter Vermeer.[50]

In Vermeer's painting of the young woman and her visitor (her suitor perhaps), sublimity has been brought down to earth. The ordinary objects of domestic life and the gestures of the human beings who live among them now glow with a reality that the limits we conventionally assign them can no longer contain. There is more to the world than we had ever noticed before—more even than Vermeer can capture with his luminous forms. But the measureless reality of the light that falls through Vermeer's window is not that of a God beyond the world. It is not like the light that falls on the alleyway in Caravaggio's painting of the beheading of John the Baptist. *That* light comes from a place beyond all worldly times and places, and the sublimity it bestows on what happens here on earth is a consequence of the fact that God is always watching and judging from afar. Its chiaroscuro underlines the division between light and dark, good and evil, saintliness and sin that constitutes the heart of the Christian drama of redemption. But in Vermeer's painting, the diffuse light that bathes everything with equal transparency is that of the world itself and though it too makes common things sublime, the infinite significance they acquire as a result is one they possess on their own. It is not the gift of a God apart from the world but the aura that surrounds the meanest of things once we learn to see how much more there is to them than even the greatest mind can conceive. It is the glow of a world that is infinitely real—one that comes from within. It is not reflected from another source on whose otherworldly power it depends. The belief that the world can only be lit by a creator God who declares that there shall be light is the source of the aesthetics of sublimity from which Vermeer's transfiguration of ordinary things derives, but in Vermeer's painting, the God who first made the world sublime rather than merely beautiful is not simply offstage, as he is in Caravaggio's. He has vanished altogether and bequeathed his divinity to the world itself, which is now flooded with the light of its own infinite being. This is the light that streams through Vermeer's window. It is the painterly equivalent of the philosophical conception of the world as both infinitely and inherently real—*deus sive natura,* in the sense given this phrase by Spinoza, who was born a month after Vermeer and lived only two years longer.

Some call Vermeer's style and that of the other Dutch painters of the period "realistic" to denote the mundane nature of the scenes they depict and the accuracy with which they portray them. But the term is too broad to capture the novelty of Vermeer's art. The painters of the Italian Renaissance were realists too, in the sense that they took mimetic fidelity to be an unquestioned norm. Alberti speaks for all his contemporaries when he declares that a painter must study nature closely in order to be able to render it truly. And even though their paintings often had an explicitly religious content—and where they did not, drew on classical or mythological sources—the artists of the south sought to portray their subjects in a realistic fashion. The frescoes in the Brancacci Chapel contain a wonderful tableau of the street life of early fifteenth-century Florence and the tavern scene that Caravaggio depicts in both versions of *The Supper at Emmaus* could hardly be more down-to-earth.

But both of these works were shaped by Christian beliefs. Their realism had a specific theological setting. What is really new in Vermeer is the absence of the theology that conditioned the work of his Italian predecessors. This must not, however, be confused with the absence of any theology whatsoever. Vermeer's paintings possess a spiritual value that cannot be explained except on the assumption that they are more than accurate representations, more even than beautiful ones—that they command our attention because they confer on the passing moments of everyday life a reality and permanence the viewer can glimpse but never exhaust. It is impossible to regard Vermeer's painting of the smiling woman and her well-dressed admirer as devoid of spiritual value—as a mere illusionistic trick—and equally impossible to account for its spirit except by reference to something larger and more lasting than any human image can contain. Here, as with Caravaggio's paintings, we are in the presence of the sublime, and to explain the experience of sublimity, a theology of some sort is needed. But in Vermeer's case, the required theology is no longer that of the Christian religion, which opposes God to the world and eternity to time. It is the theology of Spinoza and Nietzsche, and of Proust's Narrator as well, who all put time and eternity together again but with the caveat that no finite being can ever represent their unity in an adequate way.

Vermeer's born-again pagan aesthetics has been a source of inspiration for painters ever since, though there have been many reactions against it, in both a classical and Christian direction.

Some, like Poussin and his academic followers, have sought to restore the authority of an art of beauty and form. But even in Poussin's great landscape paintings, where his classical affinities are most apparent, the mysteriousness of the motif and the drama of the sky combine to give the scene a sublimity that is wholly incompatible with an aesthetics of limit and balance. And In-gres' riveting *Portrait of Monsieur Bertin*—the supreme example of an art that the painter himself defined in classical terms—is remote from the ancient equation of beauty with form, for what holds the viewer's attention is not the order and harmony of the painting but its intimation of an inexpressibly unique personality whose representation has been the aim of modern portrai-ture from the Italian Renaissance on.

Others, like certain of the Pre-Raphaelites, have reacted against what they perceived to be the spiritual emptiness of a disenchanted world by attempt-ing to breathe life back into the tired images of Christian belief. Rosetti's *The Girlhood of Mary Virgin* (1848) and Millais' *Christ in the House of His Parents* (1849–50) are early examples. Yet though both paintings are filled with reli-gious symbols of a familiar kind, the most striking thing about them is the homeliness of their settings—so much so that in the latter case, Millais was accused of having debased the holiness of the savior by depicting him in such crude and plebian circumstances. Millais' painting "domesticates" its subject. It blurs the line between the God-child and the ordinary objects that surround him in his father's workshop, so that these come to be endowed with a kind of sublimity too. Even in a work as self-consciously Christian as this one, it is impossible to miss the influence of Vermeer's idea of the sublimity of common things and of the decidedly unchristian metaphysics from which it derives.

But these classicizing and Christianizing movements run against the main current of Western painting in the three and a half centuries since Vermeer taught us to see things in the measureless light of the world, and if his Spi-nozistic aesthetics of sublimity can be detected even here, its influence else-where is more obvious.

It is difficult to imagine, for example, a more concise statement of Ver-meer's aesthetics than Constable's famous description of his art as an at-tempt to give "one brief moment caught from fleeting time a lasting and sober existence,"[51] or a more poignant illustration of it than his paintings of clouds. These are the pictorial equivalent of Wordsworth's poetic celebration of the divinity of "Nature," which is not borrowed from a God beyond the world but contained within it. Constable's German contemporary David Caspar Friedrich painted landscapes whose sublimity is still more explicit, yet like that of Constable's gentler scenes, is produced by an experience of the world's inexhaustible beauty or power, which both attracts and overwhelms us. The Romantic landscape painters of the late eighteenth and nineteenth centuries sought to depict the sublimity of the world on a colossal scale. But even their most extravagant works—the seascapes of Turner, for example, and New World vistas of Bierstadt—are shaped by the same aesthetic sensibility that already informs Vermeer's luminous interiors whose humble contents overflow with a reality as boundless as the sea and sky themselves.

Looking forward, Turner's swirling compositions anticipate the paintings of the Impressionists at the end of the nineteenth century.[52] It is easy to see their stylistic affinity, but the connection between them is much deeper than this, for like their Romantic predecessors the Impressionists were committed to the ideal of worldly sublimity that Vermeer quite literally brings to light and Constable defines with poetic precision.

It is sometimes said that the Impressionists caused a revolution in painting by giving it a more subjective direction. Rather than seeking to reproduce objective realities by means of a mimetic art whose aim is to convert three-dimensional spaces to the two of the canvas with as much fidelity as possible, they sought to convey a sense of their own subjective experience of these realities instead. This is certainly true, but the Impressionists' "revolution" in painting is best understood not as a departure from the aesthetic ideals of the Romantics, or even of the genre painters of the Dutch Golden Age, but as an intensification of them.

Without abandoning Constable's formulation, the Impressionists put greater stress on each of its two components. They took even more seriously the "fleeting" character of every moment and sought with still greater determination to confer a "lasting" existence on the least permanent of things, like the shadows on the façade of a cathedral, which begin to disappear the moment they become visible at all. The Impressionists painted in order to save the eternity in time. Their works convey a heightened sense both of the transience and permanence of the ordinary moments they record, which like the Narrator's taste of his aunt's madeleine, are at once unique in all the world, because they belong to the career of a perspectival (subjective) being, *and* have their place in the eternal fabric of the world whose deathless (objective) reality is composed of countless such perspectives, each of which captures its timeless presence from a finite point of view and therefore, of necessity, in what Spinoza calls a "mutilated" fashion.[53] The Impressionists were Proust's contemporaries and their paintings show us what the Narrator's theory of art looks like when it is translated from the realm of signs to that of images.

The Impressionists set the stage, and the agenda, for painting in the first half of the twentieth century. First Cezanne and then the analytic Cubists decomposed familiar objects—a bowl of fruit, a violin—in order to baffle our conventional experience of them, render the familiar world strange and, by multiplying perspectives, remind the viewer of the superabundant reality of even the commonest things, which transcends any finite set of postures the painter or anyone else might adopt. The Surrealists, who had a large influence on those who later came to think of painting not in representational terms but as the "expression" of an act, pursued a similar goal. The plentitude of experience is concealed, they insisted, by the superficial forms of conscious life whose limited reality must be penetrated in order to reach the wider Dionysian realm of being that lies beneath their Apollonian shapes. And even those artists like Marcel Duchamp, who deliberately mocked all historical standards of beauty by presenting the unlovely objects of ordinary life as works of art, did not so much reject the aesthetics of sublimity that inspired the beautiful paintings of the Impressionists, as extend it in an ever more self-conscious and at times quite frantic search for a mode of representation that does justice to the belief that the task of art is to depict the essential meaning of our experience of the sublime, which in an age of disenchantment lies in the thrilling if humbling encounter with a world whose boundless reality is present in a urinal too. Perhaps even Andy Warhol's *Brillo Box* may be considered a contribution to this restless campaign. It would in any case be hard to find a simpler expression of the aesthetics of sublimity that has driven modern art from Vermeer on, than the question Warhol's fellow pop artist Roy Lichtenstein once put to the philosopher Arthur Danto: "Isn't this a wonderful world?"[54]

The modern aesthetics of sublimity grew on the soil of Christian belief. It reflects—as the cognate idea of genius does too—the metaphysical shift that occurred when individuality came to be viewed not as a barrier to reality but an intensification of it instead. With the great Dutch painters of the seventeenth century, sublimity shed its Christian clothing. It became a worldly ideal, and in this form has had an effect on painting ever since—from Constable's clouds to Warhol's *Brillo Box,* as jarring as their juxtaposition may seem.

Yet this ideal is not merely the rejection of the otherworldly metaphysics of the Christian religion. It is the affirmation of a different metaphysics as well. This other metaphysics starts with an idea of divinity too. It equates the world, as Aristotle did, with the everlasting and divine, but extends its divinity to the most ephemeral of things. The modern aesthetics of sublimity, which rejects the sufficiency of beauty *and* the dependence of the sublime on a God beyond the world, rests on the born-again pagan theology of Spinoza and Nietzsche. Only this has the power to explain why modern art has spiritual value.

The same is true of the novel. The novel is the quintessentially modern form of literature and its aspiration to reach matters of ultimate importance is defensible only on the basis of the theology that Proust's Narrator expounds after stumbling over the paving stones in Mme de Guermantes' courtyard. But in the plastic arts, and in painting in particular, this theology is less secure. It competes with the antitheology of nihilism, which today perhaps even has the upper hand. This antitheology is the decayed remnant of Christian belief. It represents the lingering influence of the very theology it purports to reject, which thereby casts a continuing shadow over the words and works of even its most stridently secular supporters. What are the assumptions on which this nihilistic view of the value of art is based, and why is it so widely accepted today?

CONTEMPORARY ART

Hans Belting asks whether the history of art is over. He is not the only one to do so.[55]

Even in its most experimental phases, Belting claims, the art of the prewar period remained connected to the traditions and ideals of the past, if in a generally negative way. Many of the greatest prewar painters were critics of the view that the value of a painting lies in its faithful depiction of realities that exist independently of the painting itself. But their obsession with the limitations of the past itself constituted a connection to it, a chapter in the history of art, which has undergone many periods of critical revision, yet can still be told, as it often is, in a continuous narrative from Cimabue and Duccio to Picasso, Mondrian and Magritte.

In this respect, Belting contends, the second wave of modernism, which began after the Second World War, differs fundamentally from the first. We call this period "contemporary" because we are still in it.

Contemporary art is characterized by a profusion of different styles and techniques, ranging from the abstract panels of the Rothko Chapel to Chuck Close's hyperrealist portraits, in which pop art, appropriation art, video installations and performance art all have an accepted place. Those who appreciate contemporary art welcome this diversity as an expression of artistic freedom. They say that the definition of art has at last been freed from the dead hand of the past. Today, there are no longer any limits on what can count as a work of art. All the old conventions, the traditional expectations, the so-called standards of taste, have given way to an unprecedented spirit of invention unconfined by any recognized boundaries.

When Marcel Duchamp displayed a urinal in Alfred Stieglitz's studio in 1917, as (or as if it were) a work of art, the meaning of art as a distinct category of object and experience became radically unstable. But it was only in the postwar years that the question "What is art?" came to seem the only really important one that any work of art addresses, and therefore the defining mark of art itself, which is distinguished from everything that is not art by its self-conscious attention to this question. Those who feel at home in the chaotic diversity of contemporary art regard the triumph of Duchamp's question as a liberation from all earlier aesthetic ideals, which however different from one another each assumed an answer to the question and in this sense begged it. Contemporary art has left these ideals behind, and with them, the whole long history of art that is tied to and limited by them. In the view of its most ardent defenders, this is what gives the art of the postwar period its unique power and greatness, though not every philosopher and critic agrees, since from a less sympathetic point of view the abandonment of every definition of art may be said to empty the very concept of meaning and to render all discussion of the purpose of art pointless as well.

In the spirit of contemporary art, many of its defenders have simply given up the attempt to define its ruling principle, or describe it in wholly vacuous terms, as Arthur Danto does when he declares that "works of art are *embodied meanings*" (which countless other things are too).[56] In this respect, Meyer Schapiro's sympathetic account of postwar art is uniquely compelling and worth considering in some detail.

Schapiro was one of the greatest art historians of the twentieth century. He was deeply knowledgeable about every period of Western art. He wrote classical essays on everything from Romanesque architecture to the paintings of Cezanne. Given his profound devotion to the past, one might have expected him to view the chaos of contemporary art with a conservative eye and to regard the claims made on its behalf with skepticism or even disdain. But in fact Schapiro offers a strong endorsement of contemporary art that is distinguished by its philosophical clarity and by Schapiro's ability to connect the course of modern art as a whole to the effects of the rationalization process that he, like Weber, associates with modernity in general. Only Clement Greenberg's famous defense of modernism possesses a comparable degree of intellectual coherence and Schapiro's is by far the richer and more far-reaching of the two.[57] But what makes it of special interest is the directness with which Schapiro endorses the nihilistic metaphysics that many, less philosophically astute admirers of contemporary art implicitly assume.

According to Schapiro, the Impressionist painters of the late nineteenth century had two related goals. One was to depict the world in an accurate fashion. The other was to convey their subjective impressions of it to the viewer. For the Impressionists, these two goals were related in a deep rather than adventitious way because, in their view, the world itself exists for us only as something that is felt or experienced. The moods we feel when we view a scene and the associations it stirs in us are not something we add to a world that is already complete. They are an essential part of what the world really is. A painter who fails to express them produces a picture that is less objective than one who succeeds in capturing the feelings of delight, surprise, loneliness and the like that belong to the scene with as much reality as the objects, faces and gestures that arouse them.

The Impressionists were encouraged by various contemporary philosophers who emphasized the foundational role that our emotions and attitudes play in the constitution of anything that can be called a "world" at all.[58] But though they asserted their beliefs with a programmatic zeal that at times gave their work a revolutionary appearance, the Impressionists' basic conception of the function and value of painting was no different than that of early nineteenth-century Romantics like Turner and Constable. Indeed, one might say that the Impressionists' conviction that emotion and feeling are an integral part of the world goes back to the very origins of modern painting, for the Trecento masters whose sacred images had no meaning apart from the piety they sought to express with them, proceeded on a similar premise. In this respect, whatever novelty they claimed for their approach, the Impressionists remained committed to two ideas that, through countless permutations, have shaped the direction of Western painting from the Renaissance on: first, that a painter must strive to represent the world as it really is; and second, that his own subjective state belongs to the world and cannot be excluded from it without sacrificing the very objectivity he hopes to achieve in his work.

As Schapiro tells the story, the real break came after the Impressionists, when painters abandoned the mimetic goal of representing the world with objective fidelity, and repudiated the connection between objectivity and subjective response that every painter from Cimabue to Monet had taken for granted. Instead, they insisted, all a painter can do is act out or express the inner state that moves him to paint. On this view, it makes no sense to praise or criticize a work on the grounds that it succeeds or fails as an accurate depiction of the world or of the artist's subjective experience of it. Objectivity ceases to be a meaningful measure of evaluation in either respect. The only standard that remains is that of authenticity. Has the artist authentically expressed him- or herself in the work, or dissembled by pretending to enact a state of mind other than the one he or she genuinely feels? Only the honesty of an expression gives it value. Everything else is kitsch.[59] In this way the distinction between beauty and ugliness loses its meaning and is replaced by that between sincerity, on the one hand, and sentimentality, propaganda and advertising, on the other, as the basis for determining what counts as art, and for valuing those works that do.

Whatever role philosophical ideas may have played in this epochal shift, Schapiro assigns the principal responsibility for it to social factors instead. We live in a world, he says, that increasingly resembles a machine. Our actions are governed by countless laws and procedures that demand conformity and punish those who refuse to submit. Though he doesn't use the expression himself, Schapiro's description of the modern world resembles Weber's characterization of it as an "iron cage."[60] In our caged existence, the genuine expression of "spontaneity" becomes ever rarer and more valuable as a result. Indeed, the rationalization of all aspects of social life makes the expression of spontaneity the supremely meaningful manifestation of the worth of human beings amidst the machines that now rule their lives. According to Schapiro, it is the special task of works of art—"the last, hand-made objects within our [mechanical] culture"—to express the value of the individual's capacity for spontaneous invention, which in other areas of life has been suppressed by the demands of our minutely regulated existence. It is therefore above all in the sphere of art that we today look for the affirmation of the value of what Schapiro variously calls "spontaneity," "liberty" or "freedom"—for the expression of "creativeness, sincerity and self-reliance" in what Walter Benjamin terms the "age of mechanical reproduction."[61]

There are different ways of doing this, but they all emphasize the expressive, as opposed to representative, function of art. Jackson Pollack's drip paintings, for example, are "a trace or track of the artist in producing the work," a memento of the creative frenzy that inspired it, from which the value of the finished work is said to derive. Andy Warhol's *Brillo Box* faithfully imitates a commercial object but its artistic value has nothing to do with its mimetic fidelity. *Brillo Box* is a work of art because—and only because—it manifests a freedom of judgment (both admiring and derisive at once) which the consumers who merely buy and use Brillo boxes never experience. Even Rothko's color panels, whose absence of representational content distinguish them so strikingly from Warhol's pop art, likewise derive their value from the spontaneity of the mental processes they set in motion—from what, to borrow from Kant, one might call the free play of imagination and understanding, which abstract forms are especially well suited to enliven.[62] Schapiro calls this "the humanity of abstract painting."[63]

In his view, what unites this diversity of styles is their shared devotion to a metaphysics of freedom.

From Plato on, Western art has been shaped by a mimetic ideal. But the art of the postwar period turns this ideal upside down. It regards the attempt to depict the true nature of things as antihumanistic on account of its devaluation of the spontaneity of freedom, whose assertion becomes more important in proportion to its suppression in a world of rigid routines. Some artists employ mimetic techniques to express their freedom. Others reject these techniques for the very same reason. But this difference of approach is unimportant. What really matters is the common goal of demonstrating the freedom that every "form-creating activity" involves.[64] This is the unifying spirit of contemporary art. The only sin against it is that of dishonesty, for the artist who merely pretends to express himself, but in reality copies another, or takes his cue from the needs and interests of his audience, not only fails to act freely, but what is worse, creates the appearance of doing so in a way that makes a mockery of freedom itself.

The artistic culture that has arisen on the basis of this anti-Platonic aesthetics of freedom has several striking characteristics. Schapiro notes three in particular.

The first is a constant search for new ways to express the spontaneity that on this view is the ultimate source of all aesthetic value. As soon as a particular style gains recognition and approval, it ceases to be a vehicle for the expression of artistic freedom and becomes a threat to it instead. Those who follow it are no longer acting spontaneously. They have sacrificed their freedom to convention and social expectation. To restore value to their work, they must break out of this inauthentic rut. The result is a series of "endless reactions against existing styles," a state of permanent revolution, in which artists compete to show their disdain for established practices and techniques.[65] And because the easiest—perhaps the only—way to show such disdain is to point out that those who went before were the prisoners of conventions that they themselves failed to see, like the man who never notices that he is looking at the world through a distorting lens, the ruling spirit of contemporary art is one of irony, which can be gentle or ferocious depending on the temperament of the artist in question. This was already clear, a century ago, when Duchamp drew a mustache and beard on the *Mona Lisa.*

A second consequence of the attribution of aesthetic value to spontaneity alone is the erasure of all traditional distinctions between good and bad art, indeed between works of art and everything else. In principle, Schapiro writes, "any mark made by a human being" is an expression of the spontaneous power to create that every genuinely human action presupposes. In this respect, the works of children, madmen and primitive craftsmen may potentially be regarded as works of art too.[66] Those who made them were perhaps in the grip of a magical picture of the world that has no room for the idea of human freedom. Yet their works are as much an expression of human agency as a painting by Rembrandt, and become works of art merely by calling attention to this fact—for example, by exhibiting them in a gallery or museum. Once this is done, they stand on a par with all those works that we conventionally assign to the sphere of art and must not be judged inferior to them on account of their content or mimetic accuracy, since the only thing that makes anything a work of art is the spontaneity of the "form-creating activity" that gives it whatever shape it possesses. The result is a radical leveling of aesthetic values.

Third, this same emphasis on the value of form as distinct from content explains the systematic strategy of disenchantment that so many contemporary artists pursue. We are often enchanted by the content of a work. We find it beautiful, and admire it on account of the skill or ingenuity with which it represents its subject matter, which is something other than the work itself. But in doing so, we lapse back into a precritical, dreamlike state and forget that so far as its aesthetic value is concerned the work's content is a matter of indifference. The artist awakens us from our slumber by drawing our attention to the artificial nature of the work itself—to its form as the product of a spontaneous act of construction or composition. Clement Greenberg's insistence on the importance of the flatness of a painting, as opposed to its illusory depth, is one well-known expression of this strategy of disenchantment, whose approach Schapiro endorses as the one best suited to preserve a respect for human freedom in an age that subordinates it ever more completely to the requirements of the machine.[67]

But if Schapiro describes these developments in a generally approving way, they have a dark side too. Perhaps their most destructive consequence is the erosion of all standards of taste. These require that there be, in theory at least, a principle for distinguishing between better and worse art, and once the status of an object (or act) as a work of art is defined in terms of its expressivity alone, it is hard to see how any principle of discrimination can be derived from such a definition, other than that of authenticity, which is difficult if not impossible to apply in an objectively meaningful fashion. Theorists and critics of course try, but so long as spontaneity is assumed to be the ground of all aesthetic value, their proposed principles are subject to the same ironic treatment as more traditional ideals of artistic excellence, and lack the authority that the judgments of recognized connoisseurs once possessed because anyone, even a nonexpert, may see spontaneity where others do not and nothing in the content of a work can ever decide such disputes (unlike an argument about the iconography of a Renaissance painting).[68]

The result is a vacuum of agreement regarding the value of different works. Some viewers of course prefer certain works, and others admire different ones. But these preferences have no intellectually defensible basis, nor can they, so long as the works of pranksters and graffitists are said to be just as valuable as those of more conventional artists on the grounds that they, too, express the spontaneity that gives every work of art its aesthetic worth. Once its content has been dismissed as a source of value, judgments about the expressivity of a particular work cannot be defended on normative grounds. The only basis for doing so is the factual one that others agree in the judgment—in particular, those with the power to decide which works are singled out as especially significant. That this is so has been acknowledged, at a theoretical level, by the prominence of the so-called "institution" theory of art which defines a work of art as one that museums and galleries choose to display. At a more practical level, the market in contemporary art, where sales prices eclipse those of works from every other period, has made it increasingly clear that the greatness of such works is largely defined by the price they command.[69] In either case, the distinction between what is outstanding and what is not rests less on educated connoisseurship and more on the raw exercise of power, and while this has always been the case to some degree (as art historians whose general outlook has been shaped by the milieu of contemporary art have been quick to point out),[70] the aesthetics of expressivity, which demotes the value of a work's content to zero, has radically shifted the balance in the latter direction, so that today the vacuum of judgment, to which this aesthetics gives rise, is more openly and unashamedly filled by power than ever before.

This is the predictable result of a theory of aesthetic value that is essentially nihilistic in character.

For Schapiro, the value of a work of art is the result of an act of valuing. Its sole source is the freedom or spontaneity of the artist. The material object in which his freedom is "expressed" has no intrinsic value of its own. Those who insist that the value of a painting lies in its materiality—in the physical stuff of which it is made—do not challenge this view but support it. Their point is that the value of a work of art has nothing to do with the relation between the work and something else that it represents. But without the spontaneous act that confers meaning on the materials of which the work is composed, these would be meaningless bits of stuff devoid of aesthetic significance. They only acquire such significance through an act of valuing, which alone has the power to assign meaning to a world that otherwise lacks it.

But if that is true, then there is no basis for claiming that one work of art is better than another, just as there is no basis for discriminating among the choices people make as to how to live their lives if one begins—as Weber does—with a similarly nihilist conception of value. For there to be a standard of this kind, there would have to be something independent of the mere act of valuing that possesses an inherent value of its own, but this is precisely what the premise both of Schapiro's aesthetics and Weber's ethics rules out as a matter of principle. In the classical aesthetics of beauty, the eternality of the world itself, which is visible in the forms of things, provides a standard of this sort. In the Christian art of the Renaissance, the God who weighs everything in the world from a point of view beyond it supplies an objective measure by which the efforts of artists to express his sublimity may be judged. Their creativity is free in a way that the pagan conception of art cannot explain, and valuable on that account. But it is not the final, let alone sole, source of artistic value, for its own worth must ultimately be evaluated by the artist's success in representing the infinite reality of the divine being who has created the world and everything in it.

Nihilism in general is the result of continuing to insist on the value-conferring power of human freedom, which in Christian theology is modeled on God's own, while simultaneously denying the existence of an otherworldly God from whose perspective the free acts of human beings may be judged in an objectively valid manner. In ethics, the result is Weber's heroic but despairing morality of groundless commitment. In art, it is the radicalized expressivism of Schapiro and others, who in order to justify the ruling spirit of contemporary art, have been driven to a position which, like Weber's, destroys the basis for taste, judgment and even for the idea of genius itself, which though it is still routinely invoked by artists and critics alike, makes no sense without the possibility of a philosophically justifiable rank ordering that expressivism eliminates once and for all, and whose absence today is only thinly disguised by the pseudo-ordering that money and institutional power provide in its place.

Genius implies rank. If there is no philosophical basis for ranking works of art, then some other must be found—their auction price, for example. But this provides no warrant either for approving or disapproving the rank order that results. All judgments of this sort require a normative ideal of some kind—one that is independent of the mere fact that some works command a higher price than others. Only an ideal of this sort affords the critical detachment to decide whether the market in contemporary art is a reflection of enduring values or irrational exuberance instead.

In both the Christian art of the Renaissance and the born-again pagan art of Vermeer and his successors, down to the Impressionists and even their early twentieth-century critics, the idea of sublimity provided an independent basis for measuring the degree to which a work of art approaches its divine target. It thereby gave the idea of genius an objective foundation. The first idea served as the objective correlate of the second and grounded the rank ordering it presumes. But the concept of sublimity, though of Christian origin, is rendered meaningless by a nihilistic aesthetics that exaggerates the Christian idea of freedom while insisting that God is not to be found either in the world or beyond it. Without the light of God—whether Caravaggio's or Vermeer's—the experience of the sublime, which lies at the juncture of time and eternity, becomes wholly unintelligible. And when it does, the idea of genius loses its anchor as well.

By contrast, in the field of literature, and in particular in that of the novel, the idea that the essential goal of art is to find and save the eternity in time remains very much alive. Nabokov makes this point explicitly at the end of *Lolita* when he has his diseased hero declare that his aim in writing his memoir has been to rescue his undistinguished child lover from the pointlessness of time by composing a word painting that will confer on her a semblance of the eternity of "aurochs and angels." This is the theology of Proust's Narrator and of the eternal return of Leopold Bloom's long and adventurous day. It is the theology that underlies Dorothea Brooke's ethic of sympathy and George Eliot's conception of the purpose of the novel in which she gives Dorothea a leading role. In all these works, the sublime is close at hand. Each draws its power from the reader's sense that the ordinary experiences of its characters have a share in the timeless and enfolding story of the world, of which we never catch more than a fleeting glimpse, but whose sanctifying presence in the ebb and flow of time a novelist of genius is able to express more adequately than others.

The conception of sublimity on which Eliot, Proust, Joyce and Nabokov rely is not a Christian one. It is that of a world whose infinite and eternal reality is its own. This distinguishes the world of the modern novel from that, say, of Dante's *Commedia,* which from the lowest circle of hell to the highest ring of awestruck saints, draws its sublimity from an unseeable and unsayable source beyond it, like the gestures of the figures in Caravaggio's first painting of *The Supper at Emmaus.* Yet the god of the world that enlightens Leopold Bloom's neurotic love for his wife, and hers for him, and saves both to love for another, endless day, is just as sublime. It is greater than any mind can grasp and equally invulnerable to time. Its sublimity is the halo that surrounds even the commonest things on account of their own timeless reality. Without it, the most serious aspirations of the greatest modern novelists would make no sense at all.

Nothing could be further from the nihilistic antitheology that today has such a strong grip on the theory and practice of painting. What explains the fact that, in contrast to the art of the novel, that of painting has become a less serious medium for the representation of the highest spiritual values, on account of this antitheology, which renders the ideas of genius and sublimity largely meaningless?

Hegel declared that art of any kind is incapable of adequately representing the spirit of the modern age. Only philosophy and law can do this, he said.[71] But if, as Hegel supposed, the problem is that the finitude of every embodied representation of Absolute Spirit causes it to fall short of the mark, then the same may be said about these latter disciplines too. At most, they are capable of representing Absolute Spirit in an increasingly refined but always inadequate way. The continuing spiritual vitality of the novel, which Hegel recognized as a distinctively modern form of art, further suggests that art in general still has the power to do the same. So why has painting lost it?

Here is one answer. It is entirely speculative.

The first wave of classical modernism, which was still connected to the tradition against which it rebelled, was separated from the second, whose force is not yet spent, by Nazism and the fight against it. The Nazis were fierce critics of modern art. But more important, they sought to elevate the art they admired to an unprecedented position of moral and political importance. This was especially true of painting and film.

The Nazis defined their movement in aesthetic terms—as the protection of health and beauty against degeneracy and disease. They identified these categories with the distinction between Aryan and Jew. It is easy to dismiss this aspect of Nazism as a cover for other, more political aims, but Hitler's relentless assault on the Jews in the later years of the war, even when this required the diversion of vital military resources, suggests that for him, at least, the destruction of the Jews remained his highest priority, and one that he and his leading propagandists conceived from the start as an aesthetic-hygienic objective. In their posters, photographs and movies, the artists who served the Nazi cause sought to advance this objective by welding the ideas of moral and political legitimacy to an ideal of physical beauty, conceived in a particular, racially stereotyped way.

The result was an aestheticization of political values that ran against the current of Enlightenment thinking, whose basic tendency is to drive a wedge between the superficial looks of human beings and the invisible source of their worth as persons. Leni Riefenstahl's films make this stunningly clear. Every frame shouts, "Look at these beautiful men and women! This is what we are fighting for—the square jaw, the straight nose, the heroic blond hair, the beauty of their faces and figures. This is all defiled by race mixing and devalued by philosophy. We must be prepared to kill and die for its sake."[72] There were other, grosser versions of this same idea and nothing in Riefenstahl's films yet suggests—what would soon become Nazi policy—that the protection of the beauty of one race demands the enslavement or extermination of others. But their message is plain enough. The love of beauty is not merely for a few well-educated connoisseurs like Bernard Berenson, clucking over pretty pictures in a gallery. It is a public passion and serious unto death.

Among the smoking ruins of European culture that the defeat of the Nazis left behind was the idea that visible beauty can ever possess an ultimate value of this kind. After 1945, no visual artist could suggest otherwise by making a picture that claimed to touch the deepest longings of the human spirit, except, of course, on the condition that these are conceived in the empty way that expressivism and the nihilistic aesthetics that supports it does, as the longing to display the freedom that every form-creating activity involves, which must never, under any circumstances, be confused with what the eye can see. The Nazis' elevation of a corrupt ideal of beauty to a position of life-and-death importance may thus itself have been one of the causes, and perhaps not the

least significant, of the nihilism that informs so much contemporary painting, whose lack of seriousness about beauty is a price we are still paying for
their murderous devotion to it.

As I say, this is entirely speculative, and others will of course disagree with
my characterization of contemporary art. Moreover, though the view that I
have offered is a strongly negative one, no reasonable observer could possibly
conclude that postwar painting is wholly unserious about matters of the deepest spiritual importance. In particular, there are painters whose work seems
to me to reflect a conception of aesthetic value that is closer to the born-again
paganism of Nabokov's "aurochs and angels" than to the nihilistic philosophy of art that Schapiro defends.

I would offer the following as examples (again, judgments will differ): Lucian Freud's fleshy portraits, whose mortal subjects seem to have no secrets
left to keep; Anselm Kiefer's meditations on Paul Celan's poetic tribute to the
victims of the Nazi death camps; and Gerhard Richter's monumental seascapes, which grandly evoke what Herman Broch calls the "sunny yet deathly
loneliness of the sea." These are all paintings of unquestionable seriousness
whose aesthetic value depends on the weightiness of their themes as well as
the genius of the artists who made them. No one would confuse any of these
paintings with the representational works of an earlier period. Each has a contemporary flair. Yet all belong to the tradition of mimetic art and owe their
seriousness to the sublimity of their content as well to the beauty of their form.

There is, moreover, a thematic connection among them, for all these paintings remind the viewer, in one way or another, of the vulnerability of the
individual human being. Lucian Freud's subjects are beset by the vicissitudes
of the body, whose sags and folds are the visible signs of the downward force
that drags us back to earth and threatens to make a mockery of the upward
striving that is the essence of all human dignity. Kiefer's paintings recall a
place and time where millions of men and women were turned into an indiscriminate pile of ash by a criminal machine whose goal was the production
of death. And Richter's seascapes, which contain no figures at all, move the
viewer to reflect that the beauty of the world is merely the other side of its
indifference to human concerns.

In all these paintings, an immense force is at work that threatens to obliterate the separateness and value of the individual human being. This is most
explicit in Kiefer's paintings. But Richter's invite a similar response, for no
individual, human or other, can withstand the dissolving power of the sea.
And Freud's portraits underscore the presence in the lives of his subjects of

that intimately destructive power we know firsthand from the experience of our own decaying bodies.

These forces are incomprehensible. None of them can be understood or explained. We long to grasp them but every effort to do so fails. In this sense, they are not beautiful but sublime, for beauty exists only where the eye and mind find rest in a completed and comprehensible whole, whereas sublimity is the intimation of a reality that surpasses our human powers of representation and thought, yet whose very transcendence we are able to denote in art and philosophy. The paintings of Richter, Kiefer and Freud all point to the sublime in this sense, and thus raise the question of how it is possible for the individuality of anyone or anything to retain its value in a world of incomprehensible forces that corrupt and soon destroy it.

This is similar to the question raised by Nabokov's novel. How can the brief life of its empty-headed heroine (if that is the right word) be given a measure of durable dignity? Nabokov's answer is, through the saving power of art, whose works, though themselves subject to the sovereignty of time, are inspired by the conviction that every life and every event, even the passage of wind on the sea, is part of the timeless story of the world, which has neither beginning nor end, yet cannot be adequately told if a single one of its finite moments is ignored or disparaged. This is the born-again pagan aesthetics of Lolita. Something like it may perhaps be said to inspire the art of the three painters I have mentioned.

A well-known work of Lucian Freud's will serve as an example. It is called *Benefits Supervisor Sleeping,* and was painted in 1995. Twenty years later, it sold at auction for more than $56 million.

The painting is nicknamed "Big Sue." It is the portrait of an obese, middle-aged woman named Sue Tilley, asleep on a tattered sofa. She is naked and her ample flesh spills everywhere. One wonders that the frame of the picture can contain it.

The title of the picture implies that its subject is the occupant of a middle-management position in a large state bureaucracy. She is an ordinary person with an ordinary job, and here she is portrayed in the most ordinary human activity of all, for even kings and queens must sleep. There is nothing beautiful about her. Some may perhaps even find her figure repulsive, and be reminded by contrast of the lovely reclining forms of Titian's *Venus of Urbino* and Ingres' *Odalisque,* or even Manet's *Olympia,* all of which "Big Sue" calls to mind. Viewers used to pictures of exceptionally thin models and endless diet campaigns, which equate thinness with the virtue of self-control, may even be inclined to dismiss "Big Sue" as a caricature whose purpose is to make fun of its subject, both in physical and moral terms.

But nothing could be further from the truth. Freud's painting is clinically harsh but not unfeeling. The rolls of Sue's stomach and her pendulous breasts are portrayed as a doctor might, with a diagnostic eye that strives to see things as they really are, and refuses to amend them for beauty's sake. But also like a doctor's eye, the painter's is filled with a spirit of sympathy. If "Big Sue" conveys one thought, it is that we may be able to look at another person with the guards of wakefulness and clothing let down—to see her with a direct-ness that perhaps even she cannot achieve—and be moved by feelings of friendship that are enhanced rather than destroyed by the honesty of our ap-proach. In this respect, it may not be too farfetched to say that the spirit of "Big Sue" is psychoanalytic, for the analysand also looks naked and misshapen under the eye of the analyst, who knows that the price of freedom is honesty and pursues it ruthlessly, yet for the sake of a deeper friendship between them. Even the couch on which the painter's subject sprawls is perhaps a reminder of the sofa on which his grandfather Sigmund asked his patients to lie down and tell him their secrets so that they could learn to be better friends.

This is the spirit of Nabokov's novel as well. There is nothing lovely about Lolita—she is a pimply, ignorant child—and her lover is more than mis-shapen; he is a monster of depravity. But when Humbert Humbert says that he has written his memoir to give Lolita a lasting life in art, the sympathy he expresses for her, even if it is delusional, is the clearest statement in the novel of its author's own intentions. Nabokov leads the reader toward a form of friendship for his characters that lies beyond good and evil and the distinc-tion between beauty and ugliness. It is a form of solidarity based on the recog-nition that no one is too unlovely or corrupt to be immune to the saving power of art, whose aim is not to make things beautiful but real—to bring what would otherwise be forgotten or dismissed with disgust into the light of eternity where everything can be seen to have more reality than one could possibly guess.

"Big Sue" is like Lolita. Without Freud's portrait, she would be com-pletely forgotten, an anonymous member of the nondescript army of petty officials, with a body that ought to be kept under wraps. But here she is, in all her abundance, and the viewer's reaction is likely to be, "Look how much there is to her!" How much flesh, of course, but how much humanity too, for the fat woman asleep on the sofa is closer to one's feelings—can I say to one's heart?—than the viewer might have expected. She seems overwhelmingly real. There is more to her than the painting can capture, which is how one feels about Lolita too, whose life spills over the frame of Humbert's self-serving memoir. Looking at the painting, one has the experience of seeing something coarse, even vaguely dissolute, but recognizing for the first time how real it is—and feeling an unexpected sympathy toward it for precisely this reason.

This is the opposite of nihilism.

The Christian philosopher equates reality with eternity, as his pagan predecessors did. But because he distinguishes between the world and God, and believes that God alone is eternal, he knows that nothing in the world can be real in an ultimate sense. The nihilist embraces this conclusion, yet insists there is no God of the sort to whom the Christian prays. He is therefore driven to the conclusion that there is nothing either in the world or beyond it that is eternal and therefore real. Nihilism drains the world of its reality and has nothing to fill the resulting void but an endless series of equally groundless value judgments, whose claim to legitimacy is satisfied by the mere act of expressing them. This nihilistic philosophy has many manifestations. In the field of art, it encourages the view that a work has aesthetic value so long as it demonstrates the artist's freedom to shape some fragment of material reality in accordance with his or her personal values. It undermines any basis for ranking works of art except in terms of their institutional cachet or market price. And it promotes the idea that an artist can best show his creativity by mocking the pretensions of others to have made works that represent the world as it is in itself.

"Big Sue" makes the world more real, not less. It reminds us that everything in the world is overflowing with reality, even those things from which we look away when we meet them outside a work of art. In this sense, its subject, though far from beautiful, is utterly sublime, for what the painter wants the viewer to see is that there is more to Sue Tilley than his eye can ever take in.

Caravaggio aimed at a similar effect. He also invested the human subjects in his great religious paintings with a superabundant reality that exceeds the viewer's powers of vision and understanding—in contrast to the beautiful forms of classical art whose aesthetic value depends on our ability to see them all at once. But for Caravaggio, the source of the sublimity of worldly things lies beyond the world itself, in the God of whose eternal reality no human being can ever be more than a mortal image. There is no hint of this in Freud's portrait of Sue Tilley. Her overflowing reality is the world's own, like that of the young woman in Vermeer's painting.

Vermeer's aesthetic is neither classical nor Christian, and most certainly not nihilistic. His aim is not to negate the reality of the world by reducing it to the status of a value judgment, but to make it incomprehensibly deep—to show that even ordinary things are sublime. Vermeer's conception of sublimity is unthinkable without the Christian religion, to whose theology we owe the very idea. But his art no longer depends on the assumption (to which even the nihilist is still attached) that only a God beyond the world could be eternal and divine. It rests instead on the deification of the world that Spinoza expounds in his sober ethic of joy. "Big Sue" belongs to this tradition.

Freud's painting is a joyous work. It celebrates its subject and arouses friendly feelings toward her—not because, in the language of the law, she is "a person entitled to equal respect regardless of her condition," but on account of that condition itself. Sue Tilley is not beautiful or heroic or anything of the sort. But she is more than a benefits supervisor or overweight middle-aged woman. These are general categories. Sue has more reality than they can exhaust. This of course is true of every individual, though we rarely notice it. We live by means of judgments that place the people and things in the world into categories of various kinds—moral, social, practical and the like. For finite beings such as we, there is no other way to survive. But a great work of art gives us a glimpse of the unfathomable reality of its subject and recalls, for a moment at least, the sublimity of the world, which we mostly forget in the ordinary business of living. The light in which we see this, however briefly, is the one that falls through Vermeer's window, and since it lies outside the artist, in the world itself, it provides the objective correlate that viewers and critics need to distinguish between genius and mediocrity, which Meyer Schapiro's nihilistic aesthetics is incapable of doing.

The aesthetics of sublimity that explains the greatness of "Big Sue" starts from very different premises. This and works like it give one reason to hope that in the world of contemporary painting, which still bears the scars of the Nazis' politicization of beauty, the aesthetics of nihilism must eventually yield to a more serious and satisfying conception of the calling of art. Artists and critics will disagree as to what this might be. But one possibility is a reaffirmation of the born-again paganism of those painters who, beginning in the seventeenth century, carried the idea of sublimity out of the Christian world in which it was born, into one that is neither godless, as the nihilist claims, nor lit by the light of a God beyond the world, as every Christian believes, but divine in itself, as Spinoza and Nietzsche maintain. Spinoza and Nietzsche map this world in the "grey on grey" of philosophy. Lucian Freud paints it in livelier colors. But the theology that inspires "Big Sue" is the same as theirs, and the fact that the modern novel affirms it with such authority in one realm of art, supports the hope that in time, at least, it may prevail in others as well.

CHAPTER 36

Theological, Not Political

JOHN RAWLS' CHRISTIAN DEFENSE
OF LIBERAL DEMOCRACY

Modern Western science gets its start at the end of the thirteenth century. The Condemnation of 1277 has been called its "birth certificate." It is the product of a reinterpretation of the classical ideal of truth from the standpoint of Christian belief. The art of the modern West, which begins with Duccio and Cimabue, is the result of a parallel reworking of the classical ideal of beauty from the same point of view. In each case, the outcome has been a new system of values that is neither classical nor Christian but a fusion of the two.

Today, these values exist independently of the religion that inspired them and for centuries conditioned their growth. Scientific and aesthetic ideals that once rested on Christian assumptions now no longer require their support. But this does not mean they need no God to sustain them. Secularization is not the end of theology.

Now as in the past, the meaning of truth in science and of beauty in art depends on their relation to what Kant calls the "unconditioned" and Aristotle "the everlasting and divine." To explain the intelligibility and beauty of what happens in time, in a way that satisfies the irrepressible demands of reason itself, its finite reality must be related to something that cannot be conceived in temporal terms. The need for some such connection is "transcendental" in Kant's sense. The very possibility of human experience depends upon it. But neither Aristotle's God nor the God of Abraham is any longer available to play this role. A new God is therefore needed—or rather, a new one has been found. Modern science and art already have the theology they require. Einstein and Proust sketch its outlines, and everything that I have said in the preceding nine chapters has been merely an elaboration of their born-again paganism, on which our modern conceptions of truth and beauty depend as fully as their classical and Christian predecessors did on the now discredited theologies that once sustained them.

In this chapter and the next, we turn from science and art to politics, or rather we return to it, for it was with politics that we began.

The modern Western state is what Hans Kelsen calls a *Rechtsstaat*,[1] a political community organized around the recognition and protection of rights specified by law. Its governing norm is that of entitlement. As the sphere of entitlement has grown, those of luck and gift have shrunk. It is no longer thought legitimate to leave the benefits and opportunities that citizens enjoy to charity or chance, so far as their distribution is subject to collective control. This has made it increasingly difficult to affirm in a public way the value of love and gratitude as conditions of human well-being.

Love cannot be commanded or bought. No one ever has a right to the love she receives. Gratitude for the love of others thus expresses the acceptance of a limit on our powers of control that is less remediable than those that hamper our ability to ensure that the rights we possess are enforced. Viewed in these terms, the modern expansion of the realm of entitlement at the expense of that of gift represents an enormous increase in the capacity of human beings to control the circumstances of their lives, in an area of peculiar vulnerability.

One moral and political ideal, more than any other, has underwritten the expansion of the sphere of entitlement. This is the ideal of autonomy. Autonomy means the ability to determine one's own fate. So long as it is subject to limits of any kind, our power to do this remains incomplete. It is not yet what we wish and demand that it be. In order to approach more closely the condition of self-sufficiency that the concept of autonomy invites us to accept as the standard of moral and political judgment, these limits must continually be pushed back. They include the limits that arise from the nature of love itself.

The meaning of "autonomy" has traditionally been conceived in terms of the idea of the will—of what Kant calls our power of "spontaneous" self-legislation. This is a Christian idea. It is modeled on the freedom of God. Kant still considered the connection between human autonomy, on the one hand, and the will of God on the other, to be an important, indeed necessary one, at least so far as what he calls "the highest good" is concerned. This is no longer the case for most of the many philosophers and political writers who today embrace the concept of autonomy as a moral ideal. For them, it is a purely secular concept. Yet it remains tied to the presuppositions of the theological worldview that gave birth to it in the first place, and that continues to shape our understanding of the human condition and of the place of love and gratitude in it.

The longing for control is perennial. Human beings always wish to have more than they do. But in the modern West, this longing has assumed a peculiarly extravagant form—one that is aggravated and amplified by a loathing for the human condition itself. It is one thing to wish to have more control. It is another to regard one's lack of absolute power as something contemptible and degrading. For those who view their finitude in these terms, any form of dependence, including the one that love entails and gratitude embraces, will be more than a source of frustration or anxiety. It will be an insult and spur to revolt.

In chapter 2, I suggested that the anger that gives the modern Western demand for control its uniquely intense character is a result of the peculiar theodicy of the Christian religion, within whose spiritual milieu the civilization of the West has evolved. I further suggested that this same religion is the source of the modern idea of autonomy, which the envious children of God have used to exact their revenge against him for being made to feel so ashamed of themselves. I claimed that for both logical and psychological reasons, the Christian understanding of man's relation to God systematically undermines itself in ways the other Abrahamic religions do not, and described our loveless world of rights as the product of the self-destruction of the religion of absolute love. Much of the book at whose end we have nearly arrived has been an attempt to vindicate these extravagant claims.

Chapter 2 concluded with a question, to which the answer is long overdue. I asked if it is possible to honor our sense of the infinite value of every human being, to which the idea of autonomy gives forceful expression, while restoring love and gratitude to an honored place in public life. This is no small undertaking. It requires a different understanding of the human condition than the one implied by the ethic of entitlement and the principle of autonomy on which it is based. It demands that we see and judge our finitude from a point of view other than that of the transcendent God of the Christian religion. But can this be done in a way that preserves our respect for the equal worth of every human being, and for the system of rights that today is its most powerful political manifestation? I now return to this question after a long but unavoidable detour.

In this chapter, I describe in greater detail the all-too-Christian theology that lies behind the modern idea of autonomy on which many of the most thoughtful defenders of liberal democracy rest their moral or spiritual justification of it. I concentrate on the philosophy of John Rawls. I first identify the conception of the human condition that underlies his interpretation of the meaning of autonomy. I then show why those who embrace this conception lack the metaphysical resources to explain how diversity can be a good in itself, and patriotism anything more than the cloudy expression of a cosmopolitan morality from whose point of view no local attachments of any kind can ever possess an intrinsic worth of their own.

In the next and final chapter of the book, I attempt to show that only a different theology, neither pagan nor Christian, has the resources to overcome these two limitations: to account for the importance of rights without appealing to the supernatural idea of a kingdom of ends; and to explain why gratitude of a horizontal, human kind—as distinct from the vertical sort that Augustine and his followers insist we owe to God—is an essential condition of our well-being as finite modes of the immortal God of the world. This is the same theology that in earlier chapters I offered as the key to understanding the distinctive aspirations of modern science and art. There, I found inspiration in the writings of Spinoza and Nietzsche. In the concluding chapter of my *Confessions,* where the question is how best to understand the spiritual aims of modern democratic life, I take my lead from Walt Whitman.

"THE PERSPECTIVE OF ETERNITY"

In broad terms, liberal democracy may be defined as a system of government based on the principle of universal suffrage, qualified by the norm of majority rule and constrained by the recognition of certain basic rights that cannot be modified by ordinary political means. This general definition leaves a great deal of room for debate about the best way to organize such a regime. Which rights are fundamental and ought to be beyond the power of a majority to change? When is a supermajority appropriate? Is a presidential system better than a parliamentary one? But all these disagreements assume the supremacy of two fundamental values and every defender of liberal democracy appeals to them to explain the superiority of his or her preferred version of it. These are the values of freedom and equality.

In *A Theory of Justice,* John Rawls offers a canonical account of the meaning of freedom and equality and explicates their relevance for a wide range of questions about the design of what he calls the "basic structure" of society. Others have since used different arguments to support a broadly similar set of conclusions, but none matches the breadth and lucidity of Rawls' achievement. We may not often pause to reflect on the philosophical prejudices that underlie the ideals of liberal democracy, but for anyone who does, *A Theory of Justice* remains the high road to their understanding.

I use the word "prejudice" deliberately. The ideal to which many of the most thoughtful defenders of liberal democracy appeal is that of a community of "free and equal persons," as Rawls terms it. In the West today, no political ideal is more widely shared than this. Yet its moral force depends on a largely undefended view of what it means to be a person, and this in turn on an even more deeply suppressed understanding of man's relation to God.

Rawls defines a person as a being with the capacity for rational self-direction. His definition follows Kant's quite closely. Kant describes the power in question as that of "autonomy" and locates it in the faculty he calls the "will." For Kant, the moral and political consequences that flow from the idea of the will are still tied, in a vestigial way, to the creationist theology from which Augustine derived it.

In Rawls' case, this theological background has disappeared from view. For him and the many other political philosophers who today invoke the idea of a community of free and equal persons as a fundamental norm, the concept of autonomy is a strictly secular ideal. Yet Rawls' answer to the question of what makes one a person whose actions are entitled to equal respect still rests on the creationist assumption that *whatever* possesses *ultimate* value, for moral and political purposes, does so *only because* it owes its existence to the acts of an autonomous agent whose spontaneity is modeled on that of the God who brought the world into being from nothing.

In *A Theory of Justice*, Rawls explicitly associates his own political philosophy with the Kantian idea of autonomy. He interprets his conception of justice as a procedural expression of Kant's idea. In response to critics who charged that the argument of the book rests on an inadequate understanding of what it means to be a human being, Rawls later sought to distance himself from his own earlier Kantian interpretation of it. He claimed that *A Theory of Justice* was meant to be neutral between the Kantian and other accounts of human nature. He said that his goal had been to secure agreement among those with conflicting metaphysical views, not to resolve their disputes or beg the questions these raise by assuming an answer to them. He described the aim of the book as "political, not metaphysical."

Yet despite his later disclaimers, Rawls' critics were right. The argument of *A Theory of Justice* does indeed assume a particular view of the human condition. Moreover, the authority of the view it presupposes depends on its implied answer to the question, What is of eternal value in man? *A Theory of Justice* is not merely a metaphysical work. It is a theological one too.

As an undergraduate at Princeton in the early 1940s, Rawls wrote a senior thesis entitled, "A Brief Enquiry into Sin and Faith: An Interpretation Based on the Concept of Community."[2] At the time, he was preoccupied with theological issues, and even briefly considered a career in the ministry, though he later abandoned his faith. In biographical terms, *A Theory of Justice* marks a midpoint of sorts on the arc of Rawls' career, between the avowedly Christian outlook of his youth and the emphatically anti-metaphysical stance of his later years.

By subsequently denying that the argument of *A Theory of Justice* depends on the truth of any account of human nature, Rawls sought to disentangle the practical problem of reaching agreement on the most fundamental issues of domestic and international law from the philosophical demand for a true account of this kind. This may make sense as a political strategy, but anyone who hopes to defend liberal democracy on philosophical grounds must be prepared to offer some explanation of why human beings possess the value they do—or risk simply assuming one without justification. Rawls' later claim that the goal of *A Theory of Justice* was "political, not metaphysical" thus amounts to a disavowal of the book's deepest intellectual ambitions, and of his earlier conviction that the long-term stability of liberal democracies depends on their citizens possessing a self-conscious understanding of the source of their respect for themselves and others as autonomous agents.

If we are to take these ambitions seriously, we must pay attention to the conception of human nature on which Rawls' defense of liberal democracy rests. It cannot be removed like an unwanted wart. And we must pay especially close attention to the theological provenance of this conception, for though the relatively bloodless version of Kantian morality that Rawls invokes to explain and defend it shows no trace of the fervent Christianity that shaped his youthful understanding of God's relation to man, the reasons for Rawls' continuing belief in the dignity of every human being are intimately tied to a Christian view of the relation between time and eternity—just as they are, more explicitly, for Kant. That even Rawls himself still felt the theological dimension of the secular Kantianism he embraces in *A Theory of Justice* is suggested by his striking remark, in the very last paragraph of the book, that to view the problems of politics from the vantage point of the "original position" is to see them from "the perspective of eternity," and that "to act with grace and self-command from this point of view" is the essence of "purity of heart."[3]

The original position is Rawls' most famous invention, and though it resembles the idea of a state of nature that plays an important role in the tradition of contractarian political thought, it has certain distinctive features that bring out—indeed, that are meant to bring out—the view of the human condition that forms the backdrop to Rawls' account.

The original position is a device for framing our reflections about the basic structure of society in a morally appropriate way. Anyone can take up this position at any time. It is a thought experiment that each of us is meant to conduct on our own, like the one that Descartes invites his readers to imitate, when, sitting alone in front of the fire, he asks whether he can be confident that any of his beliefs are true.

Descartes' inquiry proceeds on the basis of a very strong assumption. Any perception or idea whose truth I *can* doubt, Descartes declares, shall for the purposes of my investigation be treated, provisionally at least, as *being false*. The deliberations of anyone who adopts Rawls' original position rest on a similarly strong premise. Only those arrangements to which I would agree, were I to consider the alternatives from this point of view, are to be deemed acceptable. When I leave the imaginary world of the original position and reenter the real one of classes, parties, elections and the like, a host of other concerns immediately become relevant, just as they do for anyone who follows Descartes' method and then, upon reentering the realm of practical life, puts its strictures aside. But the question of what "really" matters in the construction of a political regime—of what "really" counts so far as its legitimacy is concerned—must be decided from the standpoint of the original position alone, in the same way that the question of what gives our true beliefs their truth can only be answered if one takes it up in the way Descartes does, from the artificial but clarifying perspective of radical doubt.

Descartes has often been criticized on the grounds that his method is not neutral but already implicitly assumes a particular conception of truth—the very one it is intended to justify. Rawls explicitly acknowledges that this is the case with respect to the original position. It is meant, he says, to express a specific moral ideal and then in turn to strengthen and extend it. But Rawls insists this is a virtue of his argument, which proceeds by the circular method he claims all such arguments must, moving from intuitions to conceptions and back to intuitions in a self-reinforcing circle that eventually produces what he calls "reflective equilibrium." This makes it all the more important to understand just how his description of the original position already embeds, if only in a provisional way, the moral ideal that the process of reasoning from it is meant to confirm by clarifying the consequences of taking it seriously.

The original position imposes a series of constraints on the choice of a basic principle for the distribution of liberties, opportunities and material resources. To take up the original position as a thought experiment is to accept the appropriateness of these constraints on one's reflections about the strengths and weaknesses of different principles for distributing these various goods. Rawls takes great care to specify the constraints he thinks appropriate, and rightly so, for once these are in place the results of the deliberation they frame follow with deductive necessity, or something very close to it.

The constraints that Rawls imposes are epistemic. They are limits on what anyone who adopts the original position is permitted to know when choosing a principle for the basic structure of society. Broadly speaking, there are two reasons why Rawls believes the particular limits he imposes are essential to the choice of such a principle. The first is that they make it *possible*, and the second is that they guarantee it is made on terms that reflect our considered judgment of what is *fair*.

In order to decide on a principle for the distribution of liberties, opportunities and resources, one must first know that cooperation among human beings "is both possible and necessary."[4] If it is not, there is no point to deliberating about the choice of such a principle. It is also essential that one have a manageably short list of principles to consider, for otherwise the task of choosing among them becomes endless. Rawls draws his "short list" from the tradition of political philosophy.[5] Finally, if the choice of a principle for the arrangement of the basic structure of society is to be sufficiently well informed to be made in a meaningful way, the person making the choice must know not only that the "circumstances of justice" obtain, but that human beings have certain psychological and other characteristics that motivate them to behave in particular ways regardless of the nature of their society, and that economic and political organizations of all sorts obey certain universal "laws."[6] Rawls calls these "the general facts" about "human psychology" and "human society."[7] It is necessary to know them in order to predict and evaluate the consequences of adopting any of the basic principles on Rawls' short list.

These are all positive bits of knowledge that anyone who assumes the original position must possess if the choice of such a principle is to be tractable and responsive to the most elementary features of the human condition. They enable one to make the choice in a deliberate way. But it is not enough that the choice be deliberate. It must be fair as well, and to assure that it is Rawls insists that there are also many things one may *not* know in the original position.

If the first goal (of tractability) is met by *adding* to the stockpile of knowledge that anyone who adopts the original position may be assumed to possess, the second (of fairness) can only be met, according to Rawls, by *subtracting* from this same stockpile—by bracketing various items of knowledge that one already possesses and setting these aside as irrelevant to the most basic questions of political morality. To deliberate in a fair-minded way about the arrangement of the basic structure of society, certain sorts of knowledge about oneself and others must be hidden behind what Rawls calls "a veil of ignorance."[8]

These include knowledge of one's "class position or social status," "natural assets and abilities," "conception of the good," psychological propensities (including one's "aversion to risk or liability to optimism or pessimism"), and the "level of civilization and culture" of the society to which one belongs.[9] This is an impressive list. It rules out much of the information on which we ordinarily base our deliberations about all sorts of personal and political matters. But the most important thing about the list is not its scope. It is the principle that connects the various items on it, which have not been chosen at random.

In contrast to the "general" facts that anyone in the original position is permitted, indeed required, to know, those that are hidden behind the veil of ignorance are "particular" facts that serve to distinguish one person from another in ways that anyone who agrees to deliberate from the standpoint of the original position concedes are illegitimate grounds for deciding how the basic rules of social life should be framed. These facts individuate human beings in a manner that we ought to disregard in designing the basic structure of society. Putting them out of mind does not mean that those living within whatever framework is selected cease to be individuals and are merged into an indistinct collectivity. (According to Rawls, that is how utilitarianism wrongly invites us to treat them.) They remain individuals, to be recognized and honored as such, but the individuality we attribute to them and to which we assign moral worth is not defined by any of those "particular" facts about ourselves and others that the veil of ignorance prevents us from taking into account.

The justification for excluding these facts from consideration is partly pragmatic. If the parties know their strengths and weaknesses, it will be more difficult for them to reach a stable agreement regarding the basic structure of society. The strong will seek to exploit their advantage through "force and cunning" and the weak will attempt to protect themselves by forming defensive coalitions of various kinds. Under these circumstances, even a unanimous agreement among the parties can be no more than a temporary truce, subject to disruption by subsequent fluctuations in their relative power. To give the principles that emerge from the original position the durability they require in order to have the greatest chance of surviving for a reasonable period of time, they cannot themselves be based on the actual distribution of power that happens to exist at the moment of initial agreement. The veil of ignorance makes this impossible. So long as those living in a society founded on principles agreed to behind such a veil continue to recognize their authority, they will be better equipped to resist the temptation to renegotiate the terms of their relations as the balance of power among them shifts. And if one asks why principles agreed to under such hypothetical conditions should continue to be viewed as authoritative even after the veil has been lifted, part of the answer is that only they possess this practical advantage.

But that is not the whole answer. It is not even the most important part of it. For Rawls, the authority of the veil of ignorance is above all a function of its connection to a moral ideal, which the veil is meant to express in a vivid and workable way.

This ideal rests on a picture of the human condition whose outlines are as follows.

Human beings have many different interests. Some are universal; others vary from one individual to the next. They also have many different abilities that can be used to satisfy the various desires to which their interests give rise. Again, some of these are universal or nearly so, while others are more restricted or even unique. The variety of their interests and abilities distinguishes human beings from other animals, whose needs, desires and capacities are less diverse.

But it is not our greater diversity that sets us apart from other living things in a morally salient way. That is just a fact about us from which nothing of moral consequence follows. In Rawls' view, the moral standing of human beings is explained not by the scope and variety of our interests and talents but by our capacity to weave them into what he calls a "plan of life."

Human beings do more than live their lives. They live them according to a more or less well-thought-out plan. To be sure, our goals always remain inchoate and unfulfilled to some degree. Yet however sketchy the plan, however often it is revised, and however far short it falls of achieving its aims, its organizing presence in the life of a human being is what gives that life its moral dignity. To express this idea, Rawls adopts Royce's definition of a "person" as "a human life lived according to a plan."[10] In Rawls' view, the capacity to form a plan of life is what makes us moral beings accountable to ourselves and others for our actions and hence capable of winning or losing respect in our own eyes and in those of other persons like us.

A plan of life can only be pursued within the territory fixed by our interests and talents. These define what might be called the "jurisdiction" of all human planning. Moreover, the plans of life we construct for ourselves generally reshape our interests and talents, which become something different in the process. Because there can be no meaningful human planning outside the sphere of our interests and talents, and because these are themselves so often transformed by the plans we make for and with them, the distinction between the power of planning and the material that provides the substance of our plans is an artificial one. But the veil of ignorance, which conceals the latter from view, is intended to highlight precisely this distinction and to underscore that the former alone explains why human lives have the special moral value they do.

The veil of ignorance deprives us of all information about the material we have been given to form a plan of life. It leaves us, though, with the knowledge that we have the capacity to form such a plan; that we have an interest in doing so (which necessarily differs from the interest we have in satisfying any of our other desires, about which we know nothing at all); and finally, that the enterprise of framing a plan of life must be carried out within the confines of need and ability that constitute the finite field of all human planning. This particular set of epistemic conditions is meant to put a spotlight on the one and only feature of the human condition that in Rawls' judgment ought to matter from a moral point of view, and to which he assigns a unique value for the same reason Kant does.

Kant's term for the power in question is "practical reason." He defines this as the capacity to "act in accordance with the conception of a law."[11] Practical reason is practical because it is directed toward action rather than contemplation, and rational because the action in question not only follows a rule (as every intelligible action must) but is guided by the concept of a rule that for the actor serves as a reflective standard of judgment and appraisal.

This is precisely what Rawls means by a plan of life. A life lived according to a plan is one that is oriented toward a standard of this sort. It therefore presupposes the ability to formulate such a standard in the first place. This is nothing more than the power to reason—to form those unreal mental objects we call abstractions, which whatever their relation to the things that fill the world around us, are not to be found among them. A being that possesses this power is in a position to "take a stance" toward the world—to think about it and make plans to act upon it from a point of view that is inaccessible to every being that lacks the power in question. Indeed, it is not merely in a position to do so. It cannot help acting in this way. It is always already living planfully, whatever the content of its plan may be and regardless of whether others consider the plan a good one or not. Living in accordance with a plan of some kind is not optional for a being with the power to do so.

Having this power makes one a member of what Kant calls "the kingdom of ends"—the community of beings that may be held to account for their actions. Outside this kingdom, there is no such thing as moral responsibility. For Kant, the fundamental question of morality is how a being with such responsibilities should meet them. His answer is, by acting in accordance with a standard that respects one's status as a member of the kingdom of ends.

Finite members of this kingdom (that is, all rational beings other than God) must rely on their desires and skills for the content of the rules they adopt. These determine their choice of goals and of the means to pursue them. Some of these goals are common to all human beings; others vary from one individual to the next. The same is true of skills. With limited exceptions, every human is able to grasp a stone and throw it, but some can throw one much farther and faster than others. The result is a great diversity of practical rules and plans of life—as great as that of the desires and skills they employ. Yet these are not the source or ground of one's membership in the kingdom of ends. That depends solely on the power that rational beings alone possess to form a plan for the pursuit of their desires, using whatever resources happen to be available to them. Every being that has this power enjoys the privileges of membership in the kingdom of ends (including the right to be treated with respect by others as a being of this kind) and none can avoid the duties that come with it.

It follows, according to Kant, that the question of whether one has met these duties can never be decided by examining the content of the rule or "maxim" one adopts, since this always derives from a source independent of the power that gives rise to these responsibilities in the first place. It must be settled by looking to see if the rule in question ascribes its own normative force to its status as a rule, and nothing more. Only those rules that make this the sole criterion of their own authority honor the capacity for abstraction that compels those beings that possess it, and them alone, to ask if the plans they adopt to guide their lives are not merely effective but worthy of respect as well.

In an earlier chapter, I tried to show how this idea leads Kant to a formalistic ethics whose implications he labors to make more concrete by means of an artificial test he calls the "categorical imperative." Rawls' veil of ignorance performs a similar function and derives its moral force from the same basic idea.

Like Kant's categorical imperative, the veil of ignorance compels those who adopt it as a device for testing the moral adequacy of the various principles they are considering, to view themselves and others in formalistic terms. Behind the veil, one does not know anything about one's desires and skills. It is therefore impossible to know anything about the content of one's plan of life. All one knows is that one has the power to form such a plan, as do the others with whom one must come to an agreement, and that each is compelled to pursue his or her plan under conditions of "moderate scarcity" and the "circumstances of justice." All one knows, in other words, is that one is what Kant calls a finite rational being, and because every differentiating detail of one's finitude has been concealed by the veil of ignorance, anyone who accepts the constraints imposed by the veil has no choice but to proceed on the assumption that any principle for the arrangement of the basic structure of society must be evaluated from the vantage point of one's standing as a rational being alone, regardless of how the power of reason is later put to work in framing a plan of life based on one's actual desires and skills.

For Rawls, like Kant, the relationship between this power and the interests, dispositions and talents it shapes is one of form to content.

Every human life is lived according to a plan. This is what makes it the life of a person rather than an animal or plant. In this sense, all human lives exhibit an identical form, though the content of the plans that guide them varies depending on the material with which each person must work. But while this material accounts for the great diversity of the lives that human beings actually live, the design of the original position ensures that it does not figure in the choice of principles for the governance of our most basic social and political relations. The only thing that ought to matter in this regard is the formal equality of all persons conceived as beings with the power to plan. It is this and this alone that gives their lives an intrinsic worth that demands universal respect. Kant seeks to make this idea operational by means of the categorical imperative. Rawls' veil of ignorance does the same thing, though perhaps in a rhetorically more convincing way, by encouraging us to regard the moral principle the veil expresses as happily coincidental with the constraints on deliberation that self-interested individuals would accept in order to solve an elementary bargaining problem.

This interpretation of the meaning of the veil of ignorance is one that Rawls himself proposes in *A Theory of Justice*. For Rawls, the idea that gives the original position its moral (as distinguished from merely strategic) importance is that of autonomy. Autonomy is the power to give a law to oneself (to frame a plan of life). That one should respect this power, in oneself and others, is Rawls' deepest value, and the source of the value he assigns, in a derivative way, to the political norms of liberty and equality. These often clash as a practical matter. But both rest upon the shared conviction that we are all entitled to *equal* treatment *because* each of us possesses in identical measure the *liberty or autonomy* that justifies our mutual demand for respect. What "equal treatment" requires is a notoriously difficult question. But from the point of view of the moral ideal that underlies Rawls' political philosophy it is a second-order question of implementation.

How should we conceive of the power of autonomy that is the root of all moral value for Rawls, as it is for Kant?

In Kant's case, the answer is clear. Autonomy is the power of spontaneous "self-affection" that enables those who have it to start a causal chain of their own—to be an original ground of effects and not merely the product of antecedent ones, like everything in the natural world, including even autonomous beings insofar as we view them as occupying a place in the natural order and as subject to the rule of strict determination on which the very possibility of such an order depends. Kant's term for the faculty in which this power resides is the "will."

We can have no direct knowledge of the will. All our knowledge of the world depends on the heteronomous principle that one thing is intelligible only insofar as we are able to locate its cause in another. The idea of a self-caused cause violates this principle in an elementary way. Yet Kant insists that we must assume the existence of the will, inexplicable though it be, if we are to make any sense at all of our moral experience, and of the phenomenon of duty in particular.

The most that one can say about the human will is that its defining characteristic is the same as that of God's equally unintelligible power of creation from nothing. In the case of human beings, this power must be exercised within limits that are incompatible with the idea of an omnipotent deity. Still, it is only their possession of a power of self-determination as free as God's own that qualifies human beings for membership in the kingdom of ends and gives them a godlike position that is unique among created beings, even if their freedom is confined within bounds that they have no choice but to accept.

The nerve of Kant's morality is the idea that human beings ought to act in a way that honors this godlike side of their being, instead of debasing it by placing their freedom in service to given, and hence unwilled, needs and desires, however refined these may be. In this sense, Kant's basic ethical norm is not a natural one, like Aristotle's, but a *supernatural* one, whose interpretation and justification are inspired by the creationist metaphysics of the Christian religion, though the authority of the moral law itself does not depend, Kant claims, on any theological assumptions (in contrast to the idea of the highest good, which is inconceivable unless we "postulate" an omnipotent creator and the immortality of the soul).

Rawls is far more circumspect regarding the inspiration for his understanding of the concept of autonomy. He makes no effort to ground it on metaphysical, let alone religious, beliefs. Rawls associates the idea of autonomy with that of freedom, but only in a loose and casual way. He offers no account of freedom itself and his method of analysis is much less rigorous than Kant's.[12] Yet despite his own later protestations, Rawls' account of the original position in *A Theory of Justice* rests on a supernaturalist metaphysics as well, characterized by a principled distinction between the desires and skills we possess as the result of what he calls a "natural lottery,"[13] on the one hand, and, on the other, the transcendent power to form a plan of life that represents the creative, spontaneous and morally decisive part of our hybrid constitution as finite rational beings.

The first are accidental. They are given to us by fate. Together, they constitute the natural side of human existence. The second stands above them. It regards all our given characteristics from the vantage point of a creative power which, though it must act within the limits they define, is not itself an accident of nature in the way that they are. It is a supernatural power, though Rawls does not use this word to describe it.

The capacity to form a plan a life is defined by its independence from all those elements of the human condition that are given to us instead. Its essence is its freedom or spontaneity. In Kant's view, this is what qualifies one for membership in a supernatural kingdom of ends. For Rawls, it is both a necessary and sufficient condition for adopting the original position as the only morally appropriate perspective from which to evaluate the fairness of the basic structure of society. What Rawls calls the power to form a plan of life is Kant's will by another name, and the community of those who deliberate about the terms of their cooperation from behind a veil of ignorance is his version of Kant's kingdom of ends.

The supernaturalism of Rawls' conception of the original position is brought out with special clarity by his suggestion that anyone who adopts it ought to agree to treat the natural abilities that different individuals possess as a common pool, to be utilized for the benefit of all. Ordinarily, we regard these as a source of individuality. Their diversity is what makes us different from one another. By collectivizing our natural traits, even in theory, we lose the differences among them as a basis of distinction. But this does not mean that we cease to be individuals in every, or even the most important, respect. Those who agree to treat their natural advantages and disadvantages as a shared resource do so as persons whose distinctness from one another is preserved by their separate capacities for reflection, judgment and planning, which each possesses as a freestanding agent. Rawls assumes that this is the only principle of individuation that one may legitimately employ in deliberating about the basic structure of society. He further assumes that by adopting it we avoid the worst feature of utilitarianism, which he describes as its failure to take the distinction among persons seriously,[14] while simultaneously vindicating the moral devaluation of the natural side of our being that is implied by the idea of talent pooling. More than any other, perhaps, this idea underscores the way in which Rawls' original position functions as an ingenious, choice-theoretic device for expressing the same principle that Kant endorses as the fundamental premise of his moral philosophy when, at the beginning of the *Grounding for the Metaphysics of Morals,* he declares that "nothing can possibly be conceived, either in the world or even out of it, which can be called good without qualification except a good will."[15]

Kant's idea of the human will is modeled on God's. It is the divine element in us. It is the only part of the human soul that exists outside of the

natural order and hence outside of time and thus alone possesses a value beyond price. The will is our passport to the kingdom of ends. It gives us a foothold in eternity, and we must do our best to conduct our temporal affairs in
a way that honors its supreme worth. This is the Augustinian residue in Kant's
moral philosophy and even in Rawls' more thoroughly secularized version of
it, one still hears an echo of the theology that inspired the idea of autonomy
on which he also relies for the moral authority of his position.

Nowhere is the echo louder than in the concluding paragraph of *A Theory
of Justice*.

The original position is merely a thought experiment. But it is the right
one to conduct if we want to think about the most basic problems of political life in a morally defensible way. Moreover, it is an experiment that we can
undertake whenever we wish—from whatever position we happen to occupy
at any given moment in time. When we do, however, we cease to view ourselves and others from the point of view of this or that particular moment.
Indeed, we cease to view things from any temporal point of view at all. Instead, Rawls says, we now see them *sub specie aeternitatis*.[16] We can never escape from time. But a commitment to evaluate the political arrangements
under which we live and to direct our lives in accordance with the principles that are most defensible from the standpoint of the original position,
amounts to a decision to do the best we can to live, in time, from the perspective of eternity.

This is another way of saying that we ought to live in a fashion that honors the eternal part of ourselves, and though we can only do this as temporal
beings, the part we honor by striving to live in this way lies beyond the horizon of time and can never be touched or corrupted by anything that happens
in it. This is the divine part of our nature, and for Rawls, like Kant, the God
of which it is the temporal image is the creator God of the Christian religion,
whose divinity is defined, in contrast to that of Aristotle's or Spinoza's God,
by his supernatural separation from the world he creates.

It is striking that Rawls ends a book that otherwise strives to sustain such
a resolutely secular tone, by invoking the idea of eternity and hinting, at least,
at its saving power. Yet perhaps this is not so surprising after all, for to a reader
who has reached the end of his remarkable work, and considered carefully
the values that guide Rawls' construction of the original position, it must be
clear that these are tied to an idea of eternity, which no serious political
philosophy can do without, and that Rawls' own conception of eternity is
still shaped by the Augustinian God that he accepted in a more explicit way

earlier in his life and whose ghost stalks the disenchanted pages of *A Theory of Justice.*

DIVERSITY

There is no diversity behind the veil of ignorance. Everyone is exactly alike. Or rather, those who agree to evaluate the basic structure of society from behind the veil acknowledge that it is morally imperative to proceed *as if* everyone were exactly alike. To ensure that the differences among people are given no improper weight, the veil makes them invisible. But this is only a dramatic way of emphasizing what anyone who accepts the principle of autonomy already knows—that to treat human beings as free and equal persons means, in the first instance, to disregard the variations of desire, interest, talent, gender, race, ethnicity and belief that account for the diversity among them, so that none of these can be a legitimate basis for the distribution of rights and resources.

Yet merely disregarding the diversity of human beings for moral purposes does not mean it disappears. When the veil is lifted, those who accepted its constraints in order to arrive at a defensible conception of fairness find themselves surrounded once again by the spectacular heterogeneity the veil had concealed from view. Indeed, knowing, as a general matter, that the society for which they are to choose a basic structure will be diverse in many ways is one of the motives those behind the veil have for choosing the rules they do.

The diversity of liberal democratic societies is of special significance in this regard. In part that is because such societies tend to be exceptionally diverse. Even the most rigidly hierarchical caste system is characterized by a variety of statuses and roles. But in a liberal democracy, where every individual has the right to pursue his or her own plan of life, the diversity that results is greater by far. It unfolds in countless different directions, unhampered by the restrictions that limit its growth in other regimes.

The greater diversity of liberal democratic societies is not, however, merely an accidental by-product of the freedoms they afford their citizens. It is something they encourage and honor. It is, for them, a value of the highest importance, one they actively promote and consciously celebrate—which is why Socrates claims that only tyrannies are worse than democracies, for the belief that diversity has any value at all is in his judgment a metaphysical mistake.[17]

Those who defend liberal democracy on the grounds that among all the possible forms of government it is the one that best respects the moral equality of human beings thus face a special challenge. On the one hand, the principle of autonomy requires that we ignore the differences among human beings that account for their diversity. On the other, the freedom and equality this principle entails are themselves justified, in part at least, by the diversity they allow and encourage. Diversity is thus both to be disregarded and valued. How can that be?

To be sure, this is a difficulty that presents itself in an acute form only for those who defend liberal democracy by appealing to the idea of autonomy. But that is today a very large group, of whom Rawls is merely a particularly thoughtful representative. Anyone who shares his conviction that liberal democratic government is best justified on the grounds of a moral ideal that compels us to ignore the differences among human beings, yet is also to be prized for the diversity that a commitment to this same ideal produces, must explain how it is possible to reconcile these beliefs.

To do so, it is first necessary to understand why diversity has any value at all. We know why we value autonomy, on Rawls' and Kant's view of it. The autonomy of the individual is infinitely precious because it secures his or her membership in a supernatural kingdom of ends. The belief that no measure of worldly success can possibly be as valuable as this rests on a political theology inspired by the idea of a God whose divinity is defined by his transcendence of the world, however free of all contaminating religious beliefs the secular ideal of autonomy now seems to those who embrace it. But why do we value diversity?

Broadly speaking, there are three answers to this question. One says that diversity has an evidentiary value; another that its value is instrumental; and the third, that diversity has an intrinsic worth of its own. The first two are compatible with the idea of autonomy. But the third is not. And this is a serious problem because it is only the third that adequately expresses the reverence for diversity that most defenders of liberal democracy claim to feel for the splendor of the differences that result from a commitment to the ideal of a community of free and equal persons.

The first view can be disposed of quickly. It claims that diversity is a value because its presence is evidence that the society in question is a just or fair one. The presence of diversity supports the belief that the process that has produced it has not been distorted by prejudice in a way that is incompatible with a commitment to the equality of human beings conceived as autonomous moral agents. By the same token, the absence of diversity raises a suspicion, at least, that the process has been compromised by bias, and that those disadvantaged by it would be better represented than they presently are among the applicants admitted to selective colleges, the chief executives of leading companies, and the members of Congress, *if* the process that led to their selection had not been distorted by prejudicial beliefs and practices that are indefensible from the standpoint of the ideal of autonomy. This leads to the conclusion that an increase in diversity, whether it is merely encouraged or legally required, is desirable as a remedy for injustice, and when an increase of this kind has been achieved, it is praised as something good because it is presumed to show, in a credible way, that some progress has been made toward a fairer society. From this perspective, diversity is valuable as a sign or signal of fidelity to an ideal that requires us to discount diversity as a source of value. On this view, the value of diversity is entirely derivative from that of the ideal. If this were the only way we had of explaining the value of diversity, a just society whose members were all exactly the same would be as deserving of our admiration as one that was equally fair but diverse.

What I call the instrumental justification of diversity does not lead to this conclusion. Even if everyone were alike, the welfare of each can be increased by a division of labor. So long as resources are scarce, specialization has the potential to improve the well-being of all. This is true whether or not the individuals involved differ with regard to their interests and abilities. If they do, however, the gains from specialization are almost certain to be greater. If everyone had exactly the same abilities, each could refine them to the same degree at an identical cost. But if people possess different abilities, the ratio of investment to yield will also differ from one individual to the next. Specialization will be even more rewarding. It will produce an even greater social surplus than it would in the absence of such diversity. Anyone deliberating behind a veil of ignorance about the character and composition of the society she is to join would therefore prefer one that is diverse, for strictly economic or instrumental reasons.

Both the evidentiary and instrumental explanations of the value of diversity are plausible so far as they go. But they leave something important out of account, for neither justifies the belief that diversity is good in itself, apart from its value as a sign that various rules and procedures are fair, or as a means for promoting the aggregate well-being of society. Neither explains why, in addition to these external benefits, it is appropriate to view diversity as an intrinsic good as well. Yet this is an important, indeed crucial, feature of the democratic reverence for diversity, which expresses the belief that, to some extent at least, a liberal democratic society exists *for the sake* of diversity—

that diversity is one of the *ends* it is established to achieve, and not merely a means to some other goal, like greater fairness or an increase in wealth. It is possible, of course, simply to ignore this aspect of diversity. But that diminishes the worthiness and grandeur of democratic life, as many today conceive it.

To justify this view, it is necessary to explain how diversity can be a good in itself. Rawls himself recognizes the need for such an account and attempts to provide one. It begins with what he calls the "Aristotelian Principle."[18]

It is natural, Rawls says, for human beings to take pleasure in the cultivation of their abilities—to enjoy being able to perform ever more demanding and complex tasks with the powers they possess. This requires training, education, and the like, which in turn depend on the support and encouragement of others. Because it is impossible for any individual to develop to their fullest all the powers he or she possesses, a choice must be made among them. To develop one or some, others have to be neglected. The choice is typically made on the basis of one's interests and talents—of what one enjoys and does well. Because there is great diversity in both regards, the result of following the Aristotelian Principle (which we do by nature, not command) is an equally great diversity of specialized accomplishments, each of which may be thought of as the realization of one small bit of the entire arsenal of human abilities, in which everyone shares to some degree, but that are distributed unequally among different individuals.

Rawls compares the resulting diversity to that of an orchestra.[19] By developing their diverse talents, the members of an orchestra produce an overall effect that would be impossible if each specialized in playing the very same instrument. This is a collective good, like the social surplus that is produced by any division of labor. But more than that, Rawls says, the performance of the orchestra gives each of its members a reason to take pleasure in the separate achievements of the others, because each of these is developing a talent that everyone possesses, if only to a small degree, and therefore satisfying the Aristotelian Principle on behalf of those who lack the talent in question, or have others whose development precludes the refinement of this one. This gives us a reason to enjoy, for its own sake, the diversity an orchestra requires—or more exactly, in which it consists.

In this sense, diversity is an intrinsic good, and the image of an orchestra is meant to explain why. It is an image that reminds the reader of Rawls' earlier suggestion that behind a veil of ignorance, the diversity of human interests and talents must be treated as a common fund, to be exploited for the

advantage of all. But the image of an orchestra puts this diversity in a positive light, and instead of suggesting that we ignore it as a basis for the distribution of rights and responsibilities, encourages us to view it as a source of
greater self-fulfillment for everyone involved. From the standpoint of the ideal
of autonomy that underlies Rawls' description of the original position, diversity must be denied all intrinsic worth. It now appears, in light of the Aristotelian principle that gives the image of the orchestra its normative appeal, to
be a good that we have reason to value for its own sake, because it contributes
to, or rather constitutes, a collaborative state of human flourishing that none
of us can attain on our own, but are naturally inclined to enjoy as an end in
itself, unless crippled by envy.

The combination of these two ideas is very appealing and many no doubt
share Rawls' conviction that it is possible to join them without contradiction.
The first he associates with the philosophy of Kant and the second with Aristotle's moral psychology. From one perspective, diversity has no inherent moral
value. From the other, this is precisely the kind it possesses. It is obvious that
these are importantly different points of view, represented by the image of
the talent pool and orchestra respectively. Yet it may not seem that there is
any fundamental obstacle to combining them in the way that Rawls does,
even though they appear to imply contradictory answers to the question of
whether diversity is a good in itself.

At a minimum, though, anyone who holds both sets of values must explain the relation between them. Clearly, they cannot be of equal rank. If they
were, the intrinsic value of diversity might outweigh the importance of denying it all such value in the choice of a basic structure for society. The outcome
would depend on empirical considerations. But that is unacceptable.

It follows that the relation between the first and second set of values must
be hierarchical. Indeed, even this is not enough to guarantee the primacy of
the perspective that we are required to adopt in assessing the basic structure
of society. To ensure that the principle of respect for the equality of persons
is adequately protected, the relation between these two points of view has to
be lexical. What this means, in theoretical and practical terms, is that diversity can be accorded an intrinsic value only after the principle of respect,
which rests on the assumption that it has no value of this kind at all, has
been fully satisfied and comprehensively embedded in a system of rules for
the governance of our political and social relations. Only then is it appropriate to inquire how society might be organized so as to achieve the aesthetically
inspired ideal of collaborative fulfillment suggested by the image of the or-

chestra, whose appeal depends on assigning the differences among human beings an inherent worth of the sort the moral point of view denies them completely.

This is how Rawls seems to conceive the relation between these two very different attitudes toward diversity. It is also the best way of understanding Kant's view of the relation between them, for though his lapidary statement that only a good "will" is good "without qualification" assumes that other things can be good too, it implies that the goodness of a good will always enjoys an *absolute* priority over every other sort. Indeed, for anyone who adopts the idea of autonomy as a moral touchstone, no other conclusion seems possible.

Again, this may not appear particularly troubling. Why should it not be possible to adopt both points of view, despite their opposing attitudes toward the value of diversity, so long as we assign the first an unconditional priority which assures that *all* of its requirements must be met before we can legitimately attend to *any* of the other's? But there is a philosophical problem which those who hold this view cannot avoid, and that cannot be solved so long as one subscribes to the picture of the soul that underlies the ideal of autonomy, whether its presence is acknowledged or not.

The problem may be put in the following way.

Considered strictly as beings with the power to plan, we are all alike. If our plans, and lives, are different, that is because each of us is working with a unique set of endowments. Some are strengths and others liabilities. Each of our endowments is the product of many different factors, social, psychological, hereditary and the like. Together, they are given to us as the particularizing conditions of our existence as individual human beings.

If our circumstances were identical, there would be less or no diversity among us. More important, if we had no given endowments of any kind at all—if we could frame our lives with the same freedom that, on a Christian view, God creates the world as a whole—human diversity would disappear altogether. Under these inconceivable conditions, there would be no rational basis for choosing to live one way rather than another. All would choose to live the way that God does. The choice of a distinctive life makes sense only on the assumption that, unlike God, we are each compelled to build our lives from a set of materials that we may alter, embellish, refine or disregard, but cannot exchange for any other.

The diversity of human lives thus depends on the heterogeneity of the conditions under which it is given to each of us to live as we think best. If diversity is to have an intrinsic value, we must therefore ascribe it, in some fashion, to these conditions themselves. So long as the value of diversity is thought to be merely evidentiary or instrumental, no real threat is posed to the ideal of autonomy. But if one insists, as many defenders of democracy do, that this is not enough, and that diversity ought to be regarded as an end in itself too, an insuperable difficulty arises, for the very possibility of assigning a value of *this* sort to the given conditions of human life is precisely what the ideal of autonomy rules out as a matter of principle.

Those who adopt this ideal are not required to concede that diversity has no value of any kind at all. But to say that it has *inherent* value—that we should love and honor it for its own sake—conflicts with the assumption on which the moral authority of the concept of autonomy depends. This is the assumption that whatever value the distinctions that give rise to human diversity may have, they possess only in a *derivative and dependent* way, on account of their incorporation in the plans of life constructed by rational agents whose power to form such a plan is the sole independent source of value that can conceivably exist either in this world or (as Kant says) "out of it."

If it is objected that these are merely two different perspectives that need not clash so long as each remains within its proper jurisdiction, it ought to be clear to anyone who considers the matter carefully that this is not a very convincing reply. First, these two perspectives do not have an equal claim to our allegiance. One has absolute priority over the other. Second, there is no third perspective, superior to both, from which conflicts between them can be settled. These must be decided from one point of view or the other, and the principle of absolute priority requires that all be heard and adjudicated from the standpoint of the ideal of autonomy.

This is not an accommodation or harmonization of two different perspectives. It creates no stable division of moral authority between them. It is a formula for domination and an occasion for war, whenever anyone proposes that the differences among human beings, and the given conditions of life from which they spring, should be accorded a value of their own. To claim that from one point of view (represented by the pooling of talents) diversity can have no inherent value, while maintaining that from the other (exemplified by Rawls' multitalented orchestra) it must be assigned a value of exactly this kind, thus amounts to a permanent and irresolvable contradiction, so long as one remains within the moral and political framework that Rawls and many others accept as the best, indeed the only way to account for the legitimacy of modern liberal democratic states.

The root of the problem lies in the dualistic nature of the metaphysics on which the ideal of autonomy rests. In Kant's philosophy, the dualism is explicit. In Rawls' it is more muted. Indeed, Rawls would like to avoid making his theory dependent on any metaphysical commitments at all. But the veil of ignorance enforces a dualism as rigorous as Kant's by separating the power to plan from the countless diverse traits on which human beings are forced to rely in forming the plans they do, and which the veil hides *precisely because* they have no value in themselves and ought not to count at all in deciding what is fair or just in a community of free and equal persons.

Kant assigns all the latter characteristics—our gender, race, ethnicity, talents, disabilities, beliefs and the like—to the natural side of our mixed constitution. It is on account of these that we are not merely rational beings but *finite* rational ones, who must strive to live as morality requires within the limits set by the given circumstances of our lives. But these possess no value of their own. They merely fix the terms of the moral challenge we confront. To meet that challenge, we must strive to live up to an ideal we set for ourselves, not as natural beings, but as supernatural ones whose worth is defined by our membership in a kingdom of ends to which we are admitted on account of our possession of that spontaneous power of self-affection which, though called by different names, is the more or less adulterated image of God's power of creation.

All of this is explicitly stated by Kant. In Rawls' case, it belongs to the background of his thought. It molds his interpretation of the original position like the gravitational field of an invisible star. Yet so long as one subscribes, even if only implicitly, to Kant's dualistic metaphysics and to the supernaturalist theology from which it derives, there is no way to reconcile the belief that diversity is a good in itself, with the claim that democracies depend for their legitimacy on an acknowledgment of the equal rights of all their citizens conceived as free and autonomous beings.

For that, a new theology is required: one that does not depreciate what Kant calls our "heteronomous" nature and the finitude he associates with it, but "appreciates" it instead. This may sound like an extravagant philosophical claim that has nothing to do with the problems of practical life. But that is wrong. If we cannot explain *both* our commitment to equal rights *and* our reverence for diversity as an end in itself, we live in ignorance regarding the compatibility of two of our most cherished ideals. And that is not merely an intellectual failing but a practical danger as well, for those who do not understand why they value what they do, and how their values can be harmonized, are bound to be less well-equipped to protect and perfect the civilization they love.

HOMELAND

A political morality founded on the ideal of autonomy cannot account for the intrinsic value of diversity. It also cannot explain why patriotism has any inherent dignity of its own. The dualist metaphysics on which the ideal of autonomy relies for its authority rules this out as well.

A patriot is one who loves her country with special zeal, on account of its history, culture, values, language and the like. The strength of this love varies. It ranges from sentimental attachment to sacrificial devotion. Often today, it is entwined with a commitment to universal ideals that transcend the country in question. The citizens of most modern democracies love their countries, in part at least, *because* of their commitment to universal principles that apply to all people everywhere. Indeed, any form of patriotism that does not include a commitment of this kind is today likely to be viewed as ethically dubious and politically dangerous.

The difficult question is whether there is anything in the patriot's love of her homeland that is of real value beyond the loyalty it expresses to certain abstract ideals. So long as one's country remains within the bounds fixed by the universal principles of justice, and shows respect for human rights, it is permissible, perhaps even praiseworthy, to feel a special affection for its distinctive culture and history. But the scope and application of these principles are often disputed. When this happens, a question arises regarding the point of view from which the dispute should be resolved. Should it be the point of view of the world community or the necessarily more limited perspective of one's own country instead? To the extent that one gives *any* weight at all to the latter point of view *for no other reason* than that it is one's country, to whose history and traditions one feels a local allegiance that is not the result of reasoned deliberation from a cosmopolitan perspective but of the accidents of birth and acculturation, one necessarily assumes that these arbitrary facts are capable of possessing an inherent dignity of their own in addition to whatever instrumental value they may be assigned from a universalistic point of view.

In extreme cases, this judgment is sometimes expressed by the slogan, "My country right or wrong." But that is a misleading formula because it implies an indifference to universal moral concerns that undermines the legitimacy of patriotism altogether. A better one would be, "Within the range of reasonable dispute, I support my country's position *just because* I love it more than any other." This is true even if I condemn my country's failure to honor its commitment to the universal principles of justice more ferociously than I censure the similar shortcomings of other nations, *so long as* the special urgency I feel to restore its moral standing is founded on an attachment that has no justification other than the accidental fact of my particular connection to it. Yet from the vantage point of a cosmopolitan philosophy that starts by assuming that the legitimacy of every government depends on its respect for the dignity of human beings conceived as free and equal moral agents, the belief that accidents of this sort can have *any* intrinsic normative significance is impossible to justify. To the extent that it rests on this belief, patriotic devotion is as indefensible from this point of view as the claim that diversity is a good in itself.

This is not to say, of course, that patriotism can have no value of any kind from a cosmopolitan perspective. It is easy to preserve a place for patriotic feeling, on certain grounds at least, within a justificatory scheme based on the idea of autonomy. The following thought experiment suggests how this might be done.

If representatives of all the different peoples on earth could be gathered behind the equivalent of a veil of ignorance, they might well agree that everyone would be better off if the world were divided into a plurality of states and if those living within the territory of each devoted themselves with particular passion to its material, cultural and artistic development, much in the way that the members of a family put its welfare first. The representatives at such an imaginary world congress might reasonably conclude that a division of labor of this sort would be likely to produce greater material and cultural riches for humanity as a whole than an attempt to manage the resources of the planet in some more centralized way. And they might also concede that in time the histories and traditions of those living in these various units would inevitably diverge and each acquire a special value for the men and women born and brought up in them, so that a division of labor along the lines I have imagined would be bound to give rise to patriotic feelings, perhaps even quite intense ones. But they could accept these as an aid to stabilizing this division itself, and hence of promoting the welfare of all human beings, so long as the patriotic attachment of each people to its country was confined within a global system of universal norms that prevented it from becoming a source of xenophobia and war.

Viewed from a cosmopolitan perspective, the patriot suffers from a certain kind of blindness. She cannot see and appreciate the value of other cultures in the way she sees her own. Yet her experiential and affective limitations may be exploited as a means for increasing the well-being of everyone on the planet, despite the patriot's parochial preoccupation with the fate of one country alone. Even the fiercest cosmopolitan need not deny that patriotism has an instrumental value of this kind. Still, it would be a mistake to infer that there is anything *inherently* valuable about it. That human beings are limited in their ability to take the welfare of others into account, and tend to give greater weight to that of those who are close to them in looks, location and descent, is merely a fact that must be accommodated in designing a global system that best serves the interests of men and women everywhere, each of whom is equally entitled to a fair share of the surplus that results.

From the patriot's perspective, however, a justification of this sort is likely to seem less a victory than a defeat, for though it leaves room for the love she feels for her homeland, it deprives her country's special history and culture of the inherent value that to the patriot herself is the source of her attachment to it. Like a father who is told that the love he feels for his children is valuable because it helps to stabilize a division of parental labor that is good for mankind as a whole, the patriot whose loyalty to her country is justified on cosmopolitan grounds is likely to feel that its most important feature has been erased.[20]

Is there a way to avoid this result? Is it possible to reconcile the cosmopolitan ideal of autonomy with the love of one's homeland, understood as devotion to a distinctive way of life that is cherished for its own sake and not merely because it contributes, behind the patriot's back, to the promotion of a universal good that assigns no intrinsic value to any way of life at all? Rawls' image of an orchestra suggests an answer here too.

The languages, cultures and traditions of different peoples can be likened to the instruments of an orchestra. Each develops the "musicality" of humankind in a special way. No one people is able to develop them all. The symphony that results is beyond the power of any to produce on its own. It is a surplus whose production requires a cooperative division of labor. Each member of the orchestra (here, each people) has reason to take delight in the accomplishments of every other as something valuable in its own right, just as each delights in the development of its own peculiar gifts according to what Rawls calls the Aristotelian Principle.

Thus, an American may take pleasure in the history and literature of his or her own people to a degree that few Russians ever experience. But the American can still value Russian patriotism as a love for something good in itself—for one of the motifs in the complex song of humankind—and vice versa. On this view, the variety of human cultures and histories, and the special love that each people feels for its own, is more than an instrumental good. It is, for each, an intrinsic good, and one that every other people recognizes and values as such, even though they can never feel the same special attachment to it.[21]

This image comes closer to expressing the patriot's belief that no instrumental argument can ever fully capture the love she feels for her country. But do the philosophical premises of cosmopolitanism allow it? The problem is the same as the one we encountered earlier when considering the value of diversity.

The patriot is attached to a particular country, distinguished from others by its history, geography and culture. His attachment may be more or less reflective. It may express itself in various ways, including a zeal for reform. There are also many different paths to patriotism. Some feel a special affection for their country because they were born there; others, because they came as immigrants or were inducted into its way of life through marriage and the like. But by whatever route he arrives at it, the patriot's love of his country assumes that the unique characteristics that set it apart possess a value of their own. Anyone who denies this makes patriotism unintelligible from the patriot's point of view.

But this is just what the morality of autonomy does. It denies that any fact can ever have a value of this sort. From its vantage point, the accidental circumstances on which the patriot's love of his homeland are founded have no more inherent worth than those that determine his gender, race and talents. If the patriot's feelings are to be justified from this point of view, it must therefore be on an assumption that contradicts the premise on which these feelings themselves are based. Every instrumental justification of patriotism that is constructed from a cosmopolitan perspective has this result. Nor does the idea of a global symphony of cultures solve the problem. Instead of answering the question of how to reconcile the patriot's perspective, from which certain accidents appear to have a value of their own, with that of a cosmopolitan morality that declares they can have none, it simply begs it. In fact, so long as one adheres to this morality, no reconciliation between these points of view is possible, for the same reasons we noted earlier in considering whether the belief that diversity is a good in itself can be squared with the assumptions of Rawls' original position.

Here, as there, the impossibility of reconciling these perspectives is a consequence of the dualism that defines the morality of autonomy itself.

The concept of autonomy, and the cosmopolitan philosophy of international relations that today is one of its most prominent expressions, rests on a picture of the individual (whether a person or community) as a self-determining agent that happens also to possess various natural and social characteristics that confine its range of action but are able neither to create nor to destroy the freedom that alone gives the individual in question its moral standing. When this transcendent power is made the necessary and sufficient condition of the agent's right to be treated with equal dignity and respect, all its other, given attributes are drained of their inherent worth. They do not disappear, of course, nor do they cease to have any value at all. But it cannot be the sort of value that is assumed when one says that diversity is good for its own sake, or defends the patriot's devotion on the grounds that it springs from the love of something whose protection and preservation is an end in itself. These kinds of claims are ruled out by the dualistic conception of the person on which the morality of autonomy depends. Their disallowance is the latter day, secular fruit of the division between the natural and the supernatural that is the original, theological inspiration for this moral and political ideal.

What is wanted in the domestic sphere is a philosophy that justifies a robust regime of rights, such as we have come to view as essential to the legitimacy of any liberal democratic state, *and also* allows for the recognition of diversity as an end in itself. What is needed in the international realm is something similar: a philosophy that provides a compelling justification for the cosmopolitan belief that all people everywhere are entitled to certain fundamental privileges and protections, *yet also* leaves room for the patriot's love of her homeland, as she herself understands it.

Neither the one nor the other is possible so long as our philosophical imagination is constrained by a dualistic metaphysics that is the spectral residue of Christian belief. If we want rights and diversity and patriotism all at once, in a philosophy that does justice to each, we need a new metaphysics, and to construct one that is adequate to the task, we need a new theology too. That may sound like an odd thing to say. Do we not live in an age of disenchantment in which all talk of God has been banished from the public domain? Max Weber emphatically declared this to be the case a century ago. Yet today, as in the past, only a philosophy that connects the individual to something that cannot be measured or valued according to any temporal standard, will ever be able to explain why each human being has a worth beyond price. Kant understood this, and so did Rawls. Their theology is the wrong one. But the cure is not to give up on the idea of God altogether. It is to find a better one instead.

Kant and Rawls account for the sanctity of the individual on the grounds that each of us possesses a power akin to that of the God who brought the world into being from nothing. Is it possible to explain the divinity of human beings in a way that honors the reverence for them that is implied by Kant's claim that we are all entitled to respect as members of the kingdom of ends, and Rawls' contention that to view things from the vantage point of the original position is to see them under the aspect of eternity, *without* the anti-naturalistic consequences that follow from their Christian understanding of the character and source of this divinity itself? That might seem a more difficult task, even, perhaps, an insuperable one, if we did not have before us the example of a writer whose work already contains the theology we need.

I am thinking of Walt Whitman.

CHAPTER 37

Democratic Vistas

WALT WHITMAN AND THE DIVINITY
OF DIVERSITY

Walt Whitman was a poet, not a philosopher. He never presented his ideas in the systematic way that philosophers generally do. Nor was he a theologian in the conventional sense of the term, though words like "God," "divinity," "eternity" and "immortality" appear so often in his poetry that even a casual reader is likely to agree with Harold Bloom's description of the first edition of *Leaves of Grass* as a work of "secular Scripture."[1] Moreover, if it is plausible to think that Whitman's poem does in fact contain a theology, it is perhaps just as reasonable to regard his long prose essay, *Democratic Vistas,* as the sketch of a political philosophy, despite its eccentric approach to the subject.

Still, with a handful of exceptions, few today regard Walt Whitman as a serious political thinker.[2] In part, that is because he writes in a rich and unorthodox style. But there is a deeper reason why Whitman's views seem so remote from the world of contemporary political thought.

John Rawls' celebrated defense of liberal democracy rests on the idea of autonomy. This is the key to his conception of a community of "free and equal persons." The idea of autonomy in turn presupposes a distinction between the natural characteristics of human beings and their supernatural power to shape these into a plan of life of their own choosing. Rawls enforces this distinction by means of what he calls "a veil of ignorance." The details of his theory have been criticized on various grounds. But many political philosophers still follow his lead in assigning the idea of autonomy a pivotal role in their defense of liberal democratic values, and those that do implicitly rely, as Rawls himself does, on a dualistic metaphysics whose roots lie in the theological distinction between the world of finite reality and the transcendent God who creates it by a spontaneous act of will.

There is no hint of this theology in Whitman's writings. Instead, he offers a radically different one whose central teaching is that God and the world are one. Whitman's theology denies the most fundamental premise of every supernaturalist morality, including the contemporary, secularized version of Christian belief that continues to shape the intramural debate among those who seek to explain the meaning and value of our modern democratic civilization by appeal to the idea of autonomy. It is therefore bound to seem peculiar, even unintelligible, from the latter point of view.

The most notable feature of Whitman's theology is the absence from it of any distinction between God and the world. This is sometimes described by saying that Whitman is a "pantheist."[3] But if what one means by pantheism is any view that affirms the identity of God and the world, the term is overly broad, for it can then be applied with equal justification to Aristotle's theology too.

For Aristotle also, the world is divine. There is no God beyond it. In this sense, both he and Whitman are naturalists, not supernaturalists. Yet there is a crucial distinction between their theologies. Not everything in Aristotle's world is divine. Most significantly, individuality as such is not. But Whitman allows no exclusions of this kind. He insists that the uniqueness of every individual is part of the world's divinity too. For him, the God of the world is infinite and all-embracing, not limited, as it is for Aristotle, to the eternal forms of things. Indeed, there is nothing more striking about Whitman's poetry, or more characteristic of the theology that supports it, than his celebration of individuality as something divine in itself. This is the transfigured residue of Christian belief that distinguishes Whitman's conception of God from its pagan counterpart. Something more refined than "pantheist" is needed to capture this distinction. Any reader who has followed me thus far will be unsurprised to learn that I think a better title is "born-again pagan."

Our first task is to understand the main elements of Whitman's theology. It will then remain to see how his idea of God helps us answer the two questions we left suspended at the end of the previous chapter. Is it possible to explain the intrinsic value of diversity in a way that is consistent with a commitment to equal rights? And can a democrat be a patriot too? The morality of autonomy rests on a dualistic metaphysics that makes it impossible to answer these questions in a coherent way. The aim of this chapter is to show that Whitman's born-again paganism gives us the resources we need to do so, and then to explain why a modified version of what Aristotle calls political friendship is essential to the preservation of every democratic community inspired by a reverence for diversity, and by the belief that through our deepening appreciation of it, we draw closer to the infinite God of the world.

"NO TWO ALIKE AND EVERY ONE GOOD"

In what follows I shall focus mainly on the first edition of *Leaves of Grass* (1855). Whitman continued to add to his poem and to revise it for the rest of his life, but all its great themes are present in the first edition, which has a coherence and closure that the final or "deathbed" edition lacks.

We can start with an aspect of Whitman's poetry that brings out with special clarity the difference between his own naturalist theology and Aristotle's.

In his discussion of mimetic art, Aristotle observes that only certain human beings are worthy of serious artistic attention. These are the ones who stand above the rest on account of their birth or character. They alone are suitable subjects for a tragic play or epic poem. Common men and women are not. There is not enough to them to sustain more than a fleeting and superficial curiosity.

This judgment reflects the ideal of human fulfillment that underlies Aristotle's account of ethical life. According to Aristotle, human beings differ in the degree to which they actualize the powers that define the form of humankind. Those that do to a greater degree are more real, and hence of greater interest to us, even, indeed especially, when their lives involve suffering on a commensurately larger scale. About them one can say, "There is a serious (i.e., real) human being." Ordinary people lack such reality. There is "nothing to them" and no serious-minded person would be concerned with their affairs except for comic relief.

Nothing could be further from the spirit of *Leaves of Grass*. There is no man or woman who falls outside the range of Whitman's poetic concern. He takes every one of them seriously, observing each with the same wonder and admiration, judging all with equal regard, "not as the judge judges but as the sun falling around a helpless thing."[4] The most common person engaged in the most prosaic activity is enough to hold his gaze forever. "I could come," he says, "every afternoon of my life to look at the farmer's girl boiling her iron tea-kettle and baking shortcake."[5] Whitman is constantly pausing to observe the ordinary lives of ordinary people with a sympathetic concentration that compels the reader to conclude that something very real and important is happening here.

But these are not the moments that most dramatically convey the breadth of Whitman's understanding of who counts as a serious human being. It is not just ordinary people who do—the farmer's girl and store clerk and factory hand. All the wretched of the earth are worthy of the poet's attention too.

Whitman notices a prostitute, with her "tipsy and pimpled neck." "The crowd laugh at her blackguard oaths, the men jeer and wink to each other." But "I do not laugh at your oaths nor jeer you," he writes. And then, in one of the most remarkable shifts in the whole of the poem, Whitman immediately turns from her abused and degraded condition to the very peak of worldly power, to "the President" in "a cabinet council . . . surrounded by the great secretaries." The latter are as well-regarded as the prostitute is despised.[6] But the poet does not share this conventional judgment. His thoughts are "for the illiterate" as much as "for the judges of the supreme court."[7] No one is unworthy of inclusion in his song. He asks the reader, do you think the "President greater than you?" and answers, you will not be left out of my poem "because you are greasy or pimpled—or that you was once drunk, or a thief, or diseased, or rheumatic, or a prostitute—or are so now—or from frivolity or impotence—or that you are no scholar, and never saw your name in print."[8]

The poet pauses "by the city dead-house by the gate" to observe the "corpse" of a prostitute, her body left "unclaim'd." In the "fearful wreck" of her discarded remains, he sees a "wondrous house," once full of life, greater than "all the dwellings ever built," even the "white-domed capitol with majestic figure surmounted, or all the old high-spired cathedrals."[9] Is there greatness and meanness in the world? Is there goodness and evil? Well then, Whitman declares, "I am not the poet of goodness only . . . . I do not decline to be the poet of wickedness also."[10] His poem is "for the wicked just the same as the righteous." "I make appointments with all," he says. "I will not have a single person slighted or left away, the keptwoman and sponger and thief are hereby invited . . . . the heavy-lipped slave is invited . . . . the venerealee is invited, there shall be no difference between them and the rest."[11]

This attitude extends to nonhuman things as well. Nothing in the entire world is too small or its career too short to escape the poet's reverent gaze. "A mouse is miracle enough to stagger sextillions of infidels."[12] "A morning-glory at my window satisfies me more than the metaphysics of books."[13] "The narrowest hinge in my hand puts to scorn all machinery."[14] And, of course, most famously, "a leaf of grass is no less than the journeywork of the stars."[15]

Every individual, human or not, has an equal claim on the poet's attention, and no amount of study or reflection can do it justice. There is more to each than the poet can possibly say. Reading Whitman, one often feels that he has just looked up from his leaf of grass to notice the field to which it belongs, and beyond that, a world filled with countless individuals of endlessly varied sorts, each clamoring to be noticed and given a place in his poem.

The poet's experience, and the reader's too, is thus one both of exaltation and exhaustion, for if the poet tried to celebrate every individual in the world, as he is called to do, there could be no end to his work—or even a proper beginning. One is perhaps most acutely aware of the limits of Whitman's poetic calling in the endless lists he compiles. These irritate some readers, but convey with mounting energy the poet's urgent sense that he must somehow get around to every individual person, place and thing and do justice to the qualities that make it one of a kind. Every thing is what it is and not another. This is the philosopher's principle of the identity of indiscernibles.[16] For the poet it means that the individuality of each is worthy of observation and study, and none should be neglected or despised merely because it has the particular identity it does. "Do not call the tortoise unworthy because she is not something else."[17]

In Kant's view, too, human beings, at least, are all equally precious. But this is not because of the attributes that distinguish them from one another. For Kant, what gives each a value beyond price is the power of practical reason, which is the same in all who possess it. That is why his morality of autonomy is incapable of assigning an intrinsic value to human (or any other) diversity.

The contrast with Whitman could not be sharper. The idea of autonomy has nothing to do with the poet's passionate belief in the value of the individual. This does not derive from some common power or property that all individuals possess independently of the idiosyncrasies that set them apart. It resides in these idiosyncrasies themselves. For Whitman, diversity is therefore a value in its own right. Indeed, it is a value of such importance that one might call him a prophet of diversity, for whom the celebration of it as an intrinsic good is the supreme task of poetry and politics alike. "I resist anything better than my own diversity,"[18] he writes, referring to the endless and often contradictory curiosities with which he responds to the diversity of the world itself—to that limitless plenum of individual beings, "no two alike, and every one good,"[19] whose infinite variety is the cause of his wonder and the subject of his song.

Kant's idea of autonomy presupposes a distinct theology. It assumes a particular view of the relation between time and eternity. Whitman's reverence for diversity does so as well. But there is a profound difference between these two theologies, from which many other moral and political differences follow. To appreciate how remote Whitman's theology is from that of Kant and his contemporary followers, it is useful to begin by reflecting on the meaning of his arresting statement that "there is no object so soft but it makes a hub for the wheeled universe."[20] What does this image imply?

For Whitman, every individual is "a hub" in two respects. First, it offers a point of view on the world as a whole. There is nothing so "soft"—so inconsequential or quick to disappear—that it cannot serve as an organizing perspective from which everything else "falls into place."

Second, everything in the world is needed for its operation in the way a wheel depends on its hub. Without a hub, the wheel cannot go around. Without the "object" that serves as its center, the "wheeled universe" cannot revolve either. Every individual is therefore not only a perspective on the world, but an essential component of it whose elimination or destruction would bring the world to a stop. If it were removed, the universe would "go off the rails."

To what he calls the "universe" in this particular passage, Whitman gives many other names. Sometimes he calls it the "cosmos" or the "earth." Occasionally, he uses the abstract philosophical term "Being" to describe it.[21] These expressions are synonymous. Each refers to the all-encompassing totality of things that for Whitman constitutes the whole of reality. Whitman is a monist and a naturalist. For him, there is only one world and everything that exists has a place within it. "A few quadrillions of eras, a few octillions of cubic leagues, do not hazard the span, or make it impatient, they are but parts . . . . any thing is but a part."[22] The world is internally diverse, indeed infinitely so. But there is no reality outside of or beyond it, nor does it depend on any supernatural power to bring it into being or keep it there. "There is no stoppage, and never can be stoppage."[23] The reality of the world is self-contained and self-sustaining. "The earth is not an echo."[24]

Each of the countless things in the world exists only for a time. None of its parts lasts forever. This is true of the poet himself. One day his life will come to an end. But the world itself is immortal. It has neither a beginning nor an end in time, and because it is eternal, it is "perfect" and "good."[25]

Both Aristotle and Augustine equate eternity with perfection and goodness as well. The differences between them arise because one puts eternity in the world and the other outside it. Whitman is on Aristotle's side in this debate. He is a naturalist, not a supernaturalist. Yet like all the greatest thinkers, pagan and Christian alike, he knows that no human being can ever be fully satisfied with what Kant calls "merely temporal" things. "To show us a good thing or a few good things for a space of time—that is no satisfaction; we must have the indestructible breed of the best, regardless of time. If otherwise, all these things came but to ashes of dung; if maggots and rats ended us, then suspicion and treachery and death."[26] "Sauntering the pavement or crossing the ceaseless ferry, here then are faces; I see them and complain not and am content with all. Do you suppose I could be content with all if I thought them their own finale?"[27]

The flowing spectacle he sees about him has meaning and value for Whitman only because it is connected to what exists "regardless of time." "The clock indicates the moment . . . . but what does eternity indicate?"[28] Like Aristotle, Whitman finds the eternity he needs to save the faces on the ferry from the "annihilation"[29] of time, in the world and not outside it. But his conception of eternity is more radical than that of the pagan philosopher.

For Whitman, the eternality of the world is present in the individuality of things and in the passing moment. Aristotle consigns these to nothingness. His metaphysics compels him to do so. In his view, the world contains a real element of nothingness (to put it paradoxically), on account of the matter in which the eternal forms of things are embodied. Because time, motion and individuality are all tied to matter, they can have no real share in the eternity that form alone enjoys.

Whitman emphatically rejects this conclusion. Indeed, it is the uniqueness of things and the brevity of their appearance that he is *most* determined to save from nothingness—from "maggots and rats" and the "ashes of dung." Nothing is more characteristic of his view of the world than Whitman's insistence on the immortality of the individual and the eternity of the moment.

"I swear I see now that every thing has an eternal soul! The trees have, rooted in the ground . . . . the weeds of the sea have . . . . the animals. I swear I think there is nothing but immortality!"[30] "[I] peruse manifold objects, no two alike, and every one good, the earth good, and the stars good, and their adjuncts all good. I am not an earth nor an adjunct of an earth, I am the mate and companion of people, all just as immortal and fathomless as my-self; they do not know how immortal, but I know."[31] "Is it wonderful that I should be immortal? As every one is immortal, I know it is wonderful."[32] "Off the word I have spoken I except not one . . . . red white or black, all are deific."[33] "You must habit yourself to the dazzle of the light and of every mo-ment of your life."[34] "This minute that comes to me over the past decillions, there is no better than it and now."[35] "Each moment and whatever happens thrills me with joy."[36] "There was never any more inception than there is now, nor any more youth or age than there is now; and will never be any more perfection than there is now, nor any more heaven or hell than there is now."[37] "Why should I wish to see God better than this day? I see some-thing of God each hour of the twenty-four, and each moment then, in the faces of men and women I see God, and in my own face in the glass, I find letters from God dropped in the street, and every one is signed by God's name, and I leave them where they are, for I know that others will punctually come forever and ever."[38]

"The whole theory of the special and supernatural and all that was twined with it or educed out of it departs as a dream. What has ever hap-pened . . . . what happens and whatever may or shall happen, the vital laws enclose all . . . . they are sufficient for any case and for all cases . . . . none to be hurried or retarded . . . . any miracle of affairs or persons inadmissible in the vast clear scheme where every motion and every spear of grass and the frames and spirits of men and women and all that concerns them are un-speakably perfect miracles all referring to all and each distinct and in its place."[39]

This leads Whitman to the remarkable conclusion that "there is really no death."[40] Of course the poet knows, what each of us could say about ourselves, that "I was not palpable once but am now . . . . and was born on the last day of May 1819 . . . . and passed from a babe in the creeping trance of three sum-mers and three winters to articulate and walk."[41] He also knows that "you and I flow onward" and "in due time" shall take "less interest" in the world.[42] "I shall go with the rest," and die like those before me.[43] But death is not the extinction people believe. It is not even really death. Standing on the grass that forms "the beautiful uncut hair of graves," Whitman asks, "what do you think has become of the young and old men" who are buried here? What has become "of the women and children?" His answer is that "they are alive and well somewhere." "All goes onward and outward . . . . and nothing collapses, and to die is different from what any one supposed, and luckier."[44]

But where does he think the dead are alive? Not in some other world, for there is none. They live on here, in the deathlessness of this world, to which their individual careers make a unique contribution whose significance exceeds what even the greatest poet can know or say about it, and that is as unaffected by the passage of time as the reality of the world as a whole. "I do not think that seventy years is the time of a man or woman, nor that seventy millions of years is the time of a man or woman, nor that years will ever stop the existence of me or any one else."[45]

We are all finite beings. We each have a limited place in the endless procession of things. Yet if we view our lives and those of others under the aspect of eternity, we have an intimation, at least, that their uniqueness and brevity, which seem to cut us off from the world and God, in truth joins us to them on account of these very qualities. We belong to the God of the world, and it to us, not despite but because of our individuality. It is because we are each one of a kind that our diverse contributions to the story of the world are required for its completion, and because of this that we have an indefeasible share, while we live and after we die, in the world's own deathless reality. No one can see this completely or rid himself entirely of the fear of dying. But those who are able even to grasp the point of trying will be rewarded with some understanding, at least, of what Whitman means when he says that "no array of terms can say how much I am at peace about God and about death."[46] This is the joyful reward of his theology, which promises neither an eternal life in heaven, nor a contemplative union with the God of the world that requires us to consign our individual selves to the nothingness of the grave, but something at once more extravagant and more modest: a glimpse of God here and now, in every face and minute, subject to the limitations of insight and feeling that confine the experience of all finite beings, ourselves included.

This makes it possible, indeed necessary, to view diversity in a different light than either Aristotle or Kant can.

For Aristotle, the diversity of the world is inherently valuable, just as the world itself is. The diverse movements of different kinds of things constitute their various ways of sharing in the eternality of the world as a whole. But the intrinsic value of diversity stops, for Aristotle, at the species level. The diversity of individuals has no share in the eternal and divine. It is literally nothing. It has no being and can therefore have no worth.

For a Christian like Kant, the diversity that distinguishes one individual from another is part of God's plan too, and therefore cannot be dismissed as something that lacks reality and value. But the value it possesses is not intrinsic to it. It is due entirely to its inclusion in God's design. It therefore possesses the same kind of derivative value as the content of a person's plan of life, which also has the value it does only because it has been affirmed by the person in question, through an act of will that mimics God's decision to create the world in the first place.

Only a being whose existence is not compromised or qualified by time can possess an unconditional value. The God of the Christian religion, who creates the world, and the person who chooses a plan of life in an analogous way, are both beings of this sort. They are both members of a kingdom of ends that has no existence in time (the first as sovereign and the second as subject). But their relation to the diversity of what they create is an *extrinsic* one. It is not *in* them. It is created or endorsed *by* them, and possesses whatever value it does only on account of the free act of a being whose standing as an immortal member of the kingdom of ends would be exactly the same if the diversity in question did not exist.

Thus neither on an Aristotelian nor a Kantian view of the world is the diversity of individuals of value in itself. Whitman's theology supports, indeed demands, a different conclusion. Because he conceives the world to be eternal, and like Spinoza and Nietzsche, extends its immortality to the individuality of things, their diversity has to be regarded as an aspect or expression *of* the world, and therefore must possess the same inherent value that the world itself does, as the one all-inclusive timeless "Being."

The belief that diversity has a value of this sort and should be celebrated for its own sake is one of the pillars of modern democratic life. But only Whitman's theology provides a foundation for it. Aristotle, Aquinas, Kant, Spinoza, Nietzsche and Whitman all agree that nothing can have any value at all unless there is something that is valuable in itself; that for the value of anything to be self-contained, it must be unconditioned; and that only what is eternal possesses a perfectly independent value of this kind. Their acceptance of the logic of this argument transcends the otherwise considerable differences among them. But only the last three conceive eternity in a way that makes it possible to explain why the diversity of individuals has a value of its own, and only Whitman connects this idea to the aspirations of democratic life.

We shall explore this connection further in a later section. But first it is important to consider another theme in Whitman's poetry that seems, on the surface at least, in tension with modern democratic ideals. I am referring to his understanding of the role of the poet himself.

WHAT THE POET SEES

The poet is a human being like other men and women. He has a body and appetites too. He is carried along by the same current of erotic desire. In this sense, "others are as good as he." But the poet is different because he knows that he is divine and that everyone else is as well.[47]

Most people are absorbed in their romances and jobs and political quarrels. They do not see the divinity in themselves or one another. Time and death appear more real to them than they really are. In this respect, they are profoundly shortsighted.

By contrast, the poet is a "seer." He grasps the eternity that is equally present in the greatest and least of human beings. This is not an eternity that looks "like a play with a prologue and denouement," as it does to an orthodox Christian.[48] It is "in" the men and women the poet observes. He sees them not as "dreams or dots" but eternity itself, whose presence is inseparable from the individual personalities and preoccupations that define the "local habitation" within whose horizon of worry and ambition every one of them is almost always absorbed.

The poet's vision is not confined by any horizon of this kind. It is unconstrained by the petty concerns that limit the sight of everyone else, from the prostitute to the president. The poet is a "kosmos," a world unto himself.[49] He "contain[s] multitudes."[50] He is everywhere at once and sees the god that is resident in all things with a transparency that others cannot achieve because they are blinded by the prejudices that every individual perspective on the world inevitably entails.

The poet is their "tongue," putting into words what they are unable to articulate. "The insulter, the prostitute, the angry person, the beggar, see themselves in the ways of him . . . . he strangely transmutes them, they are not vile any more . . . . they hardly know themselves, they are so grown."[51] The poet is therefore the most powerful man in the world, more powerful even than the president.[52] He possesses a greatness of soul that others lack. He stands at the peak of what Nietzsche calls the "rank order" of being because his poetic interpretation of the world is the most inclusive one possible and therefore the truest, in Nietzsche's sense.

The world would be incomplete if any individual were to disappear from it. But the poet is indispensable in a special way. In particular, he plays a unique role in the expression and fulfillment of our democratic ideals. That is because he alone has the power to show us the spiritual foundation on which these depend if democracy is to be more than a mere accommodation of competing interests or a set of procedures for regulating the conflict among them. The grandeur of democracy lies in its recognition of the value of every individual, and only the poet is able to bring into the realm of articulate speech the eternity that makes every man and woman a divine being, not despite but because of the peculiarities, the deformities even, that set him or her apart from everyone else.

The success of our civilization therefore depends on the poet in a way it does on no one else. What statesmen and philosophers were in an earlier age, the poet is in ours. He is the leader, the voice, the prophet whose direction we must follow if our lives are to be anchored in something more than temporal expediencies that can never satisfy the yearning for a "finale" unconditioned by time. We need the poet in order to live lives of greater depth than the merely comfortable ones that Nietzsche ridicules in his withering description of Europe's "last man." Whitman makes this point repeatedly. It is one of the *leitmotifs* of his poem. But his portrait of the poet as a man or woman of superior power and pride[53]—as a great-souled human being who stands outside the circle of narrow obsessions that preoccupy the rest of us, most of the time—has an undemocratic look, to put it mildly. Can it be reconciled with the egalitarian thrust of Whitman's poetry and his celebration of diversity as an end in itself?

It is clear, at least, that the poet's greatness of soul bears no resemblance to that of Aristotle's man of exemplary virtue. The latter comes closer than his inferiors to realizing a common human ideal. In this sense, he is more real than they, as measured by the one standard that applies to them all. He therefore looks down on those below him as nonentities. He is separated from them by what Nietzsche calls a "pathos of distance." This is the source and spirit of his pride. It is wholly incompatible with the premises of modern democratic life.

Whitman's poet more closely resembles the artist that Nietzsche holds up as the highest type of human being, though here too there is a difference.

Nietzsche and Whitman agree that the world is eternal and that its divinity extends to the least of things—to the spider in the moonlight and the "callous shell" of the "quahaug."[54] Both also agree that the poet's or artist's view of things encompasses more of the God that is present in them, and therefore offers a truer portrait of the world than the perceptions and judgments of other human beings. This is the source of the power that sets the poet apart from those whose lives are the subject of his song. It is the ground of what Whitman calls the poet's "new chant of dilation or pride,"[55] which displays his superiority to all who see and say less than he. Nietzsche strongly agrees. The artist soars above other men on account of the greater comprehensiveness of his picture of the world. Lesser human beings have their place within it. The breadth and beauty of the frame he strives to draw around them is an expression of the artist's will to power, from which his greatness springs, along with that of everything else in the world that stands high in the rank order of being.

For Nietzsche, this has antidemocratic implications. The artist is a master of men. Others should defer to his creative will, and allow themselves to be arranged in the compositions that he alone has the strength to conceive and construct. Some of the most disturbing passages in Nietzsche's writings assert this view with dramatic bravado. But this is precisely where Whitman differs most fundamentally from Nietzsche, for though his idea of the poet as a superior human being rests on a theology that resembles Nietzsche's in certain basic respects, it is meant to be not only compatible with democratic values but essential to their realization.

In Nietzsche's view, the power of the artist is the important thing. Lesser human beings should be subordinated or sacrificed to his demands so that the artist's own glory may shine. Whitman's conception of the relation between poet and people is exactly the reverse. It is true that the poet's power is unique. All others are included in his singularly comprehensive vision of things. But Whitman's poet exists for the sake of the people, not the other way around. He may be more powerful than they, but he sings so that their power may grow, not to aggrandize his own. He understands that every human being is an artist and, potentially at least, as capable of understanding that all things are eternal, each in its own unique way. In Whitman's view, the supreme artistry of the poet is meant to extend that of the ordinary men and women he finds about him, not to draft them into a project of his own devising. Nietzsche at times suggests that every great artist enslaves. Whitman's poet does the opposite. He is a liberator who frees the rest of us to live more poetically—to be more mindful of the divinity of a world that shows its eternal being under a different guise in every face, that of "Cudge that hoes in the sugarfield" as much as "the President at his levee."[56]

The "maker of poems" is the "Answerer." His birth is a "rare" event. Such a one is not born "every century nor every five centuries."[57] But the answer he gives to the question of how we should understand the "whether and when" of human life is intended to set us all free. The poet knows that each moment of his own life is eternal, and he knows, what others do not, that the same is true of theirs as well. This is the good news that he delivers with his "barbaric yawp"[58] and those who receive it "perceive themselves as amid light."[59]

The poet teaches them that they are just as divine as he, "none more and not one a barleycorn less,"[60] that all are equally "deific,"[61] though each in an unduplicable fashion. Once they have discovered their divinity, thanks to the "hymns" of the poet, "the rest" can "never shame them afterward, nor assume to command them."[62] This is a profoundly democratic message. It not only puts the poet in alignment with the spirit of our age, but makes him the means by which its values are secured at the deepest level. Theories of equality that start with the observation that all men and women have similar needs, or the same power of reason, or some other common trait, are shallow by comparison with the poet's teaching that each is immortal and therefore perfect in his or her own special way. There can be no firmer or more lasting basis of equality than this. Every other justification of democracy is therefore bound to seem superficial when measured against the poet's—not useless or false, but less compelling as an explanation of the "wonder" we feel at the spectacle of human diversity, and of the democratic belief that its promotion is something good in itself.

"Of these States," Whitman says, "the poet is the equable man." He is "the equalizer of his age and land." He "is the arbiter of the diverse," bestowing on "every object or quality its fit proportion," seeing more than his fellow citizens do but knowing that each of them is a poet too. The poet is "the key" to our democracy because he alone has the power to open our eyes to the pervasive divinity that is the true ground of the ideal of equality on which our way of life depends. The greatness of Whitman's poet is therefore tempered by an extraordinary affection for others, each of whom he regards as his divine equal, not as material to commandeer for a work of his own. Indeed, his greatness and affection are the same. Every truly noble man or woman is for Whitman a democrat at heart.

Aristotle's great-souled man does not have a democratic bone in his body. The idea of a noble democrat is for Aristotle a contradiction in terms. Nor does Nietzsche's artist have any democratic sympathies either, though the metaphysics on which Nietzsche bases his equation of art with nobility differs fundamentally from Aristotle's pagan theology of form.

Nor, finally, is there any room for the idea of nobility in a political morality that rests on the idea of autonomy. Unlike both Aristotle and Nietzsche, the champions of autonomy are strong defenders of liberal democracy. They insist on the equality of persons. But the capacity for self-legislation which they make the foundation of moral respect is an all-or-nothing thing. It does not admit of grades or degrees. There is no room, in the kingdom of ends, for the development of this capacity from a mere potential into a realized power, and no way of connecting this realm, in a principled way, to that of the natural world, where growth and development are pervasive.

Only a metaphysics like Aristotle's or Nietzsche's, which assumes there is but one world with a hierarchy of states of fulfillment, can accommodate the idea that a human being may be more or less perfect, depending on his or her level of spiritual attainment. Only a metaphysics of this kind can explain why nobility has a value of its own. And only Whitman's version of it is compatible with a reverence for democratic values, because in contrast to Nietzsche, Whitman makes the poet's realized capacity for seeing and celebrating the infinite beauty that resides in ordinary men and women the defining mark of his nobility. In this way, the poet's love of the people, in all their untidy diversity, becomes the substance of his greatness of soul. The celebration of poetry as something out of the ordinary is reconciled with the splendor of every face on the Brooklyn ferry, and the work of the poet made essential to the defense of the democratic belief that diversity is an end in itself.

RIGHTS RECONSIDERED

Walt Whitman's theology strongly supports the modern democratic principle of universal suffrage. Because all men and women are equally "in" God to the same degree, there can be no justification for excluding some from public life, or for allowing a few to rule the many. If one starts with Aristotle's idea of divinity instead, none of this will seem troubling. Aristotle justifies natural slavery and aristocratic rule on the grounds that some men realize to a greater degree than others the common form in which our species-being consists. Whitman's theology blocks this judgment at the deepest level. That is because his God is present in the individuality of every man and woman. This elevates the principle, "one person, one vote" to a position of spiritual authority that neither Plato nor Aristotle could have imagined.

Can the same be said about the principle of equal rights?

Every liberal democratic society accords each of its citizens certain basic rights that cannot be abridged by majority vote. The principle of equal rights constrains that of equal representation and trumps it. Both principles rest on a belief in the equality of human beings, though they express this belief in ways that often clash. Does Whitman's theology provide support for the first principle as well as the second, and explain the conflict between them?

There are two conventional arguments for the establishment of a system of rights. One is based on the concept of interest and the other on that of respect.

The first starts by assuming that the principle of equal representation is the only workable solution to a bargaining problem. Everyone stands to gain through social cooperation. But the division of the surplus that results is certain to be disputed. Each will therefore look for ways to increase his or her share of it. If cooperation is not to collapse, the distribution of shares must be resolved by mutual agreement through a decision-making process of some kind. Since the very question in dispute is whose interests should be preferred, any rule for participating in such a process that gives the views of one participant greater weight than those of others will be rejected out of hand. Hence even if each believes that his or her own interests are the worthiest or most urgent of all, everyone has reason to accept *ex ante* the principle, "one person, one vote."

But once such a process is in place, individuals and groups are able to form coalitions to expropriate the shares of less powerful members, up to the point where the benefits of collaboration for the weaker participants just exceed its opportunity costs. If this happens, the advantages of having an equal vote disappear for those whose shares are taken. Knowing in advance that this is a real risk, the participants will all agree that each possesses certain assets (including liberties or freedoms) that cannot be taken away even with his or her consent (to protect against the danger of being put in the position of having to choose between relinquishing these assets and something even worse). The result is a system of rights that limits the permissible bargaining space within which debate over the division of the social surplus is now allowed to proceed.

Many find this a convincing explanation and there is nothing wrong with it so far as it goes. But for those who believe that liberal democracy is more than a rational compact among warring egos and insist that it expresses a moral ideal as well, this first, interest-based account of rights is bound to seem incomplete. This is the deficiency that Rawls' theory of justice is meant to repair.

We have examined Rawls' theory in detail. There is no need to recapitulate it here. For our present purposes, it is enough to note the following.

All human beings have needs and interests. The political process is a forum in which we pursue these in a cooperative fashion and seek to resolve the conflicts that arise when we do so. Yet we are also members of the kingdom of ends. When we view ourselves in this light, it is not our needs and interests that matter, but the capacity for critical reflection that gives whatever choices we make their moral dignity as the expression of a supernatural power that transcends all our characteristics as natural beings.

It is imperative that our moral dignity be protected at all costs. This must never be sacrificed to the accidents and exigencies of a political process that is set up to satisfy our interests and needs. It is appropriate that this process be based on the principle of equal representation. No other principle is compatible with the moral equality of the participants as members of the kingdom of ends. But that is not enough. The process must also be constrained by a system of rights that limits what can be done even by a supermajority. Some political outcomes are offensive to the dignity of certain members of the community because they express a view of them that denies their equal moral worth as rational beings—for example, by discriminating against them on the basis of race or gender. The moral integrity of democratic government therefore requires that the principle of equal representation be supplemented by a system of rights that protects every citizen against any form of discrimination that is incompatible with the recognition of his or her equality as an autonomous agent (an abstract standard that is often exceedingly difficult to apply in practice).

A political philosophy that explains the principle of equal rights by appeal to the idea of respect, introduces a moral dimension that is missing so long as one seeks to justify it on the basis of interest alone. But the morality it adds has a limited reach. It may be invoked to defend the enforcement of those side constraints that keep the political process within legitimate bounds and to support the protection of civil rights generally. Apart from this, however, it has little or nothing to say about the moral value of the decisions that individuals make, in the political arena or outside it, as to how best to live their lives. In particular, it assigns no inherent value to the diversity of these decisions themselves. From a Kantian or Rawlsian perspective, this is just the result of many morally equal persons acting in a nondiscriminatory fashion on the basis of divergent interests that possess no intrinsic moral worth of their own.

Whitman's political theology does not have this limitation. His identification of the individuality of persons and things with the immortal God of the world ensures that their diversity possesses a value of the greatest conceivable kind. But Whitman also emphatically endorses the egalitarian political norms that Rawls' morality of autonomy so strongly supports. He condemns every form of political or social subordination and insists that no one should ever think of him or herself as the natural inferior of another. This is unsurprising, given Whitman's belief in the divinity of every human being. But how, in particular, is the value of a system of *rights* to be explained on the basis of his theology? There is nothing in Whitman's writings that might be called even the beginning of a theory of rights. So we must make the effort to construct one in the spirit of his born-again paganism, which conceives the divinity of human beings not in the supernaturalist terms that Kant and Rawls do, but in the tradition of Spinoza and Nietzsche instead.

We can start by noting the obvious. If Whitman's theology assumes that every man and woman is *in* God, it also rules out the possibility that any individual can ever encompass the *whole* of the world's divinity. Each of us is inherently divine, but in a distinct and therefore limited way. In the first respect, I am as immortal as the world to which I belong. In the second, I am destined, as Whitman says, to pass from the stage, and while I live remain subject to errors and illusions of all kinds.

These are not, moreover, separate components of my being. I am not an infinite being *attached* to a finite one—an eternal soul joined to a wasting body. In reality, these are identical, though that is hard to grasp. Could I see the world with the poet's eye, I would understand that my individuality, which is the source of my liability to prejudice and error, is itself a part of the divinity of the world as a whole.

The difference between my mortality and my immortality is therefore not a real one. It is not grounded in the nature of things. It is a difference of outlook—a distinction between two ways of viewing the same thing. Spinoza describes this as the difference between conceiving something under the aspect of eternity, on the one hand, and that of time on the other. For Whitman, it is the difference between viewing the world from the nonjudgmental standpoint of the poet who sees God in every man and woman, however ordinary or even disgraced, and seeing it from the partisan perspective of a human being who is simply going about the business of life.

We are constantly shifting back and forth between these two points of view. At moments, we have an intimation of the infinite reality of every human being, ourselves included. We glimpse the God in which we and others have a place not despite but because of our differences. But these moments are rare.

Most of the time, we are preoccupied with needs and interests that put us in conflict with others. We love our friends, fear or hate our enemies, and make all the mistakes that a preoccupation with our parochial concerns is bound to produce. It cannot be otherwise. As beings whose divinity *is* their individuality and not something separate from it, we are always capable of seeing the God in us and others more clearly than we do at present, yet at each stage are confined by limitations we can never overcome. That this is so is reason for both caution and joy.

In the realm of science, the appropriate combination of these attitudes is nicely expressed by Spinoza's image of the worm in the blood. The world is infinitely intelligible. There is nothing in it that surpasses understanding. But since every attempt to comprehend the world must do so by means of laws whose generality leaves something out of account, the pursuit of understanding can never come to an end. The intelligibility of the world will always exceed our knowledge of it. We tend to forget this, however, and, like a worm in the blood, identify our partial and limited comprehension of things with the whole of their reality. To guard against this inevitable mistake, we need to remind ourselves, especially at moments of joyful discovery when our knowledge and power are growing, that we remain infinitely short of the goal we long to reach.

Rights play an analogous role in political life. A democracy that extends the vote to all gives everyone an opportunity to share in the power of government. But when this power is actually acquired by one group or party or class, those who have it are more likely to confuse their own peculiar interests and partisan conception of the public good with that of the community as a whole, and be tempted to impose their view of things on those whose needs and values differ. Greater power increases the risk of this confusion, in politics as well as science.

To some extent, of course, the exploitation of political power is perfectly normal and largely unobjectionable. Why else would one pursue it if not to advance a favored cause, often at the expense of others? But the establishment of a system of rights helps to protect against the worst abuses of political power, which are aggravated by the inevitable tendency to identify the general good with one's own interpretation of it.

The existence of a system of rights limits the power of those who happen to be in control of the government at any moment in time. It guarantees that no one can be stripped of his or her freedom to own and transfer property; to move about as he or she wishes; to speak and publish without fear of suppression or reprisal. It guarantees that each shall be treated by police, prosecutors and judges on the same terms as everyone else; continue to have an equal say in the election of representatives; and never be compelled to accept, even voluntarily, a condition of permanent subjection to others. The list is long and the precise content of each item on it a matter of endless debate. But the general meaning and function of a system of rights is plain enough. Its purpose is to provide a bulwark against the excesses of enthusiasm—to temper the confidence of those who believe they have grasped the truth completely and are therefore justified in doing to less enlightened men and women whatever it allows or demands. A system of rights is an institutionalized expression of the principle of modesty in political life. If the first task of a new democracy is to assure that everyone gets the vote, the second, which must be undertaken simultaneously, is to establish a system of rights that protects against the dangers of immodesty to which all political power, and especially that of a democratic majority, exposes those who possess it.

One can therefore justify the need for a system of rights on the grounds that it serves as a buffer against the natural tendency of human beings to confuse their finite view of the world with the infinite reality of the world itself. One can also defend it in a Rawlsian spirit as an expression of the moral principle that all persons must be treated with equal respect on account of their membership in a supernatural kingdom of ends. But there is a fundamental difference between these two justifications. The first permits, indeed demands, the recognition of diversity as a good in itself. The second does not. And this has important implications for how one views the relationship between the existence of a system of rights and the highest aims of democratic life.

A democratic government must assure that "all possess the right to vote."[63] It needs to provide "for the police, the safety of life, property, and for the basic statute and common law, and their administration." These are "always first in order."[64] Moreover, it must do what it can to promote "the safety and endurance of the aggregate of its middling property owners."[65] None of this is easy or uncomplicated. "Universal suffrage" in particular creates "appalling dangers." It makes government hostage to "the people's crudeness, vice, caprices."[66] And so long as "certain portions of the people [are] set off from the rest by a line drawn," or "not privileged as others, but degraded, humiliated, made of no account," the protections afforded by the law remain dangerously incomplete.[67] This requires constant vigilance and continuing reform. It is a task that can never come to an end and must in one sense precede all others, for until a stable political and legal framework has been put in place, no democracy has even the chance to endure.

But though it must come first chronologically, the establishment of a framework of this sort is not the "mission" of democratic government.[68] It is not the end for which democracies exist. "To be a voter with the rest is not so much."[69] Nor is material prosperity, widely distributed and within the reach of all, however important this may be to their welfare and morale. These are goods, but they are not the *final* good for whose sake universal suffrage, a system of rights and protection of the middle class must be secured. The highest good of democratic life is something that Whitman repeatedly describes as a "religious" principle instead.[70]

In a democracy, human beings appear as an "aggregate,"[71] an indistinguishable mass. They are not divided into distinct classes or castes, as in feudal or aristocratic regimes. But every single member of this mass is distinguished by his or her "precious idiocrasy and special nativity."[72] Each is utterly unique, distinct from all the rest, "soaring its own flight, following out itself."[73] This is the source of that "perfect individualism" that "deepest tinges and gives character to the idea of the aggregate."[74]

"In the moral-spiritual field," Christ stood for the idea that "in respect to the absolute soul, there is in the possession of such by each single individual, something so transcendent, so incapable of gradations (like life), that, to that extent, it places all beings on a common level, utterly regardless of the distinctions of intellect, virtue, station, or any height or lowliness whatever."[75] Whitman embraces this idea, but with a crucial modification. For those who follow Christ's teachings, the "absolute soul" that gives each individual a value beyond price is something separate from the body. It is the same in everyone because, once worldly differences are set aside, nothing remains but the uniformity of spirit that exists apart from the realm of bodily being. For Whitman, there is no distinction between body and soul—any more than between God and the world. The "transcendent" personality of the individual is *in* his or her peculiar bundle of interests, passions and talents, not *beyond* it, and if all stand on a "common level," that is because the divine "something" that every man and woman possesses is in each case unique.

The supreme goal of democracy is to promote the development of the uniqueness of every individual—in Whitman's words, to "vitalize man's free play of special Personalism."[76] The "moral-spiritual" ideal of a regime devoted to this end may therefore be described as one of individual perfectionism.[77]

To understand what this means, it is helpful once again to contrast Whitman's idea of perfection with Aristotle's.

For Aristotle, perfection means approximation to a type—the fulfillment of one's nature as a being with a makeup of a certain kind. It follows that all great-souled men are alike. Their greatness lies in their outstanding virtue, which consists of various habits that are identical in all who possess them. It has nothing to do with their "special nativity."

Whitman also believes that every human being has the potential for greatness, though only a few realize it to a significant degree. Most are consumed by their daily activities and do not see the immortality that surrounds them on all sides. Many are deformed by prejudice, hatred and the like. Only the poet understands how immortal they all are, the wicked along with the good. He alone comes close to fulfilling the potential for divinity that even the worst possess. He stands at the top of the order of excellence, like Aristotle's great-souled man.

But for Whitman, the God that resides in each of us is not a form that all men share in common. It is an "idiocrasy" that distinguishes each from the rest. Far from being sloughed off on the way to perfection, as Aristotle imagines, it is the very thing whose divinity must be grasped and perfected, so far as one can. This last idea is an inheritance from the tradition of Christian belief. When it is joined to the naturalist belief that God and the world are the same, the result is Whitman's "idea of perfect individualism."[78]

This idea confers a higher spiritual value on democratic life.[79] Its pursuit is the end for which democracy exists. But how is progress toward it to be measured? Aristotle's perfectionism assumes a common standard of achievement. By individualizing the idea of perfection, Whitman rules out the possibility of a standard of this kind. Yet that does not mean he has no criterion of any sort for measuring the degree to which different men and women succeed in realizing their "special nativity."

In broad terms, their success is measured by how closely they approach the standpoint of the poet. In contrast to Aristotle's great-souled man, who looks down on others with aristocratic hauteur, "the greatest poet hardly knows pettiness or triviality." "If he breathes into any thing that was before thought small it dilates with the grandeur and life of the universe."[80] This is Whitman's benchmark of perfection. He defines it as a combination of sympathy and pride. "The greatest poet does not moralize or make applications of morals . . . he knows the soul. The soul has that measureless pride which consists in never acknowledging any lessons but its own. But it has sympathy as measureless as its pride and the one balances the other and neither can stretch too far while it stretches in company with the other. The inmost secrets of art sleep with the twain."[81]

We must learn to take pride in our distinctness—to "own" those qualities that set us apart from others. This can happen only if we see ourselves through the eyes of the poet, for whom our individuality is something divine. But we must learn to recognize the same immortality in everyone else—to see that their individuality is just as divine as our own. If we fail to take pride in ourselves, we become vulnerable to the pathologies of self-hatred. We are filled with envy and the longing to be someone else. By the same token, if we are swollen with self-regard and incapable of seeing the greatness of others—if our deficiency is one of sympathy rather than pride—our lives are diminished by the symmetrical pathologies of prejudice and xenophobia. "Whoever walks a furlong without sympathy walks to his own funeral, dressed in his shroud."[82] The pursuit of perfection is the struggle to achieve both attitudes at once.

This is a peak that can never be reached. Our limitations are too great for us ever to attain it. But we can make continual progress toward the cosmic vision of the poet, and as we do, each increase in our powers of perception and appreciation is accompanied by joy. The experience of joy in this sense is the highest good that democratic life has to offer. It is the source of its spiritual greatness, and those who pursue it discover opening before them the prospect of an ever-deepening encounter with "Being" which, though shadowed by disappointment and certain to end in defeat, "dilates" without limit, as they soar together toward the God of the world in which each has his or her "pride and centripetal isolation."[83]

A system of rights secures the space for the pursuit of this ideal. It protects against the ever-present danger that some, whose sympathy has not kept step with their pride, will seek to expropriate or humiliate those they regard as their enemies or inferiors. Nothing can ensure that pride and sympathy grow "in company," as the poet says they must. Where the first outstrips the second, laws and the police provide a barrier against harm. But this is not an end in itself. The "core of democracy" is its "religious element."[84] The freedoms of democratic life and the rights that guarantee them exist so that the men and women who enjoy their protection may better see their own divinity and relish that of others. They exist so that each may appreciate that everyone is "just as sacred and perfect as the greatest artist."[85] And because their perfection is in the "spread" of the "body"[86] that joins each to the "earth" in a singular way, its recognition and enjoyment produces a reverence for diversity as an end in itself that is impossible so long as one equates the divinity of human beings with their possession of an unearthly power of self-legislation whose proper acknowledgment demands that everything else about them be hidden behind a veil of ignorance.

The theology on which this latter view is based allows for a morally inspired account of the basic structure of liberal democracy. But it cannot explain the love of diversity as an intrinsic good of the most exalted kind. This is the end for the sake of which democratic government exists. To explain it a different theology is required—one that supports the need for universal suffrage, and laws, and rights, and the apparatus of the state, but which places all these in service to "a sublime and serious Religious Democracy"[87] that gives its citizens the God they need to be able to say, on occasion at least, as the poet does all the time, "each moment and whatever happens thrills me with joy";[88] "the frames and spirits of men and women and all that concerns them are unspeakably perfect miracles all referring to all and each distinct and in its place";[89] my "thoughts are the hymns of the praise of things."[90]

Before they can say or even think any of this, people must be free from hunger and pain. They have to be unburdened by laws that humiliate and demean them. They need to be secure in their rights. Yet beyond all these preliminary goods, there is another and still greater one. Its pursuit is the highest good of democratic life. But even to see it, we must leave the religion of autonomy behind. We have to abandon "the whole theory of the special and supernatural"[91] and follow Walt Whitman's lead toward the religion of the "earth," in whose divine diversity every single human being has his or her immortal place. This is "the finish beyond which philosophy cannot go."[92] Only when we reach it do the democratic vistas that lie before us begin to appear in their true range.

PATRIOTISM AND ROMANTIC LOVE

Walt Whitman loves every man and woman in the world. There are no limits to his longing to see and touch them, to join his flesh to theirs. He would "turn the bridegroom out of bed and stay with the bride" and "tighten her all night" to his "thighs and lips."[93] He is drawn with indiscriminate passion to the male as much as the female, the bad along with the good, "the homely as well as the handsome."[94] He makes love to them all with his words.

Whitman's poetry throbs with a cosmic Eros unhampered by convention; unconstrained by time or place; unlimited by the stature or condition of its object. The same polymorphous passion animates his love of democracy, which rests on the assumption that every human being possesses the kind of unique appeal that only a lover can see.

But if Whitman is a promiscuous "lover" of the "earth" and all it contains, he is also "an American"[95] who loves his country in the discriminating way that one friend loves another. He is a patriot who feels a special attachment to his homeland.

In part, that is because he views America as the best example in the world of government "of, by and for the people." In the years ahead, Whitman says, the idea of democracy will be embraced on an ever-widening scale. There can be no reversion to the "feudal" and "ecclesiastic" forms of earlier ages. Democracy is on its way to becoming the universal condition of humankind. Still, he insists, "the individuality of one nation" must "as always" lead the way.[96] It falls to America to do this. America must show the world what a civilization founded on the principle of democratic rule can be. Whitman's belief that America has a historic role in this regard is one source of his special devotion to it.

But it is not the only or even the most important one. For Whitman, America is more than the leading example of a universal political ideal. It is a country with its own unique physiognomy and character, and it is mainly on account of these that he loves it as much as he does. He loves America's geography—its rivers and mountains and farms and cities, from Maine to Louisiana to the Oregon coast. He loves the peculiar character of its people, their restlessness and commercial bustle. He hears its special voice—the sound of America "singing."[97] And he loves America's heroes, who have given their lives for its sake. He takes joy in retelling their stories.[98]

In short, Whitman loves America the way a lover loves his beloved: not as the embodiment of some general trait but as an individual with "looks" unlike those of any other, which excite a passion in the lover that can never be explained by any list of attributes, because it is directed toward something unique. This is the deepest source of Whitman's patriotism. It is not merely different from his admiration for America as a leader in the global movement toward democracy but in tension with it, for while the latter puts the emphasis on a principle, and defines the value of American exceptionalism in terms of something abstract, the former reverses the order of affection and puts the love of America as an individual first.

This raises an obvious question. How can Whitman be an indiscriminate lover of every person, place and thing, and yet be attached to one country and its people with the special passion he feels for America alone? Whitman's ideal of democracy assumes that every human being ought to be viewed with the eyes of a lover. But patriotic love is exclusive. It is discriminating by nature. It assigns a value to one thing that it ascribes to no other. If Whitman's religion of democracy rests on a cosmic love that regards the whole earth and everything in it as equally perfect and good, his patriotic love of America is founded on an attachment whose focal intensity seems incompatible with the refusal to stop "one place" rather than "another"[99] that for Whitman is the spirit of democratic life. How can these two sorts of love be reconciled? Is it possible to be a democrat in Whitman's sense and a patriot too?

We have seen how the tension between the universal ideal of human equality, on the one hand, and the exclusive loyalty we feel toward those with whom we share a particular political fate, on the other, is resolved by a cosmopolitan philosophy that rests on the assumption that the equality of human beings is a consequence of their membership in a kingdom of ends defined by its separation from all worldly appearances. From this perspective, the fact that one happens to belong to a particular people is an accident with no more intrinsic value than the color of one's hair. Distinctions based on national identities may thus be accorded a measure of authority only insofar as their recognition helps to promote the establishment of a regime of universal human rights predicated on the equal moral dignity of all men and women. It may be easier to enforce a regime of this kind through a localized division of labor in which the responsibility for protecting human rights is shared among a number of smaller political communities, to each of which its own citizens feel a special loyalty. But from a cosmopolitan point of view, it can never be legitimate to love one's country *just because* it has the peculiar historical, cultural and physical looks that it does.

Those who do are guilty of more than a metaphysical mistake. Their patriotism is a principal source of the aggression and xenophobia that have caused so much human suffering over the ages. Cosmopolitanism is appealing because it offers an antidote to these pathologies. Yet the renunciation of patriotic love as anything more than an instrument of universal moral advancement destroys its meaning from the patriot's point of view. Many may be prepared to make this sacrifice. But for those who love their countries with a patriot's heart, the embrace of a cosmopolitanism inspired by Kant's ideal of moral dignity is likely to be accompanied by a sense of loss, even, perhaps, of betrayal.

By contrast, Whitman writes as if his own form of democratic patriotism involves no sacrifice of this kind. He seems confident that his love of America in particular and of mankind in general are not only compatible but reinforcing. Yet he never tells us how these two forms of love, one exclusive and the other all-embracing, can be reconciled without treating the first as a means to the second, in the way that cosmopolitanism does. But the answer is not far to seek. The same theology that explains why for Whitman diversity is a good in itself also accounts for his conviction that one can be a lover of humanity as a whole, and at the same time passionately devoted to a particular people or place.

It is easiest to see this if we begin by recalling what was said earlier, in a different context, about the nature of romantic love, which bears a suggestive resemblance to the democrat's love of her homeland.

For Plato, the love of a man or woman is always, at bottom, the love of a general form the beloved embodies in a blurred and transient way. According to Plato, it is a mistake to think that there can ever be anything loveable about an individual as such. For Aristotle too, the best sort of love that one human being can feel for another is of something general, namely, the good character that all men of virtue possess, as distinct from the idiosyncrasies that set each apart from the rest.

The idea of divine creation upsets the metaphysics on which Plato's and Aristotle's pagan conception of love is based. If God created the world from nothing, then the individuality of the man or woman I love is as much a sign of God's divinity as the general laws that govern the world as a whole. It follows that by committing myself to this one individual and "forsaking all others," I am not turning away from God, but loving him as he appears in the guise of one of his unique creatures.

Still, it would be a mistake, or rather a sin, to think that what I find so attractive in my beloved is something that any human being possesses on his or her own. That is idolatry. The Christian conception of love assigns a value to the individuality of the beloved in a way that Greek metaphysics forbids. But at the same time it requires us to view the love we feel for other men and women as an instance or expression of our love for the eternal God who created us all, and teaches us to accept, as Dante eventually does in the *Paradiso,* that the first will be left behind when we come home to God in the life after this one.

The romantic idea of love is the Christian one without the God that sustains it.

A romantic lover loves the one he does because the beloved is one of a kind. It follows that no list of properties can ever adequately express the meaning of such love. There will always be more for the lover to say. If, as Plato supposes, the love in question were directed at some set of ideal traits, it would be possible, in principle at least, to give a full account of it. But the beloved is loved because he or she is unique. All the concepts the lover might use to describe his feelings are general in nature. They must therefore always fall short of the mark.

This distinguishes the romantic from the Platonist. But the romantic is not a Christian either. He feels no need for a God beyond the world to explain his attachment to the one he loves. Indeed, from a romantic point of view, the Christian idea of love is uncongenial. It depreciates the earthly love that individual human beings feel for one another by inviting us to view it as an inferior version of the heavenly love that awaits us at the end of days. The romantic insists that his love stands on its own. He swears that he has glimpsed something infinitely precious in the man or woman he loves. He knows that he shall never have more than a glimpse of this, or love it as well as he longs to do. Yet he declares that his goal is to be as close as one lifetime permits to the individual whose inexhaustible presence has captured his heart. For the romantic, there is no end beyond this, and the suggestion that his imperfect love ought to be measured against the perfect one that both the Platonist and Christian imagine is bound to seem a kind of infidelity.

Each of these three conceptions of love defines its target as something eternal. In this sense, all three are theological. They differ because they define the divine goal of love in different ways. This is obvious in the case of the classical and Christian conceptions. But the romantic idea of love rests on a theology too. Its most rigorous formulation is that of Spinoza, who equates God with the world but extends its divinity to the individuality of things, as distinct from the general properties they share with others of their kind (or appear to share, from the limited perspective of any finite observer).

On this view, the unique identity of every individual is also part of the divinity of the world. None is more or less "in" God than any other. To love God adequately it is therefore neither necessary to leave individuality behind, as the Platonist maintains, nor to separate the divine target of one's love from its human object, in the way the Christian distinction between creator and creature compels us to do.

The Spinozist distinction between substance and mode rules out a separation of this kind. It fuses the finite and the infinite in such a way that the first can only be understood as the inadequacy with which every individual component of the world represents its participation in the eternality of the world as a whole, under the limiting categories of time. This is the theology of romantic love, which is defined by the longing for a consummation that one can approach ever more closely so long as life lasts, yet never fully express or even conceive.

One of the most characteristic experiences of those who live and love by this ideal is the feeling that their attachment to the beloved is both fortuitous and fatal. On the one hand, it is easy to imagine that one might have fallen in love with someone else. On the other, it is unthinkable that things could have turned out differently. Life without this particular man or woman is inconceivable, so that the luck of finding him or her, among so many, seems a piece of fate.

This contradictory pair of beliefs becomes less puzzling if we keep the theology of romantic love in mind. On this view, the individuality of every human being is a part of the divinity of the world. Each therefore provides as good a point of access to it as any other, so that the choice of one rather than another seems arbitrary. Yet only by devoting himself exclusively to a single human being can the lover even begin to see, however incompletely, that the God of the world is present in the individuality of things and not merely their common forms. For the romantic lover, the uniqueness of the beloved thus comes to be associated with the perfection and necessity of the world as a whole and to share these attributes too, though even the most observant and devoted lover can never see them except in what Spinoza calls a "mutilated" way.

This last aspect of romantic love sets it apart most fundamentally from its Platonic and Christian counterparts. For a Platonist, to love an individual *on account of* his or her uniqueness makes no sense at all. For a Christian, to love another human being because he or she is *part* of God is a form of idol worship. Yet romantic love demands just this combination of beliefs. The beloved is a one-of-a-kind part of the God of the world.

The same theology that distinguishes romantic love from these other two is also the source of its most striking vulnerability. The fusion of divinity and individuality on which such love depends can corrupt it by encouraging the thought that no one else's love is as good or great. The acknowledgment that it is threatens the exclusiveness of the attachment on which the romantic lover has staked his pursuit of the eternal and divine. The more deeply I come to appreciate the divinity of the one to whom I give my love exclusively, the stronger my imagination must be to see that others view the ones they love in the very same light. And of course the passions of jealousy and envy make matters worse, the first by threatening the expectation of reciprocal exclusiveness on which romantic love is based, and the second by lowering the value of my own love through a demeaning comparison with that of others.

Yet this does not always happen. Indeed, the reverse is more often the case. As a rule, the experience of loving one person above all others is more likely to be strengthened than compromised by the discovery that others do the same. Most romantic lovers love a good love story. That is one reason why the novel, which as a literary genre is preoccupied with the ups and downs of romantic love, is so popular in an age that understands the meaning of human intimacy in these terms. So far as romantic love is concerned, the tension between its celebration of exclusivity and the recognition that every man and woman in the world is worthy of being loved with such devotion, seems on the whole rather modest. For many romantic lovers, these attitudes are not opposed at all but mutually supportive.

The same is true, potentially at least, for those who embrace Walt Whitman's brand of democratic patriotism.

The patriot is moved by a special attachment to her homeland. She loves it not in the way a cosmopolitan might, as the instrument or illustration of a general idea, but for its own particular looks. Her devotion to her country has some of the exclusivity that all romantic love does. Yet as a democrat she is moved by the belief that every human being is an equally immortal expression of the all-encompassing divinity of the world in which each has a singular place. For her, this is what gives every democracy, including her own, its spiritual value, and makes it something more than a voting rule or system of civil and political rights.

The patriot knows that she cannot love every community on earth with equal ardor. She understands that the God of the world can only be approached from a local point of view. But she also knows that those who do not belong to her community are in the same position too, and unless blinded by ignorance and hate, will be inspired by their devotion to the countries they love in the same way that a romantic lover is inspired by others who love as exclusively as he. She knows that the divinity of the world can never be exhausted or even depleted by any partisan interpretation of it, and is filled with joy rather than fear by the presence of "foreigners" who love their countries with as much fervor as she loves her own.

The crucial thing is that her patriotism and theirs be imbued with Whitman's democratic religion, which affirms the immortality of every individual, not as an indistinguishable member of some supernatural kingdom of ends, but an utterly unique expression of the God of the world in which every finite being inheres. This is a supremely difficult consensus to achieve, and immeasurably harder in political than in personal life. In part, that is because political communities wield vastly greater power than the tiny ones constituted by a romantic lover and his beloved. The more power a community possesses, the greater the temptation becomes to make the attachments that bind its members together a basis for judging the value of the different loyalties on which other communities are based. And of course the temptation to do this increases exponentially so long as others are inclined to do the same (as they always are to some degree). To be sustainable even in one country, the spirit of democratic patriotism must therefore eventually be present in all.

This is a distant ideal. Who knows when we shall reach it? In the meantime, the most we can reasonably hope to achieve is the establishment of an international order based on a widening respect for human rights and the gradual delegitimation of aggressive war, reinforced by a belief in the value of toleration as a principle governing relations among peoples as well as persons. We are far even from this, which must be our first priority.

But however urgent these goals may be, we should not confuse them with the highest end of democratic life. That lies beyond the ideals of toleration and respect, which are compatible with a disinterest in the distinctiveness of others, or even an antipathy to it. The supreme goal of democratic civilization is the endless strengthening of what Walt Whitman calls his "amative" spirit—a cosmic love for the divinity of each and every individual, moderated by the sober recognition that, as finite beings, we can begin to approach the God that dwells in all things only through that concentration of attention and affection that in personal relations we call romantic love, and in political ones patriotic devotion. This is the "religion" of democracy. It leaves room for a form of patriotism that is compatible on its own terms with the most devout commitment to universal equality, and explains why the democrat's love of her homeland is a locus of human fulfillment. Toleration and respect are merely a way station on the path to this higher ideal, and those who confuse the first with the second lose sight of where we should be going and why.

FRIENDSHIP FOR DEMOCRATS

The difference between these points of view is theological.

Those who regard the establishment of a regime of rights as the highest goal of political life explain the dignity of human beings by their possession of a capacity for self-direction that transcends the natural world and allows them to act from a position outside it. From this point of view, the characteristics that account for our diversity have no value of their own. What is divine in us is not in them. They are a hindrance to the recognition of our better selves, and an embarrassing reminder of how far we are from the God we distantly resemble. That on an orthodox Christian view we depend on God's grace to overcome our shameful condition, and for our salvation from it owe thanks to God in a measure we can never adequately express, intensifies the feelings of self-loathing that result from the devaluation of everything finite in our composite nature. Even in the fully secularized versions of this theology that have so many defenders today, feelings of this sort are still at work, though their strength is masked by a superficial cheerfulness that belies their continuing influence.

The morality of autonomy enables us to overcome the finitude of our condition in the only way we can—by denying that it has any meaning or value of its own. It brings us as close to a position of omnipotence as we shall ever be in the realm of political life and thereby fulfills the not-so-secret wish to take God's place. In the West, this wish has acquired an unprecedented intensity on account of the demands the Christian religion makes on its own adherents. The modern *Rechtsstaat* is an expression of this wish. It is the most far-reaching method of social and political control that human beings have ever devised. But the same theology that has been such a powerful stimulus to its construction has also been a source of spiritual misery too, for it has left us with no way of valuing ourselves except by imagining the human world, with all its splendid diversity, from a point of view that is theologically hostile to it.

For a theological problem, there is only a theological cure. The one that is needed is clear. God must be put back into the world. The supernaturalist theology that lies at the root of the idea of autonomy must be replaced by a naturalist conception of the eternal and divine.

It is hopeless to think we can do this by resurrecting Aristotle's God. His pagan theology affirms the divinity of the world and human nature, but at

the expense of our "special Personalism," whose value disappears in his conception of God as form. This is no longer something we can accept. The only
theology that today is capable of restoring the greatest possible value to what
men and women do on earth is one that places the God of the world in their
individuality as such.

This is Walt Whitman's theology. It supports the principle of political
equality in a way that celebrates rather than obscures the inherent value of
human diversity. It explains the idea of human rights without denigrating
human nature. It allows for a form of joy that compensates for the disappointment that comes with it. And it holds the key to understanding the meaning
of political friendship in a modern democratic state.

Aristotle defines political fraternity as the spirit of devotion that holds the
members of a city together, over generations of time, in a common venture of
lawmaking, whose aim is to secure a space of rationally constructed order in
a world that otherwise operates according to natural principles that no one
consciously conceives or intentionally maintains. It is only in an artificial space
of this sort that human beings are able to acquire the virtues and study philosophy, the two distinctively human ways of sharing in the everlasting and
divine.

A city is the work of many hands. No one can build or sustain a city by
himself. We are therefore dependent on others for the existence and preservation of the space in which it is alone possible for us to live the best lives that
we can. The appropriate attitude toward those on whose care and nurture we
depend for this is one of "gratitude for goodness received." Such gratitude is
offered not in satisfaction of a debt but as an act of love on the part of those
who give it. And it can be adequately expressed through acts of caretaking
on behalf of others, who depend as much on our imperfect human love as we
do on that of those who came before us in the life of the community to which
we belong.

A modern democrat inspired by Whitman's ideals feels bound to her fellow citizens by a similar spirit of solidarity. She believes in the sacredness of
the multigenerational project that they have undertaken together. She knows
that its true end lies not in security and wealth but human perfection instead.
With them, she seeks to raise the ideal of democracy from a legal to a religious
one, by means of what Whitman calls a "prudence suitable for immortality."[100] She feels grateful to her predecessors for the contributions they have
made to the enterprise in which they are engaged, and reasonably hopes to
do as much and as good for those who follow. She is not weighed down by

the thought that her thanks are due to a God for whose gifts she can never be thankful enough.

These two conceptions of political friendship—the Aristotelian and Whitmanian—nevertheless differ in important ways. The most basic concerns their relation to diversity.

Every political community is internally diverse. But this is not, in Aristotle's view, the reason why its members are friends. They love one another because they are joined in a venture that allows them to pursue a good life whose defining characteristics are the same in every city. The virtues of a great-souled man do not change from place to place, nor do the truths of philosophy. Diversity may be an inevitable fact of political life, but its recognition and enjoyment is not the end for which such communities exist. It is not an element or ingredient of the good their members seek to achieve. It does not inspire the affection they feel for one another; if anything, it is more likely to undermine the spirit of solidarity by weakening their shared understanding of the nature of the good for whose sake they have established a common life together.

Whitman's view is different. The members of a democratic community ought to love one another, he says, *on account* of their diversity. For them, diversity is more than a fact. It is a value of supreme importance. It is what their democracy is *for*. A democracy exists *in order that* its citizens may perfect their individual temperaments, interests and talents, and take increasing pleasure in the diversity that results. The idea that everyone (or at least the best) should conform to a fixed pattern of living is antithetical to this belief. All should strive instead to live like the poet, whose love of diversity is the inspiration for the ties of friendship that join them. The more they are able to see the differences among themselves in the spirit he does, the closer they become. In this sense, one might say that for Whitman, political friendship is founded on diversity, whereas for Aristotle it exists despite it.

This difference is related to another.

Whitman's democratic ideal can never be fully achieved. It is always a work in progress. The friendship of those bound together by their devotion to it is therefore a commitment to pursue an endless task of individual and collective perfection. Once the divinity that human beings strive to experience in the realm of political life is equated with their diversity, it is no longer possible for any community of finite beings to fully attain it. The good for whose sake such communities exist becomes a regulative ideal and the solidarity of those in them a function of their shared attachment to it.

This contrasts in a fundamental way with Aristotle's conception of the good of political life and of the friendship founded upon it. His is a good that can be perfectly realized at any moment in time. That is because it is defined in formal terms. It follows that the goal of politics is not an endless progress in perfection but stability instead, and that the friendship of those devoted to the protection and perfection of their city rests on the ideal of a changeless regime. Nothing could be further from the aspirational dynamism of a democracy enlivened by Whitman's ideals.

A third difference is worth noting.

Political friendship is always local. It exists among the members of a particular community—Athens, not Sparta or Corinth; America rather than France or Japan. As a result, it is always possible that a conflict may arise between the loyalties such friendships engender and responsibilities of a more general kind. Aristotle recognizes this possibility and discusses it at length.[101]

The distinctive laws and traditions of the city to which a good man belongs do not enter into Aristotle's definition of the virtues he possesses. But it is precisely these laws and traditions that a good citizen is prepared to defend with his life. His willingness to do so is what *makes* him a good citizen and anchors the friendship he feels for others who are willing to do the same. The obligations entailed by a friendship of this sort sometimes conflict with the requirements of virtue in general. This is the predicament of a good man caught in a bad regime.

A modern democrat may of course find herself in the same situation. Nothing guarantees that the laws of her country will always be fair or its culture inspired by the combination of pride and sympathy that Whitman extols. But Aristotle's metaphysics creates a conceptual conflict between political friendship, on the one hand, and human excellence on the other that Whitman's democratic ideal avoids.

Because he defines virtue in formalistic terms, any friendship based upon the culture and history of a particular community can only be accidentally related to the meaning of human perfection itself. For Whitman, by contrast, these are internally connected, ideally at least, in a healthy democratic regime. They are joined by his theology, which confers on the individual as such a spiritual value that Aristotle's equation of being with form rules out. This makes it permissible, indeed necessary that human beings seek their perfection not beyond or alongside the localized love they feel for particular individuals, but *in and through* it. This is the essence of romantic love in all its

forms, including the sort a democrat in Whitman's sense feels for her homeland and those with whom she shares it. Here too, the criteria for being a good
citizen and a good human being may come apart for all sorts of practical
reasons, but there is no *metaphysical* conflict between them of the kind that
Aristotle's nonromantic ideal of perfection entails.

The modern, democratic form of political friendship that Walt Whitman's
poem encourages and exemplifies thus differs importantly from the Aristotelian conception of it in several related ways. All of these are explained by the
shift from a pagan to a born-again pagan theology that equates the divinity
of the world with its endless diversity. But Whitman's idea of political friendship nevertheless resembles its ancient counterpart in one crucial respect, for
it too is essentially humanistic.

The citizens of a modern democratic state whose laws and culture are inspired, however incompletely, by Whitman's poetic ideal are engaged in a
project of infinite duration. Their goal is not merely to pacify one small corner of the earth and to guarantee the rights of those who occupy it. It is to
establish a way of life that enables its participants to realize, so far as they are
able, their potential to see the immortality that dwells in the uniqueness of
each and every one of those with whom they share the venture.

In this respect, democracy is like romantic love, except on a larger scale.
In a two-party romance, each experiences the other's love as a gift to which
the only appropriate response is one of thanks. In an analogous way, the citizens of a modern democracy feel bound to one another by special ties of
affection and likewise regard the bonds that join them as an expression of
love, not the product of a bargain or exchange.

The second sort of love is weaker and more diffuse than the first. Yet just
for that reason it is able to take in those who are absent or dead, with a passion that resembles, in a diluted form, the one that at its most intense is the
defining characteristic of every two-party romance. Moreover, those who feel
grateful for the love they have received are always in a position to do as much
and as good for their successors, whose line extends into an endless future.
Of course, their love for their successors is bound to be as fitful and imperfect as their predecessors' was for them. That is because everyone involved is
a human being. But this is not a badge of shame. It is not the sign of something fundamentally flawed in our condition, and there is no standpoint beyond the world from which we might judge it to be such—a perspective of
the sort that many philosophers urge us to adopt when they insist that the

ultimate goals of political life can only be justified on the basis of a moral theology that devalues the natural circumstances of human flourishing, including our dependence on the gift of love.

Yet if there is no vantage point beyond the world from which to declare our humanity a disappointment or disgrace, there is a worldly standard that enables us to measure how well we succeed as the friends of those, dead, living and unborn, with whom we find ourselves engaged in our particular adventure in democracy. It is a standard that is internal to the human condition itself. One might call it the horizon of our humanity—the perfection of the divinity that is in us already, waiting to be realized, though we shall never do so completely. Seen from this point of view, our finitude is not something foreign to God. It does not stand outside the circle of eternity. It is the way God looks under the aspect of time. Put the other way around, it is the way our limitations look under the aspect of eternity. This is how the poet of democracy strives to see all things. Even he falls short in the end. Yet those who embrace his ideals and work to sustain them experience the world as a home, and know the joy of being in it, so long as their desire to comprehend their unique and immortal place in the infinite and eternal order of things continues to be more richly fulfilled.

This is the only sort of homecoming that a finite being can ever know. It is less complete than the one that Aristotle's philosophy offers. It is fraught with a disappointment that is antithetical to the substance and spirit of his pagan theology, which no thoughtful man or woman today can responsibly embrace. But it is also not the homelessness of the Christian pilgrim or his nihilistic descendent.

The morality of autonomy that many today regard as the best justification for our modern world of rights is a secularized version of Augustine's theology of pilgrimage. It is infected with the same embarrassment at our condition that underlies Augustine's conception of man's relation to God. And its continuing authority as a political ideal helps to explain why the gratitude we need in order to be able to love the world as well as we can has been devalued as part of a general campaign to free ourselves from the burdensome limits of our own human nature, which prevent us from becoming the other worldly God we long to be.

This latter-day Augustinian morality is a recipe for despair. It defines the ground of value in a way that makes it unintelligible in principle, since autonomy cannot be understood without ceasing to be what it is. It separates this ground from the world by a metaphysical divide that makes it impossible to explain how what Wordsworth calls "the splendor in the grass" can ever have any value of its own. And it condemns us to self-loathing on account of its demand that we judge our worth from a point of view completely foreign to the human condition. This is the unhappy state to which many critics of modernity believe we are condemned. But that is only because they do not see that their judgment is shaped by the supernaturalist theology whose demands are still spectrally present in the regnant public morality of our day.

Nor do they see that in Walt Whitman's religion of democracy we have ready at hand a different theology that avoids all these ills.

Like Spinoza's more philosophical version of it, Whitman's ethics of endless empowerment avoids the separation of intelligibility and value that inevitably follows if one locates the ground of value in a power of choice whose defining characteristic is an absolute spontaneity that is lost the minute its decisions become even potentially understandable. For Whitman, the value of an action or life is measured by how much of the eternity that resides in all things it comprehends and enjoys. Its value is a function of enlightenment. No one can ever be fully enlightened. There will always be a gap between the perfection we seek and what we are able to accomplish with our limited resources. But this gap is different from the one that the Christian idea of the will and its secular expressions guard so fiercely. The latter anathematizes even the effort to understand the ground of value by defining it in such a way that its power to confer value on anything at all is equated with its own unintelligibility. The former, by contrast, explains our inability to comprehend the source of all values as a natural consequence of our limitations as finite beings, which it is equally natural for us to strive to overcome by increasing our understanding and enjoyment of a world whose divinity and intelligibility are one and the same.

This opens the way to a humanism that remains beyond reach so long as we weigh ourselves on the scale of a God apart from the world, from whose point of view we shall always be ingrates, unable to return in adequate measure the one love that really matters. Walt Whitman's born-again paganism does not make us better than we are. What theology could? It sees that people suffer; gives encouragement to those who work to improve things; and acknowledges the disappointment that inevitably accompanies our yearning to draw closer to the infinite God of the world. But it offers these judgments from a human point of view that neither denigrates our condition by comparing it with that of an omnipotent creator, nor elevates it by promising that one day, in a life to come, we shall be perfectly healed and our love of eternity wholly fulfilled.

For an unrequited gratitude to God, it substitutes the familiarly fallible forms of thankfulness that men and women feel for one another as helpmates in the endless project of enlightenment that constitutes the soul of the modern age, which, so far from being disenchanted, is suffused with a sense of connection to the everlasting and divine. This is the homecoming for which we yearn. It is neither more nor less than anyone may reasonably desire, as a finite being in an infinitely wonderful world. And most surprising, perhaps, to those who believe that modernity represents our estrangement from God, it is a homecoming we have already achieved, like that of Leopold Bloom at the end of his long and tiring day.

DAYS AFTER TOMORROW

What does any of this mean for the practical problems we face today? It is hard to see how a new theology could help us understand and address them.

In the early years of the twenty-first century, religion has become a more dangerous and destructive force in global politics than many would have thought possible twenty-seven years ago, when the Berlin Wall came down and the Cold War with it. What we need in our public life today, it seems, is less theology, not more. Perhaps in some unimaginably distant future, religion will no longer divide us into warring camps. But that day is far off. What we urgently need now is a practical inventiveness remote from the speculative precincts of theology—including Walt Whitman's benign but ethereal religion, which is likely to seem, even to those who admire it most, useless as a guide to understanding or addressing any of the difficulties we now confront. Their complexity and global scale have no precedent in human history. In our attempt to devise intelligent and effective responses to them, can it possibly matter how, or even whether, we think about the meaning of God?

But perhaps it does matter, more than the realist thinks. I offer climate change as an example.

The problem of climate change has two unique features that make it unlike any other that human beings have faced before. The first is that, though its effects may well be catastrophic, they appear so gradually as to fall below the threshold of political attention at any given moment in time. The time horizon that is needed to comprehend the gravity of the problem and to frame a meaningful response to it is vastly greater than our normally shortsighted political imagination allows.

The second is that everyone on earth is touched by climate change. There is no one whose life is unaffected by it. Nor is there anyone whose actions do not contribute to it in some measure, whether as a producer or consumer of goods whose manufacture adds to the carbon in the air we all breathe. The problem is global and any conceivable solution to it must be global as well.

Together, these two features of the problem explain why our current political arrangements are so ill-adapted to deal with it. The short time horizon within which politicians everywhere act and decide, together with the division of the world into sovereign states that put their own interests before those of mankind in general, make the problem of climate change peculiarly resistant to diagnosis and cure. The difference between this problem and the one posed by the existence of nuclear weapons is instructive in this regard.

With the advent of nuclear weapons, it became clear that the continued existence of life on earth was now up to us. We saw that we were living in a new age that some have named the "Anthropocene," in which the survival of nature has for the first time become a human responsibility.[102] So far as nuclear weapons are concerned, we have done a reasonably good job of meeting this responsibility. But that is only because their effects have been demonstrated with a vividness that is impossible to ignore, and because their possession has been limited to a handful of nations, so that the existing system of sovereign states has made it easier, rather than more difficult, to control them. In both respects, the problem of climate change will be far harder for us to address within the framework of our political institutions, as these now exist.

Of course, for the moment, we have no choice but to try. We must look for ways to ameliorate the problem, in the world as it presently stands. Even this requires a great deal of political imagination. For the foreseeable future, though, our efforts are likely to be hobbled by the provincialism that is an inevitable consequence of the modern state system. This means that international cooperation will tend to focus on distributive issues, and in the absence of a global authority with the power to resolve them, these are bound to be an obstacle to what, from a planetary point of view, represents a more intelligent response to climate change. The fact that the leaders of each country can retain their own power only by providing short-term benefits that their constituents are able to see and measure naturally makes matters worse.

No one should expect any of this to change soon. For the time being, the most we can hope for are multilateral treaties, trade taxes on carbon inputs, national investment in new, environmentally superior technologies, and the like. But if we are to take even these preliminary steps "with all deliberate speed," our attitude toward the problem must change as well.

For anyone who thinks about it even for a moment, three things should be clear. The first is that the technological revolution that produced the problem of climate change was itself made possible by a new science of nature that has extended our knowledge of the world to an unprecedented extent and is today the universal possession of humankind. The second is that the only solution to the problem is more and better science, which must proceed on the assumption that the world is intelligible all the way down, and that the limits of the science we now have lie in our inadequate understanding of the infinitely complex nature of things. The third is that we must pursue this goal, which has no end in time, as the inhabitants of a planet that does.

The prospect of climate change has made us acutely aware of the mortality of our planet. Before, its death seemed so far off that we ignored it; now it seems much closer and more real. Climate change therefore reminds us that we share not one but two things in common: the science we must employ to meet it, and the finitude that creates the problem in the first place, which no amount of science can ever overcome.

Each of us, rich or poor, educated or not, is a member of the scientific community. Only a few may become so in an active sense, but none are excluded altogether. Science is the prerogative or privilege of no one in particular and everyone has an equal share in its discoveries, which even the greatest geniuses make only because their minds, like those of everyone else, are part of a world whose order is open to all.

Yet also like everyone else, the most brilliant scientists are able to know the world only obscurely, because no finite being can do more than that. We are finite participants in an infinite reality and while we live, we must strive to see the God of the world as clearly as we can. This is the heart of Spinoza's ethics. He thought of it as an ethics for rare souls. But Whitman believed that ordinary men and women ought to have the same ideal. He called it democratic and made it the basis for a modern form of patriotism that celebrates the divinity in every human being, while acknowledging those special ties that bind us to those with whom we share a particular portion of the earth.

Paradoxically, this attitude may today be easier to sustain on a planetary than a national scale. Science is the way we now experience eternity in a world from which the older gods have vanished. Our participation in it, as inventors or consumers, hallows all of us alike. Yet the changes in our atmosphere that we have caused by our own actions, and whose effects we must now use science to repair, make it clearer than it has ever been before that our condition is mortal in an irremediable sense. Science connects us to the eternal and divine. It seeks an unconditional knowledge of things in which the earth long ago lost its privileged place. But we must learn to use it here, on behalf of the homeland we share. We must become science-loving, eternity-dwelling, patriots of the earth, who reject both the obscurantist views of those who say that science is the enemy of God, and the comforting but juvenile thought that our mortality here is merely the prelude to eternal life somewhere else.

This is a novel, indeed unprecedented way of thinking about our global relations and responsibilities. If one were looking for a model, Spinoza's image of the worm in the blood would be a good one. So would Whitman's poet, who sings the divinity of all things in the local vernacular of the country he loves. And while it may seem far-fetched to suggest that a similar way of thinking is beginning to emerge in response to the problem of climate change, many of the young people who will lead the global campaign to address it in the years to come appear at times to see things in this light. While that by itself cannot bring about a dismantling of the current state system—nor is it obvious that we should wish it to—it can and will change the spirit in which we practice our politics on an international level, and bring us closer to the born-again paganism that Spinoza and Whitman recommend as the best way to be near to God, within the limits of the human condition.

Changes of this sort are deep and slow. Others must come first. But life without God is not only unbearable. It is unthinkable. We cannot make sense of what happens in time unless we are able to relate it to something that does not. This is the meaning of God in the most basic and permanent sense of the word.

The need for God in this sense is as imperative today as in the past. But unless we can meet it in a way that supports and is supported by our most deeply held political, scientific and aesthetic beliefs, we shall never be content. Yet it is possible to do this. Indeed, it has already been done. Spinoza, Nietzsche and Whitman show us how.

Many, perhaps, still need the reassuring comfort of a personal God who directs and judges our lives from a standpoint beyond the world. But gradually, steadily, and one day finally, this God will be replaced by another, just as he replaced the God of the Greek philosophers. That revolution took centuries to accomplish and this one may too. But one day, days after tomorrow, the particular moment in which we now live will seem, as Nietzsche said, the twilight of a discredited theology whose own travails have already given shape, in the womb of our most cherished modern beliefs, to a new God that fulfills our longing to be, as fully as we ever can, at home in the world again, joyful in the shadow of death, which comes to us all, and even to the planet that carries us along on its own mortal ride.

"Downward to Darkness, on Extended Wings"

My mother died while I was writing this book. She was ninety-six and had lived a mostly happy, mostly healthy life.

A week before she died, my mother was sleeping, as she did much of the time. She awoke with a start and grabbed the arm of the woman who was sitting by her bed. My mother looked at her intently and spoke with an urgency that suggested she had something important to say. "The world comes back," my mother said. Then she said it again. And that was it. The message had been conveyed.

My mother lived another week. I held her hand when she died. But she was beyond the point of being able to explain what she meant by these emphatic and mysterious words. Everyone in my family has an interpretation of them. The mystery of their meaning was my mother's last bequest.

Perhaps the most reasonable interpretation is that my mother's final days were crowded with memories of the earlier worlds of her life—the world as it had been when she was young, or middle-aged, or old but not yet dying. All these worlds came back to her at the end. Indeed, at times they were more than memories. They were as real as the room in which she lay.

But I have another interpretation. My mother was obsessed with the mystery of life. She was not a religious person, in the conventional sense of the term. But she was struck by the essential strangeness of our condition. That once we did not exist, and soon no longer will, that we live in the brief space between two eternities: can anything be odder than that?

When my mother said, "The world comes back," perhaps what she meant is this—that the world, from which we are separated at birth, returns to reclaim us at death, that it leaves no stragglers behind. Melanie Klein, with whose reflections I began this book, puts it in the following way. Before we are born, we are the world. Then, for a time we are separate from it and struggle against it. And then, when we die, we become the world again. "The world comes back." And of course it is only in the interval, in the time between birth and death, that the world that released us and will soon reclaim us is an object of wonder, and we ourselves along with it.

What can be more wonderful than life? For the most part, we pay no attention to it. It is the most familiar thing in the world. But we have all found ourselves reflecting, from time to time at least, on the incomprehensible fact that our lives are bounded on both sides by nonexistence, and wondered how it can be that we possess such marvelous powers of thought and feeling, which carry us to the ends of the universe, but only for a lifetime, whose boundaries are narrow and fixed. The meaning of everything we do and experience with these powers is a function of the mortal limits within which we possess and enjoy them. If our mortality were somehow erased, the meaning of human life would vanish. We cannot even imagine what this would be like. The whole of Kant's philosophy is a meditation on this fact. His thoughts are often difficult to follow. But the mystery that provoked them is our most common possession, and the one that gives our lives their depth and wonder.

In this sense, it is death that makes life wonderful. This is one way of understanding what Socrates meant when, approaching death himself, he told the young men gathered around him that philosophy is the practice of being dead.

Socrates had something specific in mind. He wanted to convey, in a vivid way, the idea that so long as we judge things according to our senses, we shall never grasp the truth about them. This belongs to the immortal forms in which visible things have only a limited and passing share. To see these forms, we must die to the world of the senses. We have to learn to live as if we were no longer alive.

When Socrates said that a serious person who wants to understand anything at all must practice being dead, he therefore meant to promote a particular set of metaphysical beliefs. But we can reject these beliefs (indeed, I think we must) and still appreciate the wisdom of his remark, for it is only by taking death seriously that life becomes serious too. It is only when we ask "What does it mean to die?" that we are moved to look up from the preoccupations of life and notice how mysterious it is. No one can do this uninterruptedly. Rochefoucauld famously remarked that thinking about death is like looking at the sun. But no one can avoid the question either, or fail to see that it gives life a depth that cannot otherwise be guessed.

The question "What does it mean to die?" is equivalent, then, to another that seems its opposite, "What does it mean to live?" Asking how one should think about death and orient him- or herself toward it is only the most serious way of asking how one should live. If we do not often think about death that means we do not often think about life with the seriousness it deserves. The failure to do this is not a philosophical shortcoming. It is something more personal than that. The question of how one ought to live is the most personal question that anyone can ask. The sign of this is that the failure to take it seriously is a loss of a kind that only the one who fails to ask it can possibly suffer.

Having taxed the reader's patience with a long and abstract book, I want to conclude with a few words about this more personal question.

There are two ways of thinking about life and death that will be familiar to my readers. Many, perhaps most, subscribe to one or the other. There is also a third, less familiar way of understanding the relation between them. It is the view that was taught by the main schools of ancient philosophy. One sometimes hears its echo today. None of these three ways of thinking about death from the vantage point of life, which is the only perspective we have on it, seems to me an adequate response to the mystery they seek to explain. The question is whether there is anything else.

Let us consider the last of these three first.

Plato and Aristotle disagreed about many things. But they both believed that it is possible to grasp the meaning of eternity while one is still alive. Our lives have a beginning and end in time. Yet while we live, our minds, if we use them properly, enable us to grasp the timeless order of things. This does not release us from death. But it makes it insignificant. When we think, we are beyond death. We dwell with what is deathless. Indeed, we become deathless ourselves. Aristotle puts the point succinctly. The best life, he says, is one devoted to thought, and when a man reaches the peak of thinking he becomes the God of the world on whom his attention is trained. Of course, he cannot remain there forever. This is what mortality means. But it means nothing more than that. In particular, it does not mean the loss of anything of real consequence because one has already taken complete possession of the thing that matters most—however brief the possession may be. There is nothing to be understood about the eternal order of the world that one does not fully comprehend in the moments of contemplative achievement that define the lives of those who succeed in solving the mystery of life and death.

The Stoics and Epicureans and Neoplatonists all taught something similar. Amidst the wonderful refinements of ancient philosophy, this common theme can be heard to its end: that the limits of mortality have no significance for us because even within them we are able to completely understand the immortality of the world, in relation to which our birth and death have no meaning.

The ancient philosophers thought of this as an intellectual achievement. They viewed it as a triumph of mind. Others, then and later, have seen it in more emotional terms, as a triumph of feeling—as an inexpressible mood of expansive well-being in which one senses, for a moment at least, one's identity with the world as a whole. In this second, mystical version of their teaching about the meaning of life and death, the ancient philosophers have had successors in all the Abrahamic religions, though the views of these religious mystics, which combine intellectual and emotional elements in varying proportions, have generally been regarded as heretical from the point of view of more orthodox believers. The many different, often nondenominational forms of mysticism that even in our disenchanted world still attract their share of followers ensure that this way of thinking about life and death remains a serious option, as it will always be.

The defect in all these views, it seems to me, is that they put too much confidence in the possibility of overcoming the gap between mortality and immortality. They all assume that it is possible, briefly at least, to get eternity into time, without remainder. This is especially clear in Aristotle's case, which is why I have devoted so much attention to his views.

If, as Aristotle says, the eternity of things resides in their forms alone, and if our minds are able to comprehend these forms without the matter in which they are embodied, then they can encompass the whole of eternity. Our minds can grasp all the immortality there could ever be, and for a short time at least become one with the God of the world. But this underestimates how much immortality there is. The Abrahamic religions have taught us to believe that individuals have a timeless value too. Today, this idea plays a foundational role in every branch of modern culture. Even those who scoff at the true believers who still pray to a God beyond the world embrace the idea that every individual is infinitely precious. Aristotle's distinction between form and matter allowed him to confine the immortality of the world to a certain aspect or dimension of it, and thereby to assume that our human minds are able to wrap themselves around it completely. But the doctrine of creation, which dissolves this distinction, releases immortality from these narrow limits, and ensures that the gap between the finite and the infinite can never be closed. In this way, it undermines the confidence of every view, philosophical or mystical, that affirms the possibility of transcending the limits of life while we live.

There is an obvious response to this dilemma. The idea of an omnipotent God beyond the world, which is the source of the problem, itself suggests a solution to it.

We can never get our mortal minds completely around the infinite and immortal order of things. Yet it is possible to view what limited insight we have into this order, while we are alive, as an intimation or anticipation of the complete understanding we shall one day possess in another life to come. The disappointments of life are not final or irremediable. The consummation that Aristotle thought possible here on earth is merely postponed, not destroyed altogether. Nearly all of those who today believe that the gap between mortality and immortality can be overcome, and death transcended, accept some version of this idea. It is a deep and compelling idea, and millions of men and women embrace it in some form. It is perhaps the most popular view of life and death in the world today.

But it also seems to me defective. The defect is not that it rests on an unprovable assumption. Every other theory about the world does so as well, though it is worth emphasizing that the assumptions on which scientific theories are based are merely provisional premises whose authority must eventually be redeemed by rational methods, whereas the belief in a life after death is not a conditional assumption awaiting further proof, but an absolute barrier to inquiry, at least so long as we are alive.

The deeper defect of the view that the gap between our longing for immortality and its deathless object will indeed be closed, but not until we are dead, is that it disparages life itself in a fundamental way.

To those who hold this view, this may seem like an odd thing to say. After all, if the attainment of the immortality we seek, but from which we are at present excluded, depends on what we do in this life, don't our actions here on earth acquire a significance infinitely greater than any they might otherwise possess? Doesn't the idea of an immortal reward after death imbue every second of our mortal lives with an inconceivably large meaning and value?

The answer, of course, is that it does, but only as a means to an end. On the view we are now considering, each of us has reason to pay the closest attention to what we are doing and experiencing at every moment, but only because our actions and experiences count toward something that lies outside their range. It is a terrible mistake—the worst one, really—to think that these have any value in themselves. Even those who devote their lives to others and work selflessly on their behalf make this awful mistake if they believe their good works have any value of their own. They have value, to be sure, but only as an instrument, or sign or confirmation of something beyond the horizon of life on earth, which as a consequence loses all of the value it might conceivably possess as something good, worthy or beautiful in itself. For some, I know, it is a sign of spiritual strength to be able to maintain this view of life amidst its splendid distractions. But I reject it, not because it is so hard to sustain, but on account of its impoverishment of life itself, whose spiritual grandeur disappears when it ceases to be thought of as having any value of its own and comes to be viewed in the way Augustine did, as a pilgrimage toward a world beyond this one.

Many still accept some version of this idea. Most Americans at least claim to, and the fundamentalist movements that are gaining strength in various parts of the world today are all inspired by the belief that eternity awaits us in a life to come. If we are patient and act righteously while we live, their followers say, we shall be rewarded with life everlasting. Death will be canceled and its meaning annulled. For them, this is the meaning of life.

But there are others, myself included, who find this view dispiriting, and for some of those who do, though not for me, the only reasonable alternative appears to be to wean themselves completely from any lingering attachment to the idea of immortality in whatever form it takes.

The champions of this view insist that God is a myth and eternity an illusion. They urge us to live honestly, by which they mean without belief in either. Sometimes they call themselves atheists. Their enemies call them nihilists. In the West, there have been forceful defenders of this view for centuries. Their growing number and increasing authority is one symptom of the immensely complex process that Max Weber describes as the disenchantment of the world, which has both been hastened by, and strengthened in reaction to, the fundamentalist faith in eternity that for some atheists, at least, is the cause of most human folly and misbehavior.

This is not a tenable view either.

In the first place, too much of what we do and think makes sense only on account of its connection to eternity. The work of science, for example, is intelligible only if we think of it as moving toward an understanding of the world that rests on laws whose validity is timeless. The very idea of a law implies this.

Even in the realm of personal relations—to take an example of a very different sort—the idea of eternity plays a crucial role. It is true, of course, that the poignancy and passion of the love we feel for others would no longer exist if we and they were somehow, magically, freed from the limits of time. In a life everlasting, nothing about our relations with those we love would continue to mean what it does for us as mortal beings. In this sense, time is a condition of the meaning of human love. But it is not the only condition. Another is that the ones we love mean more to us than any finite set of experiences and expressions can possibly contain. The temporal limits within which all such relations begin and end are essential to their meaning. But so is the sense of the incommensurability between these limits and the goal of love itself—between time and eternity. Without that, human love ceases to be what it is, just as science does if we subtract the idea of eternity from the notion of lawfulness that is the ruling principle of all scientific inquiry.

In the second place, without the longing for eternity, human life becomes less serious. Of course it will be said that there is a great deal to be serious about even after we have given up on the idea of eternity. But this underestimates the extent to which the seriousness of all these other things depends on their covert connection to the belief that their value, beauty and intelligibility cannot be exhausted in any finite period of time. If that were not true, death would have a different meaning. If we could exhaust the value of the world in the short time that we live, why should it matter that our lives come to an end? It matters because we cannot do this. Life is the experience of what it can never encompass. Time is for us the experience of an eternity it cannot exhaust. It is this disproportion that makes life so serious—indeed, that makes it serious at all. Those who dismiss the idea of eternity as a childish dream demean our lives. They make them less than human. In this sense, they support an antihumanistic view of life.

What then remains? The ancient path to the contemplative transcendence of death has been closed. The belief that we can surmount death by preparing for a reunion with God in a life to come drains this one of all intrinsic value. And the atheist, who rejects both alternatives and instructs us to give up on the wish to reach or touch something that cannot be contained within time, asks us to abandon the human condition and accept something less serious in its place.

Yet there is one more view of life and death to be considered. It is different from these other three, and grander, though not so grand as to misstate the mortal facts about our situation. It is my own view, and in this book I have tried to make it as plausible and attractive as I can.

Readers will guess what I am about to say but it is worth saying one more time.

We are awash in eternity. God is present in every thing and every moment. In this sense, the atheist has it backward. The real challenge is not to disabuse ourselves of the idea of eternity. It is to open our eyes to it: to see how fully present it is even in the least of things.

The fundamentalist has it wrong too. There is no God beyond the world. The world itself is divine. To reach eternity, it is not necessary to go outside the world; indeed, this cannot be done.

But the divinity of the world not only resides in it. It reaches down to its smallest details. Eternity may lie ready to hand, but there is more of it than we can ever grasp. It is an ocean, and our minds and hearts small cups. There is no way to comprehend it completely, in a moment of contemplative or mystical bliss.

Still, this does not mean we cannot expand our understanding and appreciation of it. We can, and do, and as we do, our power grows. We draw closer to the infinite God of the world. Death is a disappointment because it brings this movement to an end. But it does not make the movement itself pointless, or deprive us of the joy we feel as we take in more and more of the eternity around us. Our encounter with eternity is brief. Death comes all too soon. But it cannot cut us off from the everlasting and divine because we are already in it. We are born to disappointment but not to despair. Our condition is one of joy, however long it lasts. But just because life does not last forever, that is no reason to abandon the pursuit, at ever higher levels, of the joy of being present in a world that is immortal though we ourselves are not.

Wallace Steven's great poem "Sunday Morning" expresses a similar view of life.

The poem is a dialogue of sorts between the poet and an unnamed woman. She is a Christian. It is Sunday morning. She is at home, enjoying "late coffee and oranges in a sunny chair." The "holy hush of ancient sacrifice" has dissipated, and in the quiet that follows her mind wanders "over the seas, to silent Palestine, dominion of the blood and sepulcher."

The woman is comfortable in the world, yet still feels the "need of some imperishable bliss" she cannot find in worldly things. She needs a paradise beyond this earth in order to believe that what happens here has meaning and value. "She says, 'I am content when wakened birds, before they fly, test the reality of misty fields, by their sweet questionings; but when the birds are gone, and their warm fields return no more, where, then, is paradise?'"

The poet replies that the earth itself is enough. "Why should she give her bounty to the dead? What is divinity if it can come only in silent shadows and in dreams? Shall she not find in comforts of the sun, in pungent fruit and bright, green wings, or else in any balm or beauty of the earth, things to be cherished like the thought of heaven?" He acknowledges that everything on earth eventually dies. But this does not render it less beautiful. Instead, he declares that "death is the mother of beauty," and then repeats this remarkable phrase a few lines later.

In the final stanza of the poem, the woman hears "a voice that cries, 'The tomb in Palestine is not the porch of spirits lingering. It is the grave of Jesus, where he lay.'" This provokes the poet to the last and most extraordinary statement of his belief in the divinity of the earth.

"We live," he says, "in an old chaos of the sun," and wherever we look we see wonderful things. "Deer walk upon our mountains, and the quail whistle about us their spontaneous cries." The poem nearly concludes on this note of soaring joy. The world is such a beautiful place. Who could ever ask for more? We do not need the "grave of Jesus" to sanctify or redeem the world. It is redeemed already. "Divinity must live within itself." Every moment is an encounter with the God of the world. Our feelings mark its presence. It is there in each of our experiences, the ordinary ones as much as the uncommon, in "passions of rain, or moods in falling snow; grievings in loneliness, or unsubdued elations when the forest blooms; gusty emotions on wet roads on autumn nights; all pleasures and all pains, the bough of summer and the winter branch." There is more to the world that our minds and hearts can contain. O, joy without end!

But the very last image of the poem adds a sobering note. "In the isolation of the sky, at evening, casual flocks of pigeons make ambiguous undulations as they sink, downward to darkness, on extended wings."

Day, and life, come to an end. Like the pigeons we too sink down to darkness. We live in joy amidst the unfathomable splendor of the world. If we pay attention to it, we shall be rewarded with a widening eye and more generous spirit. Yet the joy cannot last forever, which perhaps explains those "ambiguous undulations." Might it be that they are ambiguous because no other word describes the condition of mortal beings in a deathless world—the pigeons' condition as well as our own? That is unclear, but what is certain is that, though we must all one day "sink down," and leave the world we love so much, we ought to do it on "extended wings," with gratitude for what we have glimpsed and a reverence for what we have not, which is a way not only to die, but more importantly, to live.

Notes

ABBREVIATIONS

AND   Carl Schmitt, "The Age of Neutralizations and Depoliticizations," in *The Concept of the Political,* expanded ed., trans. George Schwab (Chicago: University of Chicago Press, 2007).

CF   Joseph de Maistre, *Considerations on France,* trans. Richard A. Lebrun (Montreal: McGill-Queen's University Press, 1974).

CP   Carl Schmitt, *The Concept of the Political,* expanded ed., trans. George Schwab (Chicago: University of Chicago Press, 2007).

CPR   Immanuel Kant, *Critique of Pure Reason,* ed. and trans. Paul Guyer and Allen W. Wood (Cambridge University Press, 1998). All page references are cited according to the established practice.

CPrR   Immanuel Kant, *Critique of Practical Reason,* in Immanuel Kant, *Practical Philosophy*, ed. and trans. Mary J. Gregor (Cambridge: Cambridge University Press, 1996).

GPC   Joseph de Maistre, *On the Generative Principle of Political Constitutions,* in *On God and Society: Essay on the Generative Principle of Political Constitutions and Other Human Institutions,* ed. Elisha Greifer, trans. Elisha Greifer and Lawrence M. Porter (Chicago: Regnery, 1959).

NE   Aristotle, *Nicomachean Ethics,* trans. Martin Ostwald (Indianapolis: Bobbs-Merrill, 1962).

RBMR   Immanuel Kant, *Religion within the Boundaries of Mere Reason,* in *Religion and Rational Theology,* ed. and trans. Allen W. Wood and George di Giovanni (Cambridge: Cambridge University Press, 1996).

PT   Carl Schmitt, *Political Theology: Four Chapters on the Concept of Sovereignty,* trans. George Schwab (Cambridge, MA: MIT Press, 1985).

SCG   Thomas Aquinas, *Summa Contra Gentiles: Volumes 1–4 in Five Books,* trans. Anton Charles Pegis (South Bend: Notre Dame University Press, 1997).

SP   Joseph de Maistre, *St. Petersburg Dialogues, or Conversations on the Temporal Government of Providence,* ed. and trans. Richard A. Lebrun (Montreal: McGill-Queen's University Press, 1993).

ST   Thomas Aquinas, *Summa Theologiae,* in the *Complete Works of Thomas Aquinas,* vols. 13–20, trans. Laurence Shapcote (Lander, WY: Aquinas Institute for the Study of Sacred Doctrine, 2012).

CHAPTER 1. THE GOOD OF GRATITUDE

1. Aristotle defines justice as a virtue exercised in relation to others. *NE,* 1130a 12. By contrast, he characterizes the virtue of temperance or moderation as one of *self-* control. *NE,* 1117b 25–1119a 20.
2. John Rawls, *A Theory of Justice,* rev. ed. (Cambridge, MA: Harvard University Press, 1999), 3.
3. "What are bands of robbers themselves but little kingdoms? The band itself is made up of men; it is governed by the authority of a ruler . . . and the loot is divided according to an agreed law." Augustine, *The City of God,* trans. R. W. Dyson (Cambridge: Cambridge University Press, 1998), 147.
4. Aristotle makes this point regarding the related virtue of friendship: "Friendship seems also to hold cities together, and lawgivers to care more about it than about justice . . . . [W]hen people are friends, they have no need of justice, while when they are just, they need friendship as well." *NE,* 1155a 23–27.
5. Seneca, *On Favours (De Beneficiis),* in *Seneca: Moral and Political Essays,* ed. John M. Cooper and J. F. Procopé (Cambridge: Cambridge University Press, 1995), 4.18, 1–4. "Our safety depends on the fact that we have mutual acts of kindness to help us. . . . Take away this fellowship and you tear apart the unity of mankind that sustains our life." See also Adam Smith, *The Theory of Moral Sentiments,* ed. D. D. Raphael and A. L. Macfie (Indianapolis: Liberty Classics, 1982), 68.
6. Plato, *The Republic,* in *The Collected Dialogues of Plato,* trans. Paul Shorey (Princeton: Princeton University Press), 588b–592b.
7. Though this idea is generally credited to Freud, it is not found anywhere in his writings. Instead, it is cited by Erik Erikson in his work *Childhood and Society,* 2nd ed. (New York: Norton, 1963). Freud did, however, speak of love and necessity as the

twin foundations of society: "The communal life of human beings had, therefore, a two-fold foundation: the compulsion to work, which was created by external necessity, and the power of love. . . ." Sigmund Freud, *Civilization and Its Discontents,* in *The Standard Edition of the Complete Psychological Works of Sigmund Freud,* 24 vols., ed. and trans. James Strachey (London: Hogarth Press, 1953–74), 21:101.

8. See, e.g., Cicero, *Pro Plancio,* in *The Orations of Marcus Tullius Cicero,* trans. C. D. Yonge and B. A. London (London: George Bell and Sons, 1891), sec. 80: "For this one virtue [gratitude] is not only the greatest, but is also the parent of all the other virtues."

9. Robert Emmons, *Thanks! How Practicing Gratitude Can Make You Happier* (New York: Mariner Books, 2008). There is also a growing body of psychological research devoted to gratitude. For an overview, see Philip C. Watkins, *Gratitude and the Good Life: Toward a Psychology of Appreciation* (Dordrecht, Netherlands: Springer, 2013).

10. For more on Klein, her life, and her thought, see Phyllis Grosskurth, *Melanie Klein: Her World and Her Work* (New York: Knopf, 1986); and Meira Likierman, *Melanie Klein: Her Work in Context* (London: Continuum, 2001).

11. Melanie Klein, "Envy and Gratitude," in *The Writings of Melanie Klein,* vol. 3, *Envy and Gratitude and Other Works, 1946–1963* (New York: Delacorte, 1975), 176–235.

12. Ibid., 3:179.

13. Ibid., 3:192 ff.

14. See D. W. Winnicott, "Transitional Objects and Transitional Phenomena; a Study of the First Not-Me Possession," *International Journal of Psycho-Analysis* 34, no. 2 (1953): 89–97; here, 94: "There is no possibility whatever for an infant to proceed from the pleasure principle to the reality principle or towards and beyond primary identification (see Freud, *The Ego and the Id,* p. 14), unless there is a good enough mother. The good enough 'mother' (not necessarily the infant's own mother) is one who makes active adaptation to the infant's needs, an active adaptation that gradually lessens, according to the infant's growing ability to account for failure of adaptation and to tolerate the results of frustration. Naturally the infant's own mother is more likely to be good enough than some other person, since this active adaptation demands an easy and unresented preoccupation with the one infant; in fact, success in infant-care depends on the fact of devotion, not on cleverness or intellectual enlightenment."

15. Klein, "Envy and Gratitude," 3:179.

16. Ibid.

17. Ibid., 3:176.

18. Ibid., 3:181.

19. Melanie Klein, "Our Adult World and Its Roots in Infancy," in *The Writings of Melanie Klein,* 3:254.

20. In his late work, Freud generalizes from our conservative tendency for repetition to a so-called "death instinct." See Sigmund Freud, *Beyond the Pleasure Principle,* in *Standard Edition,* 18:19–23.

21. Klein, "Envy and Gratitude," 3:202.

22. Ibid., 3:190, 202.

23. Ibid., 188–89.

24. Ibid., 3:189.

25. See Thomas Hobbes, *Leviathan,* ed. Richard Tuck (Cambridge: Cambridge University Press, 1996), 71: "To have received from one, to whom we think our selves equall, greater benefits than there is hope to Requite, disposeth to counterfeit love; but really secret hatred . . . . [O]bligation is thraldome; and unrequitable obligation, perpetual thraldome; which is to ones equall, hatefull."

26. Klein, "Envy and Gratitude," 3:203.

27. Robert Frost, "The Lesson for Today," in *The Witness Tree* (New York: H. Holt, 1942), 52.

28. See Bernard Williams, "Moral Luck," in *Moral Luck,* ed. Daniel Statman (Albany: State University of New York Press, 1993), 35–57.

29. Max Weber, "The Social Psychology of the World Religions," in *From Max Weber: Essays in Sociology,* ed. and trans. H. H. Gerth and C. Wright Mills (New York: Oxford University Press, 1958), 271–77. The fortunate man "needs to know that he has a *right* to his good fortune. He wants to be convinced that he 'deserves' it." Ibid. at 271.

30. Max Weber, "Religious Rejections of the World and Their Directions," in Gerth and Mills, eds., *From Max Weber,* 359.

31. Homer, *The Iliad,* trans. Robert Fagles and ed. Bernard Knox (London: Penguin, 1998), 3.432–40.

32. See Jasper Griffin, *Homer on Life and Death* (Oxford: Clarendon Press, 1980), 189 ff.

33. The phrase is Weber's. See Max Weber, "Science as a Vocation," in Gerth and Mills, eds., *From Max Weber,* 155.

34. Article 1 of the United Nations Universal Declaration of Human Rights states only that human beings "are born free and equal in dignity and rights" and "are endowed with reason and conscience." Difficulties in defining personhood have led some philosophers to claim "the logical primitiveness of the concept of a person." Peter Strawson, "Persons," in *Essays on Other Minds,* ed. Thomas O. Buford (Chicago: University of Illinois Press, 1970), 328.

35. "How is it possible," Johnson asked, "that all these people could be so ungrateful to me after I had given them so much? Take the Negroes. I fought for them from the first day I came into office. . . . I asked so little in return. Just a little thanks. Just a little appreciation. That's all." Lyndon Johnson, quoted in Doris Kearns, *Lyndon Johnson and the American Dream* (New York: Harper and Row, 1976), 340.

36. As is evident in Hobbes' political philosophy: "The Passions that encline men to Peace, are Feare of Death; Desire of such things as are necessary to commodious living; and a Hope by their industry to obtain them. And Reason suggesteth convenient Articles of Peace, upon which men may be drawn to agreement." *Leviathan,* 90.

37. Klein, "Envy and Gratitude," 3:176–235.

CHAPTER 2. A WORLD OF RIGHTS

1. Rawls, *A Theory of Justice,* 64.

2. See Peter L. Bernstein, *Against the Gods: The Remarkable Story of Risk* (Oxford: Wiley, 1998).

3. See Philip S. Gorski, *The Disciplinary Revolution: Calvinism and the Rise of the State in Early Modern Europe* (Chicago: University of Chicago Press, 2003).

4. Claire Gaudiani, *The Greater Good* (New York: Holt, 2003).

5. Sanford Levinson, *Written in Stone* (Durham: Duke University Press, 1998), 122–23. The absence of an inscription shocked many Americans so severely that "a more conventional and heroic statute was added at the site at the insistence of veterans' groups who found Maya Lin's great memorial too unheroic." Ibid. In contrast, Levinson notes that an Austin, Texas, monument erected as late as 1904 pointedly thanks fallen Confederate soldiers, despite the moral implications of such an expression of gratitude. Ibid., 53–58.

6. Edmund Burke, *Reflections on the Revolution in France* (New York: Penguin, 2004), 149–53, 299–300.

7. Such gratitude, which leads men to consider "liberties in the light of an inheritance," ensures that "the spirit of freedom, leading in itself to misrule and excess, is tempered with an awful gravity" and "prevents that upstart insolence almost inevitably adhering to and disgracing those who are the first acquirers of any distinction." Ibid., 121.

8. "Against these [the rights of man] there can be no prescription; against these, no agreement is binding." Ibid., 148.

9. See Adam Smith, *The Theory of Moral Sentiments*, 67–77.

10. Marcel Mauss, *The Gift*, trans. W. D. Halls (London: Norton, 1990).

11. Ibid., 13 ("To refuse to give . . . is tantamount to declaring war").

12. See Burke, *Reflections on the Revolution in France*, 192–93.

13. Rawls, *A Theory of Justice*, 251–58.

14. Rawls acknowledges that the original position is "a purely hypothetical situation characterized so as to lead to a certain conception of justice." *A Theory of Justice*, 11.

15. Alexander Bickel, *The Morality of Consent* (New Haven: Yale University Press, 1975), 24–25.

16. Plato famously insisted on the parallel between the virtues of city and soul; see *Republic*, 441c–442d. Aristotle also emphasized the relationship between private and public virtue. See Aristotle, *Politics*, ed. R. F. Stalley and trans. Ernest Baker (Oxford: Oxford University Press, 2009), 1280b l.

17. See René Descartes, *Discourse on the Method*, in *The Philosophical Works of Descartes*, trans. Elizabeth Haldane and G. R. T. Ross (Cambridge: Cambridge University Press, 1967) 1:119.

18. Aristotle, *De Anima*, trans. D. W. Hamlyn (Oxford: Oxford University Press, 1993), 415b 3.

CHAPTER 3. "ENDLESS GRATITUDE SO BURDENSOME"

1. Weber, "Science as a Vocation," 155.

2. Precisely what Weber means by "fate" is ambiguous. Weber's inclusion of reason as a "fateful force" suggests that the process of rationalization, which is the essence of control, is itself beyond our individual and collective power to control. See Anthony T. Kronman, *Max Weber* (Stanford: Stanford University Press, 1983), 170.

3. Weber, "Science as a Vocation," 153.

4. Joseph Schumpeter, *Capitalism, Socialism and Democracy* (London: Routledge, 1994).

5. For Weber's discussion of capitalism, see chap. 2 of *Economy and Society*, ed. Guenther Roth and Claus Wittich (New York: Bedminster Press, 1968). For Weber's thoughts on public administration, see ibid., chap. 3, part 8, "Collegiality and the Division of Powers," and part 10, "Direct Democracy and Representative Administration." Also especially relevant is chap. 11, "Bureaucracy."

6. For a modest sample, see Max Weber, *The Sociology of Religion*, trans. Ephraim Fischoff (Boston: Beacon Press, 1964). This is a separate edition of chapter 6 of *Economy and Society*.

7. See, e.g., Edward Grant, *The Foundations of Modern Science in the Middle Ages: Their Religious, Institutional and Intellectual Contexts* (Cambridge: Cambridge University Press, 1996); and Margaret Osler, *Reconfiguring the World: Nature, God, and Human Understanding from the Middle Ages to Early Modern Europe* (Baltimore: Johns Hopkins University Press, 2010).

8. Friedrich Nietzsche, *Writings from the Late Notebooks*, trans. Kate Sturge (Cambridge: Cambridge University Press, 2003), 83–86.

9. An idea that no real counterpart in the religions of Asia. See Weber, *The Sociology of Religion*, 166 ff.

10. The idea of redemption through sacrifice of the first born, which plays a prominent role in the Hebrew Bible, may be said to prefigure the Christian doctrine of the Incarnation, but as with many other themes in the Hebrew Bible (and in the prophetic writings especially) this idea assumes a far more radical and self-conscious form in the Gospels and the Letters of Paul, the foundational texts of the Christian religion. See Jon D. Levenson, *The Death and Resurrection of the Beloved Son: The Transformation of Child Sacrifice in Judaism and Christianity* (New Haven: Yale University Press, 1995).

11. John Milton, *Paradise Lost*, ed. Stephen Orgul and Jonathan Goldberg (Oxford: Oxford University Press, 2005), bk. 4, lines 42–53.

12. Ibid., bk. 4, lines 960–65.

13. Ibid., bk. 9, line 790.

14. Ibid., bk. 1, lines 1–5.

15. For a case study, see Wolfson's book on Philo of Alexandria, which demonstrates the extent to which Philo's integration of Jewish religion and Hellenistic philosophy informed Christian theology for nearly two thousand years. Harry Austryn Wolfson, *Philo: Foundations of Religious Philosophy in Judaism, Christianity, and Islam*, vol. 1 (Cambridge, MA: Harvard University Press, 1947). Wolfson's unified, metaphysically inspired interpretation of the connections among these three religions has greatly influenced the present work.

16. For more on the relationship between God and the world in pagan thought, and especially the conception of God as craftsman in Plato's *Timaeus*, see M. B. Foster, "Christian Theology and Modern Science of Nature," *Mind* 44 (1935): 439–66.

17. *CPR*, A109: "These appearances are . . . an object that can no longer be intuited by us, and may therefore be called the nonempirical, that is, the transcendental ob-

ject=X." In a similar vein, Kant argues that the existence of God himself is a "postulate of pure practical reason" that must necessarily be presupposed for a system of morality to exist. *CPrR*, 103–11.

18. This idea of positional reoccupation is also central to Hans Blumenberg's narrative of modernity. Cf. Blumenberg, *The Legitimacy of the Modern Age* (Cambridge, MA: MIT Press, 1985).

19. *CPR*, 448/B476.

20. See *RBMR*, 151–52.

21. Weber, "Science as a Vocation," 155: "Precisely the ultimate and most sublime values have retreated from public life either into the transcendental realm of mystical life or into the brotherliness of direct and personal human relations. It is not accidental that our greatest art is intimate and not monumental, nor is it accidental that today only within the smallest and most intimate circles, in personal human situations, *in pianissimo,* that something is pulsating that corresponds to the prophetic *pneuma,* which in former times swept through the great communities like a firebrand, welding them together."

22. *CPR*, Bxxxii.

23. See Georg Lukacs, *The Theory of the Novel,* trans. Anna Bostock (Cambridge, MA: MIT Press, 1971), 29–34. For the Greeks, Lukacs says, "the soul stands in the midst of the world; the frontier that makes up its contours is not different in essence from the contours of things: it draws sharp, sure lines, but it separates only relatively."

24. Baruch Spinoza, *Ethics,* in *The Collected Works of Spinoza,* trans. Edwin Curley (Princeton: Princeton University Press, 1985), 5p42s.

CHAPTER 4. GREATNESS OF SOUL

1. I feel compelled to add a note regarding the use of the word "man" and of masculine pronouns in this and the chapters that follow. In the first three chapters of the book, when discussing modern writers and modern problems, and especially when expressing my own views, I have alternated men and women in my examples. I have used "he or she," "he and she," and similar gender-neutral forms, as often as grammar allows. In later chapters, when I return to the modern world, and develop my own views at greater length, I resume this usage to allay the perception that my book is about men, as opposed to human beings in general. No view could be further from the argument of the book as a whole.

But in the historical chapters on Aristotle, Plato, the Stoics and the main writers in the Christian tradition, it would be jarring (to my ear at least) to introduce a consciously gendered usage that is strikingly inconsistent not merely with that of the writers in question but with the substance of their views as well. Alternating sexes here would be odd. Substituting the passive voice is weak. And abstractions like "humanity" or "humankind," though I use them sparingly, are bloodless by comparison with the older word "man." In these chapters—especially those on Aristotle, whose preference for the masculine has metaphysical roots—I am attempting to describe a world remote from ours in a spirit sympathetic to its own ruling values. I hope my readers will join me in the venture.

2. *NE*, 1098b 31.

3. That pride is the root of all sin is an idea central to Augustine's theology. See, e.g., Augustine, *Augustine Catechism: Enchiridion on Faith, Hope, and Charity*, trans. Bruce Harbert (New York: New City Press, 1999), 60–63, 130; and *Augustine Through the Ages: An Encyclopedia*, ed. Allan D. Fitzgerald (Grand Rapids, MI: Eerdmans, 2009), 679–84.

4. *NE*, 1123a 34–1125a 35.

5. *NE*, 1124a 1.

6. *NE*, 1123a 25.

7. *NE*, 1120b 7ff.

8. *NE*, 1120a 5.

9. *NE*, 1120a 1–2.

10. *NE*, 1120b 16.

11. *NE*, 1120a 33.

12. *NE*, 1119b 33.

13. *NE*, 1121a 25.

14. *NE*, 1122a 22.

15. *NE*, 1122b 30.

16. *NE*, 1122b 16.

17. *NE*, 1122b 17.

18. *NE*, 1122b 18.

19. *NE*, 1121a ff.

20. *NE*, 1123a 20–25.

21. *NE*, 1123 a 28–32.

22. *NE*, 1123a 28.

23. *NE*, 1122b 7.

24. *NE*, 1122b 6–7.

25. *NE*, 1120a 2.

26. *NE*, 1123a 1–6.

27. *NE*, 1122a 23–24; 1122b 18–24.

28. *NE*, 1123a 4.

29. Aristotle, *Politics*, 1152a 7–22.

30. See Hannah Arendt, *The Human Condition* (Chicago: University of Chicago Press, 1998), esp. 96–101.

31. *NE*, 1123a 8.

32. *NE*, 1124a 1.

33. *NE*, 1125a 12.

34. *NE*, 1124b 5.

35. *NE*, 1125a 12.

36. *NE*, 1125a 16.

37. *NE*, 1124a 20.

38. *NE*, 1124a 30.

39. *NE*, 1124a 15–16.

40. *NE*, 1124b 7–9.

41. *NE*, 1115b 25 ff.

42. *NE*, 1124b 8–10.

43. *NE*, 1124b 10–12.

44. *NE*, 1124b 12–15.

45. *NE*, 1124b 17–18.

46. *NE*, 1124b 12.

47. *NE*, 1124b 32.

48. *NE*, 1125a 1.

49. On the historical background of angels in the Bible and early church, see Jean Danie-lou, *The Angels and Their Mission: According to the Fathers of the Church* (Allan, TX: Newman Press, 1957). For a brief overview, see *Encyclopedia of Christianity,* ed. John Bowden (Oxford: Oxford University Press, 2005), 42–44.

CHAPTER 5. GIVERS AND TAKERS

1. Aristotle, *Metaphysics,* trans. Huge Treddenick (Cambridge, MA: Harvard University Press, 1933), 1003a 21.

2. Ibid., 1167b 17–1168a 27.

3. Ibid., 1167b 17–18.

4. Ibid., 1167b 20.

5. Ibid., 1167b 20–25. Cf. Thucydides, *The Landmark Thucydides: A Comprehensive Guide to the Peloponnesian War* (New York: Touchstone, 1996), 114.

6. Aristotle, *Metaphysics,* 1167b 29.

7. Ibid., 1167b 31–33.

8. Ibid., 1167b 33–1168a 5; see also 1122a 34.

9. Aristotle, *Physics,* trans. Robin Waterfield (Oxford: Oxford University Press, 1996), 193b 9. Cf. Jonathan Lear, *Aristotle: The Desire to Understand* (Cambridge: Cambridge University Press, 1988), 15–26.

10. See, e.g., Aristotle, *Physics,* 193b 3.

11. Aristotle, *Metaphysics,* 1168a 5–10.

12. Ibid., 1168a 17.

13. Like the relation of slave to master; Aristotle, *Politics,* 1254a 8.

14. *NE*, 1120a 12.

CHAPTER 6. THE ETERNAL AND DIVINE

1. See Aristotle, *Metaphysics,* 1045b 28–1052a 11, 1065b 5–34. For overviews of the development of Aristotle's metaphysics, see Werner Jaeger, *Aristotle: Fundamentals of the History of His Development* (Oxford: Clarendon Press, 1950); and G. E. L. Owen, *Logic, Science, and Dialectic: Collected Papers in Greek Philosophy* (Ithaca: Cornell University Press, 1986), "The Platonism of Aristotle" and "Logic and Metaphysics in Some Earlier Works of Aristotle." Cf. Martin Heidegger, *Aristotle's Metaphysics θ 1–3: On the*

Essence and Actuality of Force, trans. Peter Warnek (Bloomington: Indiana University Press, 1995). The finest book on Aristotle that I know is Jonathan Lear's, *Aristotle: The Desire to Understand.*

2. Lear, *Aristotle,* esp. 15–25.

3. See Aristotle, *De Anima,* 413b 1–415b 9.

4. Ibid., esp. 415a 30–415b 1.

5. Aristotle, *Physics,* 217b 28–222a 9.

6. Aristotle, *De Anima,* 415b 3–9.

7. Cf. Pico della Mirandola, *Pico della Mirandola: Oration on the Dignity of Man: A New Translation and Commentary,* ed. Francesco Borghesi, Michael Papio, and Massimo Riva (Cambridge: Cambridge University Press, 2012).

8. *NE,* 1095a 17.

9. *NE,* 1025a 22–26.

10. *NE,* 1097b 23.

11. *NE,* 1097b 27–30.

12. *NE,* 1097b 34.

13. *NE,* 1098a 2. Cf. Aristotle, *De Anima,* 413a 21 ff.

14. *NE,* 1098a3–4.

15. *NE,* 1098a 3.

16. *NE,* 1098a 1.

17. *NE,* 1098a 2.

18. *NE,* 1195b 22.

19. *NE,* 1095a 15–20.

20. Aristotle, *De Anima,* 415a 26–415b 7.

21. "Prime matter" is a term coined by later scholars, but based on texts including Aristotle, *Metaphysics,* 1029a 8–26, and *Physics,* 192a 29–33.

22. Aristotle, *Metaphysics,* 1045b 28–1052a 11. Cf. Ernan McMullin, *The Concept of Matter in Greek and Medieval Philosophy* (South Bend: University of Notre Dame Press, 1966).

23. See Aristotle, *De Caelo* and *Meteorologica,* in *The Complete Works of Aristotle,* vol. 1, ed. Jonathan Barnes (Princeton: Princeton University Press, 1984).

24. Aristotle, *Physics,* 230b 12.

25. Aristotle, *De Anima,* 416b 10–20; Hans Jonas, *The Phenomenon of Life: Toward a Philosophical Biology* (Evanston: Northwestern University Press, 2001); Leon Kass, *The Hungry Soul: Eating and the Perfecting of our Nature* (Chicago: University of Chicago Press, 1999).

26. This is an idea already present in Plato; see Thomas K. Johansen, "From Plato's *Timaeus* to Aristotle's *De Caelo:* The Case of the Missing World Soul," in *New Perspectives on Aristotle's De Caelo,* ed. Alan C. Bowen and Christian Wildberg (Leiden, Netherlands: Brill, 2009).

27. G. E. R. Lloyd, *Aristotle: The Growth and Development of His Thought* (Cambridge: Cambridge University Press, 1968), 134.

28. See Lloyd, *Aristotle,* 134–40; see also Aristotle, *De Caelo,* 269b ff.

CHAPTER 7. THE BEST LIFE OF ALL

1. *NE*, 1179b 30.
2. Such a person possesses virtue while asleep but would not be called happy, because the virtue is not exercised or actual. Cf. *NE*, 1095b 31–1096a 3.
3. *NE*, 1179b 23–27.
4. *NE*, 1179b 31.
5. *NE*, 1179b 32–1180a 4.
6. Aristotle, *Politics*, 1253a 1–9.
7. Aristotle and his students at the Lyceum collected and studied 158 constitutions. Besides his discussion of constitutions in the *Politics*, 1279a 22 ff, the only extant fruit of this labor is Aristotle's summary of the Athenian Constitution. See Aristotle, *The Politics and the Constitution of Athens*, ed. Stephen Everson (Cambridge: Cambridge University Press, 1996), 211–63.
8. Cf. Karl Marx, *Capital*, vol. 1, ed. Frederick Engels (New York: The Modern Library, 1906), 198: "A spider conducts operations that resemble those of a weaver, and a bee puts to shame many an architect in the construction of her cells. But what distinguishes the worst architect from the best of bees is this, that the architect raises his structure in imagination before he erects it in reality." See also M. B. Foster, *The Political Philosophies of Plato and Hegel* (New York: Russell and Russell, 1965), 181–82.
9. *NE*, 1099b 29–32.
10. Cf. Lloyd, *Aristotle*, 6, 23, 68.
11. Cf. Aristotle, *Metaphysics*, 982b 12.
12. Aristotle, *Physics*, 194b 17–195a 27.
13. On the relation of image to original, see Plato, *Republic*, 509d–511e. See generally Jacob Klein, *A Commentary on Plato's Meno* (Chicago: University of Chicago Press, 1998).
14. On the crucial term *energeia* (usually translated as "actuality") in Aristotle and later thought, see David Bradshaw, *Aristotle East and West: Metaphysics and the Division of Christendom* (Cambridge: Cambridge University Press, 2004).
15. *NE*, 1177b 27–32.
16. Aristotle, *Metaphysics*, 1173a 5.

CHAPTER 8. FRIENDSHIP

1. *NE*, 1177a 12–1178a 8.
2. *NE*, 1176b 1.
3. See the translators' discussion of the meaning of the term in *Aristotle's Nicomachean Ethics*, trans. Robert C. Bartlett and Susan D. Collins (Chicago: University of Chicago Press, 2012), 306.
4. *NE*, 1177a 27–1177b 1.
5. *NE*, 1156b 6–10.

6. *NE*, 1157a 30.
7. *NE*, 1156b 12.
8. *NE*, 1156b 27.
9. *NE*, 1156b 6–7.
10. *NE*, 1156b 10.
11. *NE*, 1157b 8.
12. *NE*, 1157b 8.
13. *NE*, 1157b 19–20.
14. *NE*, 1169b 4–5.
15. *NE*, 1166a 23.
16. *NE*, 1166a 14–16.
17. *NE*, 1166a 23–24.
18. *NE*, 1168b 9.
19. *NE*, 1166a 10.
20. *NE*, 1166a 24.
21. *NE*, 1166b 14–17.
22. *NE*, 1166a 32; 1169b 7; 1170b 7.
23. *NE*, 1169b 3–1170b 20.
24. *NE*, 1169b 17–22.
25. *NE*, 1155a 5–10.
26. *NE*, 1169b 12–14.
27. *NE*, 1169b 29.
28. *NE*, 1169b 34.
29. *NE*, 1170a 11.
30. See, generally, *NE*, 1145a 15–1152a 36.
31. See, generally, *NE*, 1103a 15–1104b 17.

CHAPTER 9. THE FIRST COSMOPOLITAN

1. For details, see Peter Green, *Alexander of Macedon, 356–323 B.C.: A Historical Biography* (Berkeley: University of California Press, 1992); and Peter Green, *The Hellenistic Age: A Short History* (New York: Modern Library, 2008).

2. See Sheldon Wolin, *Politics and Vision: Continuity and Innovation in Western Political Thought,* expanded ed. (Princeton: Princeton University Press, 2004); and Malcolm Schofield, *The Stoic Idea of the City* (Chicago: University of Chicago Press, 1999). My understanding of Stoicism has been deeply enriched by many conversations with my teacher and friend, Kenley Dove.

3. See Schofield, *Stoic Idea,* 110 ff; and Ernst Troeltsch, *The Social Teaching of the Christian Churches,* 2 vols., trans. Oliver Wyon (Louisville: Westminster/John Knox Press, 1992), esp. 1:64–69.

4. Augustine, *On Free Choice of the Will,* trans. Thomas Williams (Indianapolis: Hackett, 1993).

5. See Eric Havelock, *Preface to Plato* (Cambridge, MA: Harvard University Press, 1982).

6. See Erich Auerbach, *Dante: Poet of the Secular World,* trans. Ralph Manheim (New York: New York Review of Books, 2001), 1–23.

7. See Griffin, *Homer on Life and Death,* chap. 5.

8. See Arendt, *The Human Condition,* 199–206.

9. James P. Holoka, ed. and trans., *Simone Weil's the* Iliad *or the Poem of Force: A Critical Edition* (New York: Lang, 2006).

10. Plato, *Republic,* 338c.

11. Ibid., 353e.

12. Ibid., 354a.

13. Ibid., 354a.

14. Ibid., 357b.

15. See ibid., 473b ff.

16. See Jacob Klein, *Greek Mathematical Thought and the Origin of Algebra* (Cambridge, MA: MIT Press, 1968).

17. Plato's psychology divided the soul into three parts. See Plato, *Republic,* 433a ff.

18. See the famous allegory of the cave, *Republic,* 514a ff.

19. See *Republic,* 516d.

20. Ibid., 473d ff.

21. Ibid., 614d.

22. Ibid., 617d–e.

23. Ibid., 619b.

24. Ibid., 621b.

CHAPTER 10. PREPARATIO EVANGELICA

1. See Dirk Baltzly, "Stoicism," in *Stanford Encyclopedia of Philosophy,* spring 2014 ed., ed. Edward N. Zalta, http://plato.stanford.edu/archives/spr2014/entries/stoicism/. For a more detailed study, cf. Susanne Bobzien, *Determinism and Freedom in Stoic Philosophy* (Oxford: Oxford University Press, 2002).

2. Epictetus, *The Handbook,* trans. Nicholas P. White (Indianapolis: Hackett, 1983).

3. Cf. Gerard Boter, *The Encheiridion of Epictetus and Its Three Christian Adaptions: Transmission and Critical Editions* (Leiden, Netherlands: Brill, 1999); and Christopher Brooke, "How the Stoics Became Atheists," *Historical Journal* 49 (2006): 387–402.

4. Epictetus, *Handbook,* par. 1.

5. Ibid., par. 32.

6. Ibid., par. 19.

7. Ibid., par. 24.

8. Ibid., pars. 29, 33.

9. Ibid., par. 44.

10. Ibid., par. 46.

11. Ibid., par. 29.

12. Ibid., par. 10.

13. Ibid., par. 1.

14. Ibid., par. 6.

15. Ibid., pars. 5, 28, 41, 45.

16. Ibid., par. 45.

17. Ibid., par. 1.

18. Ibid., par. 9 ("choice").

19. Ibid., par. 29.

20. Ibid., par. 2.

21. Martha Nussbaum, *The Therapy of Desire: Theory and Practice in Hellenistic Ethics* (Princeton: Princeton University Press, 2009).

22. Alexander Nehamas, *The Art of Living: Socratic Reflections from Plato to Foucault* (Berkeley: University of California Press, 2000).

23. Epictetus, *Handbook,* par. 33.

24. Ibid., par. 8.

25. Ibid., par. 4.

26. Ibid., par. 31.

27. Ibid., par. 27.

28. Ibid., par. 15.

29. Seneca, *On Favours,* 2.21.1.

30. Ibid., 1.2.8, 2.17.3, 2.25.3, 3.22.1.

31. Ibid., 1.4.2.

32. Ibid., 1.3.4.

33. Ibid.

34. Ibid., 1.1.2.

35. Ibid., 1.10.4.

36. Ibid.

37. Ibid., 4.19.4.

38. Ibid., 4.18.1–4.

39. Ibid.

40. Ibid., 4.18.1.

41. Ibid., 4.20.1–3, 4.21.1.

42. Ibid., 3.18.1.

43. Ibid., 3.18.2.

44. Ibid., 3.18.1.

45. Ibid., 3.21.1.

46. Ibid., 3.23–27.

47. Ibid., 3.20.1–2.

48. Aristotle, *Politics,* 1254b.

49. Seneca, *On Favours,* 1.6.1.

50. Ibid., 1.5.2.

51. Ibid., 4.11.1.

52. Ibid., 3.14.4.

53. Ibid., 4.13.3.

54. Ibid., 1.1.8.

55. Ibid., 1.15.6.

56. Ibid., 2.31.1.
57. Ibid., 1.35.5.
58. Ibid., 2.35.1.
59. Ibid., 3.2.2.
60. Immanuel Kant, *Groundwork of the Metaphysics of Morals,* in Immanuel Kant, *Practical Philosophy,* ed. and trans. Mary J. Gregor (Cambridge: Cambridge University Press, 1996), 49.
61. Seneca, *On Favours,* 4.21.1–6.
62. Ibid., 4.5.1–6.6.
63. Ibid., 4.12.5.
64. Ibid., 4.6.2.
65. Ibid., 4.7.2.

CHAPTER 11. CREATION

1. Augustine, *The City of God,* 3.
2. Cf. Plato, *Phaedo,* trans. David Gallop (Oxford: Oxford University Press, 2009), 83e, and Plato, *Republic,* 611b–612.
3. Plotinus, *The Enneads,* trans. Stephen MacKenna (New York: Larson, 1992), 1.6.71.
4. Cf. Yuri Stoyanov, *The Other God: Dualist Religions from Antiquity to the Cathar Heresy* (New Haven: Yale University Press, 2000), 102 ff.
5. Peter Brown, *Augustine of Hippo: A Biography* (Berkeley: University of California Press, 2000), 35–49.
6. Augustine's mature theology does retain certain important aspects of Plato's philosophy. In particular, Plato's theory of the forms continues to play an important role in Augustine's account of divine and human knowledge. But the theory is incorporated within a creationist metaphysics that alters its meaning in a fundamental way. For a general overview, see Étienne Gilson, *History of Christian Philosophy in the Middle Ages* (New York: Random House, 1955), 70–80. The extent to which Augustine can be called a Platonist remains a vexed question among scholars. See Philip Cary, *Augustine's Invention of the Inner Self: The Legacy of a Christian Platonist* (Oxford: Oxford University Press, 2000).
7. Genesis 1:1–3.
8. See E. A. Speiser, ed. and trans., *The Anchor Bible,* vol. 1, *Genesis: Introduction, Translation, and Notes* (New York: Doubleday, 1964).
9. For background, see Wolfson, *Philo* 1:3–86.
10. For the history of commentary on the *Timaeus,* see Jaroslav Pelikan, *What Has Athens to Do with Jerusalem? Timaeus and Genesis in Counterpoint* (Ann Arbor: University of Michigan Press, 1998).
11. See Daniel Boyarin, *Border Lines: The Partition of Judaeo-Christianity* (Philadelphia: University of Pennsylvania Press, 2004).
12. See Jaroslav Pelikan, *Christianity and Classical Culture: The Metamorphosis of Natural Theology in the Christian Encounter with Hellenism;* and Gilson, *History of Christian Philosophy,* 3–60.

13. Aristotle, *Metaphysics,* 1028a–1052a.

14. Ibid., 1032b 30.

15. Hesiod, *Theogony,* in *Hesiod and Theognis: Theogony, Works and Days, and Elegies,* trans. Dorothea Wender (New York: Penguin, 1976).

16. Plato, *Timaeus,* in *Timaeus and Critias,* trans. Robin Waterfield and ed. Andrew Gregory (Oxford: Oxford University Press, 2008), 27a ff. See also Pelikan, *What Has Athens to Do with Jerusalem?* For a more technical treatment, see Sarah Broadie, *Nature and Divinity in Plato's Timaeus* (Cambridge: Cambridge University Press, 2012).

17. Although the doctrine of "filiation" in Trinitarian theology, concerning the son's relation to the father, uses biological terms, like generation, it implies no biological relation, for the father and son are equally eternal, immaterial, and perfect. For a classic statement, see Thomas Aquinas, *ST,* 1.Q.27, "The Procession of the Divine Persons."

CHAPTER 12. WILL

1. See Lear, *Aristotle,* 141–51; and *NE,* 1107a 1–2, 1113a 32–3.

2. See, e.g., Augustine, *On Free Choice,* 13–15.

3. See, e.g., Epictetus, *Discourses,* trans. Robert Hard and ed. Christopher Gill (Oxford: Oxford University Press, 2014), 3.12 14–15.

4. *NE,* 1112b 1 ff.

5. *NE,* 1145a 15 ff.

6. The question of whether ancient philosophy already contained a less-developed conception of the will has been debated for generations. For contrasting views, compare Albrecht Dihle, *The Theory of the Will in Classical Antiquity* (Berkeley: University of California Press, 1982), with Michael Frede, *A Free Will: Origins of the Notion in Ancient Thought* (Berkeley: University of California Press, 2011). Frede contends that the idea of the will can be found in Stoic writings, and he discounts Augustine's originality in this regard. He fails, I think, to appreciate how important the doctrine of creation is to the idea of the will, and underestimates the novelty of this doctrine from the standpoint of ancient philosophy.

7. Dihle, *The Theory of the Will.*

8. See Simon Harrison, *Augustine's Way into the Will: The Theological and Philosophical Significance of* De libero arbitrio (Oxford: Oxford University Press, 2006).

9. Augustine, *On Free Choice,* 1.

10. Ibid., 3–4.

11. Ibid., 115 ff. The relationship between Augustine's comments on infants here and his developed theology of infant baptism is complex. For an overview, see Fitzgerald, ed., *Augustine through the Ages,* 87 ff.

12. This is a corollary of the Socratic view that all virtue is knowledge. See Plato, *Protagoras,* trans. and ed. C. C. W. Taylor (Oxford: Oxford University Press, 1996), 352b–d.

13. Augustine, *On Free Choice,* 119.

14. See Romans 7; and Augustine, *The Confessions,* trans. Henry Chadwick (New York: Oxford University Press, 1991), 24 ff.

15. Augustine, *On Free Choice,* 105.

16. Ibid., 67.

17. Ibid., 19–20.

18. Ibid., 21–23.

CHAPTER 13. GRACE

1. Augustine, *On Free Choice,* 27–28, 73–78.

2. Augustine, *City of God,* 541 ff.

3. Ibid., 634. Although Augustine rejects Satan's envy as the main reason for the fall, arguing in "The Literal Meaning of Genesis," 11.17 ff, in *On Genesis,* trans. Edmund Hill (New York: New City Press, 2002) that it follows pride, rather than precedes it, envy becomes important in the Augustinian tradition, most famously in John Milton; see, e.g., *Paradise Lost,* bk. 4, lines 52–57.

4. Augustine, *City of God,* 630.

5. Ibid., 634.

6. Ibid., 632.

7. Ibid., 918–19 (emphasis added).

8. Ibid., 922.

9. *Nicene and Post-Nicene Fathers, First Series,* 14 vols. (hereafter citing volume and page) (Peabody, MA: Hendrickson, 1996), 5:257, 264.

10. Ibid., 5:281.

11. Ibid., 5:xxxviii.

12. Augustine, *City of God,* 460.

CHAPTER 14. "NOT A SPARROW FALLS"

1. See Plato, *Timaeus,* 48e 4 ff.

2. The two crucial passages are Aristotle, *Metaphysics,* 1016b 31–32 and 1034a 5–8.

3. Individuation became a topic of systematic discussion in medieval philosophy. See Jorge J. E. Garcia, *Introduction to the Problem of Individuation in the Early Middle Ages* (Munich: Philosophia, 1984).

4. Cf. Jason A. Tipton, *Philosophical Biology in Aristotle's Parts of Animals* (New York: Springer, 2013).

5. See Gottfried Wilhelm Leibniz, *Discourse on Metaphysics,* sec. 9, in Leibniz, *Philosophical Papers and Letters,* ed. Leroy Loemker (Dordrecht, Netherlands: Kluwer, 1969).

6. Matthew 10:29–31.

7. *ST,* I.Q.14, A.11.

8. See Alexandre Koyré, *From the Closed World to the Infinite Universe* (Baltimore: Johns Hopkins University Press, 1957).

9. Plato, *Republic,* 329a–d. For seemingly divergent views of the body in Plato, compare *Phaedo,* 64a–65a, with *Symposium,* trans. Robin Waterfield (Oxford University Press: Oxford, 2008), 210a–212c.

10. See, e.g., Aristophanes, *Lysistrata,* in *Lysistrata and Others Plays,* trans. Alan H. Sommerstein (New York: Penguin, 2002).

11. See K. J. Dover, *Greek Homosexuality: Updated with a New Postscript* (Cambridge, MA: Harvard University Press, 1989); and John Boswell, *Christianity, Social Tolerance, and Homosexuality: Gay People in Western Europe from the Beginning of the Christian Era to the Fourteenth Century* (Chicago: University of Chicago Press, 2005).

12. *NE,* 1177b 33.

13. Plato, *Phaedo,* passim; but see 62b and 81e.

14. Something similar may be said about work, which is intimately tied to the life of the body. Aristotle regarded work as a mindless necessity. It has to be done, he said, by someone at least, but possesses no meaning or value of its own. The life of the spirit begins, for Aristotle, only where work ends—in the sphere of leisure. That is why it is best to have one's work done by slaves if that can be arranged. By defining work as the punishment for a sin, the biblical interpretation of it endows work with tremendous moral significance, negative at first, but eventually positive, when men come to see that it is possible for them to pursue their salvation by "working off" their sins. In this way, the realm of work comes to be invested with a spiritual significance comparable to that of the body, whose needs it always serves. The conclusion that either has this kind of intrinsic significance, so far as man's ultimate goals are concerned, is one that both Plato and Aristotle would have thought absurd.

15. For an overview of the subject, see Caroline Walker Bynum, *The Resurrection of the Body in Western Christianity, 200–1336* (New York: Columbia University Press, 1995). On Augustine's position, see ibid., 94 ff.

16. See Michael Inwood, "Plato's Eschatological Myths," in *Plato's Myths,* ed. Catalin Partenie (Cambridge: Cambridge University Press, 2009).

17. John 1:17 (emphasis added).

18. Aristotle, *De Anima,* 430a 10–25.

19. Immanuel Kant, *The Metaphysics of Morals,* in Immanuel Kant, *Practical Philosophy,* ed. and trans. Mary J. Gregor (Cambridge: Cambridge University Press, 1996), 378.

CHAPTER 15. THE CONTINGENCY OF THE WORLD

1. Plato, *Republic,* 475d ff.

2. See Harold Cherniss, *Aristotle's Criticism of Plato and the Academy* (Baltimore: John Hopkins University Press, 1944); Harold Cherniss, *The Riddle of the Early Academy* (Berkeley: University of California Press, 1945); and Kenneth Seeskin, "Meno 85c–89a: A Mathematical Image of Philosophic Inquiry," in *Plato, Time, and Education,* ed. Brian Hendly (Albany: State University of New York Press, 1987), 25–42.

3. Mathematical entities are an exception. Cf. Aristotle, *Metaphysics,* 1077b 18–1078a 31, and Jonathan Lear, "Aristotle's Philosophy of Mathematics," *Philosophical Review* 91, no. 2 (1982): 161–92.

4. See Edward Booth, *Aristotelian Aporetic Ontology in Islamic and Christian Thinkers* (Cambridge: Cambridge University Press, 1983).

5. Cf. Charles Kahn "Why Existence does not Emerge as a Distinct Concept in Greek Philosophy," *Archiv für Geschichte der Philosophie* 58(4):323 (1976).

6. Aristotle, *Physics*, 194b 17–195a 2.

7. Thomas Aquinas, *On Being and Essence,* trans. Robert T. Miller (New York: Fordham, 1997).

8. See Gilson, *History of Christian Philosophy,* 181–220, on the background of Islamic philosophy.

9. Aquinas, *On Being and Essence,* Prologue.

10. See, e.g., *ST,* III (supplement), Q.75, A. 1–3.

11. *ST,* I.Q.50, A.4.

12. Aquinas, *On Being and Essence,* chapter IV.

13. Ibid., chapter IV (emphasis added).

14. Ibid., chapter IV.

CHAPTER 16. THE PAGAN TEMPTATION

1. See Gilson, *History of Christian Philosophy,* 235–45. Gilson's work remains perhaps the best one-volume history of philosophy in the Middle Ages. See also Gordon Leff, *Medieval Thought: From St. Augustine to Ockham* (Atlantic Highlands, NJ: Humanities Press, 1958); and David Knowles, *The Evolution of Medieval Thought* (New York: Vintage, 1962).

2. See Christian Wildberg, "Philosophy in the Age of Justinian," in *The Cambridge Companion to the Age of Justinian,* ed. Michael Maas (Cambridge: Cambridge University Press, 2005), 316–42. Wildberg presents complicating evidence as to the effects of the imperial decree.

3. Dmitri Gutas, *Greek Thought, Arabic Culture: The Graeco-Arabic Translation Movement in Baghdad and Early ʿAbbāsid Society (2nd–4th/8th–10th Centuries)* (New York: Routledge, 1998).

4. Maria Menocal, *The Ornament of the World: How Muslims, Jews and Christians Created a Culture of Tolerance in Medieval Spain* (New York: Back Bay Books, 2003).

5. On the controversy caused by the Aristotle revival, see Stephen Gaukroger, *The Emergence of a Scientific Culture: Science and the Shaping of Modernity, 1210–1685* (Oxford: Oxford University Press, 2006), 47–86.

6. See Gilson, *History of Christian Philosophy,* 387–409.

7. *ST,* I.Q.2, A.1.

8. *ST,* I.Q.2, A.1.

9. *NE,* 1095a 30 ff.

10. *ST,* I.Q.2, A.3.

11. *ST,* I.Q.2, A.3.

12. *ST,* I.Q.3, A.3.

13. See Brian Davies, *The Thought of Thomas Aquinas* (Oxford: Oxford University Press, 1992), 70–75.

14. *ST*, I.Q.14, A.1.
15. *ST*, I.Q.84–86.
16. *ST*, I.Q.14, A.2.
17. *ST*, I.Q.14, A.2.
18. *ST*, I.Q.14, A.4.
19. *ST*, I.Q.14, A.4.
20. *ST*, I.Q.19, A.4.
21. *ST*, I.Q.14, A.4.
22. *ST*, I.Q.19, A.1.
23. *ST*, I.Q.19, A.4.
24. *ST*, I.Q.19, A.3.
25. *ST*, I.Q.19, A.1 (emphasis added).
26. *ST*, I.Q.19, A.1.
27. *ST*, I.Q.19, A.2.
28. *ST*, I.Q.19, A.2 (emphasis added).
29. *ST*, I.Q.19, A.3.
30. *ST*, I.Q.19, A.3.
31. *ST*, I.Q.19, A.3 (emphasis added).
32. *ST*, I.Q.14, A.6.
33. *ST*, I.Q.14, A.11.
34. *ST*, I.Q.44, A.2.
35. *ST*, I.Q.19, A.5.
36. *ST*, I.Q.14, A.8.
37. *SCG*, chap. 18.
38. *SCG*, chap. 19 (emphasis in original).
39. *SCG*, chap. 25.
40. *ST*, I.Q.82, A.2.
41. *SCG*, chap. 48.
42. *SCG*, chap. 42.
43. See Davies, *The Thought of Thomas Aquinas*, 274–96.
44. *SCG*, chap. 51.
45. *SCG*, chap. 51.
46. *SCG*, chap. 50.

CHAPTER 17. GOD UNCHAINED

1. See Gilson, *History of Christian Philosophy*, 387–409; Frank Wippel, "The Condemnations of 1270 and 1277 at Paris," *Journal of Medieval and Renaissance Studies* 7 (1977): 169–201; and Frank Wippel, "Thomas Aquinas and the Condemnation of 1277," *Modern Schoolman* 72 (1995): 233–72.

2. See Philotheus Boehner, "Introduction," in *Ockham: Philosophical Writings* (Indianapolis: Hackett, 1990), xi–xvi.

3. Arguably the deepest source of this claim's continuing influence is the historiography of Gilson himself. See especially Étienne Gilson, *The Unity of Philosophical Ex-*

perience (New York: Charles Scribner's Sons, 1937), which draws a direct line from Ockham to modern philosophy. For recent versions of the narrative linking nominalism, voluntarism, or both (usually with Ockham or Scotus as the source) to modernity, see Michael Allan Gillespie, *The Theological Origins of Modernity* (Chicago: University of Chicago Press, 2009); and Brad Gregory, *The Unintended Reformation: How a Religious Revolution Secularized Society* (Cambridge, MA: Harvard University Press, 2012).

4. For background, see Steven Ozment, *The Age of Reform, 1250–1550: An Intellectual and Religious History of Late Medieval and Reformation Europe* (New Haven: Yale University Press, 1980), 22–72, and 37–39 on the distinction between God's "absolute" and "ordained" power. Cf. William J. Courtenay, *Ockham and Ockhamism: Studies in the Dissemination and Impact of His Thought* (Leiden, Netherlands: Brill, 2008).

5. See Boehner, "Introduction," xix, who lists this as the first principle of all of Ockham's work.

6. See Francis Oakley, *Politics and Eternity: Studies in the History of Medieval and Early Modern Political Thought* (Leiden: Brill, 1999), chap. 9.

7. See Julius Weinberg, "Ockham's Conceptualism," *Philosophical Review* 50, no. 5 (1941): 523–28, and Alfred J. Freddoso, "Ontological Reductionism and Faith versus Reason: A Critique of Adams on Ockham," *Faith and Philosophy* 8 (1990), 317–39.

8. See Gilson, *History of Christian Philosophy,* 490; and Boehner, "Introduction," xxiii–xxvii.

9. This is complicated by Ockham's insistence that God can cause me to have an intuitive apprehension of such presence without the thing being present in fact.

10. See David W. Clark, "William of Ockham on Right Reason," *Speculum* 48, no. 1 (1973): 13–36.

11. Frederick Copleston, *A History of Philosophy,* vol. 3 (New York: Image, 1993), 105.

12. Hobbes, *Leviathan,* 246.

CHAPTER 18. THEOLOGY OF THE CROSS

1. For relevant historical context, see the preface to the *Disputation* in *Martin Luther's Basic Theological Writings,* 3rd ed., ed. Timothy F. Lull and William R. Russell (Minneapolis: Fortress, 2012), 3. Citations are to this edition except where indicated.

2. See Martin Luther, *Heidelberg Disputation,* thesis 21, p. 22. See also Alister E. McGrath, *Luther's Theology of the Cross: Martin Luther's Theological Breakthrough* (Oxford: Blackwell, 1985).

3. For the classic account of Luther's tormented development, see Erik H. Erickson, *Young Man Luther: A Study in Psychoanalysis and History* (New York: Norton, 1958).

4. Luther was first "lent" to Wittenberg in 1508, then briefly recalled to Erfurt. He permanently joined the faculty at Wittenberg in 1511.

5. Luther complains that the book "flatly opposes divine grace and all Christian virtues," in his *Letter to the Christian Nobility,* trans. W. A. Lambert and Harold J. Grimm, in Luther, *Three Treatises* (Minneapolis: Fortress Press, 1970), 93.

6. Ibid., 93–94.

7. *Disputation against Scholastic Theology,* theses 41 and 44, in Lull and Russell.

8. Ibid., thesis 50.

9. Ibid., thesis 40.

10. Ibid., theses 7, 25, and 33.

11. Ibid., thesis 4.

12. Ibid., thesis 17.

13. Cf. Augustine, *The City of God,* 608.

14. See Augustine, "A Treatise on Nature and Grace, Against Pelagius;" "On the Proceedings of Pelagius;" and "On Original Sin," all in *Nicene and Post-Nicene Fathers,* vol. 5.

15. Luther, *Disputation against Scholastic Theology,* theses 1 and 2, in Lull and Russell.

16. Ibid., thesis 6.

17. Ibid., thesis 9.

18. Ibid., thesis 10. Cf. thesis 20.

19. Ibid., thesis 34.

20. Ibid., thesis 20. Cf. thesis 10.

21. Ibid., theses 46 and 47.

22. Ibid., thesis 56.

23. Heiko A. Oberman, *The Harvest of Medieval Theology: Gabriel Biel and Late Medieval Nominalism* (Grand Rapids, MI: Baker Academic, 2000), 4.

24. Luther, *Disputation against Scholastic Theology,* theses 93–95, in Lull and Russell.

25. See, for example, Heiko A. Oberman, *Luther: Man between God and the Devil,* trans. Eileen Walliser-Schwartzbart (New Haven, CT: Yale University Press, 1989), esp. 13–49.

26. Martin Luther, *The Babylonian Captivity of the Church,* trans. A. T. W. Steinhäuser, Frederick C. Ahrens, and Abdel Ross Wentz, in *Three Treatises,* 124, 129.

27. For a more technical account of indulgences, see the essays in *Promissory Notes on the Treasury of Merits: Indulgences in Late Medieval Europe,* ed. R. N. Swanson (New York: Brill, 2006).

28. Luther, *The Babylonian Captivity of the Church,* 132.

29. Ibid., 152.

30. Ibid., 153.

31. Ibid., 167.

32. Luther claims, "Moses, in his books, drives, compels, threatens, strikes, and rebukes terribly, for he is a lawgiver and driver." See "Preface to the New Testament," in Lull and Russell, 95.

33. Cf. Martin Luther, "Concerning the Letter and the Spirit," in Lull and Russell, 53–70.

34. For an excellent account of the Peasants' Revolt, see Steven Ozment, *Protestants: The Birth of a Revolution* (New York: Image, 1993), esp. 11–31. For a more focused treatment of several radical reformers, see David C. Steinmetz, *Reformers in the Wings: From Geiler von Kaysersberg to Theodore Beza,* 2nd ed. (New York: Oxford University Press, 2001), 123–60.

35. Martin Luther, "How Christians Should Regard Moses," in Lull and Russell, 114.

36. Cf. Martin Luther, "Two Kinds of Righteousness," in *Martin Luther: Selections from His Writings,* ed. John Dillenberger (New York: Anchor, 1962), 86–98.

37. Max Weber, *The Protestant Ethic and the Spirit of Capitalism,* trans. Talcott Parsons (London: Routledge, 2001).

38. Luther, "Concerning the Letter and the Spirit," 84.

39. Luther, *Heidelberg Disputation*, theses 11, 16, 17, and 27, and proofs to 7 and 21, in Lull and Russell.

CHAPTER 19. THE HATRED OF MAN

1. Martin Luther, *Heidelberg Disputation*, proof to 25, in Lull and Russell.

2. Luther, *The Babylonian Captivity of the Church*, 180.

3. Ibid., 171.

4. Martin Luther, "Preface to the Epistle of St. Paul to the Romans," in Lull and Russell, 101.

5. Ibid.

6. Ibid.

7. All citations to Erasmus' *De Libero Arbitrio* come from *Luther and Erasmus: Free Will and Salvation,* ed. E. Gordon Rupp and Philip S. Watson (Philadelphia: Westminster, 1969), 35 ff. Here 66, 76–77, 79, and 90.

8. De Libero Arbitrio, 95.

9. Ibid., 89–91.

10. Ibid., 97.

11. All citations to Luther's reply to Erasmus, *De Servo Arbitrio,* are taken from Rupp and Watson, eds., *Luther and Erasmus: Free Will and Salvation,* 101 ff. Here, 116.

12. Luther, *De Servo Arbitrio,* 291.

13. Ibid., 291, 187, and 186.

14. Ibid., 291.

15. Ibid., 73.

16. Ibid., 262 (emphasis added).

17. Ibid., 262.

18. Ibid., 173.

19. Ibid., 289.

20. Ibid., 192.

21. Ibid., 174.

22. Ibid., 140.

23. Ibid., 143.

24. Ibid., 137.

25. Ibid., 254.

26. Ibid., 200–201.

27. Ibid., 201 (emphasis added).

28. Ibid., 260.

29. Ibid., 201.

30. Ibid., 207.

31. Ibid., 258.

32. Ibid., 236.

33. Ibid., 207.

34. Ibid., 189.

35. Ibid., 191.
36. Luther, *The Babylonian Captivity of the Church,* 158.
37. Ibid.
38. Ibid., 164.
39. Cf. *NE,* 1170b 11–15.
40. For later expressions of this view, see Blaise Pascal, *Pensées,* trans. W. F. Trotter (Letcetera, 2015), Sec. 544; and Judge William's letters in Søren Kierkegaard, *Either/Or,* vol. 2, trans. and ed. Howard V. Hong and Edna H. Hong (Princeton: Princeton University Press, 1987).

CHAPTER 20. THE ABSOLUTE SPONTANEITY OF FREEDOM

1. *CPrR,* 241.
2. Immanuel Kant, *Anthropology from a Pragmatic Point of View,* ed. R. B. Louden (Cambridge: Cambridge University Press, 2006), sec. 4, 21–22.
3. Kant, *Groundwork of the Metaphysics of Morals,* 52.
4. *CPrR,* 144.
5. Aristotle, *Physics,* 192b 10–193a 1.
6. Kant, *Groundwork,* 49.
7. Ibid., 55.
8. Ibid., 66.
9. Ibid.
10. Ibid., 78.
11. Ibid., 66.
12. Ibid., 86.
13. Ibid., 94.
14. Ibid.
15. *CPR,* A445/B473.
16. Cf. *CPR,* A141/B181
17. *CPR,* A105 ff.
18. *CPR,* A141/B181.
19. *CPrR,* 178; *CPR* A448/B476.
20. *CPR,* A19/B33.
21. Kant's God possesses the "*highest perfection*" from the moral point of view. See *CPrR,* 252 (emphasis added).
22. See, e.g., *CPrR,* 204.

CHAPTER 21. OUR BETTER SELVES

1. Legal concepts and metaphors pervade Kant's thought, which is preoccupied with the concept of *law.* Cf. Eve Stoddard, "Reason on Trial: Legal Metaphors in the *Critique of Pure Reason,*" *Philosophy and Literature* 12 (1988): 245–60.
2. Kant, *Groundwork,* 56.
3. Ibid., 82–83.

4. Ibid., 50; *CPrR,* 155.
5. Kant, *Groundwork,* 73.
6. Ibid., 75.
7. *CPrR,* 236.
8. Kant, *Groundwork,* 73.
9. Ibid., 80.
10. Ibid., 55 ff; *CPrR,* 199 ff.
11. *CPrR,* 199 ff.
12. See Immanuel Kant, "An Answer to the Question: What Is Enlightenment?" in *Kant: Political Writings,* ed. H. S. Reiss (Cambridge: Cambridge University Press, 1991), 54–61.

CHAPTER 22. GOD BECOMES A POSTULATE

1. *RBMR,* 57.
2. Kant, *Groundwork,* 61.
3. Ibid.
4. *RBMR,* 59.
5. *CPrR,* 236.
6. *CPrR,* 206.
7. *CPrR,* 228 (emphasis in the original).
8. Immanuel Kant, *Lectures on Philosophical Theology,* trans. Allen W. Wood and Gertrude Clarke (Ithaca, NY: Cornell University Press, 1986), 131.
9. *RBMR,* 59 (emphasis in the original).
10. *CPrR,* 206.
11. Kant, *Groundwork,* 83–84.
12. *CPR,* A383.
13. *CPR,* Avii.
14. *CPR,* A479/B507.
15. *CPR,* A747/B775.
16. *CPR,* A475/B503.
17. *CPrR,* 164.
18. Immanuel Kant, *Critique of Judgment,* trans. Werner Pluhar (Indianapolis: Hackett, 1987), 368.
19. *CPR,* Bxxx (emphasis in the original).
20. *CPrR,* 169.
21. *CPrR,* 241.
22. *RBMR,* 91–93 (emphasis in the original).
23. *RBMR,* 91–93. On this problem, see Samuel Loncar, "Converting the Kantian Self: Radical Evil, Agency, and Conversion in Kant's *Religion within the Boundaries of Mere Reason," Kant-Studien* 104, no. 3 (2013): 346–66.
24. *RBMR,* 76 ff.
25. See Jean-Jacques Rousseau, "A Discourse on the Origin of Inequality," in *The Social Contract and Discourses,* trans. G. D. H. Cole (New York: Dutton, 1950).
26. *RBMR,* 129 (emphasis in the original).

27. *RBMR*, 130.
28. *RBMR*, 175 ff.
29. *RBMR*, 142 (emphasis in the original).
30. *RBMR*, 208.
31. *RBMR*, 142.
32. *RBMR*, 146 (emphasis in the original).
33. *RBMR*, 181.
34. *RBMR*, 182 (emphasis in the original).
35. *RBMR*, 180.
36. *RBMR*, 180.
37. *RBMR*, 137 (emphasis in the original).
38. *RBMR*, 197 and elsewhere; compare Marx, "The Fetishism of Commodities," in *Capital,* vol. 1 163–67.
39. *RBMR*, 175 ff.
40. *RBMR*, 178 (emphasis in the original).
41. *RBMR*, 201–02.
42. *RBMR*, 151 (emphasis in the original).
43. See *RBMR*, 58–60; *CPrR*, 239–46.
44. On Descartes' radical voluntarism, see Amos Funkenstein, *Theology and the Scientific Imagination* (Princeton: Princeton University Press, 1986), 179–91.
45. On the relationship between Leibniz and Spinoza, see Matthew Stewart, *The Courtier and the Heretic: Leibniz, Spinoza, and the Fate of God in the Modern World* (New York: Norton, 2006).
46. *CPR,* A509/B537.
47. *CPR,* A663/B691.
48. See generally, *CPR,* A508/B536, A616/B644–A619/B647, A642/B670–A645/B673 and elsewhere.
49. The second part of Kant's *Critique of Judgment* is devoted to this theme. See Kant, *Critique of Judgment,* 235–381. See Hannah Ginsborg, "Kant's Biological Teleology and Its Philosophical Significance," in *A Companion to Kant,* ed. Graham Bird (Oxford: Wiley-Blackwell, 2010), 455–70.
50. *RBMR*, 207.
51. *CPR,* Aviii.
52. Weber, "Science as a Vocation."
53. Paul Berman, *Terror and Liberalism* (New York: Norton, 2004), esp. 60 ff.

CHAPTER 23. REACTION

1. Isaiah Berlin, "Joseph de Maistre and the Origins of Fascism," in *The Crooked Timber of Humanity* (Princeton: Princeton University Press, 2013), 95–177. See also Richard Lebrun, *Joseph de Maistre: An Intellectual Militant* (Montreal: McGill-Queen's University Press, 1988).
2. See, e.g., Stephen Holmes, *The Anatomy of Antiliberalism* (Cambridge, MA: Harvard University Press, 1996), 13–36. See also Richard A. Lebrun, "Introduction," in *SP,* ix–xxiii.

3. Martin Heidegger, "Nietzsche's Word: God is Dead," in *Off the Beaten Track*, ed. and trans. Julian Young and Kenneth Haynes (Cambridge: Cambridge University Press, 2002).

4. Berlin, "Joseph de Maistre and the Origins of Fascism," 173.

5. Heidegger, "The Question Concerning Technology," in *The Question Concerning Technology and Other Essays,* trans. William Lovitt (New York: Harper and Row, 1977). 27.

6. As Hannah Arendt suggested, after her post-war reunion with Heidegger. See Richard Wolin, *Heidegger's Children: Hannah Arendt, Karl Löwith, Hans Jonas, and Herbert Marcuse* (Princeton: Princeton University Press, 2001), 50 ff.

7. See Emmanuel Faye, *Heidegger: The Introduction of Nazism into Philosophy in Light of the Unpublished Seminars of 1933–1935,* trans. Michael B. Smith (New Haven: Yale University Press, 2011); Victor Farias, *Heidegger and Nazism* (Philadelphia: Temple University Press, 1989); and "Carl Schmitt: Enemy or Foe?" ed. Paul Piccone, special issue, *Telos* 72 (1987).

8. *CF,* 57 (emphasis in the original).

9. *CF,* 57 (emphasis in the original).

10. *GPC,* 17.

11. *CF,* 57.

12. *CF,* 57.

13. *GPC,* 14.

14. *GPC,* 40–41.

15. *GPC,* 55–56 (emphasis in the original).

16. *CF,* 49.

17. *GPC,* 33.

18. *CF,* 53 (emphasis in the original).

19. *CF,* 53.

20. *CF,* 53 (emphasis in the original).

21. *GPC,* xxix.

22. *CF,* 92.

23. *CF,* 98.

24. *GPC,* 40.

25. *CF,* 45.

26. *SP,* 148.

27. *GPC,* 13.

28. *SP,* 56.

29. *GPC,* 64.

30. *GPC,* 84–85 (emphasis in the original).

31. *SP,* 216 (emphasis in the original).

32. *SP,* 358 (emphasis in the original).

33. *SP,* 381.

34. *SP,* 371.

35. *CF,* 38 (emphasis added).

36. *CF,* 99.

37. *CF*, 5.
38. *CF*, 44.
39. *CF*, 7.
40. *CF*, 79–80.
41. *CF*, 80–81, 45.
42. *CF*, 5; 6; 97.
43. *CF*, 8; see also 14, 16, 31, 84, 97.
44. *CF*, 80 (emphasis in the original).
45. *CF*, 38 (emphasis in the original).
46. *CF*, 77–82.
47. *CF*, 79.
48. *SP*, 322.
49. *SP*, 105, 111–12, 117, 147, 161, 235–36.
50. *SP*, 311.
51. *SP*, 312 (emphasis in the original).
52. Joseph de Maistre, *Du Pape* (Geneva: Librairie Droz, 1966).
53. *SP*, 335 (emphasis in the original).
54. *CF*, 41.

CHAPTER 24. "FANTASTIC AND SATANIC"

1. *PT*, 53.
2. I borrow the metaphor from Jeffrey Johnson, "Introduction," in Juan Donoso Cortes, *Selected Works of Juan Donoso Cortes*, trans and ed. Jeffrey Johnson (Westport, CT: Greenwood Press, 2000), 1–44. See also Donoso Cortes, *Essays on Catholicism, Liberalism, and Socialism* (n.p.: General Books, 2009).
3. AND, 80–96.
4. Donoso Cortes, *Essays*, 17; Donoso Cortes, "Letter to Count deMontalembert," in Donoso Cortes, *Readings in Political Theory*, trans. Vincent McNamara and Michael Schwartz (Ave Maria, FL: Sapientia Press, 2007), 133.
5. Donoso Cortes, *Essays*, 114.
6. Ibid., 38.
7. Ibid., 153 ff.
8. Ibid., 37–38.
9. Ibid., 38.
10. Ibid., 84–88.
11. Ibid., 85.
12. Ibid., 47.
13. Ibid., 161.
14. Ibid.
15. Ibid., 125 ff.
16. Ibid., 19.
17. Donoso Cortes, "Letter to Count de Montalembert," in *Readings in Political Theory*, 134.

18. See generally, Donoso Cortes, "Letter to Cardinal Fornari," in *Readings in Political Theory*, 141–157.

19. Ibid.

20. Ibid.

21. Ibid., 144, 145.

22. Ibid., 146.

23. Ibid., 143.

24. Ibid., 142, 151.

25. Donoso Cortes, *Essays*, 138.

26. On this last point, see especially Donoso Cortes, "Letter to Queen María Cristina," in *Readings in Political Theory*, 125–131.

27. Donoso Cortes, "Letter to Count de Montalembert," in *Readings in Political Theory*, 138.

28. Donoso Cortes, "Letter to Cardinal Fornari," in *Readings in Political Theory*, 151.

29. Donoso Cortes, "Letters to the Count of Montalembert," in *Selected Works*, 135.

30. See generally, Donoso Cortes, "Discourse on the Situation in Spain," in *Readings in Political Theory*, 83–104.

31. Donoso Cortes, "Letter to Count Raczynski," in *Readings in Political Theory*, 118.

32. Donoso Cortes, "Discourse on the Situation in Spain," in *Readings in Political Theory*, 100.

33. Donoso Cortes, "Discourse on Dictatorship," in *Readings in Political Theory*, 56.

34. Donoso Cortes, *Essays*, 91.

35. Ibid., 130 (emphasis added).

36. Ibid., 132.

37. Ibid., 91.

38. Ibid., 91 (emphasis in the original).

39. Ibid., 109.

40. Donoso Cortes, "Letter to Cardinal Fornari," in *Readings in Political Theory*, 145.

41. Donoso Cortes, *Essays*, 90.

42. Ibid., 92, 93–95.

43. Ibid., 148.

44. Ibid., 148–49.

45. Ibid., 148.

46. Ibid., 148–49.

47. Ibid., 118.

48. Donoso Cortes, "Letter to Queen María Cristina," in *Readings in Political Theory*, 130, 131.

49. Donoso Cortes, "Letter to Cardinal Fornari," in *Readings in Political Theory*, 146.

50. Donoso Cortes, "Discourse on the General Situation of Europe," in *Readings in Political Theory*, 72.

51. Donoso Cortes, "Letter to Cardinal Fornari," in *Readings in Political Theory*, 142.

52. Donoso Cortes, "Discourse on the Situation in Spain," in *Readings in Political Theory*, 100.

53. Ibid., 96.

54. Donoso Cortes, "Letter to Count de Montalembert," in *Readings in Political Theory,* 136.
55. Ibid.
56. See Tracy B. Strong, "Foreword," xi, and George Schwab, "Introduction," xxxvii, in *PT.*
57. On all this, see *CP,* 36 ff. In his analysis, Schmitt shows the clear influence of Max Weber, especially with regard to the idea of multiple spheres.
58. *CP,* 27.
59. Hans Kelsen in particular. See John P. McCormick, *Carl Schmitt's Critique of Liberalism: Against Politics as Technology* (Cambridge: Cambridge University Press, 1997), 88 n17.
60. *CP,* 27; *PT,* 7, 12.
61. *PT,* 5 ff.
62. *PT,* 33.
63. Cf. Howard Warrender, *The Political Philosophy of Hobbes: His Theory of Obligation* (Oxford: Oxford University Press, 2000).
64. *PT,* 5.
65. *PT,* 36, 42, 48.
66. *PT,* 37.
67. *PT,* 66.
68. *PT,* 47.
69. *PT,* 49.
70. *PT,* 50.
71. *PT,* 51.
72. *PT,* 51.
73. Johnson, "Introduction," 3; Carl Schmitt, *Dictatorship* (Cambridge: Polity Press, 2014).
74. This is evident from the first pages of *PT,* 5 ff.
75. *PT,* 54–63; see also Carl Schmitt, *Roman Catholicism and Political Form,* trans. G. L. Ullmen (Westport, CT: Praeger, 1996), 8, 56.
76. See especially AND.
77. Carl Schmitt, *Crisis of Parliamentary Democracy,* trans. Ellen Kennedy (Cambridge, MA: MIT Press, 1988), 5, 49.
78. Ibid., 28.
79. Ibid., 11.
80. *CP,* 28.
81. *CP,* 57, 92.
82. *CP,* 57.
83. *CP,* 58.
84. *CP,* 62.
85. Friedrich Nietzsche, *Thus Spoke Zarathustra,* ed. Robert Pippin and trans. Adrian Del Caro (New York: Cambridge University Press, 2006), 10.
86. *CP,* 57–58.
87. *CP,* 64.
88. AND, 94.
89. AND, 81.
90. AND, 89.

91. AND, 89.

92. See Carl Schmitt, *The Leviathan in the State Theory of Thomas Hobbes: Meaning and Failure of a Political Symbol,* trans. George Schwab and Erna Hilfstein (Westport, CT: Greenwood Press, 1996).

93. Ibid., 57–59.

94. Ibid., 35–36.

95. AND, 94; see also *PT,* 63.

96. *PT,* 53.

97. AND, 80–81.

98. Schmitt, *Roman Catholicism and Political Form,* 13.

99. Paul Gottfried, *Carl Schmitt: Politics and Theory* (Westport, CT: Praeger, 1990), 29 ff.

CHAPTER 25. THE OBLIVION OF BEING

1. Paul Celan, "Todtnauberg," in *Breathturn into Timestead: The Collected Later Poetry: A Bilingual Edition* (New York: Farrar, Straus and Giroux), 254.

2. On Heidegger's life, see Rüdiger Safranski, *Martin Heidegger: Between Good and Evil,* trans. Ewald Osers (Cambridge, MA: Harvard University Press, 1999). For an excellent recent treatment of Heidegger's religious formation and its influence on his thought, see Judith Wolfe, *Heidegger's Eschatology: Theological Horizons in Martin Heidegger's Early Work* (Oxford: Oxford University Press, 2014).

3. Safranski, *Martin Heidegger,* 42.

4. Martin Heidegger, *The Phenomenology of Religious Life,* trans. Matthias Fritsch and Jennifer Anna Gosetti-Ferencei (Bloomington: Indiana University Press, 2010).

5. Hannah Arendt, "Martin Heidegger at Eighty," *New York Review of Books,* October 21, 1971.

6. Besides Faye, *Heidegger: The Introduction of Nazism into Philosophy,* and Farias, *Heidegger and Nazism,* see also Richard Wolin, ed., *The Heidegger Controversy* (Cambridge, MA: MIT Press, 1992); and Peter Eli Gordon, "Heidegger in Black," *New York Review of Books,* October 9, 2014.

7. Martin Heidegger, *Being and Time,* trans. Joan Stambaugh (Albany: State University of New York, 1996), 13–14.

8. Martin Heidegger, "On the Essence of Ground," in *Pathmarks,* ed. William McNeill (Cambridge: Cambridge University Press, 1998), 97–135. See also Heidegger's lecture course from 1929–30, *The Fundamental Concepts of Metaphysics: World, Finitude, Solitude,* trans. William McNeill and Nicholas Walker (Bloomington: Indiana University Press, 1995).

9. Heidegger, *The Fundamental Concepts of Metaphysics,* 188–212.

10. For all this, see Heidegger, "On the Essence of Ground"; and Heidegger, *The Fundamental Concepts of Metaphysics* (especially 78 ff., on boredom). See also the section in *Being and Time* on anxiety, 172 ff., where Heidegger's debt to Kierkegaard is particularly clear. On animals, see Martin Heidegger, *Basic Concepts of Aristotelian Philosophy,* trans. Robert D. Metcalf and Mark B. Tanzer (Bloomington: Indiana University Press, 2009), 32–46.

11. Heidegger's account of the dialectic of transcendence and thrownness as the essence of *Dasein* was importantly shaped by his phenomenological interpretation of Kant's analysis of spontaneity and receptivity in the *Critique of Pure Reason.* See Martin Heidegger, *Kant and the Problem of Metaphysics,* trans. Robert Taft (Bloomington: Indiana University Press, 1997).

12. See Heidegger, *Basic Concepts of Aristotelian Philosophy.* If Heidegger's concept of inauthenticity was inspired by Christian writers (Kierkegaard in particular), it was Plato and Aristotle who seem to have shaped his understanding of everydayness.

13. Rainer Maria Rilke, "Sonnets to Orpheus I," in *Duino Elegies and Sonnets to Orpheus,* trans. Stephen Mitchell (New York: Vintage, 2009), 83–134.

14. Martin Heidegger, *The Essence of Truth: On Plato's Cave Allegory and Theaetetus,* trans. Ted Sadler (London: Continuum, 2002). For his interpretation of the pre-Socratics, see the essays collected in Martin Heidegger, *Early Greek Thinking,* trans. David F. Krell and Frank A. Capuzzi (New York: Harper and Row, 1975).

15. Plato, *Republic,* 509b.

16. See, for example, Heidegger, "Moira: Parmenides VIII 34–41," and "Aletheia: Heraclitus, Fragment B 16," in *Early Greek Thinking,* 79–101; 102–23.

17. See Heidegger, "On the Essence and Concept of *Physis* in Aristotle's B, 1," in *Pathmarks,* 183–230.

18. See especially Heidegger, "The Age of the World Picture," in *The Question Concerning Technology,* 115–54.

19. Heidegger, "Nietzsche's Word: God is Dead," in *Off the Beaten Track,* 182.

20. Heidegger, "The Age of the World Picture," 81.

21. Heidegger, "Nietzsche's Word: God is Dead," 183. See also Martin Heidegger, *What Is a Thing?,* trans. W. B. Barton Jr. and Vera Deutsch (Chicago: Regnery, 1967).

22. Heidegger, "The Age of the World Picture," 83.

23. Martin Heidegger, *Introduction to Metaphysics,* trans. Gregory Fried and Richard Polt (New Haven: Yale University Press, 2014), 207.

24. Friedrich Nietzsche, *Beyond Good and Evil,* trans. Judith Norman (Cambridge: Cambridge University Press, 2002), 64.

25. Heidegger, "Nietzsche's Word: God is Dead," 170–71 (emphasis added).

26. Ibid.

27. Ibid.

28. Nietzsche, *Thus Spoke Zarathustra,* 3.

29. Heidegger, "Nietzsche's Word: God is Dead," 159.

30. Ibid., 193.

31. Ibid., 195.

32. Plato, *Republic,* 595a–608b.

33. Heidegger, *Introduction to Metaphysics;* Heidegger, "The Age of the World Picture"; Martin Heidegger, *Bremen and Freiburg Lectures: Insight into That Which Is and Basic Principles of Thinking,* trans. Andrew J. Mitchell (Bloomington: Indiana University Press, 2012).

34. For all these quotations, see Heidegger, "The Age of the World Picture," 57–85.

35. Heidegger, "The Age of the World Picture," 84–85.

36. Martin Heidegger, "The Question Concerning Technology," 14.
37. Martin Heidegger, "Letter on Humanism," in *Pathmarks*, 25.
38. Ibid., 256.
39. Ibid., 251–52.
40. Ibid., 251–52, 254.
41. Ibid., 257.
42. Ibid., 256.
43. Ibid., 258.
44. Ibid., 260.
45. Ibid., 260–61.
46. Heidegger, *Introduction to Metaphysics*, 40–41.
47. A phrase (*Die Wüste wächst*) from Nietzsche's "Dionysus Dithyrambs." See Friedrich Nietzsche, *Nietzsche's Werke* (Leipzig: C. G. Naumann, 1906), 8:419.
48. Heidegger, "The Question concerning Technology," 33.
49. Martin Heidegger, "The Origin of the Work of Art," in *Off the Beaten Track*, 1–56; Heidegger, *Introduction to Metaphysics;* Martin Heidegger, "Why Poets?" in *Off the Beaten Track*, 200–241.
50. Heidegger, *Introduction to Metaphysics*, 191.
51. Heidegger, "The Question concerning Technology," 27.
52. Ibid., 25.
53. Ibid., 19.
54. Ibid., 46.
55. Ibid., 27.
56. Ibid., 32.
57. Ibid., 28.
58. Martin Heidegger, "The Turning," in *The Question Concerning Technology*, 38.
59. Ibid., 37–39.
60. Ibid., 44.
61. Ibid., 41.
62. Ibid., 39.
63. Heidegger, *Introduction to Metaphysics*, 221.
64. Heidegger, "The Turning," 47.
65. Heidegger, "The Question concerning Technology," 15, 17.

CHAPTER 26. THE DISENCHANTMENT OF THE WORLD

1. Weber, "Science as a Vocation," 153.
2. See, e.g., Max Weber, *Economy and Society*, 1:30, 63 ff.
3. *Economy and Society*, 2:641–900; Kronman, *Max Weber*, 72 ff.
4. See Weber, *The Protestant Ethic*, xxviii.
5. Ibid., 125.
6. Max Weber, *The Religion of China*, ed. Hans H. Gerth (New York: Free Press, 1968).
7. Kronman, *Max Weber*, 150 ff.

8. Max Weber, *Ancient Judaism,* trans. Hans H. Gerth and Don Martindale (New York: Free Press, 1967).

9. *Economy and Society,* 2:623–27.

10. Weber, "Religious Rejections of the World and Their Directions," in *From Max Weber,* 323–62.

11. Christianity's self-secularization is a major motif in Blumenberg, *The Legitimacy of the Modern Age,* 3–124.

12. *Max Weber: Collected Methodological Writings,* ed. Hans Henrik Bruun and Sam Whimster (New York: Routledge, 2012).

13. See H. H. Gerth and C. Wright Mills, "Introduction," in *From Max Weber,* 32–44.

14. Kant, *Critique of Judgment,* 317–50.

15. See Frederick Beiser, *The German Historicist Tradition* (Oxford: Oxford University Press, 2011), 511–16, for Weber's connection to the neo-Kantians, and 521–28 for a treatment of his methodological works in historical context.

16. Weber, "Science as a Vocation," 147–49.

17. Ibid., 155.

18. On the necessity of thinking the unconditioned in Kant, see *CPR,* A308/B364–5.

19. *Critique of Judgment,* 64–84.

CHAPTER 27. THE WORM IN THE BLOOD

1. For details, see Steven Nadler, *Spinoza's Heresy* (Oxford: Oxford University Press, 2008). Spinoza's dislike for the doctrine of personal salvation in a life after this is strongly expressed in the *Ethics,* 5p41s.

2. Baruch Spinoza, Letter 31, in *Complete Works,* trans. Samuel Shirley and ed. Michael L. Morgan (Indianapolis: Hackett, 2002), 846.

3. Letter 6, in Spinoza, *Complete Works,* 768. See also Letter 11, 784. In addition, Spinoza seems to have been especially interested in developments in optics, which had a direct bearing on his work as a lens grinder. His lenses were among the best produced in Europe and much in demand for use in scientific instruments.

4. Thus, for example, Stephen Hawking asserts that ". . . philosophy is dead. Philosophy has not kept up with modern developments in science, particularly physics. Scientists have become the bearers of the torch of discovery in our quest for knowledge." Stephen Hawking with Leonard Mlodinow, *The Grand Design* (New York: Bantam, 2012), 1.

5. Replying to an inquiry in 1929 from New York's Rabbi Herbert Goldstein regarding his own religious beliefs, Einstein said, "I believe in Spinoza's God who reveals himself in the orderly harmony of what exists, not in a God who concerns himself with the fates and actions of human beings." "Einstein Believes in Spinoza's God," *New York Times,* April 25, 1929. See Michel Paty, "Einstein and Spinoza," trans. Michel Paty and Robert S. Cohen, in *Spinoza and the Sciences,* ed. Marjorie Grene and Debra Nails (Dordrecht, Netherlands: Reidel, 1986).

6. One is reminded of the prisoners in Plato's cave and of Glaucon's remark that their condition is a strange one—to which Socrates replies, "They're like us." Plato, *Republic,* 515a.

7. While Hobbes never explicitly endorsed atheism, and spoke of God at many points in his writings, a number of his statements have been interpreted as evidence of an hostility to Christian belief. See, for example, Hobbes, *Leviathan*, chap. 32. When Spinoza's *Theological-Political Treatise* appeared in print, Hobbes' biographer Aubrey reports that he remarked, "I durst not speak so boldly." John Aubrey, *Brief Lives*, ed. Andrew Clark (Oxford: Clarendon Press, 1898), 357.

8. For details, see Jonathan Israel, *Radical Enlightenment* (Oxford: Oxford University Press, 2001). A good summary of later reaction to Spinoza may be found in the last chapter of Michael Della Rocca, *Spinoza* (London: Routledge, 2008).

9. See the moving statement in paragraphs 1 ff. of Spinoza, *Treatise on the Emendation of the Intellect*, in *Complete Works*, 3 ff.

10. Spinoza, *Ethics*, 5p36.

11. Ibid., 5p41s.

12. Ibid., 5p33s.

13. Ibid., 5p42s.

14. Ibid., 1p33s2.

15. Pierre Duhem, *Medieval Cosmology: Theories of Infinity, Place, Time, Void and the Plurality of Worlds*, ed. and trans. Roger Ariew (Chicago: University of Chicago Press, 1984), 4.

16. Alexander Koyré, *From the Closed World to the Infinite Universe* (Baltimore: Johns Hopkins University Press, 1957).

17. Joshua 10:13.

18. "The Condemnation of 1277," Proposition 27A, in *Philosophy of the Middle Ages: The Christian, Islamic and Jewish Traditions*, ed. Arthur Hyman and James J. Walsh (New York: Harper and Row, 1967), 544.

19. On the significance of the loss of a center, see Karsten Harries, *Infinity and Perspective* (Cambridge, MA: MIT Press, 2002).

20. For details, see Harry Austryn Wolfson, *The Philosophy of Spinoza* (New York: Schocken, 1969), 1:3–31.

21. René Descartes, *Meditations on First Philosophy*, in *The Philosophical Works of Descartes*, 1:144.

22. Baruch Spinoza, *Principles of Cartesian Philosophy*, in *Complete Works*, 115.

23. Ibid., 119.

24. Spinoza, *Ethics*, 1p25s. Cf. René Descartes, *The Principles of Philosophy*, Principle LI, in *The Philosophical Works of Descartes*, 1:239.

25. For a thoughtful discussion of the principle of sufficient reason, to which I am greatly indebted, see Michael Della Rocca, "PSR," *Philosophers' Imprint* 10, no. 7 (2010): 1–13.

26. Plato, *Theaetetus*, 201d–210a.

CHAPTER 28. THE GOD OF SUFFICIENT REASON

1. Francis Oakley, "Christian Theology and the Newtonian Science: The Rise of the Concept of Laws of Nature," *Church History* 30, no. 4 (1961): 436–37.

2. Galileo Galilei, *The Assayer*, par. 7.1, in *The Essential Galileo*, ed. and trans. Maurice A. Finocchiaro (Indianapolis: Hackett, 2008), 183.

3. See Jonathan Bennett, *A Study of Spinoza's Ethics* (Indianapolis: Hackett, 1984), 92.

4. Baruch Spinoza, "Treatise on the Emendation of the Intellect," in *Complete Works*, 3.

5. Spinoza, *Ethics*, 1p15s, 2p8s.

6. Ibid., 2d4, 2p43, 2p44. See also Bennett, *A Study of Spinoza's Ethics*, 175–82; and Della Rocca, *Spinoza*, 114–15.

7. Spinoza, *Ethics*, 2p44c2.

8. Ibid.

9. Spinoza, *Ethics*, 2p16; 2p17. See, generally, Michael Della Rocca, *Representation and the Mind-Body Problem in Spinoza* (Oxford: Oxford University Press, 1996).

10. Spinoza, Letter 12, in *Complete Works*, 789.

11. Daniel Garber, *Descartes' Metaphysical Physics* (Chicago: University of Chicago Press, 1992), 63.

12. Bernard Cohen, "'Quantum in Se Est': Newton's Concept of Inertia in Relation to Descartes and Lucretius," *Notes and Records: The Royal Society Journal of the History of Science* 19 (1964): 131–55.

13. I am indebted to Jonathan Bennett's illuminating discussion of this issue. See Bennett, *A Study of Spinoza's Ethics*, 92–106. See also David Lachterman, "The Physics of Spinoza's *Ethics*," in *Spinoza: New Perspectives*, ed. Robert W. Shahan and J. I. Biro (Norman, OK: University of Oklahoma Press, 1978), 71–111.

14. Spinoza, Letter 64, in *Complete Works*, 919.

15. Don Garrett, "Spinoza's Theory of Metaphysical Individuation," in *Individuation in Early Modern Philosophy*, ed. Kenneth F. Barber and Jorge J. E. Garcia (Albany: State University of New York Press, 1994), 86–87.

16. Hobbes, *Leviathan*, 37–39.

17. Isaac Newton, "General Scholium," in *The Principia: Mathematical Principles of Natural Philosophy*, trans. Bernard Cohen and Anne Whitman (Berkeley: University of California Press, 1999), 943.

18. For an enlightening discussion of Einstein's attitude toward quantum mechanics, see Douglas Stone, *Einstein and the Quantum: The Quest of the Valiant Swabian* (Princeton: Princeton University Press, 2013).

19. See Ernst Cassirer, *Determinism and Indeterminism in Modern Physics* (New Haven: Yale University Press, 1956), chap. 4.

20. Richard Feynman, *QED: The Strange Theory of Light and Matter* (Princeton: Princeton University Press, 1985), 10.

21. Augustine, *Confessions*, 221 ff.

CHAPTER 29. "ENDLESS FORMS MOST BEAUTIFUL"

1. See Tammy Kitzmiller, et al., v. Dover Area School District, et al., 400 F. Supp. 2d 707 (M.D. Pa. 2005).

2. In a 2014 Gallup poll, 31 percent of respondents said they believe human beings have evolved, but only with God's guidance. See "Evolution, Creationism, Intelligent Design," http://www.gallup.com/poll/21814/evolution-creationism-intelligent-design.aspx.

3. See, for example, Richard Dawkins, *The God Delusion* (New York: Mariner Books, 2008).

4. Charles Darwin, *On the Origin of Species* (Cambridge, MA: Harvard University Press, 1964), 489.

5. This aspect of Aristotle's philosophy is well developed in John Herman Randall, *Aristotle* (New York: Columbia University Press, 1960).

6. Plato, *Meno*, 82b ff.

7. René Descartes, *Discourse on the Method*, in *The Philosophical Works of Descartes*, 116–18.

8. This point is elaborately developed in Hans Jonas, *The Phenomenon of Life* (Evanston: Northwestern University Press, 2001); see especially 57.

9. See Richard Dawkins, *The Selfish Gene* (Oxford: Oxford University Press, 2009), 189–201; and Daniel Dennett, *Darwin's Dangerous Idea* (New York: Simon and Schuster, 1995), 335–69.

10. Darwin, *Origin*, 352, 355.

11. Only at the very end does Darwin seem to take a more accommodating view of the idea of creation. But even here, his phrasing is cautious and qualified. Ibid., 488–89.

12. Ibid., 139, 152, 155, 167, 185, 202, 390, 406, 437, 452, 413.

13. Ibid., 52.

14. Ibid., 485.

15. H. Allen Orr and Jerry Coyne, *Speciation* (Sunderland, MA: Sinauer, 2004), 1.

16. Aristotle comes close to recognizing the phenomenon of evolution at one point, but backs away. See *Physics*, 198b–199a.

17. Dawkins, *The Selfish Gene*, 254, 256.

18. Dawkins gives several examples. See ibid., 6.

19. Aristotle, *On the Heavens*, 271a 32–33; *Politics*, 1253a 7.

20. Dawkins, *The Selfish Gene*, 31.

21. Darwin, *Origin*, 129, 413.

22. See Richard Dawkins and J. R. Krebs, "Arms Races between and within Species," *Proceedings of the Royal Society of London B., Biol. Sci.* 205 (1979): 489–511.

23. Darwin, *Origin*, 34.

24. For the classic statement, see John Maynard Smith, "Game Theory and the Evolution of Fighting," in *On Evolution* (Edinburgh: Edinburgh University Press, 1972).

25. See Dennett, *Darwin's Dangerous Idea*, 376, 380.

26. Darwin, *Origin*, 484, 488.

27. Dennett, *Darwin's Dangerous Idea*, 370.

28. See Lee Smolin, "Did the Universe Evolve?" *Classical and Quantum Gravity* 9 (1992): 173–91. Smolin offers a more popular version of his view in *The Life of the Cosmos* (Oxford: Oxford University Press, 1999).

29. See John H. Gillespie, *Population Genetics: A Concise Guide* (Baltimore: Johns Hopkins University Press, 2004), 21–58.

30. See, for example, E. C. Friedberg, "DNA Damage and Repair," *Nature* 421 (2003): 436–40; and A. D. Drummond and C. O. Wilke, "The Evolutionary Consequences of Erroneous Protein Synthesis," *Nature Review Genetics* 10 (2009): 715–24.

31. Darwin, *Origin,* 43.
32. Stephen Jay Gould, *The Structure of Evolutionary Theory* (Cambridge, MA: Harvard University Press, 2002), 457–64. As Gould acknowledges, the term "hopeful monster" was first coined by Richard Goldschmidt. See Goldschmidt, *The Material Basis of Evolution* (Seattle: University of Washington Press, 1940).
33. Spinoza, *Ethics,* appendix to part 1.
34. Ibid.
35. Aristotle, *Physics,* 199b 30.
36. Kant, *Critique of Judgment,* 64–65, 251–55.
37. See Della Rocca, *Spinoza,* 108–18.
38. Darwin, *Origin,* 219 ff.
39. Ibid., 480.

CHAPTER 30. THE NAVEL OF THE DREAM

1. Michael Della Rocca, *Representation and the Mind-Body Problem in Spinoza,* 7–17.
2. See Henri Vermorel, "The Presence of Spinoza in the Exchanges between Sigmund Freud and Romain Rolland," *International Journal of Psychoanalysis* 90, no. 6 (2009): 1235–54; Veronique Foti, "Thought, Affect, Drive and Pathogenesis in Spinoza and Freud," *History of European Ideas* 3, no. 2 (1982): 221–36; Abraham Kaplan, "Spinoza and Freud," *Journal of the American Academy of Psychoanalysis and Dynamic Psychiatry* 5 (1977): 299–326; and Lothar Bickel, "On Relationships between Psychoanalysis and a Dynamic Psychology," in *Speculum Spinozanum 1677–1977,* ed. Siegfried Hessing (London: Routledge and Kegan Paul, 1977), 81.
3. Sigmund Freud, "Notes upon a Case of Obsessional Neurosis," in *Standard Edition,* 10:239 n1.
4. His discussion of slips and parapraxes is another example. See Sigmund Freud, *The Psychopathology of Everyday Life,* in *Standard Edition,* 6:239–79.
5. Sigmund Freud, *The Interpretation of Dreams,* in *Standard Edition,* 5:525.
6. See Sigmund Freud, *On Aphasia: A Critical Study* (1891; repr., Madison, CT: International Universities Press, 1953), 55.
7. See Jonathan Lear, *Freud* (London: Routledge, 2005). My views about Freud have been deeply shaped by Jonathan Lear's brilliant study of him.
8. See, for example, Martin Svartberg and Tore C. Stiles, "Comparative Effects of Short-Term Psychodynamic Psychotherapy: A Meta-Analysis," *Journal of Consulting and Clinical Psychology* 59, no. 5 (1991): 704–14.
9. Karl Popper, *Conjectures and Refutations: The Growth of Scientific Knowledge* (London: Routledge, 2002), chap. 1.
10. Adolph Grunbaum, *The Foundations of Psychoanalysis: A Philosophical Critique* (Berkeley: University of California Press, 1984).
11. See Hans W. Loewald, *Psychoanalysis and the History of the Individual* (New Haven: Yale University Press, 1978), 19. See, generally, James W. Jones, "Hans Loewald: The Psychoanalyst as Mystic," *Psychoanalytic Review* 88 (2001): 793–809.
12. See Lear, *Freud,* 173–79.

13. Ibid.
14. See Hans W. Loewald, "Perspectives on Memory," 159–60, and "Instinct Theory, Object Relations, and Structure Formation," 208, in *Papers on Psychoanalysis* (New Haven: Yale University Press, 1980).
15. Sigmund Freud, *Three Essays on Sexuality*, in *Standard Edition*, 7:151.
16. Among many places, see Freud, *The Interpretation of Dreams*, in *Standard Edition*, 5:610.
17. Freud, *Three Essays on Sexuality*, in *Standard Edition*, 7:135–72.
18. Freud, *The Interpretation of Dreams*, in *Standard Edition*, 4:227–38 and 5:339–508.
19. *CPR*, B145.
20. Sigmund Freud, "On Narcissism: An Introduction," in *Standard Edition*, 14:73–102.
21. Sigmund Freud, "Formulations on the Two Principles of Mental Functioning," in *Standard Edition*, 12:219.
22. Sigmund Freud, *Civilization and Its Discontents*, in *Standard Edition*, 21:69–70.
23. Freud, *The Interpretation of Dreams*, in *Standard Edition*, 4:260–64.
24. For a discussion of the distinctiveness of bourgeois attitudes toward sexuality see Michel Foucault, *The History of Sexuality*, vol. 2, trans. Robert Hurley (New York: Vintage, 1990).
25. Freud, *Three Essays on Sexuality*, in *Standard Edition*, 7:197.
26. Aristotle, *De Anima*, 430a 10–20.
27. Here I must again record my debt to Jonathan Lear, whose account of the psychoanalytic relation is informed by the same humanistic spirit as Freud's own.
28. Sigmund Freud, "Analysis Terminable and Interminable," in *Standard Edition*, 23:248.
29. See Peter Gay, *Sigmund Freud: A Life for Our Time* (New York: Norton, 1988), 250.
30. I follow Jonathan Lear here. See Lear, *Freud*, chap. 4.
31. Sigmund Freud, "The Dynamics of Transference," in *Standard Edition*, 12:100.
32. Hans W. Loewald, "Therapeutic Action of Psychoanalysis," in *Papers on Psychoanalysis*, 248–49.
33. Ibid.
34. Sigmund Freud, *New Introductory Lectures on Psycho-Analysis*, in *Standard Edition*, 22:80.
35. *NE*, 1168b.
36. Spinoza, *Ethics*, 4p35s.
37. Freud, "Analysis Terminable and Interminable," in *Standard Edition*, 23:245–47.
38. Freud, *Three Essays on the Theory of Sexuality*, in *Standard Edition*, 7:158.
39. Sigmund Freud, *Beyond the Pleasure Principle*, in *Standard Edition*, 18:36–43.
40. Spinoza, *Ethics*, 3p6.
41. Klein, "Envy and Gratitude," chap. 1.
42. Freud, *Beyond the Pleasure Principle*, in *Standard Edition*, 18:56.
43. *CPR*, A26/B42.
44. Spinoza, *Ethics*, 4p67.
45. Freud, *Civilization and Its Discontents*, in *Standard Edition*, 21:64–65. See also Gay, *Sigmund Freud: A Life for Our Time*, 526.
46. Sigmund Freud, *The Future of an Illusion*, in *Standard Edition*, 21:54.

47. Ibid., 21:49.
48. Ibid., 21:50.
49. *NE*, 1139b 15–35.

CHAPTER 31. "MAN IS A GOD TO MAN"

1. Spinoza, *Ethics,* 3p1.
2. Santiago Ramón y Cajal, widely regarded as the father of modern neuroscience, once exclaimed that the "indescribable pleasure—which pales the rest of life's joys—is abundant compensation for the investigator who endures the painful and persevering analytic work that precedes the appearance of the new truth, like the pain of childbirth." Santiago Ramón y Cajal, *Advice for a Young Investigator* (Cambridge, MA: MIT Press/Bradford Books), 50.
3. Baruch Spinoza, *Theological-Political Treatise,* in *Complete Works*, 50.
4. *NE,* 1141a 10–1141b 7.
5. Spinoza, *Ethics,* 5p36.
6. Hobbes, *Leviathan,* chap. 5, 12, 76.
7. See Stillman Drake, *Galileo at Work: His Scientific Biography* (Mineola, NY: Dover, 2003).
8. *CPR,* B168.
9. Pierre-Simon Laplace, *A Philosophical Essay on Probabilities* (London: Forgotten Books, 2012).
10. Aristotle, *Metaphysics,* 1025b 3–10.
11. See Martin Heidegger, *Phenomenological Interpretations of Aristotle: Initiation into Phenomenological Research* (Bloomington: University of Indiana Press, 2001).
12. Hobbes, *Leviathan,* chap. 5, 11, 70.
13. Spinoza, *Ethics,* 4p35s.
14. Ibid., 5p42s.
15. Plato, *Symposium,* 201d.
16. René Descartes, *Meditations on First Philosophy,* in *The Philosophical Works of Descartes,* 174–79.

CHAPTER 32. THE WORLD AS AN AESTHETIC PHENOMENON

1. See Julia Cooper, *Secular Powers: Humility in Modern Political Thought* (Chicago: University of Chicago Press, 2013); and Hans Blumenberg, *The Legitimacy of the Modern Age,* 229 ff. The critique of curiosity is a deep part of the Augustinian tradition, and has been forcefully restated recently in Paul Griffiths, *Intellectual Appetite: A Theological Grammar* (Washington, DC: Catholic University Press of America, 2009).
2. Galileo Galilei, *The Assayer,* in *The Philosophy of the Sixteenth and Seventeenth Centuries,* ed. Richard Popkin (New York: Free Press, 1966), 65. Cf. Roger Penrose, *The Road to Reality: A Complete Guide to the Laws of the Universe* (New York: Vintage, 2007).

3. Erich Auerbach, *Mimesis: The Representation of Reality in Western Literature,* trans. Willard R. Trask (Princeton: Princeton University Press, 2013).

4. Ibid., 3–23.

5. Ibid., 72.

6. Ibid., 186.

7. Ibid., 43.

8. Ibid., 92, 193.

9. Ibid., 198–202. See also Erich Auerbach, *Dante: Poet of the Secular World.*

10. Auerbach, *Mimesis,* 487, 491, 547, 552. Ian Watt, *The Rise of the Novel: Studies in Defoe, Richardson and Fielding* (Berkeley: University of California Press, 1967).

11. Spinoza, *Ethics,* 4p45s.

12. See Beth Lord, ed., *Spinoza beyond Philosophy* (Edinburgh: University of Edinburgh Press, 2012).

13. See Thomas H. Brobjer, *Nietzsche's Philosophical Context: An Intellectual Biography* (Champaign: University of Illinois Press, 2007), 77. Brobjer argues that Nietzsche only knew Spinoza secondhand, through the work of Kuno Fischer.

14. Nietzsche, *Writings from the Late Notebooks,* 82.

15. Friedrich Nietzsche, *The Gay Science,* trans. Josefine Nauckhoff and Adrian Del Caro (Cambridge: Cambridge University Press, 2001), 27.

16. See, e.g., Nietzsche, *The Gay Science,* 185, 207; and Friedrich Nietzsche, *Beyond Good and Evil,* trans. Judith Norman and ed. Rolf-Peter Horstman (Cambridge University Press: Cambridge, 2001), 8, 15.

17. Friedrich Nietzsche, *The Birth of Tragedy,* ed. Raymond Geuss and Raymond Speirs (New York: Cambridge University Press, 1999), 33.

18. Nietzsche, *The Gay Science,* 104.

19. See Friedrich Nietzsche, *The Twilight of the Idols,* in *The Anti-Christ, Ecce Homo, Twilight of the Idols and Other Writings,* trans. Judith Norman (Cambridge: Cambridge University Press, 2005), 182.

20. Nietzsche, *The Gay Science,* 204.

21. See Friedrich Nietzsche, *On Truth and Lying in a Non-Moral Sense,* in *The Birth of Tragedy and Other Writings,* 139–53.

22. Nietzsche, *The Gay Science,* 104.

23. Plato, *Republic,* 595a–608b.

24. Aristotle, *Poetics,* 1453a.

25. Nietzsche, *The Gay Science,* 171.

26. Plato, *Republic,* 595a–608b.

27. Plato, *Phaedrus,* 245a.

28. See Paul Raimond Daniels, *Nietzsche and the Birth of Tragedy* (New York: Routledge, 2014), 1–40, 90–104.

29. See, e.g., Nietzsche, *The Gay Science,* 121, and *Twilight of the Idols,* 202–3.

30. See, e.g., Nietzsche, *Late Notebooks,* 130.

31. Nietzsche, *The Birth of Tragedy,* 41.

32. Nietzsche, *The Birth of Tragedy,* 12; see also 19, 105.

33. Ibid., 52.

34. Ibid., 47 ff.
35. Ibid., 50.
36. Ibid., 50.
37. Ibid., 61.
38. Ibid., 4, 38, 40, 65.
39. Ibid., 60–61.
40. Ibid., 52.
41. Nietzsche, *The Gay Science,* 200–201.
42. Nietzsche, *Twilight of the Idols,* 162–66. See also Alexander Nehamas, *Nietzsche: Life as Literature* (Cambridge, MA: Harvard University Press, 1985).
43. Nietzsche, *Twilight of the Idols,* 165 (emphasis in the original).
44. Plato, *Phaedo,* 64a.
45. Nietzsche, *Beyond Good and Evil,* 53.
46. David J. Gross, "The Role of Symmetry in Fundamental Physics," *Proceedings of the National Academy of Sciences in the United States of America* 93, no. 25 (1996): 14256–59.
47. Nietzsche, *The Birth of Tragedy,* 19.
48. Ibid., 26.
49. Ibid., 53.
50. Ibid., 27.
51. Nietzsche, *Beyond Good and Evil,* 32–33.
52. Friedrich Nietzsche, *On the Genealogy of Morality,* ed. Keith Ansell-Pearson and trans. Carol Diethe (New York: Cambridge University Press, 1994), 10 ff.
53. Ibid., 34–36.
54. For the details, see Friedrich Nietzsche, *The Anti-Christ,* in *The Anti-Christ, Ecce Homo, Twilight of the Idols and Other Writings,* 21–24. Cf. Weber, *Ancient Judaism.*
55. See Nietzsche, *The Anti-Christ,* 26–36.
56. Ibid., 37–46.
57. Nietzsche, *On the Genealogy of Morality,* 34.
58. Joseph Koerner, *Reformation of the Image* (Chicago: University of Chicago Press, 2008).
59. Nietzsche, *Thus Spoke Zarathustra,* 9–10.
60. Nietzsche, *On the Genealogy of Morality,* 19.
61. Ibid., 72 ff.
62. Nietzsche, *The Birth of Tragedy,* 104.
63. See Pierre Hadot, *What Is Ancient Philosophy?,* trans. Michael Chase (Cambridge, MA: Harvard University Press, 2004); and Pierre Hadot, *Philosophy as a Way of Life: Spiritual Exercises from Socrates to Foucault,* trans. Michael Chase (Oxford: Wiley-Blackwell, 1995), 47–70.
64. Nietzsche, *On the Genealogy of Morality,* 89.
65. Ibid., 93.
66. Ibid., 88.
67. Ibid., 81.
68. Homer, *The Iliad,* 1.47.
69. Nietzsche, *On the Genealogy of Morality,* 93.
70. Ibid., 91.

CHAPTER 33. THE SPIDER IN THE MOONLIGHT

1. John Richardson, *Nietzsche's System* (Oxford: Oxford University Press, 2002) is one of the few books to take seriously the idea that Nietzsche had a systematic metaphysics. See also Martin Heidegger, *Nietzsche: Volumes One and Two,* trans. David Farrell Krell (New York: HarperOne, 1991), and *Nietzsche: Volumes Three and Four,* trans. David Farrell Krell (New York: HarperOne, 1991).

2. Nietzsche, *Thus Spoke Zarathustra,* 88–90.

3. Jacob Golomb, "How to De-Nazify Nietzsche's Philosophical Anthropology?" in *Nietzsche, Godfather of Fascism? On the Uses and Abuses of a Philosophy,* ed. Jacob Golomb and Robert S. Wistrich (Princeton: Princeton University Press, 2002), 19–46.

4. See, e.g., Friedrich Nietzsche, *Daybreak,* trans. R. J. Hollingdale (Cambridge: Cambridge University Press, 1982), 77.

5. See Brian Leiter, "Nietzsche's Theory of the Will," *Philosophers' Imprint* 7, no. 7 (2007): 1–15.

6. Nietzsche, *Beyond Good and Evil,* 18–19.

7. Ibid., 16–18.

8. Nietzsche, *Writings from the Late Notebooks,* 27, 30, 43, 71.

9. Ibid., 154.

10. Ibid., 49.

11. Nietzsche, *Beyond Good and Evil,* 36.

12. Nietzsche, *The Gay Science,* 211–12, 217–18.

13. Ibid., 109–10.

14. Ibid., 211–12, 217–18.

15. See generally, Gottfried Wilhelm Leibniz, *The Monadology,* in *The Monadology and Other Philosophical Writings,* trans. Robert Latta (Oxford: Oxford University Press, 1898), 238–66.

16. *Gay Science,* 38–39.

17. Ibid., 116.

18. Ibid., 241.

19. See Nietzsche, *The Anti-Christ,* 56–60; and Nietzsche, *Twilight of the Idols,* 184–86.

20. Wallace Stevens, "The Idea of Order at Key West," in *The Collected Poems of Wallace Stevens* (New York: Vintage, 1982), 128–30.

21. Nietzsche, *Late Notebooks,* 135, 136–37.

22. Nietzsche, *The Gay Science,* 78, 86.

23. Nietzsche, *Late Notebooks,* 95.

24. Ibid., 38.

25. See Graham Parkes, "Nature and the Human 'Redivinised': Mahāyāna Buddhist Themes in *Thus Spoke Zarathustra,*" in *Nietzsche and the Divine,* ed. John Lippit and Jim Urpeth (Manchester: Clinamen Press, 2000), 181–99.

26. Karsten Harries, *Infinity and Perspective.*

27. Plato, *Symposium,* 210e–212a.

28. Erwin Panofsky, *Perspective as Symbolic Form* (New York: Zone Books, 1991).

29. Nietzsche, *On the Genealogy of Morality*, 10 ff.

30. Nietzsche, *Twilight of the Idols*, 171.

31. Nietzsche, *Thus Spoke Zarathustra*, 22.

32. Nietzsche, *Ecce Homo*, in *The Anti-Christ, Ecce Homo, Twilight of the Idols and Other Writings*, 72.

33. Nietzsche, *On the Genealogy of Morality*, 37.

34. Nietzsche, *The Gay Science*, 113.

35. Benedict Spinoza, Letter 64 (to G.H. Schuller), in *Complete Works*, 919.

36. See, e.g., Nietzsche, *Ecce Homo*, 99; and Nietzsche, *The Gay Science*, 157.

37. Ibid.

38. Nietzsche, *Late Notebooks*, 216.

39. Nietzsche, *Ecce Homo*, 123.

40. Nietzsche, *The Gay Science*, 194.

41. Nietzsche, *On the Genealogy of Morality*, 26.

42. Cf. Nietzsche, *Twilight of the Idols*, 170, 204.

43. Nietzsche, *The Gay Science*, 184.

44. Nietzsche, *On the Genealogy of Morality*, 152.

45. Cf. John Locke, *On Toleration* (Cambridge: Cambridge University Press, 2010).

46. Nietzsche, *Thus Spoke Zarathustra*, 16.

47. See Wael Hallaq, *An Introduction to Islamic Law* (Cambridge: Cambridge University Press, 2009).

48. Nietzsche, *The Gay Science*, 120.

49. Nietzsche, *Beyond Good and Evil*, 100–102.

50. See, e.g., Nietzsche, *Ecce Homo*, 133, 144.

51. Nietzsche, *The Anti-Christ*, 60.

52. Nietzsche, *On the Genealogy of Morality*, 66.

53. Nietzsche, *The Anti-Christ*, 64–65.

54. See Paul F. Glenn, "Nietzsche's Napoleon: The Higher Man as Political Actor," *Review of Politics* 61, no. 1 (2001): 129–58.

55. Friedrich Nietzsche, *Human, All too Human: A Book for Free Spirits*, trans. R. J. Hollingdale (Cambridge: Cambridge University Press, 1986), 85–86.

56. Nietzsche, *Late Notebooks*, 102.

57. Ibid., 181.

58. Nietzsche, *Beyond Good and Evil*, 108.

59. Nietzsche, *The Gay Science*, 30 ff.

60. Ibid., 210.

61. See, e.g., Nietzsche, *Beyond Good and Evil*, 151 ff.

62. The standard study on Nietzsche's afterlife in German politics and culture, on both the left and right, is Steven E. Aschheim, *The Nietzsche Legacy in Germany: 1880–1990* (Berkeley: University of California Press, 1992).

63. Nietzsche, *The Gay Science*, 78.

CHAPTER 34. "THE GIFT OF TRANSMIGRATION"

1. Henry James, "Preface," in *Portrait of a Lady* (Modern Library, 2002), xxi.
2. Ibid., xxiv.
3. Ibid., xxiii.
4. José Ortega y Gasset, "Notes on the Novel," in *Theory of the Novel,* ed. Michael McKeon (Baltimore: Johns Hopkins Press, 2000), 309.
5. James, *Portrait of a Lady,* xxiv.
6. Ian Watt, *The Rise of the Novel,* 60.
7. Ibid., 71, 89, 91.
8. Ibid., 21 ff. See also Georg Lukacs, *The Theory of the Novel,* 121.
9. Watt, *The Rise of the Novel,* 15 ff.
10. *NE,* 1095a 15–20.
11. Aristotle, *Poetics,* 50a 15 ff.
12. Ibid., 50b 1.
13. Ibid., 50a 22.
14. Ibid., 51b 1 ff.
15. Ibid., 53a 20.
16. Ibid., 49b 25–30.
17. Ibid., 48b 5–15.
18. Mimicry plays an important role in the nonhuman world, but is not the same as imitation in Aristotle's sense. Indeed, mimicry generally fails to accomplish its purpose if it is taken to be merely imitative. See Peter Forbes, *Dazzled and Deceived: Mimicry and Camouflage* (New Haven: Yale University Press, 2009).
19. Aristotle, *Metaphysics,* 982b 1 ff.
20. See Jacob Klein, *A Commentary on Plato's Meno,* 112 ff.
21. *NE,* 1097a 15–1098b 10.
22. *NE,* 1100a 5–10.
23. This distinction is the origin of the separation of styles codified by Horace in the *Ars Poetica.* Horace, *Ars Poetica,* in *Satires, Epistles, and Ars Poetica,* trans. H. R. Fairclough (Cambridge, MA: Harvard University Press, 2005), lines 73–98.
24. F. R. Leavis, *The Great Tradition* (Garden City, NY: Doubleday, 1954), 108–9.
25. George Eliot, *Middlemarch* (New York: Penguin, 2012), 3.
26. In this connection see Eliot's self-reflective comments on the contrast between her preoccupations as a novelist and those of Fielding. Eliot, *Middlemarch,* 153–54.
27. Eliot, *Middlemarch,* 898.
28. Ibid., 296.
29. Ibid., 897.
30. Ibid., 419. For Naumann's aestheticism, see 203–7. Cf. Søren Kierkegaard, *Either/Or,* 2:7.
31. Eliot, *Middlemarch,* 787; see also 846, 869.
32. Ibid., 227.
33. Ibid., 284.

34. Ibid., 210.

35. It is interesting to compare Jane Austen's portrait of Emma Woodhouse in this regard. The heroine of Austen's novel also moves from egoism to greater generosity. This represents a process of moral education. (Both Darcy and Elizabeth Bennet undergo a similar development in *Pride and Prejudice*.) But Emma's growth is structured by and confined within a system of social conventions that give the novel an Aristotelian orderliness that is absent in *Middlemarch*. Also, Eliot's concerns are openly philosophical; Austen's are not.

36. Eliot, *Middlemarch*, 788.

37. Ibid., 897–98.

38. Ibid., 817.

39. Ibid., 862.

40. Ibid., 523.

41. J. W. Cross, *George Eliot's Life as Related in Her Letters and Journals* (New York: Harper and Brothers, 1885), 1:281.

42. Eliot, *Middlemarch*, 90–91; see also 216, 300, 403, 450. James' treatment of Gilbert Osmond in *The Portrait of a Lady* is importantly different. We are never encouraged to see things from his point of view.

43. Ibid., 382.

44. Ibid., 126–27. After Lydgate has disappointed her, Rosamond's romantic fantasies shift to Ladislaw, 808.

45. Ibid., 705.

46. Ibid., 894.

47. Ibid., 157.

48. Ibid., 288.

49. Ibid., 857.

50. Ibid., 757 ff.

51. Ibid., 805.

52. R. W. Chapman, ed., *Jane Austen's Letters* (Oxford: Clarendon Press, 1932), 133–34.

53. I adapt the phrase from Isaac Bashevis Singer's story "The Spinoza of Market Street," also about a Spinozist of very human dimensions. Isaac Bashevis Singer, "The Spinoza of Market Street," in *An Isaac Bashevis Singer Reader* (New York: Farrar, Straus and Giroux, 1971), 71–92.

54. James Joyce, *Ulysses* (New York: Random House, 1960), 80.

55. Marcel Proust, *In Search of Lost Time*, vol. 1, *Swann's Way*, trans. Scott Moncrieff and Terence Kilmartin (New York: Random House, 2003), 252.

56. For the stones in the courtyard, see Proust, *In Search of Lost Time*, vol. 6, *Time Regained*, 256; for the first visit to Venice, see *In Search of Lost Time*, vol. 5, *The Captive and the Fugitive*, 844 ff; for the childhood dream of a visit, see *Swann's Way*, 54, 554 ff.

57. For the recollection of the earlier memory triggered by the madeleine, see Proust, *Time Regained*, 255; for the earlier memory itself, see Proust, *Swann's Way*, 59–64.

58. Proust, *Time Regained*, 257.

59. Ibid., 524.

60. Ibid., 268.
61. Ibid., 262.
62. Ibid., 260.
63. Ibid., 285.
64. Ibid., 299.
65. Ibid., 273–80.
66. Ibid., 298.
67. Proust, *Swann's Way,* 59.
68. Proust, *Time Regained,* 300.
69. Ibid., 271; see also 304.
70. Ibid., 508.
71. Hermann Broch, *The Death of Virgil,* trans. Jean Starr Untermeyer (New York: Vintage, 1995), 12, 11, 480, 344.
72. Ibid., 79.
73. Ibid., 178.
74. See, for example, Cicero, *On Moral Ends,* ed. Julia Annas (Cambridge: Cambridge University Press, 2001), 49, 77, 119.
75. Broch, *The Death of Virgil,* 63.
76. Ibid., 431.
77. Ibid., 140.
78. Ibid., 132–33.
79. Ibid., 121.
80. Ibid., 91.
81. Ibid., 81.
82. Ibid., 210.
83. Ibid., 144, 153, 154.
84. Ibid., 94.
85. Ibid., 142, 248.
86. Ibid., 140.
87. Ibid., 142.
88. Ibid., 85.
89. Ibid., 250–51.
90. Ibid., 141.
91. Ibid., 144.
92. Ibid., 40–47.
93. Ibid., 297. "Beyond any poem is the unsung within you, greater than what is formed is that which forms."
94. Ibid., 431.
95. Ibid., 136.
96. Ibid., 91. "The knowledge of death is closed to one who goes alone, it is open only to two who travel united," 331.
97. Ibid., 334.
98. Ibid., 346, 350.
99. Ibid., 343.

100. Ibid., 342.
101. Ibid., 340.
102. Ibid., 335.
103. Ibid., 336, 335, 370.
104. Ibid., 336.
105. Ibid., 366, 377.
106. Ibid., 384–85, 412.
107. Ibid., 380.
108. Ibid., 381.
109. Ibid., 378, 379.
110. Ibid., 379.
111. Ibid., 382.
112. Ibid., 386.
113. Vladimir Nabokov, *Lolita* (New York: Vintage International, 1997), 309.
114. Sigmund Freud, *Two Case Histories* ("Little Hans" and the "Rat Man"), in *Standard Edition,* 10:155–318.
115. Nabokov, *Lolita,* 5.
116. Ibid., 6.
117. Ibid., 284.
118. Ibid., 4.
119. Ibid., 309.
120. Ibid., 278.
121. Ibid., 282–83.

CHAPTER 35. GENIUS AND SUBLIMITY

1. Jacob Burckhardt, *The Civilization of the Renaissance in Italy* (Oxford: Phaidon, 1981), 84.
2. Ibid., 81.
3. See Keith Christiansen and Stefan Weppelmann, eds., *The Renaissance Portrait: From Donatello to Bellini* (New York: Metropolitan Museum of Art, 2011), 18, 25, 63. See also John Pope-Hennessy, *The Portrait in the Renaissance* (Princeton: Princeton University Press, 1967), 3, 30, 84, 105, 113.
4. Burckhardt, *The Civilization of the Renaissance in Italy,* 245.
5. Pliny, *Natural History: Books 33–35,* trans. H. Rackham (Cambridge, MA: Harvard University Press, 1952), bk. 35, 2.6–8.
6. Christiansen and Weppelmann, eds., *The Renaissance Portrait,* 67–69, 287–90.
7. Erwin Panofsky, *Gothic Architecture and Scholasticism* (New York: Meridian, 1976), 16.
8. Leon Battista Alberti, *On Painting,* trans. Martin Kemp (New York: Penguin, 1991).
9. My understanding of Alberti, and of the philosophical problem of perspective more generally, has been deeply enriched by Karsten Harries' wonderful book *Infinity and Perspective.*

10. Plato, *Republic,* 476b ff.

11. Plato, *Phaedo,* 67c–68c.

12. Plato, *Theaetetus,* 184b–186a.

13. Erwin Panofsky, *Perspective as Symbolic Form,* 51–72.

14. Alberti's conception of the relation between truth and perspective is powerfully expressed as a theological principle in the writings of his contemporary Nicholas of Cusa. Many have noted the connection. See, for example, Ernst Cassirer, *The Individual and the Cosmos in Renaissance Philosophy,* trans. Mario Domandi (Chicago: University of Chicago Press, 1963), 7–46; and Joseph Koerner, *The Moment of Self-Portraiture in German Renaissance Art* (Chicago: University of Chicago Press, 1993), 127–38.

15. Rudolph Witkower, *Architectural Principles in the Age of Humanism* (New York: Norton, 1971), 33 ff.

16. Plato, *Phaedrus,* 275a–b.

17. Hans Belting, *Likeness and Presence,* trans. Edmund Jephcott (Chicago: University of Chicago Press, 1994).

18. Ibid., 144–63.

19. Peter Brown, *The Cult of the Saints* (Chicago: University of Chicago Press, 1982), 90–91.

20. Belting, *Likeness and Presence,* 78–101.

21. Ibid., 102–15.

22. Ibid., 480.

23. Erwin Panofsky, *Idea: A Concept in Art Theory,* trans. Joseph Peake (New York: Harper and Row, 1968). See also Ernst Cassirer, "Giovanni Pico della Mirandola: A Study in the History of Renaissance Ideas," *Journal of the History of Ideas* 3 (1942): 123–44. For a wonderful account of the collaboration between Panofsky and Cassirer at the Warburg Institute in Hamburg, see Emily Levine, *Dreamland of Humanists* (Chicago: University of Chicago Press, 2013).

24. Panofsky, *Idea: A Concept in Art Theory,* 40–41.

25. Plato, *Republic,* 602a–608b.

26. Plato, *Republic,* 506 ff.; Aristotle, *De Anima,* 427a 28 ff.

27. See, for example, Augustine, *Eighty-Three Different Questions,* trans. David L. Mosher (Washington, DC: Catholic University of America Press, 1982); and Panofsky, *Idea: A Concept in Art Theory,* 36–37.

28. *CPR,* A50/B74.

29. *CPR,* B72.

30. Erwin Panofsky, *The Life and Art of Albrecht Dürer* (Princeton: Princeton University Press, 1943), 280.

31. Koerner, *The Moment of Self-Portraiture in German Renaissance Art,* 63–126.

32. Panofsky, *The Life and Art of Albrecht Dürer,* 281.

33. Albrecht Dürer, *Vier Bucher von Menschlicher Proportion* (Nuremberg, 1528). See also Panofsky, *The Life and Art of Albrecht Dürer,* 266–68.

34. E. H. Gombrich, *Art and Illusion* (Princeton: Princeton University Press, 1960), 173–74.

35. *CPR,* A137–47/B176–87.

36. His remarks about "culture" perhaps suggest a contrary view. See Kant, *Critique of Judgment,* 173.

37. Spinoza, *Ethics,* 4a1.

38. Ibid., 1p17.

39. Arthur O. Lovejoy, *The Great Chain of Being* (Cambridge, MA: Harvard University Press, 1936).

40. David Summers, *Real Spaces: World Art History and the Rise of Western Modernism* (London: Phaidon, 2003), 626.

41. See Meyer Schapiro, "Recent Abstract Painting" and "On the Humanity of Abstract Painting," in *Modern Art: 19th and 20th Centuries* (New York: Braziller, 1979).

42. George Dickie, *Art and the Aesthetic* (Ithaca: Cornell University Press, 1975). See also Arthur Danto, "The Art World," *Journal of Philosophy* 61, no. 19 (1964): 571–84; and Arthur Danto, *Transfiguration of the Commonplace* (Cambridge, MA: Harvard University Press, 1981).

43. Anthony A. C. Earl of Shaftesbury, *Characteristics of Men, Manners, Opinions, Times* (Whitefish, MT: Kessinger, 2010).

44. For details, see W. Rhys Roberts, *Longinus on the Sublime* (Cambridge: Cambridge University Press, 1907), 1–37.

45. *CPR,* Bxx.

46. Heinrich Wolfflin, *Principles of Art History* (New York: Dover, 1950), 18–72.

47. See Meyer Schapiro, "Style," in *Theory and Philosophy of Art: Style, Artist and Society* (New York: Braziller, 1994).

48. The ahistorical tendency of Wolfflin's use of the distinction is even more pronounced in the later work of Henri Focillon. See Henri Focillon, *The Life of Forms in Art* (New York: Zone Books, 1992).

49. On the relationship of Dutch painting to literary realism, see Ruth Yeazell, *Art of the Everyday* (Princeton: Princeton University Press, 2008).

50. See Eric Karpeles, *Paintings in Proust: A Visual Companion to "In Search of Lost Time"* (London: Thames and Hudson, 2008).

51. John Constable, quoted in Gombrich, *Art and Illusion,* 385.

52. Gombrich makes this point and Ruskin anticipates it. See Gombrich, *Art and Illusion,* 296.

53. Spinoza, *Ethics,* 2p29c.

54. Roy Lichtenstein, quoted in Arthur Danto, *What Art Is* (New Haven: Yale University Press, 2013), 43.

55. Hans Belting, *Art History after Modernism* (Chicago: University of Chicago Press, 2003), 115–25. See also Danto, *What Art Is,* 49.

56. Danto, *What Art Is,* 37 (emphasis in original).

57. Clement Greenberg, "Avant-Garde and Kitsch," in *Art and Culture* (Boston: Beacon Press, 1968), 3–21.

58. See, generally, Meyer Schapiro, "Cezanne and the Philosophers," in *Worldview in Painting—Art and Society* (New York: Braziller, 1999), 75–103.

59. Karsten Harries, *The Meaning of Modern Art* (Evanston: Northwestern University Press, 1968).

60. Max Weber, *The Protestant Ethic and the Spirit of Capitalism*, 181.
61. Walter Benjamin, *The Work of Art in the Age of Mechanical Reproduction* (Charleston, SC: CreateSpace, 2010).
62. Kant, *Critique of Judgment*, 76–78.
63. Schapiro, "On the Humanity of Abstract Painting," 227.
64. Schapiro, "Style," in *Theory and Philosophy of Art: Style, Artist, and Society*, 58.
65. Schapiro, "Recent Abstract Painting," in *Modern Art: 19th and 20th Centuries*, 225.
66. Schapiro, "The Value of Modern Art," in *Worldview in Painting: Art and Society*, 146.
67. Schapiro, "Recent Abstract Painting," in *Modern Art: 19th and 20th Centuries*, 222.
68. See, generally, Erwin Panofsky, *Studies in Iconology: Humanistic Themes in the Art of the Renaissance* (Oxford: Oxford University Press, 1939).
69. See Julian Barnes, "A Treacherous Art Scene?" *New York Review of Books*, November 21, 1913.
70. See, for example, David Howarth, *Images of Rule: Art and Politics in The English Renaissance, 1485–1649* (Berkeley: University of California Press, 1997); and Charles M. Rosenberg, ed., *Art and Politics in Late Medieval and Early Renaissance Italy, 1250–1500* (South Bend: Notre Dame University Press, 1990).
71. G. W. F. Hegel, *Aesthetics: Lectures on Fine Art*, trans. T. M. Knox (Oxford: Oxford University Press, 1975), 1:103.
72. See, generally, Susan Sontag, "Fascinating Fascism," *New York Review of Books*, February 6, 1975.

CHAPTER 36. THEOLOGICAL, NOT POLITICAL

1. Hans Kelsen, *Pure Theory of Law*, trans. Max Knight (Berkeley: University of California Press, 1967).
2. John Rawls, *A Brief Inquiry into the Meaning of Sin & Faith*, ed. Thomas Nagel (Cambridge, MA: Harvard University Press, 2009).
3. Rawls, *A Theory of Justice*, 514.
4. Ibid., 109.
5. Ibid., 106.
6. Ibid., 119.
7. Ibid.
8. Ibid., 118.
9. Ibid.
10. Ibid., 358.
11. Kant, *Groundwork*, 66.
12. Rawls, *A Theory of Justice*, 42–45. This is particularly evident in his use of the idea of "reflective equilibrium."
13. Ibid., 64–65.
14. Ibid., 23–24.
15. Kant, *Groundwork*, 49.
16. Rawls, *A Theory of Justice*, 514.
17. Plato, *Republic*, 557c–562a.

18. Rawls, *A Theory of Justice,* 372.

19. Ibid., 459–60, n. 4.

20. This feeling has inspired much of the Counter-Enlightenment reaction against the ideals of cosmopolitanism, beginning with Rousseau and reaching a peak in the nineteenth century with Herder and others. See Isaiah Berlin, *The Roots of Romanticism* (Princeton: Princeton University Press, 1999), 26–78.

21. Something like this helps to explain, in part at least, the definition of genocide as a crime against the diversity of humanity.

CHAPTER 37. DEMOCRATIC VISTAS

1. Harold Bloom, Introduction to Walt Whitman, *Leaves of Grass* (1855 ed.) (New York: Penguin, 2005), vii.

2. George Kateb and Martha Nussbaum are two prominent exceptions. See George Kateb, "Walt Whitman and the Culture of Democracy," in *A Political Companion to Walt Whitman,* ed. John E. Seery (Lexington: University Press of Kentucky, 2011), 19; and Martha C. Nussbaum, "Democratic Desire: Walt Whitman," in Seery, ed., *A Political Companion to Walt Whitman,* 96. I have learned much from both.

3. See, e.g., Roger Asselineau, *The Evolution of Walt Whitman* (Cambridge: Harvard University Press, 1960); Juan A. Herrero Brasas, *Walt Whitman's Mystical Ethics of Comradeship: Homosexuality and the Marginality of Friendship at the Crossroads of Modernity* (Albany: State University of New York Press, 2010); and D. J. Moores, *Mystical Discourse in Wordsworth and Whitman: A Transatlantic Bridge* (Leuven, Belgium: Peeters, 2006).

4. Walt Whitman, *Leaves of Grass,* 9. All citations to Whitman refer to the 1855 edition unless otherwise noted.

5. Ibid., 62.

6. Ibid., 44.

7. Ibid., 47.

8. Ibid., 98.

9. Walt Whitman, *Leaves of Grass* (1891–92 ed.), in *Walt Whitman: Complete Poetry and Collected Prose,* ed. Justin Kaplan (New York: Viking, 1982), 494.

10. Whitman, *Leaves of Grass,* 52.

11. Ibid., 48.

12. Ibid., 62.

13. Ibid., 56.

14. Ibid., 62.

15. Ibid.

16. Leibniz, *Discourse on Metaphysics,* sec. 9.

17. Whitman, *Leaves of Grass,* 40.

18. Ibid., 46, 158. See also Whitman, *Leaves of Grass,* 1891–92 ed., 319, 471, 475.

19. Whitman, *Leaves of Grass,* 34.

20. Ibid., 93.

21. Ibid., 59.

22. Ibid., 89.
23. Ibid.
24. Ibid., 113.
25. Ibid., 116.
26. Ibid., 115.
27. Ibid., 138–39.
28. Ibid., 86.
29. Ibid., 115–16.
30. Ibid., 116.
31. Ibid., 33–34.
32. Ibid., 155.
33. Ibid., 140.
34. Ibid., 91.
35. Ibid., 53.
36. Ibid., 56.
37. Ibid., 29–30.
38. Ibid., 93.
39. Ibid., 16.
40. Ibid., 34.
41. Ibid., 155.
42. Ibid., 112.
43. Ibid., 115.
44. Ibid., 33–34.
45. Ibid., 155.
46. Ibid., 93.
47. Ibid., 10.
48. Ibid., 9.
49. Ibid., 54.
50. Ibid., 95.
51. Ibid., 145.
52. Ibid., 9.
53. Ibid., 50.
54. Ibid., 59.
55. Ibid., 50.
56. Ibid., 144.
57. Whitman, *Leaves of Grass,* 1891–92 ed., 317.
58. Whitman, *Leaves of Grass,* 96.
59. Ibid., 142.
60. Ibid., 49.
61. Ibid., 140.
62. Ibid., 143.
63. Walt Whitman, *Democratic Vistas* (New York: Liberal Arts Press, 1949), 5.
64. Ibid., 20.
65. Ibid., 24.

66. Ibid., 2.
67. Ibid., 22.
68. Ibid., 20.
69. Ibid., 21.
70. Ibid., 5, 8, 11, 12, 22, 38.
71. Ibid., 32.
72. Ibid., 34.
73. Ibid., 52.
74. Ibid., 15.
75. Ibid., 20.
76. Ibid., 37.
77. Stanley Cavell, *Conditions Handsome and Unhandsome: The Constitution of Emersonian Perfectionism* (Chicago: University of Chicago Press, 1990).
78. Whitman, *Democratic Vistas*, 15.
79. Ibid., 38–39.
80. Whitman, *Leaves of Grass*, 10.
81. Ibid., 13.
82. Ibid., 93.
83. Whitman, *Democratic Vistas*, 32.
84. Ibid., 22.
85. Whitman, *Leaves of Grass*, 10.
86. Ibid., 55.
87. Whitman, *Democratic Vistas*, 51.
88. Whitman, *Leaves of Grass*, 56.
89. Ibid., 16.
90. Whitman, *Leaves of Grass*, 1891–92 ed., 475.
91. Whitman, *Leaves of Grass*, 16.
92. Ibid., 141.
93. Ibid., 69.
94. Ibid., 67.
95. Ibid., 54.
96. Whitman, *Democratic Vistas*, 55.
97. Whitman, *Leaves of Grass*, 1891–92 ed., 174.
98. Whitman, *Leaves of Grass*, 71–76.
99. Ibid., 96.
100. Ibid., 21.
101. Aristotle, *Politics*, 1276b 17 ff.
102. Christian Schwägerl, *The Anthropocene: The Human Era and How It Shapes Our Planet*, trans. Lucy Renner Jones (Santa Fe, NM: Synergetic Press, 2014).

Index

abortion rights, 80

Abraham and sacrifice of Isaac, 783

Abrahamic religions, 5, 15–16; Christianity vs. Judaism and Islam, 22, 89, 103, 104, 850, 938–39, 1082n15; contingency of world and, 689; on God, 17, 34, 595, 781; God as separate from the world, 23, 24, 781; gratitude in, 22; iconoclastic prejudice of, 942; immortality and, 1070–71; mysticism in, 1070; science and, 756; in secular world, 993; shared belief of Christianity, Judaism, and Islam, 175; Spinoza's attack on, 595; Spinoza's God compared to Abrahamic God, 611–12, 677, 697, 749–50; on uniqueness of individual, 39. *See also* Christianity; Islam; Judaism

Absolute Knowledge, 16, 17, 779

absolute power, 21, 245, 270, 340–45, 356, 359, 380, 385, 391, 461

absolute priority, principle of, 1016

absolute soul, 1044

Absolute Spirit, 6–7, 985

abstractions, 276, 346–51, 403–6, 409–11, 414, 420–21, 425, 428–29, 476, 570, 949–50, 957, 1004

accountability, claims of entitlement and, 44

Achilles, 121, 198–99, 783, 798, 809

activity, 602–3. *See also* motion

Adam and Eve, 22, 37, 100

Aeschylus, 791–92, 793, 796, 869, 912, 913

aesthetics: Aristotle and, 33, 782, 791; Christian, 943–44; classical aesthetics, 782, 945, 966, 983; Kant and, 957; Nazism and, 986–87; Socratism and, 793–97; of sublimity, 968, 975. *See also* art

affection of gift giver, 132–33

afterlife: assumptions about, 1071–73; Nietzsche and, 824–25, 1120n62; Spinoza and, 45. *See also* heaven

Agamemnon, 199, 784, 869

aggression, 743–44

Alberti, Leon Battista: *On Painting*, 933, 935–38, 955, 972, 1124n8, 1125n14

Alcibiades, 289

Alexander the Great, 193, 194

Alexander I (Russia), 473

alienation, 56

America, in Whitman's world view, 1048, 1050

ancient world. *See* pagan antiquity

angels, 126, 246–47, 250, 287–88, 525, 1085n49

anger: disappointment created by doctrine of grace and, 23; at God, 90; infant/child experiencing, 56, 85; politeness absent in social dealings as cause of, 74